ABSOLUTE WAR

Also by Chris Bellamy

Red God of War
Soviet Artillery and Rocket Forces

The Future of Land Warfare

The Evolution of Modern Land Warfare
Theory and Practice

Expert Witness
A Defence Correspondent's Gulf War

Knights in White Armour
The New Art of War and Peace

Consultant Editor, Eastern Front, to John Keegan (ed.)
The Times Atlas of the Second World War

Associate Editor to Richard Holmes (ed.)
The Oxford Companion to Military History

CHRIS BELLAMY

ABSOLUTE WAR

**Soviet Russia in the Second World War:
a modern history**

MACMILLAN

First published 2007 by Macmillan
an imprint of Pan Macmillan Ltd
Pan Macmillan, 20 New Wharf Road, London N1 9RR
Basingstoke and Oxford
Associated companies throughout the world
www.panmacmillan.com

ISBN 978-0-333-78022-0

9 8 7 6 5 4 3

A CIP catalogue record for this book is available from
the British Library.

Map artwork by ML Design
Typeset by SetSystems Ltd, Saffron, Walden, Essex
Printed and bound in Great Britain by
Mackays of Chatham plc, Chatham, Kent

For my father, Peter Bellamy,

one of the ten fastest sprinters

in the British Empire

'If . . .'

CONTENTS

List of illustrations, figures and tables ix

Key to map symbols and abbreviations xvi

Preface and acknowledgements xix

1 Flight of the rabid wolf: the long-term impact of the war in the East 1

2 Absolute and total war 16

3 'A cruel romance': the Nazi–Soviet alliance and Soviet expansion, August to November 1939 39

4 Further Soviet expansion and cooperation with Germany, November 1939 to June 1941 69

5 Who planned to attack whom, and how? 99

6 The war's worst-kept secret 136

7 Iron road east: the country, the forces 164

8 Barbarossa unleashed, and the battles of the frontiers . . . 179

9 Kremlin at war 207

10 Winning oneself to death 239

11 Midnight in Moscow 280

12 Black snow 313

13 White night: Leningrad, September 1941 to February 1944 351

14 The 'Grand Alliance' 409

15 To the edge of the abyss: the worst year – 1942 447

16 From defence to attack: the Caucasus, Stalingrad and Mars 497

17 Kursk, and a new professionalism 554

18 Destroying the *Wehrmacht*. Ukraine, Belarus and the Baltic: reasserting Soviet control 596

19 Victory 630

20 New world order 670

Select bibliography 689

Notes and references 705

Index 789

Illustrations, figures and tables

Illustrations

1 The partition of Poland: the map signed by Stalin and von Ribbentrop, 28 September 1939. (Rodina)
2 Agent report from *Starshina*, Berlin, 17 June 1941, and Stalin's comment. (Rodina)
3 German intelligence map of their own and Soviet dispositions, 21 June 1941. (BA-MA Koblenz)
4 Stalin: *Time* magazine's unlikely 'Man of the Year', 1942. (*Time*)
5 Order to evacuate Moscow, October 1941, with Stalin's amendments. (Rodina)
6 Central Committee to Zhdanov 13 June 1948. Document confirming that the twenty-eight Panfilov heroes story is false. (Rodina)
7 Elena Vasilevna, a child during the war, tells of the siege of Leningrad. Museum of the Road of Life, March 2005. (Author)
8 Lavrenty Pavlovich Beria, People's Commissar for Internal Affairs, head of the NKVD and NKGB and member of the State Defence Council. (GKO)
9 Aleksandra Kollontai, writer and Soviet ambassador to Sweden.
10 Timoshenko (left) and Zhukov (right) on pre-war manoeuvres. (Rodina)
11 Russian soldier taken prisoner in the frontier battles, 1941. (BA-MA Koblenz)
12 Bewildered Soviet soldiers surrender 1941. (BA-MA Koblenz)
13 The moral and physical components, shattered. Defeat and victory, 1941. (BA-MA Koblenz)

14 Russian prisoners taken in the renewed German drive, operation Blau, 1942. This photograph could equally have been taken in 1941. (BA-MA Koblenz)

15 Russian prisoners, the Crimea, 1942. The picture is uncannily reminiscent of some taken in Iraq in 1991. (BA-MA Koblenz)

16 Russian ski troops, 1941. (Rodina)

17 Winter offensive, Moscow, 1941. (Rodina)

18 Dovator's cavalry in the Moscow counter-offensive, 1941. (Rodina)

19 Armies march on their stomachs. A field kitchen in winter. (Rodina)

20 'Destroy the German monster': Leningrad poster, 1941–2. (Rodina)

21 Leningrad fire-fighter. (Rodina)

22 Victims of an air-raid on Leningrad. (Rodina)

23 Suspected 'collaborators' in the hands of the NKVD. (Rodina)

24 Woman sniper. (Rodina)

25 Po-2 night bomber of the 46th Guards 'night witches' regiment. (Rodina)

26 Women pilots, Novorossiysk, 1943. (Rodina)

27 Heroines of the Soviet Union N. V. Kovshova and M. S. Polivanova. (Author)

28 Women snipers, 1945. (Rodina)

29 Khrushchev and Brezhnev, 1942. (Rodina)

30 Russian map of northern Stalingrad. (Author's collection)

31 Lt Gen. Vasiliy Chuikov, commanding Sixty Second Army, drawn by Finogenov.

32 Chuikov's command bunker, dug into the Volga bank, drawn by Finogenov.

33 Chuikov and his staff holding central Stalingrad. (Rodina)

34 Still a secret weapon: a *Katyusha* multiple rocket launcher fires in the distance, drawn by Finogenov.

35 Rokossovskiy, during the Moscow winter offensive the year before. (Rodina)

36 Surrender at Stalingrad, drawn by Finogenov.

37 Paulus's interrogation, drawn by Finogenov.

38 Paulus (left) and his Chief of Staff, Lt Gen. Schmidt (right) under interrogation after Stalingrad. (Rodina)

39 Zhukov and Koniev. (Rodina)

40 Ilyushin-2 Shturmovik ground attack planes over Berlin. (Rodina)

41 German prisoners being marched through the streets of Moscow. (Rodina)

42 Rokossovskiy in the new, post-15 January 1943, uniform. (Rodina)

43 The cruiser *Paris Commune* firing in defence of Sevastopol, 1941. (Rodina)

44 Churchill and Molotov, during Molotov's visit to Britain, May 1942. (Rodina)

45 The 'big three': Churchill, Roosevelt, and Stalin at Yalta, February 1945. (IWM)

46 Revenge of the bear: after the destruction of the Army Group Centre, illustrated by the broken rifle, vengeful Russia advances on Hitler's Germany. (Illingworth cartoon, Solo Syndication)

47 Red flag over the Reichstag. Re-enactment of 2 May. (Rodina)

48 Yevgeniy Khaldei, war photographer, in Berlin. The tank behind him is the new JS-II. (Rodina)

49 Victory in Berlin. Maria Shalneva, Soviet traffic policewoman, in Berlin. (Rodina)

50 German prisoners of the Russians at the end of the war. (Rodina)

51 The writer Konstantin Simonov with the Soviet forces as a war correspondent. (Rodina)

52 Unconditional surrender: Keitel signs for Germany at one of the ceremonies. The official capitulation was signed by Jodl, the designated representative of the German 'state' – what was left of it. (IWM)

53 The 'United Nations' – the four powers that will occupy Germany – witness the surrender. Zhukov represents the Soviet Union. (IWM)

54 Stalin and his generals. (Rodina)

55 Zhukov, Rokossovskiy, Sokolovskiy and Vasilevskiy in Berlin after the award of British honours. (IWM)

56 The end of Nazi Germany – and Austria. (Author's collection)

Figures

1.1 Legacy of the war. Russian population by age, 1990.

1.2 Legacy of the war. Russian population by age, 2005.

3.1 Europe at the end of November 1940.

3.2 Soviet expansion in Europe, 1939–40, showing boundary changes.

4.1 The Russo–Finnish War, 1939–40.

4.2 The Battle of Suomussalmi, 7 Dec 1939 to 7 Jan 1940.

5.1 Soviet plan for a pre-emptive attack on German forces in the General Government area, 15 May 1941.

5.2 OKH plan presented to Hitler, 5 December 1940.

5.3 Compromise reached between OKH and Hitler, 5 December 1940.

5.4 Final plan, Hitler's Directive No. 21, *Case Barbarossa*, 18 December 1940.

7.1 The Eurasian 'funnel' and other key geo-strategic features.

7.2 Range of Soviet and German aircraft, 1941.

8.1 German and Soviet deployments, 22 June 1941 and echeloning of Soviet forces.

8.2 The frontier battles, 22 June to 9 July 1941.

9.1 Zhukov's 'block', 26 June 1941.

10.1 The Battle of Smolensk, 10 July to 10 September 1941.

10.2 Hitler's Directive No. 33 of 19 July 1941, Supplement of 23 July and Directive No. 34 of 30 July.

10.3 Hitler's Directive No. 35 of 6 September 1941.

10.4 Battle for Kiev (Kyiv), 7 July to 26 September 1941, and the approaches to the Crimea.

10.5 The Vyaz'ma–Bryansk encirclements and the German approach towards Moscow, 30 September to 5 December 1941.

12.1 The renewed attack on Moscow, Army Group Centre, November to December 1941.

12.2 The logistic 'bungee'. Warsaw–Vyaz'ma – German supply bases and forward limits of resupply.

12.3 The Moscow counteroffensive: Phase 1, 5–15 December 1941.

12.4 Coalescence of a mobile group in the enemy rear, Tenth Army in the Moscow counteroffensive, 6–20 December 1941.

12.5 German administrative areas in European Russia.

12.6 Winter operations on the Eastern Front, 5 December 1941 to 31 March 1942.

12.7 The Moscow counteroffensive: Phase 2, 16 December 1941 to 1 January 1942.

13.1 Iron ring round Leningrad.

13.2 The city of Leningrad.

13.3 Keeping Leningrad alive, and maintaining the 'iron ring'.

13.4 Partisans in the Leningrad area.

13.5 'Defensive pincers': Vlasov's Second Shock Army is trapped, January to June 1942.

13.6 The Sinyavino Offensive, 19 August to 1 October 1942.

13.7 'Wargame number five'. 'Spark'. The ring is cut, 7–18 January 1943.

13.8 After nearly 900 days – the Leningrad–Novgorod Operation, February 1944.

14.1 Arctic ice and the Allied sea routes.

14.2 Soviet industry and Allied aid, 1941–5.

15.1 The four phases of Operation *Blau*, and what the Russians expected.

15.2 The battle of Khar'kov (Kharkiv), 12–19 May 1942.

15.3 Sevastopol and the Crimea: the defences, the siege and the fall, 24 September 1941 to 4 July 1942.

15.4 Location of Soviet war industry, 1942, showing enterprises newly constructed or converted to war production, 1941–2.

15.5 Soviet deportation of ethnic groups and others, 1937–49, with focus on the Caucasus, 1941–6.

16.1 German plans for late 1942.

16.2 The Caucasus, 1942.

16.3 The German drive to the Volga and Stalingrad.

16.4 Stalingrad – the city.

16.5 Revenge of the Gods: Mars, a possible Jupiter, Saturn and Uranus.

16.6 The counteroffensive at Stalingrad: Operation Uranus.

16.7 The counteroffensive at Stalingrad: Operations Winter Storm (German) and Little Saturn (Russian).

16.8 Operation Mars. The failed attempt to destroy Ninth army, 25 November to 23 December 1942.

16.9 The end at Stalingrad: Operation 'Ring' (Kol'tso), 10 January to 2 February 1943.

16.10 The German last stand at Stalingrad with inset on the capture of Paulus' HQ.

17.1 Development of the war, 19 November 1942 to end 1943, and the formation of the Kursk salient:

    17.1.1 Eastern front 1942–3, showing interrelationship of certain key Russian operations.

    17.1.2 Formation of the Kursk salient (1): The Voronezh–Khar'kov Operation, 13 January to 3 March 1943.

    17.1.3 Formation of the Kursk salient (2). Ground recovered by the Germans leading to the formation of the Kursk bulge. The Khar'kov Defensive Operation (Russian), 4–25 March 1943.

17.2 The Kursk salient. Situation at the end of 4 July 1942 showing Russian and German deployments and German intentions.

17.3 The Kursk salient. Organization and extent of Russian defences and German attacks on the north and south faces.

17.4 Concentration of firepower along the Kursk perimeter.

17.5 Example of 'traffic analysis' – eastern front.

17.6 The battle at Prokhorovka field.

17.7 The 'war of the rails' around Kursk, 1943, showing Partisan organization and activity in concert with main forces.

17.8 The Kursk counteroffensives: operations Kutuzov and Rumyantsev, 12 July to 23 August 1943.

18.1 Battle of the Dnepr, with inset on the Dnepr (Velikiy Bukrin) Airborne Operation.

18.2 'Right Bank Ukraine' – the Dnepr–Carpathian Offensive Operation, 24 December 1943 to 17 April 1944, and (inset) the Crimea, 8 April to 12 May 1944.

18.3 Operation 'Bagration' – the Belorussian Offensive Operation, 23 June to 29 August 1944 and Soviet deception plan.

18.4 Outline of major Russian offensive operations, 1943–5.

19.1 The Budapest Operation, 29 October 1944 to 13 February 1945.

19.2 The Vistula–Oder Operation, 12 January to 3 February 1945.

19.3 Berlin, 16 April to 18 May, 1945.

19.4 The Battle for the Reichstag, 30 April 1945.

19.5 The end in Europe. Prague, 6–11 May 1945.

20.1 The Manchurian Strategic Offensive Operation, 9 August to 1 September 1945.

Tables

7.1 Deployment of the *Wehrmacht* for Operation Barbarossa; 21 June 1941 (simplified).
13.1 Leningrad bread ration, 1941–3.
15.1 GDP ratios between the combatants, 1941–5.
15.2 Soviet war losses by year, 1941–5.
16.1 Comparison of forces available for counteroffensives west of Moscow and around Stalingrad.
16.2 Comparison of forces employed in Mars and 'Jupiter' with those employed in Uranus and Saturn, 1942.

Key to map symbols and abbreviations

GERMAN AND AXIS	RUSSIAN AND ALLIED		
→	←	**Movements**	
⬛ ▦	▢ ⬜	**Formations**	
XXXXXX ▦	XXXXXX ▢	**Theatre Command**	**Military Boundary**
XXXXX ▦	XXXXX ▢	**Army Group (German)** **Front (Russian)**	══ XXXXX ══
XXXX ▦	XXXX ▢	**Army** *or equivalent*	══ XXXX ══
XXX ▦	XXX ▢	**Corps**	══ XXX ══
XX ▦	XX ▢	**Division**	
X ▦	X ▢	**Brigade**	

⬓	◎	**Armour**	**Panzer (German)** **Tank (Russian)**
	XXX ⬦ XXI	**Russian 1941 Mechanized Corps**	
	⊠	**Mechanized / Motor-Rifle**	
	⊘	**Cavalry-Mechanized**	
⛴	⛴	**Naval forces**	
	☂	**Airborne (parachute)**	
	✊	**Partisan activity**	

Abbreviations

A   Army

AA   Air Army (Russian air force formation, usually supporting a Front)

AC   Army Corps (German)

AG   Army Group (German)

Area   Area Army (Japanese) (equivalent to an Army Group or Front)

C   Corps

CC   Cavalry Corps

Div   divisional (directly subordinate to a divisional headquarters)

Div Arty   Divisional Artillery

Front   Russian higher formation, comprising several armies, equivalent to a German or western Allied Army Group, but generally smaller

GA   Guards Army (Russian)

GCC   Guards Cavalry Corps (Russian)

Gd   (*or* Gds)   Guards: Russian honorific for a unit or formation which had performed well in combat and was honoured for so doing.

GKMG   *Gvardeyskaya Konno-Mekhanizirovannaya Gruppa* – Guards Cavalry-Mechanized Group (Russian)

GMBr   Guards Mechanized Brigade (Russian)

GMC   Guards Mechanized Corps (Russian)

GMD   Guards Mechanized Division (Russian)

GRD   Guards Rifle Division (Russian)

GRC   Guards Rifle Corps (Russian)

GTA   Guards Tank Army (Russian)

GTBr   Guards Tank Brigade (Russian)

GTC   Guards Tank Corps (Russian)

Hun   Hungarian

ID   Infantry Division

IR   Infantry Regiment

It   (*or* Ital)   Italian

KMG   *Konno-Mekhanizirovannaya Gruppa* – Cavalry-Mechanized Group (Russian)

Luft   Luftflotte (see next)

Luftflotte   German 'Air Fleet', equivalent to a Soviet Air Army

MD   Mechanized Division

OG   (*or* Op Gp)   Operational Group

Pol   Polish (supported by Moscow, as opposed to the 'London Poles', supported by the UK)

PG   Panzer Group (equivalent to an army) (German)

Pz   Panzer (German for 'mail' – armoured, usually indicated with a 'star' rating – see above)

PzA   Panzer Army (German)

PzC   Panzer Corps (German)

PzD   Panzer Division (German)

PzG   Panzer-Grenadier – mechanized infantry

RC   Rifle Corps

RD   Rifle Division

Recce   Reconnaissance (US 'Recon')

Regt   Regiment

Rom   Romanian

RR   Rifle Regiment

SA   Shock Army (Russian)

SS   *Schutzstaffeln* – Hitler's elite bodyguard, deployed alongside the *Wehrmacht*

TA   Tank Army (Russian)

TBr   Tank Brigade (Russian)

TC   Tank Corps (Russian) (really equivalent to a division, but used for mobile attacks and counterstrokes)

TD   Tank Division (Russian).

UR   *Ukreplënny rayon* – 'fortified region'

Preface and acknowledgements

> If the mind is to emerge unscathed from this relentless
> struggle with the unforeseen, two qualities are indispensable:
> *first, an intellect that, even in the darkest hour, retains some*
> *glimmerings of the inner light that leads to truth; and second,*
> *the courage to follow this faint light wherever it may lead.*
>
> – Clausewitz, *On War*[1]

This book aims to provide, in one volume, a modern history of the
greatest and most hideous land–air conflict in history. A war that
was total, because it was fought by all elements of society. And a war
that was absolute, because both sides aimed 'to exterminate the
opponent, to destroy his political existence',[2] and in so doing perpe-
trated extremes of heinous violence and cruelty, shedding almost all of
the customary restraints that had traditionally applied in wars between
'civilized' nations. That conflict, which ended sixty years before this
book's completion, was a decisive component – arguably the single
most decisive component – of the Second World War. It was on the
eastern front, between 1941 and 1945, that the greater part of the land
and associated air forces of Nazi Germany and its allies were ultimately
destroyed by the Soviet Union in what, from 1944, its people – and
those of the fifteen successor states – called, and still call, the Great
Patriotic War.

That war clearly cannot be treated in isolation, however, from the
wider fabric of the Second World War, or from the long period immediately preceding it – nearly two years, from 23 August 1939 until 22 June
1941 – when Germany and the Soviet Union were effectively allies. Nor
can it be understood without note of the situation in the Far East and
the subsequent Soviet defeat of a million Japanese troops in Manchuria.

Therefore the book is not just about the 1941–5 Great Patriotic War, but is also – and has to be – about the Soviet Union's wider participation in the Second World War. The book tells the military story from both the Soviet and the German side, but in terms of the war's legacy it focuses on the impact on the Soviet Union and Russia. Paradoxically, in the long term, they, the winners, lost, and the losers won.

Ambitious though such a project is, it builds on the work of many others, notably that of my Edinburgh University Ph.D. supervisor, the late John Erickson (1929–2002), whose two magisterial volumes *The Road to Stalingrad* (1975) and *The Road to Berlin* (1983)[3] will remain the definitive work in English and, indeed, probably in any language on the type of war the Soviet Union and Germany waged and how it was won. However, since John completed the second volume, we have seen the reunification of Germany, the collapse of communism in central and eastern Europe, and the break-up of the Soviet Union into fifteen states. A new world order has replaced the bipolar cold war which had resulted, in large measure, from the Soviet Union's victory in 1945. In the last twenty years, therefore, much new material and many sources for historical research have become accessible, not only in Germany and Russia, but also in former Soviet states which are now members of Nato and the European Union. I am particularly grateful to my colleagues in the Baltic States of Estonia, Latvia and Lithuania for their help in researching what was, for many, a horribly painful period in their history.

The sixtieth anniversary of the 1945 Allied victory, in 2005, provoked many new studies, as had the fiftieth. This book's publication has not been timed to mark an arbitrary anniversary, however. It is the inevitable result of a surfeit of new information, which has been building for more than twenty years. There is now enough new material, not just relating to specific issues and events, but across the board, to make a new general history both timely and necessary. We knew, pretty well, how the war on the eastern front was *won*. But now we know infinitely more about how it was *run*. We knew that both sides were sustained by a mixture of draconian repression and naive patriotism, mixed in with a desire to survive, a desire not to let down one's comrades, and a desire to do a good job – and maybe to be seen to do it. But we now know far more about the complexities and contradictions of those mixed emotions and motivations. Above all, the Soviet side was motivated by burning hatred and a desire for revenge, and that shaped the troops' behaviour when they entered Germany.

Because the canvas is so broad, it has not been possible to drill down into every newly accessible archive in more than twenty modern countries whose people and territory were involved in, and fought over during, the greatest war of all – the war on the eastern front. To do so would take many large teams of researchers several lifetimes. Such teams have, however, produced volumes of newly released documents, which are not (yet) available in English, and which I have used extensively as primary sources. We also have, for the first time, a formidable German history, made possible by German reunification, again compiled by a distinguished team of scholars from the Military History Research Institute: *Germany and the Second World War*.[4] Although not an 'official history', its provenance and authoritative tone, again the work of a large team of scholars, make it one, in all but name. From another team of researchers working for Colonel-General Krivosheyev we have, for the first time, fairly authoritative (though not undisputed) figures for Soviet casualties and combat losses, not just for the armed forces (army, navy and air forces) but for the Interior Ministry, border guards and state security troops who played a pivotal role in the Soviet war effort.[5] I have therefore called this a 'modern' history because it would be presumptuous to say it is totally 'new'. I have eschewed operational detail where it is well known and easily accessible in other books in English. I have concentrated on the new evidence and new debates: who was planning to attack whom, and when; how much Stalin knew; what was the critical point of the war; how important was British and American aid; how things could have been done differently; the role of the NKVD. For that reason, the book concentrates on the middle years: 1941–3. Where I have found that previous histories have repeated myths, I have exposed them. But it is also a 'modern' history because it approaches the issues from the viewpoint of twenty-first-century security concerns. The Great Patriotic War tells us a great deal about inter-agency cooperation in guaranteeing security, homeland security and resilience, and the fine balance to be struck between national security and the human security of the state's inhabitants. And the reader may find more here on the environment, and the role of women.

The war on the eastern front continues to excite enormous interest. Anthony Beevor's *Stalingrad* and *Downfall*[6] and Max Hastings' *Armaged-*

don[7] are new studies of specific campaigns – the latter two dealing with the final defeat of Nazi Germany and the Battle of Berlin. Most histories of the Great Patriotic War until now have concentrated on the military operations and the role of the German and Soviet armed forces in them. The charismatic leading players, with their fascinating similarities and contradictions – notably Hitler, Stalin and Churchill – naturally also attract attention. However, such an approach has its limitations. Focusing on the Red Army, for example, excludes even more of the picture than would an account of the German side from the point of view of the *Wehrmacht* while ignoring the SS. Although scholars naturally want to go into the archives themselves, they would be unwise not to make use of the enormous volumes of documents now being published in Russia. In 2002, in the *Biblioglobus* bookshop in Lubyanka Square, I purchased the first volumes of *Organs of State Security in the Great Patriotic War*, published in 1995 and edited, again, by a large and expert team headed by Lieutenant-General Stepashin.[8] The release of these documents would have been unthinkable in the Soviet period. Probably the most striking revelation was how important and involved the People's Commissariat for Internal Affairs (NKVD) and People's Commissariat for State Security (NKGB) were in every aspect of operations. I was particularly struck by how much intelligence of a purely professional military nature came from these organizations, rather than the Main Intelligence Directorate of the Red Army General Staff. The role of the People's Commissariats for Internal Affairs (*Narodny Kommisariat Vnutrennykh Del*) – NKVD, and for State Security (*Narodny Kommisariat Gosudarstvennoy Bezobasnosti*) – NKGB, and the use of penal battalions (*shtrafbats*), plus information on the Soviet citizens who, for whatever reason, fought 'under enemy banners'[9] – are all crucial areas which were completely inaccessible to foreign scholars, and indeed to most Soviet scholars (and certainly those publishing openly) during the Soviet era.

Other extremely valuable collections include two volumes of documents relating to the Battle of Moscow,[10] once again edited by a large team headed by General V. A. Zhilin, which include the daily Soviet General Staff summaries, daily German reports, and captured German documents. Similarly, the two volumes of *The Unknown Siege*[11] deal with the Siege of Leningrad. Olma Press, Moscow, has done us a superb service by also releasing, in 2002, the complete, unexpurgated memoirs of Zhukov (two volumes)[12] and Rokossovskiy (one volume).[13] The latter is particularly useful, and the parts of the manuscript in his family's possession deleted by the Soviet censor are helpfully highlighted in italic. It is easy to see why some of those parts, containing frank and trenchant criticism of Zhukov and the Stavka were cut out.

As the portcullis appears to have come down on further Russian archival revelations, at least temporarily, new, Russian, secondary sources of outstanding quality have continued to appear. Pre-eminent among these are Viktor Cherepanov's 2006 *Power and War*, a study of Stalin's State control mechanism,[14] and the outstanding new 2005 atlas of the *Great Patriotic War* edited by Lt Gen Maksimov, with Army General Lobov and Major-General Zolotarëv as consultants, with the resources of the Military-Cartographic Department of the Russian Federation Armed Forces' General Staff, and computer-generated graphics.[15] The best collection of pictures and accounts from the 1945 victory parade – *Parad Pobedy* – so far was published in 2005, complete with DVD.[16]

A work on this broad canvas can only be accomplished by using the work of other scholars in the field who have drilled deep. Pre-eminent among the new studies are, firstly, Catherine Merridale's superb *Ivan's War*,[17] which is the result of more than three years' work including interviews with some 200 Soviet war veterans. Recognizing that it was on the eastern front that the war was really won, and that the crucial evidence for what made the Red Army fight was in danger of disappearing, Professor Merridale has looked widely and deeply at the social history of the Red Army at war. The book is just in time to capture the oral testimony of men and women who fought in it but, sadly, may soon pass on. The other best recent works using archival sources are those of Konstantin Pleshakov, on the critical days leading up to the war and the frontier battles,[18] Gabriel Gorodetsky, on Stalin's diplomacy and what he knew[19] and Simon Sebag Montefiore's graphic account of Stalin's regime.[20] Norman Davies's *Rising '44* is a magisterial and scholarly treatment of the 1944 Warsaw rising.[21]

On more specific issues, Lennart Samuelson's *Plans for Stalin's War Machine*,[22] Edwin Bacon's *The GULag at War*[23] and Reina Pennington's work on women in the Soviet war effort[24] are examples of outstanding research into key, previously unexplored areas. Michael Ellman's work on the other casualties – the civilian victims of Stalin's repression[25] – and Mark Harrison's on the Soviet war economy[26] have also illuminated key areas.

I have used these works, but have not attempted to duplicate any of them. This study examines the operational, military-strategic, politico-strategic (within the Soviet Union) and grand-strategic (coalition) aspects of the war. I have focussed on the major debates and controversies in the light of the latest evidence, and have dismantled a few myths. By way of subplots, there are two senior individuals who appear in all the right places throughout the story, and who have left frank memoirs. One is a soldier. The other is a diplomat.

This book began life a decade ago when Michael Sissons, my agent, asked how I felt about writing 'a new history of the Great Patriotic War'. In the decade that followed life took unexpected and sometimes unwelcome turns, but Michael kept me on course. Like a consummate supervisor Michael stayed 'hands-off', with the occasional brief and pithy note. Thank you, Michael, and thank you Pan Macmillan, London and Knopf, New York, particularly Georgina Morley at the former and Ash Green at the latter. Ash suggested that if the project was to be manageable I should resist the temptation to revisit the military-doctrinal debates of the 1920s and 30s and start with the Nazi-Soviet Pact, which coincided pretty well with the start of the Second World War. That was absolutely right. George has been a terrific editor, and wondrously patient. I should also like to thank Georgina Difford, Editorial Manager, Rachel Wright, who has been a meticulous copy editor, and Martin Lubikowski, the cartographer.

In fashioning the book in its final form, I was above all assisted by Dr Sergey Kudryashëv in Moscow. Editor of *Istochnik* and a friend of John and Ljubica Erickson, he researched *The Eastern Front in Photographs* for them. Sergey helped me with access to Russian archives and also with more hitherto unpublished photographs for this book, including some remarkable documents. Kristine Doronenkova from the Latvian Defence Ministry helped with the latest information on the Nazi–Soviet treaties and the secret protocols which consigned the Baltic States, much of Poland and Bessarabia to the Soviet Union, and Dr Janina Sleivete in Lithuania and Tatiana Anton in Moldova also provided indispensable material on the true story of the states annexed by the Soviet Union in 1940. In the UK, Dr Anna Maria Brudenell helped with research at the National Archives, and Imperial War Museum, and with more photographs, including the German archives at Koblenz.

However, the foundation for the book was laid twenty years before Michael's suggestion. My fascination with Russia's mighty and extraordinarily resilient land, culture and people was fired in 1976, by a young lecturer called Chris Donnelly, addressing a tired and depressed bunch of 'student officers', one winter afternoon at the Royal Military Academy, Sandhurst. The great rivers in Siberia, flowing into the Arctic, are more than thirty miles wide, Chris commented. 'Anybody here in the Artillery? You haven't got a gun that can fire that far.' Point taken. Although we can now see that our perception of the former Soviet 'threat' was grossly exaggerated, it was powerful stuff. I was hooked.

A decade later, in October 1987, I boarded a train at King's Cross, and headed north into the unknown to begin my doctorate at Edinburgh University under John Erickson's supervision. John, also a consummate supervisor, unwilling to intrude in my research, became my mentor and friend. My thanks to John and his widow, Ljubica, for their friendship and help, and to Kathie Brown, John's Steph (see below). And also to Dr Carl Van Dyke, a fellow research student at Edinburgh, whose groundbreaking work on the 1939–40 Soviet–Finnish war and subsequent reforms has been crucial to this book. Carl explained, I think, why the Red Army's performance improved so dramatically three years later.[27]

Charles Dick, who took over from Chris Donnelly as head of the Soviet (later Conflict) Studies Research Centre, also helped, with his encyclopaedic and profound knowledge of the Great Patriotic War, and of the Russian approach to war more generally. His detailed research is reflected in this book. In the same area, I owe a special debt to Colonel David Glantz, editor of the *Journal of Slavic* (formerly *Soviet), Military Studies*, another leading world scholar of Soviet and German military operations. David's work on the subject is voluminous, and has proved an essential corrective to much Soviet writing that was, to say the least, economical with the truth.

Special thanks go to Sir Rodric Braithwaite, formerly Her Majesty's ambassador to Moscow from 1988–92, and then a chairman of the Joint Intelligence Committee. Rodric, who was authoring his book on Moscow in the war, pointed out that huge numbers of archival documents were being published, and wisely counselled me to hit Moscow's bookshops, an insight that paid dividends. He also alerted me to new research on the Soviet punishment battalions – *shtrafbats*.[28]

Heather Taylor introduced me to Sir Rodric and also to her contacts in Kursk, which became the focus of six field trips to Russia with those of my Cranfield students brave enough to undertake the Russian elective on the Global Security M.Sc., covering St Petersburg, Kursk, Moscow, and Volgograd (formerly Stalingrad).

I am particularly indebted to all those who took that Russian elective, who made me realize what I did not know, and challenged everything. Tom Hamilton-Baillie, Rupert Thorneloe and Mark Wilkinson, in particular, thank you. I will never forget the night we sat on the banks of the Volga at Volgograd, staring across the kilometre-wide river towards Asia, drinking beer and eating ice cream in the snow. As Churchill said of the Russians, a people who eat ice cream in the middle of their winter will never be beaten. And I especially remember the wisdom of a Czech student, Colonel Miroslav Kvasnak. Astonished by the Russians' continuing obsession with their past, and with the suicidally costly victory in the Great Patriotic War, he said: 'It's like driving a car, where the rear-view mirror blots out the windscreen.' How absolutely true. In a moment of icy clarity, he – and I – saw that before Russia can really move on, it must first address and lay to rest the mysteries and uncertainties of its Stalinist past. To all my Global Security students: thank you.

I am also indebted to Philip Blood, whose Cranfield University Ph.D. I examined in 2003. He provided valuable new information and a real contribution to knowledge on *Bandenbekämpfung* – the German anti-partisan campaign, which, he discovered, was coordinated across Europe, although his study was primarily concerned with the war in the East.[29]

Colonel Christopher Langton, formerly Military Attaché in Moscow, helped with advice on Soviet Russia's internal struggle on the home front, particularly the role of the NKVD, which constitutes one of the hitherto neglected areas on which I have chosen to focus. I am greatly indebted to Steven Walsh, who signed up with me as a Ph.D. candidate, and whose work on Rokossovskiy, which I fully acknowledge, also provided new insights. John Hughes-Wilson helped with intelligence questions, particularly on the Battle of Kursk.

Of my own teachers, I thank, in particular, all those at the Polytechnic of Central London, now the University of Westminster, where I took my Russian degree, part-time, from 1981–7. Among them was Boris Bondarenko. Boris Bondarenko nearly became one of the 'victims of Yalta' – those captured by the Germans who, at the end of the war, were sent back to the GULag and death. Boris, I understand, jumped the train on the advice of a British officer, and became a brilliant teacher of Russian, first to British soldiers, and then at the 'Poly'.

Peter Caddick-Adams, another of my Ph.D. students, colleague and friend, provided many gems. It was his idea to pay a visit to the Directorate of Military Survey which, he had heard, was having a clear-out of old maps. Among the many treasures saved from the fire that day was the marked-up Red Army map of Stalingrad from the beginning of October 1942, reproduced in this book as Plate 30. Peter also stumbled across a slim volume containing Finogenov's superb pencil sketches from Stalingrad, some of which are reproduced in this book, in a second-hand bookshop.[30] I believe the Internet still has a long way to go before it can substitute for second-hand bookshops.

At Shrivenham, I am very grateful to the staff of the Joint Services Command and Staff College Library for their help. My other Cranfield friends and colleagues, Bella Platt, Steph Muir, Tom Maley and Professor Richard Holmes, enabled me to survive to write the book. Bella Platt mastered the FTP photographs and dealt with sources which were mine only for a short time. Steph not only handled the administration of the Global Security M.Sc., which grew from thirteen students in 1999 to thirty-three by the time this book was near to completion, but, it is fair to say, ran my professional life. Without her, I would not have been able to generate the time to complete the book. Tom helped by acquiring relevant books in this area as they rolled off the presses – and there were many. And thanks to Richard – for his constant grace, humanity, friend-ship and advice, particularly on the pitfalls, pluses and minuses of archival sources, but for much else besides. Richard helped me balance the moral, physical and conceptual components of this great and impassioned drama. Whether I have got the balance right, the reader will judge.

Producing a book like this is a major logistic challenge and I also thank Scott Brown, Jackie Rhodes and Liam Wellsteed of our IT Department at Cranfield for setting the FTP address to receive high-resolution scans from Sergey, installing WinRAR and other software, replacing the prehistoric 3-gig hard disk on my own computer with a 20-gig warp-drive, and much else. Without you, guys, this would not have happened. Thank you.

Finally, my wife, Heather, knows how much responsibility she bears for seeing this book to completion. For some of the time she was away working for Save the Children, seconded to the UNHCR in Chad, on the south side of the Sahara desert, as a child protection officer. I had not quite finished the book when she got home to a house in which Sergeant Pavlov would have felt at home, but she immediately turned her superb administrative and logistic skills to getting the full and final version done. Here's to you, honey, and to all your colleagues, building peace where there was once war. And finally, any mistakes are my responsibility alone.

Transliteration, and names of people and places

The system used for rendering names and occasional Russian terms from the Russian (Cyrillic) to the western alphabet is the Nato one, which is also the system used by the US Board on Geographical Names. However, where the Russian ending –ЫЙ would give the ungainly –yy, I have simplified it to –y, although I have stuck to the Nato system for –ИЙ, which gives –iy, as in Rokossovskiy. Also, where a commonly used English version of a name is familiar, I have gone with that: so Beria, rather than Beriya; Koniev rather than Konev or Konyev.

Place names are challenging, too. The frontier changes of twentieth-century history, ending with the break-up of the Soviet Union into fifteen independent states at the end of 1991 – all with their own languages – has left a legacy of perhaps four names in certain places. Thus, the German Lemberg became Polish Lwów, Russian L'vov, and now Ukrainian Lviv. The Russian name Kiev is now Ukrainian Kyiv. Kishinëv is now Moldovan Chisinau. And some names have changed completely (again). Leningrad was formerly, and is again, St Petersburg. Kalinin was formerly, and is again, Tver'. Stalingrad was formerly Tsaritsyn, and is now Volgograd. Kuybyshev, the reserve capital, to which Government and foreign delegations were evacuated as Moscow was threatened, was formerly and is again Samara. On first mention I give all the names most likely to be encountered in various sources, and thereafter the name in use at the time.

Military units and formations

In accordance with widely accepted, though by no means universal, practice, smaller units and formations are indicated by numerals: 150th

Division. Corps are indicated by Roman numerals: VIII Mechanized Corps. Armies and their equivalents (German Panzer Groups, for example), and fronts (Russian) or army groups (German) are written in full: Eighth Army, First Belorussian Front, Army Group Centre. When referred to collectively or in general terms, divisions, corps and armies are not capitalized. When an individual formation is referred to it is treated as a proper name: Eighth Army.

1

FLIGHT OF THE RABID WOLF: THE LONG-TERM IMPACT OF THE WAR IN THE EAST

By the late 1960s a new wave of the rabies virus had sped westward through Europe's wild mammal population and reached the English Channel. Rabies is endemic in many parts of the world. A bite with infected saliva transmits the virus – which can kill horribly – to domestic animals, or to humans. The United Kingdom authorities feared the disease might leap the natural defensive barrier of the Channel and reappear in the UK, which had long been rabies-free because of strict quarantine regulations. Scientists agreed that the virus, transmitted in the wild mainly by wolves and foxes, had been spreading westwards through Europe since the end of the Second World War in 1945. In 1967, there were 2,775 reported cases in West Germany, and the first 199 cases in Switzerland. In 1968 it reached France, with 60 cases reported.[1] It was clear that the epizootic – the animal equivalent of a human epidemic – had headed remorselessly westward, rather than east, north or south, since the war. Why?

It started when rabies-crazed wolves and foxes had fled the fighting on the Second World War's eastern front, as the Germans were pushed westward by the advancing Red Army from 1943 to 1945.[2] The 'Iron Curtain' between East and West established after the war is known to have been an effective barrier to animals, as well as to people.[3] The maddened creatures carrying rabies had clearly moved west before the Iron Curtain descended at the end of the war, and, understandably, kept going. And now, a quarter of a century later, the environmental effects of that war were lapping at the Channel and threatening the UK.

If the fighting on the eastern front had that effect on mad wolves and foxes, and on the natural environment, what effect must it have had on the millions of people from the sophisticated, educated and civilized nations of central and eastern Europe? A war 'hideous beyond imagining', not only unprecedented in its scale and violence, but 'befouled by and drenched in criminality'?[4]

In the late 1960s, the rabies scare was not the greatest concern for western European and UK security, however. The biggest threat – and it was very real then – was that of global thermonuclear war. Whoever might have started such a conflict, the missiles falling on western Europe, the UK and the US would probably have come from the Soviet Union. And the Soviet Union had become a world nuclear-missile-armed power as a direct result of the war in the East.

This book is the story of that war. The greatest, most costly and most brutal war on land in human history. It was fought between the Soviet Union and Nazi Germany for 1,418 days, from 22 June 1941 to 9 May 1945, on a front from the Arctic Circle to the Caucasus, from the Barents Sea to the Black Sea, up to 3,200 kilometres long. Three months to the day after it ended, as promised, on 8–9 August 1945, the Soviet Union attacked a million-strong Japanese army in Manchuria and made it surrender in eight days, although fighting continued in Manchuria and the Kurile islands until 1 September.[5]

Soviet casualties in that 1941–5 period are now estimated at 27 million direct deaths, military and civilian. That is nearly half the total losses resulting from the Second World War. But the 'global loss' to the Soviet population – the difference between the population after the war and the population as it should have been, had the war not taken place, may be 48 to 49 million. Germany probably lost 4.3 million military dead as a direct result of the battles in the East.[6] And these figures do not include the invisible legacy of wars, which we are only now coming to recognize: the psychological casualties, and the victims afflicted by nervous disorders and post-traumatic stress, and the consolations those people seek.

Another gruesome by-product of the war in the East was an intensification of Nazi persecution of the Jews and the 'final solution', which only reached its final, obscene dimensions after 1941. The Holocaust had begun before this – alert British newspapers were reporting deportation of German Jews in the 1930s, although many Jews were able to emigrate. However, the German Barbarossa offensive through central and eastern Europe brought millions more Jews under

German control. Hitler had identified the Bolsheviks, who ruled the Soviet Union, with the Jews, even though the Soviet government's attitude to its own Jewish population showed it to be unashamedly anti-Semitic. But now Hitler's delusions were compounded by a perverted and superstitious logic. With so many Aryans being killed on the eastern front, extermination of the Jews and other 'undesirables' had to be stepped up to balance the books. The Red Army and the NKVD were not squeamish, but when they liberated Auschwitz in January 1945, even they were flabbergasted.[7]

From 1944 the Soviet Union called its victorious war against Nazi Germany from 1941 to 1945 the 'Great Patriotic War', an exponentially greater sequel to the 'Patriotic War' of 1812 against Napoleon (although the latter term was used until then). Many comparisons have been and can be made between the two wars, with Russia, itself autocratic and authoritarian, fighting two of the most flamboyant dictators in history – Napoleon, then Hitler. However repressive the indigenous regime, whether under the Tsar or the red star, the majority of the people (though far from all) rallied to it, preferring home-grown despotism to anything imposed from abroad. (There is a lesson here for those who like exporting their idea of democracy today.) Both conflicts saw 'war to the knife', as well as the biggest conventional battles of the age. The Russians scorched the earth as they withdrew, buying victory at terrible cost. And then came revenge, culminating in occupation of the enemy capital. After the defeat of Nazi Germany, at the Potsdam conference in July 1945, Averill Harriman, the US Ambassador to Moscow, congratulated Josef Stalin on the achievement of his forces in reaching the Nazi capital, Berlin. 'Alexander I got to Paris,' replied Stalin, laconically – a reference to the occupation of Paris by Russian troops in 1815.[8]

Napoleon's ill-advised invasion of Russia in 1812 was only one of a number of campaigns which sealed his fate in a coalition world war. The Soviet Union's role in the Second World War, likewise, was only one part of the complex jigsaw of victory.

The Second World War was not a single conflict, but formed from a number of quite separate wars which fused as the world's leading military and economic powers were drawn in. The first war, which began with Germany's invasion of Poland (with Soviet approval) on 1 September 1939, was an old-fashioned 'cabinet war' for the European balance of power. The second war involved Germany's ally, Italy, and was about Italian attempts to establish dominion in the Mediterranean and north Africa. The 1939–40 Soviet–Finnish war and the occupation of the Baltic States and Bessarabia in 1940 were also relatively conventional affairs, their purpose being to secure Leningrad, the Soviet Union's second city, and other parts of the Soviet Union's western frontier. The Soviet Union's tightening grip on eastern Europe precipitated the third major war, the greatest and bloodiest, and the subject of this book. Hitler needed the natural resources, manpower and living space of the Soviet Union to secure Germany's position as a world power. But Nazism had also grown as a response to the perceived threat from communism, and that conflict, too, was played out in this vast theatre. It was the collision of two dictatorships in a land that had spread in a vast plain across half the world, which the geopoliticians believed to be the Eurasian 'heartland'. The fourth great war, between Japan and the other imperial powers, had its origins in Japan's invasion of China in 1937, but became part of the world war on 7 December 1941.[9] Reluctant though the isolationist United States had been to become engaged in the entangling alliances, within four years it emerged from the war as one of two world military, scientific and economic 'superpowers'. The other one was the Soviet Union.

Without British and US dominance at sea, the strategic air campaign and the war in the Pacific, it is very possible that the Soviet Union would have been defeated in 1942 or that, at the very least, the war in the East would have gone on much longer.[10] Nevertheless, during the critical period of late 1941 and all of 1942, American power was only starting to be engaged and the Allied strategic bombing offensive against Germany was just beginning to get under way, as the latter's greatest exponent, Air Chief Marshal Sir Arthur 'Bomber' Harris, confirmed.[11] Of all the interwoven strands, the war on the eastern front was probably the crucial military, economic and political struggle of the Second World War. It certainly was between mid 1941 and mid-to-late 1943, as the war's outcome hung in the balance.[12] After that, the western Allies were ashore in mainland Europe following the invasion of Sicily, which coincided with the last major German offensive in the East at Kursk, and the Japanese were being pushed back in the Pacific. The failure of Barbarossa, which became apparent during 1942, created the conditions for the initiative to pass to the Allies at the end of 1942.[13] For that reason, this book pays particular attention to that period and especially to 1942.

It was not for nothing that, as early as January 1943, with uncanny prescience, the American *Time* magazine named Josef Stalin as its 'man of the year' for 1942 (see Plate 4).[14] With hindsight, the Soviet dictator seems a bizarre choice for Americans to have made. But it underlines the scale of the Soviet achievement in that precarious year.

Winston Churchill, the British war leader, who hated communism and was no lover of the Russians, similarly acknowledged their pivotal role in the war. In a speech to the UK Parliament in 1944 his analysis was razor sharp:

> The advance of their Armies from Stalingrad to the Dniester
> river, with vanguards reaching out towards the Pruth, a
> distance of 900 miles [1,440 km], accomplished in a single
> year, constitutes the greatest cause of Hitler's undoing. Since
> I spoke to you last not only have the Hun invaders been
> driven from the lands they had ravaged, *but the guts of the
> German army have been largely torn out by Russian valour and
> generalship.* The people of all the Russias have been fortunate
> in finding in their supreme ordeal of agony a warrior leader,
> Marshal Stalin, whose *authority enabled him to combine and
> control the movements of armies numbered by many millions
> upon a front of nearly 2,000 miles.*[15]

In one sentence of his address Churchill had encapsulated the scale and significance of the Soviet effort, and in one word, 'generalship', the Soviet mastery of the higher conduct of war, at the operational and strategic levels. In the second sentence he alluded to the unwholesome but undeniable fact that only the authority wielded by the Soviet dictator and his security apparatus could coordinate a war effort on this scale in such a country.

But not only was the Great Patriotic War (with the Manchurian campaign as its ultimate postscript) the greatest land conflict, with a significant air component, in the history of the world – a conflict which sealed the destruction of Nazi Germany. It also fixed the course of the next half-century of world history – the bipolar world order which dominated international relations until the 1990s. In 1942, the British government had been planning for action 'in the event of a Russian collapse'.[16] By April 1944 the Foreign Office assessed, rightly, that the Soviet Union would emerge from the war 'as the strongest land power in the world and one of the three strongest air powers'. But, even more importantly, it would be 'the very successful exponent of a new economic and political system and a new type of multi-national state'. Finally, it would be the great Slav power, as in the past, and the heir to much of the greatness and heritage of the old Russia. 'She will have very great prestige and very great pride in herself.'[17] The war therefore stamped greatness on the Soviet Union. Its legacy is still imprinted on the United Nations, on other international cooperative security arrangements such as Nato, the Organization for Security and Cooperation in Europe, and other alliances, treaties, disarmament processes and ways of doing business. Russia's position as one of the five permanent members of the UN Security Council, and its great military and diplomatic power status in the world today, though diminished compared with that of the Soviet Union, is undeniably a result of its victory in the Great Patriotic War. Before that, it was very much a pariah in the international community, viewed rather like a 'rogue state' today.

The war therefore defined the Soviet Union, and modern Russia. Although the USSR had been conceived in the November 1917 Bolshevik revolution, it did not fully coalesce until 1924. As a fully united political entity, it was therefore only seventeen years old when the Great Patriotic War started. Even more than the forced industrialization and collectivization of the 1920s and 1930s, the great purge from 1937, the cold war and the space race, that most terrible of wars was the defining four years of Russian and Soviet history. Like the American Civil War, which fused the USA from a collection of individual states into a single nation, the Great Patriotic War made the Soviet Union a space-bound superpower.

However, the effort expended during those four years and the succeeding struggle against the West – which followed without any respite – ultimately broke the Soviet Union. It was an environmental and demographic catastrophe. Modern Russia, the successor state, one of fifteen nations created by the break-up of the USSR at the end of 1991, was a long-term casualty of the Great Patriotic War. Most of the significant battles of the Great Patriotic War, apart from Moscow, Stalingrad, Kursk and the siege of Leningrad, took place outside Russia – in Ukraine, in Belarus, and in countries that are now part of Nato – in the Baltic States, in Poland, in reunited Germany. The war was fought *out of Russia*, but much of it on *non-Russian* territory. Ultimately, that may have helped fuse Russian identity, at the expense of *Soviet* identity and unity, leading to the break-up of what is now called *former Soviet space*.[18]

During the Soviet period, the Soviet history of the Great Patriotic

War, while presenting a formidable veneer of scientific objectivity, was full of deep and dark holes and omissions. Since the break-up of the Soviet Union at the end of 1991, the reassertion of national identity by former Soviet republics (especially the Baltic States), the reunification of Germany, and the opening of the Soviet archives to western scholars, it has become possible to rewrite the history. Much was concealed – notably the stupendous Soviet casualties. Those losses, which the Soviet leader Nikita Khrushchev modestly put at 'in excess of 20 million' in the 1960s,[19] are now estimated at 26 to 27 million, including civilians, of whom 8,668,400 have been confirmed as 'irrecoverable losses' among the armed services (army, air force, navy, border guards and Interior Ministry). The latter figure, revealed in a groundbreaking study published in 1993, includes dead on the battlefield, missing in action and prisoners who did not return.[20] David Glantz successfully identified a great battle – the Soviet Operation Mars – that took place at the same time as Stalingrad and was comparable to it in size, but was simply written out of the Soviet histories, because they lost.[21]

Soviet military and economic cooperation with Germany during the 1920s and 1930s, and especially during the period of the non-aggression pact from 23 August 1939 to 22 June 1941 – equating to one-third of the entire Second World War – has been neglected in Russian sources, as has the partial, though decisive, impact of western Allied aid and lease-lend. Also neglected has been the role of the Interior Ministry forces – the *Narodny Kommissariat Vnutrennykh Del* (People's Commissariat for Internal Affairs – NKVD), border guards and other 'organs of state security', and the strength of resistance to Soviet rule. Nor was that resistance confined to the non-Russian republics, notably Ukraine and the Baltic States. It also posed a real threat to the government in Russia itself. Many people fled to the woods rather than wait for a visit from the NKVD and, as the research will show, the Soviet government's fears about being overthrown from within as it reeled under the impact of unprecedented attack from without were well founded. Its security measures were far from unjustified, or merely paranoid. If Russia wishes to move on, and confront future challenges safely, it must first confront and unravel its Stalinist past.

Of all these issues, perhaps the most critical today is the demographic impact of the Great Patriotic War on the Soviet Union and modern Russia. The facts are uncertain and highly contentious, not least because we have no firm figure for the number of people who were in the Soviet Union when the Great Patriotic War started in 1941. That is, in part, because of the huge loss of life – conservatively estimated at 7 million – in the Ukrainian famine of 1932–3, and the results of Stalinist repression, climaxing in the purges from 1937. In 1914 the Russian Empire probably had 150 million people and was believed to have 'inexhaustible manpower', compared with European adversaries. Four Soviet censuses were taken in the interwar period: 1920, 1926, 1937 and 1939. The population reported in 1926, by which time some stability had returned to the war-ravaged country, was 148.8 million. The demographers estimate the average annual increase at 2.3 per cent. At the most conservative estimate, adding 2.3 per cent per year, rather than compounding the percentage, the population in 1937 should have been 186.4 million. Compounding the percentage would make it 191 million. In fact, the 1937 census population was only 156 million – 30.4 million short of the lower figure, representing a population increase in eleven years of just over 7 million. It is well-nigh impossible to say how many of those dead or non-existent souls should be attributed to deaths in prisons and camps and how many to the famine.[22]

Stalin did the obvious thing, and on 26 September 1937 *Pravda*, the offical Soviet newspaper, denounced the results as 'extremely crude violations of the elementary principles of statistical science'.[23] In other words, they had produced the wrong answer. Stalin ordered a new census to be conducted, in early 1939.

The 1939 census, conducted by nervous officials, produced a more acceptable result of 167 million, although the Soviet authorities then added another 3 million to reach 170 million, the most widely accepted estimate for the Soviet population at the start of the Second World War.[24] Although less than it should have been, from the war-fighting point of view the figure still compared favourably with 80 million people in pre-war Germany, 130 million Americans and 46 million in the United Kingdom. The spoils of the Molotov–Ribbentrop Pact – the occupation of 'western Ukraine' and 'western Belarus' in September 1939 and the formal incorporation of Moldova, Estonia, Latvia and Lithuania in 1940 – probably increased to more than 190 million the population the Soviet government could claim to govern. By the start of the Great Patriotic War, on 22 June 1941, it seems fair to estimate the population in the territory between central Europe and the Pacific Ocean nominally controlled by the Soviet government at 196 to 197 million, although many of those would not have recognized Soviet rule, and some areas, particularly in the Baltics, were already restive. The German estimate, which must have included the population of the annexed territories, was 180 million.[25]

The figure of 196.7 million, based on 'adjusted 1939 census data', is the basis for the claim that there were 26 to 27 million 'excess deaths' during the war. That is not the same as deaths directly attributable to the war, as, by definition, it includes victims of internal repression.[26] Speaking on the occasion of the forty-fifth anniversary of victory, in 1990, President Gorbachëv gave a figure of 26.6 million, although an article in *Vestnik statistiki (Statistical Journal)* a few months later, explaining how the figures were arrived at, said it would be more accurate to say between 26 and 27 million.[27] If the 196.7 million is an overestimate of the June 1941 population (as it could well be), then Soviet war losses could be fewer. Conversely, and this is the main area of doubt, the number of people in the territories annexed in 1939–40, which remained part of the USSR after the war, could have been greater, in which case 'Soviet' war deaths would also have been more numerous. This assessment of 'excess deaths' during the war does not take account of losses among people whose territories were included in the Soviet Union after 1945. These totalled nearly 1.9 million, mostly Finns in annexed Karelia, Germans from Königsberg, which became Kaliningrad, and Japanese from south Sakhalin.[28]

Establishing Soviet military losses is a little easier, though still an uncertain and disputed science. In *Grif sekretnosti snyat (The 'Secret' Stamp is Lifted)*, Colonel-General Krivosheyev's team produced a credible and broadly accurate analysis.[29] The figures are awesome. The total mobilized man- and woman-power during the war was 34,476,000, including the 4,826,907 men under arms – whether in the army, navy, air force, NKVD or border guards – in June 1941. During the war another 29,574,900 men and women were mobilized. Of those, there was a 'turnover' of 21,700,000. More than half were 'irrecoverable losses', although there are three sets of figures for those. The first set, 11,444,100, is the number who became *hors de combat*, for whatever reason, during the conflict. That is, killed in action; died of wounds, illness or frostbite; shot by their own side for cowardice or other crimes; taken prisoner by the Germans; or just disappeared. The second, 8,668,400, is the final demographic loss – the dead on the battlefield or in German captivity. But nearly 3 million who had been written off as part of the first figure came back, though not necessarily to a hero's welcome. These included soldiers in encircled formations who then reappeared, often to face interrogation and the GULag, and 1,836,000 prisoners released from German prisoner-of-war and concentration camps, who were thrown back into the fighting. The third figure, 12,400,900, I shall call the 'bean counters' figure. People were often posted missing with more than one organization. Given our modern experience of computers, the fact that only an extra million combatants were added to the record because of double counting must count as a triumph for Soviet efficiency.[30]

The other 10 million 'irrecoverable losses' cover 3.8 million wounded, sick or medically discharged. However, the figure also includes 3.5 million redeployed to factories or to local air defence units, and nearly 1.5 million transferred to other security organizations. In terms of the war effort that means more than 6 million who should therefore, perhaps, not be considered 'irrecoverable', reducing the overall figure to 15,500,000.[31]

The numbers so far relate to the Great Patriotic War against the Germans and their allies in the West. The seasoned Red Army's lightning campaign against the Japanese, which began three months after victory in Europe, cost 12,031, of whom 9,780 were killed in action or died of wounds, 911 went missing and 1,340 died outside combat, whether from disease, accident, suicide or disciplinary action.[32]

The figures revealed by the removal of the 'secret' classification do not include 'militia' units (*narodnoye opolcheniye*), hastily raised and thrown into action with minimal training. There were 4 million militia, although 2 million were incorporated into the Red Army and should, therefore, be included in the above figures. Deaths among the other 2 million come out of the overall 26 to 27 million; likewise railway workers, who played a critical role in getting most of the troops – and their supplies – to the front, firefighters, merchant seamen and fishermen.

Most extraordinarily, perhaps, Krivosheyev's study does not identify how many of those army, navy, air force, border guard and Interior Ministry fighters were women. Estimates of the number of women in front-line fighting jobs during the war vary from 490,235 to 800,000. They include snipers, tank commanders, aircrew – including the famous 'night witches' night-bomber squadrons – military police, signallers, interpreters, doctors and nurses. As far as the Soviet authorities were concerned at the time, they were combatants, just like the men with whom they lived, fought, won medals, often died, and were buried, as can be seen from the feminine endings to the names on the blue concrete crosses topped by red stars in Soviet war cemeteries from Moscow to Berlin. The Soviet use of the other (arguably sometimes deadlier) half of the population for the war effort attracted huge western interest at the time. It gets appropriate attention in this book.[33]

Out of the 197 million people in the USSR in 1941, between 40 and 42 million were Ukrainians. Ukraine is now an independent country, one of the fifteen post-Soviet states. After the so-called 'Orange Revolution' in 2004–5, its independence and western European orientation seem assured. During the Great Patriotic War, torn between Soviet rule and invasion by Nazi Germany, Ukraine probably suffered more than any other part of the Soviet Union or post-Soviet state. The famous American journalist Edgar Snow, who visited Ukraine in 1943 and again in 1945, cited a senior Ukraine official as saying that 10 million people – a quarter of the total population – were lost in the war, and that figure excluded those men and women mobilized into Soviet or German armed forces.[34] Others put the loss as high as 11 million, even 13.6 million.[35]

In the wake of a war, nature usually has a way of compensating. As Napoleon said, chillingly, after the terrible Battle of Borodino against the Russians in 1812, 'one Paris night will replace them'. Social conventions are discarded, new opportunities arise, and men and women long separated make up for lost time. In the West, there was an indisputable 'baby boom'. However, in the Soviet Union and its successor states the loss appears to have been too great to compensate.

If the population really was 197 million in June 1941, then by the end of 1950, at Imperial Russian or early Soviet levels of increase, with high infant mortality, the population should still have been 201.5 million at the absolute minimum, or, applying the 2.3 per cent increase cumulatively, a maximum of 247 million. In fact it was 181,760,000, rising to only 208,827,000 by 1959, the next reliable census. Demographers calculate the 'global loss' of population, resulting not only from excess deaths during the war, including the direct war deaths, but also the overall impact on population, resulting from couples who never met and babies not born, to have been in the order of 48 million.[36]

Even in the part of the country – European and Asiatic Russia – not occupied by the Germans, the war economy took everything. The effect of the industrial migration – uprooting whole factories and relocating them in the East – and of an estimated 15 million internally displaced people fleeing eastwards from the German advance, has never been calculated.[37]

Conversely, after the tide turned, the effect on the German population was similarly extreme. Grand-Admiral Dönitz – who succeeded Hitler as Führer for one week – had masterminded the 'sea bridge', the greatest seaborne evacuation in history, moving 2 million people from the Baltic coast as the Soviets closed in, and shipping them west. Only about 1 per cent became casualties, but that included the greatest maritime disaster in history, when the Soviet submarine S13 torpedoed the German liner *Wilhelm Gustloff* off Gdynia on 31 January 1945. More than 6,000 refugees and servicemen and women certainly died in the icy waters of the Baltic – four times as many as on the *Titanic* – but new analysis using computer modelling suggests the number on board may have been over 10,000. This means that, with 996 survivors, there could have been more than 9,000 deaths.[38] For both sides, this was a war of superlatives, and a war of extremes.

The Great Patriotic War unquestionably contributed to the Russian population crisis evident in the early twenty-first century. That can be clearly seen in Figure 1.1, which shows the 'population pyramid' for the Russian Federation in 1990, and in Figure 1.2, which shows that for 2005.

The people aged forty-five to forty-nine in 1990 were born during the Great Patriotic War. There is a clear constriction in the pyramid. Even more remarkable – and telling, however, is the imbalance between men and women born before that. This reflects the huge losses sustained among males in the war. There is a major imbalance between men and women born from 1921 to 1925 – those of age for front-line combat service in the Great Patriotic War – and the imbalance is even greater in the preceding two age groups, those born between 1911 and 1920, although by this time the tendency of women to live longer than men is probably also a major factor.

As one might expect, after the war there is a significant, though not massive, increase in the birth rate. However, if we look at the twenty- to twenty-four-year-old age group, born between 1966 and 1970, we see that the pyramid contracts again. A 'generation' used to be reckoned at about twenty-five years, and fewer parents means fewer children.

If we move forward to 2005, shown in Figure 1.2, we can see that the effect of the Great Patriotic War repeats itself.

The 'pyramid' again contracts around those born in 1941–5, their

1.1 Legacy of the war. Russian population by age, 1990

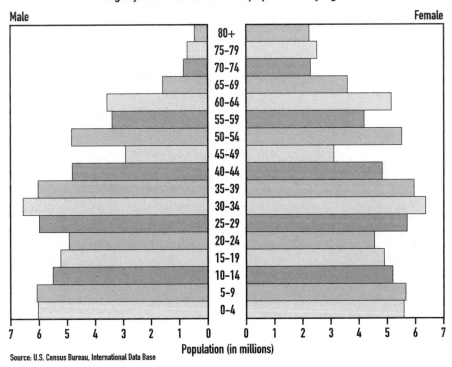

Source: U.S. Census Bureau, International Data Base

children, typically those born in 1966–70, and their children, born in 1996–2000. And, again, the imbalance between men and women born before that is striking, although once more age itself – rather than German and Russian bullets – is now becoming a factor. Although the low birth rates among the latest generation and modern Russia's demographic crisis can be ascribed to many factors, notably Russia's downward-spiralling combination of 'first world birth rates and third world death rates', the recurring demographic impact of the Great Patriotic War is clear to see.[39]

The economic impact of the war also dwarfs the imagination. The most productive part of the country had been occupied by the Germans and, if it had not been laid waste as the Soviet forces withdrew, was laid waste as the Germans withdrew when the Soviets came back. At its furthest extent, the German occupation extended across nearly half of the European territory of the Soviet Union, and about an eighth of the total. The occupied area contained two-fifths of the grain and four-fifths of the sugar beet produced in the USSR, plus about a quarter of the

1.2 Legacy of the war. Russian population by age, 2005

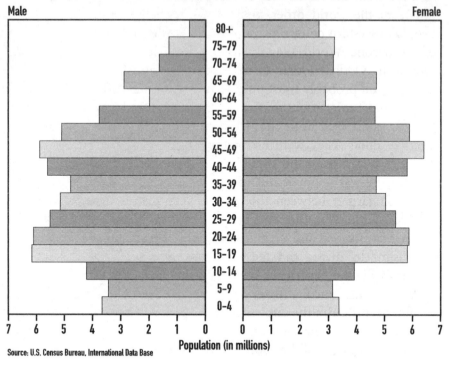

Source: U.S. Census Bureau, International Data Base

nation's farm animals, tractors and combine harvesters. In occupied areas of the Soviet Union the invaders and defenders, between them, destroyed 1,710 towns, 70,000 villages, 32,000 industrial plants and 65,000 kilometres of railway track.[40] In the Russian republic alone 23,000 schools were razed to the ground. Damage to basic industry was particularly severe. Between half and two-thirds of Soviet basic industrial capacity was put out of action. Mines which had produced 100 million tons of coal and 20 million tons of iron ore were wrecked and factories which had produced 19 million tons of steel were totally or partially destroyed. In 1945 total Soviet production, the vast majority of which had to go to the war effort, was 19 million tons.[41]

Sixty years on, the demographic, environmental and political impact of the Second World War has largely been absorbed in the West, and in the Pacific. Former adversaries: the United States, the United Kingdom, Germany, France, Italy, to name a few, are allies within Nato and interdependent economic partners in the European Union. China and Japan are no longer enemies. The cold war division of Europe, which resulted from the Allied victory, is no more. Yet Russia, while a major power in the world order, remains somewhat isolated. And whereas people in western countries properly acknowledge the tragic experience of the Second World War, as it slips from living memory they have moved on. Oddly enough, or perhaps not so oddly, the western people who are still probably most obsessed with 'the war' are the British. The British and Soviet economies were the two most highly mobilized for the war effort, and both countries felt, for a long time, that they were fighting alone. They were not – the British were receiving enormous amounts of aid from the United States under lease-lend before the US entered the war – but it must have felt that way. There are therefore some similarities between the Russian and British experiences of the Second World War but also vast differences, notably that the Soviet Union was invaded and 27 million people – one person in seven – died. No visitor to Russia can fail to be overwhelmed by the continuing emphasis on the experience of the Great Patriotic War. From central Europe to the Pacific, from Murmansk down to Grozny, the war memorials proclaim the same message: '*Nikto ne zabyt. Nichto ne zabyto.*' ('No one is forgotten. Nothing is forgotten.') The sad fact is that many people and things will be. But by looking at the scope and scale of the conflict, its hideous cruelty, arbitrariness and injustice, and by understanding that there was good and bad on both sides, we can begin to move on.

2

ABSOLUTE AND TOTAL WAR

'A world war, and a war of an extension and violence hitherto undreamt of.'[1] Just over half a century before the outbreak of the Second World War, Friedrich Engels said that no other kind of war was possible for Germany. He foresaw not only the catastrophe of 1914–18, a quarter of a century away, but also, albeit in more shadowy form, the distant shape of the Second World War. His vision would apply to Soviet Russia, as well as to Germany, and the 1941–5 war on the eastern front was its extreme fulfilment.

That war breaks all records, before and since, for the length of the front, the depth of advance and retreat, the duration of continuous fighting and the size of the armies engaged. But it was also a war of consummate brutality against civilians, prisoners of war and enemy wounded, something which Engels probably did not envisage, even though he wrote before the signatories to the 1907 Hague and 1929 Geneva Conventions attempted to impose some limits on the horrors of war and its immediate aftermath. But on the eastern front between 1941 and 1945, both sides discarded the Conventions anyway. Because the Soviet Union had never signed the July 1929 Geneva Conventions on the treatment of wounded and prisoners of war, as well as for other reasons, the Germans did not abide by them either.[2]

The savagery of the fighting and the gruesome atrocities had been seen before, but this was not the bloodthirsty ancient or medieval world, or even the sixteenth or seventeenth century. The people who fought this war had not been brought up without squeamishness, or as savages. On the contrary, they were the children of two of the most culturally, scientifically and technologically developed civilizations the world had ever seen. In the early twentieth century Germany and Russia – later the Soviet Union – excelled, as they had for centuries, in literature, music, the arts, science, technology, exploration and sport. But unfortunately, 'the maximum use of force is in no way incompatible with the simultaneous use of the intellect', as Carl von Clausewitz (1780–1831), the great Prussian military thinker and philosopher, had ominously observed.[3] And unfortunately for others, the greatest civilizations of the time are usually also the most efficient killers. We may admire the Romans' literature, law, logic, logistics and engineering, but their dominance ultimately rested on being a military superpower. Their army operated like a chainsaw and if they did not enslave any surviving prisoners, they often crucified them. In the twentieth century, which should have been a more civilized age, warfare, to borrow Churchill's phrase about a new dark age, was made even 'more sinister, and perhaps more protracted, by the lights of perverted science'.[4]

Absolute war

Clausewitz was a young Prussian general who advised the Russians, and was present at many battles in the Russian 1812 campaign – the 'Patriotic War'. His insights, shaped by the culture of both sides, are therefore especially relevant to the German–Soviet war 130 years later. Clausewitz is often mentioned, occasionally quoted, but, unfortunately, seldom read. The description of conflict dynamics in the book, *On War* (which his heartbroken wife, Marie, put together from his uncompleted drafts after his premature death) is exemplary. In conflict, the two sides constantly 'up the ante'. Each tries to outdo the other until the opponent gives in. Conflict dynamics are therefore a reciprocal process, which, if unchecked, will cause violence to escalate, until one side decides that it cannot continue the struggle. 'War', Clausewitz wrote, 'is an act of force and there is no logical limit to the application of that force. Each side therefore, compels the opponent to follow suit; a reciprocal action is started which must lead, in theory, to extremes.'[5] That is what happened on the eastern front.

The tendency to extremes is compounded by uncertainty, because war is a contest between two living wills.[6] As long as the opponent remains in existence, he is a potential threat. Until the enemy is incapable of resistance, therefore, he may surprise you and so still to some extent dictates the terms. And, finally, effort in war comprises two interrelated and inseparable factors: the means at your disposal and the strength of your will.[7] In the Great Patriotic War, the total means at the Allies' disposal was certainly far greater than that at the Germans'. On the eastern front, the means at the Soviet Union's disposal were initially greater than the Germans'. Those means were savagely cut back when, in a relatively short time, the Germans overran an area the same size as that conquered by Alexander the Great, but as a result of the evacuation of industry to the East, covered in Chapter 9, the Russians recovered again.[8] The will of the Soviet peoples may also have wavered, but ultimately proved greater, and was expressed in the greater determination to mobilize all aspects of the nation's resources.

'If we were to think in purely absolute terms', wrote Clausewitz, 'we could proclaim that ... since the extreme must always be the goal, the greatest effort must always be exerted.'[9] Furthermore, 'any additional expenditure of time – any suspension of military action – seems absurd'.[10] 'Operational pauses' would be out. However, there are always modifications in practice. International laws and customs are one, although Clausewitz tended to dismiss these because they are primarily enforced by the state and the law, and are therefore largely removed in war.[11] That was certainly true on the eastern front. Further constraints arise from the fact that all the warring sides' resources cannot be mobilized immediately or applied simultaneously, from the nature of the resources – the fighting forces, the country, with its physical features and population, and its allies.[12] And, finally, from 'friction'. From the inescapable law of nature that, if anything can go wrong, it will.[13] In the 1941–5 war on the eastern front each side had the total destruction of the enemy as its objective. The 'modifications in practice' derived from the limitations of logistics, terrain, climate; and technological, human and animal (particularly horses') limitations and endurance, rather than from laws and customs of war.

Would war ever attain this ultimate, absolute form, Clausewitz asked.

> Yes it would if: (a) war were a wholly isolated act, occurring suddenly and not produced by previous events in the political world; (b) it consisted of a single decisive act or a set of simultaneous ones; (c) the decision achieved was complete and perfect in itself, uninfluenced by any previous estimate of the political situation it would bring about.[14]

Clearly, the war on the eastern front was not an isolated act, but part of the complex tapestry of the Second World War, and its nature and course were ordained by the forces that brought it into existence. Nor did it consist of a single decisive act or several simultaneous ones. It discharged its energy over 1,418 days, the German advance pulsing forward at different speeds in different directions, culminating at Stalingrad and the Caucasus, and then waning before the waxing power of the Red Army. As Clausewitz also noted, 'the proportion of the means of resistance that cannot immediately be brought to bear is much higher than might at first be thought. Even when great strength has been expended on the first decision and the balance has been upset, equilibrium can be restored.'[15] Even after staggering defeats and the loss of 3 million prisoners, equilibrium was restored at the gates of Moscow. The war's political nature also changed. For the Soviet Union, it started as a fight for survival, but finished with the conquest of much of eastern and central Europe. Destruction of the *Wehrmacht* remained the Soviet Union's primary object, but to do this within the context of a great coalition war required constant adjustment and compromise with allies. Sometimes, they got it wrong. Had Stalin been prepared to trust the western Allies to stick by the agreement to divide Germany down the Elbe, he might not have felt the need to race for Berlin so recklessly, with the highest daily casualties of any Soviet operation in the war (apart from the catastrophic 'frontier battles' when the Germans unleashed Operation Barbarossa in June 1941).[16] And had Stalin known that the Americans were about to drop atomic bombs on Hiroshima and Nagasaki, perhaps he might have brought forward the invasion of Manchuria scheduled for, and delivered on, 9 August 1945.

Subject to those inevitable 'modifications in practice', the war on the eastern front was probably the most 'absolute' war ever fought, on both sides. It was also the prime example of Clausewitz's famous 'Trinity':[17] primordial violence, hatred and enmity; the play of chance and probability; and the political direction to which it is, and must remain, subject. The first of the three principally concerns the people. Violence by one side bred violence on the other. Soviet forces breaking into Germany in 1945 were spurred on by exhortations to exact revenge. The second – juggling the odds in a chaotic game of chance – was the responsibility of the commanders. There can be few better examples than Hitler's unwise insistence that Sixth Army should continue chewing their way into Stalingrad as the Soviet command remorselessly built up forces for the counter-attacking pincer movement, which they sprung on 19 November 1942, coinciding with the first heavy falls of snow. The third element of the Trinity – the political aim, and the way it may change – is subject to the government alone. On the Soviet side, the interplay between the Red Army senior commanders, the security and intelligence services and the Main Defence Committee (GKO), which included the heads of foreign and economic policy, provides a good example of this.

The first element of the Trinity – primordial violence, hatred and enmity – was fuelled by the lack of legal restraint on both sides. The first general attempt to restrict the abuse of prisoners and wounded and to protect the civilian population by defining distinctions between combatants and non-combatants culminated in the Hague Conventions of October 1907, and especially Convention IV, the *Laws and Customs of War on Land*. Imperial Russia signed them – indeed, it had played a major part in bringing such agreements about – but as early as 1917–18 the new Soviet government refused to accept that soldiers of the Workers' and Peasants' Red Army would surrender to their 'class enemies', and no longer regarded itself as a signatory. The USSR did not acknowledge itself as the successor state until 1955.[18] Meanwhile, in 1929 forty-three parties signed the 'Third Geneva Convention' – in fact, two Conventions – covering military personnel who fell into enemy hands, one relating to prisoners of war, the other to the care of the wounded. These Conventions were immensely important and provided protection for some of the prisoners taken during the Second World War. The United States, Germany, Italy, France, Britain and its Dominions all signed them. Unfortunately two major players in the Second World War did not. Those were Japan and the Soviet Union.[19] The USSR did, however, sign the 1925 Geneva protocol prohibiting the use of poison gas and bacteriological warfare, and the 1936 London *Procès-verbal* (diplomatic jargon for a written report) on the rules of submarine warfare against merchant ships.[20]

After the war started in 1941 the Soviet Union claimed, somewhat speciously, that its only reason for not signing the 1929 Geneva Conventions was article 9. This article, which specified that prisoners of war should be racially segregated into separate camps, would be a violation of the Soviet constitution.[21] Another slight problem was that the Swiss government had not recognized the Soviet government. Whatever the real reason, the fact that the Soviet Union had not signed the 1929

Geneva Conventions certainly played into the hands of the Nazi regime, although even if it had signed, the Nazis would probably have pursued their genocidal policies against combatants, non-combatants and prisoners of war anyway. As it was, the USSR had not signed the Conventions and therefore Germany clearly felt itself under no obligation to respect them on the eastern front either.

On 9 August 1941, Averill Harriman told the US Secretary of State, Cordell Hull, that the Soviet Union had said it would observe the 1907 Hague Convention, the 1925 Geneva Protocol on chemical and bacteriological warfare and one of the two 1929 Geneva Conventions, namely the one relating to care of enemy wounded and sick.[22] The Soviet government had issued a note saying it would observe the Hague Convention on 17 July, and even earlier, on 1 July, the Council of People's Commissars had issued a decree on 'The Position of Prisoners of War', which was in line with the Hague Conventions, even though it was hardly ever observed, at least in the earlier part of the war.[23] However, and this was the rub, the Soviet Union said it would only observe those agreements 'with respect to Germany insofar as they are observed by Germany'.[24] This was not what the Americans wanted to hear, because, although they were not yet in the war, they knew that one day they might be. If the Soviet Union maltreated German prisoners, the Germans might retaliate, and the practice might spread to other prisoners of war – who might by then include Americans. Repeated enquiries about the Convention relating to healthy prisoners of war went unanswered. The USSR was not going to agree to that because, unlike the 1907 Hague Convention, it specified that prisoners' names should be released, that they should be able to correspond with relatives, and that prison camps should be inspected by neutral observers from the Red Cross.

To apply that idea on the eastern front was unthinkable for both Soviets and Germans. The Soviets believed that any of their combatants who allowed himself to be captured was probably a traitor and a counter-revolutionary. After the Soviet–Finnish war of 1939–40 many of the 5,000 Soviet soldiers who had fallen into enemy hands were deported and never seen again.[25] Article 58 of the Soviet Criminal Code forbade Soviet soldiers – even the wounded – to allow themselves to be taken prisoner. The Red Army was the only one in the world where being taken prisoner counted as desertion and treason.[26] The Soviet government and military command had absolutely no interest in what happened to Soviet people in German captivity. When prisoners of war who had survived were released at the end of the war, they were usually sent to the GULag or shot, and the same fate even befell many who had fought and crawled their way out of German encirclement during the war. Furthermore, in summer 1941, it soon became obvious that vast numbers of Soviet troops had surrendered without firing a shot, and that 75 per cent of Balts and Ukrainians, according to official German estimates, regarded the Germans as liberators.[27] Logging their names and letting them write to their families was unthinkable, even assuming the Germans would have allowed it. But the Germans had no intention of according humane treatment to Soviet troops whom they regarded as subhuman *untermensch*, let alone giving them the protection of a treaty which, for whatever reasons, the Soviet government had not signed.[28]

The Germans, likewise, had little interest in the welfare of any of their soldiers who fell into Soviet hands. The Germans had expected the Soviet forces to collapse fast. The fact that considerable numbers of German troops were taken prisoner was highly embarrassing. Clearly, the Russians were better fighters and had better generals than the Germans had thought. A public roll of prisoners' names, and letters reaching their families in Germany, possibly saying that they were well treated by the subhuman Slavs (even if they were not) were clearly not in Hitler's interest, either. For both totalitarian regimes in conflict on the eastern front, once a combatant ceased to be of use on the battlefield, his or her fate at the enemy's hands was a matter of supreme indifference. Indeed, the very expression 'irrecoverable losses' reflects that sentiment.

Neither side, therefore, had any intention of complying with the letter or the spirit of the 1907 Hague and 1929 Geneva Conventions. Furthermore, the provision in the latter for independent inspection of prison camps made it a complete non-starter. Although the Germans did allow Red Cross inspectors into a few carefully selected, model concentration camps, they were not going to open to inspection the prisoner-of-war and concentration camps into which millions of Soviet soldiers had been herded. And the Soviets were certainly not going to go public with the GULag.

The scale, extent and awesome logistical problems of the war on the eastern front compounded this indifference. In summer 1941 the Germans were astonished by the numbers of prisoners they took. Three German army groups – South, Centre and North – attacked the Soviet

Union in June 1941. We know, from an exercise conducted in early 1941, that Army Group South assumed it might take 72,000 prisoners in the first four days, with a further 122,000 over the next six days.[29] Assuming similar plans for the other army groups, that gives a realistic expectation of up to 600,000 prisoners on the entire Eastern Front by early July. The Germans were banking on a quick victory, and, not unreasonably, they thought that would do the trick, although those numbers of prisoners would cause problems, and prisoners of war, like the German *Wehrmacht* itself, were expected to scavenge from the land. But by mid August some 1.5 million Soviet troops had surrendered, and more than 3 million by mid October. In the great encirclement battles of Bialystok, Minsk, Smolensk, Uman, Kiev, Bryansk and Vyaz'ma alone – that is, before 18 October – 2 million Soviet soldiers had 'gone in the bag'. The total of 3 million was almost ten times the figure of 378,000 admitted by Stalin on 6 November, on the eve of the twenty-fourth anniversary of the 1917 'October' revolution. By the end of 1941, 3.8 million Soviet servicemen and women had surrendered or been captured.[30]

Even if the Germans had wanted to apply the generous provisions of the Geneva Conventions – that prisoners of war should be fed and accommodated to the same standard as one's own rear echelon troops – they were simply unworkable in these circumstances. The infrastructure in the western USSR was relatively primitive, and the Germans had their own very serious logistical problems. As for moving the prisoners back to Germany, the camps there could hold 790,000 prisoners, including those from countries who had signed the Geneva Conventions.[31] The same considerations applied to the hard-pressed Soviet system. It would have been unthinkable to divert precious resources to build camps and to transport prisoners on railways needed to maintain the war effort. Instead, they made them walk. The contrasting treatment of relatively small numbers of German or western Allied aircrew shot down near urban and industrial targets owed something to the Geneva Conventions, but the practicalities of dealing with them were also very different.

German policy toward Soviet prisoners and civilians in the occupied territories had been formulated even before fighting started in the East. There were three key orders, each of which was the result of complex evolution: the 'Führer decree' of 13 May 1941, which limited military jurisdiction in occupied areas, passing responsibility for dealing with criminals and insurgents to the tender mercies of the SS; *Guidelines for the Behaviour of the Fighting Forces in Russia*, issued on 19 May 1941; and the most notorious document, which grew out of the others and was very much a clarification of one key area, the famous 'Commissar Order' (*Kommissarbefehl*) of 6 June 1941.

On 3 March 1941 Hitler ordered the Supreme Command of all the German Armed Forces – *Oberkommando der Wehrmacht (OKW)* – to revise a draft covering the administration and exploitation of the territory he expected to conquer.

> The impending campaign is more than a clash of arms; it also entails a struggle between two ideologies. To conclude this war is not enough, given the vastness of the space, to defeat the enemy forces. The entire territory must be dissolved into states with their own governments . . . The Jewish-Bolshevik intelligentsia, as the oppressor in the past, must be liquidated.[32]

In fact very few Jews held senior positions in the Soviet administration and the best-known Jewish intellectual, Leon Trotsky (who was not a Bolshevik), had been murdered on NKVD orders with an ice-axe through his head in Mexico City the previous year. Such details did not concern Hitler, however. In addition to the liquidation of the 'Jewish-Bolshevik intelligentsia' he also demanded a limitation of military jurisdiction. He may well have suspected that the officers and gentlemen who ran the *Wehrmacht* would be less zealous about exterminating civilians than doing their job, which was fighting the Red Army. The order on military jurisdiction of 13 May owed a good deal to German experience on the Eastern Front in the First World War, where the Russians had committed atrocities and deported Germans from East Prussia in 1914, and the Germans had imposed harsh security measures against 'bandits' – some of whom were anti-German partisans – in occupied Poland between 1915 and 1919.[33]

The Führer decree of 13 May 1941 was passed on to the army by its commander-in-chief, Walther von Brauchitsch, on 24 May. Fearful that the relaxation of the constraints on German troops' behaviour against prisoners and the local population might lead to a breakdown in military discipline, Brauchitsch added an appendix emphasizing that the *Wehrmacht*'s main job was to fight the Red Army and that 'search and purge' actions should be avoided. In an appendix to the second part of the

Führer decree he stressed that officers should continue to 'prevent arbitrary excess by *individual* members of the army, so as to be in good time to prevent the degeneration of the troops'.[34] Individual enthusiasm had to remain subordinated to the will of the command. On 10 and 11 June Brauchitsch's assistant, the General (Special Duties), Lt Gen. Eugen Müller, personally told the staffs of armies and army groups that any 'sense of justice must, in certain circumstances, yield to the requirements of war'.[35] The 1907 Hague Convention had recognized the right of a population to take up arms spontaneously against an aggressor. On the eastern front, as everywhere German forces were employed, that was out of the question. Guerrillas, *francs-tireurs*, agitators, distributors of leaflets and saboteurs had no rights at all, and should be punished instantaneously.

The *Guidelines for the Behaviour of the Fighting Forces in Russia* were worked out in mid May and distributed on 19 May.[36]

> *Bolshevism is the mortal enemy of the National Socialist German people. Germany's struggle is aimed against that disruptive ideology and its exponents.*
>
> The struggle demands ruthless and energetic action against *Bolshevik agitators, guerrillas, saboteurs, Jews* and the complete liquidation of any active or passive resistance.
>
> Extreme reserve and most alert vigilance are called for towards all members of the *Red Army* – even prisoners – as treacherous methods of fighting are to be expected. The *Asiatic* soldiers of the Red Army in particular are inscrutable, unpredictable, insidious and unfeeling.
>
> After the capture of units the *leaders* are to be *instantly separated* from the other ranks.[37]

The idea that depriving Soviet people of their leaders would render them incapable of organized action and the emphasis on eliminating the Soviet 'boss class' recur throughout German instructions. The conflation of 'Bolsheviks, guerrillas, saboteurs and Jews' must also have had spectacular results for mishandling of prisoners, and for eliminating and alienating many people who might well otherwise have espoused the German cause. And there were many cases where the massacre of Jews was reported as 'anti-partisan operations'.[38]

The most notorious document, the *Guidelines on the Treatment of Political Commissars*, was largely a clarification of the preceding instructions. It reveals the extraordinarily bad state of German military intelligence. Although the Germans and the Soviets had worked together since the 1920s and were effective allies from 23 August 1939 until 22 June 1941, the German forces were wrongly briefed about who commissars were. According to the official intelligence manual, *The Wartime Forces of the USSR* of 15 January 1941, anyone wearing a red star with a gold hammer and sickle on their sleeves was a 'Commissar'. In fact, at company, battery or squadron level there was only a political officer – a *politruk* – who was merely an adviser and did not have to countersign orders. The *Kommissarbefehl* of 6 June 1941 referred, somewhat conveniently, to '*political commissars of all kinds*', though not out of embarrassment about German intelligence failings.[39] Hitler insisted that commissars were not to be regarded as soldiers under the Geneva Conventions, which was completely illogical. Not only were true commissars a functioning part of the military command system, but, given that they were wearing uniform and carrying authorization to accompany an armed force, they were fully entitled to its protection. Once again, such niceties counted for nothing on the eastern front.

The *Kommissarbefehl* ordered that all prisoners resembling 'commissars' who were suspected of resistance, sabotage, or instigation of these, should be treated according to the jurisdiction decree. Red Army commissars were not to be treated as soldiers (which they were), but were to be 'separated' from other prisoners of war and 'finished off'. Two days later, Brauchitsch ordered that this should be done after their separation, outside the combat zone proper and under the order of an officer. Again, the *Wehrmacht* feared the breakdown of discipline if German soldiers received carte blanche to murder anyone they liked.[40]

The limitation on military jurisdiction required special categories of prisoners of war, including commissars and Jews, to be transferred to Special Units (*Einsatzgruppen*) of the Security Service (SD) and German Security Police. There is plenty of evidence to show that army units not only cooperated by transferring prisoners but also tried to improve implementation of the directives. However, when the German advance slowed, the Army High Command (OKH) supported initiatives to get the Commissar Order cancelled, because, they said, it was counterproductive. Soviet resistance was getting stiffer, in part because Soviet troops were unwilling to give themselves up as word spread about what they, and certainly their political officers, might face. On 5 November Field Marshal Fedor von Bock objected to transferring prisoners of war to the *Einsatzgruppen* and emphasized that the army's responsibility for POWs could not be shared with other authorities.[41]

The highest-profile protest came from Admiral Wilhelm Canaris, head of the German Armed Forces' (OKW) Intelligence, the *Abwehr*. On 8 September he protested at an OKW Directive which openly referred to a possible mass execution of Soviet prisoners. In a statement on 15 September, later used in his defence at Nuremberg, he reiterated that

> ... war captivity is neither revenge nor punishment but solely
> protective custody, the only purpose of which is to prevent
> the prisoners of war from further participation in the war.
> This principle was developed in accordance with the view
> held by all armies that it is contrary to military tradition to
> kill or injure helpless people.[42]

Field Marshal Wilhelm Keitel, head of OKW, disagreed, noting in the margin that the Admiral's views reflected 'traditional ideas of gentlemanlike warfare; but this war is an ideological war of extermination'.[43]

In spite of the scruples of some Germans, the war of extermination continued. On 30 March 1941, Hitler had explained his rationale to his commanders-in-chief. Colonel-General Franz Halder, the Chief of the German Army General Staff, recorded what he said:

> Crushing denunciation of Bolshevism, identified with asocial
> criminality. Bolshevism is an enormous danger for our
> future. We must forget the concept of comradeship between
> soldiers. A Communist is no comrade before or after the
> battle. This is a war of extermination. If we do not grasp this,
> we shall still beat the enemy, but 30 years later we shall again
> have to fight the Communist foe. We do not wage war to
> preserve the enemy ... This need not mean that the troops
> should get out of hand. Rather, the commanders must give
> orders which express the common feeling of their men ...
> Commanders must make the sacrifice of overcoming their
> personal scruples.[44]

Faced with German forces bent on extermination, the Soviet army and security forces retaliated in kind. From the very start of the war, the Soviet authorities also stressed that this war had a totally different character from any other. 'The war with fascist Germany must not be regarded as an ordinary war,' Stalin said in his radio broadcast of 3 July. 'It is not only a war between two armies. It is, at the same time, the war of the entire Soviet people against the fascist German troops ... that know no compassion for the enemy.'[45]

Ilya Ehrenburg, a famous Soviet writer, epitomized Soviet attitudes to German prisoners. He wrote war commentary in the press from the beginning of the war. Just as the Soviets were 'subhuman' to the Germans, Ehrenburg wrote, 'we do not regard them as human beings'.[46] The Germans were 'wild beasts', 'worse than wild beasts', 'Aryan beasts' and 'starving rats'. A colonel 'shows his old rat's yellow fangs'.[47] Given the conduct of the Germans, such propaganda obviously worked.

In the early phases of the war, German prisoners were usually shot, either immediately on capture or after initial interrogation. German records, including statements from Soviet prisoners of war and intercepted radio messages, indicate that the procedures were similar in widely separated parts of the front, indicating that they were not spontaneous actions by individual units. The executions were usually authorized, or at least condoned, at company, battalion and regimental level. In many cases they were carried out on the order of commissars – which, given Hitler's Kommissarbefehl, is perhaps not surprising. But on 21 February 1942 a captured Soviet colonel reported that a Luftwaffe officer had been shot in the presence of an army commander, Lt Gen. Kuznetsov, and other senior officers.[48] While that might have been an isolated incident, the Wehrmacht Investigation Office for Breaches of International Law collected several thousand reports. These included the shooting of 180 German soldiers at Broniki on 30 June 1941, between 300 and 400 Romanian and a number of German soldiers on orders from Major Savelin, commanding 225th Rifle Regiment, at Surozhinets on 2 and 3 July 1941, and 80 German soldiers shot in the 26th Rifle Division area on 13 July.[49]

Soviet records indicate that 90 to 95 per cent of German prisoners taken in 1941–2 did not survive, for various reasons. This does not seem to have been the Soviet high command's intention. As we have seen, the notes on treatment of prisoners of 1 and 17 July specified that they should be treated in accordance with the Hague Conventions. The Red Army's Chief Military Health Directorate recommended appropriate hospital treatment for sick prisoners. In August the Chief of the Red Army General Staff, Marshal Boris Shaposhnikov, the only senior officer who had served as an officer in Tsar's army to survive the purges which began in 1937, was outraged to learn that 'individual enlisted personnel' were inclined to take 'personal valuables, money and documents' from prisoners. This should stop.[50]

Even more deplorable, however, was murder. The Germans captured a number of documents which showed that the Red Army command was trying to stop the killing of prisoners, which, of course, confirms that it was happening. Often the prisoners would be assembled and marched away from the front line areas, and were then shot 'en route'.[51]

In his speech of 6 November 1941, on the twenty-fourth anniversary of the Great October Revolution, Stalin did not appear to discourage the practice. 'From now on it will be our task ... to annihilate all Germans who have penetrated as occupiers, down to the last man.' After the usual 'tumultuous applause' he continued, 'No mercy to the German occupiers! Death to the German occupiers!' after which there was (as usual, when Stalin, who had trained to be a Russian Orthodox priest, was performing) more 'tumultuous applause'.[52]

Stalin's appeal was understood to mean that all Germans, whether fighting, wounded or taken prisoner, were to be killed. As a direct result one of the worst incidents occurred after the successful Soviet amphibious landing on the Kerch' peninsula at the end of December 1941, when the Crimean Front drove the Germans back west of Feodosiya, thus relieving pressure on Sevastopol, which was under German siege. Some 160 German wounded who were left in the hospital when the German forces pulled out had their heads smashed in with blunt instruments, were mutilated, thrown out of the windows, or killed by the simple Russian winter expedient of pouring cold water over them or throwing them in the sea to freeze to death.[53]

However, Red Army commanders were already realizing that such barbarism was counterproductive. Atrocities against prisoners usually increased the enemy's determination to fight to the death, and prisoners were useful sources of intelligence. In Order No. 55 of 23 February 1942, Stalin countermanded his earlier order. 'The Red Army takes German soldiers and officers prisoner when they surrender.'[54]

Thereafter, it appears that the Red Army command was seldom guilty of outright violations of international law, although there were exceptions, particularly during the Battle of Stalingrad. The same restrictions do not appear to have applied to the NKVD, or to the counter-intelligence directorate known as *Smersh – Shmert' shpionam – *'Death to Spies', which replaced the NKVD's Third Directorate on 14 April 1943. Zinaida Pytkina, formerly a woman officer in *Smersh*, interviewed for a television documentary in 1999, told how she had shot a young German major whose interrogation had been completed. A grave had been dug outside the interrogation building. The officer was made to kneel down, and Pytkina drew her pistol. 'My hand didn't tremble. It was a joy for me ... The Germans didn't ask us to spare them and I was angry ... I fulfilled my task. And I went back into the office and had a drink.'[55]

Pytkina's murderous assignment was not, strictly speaking, counter-intelligence or counter-espionage, which underlines the overlap between the functions of the various organizations. But it is a reminder that the war on the eastern front was also the most extensive intelligence and counter-intelligence war in modern history. The latest research suggests that the Soviet security services employed up to 150,000 agents across a 2,400-mile front, which enabled them to neutralize the majority of more than 40,000 German agents deployed against them. The combination of Soviet military deception (conducted by the Red Army, air forces and navy) and the state security organizations' destruction of the *Abwehr*'s human intelligence network had a profound impact on every battle. The Germans frequently underestimated Soviet strength and resilience and were deceived about Soviet plans.[56]

The interaction between the combatants in any war has a decisive impact on its development. Reciprocity is crucial, and it was so in the Great Patriotic War. Horrific brutality by one side was met by horrific brutality on the other. That applied to civilians in occupied territory, as well as to regular troops. The Germans expected no favours from the partisans, and in those areas the people of the occupied territories suffered. Conversely, where there was no partisan activity, the occupying troops could be relatively benign. Elena Vasilevna was born in 1929 and lived in a German-occupied area west of Leningrad as a young girl and teenager. In 2005 she was still working as a guide in the 'Road of Life' museum east of St Petersburg (as Leningrad had been renamed). 'There was very little partisan activity in our area,' she recalled, 'so the Germans were quite nice to us. We worked for them ...' Sixty years after the war, such frankness was possible.[57]

The Soviet troops who moved into Germany in 1944 and 1945 were deliberately spurred on to exact revenge. In the excellent Museum of the Defence of Moscow there are photographs of burned-out houses and the remains of Soviet civilians apparently butchered by the German invaders in 1941. Sixty years after the vengeful Soviet forces burst into Germany, a German was visiting the museum with the author.

'Have you seen the German reports on what the Soviet troops did when they invaded Germany?' my German friend asked the guide. 'I put it to you', my friend said, 'that every one of those pictures could be matched with one from eastern Germany later in the war.'

'That may be,' our guide said. 'But war is war.'[58]

If you want to understand war, study this one.

Sparse though the influence of 'international law and custom'[59] was, it did sometimes apply. Perhaps the most extraordinary example of old-school, punctilious diplomacy occurred at the outbreak of the world's most savage, absolute and total war. The German diplomats in Moscow, and the Soviet diplomats in Berlin, were trapped, although the Germans had moved all non-essential staff out of Moscow well before Operation Barbarossa broke on 22 June 1941. Valentin Berezhkov, a young and extremely talented Soviet diplomat who worked with Foreign Minister Molotov and translated for Stalin on occasion, was in the Berlin embassy. Many Soviet citizens who were still in Germany (as the two countries had a non-aggression pact and were working together until that night) were arrested and sent to concentration camps. But the diplomats, after an extremely tense couple of weeks, got out. On 2 July they left Berlin, heading for Prague, Vienna, Belgrade and Niš, still in German-occupied Yugoslavia. After a tense time at Niš, constantly under SS guard, they were moved on into Bulgaria, through Sofia, and met a Soviet diplomatic delegation from Istanbul at Edirne in neutral Turkey. From there, they made their way back to Moscow.[60] Even in the most absolute of wars, channels of negotiation had to be kept open. Otherwise, nobody could surrender.

Total war

Just as Engels had predicted a war of unprecedented scope and violence – absolute war – so, four years later, in 1892, he had predicted a war in which industrial might would be paramount. 'From the moment warfare became a branch of *la grande industrie*', he wrote, '*la grande industrie*, without which all these things cannot be made, became a political necessity.'[61]

In any future war, it would be necessary to mobilize industry, indeed the whole of society, to feed the battle fronts. There had been remarkable examples in the past: the women of Carthage cutting their hair to make bowstrings springs to mind. But now industry and the population as a whole had to be mobilized, including the large-scale employment of women in industry and even in the armed forces. When Clausewitz wrote of *der totale Krieg*, he did not mean that. He meant the 'absolute war' tending to the extreme described above. It was the German Field Marshal Erich von Ludendorff who first used 'total war' in the sense it is now used, to describe the First World War, writing in 1935.[62] 'A war of engines and reserves.'[63] The Great Patriotic War was that, as well.

In the First World War Russia was unable to match the industrial capacity of its principal adversary, Germany, although its industrial achievement was impressive, as was its military achievement until the October 1917 Revolution removed it from the war. Between 1914 and 1917 Russian machine gun production increased nearly ten times, production of rifles four times, and rounds of ammunition twice. But four-fifths of the heavier artillery and three-quarters of the machine guns were still imported from the UK, USA and France over perilous sea routes.[64] As Norman Stone has noted, the industrial effort had its own political and social consequences in 1917.[65] It was obvious, as Lenin famously said, that no revolution was worth anything unless it could defend itself.

Soviet preparations to avoid a repeat of Russia's fate in the First World War – preparations for total, modern, industrialized war – began in 1924–5. The visionary was Mikhail Vasilevich Frunze (1885–1925), a Soviet politician, agitator, military commander and military theorist, who died under the surgeon's knife in autumn 1925 in what was subsequently called a 'medical murder'.[66] Frunze may or may not have been consoled by the iconic status he was subsequently given by the Soviet regime. In 1924, in the introduction to a friend's book on industrial mobilization for war, he wrote:

> In a conflict of first-class opponents, the decision cannot be won by one blow. War will take the character of a long and fierce conflict ... Expressed in the language of strategy, this

means a change from the strategy of lightning blows to a strategy of exhaustion.

Thus the bond between the front and rear in our days must become much more close, direct and decisive. The life and work of the front at any given moment are determined by the work and condition of the rear.[67]

As People's Commissar for Military and Naval Affairs – War Minister – Frunze carried through the 1924–5 Frunze reforms. In June 1925, three months before his death, his plans became law. So, in the relatively peaceful 1920s, Soviet Russia embraced total mobilization, something which would have been politically incorrect and unthinkable in just about every other developed country at the time, including Germany. The 1925 law specified appropriate expansion of war industry and the organization of other industry so that it could meet all the Soviet Union's needs, even in wartime: perfection of military equipment, and equipping the Red Army with it; improvement of the rail and road transport networks and of auto transport; development of all types of communications; horse-breeding; improvement of the physical training of the population, military training for all workers and peasants, and especially youths and students; and an increase in general knowledge of military matters and the fundamentals of rifle shooting throughout the entire population. Finally, the law noted the importance of aviation and chemical warfare. The aviation industry was to be expanded and training in chemical defence was encouraged, leading to the creation of *Osoaviakhim* – the Society for Aviation and Chemical Defence, which trained many pilots, including women, who would serve in the Great Patriotic War. Finally, Frunze stressed that 'these planned measures cannot be accomplished by the efforts of the War Office alone. Hence the [Third USSR]Congress [of Soviets] obliges all Commissariats of the USSR and of the Soviet Republics to take a very active part in conducting them, particularly the Supreme National Economic Councils . . .'.[68]

In December 1925, shortly after Frunze's untimely death, the XIV Congress of the All-Russian Communist Party proclaimed the industrialization of the country as its main target, melding the objectives both of the military and of the industrialists. At this critical juncture, the key military brain who replaced Frunze was the fascinating, brilliant and charismatic Mikhail Nikolayevich Tukhachevskiy (1893–1937). Tukhachevskiy was a former lieutenant in the Semënov regiment, the second senior foot guards in the Tsar's Imperial Guard. Had he been British, he would therefore have been a Coldstream Guard. Having obtained the highest marks ever at the Aleksandrovskiy War College in 1914, and donning his small lieutenant's stars in haste, he headed for the front but was soon captured by the Germans. In 1917 he escaped and became, to all appearances, a dedicated communist. He has been widely studied as a military commander, strategist and theorist, but also played a major role in the development of the Soviet war economy. He made violins as a hobby, and therefore had a bent for technology and engineering which fitted well with his role as developer of the Soviet war economy and new military technology.[69]

In late 1925 or, at the latest, by early 1926, the Soviet armed forces and the government had decided that the country must acquire a modern armaments industry. With no immediate threat of war – apart from a brief scare in 1927 – they could afford to play it long. The most promising angle was cooperation with German industry and the Reichswehr, which were severely constrained by the terms of the punitive 1919 Versailles treaty which limited the Reichswehr to 100,000 men and banned the development of military aircraft, tanks, battleships and other top-of-the-range military assets. But in the vast spaces of the Soviet Union, German forces could exercise unobserved by the signatories of Versailles. Trotsky initiated cooperation with German industry and the Reichswehr in 1921–2, and the Junkers aircraft company started production of aircraft and engines at Fili, the village – now suburb – west of Moscow, in 1922. In 1926 the factory was expanded. The location was ironic. It was at Fili that, in 1812, Field Marshal Kutuzov had held a council of war and took the decision to abandon Moscow to Napoleon to preserve the Russian army in being, a scene memorably portrayed in Tolstoy's War and Peace.[70] In 1928 a German delegation, headed by General Werner von Blomberg, visited the western Soviet Union to discuss further military cooperation. Blomberg's report shows he was most impressed with Tukhachevskiy – 'cultured, likeable. A person to note.'[71] But this visit may have been a factor in Tukhachevskiy's downfall in 1937, when he was accused of being an agent of a foreign power – presumably Germany.

The subsequent development of Soviet industry was heavily one-sided, and this had implications early in the war. In 1928, the first year since 1913 for which reliable figures are available, 60 per cent of Soviet industry was light, against 40 per cent heavy. In 1940, on the eve of the war, the proportions were reversed. Stalin followed Frunze's plan. He gave top priority to civilian industries which could be easily converted to war production. Instead of a reserve of munitions (which might be obsolete or past their sell-by date when war came), the USSR created a reserve of heavy industry enterprises to produce them. Tanks, aircraft, guns, warships, bullets, shells and bombs were all built by heavy industry. Tukhachevskiy also stressed the need for flexibility to convert from civilian to military production. The same factories that built tractors could build tanks. And so they did.[72]

The other principal figure in the evolution of Soviet preparations for total war was probably Aleksandr Svechin (1878–1938). Svechin had reached the rank of major-general in the Tsarist Army, one of very few former Imperial generals to continue service with the Red Army. He appears not to have got on with the flamboyant former Imperial Guard lieutenant Tukhachevskiy. Svechin's intellect was intimidating and probably made him more enemies than friends. In 1925 he completed the first edition of his classic *Strategy*, which was republished in 1927.[73] *Strategy* was the blueprint for the Soviet conduct of the Great Patriotic War. It forecast a war in which the Soviet Union would have to sacrifice territory; a war in which armies, more widely spread than before, would become 'a giant broom', occupying the entire breadth of the theatre of operations. War could no longer be concluded with a single, short blow, but would be prolonged, comprising many operations. 'Exhaustion' (*izmor*) would play a decisive role. That was not to say that destruction of enemy armed forces was not the principal objective, merely that it would take longer.[74]

Svechin's most critical insight was probably the need for an integrated – inter-agency – approach, combining the functions and expertise not just of the three armed forces but of all the security agencies. Like Frunze, he stressed the interaction of the front and the rear.[75] Long wars put more stress on the internal workings of the state. War was not, as some had regarded it, medicine for a state's internal illness, but a serious examination of the health of its internal politics.[76] The 'rear' was as important as the 'front':

> The Department of Internal Affairs [NKVD] must have its
> own mobilisation plan, which must take into account the
> steps necessary to maintain firm order in the national
> territory during the period when huge masses are torn away

from their work in the country and proceed to collection
points to flesh out the armies, and the population of the
towns doubles to meet the requirements of war industry. The
crisis . . . will be compounded by enemy propaganda,
sharpened by the activities of enemies of the existing system,
by the hopes which individual national and class groups will
have as the ruling class grows weary under the impositions of
war. It is essential to think through the measures necessary to
maintain order along lines of communications most
thoroughly, to take into account all dubious [politically
unreliable or disaffected] elements, desertion, enemy
intelligence and propaganda, measures for censorship, and so
on. And also, if necessary, to substitute special formations
made up of reliable elements for military units leaving for the
front, or to strengthen the police. Aviation, the radio, the
need for an unbroken flow of huge masses of troops to the
front, supplying them with munitions, home leave from the
active army which was previously unknown [it still was,
largely, in the Red Army in 1941–5]. All these factors now
merge the front and the rear.[77]

It was emphatically the blueprint for the Soviet conduct of the Great
Patriotic War. The urban populations swelled by the demands of war
industry and refugees were exemplified by Leningrad. The special
detachments comprising 'reliable elements' were the 'destroyer battalions' that, for example, ruthlessly stopped people fleeing Moscow in
the near-panic of October 1941.[78] *Strategy*, the blueprint for protracted,
total war, remained the only book to possess that magic word as its title
until 1962, when Marshal of the Soviet Union Vitaliy Sokolovskiy's
Military Strategy was published – the world's first blueprint for nuclear
missile war.[79]

Although Tukhachevskiy attacked Svechin, he actually lifted many
of Svechin's ideas. On 16 July 1930 Tukhachevskiy delivered a seminal
paper to the Communist Academy (Komakad). He dismissed the idea
of 'little wars' as he and his colleagues had dismissed the idea of 'little
armies', and repeated what Svechin had said three years before.

The scale of a future war will be grandiose . . . in a future war
the mobilisation of industry will, first of all, take place in a
much shorter time than before and, secondly, in this short

time industry will produce much more military hardware than in the past war ... The future (*gryadushaya*) world imperialist war will not only be a mechanised war, during which huge material resources will be used up, but, together with this, it will be a war which will embrace multi-million-strong masses and the majority of the population of the combatant nations. The frontiers between the front and the rear will be erased more and more.[80]

On the outbreak of the long-predicted total war, in 1941, the NKVD was used to implement the vision of Svechin and Tukhachevskiy, although both had died – or, at any rate, disappeared – as its victims in 1938 and 1937, respectively. The NKVD were in charge of the GULag – eighty 'concentration camp systems', plus political prisoners and prisoners of war transferred to them by the military. As soon as the Germans attacked, Stalin used the NKVD to execute all people suspected of espionage and to arrest persons considered politically unreliable. Far from a relaxation of the 'terror', the outbreak of war meant more arrests. Although some suspects were probably arrested in Moscow and Leningrad, the outlying republics in the Germans' path which in many areas were already resisting Soviet rule – eastern Poland, the Baltic States, Belorussia and Ukraine – were particularly hard hit. In the first few days mass shootings took place, primarily of Poles, Ukrainians and Baltic nationals. Before they pulled back, the NKVD shot political prisoners. The logic was presumably that, if 'liberated', as they might have seen it, by the Germans, these people were potentially high-value German agents and opponents of the USSR. Massacres took place in Brest, Minsk, Kaunas, Vilnius and Riga. But shootings also occurred in Smolensk and Kiev, and even in the Russian Republic itself. According to a US Congressional Committee in 1954 which may, admittedly, have been influenced by cold war paranoia, 80,000 to 100,000 people were shot by the NKVD before the Germans got to them, although the author would treat that estimate with caution.[81] The NKVD and the German SS Security Police Service behaved in similar fashion. In Kiev, the NKVD and other Soviet security agencies executed 4,000 Ukrainian and Polish political prisoners, as well as some German prisoners of war, some of whom were tortured. When the Germans arrived they at first tried to contain the anti-Semitic attacks which erupted. But then the German Security Police and the SS Security Service arrived, and killed another 7,000 people, allegedly as 'reprisal for inhumane atrocities'. In fact they were mostly Jews and had nothing to do with the earlier pogroms. In any areas recovered by Soviet forces, even temporarily, the Soviet security troops also shot any Soviet citizen suspected of contact with the German troops. When Khar'kov was temporarily back in Soviet hands, 4,000 people were shot, including girls and young women who had befriended German soldiers.[82]

The conditions for absolute and total war had been developed during the 1920s and 1930s, and reached a climax of intensity in early 1941. With hindsight, it looks as if war between Nazi Germany and Soviet Russia was inevitable. But it did not seem that way to everyone in 1939, as the world's two greatest dictatorships, far from falling on each other in a vicious war, embraced each other in a non-aggression pact.

3

'A CRUEL ROMANCE': THE NAZI–SOVIET ALLIANCE AND SOVIET EXPANSION, AUGUST TO NOVEMBER 1939

At three in the morning, German time, on 22 June 1941, Soviet Ambassador Vladimir Dekanozov was summoned to the German Foreign Ministry in the Berlin Wilhelmstrasse. When the Soviet delegation reached the Ministry, there were floodlights and a small crowd of journalists, photographers and film cameramen. Exactly one hour after the telephone call, they were in the not unfamiliar surroundings of the office of the Foreign Minister, Joachim von Ribbentrop. He had obviously been drinking. Ribbentrop told Dekanozov he had information that the Soviet Union had been preparing to attack Germany and that Germany had therefore had to take measures to guarantee its own 'security'. The concentration of Soviet troops on Germany's 'eastern border' necessitated 'military countermeasures'. An hour before, he said, German forces had crossed into the Soviet Union. After nearly two years of apparently fruitful economic and political collaboration between Germany and the USSR, it was war. Dekanozov turned his back on the Germans, and the Soviet delegation walked away.

Then, according to Valentin Berezhkov, the young Soviet interpreter, Ribbentrop chased after the withdrawing Soviet delegation, saying that he had been against Hitler's decision, and that he had tried to talk the Führer out of his 'madness' (*Wahnsinn*). 'Please inform Moscow that I was against the attack,' were the last words Berezhkov heard him say.[1] None of the others present reported this alleged outburst in exactly the same way, but, given the magnitude of the news they had just received, perhaps that is not altogether surprising (although the Soviet diplomats had been aware of all the reports indicating a German attack was imminent). It seems almost too remarkable and untypical of such occasions for Berezhkov to have made it up, and one of Ribbentrop's officials reported the same sentiment, if not the same words. Having worked since 1939 to build Nazi–Soviet cooperation, it is understandable that Ribbentrop should feel this way. He had almost certainly grown to know and respect the Russians – who, until now, had been colleagues, if not full allies. 'Perhaps', mused Berezhkov, 'Ribbentrop had premonitions of a disgraceful end on the gallows.'[2] But he was not the only German to ask for his opposition to the invasion to be remembered in the ensuing days. And anyone familiar with history might, with good reason, wonder whether this time Germany was biting off more than it could chew.

The biggest and worst war in history had become inevitable when Adolf Hitler became Chancellor of Germany in 1933. However, the fact that Hitler would attack Stalin first, rather than the other way round, and the timing of the attack, were not inevitable until very late in the day.[3] Wars, as Philip Bobbit observed in *The Shield of Achilles*, 'are like deaths which, while they can be postponed, come when they will come and cannot be finally avoided'.[4] This one, while postponed in 1939, was ultimately even less avoidable than most. The deeper we delve into the causes of most wars, the more of them we discover. Tolstoy, writing on the causes of the war of 1812, mused on how incomprehensible it was that millions of people killed and tortured one another for the reasons given by historians: because of Napoleon's ambitions, Tsar Alexander's firmness, the astuteness of British foreign policy, or because the Duke of Oldenburg was upset. Had there been no Duke of Oldenburg, Tolstoy reasons, had Napoleon not taken offence at being asked to retire west of the Vistula, or had large numbers of his corporals and sergeants refused to sign up for a second campaign, there would have been no war.[5] But all these causes, myriads of causes, ultimately coincided to bring about what happened.

The only thing that could have stopped the war between history's most extreme political regimes, National Socialism and Soviet communism, would have been the non-appearance of Hitler. National Socialism emerged in opposition to communism or 'Bolshevism'. Hitler's writings, including *Mein Kampf* and other statements, constantly rail at the 'Jewish-Bolshevik menace'.[6] And the unlimited control which both dictators exercised over their people, the media and over unprecedented resources and technology, made events less susceptible to other people's actions, to accident and free will, than probably at any other time or place in history.[7] In analysing German and Soviet aims and intentions, we are heavily dependent on the personal whims and psychology of the leading individuals.

Until 1933, history could well have taken a different course. Germany, defeated in 1918, suffered punitive peace terms under the Versailles Treaty of 1919, and its armed forces were limited to 100,000, with constraints on key technologies including battleships and military aircraft. In the 1920s, however, the German state and its armed forces, the Reichswehr, found an ally in a fellow pariah state. The Soviet Union had emerged after the Russian Federated Socialist republic had survived half-hearted attempts by the victors of the First World War to strangle it at birth, and linked up with other Soviet republics.[8] In April 1922 the victorious Allies called a conference at Rapallo, Italy, to discuss economic and political collaboration between all nations, including Germany, defeated in 1918, and the newly formed Union of four Soviet republics. The German and Soviet delegations withdrew to a neighbouring village and, to the horror of the other delegates, signed an agreement to 'give each other mutual assistance for the alleviation of their economic difficulties'.[9] The road to German–Soviet collaboration was open.

By the late 1920s German and Soviet military experts were working together, safe from the prying eyes of the First World War victors, on manoeuvres in the wide spaces of Ukraine.[10] Nor was this German–Russian affinity entirely new. For nearly three centuries, since the reign of Tsar Aleksey Mikhailovich, Peter the Great's father, from 1645 to 1676, German military methods and style had enjoyed recurring favour in Russia. The two armies could be said to form part of a common, north-east European military tradition.[11] Clausewitz himself had been with the Russians in the 1812 campaign. And during the nineteenth century, the shrewder German leaders, including Bismarck, had pragmatically sought the friendship of the great power to the east. In the 1920s, the Soviet Union had an unlimited appetite for German – and, indeed, for any kind of – technological expertise. Until 1933, long-term cooperation between Germany and the Soviet Union was far from unthinkable.

Hitler's accession changed that, but cooperation was still necessary in the short term. Nor, at the time, did it seem so absurd. Politics, like the world, is round. If you go far enough west, you reach the 'far east'. And, if you travel far to the political 'left' or 'right', you end up in the same place: some form of totalitarian dictatorship where state security is not only paramount, but actually threatens the very people whose lives, liberties and aspirations the state exists to protect.

So it was with National Socialism under Hitler and Soviet communism under Stalin. There were striking similarities between the two states, both energetically rearming after the catastrophes of the First World War and the Russian Civil War. On the one hand, there were militarized youth movements: the *Hitlerjugend* in Germany and the *Komsomol* (the Young Communist League) in the USSR, and a culture of outdoor, muscular athleticism, which was also present in parts of the the British Empire and in the USA. At the other extreme, there was the use of slave labour – far more so in the USSR than in Germany, at this time. But most people in both countries seem to have been blissfully unaware of the dark undercurrents swirling beneath the apparently progressive world in which they lived. Even the urban population lived much closer to nature than ours does now, and memoirs of life in Germany and the USSR just before the war are full of summer camps, of picnics and good food, cultivated in allotments and kitchen gardens. They worked hard, studied hard to better themselves, played hard, fell in love and had children young.[12]

Nor did the leaders who exercised unprecedented power over these self-confident superstates appear so different from one another. In Alan Bullock's words, they had led 'parallel lives'.[13] Both had come from lower-middle-class origins at the extremities of the empires they came to rule. Hitler (1889–1945) was not from Germany at all, but from Austria-Hungary: Stalin (1878–1953), as his real surname reveals, was from Georgia. Both were therefore 'outsiders', easily detectable from their accents. 'Stalin' was a pseudonym taken from the word *stal'* – 'steel', as was common among Bolshevik revolutionaries. He was born Dzhugashvili, and his official date of birth was not the real one, either. According to the birth certificate in the Cathedral of the Assumption at Gori, Iosef Dzhugashvili was born on 6 December 1878 in the Old Style calendar used in Russia until 1918, or 18 December in the modern calendar. However, in 1922 his secretary was making out a new CV for him and, for some reason, gave his date of birth as 21 December 1879. That day was celebrated as his fiftieth birthday in 1929 and seventieth in 1949. Only when the Central Party Archive was opened in the 1990s did the discrepancy come to light.[14] Hitler, on the other hand, died with the name that appeared on his birth certificate.[15] Both men developed consummate presentational skills – Hitler, in part, because he was an artist and designer (albeit in dubious taste) with an eye for arresting graphics. These are particularly striking and powerful when viewed in the colour film taken at the time, which is now far more widely available. Stalin trained to be a Russian Orthodox priest, and his conduct of ceremony had an ecclesiastical quality. Both leaders encouraged and exploited a 'cult of personality'.

Most importantly, in spite of the intense hatred between them, and for everything the other one stood for, it seems clear that Stalin and Hitler had huge respect for each other. This was certainly a key reason why Stalin refused to believe that Hitler was about to stab him in the back as the 'cruel romance'[16] approached its inevitable demise.

Hitler's views on the Bolshevik regime were set out clearly in *Mein Kampf*. The 'real organizer of the Revolution and the international wire-puller behind it', wrote Hitler, was 'the international Jew'. The Russian became 'the slave of his Jewish dictators who, on their side, were shrewd enough to name their dictatorship "the Dictatorship of the people"'.[17] As for the feasibility of a German–Soviet alliance:

> From the purely military viewpoint a Russo–German
> coalition waging war against Western Europe, and probably
> against the whole world on that account, would be
> catastrophic for us. The struggle would have to be fought
> out, not on Russian but on German territory . . . Therefore
> the fact of forming an alliance with Russia would be the
> signal for a new war. And the result of that would be the end
> of Germany . . . Those who are in power in Russia to-day
> have no idea of forming an honourable alliance or of
> remaining true to it, if they did. It must never be forgotten
> that the present rulers of Russia are blood-stained criminals,
> that here we have the dregs of humanity which, favoured by
> the circumstances of a tragic moment, overran a great state,
> degraded and extirpated millions of educated people out of
> sheer blood-lust and that now [November 1926] for nearly
> ten years they have ruled with such a savage tyranny as was
> never known before . . . the international Jew, who is to-day
> the absolute master of Russia, does not look upon Germany
> as an ally but as a State condemned to the same doom as

> Russia ... The struggle against the Jewish Bolshevisation of
> the world demands that we should declare our position
> towards Soviet Russia. We cannot cast out the devil through
> Beelzebub ... the future goal of our foreign policy ought not
> to involve an orientation to the East or West; but it ought to
> be an eastern policy which will have in view the acquisition
> of such territory as is necessary for our German people.[18]

The last sentence encapsulates Hitler's desire for *Lebensraum* (living space), based on the theories of earlier geopoliticists, notably Karl Haushofer (1869–1946). Hitler knew Haushofer by 1922, through Rudolf Hess, who had been Haushofer's pupil.[19] The world's 'heartland', according to the British geopoliticist Sir Halford Mackinder (1861–1947) lay at the centre of the Eurasian land mass, in eastern Europe and central Asia, and Haushofer had seized on his views.[20] Whatever the origins of Hitler's beliefs on the exploitation of the 'heartland' for Germany's role as a world power, it seems unlikely that any considerations of realpolitik could change views as strongly held as those expressed in *Mein Kampf*. But Hitler's colleagues, including the Foreign Minister, Joachim von Ribbentrop, were not so ideologically constrained. Ribbentrop's foreign policy goals were more traditionally German, including hegemony in central Europe, which might involve cooperation with the Soviet Union, economic penetration of south-east Europe, and colonies overseas. Whereas Hitler saw the Soviet Union, albeit perhaps only in the long term, as a target for German expansion and the acquisition of *Lebensraum*, Ribbentrop was prepared to cooperate with the Soviet Union – when it suited Germany.

From spring 1937, Ribbentrop was increasingly inclined to pursue that cooperation, notwithstanding the views of Hitler, his boss. Group Captain Malcolm Christie, the former Air Attaché in Berlin, was the first to report that Ribbentrop had developed a plan to devise conditions under which the four 'fascist states' – Germany, Russia, Japan and Italy – could collaborate at the expense of the British Empire. To do this, there had to be large-scale removal of Jewish functionaries by Stalin, which was under way by 1938.[21]

But even before the first signs appeared of the short-term cooperation between Nazi Germany and the Soviet Union, a real indication that the two dictatorships might just as easily cross swords came in the form of a proxy war. The Spanish Civil War began when a socialist Republican government took power in Madrid in 1936 and, in July, faced a rebellion by right-wing Nationalists, led by General Francisco Franco who brought troops across from North Africa. Hitler and Benito Mussolini, Italy's dictator and the the real founder of fascism, supported Franco. During the three years of bitter and protracted fighting which followed, the Soviet Union actively assisted the Republicans – the legitimate government – with arms, 'volunteers' and military advisers. The Republican cause also attracted left-wing volunteers from other countries including Britain and the United States, whether as fighters or news reporters.[22]

The Spanish Civil War was in many respects a dress rehearsal for the Second World War, although some of its lessons were wrongly learned. The German Condor Legion's attack on the northern city of Guernica, for example, probably led air force planners to overestimate the likely damage to civilian morale of attacks on urban areas. New equipment, including the famous German Me-109 fighter plane, was first used in anger. It was also the first major war in which blood transfusion, following the identification of blood groups, was widely used in treatment of the injured. From October 1936 to January 1939 the Soviet Union supplied the Spanish government with 648 aircraft, 347 tanks, 60 armoured vehicles, 1,186 artillery pieces, 20,486 machine guns and 497,813 rifles. About 3,000 Soviet volunteers also went to Spain, of whom 158 were killed.[23] The 'volunteers' included a number of senior Soviet officers travelling incognito under suitably radical pseudonyms, who became eminent commanders in the Great Patriotic War. Of particular note was volunteer 'Voltaire', alias Nikolai Voronov, who, as the Red Army's chief of artillery, later became commander of the largest artillery force the world has ever seen. Stalin debriefed the Soviet military advisers personally as soon as they arrived back in Moscow. Voronov's memoirs of Spain are perceptive, and sometimes amusing. One of the important lessons he brought back was that ordinary field artillery in the direct-fire role was very effective against tanks: specialized anti-tank guns were unnecessary. Among the exhibits at the Artillery Museum in St Petersburg is a silver pen with an inscription indicating it was given to him by a Spanish lady, Dolores Ibarruri – the well-known Spanish communist leader. Voronov believed his pen was a lucky talisman, and so it proved. On one occasion, he was in a car accident, and believed it saved his life. On another, during the war with Germany, a small shell fragment hit the pen and was deflected, leaving a visible dent, but Voronov was unscathed as a result. She does not feature in his memoirs, so the nature of their Spanish Civil War relationship is unclear.[24] If the pen was lucky, Dolores's son was less so. He died commanding a Soviet machine-gun company. At Stalingrad.

For the victors of the First World War, the Soviet Union was potentially a greater threat than a resurgent Germany. In the 1930s, apart from the short-lived Republican government in Spain, the Soviet Union was the only truly 'socialist' country in Europe, if 'national socialist' Germany is excluded. Socialism, or communism, was still very much a transnational ideology, and the activities of the Communist International – Comintern – caused great concern. Until the Great Patriotic War – until 1943, in fact – the Soviet national anthem was not the splendid tune we know from subsequent Olympic Games, which was readopted, with different words, by the new Russia's President Putin, but the Internationale.

Events in the Soviet Union in the late 1930s did not encourage western democracies to trust the Russian bear. Foreign observers were stunned when, in summer 1937, the arrest and immediate execution of a number of senior Red Army officers was announced. Top of the list was Marshal Tukhachevskiy, who had impressed British and German generals as their host in the USSR and as the Soviet representative at the funeral of King George V in January of the previous year.[25] In all, 3 out of 5 Marshals of the Soviet Union died, 3 out of 5 Army Commanders (*komandarm*), First Class, all 10 Second Class, 50 out of 57 Corps Commanders (*komkor*), 154 out of 186 Divisional Commanders (*komdiv*), 401 out of 456 colonels, plus almost all corps and divisional commissars.[26] Although these staggering figures and the precise extent of the purges were not revealed until the very end of the Soviet era, enough was known to suggest, first, that it would take the Red Army, navy and air force a long time to recover from this abattoir of its top talent. This was undoubtedly a major factor in Hitler's ultimate decision to go to war in 1941. Secondly, the democracies might ponder whether Hitler's National Socialism might be preferable to Stalin's communism, and Hitler was well able to use the story of the purges to reinforce his own image as the opponent of Bolshevism. But privately, Hitler admired and identified with Stalin's approach.

On 30 September 1938 the British Prime Minister, Neville Chamberlain, appeared at the door of the British Airways aircraft in which he had returned to London, waving the now infamous piece of paper which promised 'peace in our time'. The 1938 Munich agreement, which ceded parts of Czechoslovakia to Hitler, undoubtedly convinced Hitler that the western democracies were weak and could be bought off. Conversely, Stalin's close associates confirmed that the Soviet leader was increasingly convinced that the western democracies were not serious in their opposition to Hitler.[27] The Soviet Union's ruling elite probably, and not unreasonably, thought that the West was willing to let Hitler get away with anything as long as he delivered on the promise, made in *Mein Kampf*, to eliminate Bolshevism. The Munich agreement was a big shock to the Soviet Union which, like Russia today, placed great emphasis on international 'collective security' arrangements. The Soviet Ambassador in London, Ivan Maisky, warned that international relations were now entering the 'era of brute force, savagery and the policy of the mailed fist'. Further analysis warned that British policy had only two aims: 'peace at any cost and, secondly, collusion with aggressors at the expense of third countries'.[28] It may have been at this time – 1938 – that Stalin began to contemplate an agreement with Germany's Führer.

From January 1939 the British began to receive reports that Ribbentrop was already considering an approach to Moscow. In April, he reportedly told the commander-in-chief of the Lithuanian armed forces that Britain was about to suffer a diplomatic and political defeat 'such as she had never before experienced in her history'.[29] This could well have been a reference to a Nazi–Soviet pact or alliance. The consequences of a rapprochement with Germany and Italy, resulting in the Soviet Union joining the anti-Comintern 'triangle' of Germany, Italy and Japan, in an alliance directed against the British empire, could be terrifying. As Sir Robert Vansittart, the Permanent Under-Secretary at the British Foreign Office, commented: 'There is enough boodle in the British Empire for all of them, and we might then have a fourfold combination to face, which would be quite impossible.'[30]

Hitler, meanwhile, judged that he had a better chance of winning in the West than in the East (see Figure 3.1). All the evidence suggested that France, the great victor of 1918, had lost its fighting spirit, and the construction of the fortified Maginot Line, effectively a chain of battleships buried in the ground, which he resolved to outflank, confirmed this view. The evidence from Britain also suggested that the country was unwilling to engage in battle, which, as other dictators have discovered before and since, it was – until there was no other option and it was put to the test.

By early August 1939 Stalin had decided it was futile to hope for

3.1 Europe at the end of November 1940

ATLANTIC OCEAN

REYKJAVIK
ICELAND

Narvik

SWEDEN

Faroes
(British Occupied)

Shetland
Islands

Trondheim

NORWAY

Bergen

OSLO

STOCKHOLM

Göteborg

Orkney
Islands

North
Sea

DENMARK

COPENHAGEN

Baltic Sea

Danzig

Glasgow

GREAT
BRITAIN

Hamburg

BERLIN

Posen

IRELAND

DUBLIN

Manchester

NETHERLANDS

Amsterdam
THE HAGUE

BRUSSELS

Hanover

Leipzig

Elbe

LONDON

Cherbourg

BELGIUM

Cologne

GERMAN

Rhine

Prague

Brest

LUXEMBOURG

Prot. Bohemia & Moravia

PARIS

Nancy

Nantes

Loire

Stuttgart

REICH

Munich

Danube

VIENNA

FRANCE

BERNE

SWITZERLAND

Graz

VICHY

Lyons

Bordeaux

Rhône

Milan

Po

Venice

Zagreb

Zara (Ital.)

PORTUGAL

SPAIN

Toulouse

Genoa

Marseilles

Adriatic Sea

Porto

ITALY

Corsica

ROME

LISBON

MADRID

Barcelona

Valencia

Balearic Islands

Sardinia

Tyrrhenian
Sea

Naples

Taranto

Seville

Mallorca

Tangier

Gibraltar (Brit.)

Spanish Morocco

Mediterranean Sea

Messina

Sicily

RABAT

Oran

ALGIERS

TUNIS

Malta

MOROCCO
(French)

ALGERIA
(French)

TUNISIA
(French)

Kirkeness
Murmansk

Tornio
Oulu

FINLAND

Arkhangel'sk

Northern Dvina
Vychegda

Kotlas

Sukhona

Vaasa

HELSINKI
Leningrad

Vologda

Volga

Kazan

Tallinn
Narva
Novgorod
Gorkiy

SOVIET

Kuybyshev

Orenburg

Riga
Western Dvina

MOSCOW

Ural

Kaunas
Vilna
Smolensk

UNION

Königsberg
Minsk
Voroezh

Don
Volga

Guryev

Białystok
Gomel
Kursk

WARSAW
Brest–Litovsk
Khar'kov
Stalingrad

General
Government
of Poland
Kiev
Donats

Astrakhan

Kraków
Lemberg
Dnieper
Dnepropetrovak
Rostov

*Caspian
Sea*

SLOVAKIA
Cernovicy
Dniester
Odessa
Krasnodar

Kassa
Iasi

HUNGARY
Prut

Szeged
Tiflis

ROMANIA
Batumi

BELGRADE
BUCHAREST
Constanta
Black Sea

Danube

YUGOSLAVIA
BULGARIA

Tabriz

Skopje
SOFIA
Istanbul

IRAN

TIRANA
Salonika
ANKARA

ALBANIA
TURKEY

GREECE
*Aegean
Sea*
Izmir
Adana

*Ionian
Sea*
Adalia
SYRIA
(French mandated
territory)
BAGHDAD

ATHENS

IRAQ

Dodecanese
Cyprus
BEIRUT
Damascus

Crete

Euphrates
Tigris

Legend:

- Germany and annexed territories
- German-occupied territories
- Italy and annexed territories
- Countries allied to Germany and Italy
- Neutral states
- States not officially parties to the war
- Soviet Union and annexed territories
- Great Britain and colonies

500 kilometres
300 miles

N

any serious agreement with London or Paris, but he made one more effort to engage the British and French in negotiations. The British and French delegations arrived in Leningrad on a passenger ship, the *City of Exeter*, without authority to sign any documents. Stalin and his team were not impressed. On 11 August the visitors arrived in Moscow for talks about combined (multinational) action to repel any German aggression. Their lack of authority to sign documents soon became apparent. The People's Commissar for Defence (Defence Minister) Kliment Voroshilov asked whether there was any agreement with Poland to let Soviet forces pass through its territory in the event of war between the western powers and Germany. The head of the French delegation, General Doumain, said he did not know the Polish plans. Asked what they could contribute to the land battle – for such esoteric concepts as command of the sea were of little immediate value to the Russians – the British replied sixteen divisions immediately, plus another sixteen later. Given that the British Army at the time comprised six divisions, against 140 German and, according to British and French intelligence, 120 Soviet, this promise was, frankly, incredible. The Soviet side also asked about British and French plans for Belgium. Again, they received the helpful (and disingenuous) answer from the French that they would only enter Belgium if the Belgians asked them to, and that the French had no idea whether the Belgians would. In the face of such consummate diplomacy, on 14 August 1939 Marshal Voroshilov declared that 'without clear and unambiguous answers to these questions, further negotiations are pointless. The Soviet military delegation cannot recommend that its government participate in an undertaking so clearly doomed to failure.'[31]

Compared with this sorry state of affairs, the proposal which had come from Germany seemed to be a breath of fresh air. On 2 August, no doubt on direct instructions from Hitler, the German Foreign Minister, Joachim von Ribbentrop, told Georgiy Astakhov, the Soviet Chargé d'Affaires in Berlin, that Hitler wanted a 'new kind' of relations between Germany and the Soviet Union. Astakhov asked him to be more specific. In a cable sent on the afternoon of 3 August reporting these discussions to Count Werner von Schulenberg, the German ambassador in Moscow, Ribbentrop added that he had told Astakhov that Germany was prepared to 'reach an agreement with Russia [*sic*] regarding the future of Poland'.[32]

On the evening of 3 August Schulenberg went to see Molotov, in

Moscow. He reiterated that Germany wanted 'to reach an understanding regarding spheres of interest'. Molotov was cautious. The Soviet Union and France had jointly agreed to assist Czechoslovakia in the event of aggression, and when the threat became real in autumn 1938, mobilization orders had been issued in the western Soviet Union. France, however, had been party to the Munich agreement, from which the Soviet Union had been excluded. In addition to the Munich agreement, Molotov cited a number of other 'unfriendly' actions by Germany: the anti-Comintern pact and support for the Japanese in their actions against the Soviet Union in Asia, which were curtailed by Zhukov's great victory at Nomonhan, on the River Khalkin Gol.[33]

Schulenberg got the impression that the Soviet Union had 'decided to conclude an agreement with Britain and France', and recommended that Berlin try harder.[34] Hitler had already set the invasion of Poland for 1 September, and was therefore in a hurry. Stalin was much cooler, but increasingly inclined towards an agreement with Germany. On 14 August Schulenberg was told to inform Molotov that 'German–Russian relations have reached a turning point and . . . there is no real conflict of interest between Germany and Russia.'[35] It was at this meeting that the idea of a non-aggression pact was first raised.

Both sides had a lot to gain. Hitler, working through Ribbentrop, needed to ensure that there would be no risk of war with the Soviet Union when he invaded Poland. Stalin, working through Molotov, was aware that Britain and France were not going to provide any guarantees to the Baltic States – Estonia, Latvia and Lithuania – like their guarantee to Poland. That therefore gave Hitler an easy route to invade the Soviet Union. If Hitler could be persuaded to give the Soviet Union a free hand in the Baltics, that vulnerability would be removed.

On 16 August Hitler confirmed that he was prepared to sign a non-aggression treaty with the Soviet Union, and that other 'current issues' – the partition of Poland and the fate of the Baltic States – would be 'clarified'. It was also stated that Ribbentrop would be on standby to fly to Moscow at any time from 18 August. Stalin was not in such a hurry, and in his reply he stipulated that he also wanted a treaty on commerce and credits and an 'additional secret protocol'. At this stage Astakhov, the Chargé d'Affaires in Berlin, was recalled, and subsequently disappeared. It later transpired that Stalin had him shot, because he knew too much.[36]

As 'D-Day' for the invasion of Poland approached, Hitler became more and more agitated. On 19 August Schulenberg was ordered to see Molotov as soon as possible and to inform him that although Germany would prefer to conduct negotiations in the normal diplomatic way, the 'unusual situation of the moment' made this impossible. In fact, exasperated by the old-world diplomacy carried on by Britain and France, Stalin already realized that his fellow dictator was a man with whom he could do business. Schulenberg was also told to say that German–Polish relations were deteriorating rapidly and might result in an armed clash any day. If that happened, the Führer was keen that 'Russian interests should be taken into account'. Stalin saw that here was the opportunity to do an advantageous deal with Hitler, and Molotov, who had been holding out for a commercial treaty as top priority, was told to summon Ambassador Schulenberg immediately. At first the Soviet side offered to sign the commercial treaty on 20 August, and then to welcome Ribbentrop to Moscow on 26–27 August.[37] This was too close to the Polish invasion. The trade agreement was signed on 20 August. Then, the same day, Hitler dictated his first letter to Stalin, the leader of the 'world Bolshevism' which he so hated. He accepted the draft non-aggression treaty proposed by Molotov, but said it was necessary to 'clarify the issues related to it at the earliest possible date'. The tension between Germany and Poland had become 'intolerable', so Hitler asked Stalin to receive Ribbentrop on Tuesday 22 August, but no later than Wednesday 23 August.

> The Minister of Foreign Affairs has full and unlimited
> authority to draft and sign both a non-aggression treaty and
> a protocol. In view of the international situation, the Minister
> of Foreign Affairs cannot stay in Moscow longer than one or
> two days at most. I would be pleased to receive your early
> reply. Adolf Hitler.[38]

For Hitler, this was a short-term fix, designed to clear the decks for the invasion of Poland. In no way did it compromise his long-term aim of eliminating Bolshevism. Indeed, by bringing the frontiers of German and Soviet occupation together, it made a subsequent armed clash between the superstates more likely. Stalin interpreted Hitler's message as a framework for longer-term cooperation. Hitler had alluded to the 'political course [of German–Russian cooperation] that over centuries benefited both states'. And this was a far better way of doing business than the dull, imprecise messages he had been getting from London and

Paris. He did not rule out the idea that he would eventually have to fight Hitler, but he clearly saw the pact as putting off hostilities for some time. Stalin must have been aware of the damage his purges had inflicted on the Red Army's ability to fight a major war. Furthermore, if he spurned Hitler's offer, it would give Hitler the opportunity to accuse the Soviet Union of planning to launch aggression. Hitler's anxiety to conclude the Pact and to tidy up the fate of Poland suggested that he was going to attack there, which would inevitably bring Britain and France into the war. There was no guarantee that a war with those countries would be resolved quickly – or even that Hitler would win it. For Stalin, at that time, the Pact seemed a very good idea.

Schulenberg was summoned to see Molotov at 17.00 on 21 August. Molotov handed him Stalin's response to Hitler's telegram, confirming that the Soviet government would receive Ribbentrop on 23 August. A short communiqué would be published late the next morning, announcing the suggested conclusion of the Pact and the 'awaited' arrival of the German Foreign Minister. Molotov requested Germany's agreement by midnight on 21 August.[39] Schulenberg then forwarded Stalin's concise reply. In the light of what happened between 1941 and 1945, it is worth quoting in full:

> To the Chancellor of Germany Mr Adolf Hitler.
> Thank you for your letter.
>
> I hope that the German–Soviet non-aggression pact will be a decisive turning point in improving political relations between our countries.
>
> The peoples of our countries need peaceful relations with each other. The agreement of the German Government to conclude the non-aggression pact creates a foundation for liquidating political tension and for establishing peace and comradeship between our countries.
>
> The Soviet Government authorizes me to inform you, that it agrees to Mr Ribbentrop coming to Moscow on 23 August.
>
> I. Stalin.[40]

Ribbentrop duly arrived in Moscow, bearing a letter which Hitler had signed at his mountain retreat, the Berghof at Obersaltzburg, the previous day. The letter authorized him to carry out negotiations and to conclude the pact concerning 'non-aggression, and also concerning other linked questions which emerge as a result of these negotiations, in order that the Pact and these agreements should come into force immediately after their signature'.[41] The first meeting with Stalin and Molotov lasted three hours, after which, just after eight in the evening, Ribbentrop cabled the German Foreign Ministry asking for clarification on just one point concerning the Additional Secret Protocol. The Soviets wanted confirmation that the Latvian ports of Libau (Liepaja) and Vindava (Ventspils) would be in their sphere of influence (see map in Figure 3.2).[42] This was hardly a contentious issue, since the 23 August agreement assigned Latvia to the Soviet sphere, and Hitler's agreement was forthcoming, by telephone.[43] The documents were signed at a solemn ceremony in Stalin's presence, and then the drinking started. The cocktail party lasted until dawn, and only after that was Ribbentrop able to report success. The Germans had brought with them an exhibition of Albert Speer's designs for the new Berlin, based on Hitler's grandiose construction plans. Hitler's original drawings were displayed on separate stands, and then translated into Albert Speer's more perfect images, enlivened by sophisticated lighting effects. The atmosphere, by all accounts, was exceptionally warm. The vodka and champagne flowed, and Stalin was charming. In conversation, it emerged that the key difference between Nazi Germany and Soviet Russia remained the anti-Comintern Pact, concluded between Italy, Germany and Japan. That Pact, Ribbentrop said, half in jest, was concluded not against the Soviet Union, but against the western democracies. That was an absurd statement, but Stalin pretended to agree, adding that it 'scared the City of London mostly – and the small shopkeepers in Britain'.[44] Stalin then raised his glass in a toast to Hitler, while Molotov toasted Ribbentrop and Schulenberg. And then, before departing, Stalin said to Ribbentrop 'The Soviet Union is very serious about the new Pact. I give you my word of honour that the Soviet Union will not cheat on its partner.'[45]

Whatever Stalin's long-term plans, the Soviet Union did not cheat on its 'partner'. But Hitler had probably already resolved to do so. Hitler's obvious intent in *Mein Kampf* was fulfilled. He had said the Soviet Union could not be trusted to keep its promises. At the end of the day, it was he who did not.

The Molotov–Ribbentrop Pact of 23 August 1939 comprised seven articles which were published in *Pravda* the next day. Both states would refrain from any aggressive action against each other or against neigh-bouring states. In the event of either party being attacked by a third, the

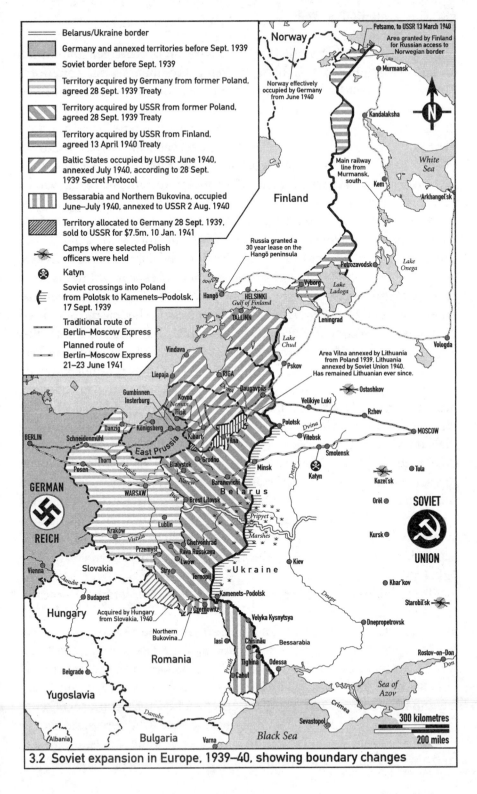

Legend:

- Belarus/Ukraine border
- Germany and annexed territories before Sept. 1939
- Soviet border before Sept. 1939
- Territory acquired by Germany from former Poland, agreed 28 Sept. 1939 Treaty
- Territory acquired by USSR from former Poland, agreed 28 Sept. 1939 Treaty
- Territory acquired by USSR from Finland, agreed 13 April 1940 Treaty
- Baltic States occupied by USSR June 1940, annexed July 1940, according to 28 Sept. 1939 Secret Protocol
- Bessarabia and Northern Bukovina, occupied June–July 1940, annexed to USSR 2 Aug. 1940
- Territory allocated to Germany 28 Sept. 1939, sold to USSR for $7.5m, 10 Jan. 1941
- Camps where selected Polish officers were held
- Katyn
- Soviet crossings into Poland from Polotsk to Kamenets–Podolsk, 17 Sept. 1939
- Traditional route of Berlin–Moscow Express
- Planned route of Berlin–Moscow Express 21–23 June 1941

3.2 Soviet expansion in Europe, 1939–40, showing boundary changes

other party would not assist that third party. Both governments would consult each other on all matters relating to their mutual interests. Neither would participate in any alliance prejudicial to the interests of the other. In the event of any disagreement or conflict between the two parties, those would be resolved by exclusively peaceful means and, if necessary, by arbitration. The Pact would be valid for ten years and, if neither party reneged on it a year before that time was up, it would automatically be extended for another five years. And it would come into force immediately.[46]

The Additional Secret Protocol, which was superseded by a subsequent protocol agreed on Ribbentrop's next visit to Moscow on 28 September, fixed the northern demarcation line between the German and Soviet spheres of influence as the northern border of Lithuania. The spheres of influence between Germany and the USSR were more widely established as the Rivers Narew, Vistula and San. This meant that after Germany's invasion of Poland, the Soviet Union would acquire the eastern part of the country, known as 'western Belarus' and 'western Ukraine'. Whilst this partition – and the Soviet names for the territories thus acquired – may appear grossly cynical, the areas concerned were heavily populated by Slavs, and the Soviet position was that the 'Curzon line', which formed the border of the new Poland, had been imposed at the end of the Great War at a time of great Soviet weakness and disadvantage. Most of Poland had also been part of the old, pre-1917 Russian Empire. Finally, 'as far as south-east Europe is concerned', the Additional Secret Protocol established Soviet interest in Bessarabia (modern Moldova). (See Figure 3.2.) Germany, for its part, affirmed its 'complete lack of interest' in the area.[47] Thus, subject to the 28 September 1939 amendment, the reorganization of eastern Europe in 1939–40 was cast in stone.

The Additional Secret Protocol to the 23 August Molotov–Ribbentrop Pact had placed Finland, Estonia and Latvia in the Soviet 'sphere of influence' but left Lithuania for the Germans. The Secret Protocol to the 28 September Treaty on Friendship and the USSR–German Frontier 'corrected' that position, and placed Lithuania within the Soviet sphere (see Figure 3.2). When the secret protocols were revealed, in 1989, attention focused on the 23 August pact and associated protocol, and the fact that Lithuania was, at that stage, outside the Soviet sphere of influence led some to question the authenticity of the new evidence. In fact, the scholars – and Mikhail Gorbachëv's advisers – had simply overlooked the later 28 September treaty and associated secret protocols.[48]

Meanwhile, on 1 September, German forces – five armies, totalling 1.5 million men – had attacked Poland. Although the 23 August Pact had agreed the demarcation line, the Soviet forces were not ready to move into Poland. Stalin had never been in as much of a hurry as Hitler, and Hitler's troops could do – and did – most of the fighting. The Germans had penetrated the Polish frontier areas by 5 September, by which time Britain and France had declared war, and by 7 September were within 40 kilometres of Warsaw.

On the evening of 3 September, Ribbentrop sent an uncharacteristically panicky cable to Schulenberg in Moscow. 'Very immediate. For the Ambassador personally. Top Secret! ... only to be deciphered by him personally! *Extremely* Top Secret.'[49] Ribbentrop said the Germans hoped to completely defeat the Polish army within several weeks. Then they would occupy the areas which, it had been agreed in Moscow, lay within the German sphere of influence. However, until then they would also have to act against Polish forces in the Soviet sphere of influence. Would Schulenberg please inform Molotov of this and see whether the Soviet Union would allow the 'Russian Army' [*sic*] to move against the Polish forces at an appropriate moment.

Molotov saw Schulenberg at 12.30 on 5 September, replying that 'concrete action' – in other words, the committal of Soviet forces – was required, but that excessive haste might be counterproductive and help their mutual enemy. Therefore, if either German or Soviet forces needed to cross the demarcation line in the course of operations, that would not affect the ultimate implementation of the agreed plan. The Soviets were quite happy to have the Germans do most of the fighting – at first. It is probable that the risk of friendly fire incidents – of German and Soviet troops firing on each other by mistake – provided an additional reason to hold back, especially given the poor state of training of the Soviet troops and many of their officers. On the other hand, if the Soviet forces did nothing, and the Germans occupied eastern Poland all the way to the original Soviet frontier, it might prove very difficult to dislodge them. German requests that the Red Army should advance also implied a threat to occupy the Soviet 'sphere of interest' if it did not. At this point mobilization of an additional 1.5 million Soviet troops was under way. On 9 September Schulenberg reported that the Soviet offensive would begin 'in the next few days'. But the following day he reported that the Soviet forces would need two to three weeks for their preparations, although they had already mobilized 3 million men.[50] Either Molotov was playing a cynical game, or he really had little idea what the Red Army was up to, or the Soviets were trying desperately to organize a military response. Reports of the state of the Soviet forces which moved into Poland suggest the latter is probably the case. The Soviet response to the German invasion of Poland, which caught the former unawares, was not totally dissimilar to its response on 22 June 1941, though on a far smaller scale and without the utterly catastrophic consequences.

A week later, on 16 September, Molotov said the Soviet military intervention would begin 'tomorrow or the day after'. But then Stalin summoned Schulenberg and, at 2 a.m. on 17 September, in the presence of Molotov and Voroshilov – the People's Commissar for Defence – told him that the Red Army would cross the border at 6 a.m., along a line from Polotsk to Kamenets-Podolsk. Therefore in order to avoid 'incidents' – 'friendly fire', again – he asked German aircraft not to fly east of the line Bialystok–Brest–Litovsk–Lemberg (L'viv). Henceforward, Marshal Voroshilov, the Defence Minister, would deal directly with Lieutenant-General Köstring, the German military attaché, on all military matters.[51]

In accordance with long-standing Soviet plans, the Chief of the Soviet General Staff, Marshal Boris Shaposhnikov, ordered the Kiev Special Military District commander, Army Commander First Rank Semyen Timoshenko, and Army Commander Second Rank Kovalëv, commanding the Belorussian, to form *front* (army group) commands, a higher formation introduced by the Imperial Russian Army in the First World War. (In passing, it is easy to see why the Soviets reintroduced the more concise rank of 'general' the following year.) The military districts – the 'peacetime' organizations established by War Minister Milyutin in the 1860s – became the Ukrainian and the Belorussian Fronts, respectively. The Ukrainian Front, to the south, with 265,000 troops; and the Belorussian, to the north, with 200,000, moved into Poland. The boundary between them ran through the southern edge of the Pripyet marshes.

The first troops across, at 05.40 on 17 September, were cavalry and tanks in 'mobile groups', and they brushed aside the Polish border guards. By 25 September, a week later, they had reached the demarcation line along the western Bug and San rivers. Only one 'friendly fire' incident with German troops is recorded.[52] Many Poles surrendered to the Germans rather than confront the Soviet army. The Soviets therefore faced minimal resistance. The Poles were already broken by the German onslaught, and the Red Army encountered only isolated pockets of troops: remnants of Polish army formations, 'nationalist paramilitaries' – Polish partisans, and *gendarmerie*. The main Polish forces were not engaged, although, even so, they allegedly accounted for 330 Soviet tanks, in spite of being short on anti-armour weapons.[53] However, the Red Army lost a relatively modest 996 officers and men killed and missing, and just under 2,400 sick and wounded. Russian statistics list only members of the Red Army: NKVD troops arrived later to cement the Soviet occupation of 'western Ukraine' and 'western Belarus'.[54]

Although fears of 'friendly fire' were largely unfulfilled, there was one confrontation between German and Russian generals. Although the demarcation line was provisionally fixed on the River Bug, General Heinz Guderian may have thought that possession was nine-tenths of the law, and a train carrying his tanks continued heading eastwards, but was stopped because Soviet tanks had smartly parked across the tracks. Guderian was photographed arguing with Semyon Krivosheyn, the Soviet general and a veteran of very recent action at Khalkin Gol. Guderian demanded that Krivosheyn remove his tanks. 'Sorry, general,' the Russian replied, 'but our tanks are out of fuel.'[55]

On 8 September, Beria, the People's Commissar for Internal Affairs, had ordered exercises involving NKVD personnel and border guards in the Ukrainian and Belorussian Republics to begin the following evening. Some 50 Ukrainian NKVD agents and 150 political officers from the border guards ('operational–political workers') were to convene in Kiev by 22.00, and the same number of each in Minsk by the same time. In addition, another 30 NKVD agents were to be brought to Kiev from Leningrad, and 10 from the NKVD of the USSR, presumably from Moscow. A further 15 USSR NKVD agents would deploy to Minsk. The heads of the Ukrainian and Belorussian NKVD, the newly appointed 34-year-old Ivan Serov and 39-year-old Lavrenty Tsanava, respectively, were to set up 'operational-Chekist groups' to work with the army groups (fronts) in the areas about to be occupied. The *Cheka* had been the name for the Soviet internal security service from 1918 to 1922, and was still used informally, although it had become OGPU[56] in 1922 and the NKVD in 1934. Five such *operchekistskiy* groups would be set up in the Kiev Special Military District and four in the Belorussian, numbering 50 to 70 and 40 to 55, respectively.[57]

Beria issued orders for NKVD operations in the 'liberated regions of the western districts of Ukraine and Belarus' on 15 September, two days before the Soviet forces, initially the army, moved in.[58] Now referred to, less anachronistically, as NKVD Operational Groups (*opergruppy*), their job was, first, to occupy all communications installations including telephone exchanges, telegraph offices, radio stations and post offices, and to put 'reliable people' in charge of them. Next, they would seize all state and private banks, vaults and any repositories for valuables, and record the assets they found. They would work with the political departments of the army to seize all printing presses, newspaper offices and stocks of paper, and 'sort out newspaper publishing'. They would seize all state records, especially police records and the files of the Polish intelligence services. The *opergruppy* would then arrest 'the most reactionary members of the Government (heads of local police, gendarmerie, foreign and military intelligence, military commanders and their immediate staff), the leaders of anti-revolutionary parties, including émigré White Guards and members of the monarchist organizations BRP and ROVS'.[59] Prisons were to be seized, and the prisoners carefully investigated. Those imprisoned for anti-government agitation should, after careful checking, be released and employed on political work among the population. A new prison administration was to be set up, headed by one of the NKVD agents who would ensure a 'strict regime'. Those now arrested would have their affairs carefully investigated so as to reveal underground organizations which might conduct terror and sabotage. Power stations, waterworks, granaries and grain elevators should be secured, and a constant watch kept for theft, looting, banditry and speculation. Rifled firearms (not smooth-bores, such as shotguns), explosives and radio transmitters were all to be confiscated. However, Beria ordered, 'avoid confiscating forage and food from the population. You will buy forage and food supplies which you need from the population in cash, in Soviet roubles, having told them that the [paper] rouble is worth the same as gold.'[60]

Although issued only two days before the move into former Poland, Beria's orders are perceptive and would repay study by those planning 'regime change' in other people's countries. NKVD border guards were involved in the initial move into Poland on 17 September,[61] and on

19 September the first report from what is, again, referred to as an *operchekistskiy* group appeared, relating action the previous day. The 'state-builders' were right behind the forward troops. They reached Tarnopol (modern Ternopil, now in Ukraine), 46 kilometres from the 1939 frontier, at six in the evening, five hours behind the first NKVD detachment. The Red Army had got there the previous day, but had obviously not been aware of Beria's intent. There were several thousand prisoners, and it soon emerged that the Red Army, having captured the prison, had smashed it up, let all the prisoners go and destroyed a lot of the documents. Some of the escaped prisoners were recaptured quite quickly. The Red Army's orders were to move on as fast as possible in the direction of Lwów, and they were doing so, leaving the city without any visible army command. The Red Army soldiers did not know where the headquarters was and the designated commander in the city, Major Vervitskiy, deputy commander of 289 Rifle Regiment, was nowhere to be found. Unsurprisingly, perhaps, he is next heard of as head of a logistics department of Sixth Army. And after that ... nothing. The NKVD had their orders, which centred on careful scrutiny and assessment of the prisoners. After dark on the 18th, in the words of the report, 'some unit of the Red Army or other' deployed as if to oppose the border guards, who had just arrived. Then they opened fire with rifles and machine guns 'in a disorderly way ... in panic'.[62] Meanwhile the *operchekistskiye* got on with their job, arresting about 200 police, gendarmes and other key people. However, they could not be taken to the prison because the Red Army had 'smashed in all the doors'.[63] They then got word that a group of up to forty 'suspicious' people – Polish officers – was gathering outside the city, and a group was despatched 'to liquidate them'. The report was signed by Vsevolod Merkulov, head of the State Security Directorate of the NKVD, which would become the NKGB in 1941, and by Serov, head of the Ukrainian NKVD. They said they needed more men in the 'Chekist' groups than they had originally thought, and that the Red Army would have to take responsibility for order and guarding prisoners in captured towns.[64]

As the NKVD teams, under Beria's direction, began the 'liberation' of civilians in 'western Ukraine' and 'western Belarus', the Polish troops who had not surrendered to the Germans were taken prisoner by the Soviets, who were surprised by their numbers. A year after the Red Army move into Poland, the prisoners taken were numbered at 230,000, including 190,460 by the Ukrainian Front alone.[65] British diplomats estimated that, of these, 180,000 were moved to camps in Russia.[66] But, as so often happens with accounts of the Soviet role in the Second World War, the numbers grow. According to the refined Russian records, published in 1993, the Ukrainian Front to the south took prisoner 392,334 Poles between 17 September and 2 October, while the Belorussian Front, in the smaller area to the north of the Pripyet marshes, took 60,202. Total – 452, 536.[67]

The surrender of Lwów (L'viv) to the Red Army on 22 September exemplifies the long-standing Polish dilemma, trapped between the Germans and the Russians,[68] and also demonstrates how the Russians operated. The Poles wanted to go on fighting the Germans, and in negotiations between Polish General Langner and Marshal Timoshenko's deputy, the Russians promised they would be allowed to go to Romania or Hungary and thence to France, where they could join compatriots already there, and continue fighting the Germans. Those who did not want to leave the country but just wished to go home were promised food for the journey. Given that the Russians were collaborating closely with the Germans, it was unlikely these promises would be fulfilled – but the Poles probably did not know that. The majority of the Polish officers, certainly, were deported to special camps in Russia.[69]

The Russian state security archives reveal some intriguing collaboration with the Germans. On 16 October Beria wrote that the command of the Belorussian Front had been offered 20,000 Polish soldiers taken prisoners of war by the Germans. The prisoners were Belorussians and Ukrainians by nationality and their families came from territory now occupied by the Russians. Some 3,000 would be sent to Drogichin and 6,000 to Brest-Litovsk. Beria ordered them to be 'welcomed in an organized fashion', fed at intervals along the journey, and then given free transportation home. But there was a rub to his apparent generosity. 'In the process of receiving them,' he wrote, 'take account of people who look like officers, spies and suspicious people.' And then: 'make a report' (*ispolnite doneseniye*).[70]

Most of the surviving reports of the Red Army moving into Poland and, later, into the Baltic States, came from Poles and Estonians who were 'always apt to be prejudiced against the Russians', and British Intelligence warned in November 1939 that the picture might therefore be 'somewhat unfair to the Red Army'. This was the first time the Red Army had been seen in any numbers outside the original Soviet Union, in Europe, and observers believed the Red Army Command tried to use its best troops at the start of every operation. Even so, some observers commented on the 'low standard of intelligence and slovenly appearance of the officers, although some individual officers of armoured units made a satisfactory impression'. In Lwów, the Red Army officers 'created a great impression among the Poles, themselves no mean trenchermen, by the alacrity with which they rushed into the restaurants and consumed vast quantities of food'. The other ranks who moved into Poland were often 'small and thin' and showed signs of previous undernourishment, although they made up for it by rivalling their officers in the amount of food they consumed.[71] On the whole, the officers had 'good control over their men and suppressed *drastically and effectively any tendency towards looting*'. That almost certainly means that officers shot soldiers who breached military discipline. As a result there was 'little looting or drunkenness, strict measures having been taken to prevent trouble of this sort'. Most of the troops appeared 'apathetic' about their own operations although there was, interestingly, 'some apparent desire to fight the Germans'.[72] The advance into Poland went fast – 35 to 40 miles (56 to 64 kilometres) per day – and although the Soviet columns carried a large amount of fuel with them, it ran out rapidly. The tanks stuck to the roads as much as possible and there were apparently few breakdowns, but an attempt to move across country near Lwów was described as a 'dismal failure'. Anyone who knows the Russians may empathize with the British Intelligence officer:

> Russian military administration remains much as it used to be. Train timings are chaotic, motor transport is seldom available at the right time and place, petrol supplies break down, and no one has any clear idea at what time anything is going to arrive. In spite of it all *something* happens . . . the Red Army was faced with hardly any opposition, so . . . the defects in administration did not have their full effect, but even so one is left with the impression that the Russian genius for piecemeal improvisation will always carry them through to a strictly limited extent.[73]

Although Germany and the Soviet Union both clearly intended to abide by the Molotov–Ribbentrop Pact, a further agreement was necessary to tidy up the partition of Poland. On 20 September Schulenberg cabled Ribbentrop to say that Molotov had asked for further talks in Moscow. On 25 September Schulenberg was again summoned to the

Kremlin, at 20.00, and told that Stalin was against leaving any portion of Poland as an independent country. Therefore, Stalin proposed handing over the Lublin area, and part of the Warsaw area west of the Bug, to Germany if the Germans gave up their claim to Lithuania. Stalin stressed the importance of Estonia, Latvia and Lithuania, but, Schulenberg noted, 'did not mention Finland'.[74]

Pravda was regularly printing maps showing the demarcation line between the German and Soviet forces in Poland.[75] Ribbentrop arrived in Moscow at 18.00 on 27 September to discuss 'questions linked with events in Poland'. Once again, the initial meeting lasted three hours, from 22.00 until 01.00 the next morning – 'one of the night', as the Russian language so eloquently describes that itching, aching, post-witching hour. Stalin, like many great leaders, was a nocturnal creature. Negotiations resumed at 15.00 the next day, 28 September, and lasted until 18.30. After a brief supper at the Kremlin, Ribbentrop was taken to one act of *Swan Lake*, while Stalin conferred with his lieutenants. Negotiations resumed at midnight, with the German–Soviet Treaty on Friendship and the Frontier between the USSR and Germany signed at 05.00 on 29 September, although it was dated 28th. Then the delegations retired to the German Ambassador's residence for a reception until 06.30 – dawn.[76]

The Treaty established the new frontier between their 'state interests on the territory of the former state of Poland', according to the attached map and the Additional Secret Protocol. Both sides recognized this frontier as final and rejected any interference by third parties in its determination. What happened to the west of the line was Germany's business and, to the east, the Soviet Union's. Both governments would do everything possible to further develop friendly relations between their peoples, and the Treaty would come into force immediately.[77] Besides the published Treaty, there were three additional protocols. The first Confidential Protocol said, fairly innocuously, that people 'of German descent' finding themselves in the Soviet sphere of influence could move to Germany and that their rights were safeguarded, and, similarly, that Belorussians and Ukrainians in the German area could move to the USSR. What that really meant was that the secret police on both sides could demand the extradition of anyone they wanted. Then there were the two 28 September Additional Secret Protocols. The first said that the Secret Protocol to the 23 August Pact had to be 'corrected' (*ispravlën*) on its first point. The territory of Lithuania, the new Secret

Protocol explained, lay within the USSR's sphere of influence and the Lublin area and part of the Warsaw area of the former state of Poland lay within Germany's. A small part of Lithuanian territory, south of a line on the map between Gumbinnen and Grodno, would be transferred to Germany.[78] Fifteen months later, very quietly, Germany dropped its claim to that area of Lithuanian territory if the Soviet Union paid it 7.5 million gold US dollars, equivalent to 31.5 million Reichsmarks. On 10 January 1941 Molotov and Schulenberg signed the secret deal in Moscow.[79]

A second Secret Protocol said that neither party would permit 'Polish agitation' on its territory which might damage the other, and that both parties would suppress all sources of such agitation and keep the other informed about what they were doing.[80] These protocols not only affected 'Polish agitation', but anyone wanted by either country for any reason. By the summer of 1941 the Soviet state security services had extradited about 4,000 people to Germany, including the families of German communists who had been arrested and shot in the Soviet Union during the purges, and German workers who had moved to the Soviet Union during the economic Depression in the West in the 1930s. Most of these were immediately sent to concentration camps. For their part, the Nazis deported people wanted by the Soviet state security agencies, principally the NKVD.[81]

Stalin's insistence that Poland should disappear from the face of the earth and that no part of it should remain independent had been confirmed in a note by the Commissariat for Foreign Affairs on 17 September, the start of the Soviet occupation. It had tragic consequences for many of the Polish troops who had surrendered. They had been told they would be allowed to leave for the West via Romania, and expected to be treated as prisoners of war according to the 1929 Geneva Conventions, not realizing that the Soviet Union had not signed it (see Chapter 2). According to proclamations by the Soviet General Staff and by Marshal Timoshenko, commanding the Ukrainian Front, they had come over to the Red Army voluntarily, and should be treated as friends. But the Soviet press and NKVD reasoned that if there was no longer a Polish state, they were no longer prisoners of war, but merely 'members of armed bands' – like bandits. This little technicality provided the Soviet security services with any justification they might need to dispose of former Polish soldiers and officers. The road to the Katyn massacre the next spring was clear.[82]

Once the German–Soviet Treaty and secret protocols were signed, champagne was served. Then a map was brought in with the dividing line between the two totalitarian states in the last partition of Poland marked on it. The allocation of the Baltic countries to the USSR was too secret to be marked, even on this map, but the line started north-west of Grodno (Hrodno), ran west to join the East Prussian border, as far as the Masurian Lakes, then south along the Pisa, cutting south-east again at Lomza, from the Narew to the western Bug river (the eastern Bug is in Ukraine, between the Dnestr and the Dnepr). The German–Soviet border then followed the Bug past Brest-Litovsk, and then south-south-east to Chervonhrad. There it left the western River Bug, ran west, north of Rava Russkaya (Rus'ka), to join the River San. Here, Stalin made a slight amendment to the frontier, taking Soviet territory a touch further north of Rava Russkaya, which he marked in blue pencil and initialled separately. Then the border ran south again, along the San, past the great First World War fortress of Przemysl, to the Hungarian border.[83] Germany received 190,000 square kilometres with 22 million people: the Soviet Union 200,000 square kilometres with 13 million people.[84]

Stalin spread the map out, took his big blue pencil and signed his name with an uncharacteristic flourish that swept from just south of Warsaw to the Pripyet marshes. Ribbentrop's signature was more controlled, but he used a red pencil – normally Stalin's preserve – and appended the date: 28/IX/39.[85] Plate 1 shows a photograph of the map, held in a 'closed archive' in Moscow.

Until now, Soviet troops had only moved into Poland. Another report signed by Merkulov on that very day recorded that on 27 September 'Operational-Chekist' group no. 1 had arrested 923 people, including 126 former Polish army officers, 513 people of political significance, 28 paramilitary police ('gendarmes'), 31 'police secret agents' and 44 members of the upper-middle classes. Group no. 4, operating in the Stry area, south of Lwów, had identified 700 oil wells – part of the registration of assets. Some 3,000 railway wagons with various petrol products, and including more than 200 containing high-grade fuel, were seized.[86]

But although the formal occupation and annexation of the Baltic States took place the next summer, Stalin was already demanding military facilities in the still independent states – the thin-end-of-the-wedge strategy. On the day before the 28 September treaty with Germany, Stalin had presented the Estonian Foreign Minister, who had hoped to sign a commercial agreement, with a proposal for a military alliance involving Soviet use of Estonian naval and air bases. The Estonians had no feasible option but to agree. On 28 September the 'Soviet-Estonian Pact on Mutual Cooperation' was signed in Moscow.[87] With the signature of the boundary treaty the next morning, Latvia and Lithuania soon followed the same path. Stalin suggested that 50,000 Soviet troops be based in Lithuania, which was negotiated down to 28,000. He now told the Latvian foreign minister that 'spheres of influence' had been agreed, and that it was necessary to comply, adding duplicitously that both Germany and the United Kingdom were ready to attack the Soviet Union if either won the war – not that such an outcome was remotely likely in the near future. On 18 October 1939, Soviet troops therefore moved into the Baltic States with the agreement of the 'host' governments.[88]

The impression created as the Soviet 'allies' moved in was similar to that created in Poland. An Estonian officer on traffic control duty during the movement of Soviet troops said that a Russian officer who asked the way was 'so bad at map reading that he could easily have sent him back to Russia'. While one must be careful about the reports, those moving into the Baltic States were described as 'real criminal types'. The British Military Attaché reported that part of a Soviet armoured brigade had lost seven tanks, five trucks and three caterpillar tractors broken down along a 40-kilometre stretch of quite good road. The locals cannot have been too hostile, however. A story did the rounds about a Red Army officer who, when shown the billets allocated to his men in an Estonian town, said they were far too good and that something much worse must be found. The standard of living in Latvia was high in comparison to the Soviet Union, especially its eastern parts, and, in order to explain this, soldiers from the Urals and other remoter parts were told they were being transferred to a 'particularly favoured part of the Soviet Union', which it was not. It would soon become part of the Soviet Union, but certainly not a favoured one.[89]

As a result of the observations in Poland and the Baltic States, most foreigners believed that 'the value of the Red Army for war remains low'. But many of the reports were of doubtful value. British Intelligence concluded that 'the strength of the army lies in its numbers and in a considerable quantity of good equipment'. One man in ten appeared to be carrying an automatic rifle, for example – very unusual in 1939. However,

> The weakness of leadership and of the administrative machine are evidently still very serious, and combined with the apathy and loss of initiative of the rank and file, must render the army a somewhat amorphous mass which may be capable of taking hard blows but is not capable of delivering them, at any rate when faced with a large scale organised opposition.[90]

They were about to meet it.

4

FURTHER SOVIET EXPANSION AND COOPERATION WITH GERMANY, NOVEMBER 1939 TO JUNE 1941

Finland, like the Baltic States, had long been seen as a 'complex issue' for Soviet security, and, although the Finns had long and close ties with Germany, the Molotov–Ribbentrop Pact placed it in the Soviet 'sphere of influence'. In 1936 Tukhachevskiy, then Chief of the Soviet General Staff, had accused the Finns of building air bases that the Germans could use to bomb Russia. In his 'testament', written before his reported execution in June 1937, Tukhachevskiy said that in the event of war with Germany the Soviet Union would have to occupy the Baltic States, but referred to Finland only as an 'independent issue of great complexity'. But the following year the NKVD's man in Helsinki warned the Finnish Foreign Minister that if Finland had not guaranteed its neutrality in the event of any war with Germany, then the Soviet Union would invade Finland, and Sweden as well.[1] Finland commanded the northern shore of the shallow Gulf of the same name, leading to Leningrad (formerly and now again St Petersburg). Leningrad was the former Russian capital, the Soviet Union's second city, a massive industrial centre, and the country's greatest sea port. If Finland's neutrality were compromised by either of the sides in the war that started on 1 September 1939, Finland could be used as a springboard for an attack on the Soviet Union. Leningrad was painfully close to the border, and so was the Leningrad-to-Murmansk railway which, if the Baltic and Black Seas were closed to Soviet shipping, would be the country's only link with a navigable sea in the west.

When Soviet forces moved into Poland on 17 September Molotov reassured Finland that he would respect the country's neutrality. In 1933 the Soviet Union had renewed its non-aggression pacts with Finland and the Baltic States. On 12 October a Finnish delegation arrived in Moscow for discussions in which Stalin and Molotov, advised by naval officers, sought to extend Soviet control over the Gulf of Finland. The demands were far-reaching, including cession to the Soviet Union of all the islands in the Gulf, especially the Björkö archipelago (now in Russia as the three Berezovy islands), and a Soviet base at the west end of the Gulf, on the Hangö (Hanko) peninsula (see Figure 3.2). Asking Finland to give up the Björkö islands, the Finnish Foreign Ministry's 'White Book' recorded, was a bit like asking the United Kingdom to give up the Isle of Wight, while the Hanko peninsula was more like the Orkney and Shetland Islands. If the latter was an exaggeration, the proposal was certainly equivalent to a foreign power setting up a base in Cornwall to control access to the English Channel.[2] The Finns, understandably, refused and after a second round of negotiations on 23 October, Stalin ordered the Main Military Soviet to update its plans to invade Finland. Whatever the foreign observers had thought, Stalin was evidently impressed, and misled, by the speed of the Red Army's advance through Poland, and suggestions that the lack of resistance was partly due to their being seen as liberators. He thought the Finns might feel the same way. The Red Army's success against the Japanese at faraway Khalkin Gol was another, perhaps more genuinely encouraging indicator, although the circumstances, terrain and climate were all quite different. And, at the end of the day, the population of Finland was 4 million: just over 2 per cent of that of the Soviet Union.

The invasion of Finland was to be conducted by the Leningrad Military District, on its own. The General Staff was 'not to have a hand in this; it is to concern itself with other matters'.[3] Not until January 1940, after humiliating setbacks, did the Military District become the North-West Front.

On 26 November the snowy quiet of the Karelian isthmus, near the border post of Mainila, was broken by seven rounds of artillery fire. Molotov blamed the Finns and demanded they withdraw 20 to 25 kilometres from the border. The Finns blamed the Russians, but were prepared to cooperate in an investigation, under the terms of their non-aggression pact. The next day, however, Molotov's deputy informed the Finnish Ambassador that the Soviet Union was severing diplomatic relations. At a quarter past midnight on 30 November the Defence Commissariat ordered the Leningrad Military District to launch its invasion later that day. Its commander, 42-year-old Kirill Meretskov (1897–1968), issued an order explaining that they were attacking not the Finnish people, but the government, which had provoked war with the Soviet Union. As Carl van Dyke has observed, it was neither an exhortation to the Red Army troops to fulfil a grandiose internationalist duty, nor a justification for limited territorial expansion. It was somewhere between. The war with Finland started as a preventive war, similar to the occupation of eastern Poland. It was to insulate the Soviet Union against military action either by Germany or by Britain and France.[4] It did not achieve that end, but it did achieve some territorial expansion, which may have saved Leningrad in 1941. Still more importantly, however, the terrible losses inflicted on the Soviet forces brought about essential military reforms which would come to fruition when they were most needed, in 1942–3.

The Finns expected a Soviet attack in the Karelian isthmus, between the Gulf of Finland and Lake Ladoga, and also along the north side of the Lake (see Figure 4.1). They had therefore fortified the isthmus with a belt of permanent field fortifications known as the 'Mannerheim Line' after the Finnish commander. Although nowhere near comparable with the Maginot or Siegfried Lines along the Franco-German border, the 'line' caused the Soviet troops enormous problems. At its widest, the 'Mannerheim Line' was 135 kilometres in extent and 90 kilometres deep.[5] There was an obstacle zone extending several kilometres back from the border, with minefields covered by machine-gun nests, then a main defensive zone comprising pillboxes – known to the Russians as DOTs (*dolgovremennaya ognevaya tochka* – permanent fire point), machine-gun posts, anti-tank barriers and other obstacles, linked by trenches. It was not necessary to fortify the entire 70-kilometre extent of this line because of the large number of swamps and lakes. Behind it were two more zones: the second defensive zone comprising 40 pillboxes and the rear zone comprising 18 (see map, Figure 4.2). These four zones were defended by six infantry divisions, while the other two Finnish divisions were deployed around Sortavala, on the north side of Lake Ladoga. The Finns did not expect any large-scale threat along the extensive border, which at that time extended northwards beyond Petsamo, now Pechenga, to the Barents Sea.[6]

On the Soviet side, Meretskov deployed 4 armies along the 1,000-kilometre front from the Baltic to the Barents Seas. The Leningrad Military District, responsible for running the war, had at its disposal

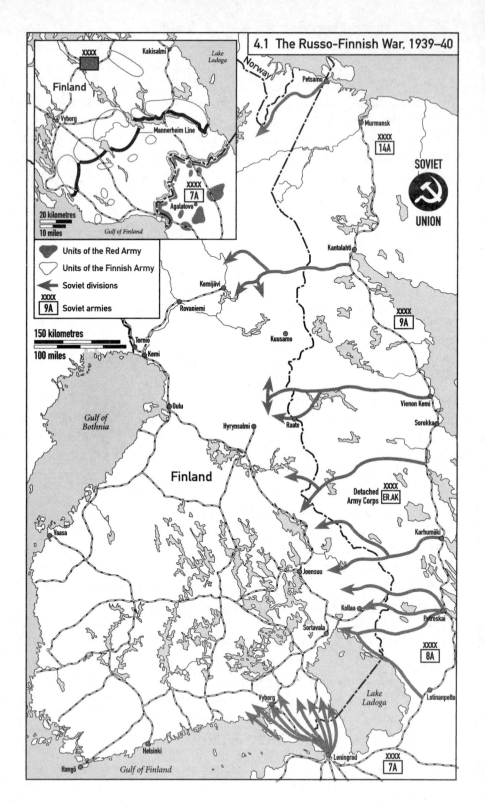

4.1 The Russo-Finnish War, 1939–40

Inset map (top left):

Finland

Kakisalmi

Lake Ladoga

Vyborg

Mannerheim Line

XXXX 7A

Agalatovo

Gulf of Finland

20 kilometres

10 miles

Legend:

Units of the Red Army

Units of the Finnish Army

Soviet divisions

XXXX 9A Soviet armies

150 kilometres

100 miles

Main map labels:

Norway

Petsamo

Murmansk

XXXX 14A

SOVIET UNION

Kantalahti

Kemijävi

Rovaniemi

Kuusamo

XXXX 9A

Tornio

Kemi

Vienon Kemi

Sorokka

Gulf of Bothnia

Oulu

Hyrynsalmi

Raate

Finland

Detached Army Corps XXXX ER.AK

Karhumäki

Vaasa

Joensuu

Kollaa

Petroskai

Sortavala

XXXX 8A

Lake Ladoga

Lotinanpelto

Vyborg

Helsinki

Hangö

Gulf of Finland

Leningrad

XXXX 7A

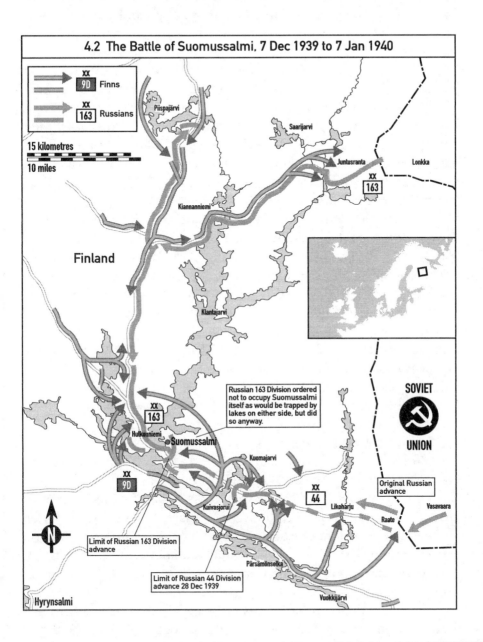

4.2 The Battle of Suomussalmi, 7 Dec 1939 to 7 Jan 1940

Finns
XX
9D

Russians
XX
163

15 kilometres

10 miles

Piispajärvi

Saarijarvi

Juntusranta

Lonkka

XX
163

Kiannanniemi

Finland

Klantajarvi

Russian 163 Division ordered
not to occupy Suomussalmi
itself as would be trapped by
lakes on either side, but did
so anyway.

SOVIET

UNION

XX
163

Hulkonniemi

Suomussalmi

Kuomajarvi

XX
9D

Original Russian
advance

Kuivasjorui

XX
44

Likoharju

Vasavaara

Raate

N

Limit of Russian 163 Division
advance

Limit of Russian 44 Division
advance 28 Dec 1939

Pärsämönselka

Hyrynsalmi

Vuokkijärvi

about a quarter of the Red Army's total 1939 order of battle. That meant 450,000 men, 23 rifle divisions, 2,000 tanks and 1,000 aircraft – nearly double the 12 divisions on which the Finns had based their calculations. In the Seventh Army on the Karelian isthmus alone Meretskov had 12 rifle divisions, 1 mechanized corps – equating roughly to an armoured division – 3 tank brigades and 12 artillery regiments. This meant 200,000 men, or just under half of the Leningrad MD's total forces. As the war progressed, the Soviet troops across this wide, inhospitable expanse of snow with 60,000 lakes had to be reinforced and the average monthly deployment, including the Baltic fleet, from December 1939 to March 1940 was a staggering 848,570 – one-fifth of the entire population of Finland.[7]

Breaking through the Mannerheim Line and operations north of Lake Ladoga would depend, to a great extent, on artillery. The Chief of Red Army Artillery, Nikolai Voronov, just back from the rather different climate of Spain, was summoned to the Kremlin. Meretskov, Gennady Kulik and Lev Mekhlis, both People's Commissars of Defence, were waiting. How many shells would be needed, Kulik asked?

'Everything depends on the situation,' Voronov replied warily. 'Are you planning to defend or attack? With what forces and in what sectors? By the way, how much time is allotted to the operations?'

'Between ten and twelve days.'

'I will be happy if everything can be resolved within two or three months,' replied Voronov.

Everyone else laughed.

'Voronov,' said Kulik, 'you are ordered to base all your estimates on the assumption that the operation will last twelve days.'[8]

Voronov was right. The war would last 105 days. The assumption that the operation would last only twelve days was one reason for an unforgivable omission. The Soviet troops were not equipped with warm winter clothing. They were still wearing summer uniforms. That was one lesson that they, and the Germans in 1941, would learn to their cost.

The other three Soviet armies were deployed in the remote and largely uninhabited region north of Lake Ladoga, and since the beginning of 1939 new depots, roads and railways had been built to facilitate their survival and movement. These included a secret road built to carry Soviet forces to the important road junction of Suomussalmi, which became the scene of a spectacular Red Army defeat.

The 1939–40 Soviet–Finnish war, known as the 'Winter War', began when Seventh Army was committed on 30 November. By 6 December Meretskov's forward tanks had only just crossed the obstacle zone and reached the anti-tank obstacles of the main zone. While Seventh Army tried to chew its way through the Mannerheim Line in the south, Soviet troops in the north captured Petsamo. But in the middle, trying to cut Finland in two at the waist, the Red Army encountered its biggest disaster. The Soviet 163rd Rifle Division headed south down the newly built secret road, but encountered Finnish resistance. On 14 December Ninth Army's commander, A. Dukhanov, sent 44th Division, commanded by A. Vinogradov, north to help it out.

On 20 December 44th Division began its move west along the Raate road towards Suomussalmi. A day later, Ninth Army headquarters helpfully sent it orders in clear over the radio.[9] Now informed of the planned junction of the two divisions, the Finns had the information they needed to prevent it. Although greatly outnumbered, the Finnish commander Col. Siilasvuo decided to break the two divisions apart, and succeeded. The Finns cut the road up which 44th Division had advanced, and held them off, turning on the now withdrawing 163rd. The Soviet troops, stuck to the roads with their heavy equipment, were separated into small groups and encircled by the Finns moving fast through the forest on skis. Then they were shot to pieces. These became known as *motti* battles, from the Finnish word for a 'little log of firewood', although like many tactical devices this one emerged by accident.[10] The Soviet 163rd Division's artillery, tanks and transport were strung out over an 8-kilometre stretch of road. The Finns broke it up and then worked away at the 'logs', one by one. By 9 January, the destruction of 163rd Division was complete. The *motti* tactical encirclements worked well, as did carefully targeted attacks on key components, notably the field kitchens without which, in the severest winter for a quarter of a century, no troops – even Russians – could be expected to fight for very long.

The Finns then turned their attention to 44th Division. On 4 January the commander, Vinogradov, asked permission to pull back. By this time, not surprisingly, Ninth Army had a new commander, *Komkor* (now Lt Gen.) Vasiliy Chuikov, who would later hold the city centre at Stalingrad and one day be a Marshal. Chuikov, in turn, requested permission from the chain of command – not the Leningrad Military District, this time, but the Stavka, the supreme High Command – for

Vinogradov to withdraw, but it took two days to come through.[11] When Vinogradov's division reached the relative safety of the Soviet–Finnish border on 7 December, it had lost 1,001 dead, 1,430 wounded, 82 suffering from frostbite (a disciplinary offence in the Red Army) and 2,243 missing.

The disaster at Suomussalmi was too bad to be left to the Military District to sort out. Lev Mekhlis, the Chief of the Red Army's Main Political Administration, was sent to find out what had happened, although he was more interested in making examples. Vinogradov and his staff were arrested and accused of leaving war materiel on the battlefield and failing to secure the Raate–Suomussalmi road properly. Vinogradov, his Political Commissar and Chief-of-Staff were shot in the presence of the other staff officers.[12]

The events at Suomussalmi and the Soviet response provide valuable pointers to what would happen in 1941. Chuikov and others at Ninth Army did not blame Vinogradov alone. Chuikov's Chief-of-Staff, D. Nikishev, produced a percipient analysis. Far from being in any sense technologically backward or ill equipped, the Red Army was, if anything, too reliant on heavy equipment, but did not know how to use it. The Red Army had been unable to free itself from what he called 'road strategy' because it had not devised tactical doctrine suitable to the terrain of north Finland. The relatively good roads and other communications in Poland and the Baltic States suited it much better. 'Our units,' he wrote, '*saturated by technology* (especially artillery and transport vehicles), are incapable of manoeuvre and combat in this theatre: they are *burdened and chained down by technology* which can only go by road.' It was a cry that will be familiar to many 21st-century readers. The troops, he continued, 'are frightened by the forest and cannot ski'.[13]

In the south, the penetration of the Mannerheim Line had been far too slow and Mannerheim had counter-attacked on 23 December. On 28 December, the People's Commissariat for Defence ordered the Leningrad Military District's armies to go over to the defensive. 'The war with Finland', the directive explained, in a style suggestive of Stalin's pencil, 'is a serious war, distinctly different from our autumn campaign in Poland.'[14] After four weeks, there would be no 'Blitzkrieg', as the Germans had accomplished in Poland, with the Soviet Union stumbling unprepared to exploit their success. The Leningrad Military District's attack on a broad front had failed. Shaposhnikov had suggested concentrating the available offensive power on a narrow front, and Stalin now agreed. On 7 January the North-West Front was created. It would be commanded by Timoshenko, who had directed the Ukrainian Front into Poland. The new front, unlike a combined-arms army, was responsible not just for coordinating infantry, tanks, artillery, engineers and other forces, but for coordinating the operations of all three services: land, sea and air. Timoshenko summoned people he knew from the Kiev Special Military District, from the General Staff Academy, the Frunze Military Academy, and the Leningrad Military District.[15]

On 1 February 1940 the Soviet forces began five 'demonstration' operations on separate sectors of the Karelian isthmus, prior to a new general offensive on 11 February. On each of the five demonstration sectors divisional commanders were given authority to select their own objectives and train their troops to overcome them, an idea inspired by the successful German use of *Auftragstaktik* or 'mission command'. Under this system, still espoused by modern armies,[16] subordinate commanders are not told *how* to do it: just what to do, and allowed to get on with it. When it works, it contributes greatly to operational flexibility and also to a force's resilience in the face of the unexpected, and particularly breakdowns in communications. But it takes years of training and practice to educate – and that is the real word – all levels of a force command to accomplish this. Timoshenko, commanding the new North-West Front, was understandably sceptical, but he was prepared to give it a go. Because the Soviet forces had failed to break through the Mannerheim Line before, they were reinforced with powerful artillery forces including massive 356mm coastal artillery guns on railway carriages to bombard Vyborg and divisional headquarters and ammunition depots. If the attempts at tactical subtlety failed, the Finnish fortifications would just be blown out of the ground.

Under the sheer weight of firepower and numbers, Finland was forced to sue for peace on 6 March. On 3 March the Red Army launched an offensive across the ice of Vyborg Bay, and the Finnish High Command warned that the front would soon collapse. Either there had to be foreign intervention by the vacillating British and French, or peace would have to be concluded. In late February there had been reports of the Finns using chemical weapons against some of the encircled *mottis*, especially against the 5th NKVD Division, and Mekhlis asked Stavka for permission to reply in kind, which was refused. If there was any truth in these reports, it was a sign that the Finns were getting desperate. But, for the first time, they were able to bomb targets in Seventh Army's rear areas using aircraft just received from abroad. The Soviet forces advancing along the Gulf of Finland coast were exhausted, and delayed by deliberate flooding. By 12 March both sides' efforts had culminated in a state of complete exhaustion.

On 6 March a delegation led by Finnish Prime Minister Risto Ryti flew to neutral Stockholm, and thence to Moscow where it arrived the next day. After several days of fruitless negotiations, on the evening of 12 March Ryti's delegation signed a treaty ceding all the territory demanded in the negotiations before the war, plus some more. It came into effect at 11.00 the next day. 'The territorial concessions offered by Finland must be greater than those proposed ... in October and November 1939', Molotov insisted. The Soviet Union took Finland's second biggest city, Viipuri (Vyborg), the strategically important area of Hanko, Petsamo (Pechenga), the largest Arctic Ocean port, the entire coast of Lake Ladoga, and the entire Karelian isthmus, home to 12 per cent of Finland's population. The latter had the option of becoming Soviet citizens, or leaving. All of them, without exception, headed west, leaving 40,000 farms behind them, many burning.[17]

But the Finns' heroic resistance thwarted the underlying Soviet intention to overrun their country in its entirety. As Stalin said later, 'Finland wasn't relevant to the basic needs of the world proletarian revolution.'[18] He had what he needed to protect Leningrad and improve access to the Gulf. The rest of Finland was not worth a guerrilla war which would probably continue indefinitely.

Initial reports indicated that the Finns suffered about 24,000 fatal casualties. Later, these figures were revised to 48,243 killed and 43,000 wounded.[19] The Soviet Union's total casualties were reported as 200,000, although at the time some reports, which we now know to be grossly exaggerated, suggested 500,000 or even 750,000 killed.[20] In 1949 to 1951 the USSR Ministry of Defence drew up the most accurate figures for Soviet casualties now available, which amounted to 126,875 'irrecoverable losses' – officers, men and civilian workers killed in action, dead or missing. About four times that number were wounded or sick, including frostbite cases who recovered. This high number of recoveries was largely due to the proximity of Leningrad with its excellent hospitals and medical facilities and to good casualty evacuation arrangements.[21]

The 1940 reforms

The lessons of the Soviet–Finnish winter appeared to bear out Timoshenko's own views, and those of many observers in the first year of the Second World War. France, it must be remembered, had not yet fallen, and many regarded the rapid German 'Blitzkrieg' (never an official German military term) into Poland as an aberration, attributable to Polish weakness. During the 1930s, the Red Army had experimented with Tukhachevskiy's grandiose plans for 'deep battle', involving simultaneous destruction of the enemy to great depths and rapid manoeuvre into the spaces which had been opened up. Much of the evidence from Spain, and now from Finland, led Stalin to support Timoshenko's view that what really worked was a 'wall of fire'. 'In previous years', Stalin said, 'we paid too much attention to ostentatious manoeuvres,' an allusion to the grand 1935 and 1936 summer manoeuvres, which attracted much interest in the West, and the grand plans of the now disappeared Tukhachevskiy.[22] Behind this curtain of fire, small-scale tactical manoeuvre, penetrating 'gaps in the enemy's fighting order', was possible.[23] But even doing this on a small scale required great improvements in training, and particularly in radio communications. Stalin seems to have greatly underrated the value of radios, in part, and not without reason, because radio communications were open to interception. The whole question of inter-arm cooperation was crucial, in particular between infantry, armour and artillery, and between ground forces and air. There was a proposal to improve the tactical effectiveness of Soviet aviation by adopting the German technique of dive-bombing, and on 22 April 1940 there was a suggestion that a group of Soviet pilots be sent to Germany to learn the technique.[24]

The Soviet–Finnish war therefore reinforced many ideas that were already around. On 13 August 1939, as the Molotov–Ribbentrop Pact was imminent, Defence Commissar Voroshilov had stressed the need for bright, well-trained soldiers. 'Neither an illiterate nor even a well-educated person can nowadays effectively exercise even the functions of a simple communications operator without having undergone basic training, let alone the junior officer corps.'[25] Voroshilov said he was going to lengthen the training period for junior commanders to three years. Even if that had happened immediately, it would have taken until the end of August 1942 for the first of the new wave of junior officers to qualify. The timing is highly significant. Even with the shock of 22 June 1941, and the simultaneous interruption and acceleration of military training programmes, we would not expect to see the results of this initiative and then of the Finnish war to show significant results until 1942. And that was when Red Army performance against the Germans really began to improve.

The need for *Auftragstaktik* – for 'mission command' – and the training implications was perhaps the most significant lesson reinforced amid the frozen swamps, snow and forest of Finland. Clearly, tactics had to be adapted to terrain – what worked in the Ukrainian steppe would not necessarily work in the Arctic or, as the Red Army later quickly discovered, in the Carpathians. If badly handled, tanks, trucks and mechanical artillery traction could be as much of a liability as an asset. Timoshenko wanted an army that could fight like the Finns, but, even if that was attainable in the case of a few units, it would take years to develop. During the Soviet–Finnish war, Stalin ordered the formation of new ski brigades for reconnaissance. Although many contemporary observers continued to deride the Red Army's preparation for modern war, those who followed the fighting in the Karelian isthmus carefully, notably the British military theorist and commentator Basil Liddell-Hart, recognized a 'surprising degree of organisational adaptability'.[26]

The Red Army's lack of preparation for fighting in the winter was partly due to the grossly optimistic estimates of how long the campaign would take, and that was a lesson well learned. 'The troops were ill-prepared for operations in forests and for coping with freezing weather and impassable roads,' wrote Marshal Voronov. 'Artillery material was of particular concern. During the freezing weather in Finland, the semi-automatic mechanisms in the guns failed. New types of lubricants had to be developed immediately.' There was a particular problem with the 152mm howitzer, and so 'large-scale research work had to be carried out'. The necessary changes highlighted by the Soviet–Finnish war would take time, but they were in place a year and a half later.[27] In 1941 it was the Germans who would freeze in summer uniforms, along with their fuel and lubricants, as the Red Army moved forward in quilted jackets, fur and snow camouflage, with equipment that worked at tens of degrees Celsius below zero.

One of the key lessons learned was the importance of camouflage. Meretskov, commanding the Leningrad Military District, saw this for himself when he and Pavlov, commanding Seventh Army, moved forward to within 500 metres of Finnish defences at Kiviniemi and watched them for two hours without being able to locate the precise firing points. Later, he and his political commissar observed a pillbox at Hill 65.5 firing from even closer range, but again could not locate it accurately.[28] Conversely, Soviet camouflage, particularly that of airfields, was often observed to be deficient.

In operational and military terms, the Soviet–Finnish war showed, once again, that there was no straightforward choice between 'manoeuvre' – avoiding the enemy's main forces, if you can, using surprise, cutting off communications – and 'attrition'. Attrition means killing people and destroying things. Against the Mannerheim Line, there was little choice. But when the opportunity arose to encircle Viipuri (Vyborg) by attacking across the ice of the Gulf of Finland, on 3 March, Timoshenko took it.[29] But fetishizing manoeuvre for its own sake would cause disaster. 'Today we are too fascinated with manoeuvre wars and we underestimate the struggle to break through defensive fortifications like the Maginot and Siegfried lines and others like them,' wrote Mekhlis in a report of 23 May 1940.[30] But defensive barriers could also be very useful to the Red Army itself. The experience in Finland indicated that a defender could easily absorb deep penetration by armoured and mechanized formations. 'Long term fixed fortifications within the defensive zone provide even greater power to the defender and allow the largest possible number of troops for a [counter] offensive.'[31] The recipe for Kursk was clear.

Although they suffered huge losses moving into Finland, the Soviet forces never faced any concerted attack on their own strategic bases until the very end. Politically, this is often a good idea for a country attacked, although it denies potentially lucrative opportunities. 'The enemy conducted not one strike against our bases,' reported Deputy Commissar for the Navy Isakov. 'This has colossal significance because if any base or port commander ... draws the conclusion that his ports and bases will work without jamming, this will not be the case in a large war.'[32] In this case, the 'enemy', for military and political reasons, refrained from attacks on Soviet (Russian) home territory. But big military operations are not usually performed on a patient who is strapped down.

At the politico-strategic level, the key lesson was that you cannot always count on assistance to be received in the invaded country, a lesson the British and US governments learned again in Iraq in 2003. The Soviet planners had counted on the collapse of Finnish morale, political will, and the Finnish government. There was no way this was going to happen. In 1941, the Germans, had they been clever, could possibly have exploited their initial welcome and won over the populace of much of the western Soviet Union. They failed, through their own brutality and colossal insensitivity. 'In the absence of moral-political collapse in the enemy's army and domestic population,' the Soviet General Staff concluded, 'the enemy's army will continue to preserve its ability to resist.'[33]

Lessons from learned and the last, lethal embrace

At the end of March 1940 the Central Committee of the Communist Party devoted much attention to examining the lessons of the Winter War, and other conflicts which can be regarded, with hindsight, as 'dress rehearsals' for 1941. The Party demanded an examination of, in particular, the combat experience accumulated at Lake Khasan in 1938, at Khalkin Gol in August 1939, and in Finland.[34] The events at Lake Khasan, where the Soviet Union, Japanese-occupied China and Korea met in summer 1938, arguably marked the nadir of the Soviet security forces' fortunes. The purges were at their height: the border guards did not belong to the Red Army, but came under the NKVD. At first both sides took care not to station troops near the disputed area, but then an NKVD general familiar with Soviet defences in the region defected to the Japanese. The Soviets decided to fortify the hills around the lake, thus claiming them for the Soviet Union, and NKVD patrols pushed deeper into Manchuria. The Japanese responded by capturing the heights. The Red Army Commander of the Far Eastern Military District, Vasiliy Blyukher, initially hesitated because he was unsure whether the heights really belonged to the USSR, but then Stalin ordered him to attack. Although the Soviet forces outnumbered the Japanese by three to one, between 29 July and 11 August the Japanese beat off every assault, inflicting 5,000 casualties including 717 killed and 75 prisoners and missing.[35] Having demonstrated (they thought) that they could take and hold any position they wanted, the Japanese then withdrew. Although the Soviet command threw in aircraft, tanks and infantry, the coordination was abysmal. However, the failure to achieve all-arms cooperation, rather than encouraging efforts to get it right, undermined the development of such techniques and led to demands for an increase of infantry firepower. If coordination between arms of the Red Army had been bad, that between the Red Army and the NKVD border guards was worse. Stalin had Blyukher arrested and shot.[36]

The Battle at Khalkin Gol (Nomonhan) a year later showed how fast the Red Army could learn, especially under a gifted commander. The Japanese had occupied a disputed area between Nomonhan, where the Soviet Union and its Mongolian allies believed the border to be, and the River Khalka, where the Japanese thought the border was. Komkor Georgiy Zhukov, commanding LVII Special Corps, later renamed First Army Group, concentrated 57,000 troops on the west side of the river, 650 kilometres from the nearest railhead. Facing him was Sixth Japanese Army, totalling 75,000 men, although not all were engaged. Zhukov constructed defensive positions, in part to deceive the Japanese and Manchukuoan troops facing him into thinking he would not attack. Then on 19 August Soviet and Mongolian troops started moving forward on both flanks. This was 'deep battle' in the old style. Cavalry, tanks and mechanized brigades established an inner front, to seal the Japanese and Manchukuoan forces in the disputed area, and then infantry got to work to destroy the trapped enemy. The Japanese divisional commander and 400 survivors managed to escape. It was a masterly battle – Shtern, now the commander of the Far East Army Military Soviet, said it would become 'the second greatest battle of encirclement, after Cannae [in 216 BC] in all history'.[37]

With a large part of Sixth Army cut off and then killed in the Khalkin Gol pocket, on 3 September the Japanese Emperor ordered the incident to be resolved diplomatically. Khalkin Gol was an undeniable success, but won at great cost. The latest Russian figures for Soviet and Mongolian casualties are 6,831 killed, 1,143 missing and 15,925 wounded and sick – a total of nearly 24,000. However, Zhukov had won, spectacularly. But everyone's attention was diverted by events in Europe and the purges, still in progress, discouraged open analysis and debate on the lessons. As a result, the political, as well as military, effectiveness of huge encirclements of this type, which were still out of fashion, was underplayed. And the fact that Zhukov had won, however he achieved his victory, once again meant there was little appetite for radical reforms.[38]

Khalkin Gol also led to an unofficial expansion of the Soviet Union eastward. In its January 1941 assessment of the Red Army *Order of Battle*, reflecting on the previous year, British Intelligence noted that 'Soviet regular troops are now so firmly in occupation of Outer Mongolia that there is no longer any pretence that this area does not come under the direct control of the Trans-Baikal Military district.'[39]

Of the 'dress rehearsals' analysed on the Central Committee's orders, the Soviet–Finnish War had most impact at the time. The reforms made were quite radical, and included: creation of the North-West Front, to command joint forces – sea, land and air; Timoshenko's willingness to experiment with 'mission command' (directive control) and borrow ideas from abroad, especially the Germans; and Stalin's concentration of the Party, state and military leadership to ensure the crisis was brought to an acceptable conclusion. The technical, tactical and organizational reforms made by the Soviet military during the war and afterwards make it clear that, as Carl van Dyke observed, the war 'stimulated a profound reform of Soviet military doctrine and institutions, reforms which came to fruition only by the second half of the Great Patriotic War'.[40]

No one could be expected to guess whether any future great war would be a Finland or a Khalkin Gol or, as it turned out, a thousand variants of each, and many more besides. Meanwhile, however, the military command structure, morale and training all required attention. At the beginning of May, as a very gentle acknowledgement of mistakes made during the war, Voroshilov was removed from his position as Commissar for Defence, although Shaposhnikov remained as Chief of the General Staff. Voroshilov was replaced by Timoshenko, undoubtedly the 'man of the moment'. In August, Meretskov briefly replaced Shaposhnikov.

Timoshenko, promoted to Marshal of the Soviet Union on 7 May 1940, immediately initiated a series of reforms. The summer 1940 training programme was based entirely on combined-arms attacks on fortified positions, in order to reintroduce the Red Army to combined-arms warfare techniques. During the Finnish war the lack of discipline and apparent lack of authority of officers over their men had been widely commented on. Timoshenko had to tread warily, because a former Marshal of the Soviet Union, Tukhachevskiy, had paid for increasing the power and prestige of the officer corps with his life. But only by restoring the privileges and distinctions of rank could the crushing effect of the purges on the soul and spirit of the armed forces begin to be dissipated. And only that way could the requirement that orders be obeyed 'without reservation, precisely and promptly' be guaranteed. Indeed, because the Red Army aspired to be classless and meritocratic, distinctions of rank had to be even more marked than in the forces of capitalist countries, where social stereotypes and conventions could convey the 'pecking order' more subtly. Discipline must be 'higher, firmer and marked with severer and harsher requirements than discipline in other armies based upon class subjugation'.[41] With this in mind, the 1940 disciplinary code gave 'commanders' (the term 'officer' was still used warily) full authority to punish disobedient subordinates. Soldiers lost their right to make complaints against officers.

To reinforce the authority of senior officers, the old titles of general and admiral were brought back, with a system of stars, similar to the American one, as insignia, although senior political commissars retained the diamond-shaped studs which had previously indicated 'starred' officers – one for a brigade commissar, and so on. But for military commanders, instead of *kombrig, komdiv, komkor* and *komandarm* second- and first-class, there were major-generals, lieutenant generals, colonel-generals – a rank which had not existed in the Tsarist army – and army (full) generals, with equivalent ranks for specialist arms plus, unchanged, the marshals of the Soviet Union which had existed since 1935. There were also rear-, vice- and full admirals. In June, more than 1,000 officers were promoted to the new ranks, including Zhukov and Meretskov as full generals. Meretskov was already Chief of the General Staff, while Zhukov took over command of the Kiev Special Military District. There were 479 new major-generals including many who would distinguish themselves commanding armies and fronts in the Great Patriotic War.

One of them was a former colonel just released after four years in the GULag. He was lucky to have survived his detention in a camp on Kamchatka in the Far East. After his release, he was sent to a resort on the Black Sea to put on weight before being measured for his new general's uniform, and saw a good dentist who fitted him with a set of steel teeth to replace the nine which had been kicked out by the NKVD during his arrest and detention. They had also broken several ribs and smashed his toes with a hammer. Throughout his career, until his arrest, he had always been senior to Zhukov. At the victory parade in Red Square in 1945, he would have to take second place to Zhukov, riding a black horse in deliberate and dramatic contrast to Zhukov's white charger. His name was Konstantin Rokossovskiy, and he would become known to the Germans as 'the dagger'. He was the most tactically deft commander in the Red Army during the Great Patriotic War.

The most significant single reform came on 12 August when dual command – where the military commander worked jointly with a political officer or commissar – was ended. Unitary command was reintroduced and the Red Army, navy or air force commander became the 'sole leader' of the fighting forces. The political officers and commissars were still there, and played an important role, but at last the military commander was boss.[42]

Meanwhile, in April 1940 the so-called 'phoney war' in the West – which had certainly not been phoney at sea – came to an end. On 9 April 1940 German forces attacked Denmark and Norway. Denmark capitulated immediately, but fighting in Norway, where the Norwegians were joined by British and French forces, continued until 9 June. The occupation of Norway by Germany caused Stalin to breathe a huge sigh of relief. He had hurriedly concluded the Soviet–Finnish war, in part, to pre-empt action by the western entente, which had indeed considered moving forces through Norway to help the Finns. Now, the British and French were firmly excluded from the Baltic. So far, everything was going Stalin's way. But it would not last.

The Soviet Ambassador to Sweden, Aleksandra Kollontai, played a key role in events in Scandinavia. An eminent writer, and a woman of class, she seems quite incompatible with the coarse and surly men like Stalin and Beria who ran much of Soviet government and diplomacy. She was also very anti-German, and an opponent of the Molotov–Ribbentrop Pact, although Stalin later used her, rather cleverly, to try to convince the Germans that he remained their best friend. She was unique among Soviet diplomats in speaking her mind. In spite of that, and of her cosmopolitan intellectual background, she survived. After Norway fell to the Germans, she helped a number of young Norwegian men who were training to be pilots to leave Norway for neutral Sweden. From there, she arranged visas for them to travel to Russia, and across eastern Europe and Asia on the trans-Siberian railway. As citizens of a

German-occupied country, they were relatively safe under the terms of the Molotov–Ribbentrop Pact. Some of them eventually reached Japan, still neutral, and left before the bombing of Pearl Harbor on 7 December 1941 brought Japan into the war. They travelled safely across the Pacific to the United States, north to the British Dominion of Canada, and then across the Atlantic to join the Royal Air Force. After the war, they returned to their own country. At least one of them became a general in the Norwegian air force, and told the author the extraordinary story of his escape into Russia, and all the way around the world.[43]

Meanwhile, right behind (and, indeed, sometimes exchanging shots with) the Red Army, the NKVD had moved into the new Soviet territories in the former state of Poland. Throughout Russian history, the Poles had resented rule from Moscow or St Petersburg and during the interwar period had enjoyed something of a western, capitalist lifestyle. The country was also strongly Roman Catholic, which presented an ideological threat whether you were Russian Orthodox or communist atheist. There can be little doubt that a decision was taken at the highest level to eliminate the Polish officers who had fallen into Soviet hands. Of the quarter-million Polish prisoners deported to Russia, 14,920 regular officers and reservists, who included many eminent professional men, were creamed off and sent to three special camps at Kozel'sk, Starobelsk and Ostashkov. All were desecrated former monasteries.[44]

From October 1939, a lengthy interrogation process began. The captured Polish officers, cadets and intellectuals were repeatedly interviewed, fingerprinted, humiliated, and taunted with promises that they would soon be released to join their comrades-in-arms to fight Germany. The process lasted six months, until March 1940, when the NKVD started to empty the camps. The NKVD was assessing the leadership potential of its prisoners, and whether they might possibly be 're-educated'. About 400 were removed from the camps because the Russians had other plans for them, and some of these survived, although they had no clear idea of why they were selected. Only 448 prisoners were ever seen alive again, after joining the Polish army in the USSR. Of the remainder, nothing was heard after April 1940. It is not possible to say with any certainty what happened to the 4,000 prisoners held at Starobelsk or the 6,500 at Ostashkov, but those at Kozel'sk were shipped out, about 300 each day, and taken to the forest of Katyn near Smolensk. There, they were shot dead individually in the back of the head at the base of the skull, and thrown into mass graves. Some of the bodies had their hands tied behind them and had wounds from Soviet bayonets, which were square in cross section, the four-bladed spikes causing unmistakable wounds. After the mass graves were filled with bodies, they were covered with earth and planted with young pine trees.

The NKVD authorities, and the Soviet government, could have had no idea that their skilful handiwork – and the NKVD executioners were clearly very professional – would be revealed relatively soon. Two years later the Germans, who now occupied the area, having heard local rumours, began to dig the area once the ground had thawed. They found 4,143 bodies, a total which later rose to 4,253, dressed in well-fitting uniforms with overcoats and winter underwear, and plenty of documents. The find, announced in a radio broadcast on 13 April 1943, was a potential propaganda coup for the Germans, but the Soviet Union claimed the Germans had done it. It was obviously unwise for the British and Americans to press the point at the time, and the subsequent investigations became a test of the uneasy wartime alliance. It is now established beyond any reasonable doubt that the killings took place in March or April 1940, when the Soviet Union controlled the area, and that the NKVD did it on orders from Moscow. However, this appalling war crime went unpunished, because the Soviet Union was on the winning side in the Second World War.[45]

Although the fate of the Baltic States (see Figure 3.2) had been sealed on 23 August and 28 September 1939, and Soviet troops had moved in to garrison forward bases in October, it was not until 15 June 1940 that full-scale Soviet occupation began. The countries all enjoyed a relatively high standard of living, but were effectively small dictatorships. Their leaders estimated that they might hold out for a week against a determined Soviet assault. This was probably a reasonable assessment. Germany had ceded the Baltic States to the Soviet Union's 'sphere of influence' the previous year, and would not therefore be coming to their defence. The western entente was now broken, with the fall of France imminent. German troops entered Paris on 14 June, although France did not surrender until 22 June. Soon, Britain itself would face an invasion threat. There had been undoubted improvements in Red Army performance during and after the Finnish war. And Red Army units were already based on their territory.[46]

By 17 June Soviet troops had occupied Latvia but, as in the other Baltic States, many hoped the country might preserve some formal independence. The People's Government of Latvia, formed by Soviet emissary Andrey Vyshinskiy and under the Presidency of Professor Augusts Kirhensteins, promised its citizens a democratic Saeima, or parliament. On 14 and 15 July hurried elections were held, but communists, approved by Moscow, were the only candidates. All attempts to put up alternative candidates failed and the new parliament voted for Latvia's incorporation into the Soviet Union. The elections for the Lithuanian parliament (Seimas) were similarly manipulated, and in its first session, it discussed incorporation into the USSR. The 'Declaration of Lithuania's entering the Union of Soviet Socialist Republics' was approved. Although Lithuanians working abroad, including diplomats, declared the Resolution to be unlawful, because the Seimas that had passed it was unlawfully elected, Lithuania also passed under the de facto rule of the USSR. In Estonia, the Soviet occupation and the disarming of the volunteer national defence organization, the Defence League, on 17 and 19 June were followed by a coup on 21 June. The Soviet Union again set up a puppet government, and declared elections for 14 and 15 July. Opposition groups succeeded in putting up 78 candidates but 57 candidates' applications were declared void, 20 withdrew, as a result of public or private intimidation, and one candidate was arrested.[47] The lessons for organizing elections in our own century are clear enough, but in 1940 there was no Organization for Security and Cooperation in Europe to supervise them and declare that they were 'free and fair', or, in this case, not free and not fair. The United States always refused to recognize the countries' incorporation into the Soviet Union, as maps from the cold war make clear.[48]

By the end of the year the three former Baltic States constituted a new Pri-Baltic Military District. The Kalinin MD was abolished and divided between the Moscow and Western MDs. The areas ceded by Finland, including the Hangö peninsula, formed part of the Leningrad MD.[49]

Slightly different factors affected Northern Bukovina and Bessarabia – modern Moldova. More than any of the other acquisitions in 1940, these were motivated by military-strategic considerations. The important Soviet port of Odessa was only 40 kilometres from the Romanian border – a situation not dissimilar to that of Leningrad before the Finnish war. But whereas the British were excluded from the Baltic, they had a major interest in the eastern Mediterranean and the Black Sea. The area had been ceded to Russia by Turkey in 1812, but given to Romania after 1919. Occupying the area (or, in the Russian view, re-occupying it) would take the Soviet frontier to the north edge of the mouths of the Danube. Besides shielding Odessa and Sevastopol, it would deny any potential invader the perfect springboard for an attack into the Ukraine. The railway lines between Ukraine and Bessarabia ran through Northern Bukovina. The third article of the secret protocol to the Molotov–Ribbentrop Pact placed Bessarabia in the Soviet sphere of influence, but did not mention Bukovina.

In February 1940 Stalin approached King Carol of Romania to propose a non-aggression pact. On 29 March Molotov suggested to the Supreme Soviet that the USSR might annexe Bessarabia. In May and June Germany, Italy and the USSR held secret negotiations about the area. As Romania swung towards Germany, but with the fall of France and an invasion of Britain imminent, Stalin decided it was time to strike. Reports from the Soviet Army's Main Intelligence Directorate (GRU) indicated that an attack on Britain might take place at the end of June.[50] On 22 June Ambassador Schulenberg was summoned to see Molotov and told that the Soviet Union was considering a move into Bessarabia. Still locked into a major operation in the Battle of Britain, Hitler was not in a position to dictate to the Soviet Union. Instead, he acted as a mediator, and advised King Carol to give up Bessarabia. On the night of 26 June Molotov summoned Ambassador Davidescu and told him it was time to 'return' Bessarabia and also to transfer northern Bukovina to the Soviet Union, on the grounds that 'most of the population of Bessarabia were Ukrainians'. Whereas the Germans knew about Bessarabia, the demand for northern Bukovina was a complete surprise, both to the Romanians and the Germans. Molotov gave Romania one day to consider the ultimatum. Romanian troops were to leave the area in three days, and the Red Army already had orders to cross the frontier on the Dnestr river. King Carol did not take the news well, and tried to get the British involved, playing on traditional British fears that the Russians might get Constantinople (Istanbul) and the Straits. But, once again, Stalin outplayed him.

The Romanian army was in no position to oppose the twenty-four Soviet divisions, two of them deployed on the Dnestr and on the border with Bukovina. As with the Baltic States, resistance appeared hopeless, and the Romanians withdrew, without destroying any key installations at this stage. According to NKVD records, two Regiments of the Red Army's 169th Division forced the River Dnestr at 15.30 on 28 June in the area of Yampol' (Yampil). By 16.40 artillery and tanks were across.

Other units crossed in the Velikaya Kosnitsa (Velyka Kysniytsya) region at 20.50, and so on, rolling from north to south down to the Bendery (modern Tighina) area during the evening. The Romanian sector commander, Major Onichanu, with interpreters and two sailors, made contact with the Russians on board a launch on the River Dnestr at 12.20, and after discussions with Major-General Nikolay Kiryukhin, the Romanians pulled out of Tighina and Kishinёv (Chisinau) during the rest of the day.[51]

On 3 July a new Soviet frontier was set up on the River Pruth. On that day Serov reported that his *operchekistskiy* groups had arrested a total of 760 people. Under interrogation, 'as a rule', they admitted they had been recruited by Romanian intelligence. On the night of 3 July Romanian army units blew up road and rail bridges across the Pruth in the Kagul (Cahul) area, on the southern part of the new frontier. During the previous few days, Serov reported, large numbers of people had been gathering on the right (west) bank of the Pruth. He said they had been taken there by the Romanian army, and now wanted to return to Bessarabia, but that the Romanians were trying to stop them. There was an especially large concentraion across the major railway bridge leading to Yassy (Iasi).[52]

On the same day, with the new border installations set up by NKVD border troops, Marshal Timoshenko, the Commissar for Defence, wrote to Army General Zhukov, commanding the Southern Front, requesting that they be moved out as soon as possible and replaced by 'field units of the Red Army'.[53] The USSR acquired 44,500 square kilometres of territory and 200,000 people in Bessarabia, and 6,000 square kilometres with 500,000 people in northern Bukovina. Into the area, which became the Odessa Special Military District, moved fifteen infantry, motorized and cavalry divisions and seven tank and airborne brigades. However, Stalin's action had pushed Romania firmly into alliance with Hitler.[54]

Creating the Moldavian Soviet Socialist Republic of the USSR was a fairly lengthy process, which began on 11 July. A small Moldavian Autonomous Republic had been part of Ukraine, and the new territories were grafted on to it to form the new MSSR with its capital at Kishinev (Chisinau).[55] Only in November was the border between the new Republic and Ukraine finalized. Ten thousand families were moved from Ukraine into the new territories during the autumn, but as early as August 1940, some 53,356 young men and women had been mobilized and sent to other parts of the Soviet Union. As in the Baltic States, mass deportations started in summer 1941, with more than 5,000 Bessarabian families forcibly transported on the night of 13 June.[56]

The movement of German troops into Finland and Romania was one of the factors which began to sour German–Soviet relations. But although Hitler spoke of a spring 1941 attack on the Soviet Union during a conference on 31 July 1940, he later colluded with Ribbentrop's plan to engage the Soviet Union with the tripartite pact between Germany, Italy and Japan, and turn it into a four-power pact.[57] Ribbentrop wrote to Stalin inviting Molotov to Berlin to discuss 'possibly with the representatives of Japan and Italy – the basis of a policy which would be of practical advantage to all of us'.[58] Had such a four-power alliance materialized, Britain and the United States would have faced a formidable coalition of Germany, the USSR and Italy dominating Eurasia while Japan, contiguous with the USSR, would have extended the four-power coalition's reach into the Pacific. There were also plenty of client states including fascist Spain, Vichy France and German satellites in south-eastern Europe. It might also have been difficult for Turkey, which remained neutral during the Second World War, to remain outside the ambit of the four-power pact.

In the evening of 9 November 1940 a special train left the Belorussia station in Moscow. Special carriages of west European type (though running on the Russian broad gauge which was to cause the Germans so many logistic problems the next year) carried Molotov and his staff, including Berezhkov, on his second visit to the West. Berezhkov had been to Germany in the summer on a visit with Foreign Trade Commissar Mikoyan to discuss shipments of German equipment to the Soviet Union in exchange for critical raw materials, especially oil, grain and manganese. Now they were going to talk about the possibility of a four-power pact to break the British Empire.

As a fluent German speaker and trained engineer, Berezhkov was the ideal person to act as Molotov's interpreter. On 12 November he met Hitler. Having just conquered France, Hitler was 'haughty and arrogant'. 'In this respect he was the complete opposite of Stalin,' recalled Berezhkov, 'who amazed everyone with his ostensible modesty and total lack of desire to impress. Unlike Hitler, Stalin thought that if his limitless power over millions of his subjects was evident, there was no need to advertise it.'[59]

Berezhkov began to interpret, but Hitler was taken aback by his Berlin accent.

'Who are you? A German?' asked Hitler.

'No,' said Berezhkov. 'I am Russian.'

After the meeting, Hitler told Molotov he considered Stalin 'to be a historic personality. I also flatter myself with the thought that I will also go down in history. That is why it is natural for two political leaders like us to meet. Please, Mr Molotov, transmit to Mr Stalin my greetings and my proposal that we hold a meeting in the not too-distant future.'[60]

Molotov passed the message on, and it may have played a part in Stalin's miscalculations about Hitler's intentions or, at any rate, the timing of any attack on the Soviet Union. In fact, the dictators never met.

The next evening Molotov and the Soviet diplomats were in Ribbentrop's study, slightly smaller than Hitler's, but luxurious, filled with tapestries and old masters which Berezhkov surmised might be recent trophies from France.

'But that lampshade? Now I wonder . . .'[61]

The German Foreign Minister pulled out a piece of paper with the German government's proposals on it. At that point an air-raid siren sounded. British bombers were heading in their direction. Berezhkov said the British knew Molotov was in Berlin (which they did), and surmised that they had launched a significant air raid to prove they were still capable of fighting and to show the Russians what they could do. The next year, Stalin asked his new ally Churchill why he had bombed 'my Vyacheslav', and Churchill played along, nodding and saying that 'a golden opportunity should never be passed up'.[62] In fact, according to the operational records of Bomber Command, on the night of 13–14 November sixty-nine aircraft were ordered to attack the Reich's Chancellery – which had Hitler's bunker underneath it – the Admiralty, Schlesischer Station, two power stations and two railway marshalling yards.[63] The British probably did not know exactly where the two foreign ministers would be and the bombing techniques of the time precluded any form of precision. Although the Berlin targets were therefore military, Churchill himself admitted that another aim was to impress the Russians. 'We had heard of the conference beforehand', he wrote, 'and though not invited to join the discussion did not wish to be entirely left out of the proceedings.'[64] Berlin was a very long way for the relatively small two-engined Wellington bombers to go. The following night, 14–15 November, German bombers tore the heart out of the British city of Coventry, although that raid had been planned well before.

With British bombs falling on central Berlin, Ribbentrop, Molotov and their teams headed down to the sumptuously furnished bunker, where they discussed what might be done in the event of Britain's imminent defeat.

'If Britain is defeated,' said Molotov, who was not renowned for his sense of humour, 'why are we sitting in a shelter? And whose bombs are falling so close their explosions can be heard even here?'[65]

The draft treaty would turn the pact of three into a pact of four. The four states – Germany, Italy, Japan and the Soviet Union – shared the desire to cooperate 'in ensuring their natural spheres of interest in Europe, Asia and Africa'. The treaty would enter into force on signature, like the earlier German–Soviet treaties, and would run for ten years. Two secret protocols were appended. One of them defined the 'spheres of interest', and allocated the Soviet Union the southern direction, 'toward the Indian Ocean'. This harked back to Imperial Russian ambitions of the previous century, promising to fulfil long-standing and deep-rooted Russian interest in warm-water ports and in India, still part of the British Empire. The second secret protocol dealt with Turkey and replacing the Montreux convention with a new treaty more favourable to Soviet interests.[66]

Fortunately for the western democracies, it did not happen. On 4 November it had been made clear that preparations for the invasion of the USSR were to continue in spite of the imminent visit of the Russian Foreign Minister, and Directive 18, on the conduct of the war in the East, was issued the very same day that Molotov arrived in Berlin. 'Political discussions have been initiated with the aim of clarifying Russia's attitude for the coming period. Regardless of what outcome these discussions will have, all preparations for the East which already have been orally ordered, are to be continued.' It is virtually certain that details of these military plans were kept from the Foreign Minister. However, it is probably wrong to think that German–Soviet negotiations were totally doomed at this stage. The directive focused mainly on the Balkans and Greece, with preparations for operations against the Soviet Union as a marginal, 'just in case' issue.[67]

It seems unlikely that Ribbentrop was aware of Hitler's growing determination to destroy Soviet Russia before the conference at the Berghof on 8–9 January 1941, when the Führer left no one in any doubt of his ambition. Meanwhile, negotiations about mutual economic support continued, and Berezhkov remained in Berlin to assist.

By the time of the Molotov–Ribbentrop Pact, the German High Command's war economy staff had already recommended that Germany could only manage a war if it availed itself of the resources of the Romanian oil fields and the deposits in southern Russia and Ukraine.[68] Either they would have to take the areas by force or do business with the Soviet Union. The Pact opened the way for the latter. Germany need not fear blockade, Hitler explained on 22 August 1939, because Russia would supply 'grain, cattle, coal, lead and zinc'. In September another study concluded that while Germany could manage in the short term, in the longer term it needed grain and three strategically important raw materials: manganese ore, petroleum products and raw phosphates. This opened the way for German experts and technologies to boost Soviet economic performance. In October 1939 Germany asked the Russians to double the grain supplies already agreed, from a million to at least 2 million tons.[69] Realizing the German needs, the Russians countered by demanding imports of the most modern military technology. The aim here was not just to acquire a few pieces of German equipment, but to obtain technology which they could develop for their own wider use. On 11 February 1940 an economic agreement was signed for the delivery of Soviet raw materials worth 600–700 million Reichsmarks. In return Germany had to agree to large-scale deliveries of German armaments, and also some of its most secret and modern technology, which German industry did not like. The biggest problem beset IG-Farbenindustrie, who were asked to hand over their newly developed process for manufacturing toluene, which could then be used to produce higher-octane aviation fuel. A Luftwaffe representative explained that the German air force's technological lead was largely due to possession of higher quality fuel, whilst the Soviet aircraft had to operate on greatly inferior fuel. The Russians also asked for Buna synthetic rubber which, like natural rubber, was in short supply and would reduce deliveries to the *Wehrmacht*.[70] Germany needed Russia's raw materials, but was increasingly reluctant to give what the Soviet Union demanded in return. The solution was becoming obvious.

Meanwhile, on 10 January 1941, a further German–Soviet economic agreement was concluded. Through the Soviet Union, Germany was able to trade with Iran, Afghanistan and the Far East. The Soviet Union pledged that it would supply Germany with the raw materials most important for military purposes, 'above all, petroleum products, cotton, manganese ore, platinum and manganese oxide'. It would also safeguard

Germany's food situation with no less than 2.5 million tons of grain, and provide 2 million Reichsmarks' worth of lumber. German exports had to be guaranteed up to 11 August 1941, because the Soviet side had committed itself to very large early deliveries of raw materials, which Germany could not match with its deliveries in the same period. The Germans would respond with manufactured goods including weapons and military hardware, which the Soviets wanted to supervise. It was suggested that the Russian officials might supervise production on a given day each week. This arrangement affected not just the territory of the Reich, but occupied territories as well. If there was any problem with Soviet demands for military hardware, Reichsmarschall Göring's decision should be obtained.[71]

In exchange for deliveries of oil and strategic metals, the Soviet Union bought a cruiser, the *Lutzov*. In April 1940 the Soviet delegation approached Gustav Krupp, head of the famous armaments firm, complaining that work on fitting it out was far behind schedule. The Germans used every excuse, including their planned invasion of Britain, which was not unreasonable. It seems clear that Hitler had no intention of allowing a state-of-the-art cruiser to be completed for the Russians. By the end of 1940 only the two bow turrets were in place, and the cruiser was not finished before the German attack on the Soviet Union. After the first few days of the war, the Luftwaffe sank it.[72]

In February 1941 the Soviet deliveries to Germany fell off, and the Germans threatened to reduce their deliveries proportionately, but in March large deliveries of grain and raw materials resumed.[73] In January and February imports of raw materials from the USSR totalled only 17 million and 11 million Reichsmarks respectively, the largest and most important item being 200,000 tons of Bessarabian grain. In March deliveries rose 'by leaps and bounds', especially grains, petroleum, manganese ore and non-ferrous and precious metals. A contract to deliver 1.4 million tons of grain by September 1941 was also concluded at favourable prices. The Soviet Union had already shipped 110,000 tons of grain and promised firmly to deliver 170,000–200,000 tons in April. The German counter-deliveries were being made on schedule, but further ahead it would 'not be possible to adhere to the ... delivery periods because of a shortage of labour and priority of the military programmes'. German traffic through Siberia continued to proceed 'favourably, as usual', and the Soviet government 'even put a special freight train for rubber at our disposal at the Manchurian border'.[74] By

11 February 1941, Soviet deliveries amounted to 310 million Reichs-marks' worth, and the Germans, whose deliveries always followed behind, agreed to have made deliveries to this value by 11 May.[75]

On 21 April the Deputy Commissar for Foreign Trade, Krutikov, complained that Germany was not providing enough rolling stock to transport Soviet imports into Germany from the border (where the railway gauge changed), and that not enough freight cars were being made available for German deliveries to the Soviet Union, either. The Soviets planned big shipments which were frustrated by transport difficulties on the German side. Presumably, by this time, preparations for the invasion of the Soviet Union were part of the problem. In April the Soviet delivery programme was 200,000 tons of grain, 91,000 tons of petroleum products and 20,000 tons of manganese ore, plus substan-tial amounts of phosphates, non-ferrous ores and so on. Krutikov even suggested that these quantities might be increased.[76]

The final tally of Soviet deliveries came on 15 May. In April 208,000 tons of grain had been delivered, 90,000 tons of petroleum, 8,300 tons of cotton and 6,340 tons of non-ferrous metals, all of strategic value: copper, tin and nickel. The transit route for German goods through Siberia was still operating, which was critical to the German war effort because of the need for rubber from the Far East. Some 2,000 tons of raw rubber reached Germany in April by regular Soviet trains and another 2,000 by special trains. The total deliveries so far in 1941 were 632,000 tons of grain, 232,000 tons of petroleum, 23,500 tons of cotton, 50,000 tons of manganese ore, 67,000 tons of phosphates and 900 kilograms (nearly a ton!) of platinum. The quantities of raw materials contracted for were being delivered punctually, despite the heavy burden this placed on the Soviet system. On the other hand, problems were being caused on the German side because of rumours of an impending Soviet–German conflict. These were causing grave anxiety to German industry, which was eager to withdraw from its engagements in Russia and refusing to despatch personnel to work in Moscow to ensure completion of the contracts.[77]

The 'cruel romance' had resulted in enormous deliveries of crucial food and raw materials to Germany, and in major territorial gains for the Soviet Union. In 1974, thirty years after the war and more than twenty after Stalin's death, Molotov told a story of what had happened when a new school map of the USSR, with the new borders, was brought to Stalin's *dacha* – the country cottages outside the big cities where

Russians and other Soviet nationalities love to spend their weekends.
'Well, let's see . . .' said Stalin:

> . . . everything looks all right in the north. Finland has been
> very naughty to us, so we moved our border away from
> Leningrad. The Baltics – these traditional Russian lands –
> belong to us again. The Belorussians are all living together
> now, the Ukrainians, together, and the Moldovans, together.
> Looks all right in the west.[78]

To achieve this, Poland, Estonia, Latvia and Lithuania had been
eliminated as states, while large parts of Finland and Romania had been
transferred to the Soviet Union (see Figure 3.2). On the sixtieth
anniversary of victory in Europe, in May 2005, the restored Baltic States
demanded that President Vladimir Putin of Russia apologize for their
annexation. He said the Soviet Union had apologized in 1989, and
refused to do so again. Although the Soviet Union's advances would
soon be reversed by the German and Romanian armies, the brief period
of Soviet occupation in 1940–41 provided a model, and would serve as
justification, for the return of those areas to Soviet rule after the Second
World War.

For the moment, the Soviet Union had acquired a valuable cushion
of territory, from 100 to 300 kilometres thick, along its western border.
But at the same time, it had acquired a terrible vulnerability. Along
1,000 of the 1,500-kilometre length of its western borders between the
Baltic and Black Sea, it was now in direct contact with the territory of
the Third Reich, and along the remainder, with Hitler's ally Romania.
North of the Baltic, there was a 1,000-kilometre border with Finland,
which was no friend. If either dictatorship wished to attack the other,
and drive for its jugular, there was now nobody else to get in the way.

5

WHO PLANNED TO ATTACK WHOM, AND HOW?

Hitler's decision to launch the greatest and most ambitious military operation in world history, Operation Barbarossa, on the real 'longest day' – 22 June 1941 – can only be explained in terms of Leo Tolstoy's 'myriads of ... diverse and complex causes'.[1] These range from the global and grandiose to the pragmatic, even pedestrian. The politics of the post-war world have induced certain historians to favour particular causes as pre-eminent, but Hitler's decision to attack the USSR can only be explained by treating all the causes as equally important in their own way.[2]

Hitler's obsession with 'Jewish Bolshevism', set out in *Mein Kampf*, and the ideological polarity between National Socialism and Soviet communism were clearly one. But they must be set against the very real feeling, held by both Stalin and Hitler, that the other was someone with whom he could do business. Germany's perceived need for *Lebensraum*, which owed something to the geopoliticians, was undoubtedly a cause. So was the very real German need for raw materials, explored in Chapter 3, to wage a war already under way, which might – and later did – expand to global dimensions, embracing the United States. Then there were politico-strategic considerations within the context of a wider European, but not yet global, war. The defeat of France in June 1940 and Britain's continued resistance afterwards placed Hitler in a strategic quandary. He needed Soviet resources to fight the British Empire and possibly the United States. But, as noted in Chapter 3, Germany was reluctant to pay for them. Destroying Soviet Russia would also strike at Britain indirectly by removing one of its last hopes for a great ally. The constant efforts of Britain, Germany and the Soviet Union to play each other off against the third in the European ring have to be balanced against, and seen in the context of, longer-term objectives. The Soviet Union, it had to be remembered, was getting stronger, and might still turn on a Germany weakened by continued engagement with Britain. And the United States, already a massive contributor of growing amounts of war materiel to the British effort (which greatly concerned Hitler), would probably not stay out of the war as a direct combatant forever.

There were also the very real and immediate issues in the Balkans, connected with Britain's interest in the eastern Mediterranean and the Middle East. Germany's relations with Romania were designed to increase German influence in the Balkans, but Hitler was not prepared to accept a similar Soviet relationship with Bulgaria. Barbarossa was delayed – almost certainly with disastrous consequences for the Germans – because of the 27 March 1941 coup in Yugoslavia, and Hitler's subsequent invasion to deal with it. Finally, and inextricably linked with the question of Britain, Germany and the USSR playing one another off against each other, there was a real dilemma in the realm of military strategy and intelligence. Might Hitler betray the 1939 Pact and attack Stalin? Or might Stalin attack Hitler before Hitler attacked him? But that water, in turn, was muddied by Stalin's obsessive wariness that the British were trying to provoke him into a war with Germany, and also his fear that the British would make peace with the Germans and join them against the USSR. Rudolf Hess's mission to Britain on 10 May 1941 lent further credibility to this view, and diverted Stalin at a critical moment. Stalin's suspicions of the British led him to disregard the intelligence which they furnished as well as that supplied by his own very competent intelligence services. There is no option, therefore, but to consider these intertwined and interacting 'myriads of causes' together.

Stalin had not pushed Finland too hard earlier in 1940 because, if he did, he might trigger a response from the British–French entente and thus find himself embroiled in the conflict on Germany's side, which he did not want. But in June 1940 all that changed. On 22 June 1940 – another long day – the French capitulated at the same place, near Compiègne, and in the same railway carriage in which the Germans had signed the Armistice ending the First World War in November 1918. The British had withdrawn from the continent by 4 June 1940, evacuating 338,226 men from Dunkirk, two-thirds of them British. The Germans attempted to achieve air superiority prior to launching an invasion, but failed in the Battle of Britain, and on 17 September Operation Seelöwe (Sea Lion) was postponed – indefinitely. From Hitler's (and Stalin's) perspective, France was out of the war as a single nation-state, at least for the moment, and operations against Britain would, for the foreseeable future, take place at sea and in the air, and outside Europe.

For Stalin, this was a critical turning point. Until now he might, with reason, have expected a protracted and exhausting land struggle in the West, similar to the First World War, which would weaken both Germany and the British–French entente, while the Soviet Union waited, gaining strength on the sidelines. Now, that was not going to happen. And by defeating the mighty French army so fast, the *Wehrmacht* had proved itself to be even more formidable than anyone had expected. In any battle between forces equal in numbers of men and equipment, the *Wehrmacht* would tear its opponents to pieces. One of the reasons for the German success was the concentration of armour into fast-moving Panzer divisions – the precise opposite of the lesson the Russians had just learned from Finland. This was all very bad news for Russia.

On 14 June, even before the fall of France, Sir Stafford Cripps reported that the Russians were alarmed by German successes in the French campaign. Cripps was a socialist politician newly appointed as ambassador to Moscow in a perhaps naive attempt to woo the Soviet government. He told Molotov that 'according to our information' Germany would turn east if France collapsed, a warning repeated by Churchill on 26 June.[3] Whilst these warnings were undoubtedly sincere, they were not based on military intelligence. On the contrary, the MI branches said Germany would continue to give priority to Sea Lion, while the Foreign Office was less certain, and anticipated a German thrust into Ukraine, though not immediately.[4] On 5 August the British Joint Intelligence Committee, responsible for reconciling the views of the various ministries and intelligence agencies, concluded unanimously that Germany and the Soviet Union had the best of reasons for avoiding an open clash – at least for the moment.[5]

The events of summer 1940 are the first big argument against the theory, initially propounded in 1985, that having let Hitler start the Second World War, Stalin planned to attack Germany in 1941. The hypothesis, which caused furious debate and is widely scorned, was first put forward by a former major in the Soviet Main Intelligence Directorate – GRU – writing under the pseudonym Viktor Suvorov. His real name is Rezun. 'Suvorov' defected to the West in the late 1970s. Under his prestigious pseudonym,[6] and under sentence of death in the Soviet Union, he argued that Stalin had a long-term, grand strategic plan to spread communism around the world. From the precarious safety of exile, Suvorov claimed that Stalin had used Hitler as his 'icebreaker', to weaken the western democracies before Stalin himself overran Europe, starting with Germany. Hitler's attack on the Soviet Union could therefore be seen as a preventive – or even pre-emptive – war, eventually launched on 22 June 1941, prior to a Soviet attack scheduled, according to Suvorov, for 6 July.[7] Pre-emptive war – action to forestall or deflect a threat which is 'imminent and overwhelming' – has a respectable pedigree in international law. Preventive war – acting to prevent a threat from materializing which does not yet exist – enjoys less legal favour.[8] In the wake of the 'preventive war' against Iraq in 2003, the issue is particularly current at the time of writing. But, that aside, it is also crucial in the context of 1941.

There are three possibilities. The first is that, the moment war started, the Soviet Union intended to carry it to enemy territory, and to fight it as offensively as possible. That would be fully consistent with the military doctrine enshrined in the 1939 field service regulations. 'If an enemy imposes war upon us, the Workers' and Peasants' Red Army will be the most offensively-minded of all attacking armies in history.'[9] Secondly, the Soviet Union could have been going slightly further, and was simply preparing a limited pre-emptive strike to forestall the German attack which its General Staff, intelligence services and even Stalin himself knew was coming – eventually. That might help explain certain anomalies about Soviet deployments and the speed and scale of the initial German successes. If the Red Army was caught on one foot as it was itself preparing to strike, it would be more vulnerable than if hunkered down in defensive positions. That would certainly explain Stalin's paranoia about not provoking the Germans as he put his own ducks in a row. The third, most ambitious thesis, championed by Suvorov, is that Stalin engineered the Molotov–Ribbentrop Pact to provoke conflict between the western powers, enabling Hitler to start the European war which became the Second World War. Then he would exploit the mutual destruction of competing powers, and overrun Europe. If one then accepts that Hitler launched his 1941 attack to pre-empt Stalin and save western civilization, that shifts the blame for starting the Second World War, as well as the war on the eastern front, away from Hitler and towards Stalin. In historical terms, this is a shift which rates very high on the Richter scale. One can see why most Russians reject it absolutely.

Suvorov's thesis was first put forward in the *Journal of the Royal United Services Institute* in June 1985, and rebutted by Professor Gabriel Gorodetsky of Tel Aviv University in the same journal the next year. In 1990 *Icebreaker* appeared in Britain, where its reception was lukewarm, and in 1992 in Russia, where it burst like a bombshell. Any question of the USSR's preparations for an 'offensive', preventive or pre-emptive war could not have been contemplated in the Soviet Union.[10] Suvorov's thesis, unsurprisingly, attracted a number of supporters in Germany.[11] Some serious historians in the West and in Russia slated Suvorov, however: Gorodetsky followed his rebuttal in *RUSI Journal* with his excellent *Grand Delusion*, published in 1999. John Erickson was damning: 'the Suvorov fantasies and fictions do not bear comparison with a horrendous reality'.[12] Furthermore, as Erickson pointed out, 'Generous spirits might accord a degree of credibility to Suvorov's interpretation of Stalin's strategic design before June 1940, but the fall of France wrought havoc with the Soviet leader's plans and equally demolishes Suvorov's theory of his intent. "The Germans will now turn on us. They will eat us alive," was Stalin's frantic comment.'[13]

The present author knows Rezun, alias Suvorov, and for six years before completing this book has regularly invited him to address students to explain and defend his thesis. The thesis is skilful and persuasive. Suvorov's mother was a doctor in one of the GULag camps and she reported GULag inmates being transported westwards to flesh out the Soviet armies weeks before 22 June 1941. The gaunt appearance of many of the captured Soviet troops suggested they might be former labour camp inmates, although, it will be remembered from Chapter 3, some of those moving into Poland in 1939 also appeared malnourished. The majority of Soviet tanks captured in summer 1941 were light, with narrow tracks, better designed for movement along the good roads of Germany than the poor Russian roads, swamps and snow. The conscription law of 1939 had greatly increased the size of the Soviet army, but if that intake of troops was not employed soon, they would all have to be discharged. Viktor showed the author a copy of a German–Russian military dictionary, published in vast numbers in the Ukrainian Military District shortly before the German 'surprise attack'.

But all Suvorov's evidence appears circumstantial. Is there one jot of hard evidence of a Soviet intention to launch an attack in 1941, and of German knowledge of it?

The official German explanation for war at the time was that 'Russian concentrations on the eastern border of Germany had forced the Reich to military countermeasures'.[14] Ambassador Schulenberg told Molotov that 'The Soviet government, contrary to the obligations it assumed ... has concentrated all its forces in readiness at the German border.'[15] These statements have been largely ignored or dismissed as the inevitable diplomatic 'cover' for the attack: 'They would say that, wouldn't they?'

However, we know from documents which have become accessible since 1990 that the Soviet command did have plans for an attack on German forces in occupied Poland, and that the Soviet deployment did look rather offensive. There were in fact four plans: July 1940, 18 September 1940, 11 March 1941 and 15 May 1941. These were all published in the Russian specialist *Military-Historical Journal* in 1991–2.[16] But the existence of plans is no proof of political intent to implement them, and certainly not immediately. It is the job of any General Staff to have plans for any eventuality. The July 1940 plan was signed by Timoshenko as Defence Commissar and Shaposhnikov as Chief of Staff, but had largely been developed by a young general, Aleksandr Vasilevskiy (1895–1977). The plan was extremely carefully worded and began with the assumption that Germany could attack first. In view of the main German attack being expected north of the River San, the main forces of the Red Army would be deployed north of the Pripyet marshes (Poles'ye). Then the wording suggests a crucial difference. The main task of Soviet forces would be destruction of the German forces *in the process of concentrating (sosredotochivayushchimsya)* in East Prussia and around Warsaw. An auxiliary attack would be made against German forces in the Ivangorod, Lublin, Grubeshov, Tomashov and Sandomierz areas. The North-West Front would also attack German forces in East Prussia 'with the final aim, in concert with the Western Front, of destroying [the enemy's] grouping in East Prussia and to take control of the latter'. The only 'active defence' mentioned is in the south, 'to cover western Ukraine and Bessarabia and to neutralise the larger part of the German Army'.[17] The wording suggests some form of pre-emptive attack, certainly in the north.

Stalin rejected this draft, because he believed the main German thrust would come in the south, through Ukraine, and that any pre-emptive strike would therefore be best directed there. Vasilevskiy was told to rewrite the plan, but after October work on it appears to have ceased, quite possibly because Stalin decided that, although he would have to take Hitler on, he was not going to do so very soon.[18]

None of the General Staff plans from July 1940 to May 1945 envisaged much of a role for the Soviet navy. There are only short sentences about possible amphibious operations against the Germans in the Baltic and Japan in the Far East. Given the actual events of 1941, the consequences were not too serious. The Germans rapidly overran or invested most of the Soviet bases in the Baltic and Black Seas,[19] and as a result Soviet surface warships used their guns in support of land forces and many sailors were deployed as infantry. Had the Soviet navy made a break for it, and headed for British ports, it could have played a useful role in the war at sea. But right up to Barbarossa, cooperation with the British was almost unthinkable. Culturally and politically, the Soviet navy was bound to be subordinate to the requirements of the land campaign, and tied to the stubborn defence of Russian land.

In January 1941 the Soviet General Staff ran two major war games set, ominously and prophetically, in the following July. Some thirty-two officers and generals took part as 'players', with a staff of fifty-five to run the game. According to Assistant Chief of the General Staff, Matvey Zakharov, the scenario 'resembled the events which unfurled on our frontiers in June 1941 in many ways'.[20] Zakharov describes the war games in great detail. In the first game the 'western' (German) side, with 160 divisions, launched its offensive on 15 July, with its main thrust south of Brest. The initial objective was the line Baranovichi–Dvinsk–Riga, to be reached by 15 August. However, the game concentrated on the northern part of the theatre and East Prussia, where the 'western' side launched a diversionary attack with sixty divisions.

The terrain and fortifications in East Prussia would make any counteroffensive there a protracted and costly undertaking, whereas Zhukov's counteroffensive in the south-west was very successful. This tended to suggest that the southern part of the theatre should receive priority reinforcement. Whereas the first game concentrated on the particular problems to be encountered in the marshy and forested area north of the Pripyet marshes, the second, run from 8 to 11 January, was set on a much broader canvas with mountain, steppe and many significant water obstacles.[21] Zhukov was able to get between the forward German forces and their bases to the rear, in a classic 'deep operation', but, significantly, the 'eastern' (Soviet) side ran out of steam on account of the vast distances. The Thirteenth and Fifteenth Armies penetrated to depths of 100 to 120 kilometres, concentrating on narrow sectors of the very wide fronts they had to cover – 300 kilometres for Thirteenth Army and 540 for the Fifteenth. The difficulty of operating, and of controlling movement and logistics, over such vast distances was a key lesson for the coming war on the eastern front, as Zakharov explained with reference to the smaller, first game:

> [it] showed that the operational-strategic vision of many
> high-level commanders was far from perfect and required
> further assiduous and determined efforts to sharpen up the
> command and control of powerful formations and deep
> understanding of the character of conventional operations,
> their organisation, planning and subsequent carrying through
> in practice.[22]

Zakharov was in no doubt that the war game 'did overestimate our defensive abilities somewhat', and therefore 'did not provide realistic propositions about the character of actions by forces in the opening period of a war'.[23] The 'wash-up' on the two war games was held on 13 May 1941, in the Kremlin. The lessons were confused, and when Stalin asked who won, no one could say. Meretskov was immediately fired as Chief of the General Staff, and replaced by Zhukov who had impressed Stalin. Although Zhukov's style was overwhelmingly offensive, he advocated the creation of fortified regions *(Ukreplënnye Rayony – URs)* some way back from the frontier to act as bases on which the defending forces could pivot as they concentrated for their enormous counter-attacks.

However, it is significant that neither war game appears to have envisaged a pre-emptive or preventive strike: merely an immediate and aggressive counter-attack.

The final war plan, produced by Zhukov, who had taken over from Meretskov as Chief of Staff on 15 May 1941, was a development of the three earlier plans, but there was one key difference. The 11 March plan had remained defensive, overestimating the German threat but deploying 171 divisions to meet a German attack, once again assumed to come from the south-west with the prime objective of seizing Ukraine.[24] However, the 15 May plan emphatically *did* involve a Soviet pre-emptive strike.

The plan was a fifteen-page document in Vasilevskiy's handwriting,

addressed to Stalin. On the top right-hand corner it bore the caveats
'Top Secret. Very Urgent. Exclusively Personal. The only copy'.[25] Against
the 100 German divisions believed to be in the former territory of
Poland, now known as the General Government, west of the Bug,
Zhukov planned to launch 152. This was a fragile superiority in view
of Soviet deficiencies in training and command and incomplete re-
equipment. The plan, shown in Figure 5.1, aimed to split the Germans
from their southern allies and encircle the main group of forces in the
Lublin area.

By Day 30 the Red Army should reach the 'first strategic objective',
the curved line running roughly north-east to south-west through
Ostrolenka, the River Narew, Łowicz, Łódź and Opole (Oppel'n). Then
the second phase would begin: an attack from the Katowice area
northwards to cut off any remaining German forces and to occupy all
the territory of the former state of Poland, and German East Prussia –
the 'subsequent strategic objective'.[26]

The May scheme for a pre-emptive strike cannot be dismissed as
one of a number of pure contingency plans. It was presented on 15 May
to Stalin who acknowledged he had seen it. Knowing how the Soviet
system operated, this indicates approval, albeit not authority to
implement it immediately.[27] The switch from immediate counter-attack
to possible pre-emption must be seen in the light of the intelligence
which, by this time, was raining down on the senior military command.
The opening paragraph of the unsigned Vasilevskiy draft, to which
Zhukov added marginal corrections, read:

> Germany . . . is in a position to circumvent us by mounting a
> surprise attack. To prevent this, I think it is essential not to
> allow the German High Command to seize the initiative on
> any account, to forestall the deployment of the enemy, and to
> attack the German army at the moment when it is in the
> middle of deployment and before it has successfully
> completed the organization of the front and the co-
> ordination of the movement of the various forces.[28]

The two Fronts which would attack: the Western, towards Warsaw,
and the much stronger South-Western, from Ukraine, had 164 divisions
in total, although the plan mentions 152. The South-Western Front's
119 divisions were to be grouped into eight armies, but only four
existed, although they were already very close to the border. The

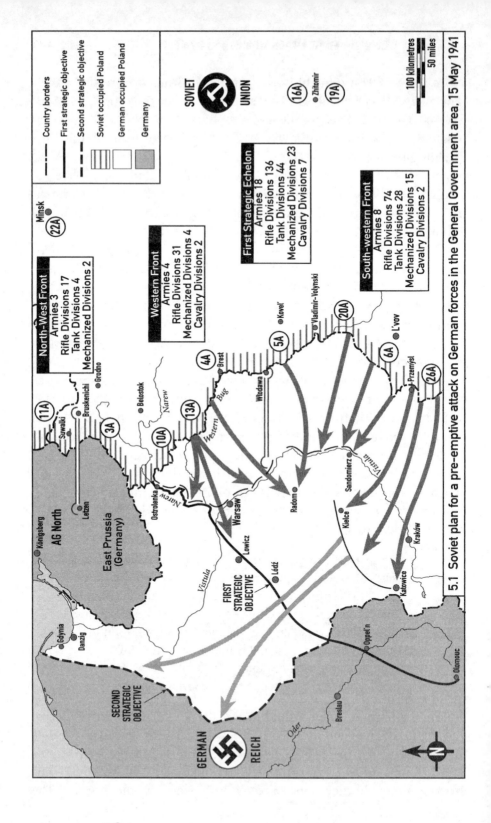

Legend:
- Country borders
- First strategic objective
- Second strategic objective
- Soviet occupied Poland
- German occupied Poland
- Germany

North-West Front
Armies 3
Rifle Divisions 17
Tank Divisions 4
Mechanized Divisions 2

Western Front
Armies 4
Rifle Divisions 31
Mechanized Divisions 4
Cavalry Divisions 2

First Strategic Echelon
Armies 18
Rifle Divisions 136
Tank Divisions 44
Mechanized Divisions 23
Cavalry Divisions 7

South-western Front
Armies 8
Rifle Divisions 74
Tank Divisions 28
Mechanized Divisions 15
Cavalry Divisions 2

SOVIET UNION

AG North
East Prussia (Germany)

GERMAN REICH

FIRST STRATEGIC OBJECTIVE

SECOND STRATEGIC OBJECTIVE

100 kilometres
50 miles

5.1 Soviet plan for a pre-emptive attack on German forces in the General Government area, 15 May 1941

Western Front was closer to readiness, with three out of the four armies suggested in the 'scheme' (*zamysel'*) – rather than a fully developed plan – at the frontier and a fourth being assembled behind. But the plan also required five armies to be available as a High Command Reserve, and they did not exist yet, either.[29]

No date was given for the implementation of what was still a 'concept', but there are suggestions in the document that plans were to be finalized in 1942. Some of them, including the establishment of new hospitals and logistic bases, would take some time to complete.[30]

With hindsight, Zhukov later recognized that, if implemented as a pre-emptive strike – certainly in 1941 – the 15 May plan would almost certainly have been a disastrous failure.[31] The *Wehrmacht*, after its victories in Poland, Norway, the Low Countries and France, not to mention the more recent ones in Yugoslavia, Greece and Crete, was a superbly honed fighting machine directed by a consummately professional General Staff. The Germans not only had more experience of successful offensive and mechanized operations than any contemporary army: they also knew how to mount a tenacious and effective defence if they had to. With a mere three-to-two superiority the lumbering Red Army, if committed to a pre-emptive strike in Poland, would, in all probability, have marched or driven to total destruction. Even Stalin could not afford to throw away 152 – or 164 – of his best divisions, and he knew it, probably better than his military commanders. The Germans would have torn the Red Army's pre-emptive attack apart, with fatal consequences for the Soviet Union – and, probably, therefore, for Britain, too.

To formulate and execute a plan like Zhukov's 15 May pre-emptive strike would tax an army and General Staff at the height of its power. Whereas the arrows in Figure 5.1 make such an operation look simple, the planning, organization and particularly the logistics involved in coordinating the synchronized movement of such a force are supremely complex. The planners clearly recognized this, with, for example, the emphasis on setting up new logistic bases and hospitals. The Red Army had lost hundreds of its most able officers in the purges from 1937. Those, it will be remembered, had taken out 3 out of 5 Marshals – including Tukhachevskiy, probably the most brilliant military brain in the Soviet Union, and perhaps in the world, at the time, and the only Soviet senior commander with experience of leading an invading army into a foreign country. The purges also removed 13 out of 15 army commanders, 50 out of 57 corps commanders, 154 out of 186 divisional commanders and 401 out of 456 colonels. In all, 25,000 officers, including 6 out of 7 colonels and generals. If those proportions were applied to the most professional armed forces in the world now, in one experienced general's words, 'you wouldn't have enough left to run a whelk stall'.[32]

This argument is *not* to support the German leader's and General Staff's overconfidence in their ability to achieve a rapid victory on account of the self-inflicted damage done to Soviet armed forces by the purges. On the contrary, once the Russians were attacked they learned, incrementally. There is a huge difference between rolling with a punch, digging in, and coming back – as they did – in a fifteen-round fight, and knocking the opponent out with the first blow. The real effect of the purges was *not* to render the Soviet Union incapable of the former, as Hitler and his advisers mistakenly believed. But it certainly precluded the latter.

Zhukov's 15 May plan, therefore, did not seek the destruction of the German state or armed forces. It certainly did not anticipate a triumphal march across Germany, occupied France, and, perhaps, on to Britain. It was merely designed to interrupt preparations for a German offensive which Zhukov well knew, from the intelligence reports he was receiving, was 'imminent' and 'overwhelming'.

The *circumstantial* evidence for a planned Soviet offensive against Germany, however, must be examined, if only because those who incline towards Suvorov's thesis cite it so strongly. The first piece of circumstantial evidence is that the Soviet Union – and the Red Army – were utterly determined to act as offensively as possible. At the Eighteenth Communist Party Congress in March 1939, one delegate, the well-known writer and playwright Vishnevskiy, noted that Stalin's speech implied 'a deliberate and careful attack against the capitalist world'.[33] Another speech, by Mekhlis, head of the Red Army Political Directorate, stressed that if the USSR became involved in a major war, it would have to 'shift military operations to enemy territory, carry out our international duty, and multiply the number of Soviet republics'.[34] On 25 June 1940, the editor of *Red Star*, the official Red Army newspaper, told the Union of Writers that Soviet military doctrine was, as before, offensive, aiming to 'beat the enemy on his own territory'. People therefore needed to understand that 'the Red Army is an instrument of war, not an instrument of peace ... we must, if necessary, be the first to strike'.[35]

During the 1930s, and even at the time of Stalin's maximum paranoia about not provoking Germany, a number of plays and films presaged war with Germany. These included Vyshnevskiy's own *Battle in the West* (1932–3), which pre-dated Hitler's accession. Eisenstein's classic *Aleksandr Nevskiy*, made in 1938 and set in the thirteenth century, was a fairly unsubtle warning that the danger posed by the *Nemtsy* – Germans – from the west, in this case the Teutonic Knights, was greater than that by the Tartars from the east. Before the Molotov–Ribbentrop pact, a number of works predicting armed conflict between the Red Army and the *Wehrmacht* appeared, including N. Shpanov's *The First Blow* and the resulting film *If War Comes Tomorrow*. Yet immediately after the Pact, V. Azovskiy's *The Double Blow*, on the same theme, was banned.[36] During a lunch on 7 November 1940, however – the anniversary of the 1917 Revolution – Stalin told his top management that the USSR's enemies were 'all capitalist states, including those which pose as our friends'.[37]

The Molotov–Ribbentrop Pact had understandably created confusion among the Soviet people, who for years had been fed on a diet of anti-German and anti-fascist propaganda. Vyshnevskiy received the news with 'incomprehension', but rapidly saw that the deal with the Germans had its advantages. In his diary he noted that the Pact gave the USSR the opportunity to be, perhaps, the last to enter the war and to use the time to make plans and amass forces for a pre-emptive strike.[38]

After the fall of France the Soviet leaders became alarmed. On 1 August 1940 Molotov reiterated the need for constant vigilance so as not to be taken by surprise. 'The nation', he said, 'must be kept in a state of constant mobilization readiness.'[39] This warning was sharply at odds with the prevailing media coverage of Soviet–German relations, but was repeated several times in 1940. By spring 1941 the atmosphere had changed. Although Stalin violently dismissed warnings of imminent German attack, on 24 April he called the writer Il'ya Ehrenburg, who became a leading propagandist during the forthcoming war. The censor had just banned the second part of *The Fall of Paris*, a novel Ehrenburg was writing about the fall of France, because it might appear unfavourable to the Germans. Stalin said Ehrenburg should continue working on the novel, a sure sign that he foresaw a change in Soviet–German relations. But, although Stalin anticipated such an outcome, and might have wanted it in the future, like Saint Augustine, he was praying: 'but not yet!'[40]

Given the continuing sensitivity of this issue in Russia, our best hope for hard evidence of Soviet offensive intent might lie in the German archives, especially given the German planners' obvious interest in what the Russians were up to. There is evidence to support either argument. After Hitler made his intention to attack Russia known to his planners, from 21 July 1940, two major studies were undertaken by Major-General Erick Marcks and Lt Col. von Lossberg. Lossberg's 'Operational study east', completed on 15 September 1940, considered three Red Army options. An attack into 'incipient' German deployments (pre-emptive); rolling with the German attack in the frontier areas, but hanging on to the Baltic and Black Sea flanks; and withdrawal into the depth of Russia in order to wear down the German attackers with all the burdens of extended communications and logistics, à la 1812, prior to a strategic counterstroke at a later date.[41] The first option – the Soviet pre-emptive strike – was, in Lossberg's view, unlikely because of the poor state of Red Army command and training. The latter, although the most unfavourable to Germany, was unlikely because the Soviet Union could hardly be seen to give up the most vulnerable and also productive parts of its territory – the Ukrainian 'bread basket', even though that was something of a myth – without a fight. The most likely option, Lossberg believed, would be for the Red Army to meet the German attack in the western Soviet Union. That is what actually happened.[42]

Marcks knew about the massive concentrations of troops in what was now the western Soviet Union, but thought they were not preparations for an attack but, rather, to secure the newly occupied territories. On 10 September 1940 he sent his report to a close personal friend, Lt Gen. von Tippleskirch, for evaluation. Tippelskirch's comments did not do Marcks's thorough and perceptive work justice, but he agreed that 'a war between Germany and Russia [would] not be triggered off by the Russian side during the next year'.[43] Neither Marcks, Tippelskirch nor Lossberg, therefore, regarded the Soviet Union as able, willing or likely to attack Germany.[44]

German views did change, however, as the final date for Barbarossa drew closer. As early as March 1941 Field Marshal von Bock received agent reports that Soviet manoeuvres in the Baltic might indicate preparations for an attack on Germany. At the end of that month the Supreme Command of Army Group B – later Army Group Centre – requested orders on what to do in the event of a Soviet attack, although they regarded it as unlikely. Then, in early April, the German Chief of the General Staff, Colonel-General Halder, wrote that 'the Russian deployment actually does permit a rapid shift to the attack, which could become very uncomfortable for us'.[45] But then, in June, he described the Soviet deployments as defensive, and, once again, his concerns probably referred to a counter-offensive rather than a pre-emptive strike.[46]

The single most persuasive evidence of some sort of pre-emptive or even offensive deployment is the German intelligence map of 21 June 1941, reproduced as Plate 3.[47] The map shows the bulk of the German forces in an offensive deployment in East Prussia and forming a salient west of Warsaw. On either side of the latter Soviet forces are deployed well forward, in what several professional soldiers have agreed with the author is an apparently offensive deployment, including mechanized corps, cavalry corps and tank brigades.[48] Behind the 200-kilometre border between Hungary and Soviet Ukraine, which then ran along the Carpathian mountain chain, there is a mountain corps (I) comprising four mountain divisions (28th, 47th, 96th, 192nd). That suggests that rather than letting the Hungarians advance through the Carpathians, which would constrain their lines of communication, and then engaging them in the flat country to the north-east, the Russians were contemplating moving into the mountains.

A comparison with the scheme of attack in Zhukov's 15 May 1941 plan (Figure 5.1) is revealing. In the 15 May plan, the Western Special Military District has become the Western Front and the Kiev Special MD the South-West Front. The aim in the plan was to encircle the large concentration of German forces south-south-east of Warsaw. From the German intelligence map, this appears a possible objective for the Soviet forces. However, it appears to the author that the numbers of Soviet formations, given their far lower quality, lack of battle experience and incomplete equipment, would have been quite inadequate to take the offensive against the *Wehrmacht*, as constituted in 1941, with any prospect of success.

However, there is now absolutely no doubt that in April 1941, even before Zhukov's scheme, the Soviet Union had begun a covert mobilization. A new mobilization plan – MP-41 – had been drafted by Major-General Vasilevskiy in January and approved in February. It was expected to be ready by May. In some sectors the plan would not be complete until 20 July, and *full implementation of the plan would take place once hostilities had started*.[49] However, an interim – and covert – plan was put into action in April. Even the most conservative and, one might reasonably deduce, anti-Suvorov, Russian authorities now acknowledge it. In an authoritative and officially sanctioned work, *Military Strategy* by S. N. Mikhalev, edited by Major-General V. A. Zolotarëv, published in 2003, mobilization had 'in fact begun on 1 September 1939, with the adoption of the law on universal military service'.[50] For twenty-two months, until June 1941, the paper strength of the Soviet forces more than doubled, from 1,943,000 to 4,629,000. In April 1941 a 'covert mobilization' began, under cover of major exercises. In all, by 22 June, 805,300 men had been called up. Of them, 310,000 were directed to reinforce the five western military districts (Leningrad, Baltic Special, Western Special, Kiev Special and Odessa). That, Mikhalev says, meant that in the couple of months before the war, another 11.4 per cent of poorly trained personnel poured into those military districts. These reinforcements had not completed the regulation six months' training.[51]

On 7 April 1941 the British Military Attaché in Moscow reported that men born in the second half of 1921 and not due to be called up until the autumn were being called to the colours but not, it appeared, in large numbers.[52] On 11 April he observed:

> what is taking place now is that numbers of men are being
> called up individually, not by classes. These include many but
> not all those born in second half 1921 who normally would
> not be called up until next autumn. There are also some
> individuals I know of age 23 and [previously] uncalled . . .
> called up this week. Also some N.C.O. reservists of 32. The
> whole thing is being done quietly and without publication of
> any official decree and it is therefore impossible at present to
> give estimate numbers involved except there seem a good
> many in Moscow.[53]

This was a limited, covert mobilization, conducted by the People's Commissariat for Defence and the Red Army General Staff, with government assent, under cover of 'large training exercises'.[54] The observant British Military Attaché noted on 20 May that he was not being allowed to visit a Soviet unit 'for technical reasons', but that numbers of troops were moving out to 'summer camps', and requested that the Foreign Office be informed.[55] The following day *Red Star* carried a small editorial mentioning the mobilization of reserves – 'hundreds of thousands' – for 'reserve training'.[56]

The Germans had also observed the covert, partial mobilization. On 14 March 1941 *Fremde Heere Ost* (Foreign Armies East) reported that it expected four classes of men – two years' worth – to be called up, but it could not tell whether existing units were being brought up to wartime strength or whether new formations were being raised. There was large-scale movement from the Moscow Military District westwards, to the area around Minsk and Smolensk, and also westwards in the Baltic region. Practice air raid alerts and blackouts were conducted in certain towns, officers' families were being moved from border areas back into Russia, and the population was openly talking about the possibility of war. On 20 March another report warned of the possible appearance of new mobile corps in the central and southern areas of the 1,500-kilometre front. On 25 May, just a month before Barbarossa, Hitler warned the *Wehrmacht* planners that the Russians might take 'preventive measures' over the next few weeks and that the German General Staff should ensure they could defend against them.[57]

On 5 May 1941 Stalin made a speech to the new graduates of the Frunze Military Academy in Moscow. This was not an officer training school, like Sandhurst or West Point, of which the Soviet Union had scores, and Russia still does, but, at that time, the most prestigious staff or war college, attended by promising captains and majors. What Stalin said had to be put together from German interrogation of captured Soviet officers who were present. The carefully reconstructed text records Stalin saying that now, having rebuilt the Red Army and equipped it with technology for modern war, 'we must shift from the defensive to the attack. If we are to defend our country, we are obliged to do so offensively.'[58] This can be cited as circumstantial evidence that some sort of imminent Soviet offensive was planned, but might equally refer to developments further in the future. It could also be a reference to a true offensive, to a pre-emptive strike or to an immediate counter-attack. It is inconclusive.

Until documentary proof of intent is found, therefore, the jury is still out. Among the most persuasive proponents of the thesis first put forward by Suvorov, although not subscribing to his full 'icebreaker' theory, is Heinz Magenheimer. In his book, published in 1997, he concluded that:

> on 22 June the Wehrmacht launched its attack into the centre of an offensive deployment that was largely completed . . .

> Even if there is no documentary proof for the exact date of a
> Soviet attack, the circumstances of the deployment and the
> pressures of time on deployment, logistics and mobilization,
> all indicate a deadline in the latter half of the year, no later
> than the beginning of autumn . . . the possibility of an attack
> by the Red Army as late as 1942, as was long maintained by
> historical opinion, can very probably be discounted.[59]

Furthermore:

> The gigantic numbers of prisoners and weapons captured
> during the initial days and weeks of the offensive . . . do not
> permit any other conclusion than that the Wehrmacht thrust
> into the centre of an overpowering offensive deployment with
> armoured and mechanized troops massed on the borders.[60]

Others, like Gabriel Gorodetsky and the late John Erickson, have
dismissed these ideas. They point out that there is not only no documentary proof of offensive plans on the Soviet side, until the very last
plan for a limited pre-emptive strike on 15 May, but also no consistent
evidence of German knowledge of such plans. As late as June 1941,
Erickson points out, Halder, the German Chief of Staff, described Soviet
deployments as 'rein defensiv' (purely defensive), and dismissed the idea
of any major Red Army offensive as 'nonsense'. Halder had been
concerned that the Soviet Union might become a danger to Germany
and in November 1939 had commissioned Major-General Karl Hollidt
to undertake a study into security in the East against Russia. However,
neither this, nor another study by Colonel-General Ludwig Beck,
Halder's predecessor, assessed an attack by the Red Army as imminent.[61]
Erickson believed that Hitler was concerned by Soviet concessions to
Germany, which might deprive him of a pretext to attack.[62]

The author believes that Stalin was getting ready to attack Germany
at some point, but inclines to the more traditional view that 1942 would
have been the preferred option. Not until then would the physical
component of Soviet military power – new tanks, guns, multiple rocket-
launchers, sub-machine guns (avtomaty) and aircraft be ready. Nor
would the conceptual and moral components – the replacement of the
27,000 trained and senior officers killed in the purges, and the improvement of junior and middle level command – be accomplished. It was
not inconceivable that by some point in 1942 the British Empire and,

possibly, the United States would be draining German strength in land battles – as, indeed, they were. In the interim, everything had to be done to postpone – and certainly to avoid provoking – a German attack. If the Germans *did* attack then there is no doubt that the preferred option was an immediate counter-attack. The events of 22 June support this. On the night of 22 June 1941 – after Barbarossa was launched – the North-West, West and South-West Fronts all received People's Commissariat of Defence order no. 3, ordering them to destroy the enemy and carry the war into his territory.[63] As evidence of an imminent German attack accumulated, the possibility of a pre-emptive, spoiling attack was raised, and featured in the 15 May 1941 Soviet plan. But, although Stalin apparently approved the plan, the fact that a General Staff has a plan is no proof of any political intent to use it immediately. Suvorov's thesis that Stalin planned to attack as early as 6 July 1941 does not appear credible.

If the Russians were planning to attack before 1942, as Magenheimer believes, for example, then a more credible, but also radical possibility suggests itself. The first great Soviet offensive of the war was the counteroffensive at Moscow, which was launched between 5 and 8 December 1941 (see Chapter 12). The Germans were pushed back, in places, up to 350 kilometres. If the same operation had been launched as a surprise attack against German-occupied Poland and East Prussia, from the pre-22 June 1941 border, it would have overrun the territory envisaged in Zhukov's 15 May plan. To attack in winter might well have suited the Russians, especially given the improvements made after the Finnish war. Had Hitler not moved first, December might have been a very good time. And it would have coincided with the Japanese attack on Pearl Harbor, on 7 December 1941, which brought the United States into the war.

Probably the most credible new theory, and the most persuasively argued, based on the known fact of the 15 May pre-emptive strike plan, and on what happened from 22 June, is Constantine Pleshakov's, set out in *Stalin's Folly*, published in 2005. Pleshakov suggests that on the night of 21–22 June 1941, the 'plan', which was still really only a *zamysel'*, or concept, was implemented because there was no other. Having come up with a concept for a pre-emptive strike, or even something more preventive – and therefore 'aggressive' – for 1942, and without a firm plan for the immediate future, Stalin had no option but to order the plan into operation with forces as yet in the wrong place,

and woefully under strength. The circumstantial evidence for this –
including Rokossovskiy's comments about strange orders he received
early on 22 June, anticipating the completion of preparations which had
scarcely begun – strongly supports this hypothesis.[64] Andrei Mertsalov
is of the same view.

> It is completely normal that Staffs work out different variants
> of operations . . . They are certainly not always conditioned
> by the political aims of the Government. In the case of the
> Soviet General Staff, the matter is not just the fact that they
> planned for attack. What is dreadful is that these or other
> optimum variations were tackled too late and amongst too
> narrow a circle; thus to realise and execute these plans on 22
> June was impossible as they were not ready.[65]

But, as Pleshakov suggests, until we have firm documentary evidence of
what Stalin said between 19.05 and 20.15 on 21 June, we cannot be
sure.

All this, however, has brought us even further into the realm of
'counter-factual' history, of 'what if?' No matter how intriguing the
possibilities, what really happened is fascinating enough.

On 21 July 1940 Hitler held the first of two key conferences. The
second took place on the 31st, and it is important to understand what
happened at each. On 21 July, Hitler summoned the commanders-in-
chief of the army, Colonel-General Walther von Brauchitsch, and of
the navy, Grand-Admiral Erich Raeder, to discuss the development
of the war. The main focus was the war against the United Kingdom,
but the United States and the Soviet Union had to be borne in mind as
possible future allies, upon whom Britain was undoubtedly counting.
Eventually, Hitler ordered that consideration should be given to the
'Russian problem'. The next day Brauchitsch briefed his Chief of Staff,
Colonel-General Franz Halder. The day after that Halder ordered Major-
General Erich Marcks, the Chief of Staff of Eighteenth Army and a
brilliant planner, to be ready to meet him at Eighteenth Army's headquarters at Fontainebleau in occupied France. On 29 July, Hitler privately
told Artillery General Alfred Jodl, head of the tri-service *Oberkommando
der Wehrmacht* (OKW) Operations Bureau, that he had decided to attack
the Soviet Union in May 1941 and that preparations should begin.[66]

On 31 July 1940, Hitler summoned his top commanders to a
conference on the overall war situation at the Berghof, his breathtaking

Bavarian mountain retreat at Berchtesgaden, near the Austrian border. The Berghof was originally an inn near the bottom of the mountain, but Martin Bormann used slave labour to instal a lift shaft inside the mountain and create the 'Eagle's Nest' on the top. A picturesque country pub therefore gave its name to a complex which expanded as more and more Nazi cronies moved into the neighbourhood. The Berghof and Eagle's Nest feature prominently in Hitler's home movies, complete with SS Guards resplendent in black and silver, Hitler's pretty blonde mistress, Eva Braun, and Hitler playing with his German shepherd dogs on the flagstones of the terrace.

In this idyllic setting Hitler announced his intention to attack the Soviet Union in the spring of 1941. The first to respond was Grand-Admiral Raeder, who left as soon as he had made his report on the state of preparations for landing in England. Hitler realized that a successful landing would depend on weather conditions (which made mid September the latest possible date) and on the Luftwaffe seizing command of the air. If Sea Lion failed, or had to be postponed until the following May, he asked, what was most likely to bring the United Kingdom to its knees? He believed the UK's determination was based on hopes that the Soviet Union and the United States would join the war against Germany. If the Soviet Union was destroyed, then that would greatly enhance Japanese strength in the Pacific, and deter the United States from joining the war – or, at least, give it quite enough to deal with without taking on Germany as well.[67]

Hitler's decision to destroy the Soviet Union therefore became fully clear to his military commanders (but not to Foreign Minister Ribbentrop) on 31 July 1940. That course of action would also give him *Lebensraum* for the German people and the mineral and food resources he needed to continue the war against Britain. After Raeder left, Hitler's advisers on the 'eastern question' were Wilhelm Keitel, Chief of Staff of the OKW, which controlled all the German armed services; Jodl, his Chief of Operations, and Brauchitsch and Halder, Commander and Chief of Staff of the Army, respectively, from the *Oberkommando des Heeres* (OKH). Whereas Brauchitsch had earlier presented a plan for limited seizure of Soviet territory, Hitler demanded that the Soviet Union must be crushed in a single blow. May 1941 was the provisional date. After that there would be five months left for operations before the Russian winter set in. Hitler suggested two thrusts: one towards Kiev, and the other via the Baltic States and then towards Moscow. The two thrusts would eventually converge, east of Moscow. Hitler calculated that Germany needed 180 divisions in total to secure Europe, including 120 for the war in the East. This meant that another 40 would have to be raised.[68] This contrasted with Hitler's earlier message to Brauchitsch, on 28 May, that once Britain was defeated or made peace, von Brauchitsch's army could be reduced to a total of between 72 and 76 divisions, releasing manpower for the air force, navy and industrial economy.[69] This prospect no doubt upset German land force commanders, who were no more immune to single-service rivalry than their successors around the world today.

Halder later claimed that he was 'shocked' by Hitler's apparently sudden decision, but given that he had started planning on 22 July this seems unlikely. Until then Brauchitsch and Halder had agreed that it was wise to stay friends with the Russians, but they did not argue with Hitler on 31 July.[70] In spite of his 'shock', however, Halder proceeded smoothly. The next day he summoned Lt Gen. Rudolf Bogatsch, the Luftwaffe commander supporting the ground forces, and started looking at raising an extra 40 divisions, and training more staff officers to handle the new 180-division army. Instead of being halved in size from 140 to 72 divisions, the German army was to be increased to 180. One suspects that Brauchitsch and Halder may secretly have been delighted that the German land forces now had something serious to do. The decision to launch an air–land operation against Russia was also popular with elements of the Luftwaffe. The Luftwaffe had never been designed for independent strategic bombing of the type in which it was now engaged against Great Britain. Many of the Luftwaffe commanders had served in the army and believed that the most efficient use of air power was in close concert with ground forces, as demonstrated in Poland, the Low Countries and France. On 4 January 1941 General Hans Jeschonnek, Chief of the Luftwaffe General Staff, enthusiastically supported the decision to attack Soviet Russia, after the disappointing results of the strategic air campaign against Britain. 'At last', he said, 'a proper war again.' The Luftwaffe had done little to influence Hitler's decision to attack the Soviet Union, except insofar as its self-confidence in air–ground operations and its underestimates of Soviet air power strength confirmed him in his decision.[71]

Soviet Russia was therefore to be utterly destroyed as a political and social entity in a single blow. The conquest of vast swathes of territory rich in grain, oil and ore was not enough. Marcks arrived in Fontainebleau on 29 July and Halder briefed him, even before Hitler's decision was communicated to his senior commanders on the 31st. Halder believed that Moscow was the Soviet centre of gravity, that its capture would conclude the war and that, therefore, the shortest approach to the Soviet capital should be chosen. The principal obstacle to the attack would be the Pripyet marshes – in Russian, *Poles'ye*, also known as the Pinsk marshes. Marcks therefore planned to attack the central point on the front – the 'land bridge' bounded by the western Dvina to the north and the Dnepr to the south, via Minsk, Orsha and Smolensk. Stalin expected the main attack *south* of the Pripyet marshes. Marcks's plan indeed aimed for a final objective along the lower (southern) Don, Middle Volga and northern Dvina – in other words, a big bulge to the south.[72]

However, Moscow, as the political, economic, intellectual, transport and emotional capital of the Soviet Union, had to be taken. That would lead to the destruction of the Red Army and of Stalin's other security apparatus: principally, at that time, the NKVD. But the best way to reach Moscow, Marcks thought, would be *north* of the Pripyet marshes, because the roads were better. The open country south of the marshes would be suitable for armoured operations but the lack of good roads, vital for logistics, and the major obstacle of the Dnepr would make it unsuitable for fast-moving military operations.[73]

Marcks expected the Russians to oppose the invasion primarily in the south. For this and other reasons, he therefore agreed with Halder that the German army should thrust towards Moscow, as Napoleon had done in 1812.[74] Two more reports to Halder followed, dated 5 and 6 August, and then Marcks tabled *Operations Outline East* (*Operationsentwurf Ost*), which utilized work by the intelligence department of Foreign Armies East (*Fremde Heere Ost*), and by the military geography department of the Army General Staff. Ironically, on the importance of the 'land bridge' and the unsuitability of the terrain south of the lower Berezina, it also referred to *Advance Beyond the Vistula*, the account of the Soviet campaign against Poland in 1920 by the now purged and disappeared, if not necessarily dead, Marshal Mikhail Tukhachevskiy.[75]

On 3 September 1940 Lt Gen. Friedrich Paulus (not *von* Paulus, as often described)[76] took over responsibility for planning the war on Russia.[77] Paulus later surrendered to the Russians at Stalingrad at the end of January 1943 (see Chapter 16). As Oberquartiermeister I, Paulus was responsible for all planning work on the Army General Staff, and in planning the attack on Russia he drew heavily on the work of Marcks and Lt Col. Feyerabend, who did much of the work on the organization of German forces for the eastern campaign.

On 28 October 1940 Benito Mussolini, the Italian dictator and Hitler's ally, attacked Greece, which temporarily diverted attention from planning for Russia. Hitler was furious because Mussolini's initiative gave Britain a pretext to intervene and heightened Soviet suspicions about Germany's policy towards Bulgaria. On 4 November 1940, Hitler, contemptuous of the Italians' ability to win a campaign, ordered OKH to begin planning for an attack on Greece. In early November, therefore, Halder began to doubt the continued primacy of *Operationsentwurf Ost – Operations Outline East*. Hitler's Directive No. 18 of 12 November appeared to assign secondary importance to Russia, behind the invasion of Britain, and the capture of Gibraltar, Cape Verde and the Canary Islands.[78] The German army commanders continued to get this impression at the next conference with Hitler on 1 December. The Balkan campaign, scheduled for March 1941, was to be concluded before any attack on Russia. Hitler hinted at the date of the planned attack on Russia by saying that the Red Army would still be grossly inferior in armament and combat readiness whilst the *Wehrmacht* would be at its peak next spring. He said the Red Army was to be split up by big encirclement operations and 'strangled in parcels'. Halder then summarized his plans so far. The backstop for defending the core of the Soviet industrial areas was the Dnepr–Dvina line and the Red Army therefore had to be prevented from establishing any firm line of defence west of those two rivers. A particularly strong Army Group Centre, already emerging as the centre of gravity of the German armies in the East, would strike from Warsaw north of the Pripyet marshes towards Moscow. Army Group North would go for Leningrad, Army Group South for Kiev. The final objective would be a line roughly stretching along the Volga and then north to Arkhangel'sk (Archangel). Hitler made no comment on this, or on whether the three great army groups should converge on Moscow or east of it. Hitler assumed that his broad directives would be followed; Halder, that the devil was in the detail and that his decisions would be proved right. A conflict of ideas and objectives was therefore ingrained in the plans from the start. On 5 December OKH, the army command, presented its broad plan to Hitler, which proposed focusing on Moscow, as shown in Figure 5.2. The Red Army would concentrate to defend

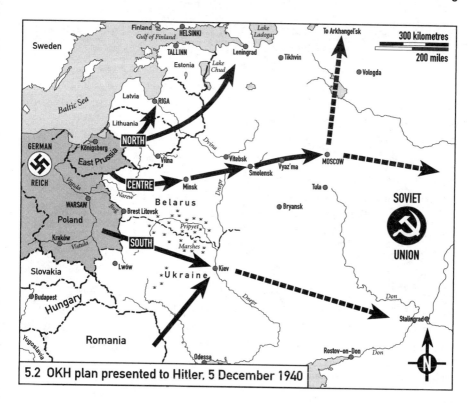

5.2 OKH plan presented to Hitler, 5 December 1940

Moscow, the capital and hub of the rail network, and there it would be destroyed.[79]

Hitler disagreed, believing that the Russians would give ground before Moscow but try to hold on to the Baltic and Black Sea ports and the economic assets of Ukraine. The compromise agreed is shown in Figure 5.3. Once the 'land bridge' – the watershed between the Western Dvina and Dnepr – had been seized, Hitler would determine whether to press on towards Moscow or to strike north towards Leningrad or south to Ukraine.[80]

On 12 December Lossberg submitted the first draft of the historic Directive No. 21. Jodl revised the text, building in the occupation of Petsamo, on the Barents Sea, in order to secure the Arctic sea route. On 14 December the plan went back to Lossberg for further revision, and then on 16 December it went back to Jodl with a note saying that Luftwaffe comments were expected. Whereas the ground forces would be predominantly involved in a one-front war, the Luftwaffe would continue to be employed on two fronts with the air war against Britain,

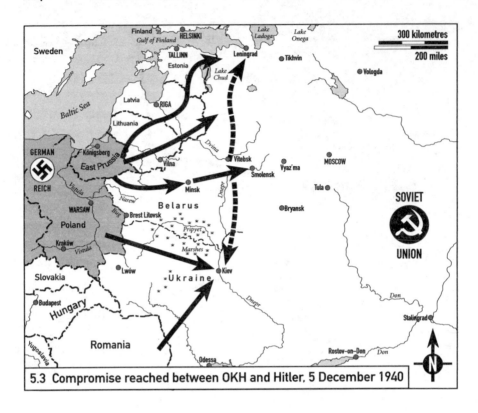

5.3 Compromise reached between OKH and Hitler, 5 December 1940

its navy and convoys. On 17 December Jodl reported to Hitler, and Hitler personally dictated his final touches. These included the continued obsession with Leningrad and the north. After the Soviet forces were smashed west of the Dnepr–Dvina line, Army Group Centre would move north to join Army Group North and complete capture of the Baltic States and coastline. Only when this more urgent mission was accomplished would operations resume to capture Moscow, which was merely 'the most important transport and armament centre'.[81] Its capture would be a 'decisive success', politically and economically, but there was no suggestion that it might also result in the destruction of coherent resistance by the Red Army, as Halder believed. Hitler may well have been influenced by what happened in 1812, when the Russians abandoned it. But in 1812, Moscow was not the capital.

The final plan enshrined in Directive No. 21 is shown in Figure 5.4. The initial axes of advance are marked with the number 1. Once Smolensk, on the 'land bridge', was reached, Army Group Centre would halt and then half its forces (3 Panzer Group) would swing north to

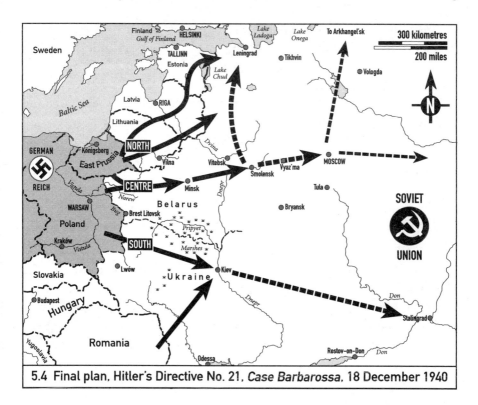

5.4 Final plan, Hitler's Directive No. 21, *Case Barbarossa*, 18 December 1940

reinforce Army Group North attacking Leningrad (2). The other half would remain in readiness to move south into Ukraine. Then Army Group South would occupy Ukraine (3). When Leningrad and Ukraine had been taken, the advance on Moscow would resume (4). Then the campaign would end with the advance to the final, still vaguely defined objective, the rough line from Rostov along the Volga and then north to Arkhangel'sk (5). Hitler and his army group commanders agreed on one thing at least: the Red Army had to be destroyed west of the Dnepr–Dvina line to prevent it escaping into the vast Russian interior or to consolidate on the so-called 'Stalin line' (see Figure 8.1), back inside pre-1939 Soviet territory. Obligingly, the Red Army deployed its main strength right forward, on the frontier, for the reasons debated above.

Halder was able to insert one final phrase. Before the section on army operations, it read 'approving the intentions reported to me'.[82] That meant that if Hitler changed his mind on how to implement any of the intentions expressed, the door was still open for debate. The seeds for the shifts in emphasis which would hamper the progress of the

German invasion were therefore already sown. Not only were there constant changes during the planning stage, which is understandable, but there were also three changes after the plan was put into action on 22 June 1941. The German invasion of Russia is a classic example of failure to abide by the first British principle of war: 'selection and maintenance of the aim'.[83]

A codename to remember

The *aim* was actually crystal clear. It was the objectives leading to the aim which constantly changed. On 18 December 1940 Hitler signed Directive No. 21, 'to crush Russia in one rapid campaign even before the conclusion of the war with England [sic]'. Only nine copies of the forty-nine-page document, in its top secret cover, scarlet with a diagonal yellow line, were produced. They were to be carried 'by hand of officer, only'. And, on the cover, only now, the supremely evocative, crusading codename for the greatest operation in the history of war ... 'Barbarossa'.

Frederick I 'Barbarossa' (c. 1123–90) had succeeded his uncle as Holy Roman Emperor in 1152. The nickname came from his red beard. He was a bold and skilful commander and astute ruler. After taking part in the Second Crusade in 1188, he led the largest ever medieval crusading army back towards Palestine in 1189, but was drowned crossing the River Calycadnus (in modern Turkey) in June 1190. He became the German equivalent of the British (Celtic) King Arthur. Legend has it that his body, which was, pungently no doubt, carried along with his army after his death until it rotted to pieces, now sleeps beneath a mountain at Kyffhäuser, on the Rhine. One day, the story continues, Barbarossa's red beard will grow out again, from beneath the mountain, and he will rise, responding once more to the call to arms. It was a brilliantly evocative and apposite codename for the 1941 offensive, 'arrogant in its recall of medieval splendours and menacing in its hints of medieval cruelties'.[84] *Case Barbarossa*, to give it its full title, was, in part, a 'crusade' against an ideology, and a social system. As we saw in Chapter 2, it was also a racial war of annihilation, predicated on genocide. It was a war for living space, and for economic autarky. But just as Frederick Barbarossa drowned in a river, in what his Islamic (Kurdish) adversary Saladin regarded as a miracle, Operation Barbarossa drowned in the immensity of the spaces it sought to conquer, in mud, rather than fast-flowing water, but above all in ice and, finally, in fire, before a storm of steel.

The British muddy the waters (further)

On 2 November 1940 a Most Secret British Intelligence report began, 'There have recently been indications that we may shortly be in a position to exchange military information and, perhaps, views with the Soviet General Staff.'[85] The British had clearly got wind of Hitler's 31 July decision, whether through agent reports or decrypts. But even a 'Most Secret' report could only hint at 'indications'. In July the Secret Intelligence Service – SIS – had reported that the Soviet Military Attaché in Berlin had warned of German intentions to attack Russia, but another agent believed that war was 'out of the question at present'.[86] The Germans kept their plans for the expansion of the army to 180 divisions and eastward deployment highly secret. By mid October 1940 Army Group East had been set up in Poland and OKH had moved from France to its location for the rest of the war at the great former Imperial German complex at Zossen-Wünsdorf, south of Berlin.[87] OKW – the joint armed forces command – would look after operations in the rest of the world. OKH, the army command, would have exclusive control of Barbarossa, another quirky piece of Hitler organization. Hitler refused OKH requests for more forces, apart from resurrecting the thirty-five divisions disbanded after the fall of France and creating ten new motorized and ten new Panzer (armoured) divisions, the latter by the simple expedient of halving the tank strength of the existing divisions.

Eccentric they might have been, but these indications were also well concealed. British Intelligence, cautious as ever, could report on 31 October only that 'Germany is preparing for a campaign in areas suitable for operations by mechanised forces on a large scale ... These areas might equally be Russia or the Middle East.'[88] British attention, understandably, focused on the Balkans and Greece.

However, from November, the world's media, never slow to detect fire where smoke had appeared, began to talk of a coming Soviet–German war. Foreign diplomats in Moscow reported German moves to the east and SIS reported that Germany would attack Russia in the spring.[89]

For the Germans, the best possible deception would be to give the impression that they were planning an attack on the United Kingdom. That is what they did. In March 1941 some twenty-one divisions, mostly of ropy quality, were moved from eastern Europe to Belgium. British military intelligence was initially confused, then intrigued, but not totally fooled, and some judged that the move of these second-rate forces westwards was an indication of an intent to attack Russia. However, using the usual worst-case scenarios, British Intelligence still, pessimistically, planned for an attack on its own territory.[90]

Meanwhile, the Americans, who were still neutral in the war, and would remain officially so for a full five-and-a-half months after Hitler's attack on Russia, had received some useful information. According to some published US accounts, the US Commercial Attaché in Berlin was informed by a senior Nazi Party member of German planning. The reports covered Hitler's initial 31 July 1940 suggestion, via the Barbarossa Directive 21 of 18 December, to Hitler's conference on 9 January 1941. According to the same accounts the US authorities received the information on 21 February 1941 and passed it to the Soviet Ambassador in Washington on 1 March. The US Ambassador in Moscow, Laurence Steinhardt, who may have consulted with Cripps, advised that the Russians would obviously distrust any such warning against their current 'ally', and regard it as a provocation.[91]

The difficulties of appreciating the available information within the context of the wider war were later summarized by the British Prime Minister and war leader, Winston Churchill.

> Up till the end of March I was not convinced that Hitler was
> resolved on mortal war with Russia, nor how near it was.
> Our intelligence reports revealed in much detail the extensive
> German troop movements towards and into the Balkan states
> ... But none of these necessarily involved the invasion of
> Russia and all were readily explainable by German interests

> and policy . . . That Germany should at that stage and, before
> leaving the Balkan scene, open another major war with
> Russia seemed to me too good to be true . . . There was no
> sign of lessening German strength opposite us across the
> Channel . . . The manner in which the German troop
> concentrations in Romania and Bulgaria had been glossed
> over and apparently accepted by the Soviet government, the
> evidence we had of large and invaluable supplies being sent
> to Germany from Russia [see Chapters 3 and 4], . . . all made
> it seem more likely that Hitler and Stalin would make a
> bargain at our expense rather than war upon each other.[92]

Up to this time, German talk of war with Russia, or of military preparations with an eastward orientation, could be, and usually was, explained as part of a 'war of nerves'. Rumours or threats of German military action were designed to put diplomatic pressure on the Soviet Union to maintain and improve its economic contribution to the German war effort, and to dissuade it from interfering in Germany's plans for the Balkans.[93]

On 25 March 1941 Yugoslavia joined the Axis, which had started with the 'Tripartite Pact' between Germany, Italy and Japan. It now became, for two days, a seven-party pact. Romania, alienated by the Soviet occupation of Moldova, and Hungary had been bound into the pact in autumn 1940, and Bulgaria on 1 March 1941. Yugoslavia made seven. But only two days after Yugoslavia joined, there was a military coup in Belgrade. The new military government immediately went to Stalin for help, but only secured a meaningless 'treaty of friendship' on 5 April. Given Stalin's obsessive avoidance of doing anything which might upset the Germans, this was hardly surprising.

At this point, however, British Prime Minister Churchill claimed to have had an insight which 'illuminated the whole Eastern scene like a lightning flash'.[94] In conditions of the strictest secrecy, the British 'Government Code and Cypher School' at Bletchley Park had been deciphering German coded radio transmissions sent between military units using the Enigma coding machine. The British could not yet decipher all the German messages, including German army traffic, or the much more complex (twelve-rotor) Lorentz system used for high-level communications between armies, army groups and OKH. But they were deciphering Luftwaffe communications and also the railway

Enigma.[95] Information on army movements from both sources was fragmentary, and required skilled interpretation. The intelligence gleaned from this source was classified as 'Most Secret' with an additional stamp, 'Ultra', which helped suggest it came from an ultra-reliable and sensitive human source (humint) rather than signals intelligence (sigint), as was in fact the case.[96] One of the reasons why the British were slow to pick up the German turn to the east was that many communications about that deployment were made by landline within German territory, which was not vulnerable to interception.

However, the intercepted radio traffic indicated that on 26 March, the day after Yugoslavia joined the Axis, three out of the five German armoured divisions, and two motorized divisions, including one SS, had been ordered north to Cracow (Kraków) in Poland, close to the new Soviet border, but were then recalled as soon as the Germans learned of the coup in Belgrade. The first intercept was shown to Churchill by Major-General Sir Stewart Menzies, the Chief of MI6, the Secret Intelligence Service, on 28 March 1941. Menzies, now aware of the 27 March coup, said it would be 'of interest to see if it [the movement] is still carried out'.[97]

Churchill later claimed that this was the moment of epiphany when he suddenly had a vision of what was going to happen in the East.

> The sudden movement to Cracow of so much armour
> needed in the Balkan sphere could only mean Hitler's
> intention to invade Russia in May. This seemed to me
> henceforward certainly his major purpose. The fact that the
> Belgrade revolution had required their return to Romania
> involved perhaps a delay from May to June.[98]

Churchill's account may telescope events a little. He may still have been thinking that Hitler's main objectives were the Balkans and the Middle East and that effective resistance there would divert him to Russia. That was a powerful argument to persuade the Greeks, Turks and Yugoslavs to resist Hitler effectively. This is the import of his whimsically coded message to his Foreign Secretary, Anthony Eden, on 30 March 1941.

> The bad man concentrated very large armoured forces etc to
> over-awe Yugo and Greece and hoped to get former or both
> without fighting. The moment he was sure Yugo was in the

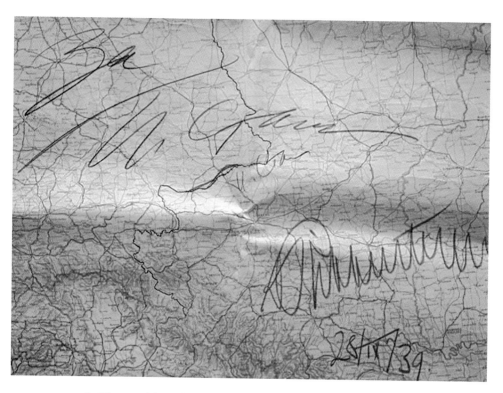

1. The partition of Poland: the map signed by Stalin and
   von Ribbentrop, 28 September 1939.
2. Agent report from *Starshina*, Berlin, 17 June 1941,
   and Stalin's comment.

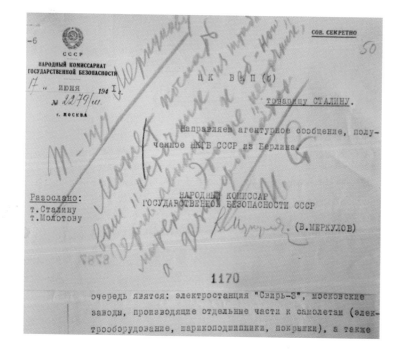

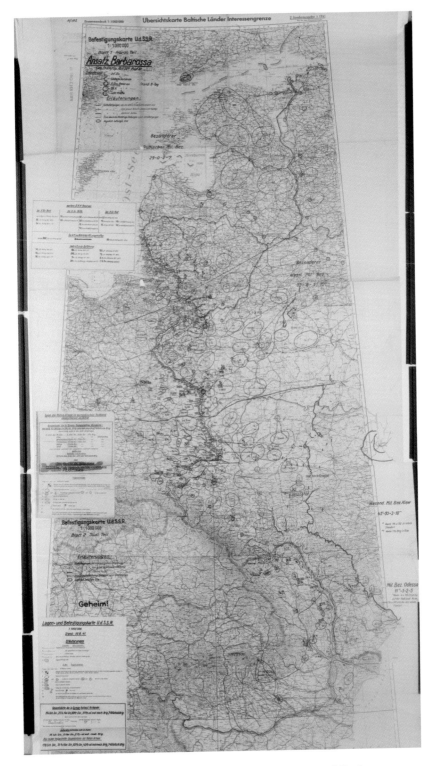

3. German intelligence map of their own and Soviet dispositions, 21 June 1941.

4. Stalin: *Time* magazine's unlikely 'Man of the Year', 1942.

5. Order to evacuate Moscow, October 1941, with Stalin's amendments.

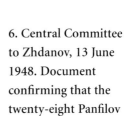

Т.т.СТАЛИНУ И.В., МОЛОТОВУ В.М.,
БЕРИЯ Л.П., МИКОЯНУ А.И.,
МАЛЕНКОВУ Г.М.,ВОЗНЕСЕНСКОМУ Н.А.,
КАГАНОВИЧУ Л.М., БУЛГАНИНУ Н.А.

Жданов.

13.У1.48г.

Сов.секретно.

ЦК ВКП(б) товарищу ЖДАНОВУ А.А.

В ноябре 1947 года военной прокуратурой Харьковского
гарнизона был арестован за измену Родине Добробабин Иван
Евстафьевич.

Расследованием установлено, что, будучи на фронте, Добробабин добровольно сдался немцам в плен, а весной 1942 года
стал служить у них в качестве начальника полиции с.Перекоп
Валковского района Харьковской области.

В марте 1943 года, после освобождения Валковского района,
Добробабин был арестован советскими органами, но из-под стражи
бежал, вновь перешел к немцам, опять поступил в полицию и
продолжал вести активную предательскую деятельность.

При аресте у Добробабина была найдена книга о „28 героях
панфиловцах" и оказалось, что он значится одним из главных
участников героического боя, за что ему и присвоено звание
Героя Советского Союза.

Допросом Добробабина установлено, что в районе Дубосеко-
во он действительно был (там и сдался немцам в плен) , но
никаких подвигов не совершал и все, что написано о нем в
книге о героях панфиловцах, не соответствует действительности.

Далее было установлено, что кроме Добробабина остались
в живых Васильев Илларион Романович, Шемякин Григорий Мелентье-
вич, Шадрин Иван Демидович и Кужебергенов Даниил Александро-
вич, которые также числятся в списке 28 панфиловцев, погибших
в бою с немецкими танками.

6. Central Committee to Zhdanov, 13 June 1948. Document confirming that the twenty-eight Panfilov heroes story is false.

7. Elena Vasilevna, a child during the war, tells of the siege of Leningrad. Museum of the Road of Life, March 2005.

8. Lavrenty Pavlovich Beria, People's Commissar for Internal Affairs, head of the NKVD and NKGB and member of the State Defence Council.
9. Aleksandra Kollontai, writer and Soviet ambassador to Sweden.
10. Timoshenko (left) and Zhukov (right) on pre-war manoeuvres.

11. Russian soldier taken prisoner in the frontier battles, 1941.

12. Bewildered Soviet soldiers surrender 1941.

13. The moral and physical components, shattered. Defeat and victory, 1941.

14. Russian prisoners taken in the renewed German drive, operation Blau, 1942. This photograph showing the appalling fate that met Russian prisoners could equally have been taken in 1941.

15. Russian prisoners, the Crimea, 1942. The picture is uncannily reminiscent of some taken in Iraq in 1991.

16. Russian
ski troops, 1941.

17. Winter
offensive,
Moscow, 1941.

18. Dovator's
cavalry in
the Moscow
counter-offensive,
1941.

Axis he moved three of the five Panthers towards the Bear
believing that what was left would be enough to finish the
Greek affair. However Belgrade revolution upset this picture
and caused orders for northward move to be arrested in
transit. This can only mean in my opinion intention to attack
Yugo . . . or . . . act against the Turk. It looks as if heavy
forces will be used in Balkan peninsula and that Bear will be
kept waiting a bit.[99]

On 3 April Churchill sent a message to Stalin. At first sight it looks
like a simple warning, but it is subject to different interpretations. Given
Stalin's mood, it proved counterproductive.

I have sure information from a trusted agent [Ultra] that
when the Germans thought they had got Yugoslavia in the
net, that is to say, after March 20, they began to move three
out of the five Panzer divisions from Romania to southern
Poland. The moment they heard of the Serbian revolution
this movement was countermanded. Your Excellency will
readily appreciate the significance of these facts.[100]

To Churchill's fury, the 'short and cryptic' message, of which he was
obviously very proud, and which he wanted delivered to Stalin 'personally', did not reach the Soviet leader until 19 April. One reason was that
Cripps, the Ambassador in Moscow, thought the Russians would find it
provocative. Cripps himself had no doubt that Germany was planning
to attack, and soon. The problem was how to tell Stalin what he did not
want to hear. The import of the message was also ambiguous. As Sir
Alexander Cadogan, the Permanent Secretary at the Foreign Office,
pointed out, the fact that the Germans had to bring three crack divisions
back to deal with a relatively minor opponent showed that their forces
were not unlimited, which in turn argued against taking on the Bear.[101]
In fact, the operations in Yugoslavia and Greece tied up relatively few
German forces – fifteen divisions out of 152 allocated to Barbarossa.
The German build-up was proceeding quite slowly, so that only one of
the five divisions diverted to deal with the results of the Belgrade coup
had already started moving eastwards. Martin Van Creveld, the distinguished military historian, believed that Greece and Yugoslavia only
resulted in a negligible delay in the build-up for the attack on Russia.[102]
The Germans bombed Belgrade on 6 April, killing 17,000 people, and
on 10 April Yugoslav resistance began to cave in when two Croatian

divisions, 4th and 7th, mutinied and went over to the Germans. Belgrade fell on the 12th, and on 14 April the short-lived government asked for an armistice. Resistance in the mountainous areas of Yugoslavia began almost immediately, but tied down relatively few German troops. The Germans poured on into Greece, pushing out British forces who completed their evacuation on 30 April. In total, therefore, Yugoslavia and Greece diverted a relatively small number of German divisions for about a month. 'Negligible' the delay may have been, but a slip of a month was still critical. There was a month less before the Russian winter, and agents who had correctly reported the original 'B-Day' of 15 May were now discredited.

Meanwhile, having received Churchill's despatch of 3 April, Cripps explained that delivering any message to Stalin 'personally' was not on the cards, and Churchill agreed that it should be given to Molotov instead. This message crossed with another one from Cripps saying that the Russians were, understandably, making great play of their 5 April 1941 agreement with the Yugoslav military junta.[103]

On 19 April Cripps eventually delivered Churchill's message to Andrey Vyshinsky, Molotov's Deputy Foreign Minister, and also a message of his own. Cripps said that in view of

> the many indications we have received from usually reliable
> sources . . . a seizure by force of the sources of supply in the
> east is not a hypothesis at all, but part of the planned
> German development of the war for the spring of this year.[104]

In the interim, British military intelligence had begun to come round to the view already held by Churchill and Cripps. On 15 and 16 April the War Office concluded that the reports were consistent either with the 'war of nerves', or an intention to invade.[105] The Foreign Office, however, warned, correctly, that approaches to the Soviet government would be useless 'since they will be taken as proof that our position was desperate and thus reinforce the tendencies of Molotov to compromise with the Germans'.[106]

The Americans, who were still neutral in the war, had better intelligence sources in Germany and south-eastern Europe than the British did. As noted above, by early March the Americans had strong indications of German offensive intent towards the East, and they considered an approach to the Soviet government. Laurence Steinhardt, the US Ambassador to Moscow, found himself in the same position as

Cripps. However, he told Secretary of State Cordell Hull that there was no point warning the Russians because they would not believe it, regarding it as 'neither sincere nor independent'.[107]

The Hess enigma

Russian suspicion of British motives was not allayed by the extraordinary events of 10 May. Rudolf Hess had long been a close colleague of Hitler and was now his Deputy. He had also been a pupil of Professor Karl Haushofer, the famous geopolitician (see Chapter 3). Hess, a skilled pilot, dressed as a Luftwaffe captain, but wearing a particularly well-tailored and clearly new uniform, took off from Augsburg at 17.45 in the superb Messerschmitt' BF 110 which he had managed to steal, heading for Scotland. Known as the Me-110 to the British, this was a long-range twin-engined aircraft which could outrun single-seat fighters. He reached Scotland just after dark, chased initially by two Spitfires and then by a black-camouflaged Defiant night fighter. Having crossed the North Sea and the heavily defended British east coast, he baled out over Eaglesham, just south of Glasgow, aiming for the Duke of Hamilton's estate. It was an extraordinary feat of navigation, which led Stalin, and conspiracy theorists since, to surmise that British intelligence (MI6) must have been involved, guided him in, and that some sort of secure corridor must have been set up. In Churchill's much later conversation with Stalin during his visit to Moscow in October 1944, the Prime Minister dismissed Hess as crazy. Stalin then proposed a toast to the British [Secret–Foreign] Intelligence Service, which had induced Hess to come to Scotland. Stalin believed Hess could not have made it without signals and that, therefore, the Intelligence Services must have been behind the flight. In fact, Hess's arrival on 10–11 May 1941 took the British completely by surprise.[108] If they had been expecting a high-class visitor, and a guest of MI6, they would have treated him better – especially in Scotland.

Obviously, Hess was trying to secure a separate peace between Germany and the UK. The real question is whether he did it on his own initiative or at Hitler's behest. For our purposes, the only relevant issue is what the Russians made of it. In the climate of the time, they were understandably supremely suspicious. According to the fairly credible 'memoirs' attributed to Nikita Khrushchev, when the news of Hess's bizarre flight reached Moscow, Stalin agreed that he was on a secret mission from Hitler to negotiate with the British. That way, Hitler's war with the UK could be curtailed to free Germany for the push eastwards. However, Stalin was not altogether pessimistic. Hess's mad mission might also indicate a split in the German leadership which could result in improved Soviet–German relations – at least for the time being. For that reason, Moscow decided to play down Hess's potential role as a negotiator for Hitler or as some form of tool in any British search for a separate peace.[109]

The Russians pored over the British official statement. It was examined by the newly independent NKGB Foreign Intelligence Service – People's Commissariat for State Security, formerly (until 1 March 1941) the Main Directorate of State Intelligence (GUGB) of the NKVD.[110] They wrote, as usual, in the margins in coloured pencil. They were not unduly bothered about the possibility that Hess was acting on Hitler's orders, but heavily underlined the parts suggesting that the flight indicated 'differences of opinion' in the Nazi party. Swedish comments about internal discord in Nazi political, economic and industrial circles were also highlighted. The NKGB seemed inclined to favour the idea that Hess's trip coincided with rumours about a possible meeting between Stalin and Hitler and that Hess had sought a meeting with the British before Hitler met Stalin. Hess was making 'a personal attempt to conclude peace'.[111] Another important point was that the head of the Luftwaffe, Reichsmarschall Hermann Göring, was known to favour a separate peace with Britain. And if you wanted an Me-110 . . . who would have been better placed to provide it?

Although the NKGB seemed to favour the interpretation that Hess was a loose cannon, the Russians continued to believe that he had parachuted into Scotland on Hitler's orders, and speculated that there might have been a British invitation, which there was not. However, they were also gracious enough to believe that Hess, Hitler or both had miscalculated the British response, which was to pass Hess from a ploughman to the Home Guard, to the regular army, and eventually to the Tower of London. His political importance at this stage made him a subject of intense interest to Stalin once he and Churchill became allies, and undoubtedly resulted in his harsh treatment after the war, when

Hess was handed over to the Soviet Union and imprisoned in Spandau jail. Soviet fears that the British were up for a separate peace were only dispelled to some extent on 22 June 1941 when Churchill made a passionate speech in support of his new, uncomfortable ally, but the Russians remained suspicious of British intentions into 1942 (see Chapter 14), for good reasons. Meanwhile, Hess's flight diverted the attention of Stalin, his close associates, and Soviet intelligence just six weeks before the German attack. The Hess mission sowed further doubt within the Soviet government and High Command about British reliability and intentions, and the veracity of any intelligence they might have been providing.[112] At the risk of starting another hare, maybe that could have been another reason for the Germans to let Hess, a loose cannon, roll in an Me-110 from Augsburg to Scotland.

6

THE WAR'S WORST-KEPT SECRET

In spite of Stalin's desperate desire to avoid provoking the Germans, and his natural tendency to favour peaceful economic cooperation, rather than to invite invasion, his intelligence services had been far from idle. Their reports are now published. On 9 July 1940 the Chief of Foreign Intelligence of the State Security Directorate (GUGB) of the NKVD wrote to the Main Intelligence Directorate of the Red Army (GRU) asking their opinion of agent reports of German preparations for war with the Soviet Union. The reports are disparate. First, the former British King Edward VIII and the wife for whom he had forsaken the throne, the American divorcée Wallis Simpson, had met Hitler in Madrid, and discussed a separate peace with Germany and cooperation against the Soviet Union. Second, the Germans were about to attack the UK in a big way. Third, the German Military Attaché in Bucharest had discreetly referred to Bessarabia and Soviet Moldova being severed from the USSR, of which they had officially become part six days before. Fourth, the Germans were bringing up vast quantities of stone and cement to build new 'strategic highways' – autobahns – in 'the territory of former Poland' – an interesting phrase, since Stalin had determined that any vestige of Polish national identity should be erased (see Chapter 3). These were right up against Soviet territory. Fifth, two steamers, presumably with reinforcements, had been sent to Königsberg and thirty-seven German troop trains (*eshelony* – often mistranslated) had been spotted moving from Bohemia to former Poland. Sixth, fortifications were being built between Silesia and 'Poland', and also in Moravia. Seventh, in the 'Protectorate', occupied by Germany, registration was taking place of former officers and NCOs who knew Russian, Serbian, Croatian, Bulgarian and Romanian. Also, Ukrainian emigrants in Prague had been ordered to increase anti-Soviet propaganda. The GUGB of the NKVD asked the GRU of the Red Army what they should make of it all.[1]

On 14 and 15 July 1940 there were more reports of 'concentration' of German forces on the borders of Lithuania and Belarus.[2] On 18 September 1940 the People's Commissariat for Defence reported to the Central Committee of the Communist Party that Germany had between 205 and 226 infantry divisions, including 8 motorized, and 15 to 17 Panzer divisions – 243 in all. Of these, 85 infantry and up to 9 Panzer were deployed to the east, facing the Soviet Union, or the south-east, in the Balkans. In the event of war between Germany and the USSR, it was estimated that 173 German divisions with 10,000 tanks and 13,000 aircraft could be deployed against the USSR, alongside 15 Finnish divisions, 30 Romanian, and 15 Hungarian and, from those allies, another 550 tanks and 2100 aircraft. At this stage the Germans were expected to launch their main attack in the north with 123 divisions, with only 50 providing a supporting attack in Ukraine.[3]

As the German deployment unfolded through 1941, Soviet agents observing all the railway junctions close to their own border enabled the NKVD and NKGB to build up extraordinarily detailed intelligence on German movements. At the politico-strategic level these were supplemented by a string of high-quality agents. One of them was Arvid Harnack (1901–42), a Reader at Hesse University working in the German Economic Ministry, codename '*Korsikanets*'('Corsican'). He provided a stream of valuable information from 1940 until his arrest by the Gestapo on 22 December 1942 and subsequent execution. An NKVD report to the People's Commissariat for Defence dated no earlier than October 1940 cited a meeting between 'Corsican' and a Staff Officer of the German High Command who told him that war with the Soviet Union would start at the beginning of the next year, and another source gave it six months.[4]

As 1941 dawned, the Soviet Defence Commissariat and the General Staff were in no doubt of the menace growing to the west. 'We usually worked past midnight and, in practice, had 15 or 16 hour days,' recalled Zakharov. 'The headquarters of the frontier military districts worked at the same intensity.'[5] While the military planned for the conventional, external war, the security services were reorganized to fight the war on the 'inner front' of which Svechin had warned (see Chapter 2), and also to improve the flow of intelligence. On 3 February the Politburo considered dividing the existing NKVD in two. Until now, it had responsibility for 'state security' issues – foreign intelligence – as well as maintaining order in society, the security of state borders (the border guards who had been so actively employed in the extension of Soviet territory in 1939–40), security of especially important industrial sites, railways, prisons, fire services, local air defence, highway security, and the whole GULag empire (described as labour camps and the organization of work by convicted criminals), major economic works and the exploitation of new regions, especially in the far northern districts of the USSR.[6]

The recommendations were accepted and Beria signed the confirmatory order on 1 March 1941. The NKVD was split in two, although the responsibilities clearly overlapped to some extent. The NKVD, as the internal security ministry was still known, would guarantee 'personal security' and the possessions of individuals, and social order; defence of the state frontiers, and control of an area 22 kilometres inside the frontier; local and air defence; security in prisons, 'corrective-labour camps' and 'colonies'; correction and re-education; dealing with antisocial behaviour by children who were neglected and out of control; the reception, transport, security, custody and most efficient utilization of prisoners of war and convicted persons; the operations of NKVD *operchekistskiy* detachments and NKVD field forces used in state-building operations in the newly occupied (and any future occupied) territories; fire services; registration of those called up for military service; and the construction, repair and maintenance of roads of [Soviet] Union importance.[7] In 1940 there had been about 65,000 NKVD border guards. The NKVD field forces operated as separate units and formations. The political 'leaders' (officers) and commissars (from battalion commissar, equivalent to major, upwards), within army units and formations were part of the army and not of the NKVD.[8]

The responsibilities of the NKVD, with its emphasis on 'personal security' factors, and other community matters – such as anti-social children – strikes a remarkably modern chord at the time of writing. The new NKGB's responsibilities were more traditional: the conduct of intelligence work abroad (spying); counter-espionage, counter-insurgency and counter-terrorism within the USSR; the liquidation of any remaining anti-Soviet and counter-revolutionary elements within the USSR, including industry, transport, communications and agriculture; and VIP security for government and Party members.[9]

The NKGB was relieved of any other work not directly connected with state security, as described above. The tasks of countering espionage and sabotage within the armed forces – formerly the responsibility of Special Department of the State Security Directorate of the NKVD (the GUGB) – and subordinate elements, were given to the Third Directorate of the Defence Commissariat. The order was signed by Beria, who remained People's Commissar for Internal Affairs, and the smooth Vsevolod Merkulov (1895–1953), the new head of the NKGB.[10]

On 11 March 1941 Merkulov's new foreign intelligence commissariat duly noted a 6 March background briefing given by Cripps to six top British and US media correspondents in Moscow.[11] Soviet–German relations were getting worse, and on 1 March, following the move of German troops into Bulgaria, Vyshinskiy had embarked on a course which could threaten Soviet interests if Bulgaria were fully occupied. Cripps cited the 'most reliable diplomatic sources in Berlin' as evidence that Germany planned an attack on the USSR in 1941, probably in the summer. Hitler might still pursue a separate peace with Britain, involving the restoration of independent government in France, Belgium and the Netherlands and seizure (*zakhvat*) of the USSR. Influential circles in Britain and Germany (and, indeed, the US) wanted the USSR destroyed and once such a peace was concluded Hitler would attack Russia very quickly. Merkulov knew this was not what Stalin wanted to hear, and therefore stressed Cripps's comments that the Red Army was getting stronger, and that was why Hitler wanted to attack sooner rather than later. The report ended with Cripps's view that the Red Army was 'significantly better' than Eden, the British Foreign Secretary and Sir John Dill, the Chief of the Imperial General Staff, believed.[12]

In April and early May Schulenberg, the German Ambassador to Moscow, spent two weeks in Germany and tried to dissuade Hitler from the war with the USSR that was being talked about in the highest military and political circles. He failed, but on his return to Moscow tried to persuade Stalin that it was still possible to restore trust between Germany and the USSR. In this, perhaps with fatal consequences, he succeeded. Broadly, Soviet intelligence reports suggested that the German leadership was split, with one faction, led by Göring, favouring war with the USSR and the other, including Hitler and Ribbentrop, ready to do business. Anthony Blunt, of the British 'Cambridge Five' working as NKGB agents, provided his controllers with some of the Foreign Office weekly intelligence summaries. The one for 16 to 23 April 1941 stated that German preparations for war against Russia continued, 'though so far there is no absolute evidence that the Germans intend to attack the Soviet Union in summer 1941'.[13] This encouraged Stalin's hopes that he could still work with Hitler.

For their part, the Russians endeavoured to persuade the Germans of the Red Army's strength and readiness. In mid April Stalin ordered his security services to escort the German Military Attaché on a tour of the massive new industrial plants in Siberia, which greatly impressed him. It was against this background that Stalin's 5 May speech to the Frunze Academy must be seen. It was part of a double-sided strategy of deterrence on the one hand, and appeasement on the other. Andrey Zhdanov (1896–1948), Stalin's protégé, even begged him to call off the May Day parade, in case the Germans saw it as provocative. Instead, Stalin ordered it to go ahead as part of the deterrence side of the coin.

Between 6 September 1940 and, at the latest, 16 June 1941, the NKGB received no fewer than 41 reports from 'Corsican' and its other most useful Berlin agent, codenamed 'Starshina' – 'Sergeant-Major'.[14] He was Harro Schulze Boysen (1909–42), an *Oberleutnant* on the air force Staff.[15] Although 'Sergeant-Major''s information is reliable, accurate and detailed, however, it reflects only a fairly low-level view from within the Air Ministry and served to reinforce the (erroneous) view that Göring was pressing for war against the wishes of Hitler and the majority of the German officer corps. In fact, Göring was doing what any head of service would do and pressing for more resources and more of a role on the big day. One of the reports from 'Sergeant-Major' may have influenced Stalin to adopt the 'deterrent approach'. In April, the Berlin agent reported that the German delegation visiting the Soviet aircraft industry had been taken aback by its efficiency and scale of production. They were shown a 1,200-horsepower engine and a mass of more than 300 new Ilyushin-18 aircraft, with another hundred on the state-of-the-art production line.[16] He was referring to the visit from 7 to 16 April of the Air Attaché, two Luftwaffe engineers and representatives of Daimler-Benz, Hensschel, Mauser and other firms. They had been shown plants in Moscow, Rybinsk, Perm (Molotov), in the Urals and elsewhere. Artem Mikoyan, brother of the People's Commissar for Economic Affairs, warned the Germans that they had been shown 'everything we have and are capable of. Anyone attacking us will be smashed by us'. One of the aircraft engine factories, the German engineers reported, was bigger than six of Germany's principal engine plants put together. Göring was furious, accusing them of defeatism.

Hitler, however, was impressed. Stalin's policy of deterrence fed Hitler's penchant for pre-emption. 'Now you see how far these people have already got. We must start at once.'[17]

The same *Starshina* report also warned that the Germans would start their attack with dive-bombing to cut the supply routes, which ran south to north, and the reinforcement routes, from east to west. The first priority would be to attack airfields because the Germans believed, correctly, that Soviet ground-servicing of aircraft was poor and that destroying planes on the ground was the best way of paralysing air defence.[18]

On 20 June 1941 the NKGB compiled a 'Calendar' of the 41 reports from the two agents. However, Merkulov, head of the NKGB, mindful of keeping his own head, refused to sign it or to present it to Stalin.[19]

In the latter part of April the German deployment had got seriously under way, and the number of German reconnaissance flights had increased. Between 27 March and 18 April 1941, there were eighty observed flights, leading to a 21 April protest from the Russians to the German Chargé d'Affaires. On 15 April a German plane landed near Rovno and the Russians found a camera, rolls of exposed film 'and a torn topographical map of the districts of the USSR, all of which [gave] evidence of the purpose of the crew' of the aircraft.[20] The Soviet warning to Germany was conciliatory in the extreme, however, reflecting Stalin's paranoia about provoking the Germans. It reiterated the mild admonition of 28 March, when the Defence Commissar had told Göring that Soviet border troops had, exceptionally, been ordered not to fire on German planes, 'so long as such flights do not occur frequently'.[21]

Army General Zhukov, the new Chief of the General Staff, arrived to face a growing wave of reports. His intelligence chief was Fillip Ivanovich Golikov (1900–80), who had been head of 5th (Intelligence) Department of the Red Army – the Main Intelligence Directorate, since July 1940. In early April Golikov identified a clear German move towards the central part of the front, near Warsaw, where eighty-four divisions had been identified. In a second report on 15 April he identified:

> A major transfer of troops . . . by railway, roads, motor
> columns and organised marches between 1 and 15 April,
> from the heart of Germany, from the western districts of east
> Prussia and from the General Gubernia [German-occupied

former Poland] towards the Soviet borders. The
concentrations are mainly in East Prussia, in the vicinity of
Warsaw and in the districts south of Lublin. Within 15 days
the German Army in the eastern borders has increased by
three infantry divisions, two motorised ones and 17,000
armed Ukrainian nationalists and one formation of
paratroopers. There were 78 divisions in East Prussia and
former Poland alone.[22]

At the end of April 1941 Golikov sought the advice of General
Tupikov, the Soviet Military Attaché in Berlin. Tupikov's 150 telegrams
and a score of reports to the Army's Main Intelligence Directorate
mirrored the reports the NKGB had been receiving. The overwhelming
impression was of a continuous build-up of German troops facing the
Soviet Union, weighted towards northern and central sectors, rather
than towards Ukraine and the south, where Zhukov expected the main
blow to fall. However, as the weight of the *Wehrmacht* shifted eastwards,
many still believed it was 'sabre-rattling' to pressurize the Soviet Union
into making further economic contributions to the German war effort.[23]
Another valuable source whom Stalin also disregarded was the NKGB's
man in Tokyo, Richard Sorge. But Sorge's reports, though apparently
prescient, still left Stalin with room to believe that he faced diplomatic
pressure rather than imminent attack. In May, Sorge warned that Hitler
had determined 'to crush the Soviet Union and keep the European part
of [it] in his hands as the raw material and grain resources necessary for
the German control of Europe'. But this was modified to suggest that
war would still only become inevitable if the Russians were uncoopera-
tive.[24] The British thought the same. To the very end, the British
departments thought Germany was using diplomatic and military pressure to intimidate the Soviet government and expected German demands
or an ultimatum.[25]

On 5 May 1941, the same day as Stalin's Frunze Academy speech,
Merkulov, head of the NKGB, signed a report to the Party Central
Committee, Council of People's Commissars, State Defence Committee
and NKVD warning that military preparations in Warsaw and the
territory of the 'General Government' area were proceeding openly, and
that German officers were talking openly of an 'impending
war'(*predstoyashchey voyny*) between Germany and the Soviet Union.
War would start immediately after the spring exercises and officers

confirmed that their men believed that German capture of the Ukraine was guaranteed by a 'fifth column' [of Ukrainian partisans] working on Soviet territory.[26] On the same day Golikov confirmed that there were between 103 and 107 German divisions facing the USSR, including 6 in the Danzig–Poznan region. There were 23 to 24 in East Prussia; 29 facing the Western Special Military District; 31 to 34 facing the Kiev Military District; 4 facing Ukraine in the Carpathians; and 10 or 11 facing Moldavia and in northern Dobrudzha (Bulgaria). Therefore, the number of German divisions facing the USSR had increased by 37, from 70 to 107, in two months. When the Soviet Foreign Ministry questioned the Germans about these massive deployments, they were told they were training in former Poland in preparation for the invasion of the British Isles because training areas this far east were out of range of RAF interference, whether by attack or reconnaissance. The fact that German tanks were observed to train with snorkel devices supported the story. In fact the tanks were not remotely capable of operating in the sea. Their real objective was the River Bug, the border between the two titans' territory.[27]

Reports also flowed in of airfield construction close to the Soviet borders.[28] On 21 May 1941 GRU issued precise guidelines to the NKGB about the information it needed on German deployments. The German command was reinforcing its troops on the USSR's borders and carrying out 'massive transfers of forces from the interior regions of Germany, occupied countries of western Europe and the Balkans. Of this reinforcement there is no doubt.'[29] GRU needed to know where the German units and formations came from (France, Belgium, Yugoslavia, Germany . . .); when and through which points they had passed; what sort of forces they were (infantry, artillery, armour . . .); at what level (regiment, division . . .); more precise identification of the unit or formation (the number of the regiment or division); which corps or army they belonged to; and when and where they were going. GRU also wanted facts about road-building in the border area, including the breadth of the roads, the thickness of concrete, and what kind of vehicles had been used in their construction.[30] Three days later the NKGB passed the guidance on, in slightly abbreviated form, to its own people in Belarus, Lithuania, the Karelian-Finnish Republic and Moldova.[31]

Against this background, Zhukov, undoubtedly assisted by the Deputy Head of the Planning Division, General Nikolay Vatutin, produced the 15 May 1941 draft pre-emptive strike plan. As we have seen, the aim was not the destruction of Germany or its armed forces, but a strictly limited strike to knock them off balance as they were deploying to attack. Magenheimer interprets Stalin's initial on the document as a sign of approval.[32] Gorodetsky believes Stalin 'rejected it outright', as it would jeopardize his attempts to avoid provoking Germany and to bring about a political solution.[33] In the light of Ribbentrop's words to Dekanozov on 22 June about the need to take 'military countermeasures' in the face of threatening Soviet deployments, Stalin had a point. The plan was noted, and shelved.

More defensive measures were under way, but would not be finished before the German attack. In 1938 the Soviet Union had begun to build the so-called 'Stalin Line' inside its old borders. Thirteen fortified areas were constructed in 1938 and another eight were added before the German invasion of Poland. With the acquisition of 'Western Ukraine', 'Western Belarus' and Moldova, the Stalin Line was seen as too far to the rear, and a new 'Molotov Line' was begun some 300 kilometres west of the former border, though still a little way inside the expanded Soviet territory. By 1941 the Red Army military council and Politburo were getting concerned about slow progress.[34]

By early June 1941 the volume of the reports reaching the NKGB, which had been placed on a war footing on 26 April,[35] had become overwhelming, but only a small amount was getting through to Stalin. On 12 June Beria told the Central Committee and the Council of People's Commissars that since October 1940 there had been 185 German intrusions into Soviet air space and that 91 of these had been in May and the first ten days of June. Even more sinister, there had been 'a number of incidents' of German intelligence agents dropped into Soviet territory equipped with 'portable radio transmitter-receivers, weapons and hand-grenades'.[36] A number of other reports received by the NKVD and NKGB the same day were summarized for Stalin. Perhaps the most blatant indicator was a report that twenty-three senior German officers had visited the border area and photographed the Soviet side. But the German build-up was again presented as presaging an ultimatum.[37]

At this point, Ambassador Cripps was called home to London for 'consultation'. The Foreign Office and the War Office had both been upset by the Labour knight's bruising style and occasional indifference to its instructions.[38] He firmly believed Germany was about to attack the USSR and told the Russians so, but the Foreign Office feared that might reinforce the view that Britain was trying to drag Russia into the war, and therefore drive it further into the arms of Germany. The British media took the latter view. The Foreign Office had also neglected to take account of Russian sensitivities. While the British feared a real military alliance between Germany and the USSR, they failed to see that the Russians feared a separate peace between Britain and Germany, and that Cripps's recall might be seen as connected with this. Cripps's departure coincided with the evacuation of a number of British diplomatic personnel, as fear of a Soviet–German war – or (in the British case) of the Soviet Union joining Germany in the war – increased. Cripps's wife accompanied him, but their daughter was evacuated to the then relatively benign environment of Tehran in Persia.[39]

As a result of the military intelligence flowing in, and Stalin's fear of provoking the Germans, on 14 June 1941 the Soviet news agency TASS[40] issued a communiqué to reassure Germany that the Soviet Union remained friendly. It denied rumours of German aggressive intentions, which it blamed on forces 'hostile to the Soviet Union' – that is, Britain, although Britain was not named. In view of Stalin and his supporters' supine acceptance of German activity, the communiqué was received with contempt in Berlin. The British considered it 'grovelling', but it had the serious effect of maintaining British fears that a further German–Soviet pact was likely or that, if attacked, Russia would not fight.[41]

On 9 June Marshal Timoshenko, the Defence Minister, and Army General Zhukov, the Chief of the General Staff, met Stalin. Stalin was by now in his most paranoid, unbending and unreceptive mood, convinced of British and German attempts to trap him into a war he was not ready to fight, and seeing 'disinformers', 'traitors' and 'wreckers' in every shadow. Presented with GRU intelligence, some of which had come from the NKGB, Stalin allegedly threw it back, saying, 'I have different documents.' He allegedly joked about the information provided by Sorge who had forecast the invasion for 22 June. If he really said, 'Are you suggesting I believe him, too', it would have been consummately ironic, but we cannot be sure that he did.[42]

Stalin's behaviour shows the classic symptoms of someone who is in 'denial'. Humanistic psychologists recognize a phenomenon where people who have an overinflated idea of their own abilities or importance slip (subconsciously) into a state where they do not look for, or dismiss, information which contradicts their formed view.[43] Those who were in the best position to talk Stalin out of denial were too close and too dependent on his patronage to dare to do so. One has to really admire the courage and intellectual honesty of people like Zhukov, Timoshenko, Merkulov and even, perhaps, Beria, who has been so universally damned by historians, for continuing to present facts which the prevailing paradigm was becoming unable to explain. Put simply, that paradigm was, 'the Germans are our friends. This is the British trying to drag us into the war. If the reports are true, it is just to put pressure on us in negotiations.'

This was Stalin's mood when, on 16 June 1941, he received reports based on evidence provided by 'Sergeant-Major' and 'Corsican' in Berlin. The first report, signed by 'Zakhar' – Amayak Kobulov, the NKGB's agent-runner in Berlin – summarized the agents' reports, from the air staff and economic ministry, respectively.[44] The 14 June TASS communiqué saying that Germany and Russia were friends was regarded as 'ironic' and disappeared without trace from official correspondence. 'Corsican' gave details for the occupation of the western USSR, nominating Ammon, an economic consultant in Dusseldorf, to run the Caucasus; Wilhelm Burandt, currently working in France, to run Kiev; and Burger, from Stuttgart, to run Moscow. It was unknown who would run Leningrad. The other three gentlemen, however, had been given military status and left for Dresden, the 'collection point' for people heading east. Overall control would be given to Gustav Schlotterer, who was still in Berlin. The very idea of the Soviet Union 'would be erased from the geographical map'.[45]

But it was 'Sergeant-Major''s report, submitted separately, which drew Stalin's ire. It was typed, with the names of the sources left blank for insertion in manuscript – even the NKGB's most senior typist was not cleared to that level – and sent to Merkulov for signature, before despatch to Stalin and Molotov under a cover slip dated 17 June 1941 – four days and a few hours before Barbarossa. The 'Information from Berlin', reproduced as Plate 2, read as follows:

> A source, working in the headquarters of German aviation
> [the Air Ministry], informs us:
> 1. All military measures by Germany in preparation for an
> armed attack on the USSR are fully complete, and an attack
> may be expected at any moment.

2. In air staff circles the TASS communiqué of 6 June [an
error – the reference is to the widely reported communiqué
of 14 June] has been received very ironically. They underline
that in practice it has no significance.
3. Targets for German air attacks in the first instance will be:
the Svir'-Z electric power station, Moscow factories, making
parts for aircraft (electrical, ball bearings, tyres), and also
auto repair shops.
4. Hungary will play a major part in military action on the
German side. Part of the German Air Force, mainly fighters,
has already left for Hungarian airfields.
5. Important German aircraft repair shops are deployed in
Königsberg [Kaliningrad], Gdynia, Grudziąz, Breslau
(Wrocław), Marienburg (Malbork). The aviation repair shops
in Poland are at Milicz . . . in Warsaw and, especially
important, – at Heiligenkeil . . .

The report then continued with the information on the occupation
and erasure of the Soviet Union, repeated in Zakhar's summary.[46]

This was not what Stalin wanted to hear. His coarse and brutal
comment reveals his character, his way of working and his state of
denial. Across the top left-hand corner in green pencil he wrote:

> To Comrade Merkulov.
> *You can tell your 'source' from the German Air*
> *Headquarters that he can go and fuck his mother. This is not a*
> *'source', but a disinformant.*
> I. St.[47]

Small wonder that three days later, on 20 June, the Head of the
NKGB declined to pass the summary of the Berlin agents' reports to the
'boss'. There could be no clearer indication of Stalin's state of mind at
this time.

Timoshenko and Zhukov had been trying to get Stalin to put the
armed forces on full alert since 9 June. On 18 June they tried again, at a
three-hour meeting. Stalin's comments, recalled by Timoshenko, have
been widely quoted, but they provide such an insight into his manner
and his thinking that they are given verbatim. The account of Timoshenko's statement to General Lyashchenko was passed to Dr Lev
Bezymensky who made it available to Gabriel Gorodetsky for use in his

seminal account of the run-up to the war. Zhukov, ever the professional officer, made a matter-of-fact, polished presentation, explaining his troops' anxiety at the uncertain situation and asking for them to be put on full alert. Stalin erupted at Zhukov, 'Do you want a war as you are not sufficiently decorated or your rank is not high enough?' Zhukov went pale and sat down. Timoshenko explained that at present the troops were in a position neither to attack, nor defend. If attacked as they were, there would be disaster. According to a signed statement recording Timoshenko's later account, Stalin began:

> 'It's all Timoshenko's work. He's preparing everyone for war. He ought to have been shot . . .' I [Timoshenko] told Stalin what he had told everyone at the meeting with the Academy graduates [5 May], that war is inevitable. 'So you see,' Stalin said, addressing the Politburo, 'Timoshenko is a fine man, with a big head, but apparently a small brain' – at this he showed his thumb. 'I said it for the people, we have to raise their alertness, while you have to realise that Germany on her own will never fight Russia. You must understand this.' And he left.
>
> Then he opened the door and stuck his pock-marked face round it and uttered in a loud voice: 'If you're going to provoke the Germans on the frontier by moving troops there without our permission, then heads will roll, mark my words,' and he slammed the door.[48]

But what else could Stalin do? Fortifications were being built on the western frontiers, but would not become properly effective until 1 July 1941 at the earliest, and not fully so until October. New, potentially formidable armoured and motorized Soviet formations were being assembled, but were still short of equipment, supplies, men and, above all, trained officers and NCOs. Stalin had looked at Zhukov's plan for a pre-emptive strike in May, and Zhukov was still alive. The warnings became increasingly dire, but by that time all Stalin could do was try to fend off the fateful day. To use a financial analogy, he had reached his credit limit, and although expecting new funds soon, he had huge expenses to meet in the interim. Hitler was no friendly bank manager. The TASS communiqué of 14 June – just a week before Barbarossa – was obviously a final, desperate attempt to fend off attack. Stalin had played a very clever, if utterly ruthless, game, for nearly two years. Now, if the reports were true, he was pre-empted, and humiliated. He was undoubtedly embarrassed, as his conduct over the next three weeks, until 3 July, would indicate. But in spite of all the stories of denial, and of a nervous breakdown, the evidence suggests he never lost control.

It seems that, right to the end, Stalin was convinced by the 'split' theory: he believed the *Wehrmacht* was provoking war without Hitler's wish or consent. The British view that the German war preparations were intended to impose diplomatic and political pressure was not totally ridiculous, either. Although Germany had attacked Poland without warning in 1939, surprise attacks were very rare in military history. Russia's experience of the First World War, when the dynamics of mobilization precipated war, were all too familiar to Stalin. Apart from 'never attack Russia (unless you are Genghis Khan)', one of the old clichés of military history is '[overt] mobilization means war'.[49] That was running through Stalin's mind.

The same day, 18 June 1941, the NKGB reported that thirty-four members of the German diplomatic community and their belongings had been shipped out in the past week. On 20 June Sorge reported that war was inevitable, and that the Japanese were discussing what they would do the moment war started.[50] The NKVD and NKGB continued to report endless detail about German deployments, but there is little analysis of the wider form of a German attack and the main direction it would take. A lengthy NKGB report of 19 June noted, amongst a confusing welter of detail, the modification of 800 railway wagons in the Ostrowiecz factory in Warsaw to give them axles which could be separated – presumably so that they could be pulled apart to operate on the Russian broader gauge.[51]

Zhukov and Timoshenko had more useful reports from Golikov, head of GRU. On 15 May 1941 Golikov had estimated roughly 100 German divisions facing the USSR, which was the figure used in Zhukov's plan of the same day. Up to 24 German divisions were in the north; 29 in the central sector (Army Group Centre); up to 38 in the Lublin-Krakow region (Army Group South); 6 mountain divisions in Slovakia and another 4 along the Carpathian border with Ukraine (also Army Group South). Golikov also reckoned on 22 Romanian divisions, making 122 in all.[52] The figures correlate remarkably accurately with the German deployment. The German map of 21 June (Plate 3) and the OKH schematic for 'B [Barbarossa]-Day' show forces in the same balance, with the numbers slightly above 15 May levels. According to the schematic, Army Group North had 26 fighting divisions and 3 security divisions; Army Group Centre had increased most, to 48 plus 3 security divisions; Army Group South, 32 German divisions and 3 security divisions, plus 9 Romanian divisions and 6 mountain and cavalry brigades. Total: 106 German and 15 Romanian – 121 in all, plus 6 security divisions, making 127. In addition, there were OKH reserves which were not due to move until 19 June at the earliest, and in many cases after Barbarossa started.[53] The Soviet picture of the configuration of German forces on the eastern front was therefore remarkably accurate.

There was one small problem, however. The number of German troops in the west, facing Britain, or available to head overseas, was roughly equal – Golikov estimated 126 divisions, which was a powerful argument he used for maintaining that other options were feasible.

In the weeks before Barbarossa the NKVD and NKGB were engaged in other business, which had a direct impact on Barbarossa itself. From 16 May 1941 a series of orders were issued to the NKGB and NKVD to round up potential insurgent elements in the border areas – the new territories of the Baltic States, 'Western Belarus' and 'Western Ukraine', and Moldova.[54] Over the next two weeks the NKGB was fully occupied, not with countering the imminent German threat, which it knew well, but with arresting and deporting people regarded as politically unreliable. These were not the first arrests and deportations in the newly occupied territories, but they were on a scale hitherto unseen. Resistance movements usually take about a year to get going – witness Northern Ireland in 1969–70 and Iraq in 2003–4. On 17 June the NKGB reported that in Lithuania 5,664 people had been arrested and 10,187 transported, a total of 15,851 which the NKGB were quite happy to record, with a mind-boggling lack of 'political correctness' (although in the USSR it was, then, very 'politically correct') as 'repressed'. In Latvia 5,625 were arrested and 15,171 transported, and in Estonia 3,178 and 5,978. In all, 14,467 arrested, 25,711 transported and 40,178 'repressed'. Of these, 5,420 were classified as active members of counter-revolutionary and nationalist movements who were arrested, and 11,038 members of their families were 'resettled'. Guerrilla groups were forming and some of the former could have been a real threat. The remaining people – nearly 23,500 – were former civil servants, military officers, police, and people who had fled from the now erased state of Poland.[55] This was the situation in countries which had been fully independent two years before, and which were about to be invaded by the Germans. Small wonder, as we shall see in the next chapter, that the Germans did so well.

On 20 June 1941 NKVD border guards in Belarus were ordered to step up vigilance.[56] In London, Maisky, the Soviet Ambassador, who had had to pass on British warnings to Stalin tempered by appropriate scepticism, had been unsettled by the precision of British intelligence and by a meeting with Cripps on 18 June. In May, Ultra sources had given the British a clear picture of a German deployment along the whole length of the frontier, and in mid June decrypts of Luftwaffe Enigma messages revealed German war preparations at Kirkenes, in northern Norway. A 'chief war correspondent' arrived at Kirkenes on 14 June, always a good indicator, and on 19 June Luftflotte (Air Fleet) 1 was given clearance to lay sea mines before 'general crossing of the frontier'.[57] But even at its last meeting before war broke out on the eastern front, held on 16 June, the British War Cabinet remained convinced there would be an ultimatum.[58] There had been very real concern about whether Russia would resist German diplomatic pressure. Gradually, this was now giving way to near certainty that Russia would not survive any German attack for very long. On 14 June the Joint Intelligence Committee estimated that the Germans might reach Moscow in three to four weeks. If they did, there would be an interval of four to six weeks before Germany could attempt to invade the United Kingdom. If it took the Germans six weeks to get to Moscow, then the turnaround time would increase to between six and eight weeks. When Barbarossa started, that was no immediate reprieve for the British planners. On the contrary, it was three days after the unexpected German attack that the British Chiefs of Staff ordered UK forces to be brought to the highest possible state of efficiency by 1 September 1941. Four weeks to Moscow, six weeks' turnaround . . .[59]

In Berlin, Hitler held his last conference before the Russian war on 14 June 1941. The definitive Deployment Directive for Barbarossa was not finalized until 8 June, and is analysed in the coverage of the operation in the next chapter. As for German intelligence, as Plate 3 shows, the Germans had a reasonable knowledge of which Russian formations were where in the forward areas, but they completely underestimated the strength of Russian reserves, and especially the strength of the Russian air forces. On 3 July 1941 Major-General Hoffman von Waldau, a Luftwaffe general, wrote:

> The complete surprise struck at a gigantic Russian
> deployment ... the military means of the Soviet union are
> considerably stronger than studies before the start of the war
> indicated. We had regarded many statistics as propagandist
> exaggerations. The material quality is better than expected ...
> As a result we scored great successes with relatively low losses
> but a large number of Soviet aircraft remain to be destroyed
> ... The will to resist and the toughness of the masses
> exceeded all expectations.[60]

German intelligence was coloured to some extent by Hitler's views,
expressed on 5 December 1940 when presented with the army's draft
plan.

> The Russian is inferior. The army is without leadership. It is
> more than doubtful whether the correct findings of the
> [Soviet] military leadership that have been noted occasionally
> in recent times will have been properly evaluated. The
> internal restructuring of the Russian army will not be better
> in the spring ... we will have a perceptibly better position in
> leadership, matériel, troops, while the Russians will be at an
> unmistakably low point. Once the Russian army is beaten,
> then disaster cannot be forestalled.[61]

The official German intelligence assessment of the Soviet Union was
published on 15 January 1941.[62] *Fremde Heere Ost* reckoned that 11 or
12 million men were available for a wartime Soviet army but doubted
whether this figure could be reached because of the resulting labour
shortages and the shortages of commanders and equipment. In fact, it
was, not least because of the mass mobilization of women. At the end
of 1940 they estimated that the Soviet Union could deploy 121 rifle
divisions in Europe. We know that Zhukov planned a pre-emptive strike
with 152 in May. Whereas some Red Army armoured units were
impressive, as the reports from Poland indicated (see Chapter 3), they
were handicapped by training and lack of modern equipment. The
strength of the Red Army rested on the number and quality of its
weapons, and on the frugality, toughness and courage of the soldiers.
This led the Germans to expect, correctly, that the Russians would be
formidable in defence. However, they would not be able to accomplish
large-scale manoeuvre operations, which made the Germans feel safer
about rapid advances with unprotected flanks. Hitler's view that the

whole structure would come crashing down in the event of a hard blow was widely held. And yet the Germans made no serious or coherent attempt to exploit the tensions and sensitivities which existed between the hundred or so ethnic and linguistic groups within the Russian-Soviet Empire, even the most obvious ones like the resentment and bitterness of the inhabitants of the Baltic States and Ukraine. The Army High Command (OKH), which was responsible for Barbarossa, believed that it understood the essence of the Soviet war-machine. In balancing strengths and weaknesses the main problems appeared to be those which would take a long time to put right. These were a shortage of commanders at virtually all levels, right up to the most senior, inadequate training for a modern war of manoeuvre, and insufficient modern equipment for all units.[63] It was a fair assessment – to a point.

The biased views of German intelligence did not greatly degrade its tactical value after the invasion. But nevertheless the Germans underestimated the Soviet Union and overestimated themselves at the strategic level, and that was what mattered most. Marcks regretted the fact that the Russians would not do the Germans the favour of attacking first, while Colonel Eberhard Kinzel, the head of army intelligence in the Soviet Union, assessed that while Red Army regulations demanded attack, it would not dare to launch even a limited campaign against the Romanian oil fields, since 'fear of the German Army paralyses the [Red Army's] resolution'.[64]

Stalin was probably at his lowest ebb by now. In the week before Barbarossa, from mid June 1941, he appears to have retreated into heavy drinking bouts and dinners at his *dacha* at Kuntsevo. Nikita Khrushchev, the future First Secretary of the Communist Party, was in charge of Ukraine. On Friday, 20 June, Khrushchev persuaded Stalin to let him return to the Soviet Socialist republic which, relatively speaking, was to suffer the worst damage from either side in the coming war. The day before that Zhdanov, who suffered from asthma, had also left on summer holidays.[65]

The first warning of the final countdown to attack came at 19.30 on 20 June 1941, when Mikoyan, the Deputy Prime Minister who controlled the merchant navy, telephoned to say that he was getting reports from the harbourmasters in Soviet Baltic ports that German ships were leaving without having unloaded. Stalin remained unmoved. But in the light of this, and reports from the ever-observant fire brigade that the German embassy was burning documents, Stalin ordered that Moscow's air defences should be brought up to 75 per cent combat readiness.[66]

Saturday, 21 June 1941 dawned warm and sunny in both Berlin and Moscow. In Russia, the winter had been longer than usual and it had snowed just over a week before. But on that Saturday, with the cruellest irony, the sun broke through. The night of 21 to 22 June was the shortest of the year, and in Leningrad, famous for its 'white nights', there was practically none. In Leningrad, Moscow and Kiev, crowds filled the streets and parks, drinking beer and *kvass* (a soft drink similar to ginger beer) and eating ice cream. In Berlin, most Soviet embassy staff enjoyed the holiday atmosphere, sunbathing and swimming in the parks. But some knew what was coming. Among those in the embassy who well knew what to expect were Ambassador Dekanozov; Berezhkov, the interpreter; and Tupikov, the Military Attaché. So did Vorontsov, the Naval Attaché, but he had been recalled to Moscow and by noon on 21 June was back home, and found himself summoned to see Stalin that evening. 'Each of them had his own reliable sources, and all the information tallied.'[67] Ambassador Dekanozov had been trying to fix a meeting with Hitler for days, and the handful of staff who had to remain at the embassy were suddenly told to deliver a 'verbal note' to Ribbentrop. The note complained that between 19 April and 19 June there had been a further 180 intrusions into Soviet air space, penetrating up to 150 kilometres.[68] But Ribbentrop had already left town, leaving instructions that Dekanozov was to be kept at bay.

Stalin, Molotov, Timoshenko, Beria and some other members of the Politburo convened at 19.05 Moscow time on the hot, still summer Saturday and discussed what to do. Zhukov was not invited – he was at the Defence Commissariat, monitoring the situation.

The meeting lasted seventy minutes. The transcript was not available at the time of writing but it may be that during that meeting Stalin reluctantly ordered the still unfinished 15 May scheme for a pre-emptive strike against German forces as they assembled – he still did not know they were within nine hours of attacking – to be put into operation, as a precaution.[69] If that is the case, the Soviet Union was not caught off balance as it prepared to attack, as Suvorov has suggested, but was woken up with a start and hit the wrong button, with equally catastrophic results.

Then, at 20.00, Zhukov called with news from the first line-crosser, warning of a dawn attack.[70]

Since Dekanozov could not get hold of the German Foreign Minister, Stalin told Molotov to summon Ambassador Schulenberg. He was brought to the Kremlin and met Molotov at 21.30 Moscow time (20.30 German). The main reason was to protest against more overflights by German aircraft, but the opening question was to ask why members of the German diplomatic service and their wives and children had left the USSR. 'Not all the women,' replied Schulenberg. 'My wife is still in town.'[71] Molotov then asked why there had been no German response to the 'peace-loving' TASS communiqué. Schulenberg said he did not have the information to answer, but that he would pass the questions on to Berlin.

As Molotov was speaking to the German Ambassador, Army General Zhukov took a call from the Chief of Staff of the Kiev Military District, Lt Gen. Purkayev, who said that a senior German NCO (and, therefore, not someone to be taken lightly) had crossed the border and told the Soviet border guards that the Germans would attack the next morning.[72] The German soldiers who valiantly tried to give the Soviet Union a last warning were generally German communists or communist sympathizers forced into German military service. Stalin told Zhukov and Timoshenko to come to the Kremlin, where they arrived at about 19.00. He was still suspicious that this might be a provocation by the German military, operating without Hitler's knowledge or orders.

Hitler had in fact told his generals of his wishes on 31 July 1940, and that intent had been set in stone by Directive 21 on 18 December. His feelings on the eve of Barbarossa are best summarized in the letter he wrote to Mussolini that day. He told his Italian ally that there was a tremendous concentration of Russian forces in the east. The British were counting on the Russians, and also on the Americans, whose lease-lend supplies would start to make a real difference in 1942. Therefore, Hitler said, he had 'finally reached the decision to cut the noose before it can be drawn tight'. He would 'put an end to the hypocritical performance of the Kremlin'. In conclusion, he wrote:

> Since I struggled through to this decision, I again feel
> spiritually free. The partnership with the Soviet Union, in
> spite of the complete sincerity of the efforts to bring about a
> final conciliation, was nevertheless often very irksome to me,
> for in some way or other it seemed to me to be a break with
> my old origin, my concepts, and my former obligations. I am
> happy now to be relieved of these mental agonies.[73]

For tens of millions of loyal Soviet and German citizens, and millions more caught between them, agonies, both mental and physical, were about to begin.

The events of the next few hours on the Russian side are difficult to timetable, not only because memories of that night vary, but because two (indeed, potentially three) time zones are involved. Moscow was (and still is, normally) *two* hours ahead of Berlin. With the advance of both empires to the Bug, the intervening time zone had fallen out of use. However, as a daylight-saving measure, most necessary in the wartime summer of 1941, the Germans put their clocks forward an hour. Thus German timings for June 1941 are in German summer time, one hour behind (an hour sooner than) Soviet time.[74] At about midnight, Moscow time, there was a report that a second deserter had swum one of the frontier rivers and, it was reported up the Soviet chain, told the NKVD border guards that the attack would start at '04.00'. That is correct, if 04.00 is the Moscow time equivalent – as it would be.

'H'-Hour for Operation Barbarossa was in fact 03.30 hours German summer time, 04.30 Moscow time, on Sunday 22 June – the time to which all the orders for an attack by more than 3 million men on a 3,000-kilometre front were related. But special forces, advance patrols, artillery and air attacks went in or opened fire before 'H'-hour, at 'H minus' . . . whatever. The German attack on all fronts began to unroll at around H minus 30, at 03.00 German summer time, 04.00 Moscow time.[75] Zhukov was summoned to the Kremlin where he joined Timoshenko to meet Stalin at 20.50 on Saturday night, 21 June. Timoshenko wanted to issue a full Directive ordering the forces into action, but Stalin was still wary. Eventually, a formula was agreed. Zhukov and Timoshenko left at 22.20, with a hopelessly abbreviated, watered-down and in many ways ambiguous order, later termed NKO Order No. 1, which was finally issued to the military districts by 00.30 (see below).[76]

At about half past midnight Zhukov telephoned Stalin with another report from a German line-crosser. He is sometimes identified as Corporal Alfred Liskow, a communist furniture-maker from Bavaria, although Liskow had actually crossed at about 21.00 near Sokal, just north of L'viv.[77] Elsewhere, he is identified as Wilhelm Korpik, a German communist labourer from Berlin. Both sources, if they were different, said they had received orders that there would be a German attack at 04.00, Moscow time, 03.00 German time – H minus 30. This information tallied with that provided by a Lithuanian deserter who crossed into the Soviet XVI Corps area, near Kaunas, in the Baltic Military District, 600 kilometres to the north.[78] Stalin ordered the 'German deserter' to be shot for disinformation, but it is not clear which one suffered this fate. Liskov's interrogation continued until the morning, when the German guns opened fire. But, while potentially useful as confirmation, all these reports were too late to influence the Soviet deployment. The Soviets knew what was coming, but it was now too late to do anything effective about it – the true military definition of being taken by 'surprise'.

Back in Moscow, all those present in the Kremlin and at Kuntsevo that night disagree about the precise timings. According to Stalin's diary secretary's notes, Timoshenko, Zhukov, Malenkov and Mekhlis left Stalin at 22.20, and Molotov, Voroshilov and Beria at 23.00.[79] If that is right, Stalin and the Politburo therefore left the Kremlin sometime shortly after 23.00 – early for them. Stalin carried on carousing at his Kuntsevo dacha until perhaps 02.00. Hitler, far away in Berlin and a time-zone behind, also took a brief nap around this time.[80] Given Stalin's state of mind, the white midsummer night and the constant stress, the political leadership had headed off earlier than usual.

Timoshenko and Zhukov had already returned to the Defence Commissariat, whence they issued the order alerting the Soviet forces, dated 21 June 1941. They predicted the possible attack for the following night – 22–23 June, although they well knew that an attack was imminent that very night. Maybe, that way, they could alert the forces without appearing to indulge in unnecessary 'provocation'. Once the war started, they probably reasoned, Stalin would have other things on his mind. The order ran:

> 1. During 22–23 June 1941 a sudden attack by the Germans on the fronts of the Leningrad, Baltic, Western, Kiev and Odessa Military Districts is possible. The offensive might start with provocations.
> 2. The task of our forces – is not to be drawn into any provocative action which could cause serious complications.
>   Simultaneously the forces of the Leningrad, Baltic, Western, Kiev and Odessa Military Districts are to be at full military readiness to meet a possible sudden strike (*udar*) by the Germans or their allies.

I ORDER:

a) In the course of the night of [21-] 22 June 1941, in secret, occupy the firepoints of the fortified regions on the state frontier;

b) Before dawn on 22 June concentrate all aviation on field aerodromes, including direct support, and to camouflage it carefully;

c) All units to combat readiness. Forces to be dispersed and camouflaged.

d) All air defence to combat readiness, [but] without bringing up additional personnel. All measures to be taken to black out towns and military targets.

e) No other measures to be taken without special permission.

Timoshenko

Zhukov[81]

The order went out just after midnight, but was reaching the army commands only an hour before the German assault began. It was also highly confusing: the forces were to be at 'combat readiness', but yet must not do anything to 'provoke' the Germans. The order must be one of the worst 'Rules of Engagement' (in modern parlance) ever issued. The order to concentrate aircraft on their front-line airfields while forbidding them to respond aggressively was inviting the Luftwaffe to indulge in a duck-shoot – which they soon did. At sunrise, the Luftwaffe struck 66 Soviet airfields in the forward areas, where the aircraft had been obediently concentrated, with 270 dive-bombers, 500 other bombers, and 480 fighters which, in the absence of any effective fighter opposition, could also strafe ground targets. The Luftwaffe destroyed 1,200 Soviet aircraft on the first day of the war.[82]

While the indecisive order was being drafted Admiral Kuznetsov, the navy commander-in-chief, came in. Bemused, he asked Zhukov if 'use of weapons' was authorized. Zhukov, with the curtness for which he was often criticized, snapped 'yes'. Kuznetsov, in a very naval way, took his leave, and headed back to his own headquarters to order all fleets and shore bases to 'readiness state 1' – the highest alert state. His order went out at 02.40, Moscow time, and the unambiguous signal reached the shore batteries and grey warships far faster than the confused land and air force equivalents. While the army and air forces fumbled in darkness and confusion along an 1,800-kilometre front from the Baltic to the Black Sea, at either end the navy, at least, knew what to do.[83]

The best evidence confirming the timings comes from the diplomats, including Berezhkov's account. Ribbentrop saw Dekanozov and Berezhkov at 04.00 German summer time, 05.00 Moscow time, by which time the German offensive had been under way for an hour.[84] In the meantime, Schulenberg, the German Ambassador in Moscow, had been ordered to try to meet Molotov. The top secret telegram from Ribbentrop began by ordering him to destroy all cipher material and the radio set, and then to pass the message that Soviet troop concentrations had forced Germany to take countermeasures. The last sentence is the most extraordinary, albeit the most correct, under the circumstances. 'It is incumbent upon the Government of Soviet Russia to safeguard the security of the [German] Embassy personnel.' Although the fateful telegram bears no number or time of despatch, Gustav Hilger, the Counsellor in the German embassy, recalled that it was received at 03.00, Moscow time. It would take Schulenberg an hour to get to Molotov, at the very least. The intention was clearly that the message should be delivered no earlier than around 04.00, Moscow time – 03.00 German summer time – as the first artillery salvos started landing on Soviet positions. However, it was not until 05.30, Moscow time, that Schulenberg was able to face Molotov.[85]

General Heinz Guderian, commanding Panzergruppe 2 of the German Fourth Army across the River Bug, reached his command post at 02.10 German time, 03.10 Moscow. All the accounts from German attacking forces in Army Group Centre give the time of the first air attacks as H-30 minutes, 03.00 (German summer time, 04.00 Moscow time). The artillery opened up at H-15 minutes, 03.15 hours.[86] Two minutes after that the first report came in to Zhukov, who was at his post in the Defence Ministry. It was from the Black Sea fleet, to report a large formation of bombers at 04.17 Moscow time (03.17 German summer time), heading for the great naval base at Sevastopol. The Western Front, facing Army Group Centre, called Zhukov at 04.30, Moscow time, having been under bombardment for about fifteen minutes.[87]

The Soviet navy therefore fired the first shots back at the Germans. The first reports of air attacks and bomber swarms came in from Sevastopol – the base for the Black Sea fleet, which was the first to open fire. The warships in Sevastopol harbour had all received orders from their commander, Vice-Admiral Oktyabr'skiy, following Kuznetsov's 02.40 order. At 04.13 Moscow time, 03.13 German time, the searchlights were switched on and within a few minutes naval guns and shore batteries opened up against the incoming German bombers.[88]

Eventually, Schulenberg reached Molotov, in the Kremlin. At 05.30 Moscow time he met Molotov and delivered the contents of the top secret telegram he had received.[89] The Soviet Union had:

> concentrated all its forces in readiness at the German border. Thereby the Soviet Government has broken its treaties with Germany and is about to fall on Germany's back while Germany is in a struggle for her life. The Führer has therefore ordered his Wehrmacht to oppose this threat with all the means at its disposal.[90]

This was not a formal declaration of war. Probably deliberately, it could still give Stalin hope of room for manoeuvre. The top secret telegram told Schulenberg not to 'enter into any discussion of this communication'. But Molotov, flabbergasted, wanted to know what it meant. Was it war?

Schulenberg gave in. In his opinion, he said, 'It's war. The German forces have crossed the border of the Soviet Union on orders from the Führer.'[91]

All Molotov could say was what most of us have said when shocked, surprised and fooled: 'We have not deserved this.'[92]

By five in the morning, Moscow time, a little less than an hour after the first sweeps by German aircraft, military commanders were trying to contact Stalin. Admiral Kuznetsov, the navy commander, whose forces had been the first to open fire, was among the first. He called Stalin's dacha, which was supposed to be a secret location. An NKGB officer answered the phone, and denied that Stalin was there. Kuznetsov realized he had met a brick wall, so he called Timoshenko instead. Zhukov was also trying to get through. Col. Gen. of Artillery Nikolay Voronov, who had been made head of the nation's anti-aircraft artillery – PVO,[93] or ground-based air defence – a week before, came in to report to Timoshenko, asking permission to engage attacking planes. He was ordered *not* to respond to the air attacks, although Sevastopol naval base had opened fire three-quarters of an hour before.

Meanwhile, Zhukov had got through to Stalin's Kuntesvo dacha. Stalin had been wakened, and Zhukov waited for several agonizing minutes before he heard Stalin's voice. He reported that the Germans were attacking, and asked permission to counter-attack. There was silence. Just the heavy breathing of the 63-year-old autocrat of the Soviet Union, who was no doubt somewhat the worse for vodka and Georgian wine, and very little sleep (not that he ever had much sleep). But then Stalin told Zhukov to bring Timoshenko to the Kremlin and have the Politburo summoned.[94]

Stalin had been fooled. The superb intelligence provided by his own services, and also sincerely given by the British, had been ignored or misinterpreted, although for understandable reasons. Everyone expected some sort of ultimatum, and in the face of Soviet efforts to satisfy Germany an attack seemed hardly logical. The invasion of Yugoslavia and Greece in April and May, besides delaying Barbarossa, also provided some plausible explanation for the movement of German forces east and discredited the sources who had correctly reported the original 'B-Day' as 15 May. There had, perhaps, been too many false alarms.[95]

On the face of it, this was a great 'intelligence failure'. But it was not really an *intelligence* failure. It was, like 'intelligence failures' since, a failure of political interpretation. The real, and very big, intelligence failure was that of the Germans – one of the two greatest in world history, the other being the Japanese attack on Pearl Harbor later the same year. With regard to the latter, Japanese Admiral Yamamoto later said that all they had done when they attacked the US on 7 December was awaken a 'sleeping dragon', who would exact a terrible revenge. Similarly, on 22 June, the Germans, as arrogant as the flamboyant codename they had given their operation, had attacked an already very testy bear in its deep and tortuous cave. Once committed, however, with the British and, shortly, the Americans at their back, where was the way out? The Germans catastrophically underestimated their opponent. And they, too, would face a terrible revenge.

The Soviet forces were not really caught by 'surprise', either tactically or strategically. They had been shackled by Stalin's mistaken judgement. The most important form of 'surprise' was institutional. They were in the middle of reorganization, retraining and re-equipment. Their formations were gearing up for a war still some way ahead, possibly in 1942.[96]

Unlike the navy, the Soviet troops on the 1,800-kilometre land border with Germany and Romania still had no effective orders. Even the alert issued by Zhukov and Timoshenko around midnight was only just beginning to filter through. Disperse, deploy, camouflage – but do not fire back. But as the sun rose early on 22 June, Soviet officers who had spent their lives in informed and erudite awe, sharpened by terror, of the dictatorship to which they belonged, were not unaware of the issues. Hitler and his military high command had underestimated them. On the River San, Brigade Commissar (Colonel) Nikolay Popel' was Chief Political Officer of VIII Mechanized Corps, on the River Dnestr, part of Twenty-Sixth Army, facing German Army Group Centre. He worked to Lt Gen. Dmitriy Ryabishev, the Corps Commander. The neighbouring Combined-Arms Army, Sixth, was based in L'viv (Lwów – Lemberg) to the north (see Figure 8.2), commanded by his friend from the Finnish war, Lt Gen. Muzychenko. Like all the mechanized corps, VIII 'was not ready to fight. We had not finished reforming and had not managed to find all our new equipment. We lacked repair equipment and spare parts. How could our minds reconcile themselves to beginning a war in such unfavourable conditions?'[97]

On 21 June, Popel' had been visiting one of the divisions in the corps area and, on the way back, used the opportunity to visit his old comrade in L'viv. He told Lt Gen. Muzychenko of a recent dispute between his own boss, the corps commander, Ryabishev, and Colonel Varennikov, the Chief-of-Staff to Twenty-Sixth Army, his own army command. Varennikov had dismissed Ryabishev's concerns about the huge German concentrations on the other side of the San. 'I guarantee there'll be no war for another year,' he had allegedly said – 'you can cut my hand off if there is.' After visiting Muzychenko, and returning to a late Saturday evening with a visiting Red Army song-and-dance ensemble, Popel' was at home relaxing under a warm shower at 3 a.m. – Moscow time – on Sunday, 22 June. His wife rapped on the door and said he was wanted on the telephone. It was the Operations Duty Officer, who said he should come to Corps headquarters immediately, and that he was sending a car.

Despite the conviction that war with Hitler was inevitable, 'which had never left any of us in recent years', Popel' recalled, 'the approaching reality of the war itself was a catastrophe which we could not even conceive'. At 04.30, Moscow time, Army Chief-of-Staff Varennikov, still miraculously in possession of his hand, called. German artillery was firing along the whole extent of the front, he said, and Przemysl, about 80 kilometres in front of the VIII Mechanized Corps area (see Figure 8.2) was under close-range fire. But, Varennikov warned: 'Do not fall for provocation. Do not open fire on German aircraft. Wait for orders!'

Then two waves of German aircraft came in. 'They bombed with precision: the railway station, the approach roads, the oil refinery, our barracks (the Germans did not know that they had been emptied some days before).' The second wave bombed the town centre, including the officers' families' apartments. Ryabishev seized Popel' by the hand, shouted that he wanted to be connected to the anti-aircraft brigade, and they raced for the corps commander's office. Ryabishev shut the door firmly. He looked Popel' in the eyes. The corps commander still needed his political officer's assent to give an order, but this time it was easy. The orders from above were still not to fire on the attacking German aircraft. But now the training, instincts and trust, in the face of a cataclysm beyond imagining, all kicked in.

> We had already known each other more than a year . . . We did not need long explanations. I nodded silently. Ryabishev lifted the telephone, hesitated a second, then gave the command.
>
> *Open fire on the enemy aircraft!*[98]

Recalling the chaos of the time, Voronov, the new chief of all the country's anti-aircraft artillery, later made an extraordinary statement. At about 07.30 that morning, 22 June, he said there was 'encouraging news'. *Encouraging news?* 'Yes,' said Voronov. Even *in spite of orders*, the Russians were fighting back.[99]

7

IRON ROAD EAST:
THE COUNTRY, THE FORCES

The country

If you want a feel for the clatter of steel that drove the Great Patriotic War, and for the size of the country, albeit a comparatively comfortable one, take the *Chernomorets* – the 'Black Sea train' – south from St Petersburg. You do not have to go all the way to Sevastopol, or on to Rostov-on-Don. After sixteen hours on the solidly built sleeper, moving fast through the night and the next morning, with the occasional stop, including ones at Moscow, Tula and Orël, you reach Kursk at about midday. Sixteen hours on a fast train, and you have covered about *half* of the *main part* of the eastern front, of the part between the Baltic and Black Seas, and arrived at a key point at its centre – the scene of the titanic battle in 1943.[1] The scale of the battle front, and the key role of rail transport in the logistic battle, are both indelibly imprinted on the mind.

Certain trains feature constantly in accounts of the war. The last train carrying Soviet supplies for Germany under the Nazi–Soviet Pact arrangements rolled westwards across the border at Brest-Litovsk less than an hour before the invasion, at around 02.00 German time, past German soldiers who were poised to attack. It was not until dawn that the Soviet transport administration ordered all loads destined for Germany to be held, and a count of all the traffic to be returned by 18.00 that evening.[2]

There is also a ghost train. The story goes that the Berlin–Moscow passenger express rolled the other way, after midnight, through Brest-Litovsk, 'as normal'. But that story, intriguing though it is, is completely untrue.[3]

The Berlin–Moscow 'express', which actually took more than forty hours to make the journey – another measure of the scale of theatre of war – had never passed through Brest. At the time of writing, in the early 2000s, it left Berlin at 18.12, which would have been uncannily appropriate, but in 1941 it left at 18.42. Traditionally, it had travelled northeast, through Insterburg in East Prussia and then into Lithuania (where its border stop at Kibart, often with a number of VIP passengers, was quite a local event). It then headed on to Kaunas (Kovno), before turning east through Daugavpils in Latvia and into Belarus (see Figure 3.2).[4] This route appears to have been changed after the German–Soviet occupation of Poland. The train that left Berlin at 18.42 on 21 June was routed via Warsaw, Malkinia and Czyzew, Bialystok and Minsk to Moscow.[5] Czyzew was the border entry point for Soviet territory. The country round about is sandy plain, dotted with pine woods and marshes. Here, the train officially stopped for an hour and 24 minutes. That time was needed to change from German standard gauge (1.435 metre) to the wider Russian gauge (1.520 metre) rolling stock. But in 1939–41 the Soviet border guards and customs took the opportunity to search everyone and all their baggage thoroughly. Even Berezhkov, an important – if young – Soviet official, returning from Berlin in 1940, was dismayed when he heard the order 'everybody ... off the train with their luggage for customs clearance'.[6] Although he had been overjoyed to come home, by the time they had searched everything, given him a hard time, confiscated his new German radio, two German watches, and given him a receipt, 'there was no trace left of the blissful state of mind in which I had arrived'.[7]

In all probability the DmW23 train, an express with part reserved for the *Wehrmacht*, never passed through German controls at Malkynia, which later became the station for Treblinka concentration camp,[8] or arrived in Soviet space at Czyzew. Having left Berlin at 18.42 on 21 June, it reached Warsaw at 05.30 the next morning (German time), when the war had already been under way for two-and-a-half hours. In all probability, it stopped there. It should have reached Czyzew at 10.04 on the morning of Sunday, 22 June. By that time, the Soviet border guards and customs were long gone, either fled or dead. On the other hand, the 'express' train that left Berlin on Friday 20 June should have been several hours past Minsk en route for Moscow by the time war started. It had rolled out of Czyzew at 11.28 German time – 12.28 Moscow time – on 21 June – just after noon, and maybe that is the cause of the confusion.[9]

As Churchill observed in his brilliant account of the eastern front in the First World War, the prime characteristic of the theatre was and is its size. His observation that 'in the West the armies were too big for the country; in the East the country was too big for the armies' applies equally to the Second World War.[10] This simple geostrategic fact is illustrated in Figure 7.1. For illustrative purposes, we might assume that a Second World War division could dominate and impede movement in an area perhaps 10 kilometres square, although divisions might be concentrated on far smaller sectors or dispersed across wider ones.[11] On 22 June 1941 there were 171 Soviet divisions in the first strategic echelon, and 202 on the Soviet–German front as a whole.[12] The initial German attack was with 100 German and Romanian divisions, but there were 180 on the front as a whole.[13] Thus, overall, we are talking about 400 divisions on the opposing sides.

Fighting in the 'cockpit of Europe' – north-western France and the Low Countries – such a force might completely occupy and bog down in the area shown. But as you move east, the territory gets bigger. Even within the area of initial German advance, the funnel is apparent. The starting frontage for German forces and their allies was 1,600 kilometres: by the time they had penetrated the second operational echelon, roughly from Odessa to Leningrad, the oscillating front line was 2,400 kilometres – already a 50 per cent increase.[14] By the time the Germans reached the maximum extent of their advance, from the Caucasus up to Stalingrad, back to before Moscow, and up to Leningrad, such a force is widely dispersed. Had they made it to the Arkhangel'sk–Astrakhan line, they would still have been very dispersed. There was a 'density problem'.[15] The country was too big for the armies, and that effect was multiplied by the relative paucity of railways and good roads. Only 80,000 kilometres of railways and 64,000 kilometres of hard-surfaced all-weather roads traversed such a country.[16]

The millions of men and women employed were dwarfed by the scale of the landscape. The flanks and rear of any German or Soviet formation advancing were always vulnerable to some other massive force moving in from an unexpected angle and suddenly appearing in unknown strength. Even more than in the First World War, both sides were dependent on copious supplies of sophisticated manufactured goods, especially ammunition and spares and, of course, fuel. And, even more than in the First World War, these vast spaces, especially the swamps and forests, provided fastnesses where large partisan groups

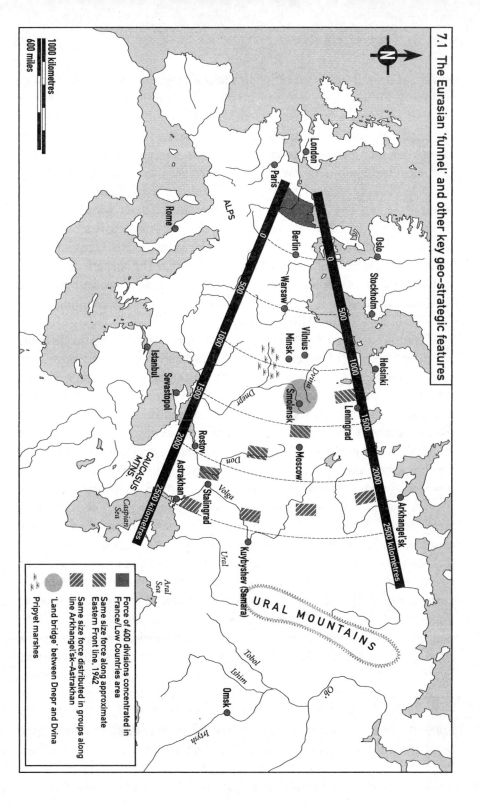

Legend:

- Force of 400 divisions concentrated in France/Low Countries area
- Same size force along approximate Eastern Front line, 1942
- Same size force distributed in groups along line Arkhangel'sk–Astrakhan
- 'Land bridge' between Dnepr and Dvina
- Pripyet marshes

1000 kilometres
600 miles

could concentrate and whence they could move out to attack German communications.[17]

East of Warsaw and the Vistula river the country becomes increasingly marshy and wooded until, 130 kilometres east of what is, once again, Poland's proud capital, any invader is confronted by the 480-kilometre wide and deep barrier of the Pripyet marshes (see Figures 3.2 and 7.1). This region, which in 1941 was still one of 'primeval bog and forest', is as large as Scotland or South Carolina. The roads and railways in this area are effectively causeways, and the villages were to some extent islands surrounded by treacherous swamps.[18] All German operational ideas were based on the assumption that the armies in the east would have to be deployed in at least two groups, north and south of the Pripyet marshes.

The first German 'Military-geographical study of European Russia' was completed by 10 August 1940. The main targets were Ukraine, which produced 90 per cent of the USSR's sugar beet, 60 per cent of its coal, 60 per cent of its iron and 20 per cent of its wheat, plus Moscow, the capital, and Leningrad.[19] As we saw in Chapter 4, the competing attractions of these objectives played havoc with the selection and maintenance of Hitler's aim. Marcks favoured a direct thrust for Moscow starting north of the Pripyet marshes and through the only feasible route, via Smolensk, where the Dnepr and western Dvina both bend eastwards to form the 'land bridge' – the 'Smolensk–Moscow upland' (see Figure 7.1). Assessments of the soil structure and vegetation were begun. While the sparsely wooded, open terrain south of the marshes might at first sight appear ideal for armoured operations, the lack of roads and the massive Dnepr river would restrict freedom of movement. Even where the Dnepr did not run straight across the German front, its numerous tributaries did and these were expected to form part of lines of defence. The Germans expected the Red Army to consolidate on the Dnepr–Dvina line, about 400 kilometres from the start line, and therefore devoted great effort to trapping the Soviet forces before they could withdraw to it.[20]

Because good roads were so few and far between, they were to be exclusively used by armoured and motorized units, while troops on foot and with horses were to use secondary tracks and open country. High priority was attached to the seizure of road junctions and river crossings by fast-moving mobile forces, and Marcks demanded preparations to be made for such conditions with modifications to organization, training, equipment and leadership. Because the Russian rail gauge was wider, it would take time before a smooth flow of supplies by rail could be guaranteed. Until then, the Germans had to move heavy supplies forward using whatever Russian gauge rolling stock they could capture. Therefore, as Halder said in his report to Hitler on 3 February 1941, 'Motor vehicle must accomplish everything.'[21] The overwhelming priorities were ammunition and fuel. As far as food was concerned, the German forces were expected to live off the land, which proved increasingly difficult since the Russians soon started to destroy crops as they withdrew.[22]

The forces

The German army in June 1941 was far from all-mechanized, and would remain so throughout the war. The *Panzer* – 'mail', or armoured – divisions which had been so successful against France in 1940 had been halved in size, to make more of them. Instead of 10, there were now 19 available for the start of Barbarossa, plus 1.5 to 2 in North Africa.[23] The German Order of Battle for Barbarossa down to divisional level is shown in Table 7.1 and the main concentrations of force in Figure 8.1.

The vast bulk of the German army marched, with horse-drawn artillery and supplies. For Russia, with its few roads, this was no bad thing, and the German planners took account of it. Nonetheless, the fast-moving armoured and motorized formations often had to stop to wait for the rest to catch up and when they thought they had encircled the Russians, the Russians often managed to escape.

The best estimate for German tank numbers on the eastern front on the morning of 22 June is 3,330. Most of them would appear pathetically lightly armoured and armed by our standards, and, indeed, by the standards which applied later in the war. The most important advantage enjoyed by the German Panzer divisions was that every tank had an excellent radio, whereas only one Soviet tank in three (the platoon commander) did. Guderian, who developed the German Panzer forces in the 1930s, had been a signals officer, and it showed.

Paradoxically, the German infantry had better guns for taking on

Table 7.1 – Deployment of the *Wehrmacht* for Operation Barbarossa; 21 June 1941 (simplified)

OBERKOMMANDO DES HEERES (OKH)
Army High Command, responsible for command of the entire Eastern Front

Panzer Groups (Armies), corps and divisions are shown in **bold italic**, motorized corps and division in *italic*

To be moved up: by 4 July XXXX – motor transport, *60 mot* / after 4 July – 46, 93, 96, 98, 260, 94, 183, 73, *5 pz* 294, *2pz* / autumn – 707, 713

ARMY GROUPS	ARMIES	CORPS	DIVISIONS
AG NORTH	**Eighteen**	XXVI	291, 61, 217
Res:		XXXVIII	58
XXIII		I	11, 1, 21
254, 251, 206			
	Panzer Group Four	*XXXXI (XLI) mot*	*1 pz, 269, 6 pz, mot*
Security divisions:	Res: *SS Totenkopf*		*6 pz, 36 mot*
207, 285, 281		*LVI mot*	*290, 8 pz, 3 mot*
	Sixteen	X	30, 126
	Res: 253	XXVIII	122, 123
		II	121, 12, 32
AG CENTRE	***Panzer Group Three***	VI	26, 6
Res:		*XXXIX mot*	*14 mot, 20 mot, 20 pz, 7 pz*
LIII		V	35, 5
293		*LVII mot*	*18 mot, 19 pz, 12 pz*
Security divisions	**Nine**	VIII	161, 28, 8
403, 221, 286		XX	256, 162
		XXXXII	129, 102, 87
	Four	VII	258, 23, 7, 268
		XXIII	17, 78
		IX	263, 137, 292
		XXXXIII	252, 134, 131

Table 7.1 (cont.)

ARMY GROUPS	ARMIES	CORPS	DIVISIONS
AG CENTRE	*Panzer Group Two* Res: 255	*XXXXVI mot*	*Regiment Großdeutschland* *10 pz, SS 'Das Reich'*
		XXXXVII mot	*29 mot, 167, 17 pz, 18 pz*
		XII	31, 45, 34
		XXIV mot	*10 mot, 3 pz, 4 pz,* 1 cavalry
			267
AG SOUTH Res 99 light Security divisions 213, 444, 454	*Panzer Group One* *Res 16 mot, 25 mot,* *13 pz, SS 'Adolf Hitler'*	*XIV mot*	*SS Viking, 16 pz, 9 pz*
		III mot	*14 pz, 298, 44*
		XXIX	299, 111
		XXXXVIII mot	*11 pz, 75, 57*
	Six Res LV, 168	XVII	56, 62
		XXXXIV	297, 9
	Seventeen Res 100 light, 97 light	XXXXIX	262, 24, 295, 296, 71
		Mountain	1 mountain, 68, 257
		LII	101 light
	Eleven Res, General, Command Rom, cav corps, 22	Romanian Mountain Corps	4 Rom mtn bde, 1 Rom mtn bde, 2 Rom mtn bde, 8 Rom mtn bde, 7 Rom mtn bde
		XI	239, 76, 6 Rom inf div, 8 Rom inf div, 6 Rom cav bde
		XXX	5 Rom cav bde, 14 Rom inf div, 198
		LIV	170, 15

In addition, Romanian Third and Fourth armies and four corps commands, divisions, brigades and other small units not subordinate to OKH on 22 June 1941

Source: *Germany and Second World War*, Vol. IV, Maps, 2, *Schematische Kriegsgliederung Stand: B-tag 1941 (22.6), 'Barbarossa'.*

enemy armour than their armour did: a long-barrelled 50mm anti-tank gun and the 88mm anti-aircraft gun. German tactics reflected this. Good reconnaissance would identify a weak point in the enemy front, and tanks would be pushed through it, to seize vital ground ahead, often supported by the siren-screaming, bent-winged Junkers-87 Stuka dive-bombers. Then infantry would be brought forward to hold that ground, with anti-tank guns. If the enemy counter-attacked, the defending German infantry and anti-tank guns had a certain advantage. Meanwhile the German tanks hung back, and waited to execute the next movement. Close support from the Luftwaffe was crucial in the initial breakthrough, but the role of German artillery, deployed well forwards and often firing direct (at targets the guns could see themselves), as opposed to indirect (at coordinates on the map), should not be underestimated.[24]

The Luftwaffe had emerged as a pre-eminent close-support air force, but lacked heavy, long-range planes to conduct 'strategic' bombing – attacks on the enemy's industrial and psychological heartland, or what the Russians called, and still call, the 'deep rear'. Estimates of the number of aircraft deployed on the eastern front vary from 2,770 to 2,840. As German industry had not made up for losses incurred in the Battle of Britain in 1940 to early 1941, the Luftwaffe had 200 fewer bombers for the attack on the USSR than it had for the attacks on the much more concentrated targets (see Figure 7.1) of France, the Low Countries and the UK.

In all, the Luftwaffe had a total of 3,904 aircraft in the East, of which 3,032 were operational. In addition there were about 900 aircraft from Germany's allies – 70 Italian, and the rest Romanian and Hungarian.[25]

The latest Russian estimates of German ground forces' strength in the east on 22 June – 3,512,600 men[26] – are only slightly above those in the most reliable German- and English-language sources, which vary from 3,206,000 to 3,500,000.[27]

As part of the deception plan, the Luftwaffe carried out its final, climactic attack against the British Isles on the night of 10 to 11 May 1941, when 500 bombers attacked London. More than 3,000 people were killed or injured, 2,000 fires were started, 5 London docks and 71 other major installations were hit and most of the main railway stations were closed for weeks. Thereafter, Luftwaffe attacks rapidly slackened to fifty or sixty per day. In the period from August 1940 to June 1941, however, the offensive against Britain and British air attacks on the Continent had cost the Luftwaffe 3,700 aircraft written off and 2,300 damaged, 3,700 aircrew killed, 3,000 missing – mostly prisoners – and 1,500 wounded. Although the Luftwaffe still began the war against Russia in good shape, the loss of experienced flying crews with peacetime training would have a significant effect later on. In order to maintain the necessary superiority over Russia, the Germans could use only negligible forces against Britain. That meant British factories were free to produce formidable new aircraft including the four-engined 'heavies' introduced in 1942 with little interference, thus laying the foundations for the massive strategic air offensive against Germany.[28]

The Germans had never seriously espoused the idea of long-range strategic bombing and this placed them at a disadvantage in attacking the Soviet Union. The Luftwaffe had long demanded a long-range aircraft – the 'Uralbomber' – but in November 1940 production of the Heinkel 177 long-range bomber was postponed for three months and limited to just a few a month. Not until January 1942 did a few more aircraft start to roll off the production line.[29] The German medium bombers – the Dornier 17 'flying pencil', Junkers-88 and Heinkel 111 had been state-of-the art in the late 1930s, but were now approaching obsolescence, while the Junkers-87 Stuka dive-bomber could survive only when there was no serious air opposition. The range of the aircraft available to both sides is shown in Figure 7.2. Even with just half their normal bomb-load, the medium bombers could only fly 900 to 1,000 kilometres. Ground-attack aircraft, dive-bombers and fighters could penetrate only 375,200 and 180 kilometres into Soviet-held territory, unless fitted with extra fuel tanks. The planned attack on the Svir electric power station, north-east of Leningrad, noted in the *Starshina* report passed to an unappreciative Stalin on 17 June (see Chapter 6), for example, was at the very limit of the medium bombers' range. Only the major industrial centres in Ukraine and Leningrad were within range of German air attack from their starting bases, while Moscow and the great armaments manufacturing centre of Tula were right at the outer limit. The reserve capital of Kuybyshev, Saratov, Stalingrad and Baku would come within range after spectacular German advances, but the great industrial complexes of the Urals always remained targets too far.[30] In late 1940, the German air force appears either to have been unaware of Hitler's plans for the East, or not to have taken them seriously. When it did start planning, like the army, it staked everything on a quick victory with existing technology.

German intelligence on the Soviet ability to wage war was, as we

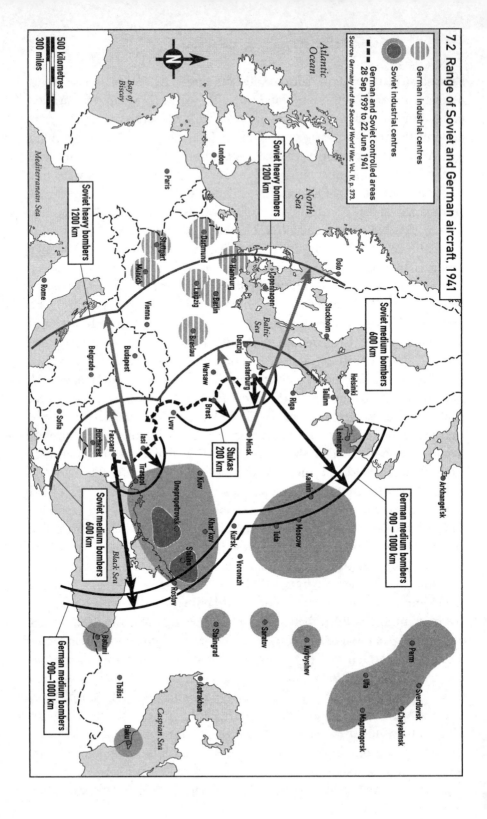

7.2 Range of Soviet and German aircraft, 1941

German industrial centres

Soviet industrial centres

German and Soviet controlled areas
28 Sep 1939 to 22 June 1941

Source: *Germany and the Second World War*, Vol. IV, p. 373.

500 kilometres

300 miles

Soviet heavy bombers
1200 km

Soviet heavy bombers
1200 km

Soviet medium bombers
600 km

Soviet medium bombers
600 km

Stukas
200 Km

German medium bombers
900 – 1000 km

German medium bombers
900 – 1000 Km

Atlantic
Ocean

Bay of
Biscay

Mediterranean Sea

North
Sea

Baltic
Sea

Black Sea

Caspian Sea

London

Paris

Rome

Stuttgart

Dortmund

Munich

Hamburg

Leipzig

Berlin

Vienna

Breslau

Copenhagen

Oslo

Stockholm

Helsinki

Tallinn

Riga

Danzig

Insterburg

Warsaw

Brest

Lvov

Minsk

Leningrad

Kalinin

Moscow

Tula

Kursk

Khar'kov

Stalino

Voronezh

Rostov

Dnepropetrovsk

Kiev

Iasi

Tiraspol

Focşani

Bucharest

Sofia

Belgrade

Budapest

Batumi

Tbilisi

Astrakhan

Stalingrad

Saratov

Kuybyshev

Perm

Ufa

Sverdlovsk

Chelyabinsk

Magnitogorsk

Baku

Arkhangel'sk

Svir

174

have seen in Chapter 4, profoundly wrong. The Germans had a good picture of the Soviet forces deployed well forward, which suited their plans, but virtually no picture of the second operational echelon, and none of the second strategic echelon (see Figure 8.1). In June 1941 the Red Army was in the process of a major shift in deployment, absorption of new equipment (most of which was not yet available), and recovery from the purges which had started in 1937 but were still going on.

On 22 June 1941 the Soviet armed forces, at a best guess, numbered 4.7 to 4.9 million in all, in 20 armies, broken up into 303 divisions. Of this total force, about 2.5 million men in 171 divisions were on the western frontiers of the recently expanded (see Chapters 3 and 4) Soviet Union.[31] Once again, Soviet and modern Russian sources appear fairly credible in terms of numbers of troops, German and Soviet, but differ wildly from German and other sources on numbers of aircraft and tanks.

The Soviet State Defence Plan-41, prepared in early 1941, envisaged four fronts (army groups) – North-Western, Western, South-Western and Southern, based on the Baltic, Western and Kiev Special Military Districts and the Ninth Separate Army, respectively. These four fronts would comprise 186 divisions in the first strategic echelon. The second strategic echelon would comprise a further 51 divisions in five armies under the centralized control of Stavka – the Supreme High Command. The fact that Stavka was not formed until 23 June, the day after the German attack, further suggests that, at the highest level, war was not expected immediately.[32] The first strategic echelon would comprise three operational echelons or belts – a light covering force on the frontier, and then two further echelons to provide 'defence in depth'.

However, as we saw in Chapter 6, mobilization problems prevented DP-41 from being fully implemented. By 22 June, 171 divisions and 20 out of the 28 giant Soviet mechanized corps were available to make up the first strategic echelon. They were deployed in the western military districts (Leningrad, Baltic, Western Special, Kiev Special, Odessa and the Crimea). In addition, five armies comprising 57 divisions were assembling on the Dnepr and Dvina rivers to form the second strategic echelon (see Figure 8.1). This was the result of the movement of forces westward during the preceding two months.[33] Whereas the second and third operational echelons would conduct counter-attacks and counter-strokes against advancing German forces, the second strategic echelon would ultimately deal the knock-out blow and carry the war back to Germany. In May and June, Twenty-Second Army from the Ural Military District (MD) deployed south of Velikiye Luki, Twenty-First Army from the Volga MD south of Gomel', and Nineteenth Army from the North Caucasus MD on the Dnepr south of Kiev, all on the old and now cannibalized 'Stalin Line'. Twentieth Army began forming in the Moscow area. The second strategic echelon is a crucial part of Suvorov's argument for offensive intent. However, these seem merely prudent defensive measures designed to permit robust counter-attack, as Soviet doctrine clearly envisaged.

The mechanized corps would be crucial to this vision of operational counterstrokes by the first strategic echelon and then a strategic one by the second. But they were not ready. As Popel's graphic account of VIII Mechanized Corps' experience makes clear (see the end of Chapter 4), the Germans had caught the Red Army in the middle of a major restructuring. After the triumph of German armoured forces in the West in 1940, the Red Army began to assemble these giant formations, each with a strength, on paper, of 36,080 men and 1,031 tanks.

The Soviet infantry ('rifle') divisions were similarly short on men, weapons and vehicles. Each was supposed to have 14,483 men, but in fact their strength varied from 8,400 to 12,000 men, with most between 8,000 and 10,000. Ironically, the weakest divisions were located in the Kiev Special Military District, where the main German attack was expected, and the recently occupied Baltic Special MD. The biggest shortfall, however, was in 'soft-skinned' motor vehicles – trucks. Each rifle division had only 10 to 25 per cent of the motor vehicles it should have had, because any new vehicles available were directed towards the massive newly formed mechanized corps.[34]

Of all the Soviet ground forces, the best-equipped and most professional arm was the artillery. With an unbroken tradition of excellence throughout Russian history, the Russian artillery deployed superb guns, some updated 1930s versions of excellent Tsarist weapons, others new models, under very professional officers. The BM-13 *Katyusha* rocket-launcher, firing a salvo of sixteen rockets with 132mm calibre warheads, was just beginning to appear, deployed in great secrecy, and would first be used in July at the key rail junction at Orsha, at the gate to the Smolensk land bridge.[35] Whereas the Germans parcelled out their artillery for close support, the Russians had so much of it that they could, and did, do that at regimental and divisional level, but were also able to retain large concentrations of medium and heavy artillery for concentrated firepower strikes under control of corps, armies and fronts.

The Soviet air forces were likewise rearming. They were the largest in the world, with, at the most conservative estimates, nearly 20,000 aircraft overall, of which at least 7,133 were based in the westernmost military districts.[36] On 22 June the Luftwaffe operations staff believed that there were 5,800 aircraft in the western part of the Soviet Union, of which only 1,300 bombers and 1,500 fighters were ready for combat. Radio intercepts, however, had indicated that there were 13,000 to 14,000 aircraft in western Russia, which *could* have been a result of electronic deception.[37]

The newer types included the Ilyushin (Il-)16 fighter, of which there were an estimated 1,762 in the western frontier districts on 22 June, but the newest – the Mikoyan-Gurevich (MiG)-3 and the Ilyushin (Il)-2 Shturmovik ground-attack plane, the Red air force's unique, armoured 'flying tank', had just entered service in spring 1941 and were still in short supply, while the excellent Petlyakov (Pe)-2 twin-engined dive-bomber was not yet available. The Luftwaffe had confidently brushed off realistic predictions of a three-to-one Soviet numerical superiority and the possible appearance of new types in the belief that the war would be over before the Russians could get sufficient experience to fly them. And, as with tanks on the ground, most Soviet aircraft did not have radios fitted in 1941. Compared with the experienced pilots of the Luftwaffe, the Red air force's newest rookie pilots in the forward areas may have had as few as four hours' experience of flying their machines.[38] Not only did this make them easy meat for experienced Luftwaffe pilots; it also made them more likely to fire on their own aircraft. Some air force divisions were subordinated to ground armies or fronts, others to the General Staff, and others to regional air defence, which was the responsibility of the NKVD. This made coordination – and firing at the right planes – all the more difficult.

Although the Soviet air force had longer-range, heavy bombers, which could strike at targets in Germany proper (see Figure 7.2), the only significant Soviet strategic air attacks were against the Romanian oilfields.[39] Soviet priorities reflected the prevailing view, expressed by Ilyushin at the end of the war, that 'in the main, the air forces must be used for combined operations with the ground forces and the navy'.[40] The Shturmovik was built with this in mind, anticipating the philosophy embodied in the US A-10 tank-buster forty years later. The Shturmovik's engine, cockpit and fuel tanks were all protected by steel armour and the pilot's windshield was of 66mm-thick bullet-resistant glass. It could attack ground targets with machine guns, 32mm cannon, bombs and rockets, and could survive ground fire that would be lethal to any other aeroplane.[41]

For the German navy the principal and overwhelming enemy was the British Royal Navy which, Grand-Admiral Raeder believed, was bound to be joined by the United States Navy. Understandably, given his blue uniform, he favoured seeking the main decision in the Atlantic and Mediterranean, and argued against a war on two fronts. But he would never persuade Hitler, and was drawn unwillingly into providing support for Barbarossa. The Germans regarded the Soviet Black Sea fleet as vastly superior to the Romanian and Bulgarian naval forces there, and the German navy could only get to the Black Sea via the British-dominated Mediterranean. The Barents Sea was too far away and German action there focused on land-based air attacks on the Soviet Murmansk and Polyarny bases, intended to interrupt any British operations in the Arctic.

The German navy's only offensive role in Barbarossa was therefore in the Baltic. The Soviet navy, while possessing large numbers of vessels including powerful surface warships, was probably not skilful enough from the point of view of initiative, command and training, to mount successful surface operations. Mining and submarine attack, however, both areas on which the Russian and, later, Soviet navies had placed great emphasis, could seriously impair German communications in the Baltic. It was also assumed that if the Soviet Baltic naval bases were overrun, the ships would try to make for Britain. Therefore, the first German minelayers set out on 18 June, and laid their mines on the night of 19th, to ensure that after Barbarossa began Soviet ships could not leave harbour.[42]

8

BARBAROSSA UNLEASHED, AND THE
BATTLES OF THE FRONTIERS . . .

Codeword 'Dortmund'

The definitive version of the deployment directive for Barbarossa had been issued on 9 June.[1] The codeword 'Dortmund' was transmitted on 20 June, confirming that Barbarossa would be launched with 'H'-Hour as 03.30, German summer time on 22 June. In addition to the relative tactical, operational, strategic, logistic and organizational disarray of the Soviet forces along the 1,800-kilometre main front, they had been deployed to counter a main attack in Ukraine, south of the Pripyet marshes (see Figures 7.2 and 8.1, and the German intelligence picture at the time, Plate 3). In fact, the main German thrust came to the north.[2]

There, Army Group Centre's task, as defined on 9 June, remained essentially the same as in Directive No. 21. This immensely strong Army Group, reinforced to drive on Moscow, was commanded by Generalfeld-marschall (Field Marshal) Fedor von Bock. With his initial headquarters at Rembertow, east of Warsaw, he had two infantry armies, Fourth and Ninth, and two Panzer groups, Two and Three, totalling 1,180,000 men with 1,770 tanks. Panzer Group Two and Fourth Army would break through around, and north of, Kobrymin and advance towards Slutsk and Minsk. Panzer Group Three would arc round north of Minsk and, with Ninth Army, meet them there. The aim was to trap and annihilate Soviet forces west of the Dnepr and south of the Dvina, and to prevent them establishing a line of resistance along those rivers.[3] Field Marshal Albert Kesselring's Second Luftflotte (Air Fleet) provided air support, with 1,500 planes – more than half the total committed to Barbarossa. Opposite Bock was the Soviet Special Western Military District under

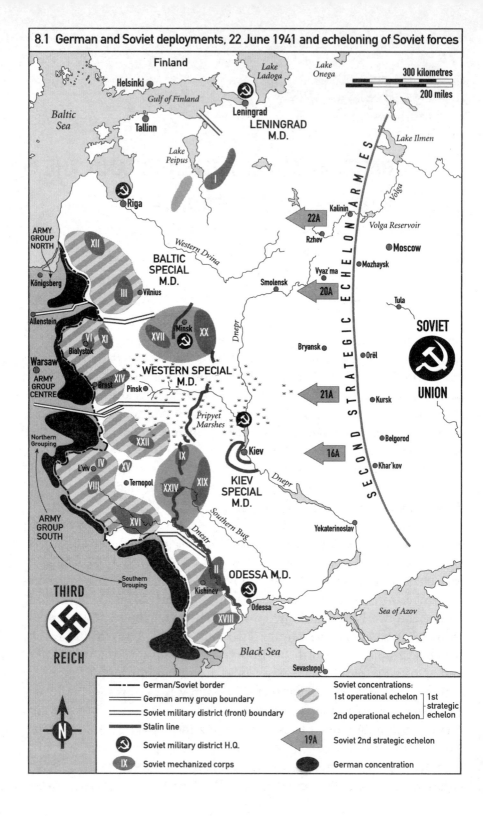

8.1 German and Soviet deployments, 22 June 1941 and echeloning of Soviet forces

the ill-fated Army-General Dmitry Pavlov (1897–1941),[4] which became the Western Front the moment war started. Its headquarters was at Minsk. Because any German main attack was expected to the south, his three armies were exposed well forward in the Bialystok salient and numbered a relatively weak 647,000 men.[5]

Army Group Centre was the military-strategic centre of gravity of the German attack, and of the entire eastern front effort. The Russians quickly appreciated this, and never forgot it. In late 1942, Zhukov's massive, failed attack at Rzhev-Sychevka aimed to destroy it. In Belorussia, in summer 1944, three years after Barbarossa, the Soviet forces finally succeeded in breaking it. Although the name Army Group Centre was retained, the back of the *Wehrmacht* was then broken.

In June 1941, the area south of the Pripyet marshes was the responsibility of German Army Group South, commanded by Field Marshal Gerd von Runstedt, from his headquarters at Rzeszów. Because of the huge extent of this sector, the Army Group was split into two main groups. Three German armies in the northern part – Sixth, Seventeenth and First Panzer Group – totalled 797,000 men. These faced the Kiev Special Military District, which became the South-West Front, commanded by Colonel-General Mikhail Kirponos (1892–1941). Because the Soviets expected the main German attack here, Kirponos, with his headquarters in Kiev, had more forces (five armies, with Nineteenth Army forming behind him), a total of 870,000 men.[6]

Further south, opposite the new Soviet republic of Moldova, were the German Eleventh Army (175,000 men) and Romanian Third and Fourth Armies. These faced the Odessa Military District, which was still forming under Major-General Ivan Tyulenev (1892–1978), with 320,000 men.[7]

The northern part of the Army Group was far stronger. The deployment directive envisaged a breakthrough near Rawa Ruska (Rava Russkaya) to reach the Dnepr south of Kyyiv (Kiev). The Group would then continue to slide south-eastwards along the river, preventing the Soviet forces withdrawing behind it, and cutting back to the north to take them in the rear. Eleventh Army was primarily to protect Romania and its precious oilfields, which were vital to the German war effort. But it would also distract and tie down major Soviet forces, which it initially succeeded in doing.[8]

Towards the Baltic, Field Marshal Ritter von Leeb commanded German Army Group North, with its initial headquarters at Waldfrieden in East Prussia. Army Group North's instructions also followed Directive No. 21 closely. Leeb had two armies, Eighteenth and Sixteenth, and the Fourth Panzer Group, totalling, with reserves, 641,000 men in the Army Group. He faced the Baltic Special Military District, which became the North-West Front, commanded by Colonel-General Fëdor Kuznetsov (1898–1961). Kuznetsov's was the weakest of the fronts facing the invading force, with three armies and two of the still forming mechanized corps.[9] Leeb's task was to destroy enemy forces in the Baltic region and occupy the Baltic ports including, ultimately, Kronshtadt and Leningrad, thus depriving the Soviet navy of any Baltic bases. Panzer Group Four and the Sixteenth and Eighteenth Armies were to reach the Dvina and Dvinsk (Daugavpils). Fourth Panzer Group and Sixteenth Army would then head for Leningrad while Eighteenth Army would cut off large Soviet forces along the Baltic coast and also head for Ostrov-Pskov area, along the old Stalin Line, again to prevent Soviet forces escaping. It would then clear Estonia and the large Baltic islands of Saaremaa (Osel), Hiiumaa (Dago) and Munu.[10]

Still further north was the Finnish Front. This Front was always subsidiary in German eyes, and the fact that it came under Army Command Norway, which was directly subordinated to OKW, and not OKH (which ran the rest of the war on the eastern front) highlighted a potential lack of synchronization.[11] The Germans planned a simultaneous but subsidiary advance alongside the Finns, who were understandably anxious to recover the territory and resources they had lost in April 1940. The Germans planned to cut the supply line from Murmansk – the likely entry point for Allied, then British, aid – and also to cut Leningrad off from the north, while the Finns were primarily concerned about recovering lost territory. Initially the Germans planned an attack towards the ports of Murmansk and Polyarny, which would become critical for Allied aid to Russia, but an amendment of 31 May emphasized the need to defend the Norwegian coast.

The Finns deployed two armies: the South-Eastern, just north of Leningrad, and the Karelian Army, further north. In the very far north the Germans deployed their Mountain Corps from Norway, 97,000 strong. Between, there was a relatively weakly manned section covered by 3rd Finnish Division and, further north, 36th German Corps. Operations in the south and centre were exclusively assigned to Finnish units, including the elimination of the isolated Soviet base at Hango.[12] Overall, on the Finnish sector – 1,000 kilometres from the Baltic to the

Barents Seas – there were 407,000 German and allied troops, 150,000 of whom were Finns and the rest German. The opposing Soviet forces, totalling 426,000 men, came under the Leningrad Military District, under Lt Gen. Markian Popov (1902–1969), which became the Northern and, later, Leningrad Fronts.[13]

Lightning meets rock . . .

The first Germans across the border were special forces of Regiment 800, known as the 'Brandenburgers'. Many of these were Russian speakers, clad in Red Army or (more likely) security force uniforms, who were parachuted into Soviet territory or smuggled in on board goods trains in previous days. Their mission was to blow up power facilities, cut communications, activate German 'sleeper' agents, ensure that bridges could not be demolished and spread false orders and disinformation. From Kobrin, east of Brest and right in the centre of Army Group Centre's attack front, the Soviet Fourth Army attempted to alert its subordinate formations after interrogating a German line-crosser, at 02.20 Moscow time. With less than two hours to go until the main German attack began, the telephone lines had already been cut in an area stretching 50 kilometres inside the border.[14]

Soviet communications security was appalling, particularly for a country which was so paranoiac about such matters. The fact that German special forces managed to crack the Soviet communications across the 1,800-kilometre front from the Baltic to the Black Sea and to paralyse communications between the 20-kilometre-wide zone held by the NKVD border guards and forward and rear Red Army formations, heading back to Army Headquarters 80 kilometres or so in the rear, was a stupendous achievement for them. It was also a disgrace for the Red Army, the NKVD and the Soviet government. The Soviet military, and Stalin, did not trust radio because it was vulnerable to interception. Their procedures were cumbersome and if war was expected (which it was not, officially), new frequencies and call signs would have to be allocated. In practice it would take a week to notify units – down to battalion level – of the frequencies and call signs. So, on the morning of 22 June, as the wartime alert went out, the radios were inoperable.[15]

The Red Army and NKVD placed much more reliance on landline, with, perhaps, good reason. However, only the last 8 kilometres or so of line, closest to Army and Front headquarters, was dug in. The rest, stretching over hundreds of kilometres, was hanging from telegraph poles along roads and railways in a country where private telephones were pretty rare. The German special forces only had to take out thirty metres or so of dangling cable between two telegraph poles, and an Army or Front was cut off. Soviet border defences were good, and, given the concentration of these relatively few lines along few road and rail routes, with any alert, the NKVD or local police could have secured them quite well. But they did not.[16]

In the Soviet Fourth Army's sector, at Koden, 40 kilometres south of Brest, the Germans needed to capture the bridge across the River Bug intact so they could get their armour moving quickly. The Soviet border guards were used to dealing with – were probably friendly with – the Germans on the other side of the bridge. 'Important business', shouted the Germans. As the Soviet border guards appeared, they were machine-gunned. The bridge was not mined, but the railway bridge at Brest was. Here, the Germans gunned down the border guards, and quickly removed the demolition charge.[17]

Across the entire front, the first Soviet troops to face the German attack, in most cases, were the border guards, part of the NKVD. They, it will be remembered (see Chapter 3), were responsible for the area up to 22 kilometres inside the frontier. They wore uniforms similar to the Red Army, but were distinguished by green collar tabs and green bands around their caps – much the same as the Russian border guards you meet at international airports nowadays. The forward Red Army divisions were behind them, between 25 and 80 kilometres east of the frontier. How well the Soviets responded in these crucial early hours depended very much on how the Red Army commanders further back had cooperated with their colleagues from the Interior Ministry on the frontier. Kirponos, commanding the Kiev Special Military District, which morphed into the South-West Front, had done this better than others, and it showed.

On Saturday 21st, German reconnaissance troops and spies had reported that the fortress-citadel of Brest-Litovsk was not expecting an attack. Zhukov and Timoshenko's early-morning order had reached the garrison, however, and although the Germans stormed across the Bug with complete surprise, they were halted in front of the citadel. The German 45th Infantry Division had been ordered to capture the city and the fortress at its core.

Brest was a classic nineteenth-century fortress, which formed four islands using the waters of the Western Bug and Mukhavets rivers. It was surrounded by earthworks (in fact, sand) nearly ten metres high and even the barracks, which could hold up to 12,000 troops, had walls a metre and a half thick and could therefore withstand all but the heaviest artillery shells. Brest fortress would become to Barbarossa what Fort Sumter had been in the American Civil War, but held out far, far longer.

After a heavy artillery and rocket bombardment of the fortress, the 45th Infantry stormed towards the citadel, but the fire had little effect on the fortifications and they were beaten back by small-arms fire from every window, loophole and embrasure. Holding the fortress were seven battalions of the 6th Orël Red Banner and 42nd Rifle Divisions of the Red Army and elements of the 17th NKVD Border Guards Detachment and the 132nd Independent NKVD Battalion – a total of about 3,500 men.[18] The presence of the NKVD was probably crucial to the decision to stand and fight, and the ability to hold. Not only were they better-disciplined, élite troops, but they could also provide an element of political initiative which was often lacking in the Red Army. Once the Germans were across the Bug and attacking the fortress, even the fanatically loyal, pro-Stalin NKVD could see that any concerns about avoiding 'provocation' had evaporated.

Although organized Soviet resistance west of Brest had ceased, for all practical purposes, by the evening of 24 June, the fortress held out. The Germans claimed to have subdued it on 30 June, after Junkers-88s had dropped an 1,800 kg bomb the previous day, but individuals and small groups of Soviet defenders fought on for two or even three more weeks.[19] Defenders survived in some numbers until 20 July. After the Germans overran most of the fortress on 30 June Major Pëtr Gavrilov, commanding 44th Rifle Regiment of 46 Division, and an NKVD officer hid from the Germans for several days and eventually made their way out, encountering twelve more Russian survivors on the way. They resolved to try to escape to the Belovezhskaya Pushcha, a wildlife sanctuary north-east of Brest – a good place to hide and make contact with the partisan groups whom they thought might be forming up

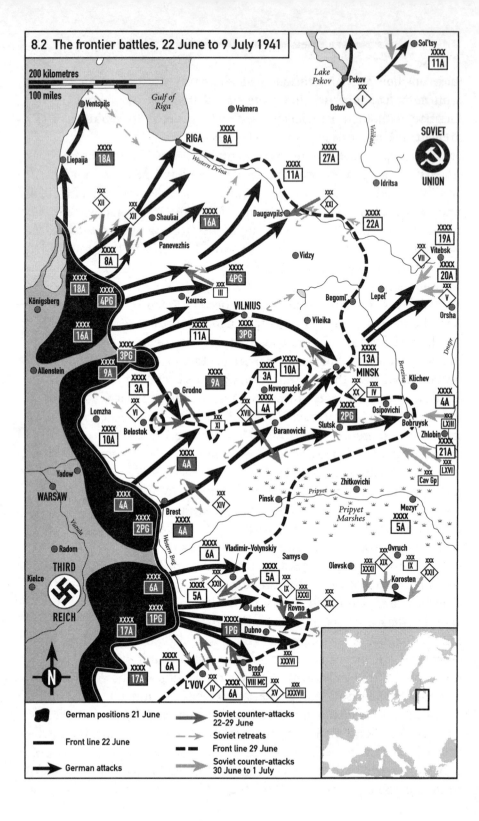

8.2 The frontier battles, 22 June to 9 July 1941

200 kilometres

100 miles

Gulf of Riga

Lake Pskov

SOVIET UNION

Sol'tsy XXXX 11A

Pskov XXX I

Ostov

Ventspils

Valmera

Ostrov

Idritsa

Velikaia

RIGA XXXX 8A

XXXX 27A

Liepaija XXXX 18A

Western Dvina

XXXX 11A

XXX XII

XXX XII

Shauliai

XXXX 16A

Daugavpils XXX XXI

XXXX 22A

XXXX 19A

Panevezhis

Vidzy

XXX VII Vitebsk

XXXX 20A

XXXX 8A

XXXX 4PG

XXX III

Kaunas

VILNIUS

Begoml' Lepel'

XXX V

Königsberg

XXXX 18A XXXX 4PG

XXXX 11A XXXX 3PG

Vileika

Orsha

XXXX 16A

Dnepr

Allenstein

XXXX 3PG XXXX 9A

XXXX 3A

Grodno

XXXX 9A

XXXX 3A XXXX 10A

Novogrudok

XXXX 13A

MINSK

Berezina

Klichev

Lomzha XXX VI

XXX XVII XXXX 4A

XXX IV

XXXX 4A

Belostok XXXX 10A

XXX XI

Baranovichi

Slutsk

XXXX 2PG

Osipovichi

Bobruysk XXX LXIII

Zhlobin

XXXX 4A

Yadow

XXXX 4A

Slutsk

XXXX 21A XXX LXVI

WARSAW XXXX 4A

Zhitkovichi

XXX Cav Gp

Brest XXXX 4A

XXX XIV

Pinsk

Pripyet

Pripyet Marshes

Mozyr' XXXX 5A

XXXX 2PG

Radom

THIRD REICH

Western Bug

XXXX 6A

Vladimir-Volynskiy

Samys

Olevsk

Ovruch XXX IX

XXX XXXI XXX XIX

XXX XXII

Kielce

XXXX 6A XXXX 1PG

XXXX 5A XXX IX

Korosten

XXXX 17A

XXXX 5A XXX XXII

XXXX 5A

XXX XXXI

Lutsk

Rovno XXX XIX

XXXX 6A

XXXX 1PG Dubno

XXXX 17A

XXXX 6A

Brody XXX XXXVI

XXX IV

L'VOV XXXX 6A XXX VIII MC XXX XV XXX XXXVII

German positions 21 June

Front line 22 June

German attacks

Soviet counter-attacks 22-29 June

Soviet retreats

Front line 29 June

Soviet counter-attacks 30 June to 1 July

there. Dodging the Germans, and hiding by day, Gavrilov evaded capture until about the 20th when he was cornered, still inside the fortress. He fought ferociously, but was knocked unconscious in the firefight. His courage may have saved him. He was taken to a prisoner-of-war camp south of the city. Witnesses reported a Soviet officer, covered in filth, with a month's growth of beard, being brought in on 23 July. We know this is true, because Gavrilov survived the war. There are also reports of individual Soviet officers and men and small groups continuing to resist until August, when the Germans flooded the cellars of the fortress to get rid of them. The last survivor may have held on for ten months, until April 1942.[20]

The 'hero-fortress' was the first rock to stand, and stay standing for twenty days, before the incoming German tide. On the first day of the war, the German (in fact, mostly Austrian) 45th Infantry Division lost 29 officers and 290 other ranks killed – a very heavy toll. By 30 July it had lost 40 officers and 442 other ranks dead and 1,000 wounded, in the subjugation of the defiant fortress. In late June a battle report from the Division reported that Brest had been held by 'a courageous garrison that cost us a lot of blood ... The Russians fought with exceptional stubbornness and determination. They displayed superb infantry training and a splendid will to resist.'[21]

German accounts are unanimous about the unexpected strength and savagery of the Soviet resistance across most of the front. In its attacks on 66 Soviet airfields, on the first day, the Luftwaffe claimed to have destroyed 1,500 aircraft, with a further 300 downed in air-to-air combat by incomparably better trained and more experienced German pilots. But in the Brest area, the Soviets attacked one of the forward German airfields at Biala Polaska, the base for 77 Stuka Dive-bomber Squadron. The defending Me-109 fighters shot down all six Russian planes. Then another twelve Russian planes came in, and they, too, were all shot down. But the Russians kept coming back, and near Grodno, managed to shoot down and kill the highly experienced commander of the 27th fighter squadron, Lt Col. Schellman, on the first day of the war.[22] Soviet quantity was already showing it had, and also inspired, a quality all its own.

In spite of the Red Army and NKVD's heroic stand at Brest, the German Army Group Centre's attack flooded past on both sides. At the Soviet mechanized corps, army, and front level the doctrine was clearly understood. Parry the German thrusts with massive armoured counter-strokes, if you can ...

The order came at 21.15 on 22 June, as People's Commissariat for Defence (NKO) Directive No. 3.[23] By late on the summer evening, therefore, the 'do not provoke' orders had changed to orders 'to counter-attack and expel the Germans'.[24] At this stage, it is clear that the best intelligence was coming from the North-Western Front, in the Baltic States area, but the order covered the entire 1,800-kilometre Baltic to Black Sea front. The order claimed that along this entire front the attacks had been 'beaten off with heavy losses', which was optimistic, to say the least. The Northern Front, as it had become, was to destroy the enemy's 'Suwalki grouping' (Army Group North and part of Army Group Centre). The Western Front (formerly Special Western MD) would attack the same grouping from the southern flank, and from the rear, and capture the Suwalki region by the end of 24 June. The Russian orders clearly missed the significance of Army Group Centre. The South-Western Front (formerly Kiev Special MD) would encircle and destroy the forces of Army Group South, with concentric attacks towards the Lublin area. The Southern Front was to stop any invasion from Romania. Most critically, though unrealistically, Timoshenko, Malenkov and Zhukov authorized Soviet forces to cross borders 'from the Baltic Sea to the state border of Hungary, and operations *without regard for the borders*'.[25] The doctrine of immediate and aggressive counter-attack was kicking in, but the chances of it working now were minimal.

On 22 June 6th Panzer Division attacked into Lithuania across bridges over the Neman (Njemen) river. Colonel Helmuth Ritgen, then a junior officer, was adjutant of second battalion, 11th Panzer Regiment, and General von Kielmansegg was on the divisional staff. The border zone was heavily wooded and partly swampy. Very soon, the Germans encountered new KV-1, KV-2 and T-34 tanks. 'It was a complete surprise,' recalled General Kielmansegg. 'Nobody in Germany knew anything about these tanks, even that they were under construction.'[26] At this point, he added, the terrain was 'thick green jungle. We could see only a short distance ahead. The lack of roads was equally bad.'

On 22 June the division pushed into Lithuania. A few hours later, Ritgen recalled,

> I witnessed an incident which characterised the fanaticism of
> the Soviet Soldier. Beyond the forest we were waiting for
> resupply for at least two hours near a cornfield. Suddenly two
> Russians jumped out of the field with their hands raised. A

sergeant waved to them to come on. At that moment they dodged, while one threw a hand-grenade and the other fired a pistol at the sergeant, who was wounded. The Russians must have hidden motionless in the field for three or more hours.[27]

On 23 June the Germans pushed forward to the Dubyssa river, and seized two small bridgeheads across it. During the night one was evacuated, while the other was held by two platoons (fifty to sixty men), but a Soviet counter-attack overran it. Kielmansegg recalled:

> The next day we found all the personnel shot, that is murdered, and atrociously mutilated. Eyes had been put out, genitals cut off and other cruelties inflicted. This was our first such experience, but not the last. On the evening [after] these first two days I said to my general, 'Sir, this will be a very different war from the one in Poland and France.'[28]

The frontier battles, 22 June to 9 July 1941[29]

Army Group Centre versus the Western Front

In the face of Army Group Centre's attack, the Soviet Fourth Army, one of the three deployed forward, was unable to establish communications with Pavlov's Western Front headquarters at Minsk or with the formations below it (see Figure 8.1). The Third and Tenth Armies did have radio communications with the Front, but had similar difficulties in maintaining contact with their subordinate formations and also with Moscow. Communications between Tenth Army, located between 50 and 80 kilometres from the forward German troops, and its subordinate formations were dependent on landline and had fallen victim to the skilfully targeted German special forces.[30] Thirteenth Army, 300 kilometres further back, in the Minsk area, and right on top of Western Front headquarters, did not, initially, have such problems.

On 22 June Pavlov's deputy, Boldin, braved the constant German air attacks to fly to Tenth Army's headquarters at an airfield outside

Bialystok, to order its commander, Golubev, to counter-attack. Golubev tried but failed and Tenth Army was soon broken up. On the left flank of the German Army Group, Third Panzer Group, under Colonel-General Herman Hoth, chiselled into the vulnerable split between Pavlov's Western and Kuznetsov's North-Western Fronts (see Figure 8.1). The Panzer Group swept past the Soviet forces and reached Vlnius by the end of 23 June. Again, Pavlov ordered Boldin to launch a counterstroke northwards, towards Grodno, to strike into the Panzer Group's flank and sever its communications. Boldin was given control of VI and XI Mechanized Corps and VI Cavalry Corps. It was a massive operational counterstroke in the best Soviet tradition. But without reliable communications and under constant German air attack, it was doomed. By the time Soviet forces reached Grodno, it had missed its target. The Panzer Group had sped past, and was 100 kilometres to the east, leaving infantry and anti-tank guns to shoot up the lightly equipped Soviet forces – a classic example of 'Blitzkrieg' operational art. What had been intended as an immense armoured-cavalry counterstroke, with three corps, failed because of command and control difficulties and, crucially, logistics. By the end of 25 June VI Cavalry Corps had suffered 50 per cent casualties, and one of the tank divisions forming part of the mechanized corps was out of ammunition.[31]

Already, the Red Army was trying to implement the impressive theory it had developed in the interwar years and practised, most recently, in the exercises early in 1941. However, for the moment, its commanders were trying to run before they could walk.

With Hoth's Third and Guderian's Second Panzer Groups now converging in a race towards Minsk, Pavlov ordered his forces to break off the engagement and withdraw to a defensive position behind the Shchara river at Slonim. When they got there, they found that the Luftwaffe had destroyed most of the bridges. In order to escape the rapidly advancing German armoured formations, Soviet troops abandoned much of their heavy equipment and supplies. The men could march, run and crawl out of encirclement, but they had to leave their equipment behind.

The Luftwaffe, which had been so spectacularly successful in the first few days of Barbarossa, played a major role in trapping Soviet forces in the Bialystok pocket. On 24 and 25 June bombers and dive-bombers of VIII Air Corps smashed a Soviet tank attack on VIII and XX Corps in the Kuznitsa-Orël'sk-Grodno and Dombrova area. These two air corps of Luftflotte 2 effectively helped prevent a larger Soviet breakout from the Bialystok pocket. Not until Guderian's Panzer Group Two was crossing the Berezina at Bobruisk and the Dnepr at Mogilev on 11 July did large Soviet bomber formations manage to penetrate the German air superiority and attack the advancing German mechanized forces. But, they, too, suffered heavy casualties.[32]

On 26 June Pavlov, in a state of near panic, reported that up to a thousand German tanks were enveloping Minsk from the north-west.[33] This was not too much of an exaggeration: Third Panzer Group had 840 at the start of the operation.[34] On 28 June Second and Third Panzer Groups met, completing the first great encirclement of Barbarossa and trapping much of what was left of Pavlov's four armies – Third, Fourth, Tenth and Thirteenth – in the huge Bialystok pocket west of Minsk.

Pavlov had tried his best, but it was not enough to save him. This was clearly the main thrust of the German attack, and a crushing defeat. Marshal Timoshenko, seen as the victor of the Soviet–Finnish war and a former defence minister, was appointed to succeed him. The unfortunate Pavlov had moved his headquarters – such as it was – east, to Mogilev (Mahilow), south of Orsha, and Timoshenko arrived there on 26 June. Leaving his troops was a final fatal mistake. Timoshenko eventually found him, eating *kasha* (buckwheat porridge) in the rain, along with two other Marshals – Shaposhnikov and Kulik, whom Stalin had dispatched to find out what was going on.[35] Timoshenko raged against Pavlov for his failures, reminded him that he had complained to Stalin about him before, and, for the moment, returned to Moscow. At some point, Pavlov was arrested – the accounts range from 1 to 6 July – and eventually shot on the 22nd, along with his Chief-of-Staff, Major-General Vladimir Klimovskikh; his former Chief of Communications, Major-General Andrey Grigor'ev; and the Commander of Fourth Army, Major-General Aleksandr Korobkov.[36]

Although numerous Soviet generals were shot for failures of various kinds during the war, Pavlov and his immediate entourage were by far the most senior command group. Nor was the process as quick and arbitrary as might be imagined. We now know it was attended by hugely legalistic bureaucracy. Even as the cataclysm threatened to spiral out of control, the wheels of Soviet Russian military justice ground quite slowly, though they ground exceeding sure. The order from the State Defence Committee, signed by Stalin, confirming the arrest and handing over for trial of the four senior generals and five others – the commander of XL Rifle Corps and four divisional commanders – was dated 16 July. They were being tried for 'disgracing their rank, cowardice, lack of effectiveness, failure to manage troop control, abandoning weapons to the enemy without giving battle, and voluntarily quitting their military positions'. The order was distributed throughout the Soviet armed forces, down to company, battery and squadron level.[37] *Pour encourager les autres* ... However, the final verdict did not come until 21 July. If the charges of failure on the battlefield were not enough, Pavlov was also accused of involvement in an anti-Soviet plot from 1936, in the course of which the fatal names of Tukhachevskiy and Uborevich were raised, although he denied those charges. Klimovskikh was also quizzed about failing to complete the construction of fortified regions in the Western Front area, only 189 out of 600 of which were ready when Barbarossa struck. The Front's Deputy Chief for Fortified Regions, Major-General Ivan Mikhaidin, had, conveniently perhaps, been killed in action on the second day of the war.[38] The Military College of the USSR Supreme Court passed sentence on 22 July. The generals were stripped of their rank, orders and decorations, their personal possessions were confiscated, and they were then shot.[39]

Before these oddly refined procedures, if not penalties, of military courts had even got under way, organized Soviet resistance had collapsed west of the Dnepr. On 30 June General Andrey Yeremenko, formerly commander of the Special Red Banner Army of the Far East, took command of the collapsing Western Front in place of Pavlov. He found Pavlov at the Front headquarters near Mogilev (Mahilyow) on 1 July, but on the following day received a call from Stalin. Stalin apologized for not having seen him in Moscow en route from the Far East and then told him that he would be sending Timoshenko to command the Front, effectively demoting Yeremenko to Deputy. Understandably enraged, Yeremenko asked for reinforcements. Stalin said he would do what he could.[40] The reality was that there were no intact armies west of the Dnepr. After meeting in the Minsk area on 28 June, and completing the destruction of encircled German forces, Hoth's Third and Guderian's Second Panzer Groups were to move towards the Dnepr. They crossed the Berezina on 1 July, and reached the upper reaches of the Dnepr at the same time. The two Panzer Groups were placed under control of Kluge's Fourth Army, a move which neither Panzer leader liked and which caused a number of arguments.[41]

By the beginning of July, Army Group Centre had advanced 600 kilometres. But contrary to expectations, the Red Army had managed to organize defensive positions in the land bridge between Orsha and Vitebsk and even to launch vigorous counter-attacks. At Borisov, Soviet armoured formations with air support attacked German crossings over the Berezina. Increasingly, the encircled Red Army units were fighting hard, which forced the Germans to divert troops to deal with them rather than pushing on as fast as possible to seize key objectives and keep the withdrawing elements of the Red Army off balance. By 7 July Guderian's Second Panzer Group was stalled on the Dnepr, and Third Panzer was largely on the defensive, concentrating its ability to attack on Vitebsk.[42]

By 9 July, according to the latest Russian statistics, which roughly tally with western sources, the Western Front had lost 341,073 of its original 627,300 strength, killed, wounded, missing and prisoners. Another 76,717 were sick and wounded, a total of 417,790 – more than two-thirds of its soldiers, and an average daily loss of 23,210.[43] They died with, or those who escaped left behind them, 4,799 tanks, 9,427 guns and mortars and 1,777 combat aircraft.[44] But several Soviet divisions, now reduced to 1,500–2,000 men each, managed to work their way out of encirclement and survived to be reconstituted and appear in the accounts of subsequent battles. Furthermore, many of the several hundred thousand Soviet troops listed as 'missing' – encircled west of Minsk – survived to form partisan units, which would remain thorns in the German side and survived, with NKVD support, to play a still decisive role in the Soviet Belorussian offensive three years later, in summer 1944.

An open door? Army Group North and the Baltic States

The attack of Leeb's Northern Army Group further north met slightly different conditions. Bock's men of Army Group Centre had immediately encountered civilians in the former Polish territories who had welcomed them enthusiastically as liberators, but the reaction was confused. Even when they got further east, into the former Soviet territories, civilians sometimes still met them in the traditional way with flowers, bread and salt, whereas, right from the start, the Soviet Army and NKVD had fought with savage determination and cunning.[45] The people of the Baltic States, which the Soviet Union had occupied about a year before, welcomed the Germans with their own national flags, open arms, and by firing on withdrawing Red Army and NKVD troops.

There was considerable confusion during the first day of the German attack into Lithuania. Halder thought the Soviet forces might have been preparing to withdraw to the Latvian border, the Western Dvina (Duena), between Daugavpils (Dunauburg) and Jekabpils (Jakobstadt), 'possibly because we are claiming Lithuania according to agreement'.[46] The secret protocols of 23 August 1939 (which had given Lithuania to Germany) and 28 September 1939 (which had 'corrected' that and given it to the Soviet Union) were clearly *so* secret that even members of the German military High Command were unaware of them.

As seen in Chapter 4, preparations for armed revolt against the Soviet authorities in all the Baltic States had begun as soon as Soviet occupation forces arrived in 1940. Although plans for a revolt were headed by the *Lietuviu aktyvistu frontas* (Lithuanian Activist Front or LAF) in Berlin, which envisaged cooperation with the Germans, the German forces moving into Lithuania on 22 June 1941 do not appear to have been aware of its existence. On the night of 13–14 June 1941 the Soviet authorities had begun deporting civilians from the Baltic States. Some 18,000, including 5,000 children, were deported from Lithuania.[47]

On 22 June, therefore, the moment the Germans attacked, the LAF immediately sprang into action. A number of government buildings were occupied in Kaunas (Kovno), which was still the capital (Vilnius, the modern capital, had been transferred from Poland only in 1939). The first was the radio station, and Leonas Prapuolenis, the LAF representative, announced the restoration of an independent Lithuanian state and the formation of a provisional government. From 23 to 25 June a series of partisan groups went into action in Kaunas, although the attacks appear to have been largely spontaneous and opportunistic.

The new Lithuanian government, headed by the Christian democrats, announced its existence in the newspaper *Į laişve* (To Freedom) on 24 June. Kazys Skirpa, the effective leader of the Lithuanian National Committee in exile, was forbidden to leave Berlin and Jozas Ambrazevicius was therefore put in charge of the brief new government. One of its first acts was to announce the restoration of private property. Since the withdrawing Soviet troops were already starting to use scorched earth tactics, this was another incentive for the people whose recently confiscated houses, shops and farms were in danger of going up in smoke, to prevent the Soviet forces from implementing their orders.[48]

In Vilna (Vilnius) the scale of the revolt was smaller, largely because there were fewer ethnic Lithuanians in what had been a Polish city. Nevertheless, on the evening of 23 June rebels captured the post office. On the next day guards were posted, the radio station was captured and yellow, red and green Lithuanian national flags were hoisted just in time to be seen by the German motorcycle battalion, as it arrived from the south at 05.00 on 24 June.[49] The impact of the Lithuanian revolt on the performance of the Red Army against the Germans was diminished by the fact that the main group which had prepared for action against the Soviet forces, led by Major Vytautas Bulvičius, had been broken in April. Nevertheless, rebel units and civilians across the country attacked Red Army and NKVD units.

According to the Germans, on 23 June local volunteers had succeeded in occupying another transmitting station, in Kaunas, and at 19.30 a representative of the Lithuanian army command broadcast a request for the Germans to bomb the city and the Soviet forces, who were withdrawing. At noon the next day, the 24th, Soviet formations withdrew further and an assault platoon of the German 123rd Reconnaissance Battalion under Lt Floret made contact with Lithuanian volunteers in Kovno. By 26 June the Kaunas transmitter, in the capital, was under guard of 501st Propaganda Company of the *Wehrmacht*, which transmitted a German broadcast that day.[50]

The Lithuanians greeted the Germans enthusiastically, with flowers and, probably more welcome to hard-fighting combat troops, coffee, milk, eggs, bread and butter laid out on tables in front of their houses.[51] The Germans appear to have been unprepared to exploit the unexpected support they received, both military and political. The Red Army, however, was about to spring surprises of a different kind. At 15.00 on 24 June Major-General Kurkin's III Mechanized Corps, which had been based just north of Kaunas, rolled forward, aiming, as pre-war Soviet doctrine demanded, for the flank of the advancing German XLI Motorized Corps (see Figure 8.1). These were the new tanks, of which the Germans were unaware.

> The Kv-I and -II 46-ton tanks raged forward. Our company
> opened fire at about 800 metres [half a mile]; it had no
> effect. The enemy advanced closer and closer, without

> flagging. After a short time they were 50 to 100 metres in
> front of us. A furious fire-fight ensued, without any
> noticeable German success. All of our anti-tank shells
> bounced off them . . . the Russian tanks rolled through the
> ranks of 1st Panzer regiment and into our rear. The Panzer
> regiment turned about and moved to high ground.[52]

Only where 88mm anti-aircraft guns were deployed, or where there were several of the medium Pz-III and -IV German tanks on hand, could the German forces resist the onslaught. Fortunately for them III Mechanized Corps was one of only two of these giant Soviet corps facing Army Group North, and it struck the Germans in the front rather than the flank. It was the only major tank battle in the Baltic States area. However, III Mechanized Corps held up the German XLI Corps for two days. The Germans encircled them, forcing the Soviets to abandon 186 tanks, including 29 KV-1s.

Although the Germans had not yet reached Latvia or Estonia, the rebellion broke out immediately after news of Barbarossa. It was therefore not so much a 'domino effect', although it might have looked that way to attacking German and withdrawing Soviet forces, but rather a simultaneous uprising across all three Baltic countries. As in Lithuania, mass deportations from Latvia had begun on the night of 13 to 14 June and 16,000 Latvians were carried off to remote regions of the Soviet Union.[53] Many Latvians decided that the only way to respond was to rebel, and a number of partisan groups started forming in the extensive forests of the area. The terrain in the Baltic States lends itself to guerrilla warfare, with few roads, and plenty of forest and marshes, known only to the locals, and not to recently arrived occupying troops.

The moment news of the German attack came, on 22 June, they were ready, if not well prepared, to act. Only about 3,000 Latvian soldiers retreated with the Red Army: the rest, either as individuals or as whole units led by their commanders, deserted, and then started to attack Red Army and NKVD units. On 2 July a unit led by Lt Voldemars took control of Sigulda. On 5 July, partisans commanded by Col. Arvis Kripens blocked the Pskov road (to Russia) and captured Smiltene. The largest groups, understandably, formed in Riga. A large grouping from the XXIV Territorial Rifle Corps began to assemble, while reinforcements flowed in from the summer military training camps set up as part of the Soviet mobilization plans. The Latvians started to form a division. But the most serious clashes with Soviet forces were on 4 July in Limbazi, on 5 July near Olaine and 9 July in Aluksne. The partisans captured all three towns before any German forces arrived.[54]

On 1 July, however, the Germans ordered the former Latvian Military Attaché in Germany, Col. Alexander Plesners, to supervise the formation of Latvian Defence Forces under German control. On 8 July the SS General Stahlecker issued orders that security in the German rear areas were his responsibility, prohibiting the wearing of non-German uniforms and ordering partisan units to disarm.[55]

The same thing happened in Estonia. A few Estonians had fled to the forests during late 1940 and early 1941, but the Soviet arrests of mid June were, once again, the real catalyst. On 14 June, about 10,000 Estonians were rounded up and deported eastwards. Again, the forests were the obvious place for resistance groups to form, and in Estonia they were called 'forest brothers'. Immediately after the German attack, Estonian soldiers began to desert from Soviet bases in large numbers. On 22 June a Forest Brother unit opened fire on Red Army trucks on a road in the Harju district, although guerrilla action at this point was sporadic. At the end of June the Soviet 22nd Rifle Corps, which had been formed from the Lithuanian armed forces, was ordered back into the Soviet Union, but large numbers of the Estonian soldiers and officers deserted. Similarly, the Estonian SSR border guards were mostly former members of the independent Estonian border guards, and most of them deserted too. Like their Soviet equivalents, they were extremely well trained, which put them among the most effective of the Estonian guerrilla groups. By early July, as the Germans approached, the rebellion was taking hold. 'These days bogs and forests are more populated than farms and fields,' wrote Juhan Jaik in 1941. 'The forests and bogs are our territory while the fields and farms are occupied by the enemy.' By 'the enemy' he still meant the Russians – but not for long.[56]

The Soviet authorities tried to recruit Estonians into the Red Army, starting on 2 July, although on that day they suffered defeat at Riga, and began to retreat through northern Latvia and southern Estonia to a new defence line running from Tartu to Pärnu (Pernau). The Germans halted their advance, so that for about two weeks southern Estonia was a no-man's-land where neither the main German nor Soviet forces operated. The Estonian partisans and NKVD squads fought small actions, with dozens killed on both sides, but this brief pause can have had little effect on the overall progress of the German invasion. The first German units crossed into Estonia on 7 July. By this time an independent Estonian government had been restored. By mid July the Germans had reached a line running from Emajõgi to Pärnu, across the middle of Estonia, and the Soviet authorities only managed to call up 32,187 Estonian men. On 10 July a revolt broke out in Tartu, which the Red Army was unable to suppress. Estonian officers who had deserted the Red Army began to form units totalling about 3,000 men. Once again the Germans had no policy for managing this unexpected phenomenon. On 29 July there was a parade of about 2,000 Estonian fighters in Tartu, but at the end the Germans announced that they would be disbanded. However, the Estonian Home Guard was declared legal again in August, to protect German rear areas against Soviet troops who had been left behind.[57]

The status of the Baltic States – for the next three years, anyway – had been decided at a meeting in Hitler's office on 16 July. They would become a region of the Reich, the Reich commissariat of Ostland (see Figure 12.5).[58] However, the simultaneous revolt of armed resistance movements in the three Baltic countries the moment the Germans attacked must have had a significant impact on the ability of the Red Army and the NKVD to resist. The seizure of major towns, the revolt of major military bases, the seizure of communications and attacks on Red Army supplies and withdrawing Soviet forces, while perhaps not utterly decisive, probably accelerated the Soviet collapse and the very rapid withdrawal of Soviet forces towards Leningrad. During the first ten days Northern Army Group had captured Lithuania and southern Latvia, and the Red Army withdrew to mid Estonia. Northern Estonia remained in Soviet hands until the end of August. In the first three weeks the Soviet North-West Front lost 90,000 soldiers, and more than 1,000 tanks.[59]

Army Group South and Ukraine

Army Group South, under Gerd Von Runstedt, had the hardest time, as the Russians were expecting the main German thrust – which it was not – in this area. The western Bug was also a formidable obstacle. With four armies deployed forward and one back, and a total of eight mechanized and one airborne corps, Kirponos was the most likely of the Front commanders to deal the Germans a crippling blow. Another two armies, Sixteenth and Nineteenth, were still forming up further back on the Dnepr, the former under Lt Gen. Ivan Koniev, who would emerge as one of the war's most outstanding commanders. The Soviet IX Mechanized Corps, one of two in Fifth Army, was commanded by Major-General Konstantin Rokossovskiy, who would be another. In the Sixth Army area was IV Mechanized Corps, the largest and best equipped of all the Soviet corps of this type in the western districts, commanded by Major-General Andrey Vlasov. Vlasov was an extremely able officer who seemed to be cut out for a distinguished career in the Red Army, and the fact that he was entrusted with the most fully fledged Mechanized Corps reflected this. However, he is best known to history for defecting to the Germans after his capture on the Volkhov Front (east of Leningrad) later in the war, and for taking charge of the 'Russian Liberation Army' on the German side. At this stage, however, there appears to have been no doubt of his loyalty.[60] The IV Mechanized Corps had 460 of the new T-34s and KVs out of a total strength of nearly 1,000 tanks – close to the full complement.

The German attack from 03.00 on 22 June destroyed 250 aircraft from the South-West Front in the first day. Von Runstedt aimed to drive his armoured chisel between the Fifth Army, isolated just to the west of the Pripyet marshes, and the Sixth, well forward north-west of L'viv, which Von Runstedt intended to encircle. Kirponos could not make contact with his Fifth Army because the German Special Forces had, again, cut its dangling, vulnerable landline communications so effectively, although he could still talk to Moscow.[61]

In all, Kirponos had eight mechanized corps – IV, VIII, IX, XV, XVI, XIX, XXII and XXIV – a tremendous potential concentration of armour, if only the Soviet command could manage to bring it together. At the end of 22 June, People's Defence Commissariat Directive No. 3 (the first to give specific orders) told him to do just that. He was to encircle and destroy the enemy grouping advancing in the Vladimir-Volynskii area and to capture the Lublin area – the first suggestion of striking back across the former border. For this, he was to use no fewer than five of his eight mechanized corps.[62]

The armoured spearhead of Von Runstedt's attack was Colonel-General Ewald Kleist's First Panzer Group, which penetrated the Soviet Fifth Army in the Vladimir-Volynskiy area on the first day (see Figure 8.2). When Kirponos received Directive No. 3 that evening, some of his forces were still 400 kilometres away from the Germans he was supposed to counter-attack and encircle, but he tried to carry out the instruction.

Rokossovskiy had received instructions from his army headquarters at 04.00 (Moscow time) on 22 June to open the sealed envelope containing 'special secret'[63] plans, which could only be authorized by Stalin or Timoshenko. He was naturally cautious, and tried to contact the Defence Ministry in Moscow, his Military District headquarters at Ternopol' (he did not yet know that war had just broken out and that it had morphed into a Front), and, finally, Fifth Army at Lutsk. He knew that the Military District headquarters had moved 350 kilometres westward, but noted that 'no one had told us why'. All communications had been cut. Mindful of the risks, then, he nevertheless opened the envelope. His Corps was ordered to proceed north-west to Rovno (see Figure 8.2), Lutsk and then Kovel'. This, although Rokossovskiy did not know it at the time, would put it absolutely within Fifth Army's axis of attack in the 15 May Zhukov pre-emptive strike plan (see Figure 5.1).

The original, 1968 Soviet edition of Rokossovskiy's memoirs had about 2,200 words cut from the author's manuscript around this point, including most of those referring to the above events. In the complete, 2002 edition, they are highlighted. Among them:

> Up to the beginning of the war our corps was up to half of its establishment for personnel, but had not received basic equipment: tanks and motor transport. Here, the stocks were no more than 30 per cent of the authorized strength. Some of the machinery had also broken down or was worn out by prolonged use. Put simply, the Corps was unready for military operation as a mechanized unit in any form. There was *no way the Kiev Special Military District [KOVO] headquarters and the General Staff didn't know this.*[64]

His Corps was still forming up, but the sealed order treated it as if it was a fully equipped, honed strike force. The implication – and it is only implied, but rather strongly, is that something was very odd. The sealed orders had not been intended for 22 June.[65] It is one of the strongest pieces of evidence to support Pleshakov's thesis that the Soviets had switched on the 15 May pre-emptive strike plan, probably intended for 1942, for want of anything better (see Chapter 5). Rokossovskiy, a big, tough man with film-star looks who had been through hell in the GULag, headed home to get ready for war and met his teenage daughter Adya on the way. He told her to get home.[66]

At 16.00 on 22 June Zhukov had left Stalin's office and boarded a plane for Kiev, where he met Khrushchev, the First Secretary of the Ukrainian Communist Party – effectively its Viceroy.[67] Zhukov and Khrushchev then drove – it was too dangerous to fly – to Kirponos's headquarters at Ternopol. Zhukov arrived there late in the evening, and, when he eventually obtained a phone, called Moscow. He was told about Directive No. 3, timed at 21.15, to which his name had been appended, even though he knew nothing of it. Zhukov swallowed his anger, and confirmed the order to Kirponos. Kirponos hoped to attack the German thrust from both sides with three mechanized corps on each – 3,700 tanks in all. This grandiose vision for an operational counterstroke obviously appealed to Zhukov, but it proved impossible to implement it in practice. Initially Kirponos ordered XXII Mechanized Corps to attack from the north and XV from the south, but by the end of 23 June it had only been possible to commit a part of 10th Tank Division.

Zhukov, meanwhile, left the South-West Front headquarters, and spent the next day and a half moving around the area trying to find out what was going on and boost morale. On the evening of 24 June he bumped into Ryabyshev, commander of VIII Mechanized Corps.

In the confusion of 22 June VIII Mechanized Corps had initially been ordered forward from its base at Drogobych to Sambor, across the River Dnestr. As with Rokossovskiy's orders, this very early move into the teeth of the oncoming tiger could have been ordered as part of the panicked and now pointless implementation of the pre-emptive strike plan. It was the beginning of a 500-kilometre odyssey that must rank high in the annals of the futility of war. By the time Ryabyshev's corps would finally meet the enemy near Brody on 25 June, half of its tanks had broken down or otherwise been lost.[68] After a ten-hour march, Ryabyshev and his men were told to turn round and head back to Drogobych. They arrived to find their families, some of them dead, in the flaming ruins of the barracks which had been attacked by German aircraft. Then the Corps was ordered to L'viv, the capital of western Ukraine. They got there on the morning of the 24th, and were ambushed by Ukrainian partisans of the Organization of Ukrainian Nationalists sniping at them from the rooftops. Here, as in the Baltic States, the Russians were unwelcome recent arrivals and on 22 June the OUN had sprung into action, prompted by the NKVD's decision to start shooting everyone in the city prison.[69] The Red Army dealt with the snipers who had shown themselves, but restoring order in L'viv was not their job, and VIII moved on east, leaving the local NKVD, reinforced by NKVD border guards who had fled from the frontier, to deal with the rising.

By late on 26 June Von Kleist's First Panzer Group was poised to strike through Rovno and on to Kiev, which, as the political and industrial centre of Ukraine, was a strategic objective. By this time, Kirponos had managed to muster enough forces for a proper operational-level counterstroke. Karpezo's XV and Ryabyshev's VIII Mechanized Corps had made contact on 25 June, and were ordered to attack the Germans from the south on the 26th. Rokossovskiy's IX and Feklenko's XIX Mechanized Corps, even though they were not all there, would attack the German spearhead from the front (the east and north). The counterstroke began that morning, and VIII and XV Corps struck the Germans in the flank, forcing them to withdraw 10 kilometres. VIII Corps recaptured the town of Leshnev, but Ryabyshev was hit in a German air attack. He was knocked unconscious, but, being an incredible survivor, came round. Once again, however, the leading Panzer division – 11 Panzer – had moved too fast for the Russians and when VIII Mechanized Corps pushed on to Dubno it ran into 16th Panzer Division which was racing behind. Again, the Russians were stopped. They were extremely vulnerable to air attack, and in order to avoid it drove off the roads and into the surrounding swamps. As Figure 8.1 shows, the attempted counterstroke took place right on the edge of the Pripyet swamp, which was hardly ideal country.[70]

Before he was knocked unconscious, Ryabyshev had told Popel', his political officer, that he would give his much-loved cavalry sabre to his grandchildren. No use now, he said. 'This is a war of iron.'[71]

The two corps from the east tried to attack the northern flank of the German thrust. Two of Feklenko's tank division ran into two German Panzer divisions, which could never be a fair contest. He was repulsed and pushed back to Rovno. Rokossovskiy knew that the orders to attack were unrealistic but, perhaps with memories of the GULag in mind, on 27 June he complied with the order from Zhukov, once his junior, and committed his IX Mechanized Corps to the attack. His tank divisions were mostly outmoded T-26, BT-2, BT-5 and BT-7 light tanks, and he did not have even as many of those as he should. He had only about a third of the official number of armoured (such as they were) and soft-skinned vehicles. But he had done the best he could, including signing for every possible vehicle and item of stores on the morning of 22 June, to the fury of the quartermasters, including 200 trucks from the Front's reserve.[72]

In his attack on 27 June, Rokossovskiy lost contact with Feklenko and, as he expected, his light tanks suffered terribly. The next day he was ordered to attack again, but instead he set up an ambush for the German 13th Panzer Division, which was approaching Rovno. For the first time in the war, the Germans ran into massed Soviet artillery fire which caused heavy losses among their armour and infantry. Rokossovskiy held his position for two days, and was then ordered to withdraw. The Russians were learning.

This ferocious and concentrated counterstroke, even though unsuccessful, delayed the German advance in the south by a good week. The German advance to Rovno threatened to cut off the Soviet forces to the south and Muzychenko's Sixth Army vacated its forward positions on the 27th, falling back to L'viv and, on the 30th, withdrew east again. Kirponos was ordered to withdraw to the Korosten', Novgorod-Volynskiy and Letichev fortified regions on the old Stalin Line by 9 July.

Kirponos's conduct of the battle was relatively skilful, certainly compared with Pavlov to his north. To cover his withdrawal he ordered XXII Mechanized and XXVII Rifle Corps of Fifth Army, which was trapped north of the German armoured attack anyway, to drive south into its flank. That delayed the Germans for another two precious days. During the withdrawal there were frequent cases of Soviet troops panicking, and Kirponos ordered the formation of 'blocking detachments', which would become infamous across the front, to shoot any soldiers who withdrew without orders. At this stage, these were drawn from the Red Army, and not provided by the NKVD.

Rokossovskiy had first encountered panic as early as 23 June, when he noticed men swarming through the fields, with wheat growing high, in peasant clothes and, more suspiciously, regulation Red Army underwear. Rumours that German special forces had infiltrated, dressed as Soviet security forces, made it more difficult for the real Soviet officers and security forces to bring to order the deserters – and the merely confused. Rokossovskiy observed that the reports of 'diversionary troops' disguised as policemen, NKVD troops and officers that flooded the country, while supposed to increase vigilance, in fact led to malicious and totally unfounded rumours and panic.

> One day a general who had lost his weapons, in a tattered
> jacket, haggard and drained of his strength, was delivered to
> our Command Post. He told how, having been sent to the

headquarters of Fifth Army by Front headquarters, in order
to find out what was going on, he had seen trucks with our
troops in, west of Rovno, racing headlong to the east, one
after another. In a word, the general [not named] detected
panic and, in order to determine the cause, tried to stop one
of the vehicles. Eventually he succeeded. In the truck there
were about 20 men. But instead of the troops answering his
questions – where they were heading, and what unit they
were from – the general was dragged into the back of the
truck and, in unison, the troops interrogated him. After a
short while, and not having given the matter much thought,
they said he was a diversionary agent in a [Soviet] uniform,
grabbed his documents and weapons, and condemned him to
death. The general managed to jump out of the truck, and
raced off the road into thick rye. He then made it to our
headquarters, through the woods.[73]

The general had had a lucky escape. Rokossovskiy ordered his troops
to restore order in the corps area, but some of the deserters, who were
still armed, would not give up easily and opened fire. Hundreds of
captured deserters were shot. Rokossovskiy also started receiving reports
of suicides. On the evening of 25 June Rokossovskiy had a major
confrontation with officers and men fleeing from the XXII Mechanized
Corps, which, he was told, had been destroyed. At first, they refused to
respond to his orders. Then he picked on one man who had obviously
'lived a bit'.

By his appearance and bearing he didn't look like an ordinary
soldier. Right next to him a young nurse was sitting. I turned
to the people sitting down, of whom there were no fewer
than a hundred. I ordered the officers to report to me.
Nobody moved. I raised my voice, and repeated the order a
second, and then a third time. Again, silence, and no
movement. I moved towards the 'encircled', and got them to
stand up. Having figured this guy was the commander, I
asked him his rank. 'Colonel'.[74]

His tone was 'indifferent', his defiance 'insolent'. Rokossovskiy, in
his own words, 'literally blew up'. He pulled out his pistol, ready to
shoot the colonel there and then. Realizing it could be the end for him,
the colonel fell on his knees and agreed to do whatever Rokossovskiy

said. By the next morning he had gathered 500 men.[75] Some 5,000 men of the Sixth Rifle Corps were sent back to the front, while 100 were shot on the spot. Rokossovskiy's towering stature and character served him well that day. He was determined to do his duty, but he was also determined not to go back to the GULag.[76]

In the hot end-of-June sun and through the oppressive nights a vision of hell swelled and rolled eastwards across the wheatfields and woods of Ukraine. Thousands, tens of thousands of Red Army soldiers, and equal numbers of civilians swarmed through the fields and forests. The Red Army had its fair share of 'real criminal types', and the forests were alive with deserters. Women fleeing with children, fearing rape and murder, were reluctant to move off the few roads, where they provided targets for German aircraft.

Just as it appeared that things could not get any worse, on 2 July the second, southern grouping of the German Army Group South attacked into Moldova. The area was defended by Colonel-General Ivan Tyulenev's new Southern Front, which had been formed only on 25 June. Von Runstedt planned to use the German Eleventh Army to swing north and help encircle the Soviet South-West Front's forces in Ukraine. Tyulenev initially overestimated German strength, and received permission to withdraw to the Dnestr. When he realized his error, he was able to establish a stable front between the Pruth and the Dnestr – the middle of the recently occupied new Soviet territory. Once again, the old Stalin Line proved useful. The Mogilev-Podol'sk fortified region on the bend of the Dnestr was garrisoned by the newly formed Eighteenth Army, formed from the Moscow Military District, and formed a block which protected the South-West Front's left flank.

The border battles in Ukraine were fierce, costing the Russians 173,323 killed, captured and missing, 4,381 tanks and 1,218 combat aircraft. Of the dead, many fell to the Germans, but the figure also includes deserters shot by loyal troops, and vice versa, and those killed by Ukrainian partisans. But in spite of the enormity of the disaster and the confusion, Kirponos and his mechanized corps commanders had attempted massive armoured counterstrokes of a kind which would have been unthinkable in France in 1940, and so had commanders on the other two fronts (see Figure 8.2).

But the price of this bloody learning process, like the scale of Operation Barbarossa, overwhelms the imagination. The 'border' or 'frontier' battles lasted from 22 June to 9 July in the Baltic (North-West

Front) and Belorussian (Western Front) areas, and until 6 July in western Ukraine and, later, Moldova (the South-Western Front and Southern Front's Eighteenth Army). The average daily losses were 23,207 in Belorussia, against Army Group Centre, and 16,106 in Western Ukraine, against Army Group South, with some also falling to Ukrainian nationalists. However, the North-West Front suffered a relatively slight 4,916 casualties per day (including 71 from the Baltic fleet) in the Baltic States, against Army Group North and the Baltic rebels. The Soviet forces retreated between 400 and 450 kilometres in the northern sector, between 450 and 600 kilometres in Belorussia, before the main blow from Army Group Centre, and 300 to 350 kilometres in the south, where they were strongest[77] – so the staggering arithmetic all made sense, to a point.

The losses were terrifying, however. An attacking force, with only a modest superiority in numbers of men, and inferior in numbers of tanks, guns and aircraft, had been able to drive the defending Russians back between 300 and 600 kilometres and inflict irrecoverable losses – killed, prisoners and missing – officially numbered at 589,537, in between fifteen and eighteen days. According to *that* arithmetic, losing more than 44,000 men a day, how much longer could the Soviet Union last?

However, by the end of July the eastern armies of the *Wehrmacht* had also lost 25,000 men dead.[78] By 13 July, just after the 'frontier battle' phase ended, in three weeks, the *Wehrmacht* had lost 92,120 killed, wounded and missing – some 3.6 per cent of its total strength, and half as many again as the 60,000 casualties they suffered taking France the year before in the same period.[79] Between 23 and 26 June the Germans had attacked 123 Soviet airfields, destroying, they reported (the accounts must always be taken with a slight pinch of salt) 4,614 planes. These included 1,438 in the air and 3,176 on the ground, at a cost of 330 German aircraft lost. By the end of the 'frontier battles', for which the statistics date from 12 July, the total had risen to 6,857 Soviet aircraft destroyed as against 550 German – which was comparable. Whilst these statistics appear astonishing, they are not so different from the one-to-ten balance which was emerging between the respective ground forces. One to twelve or thirteen, overall, but only one to five in the air.[80] The Germans had overall suffered a fraction – between a sixth and a seventh – of the Red Army, air force and NKVD's casualties, but still an awful lot in just twenty-two days. Hard pounding, this.[81] Who would pound longest?

9

KREMLIN AT WAR

Moscow

On the morning of 22 June Stalin, having been wakened by Zhukov's phone call, returned to the Kremlin before 05.45, Moscow time. The first German artillery and air strikes, 1,000 kilometres to the west, had begun an hour and three-quarters before. After telling Molotov of the attack, at 05.30, German Ambassador Schulenberg was leaving the great red-brick fairytale citadel just as members of the Soviet leadership were driving in. Molotov raced downstairs from his office to Stalin's, and by 05.45 Beria, Timoshenko, Mekhlis and Zhukov had joined them.[1] Stalin looked worn out, and Zhukov said it was the only time he saw him depressed. Eventually Stalin rallied. 'The enemy will be beaten all along the line. What do you recommend?' Stalin still cherished the illusion that the reported German attack could be a mistake, the result of spontaneous action by some wayward German generals, or that there might still be room for negotiation. 'Do not cross the border,' he said.[2] NKO Directive No. 2, signed by Timoshenko, Malenkov and Zhukov, was issued at 07.15. It carefully avoided labelling what had happened so far as a full-scale attack:

> On 22 June 1941 at 04.00 hours in the morning, without any cause whatsoever, German aircraft carried out flights to our airfields and cities along the western frontier and subjected them to bombing.
>
> Simultaneously in a number of places German forces opened fire with artillery and crossed our border.
>
> In connection with the unprecedented attack by Germany on the Soviet Union, I ORDER:

1. Troops in full strength and with all the means at their disposal will attack the enemy and destroy him in those regions where he has violated the Soviet border. In the absence of special authorization, ground troops will not cross the frontier.

2. Reconnaissance and combat aircraft will determine the concentration areas of enemy aircraft and the deployment of the ground forces. Bombers and ground-attack aircraft will destroy the aircraft on enemy airfields by powerful strikes and will bomb concentrations of his ground forces. Mount aviation strikes on German territory to a depth of 100–150 km.

Bomb Königsberg and Memel'.

Do not conduct flights over Finland and Romania without special authorization.[3]

Stalin was still clinging to the remote possibility of a diplomatic solution, and hoped that this was perhaps just a demonstration, although Molotov and the generals kept insisting it was real war. One comment to Georgiy Dimitrov (1882–1949), the Bulgarian leader of the Comintern, who arrived at 08.40, was telling. 'They fell on us *without making any claims*, making a vile attack like bandits.'[4] Stalin, like the British, had evidently expected the German military build-up to lead, at worst, to some sort of demands or ultimatum. But instead, he was faced with a totally unprovoked and unconditional attack to which there could be no political response apart from immediate and total surrender. Georgiy Malenkov, the Secretary of the Party Central Committee, and Vyshinskiy, Molotov's Deputy for Foreign Affairs, arrived at 07.30; Mikoyan, Minister for External Trade, who would play a key role in the evacuation of industry eastwards, at 07.55; and Kaganovich, Minister for Communications, who would do the same, at 08.00.

Meanwhile, Moscow radio broadcasts across the Soviet Union and abroad continued as normal, starting with news and physical jerks at 06.00. A brief halt in transmission led some to think that a special announcement was on its way, but then the optimistic broadcast continued.[5] It would be another six hours before the special announcement was ready. In the Kremlin, Stalin issued a stream of orders, while Molotov was tasked to write the announcement to the Soviet people, and to the world.

That was an understandable reaction. As the morning went on Stalin must have realized he had been fooled and humiliated. But Molotov had signed the non-aggression pact with Germany. While Stalin began to grasp key issues which would prove crucial to the country's survival, Molotov could talk to the people. At midday he drove to the Central Telegraph Office on Gor'kiy Street, where, striving to overcome his stutter, he made the announcement at 12.15.

Although Molotov's famous speech appears to greatly underestimate the Soviet casualties – saying that just 200 had been killed and wounded in the initial air raids – information from the front was extremely sparse. Molotov's conversation with Schulenberg is faithfully reported, including the German claim that Red Army units were concentrated on the eastern German frontier. The announcement stressed that there had been no declaration of war and the fact that no claims or demands had been made of the Soviet Union is mentioned twice. 'Fascist Germany' was therefore without any doubt 'the aggressor'. The point was well made. That would be more than enough for Churchill, for the British people and for the United States. Molotov then recalled what befell Napoleon in Russia during the 'Patriotic War' – a prophetic comparison which he had been very quick to make in the first few hours – and said that the Red Army and the entire people would conduct a '*new* Patriotic War, for the Motherland (*Rodina*), for honour, for freedom'. And, anticipating the outcome of what would become the *Great* Patriotic War, although he could have had no idea whether they would material-ize, he concluded with those simple but soul-searing words. They might have been his, or Stalin's own. They were insanely optimistic, but nonetheless inspirational, and very Marxist. If you say 'it will be', then it will be. Churchill said truth needed a bodyguard of lies. These sprang from a background of lies, and yet, after 1,418 days, would come true: '*Our cause is just. The enemy will be beaten. Victory will be with us.*'[6]

A few blocks away from the studio, in the eerily self-contained world of the Kremlin fortress, Stalin ordered Kaganovich to evacuate factories and 20 million people from the front-line areas, while Mikoyan was tasked to feed and supply the Russian armies. Stalin was pleased with Molotov's radio performance, but, perhaps irrationally, had already focused on General Pavlov, who was doomed to lose Belarus, as the target of his frustration and anger.[7]

London

In London, Ambassador Maisky first heard about the invasion from the BBC news. He had to postpone a meeting with Foreign Secretary Eden until he learned of Soviet policy from Molotov's address which, fortunately, came at 11.15, *double* British summer time. In Moscow, the Russians still thought the German invasion might have been launched in collusion with the British, and Maisky's main concern was to get reassurance that, following Germany's swing to the east, the British would not now sue for a separate peace. On the same day the British Chargé d'Affaires in Moscow found Vyshinskiy, Molotov's Deputy, 'exceedingly nervous'.[8]

Churchill learned of the invasion at 08.00, British time, that Sunday morning. The news had come in four hours earlier, but Churchill, who was fond of his bed, had given orders that he was not to be woken unless Britain itself was invaded.[9] His private secretary was to tell the BBC, and Churchill would broadcast at 21.00. For Churchill, the news that Hitler had turned east was an immediate, albeit perhaps temporary, relief, and the consummate politician quickly sprang on the events of the morning as a 'turning point' in the war. The fourth, he said, after the fall of France, the victory in the Battle of Britain, and the passage of the Lease-and-Lend Act between the United States and the UK. His brilliantly drafted speech on the evening of 22 June appeared to mark a sudden shift from lifelong prejudices, and Churchill did nothing to discourage that view. 'I will unsay no word that I have spoken about it. But all this fades away before the spectacle which is now unfolding.' He must have seen a translation of Molotov's speech, and picked up the same references to Russia's past history. However, his famous comment to his secretary that 'if Hitler invaded Hell I would at least make a favourable reference to the Devil in the House of Commons' did not mark a fundamental shift in relations, at least immediately. Churchill had worked out his policy towards the Soviet Union in the event of a German attack well before, and the 'spin' was self-interested. The invasion of Russia (he always called it Russia), he said, was 'no more than a prelude to the attempt to violate the

British Isles'. As shown in Chapter 4, his military chiefs agreed with him. His speech made the threat sound very general: in fact it was very specific.

> The Russian danger is therefore our danger, and the danger
> of the United States, just as the cause of any Russian fighting
> for his hearth and home is the cause of free men and free
> peoples in every quarter of the globe.[10]

In reality, Churchill and his military commanders saw the German attack on Russia as a purely temporary diversion, believing the Russians would collapse very quickly, and a fleeting opportunity to 'make hell *while* the sun shines'.[11]

Berlin

In Berlin and Moscow the remaining Soviet and German diplomats were understandably nervous, and other citizens terrified. Traditional norms of international relations should have guaranteed the diplomats' safety, at least, but the invasion of the Soviet Union and what was clearly going to be an 'absolute war', with few, if any constraints, had made even those assumptions dubious.

At 06.00, Moscow time, Berezhkov and his colleagues in the Berlin embassy, whom Ribbentrop had told of the invasion an hour before, listened anxiously to the radio to hear the Soviet take on events. There was no mention of war. Perhaps – incredibly, Berezhkov thought – Moscow might not even know yet. It did, but the Berlin embassy's telephone lines had been cut, so a member of the embassy staff headed for the main post office in a big black diplomatic car to send a telegram. He returned, fifteen minutes later, on foot. The Germans had let him go, because he had diplomatic ID, but had arrested the driver. Then Berezhkov tried, using a discreetly downmarket yellow Opel Olympia. He succeeded in reaching the post office, to find people standing around a loudspeaker listening to Goebbels' 'hysterical shrieks'. The counter clerk was incredulous: 'To *Moscow*? There's *no way* you can't have heard what's going on . . .' Berezhkov, the consummate diplomat, said he persuaded him to take the telegram and got a receipt, but the cable was never sent – or, at least, never arrived.[12]

The Gestapo stormed into the Soviet trade mission in Berlin and started to carry documents away, while the Russian staff frantically tried to burn what they could, smoke issuing from an upstairs window. The courtyard of the Soviet embassy turned into a 'gypsy encampment', Berezhkov recalls, as a few – but still far too many – of the thousand Soviet citizens still in Germany and the occupied territories sought refuge. On the next day, the Germans said they were going to intern all USSR nationals. They said they would exchange individuals for Germans still in the USSR, but there was a problem. Given that the Germans had moved first, there were still 1,000 Soviet citizens in Germany, but only about 120 Germans in the Soviet Union. The interests of Soviet people in Germany were placed under the protection of the Swedes: those of Germans in the USSR under the Bulgarians. Eventually, it was agreed that all the Soviet workers in Germany and their families would be evacuated, through Prague, Vienna and Belgrade, as far as the Yugoslav city of Niš, in order to allow the Germans to get their remaining people out of the USSR.

During these few stressful days, as Soviet and German troops butchered each other with almost unprecedented savagery in the frontier battles, Berezhkov was in the bizarre and almost unique position of being able to negotiate and even socialize with his German guards in Berlin. He established an unlikely rapport with one of the guards assigned to the Soviet delegation, a middle-aged but relatively junior[13] SS officer called Heinemann. On one occasion Heinemann asked Berezhkov out for a beer, but was spotted by six other SS officers at a neighbouring table, who asked the pair to join them.

What on earth were they to do? Heinemann, an officer in the elite SS, was socializing in Berlin with a Soviet internee, from a race which Hitler considered *untermensch* and which was being convincingly wiped from the face of the earth. Heinemann introduced Berezhkov as a relation of his wife's from Munich, called Kurt, who worked in an arms factory and could not therefore talk much about what he did. After talking about the war in the East and the British bombing raids, one of the SS officers made a toast 'to our victory'. 'To *our* victory', replied Berezhkov, and put his beer mug down on the table.[14]

Heinemann was desperate that his son, who had just joined the SS, should not die fighting the Russians, and was also short of money because he had had to pay for medical treatment for his own wife. Until the small hours of 22 June the Soviet embassy in Berlin had, at least officially, represented Hitler's greatest friends – apart, perhaps, from the Italians and Japanese – and certainly the most powerful. The embassy safes were therefore full of German cash, used for various aspects of embassy business, whether compatible or not with the diplomats' status. If they got out at all, the Russian diplomats were not going to be allowed to take more with them than a suitcase and enough cash for 'out-of-pocket expenses'. Explaining that he could not take it with him, Berezhkov therefore slipped Heinemann a thousand marks – a lot of money. In return, Heinemann helped to organize the Soviet embassy staff's evacuation. This was far more effort for Heinemann than it had been for Berezhkov to give him a backhander. On 2 July the Soviet delegation finally left Berlin, and Berezhkov had a last meeting with Heinemann. The SS officer gave him a photograph of himself, with an inscription on the back. 'It may so happen', the SS man said, 'that sometime or other I'll have to refer to the service I rendered to the Soviet Embassy. I hope it won't be forgotten.'[15] Like Ribbentrop, perhaps, Heinemann, whose ultimate fate Berezhkov never discovered, may have had a premonition of a Russian victory.

The Soviet citizens arrived in Niš under SS guard. Behind their backs, the Yugoslavs waved red flags in support of the Russians. The non-diplomats were placed in a concentration camp in an old barracks, but after a few days the diplomats were able to arrange some improvement to their treatment, although their subsequent fate is unknown. Here, Berezhkov met an old-school Swedish diplomat, Baron Botman. Botman helped arrange for the Soviet diplomatic team to be taken to the Bulgarian-Turkish frontier, where they were handed over to neutral Turkey. In Edirne they were met by diplomats from the Soviet embassy in Istanbul and by the provincial Governor. After an evening reception, the next day they took a train to Ankara where they were met by a special Soviet aircraft, which flew them back to a now unfamiliar, wartime Moscow.

> On the gable-end of one of the buildings there was a poster –
> a Russian woman with a severe face, in her raised hand the
> text of the military oath and the caption 'Mother Russia
> calls'. Several times our car had to avoid shambolic ranks of
> marching militiamen [*opolcheniye* – not *militsiya*, who are

police]. The fronts of the houses were covered with green and brown stains, and the glass in the windows was criss-crossed with paper tape.[16]

By now, it was well into July. It was war, but young Berezhkov had been extremely privileged, and incredibly lucky.

The bear's cave

Meanwhile, through the afternoon of 22 June key officials had returned to see Stalin. Khrushchev, who famously later denounced Stalin, was behind the allegation that the Soviet leader was shocked, confused, and basically 'lost it' for ten days, until he was able to face the Soviet people in his 3 July speech. The newly available evidence shows this to be completely untrue. On 22 June Stalin had twenty-nine meetings with senior people, including many of them two or three times. Having had perhaps three hours' sleep early that morning, he was exhausted and his last appointment, Beria, who had been with him on three occasions for nearly four hours in total, left at 16.45.[17] Khrushchev, Viceroy of the Ukraine, who was joined by Zhukov in Kiev late that evening, was never there. Stalin was back in his office to see Molotov at 03.20 the next morning. In the next three hours he saw seven more people: Voroshilov; Beria; Timoshenko; Vatutin; Kuznetsov, the commander of the navy; Kaganovich and Zhigarev, the commander of the air force. He then had a twelve-hour break before seeing most of them again, plus Merkulov, chief of the NKGB and Vlasik, chief of its First Directorate. This was not a man suffering a nervous breakdown, as some have suggested – not *yet*, anyway, as we shall see.[18]

Stalin had already ordered Kaganovich to begin the evacuation of industry. After some sleep, on 23 June, Stalin took another critical decision: the establishment of a supreme political-military war command, with its old Russian name, *Stavka*. Marshal Timoshenko would preside (officially) over the 'Stavka of the Main [High] Command' (*Stavka Glavnogo Komandovaniya*) – though in reality Stalin would be in charge. The other members, in order of precedence, were Chief of the General Staff Zhukov, Foreign Minister Molotov, Marshals Voroshilov and Budënny and Navy Minister Admiral Kuznetsov. It was designed 'to effect the most centralised and flexible command of the Armed Forces in the conditions of the war which had just begun'. On 10 July it was renamed the 'Stavka of the *Supreme* High Command' (*Stavka Verkhovnogo Komandovaniya*), now headed by Stalin, and it was joined by the benign former Tsarist Colonel, Marshal Boris Shaposhnikov, probably the best staff officer the Soviet forces still had.[19]

The internal security services – overreaction?

A state of war and military mobilization were both declared on 22 June, the latter to start the next day.[20] In accordance with Article 49 of the Soviet constitution, a state of war was declared 'in individual districts and across the whole of the USSR in order to guarantee social order and state security'.[21] If people thought things were bad in Stalin's Russia, they were about to get worse. One imagines that some members of the NKGB and NKVD were rubbing their hands with glee. Anybody due for release from prison or from a camp on 22 June or shortly thereafter had a nasty shock coming. All releases from camps, jails and colonies of 'counter-revolutionaries, bandits, recidivists, and other dangerous offenders' were to be stopped.[22] At 07.00 on 22 June all operational staff of the Moscow Directorates of the NKGB and NKVD were confined to barracks while the plans to secure the capital and surrounding area were put into practice. At 09.10 all the 'Operational-Chekist detachments of the NKGB and NKVD' (see Chapters 3 and 4) were mobilized for war.[23]

By 17.00 the NKGB and NKVD had arrested 14 people but had lined up another 240 for arrest including 71 German 'spies', 6 Japanese, 2 Hungarians, 4 British, 3 Italians, 2 Turks and 5 Romanians, plus hundreds of other 'criminal elements'. The Department for Combating Misappropriation of Socialist Property and Speculation was directed to identify speculators and black marketeers, while 114 defence and state factories and enterprises were placed under special surveillance, often by officials at deputy director level, and 472 checkpoints were set up. The guard on prisons, remand centres and detention camps was to be reinforced, and a camp for 1,000 inmates was set up to house the expected overflow from the prisons. In addition, foreign nationals who were interned had the privilege of being sent to a 'special camp for 300 people'. A force of 492 officers was detailed to patrol railway lines and installations. Special military and police guards were placed on fourteen key railway and other strategic bridges, while the much-loved traffic police (UShOSDOR) were to keep an eye out for any attempts to sabotage the roads and maintain a tighter grip on road traffic. The forces employed included the army, regular and reserve police, NKVD and People's Commissariat for Communications (NKPS – *Narodny Komissariat Putey Soobshcheniya*). Finally, a force of 1,525 police and special constables was to patrol Moscow's streets to maintain public order and also, no doubt, to reassure the public.[24] From the documentation, and the speed and detail with which the required numbers were established, it seems clear that Svechin's 1926 vision of the Interior Ministry having its own mobilization plan (see Chapter 2) had been fully implemented.

Besides the very efficient and necessary measures outlined above, Beria and his ever-assiduous staff in the NKGB and NKVD were also nervous about public reaction to the war. On 24 June a detailed report containing a sample of public reactions was sent to Abakumov, the Deputy Commissar for Internal Affairs. The factory worker who regretted that he was too old to join his son in chasing the fascist invaders from the frontiers of the USSR was reported approvingly, as was Tyuneyev, the railway worker who had sent his two sons to the front with orders to fight for every piece of Soviet soil. But Chervyakov, the former officer in the Tsarist Army who said there was major discontent in the Red Army was *arestovan*. So was 'Kyun' (Kühn?), 'a German', who said the Soviet government was not popularly elected. People with German names got a hard time, but Kurbanov, from Intourist's buildings department, was not arrested, even though he stated that 'the victory of Soviet power in this war is doubtful'. By 21.00 on 23 June, Kubatkin and Zhuravlëv reported that they had arrested seventy-nine people.[25] There was not much they could do to stop the Germans tearing the Red Army apart, but they could arrest people with German names.

The maintenance of public morale was a top priority, and the Russian authorities approached it in a very Russian way. In the United Kingdom during the war the main source of broadcast information and entertainment in most private homes was the radio. Even that was to be denied to the Soviet people. On 25 June the Communist Party Central Committee issued an order that all radio transmitters and receivers, of any type, were to be handed in within the next five days. Local Councils of People's Deputies, working with the People's Commissariat for Communications, would allocate storage space where radios would be held in 'temporary safe keeping until the end of the war'. The only exceptions would be certain clubs, social organizations, factories and other establishments where people could gather to listen to official broadcasts at 'strictly determined times'.[26] There would be no Russian equivalent of 'Lord Haw-Haw' – the British traitor William Joyce – breaking into Radio Moscow as Joyce's pro-Nazi broadcasts broke into the BBC.

Although special forces had undoubtedly facilitated the initial German successes, the Soviet authorities may have overestimated the threat from such '*diversanty*', and the Interior and State Security Ministries' orders over the ensuing months exhibited extreme paranoia. The order from the Belorussian Party Central Committee on 23 June to counter diversionary groups attacking bridges, roads, railways and communications[27] was already too late for the border areas, where the initial special attacks had paralysed Soviet resistance, but over the ensuing days similar instructions rippled backwards. An order went out on 24 June to the NKVD to form 'destroyer battalions' (*istrebitel'nye batal'ony*) of a hundred to two hundred men each to deal with possible diversionary attacks in the Leningrad, Murmansk and Kalinin districts, the Karelian Finnish Republic (north of Leningrad, including the areas of Finland taken in 1940), Belorussia, Estonia, Latvia, Lithuania, Moldova, the Crimea, Rostov, Krasnodar and the western part of Georgia. Beria duly passed on the order on 25 June.[28] By the end of July 1,755 destroyer battalions had been formed, totalling 328,000 men. Their main tasks were the protection of economic targets in the rear of Red Army forces. However, with the speed and ferocity of the German advance on the ground, many of them found themselves reinforcing Red Army soldiers and many were cut off, forming the nucleus of partisan groups.[29] Throughout the next weeks and months, more and more orders were issued for dealing with enemy agents and diversionary groups, but the greatest threat was from German conventional forces.[30]

Because the NKVD were responsible for capturing German special forces who landed behind Soviet lines, the Red Army did not always get the information it needed. The problems of inter-agency cooperation which beset modern military operations also affected the Soviet defence and security agencies in the Great Patriotic War. On 1 July, Lt Gen. Filipp Golikov, the chief of military intelligence, wrote a grovelling letter to Beria:

> I would ask you to give instructions for any materials and types of equipment found as part of the outfits, weaponry and equipment of captured German parachutists in the NKVD's possession to be sent to the Intelligence Directorate of the Red Army General Staff. And codes and cyphers found on them, instructions for operating radio sets, etc. We are particularly interested in the type of radio sets used by the German parachute detachment.[31]

In a well-run war, that would hardly have been necessary – and certainly not at that level. The fact that Golikov had to write to Beria may have been a function of the paralysing fear pervading the Red Army and security services of being accused of diversion, sabotage and treason. The reasons why the Red Army needed to know German codes, frequencies and procedures, and what radios they used, all seem obvious to us. But in the paranoid atmosphere of the time less senior Red Army intelligence officers might well fear that they could be accused of trying to make contact with the Germans for different reasons.

Although the NKVD were responsible for any German prisoners after they had been initially sifted in camps under the command of armies,[32] the chaotic situation on the frontiers precluded any estimate of German prisoners. There cannot have been many, especially given the Russians' initial habit of killing and mutilating Germans who fell into the hands of partisan units or even the Red Army. This criminal anarchy does not seem to have lasted very long, however. A document from the NKVD's Directorate of Prisoners of War and Internees, dated only 'June', enumerated 27,456 prisoners but of these the vast majority – 21,040 – were Poles captured in 1939.[33]

On 1 July the Council of People's Commissars issued a decree on the 'Special Status of Prisoners'.[34] Although the Soviet Union had not signed the 1929 Geneva Conventions, it later agreed to follow the 1907 Hague Convention on prisoners of war. The 1 July 1941 Soviet decree broadly followed the 1907 and 1929 Conventions, specifying that to qualify as PoWs combatants had to carry arms openly (something Soviet partisans often did not do) and that civilians accompanying an armed force such as war correspondents should also be treated as PoWs. Insulting or cruel treatment towards prisoners was forbidden; equipment, documents and insignia were not to be confiscated; and any valuables or money were to be held in safe keeping and a receipt given. The provisions for liaison with the Red Cross and Red Crescent similarly reflected those set out in international law, but were never implemented. It all sounded quite proper, but the reality was very different. The only prisoners who had much, if any, hope in 1941 were the 41,500 Poles and 4,600 Slovaks who, after major efforts by the USSR's new allies, were released to form the nuclei of Polish and Czechoslovak armies.[35] As we saw in Chapter 2, apart from those who could be 'turned', the treatment of prisoners by both sides at best fell short of the provisions of the Geneva and Hague Conventions, and even of this Soviet instruction to the NKVD. At worst, torture and murder were widely used as tools for interrogation, and sometimes just gratuitously, on both sides.

By 11 July, with the frontier battles already over, concern had shifted to areas further back. On that day NKVD and NKGB Directive 257/207 signed by Beria and Merkulov ordered an 'intensification of the struggle with diversionary agents placed in the rear areas of the Soviet Union by the enemy'.[36] Many of these orders appear to be rather pathetic statements of the obvious, but their overzealous implementation could have fatal consequences. 'Any person who has newly appeared in the vicinity of economic, military or defence installations must be carefully checked out ... new employees must be checked out with special care.' A small prize for common sense goes to State Security Captain (Lt Col.) Pëtr Aksenov, chief of the Kursk Region NKGB who, on 28 June, ordered that people should only be arrested with his and the regional procurator's (magistrate's) approval. 'I will take a very dim view of unwarranted arrests on the basis of unsubstantiated facts,' he warned. In 1943, they made him a colonel, so the system did have its saner moments.[37]

Key decisions

While the security agencies moved on the streets with an incongruous mixture of efficiency on the one hand, and near-paranoia on the other, key decisions were being made deep in the Kremlin which, even at this early stage, would shape the outcome of the war. On 24 June a 'Soviet' – a Council – for Evacuation was set up. In the wake of the Red Army's withdrawal it would 'decide the most important strategic and war-economic task – re-basing powerful human and material resources from the threatened regions to the east, to the rear of the country'.[38]

The overall operation was placed under the direction of Nikolay Voznesenskiy (1903–50), the head of the State Planning Commission, or Gosplan. The Evacuation Soviet reported to him, as a working group. Its president was N. M. Shvernik, with Aleksey Kosygin and M. G. Pervukhin as his deputies, and Anastas Mikoyan, Lazar Kaganovich and M. Z. Saburov as other members. During the next six months 2,593 industrial enterprises were evacuated, 1,523 of them classified as 'major', of which 1,360 were armaments related. Some 226 were moved to the Volga area, 667 to the Urals, 244 to western Siberia, 78 to eastern Siberia and 308 to Kazakhstan and Central Asia. With them went between 30 and 40 per cent of the workers, engineers and technicians.[39] Stalin had made what was probably his most crucial decision early.

In the Leningrad area, where the German advance was very swift, only 92 plants were 're-based' before the city was isolated. The best results were achieved, predictably, in Ukraine, where the Soviet resistance was strongest. The impressive numbers must be matched against the chaos. When the trains arrived carrying plant, machinery and fewer than half of the staff (starving, after perhaps a week or ten days on the railways – assuming they had escaped German bombing), they were pitched out into fields or clearings or, if lucky, into unheated wooden buildings. By November, the ground was starting to freeze so hard that it became impossible to dig foundations for new buildings. Nevertheless, confused and imperfect though it was, with fragments of factories and a small, exhausted proportion of the workforce arriving in the wrong order in the dead of night, the achievement is still astonishing. Some

1.5 million railway wagons carried enough of Soviet industry eastwards to begin to rebuild a war industry and economy which would out-produce the Germans and compensate for the stupendous losses suf-fered.[40] After two days of war, Stalin had focused on that inner truth. The hard definition of intellect. *Priorities.*

Did Stalin have a nervous breakdown?

But then, did Stalin 'panic', as some have alleged?[41] Stalin saw twenty people on 24 June, including Molotov and Beria once each, between 16.50 and 21.30. Stalin, Molotov and Beria were together for more than three hours from 17.05. The Boss's frenetic schedule peaked on 25 June with twenty-nine appointments that day, eleven in the small hours, from 01.00 to 05.20, and then starting again at 19.40. On the 26th he had twenty-eight appointments between noon and 22.00.[42] On those two days he saw Molotov four times and Beria six.

It was around this time that Stalin is first alleged to have put out peace feelers to the Germans. Pavel Sudoplatov, Chief of the 4th (Diversionary-Reconnaissance) Directorate of the NKGB and NKVD, was one of Beria's most trusted officers, who had organized the assassi-nation of Leon Trotsky in Mexico City the previous year. In his memoirs, published in 1994, he said that he received instructions from Beria to approach the Bulgarian Ambassador, Ivan Stamenov, on 25 July, but in evidence to the Council of Ministers dated 7 August 1953, when Beria was on trial, he claimed that the order came between 25 and 27 June.[43] It was hoped that Stamenov would pass the information – which was not a formal Soviet government offer – to his King Boris, who might then pass it to Berlin. The story goes that Sudoplatov met Stamenov in Beria's private room in the trendy *Aragvi* Georgian Res-taurant, a favourite haunt of the NKVD and NKGB in central Moscow. The four questions he posed were: why Germany had attacked the Soviet Union; whether Germany would be prepared to stop the war and under what terms; would the Germans be happy if Stalin handed over the Baltic States, Ukraine, Bessarabia, Bukovina and the Karelian isth-mus; and, if not, what else would Germany want?[44]

Stamenov reportedly replied that he thought the Soviet Union would win the war, even if it had to fall back to the Volga – which is what happened, and it is doubtful whether, assuming the meeting happened, Stamenov passed the message to his King and whether it was ever passed on to Berlin.[45] Other testimony including that of a historian who knew Zhukov suggests that Stalin was contemplating a separate peace with the Germans in October.[46]

Knowing how secret services work, meeting in a discreet restaurant, gently mooting an idea, letting the other party mull over it, and then trying again at another meeting, it is quite possible that two separate attempts were made to contact the Germans in the summer and that the idea of making a separate peace was considered again in the darkest days of October.

An equally plausible theory, however, is that Stalin did not really intend to hand over large chunks, some of them newly acquired, of the western USSR, but was throwing the possibility out as disinformation to delay the German advance, which had certainly run into serious delays by the end of July. Sudoplatov also said in his memoirs that at that time (the end of July), Stalin, Molotov and Beria had hatched a 'disinformation plan' involving Sudoplatov and the Bulgarian Ambassador.[47]

Sudoplatov said that Molotov had told Beria not to meet Stamenov personally, so as not to give the 'preliminary' conversation too much weight in Stamenov's eyes. Obviously, after Stalin's death, it was in Beria's interest to portray the approach as 'disinformation', designed to deflect and delay the German advance with the carrot of a peaceful solution which would satisfy many of German's economic war aims – though not Hitler's deep-seated determination to annihilate Soviet Russia. Khrushchev, on the other hand, was naturally inclined to implicate Beria in a plot to sell out to the Germans. However, even after Beria's arrest, Sudoplatov supported Beria's version.[48] Once again, in view of the contradictory accounts, there can be no definitive answer, but if 'disinformation' about Soviet willingness to offer peace terms was behind an indirect approach through Bulgaria, then 25 to 27 June seems too soon. However, given Stalin's earlier willingness to negotiate with the Germans, it is not inconceivable that he might have returned to the possibility in the darkest hours of late July or early October.

The other indication cited as evidence of 'panic', although it was probably far-sighted prudence comparable with the 24 June formation of the Evacuation Soviet, was the Politburo Central Committee Order No. 34 of 27 June. It ordered the evacuation of state reserves of precious metals, precious stones, diamonds and the treasures 'of the Kremlin Armoury Palace' ('*oruzheynoy palaty*'). This was a precaution against air attack more than against ground invasion at this stage. The People's Commissariat for Finances (the Treasury)(NKF), NKVD and NKGB were ordered to remove these precious artefacts from Moscow and take them to Sverdlovsk and Chelyabinsk (see Figure 7.1). The Ministry of Finance was to be given an estimate of the consignment's value in crude monetary terms (jewels, ingots and scrap), rather than its priceless historical value, while the Communications (Transport) Ministry (NKPS) would let the Finance Ministry and the NKVD know how many railway wagons would be needed to transport it. The Russian Federation People's Commissariat for Timber (*Narkomles RSFSR*) would also let the NKVD know how many packing cases would be needed. The Russians are good at logistics. Finally, the NKVD and NKF would establish how many workers and security guards would be needed to accomplish the evacuation of other treasures from museums across the country, especially the Hermitage in Leningrad.[49]

Whilst it is tempting to ascribe some cultural sensitivity to the swift evacuation of national treasures, the tone of the Politburo decree is unmistakable. Diamonds, platinum, gold, silver . . . The convertible hard currency on which a nation state ultimately depends for its survival and bargaining power, to be transported 1,500 kilometres, not just to the Urals, but to their far edge, and nearly 1,000 kilometres beyond the Germans' final land objective – which the Russians knew about from the intelligence reports their leader had previously spurned.

On 26 June, Zhukov flew back to Moscow having witnessed the disasters in Ukraine at first hand. He saw Stalin at 15.00.[50] It was not Ukraine that really concerned Stalin, however, but Belarus – where the Red Army had been taken by surprise by Germany's strongest element, Army Group Centre. What should be done, snapped Stalin? Zhukov kept his nerve, and said it would take forty minutes to come up with a solution. Like all good military plans, it was starkly simple and easy to illustrate graphically. Zhukov's suggestion is shown in Figure 9.1. Having identified the thrust, block it. There should be two concentric arcs of defence. The first, 300 kilometres long, running from Polotsk through Vitebsk, Orsha – the rail junction at the entry to the Smolensk land bridge – and Mogilev to Mozyr. It rested on the great rivers of the

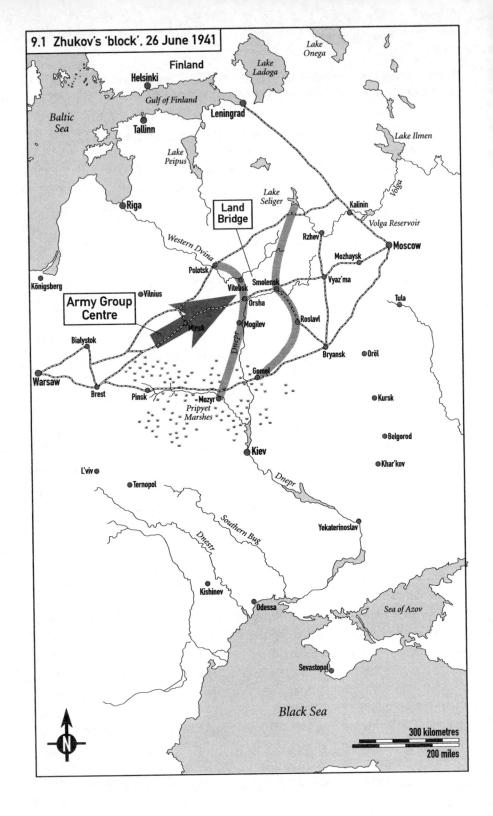

9.1 Zhukov's 'block', 26 June 1941

western Dvina and Dnepr. Some 80 kilometres further east was the second concentric ring or arc, Lake Selizharovo (Seliger) to Smolensk, Roslavl, and Gomel'.

These defensive curves, pivoting on natural defences, appealed to Stalin. The remnants of the armies destroyed in Belarus would fall back on the first line of defence, to be joined by four new armies – the Nineteenth to the Twenty-Second. The Twenty-Fourth and Twenty-Eighth Armies would form on the rear defensive line, to be joined by two new ones.[51]

In forty minutes, Zhukov had served his country well. It was obvious that the main German thrust was heading for Moscow and that was where to put the defences. For the moment, Leningrad and Ukraine had to wait. Stalin agreed to everything. Zhukov left Stalin at 16.10, but returned for an hour at 21.00.

Stalin continued his unforgiving rhythm of work and meetings until 28 June. On 27 and 28 June, however, there were no early-morning or midday meetings. They started at 16.30 and 19.35, respectively, and continued into the small hours. In 1992, the distinguished historian Dr Dmitry Volkogonov told an important Russian TV documentary, *Monster*, that Stalin was not confused or broken by the impact of the initial German attack, but only after the fall of Minsk on 28 June.[52] The absence of Stalin's diary notebooks from the official record for the couple of days after 28 June certainly supports this view. According to Volkogonov, he headed for his dacha, not wanting to see anybody.[53] His working day on 28 June ended at 00.50 on the 29th, after five-and-a-quarter hours. But there was other business to attend to.

The loss of Belarus, which finally became obvious with the first reports of the encirclement and, therefore, imminent fall, of its capital, Minsk, on 28 June, and which were finalized on the morning of 29 June, drove Stalin into a fit of rage. That evening, 29 June, Anastas Mikoyan, the key witness, recalled: 'several members of the Politburo were gathered with Stalin in the Kremlin'.[54] So Stalin *was* still in the Kremlin, although there was no official diary entry.

Mikoyan continued:

> They were all interested in the situation on the western front, especially in Belorussia, where during the previous evening German-Fascist forces had occupied Minsk. Communications with the Belorussian Military District had been interrupted.

No fresh reports about the situation in Belorussia at that time were coming though. What was certain was that there was no contact with the forces on the western front. Stalin rang up Marshal Timoshenko at the People's Commissariat for Defence. However, he could not give any concrete information . . .

Anxious about the developments Stalin suggested to us all that we [Stalin, Malenkov, Mikoyan and Beria] go to the Defence Commissariat and investigate the situation there. In the office with Timoshenko were G. K. Zhukov, N. F. Vatutin and several other generals and officers of the General Staff. The conversation was very grave. Only at that time did Stalin properly understand the whole seriousness of the assessments of the force, time-factor and consequences behind the attack by Hitler's Germany. It was decided to send responsible representatives from the Stavka to establish contact with the Belorussian Military District immediately.[55]

For the first time, Stalin and his political colleagues had stormed round to the General Staff building to visit the military command. Timoshenko and Zhukov stood their ground, nervously, explaining that the reports coming in were contradictory and that they were not yet ready to report. Stalin exploded at Zhukov, then stormed away, realizing that disaster was looming.[56] Of all the catastrophes across the three main fronts, the loss of Belarus – on the direct route to Moscow – was the most critical.

On 29 and 30 June Stalin therefore broke his usual routine, although according to Mikoyan he was not completely absent from his office in the Kremlin. Apart from the unprecedented visit to the military command he had also had to prepare or at least supervise a very important announcement for 30 June and his speech to the Russian people of 3 July. Both of them undoubtedly bear his own hand.[57]

Stalin had certainly coped on 22 June and immediately afterwards. Kaganovich, asked if Stalin had been confused, replied, 'Lies!' 'We met Stalin that night, when Molotov summoned Schulenberg. Stalin gave each of us our tasks. Me – transport. Mikoyan – supply.'[58] Volkogonov suggested that Stalin did suffer a form of breakdown a week later, on 29 and 30 June. However, the fact that Stalin did not continue his usual exhausting schedule of appointments in his office on those days does not mean that he had completely 'lost it'. On the contrary, his surprise visit to the Defence Commissariat on 29 June may well have been productive, and his next moves proved even more so. And if anyone deserved a break, it was Stalin. But, it transpired, the country could not do without him.

These two days, 29 and 30 June, were perhaps the most critical in shaping the Soviet political response to the war, as the early orders to evacuate everything eastwards had been the spark that ignited the slow but relentlessly growing fire of the war economy. At about four in the afternoon of 30 June Vosnesenskiy was in Mikoyan's office.

> Suddenly there was a call from V. M. Molotov's office asking us to go and see him. With Molotov were already several members of the Politburo [Beria, Malenkov]. They were considering a suggestion about the need to create, on the model of the Leninist soviet of Workers' and Peasants' Defence, an extraordinary wartime organ – the State Committee of Defence (GKO), which would have total control of the country.[59]

Either Stalin had to be got back to work, or there would have to be a coup. No one dared suggest the latter, but if ever there was a possibility of Stalin being overthrown, this was it. It was Beria who had suggested the creation of a State Defence Committee with Stalin as chairman. That would remove the need to make Stalin 'commander-in-chief' of the armed forces, which would give him responsibility for the continuing disasters on the western frontiers. Voznesenskiy briefly suggested that Molotov should head it, but no one, apparently, supported him. Beria knew that if Molotov took charge, Stalin – his top cover – was blown, and he would be dead.[60] According to Mikoyan,

> We, together with Voznesenskii, agreed with that recommendation. We all concurred that Stalin should head the GKO. We decided to visit him. He was in his so-called 'nearer' dacha, in the forest of Poklonnaia Gora, where he had been now for several days.
>
> We found Stalin in the small dining room, sitting in an armchair. He looked at us quizzically and asked us 'Why have you come?'. One could sense that he was worried, but that he was taking care to appear calm. Molotov, as our spokesman, said that it was necessary to concentrate the power into one organ that would be called upon to decide all

> the questions of operations and to organise the mobilisation
> of all the country's forces for the resistance against the
> occupiers. That kind of organ had to be headed by Stalin.
>   Stalin looked somewhat astonished but after a short
> pause said:
>   'Very well . . .'[61]

Stalin had probably expected a coup. No wonder Mikoyan could 'sense that he was worried'. Now, he looked surprised and relieved. The most critical moment, for him and his leadership, had passed.

Had Stalin really undergone, or come very close to, a nervous breakdown? The other possibility is that over the previous few days Stalin was testing the loyalty of the other Politburo members, and maybe military commanders as well. Hiding from the responsibilities of power has been a common pose throughout history – Ivan the Terrible, whom Stalin admired and wanted to emulate, had done the same.[62] It was a classic tactic: 'pretend inferiority and encourage his arrogance', as Sun Tzu had said.[63] We will never know for sure. Stalin's hold on power was secure, against a palace coup, at least. But then, there were the Germans.

Organizing war

That evening, 30 June, saw the creation of a war cabinet – the People's Commissariat for Defence (GKO). Like all the most important committees, it was very small, and the order creating it was extremely short.

> In view of the extraordinary situation which has arisen, and
> with the aim of swift mobilisation of all peoples of the USSR
> for the repulse of the enemy the Præsidium of the Supreme
> Soviet, the Central Committee of the Communist Party and
> the Council of People's Commissars have considered it
> necessary:
>   1. To create a State Defence Committee comprising
> comrade I. V. Stalin (President), V. M. Molotov (Deputy
> President), K. E. Voroshilov, G. M. Malenkov, L. P. Beria.

2. To concentrate all State power in the hands of the State Defence Committee.

3. To oblige all citizens and all party, Soviet, youth and military organisations to fulfil the State Defence Committee's decisions and orders unquestioningly.

President of the Supreme Soviet of the USSR M. I. Kalinin

President of the Council of People's Commissars of the USSR and Secretary of the Communist Party Central Committee I. V. Stalin[64]

The Committee therefore had absolute power over everything. Mikoyan says that they considered whether to have five or seven members, and that Stalin thought seven, including Mikoyan and Voznesenskiy, but not all agreed. To speed things up, Mikoyan suggested that he be made a plenipotentiary of GKO with GKO powers in the area of supplies for the front. Voznesenskiy was also left out at this stage, but given responsibility for production of arms and ammunition. Molotov would manage production of tanks, while Malenkov would manage aircraft production.[65] The GKO remained small, although on 3 February 1942 Mikoyan and Vosnesenskiy, the other two members of the group and both key figures in the evacuation and mobilization of industry, were brought in, and on 20 February Kaganovich, likewise. On 22 November 1944 Bulganin was made a member, replacing Voroshilov.[66] The GKO continued in operation until 4 September 1945, two days after the final, formal capitulation of Japan.

The GKO controlled the activities of all Departments and institutions in the USSR, directing their efforts to the 'universal utilization of material, spiritual and military capabilities of the country for victory over the enemy'. GKO instructions had the force of wartime law. The GKO would

> decide questions of restructuring the economy and
> mobilising the human resources of the country for the needs
> of the front and the economy, the preparation of reserves and
> regular staff for the Armed Forces and industry, the
> evacuation of industry from threatened regions, the transfer
> of industrial enterprises back into regions liberated by the
> Red Army and the restoration of the economy in the
> destroyed western regions of the country.[67]

The GKO therefore tasked the Stavka of the Main, soon to be the Supreme, High Command and, through it, the armed forces, at the 'military-political' – that is, politico-strategic – level, determined the structure of the armed forces, set up the command staff and determined how the armed forces were to be used in the war. GKO was particularly concerned with directing the activity of Soviet partisans in occupied areas of the Soviet Union. Its political-strategic focus was mirrored down at local level in more than sixty 'Urban' or 'Municipal' (*gorod-skiye*) Defence Committees (also, coincidentally, or perhaps not, GKO). These committees were set up in cities playing a key role on the front line and sometimes isolated or overrun, including Leningrad, Sevastopol, Tula, Rostov, Stalingrad and Kursk.[68]

Below the newly created GKO, and the Politburo of the Central Committee, Stavka operated. Its job was to evaluate the politico-strategic assessments of GKO, but it was essentially a military-strategic-level organization. Its main task was to create groups of forces and coordinate the operations of groups of fronts, fronts, armies and partisan forces. It also directed the formation and training of strategic reserves and resolved final questions on the armed forces' material and technical support.

Below Stavka came the General Staff which, although immensely expert and powerful, enjoyed only the same weighting as individual fronts. Thus, Stavka made its decisions after discussion with the General Staff and with the relevant front commanders, plus other relevant military, civil and communist party leaders and People's Commissariats (ministries). It was very much an inter-agency effort, and the General Staff, far from being as grand as it sounded, was simply a specialist military advisory group. Partisans, as noted, were controlled directly by Stavka, through the Central Headquarters of the partisan movement.[69]

The 'Boss' speaks

Stalin returned to his more normal routine on 1 July. The next couple of days were preoccupied with the meltdown of the Western Front, which resulted in Stalin's decision to put Timoshenko in direct command there on 2 July. Late the same night, David Ortenberg, the editor of the armed forces' newspaper *Red Star*, received a phone call telling him to 'hold the front page'. He did not have to ask what for.[70] After an absence of twelve days, which gave rise to the numerous accusations that he had 'lost it', Stalin spoke to his people on 3 July.

His speech is extraordinary, because it indicates a complete change in the way Stalin's relationship with the people was portrayed – even though in reality it had not changed at all. The opening phrases are unreal. 'Comrades! Citizens! Brothers and Sisters! Fighters of our Army and Fleet! I address you (*obrashchayushchsya k vam*), my friends!'[71]

The use of the words 'brothers', 'sisters' and 'friends' was highly significant. Stalin had led the country with promises and driven it with whips for more than a decade, but, after a suitably lengthy twelve-day pause, everyone was 'family', now. This change of approach was closely linked with a new emphasis on traditional Russian patriotism.

After the astonishing introduction, Stalin more or less accurately admitted the catastrophic losses of territory – 'Lithuania, western Latvia, western Belarus, part of western Ukraine'. So far, of course, he was talking about territory which had only come under Soviet rule in the previous two years. He quickly moved to the Russian defeat of Napoleon, and also to German defeat in the First World War. Germany had thrown 170 divisions at the USSR – a slight underestimate – but had already lost 'its best divisions and part of its air force' – which was not true. The Molotov–Ribbentrop Pact, he continued, had not been a mistake. Germany had proposed it, and should the Soviet Union have turned it down? He referred to the enslavement of Russian peoples by 'German Princes and Barons', a sentence which has slight similarities with Churchill's 22 June speech referring to 'heel-clicking, dandified Prussian officers'.[72] Stalin stressed the diversity of the peoples of the Soviet Union – Russians, Ukrainians, Belorussians, Lithuanians, Latvians and Estonians, Uzbeks, Tatars, Moldovans, Georgians, Armenians, Azerbaijanis and other 'free peoples'.[73] Stalin demanded the creation of partisan units, operating 'anywhere and everywhere, blowing up bridges, roads, cutting telephone and telegraph communications links, creating forest fires, and incinerating depots and convoys'.[74] What must still have been an unexpected bonus on the diplomatic front did not escape attention. For anyone under siege, a distant drum from outside is welcome. The Soviet war was part of a 'united front of peoples standing for freedom'. Churchill's speech of 22 June, he said, had been historic and the US government offer of help should raise Soviet morale.[75] Finally, following the example of workers in Moscow and Leningrad, a People's Militia (*Narodnoye Opolcheniye*) to support the Red Army needed to be formed in every city.[76]

The reaction was stunned, but not universally and unambiguously favourable. The NKGB immediately reported on the response. The people had certainly been listening very carefully. Factory workers appear to have roused to the call for maximum effort. Rasskazov, working in a plastics factory, said it was a 'warm speech, like a freshly minted coin. Those words – "brothers and sisters" go straight to everyone's heart.' But, the report continued, 'some elements of society' – the better-educated, it seems – appeared determined to 'discredit' Stalin's speech. The creation of a 'universal militia' for those excused military service by virtue of age or disability went down particularly badly with the comfortable middle classes, understandably. Shifman, working at the Institute for World Literature, said, 'It's destruction for everyone. The situation at the front is hopeless. The Kremlin has given instructions to create underground organisations. The situation is so critical that the Party Central Committee has decided to create a universal militia. What does that tell you about the valour of the Red Army? ... that's a step of desperation, a sign of confusion.'[77] A legal adviser, Izraelit, presumably a Jew, said that the Soviet government had 'missed the German offensive on the first day of the war, and this led to the subsequent destruction and colossal losses of aviation and personnel. The partisan movement which Stalin called for – that's a completely ineffective form of warfare. It is a gust of despair. As for hoping for help from Britain and the United States, that's mad. The USSR is in a ring, and we can't see a way out.'[78] Perel'man, an engineer, agreed that 'all these speeches – the mobilisation of the people, the organisation of a militia in the rear, bear witness to extreme hopelessness and won't save the situation. It's obvious that the Germans will soon take Moscow, and that Soviet power will not survive.'[79] Karasik, described as an 'office worker' – said that 'destruction is unavoidable, and the loss of Moscow is inevitable. Everything we've built in the course of the last twenty-five years: it's all a myth. Its destruction is obvious from Stalin's speech, from his despairing slogans.'[80] The 'analysis', signed by Kubatkin, was sent to the Moscow City and Districts Committees of the Communist Party, not the NKVD or NKGB, and perhaps for that reason, the doubters' responses were not suffixed '*arestovan*', although they must have been taking huge risks. Extraordinarily, perhaps, the critical comments might, for the first time, have been taken on board. They reflected 'different evaluations in different levels of Moscow society of Stalin's radio broadcast. However, overall, *the impression presented in the document is favourable.*'[81] The adverse comments certainly reflected informed and critical judgment. Perhaps the system was already starting to learn . . .

Strategic directions

As Stalin spoke, the eastward evacuation of crucial assets from the richest and most productive parts of the Soviet Union – Ukraine, Belarus and the Baltics – continued.[82] However, as well as moving goods east, the Soviets were still trying to move troops, ammunition and fuel west as part of a massive counter-attack plan. On the north-west and western fronts, in the twenty-four hours between 18.00 on 2 July and 3 July, 75 troop and transport trains, including 35 with personnel, were scheduled to leave Moscow.[83] Typically, a troop train might include 2,300 troops.[84] Of these 75 trains, some 38, including 19 with troops, remained 'in transit'. The critical rail junction at Orsha needed 200 fuel wagons (*tsistern*), no doubt for the continued massive armoured counter-attacks which the Soviet command envisaged. Trains heading west through Smolensk were stopped there, and unloaded.[85] It was proving impossible to move in two directions at once.

On 5 July the Council of People's Commissars and the Central Committee – effectively the GKO, although the latter was not mentioned in the report – ordered the evacuation of Soviet state archives from Moscow. They were to be taken to the remote city of Ufa, in the Bashkir (Bashkortostan) Autonomous Soviet Socialist Republic, on the edge of the Urals, 400 kilometres east of Kuybyshev and Kazan', and nearly 1,000 kilometres east of Moscow (see Figure 7.1). The archives of the Council of People's Commissars, the Higher Defence Committee, the Communist Party Central Committee, the Central Committee of the All-Union Leninist Communist Youth Union, the Chinese Communist Party, the Executive Committee of the Communist International (Comintern), the

Institute of Marx, Engels and Lenin and the Committee of State Security were all to go. Once again, the NKVD was in charge. The People's Commissariat for Communications (NKPS) would ensure that enough wagons were made available and Abakumov, Beria's deputy head of the NKVD since February 1941, would guarantee it happened. As with the Kremlin treasures, they had just five days to do it.[86]

The appointment of Timoshenko, the Defence Minister, to command the Western Front marked an undeniable, if informal, shift in the balance of power within the armed forces and the Stavka to Zhukov. For some reason, since the catastrophic events of 22 June, Army General Zhukov's star was in the ascendant. Even when Timoshenko was in Moscow, it was clear that the Chief of the General Staff was the real commander of the armed forces and Stalin's new favourite. Zhukov's spectacular victory at Khalkin Gol had not immunized him against the possibility of disgrace, torture and execution as a German spy, a fate which had befallen and would befall others. But his brusque military manner, ability to get things done, brutal disregard for subordinates' lives or feelings and complete non-sufferance of fools impressed Stalin.

The General Staff building was, and still is, right next to the Ministry of Defence in central Moscow. Zhukov occupied a two-storey suite there. It is still preserved exactly as it was during the war, now surrounded by the offices of the Arms Control Directorate. Downstairs there is a kitchen and a sitting room. Upstairs, his office contains the inevitable huge desk with a dark leather top. Stalin's picture is not behind the desk, but behind the door. The telephone is black, with three quick-dial buttons. Button one is Beria; two is Stalin; three is Mrs Aleksandra Diyevnaya Zhukova, his wife.

In order to provide unity of control over several fronts and other forces such as the Northern, Baltic and Black Sea fleets, operating along a single strategic axis in a single 'theatre of military operations' (*Teatr voyennykh deystviy*), Stalin, probably advised by Shaposhnikov, ordered the creation of three higher-level commands, known as 'Strategic Directions' (*Strategicheskiye napravleniya*).[87]

Voroshilov would command the North-West Strategic Direction which would embrace the Northern and North-Western Fronts and the Baltic and Black Sea fleets. Timoshenko would take the Western Strategic Direction, which at this stage comprised only the Western Front and supporting air and river forces. Budënny would take the South-Western Direction including the South-Western and Southern Fronts and the

Black Sea fleet. The same GKO order also made the Stavka of the Main Command the Stavka of the Supreme Command. Its president would be Stalin, who was also president of the ultimate authority, the GKO, with Molotov, Marshals Timoshenko, Budënny, Voroshilov, and Shaposhnikov and Chief of the General Staff, General Zhukov. The new Strategic Directions were to issue orders to the subordinate fronts and armies forbidding withdrawal from strategic points without permission from the 'High Command' – in other words, from Stavka, which meant Stalin. The Strategic Directions also had responsibility for coordinating partisan operations in the German rear.[88]

The original idea behind the Strategic Directions was sound. As we saw in Chapter 8, the first weeks of the war had seen many instances of Moscow losing contact with fronts and armies, and High Command representatives were sent out to find them. During the first days of the war Stalin had despatched several of his top officers, including Zhukov, to the three front commands to see what was going on. One of them, the incompetent Marshal Kulik, had headed for Tenth Army in the Bialystok pocket and gone missing for several days. An intermediate level of command therefore appeared logical. As communications improved, however, in part because the Red Army was falling back, the intermediate level proved redundant. In practice, Stalin and the Stavka constantly exercised direct command over fronts and even armies, and the new high-level commands to coordinate army groups and fleets (which in modern Nato terms would be 'six-star'!) proved completely superfluous. The fact they were even thought to be necessary is a measure of the vast scale of the theatre of war and the forces involved. During the late 1970s and 1980s, at the very end of the cold war, the Soviet Union reintroduced the level of the Strategic Direction, but, in an era when fronts on the ground and in the lower atmosphere might need to be coordinated with intercontinental missile strikes from submarines and operations in space, that made more sense.

The North-West Strategic Direction, embracing the Baltic States, Finland and the Arctic, was abolished on 27 August 1941. The South-Western Strategic Direction lasted until 21 June 1942, while the Western was abolished on 10 September 1941. On 1 February 1942 the Western Strategic Direction was reconstituted, in order to control and coordinate forces operating in that theatre more closely. It lasted until 5 May 1942.[89] From a historiographical point of view, it should be added, there are very few, if any, records and statistics presented in terms of the

Strategic Directions' responsibilities. All the accounts and figures relate to armies, fleets and fronts. The appointment of three future leaders of the Soviet Communist Party as the 'Members of the Military Council' acting as commissars to the Direction commanders reinforces the concept of the Strategic Direction as more of a politico-strategic level. Andrey Zhdanov (1896–1948) was the Party chief for the North-Western Direction, Nikolay Bulganin (1895–1975) for the Western and Nikita Khrushchev (1894–1971) for the South-Western.

Reunification of the NKVD

As we saw in Chapter 4, the NKVD had split into two People's Commissariats – the NKVD and NKGB – on 1 March 1941. The latter did foreign espionage, but also VIP security in the Soviet Union and a lot of home counter-intelligence and surveillance work, including vox pops[90] on what people thought of Stalin's 3 July speech. There was also the Military Intelligence Directorate of the Red Army – the GRU – which had to beg Beria to pass on captured German radios and codes – and the Third Directorate of the People's Commissariat for Defence, which did counter-espionage and counter-subversion within the armed forces.[91] The latter duplicated a lot of NKVD work.

On 17 July the State Defence Committee (in other words, Stalin) ordered that the 'special departments' of the Third Directorate be transferred to the NKVD. They would continue to hunt deserters and root out spies, and would draw any armed detachments they needed from the NKVD.[92] On 20 July, the Presidium of the Supreme Soviet issued an *ukaz* – an order – amalgamating the NKVD and NKGB into a single People's Commissariat, to be known, once again, as the NKVD. The change from peacetime to wartime conditions, it said, had made it 'expedient'. Given the chaotic situation in the front-line areas, plus the pressure of work, NKGB staff carried on using their former titles and documentation for some time.[93] However, they may have gained some comfort from knowing that, once again, they now formed part of a single Security Ministry, headed by the same dedicated boss: Lavrenty Pavlovich Beria.[94]

A far country[95]

As the traumatized Soviet system shuddered on its axis, the all-powerful GKO authorized a mission to Russia's old allies, the British. After combining to beat Napoleon, the British and the Russians had fallen out over Imperial Russian ambitions in the Middle East and central Asia, but came together again as allies in 1907 and during the First World War. The Russian contribution to Alliance strategy from 1914 to 1916 had been stupendous. They had fallen out again in 1918 after the 1917 Russian Revolutions. Churchill had been instrumental in trying to strangle the Bolshevik state at birth, but failed. While there was a strong 'hands off Russia' movement, the murder of the British King George V's cousin, Tsar Nicholas II, his haemophiliac heir, and his spectacularly beautiful and photogenic wife and daughters did not help the Bolshevik cause.

Suspicion, distrust and cynical manipulation were still in the air. But on 23 June the NKGB reported that the Chief of the British Air Staff, Sir Charles Portal, had suggested cabling the commands in India and the Middle East ordering them to stop planning to bomb the Baku oilfields, which, it had been feared, might be used to supply the Germans.[96] Now Lt Gen. Filipp Golikov, head of Soviet military intelligence, was in charge of a mission to the UK. His deputies were Rear-Admiral Nikolay Kharlamov, for naval affairs, and Colonel Grigory Pugachëv – a good old Russian rebel's name – for air force matters. The USSR Defence Attaché to the UK, Colonel Ivan Sklyarov, was also a member of the mission. Other members were Colonel Vasiliy Dragun – inevitably a member of the Red Army Intelligence Department, Major Boris Shvetsov, the Military Attaché's assistant, and Major Aleksandr Sizov, another spook – who had served in the General Staff Intelligence Directorate from June 1938. They went to request aid to the USSR.[97] All things considered, it was a relatively low-powered mission, but it was a start. On 12 July, with Stalin present, Molotov and Cripps, the British Ambassador to Moscow, signed a brief and very general agreement to provide each other 'help and support of any kind in the present war against Nazi Germany'.[98] In addition to Stalin, Admiral Kuznetsov, the

Commander of the Soviet navy, and Shaposhnikov, were present on the Soviet side. The British military delegation was headed by Lt Gen. Macfarlane, the British Defence Attaché, and included Cadbury, the head of the Economic Mission, plus the Naval and Air Attachés and other embassy staff. It would always be an uneasy alliance.

10

WINNING ONESELF TO DEATH

The Battle of Smolensk,
10 July to 10 September 1941

On 3 July 1941, eleven days into the war, Halder wrote in his diary that the objective of shattering the Soviet army on the western side of the Dvina and Dnepr had been accomplished. That was just a little premature.

East of those rivers, he thought the Germans would encounter 'nothing more than partial forces'. It was 'probably no overstatement to say to say that the Russian Campaign has been won in the space of two weeks'.[1] In fact the partisans stirring in the forest and the Pripyet swamps, and other large bodies of encircled troops would delay and divert the Germans' forward drive. It was particularly hard for Halder and his fellow German leaders, schooled in a world where people accepted the results of the big battles, to come to terms with this kind of warfare. Stalin's speech, on the same day, clearly showed that organized operations behind German lines were not only being prepared, but would be a major part of the Soviet war effort. For the Germans, dealing with the partisans and remnants of surrounded Russian forces was left to the army commands and subordinate headquarters. The danger represented by the partisan units operating behind German lines was not yet understood and Halder still refused to consider it a serious threat.[2] As Halder later justified it to himself in conventional military terms, on 26 July, the Red Army could not be defeated by such operational manoeuvres in big battles 'because they simply do not know when they have been defeated'.[3]

Statements by Hitler and Halder around this time show that they both considered the back of Soviet military resistance to be broken. On

4 July Hitler thought that the 'most difficult decision of the war' would be to weaken the centre in order to be able to send armoured groups to Leningrad and into Ukraine – indicating that he had no doubt of ultimate victory, merely about the order in which to approach the various objectives.[4] On 8 July, as the 'border battles' phase was drawing to a close, the Germans assessed that out of 164 enemy formations identified, 89 could be counted as destroyed, including 20 out of 29 armoured divisions encountered. The euphoria would not last.[5]

Army Group Centre's battle for the Bialystok pocket ended on 2 July, although some Soviet forces held out in the Novogrudek-Volkovysk area and tried to break out east. They finally surrendered on 5 July.[6] Panzer Groups Two and Three moved on the Dnepr, and into the 'land bridge' – the 'dry gap between the Dnepr and the Dvina'[7] – which Zhukov had decided to block. Stavka had ordered the western Dvina and Dnepr to be defended on 4 July, and on 6 July launched another massive counterstroke with V and VII Mechanized Corps of Twenty-Second Army, which crashed into XXXIX and XXXXVII Panzer Corps. After five days of ferocious and confused fighting the Soviets had lost 832 out of 2,000 tanks engaged. However, the Germans still found that they could not deal with the new T-34s and KV-1s, and the attack of Soviet Major-General Kreyser's 1st Motor-Rifle Division was stopped only by the lucky – for the Germans – appearance of the Luftwaffe's only squadron of tank-busting aircraft in existence at the time.[8]

Having devoted itself to the destruction of the Soviet air force, on the ground and, occasionally, in the air, for the first three days of the war, on 25 June the Luftwaffe had begun its second major task – direct and indirect support of the ground forces. The Russian air forces continued to attack in ways which Field Marshal Albert Kesselring, the commander of Luftflotte 2, described as 'a slaughter of innocents', while it was clear that the Russians had totally different concepts of 'the value of human life'.[9] However, in spite of spectacular success rates – though they were less successful in the air than in their initial surprise attack – the Luftwaffe could not sustain operations of such intensity and therefore now relegated combat in the air to the sideline, and concentrated on supporting the German ground troops.[10]

The Battle of Smolensk (Figure 10.1) officially began on 10 July, when Guderian's forces crossed the Dnepr. On 11 July the Soviet V and VII Mechanized Corps fell back across the river to avoid being cut off. On the same day Lt Gen. Ivan Koniev's Nineteenth Army launched a

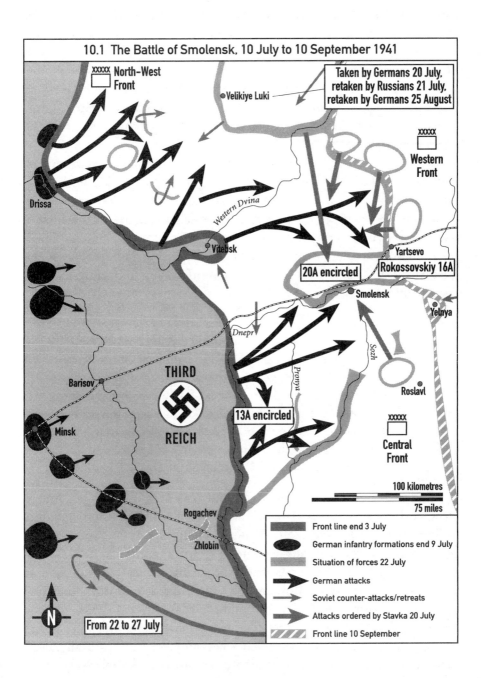

10.1 The Battle of Smolensk, 10 July to 10 September 1941

North-West Front

Velikiye Luki

Taken by Germans 20 July, retaken by Russians 21 July, retaken by Germans 25 August

Western Front

Drissa

Western Dvina

Vitebsk

20A encircled

Yartsevo

Rokossovskiy 16A

Smolensk

Yelnya

Dnepr

Barisov

THIRD REICH

Sozh

Pronya

Roslavl

13A encircled

Minsk

Central Front

100 kilometres

75 miles

Rogachev

Zhlobin

Front line end 3 July

German infantry formations end 9 July

Situation of forces 22 July

German attacks

Soviet counter-attacks/retreats

Attacks ordered by Stavka 20 July

Front line 10 September

N

From 22 to 27 July

counter-attack straight from the trains in which they had been brought up to the front, but after two days Koniev's army had fallen apart. Not a promising beginning for the general who would race Zhukov for the Reichstag.

On 12 July Stavka directed Timoshenko's two-day-old Western Strategic Direction (which, unlike the other Strategic Directions, comprised little more than the Western Front), to launch a counterstroke northwards from Smolensk and Orsha towards Vitebsk. The attack was to be supported by all the Front aircraft and also long-range bombers, which came under the control of the Strategic Direction. No fewer than six armies were to attack in a coordinated fashion. Although, once again, the Soviet plan proved overambitious, and many of the formations were well under strength – some of the divisions numbered fewer than 3,000 men each – it nevertheless made a big impression on the Germans, who called it the 'Timoshenko offensive'. According to Guderian, commanding Second Panzer,

> Since July 13th the Russians have been launching heavy
> counterattacks. Some twenty enemy divisions moved from
> the direction of Gomel' against the right flank of my Panzer
> Group, while the Russians encircled in Mogilev and Orsha
> attempted simultaneously to break out, the former garrison
> in a south and southeasterly direction, the latter toward the
> south. All of these operations were controlled by Marshal
> Timoshenko with the obvious objective of belatedly
> frustrating our successful crossing of the Dnepr.[11]

Guderian and Hoth elbowed off the Soviet counterstrokes, but at great cost to themselves. By 16 July, 18th Panzer Division had just twelve operational tanks left. The casualties had to be reduced, its commander noted, 'if we do not intend to win ourselves to death'.[12]

On 13 July German forces had reached the critical rail junction at Orsha, where the main Minsk–Moscow line crossed another line running south from Leningrad through Vitebsk. It was here, on the following day, that the Soviets revealed a new 'secret weapon'. Series production of the BM-13 multiple rocket-launcher had, ironically, been authorized on 21 June, the day before Barbarossa. The relatively crude machine, with sixteen 132mm rockets fired from two rows of rails on the back of a truck, and with an armoured shield protecting the cab, became a symbol of Russia's war. Because of the sound the rockets made, as well as the arrangement of the sixteen rails or 'pipes', the Germans called it 'Stalin's organ'. The Russians called it *Katyusha* – 'Little Kate'. The battery commander, Captain Flёrov, recalled 'results excellent. *Solid sea of fire.*' They were later surrounded and torched the new engines of war to prevent them falling into enemy hands. *Katyusha* remained a very jealously guarded secret, and pictures of the machines are very rare before and even during the Battle of Stalingrad at the end of 1942.[13]

Guderian's forces captured the city of Smolensk itself on 15 July but a large gap between the two Panzer Groups remained north and east of the city. By 20 July Guderian's thrust to the south of Smolensk and Hoth's to the north threatened to encircle the bulk of three Soviet armies – Sixteenth, Nineteenth and Twentieth – in a pocket north-east of the city. The shape of the pocket was partly determined by the marshes to the north and north-west of Smolensk. That day Zhukov ordered the Western Strategic Direction to organize a counteroffensive including four armies from Stavka's strategic reserve, in order to rescue Soviet forces which were nearly trapped. Timoshenko's forces would be divided into four 'operational groups' known by the names of their commanders. There was also a fifth, under Rokossovskiy, who had just been promoted to command Sixteenth Army after his IX Corps had successfully bloodied the Germans in the battles on the South-Western Front. Rokossovskiy's army was defending the Yartsevo area, where the main Minsk–Smolensk–Moscow railway crosses the River Vop, which flows south into the Dnepr.

The five Soviet groups would attack concentrically, towards the encircled Soviet forces. The Germans continued eastwards, and Rokossovskiy was in the thick of the fighting. He held the Germans from 18 to 23 July and counter-attacked on the 24th, all the time managing to keep in contact with the three Soviet armies in the pocket. General Kurochkin, commanding Twentieth Army, took overall command of the forces there and managed to keep the Germans back and the mouth of the pocket open until 26 July when the Germans linked up east of the city. However, the Soviet counter-attacks enabled more than 100,000 of the Soviet forces by 4 August to break out eastwards, where Rokossovskiy was holding the line at Yartsevo.[14] The Luftwaffe fought back furiously, against 'a group of enemy forces attacking across the Vop, a situation which endangered not only the army units but also the command post of the air corps [VIII] itself east of Dukhovshchina, as well as several of its airfields'.[15] The ex-convict 'dagger' was striking back hard at high-value German targets.

The Luftwaffe had tried to close the gap, but failed. Insufficient aircraft were available and paratroops, who could have closed the gap, 'were no longer to be dropped from the air after their heavy losses on Crete [May 1941]'. The gap could therefore be closed by day only, until the pocket was finally considered closed on 5 August.[16]

Tactical aviation was proving to be a key player on both sides. In spite of appalling losses, Soviet ground-attack planes flying singly or in pairs at very low level caused considerable psychological stress. The German fighters usually arrived too late to catch them and could not pursue because they were not heavily armoured (unlike the Soviet Il-2 Shturmoviks) and at very low level would meet massive small-arms fire from Soviet troops on the ground. The Germans were therefore ordered to strengthen their own low-level air defences with additional machine guns, as the Russians had done right from the start. This happened all along the eastern front. The Luftwaffe was also tasked to knock out Soviet 'monitors' – shallow-draught gunboats on the rivers – especially south of the Pripyet marshes. The fighting on the eastern front under-lined the need for the Luftwaffe's own ground support troops to be extremely well trained, since in order for the short-range aircraft to keep up with the rapidly advancing ground troops, they had to set up new airfields quickly, establish all-round defence not only against air attack but also against Soviet partisans and stragglers, and install communications. There was no 'front line'.[17]

On 29 July units of the Soviet Western Front and the Western Strategic Direction were unified in in a single 'Western Front', with Marshal Timoshenko, now deputy Commissar for Defence, as commander of both the Western Front and the Western Strategic Direction. Yeremenko became Timoshenko's deputy for the Western Front. The Central Front would report directly to Stavka.[18]

On 31 July Guderian retaliated against the most successful of the Soviet Groups, Group Kachalov, south of Smolensk, and destroyed it. However, the terrible casualties and the constant strain of repelling determined Soviet counter-attacks was beginning to tell on the German army. By 30 July the fierce Soviet resistance had had a significant strategic effect. Hitler's Führer Directive No. 33 of 19 July had reiterated his, and OKH's, determination to 'prevent the escape of large enemy forces into the depths of Russian territory and to annihilate them'. However, this directive halted the drive towards Moscow and reinforced the thrusts towards Leningrad and into Ukraine. A supplementary directive of 23 July assigned Panzer Group Three to Army Group North for the attack on Leningrad. On 30 July Hitler issued Directive No. 34 which reflected the critical effect of the Battle of Smolensk. 'The appearance of large enemy forces before the front, the supply situation and the necessity of giving the Second and Third Panzer Groups ten days to restore their formations has forced a temporary postponement of the fulfilment of the aims and missions set forth in Directive No. 33.' Therefore, it ordered, *'Army Group Centre will go on the defence.'*[19]

The colossal Soviet effort on the main axis towards Moscow had forced Hitler to divert his main effort to Leningrad in the north and Ukraine in the south. The Germans did not carry out any major attacks eastwards in the area of the land bridge for two months. Besides the ferocity of Soviet resistance and resilience, the Germans were beginning to feel the tyranny of logistics, running out of fuel and ammunition as their supply lines stretched and the Soviets' got shorter.[20] Second Panzer Group's bridgehead over the Desna at Yel'nya was 720 kilometres from the nearest railway dropping-off point ('railhead'). Even more critically, the three German Army Groups on the 1,800-kilometre Baltic to Black Sea front had suffered 213,301 casualties, prisoners and missing in the first six weeks, until 31 July, and only received 47,000 new troops.[21] The Soviets had suffered almost ten times as many irrecoverable losses – 2,129,677 – by 30 September, but, unlike the Germans', the losses seemed not to count. 'We have underestimated the Russian colossus,' wrote Halder on 11 August. '[Its] divisions are not armed and equipped according to our standards, and their tactical leadership is often poor. But there they are . . .' The Soviets were near their own bases, while the Germans were moving further away from theirs. And their troops were 'sprawled over an incessant line without any depth'.[22] The 'funnel' effect, explained in Chapter 7, was beginning to tell.

At the time, neither the Germans nor the Soviets realized how critical the battle would later prove to be. The Germans' decision to go on to the defensive could have brought welcome relief from the slaughter being suffered by the Soviet forces, but, obsessed with the pre-war doctrine of the offensive, Stavka ordered more massive counterattacks. From 30 August to 8 September three fronts launched the Smolensk counteroffensive. Timoshenko, commanding the Western

Strategic Direction and also the Western Front, would cut German communications west of Smolensk and recapture the city. He would cooperate with Zhukov, who had been fired as Chief of the General Staff on 29 July after arguing with Stalin over the need to evacuate Kiev. Zhukor was sent to command the newly created Reserve Front, which would now wipe out the Yel'nya bridgehead established by Second Panzer Group and advance level with the Western Front. Yeremenko's newly created Bryansk Front would attack Guderian's Panzer Group head-on and destroy it.[23] Stavka hoped, if not to take Guderian's attack on Kiev in the flank, at least to force it to divert its attention.

The Germans were not sure whether to hold the Yel'nya bridgehead or not. With the start of air attacks on Moscow on the night of 21 to 22 July, Luftflotte 2 could no longer carry out all tasks at the same time and Kesselring had diverted II Air Corps to support the southern wing of the Army Group. For this 'high-handed' action he was criticized. Only when he heard that the Yel'nya bridgehead might have to be given up did he agree to provide air support from 30 August until the Germans finally evacuated it on 6 September.[24] Kesselring's decision proved correct as only a tactical defensive success could be hoped for in the Yel'nya bridgehead, whilst the continued commitment of the bulk of II Air Corps to Second Panzer and Second Army enabled the Germans to destroy the Soviet wedge separating Army Groups Centre and South and to establish the jumping-off point for Guderian's swing down as one pincer of the encirclement of massive Soviet forces east of the Dnepr (see below).

Meanwhile Zhukov continued to attack, widening his Front's mission on 21 and 25 August when he ordered it to attack Velizh, Demidov and Smolensk. The Germans encircled Twenty-Second Army in the Velikiye Luki area, but the Thirtieth Army came to its aid and on 29 August smashed through German defences near Velizh. In a classic Russian move, Major-General Lev Dovator's Cavalry Group, comprising two divisions (50th and 53rd), galloped through the breach, and ran amok in the German rear areas, tying down three German divisions for more than a week.[25] The Soviet Smolensk counteroffensive battle continued until 8 September when the Russians reached the Ustrom and Striana rivers. The Germans were well dug in and the Russians suffered heavy losses. Shaposhnikov, who had taken over again as Chief of the General Staff, ordered the offensive halted on 10 September. In a classic First World War image, he noted, sadly, 'the enemy has withdrawn to prepared defensive positions and our units are being forced to gnaw their way through them'.[26]

It was at this time that the NKVD first became aware of a widespread German practice of using children and youths as spies, presumably because they thought their movements would attract less attention. On 4 September the Smolensk NKVD reported several cases of boys between 13 and 18 years old being recruited by the Germans and paid between 2,000 and 5,000 roubles to cross the permeable 'front lines' to give details of Red Army units and airfields. Movements of children and youths should therefore be 'carefully checked'.[27]

On 7 September Zhukov, commanding the Reserve Front from his headquarters at Novo-Aleksandrovsk, signed an order to all his officers and men containing a word seldom seen in Russian despatches so far:

> After unrelenting and bitter battles, brave units of our
> Twenty-Fourth Army have achieved a great *victory*. In the
> Yel'nya region German forces have been dealt a crushing
> blow. The enemy has been beaten . . .[28]

The appearance of the word *victory* was highly significant. Zhukov claimed to have defeated eight German divisions including one SS, and to have inflicted 75,000 to 80,000 casualties on the Germans, killed and wounded.[29] But the cost was terrible for the Russians as well. From 30 August to 8 September the Reserve Front alone suffered 10,701 irrecoverable losses out of 103,200 engaged.[30]

Smolensk was therefore a strategically critical battle, since it forced the Germans to change their objective from Moscow to Leningrad and Ukraine. In itself, it was the first engagement of the war which the Russians rate as deserving the title of a great 'Battle' – an operational level battle, or *srazheniye* – which, as much as any battle can be, was self-contained. During the sixty-three days of the operation, although there were short pauses, one side or the other was always struggling for the initiative. It was by far the biggest concentration of forces on either side at that point in the war. The Battle of Smolensk straddled 600 to 650 kilometres of front, and the Soviet forces retreated 200 to 250 kilometres. On the Soviet side, in addition to the headquarters of the Central, Reserve and Bryansk (from 14 August) Fronts, 9 army headquarters, 59 divisions and 2 brigades were employed.[31]

The overall casualties on both sides were staggering. From 10 July to 10 September, according to the Russian estimates, the Soviet Western

Front suffered 309,959 irrecoverable losses out of 579,400 committed to battle. In addition, there were 159,625 sick and wounded, giving a total of more than 80 per cent.[32] At first the Germans, and then the Russians, faced the endemic eastern front problem of 'open flanks'. Until now, the German attack had been forced into two lanes by the Pripyet marshes. Now, they could come together. The Soviet counter-attacks were on an even bigger scale than before, and it was the first time that Soviet troops had penetrated prepared German defences and recaptured substantial chunks of territory. It was also the first time that cavalry divisions were thrown into breaches hacked in German lines, and were able to conduct substantial raiding operations in the enemy rear.

Adjusting to circumstances

Both military systems were adjusting. The Germans changed their strategic plan in response to the resolute Soviet resistance. The Soviets adjusted their organization in response to brutal reality. It was clear that inexperienced Soviet officers could not control massive formations and that, at the lower level, there were too many tiers of command. On 15 July, five days after the Battle of Smolensk began, Stavka Directive No. 01 ordered the abolition of the rifle corps level. Field armies would control divisions directly. As so many troops had been wiped out, the armies were made smaller. Each would control maybe five or six divisions – the limit of the 'span of control' of the human brain, plus one or two cavalry divisions and several artillery regiments. The divisions themselves were also much smaller. The authorized strength was reduced from 14,400 to under 11,000, but in reality, many had as few as 3,000 men. The number of artillery guns and trucks, on paper (not in reality) decreased by 24 per cent and 64 per cent as a result. Many divisions were clearly not divisions at all and were redesignated brigades. Later, and in the next year, 1942, Stavka formed 170 rifle brigades of 4,400 men each (officially), instead of rifle divisions. The great mechanized corps, originally intended to have more than 1,000 tanks each, which had blundered into action, probably in premature implementation of an incomplete pre-emptive strike plan, were abolished. Directive No. 01 dispersed the corps' rifle divisions to rifle armies and the tank divisions became independent, with a reduced strength of just 217 tanks each – again, on paper. The losses of armour had been so high that, once again, brigades were formed, some with as few as 50 tanks.

And, paradoxically, in what is sometimes erroneously perceived as a mechanized war, cavalry units were expanded. Sometimes, cavalry could be hurled into a breach and exploited far and wide behind German lines. Cavalry units started to become particularly successful after the freeze set in, during the Battle of Moscow (see Chapter 12). Some 30 new light cavalry 'divisions' of 3,447 horsemen (officially) were created.[33] In the winter of 1941–2, when the cold and deep snow often immobilized armoured formations, cavalry could still operate.

Although the Soviet Union possessed 'strategic' long-range aviation, it had proved relatively ineffective in the opening phases of Barbarossa and there were more pressing priorities than taking the war to the German homeland. The Strategic Long-Range Air Command was abolished. Tactical aviation, subordinated to fronts, was, like the ground forces, broken up into smaller units – regiments of 30, rather than 60, aircraft.

These reforms were in part a reaction to what had happened to the Red Army and air forces on and over the battlefield. But they were also a very rational response to what inexperienced Soviet commanders could realistically control. Having acquired experience with brigades, and very 'light' divisions, the survivors – and they were few enough – might graduate to something bigger as the industry which had migrated east geared up and started to produce more and better tanks, guns and aircraft, and the new draft turned out more soldiers. It was an instinctive response, and owed as much to luck and instinct as to judgement. But there was judgement, too.

As we saw in Chapter 8, the German advance through the Baltic States moved relatively quickly, partly due to the spontaneous revolt of people occupied by the Soviet Union only the year before. In spite of the numbers of troops involved, they still did not saturate the area, and it was possible to hide in the extensive forests. Märja Talvi was six years old when the Germans arrived, living with her family on a prosperous farm south of Tallinn. She recalled Red Army troops withdrawing north up the main road, about 500 metres from the farm, and then German planes strafing them.

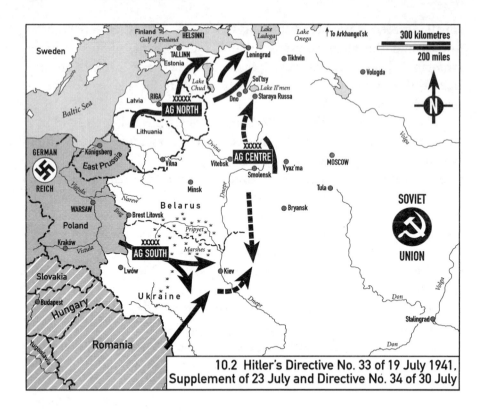

10.2 Hitler's Directive No. 33 of 19 July 1941, Supplement of 23 July and Directive No. 34 of 30 July

We were running. I was wearing a dark red skirt. We ran, and behind us the bombs were falling. We ran into the forest. We stayed there three days. We buried the best things. Then my father and uncle climbed the trees to see if the coast was clear. After three days we went back to the farm. The Germans had been there. It was obvious. They had jam – well, probably Germans, but I am not absolutely sure.[34]

On 10 July 1941 some forty-two men of an Estonian commando group called Erna, trained in Helsinki, landed by parachute in Estonia, this time in agreement with the Germans. Another seventeen landed on 28 July. Initially they signalled intelligence to the Germans and began liaison with the 'forest brothers' already operating in the area. However, on 4 August they received orders to break out of the rear areas still held by the Soviets and to cross the front line and join the Germans. Other Estonian groups also operated during August, but after the seizure of Tallinn on 28 August most of them were disbanded. Erna was disbanded on 10 October. It has been estimated that there were about 12,000 active guerrillas in Estonia in summer 1941. While this may seem insignificant compared with the numbers employed on the eastern front, these were operating behind Soviet lines and providing crucial intelligence to the Germans. The guerrillas made up about 1.1 per cent of the Estonian population, which is fairly standard for guerrilla movements: rather more than the 0.5 to 1 per cent of the South Vietnamese population who belonged to the Vietcong, and slightly fewer than the 2 per cent of Afghans who actively resisted the Soviet Union in Afghanistan.[35]

Where Estonia was occupied by German forces, guerrilla action against the Soviet forces did not cease immediately. As in the areas of Army Groups Centre and South, Red Army units were left behind and Estonian guerrillas were ideally placed to deal with them. After the fall of Tallinn, groups of Soviet forces, each several hundred strong, tried to get across the River Narva and back into Russia. The Estonian 'home guards' were engaged against such forces and also hunted down Soviet stay-behind parties. By the end of 1941, they had reportedly captured 20,989 Red Army soldiers and 5,646 Soviet partisans and intelligence agents.[36]

The main German forces continued to make fast progress through the Baltic States, but as they simultaneously moved north-north-east into Russia itself, resistance stiffened. On 13 July XXXXI Motorized Corps reached the Luga river, about 96 kilometres south of Leningrad, and on the same day the 8th Panzer Division of Leeb's Army Group North had reached Sol'tsy, about 40 kilometres east of Lake Il'men. Here there was a Soviet counter-attack organized by Lt Gen. Nikolay Vatutin, Chief-of-Staff of the Soviet North-Western Front. The Russians cut 8th Panzer off from its neighbours, 3rd Motorized and SS *Totenkopf* (Death's Head) Divisions, and trapped it for four days. Considerable German forces had to be diverted to rescue it. Vatutin's counterstroke may have held up the German advance for three weeks.[37] Ultimately, the counterstroke failed in its objective of destroying 8th Panzer, and Voroshilov, commanding the North-Western Strategic Direction, which embraced the North-Western and Northern Fronts and the Baltic and Northern fleets, reinforced Soviet positions along the Luga.

Hitler's Directive No. 33 of 19 July had shifted the main emphasis of the German attack towards Leningrad, and the supplement issued on 23 July stressed that it should be captured before Moscow (see Figure 10.2). On 8 August Leeb was ordered to encircle the city and link up

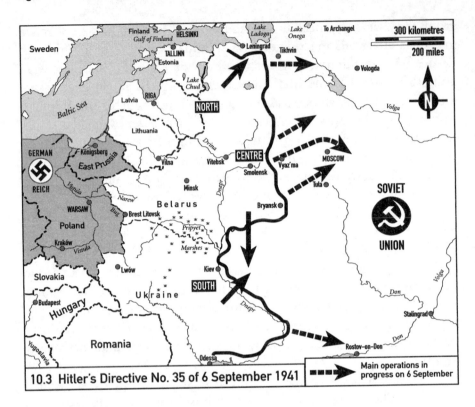

10.3 Hitler's Directive No. 35 of 6 September 1941 ▪▪▪▶ Main operations in progress on 6 September

with the Finns on the other side of the Gulf of Finland. That was what Stavka expected and it ordered yet another counterstroke to destroy German forces in the regions of Sol'tsy, Staraya Russa and Dno (see Figure 10.2). It started on 12 August but failed. When the Germans tried to retaliate with their own renewed attack on 25 August, they were delayed by heavy rain, but nevertheless, by the end of the month they had captured Demyansk.[38] By 24 August the Germans had cut the railway line from Moscow to Leningrad, a route similar in length and importance to the main lines from London to Edinburgh or Glasgow.[39]

The German Army Group North's attack was supported by Luftflotte I, which on 27 June had smashed a Soviet counter-attack by 200 tanks near Šiauliai in Lithuania. After Army Group North had moved through the old Soviet frontier fortifications on the line from Narva south through Lake Peipus (Chud) to Daugavpils, and on to the line Pochka–Ostrov–Pskov–Tartu, I Air Corps units were moved up to Daugavpils and Riga. The Russians attacked the German bridgehead over the Velikaya river at Ostrov on 6 July, losing 65 out of 75 bombers.

From then until the middle of August the Russians refrained from major air attacks. The road from Pskov, north along the east coast of Lake Peipus to Gdo, was controlled by Soviet stragglers and by Soviet units still hidden in the dark and extensive forests. Transport aircraft were therefore largely responsible for getting supplies up to the Germans advancing on Leningrad. The Soviet airfield at Bologoye, 320 kilometres east of Pskov and 300 kilometres south-east of Leningrad, was an especially important target.

Luftflotte 2, reinforced by the addition of VIII Air Corps, supported the breakthrough of Soviet fortifications at Luga and the advance of the German Eighteenth Army towards Novgorod. Hitler issued extremely precise instructions about the use of air forces, with which Reichsmarschall Göring, head of the Luftwaffe, obviously agreed. He had to. On 15 August the German I Army Corps captured Novgorod, supported by VIII Air Corps. On 28 August the Germans took Tallinn, in combination with I Air Corps under the Air Commander Baltic. Up to 23 August, Luftflotte I reported destroying 2,541 Soviet aircraft with another 433 'probables'. In addition, aircraft commanded by the Air Leader Baltic, who was in charge of maritime air operations, had flown 1,775 sorties by 31 August and destroyed 58 Soviet aircraft with a loss of 20 of their own – a far less favourable kill ratio than the Luftwaffe was used to on the eastern front.[40]

The Red Banner Baltic fleet had been encircled in Tallinn on the landward side, and the order to evacuate was not given until 28 August – the day the city fell. Around 67 vessels attempted to break out. Some 33 made it to Kronshtadt or Leningrad. The other 34 were sunk by air attack, torpedoes or gunfire, or ran into mines. But even though Luftflotte I had sunk or damaged numerous Soviet warships and merchant ships, it had not been able to prevent the withdrawal of half of the Soviet Baltic fleet to Leningrad and its island fortress shield, Kronshtadt. Luftflotte I also played an important part in the German defensive battle south of Staraya Russa, 250 kilometres south of Leningrad and 200 east of Pskov, which lasted until 24 August.[41]

Faced with the collapse of its forces before Leningrad, on 23 August Stavka split the Northern Front into two: the Leningrad and the Karelian. On 27 August it terminated the brief existence of Voroshilov's North-Western Strategic Direction and took direct charge of the Leningrad, Karelian and North-Western Fronts.

The Tsarist capital of St Petersburg, renamed Petrograd in 1914 in

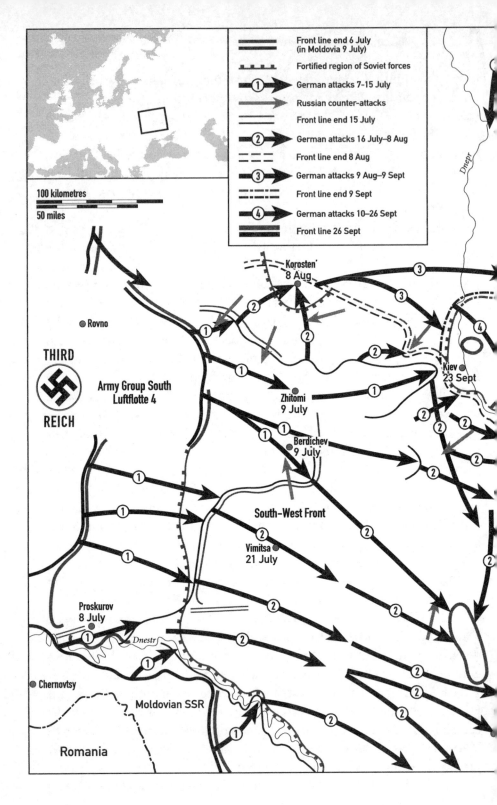

Front line end 6 July
(in Moldovia 9 July)

Fortified region of Soviet forces

(1) German attacks 7–15 July

Russian counter-attacks

Front line end 15 July

(2) German attacks 16 July–8 Aug

Front line end 8 Aug

(3) German attacks 9 Aug–9 Sept

Front line end 9 Sept

(4) German attacks 10–26 Sept

Front line 26 Sept

100 kilometres

50 miles

Dnepr

Rovno

THIRD

REICH

Army Group South
Luftflotte 4

Korosten'
8 Aug

Zhitomi
9 July

Kiev
23 Sept

Berdichev
9 July

South–West Front

Vimitsa
21 July

Proskurov
8 July

Dnestr

Chernovtsy

Moldovian SSR

Romania

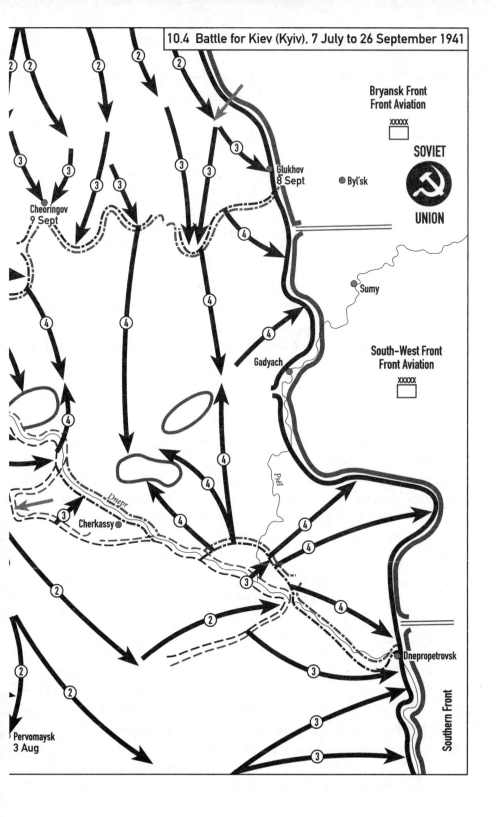

10.4 Battle for Kiev (Kyiv), 7 July to 26 September 1941

Bryansk Front
Front Aviation

SOVIET
UNION

Glukhov
8 Sept

Byl'sk

Cheoringov
9 Sept

Sumy

South-West Front
Front Aviation

Gadyach

Psël

Dnepr

Cherkassy

Dnepropetrovsk

Southern Front

Pervomaysk
3 Aug

255

an anti-German gesture, and Leningrad on that great man's death in 1924, has always had a unique character, to which the '900 days' of the great siege which was about to begin have added a terrible gravitas. During the 900-day siege, from September 1941 to January 1944, the attacking German troops still often referred to it as 'Petersburg'. As Petrograd, the stunningly beautiful 'Venice of the North', it had been the cradle of the 1917 Russian Revolutions – one reason why Hitler hated the place so much.

The first German long-range artillery shell fell on Leningrad on 1 September. By 8 September the Germans had captured Shlisselburg on the south shore of Lake Ladoga – more like an inland sea than a lake – to the east of the city. Leningrad was cut off by the Germans to the south, and threatened by the Finns from the north. A German signal that day confirmed that there was no land communication with the Russian hinterland.[42] The epic Siege of Leningrad had begun. Although the front around the city did not stabilize until the end of September, when the 'Leningrad Strategic Defensive Operation' ended, the great city's story from this point on is told in Chapter 13.[43]

On 5 September Halder wrote that as far as Leningrad was concerned, 'our objective has been achieved. Will become a subsidiary theatre of operations.'[44] There was no point in expending men and material in a costly assault on an urban area, so the Germans decided to starve Leningrad into submission instead. Had they moved faster in late July, when its defences were disorganized, they might have captured the city. But as they moved forward, they slowed down. In mid July, XLI Panzer Corps of Panzer Group Four was already within 120 kilometres of Leningrad but only had half its ammunition complement left. When General Hoepner, commander of the Group, suggested racing for Leningrad with just this one force, Army Group North said it could not guarantee to supply it. Once again, as German supply lines stretched, Soviet resistance could become more concentrated. By 11 September the Leningrad Front had 452,000 men, about two-thirds of them deployed south of the city against a comparable number of Germans. On 9 September, the day after Leningrad was cut off, Zhukov was sent to command the Leningrad Front. For the Germans, there would now be another shift in priorities. The next day, 6 September, Hitler issued Directive No. 35, orders for Operation Typhoon, the assault on Moscow. Having switched priority to Leningrad on 30 July, he now switched back to Moscow (see Figure 10.3). Stupendous though the speed of the German advances had been so far, this was not the way to win a war.

Back in July, Hitler had been determined to capture the industrial and agricultural wealth of Ukraine, but here the Germans had faced the toughest opposition. On 9 July von Kleist's First Panzer Group was still between 100 and 200 kilometres west of the Dnepr. Here, it will be recalled, von Runstedt's German Army Group South was divided into two separate groups, one facing Kirponos's South-West Front, the other, including Romanian forces, facing Tyulenev's Southern Front. Stavka assessed that the Germans' main target, with the northern grouping, was Kiev, and on 7 July ordered Kirponos (who had been doing relatively well, all things considered) to launch counterstrokes into the flanks of First Panzer which was in the lead, prising its way between Potapov's Fifth and Muzychenko's Sixth Armies. These failed, and von Runstedt then turned the whole of his northern grouping on Fifth Army. Kirponos belatedly realized that von Runstedt was trying to cut off Soviet forces withdrawing to the Dnepr before driving on Kiev.[45]

Führer Directive No. 33 of 19 July prescribed in detail how Muzychenko's Sixth and Ponedelin's Twelfth Armies were to be encircled. The German Eleventh Army, part of the southern grouping, linked up with Stulpnagel's Seventeenth Army and Keist's First Panzer Group, part of the northern grouping, to trap the two Soviet armies in the Uman' encirclement on 2 August. The Luftwaffe V Air Corps was assigned to close support of the two ground armies. In order to prevent Soviet forces escaping, railways and roads all the way to the Dnepr were attacked, although bad weather and continuous rain meant that 'it proved impossible to prevent the escape of some of the enemy forces to the east'.[46] The Germans managed to establish local air superiority in spite of big supply problems, and the Stuka dive-bombers (which could only operate in such circumstances, but were terrifying when they could) were especially important in reducing resistance in the Uman' pocket. The commitment of V Air Corps to the main axis of attack meant that it could not support Sixth Army in its battle against the Soviet Fifth, which seriously reduced the army's confidence in the Luftwaffe. The remaining Soviet troops in the Uman' pocket made a last attempt to escape on 7 August, and were then forced to surrender by 10 August. The Germans captured 107,000, including Generals Ponedelin and Muzychenko, four corps commanders, eleven divisional

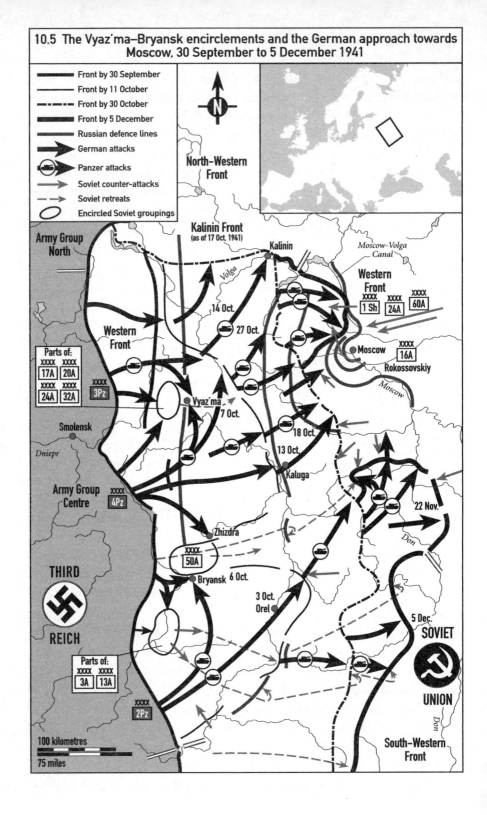

10.5 The Vyaz'ma–Bryansk encirclements and the German approach towards Moscow, 30 September to 5 December 1941

Front by 30 September
Front by 11 October
Front by 30 October
Front by 5 December
Russian defence lines
German attacks
Panzer attacks
Soviet counter-attacks
Soviet retreats
Encircled Soviet groupings

North-Western Front

Kalinin Front
(as of 17 Oct. 1941)

Kalinin

Moscow-Volga Canal

Army Group North

Volga

Western Front
XXXX 1 Sh   XXXX 24A   XXXX 60A

14 Oct.

27 Oct.

Western Front

Parts of:
XXXX 17A XXXX 20A
XXXX 24A XXXX 32A
XXXX 3Pz

Moscow
XXXX 16A
Rokossovskiy

Moscow

Vyaz'ma

7 Oct.

Smolensk

18 Oct.

Dniepr

13 Oct.

Kaluga

Army Group Centre   XXXX 4Pz

Zhizdra

22 Nov.

Don

XXXX 50A

THIRD

Bryansk   6 Oct.

3 Oct.
Orel

5 Dec.

SOVIET

REICH

Parts of:
XXXX 3A   XXXX 13A

XXXX 2Pz

UNION

100 kilometres

Don

75 miles

South-Western Front

258

commanders, 286 tanks and 953 guns.[47] Stalin issued Stavka Order No. 270, sentencing some of the captured generals to death *in absentia*. Muzychenko avoided this fate, but Ponedelin was shot after release from German captivity at the end of the war.[48]

Meanwhile, Zhukov had been unaware of Hitler's switch of the German effort from Moscow to north and south. He believed that although the Germans had been severely mauled in the Battle of Smolensk, they would resume their efforts against Moscow, but only after dealing with the threat to their flank from the south-west. On 29 July he therefore advised Stalin to evacuate Kiev and withdraw behind the Dnepr. Stalin was furious and decided to replace Zhukov as Chief of the General Staff with the meticulous old Tsarist colonel, Marshal Shaposhnikov, the following day. Hitler was even less interested in Kiev itself than he was in Moscow – merely in the resources around it. But, for Stalin, to abandon the great capital of Ukraine would be humiliating for him in the eyes of his own people and, perhaps equally importantly, his new British and potential American allies.[49]

On 18 August Halder again tried to persuade Hitler that the advance on Moscow should be continued, but his advice was rejected. The day after, Stavka ordered the South-Western Strategic Direction to defend the line of the Dnepr and hold on to Kiev at all costs. Kirpononos therefore started withdrawing forces behind the Dnepr. On 18 August Soviet sappers blew up the great dam and hydro-electric power station at Dnepropetrovsk, flooding the area downriver and complicating the withdrawal of Tyulenev's Southern Front. Even so, by the end of August the Soviets had continuous defences along the Dnepr all the way from Kiev south to the Black Sea – 700 kilometres.

But the Germans had changed their plan. Hitler regarded the Battle of Uman' as partial fulfilment of the earlier objective of encircling Soviet forces west of the Dnepr, but the Germans had failed to trap most of them, as originally envisaged.[50] A bigger encirclement was therefore needed. The place to do that was east of the Dnepr, by pinching off the bulge formed by the Dnepr and Desna rivers. That is where the great battle of encirclement and annihilation would take place, as determined by Hitler in his 22 August 'study'.[51]

Guderian's Second Panzer Group therefore seized a crossing over the Desna on 25 August and moved across on 3 September, and was now swinging round in a massive encirclement to outflank the South-Western Front. Shaposhnikov and Vasilevskiy tried to convince Stalin of the need to pull back and save the South-Western front, but to no avail. On 13 September Major-General Tupikov, the Front's Chief of Staff, radioed the Chief of the General Staff, Shaposhnikov, saying 'the catastrophe that is clear to you will occur in a matter of several days'.[52]

It did. On 16 September Kleist's First Panzer, supported by II Air Corps and Guderian's Second Panzer Group, supported by V Air Corps, made contact near Lokhvitsa, trapping the best part of a Soviet Front – an army group – in the giant Kiev pocket. Fighting in Kiev itself ended on 19 September. Soviet forces who had escaped from the pocket formed up in a quadrilateral Gadyakh–Akhtyrka–Poltava–Mirgorod, 200 kilometres due east of the gigantic Kremenchug reservoir, and about two-thirds of the way between Kyyiv (Kiev) and Kharkiv (Khar'kov), and were reinforced from the east (see Figure 10.4). The Luftwaffe mounted constant attacks against this area to try to prevent the Soviet commanders from assembling forces to break through the encirclement ring. On 16 and 17 September the German V Air Corps had to restrict its operations, however, because of the supply difficulties caused by the extremely rapid advance over a great expanse of territory.[53]

On 10 September Timoshenko took over command of the South-Western Strategic Direction from Budënny, who was assigned to command the Reserve Front (a demotion, in practical terms) in place of Zhukov, who had also been demoted after arguing with Stalin on 29 June, and who was sent to Leningrad the next day.[54] Two days later, with typical contempt for the chain of command, Stalin and Shaposhnikov signed a Stavka Directive to all Front, Army and Division commanders, and to Timoshenko, commanding the South-Western Strategic Direction, ordering the formation of 'blocking detachments' in all divisions. Each division would have such a detachment, made up of 'reliable fighters', of not more than a battalion, and typically a company. These were to be formed within the usual five days and would come under the divisional commander's direct control. In addition to its normal equipment, a blocking detachment would have some trucks and tanks or armoured vehicles. Its role was to prevent 'panic and flight'. It seems extraordinarily self-destructive that, in every division, some of the best fighting men, with more and better equipment than usual, should be employed to shoot Russians rather than Germans. However, that was seen as the way to 'reinforce the order and discipline of divisions'.[55]

Withdrawal was permitted only with express orders from the Strategic Direction or Stavka. Timoshenko and his Commissar Nikita

Khrushchev finally gave permission to withdraw, but only orally. Given the prevailing attitude to unauthorized withdrawal, Kirponos, perhaps understandably, waited until written instructions arrived from Shaposh-nikov on the night of 17 to 18 September. Even then, he was only to withdraw from Kiev and not pull back as far as the Psël river, which curves south of Kursk and bends southwards, down to the Dnepr. But First Panzer was already in that area, anyway. Shaposhnikov's orders to Kirponos on 21 September clearly showed the state of total catastrophe as a Front disappeared. In what could be dark satire set in a world of Stalinist paranoia, the punctilious Shaposhnikov 'demanded' to know whether Kirponos's formations and units had abandoned Kiev. If they had, had the bridges been blown? If they had, who could *confirm* that they had been blown?[56] There was no answer. Kirponos's South-West Front headquarters was not there.

It had reached a farm, Dryukovshchina, on 20 September. It was 15 kilometres south-west of Lokhvitsa, which is 200 kilometres east of Kiev. The Front-Army Group headquarters then retreated into the nearby Shumeykovo woods, where the German 3rd Panzer Division attacked it. Kirponos, his Chief-of-Staff Tupikov and about 2,000 staff officers and soldiers went down fighting. All of them.

From 18 September Luftwaffe planes operating out of Belaya Tser-kov supported Sixth Army's attack on the city of Kiev itself. Hitler had ordered them to 'reduce the city to rubble and ashes' and do half of the army's work for them. This made it possible to take the city itself the next day, 19 September. In the ten days from 12 to 21 September V Air Corps flew 1,422 sorties, dropped 567 tonnes of bombs, and in addition to destroying 65 Soviet aircraft in the air and 42 on the ground, destroyed 52 trains, 28 locomotives, 23 tanks, 2,171 other motor vehicles and a bridge, and cut 18 railway lines, for just 9 men killed and 17 aircraft lost.[57] Air power was crucial, but with such short-ranged aircraft, it depended on ground power to operate at all.

Just as the Germans thought they had captured Kiev, however, on 19 September, the Germans got an anonymous tip-off – possibly from the Russians themselves, given the antipathy between local Ukrainians and the former Soviet occupiers – that the withdrawing Soviet forces had left behind in key buildings explosive charges which could be detonated remotely. Those were just the sort of buildings that were very suitable for headquarters and barracks. The Germans searched every-thing but, nevertheless, five days later on 24 September, an ammunition depot next to the main post office blew up, starting a great fire. Predictably, the Germans retaliated by blaming 'partisans and Jews' and started pulling key headquarters out of the city. But in the fire a number of German officers were killed, including Colonel Baron von Seidlitz und Gohlau of the Army General Staff. Not the sort of person you would incinerate lightly and get away with it.

As a result Field Marshal von Reichenau, commanding Sixth Army, issued orders on 10 October, mirroring orders given by Hitler on 7 October. Large fortified cities should be bypassed and encircled, not taken directly until completely reduced – 'obliterated' – by bombing and shelling first. The *Wehrmacht* ignored these orders where they needed the cities as centres for transportation and command and, as the coming winter would reveal, shelter. The Kiev fire was used as an excuse for rounding up and killing all 'partisans and Jews', many of whom were shot out of hand. The Germans justified these killings by citing atrocities against German prisoners of war, and attacks on hospitals and individual sentries. However, as the new, quasi-official German history makes clear, 'the rounding up and subsequent execution of the Jewish population of Kiev cannot be justified by any reference to a military threat'.[58]

Most of the fighting in the pocket east of Kiev ended on 25 September. The end of the 'Battle of Kiev', as the Germans later called it, raised German hopes that they might be able to take the Crimean peninsula and cross to the Caucasus by the beginning of winter – although that was now less than two months away. The enormous losses inflicted on the Red Army gave rise to expectations that Operation Typhoon – the attack on Moscow – could also still succeed as the nights were drawing in.[59]

Perhaps 15,000 Soviet troops escaped from the encirclement. Overall the South-West Front, and the Central and Southern Front armies fighting with it, lost 700,544 men – irrecoverable losses, including dead, prisoners and missing, plus sick and wounded, out of perhaps 760,000. The South-West Front itself lost 585,598 out of 627,000. This was destruction on an unprecedented scale.[60] And, by wiping out of the equation four armies and more than 700,000 men, the Germans had removed a major threat to Army Group Centre's right flank as it moved on Moscow. Exactly as Zhukov had said it would.

Meanwhile the southern grouping of German Army Group South pushed the Russians back and cut off the great port of Odessa on the

Black Sea. German objectives on the Black Sea were Odessa, as the Black Sea fleet's base, the naval base and commercial port of Nikolayev which was also the hub of shipbuilding and repair, the commercial port of Kherson on the Dnepr estuary and the great naval base and fortress at Sevastopol. Seizure of Kherson would give the Germans a port, which would greatly alleviate their supply problems in Army Group South's area. Further on lay the naval base of Novorossiysk, which also straddled the main railway line to the Caucasus. The Black Sea fleet comprised one ageing but formidable battleship, 5 cruisers, 17 destroyers, 43 submarines and 81 smaller vessels.[61] The Crimea was an important objective for the air war over the Black Sea as it was, in effect, a massive, unsinkable aircraft carrier.

Odessa lay in the path of the Romanian Fourth Army, the southern-most element of Army Group South. On 19 August Stavka set up the Odessa Defensive Region, comprising the forces of the Coastal Army and the Odessa Naval Base. The Region successfully held off the German Eleventh and Romanian Fourth armies until early October when, in a brilliant operation which had many of the characteristics of a Soviet Dunkirk, the Black Sea fleet (for which the Germans had a huge respect) successfully evacuated the entire garrison to Sevastopol in the Crimea. They would fight and die there, but the defence and evacuation of Odessa from 2 to 16 October was a remarkable achievement. Thus far, the Black Sea fleet, the first to open fire, had proved itself among the most professional of the Soviet forces.

Back in mainland Europe, Army Group South, flushed with its triumph at Kiev, pondered what to do next. On 20 September its operations department was asked what Hitler's views were on a thrust by Panzer Group I towards the Sea of Azov and Rostov-on-Don. Hitler gave his consent. Eleventh Army was now in position to drive south into the Crimea through the isthmus of Perekop, and German forces were deployed to help the Romanians take Odessa, which was needed as a supply base for operations in the Crimea. This proved to be a two-edged sword, as the Soviet forces successfully withdrawn from Odessa up until 16 October were used to reinforce the defences of the Crimea.

Enter weapons of mass destruction?

The Crimea was defended by Fifty-First Army, with its headquarters at
Simferopol, in the south-centre of the peninsula. On 15 September, with
German forces approaching, its commander, Colonel-General Fëdor
Kuznetsov, received a sharply worded reply from Marshal Shaposhnikov
to a proposal he had made. Kuznetsov's task – to prevent the Germans
breaking through a critical fortified line sealing off a strategic peninsula
– suggested a First World War response, but Shaposhnikov, who had
been a colonel in that earlier war, would have none of it.

> Your plan for chemical defence envisages using agent No. 6 –
> Yperite [Mustard Gas], which is completely inadmissible and
> categorically forbidden without express authorisation by
> Stavka.
> Check this personally and eliminate this mistake . . .[62]

By the time 'Yperite' – mustard gas – had first been used in the First
World War, in July 1917, Russia's involvement in the war was already
coming to an end and Shaposhnikov's reservations had nothing to do
with his own personal trauma in that war, as Hitler's probably did.
Using chemical weapons was 'categorically forbidden', and the Soviet
Union had expressly promised to abide by the 1925 Convention on the
use of chemical and bacteriological agents (see Chapter 2). As Chief of
the General Staff, Shaposhnikov was, obviously, fully aware of the Soviet
Union's diplomatic undertakings to the United States, among others. As
a practical military man, he, and his colleagues also, knew that in spite
of the immense stress placed on chemical and bacteriological warfare
training and development in the interwar period, the Germans, with
their current mastery of the air in spite of fewer aircraft, and their better
training and discipline, would almost certainly get the better of any
chemical exchange, both from the point of delivering the filthy weapons,
and of protecting their own forces. As for what would happen to the
Russian civilian population, who had not all been issued with respirators
(gas masks), as the British had, under a chemical exchange, it did not
bear thinking about.

But Kuznetsov's proposal to use mustard gas – a persistent blister agent – is particularly interesting. Kuznetsov, who had commanded the North-West Front, Twenty-First Army and the Central Front, was not some bumpkin army commander who did not fully understand the political, diplomatic, strategic and operational implications of his proposal. On the contrary, before taking command of armies and fronts, he had been, in 1940–41, Chief of the Military Academy of the Red Army General Staff.[63] He had then commanded forces in the North Caucasus and Baltic Special Military Districts. He was not only a highly experienced commander, but also one of the Soviet Union's top surviving military-academic thinkers. This was the man who knew, better than just about anybody, that in terms of Soviet military doctrine, these were the circumstances in which to throw the rule book out of the window and go for weapons of mass destruction, the Russian term which has recently been hijacked by the Americans and British and become standard-speak for chemical, biological, radiological and nuclear weapons.[64] Kuznetsov's proposal to use chemical weapons – weapons of mass destruction – was a clear sign of how desperate things were getting.

It indicated other things as well. In doctrinal terms, an attacking German force trapped on the mines and wire of the Perekop fortifications was the ideal target for a chemical attack. In the Gulf War of 1991, the Allies' greatest fear was that they would be pinned on the southern Kuwaiti frontier defences, and that the Iraqis would then rain chemical weapons down on them.[65] Whether he expected the answer 'yes' or 'no' to his plan to use chemical weapons, army commander Kuznetsov would not have factored them into his defensive fireplan if he were not utterly confident that he had stocks of chemical munitions available and the means to deliver them effectively. Kuznetsov's proposal was deadly serious, and, now that reality had set in, would not have been made if the Red Army could not have carried it out. It was not the first time that chemical weapons would raise their 'hanging face, like a devil's sick of sin',[66] on the eastern front.

But, with the benefit of hindsight, why was Shaposhnikov's slap-down so preremptory? If there was ever a time when Soviet forces might use the chemical weapons which had been so assiduously studied and developed in the interwar period, it was now. As noted in Chapter 2, the USSR had assured Averill Harriman that it would abide by the 1925 Geneva Protocol for the Prohibition of the Use in War of Asphyxiating

Poisonous or Other Gases, and of Bacteriological Methods of Warfare.[67] The United Kingdom was a new but, in Soviet eyes, uncertain ally, and the United States had just initiated lease-lend aid to the USSR on 24 June, two days after Barbarossa. Given the Soviet regime's complete indifference to vast casualties among its own people, whether military or civilian, let alone to those among the Germans, however gruesomely inflicted, it seems unlikely that this was the prime consideration. To be sure, a state still committed to 'the offensive', and ready to throw ill-prepared forces into action at horrendous cost, might take its military experts' advice that chemical warfare would slow everything down, and make the manoeuvre they craved more difficult. That was another primary reason why the Germans and the western Allies eschewed it. But, most likely, the political- and grand-strategic disadvantages of initiating chemical warfare on the eastern front, in terms of how the British and Americans would view it, outweighed any temporary military-strategic and operational advantages it might offer for delaying and killing Germans. The answer lies somewhere in the Russian archives, no doubt, but that seems a reasonable – in fact, the only reasonable – explanation.

Attack on the Crimea

On 24 September the German Eleventh Army attacked the Perekop isthmus, which they had reached on the 17th. They had hoped to catch the Russians unawares, with an attack by two divisions, 73rd and 46th, but instead ran into strong defences on a narrow isthmus devoid of natural cover. The LIV Mountain Corps, which had been intended for operations in the Crimean peninsula itself, had to be committed on the left flank. The attack shuddered to a halt, and the Germans did not succeed in breaking through into the Crimea for another month – until 28 October. However, on 1 October the Germans captured Zaporizh-zhya (Zaporozh'ye) east of the Dnepr bend, threatening to cut off Soviet forces in the area, and the Soviet forces pulled back. Army Group South suggested to Halder that operations should be confined to eliminating Soviet resistance west of the River Don before the onset of winter, but he insisted that it push on across the river, with Seventeenth Army heading for Stalingrad and Sixth Army covering it to the north. With the disasters at Vyaz'ma and Bryansk (see below), Shaposhnikov had little option but to order the South-Western and Southern Fronts to withdraw to the line of the Mius, Northern Donets and Oskol' rivers between 17 and 30 October. Hitler feared the Soviet forces would therefore escape. On 25 October Sixth Army captured Khar'kov after five days' heavy fighting.

At this point logistic considerations were beginning to weigh very heavily on the Germans' minds as they contemplated any further advance. Although Sixth Army had orders not to enter the city but to destroy it by artillery bombardment and air attacks and thereby to encourage the population to flee, it would destroy the shelter and communications the city might provide for the coming winter. Also, any German officer would by now be aware that the Ukrainian civilian population might be inclined to welcome the Germans, rather than flee. Khar'kov was a potentially valuable railhead, but only after the line from Belgorod, which lies to the north, had been converted to standard gauge (see the opening to Chapter 7), as the Russians had destroyed or withdrawn their broad-gauge rolling stock and locomotives. On 22 October, therefore, the Army Group suggested to OKH that a three-week 'operational pause' be ordered. Halder did not like this at all, as he thought it would send the wrong message to the troops. But without railways, the Germans were utterly dependent on the roads. The problem was – what roads? On the same day, Sixth Army reported that the roads could no longer be expected to dry out. The Russians had – and have – a name for it: *rasputitsa* ('the season of muddy roads'). That would last until mid December, when really hard frosts set in. An order of III Panzer Corps dated 23 October told units to be prepared to survive on their own for several days with regard to food, ammunition and fuel. The main form of transport was the horse and cart. To give an idea of the problem for a fast-moving 'mechanized' army, between Zaporizhzhya and Mariupol, 2,500 wagons could transport 60 tonnes of supplies a day.[68]

By the end of October, then, the situation had temporarily stabilized. The Southern and South-Western fronts had fallen back level with the eastern end of the Sea of Azov, and the Crimea was cut off. But the rapid German advance had left large numbers of partisans throughout Ukraine. On 2 September the Fourth Department of the Ukrainian

NKVD reported that sixty-three partisan detachments totalling 4,855 irregular combatants – men and women – were already operating in the German rear and another eighty detachments totalling 2,409 fighters were trained for insertion 'behind enemy lines'. Another 434 detachments totalling 12,561 were trained for operations 'in place' – that is, they were stay-behind parties which would be activated when the Germans rolled past them. Finally, nine detachments totalling 285 had been inserted behind the advancing German troops 'with various tasks', unspecified. These were probably the highest-value agents with special missions. There were also 285 'trained partisan and diversionary groups' totalling 1,460 people. Altogether, 21,530 rear-area combatants either in place or ready to go.[69] As noted, the Germans had massively underestimated this threat.

The 'Finland theatre'

The German Mountain Corps Norway, reinforced by Finnish troops, had advanced into the Petsamo area on the Soviet Union's northern Arctic coast on 22 June 1941 in the imaginatively named Operation Reindeer. They quickly reached the Litsa river, where Soviet forces holding the Rybachy peninsula threatened their flank, delaying part of the more glamorous-sounding Operation Platinum Fox against Murmansk. The Russians then started to launch fierce counter-attacks and also amphibious landings on the flank in Litsa Bay. Hitler's fear of a British landing in Norway prevented him from allowing more German troops to be transferred from Northern Norway. The Germans thought that British or Soviet troops might land in their rear – a degree of British–Soviet cooperation which, with hindsight, seems inconceivable at this stage. The Germans never advanced beyond the Litsa, and on 10 October Hitler ordered Army Group Command Norway to go over to the defensive 'in view of the lateness of the season and the onset of winter'.[70]

Platinum Fox also targeted the Murmansk railway, which would be critical for British and US aid to the USSR. An attack by SS Division Nordland and the Finnish 6th Division under XXXVI Army Corps began on 1 July. The plan was to cut the line at Kandalaksha, but the German–Finnish troops first had to capture Salla, formerly and now in Finland, but which had been ceded to the USSR in 1940. The Russians had constructed strong fortifications and it took a whole week to capture Salla. By September 1941 XXXVI Army Corps had advanced about 60 kilometres and recaptured the Finnish territory taken by the USSR the year before. It then dug in for the winter. Further south, the Finnish III Corps attacked towards the White Sea in the direction of Louchi. They reached Kiestinki (Kestenga) on 8 August, but Soviet reinforcements halted them there. Army Command Norway wanted to try again but on 8 October the OKW, which was controlling this part of the war, as opposed to OKH, which controlled war on the the main eastern front between the Baltic and the Black Seas, ordered all operations to be halted for the winter.

It seems extraordinary that the objective of cutting the single railway linking the Soviet hinterland – 'bol'shaya zemlya' – with the Arctic and the outside world, was pursued so half-heartedly. Marshal Mannerheim suggested they might try again in 1942, but in reality the reasons were political. The Americans warned the Finnish government of serious consequences if deliveries of Allied aid to the USSR were interrupted by a Finnish capture of the Murmansk railway. On 27 and 28 October the Americans, still neutral, had initiated diplomatic efforts to achieve a separate peace between Finland and the USSR. Major-General Siilasvuo, the Finnish commander of III Corps, had almost certainly been tipped off about this. His forces had come closest to severing the vital link, but he did not want to be responsible for scuppering a mutually beneficial and lasting peace between his proud country and its gigantic bear of a neighbour. And without the Finns' cooperation, there was little the Germans could do – unless they wanted Finland to become an ally of the Soviet Union, which would be a disaster for them.

The same political situation influenced operations further south, towards Leningrad, Lake Ladoga and Lake Onega. The Finns fought to seize back the land they lost in 1940, reaching the west bank of Lake Onega and the River Svir by 8 December. In the Karelian isthmus, they recovered their own territory, but stopped between 35 and 70 kilometres from Leningrad, where the line stabilized between 9 and 11 November, 1941. They never pushed as hard as they could have done, something which Leningrad, now St Petersburg again, would always remember (see Chapter 13).[71]

Operation Typhoon. Vyaz'ma-Bryansk and the road to Moscow

Even before the eradication of an entire front around Kiev, Hitler had regained interest in Moscow. As early as 12 August, he issued a supplement to Directive 34 of 30 July, ordering that Moscow, as the enemy's 'government, armament and traffic centre', must be captured 'before the beginning of winter'.[72]

There was a reason, which became clear with a survey of the strategic situation produced by the *Wehrmacht* High Command on 24 August, approved by Hitler. It said that operations to crush Soviet resistance might have to continue into 1942, and that had to be borne in mind in future strategic planning.[73] Further operations with strategic aims – including possibly the capture of Leningrad and the Caucasus – might have to be delayed until then, and priority given to securing territory already conquered.

On 6 September, with Leningrad effectively isolated and the encirclement of the South-West Front under way, Order No. 35 recognized the 'prerequisites for conducting a decisive operation against Army Group Timoshenko [the Western Front] which is conducting unsuccessful offensive operations on Army Group Centre's front'.[74] Timoshenko was in fact moved to command the South-Western Strategic Direction four days later, but that was irrelevant: the Western Front remained the critical block before Moscow. Hitler used the argument that if the bulk of the Red Army was massed to defend Moscow, then that was where it would have to be destroyed. In a 'study' of 22 August Hitler had envisaged the great battle of encirclement east of the Dnepr, which took place in the 'Battle of Kiev' the next month, and clearly saw the destruction of the maximum number of enemy forces in the battle for Moscow as more important than capturing the city itself.[75] However, in the view of the new German history,

> Halder, more than Hitler . . . believed that a final effort to
> capture Moscow would lead to the collapse of Soviet
> defences. Hitler, on the other hand, drew the correct (in his

view) operational conclusions dictated by his priorities. Military-economic necessity was the decisive factor; he never considered a Cannae around Moscow. But the German leaders still hoped – even if they no longer expected with certainty – to conclude the campaign against the Soviet Union satisfactorily in 1941 in so far as they might manage to deprive the enemy of the basis to rehabilitate and redispose his forces . . .[76]

Directive No. 35 ordered Army Group Centre to 'destroy the enemy in the region east of Smolensk by a double envelopment by powerful panzer forces concentrated on both flanks' (a pincer movement)[77]. After destroying the 'main mass of Timoshenko's group of forces', the Army Group was to pursue the Soviet forces towards Moscow shielded by the Oka river to the right and the upper reaches of the Volga to the left. On 16 September Bock gave the operation its historic codename, Typhoon.

Meanwhile, in early September Yeremenko's Bryansk Front had attacked Second Panzer Group's left (eastern) flank as it was engaged in the Kiev encirclement to the south. It suffered heavy casualties and on 5 September Shaposhnikov authorized Yeremenko to form 'blocking detachments' in 'those divisions which had proved themselves unreliable'.[78] The next day poor Yeremenko received another message, from Stalin, which was almost worthy of Hitler:

> I noticed that 108th Tank Division got encircled and lost lots of tanks and equipment. This could only happen as a result of bad management on your part. You shouldn't send a division into the offensive on its own, without reinforcing its flanks and giving it air cover. If aircraft can't fly because of bad weather, you must cancel the tank division's offensive until the moment that the weather improves and the planes can support the division. In future, I demand that you do not allow such precipitate action. I also demand that you find the means to rescue the encircled tank crewmen and, if possible, their tanks as well. Also be aware that sending pilots in bad weather is not always a good idea. The *Shturmoviki* [this could refer either to the planes or the pilots who flew them] can even fly in bad weather if the cloud is above 100 to 150 metres [330 to 500 feet]. Tell Comrade Petrov [Major-General of the Air Force, the Bryansk Front's Chief of Air

Staff] that I expect him, at the very least, to take account of
the weather and, at best, to use the ground-attack fighters in
bad weather.[79]

Yeremenko survived both Stalin and the Germans – just. It was a
strangely friendly rebuke. By furiously attacking and trying to hack off
Guderian's deadly pincer, he was at least trying. He went on to
command the Stalingrad Front, the Second Baltic, and the Fourth
Ukrainian which, in 1945, swept as far as Austria. In 1955, after Stalin's
death, he was made a Marshal.[80]

With the Soviet South-West Front obliterated, Guderian's Second
Panzer Group was available to attack to the north-east, through Tula,
reinforcing the Third and Fourth Panzer Groups belonging to Army
Group Centre. The total German force for Typhoon numbered
1,929,406 men, excluding the Luftwaffe, with 14,000 artillery pieces,
more than 1,000 tanks and 1,390 combat aircraft. There were three all-
arms armies and three Panzer Groups, adding up to 78 divisions in all.
On the Soviet side, there were three fronts. When the Germans talked
of 'Army Group Timoshenko', they were probably referring to the
Western Strategic Direction, rather than the Western Front. The latter
had, in any case, by now become Army Group Koniev – the Western
Front, comprising six armies, deployed behind the eastern of the two
lines Zhukov had indicated to Stalin at the end of June. There was also
the Reserve Front, commanded by Budënny, with six armies, and the
Bryansk Front, with three armies and Operational Group Yermakov.

Guderian's Second Panzer attacked on 30 September and the Army
Group's main assault followed on 2 October. Guderian made spectacular
progress at first, reaching Sevsk on 1 October, and then splitting,
reaching Orël by 3 October and Bryansk on 6 October. The Soviet Third
and Fiftieth Armies had to dodge and fight their way out eastwards,
either side of Bryansk, to avoid encirclement. Guderian's 7th Panzer
Division captured the headquarters of the Bryansk Front 11 kilometres
south of the city. Yeremenko and his key staff escaped – just.

Once Guderian's troops reached Orël, the city called 'Eagle', on 3
October, the airfield there became a base for dive-bombers and fighters
and also a major logistic base for all the requirements of the Second
Panzer Group. It also, naturally, became a target for fierce Soviet air
attacks.[81]

Catastrophic though Bryansk had been, the real catastrophe occurred at Vyaz'ma. Here, Lt Gen. Rokossovskiy, too, had a lucky escape which tells a great deal about the atmosphere in which the Soviet commanders were operating. On the evening of 5 October he received a telegram ordering him to hand over command of his Sixteenth Army to Lt Gen. Yershakov, commanding Twentieth Army,[82] on his left, and to report on the next day with the whole of his Sixteenth Army headquarters to Vyaz'ma, where he would organize a counter-attack with five infantry divisions towards Yukhnov, to the north-west. It sounded 'strange', and Rokossovskiy did not like it. 'Leave the troops at such a time?' his chief of staff, Malinin, exclaimed. 'This is incredible!' Rokossovskiy requested that the order be confirmed in writing and signed by the Front commander, Colonel-General Koniev. That night, an airman delivered the order signed by Koniev and his political commissar, Bulganin.

Reassured but still not happy, Rokossovskiy and his headquarters headed for Vyaz'ma. But when they arrived, there were no divisions for him to command, never mind five. Rokossovskiy found the Smolensk regional party committee and the committees of Smolensk and Vyazma cities crouched in the crypt of Vyaz'ma cathedral. The garrison commander and party officials knew nothing of Rokossovskiy's orders. 'All I have is the police force,' the commander said, glumly.

At that moment the mayor rushed in. 'German tanks are in the city.'

'Who reported that?' said Rokossovskiy.

'I saw them myself, from the belfry.'

He could conceivably have misidentified Russian tanks, but Rokossovskiy knew that was most unlikely. 'Get the cars ready,' he ordered, and headed up to the belfry to see German tanks machine-gunning other cars which were attempting to escape from the city. Rokossovskiy and his staff headed out of town, at one point almost running into a German tank, and swerving down a side street to avoid it before it could open fire. They returned to their command post about 10 kilometres northeast of the city and assessed the situation. It was obvious that the Germans were doing their favourite move, and encircling Vyaz'ma, which had already fallen. On the next day, 7 October, the Third and Fourth Panzer Groups linked up to form the Vyaz'ma pocket. They had trapped Sixteenth, Nineteenth, Twentieth, Twenty-Fourth and part of Thirty-Second Armies. Both sides were learning, and, mindful of successful Soviet escapes from encirclement in the past, the Germans had stacked up Panzer divisions west of Vyaz'ma.

Rokossovskiy's first instinct, inevitably, was to return to his Sixteenth

Army troops, who were being encircled. But his headquarters had been designated for a mission, 'and we were duty bound to report and find out what it was'.[83] It looked as if the Panzers forming the inner ring of encirclement – to hold the Russians in – had met at Vyaz'ma (in fact, they met just east of the city) and that an outer ring would be established further east to keep relieving Russian forces out. The question was – where?

Rokossovskiy decided to break out to the north-east, where he reckoned the German lines were thinnest. At Tumanovo, 40 kilometres to the east of Vyaz'ma on the main railway line to Moscow, his scouts found an NKVD cavalry squadron, who gladly joined the Army headquarters and their charismatic commander. This time, Rokossovskiy was probably pleased to see the NKVD. It had not always been so.

Here, they also found several trains with food on board. They loaded what they could into the trucks, and blew up the rest. At one village, they entered a house to gather more information about what lay ahead. The locals were terrified, but welcomed the Soviet brass warmly. After they had heard where the Germans were from a small boy and his mother, a voice came from the corner.

> 'What's going on, comrade Commander?'
> It was a grey-bearded old man, the grandfather of the family.
> 'Comrade Commander, you're getting away yourselves, and leaving *us* behind. We've given all we had to help the Red Army, we'd spare the last shirt from our back if it would help. I'm an old soldier myself. I fought the Germans, and we didn't let them into Russia. What are you doing now?'[84]

Rokossovskiy felt the words 'like a slap in the face'. The old man had been wounded twice in the First World War, and was now bedridden. In the First World War, the Tsar's Army had done a lot better than the Red Army had, so far. 'If I were well,' the old man said, as the strapping 44-year-old general with nine steel teeth, red and gold chevrons on his sleeve and three stars on each collar ducked through the low door and left the humble farmhouse and family to their fate, 'I'd go and defend Russia myself.'[85]

It cut to the quick, and Rokossovskiy never forgot it. As he and his staff and those they picked up along the way trudged on, there was a report that a U2 light aircraft, used for transporting senior officers and important messages, rather like the German Fiesler Storch, had landed in a field nearby. The Chief of Sixteenth Army's Air Force, Col. Baranchuk, was sent to investigate. He came back with news that Soviet troops were still holding Gzhatsk (now Gagarin), 35 kilometres east of Tumanovo, and that Voroshilov and Molotov had been seen there the day before. In his excitement, Baranchuk never checked the pilot's name and did not interrogate him at any length. Rokossovskiy ordered the pilot to be brought to him, but by that time the pilot had then flown off – oddly enough, to the west . . .

It could well have been a German trap. Rokossovskiy and his team headed for Gzhatsk, and ran straight into German forces. An armoured personnel carrier of the reconnaissance detachment hit a mine, and the Germans opened fire, but the main body was strong enough to overcome the opposition. Eventually, on 9 October, after two nights and a day dodging German patrols and picking up stragglers, of whom quite a few had escaped from the inner German encirclement, they reached a forest 40 kilometres from Mozhaysk and made contact with Western Front headquarters. Two U2s were sent to pick up Rokossovskiy and Lobachov.

Rokossovskiy said his Chief of Staff, Malinin, was 'calm' and 'pedantic'. Those qualities may have saved Rokossovskiy's life. 'Take the order about handing over the sector and troops to Yershakov,' Malinin said.

'Why?'

'It may come in handy. You never can tell . . .'

Malinin was right. When Rokossovskiy arrived, he found a heavyweight Soviet delegation. Molotov, who was Stalin's Deputy, Voroshilov, Koniev, who had been the Front commander, and Bulganin were all there. The first two were members of the State Defence Committee – GKO.[86] After the brief preliminaries, the question Malinin had anticipated.

'How come you were at Vyaz'ma with your headquarters but without any troops of the Sixteenth Army?' asked Voroshilov.

'The Front commander said the troops I would be taking over would be waiting there . . .' Rokossovskiy replied.

'Strange . . .'

Rokossovskiy produced the written order signed by Koniev and Bulganin.

Had he not, he might well have gone down in history as just another general who panicked, retreated without orders, and deserted his troops.

Voroshilov then called in Army General Georgy Zhukov. 'This is the new commander of the Western Front,' he said. 'He will give you your new assignment.'[87] Rokossovskiy was to hold Volokolamsk, on the main road to Moscow. Koniev was formally relieved of the command on 10 October, but on 17 October, assigned to command the newly created Kalinin Front.

Rokossovskiy's luck was holding in other ways as well. He had been ordered to hand over to Yershakov, who was one of the three Soviet generals taken prisoner in the Vyaz'ma encirclement, together with Vyshnevskiy, commanding Thirty-Second Army, and Lukin, originally commanding Nineteenth Army, who had been placed in command of all the encircled elements. Could it be that the reason for the strange order to Rokossovskiy to take command of a non-existent army was that somebody – maybe Koniev, maybe someone more senior – had decided that the Red Army's most talented up-and-coming commander *must* be extracted? Speculation, but given the Byzantine circumstances of the time, not inconceivable. Yershakov was certainly not in a position to complain.

The Russians were learning, as well as the Germans. Stavka ordered Soviet forces encircled at Vyaz'ma to break out on 10–11 October and 'escape encirclement at all costs'. Whether they gave guarantees that the escapers would not be arrested by the NKVD is not recorded. Meanwhile, in the next few days German radio and newspapers proclaimed the successful outcome of the war in the East, gloating that 'the enemy is broken and will never rise again'.[88] On 11 October Luftwaffe General Freiherr Wolfram von Richthofen (who *was* a relation, of course . . .) believed that 'the Russians can now be finished off militarily, if everybody makes an all-out effort'.[89]

While Soviet forces in the northern Vyaz'ma pocket were all defeated by 23 October, large numbers of those in the southern pocket around Bryansk (including the Front commander) were able to get away, although the Luftwaffe harried them constantly. The Luftwaffe had made a significant contribution to the encirclement battles. Between 2 and 13 October II Luftwaffe Air Corps, in addition to downing 29 Soviet aircraft, had accounted for a goods train and 579 Soviet vehicles, fought off 8 cavalry and 23 infantry attacks, and captured 3,842 prisoners.[90] They were getting very good at fighting on the ground. By the end of the war, that was where the vast majority of them would be fighting.

On 13 October the Germans announced that 'the enemy encircled west of Vyaz'ma has been completely destroyed'.[91] In fact, they held down five German divisions until the end of the month. But the calamity was undeniable. The three Soviet Fronts facing Army Group Centre had totalled 1,250,000 men, with 7,600 guns, 990 tanks and 667 aircraft. They accounted for about 40 per cent of the Red Army's surviving forces between the Baltic and the Black Seas. The Germans had successfully accomplished two gigantic encirclement battles of which one, Vyaz'ma, was probably even more spectacular than Kiev. Out of 1,250,000 troops of the Western, Reserve and Bryansk Fronts, 85,000 are estimated to have escaped from Vyaz'ma and 23,000 from Bryansk, while another 98,000 from other formations also made it out – a total of 250,000. The Russian statistics give irrecoverable losses – dead, prisoners and missing – of 514,338, plus 143,941 sick and wounded, a total of 658,279. But with 1,250,000 to start with and only 250,000 escapers, the true losses could be a million – 300,000 dead and 700,000 prisoners. Three Fronts had lost 7 out of their 15 armies, 64 out of 95 divisions, 11 out of 15 tank brigades, and 50 out of 62 artillery regiments. The Soviets lost 6,000 guns and mortars and 830 tanks.[92] The October arithmetic dwarfs that of June, July, August and September. The German rule of thumb at the time was that, under wartime conditions, it took a million of population to provide enough men for two divisions. These calculations proved completely inadequate, but applying that logic, the Soviet loss of 64 divisions at Vyaz'ma–Bryansk and in the surrounding operations would have taken a population of 32 million – one-sixth of the pre-war Soviet population – to replenish.[93] It was a cataclysm.

Some small comfort could be gleaned, however, from the halt imposed on Guderian's advance from the south-west. At Mtsensk, First Guards Rifle Corps, under Lelyushenko's direction, had temporarily halted Guderian's advance, and when XXIV Panzer Corps reached Tula on 30 October, it failed to take it.

The moment the Vyaz'ma encirclement closed, Zhukov called the Stavka early on 8 October, warning that 'almost all routes to Moscow are open'.[94] He recommended that new forces should be assembled on the Mozhaysk defence line, which had been established on 16 July, about 200 kilometres back towards Moscow.[95] Over the next few days, as a quarter of a million men fought or crawled their way out of the German claws, the Russians reorganized again. What little was left of the Western and Reserve Fronts was united in a reconstituted Western Front, under Zhukov's command.

The Germans, understandably, were ecstatic, and became overconfident. OKH decided that it could attack eastwards towards Moscow and move north to eliminate the North-Western Front as well. This would give them total control of the Moscow–Leningrad railway, already cut, and help to secure the elimination of Leningrad. Hitler, meanwhile, conceived a broader, politico-strategic plan to isolate Moscow in a big ring to 'exert political pressure', but not to enter the city. As noted above, he was not interested in Moscow per se but in destroying the bulk of the enemy's armed forces wherever they might be – which would, in all probability be Moscow – and in reaching a favourable, if not exactly comfortable, position on which to base the new campaign now expected to take place in 1942.[96] Moscow was also important as the communications hub at the centre of the supply lines leading north to the Arctic Ocean, south to the Black Sea (although that was soon to be cut off), to the interior of Russia and further east into Asia, and along the middle and upper Volga.[97]

By 1 October 1941 the German Army Group Centre had lost 229,000 men, which rose to 277,000 by 16 October. Replacements amounted to 151,000 men. But the fighting power of individual units and formations had dropped substantially, and by 6 November was assessed as about 60 per cent of what it would normally be.[98]

By mid October, therefore, Moscow was under direct threat, with German forces which had encircled Vyaz'ma moving rapidly on Mozhaysk and its defence line – a line they reached by 24 October. Leningrad had been sealed off and effectively came under siege on 8 September. In the far north, Axis operations had more or less ceased with the decision on 8 October to halt any attacks there, while the line north of Leningrad stabilized on 11 November. Only between Lake Ladoga and Lake Onega did the Finns continue to push forward in late autumn, reaching the Svir by 8 December. Far to the south, in Ukraine and on the edge of the Black Sea, the front had stabilized east of the Sea of Azov by the end of October and, following a month's delay in breaking through the Perekop isthmus, the battle for the Crimea itself began at the same time. Across the eastern front as a whole, by 1 November 1941, the Germans had lost 686,000 casualties, or one-fifth of the original Barbarossa force and all the replacements received since 22 June. It now had 2.7 million men, compared with the 3.2 million on 22 June. One-third of motor vehicles were still operational and Panzer divisions were at 35 per cent of their official strength. On that day, the fighting strength of the Red Army in western Russia and what was left of Ukraine, not including the very effective NKVD, was about

2.2 million. A month later, as a result of the transfer of forces from Siberia and mobilization measures, it fielded 4 million.[99] That was as many as it lost between 22 June and 31 December, equivalent to its entire peacetime army.[100] But if the Germans were going to take Moscow they had to do so before the onset of winter. Barbarossa was beginning to fragment, not only geographically, as it broke up into a series of clearly distinct operations which will be addressed in the following chapters, but also in other ways. Above all, logistically, as the Germans outran their supplies.

11

MIDNIGHT IN MOSCOW

Fighting fire with fire

As Red Army soldiers fought and died or were captured in their millions, the ancient capital of Russia steeled itself for the coming 'Typhoon'. In the second quarter of the twentieth century, Moscow had expanded into a spacious showpiece of Stalinist progress, wrapped around an 'S' bend in the Moskva river and, in the brief Russian summer, lying between mellow, light-green hills. The first decree of the newly formed State Defence Committee, GKO, dated 1 July, gives a startling insight into what 'national security' is really about.

It relates not to armies or aircraft or ships, but to reinforcement of the Moscow fire services. The secret document ordered the Commissariat for General Machine Building to increase production of fire engines at the Moscow fire service factory to 150 and water tankers to 200, while the Commissariat for Medium Machine Building was to ensure an uninterrupted supply of ZIS-5 and ZIS-11 chassis for fire engines and water tankers.[1] Sixty years later, when al-Qa'ida attacked New York, the first service engaged in countering the effects of the attack was – the fire service. GKO's third order, on 2 July, classified top secret because it contained more operational detail, also gave orders for reinforcing Moscow's fire defences, which came under the control of the NKVD. Oddly enough, the first of the surrounding villages mentioned is Kuntsevo, where Stalin had one of his dachas.[2] Both orders were signed by Molotov.

The meticulous care with which the State Defence Committee – the war cabinet – directed every aspect of the country's response is fascinating. On 5 July the Moscow Local Air Defence Service (MPVO), responsible for clearing up bomb damage and restoring water, power, heating, gas and telephone lines, was reinforced to four regiments totalling 11,300 personnel. The big buildings in Moscow and, indeed, throughout Russia and the former Soviet Union were, and are, heated centrally. Interruption of heating in the depths of the Russian winter could quickly have fatal consequences on a large scale. The First Regiment, with equipment including 19 excavators, 14 tractors, 14 mobile electric generators and 9 cranes, numbered 5,830 and would repair buildings and remove obstructions caused by bombing. The Second, with 1,000 personnel, would repair bridges and roads. The Third would restore water supplies and the Fourth power and heating. Independent battalions were responsible for gas and communications. The NKVD was given five days to provide 300 new uniforms for Local Air Defence officers.[3]

Military measures for the defence of Moscow were first ordered on 9 July. First of all, a new Camouflage Service – *Sluzhba maskirovki* – was created, staffed by architects and artists, reporting to the Moscow Soviet and funded out of its city budget.[4] The Russian word *maskirovka* – literally 'masking' – refers not just to physical camouflage but to all forms of deception.[5] The Camouflage Service would obscure factories producing military equipment, water pumping stations, the Kremlin, the central telegraph offices, fuel storage depots and bridges. Comrade Denisov, of the People's Commissariat for the Chemical Industry, was to ensure the Camouflage Service got all the paint it needed. On the same day GKO issued a more menacing top secret order, signed by Stalin and copied to Beria, Zhukov and Major-General L. Z. Kotlyar of the Main Engineering Directorate of the Red Army (GVIUKA), on 'The Conduct of Special Work'.[6] Kotlyar was relieved of his duties as Inspector-General of Engineers and made a member of the Reserve Armies' Front. In addition to the usual minefields, 'massive explosions' were to be widely used, in particular to destroy dams and water installations. Some 2,700 tonnes of ammonite, 170 tonnes of Trotyl, 160,000 detonators, 50,000 electric detonators, and 110 kilometres of detonating cord were to be made available. The Chemical Industry Commissariat was also ordered to hand over 1,510 tonnes of ammonium nitrate, and the Agricultural Commissariat 743 tonnes. Ammonium nitrate fertilizer mixed with fuel oil (ANFO) is a very effective home-made explosive.[7]

Stalin also ordered the creation of 35 'destroyer battalions' (*Istrebi-tel'nye batal'ony*) to deal with enemy paratroops and special forces in the Moscow area, but they had another role, too – dealing with looters, deserters and panic. Each battalion was up to 500 strong with four or five trucks and, for those in the surrounding countryside, fifteen to twenty horses to help reconnoitre likely paratroop landing sites. The People's Defence Committee (NKO) – the Defence Ministry, which came under the GKO – was ordered to provide 300 sub-machine guns, 6,000 pistols and revolvers, and 55,000 hand grenades. The Destroyer battalions were controlled by the NKVD and commanded by regular NKVD officers. Each would also be stiffened by fifteen NKVD agents of known reliability.[8]

The German Luftwaffe had not yet bombed Moscow, concentrating on the priority task of supporting the German ground forces. But by 9 July the closest German forces, moving towards Orsha, were just 400 miles – 640 kilometres – from the capital, which was already well within range of German medium bombers. On 8 July two new medium anti-aircraft gun regiments, each with fifty-two 85mm guns, and two light, each with forty 37mm guns, had been formed. Stalin ordered that by 18 July he wanted 800 anti-aircraft guns in the Moscow area, and that each regiment's number of guns should be increased by fifteen or sixteen per day until this was achieved. Searchlights were to be placed between 30 and 40 kilometres from the anti-aircraft guns, and barrage balloon units, which appear to have been neglected, were to be brought up to strength. Air defence fighters were to be based around Moscow at Tula, Kaluga, Vyaz'ma, Rzhev and Kalinin. With eleven regiments of 63 aircraft each and ten regiments with 30, the total number should rise to 993. In order to disperse the aircraft more effectively, the NKVD was ordered to create twenty-four additional airfields in the Moscow area by 15 July and, by 1 October, another nine with concrete runways.[9] The Russians well knew that by then the *rasputitsa* (see Chapter 10) – the season of mud – would be setting in.

The creation of the Mozhaysk Defence Line, 100 kilometres west of Moscow, on 16 July with three Armies (Thirty-Second, Third and Fourth) defending it, plus ten divisions of People's Militia and five divisions of NKVD troops, under the command of Lt Gen. Artem'yev, the commander of the Moscow Military District, marked a 'line in the sand'. If the Germans got beyond there, Moscow would be seriously threatened.[10] This happened in mid October, after the the catastrophe at Vyaz'ma (see Chapter 10).

Molotov, who fancied himself as a bit of a journalist, took a close interest in the fortunes of TASS, the Soviet news agency which has now inherited coverage of the fifteen countries which emerged from the Soviet Union. Realizing, as all the war leaders did, that modern war was information war, as early as 23 July he issued orders designed to ensure the 'unbroken transmission of radio broadcasts of the all-Union Radio Committee and for TASS'. Five 15-kilowatt transmitters were to be moved from Moscow: four to Kuybyshev (formerly, and now again, Samara) and one to Sverdlovsk (formerly and now Yekaterinburg, where the Tsar and his family had been killed in 1918). New radio transmitting centres would be set up in both cities, paid for out of funds allocated for 1941. The NKVD would ensure that the centres would have accommodation, power and water. At this stage Molotov was leaving the options open. There were three variants. First, TASS staff would transfer to Kuybyshev but would continue to transmit from Moscow, with which Kuybyshev would communicate by telephone and and telegraph. Secondly, the entire operation would transfer to Sverdlovsk and, thirdly, to Kuybyshev. Because Sverdlovsk was on the east side of the Urals, broadcasts from there would need to be relayed to reach western Europe and the United States. Kuybyshev was clearly the preferred option.[11]

Two days before, on 20 August, Molotov had authorized 3,600 NKVD and NKGB personnel to be evacuated from Moscow. Of these, the largest component – 1,500 – were going to Kuybyshev. Another 500 headed for Ufa and 500 to the Chkalov *oblast'*.[12] The security service(s), which had officially been reunited exactly a month before (see Chapter 9),[13] were getting some key people out first who guarded the regime, and would be crucial to its survival. But, under the circumstances, that was not necessarily a bad or overcynical decision. The reunited NKVD's responsibilities were enormously wide, and included the construction of permanent defensive works. On 3 September Chernyshev, the Deputy Commissar for Internal Affairs, issued orders that all possible cooperation should take place beween the NKVD and the People's Commissariats for Heavy Metallurgy (NKChM) and Communication Routes (NKPS) to ensure the output and delivery of cement and metal reinforcing rods.[14]

It is clear that Kuybyshev, lying 800 kilometres due east of Moscow, and a more circuitous 1,100 kilometres by train, behind the great reservoirs formed from the Volga at its easternmost points, was already earmarked, if not officially designated, as the reserve capital if Moscow fell. It was the destination of key government agencies and foreign diplomatic missions when the evacuation order was given on 15 October.[15]

On 2 August Stalin issued a curt order that anyone caught causing self-inflicted injury should be shot on sight, as if they were a deserter. Rokossovskiy later called them 'left-handers' – because they generally shot themselves in the palm of the left hand or shot off a few fingers (assuming they were not left-handed). When the authorities quickly got wise to this, people started shooting themselves in the right hand. In order for right-handers to accomplish this, men would sometimes cooperate and shoot each other.[16]

But, with that peculiarly Stalinist combination of carrot and stick, three weeks later, on 22 August, the 'Boss' issued another, much more welcome order. GKO order 562, classified top secret (the order, not its result) was that from 1 September every officer and man serving in the 'army in the field' – as Zhukov had cleverly described it to get round reporting restrictions – was to get a tot of 100 grams of 40 per cent proof vodka each day.[17] They were still dying, but they might die a bit happier, and long-term health problems were not an issue. While some effort was made to keep the fighting men and women as happy as could be expected under the awful circumstances, the civilians working under drab and irksome conditions would soon become less so. On 17 September the GKO announced a programme of spare-time military training for all males between 16 and 50 years old, starting on 1 October. It was designed to ensure that everyone, even those working in other essential industries, had 110 hours of military training – in most cases refresher training, as many had done military service before.[18]

Ethnic minorities . . .

Across the Soviet Union there were small communities of ethnic minority 'Germans'. These were not citizens of the Third Reich who had been there on business on 22 June, who were interned, or, if lucky, evacuated as diplomats, but Soviet people of German origin. They might be useful to the German invaders. The largest German ethnic community comprised the 'Volga Germans', who had their own 'German Republic of Podvol'zhya'. There were also large numbers in the Saratov and Stalingrad regions. In an order of 28 August, the Presidium of the Supreme Soviet alleged that 'according to verified facts', there were 'tens of thousands of diversionary agents and spies, who, on a signal, given from Germany, could detonate explosions in the areas populated by the Volga Germans'. With logic worthy of the later Middle Ages, the Supreme Soviet order continued: 'None of the Germans living in the Volga area have informed the Soviet authorities of the presence of such a large number of diversionary agents and spies.' Therefore, it concluded, with consummate logic, they must have been concealing them, and so should be resettled into 'the Novosibirsk and Omsk regions, Altay, Kazakhstan and other neighbouring areas'.[19] Interestingly, the NKVD, who were professionals, were not impressed. On 14 September the Third Directorate of the NKVD reported that there had been no excesses or anti-Soviet outbursts in the Volga German territories. Since the start of the operation, just 190 people had been arrested.[20] The numbers deported, however, were huge. On 21 September the NKVD reported that 82,608 families – 374,225 people in all – had been deported from the 'former German Republic'. From Saratov, 11,319 families or 43,101 people had been removed, and from Stalingrad 6,541 families or 24,656 people. All told, 100,468 families – 441,982 individuals. It took 178 trains, 16 river steamers and 10 barges to move them. The Volga German Republic had ceased to exist.[21]

Once again, the effort expended on such moves appears extraordinary, given the potential value of 178 *eshelony* – trains, whether for internally displaced persons,[22] or troops – and the river transport for bringing up reinforcements to fight the Germans. With hindsight, it seems an odd sense of priorities.

On 6 September, Stalin ordered 8,617 ethnic minority Germans from Moscow and 21,400 from Rostov to be resettled in Kazakhstan. Each family member was given a baggage allowance of 200 kilograms, to include personal possessions and food for the journey – ten times as much as a modern economy-class air passenger. Given that this was Stalin's Russia at war, those conditions, while tough, were not as brutal as they might have been. By the deadline of 15 September, 7,384 people from Moscow had been moved in three trains. When they reached Kazakhstan, the Kazakh authorities were to provide trucks or wagons to take them from the railheads to the collective farms where they were to start their new lives. This first 'resettlement' was relatively civilized: the mass deportations of those accused of collaborating with the Nazi invasion, which took place in 1942–3, would not be.[23] By 20 September 1,142 'Germans' had been arrested in Moscow, and 8,449 resettled. Just 1,620 remained, including 912 whose heads of family were *not* German – 'German' women who had married Russians, for example, some old and infirm, relatives of Red Army soldiers, NKVD personnel and important specialists whom the People's Commissariats had asked to keep in Moscow.[24]

Scorched earth . . .

By 7 October the German armed forces were close to sealing the Vyaz'ma pocket, and were 100 kilometres from the Mozhaysk defence line and 200 kilometres from the capital.[25] The next day GKO – with Stalin signing, as usual – ordered the formation of a *pyatërka* – a 'gang of five' – headed by deputy Commissar for Internal Affairs Serov, with the head of the Moscow NKVD Zhuravlev and including Chief Engineer Kotlyar, and *troikas* – 'threesomes' from each region of the Moscow District headed by the First Secretaries of the local Communist Parties. Their job was to 'prepare to take the industrial enterprises of Moscow and the Moscow area out of commission'.[26] And, on 9 October, the *pyatërka* duly issued their orders: 1,119 enterprises had been identified for destruction, in two categories. In the first were 412 of 'defence significance' or, perhaps, 'dual use'. These should be blown up. In the second category, 707 enterprises, not specifically defence-related, should be 'damaged' or burned. The enterprises were detailed in an Annex which has not been made public. In addition to the defence-related enterprises, the Annex detailed food manufacturers (bakeries, dairies, meat manufacturers) plus other installations including railway stations, tram and trolleybus stops and electric power stations.[27]

On 10 October another note to Stalin from a disparate group – Molotov and Voroshilov, who were members of GKO, and Koniev, Bulganin and Vasilevskiy, who were not – warned that to cover Moscow five divisions from Twenty-Second and Twenty-Ninth Armies needed to be moved into the Mozhaysk region as soon as possible and that U2 aircraft needed to be sent to Nineteenth, Sixteenth and Twentieth Armies and to Lt Gen. Boldin's Group to expedite the escape of these armies from encirclement.[28]

Panic in the streets? Panic at the top?

In 'early October', according to a Russian historian who later came to know him, Zhukov was summoned to 'Stalin's dacha' – probably Kuntsevo. Zhukov reportedly said 'good afternoon', but Stalin, who had his back to him, apparently did not hear him. Stalin was engrossed in a conversation with Beria. Zhukov allegedly said that he overheard Stalin say, 'Get in touch through your agents with German intelligence, find out what Germany is going to want from us if we offer to sign a separate peace treaty.'[29] It was the same story as in July, when Sudoplatov claimed he was ordered to approach the Bulgarian ambassador (see Chapter 9). There might well have been two or more approaches. But Sudoplatov always maintained that the approach was 'disinformation'. If the report of Zhukov's reminiscence, and Zhukov's version itself, are true, then it sounds as if it was not a disinformation plot. It sounds as if Stalin was serious about offering the Germans everything they had captured so far, if they would leave him alone. And this was the darkest hour. The Germans had captured the Baltic States, Belarus, and much of Ukraine, including all the non-Russian territories of the western USSR. Stalin might have entertained such a surrender, but the Germans would not have accepted it, anyway.

As the reality of the Vyaz'ma disaster sank in, on 12 October the GKO ordered defences to be constructed on the immediate approaches to Moscow city. The 'third line of defence of the City of Moscow' was to be built by a quarter of a million people under forced labour conditions – *trudovoy povinnosti* – in twenty days. Many of them, as can be seen from the photographs, were women. The Moscow Soviet would be responsible for finding 200,000 of them – just about anyone not employed on tanks, munitions, other armaments or other defensive installations. The only technological help they got was an order to the

People's Commissariat for Ferrous Metals (*Narkomchermet*) to provide, within three days, 400 tonnes of steel to make spades.[30]

On 13 October Stalin ordered the evacuation of the four most prestigious Moscow theatres, a sure sign that things were getting really serious. The Lenin State Theatre, the Maksim Gor'kiy Moscow Artistic Academic Theatre, the Little Academic Theatre and the Vakhtangov Theatre were all to be evacuated. The first was to go to Kuybyshev, to join the Kuybyshev Operatic Theatre there; the second, to Saratov, to join the Dramatic Theatre there; the third, to Chelyabinsk, to work with the Dramatic Theatre there, and the last to Omsk, to work with the local theatre there. The People's Commissar for the Arts, Khrapchenko, was responsible for their evacuation and the People's Commissariat for Communications would make available forty-three passenger cars and thirty-five goods wagons for this purpose.[31] The Russians are a cultured and efficient people. But don't get on the wrong side of them.

On 14 October Stalin saw twenty-three of his senior people, starting with Molotov, Beria and Malenkov, all GKO members, who were immediately joined by Shaposhnikov and Vasilevskiy at 15.30, and finishing with Voznesenskiy at 18.15. The last time he had seen that many people was on 1 July, just after the creation of GKO and before he emerged from his 'retreat' (which had been anything but). The decision to evacuate Moscow was taken.[32] With the collapse of the Vyaz'ma pocket, the order to evacuate the capital, just 200 kilometres away, came on 15 October. The Mozhaysk Defence Line, 100 kilometres from Moscow, was the 'tripwire'. The Germans pushed in from the west, along the same route Napoleon had followed. Just short of Mozhaysk, 125 kilometres west of Moscow, on the Smolensk road, they passed the old Napoleonic battlefield of Borodino, and the Soviet defenders in the area put up a stiff fight.[33] The story goes that the defenders were shown Imperial Russian standards from the bloody but not entirely decisive 1812 battle, which were held at the military museum just south of the battlefield, constructed in 1903. However, appealing though the image may be of Soviet communists being solemnly presented with, and motivated by, the symbols of Mother Russia's military past, the author has found no documentary evidence to prove that it happened. The General Staff report for 16 October says that Western Front aviation hit enemy targets in the Borodino area, along with Yukhnov, Mtsensk, Orël, Borovsk and Maloyaroslavets. Recording events the next day, 17 October, the General Staff report mentions Dovator's Cavalry Group and, perhaps significantly, an officer-cadet battalion, formed from those who had been training to become officers but had to be committed to battle as infantry, so desperate was the country's plight. The Cavalry Group and the officer-cadets held the line from Bushino, through Borodino, to Tarutino. If there was ever a consummately appropriate place to use the officer-cadet battalion, it would have been Borodino, but the Red Army General Staff could not afford to waste time on emphasizing historical parallels, intriguing though they are in retrospect. The next day, 18 October, Mozhaysk itself fell to the Germans.[34]

On 12 October the GKO had issued orders for securing the 'Moscow Zone'. From the line about 100 kilometres out from Kalinin–Rzhev–Mozhaysk–Tula–Kolomna–Kashira, eastwards and northwards to the capital, was a 'zone under special security'. The original order to evacuate the capital is shown in Plate 5.

> In view of the unfavourable situation in the area of the Mozhaysk Defence Line the GKO orders:
>
> 1. Comrade Molotov will announce to Foreign Missions that they should today be evacuated to the city of Kuybyshev (People's Commissariat for Communications – Comrade Kaganovich – will ensure the timely departure of members of the Missions and the NKVD – Comrade Beria – will organize their security).
>
> 2. Today the Præsidium of the Supreme Soviet will be evacuated and also the Government with the Deputy Head of the Soviet of People's Commissars Comrade Molotov (Comrade Stalin will be evacuated tomorrow or later, depending on the situation).
>
> 3. Immediately organs of the People's Commissariat for Defence and the People's Commissariat for the Navy will be evacuated to Kuybyshev, and a key group of the general staff – to Arzamas [100 kilometres south of Nizhny-Novgorod and 300 kilometres east of Moscow].
>
> In the event of enemy forces appearing at the gates of Moscow the NKVD – Comrade Beria and Comrade Shcherbakov – will ensure the destruction [blowing up] of all enterprises, depots and establishments which it has not been

possible to evacuate, and also all electric power to the Metro
(excluding water supplies and sewerage).
President of the State Defence Committee I. Stalin.[35]

Whereas, after some uncertainty, Stalin stayed in Moscow, Beria
headed for the Caucasus. In Berezhkov's words, that was 'ostensibly to
coordinate the supplies of oil products for the army'. But in reality, 'he
probably wanted to sit out the time of danger far away from Moscow'.[36]

With most of the government heading for Kuybyshev, Stalin had no
appointments for the next four days – 15–18 October.[37] He moved
around the city, pretty well on his own, apart from bodyguards. The next
day, as Stalin headed in towards the Kremlin he was shocked to see mobs
looting the shops. The looting reached its peak on Thursday, 16 and
Friday, 17 October.[38] It is claimed that Stalin demanded that his car be
stopped, and spoke to the ordinary people before heading back into his
secret world. He ordered all members of the government to head for
Kuybyshev, and their families had just one hour to prepare to move.[39]
The Departments evacuated included the Central Committee of the Communist Party and its staff, Directorates of the General Staff of the Red
Army, military academies, and other People's Commissariats. The
bridges, power stations and main factories were mined, as laid down in
the 9 October order.

Friday, 17 October was payday, and that triggered many of the
incidents. Although the government had ordered everyone to be given a
month's pay – which would be useful for people being evacuated –
many factories were able to pay their workers for only two weeks and
this caused great anger and frustration. At this point, convoys drove
past carrying the possessions of people being evacuated – often government and key defence workers – and the workers turned on the trucks
and started stealing the property of the evacuees. At the Stalin car
factory 1,500 workers demanded access to the factory so that they could
be paid. The janitor manning the sentry box at the gate said 'no', and
was hit over the head with a spade, while two policemen who tried to
restore order were beaten up. At factory number 230 a group of truck
drivers started looting the premises and beat up the secretary of the
factory Communist Party and another communist official who tried to
stop them. Ten arrests were made there, but on the whole, the authorities do not seem to have come down very hard on the rioters. Many
of the former had fled – or, rather, been evacuated – already.[40]

This became clear on 20 October, when Senior Major of State Security (equivalent to a major general) Shadrin, Deputy Head of the First Department of the NKVD, reported on the building vacated by the Communist Party Central Committee '*apparat*' during the evacuation of 16 October.

> 1. ... Not one staff member of the Central Committee, who could have put things in the premises in order and could have burned the secret correspondence remained in place.
> 2. All the equipment – the heating system, the telephone exchange, refrigerators, electric power and so on – was left with no supervision.
> 3. The fire service had disappeared in its entirety. All the fire equipment was thrown about all over the place.
> 4. All the chemical defence equipment, including more than a hundred BS gas masks, was thrown about on the floor in the rooms.
> 5. In the offices of the central committee total chaos reigned. Many locks to the desks and the desks themselves were broken and forms and every conceivable type of correspondence were thrown about including secret Central Committee Directives.
> 6. Top secret material which had been brought to the boiler-house to be incinerated was left in heaps, unburned.
> 7. More than a hundred typewriters of various types, 128 pairs of shoes, sheepskin coats [*tulupy* – precious items in the forthcoming Russian winter], 22 sacks full of footwear and other garments, several tonnes of meat, potatoes, several boxes of herring, meat and other products, were all left behind.
> 8. In Comrade Zhdanov's office five top secret packets were discovered.
> At the moment the premises is being put back in order ...[41]

However, if the Party apparatus had only had an hour or so to get its people and their families out of Moscow, the rapid vacation of the offices is understandable. And Shadrin was a security officer. His job was to ensure regulations were followed. But it was a startling insight into Moscow's midnight hour, as the 'hasty'[42] evacuation of the city proceeded.

Stalin could not make up his mind whether or not to leave. There were no really serious air-raid shelters (bunkers) under the Kremlin and he moved to the best command post available which was at the Air Defence Headquarters at 33 Kirov Street (now Myasnitskaya). When the air-raid alerts sounded, he could descend by lift to the Kirov underground station, now Chistye Prudy, one stop north of Lubyanka on the Sokolnicheskaya line. In the station a special compartment was constructed, shielded from the passing trains by plywood panels. In Simon Sebag Montefiore's words, he 'dossed down ... not unlike an omnipotent tramp'.[43] Stalin was still wondering whether to leave on 18 October, three days after the evacuation order and two after the evacuation of most key people. In 1812 Field Marshal Kutuzov, the wily *War and Peace* commander, had kept his plans to abandon Moscow secret until the last moment. Stalin seems to have made the decision to stay on the evening of 18 October, and announced it on the afternoon of the 19th.[44]

Stalin's new-found identity as a despotic tramp could be the explanation for an order which he signed on 16 October 'not to prevent movement on the Metro' – the Moscow Tube or subway – 'but to reduce it, let us say, by half'.[45] Meanwhile, in the workshops of factories that were being evacuated, especially on assembly lines, every effort should made to keep partial production going while other parts of the factory were removed.

State of siege

The cornerstones to the defence of Moscow were the cities of Kalinin, formerly and now again Tver', 160 kilometres to the north-west, and Tula, the same distance to the south. As most of the government pulled out of Moscow and Stalin hung on, sleeping on a mattress on a Tube platform behind a plywood curtain, the Germans had taken Kalinin, Mozhaysk and Maloyaroslavets. The latter – 'Little, little Yaroslav' – was a key town, on that same line, 100 kilometres south-west of Moscow, which had been the scene of a major battle in 1812 when Napoleon's *Grande Armée* was withdrawing. While, as the NKVD orders acknowledge, the Red Army was operating in the forward areas, the NKVD would man the immediate approaches to central Moscow. This was logical, given their 'peacetime' role, and given that they were much better trained and equipped for fighting in urban areas, which was part of their job. But they might also have fired on the Red Army if it retreated into the city without orders. The 2nd NKVD Motor-Rifle Division was ordered to cover the approaches to Moscow from the north and north-west. The 9th, Dzerzhinskiy, Division, named after the infamous 'Iron Felix' who created the Soviet internal security forces, would cover Sector 2, on the left, to the east. The 2nd Division would cover sector 1, to the north and north-west, on a wide arc from the Yaroslavl' road, coming in from the north-east, to the Mozhaysk road from the west (excluding the latter).[46] On the next day the 9th Dzerzhinskiy Division – by any considerations, an 'elite' formation, was ordered to hold an inner ring, from Vosstaniya and Kuntsevo (exclusive) on the right to the Moscow river on the left. Their orders were to 'prevent enemy motor-mechanized units breaking through to Moscow'. So, to the north and north-west, the 2nd NKVD Motor-Rifle Division was further out, with the 9th, Dzerzhinskiy, Division behind. These were elite NKVD troops, and the backstops.

As part of the shake-up of internal security forces in the capital, the next day Mikhail Zhuravlëv, the commander of NKVD forces in Moscow, ordered the formation of a 'Moscow Motor-Rifle Destroyer Regiment'. This would combine two 'destroyer battalions' created earlier: the 498 men of the Komintern region battalion would form the 1st Battalion of the new regiment and the 462 men of the Krasnogvardeyskiy region battalion would form the 2nd Battalion. The 3rd Battalion would be formed from policemen and other NKVD sub-units. The 4th Battalion, based on the Podol'sk region destroyer battalion, was formed in December. In July 1942, the regiment became 308th Rifle Regiment.[47] The out-of-town NKVD detachments and police were formed into 'destroyer battalions' under an order of 22 October, and on the same day Zhuravlëv issued a strong demand that the destroyer battalions located in the fighting zone should be transferred to command of the Red Army. This made sense as they needed Red Army logistics to supply them with ammunition, food and fuel, but since they were not part of the Red Army, the latter was not obliged to give them anything and there were cases of the unlucky destroyer battalions going without food for days at a time.[48] Since one of their roles was to shoot Red Army soldiers if they retreated, perhaps that is not altogether surprising.

As large numbers of people and equipment were shipped east, and with the city in some disorder, it was inevitable that there would be problems getting vitally needed commodities forward. The NKVD constantly encountered stocks sitting in factories which should have been sent to the troops. On 13 October, munitions factory No. 574 sent 10,000 mines to the Maloyroslavets fortified region, which was about to be taken by the Germans, but the necessary transport did not materialize and they were returned to the factory. The next day, all transport ceased. As a result, after three days, 30,000 anti-tank mines, 2,000 85mm armour-piercing shells and 32,000 shell-cases had piled up at the factory. The pattern was repeated across the city, and continued into December.[49]

On 19 October Army Gen. Zhukov, commanding the Western Front, and Lt Gen. Artem'yev, commanding the Moscow garrison, were ordered to take charge of the defence of the approaches to Moscow. The next day, 20 October, Stalin issued GKO order 813, declaring Moscow to be in a 'state of siege'.[50] A 'state of siege' was a special state of emergency used only in strategically important centres near the battle front with the aim of achieving maximum mobilization of resources. Moscow was the first city to have this dubious distinction. Tula received it six days later, on 26 October. The Crimea was declared to be under siege three days after that, on 29 October, and Stalingrad on 25 August 1942.[51]

In Moscow, a curfew was brought in, prohibiting all movement between midnight and 05.00 hours, apart from public transport and people with special passes from the Moscow city commandant, Major-General Sinilov, who, by a strange coincidence, was also the general commanding the 2nd Motor-Rifle Division of the NKVD. In the event of an air-raid warning they would obey orders from the Moscow Air Defence Command, which would be published in the press. Sinilov also commanded the Police and Workers' Volunteer detachments, including 'destroyer battalions'. Anybody who offended against public order would 'rapidly be brought to account' and sent before a military tribunal, and 'provocateurs, spies and other enemy agents, guilty of disrupting order' would be 'shot on the spot'. The GKO wanted all workers in the capital to maintain order and calm and to cooperate with the Red Army, defending Moscow.[52] No human rights protestors were going to argue with any of this.

In some places, there was panic. Sergeant of State Security – Lieutenant – Vladimir Ogryzko, born in 1917, commanded one of the NKVD detachments. Interviewed on television in 1999, he blamed 'diversionary groups and spies who had broken through Moscow's defences' for spreading panic, but whenever order breaks down, some people take advantage. 'There were robberies – everything you can imagine happened – because as usual, the people lost their heads . . . the ill-educated ones. The scum of the earth did show its face. It seeped through.' The order to shoot anybody who resisted or tried to run away on the spot was interpreted quite literally. People trying to flee without authorization had their cars manhandled or bulldozed into ditches on the side of the road. 'If the driver was crushed,' recalled Ogryzko, 'well, even better.'[53]

The harsh measures, combined with Stalin's decision to stay in Moscow, worked. However, the panic and disorder was not ubiquitous. The situation in Moscow can be gauged from Sinilov's report for the twenty-four hours from 20.00 on Sunday 19th to 20.00 on Monday, 20 October. The authorities pulled in 1,530 people: 14 '*agents provocateurs*' – enemy agents; 26 deserters; 15 for disturbing public order; 33 vandals and 1,442 people 'absent from their units' – soldiers, NKVD, and other government and public service workers who were not where they should be. Of these, the vast majority were taken to the Moscow transit point, and then sent home. Just seven were put in jail, and twelve got 'the highest form of punishment' – they were shot.[54] Given that this was a capital in a 'state of siege' at a critical moment in the war, it does not sound like total 'panic'. Apart from the execution of twelve people, it could be any Saturday night in a large British or American city today. But, then, Stalin's Russia was used to order.

Meanwhile, around 12 to 13 October, Rokossovskiy's Sixteenth Army headquarters, safely extracted from Vyaz'ma, was ordered to take over the area between the Volga reservoir, also known as the 'Moscow Sea', which formed a huge flattened 'Y' shape 25 kilometres north-west of Klin, and Ruza, 80 kilometres west of Moscow. They arrived at Volokolamsk on 14 October to find the situation 'extremely grave'. On 16 October the Germans attacked Sixteenth Army's left flank with armour. But, even before the German attack, Zhukov suggested a counterstroke south of the Volga reservoir, against German forces concentrating in the Volokolamsk area, using a cavalry army formed from four cavalry divisions which had arrived from Central Asia and Dovator's Cavalry Corps. Rokossovskiy thought this would be a complete waste of men and horses. 'I don't know whether I convinced Zhukov,' Rokossovskiy wrote in the expurgated part of his memoirs, 'or whether the increasingly complex situation at the front influenced him. Either way, having asked me to think about his suggestion, he never returned to this question.'[55]

Kuybyshev, and a city called 'Nameless'

Among the foreign diplomats ordered to evacuate Moscow was Ellsworth Lester Raymond, a young American research analyst at the US Embassy in Moscow. 'As the battle of Moscow began,' he later recalled – in other words, starting on 16 October – 'our office was evacuated to the old Volga city, Kuibyshev [sic], where we remained till some months after the Battle of Stalingrad.'[56]

Kuybyshev did not look like the capital-in-waiting. Its population in 1941 was more than half a million, but a visitor could walk across the entire city in a couple of hours. Like a mirror image of Stalingrad, 600 kilometres down the Volga to the south-west, the old part of the city stood on a high bluff overlooking the river which, here, was a mile wide, but looking to the west, not the east. The city's population had expanded greatly since the Revolution, but more people had simply been crammed into the same space. Like many places in Russia today, there were old houses which, with a lick of paint, might have looked quite grand, but painting was not a favoured activity, in spite of the corrosive and abrasive climate. The city looked at its best draped in icicles and frozen against a midnight-blue winter sky, like a set from *Dr Zhivago*.[57] Very few new buildings had been erected, but they included a rather fine NKVD club, and a new hall of residence for railway workers near the rail marshalling yards. There were only four paved streets: the main street, two leading to the railway station, and one leading out towards the factories. A few streets had been modestly improved by laying cobblestones down the middle. There was a trolleybus service along two of the four principal streets, and during the war a bus service was begun on the other two. There were very few cars or trucks and, in addition to horses, camels were much in evidence. There were two small hotels, which Raymond thought were much like the hotels in small midwestern US cities. There were a few blocks of shops and offices on the main street, plus a few shops in the side lanes. Sanitation relied on privies, even close to the main shopping centre, and the water supply came from wells. This city of half a million people had as many shops and stores as an American one of 15,000. However, there was a music hall, an opera house and a theatre – the Kuybyshev Operatic, where the Lenin State Theatre from Moscow was to find a temporary home.[58]

There was a small macaroni-making plant, a clothes factory, a foundry and sheds for drying the fish which teemed in the great river. With the mile-wide Volga, nobody need starve or want for protein. But the only modern installations seemed to be the grain elevator and a power station. The latter was surrounded by a concrete wall and armed guards. They were NKVD, responsible for the security of power and industry. But life in Kuybyshev, the Soviet Union's reserve capital, was, Raymond recalled, like that in a sleepy American country town – 'slow, quiet and drab'.[59]

However, a year after his evacuation from Moscow, as the Battle of Stalingrad was raging in late 1942, Raymond had seen the full picture:

> A short trip outside the town explained matters only too well. Several miles from Kuibyshev's outskirts stood a second city almost as large as the town itself, but consisting of nothing but factories. This was Nameless [*Bezymyanny*], a city of smokestacks, where big factories stood side by side like houses. Several of these factories made airplane parts and assembled planes, forming a giant conveyor belt not of machines but of factories. US Air Transport Command aviators, who had visited every British and American battlefront in the world, had never seen so many military planes together as in this Nameless airport. These hundreds of aircraft were the output of the seven factories . . . This sleepy residential city was simply one giant dormitory for the many thousands of workers who trekked every day on foot or by ailing trolley to the Nameless factories. Nor was Nameless a purely wartime creation. Some of the huge industrial plants

> were evacuees from the West [of the USSR], *but many had been built near Kuibyshev before Hitler invaded Russia.*[60]

Only the Russians could create a city called 'Nameless', to go with cities called 'Terrible' (Grozny) and 'Lord of the East' (Vladivostok). They had obviously read Homer.

There was an even darker side to Kuybyshev, as well. As the Soviet forces pulled back the NKVD had either transferred those they were holding in jail to the interior of the country, or, if that proved difficult, killed them, often by throwing hand grenades into prison cells. On 3 October, Beria had 157 prominent prisoners shot, including Olga Kameneva, Trotskiy's sister and the widow of Lev Kamenev, a well-known victim of the purges.[61]

In Kuybyshev twenty-five senior officers, officials and intellectuals had been held for between three months and, in one case, nearly four years (from January 1938). On 17 October, two days after the order to evacuate Moscow, the NKVD decided to execute them. The next day, 18 October, Beria signed the order. All were arrested in accordance with the 17 October NKVD 'judgment' and charged with membership of anti-Soviet, Trotskyite organizations. Most were shot without trial on 28 October, the last on 6 November. Among them were military officers from Colonel to Colonel-General, senior officials, including a deputy People's Commissar for Trade, and a writer. Of the officers, one was Lieutenant-General of the Air Force Pavel Rychagev, just 30 years old. Shortly before Barbarossa, he had rashly criticized the aircraft his pilots had to fly, and two days after the German attack he was arrested. Four of those condemned and executed without trial were women. Zinaida Rozova-Yegorova, aged about 37, was a student at the Foreign Languages Institute. Mariya Nesterenko, aged about 31, was a major in the Red Air Force, a woman pilot. Aleksandra Fibikh-Savchenko-Petrovskaya, aged about 40, was described as a 'housewife', but happened to be married to the deputy Chief of the Red Army's Main Artillery Directorate, which oversaw not just large-calibre artillery but all ordnance development including small arms. And finally, there was Anna Slezberg, aged about 48, head of a department in the People's Commissariat for the Food Industry.[62]

All their convictions were quashed, posthumously, after Stalin's death in 1953. Most were quashed between 1954 and 1956, including all the women's, but one did not receive his pardon until November 1961.

That was Filipp Goloshchekin, who had worked for the Council of People's Commissars of the USSR, and who was arrested in October 1939 for being a member of a 'right-wing Trotskyite organization', and executed on 28 October 1941, aged about 65.[63]

It is hard to believe that any of these distinguished and able individuals, who could have been very useful to the war effort, were guilty of the crimes of which they were accused. Of the millions who perished at the hands of Stalin's regime, the names and details of the Kuybyshev twenty-five are at least preserved in the NKVD archives. In mid October 1941 sections of the government apparatus – including Beria himself – were moving to Kuybyshev. They were probably just taking up too much space. It was yet another example of the predatory, self-consuming, self-destructive character of parts of the system.

When the cat's away . . .

The People's Commissariat for Foreign Affairs had also been evacuated to Kuybyshev on 16 October, along with the foreign diplomatic missions. In early November, after the mid October panic had subsided, Berezhkov, now Molotov's assistant, and his colleague, Pavlov, were ordered to return to Moscow. They found their Kremlin offices occupied, so Molotov suggested they move on a temporary basis into Beria's, which were still vacant. The Kremlin commandant was duly called and, 'without any enthusiasm', did as the Foreign Minister and Stalin's political deputy ordered.

A visitor to Beria's suite, which had originally been occupied by the Tsar's servants, would first enter a reception room where the guards were posted. A door to the right led to the secretariat, which comprised two relatively small rooms. The door on the left opened into a big meeting room with a long table. Beyond this lay Beria's study, which was connected to a 'relaxation room'. Further on was a bedroom and small kitchen with a sink and gas stove. Although Beria could sleep here, it was a more modest suite than those of Molotov, Stalin and other Politburo members, because Beria had his main apartment outside the Kremlin, on the corner of Kachalov Street and the Garden Ring. Allegedly, that was because the head of the People's Commissariat for Internal Affairs, now reunited with that for State Security, could be secured independently of other Politburo members in the event of a terrorist attack and could then organize the rescue of the other government members if they were trapped in the Kremlin.[64] The real reason was that Beria liked to cruise the streets of Moscow at night in his armoured limousine and pick up young women and girls who, given Beria's position, could do absolutely nothing to resist his predatory advances.

Beria's suite was in perfect order, which, as with most tidy places, meant it was unlived or worked in. 'It was as if the occupant had no intention of coming back,' recalled Berezhkov.[65] All the telephones were working, including those on the Kremlin switchboard and the government intercity high-frequency link. 'We didn't feel comfortable in Beria's office suite,' recalled Berezhkov. 'The only thing we liked was its bathroom with its constantly running hot water and the Government intercity telephone.' Berezhkov and Pavlov often had to call Kuybyshev, where Vyshinskiy, the deputy Foreign Minister, and their colleagues on the British and US desks of the Foreign Ministry, were still operating. They also used the privileges of rank and luck – as anyone would – to call their wives. Having been given one hour's notice to leave Moscow with all they could carry, including, in most cases, young children, these senior members of Soviet society had been evacuated along 1,100 kilometres of railway on a circuitous route via Nizhny-Novgorod and Penza to a 'slow, quiet and drab' town on the edge of Asia, where the most exciting place was a neighbouring cluster of factories called 'Nameless'. Inevitably, Beria's phone was closely monitored. One day, it rang. 'Hello,' said Berezhkov.

> 'Who gave you permission to use Lavrenty Pavlovich's phone?'
>
> 'Who's asking?'
>
> 'This is General Serov, in charge of Government Communications. I am informed this is not the first time you have used the Government Communications system to make personal calls.'
>
> 'Berezhkov speaking here. We met in L'vov [L'viv], you may recall. I work in this office because Vyacheslav Mikhaylovich [Molotov] instructed me to, while Comrade Beria is away. I am Molotov's assistant. How come you don't know this?'

'I am in Kuybyshev at present and I guess I haven't been kept up to date,' Serov said, somewhat flustered, and hung up.[66]

Berezhkov's luck, at least, was holding. Millions of others were not so fortunate.

The last *Wehrmacht* window of opportunity before winter

But while some elements of Moscow's population were panicking, and most of the organs of Soviet government and communications were in, or trundling towards, Kuybyshev, the Germans were running out of steam. They were also bogged down in mud.

On 13 October Stavka merged the Moscow Reserve Front into the Western Front, under Zhukov, and formed the Fifth, Sixteenth, Forty-Third and Forty-Ninth Armies to defend the approaches from Mozhaisk, Volokolamsk, Maloyaroslavets and Kaluga, respectively. The Germans reached all four places between 11 and 16 October, and captured them all. But by 30 October, the German attack had ground to a halt. By that time, the *Wehrmacht* had suffered 686,000 casualties – one-fifth of the force that had launched its proud crusade in the small hours of 22 June, plus all the replacements sent since then. On 22 June the *Wehrmacht* on the eastern front had fielded 3.2 million: now it was down to 2.7 million. Only a third of all motor vehicles were operational.[67]

As noted in Chapter 10, the Soviet disasters at Vyaz'ma-Bryansk early in October had made the Germans overconfident. Army Group Centre was ordered to spread its effort to north and south, to link up with those respective Army Groups, and, as a result, lacked the necessary punch for a decisive pursuit of the reeling Soviet forces towards Moscow. The combined effects of funnel and mud had an inevitable synergy. Soviet resistance also stiffened in the second half of October, as they fell back before the capital. Soviet command arrangements became simpler as the distance of forward Soviet forces from the capital decreased, and the abolition of the Western Strategic Direction on 10 September removed an unnecessary intermediate chain of command (although Stavka had largely ignored it, anyway). German Army Group Centre ceased its offensive efforts in the last ten days of October, which was officially approved by Bock on 1 November.[68]

If the *Wehrmacht* wished to capture Moscow in the centre, Rostov in the south, and completely isolate Leningrad in the north, it had a slim window of opportunity before winter. The sucking mud would freeze in mid November, and there would be a brief spell when fast movement would be possible before deep snow fell. But no one could predict the uncertain, fickle nature of the weather. The winter of 1941–2 was the worst in central and eastern Europe for many years. On 7 November Halder prepared a plan with two variants. The 'maximum' envisaged a drive to the line Vologda, Gorkiy, Stalingrad and Maikop, which would cut off Moscow from the northern ports and the north Caucasus oil and industrial region. Even that would not end the war, but it would put Germany in a strong position to resume operations the next year. The 'minimum' variant envisaged an advance to the line running from 50 kilometres east of Lake Ladoga, to a point 275 kilometres east of Moscow and then to Rostov.[69]

On 13 November Halder and his main OKH staff officers met the Chiefs of Staff of the three eastern front army groups, and of all the armies and panzer groups at Orsha, on the railway line from Minsk to Moscow, 500 kilometres from the Kremlin. Halder wanted to discuss whether to continue offensive operations or call a halt right there and resume in spring 1942. The Chiefs of Staff were pretty unanimous that the campaign had failed in its initial objectives of defeating Soviet Russia in a swift campaign and destroying the Red Army, which had suffered the loss of its entire peacetime strength – 4 million troops[70] – and yet was still there, and fighting back ever more fiercely. The Chiefs of Staff all thought they should stop and dig in for the winter, but Halder and Bock both thought they had to make one last throw of the iron dice.[71] Privately, they too had doubts. Halder recorded the 'long-range' and 'short-range' options, described above. 'Von Bock argues', he wrote, 'that even if we were content to reach the interim objective ('the bird in the hand') [it wasn't], we would have to commence the attack immediately, for every day was bringing us closer to the critical date for deep snowfall.'[72] It was undoubtedly the last opportunity to defeat the Russians before winter.

As noted above, the Germans were planning to make their main effort from west-north-west – the sector bounded by the Moskva river (west) and the Moskva–Volga canal (north). Hitler had already approved a plan on 30 October which envisaged encircling Moscow and linking up to the east-south-east of the capital, between Orekhovo Zuyevo (east) and Kolomna (south-east).[73] Extraordinarily, to justify a final supreme effort to capture Moscow, which he had previously considered 'merely a geographical expression', Hitler now started using arguments that he had previously rejected about the criticality of Moscow as the focal communications centre. All the railways converged there, and its capture would effectively destroy the Soviet regime.[74] Meanwhile, General Thomas, Chief of the War Economy and Armaments Office, warned that even if the Donets Basin, Stalingrad, Voronezh, Moscow and Gorkiy were taken, a residual Soviet state could carry on fighting from its industrial bases in the Urals. By the time that was under threat, in the middle of 1942, the 'Anglo-Saxons' (the British and Americans) would be involved in the war. His study was not taken seriously, but he was probably right.[75]

Hitler dismissed reports of new Russian armies forming in the Ural mountain and Volga river areas, saying that was 'impossible', if only because the equipment for them would not be available. In fact, from mid October the Soviet Union was forming eleven new armies, and also began to redeploy more troops from the Far East, Siberia and the Caucasus (see below).[76]

After a pause of nearly three weeks for resupply, German operations in the east began again on 15 November, with the objective of encircling Moscow.[77] Meanwhile, on 30 October, Stalin had raised a casual question. 'How are we going to do the military parade?' That was the great, traditional 7 November Red Square parade, the celebration of the 1917 'October' Revolution, which had taken place on 24–5 October, Old Style – 6–7 November, New Style. General Pavel Artem'ev, who had been commander of the Moscow Military District and had taken command of the Moscow defence zone as the critical phase began, on 12 October, said it could not happen. Yes, it would, said Stalin. If there was a German air raid, the dead and wounded should be removed quickly, he added.[78] It *would* happen. The risk was considerable. The potential political response was devastatingly positive, and worth the risk. The 'Boss' had his faults, but this was the decision of a leader. The parade would take place, and the troops, guns and armoured vehicles would then proceed straight to the front. It was a stroke of genius. The military effect would be compounded by the media and political effect. As always, everything was kept secret until the last moment. The officers involved did not receive their final briefing until 02.00. Stalin liked surprises, as most dictators do.

On 7 November, at 08.00 hours, just after dawn, under a steely, overcast Russian sky, with rimy air on the brink of freezing and snow beginning to fall, the troops marched south-east down the 'square', towards St Basil's Cathedral and the Moskva river, beyond. Red Square,[79] which owes its name to the old Slavic word for 'beautiful', and not to communism at all, is not really a square, either. It is a wide cobbled boulevard, running past the north-east wall of the red-brick, triangular Renaissance fortress. St Basil's Cathedral is the onion-domed fantasy built for Ivan the Terrible. He was so delighted with it that he had the architect's eyes put out, so that he could not build for anybody else anything so whimsically fantastic and beautiful. Stalin admired Ivan. The Germans were coming from the north-north-west, so, once the troops, guns and armoured vehicles had passed Lenin's Mausoleum and reached St Basil's, they would turn smartly about and head in the opposite direction, up Gor'kiy Street, and then north-west, to face the Germans.

The stars of the show were the new T-34 and KV tanks. But one of the heavy KV tanks screeched to a halt and then turned the wrong way. Another followed. The tanks were all armed, ready for battle, and if anybody wanted to take out the Politburo standing on Lenin's Mausoleum, that would have been an ideal opportunity. Given the paranoia which prevailed in Moscow at the time, overreaction might have been the order of the day. Artem'ev demanded to know what had happened. The first tank, it turned out, had suffered a mechanical problem, and its commander did not want to cause any embarrassment on the big parade, so he got out of the way. Following the standard operating procedures the newly trained crews had been taught, the second tank went to its aid. This was starting to look like a professional army. The boss classes gathered on the Mausoleum found it amusing, and no one was reprimanded.[80] The big parade was an iconic image of the war, and a stroke of public-relations genius. And, that night, earlier than usual, the Russian winter snow really began to fall. That was the night of 7–8 November. On 12 November the temperature fell to −15 °C (5 °F) and the next day to −22 °C (−8 °F). It was going to be a cold winter, and there has been much debate about whether it was unusually so (see Chapter 12).

On 14 November Stalin ordered Zhukov, who, after a brief spell in Leningrad (see Chapter 13) had been moved back to Moscow on 5 October and appointed to command the Western Front on 10 October, to mount attacks to disrupt German preparations. Zhukov protested, but Stalin insisted. On 16 November, on Zhukov's orders, Rokossovskiy's Sixteenth Army and Zakharkin's Forty-Ninth attacked the flanks of the German Fourth Army. These attacks were disastrous, with heavy casualties including the massacre of 2,000 men and horses of Dovator's 20th and 44th Cavalry Divisions.[81]

However, there were signs that the Germans were reaching their 'culminating point' – the term military planners use for the point at which the weight of an army's offensive power is outweighed by the logistic constraints acting like a giant elasticated bungee cord to pull it back. At Uslovaya, south of Tula, on 8 November the 413th Rifle Division, which had just arrived, in combination with 239th and 32nd Tank Brigades, mounted an attack which, although unsuccessful, severely upset Guderian's headquarters. On 17 November parts of the German 112th Infantry Division, which lacked heavy anti-tank weapons, broke and ran before attacks by new Soviet T-34s. This was not supposed to happen in the *Wehrmacht*. As temperatures dropped to − 20°C, or thereabouts, it did.[82] But the Russians had to fight in these temperatures too, of course. The next day the German Second Panzer Group bypassed Tula to the east and then headed north-east through Venev towards Ryazan' – an 'exceptionally dangerous situation', in Zhukov's words. Moscow was being enveloped. As the Germans headed for the Western Front's headquarters at Kashira, 80 kilometres northeast of Tula and 120 south-south-east of Moscow, the Russians hurled Major-General Belov's II Cavalry Corps at the German flank. On 26 November, the Cavalry Corps, now renamed I Guards, plus the Soviet 112th Tank Division, an armoured brigade and a *divizion* (battalion) of *Katyusha* multiple rocket-launchers, with air support, succeeded in driving the Germans back 40 kilometres to Mordves (between Tula and Kashira).[83]

By late November, a force of 65,000 troops defended the city of Moscow proper: people's militia and destroyer detachments, including the Moscow Destroyer Regiment, and the two NKVD divisions.[84] The big anti-tank ditches on which thousands had laboured during the late summer were further west, now overrun by the Germans. The city's direct defences consisted of three defence lines: an outer defence belt 30 kilometres out, a second defence belt round the suburbs, 22 kilometres out, and a rear defensive belt behind (east of) the city. Within the city centre there was a complex system of barricades and defensive belts manned by internal security forces, and mounted NKVD troops patrolled the streets.

A prominent feature of the barricades in the city and suburbs were the 'ёzhy' (pronounced 'yozhy') or 'hedgehogs', made from three pieces of steel girder welded together. The giant version of these which can be seen on the main road north-west to Moscow's Sheremetevo international airport and on to St Petersburg (Leningrad) stands at the 22 kilometre line – the second line of defence. The granite-faced soldiers who stare impassively from the north-east side of the road at the Zelenovka monument, 41 kilometres out, mark the limit of the main German forces' advance. The kilometre stone, No. 41, is in the Central Museum of the Armed Forces.

Don't let the truth get in the way of a good story . . .

During the fighting on the approaches to Moscow, Volokolamsk, on the main railway line from Latvia, and 110 kilometres from central Moscow, was a key position on the Mozhaysk defence line. It was held by Rokossovskiy's Sixteenth Army, but fell to the Germans on 27 October. After the declaration of the Moscow 'state of siege' on 20 October the situation east of Volokolamsk became critical. On 24 October the Germans attacked Volokolamsk with five divisions and captured it after a seven-day battle. Then the front stabilized. It was clear to Stavka that this was going to be the main launching pad for the German attack on Moscow. As noted, Zhukov was pinning his defence on cornerstones at Kalinin (Tver') in the north and Tula in the south. Rokossovskiy was holding to the north-west of Moscow, but his forces were forced back towards Klin, 90 kilometres from central Moscow. On the next main

approach, anticlockwise, through Volokolamsk and Istra (just 50 kilometres out) there were three rifle divisions: 316th, 18th and 78th, two
cavalry, Dovatpor's 50th and 53rd, and the 1st Guards Tank Brigade.
Here they struggled to hold back Hoepner's Fourth Panzer Group.[85]

Major-General Ivan Vasilevich Panfilov (1893–1941) was commanding 316th Rifle Division. He died fighting, and his 316th Division was
renamed 8th Guards for its heroic role in the defence of Moscow. It was
in Panfilov's divisional area, at Dubosekovo (which means 'the place
where oak trees are cut down'), 7 kilometres south-east of Volokolamsk,
on 16 November, that one of the most famous tales of the Great
Patriotic War was played out. It had all the ingredients of a great story,
including the place-name.

Among Panfilov's troops, the famous 'Panfilovtsy', twenty-eight
members of 1075 Rifle Regiment went down in history. Led by junior
political officer – politruk – Lt Klochkov-Diyev, they held off superior
German forces for four hours and in the process destroyed eighteen
German tanks and killed 'dozens' of German troops. A monument to
their achievement stands on the site.

However, in 1947 the military procurator for the Khabarovsk
garrison arrested Ivan Yevstavevich Dobrovavin for treason to his
country. Fighting at the front, in 1942, Dobrovavin had given himself
up to the Germans and allowed himself to be taken prisoner. In spring
1942 he started working for them as chief of police in Perekop, in the
occupied isthmus leading into the Crimea. He was arrested by Soviet
forces (the NKVD) in March 1943 but managed to escape from
captivity, and rejoined the Germans. While under Soviet arrest (presumably the second time), Dobrovavin was found with a copy of the book
The 28 Panfilovtsy Heroes,[86] and it emerged that he had received the pre-
eminent award of Hero of the Soviet Union for his role as a leading
participant in the legendary event.

Under interrogation, Dobrovavin revealed that at Dubosekovo,
where he had genuinely been present, and had also been taken prisoner
by the Germans, he had not destroyed any tanks and that everything
written in the book about the exploits of the twenty-eight had never
actually happened. The top secret note dated 13 June 1948 and reproduced as Plate 6 was sent by Andrey Zhdanov, the Secretary of the Party
Central Committee, to Stalin, Molotov, Beria, Mikoyan, Malenkov,
Voznesenskiy, Kaganovich and Bulganin – the entire Politburo.[87] So,
from 1948, the entire Soviet leadership knew that the famous story of

the twenty-eight gallant 'Panfilovtsy' was a myth (although their General died in action – that is undisputed). But it had been too good a story at the time, and it was too good a story in 1948 as the nation was struggling to recover from the hot war and bracing itself for the cold one. And so it passed into history – until now.

Sunrise in the east?

In late September the NKGB's man in Tokyo, Richard Sorge, had reported that Japan's aggressive intentions lay to the south, to seize the rubber and oil of south-east Asia. Stalin was understandably sceptical, as he was of all intelligence reports (see Chapter 6). On 13 April 1941, the Soviet Union and Japan had signed a non-aggression pact with considerable fanfare, after the Japanese Foreign Minister, Matsuoka, had travelled to Moscow along the trans-Siberian railway. But the events of 22 June hardly inspired confidence in non-aggression pacts. From the Japanese point of view, the Pact was to protect its rear while it pursued a more aggressive policy in the Pacific, but, particularly after 22 June 1941, Stalin was not necessarily going to buy that. It is true, however, that in September Japan took the decision to go to war with Britain, the Netherlands and the US if diplomacy failed to lift the sanctions which were being imposed on it because of its presence in Indo-China and Manchuria.

Sorge was a confidant of Ott, the German ambassador in Tokyo, and had access to some valuable information. On this occasion, his information was sound, but his reports were not always accurate and have been quoted selectively by historians since.[88] On 12 October Stalin consulted with his advisers. It is frequently claimed that the intelligence from the Sorge group triggered a massive transfer westwards of troops, who proved critical in the Battle for Moscow. The truth is a little more complicated. There had already been significant transfers of troops westwards in the spring and early summer. While German sources cite the arrival of central Asian troops in the Tikhvin area as part of the Leningrad operations, the main Red Banner armies in the Far East were placed on the alert in August, but for possible *offensive* operations in the event of Japanese intervention in the war.[89] On 1 August the NKVD had intercepted a communication from the British Foreign Office to the Ambassador in Tokyo saying that if Japan attacked the USSR the British would not necessarily sever diplomatic relations because it would be easier to observe Japanese policy with diplomats still in place.[90] That reinforced Russian suspicions of perfidious Albion. More importantly, in October the NKVD reported a number of border violations on the frontier between the Soviet Union and Japan and its puppet state of Manchukuo. Most were by aircraft and ships but on 22 and 23 October three groups of Japanese soldiers crossed the frontier.[91] On 2 November the NKVD foreign intelligence department warned Beria and the General Staff that the Kwantung army had given permission for Japanese forces to capture Soviet border guard posts.[92]

It may be that this was part of a Japanese deception plan to keep the Russians – and the British and Americans – on their toes. The Soviet policy in the winter of 1941 was to send some units shattered by fighting the Germans to the Far East to re-form, and to ship fresh divisions from the Far East in exchange. Once the Siberian winter set in, a Japanese attack was unlikely in any case.[93]

Another factor was the Japanese perception of Soviet military strength and competence. Having been bled and mauled horribly at Khalkin Gol, by Zhukov, no less, the Japanese were wary of Soviet strength on the plains of Mongolia and, no doubt, in the forests of Siberia. According to German sources, the damage inflicted on the German attackers by the Red Army at Smolensk, between 10 July and 10 September, also had an effect on the Japanese. Only then did they accept the 'southern variant' plan, persuaded, quite possibly, by the continued presence of very large Soviet armies totalling about 700,000 in the Far East.[94] They were good in the jungle and at sea, but they 'did not do' deciduous and coniferous forest, steppe, desert and snow. And, apart from wood, what was there in Siberia worth taking, at least in the short term? Wisely, the Japanese turned south. But Stalin was probably never entirely sure, and certainly not before 7 December 1941, when the Japanese did their own, ill-advised version of Barbarossa, and attacked the greatest military and industrial power of the twentieth century, the United States. A bad move, as it turned out.

The reinforcements which appeared before and during the Battle of Moscow tell the story. The Germans had reckoned, based on the 'two divisions per million of population' rule of thumb, that the USSR could raise another 300 divisions. By December, it had raised twice that number: 285 rifle divisions, twelve re-formed tank divisions, 88 cavalry divisions, 174 rifle and 93 tank brigades by 31 December 1941.[95]

Excluding 9 armies formed in June under the 13 May mobilization order, between July and the end of December 1941 50 armies had been newly created or re-formed. These included 12 corps which had been made into armies and 13 armies which had been re-formed, plus 3 Fortified Regions and one Front (Army Group) which had morphed into armies. But that still left 21 new armies, after the 9 conceived before Barbarossa.[96] During October and November the Fifth Army (one of 13 re-formed) was activated east of Moscow, along with Twenty-Sixth (which had been a Rifle Corps), Tenth, south of Moscow (its third incarnation), Fifty-Sixth, and Fifty-Seventh, both new armies, in the North Caucasus. In November the Nineteenth, Sixtieth, Twenty-Fourth, Twenty-Eighth and Twentieth Armies were formed in the Moscow area, plus the Fifty-Eighth, Fifty-Ninth, Thirtieth and Twenty-Eighth east of Leningrad, the Sixty-First, east of Tula and the Thirty-Seventh, in the Don bend. Just two new armies – Fifty-Eighth and Fifty-Ninth – were formed in Siberia in November, but existing formations were transported from the Far East.[97]

Since the start of the Great Patriotic War, therefore, some 70 divisions had been brought from interior Military Districts, and 194 divisions and 94 brigades had been newly raised. Around 27 divisions had been brought from the Far East, central Asia and Transcaucasia.[98] Overall, then, the divisions brought from the Far East after 12 October were a small contribution. The creation of 9 new armies comprising 59 rifle and 13 cavalry divisions and 75 rifle and 20 tank brigades was at least as significant.[99] But, unlike the newly raised and scarcely trained new formations, the 27 divisions moved from the Far East, central Asia and the Caucasus, and especially those from the elite armies of the Far East, stood out for their quality. At this critical moment, that is what counted most. Whereas the newly formed divisions included urban workers unused to forest and skis, the Siberians had grown up with all that, and were natural hunters and skilled shots. Many were the kind of people who, in later generations, would have joined *Spetsnaz* – the Soviet and Russian special forces. *Za pugannogo – dvukh nepugannykh dayut.*[100] But, numerically, they were far less significant than conventional wisdom would have us believe.

Rokossovskiy received cavalry divisions from central Asia in mid

November. 'The horses weren't made for winter,' Rokossovskiy recalled. Neither they nor their riders were suited to the marshy, forested conditions in which they found themselves. On the other hand, the arrival of 78th Siberian Rifle Division, 'fully manned and equipped for winter conditions at wartime establishment . . . made us very happy'.[101]

Zhukov was clearly worried at this time. According to Rokossovskiy, in paragraphs excised from the Soviet edition of his memoirs – which must have been because they were critical of Zhukov – the Western Front commander effectively accused Rokossovskiy of 'panicking', as he conducted a slow withdrawal in contact – one of the most difficult manoeuvres in war, at any level – pulling back 2–3 kilometres a day. At this point Rokossovskiy's left wing was between 10 and 12 kilometres from the Istrin reservoir. Zhukov was planning another counterstroke south of the Volga reservoir, towards Klin (see Figure 12.1). He ordered Rokossovskiy's Sixteenth Army not to withdraw one step. Rokossovskiy recalled the 'short, but terrible coded message from Zhukov. "I command the Front's forces. I countermand the order about withdrawing forces to the Istra reservoir [see Figure 12.1]. I order those defending that line *not to take one step back*." '[102] And then, Rokossovskiy lets rip. 'I can't remain silent about the fact that, at the start of the war, and in the Battle of Moscow, in prominent instances, which were not infrequent, he took no account of the time, and the forces, which his instructions and orders were throwing away.'[103]

On one occasion Zhukov arrived at Rokossovskiy's Sixteenth Army headquarters (command post – KP), bringing with him General Leonid Govorov, who, a month before – 18 October – had been placed in command of Fifth Army, on Rokossovskiy's left. An artilleryman, Govorov had been crucial in breaking through the Mannerheim Line in the Finnish war (see Chapter 4). What happened then tells a lot about the relationship between extremely senior – multi-stellar – officers in the Red Army. Beneath a veneer of politeness, with a few exceptions, they all seem to have hated one another.

'Well,' Zhukov began, fingering Rokossovskiy, 'the Germans have been chasing you again, eh? You've got plenty of forces, but you don't know how to use them. You're a *useless commander*! Govorov's got more enemy forces than you have in front of him, and he holds them. I've brought him here, so he can teach you how to fight.' Zhukov was wrong about the enemy strengths, of course, Rokossovskiy explains. Zhukov went to another room, presumably to study the situation, leaving Rokossovskiy and his staff devastated, but determined to prove him wrong. Shortly afterwards, Zhukov rushed back in, his face 'terrible'.

Suddenly, the tables were turned. Now Govorov was the target. Zhukov started to shout 'in a shattering voice':

> You what? Who did you come here to teach? Rokossovskiy?
> He pushes back attacks by German armoured divisions and
> beats the shit out of them. Against you they sent some
> rubbish motorised division or other and chased you for tens
> of kilometres. Get lost! *And if you don't sort it out*...[104]

Rokossovskiy, always dignified and correct, later recorded 'and so on, etcetera'. Zhukov's management style was in complete contrast to Rokossovskiy's. While this tirade was going on, Zhukov's Chief-of-Staff delivered an unwelcome message. While Zhukov had been humiliating two of his army commanders by turns, perhaps to encourage rivalry, a German motorized division had broken into Fifth Army's area and penetrated 15 kilometres. Zhukov immediately calmed down.[105] It was time to start behaving like grown-ups.

Zhukov was clearly under enormous stress. He often said that of all the times in the Great Patriotic War, the time when he really worried was the Battle of Moscow. 'Whenever they ask me what I remember above all about the war gone by, I always answer: the Battle for Moscow.'[106] On several occasions, during this critical time in October and November, Stalin asked, 'Can we hold Moscow?' He asked Zhukov at least twice, on 17 October and 15 November, and probably many more times as well.[107] On the second occasion, Zhukov said, 'We'll hold Moscow, without a doubt.' About the same time Rokossovskiy, the rapidly rising star of the Red Army, told P. Troyanovskiy, a reporter for the Red Army newspaper *Red Star*, what he thought.

'Guaranteed. Soon the Germans will start to get washed out,' – *vydykhatsya* – 'and the time will come – we'll be in Berlin.'[108]

Zhukov focused on the immediate objective. Rokossovskiy, who had been Zhukov's senior, was already looking at the big picture.

12

BLACK SNOW

The tipping point

The Soviet command expected the main German attack on Moscow to come in the second half of November, and so it was. The Soviet accounts stress that the Red Army, backed by the NKVD, fought the Germans to a standstill by the beginning of November, and that the Germans needed two weeks to prepare for their next move. That also allowed the Russians to reinforce their forward troops and consolidate defences. They dismiss the role of the weather, arguing that they had to fight in it, too. However, it seems undeniable that the *rasputitsa* – the season of mud – severely hampered the German advance and that when the winter freeze came, which was at least as cold as anyone expected that year, the Russians were far better equipped, and their equipment far better designed, to work in the cold. And they knew it.[1]

The first news to the German people that the *Wehrmacht* had gone on the attack again was not broadcast until 24 November, after the capture of Solnechnogorsk – a town called 'Sunny' (!), 50 kilometres north-west of Moscow (see Figure 12.1).[2] The Germans had struggled down the highway from Kalinin (Tver'), through Klin, and were now heading for their final destination: a milestone called 'kilometre 41'. The grey obelisk, about a metre high, stood at that point on the road to Leningrad, north-west of the centre of Moscow. Many German accounts indicate that forward units of the lead formations got closer than that. On 27 November troops of Third Panzer Army got across the Moscow-Volga canal, running due north from the city, and seized the bridge at Yakhroma, 60 kilometres north of Moscow centre, intact. They managed to blow up the power station, which had supplied most of the capital's electricity. Stalin recognized the danger this represented – Moscow

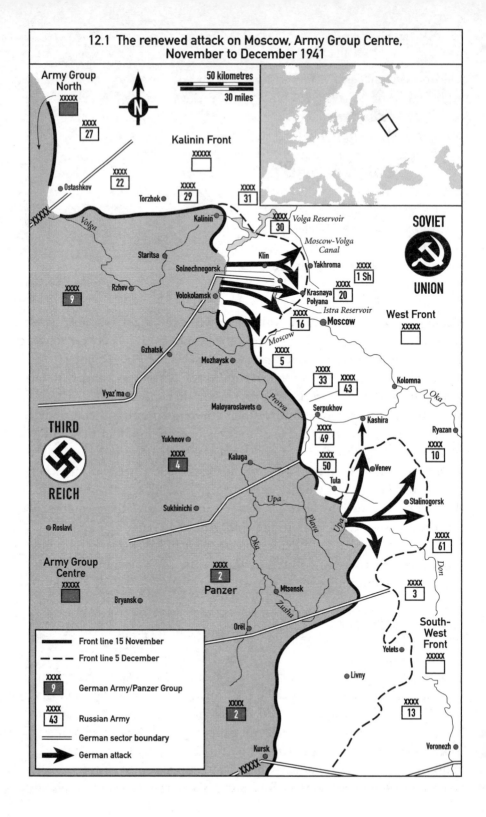

12.1 The renewed attack on Moscow, Army Group Centre, November to December 1941

Army Group North

Kalinin Front

50 kilometres
30 miles

SOVIET

UNION

THIRD

REICH

Army Group Centre

Panzer

Ostashkov

Torzhok

Kalinin

Staritsa

Rzhev

Solnechnogorsk

Volokolamsk

Gzhatsk

Mozhaysk

Vyaz'ma

Maloyaroslavets

Yukhnov

Kaluga

Sukhinichi

Roslavl

Bryansk

Mtsensk

Orël

Kursk

Volga Reservoir

Moscow-Volga Canal

Klin

Yakhroma

Krasnaya Polyana

Istra Reservoir

Moscow

West Front

Serpukhov

Kashira

Ryazan

Venev

Tula

Stalinogorsk

Kolomna

Livny

Yelets

Voronezh

South-West Front

27

22

29

31

30

1 Sh

20

16

5

33

43

49

50

10

61

3

13

2

4

9

Volga

Protva

Oka

Upa

Upa

Playa

Oka

Zusha

Don

Moscow

Legend:

— Front line 15 November

--- Front line 5 December

9 German Army/Panzer Group

43 Russian Army

German sector boundary

➤ German attack

could be encircled from the north – and ordered Zhukov to eliminate the bridgehead. All available tank brigades from across the front were focused to take part, while militia units and civilians hacked away at the rock-hard ground building fortifications along the east bank.

Meanwhile, other elements of Third Panzer were heading south-east, directly for Moscow, while Fourth Panzer was moving from the west, with the same target. Among the former, on 1 December troops of the German 240th Infantry and the 52nd Anti-Aircraft Regiment – who were needed to take on the formidable T-34 and KV tanks – reached Kryukovo railway station, the terminus of the local Moscow rail network. The signpost said 22 kilometres to Moscow. The 35th Infantry Division, advancing south of the Solnechnogorsk–Moscow road, pushed to a point 16 kilometres from Moscow's outskirts, which meant 26 from the centre. And, by a strange coincidence, standing between the Germans and Moscow was the Soviet Sixteenth Army, reconstituted and under its old commander, Rokossovskiy.

On 29 November, *Pravda* published a strikingly accurate account of fighting in this area from its special military correspondent, O. Kurganov. The enemy had concentrated his most powerful forces on the Klinsk, Volokolamsk and Stalinogorsk directions. Here, 'the most cruel battles, requiring enormous exertions of strength and will from our people took place'. In just two sectors – north and west of Solnechnogorsk – the Germans gathered four tank divisions: 2nd, 6th, 7th and 10th, and four infantry – 28th, 252nd, 106th and 35th, plus an SS division. Kurganov, no doubt with assistance from the Red Army, had identified the most determined, closest and most dangerous German thrust. 'The enemy knows', Kurganov wrote,

> that December can bring ferocious frosts, and impenetrable
> snowdrifts, and blizzards. Therefore the fascists will not spare
> one of their soldiers, one piece of equipment. They will
> throw regiment after regiment into combat – tanks, mortars,
> artillery, machine gunners, trying to break through into the
> depth of our forces' defences and, at the same time, cut
> through our road links, communications, threatening to
> encircle Moscow.[3]

This was war reporting by an expert. The Soviet General Staff reports also stressed the ferocity of the fighting, as the Germans clawed their way towards and round the capital, in the face of ever-hardening resistance and constant counter-attacks. During 1 December, there was 'cruel, defensive fighting with the enemy in Solnechnogorsk, Istrin, Mozhaysk and Naro-Fominsk directions'. The Russians counter-attacked. Exactly the same words were used to describe the battles in the area on 2, 3 and 4 December. On the first two of these days, the Russians also fought furiously to contain a breakthrough by tank and motor-mechanized forces in the Aprelevka area, which was obviously a move to take the Western Front in the left (southern) flank. On 4 December, 'cruel defensive battles' again raged in the Zvenigorodsk area, while Soviet counter-attacks took place towards Dmitrovsk, Solnechnogorsk and Naro-Fominsk.[4] Stalin later said that 4 December was the absolutely critical day.[5]

So intense was the fighting and so ferocious the firepower employed that it was said the snow sometimes fell blackened by the gunsmoke. All the photographs the author has seen show the snow its more usual white colour, but it is still a good story . . .

A young SS officer recorded the final push:

> Thus, we are approaching our final goal, Moscow, step by step. It is icy cold . . . To start the engines, they must be warmed by lighting fires under the oil pan. The fuel is partially frozen, the motor oil is thick, and we lack antifreeze to prevent the cold water from freezing.
>
> The remaining limited combat strength of the troops diminishes further due to the continuous exposure to the cold. It is much too inconvenient to shelter the troops from the weather . . . In addition, the automatic weapons of the groups and platoons often fail to operate, because the breeches can no longer move. This of course becomes very dangerous during enemy attacks or counterattacks . . .[6]

The temperature was now sometimes dropping to −45° – the temperature where Fahrenheit and Celsius are about the same. The Germans had still only been issued with ordinary uniforms and regular leather boots. Wherever possible they took Russian winter clothing – felt boots, fur mittens and caps – from Russian dead. Whether they took it from prisoners as well, the SS officer does not say, although on 21 December Hitler gave the order that they should. As a result, those wearing captured Russian winter clothing often could not easily be recognized as Germans.[7]

The forward company of the SS motorcycle battalion (Regiment 'Deutschland') reached the terminus of the Moscow trolleybus system, 17 kilometres from the outskirts and 27 from the Kremlin – close to the Second Line of Defence, now marked by the three giant steel 'hedgehogs' at kilometre 22. One intrepid motorcyclist managed to evade the Soviet troops holding the route in from the north-west, and headed on, right into Moscow. Given the German desperation to acquire Russian winter clothing, this is not implausible – careless Soviet sentries could easily have mistaken him for one of their own. The story goes that he reached the Belorussian railway station, just 3 kilometres from the Kremlin, when the alert NKVD shot him.[8]

The Germans were also attacking from the west, along the Moskva river and the road from Mozhaysk. By 3 December, troops of the 87th Infantry Division had also got to about 20 kilometres from the outskirts, to the forest east of Masslovo, where the River Istra flows into the Moskva. Through binoculars, they could see the towers of the Kremlin.[9] This was the division which had occupied Paris in 1940, but now, they probably wished they had settled for Paris. On 30 November their commander, Lt Gen. von Studnitz, reported that '... there was no question of resting and refreshing the troops, since many more casualties had resulted from exposure to the cold than from the actions of the enemy'. Due to uninterrupted commitment by day and night, 'the emotional strength of the men had become noticeably diminished'. And so hard was the ground that effective entrenching was impossible. Given that the cold was causing more casualties than enemy fire, the general considered it worth taking the risk of crowding his men into a house, in order to give them some protection from the biting cold.[10]

At 17.30 on 3 December, Generaloberst Erich Hoepner, commanding Fourth Panzer Group, reported that:

> The offensive combat power of the Corps [XII, XL Panzer,
> XLVI Panzer, LVII Panzer] *has run out*.
> **Reasons**: physical and moral over-exertion, loss of a large
> number of commanders, inadequate winter equipment.
> It is still possible to achieve limited successes through skilful
> use of local conditions. The situation as far as our forward
> line is concerned is: the lower course of the River Istra –
> River Nakhabinka – Poodolino – Klyazmin Reservoir. Any
> further offensive may lead to sapping the strength of units

and make the repulsion of Russian counterattacks impossible. On the basis of this evaluation of the situation here, and of both neighbours' [Third Panzer and Fourth Army], the High Command should decide whether a withdrawal should be undertaken. In that event I suggest the line: Narskye Prudy – River Moskva – Zvenigoorod – the Istrinsk Reservoir – Solnechnogorsk.

[signed] Hoepner[11]

With just 41 kilometres to go to the Kremlin, the Germans' energy had run out. This was the 'culminating point'. The logistical bungee cord, stretching from around Warsaw, through Minsk, and then Smolensk (see Figure 12.2), was starting to pull them back. The exhausted German forces were halted at Yakhroma on the Moskva-Volga canal and at Krasnaya Polyana at the beginning of December. Some German troops undoubtedly did get further than kilometre 41. However, the Germans ordered their troops to withdraw almost immediately, and consolidate on a 'winter line', which passed through there. So it is fair to say that the main German formations reached kilometre 41, and that was the nearest to Moscow that any of them stayed for any appreciable length of time.

The Russians did not know it at this point, but having failed to halt the Germans so far, they could not have timed their counteroffensive much better.

Since 22 June 1941 the German army on the eastern front had lost 162,314 dead, 563,082 wounded and 31,191 missing, plus prisoners. Of these, 109,600 – two-thirds – of the dead and 16,953 – more than half – of the missing were registered since the start of the offensive towards Moscow. The two formations that had advanced furthest towards Moscow, 10th Panzer and the SS Panzer division *Das Reich*, had between them lost 7,582 officers and men: 40 per cent of their authorized strength, although they would have received replacements. But they had also suffered enormous losses of equipment and many of the divisions were down to half their original strength.[12]

In early October the Stavka began, in conditions of strictest secrecy, to form a second strategic echelon of reserve armies along a line running from Vytegra–Ryabinsk–Gorkiy–Saratov–Astrakhan. On 5 October the GKO ordered the formation of Tenth, Twenty-Sixth and Fifty-Seventh Reserve Armies. Late November saw the formation of another eight:

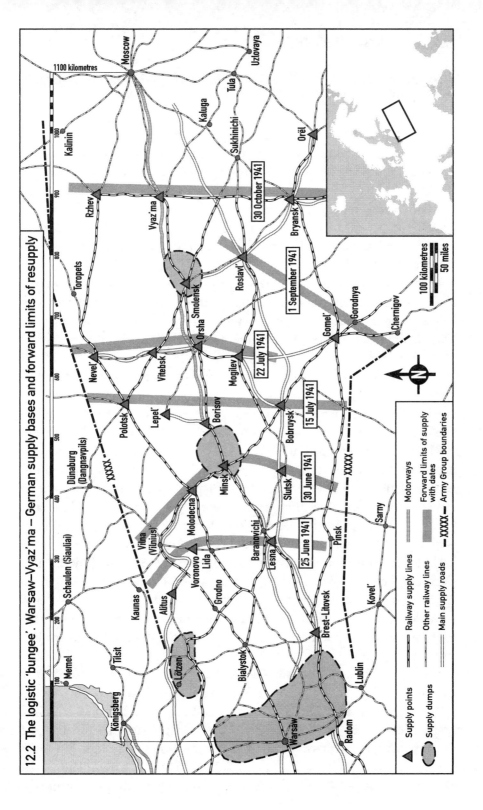

12.2 The logistic 'bungee'. Warsaw–Vyaz'ma – German supply bases and forward limits of resupply

319

First Shock, Twentieth, Twenty-Eighth, Thirty-Ninth, Fifty-Eighth, Fifty-Ninth, Sixtieth and Sixty-First. These eleven new armies would reinforce the three fronts – Koniev's Kalinin, Zhukov's Western and the north wing of Kostenko's South-Western. By 6 December the three Soviet fronts initially involved in the strategic counteroffensive had received another twenty-seven divisions, though of greatly varying quality.

On 29 November First Shock Army under Lt Gen. Vasiliy Kuznetsov (1894–1964) – not to be confused with Colonel-General Fëdor Kuznetsov who had asked permission to use mustard gas on the Germans (see Chapter 10) – and Twentieth, under Major-General Andrey Vlasov, who later fell out of favour after defecting to the Germans, were deployed at the immediate danger points to the north-east of Moscow. Vlasov was omitted from Soviet accounts of the Battle of Moscow, although his Twentieth Army had been instrumental in halting the German attacks from the north-west.[13]

The 'Shock Army' was a revived concept. Translations of German sources sometimes refer to them as 'Assault Armies'. First Shock was formed from the former Nineteenth Army in November, 1941. Unlike the 'Guards Army' titles, which were later awarded to armies which had distinguished themselves in battle, Shock Armies were designated for action on the main axes of fronts (army groups) in offensive operations. Rather than being elite on the basis of prior performance, they were elite in the sense that they could expect very heavy casualties and contained a disproportionate number of *shtrafbats* – penal battalions, as well as mobile troops and firepower. The term had first appeared in the early 1930s, as part of the deep operations theory postulated by the now departed Tukhachevskiy. First Shock Army was effectively activated on 29 November, with seven rifle brigades – divisions were too bulky and unwieldy at this critical point, and brigades were much easier for inexperienced commanders to handle – and a number of ski and artillery units.[14]

Since 22 June, and certainly since the start of the Germans' advance on Moscow, the Soviet Stavka and General Staff had been determined not only to halt the Germans, but to deal an aggressive and crippling counterblow. 'The counteroffensive had been prepared all through the defence actions,' Zhukov stressed in his memoirs, although hindsight unquestionably played a role here. Sokolovskiy concurred. The Soviet strategy had been to 'let the enemy wear himself down, bring him to a stop, and create the conditions for a subsequent shift to the counteroffensive'.[15] However, losing 4 million troops – equivalent to its entire peacetime army – 1.5 million square kilometres of land, 77 million of its people, half of its economic base and one-third of its agriculture in the process was taking military principles a bit far. As Trotsky would have said, it was making a virtue out of weakness.[16]

Stavka seriously began to contemplate a strategic counteroffensive operation in early November after the *rasputitsa* – the mud season – slowed the German advance, albeit only temporarily. From 21 October to 9 November Stavka had ordered the formation of nine of the eleven reserve armies mentioned above. As we have seen, two were thrown in to reinforce the defences after Solnechnogorsk fell on 23 November. The plan was worked up by the General Staff, headed by genteel Marshal Shaposhnikov, from 21 November. The first, vital task was to eliminate the assault groupings threatening to encircle Moscow from north and south, as Zhukov noted in a request to Stavka on 29 November.[17] The second was to force the enemy back and the third, to defeat him decisively, which probably meant encirclement.[18] 'The enemy is exhausted,' Zhukov wrote, 'but if we do not now liquidate the dangerous enemy penetrations, the Germans will be able to reinforce their forces in the Moscow region at the expense of the northern and southern groups of forces.'[19]

The Western Front, holding the central ground, was initially only to do just that. The other fronts, however, would strike to eliminate the assault groupings – the dangerous German salients bulging eastwards around Klin in the north and Stalinogorsk (now Novomoskovsk) in the south (see Figure 12.1). In the north, armies of Koniev's Kalinin Front would attack towards Turginovo and drive into the rear of Panzer Group Three at Klin, and, in cooperation with First Shock Army, from the Western Front, annihilate it. In the south, Kostenko's mobile group from the South-West Front would strike north to encircle elements of Weichs's Second German Army.

General Winter

On 6 December a German soldier wrote to his family in Vienna:

> General Winter has stopped us with his icy hand. It's very
> difficult to move forward. Frost has already reached 30
> degrees [Fahrenheit, probably: − 34° Celsius]. Every day is
> filled with anxiety for us. The Russians are west of us − now
> there's a paradox. We have also had many cases of second
> and third degree frostbite.[20]

The letter never reached Vienna. It is in the Russian archives. That
probably means the soldier died in the Russian counteroffensive which
started in earnest that day.

The Russian plan, as executed, was highly opportunistic. All the talk
about bleeding the enemy prior to a counter-attack presupposed that
the enemy would actually be stopped. The Germans were not stopped −
they were still fighting viciously and dangerously, and moving forward.
From 2 to 4 December, the Soviet command was still uncertain when
to launch the great strategic counteroffensive which Zhukov and Sokolovskiy later claimed to have been planning all along. Sokolovskiy says
the decision was made on 4 December. It is unclear whether, as with
the D-Day landings in France in 1944,[21] the weather forecasters were
directly involved in the decision, although it seems highly likely they
were. In 1942, too late to be of any use, German Intelligence circulated
comments allegedly made by Marshal Timoshenko at the time. Timoshenko had reportedly said the Russians should go over to the attack
when the first few days of cold had broken the backbone of the Germans.
That would happen when the temperature dropped to '20 degrees
Fahrenheit below zero' − in other words, − 29 °C, when the German
tanks and motorized artillery became useless. Zhukov supposedly added
that he expected the start and the course of the offensive to be
determined by the weather, and its success to depend on 'freezing off'
German equipment.[22] However, although the German intelligence
reports attribute these comments to a very reliable source, this could
just be favourable 'spin', to excuse the German defeat.

For those who have never experienced it, at about $-20\,°C$ ($-4\,°F$) you start to feel the hairs and mucus in your nose go crunchy, as they freeze.

The continental weather should have been far more predictable than that on the edge of the Atlantic. By and large, European weather systems run from west to east, so the Germans actually had the opportunity to predict the weather before the Russians.[23] However, from at least 1940, the Russians were among the world leaders in long-range weather forecasting.[24] In 1941 forecasts for the next twenty-four hours were, by and large, about as good as our own several-day forecasts in the early twenty-first century. Anything over forty-eight hours was, broadly speaking, superstition. A book published by the Hydrometeorological Publishing House in Moscow and Leningrad in 1940 reveals that while the Russians may have been unable to predict weather very precisely, they could, in addition to reasonably accurate twenty-four hour forecasts, predict on the basis of historical data that such-and-such a season would replicate a similar season in the past.[25] Given the enormous emphasis the Russians have always placed on scientific research and the respect they accord it, it is almost inconceivable that the best meteorological brains in the country were not advising Stavka to help it win the war.

The Soviet accounts insist that the weather around Moscow in December was not as cold as the Germans claimed. One cites the mean temperature recorded by Russian weather stations around Moscow as $-28.6\,°C$ ($-19.3\,°F$).[26] That is quite cold. It has been suggested that the Germans were caught in a typical – or slightly colder than usual – Russian winter and simply underestimated the difficulties that would cause. However, analysis of German records indicates that the winter *was* unusually cold.[27]

The German equipment started to fail when the temperature dropped to $-20\,°C$ ($-4\,°F$). Here the ordinary 'brown recoil fluid' in the artillery and anti-tank weapons and the lubricating oil on small arms and machine guns started to freeze. This proved disastrous when the Germans had to repel ferocious counter-attacks by Russian infantry, and sometimes the Germans were forced to rely on hand grenades alone when their automatic weapons and even rifles stopped working. At $-5\,°F$ firing pins became brittle, and started to break. The superb MG-34 light machine gun started failing to fire because of frozen lubricants, rust-inhibiting oils and frozen condensed moisture on moving parts.

Vehicle, aircraft and even locomotive engines became extraordinarily difficult to start. Tank turrets would not turn, and truck and tank engines had to be kept running constantly, which meant that a tank which did not move at all still consumed as much fuel in two days as a tank operating normally did in one. In contrast, the Soviet T-34 tank, first encountered in June but only now beginning to appear in large numbers, had a compressed-air starter which could turn the engine over in the coldest weather, while its very wide tracks spread its weight so that it could roll over ditches and hollows holding 1.5 metres – 5 feet – of snow.[28]

The Russians had decided to begin the Moscow counteroffensive on 5 December which coincided with a dramatic drop in temperature. It centred on a sector from Kalinin, 170 kilometres north of Moscow, to Yelets, 350 kilometres south, although the total frontage extended to 1,000 kilometres. At first the Western and Kalinin Fronts would be involved, with the right wing of the South-Western joining a day later, on 6 December, and the Bryansk Front from 24 December.

The aim was, initially, to isolate the German Panzer 'wedges' which were threatening Moscow – Phase One (see Figure 12.3). Then, the Russians would try to penetrate the open flanks, and destroy Army Group Centre – Phase Two.

Essentially therefore, the left of the Kalinin Front and the right of the Western Front would encircle the German 'shock grouping' – heavy in armour – north-west of Moscow, while the left of the Western Front and right of the South-West would encircle the 'shock grouping' to the south.[29]

Strikeback . . . the Moscow counteroffensive, first phase: 5–15 December 1941

On 4 December an OKH intelligence report noted, optimistically, that 'at present the enemy in front of Army Group Centre are not capable of conducting a counteroffensive without significant reserves'. The problem was – they had them. Nine new armies, twenty-seven new divisions, all kitted out for winter war. At 06.00 the next day – before dawn on 5

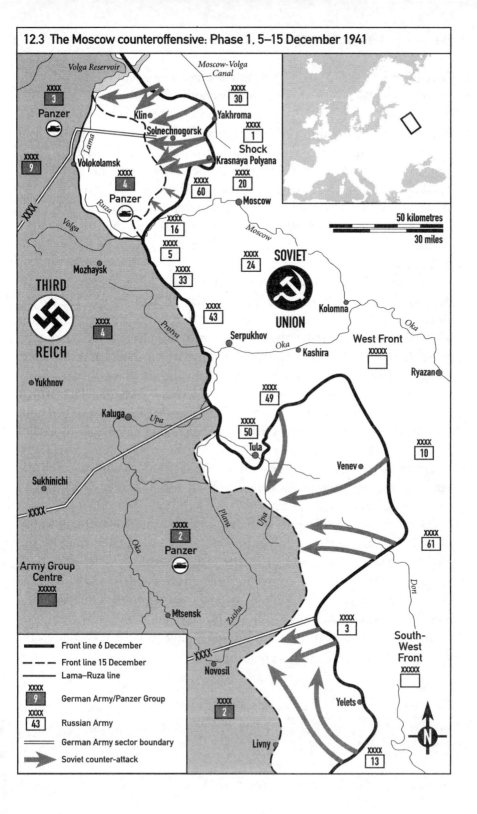

12.3 The Moscow counteroffensive: Phase 1, 5–15 December 1941

Volga Reservoir

Moscow-Volga Canal

XXXX
3
Panzer

XXXX
30

Klin
Solnechnogorsk
Yakhroma

XXXX
1
Shock

XXXX
9

Volokolamsk
Krasnaya Polyana

XXXX
4
Panzer

XXXX
60

XXXX
20

Moscow

Lama

Ruza

XXXX

Volga

XXXX
16

Moscow

XXXX
5

XXXX
24

SOVIET

Mozhaysk

XXXX
33

XXXX
4

XXXX
43

UNION

Protva

Serpukhov

Kolomna

Oka

West Front

XXXXX

Yukhnov

Oka

Kashira

Ryazan

Kaluga

Upa

XXXX
49

THIRD

REICH

XXXX
50

Tula

XXXX
10

Venev

Sukhinichi

XXXX

Oka

XXXX
2
Panzer

Plava

Upa

XXXX
61

Army Group Centre

XXXXX

Mtsensk

Zusha

XXXX
3

Don

South-West Front

XXXXX

Yelets

Novosil

XXXX
2

Livny

XXXX
13

50 kilometres

30 miles

N

———	Front line 6 December
- - -	Front line 15 December
═══	Lama–Ruza line
XXXX **9**	German Army/Panzer Group
XXXX **43**	Russian Army
═══	German Army sector boundary
➤	Soviet counter-attack

325

December – Field Marshal Bock, commanding Army Group Centre, reported to OKH: 'our strength is at an end!'[30]

During the night of 5–6 December Bock, at Army Group Centre, had approved the withdrawal of Guderian's Second Panzer Group from its salient south of Tula and of Third and Fourth Panzer Groups from Yakhroma and Krasnaya Polyana to a line just east of Klin (see Figure 12.3). He also ordered Second Army, which was now more than 50 kilometres east of Kursk, and heading towards Yelets, to halt. Otherwise it would be left out in front. He had anticipated what the Russians were about to do. They wanted to trap his 'Panzer wedges' – he was going to pull them out.

As the Germans woke on the morning of 6 December to find that their weapons would not fire because the oil had frozen, the Soviet Twenty-Ninth Army attacked southwards across the frozen Volga river west of Kalinin (Tver') and smashed into the German Ninth Army. They were on the extreme right (north-west) flank of the Soviet offensive. Third Panzer Group tried to split the attacking Russian army to its north from Thirty-First. Neither Twenty-Ninth nor Thirty-First made much progress, but Dmitry Lelyushenko's Thirtieth, on the right of Zhukov's front, penetrated Third Panzer Group's flank north-east of Klin to a depth of 12 kilometres. Far to the south, Golikov's Tenth Army attacked into the eastern rim of the German salient east of Tula, but, even further south, the German Second Army obstinately continued to move east and took Yelets.

Before noon on 6 December it was obvious that Third Panzer would have to pull armour back to counter the dangerous penetration by the Soviet Thirtieth Army and that Fourth Panzer would have to move back so as not to be left exposed. The Germans wanted to move back as slowly as possible, so they could extract all their equipment and supplies. Russian pressure slackened later in the day, but Sunday 7 December dawned clear and very cold.[31] *That* was going to be a very significant day.

The turning point of the war? 7 December 1941

During the night of 6 to 7 December 1941, Third Panzer streamed westwards, withdrawing. As the Germans withdrew west of the Moscow-Volga canal, First Shock Army followed hesitantly behind. On 6 December the Germans had recorded a temperature of −31 °F north-west of Klin, 88 kilometres north-west of Moscow.[32] By dawn the Germans had already abandoned fifteen tanks, three heavy howitzers, six anti-aircraft guns and dozens of trucks and staff cars – more than would normally be lost in a week's heavy fighting against the *untermensch* they had so despised.[33] Now, as a report from the previous dawn confirms, 'the fur-clad regiments assaulted with cries of "Ura!". Kilometre-wide chains, man next to man in several rows, advanced through the ice and snowdrifts. Behind them hummed hundreds of tank engines, which staunchly burrowed their tracks into the deep, snow-covered terrain.'[34] Engines would not start, and the grease and oil were now starting to freeze even when engines were running. First Panzer Division had been withdrawing during the night but turned round to block the Soviet attack towards Klin. By the morning it was extended over 64 kilometres, struggling through deep snowdrifts, with its tanks short on fuel.[35] The second morning of the Russian counteroffensive – and it was Russian because the Baltic States, Belarus and much of Ukraine were gone, and this in front of Moscow – brought in the most powerful Russian Army within the Western Front, led by its best general. Sixteenth. Rokossovskiy. And the furry soldiers kept coming on.

Rokossovskiy's Sixteenth Army attacked westwards from Krasnaya Polyana, from which the Germans had been withdrawing. However, the most dangerous spot for the Germans remained the penetration by Thirtieth Army. Army Group Centre desperately called for all possible reinforcements to be sent to Third Panzer. 'Even the last bicyclist'.[36] On an 1,100-kilometre front from Tikhvin east of Leningrad, in the north, to German Army Group Centre's right flank, east of Kursk, just inside Russia, bordering on Ukraine, the Russians were attacking. It may have been deliberate – once a formation is committed to the attack the enemy knows about it – that Soviet forces started breaking the radio silence which had masked and veiled their quiet assembly for the counteroffensive. German radio monitors picked up signals from two dozen more Soviet brigades and divisions than there had been on 15 November.[37]

As the icy winter dawn broke on 7 December in western Russia, halfway round the world, in the very different and far more pleasant climate of the Hawaiian islands, it was still 6 December. Hawaii is just east of the international date line, where history starts to record the sun's daily 24-hour westward journey – or, rather, the earth's eastward one. Hawaii's clocks were ten hours behind Greenwich Mean Time, eleven hours behind British wartime winter time, and thirteen hours behind Moscow. But as the sun set later that day on the freezing white snowdrifts west of Moscow, at around 16.00 hours, Russian time, and German soldiers steeled themselves for another splinteringly cold night, it was close to rising in the Pacific on 7 December. And then, as the sun came up like thunder out of the eastern Pacific, 350 Japanese carrier-borne aircraft – bombers and fighters – screamed in from the other direction to attack the great US Pacific Fleet base at Pearl Harbor, Oahu, Hawaii. Eight battleships and assorted other warships were sunk or disabled and 186 aircraft were destroyed.[38] The result: a sleeping dragon was woken[39] – much as a hibernating bear had been, five-and-a-half months earlier.

Ultimately, there were two great intelligence blunders in the Second World War, both by the Axis powers, both in 1941. Compared with them, Stalin's 'denial' of the intelligence he was receiving comes a poor third. Barbarossa was the first. Pearl Harbor was the second. Almost immediately after the Japanese attack, in a speech before the Reichstag on 11 December, Adolf Hitler declared war on the United States.[40] Although attacked by the Japanese, the United States adopted a 'Germany first' policy. The United States had authorized lease-lend aid to Russia two days after Barbarossa, on 24 June 1941. Now, if not exactly an ally of Soviet Russia, the greatest industrial power in the world, the United States, with more staggering reserves of energy, ingenuity and inventiveness, was a co-belligerent against Germany – and Japan. Russia could still lose – it was touch-and-go through 1942 – but now, given the strength and resilience of the opposition it had brought upon itself, Germany could not win. As Zhukov recorded, the crisis continued throughout 1942.[41] Having survived the initial impact, Russia could still die from shock. It nearly did, in 1942 (see Chapter 15). But it was not dead yet, and help was on the way. As the world completed its 24-hour rotation, its fullness spanned by the sun, from Orël to Oahu, from Yakhroma to Hawaii, 7 December 1941 had been a momentous day.

Some have gone so far as to say that the Moscow counteroffensive was the 'turning point of the war'.[42] With very long hindsight, possibly. But it certainly did not look like it at the time, either to the senior Russian commanders, or to the *Wehrmacht* and Luftwaffe commanders.[43] And Soviet Russia could easily have collapsed in 1942.

The *Wehrmacht* on the run

For the moment, however, the Russians had the initiative. In his diary for 7 December, Bock recorded 'a terrible day'. He cited a report of 318 frostbite casualties from one regiment in Second Army, which was probably the night of 4 to 5 December (see above). Three factors had led to 'the current serious crisis'. They were the autumn season of mud, which had paralysed movement of forces and made it impossible to exploit the victory at Vyaz'ma'; paralysis of the railways, including a shortage of rolling stock, locomotives and support vehicles, and trained personnel. Only the Russian insulated locomotives could make steam in the extreme cold. Thirdly, his forces were 'inadequate' to stand up to the enemy and his reserves of troops and equipment. The Russians had exploited Bock's transport problems by destroying all the buildings along the main roads and railways. As a result, it was 'impossible to bring up munitions, fuel, food and winter clothing. Because of the paralysis and the 1,500-kilometre depth of the advance, from the former German border to Moscow, motor vehicles were inadequate. And now the Russians had thrown their 'unexpended masses of people, without mercy, into the counter-offensive'.[44] He was not a happy field marshal.

The next morning, 8 December, the Russians crossed the Klin-Kalinin railway line and approached the Klin road junction through which Third Panzer was trying to withdraw. Colonel-General Hans Reinhardt was attempting to get his Third Panzer troops and their equipment out in a hurry, but Hoepner's Fourth Panzer would have to keep pace or be isolated. Bock, commanding the Army Group, asked Halder for reinforcements, but was told he could not have replacement battalions until January. In a reorganization worthy of the Russians, Colonel-General Reinhardt's Third Panzer was subordinated to Field Marshal Hoepner's Fourth Panzer, which, in turn, was already under Field Marshal Günther von Kluge's Fourth Army. Field Marshal Bock, commanding the army group, thought this might make the two other Field Marshals more inclined to help the harassed Colonel-General.[45] On the same day, Hitler issued a directive – such as it was – for the winter campaign. 'Large offensive operations' were to cease (they already had). But there were to be no withdrawals, either. The German forces were to dig in for the winter and, in particular, the worst month, according to all the records – January.[46] On the same day, the German Second Army, which had taken Yelets, was taken by surprise when half a dozen Soviet tanks smashed a hole in its centre and a Soviet cavalry division galloped through. Paralysed by the cold, the German armour could not respond and was, in any case, running out of fuel. The next day, another two Soviet cavalry divisions widened the gap to 25 kilometres.

As the German advance on Moscow halted and pulled back, Leeb, commanding Army Group North, correctly anticipated trouble. His army group had just grabbed Tikhvin, which controlled the approaches to Leningrad from the *bol'shaya zemlya* – the 'mainland'. On the same day – 7 December – that the Moscow counteroffensive erupted in full, General Kirill Meretskov attacked from three sides the forward German forces with a foothold in Tikhvin, 500 kilometres to the north. But by holding a critical rail link, the handful of Germans – freezing infantry and five tanks – were putting a tourniquet around Leningrad's failing blood supply. To restore it, exploiting the pressure on the Germans at Moscow, the Russian Stavka was acting in a truly joined-up fashion (see Chapter 13).[47]

The Germans were not used to losing. Given that they were close to having killed or taken prisoner 4 million Soviet troops – ten times their own losses, approximately – they were still doing incredibly well. But Bock, commanding the mighty Army Group Centre, confessed to Kluge that he was contemplating sending Hitler a 'personal telegram' about issues which went 'far beyond the military'. He was probably contemplating a withdrawal 'of Napoleonic proportions'.[48] But the Russians were disappointed by their performance in the first four days. Zhukov railed that units were continually trying to attack the Germans frontally rather than being smart and working their way round the sides. At last the Russians were getting really good equipment in substantial quantities, but their forces, conjured by a miracle from the snowy depths of the motherland, while enthusiastic, were, in the main, poorly trained and inexpertly and unsubtly led.[49]

Shortly after noon on 13 December Field Marshal von Brauchitsch, the army commander-in-chief, appeared at Bock's Smolensk headquarters. Bock had decided to pull back to the line Rzhev–Gzhatsk (Gagarin)–Orël–Kursk, and Kluge, who had disagreed, had by now fallen into line. This quickly became known as the Königsberg or K-Line. The next day Brauchitsch went forward to Roslavl while Hitler's chief adjutant, Major-General Rudolf Schmundt, arrived in Smolensk, to make sure the Field Marshals did not sell the Führer out. Schmundt called the artillery general Alfred Kodl, Chief of the OKW Operations Staff and Hitler's personal Chief of Staff, to get a decision from Hitler. The answer was a qualified no, permitting only a limited withdrawal of Third Panzer Group and Ninth Army from Kalinin and Klin, and a similar withdrawal by Second Panzer Army around Tula. Bock ordered his army group to get ready to pull back to the Rzhev–Kursk line – between 200 and 70 kilometres east of Moscow longitude, 'as far as possible'.[50]

On 16 December Hitler, who had been vacillating, finally took charge. Bock reported that his army group was close to being smashed to pieces, and was unsure whether it was more dangerous to withdraw or hold. At midnight Hitler ordered 'not a step back' – not the first or the last time either dictator would say that in this war – and announced that he was sending reinforcements. Two days later, on the morning of the 18th, the order was confirmed: 'The Führer has ordered: larger evasive movements cannot be made. They will lead to a total loss of heavy weapons and equipment.' Units were to hold, even if the Russians had broken through to their rear. Troops were to be compelled to make 'fanatical resistance'.[51]

With the order to stand fast on 18 December, Hitler effectively took all initiative from his generals' and field marshals' hands. Guderian requested an aircraft to take him to see Hitler, and told his Chief-of-Staff not to implement the orders he had received. On 19 December Kluge, who had been in poor health for some time, was granted leave. He handed over command of Army Group Centre to Kluge, while

Brauchitsch, commander-in chief of the army, also resigned. On 20 December Guderian flew to the Führer headquarters, the *Wolfsschanze* east of Rastenburg, in East Prussia. Kluge had called Halder and insinuated that Guderian's courage had failed. He had worked out that Guderian had moved one regiment from each division back 60 or so kilometres to the Oka river, which meant it was pretty obvious he was going to defy the Führer's orders and retreat. Hitler told Guderian to stand and hold.[52] Such behaviour by the German generals, if not by Hitler, would be almost unbelievable if we did not know that the Russian generals and Stalin all behaved in exactly the same way. But while Hitler ranted and raved at his generals, Stalin at least listened to his, even if the consequences could later be lethal. Paradoxically, in Nazi Germany, only generals who actually plotted against Hitler and got caught were terminated.

The Moscow counteroffensive, second phase: 16 December 1941 to 7 January 1942

After cutting off or forcing back the pincers threatening Moscow from north-west and south-south-east in Phase I, Zhukov's concept for the second phase, revealed in a directive of 13 December, was to drive the Germans back to a line about 130 to 160 kilometres west of Moscow – which was, in some places, Bock's chosen position – and to spend the rest of the winter driving the Germans back another 150 kilometres or so to the line east of Smolensk from which they had launched Typhoon in early October. To do this Zhukov wanted reinforcements and resupply for the armies already fighting and another four new armies from the Stavka reserve. Stalin, however, was thinking bigger, and told Zhukov he could not have another four armies. Instead, Zhukov launched the second phase with Fifth, Thirty-Third, Forty-Third and Forty-Ninth Armies. Fifth Army included Dovator's II Cavalry Corps. Stalin sent the new armies to the Fronts on the flanks – Thirtieth Army from Zhukov's Western Front and Thirty-Ninth from the Stavka reserve went to Koniev's Kalinin Front and gave Third and Thirteenth Armies, plus Sixty-First from the reserve, to the Bryansk Front, reformed under

Colonel-General Cherevichenko on 24 December. Koniev was to strike south and south-west to Rzhev, behind Army Group Centre and Cherevichenko north-west to Mtsensk. If they kept going, Koniev and Cherevichenko would meet in the Vyaz'ma-Bryansk area, encircling Army Group Centre.[53] The Russians were thinking big.

However, the Germans managed to get away and break contact. Third and Fourth Panzer Groups made it to the Lama and Ruza rivers and managed to consolidate and find shelter against the winter in the villages behind the protecting river lines. Major General Dovator, commanding II Guards Cavalry Corps, tried to get across the river with dismounted cossack cavalry, but was killed on 19 December near Palashkino, 12 kilometres north-west of Ruza, along with the commander of 20th Cavalry Division, Lt Col. Tavliyev. Dovator was posthumously awarded the gold star medal of Hero of the Soviet Union.[54] His attempt to exploit the Germans' discomfiture failed, but, more significantly, five Soviet armies came to a halt on the east banks of the rivers.

On this occasion, the Red Army had failed to conduct a successful pursuit – keeping the withdrawing enemy off balance and preventing him from establishing new defence lines. Zhukov had seen 'mobile groups' – typically cavalry divisions, usually reinforced with mechanized brigades – as crucial to pursuing the Germans and getting west of them, preventing them from re-establishing a defence line. Dovator's II Cavalry Corps had tried, and Dovator himself died. But other attempts were more successful. To the south, on the extreme left of Zhukov's Western Front, at the end of November, Tenth Army had regrouped in the Ryazan' area, with its main headquarters at Shilovo and a forward one at Starozhilovo (see Figure 12.4). Lt Gen. Golikov, commanding Tenth Army, began his counteroffensive on 6 December. By 19 December they were on the approaches to Plavsk, which was an important road and rail junction and lay on the main road and railway from Moscow to Orël. General Golikov decided to form a mobile group from 41st, 57th and 75th cavalry divisions in order to seize Plavsk more quickly. These three formations were dispersed over 75 kilometres at the start of the operation, and were also subordinate to two separate groupings within the army, one commanded by Lt Gen. Mishulin, the other by Lt Gen. Kalganov. The three divisions were committed on 17 December after the third line of German defences had been penetrated (see Figure 12.4). Because of the difficult terrain the cavalry was not in fact able to

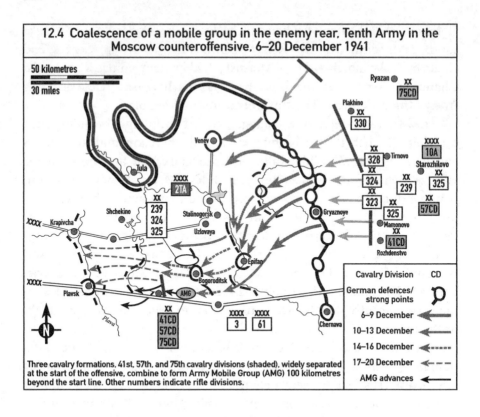

12.4 Coalescence of a mobile group in the enemy rear, Tenth Army in the Moscow counteroffensive, 6–20 December 1941

Three cavalry formations, 41st, 57th, and 75th cavalry divisions (shaded), widely separated at the start of the offensive, combine to form Army Mobile Group (AMG) 100 kilometres beyond the start line. Other numbers indicate rifle divisions.

overtake the infantry and one of the cavalry divisions – 41st – took part in the assault of Plavsk itself. Nevertheless, the idea of creating a mobile group which would coalesce behind the German 'front line' was highly ambitious. The only way Army headquarters could communicate with the cavalry divisions was by radio, and in addition to converging from two separate command groups within the Army, 57th and 75th Divisions moved across the left-hand boundary not only of Tenth Army, but also of the Western Front, into the area of the South-West Front, which became Bryansk Front on 24 December.[55] The Soviet command was not only thinking very big. It was also starting to get very flexible.

On 20 December, while Guderian was having an interview without coffee at the *Wolfsschanze* and the German commanders were proving as bitchy as their Soviet counterparts could be, Lt Gen. Boldin's Fiftieth Soviet Army pushed another mobile group through a 50-kilometre-wide gap in the German front. The mobile group comprised one tank division, one cavalry and one rifle division under Major-General Popov, and was aimed at the German Fourth Army's railhead and supply base at Kaluga. He also sent I Guards Cavalry Corps under Major-General Belov in a similar quest to get behind the Germans, heading for Chekalin, very close to the 'Königsberg Line'. Army Group Centre was beginning to be dissected. But, even at the end of December, with troops frozen, unable to attack, and able to withdraw carrying only rifles, Hitler still refused to authorize withdrawal to the Königsberg line.[56]

'Restoring revolutionary order'

By mid December 1941 the Soviet forces had already recaptured part of the Tula, Ryazan', Rostov, Kalinin (Tver'), Leningrad, Smolensk, Orlov, Kursk areas and some other districts. They still expected to recapture a lot more. But, once again, the Red Army's job was not to administer occupied or even liberated territory. On 12 December Beria signed another directive on the work of the ever-popular 'Operational-Chekist detachments' – NKVD security – this time in territory newly 'liberated from enemy forces'.[57] In all populated areas 'liberated by the Red Army', the chiefs of the NKVD for each front would immediately establish municipal or regional NKVD Departments, also known as sections. Sufficient companies of NKVD troops or destroyer battalions would be allocated to support their work, which consisted, first of all, in identifying and countering German agents and saboteurs who had been left behind. To that end, the NKVD detachments were to re-establish contact with Soviet agents in the German rear and to establish new networks of agents and informers. They would also make contact with partisan units, whether in territory still held by the Germans, or in territory liberated. With the help of agents, informers, partisans and also 'decent Soviet citizens' they would then arrest 'wreckers, traitors and provocateurs', both those who had worked for the Germans and those who had carried out anti-Soviet activities. The mission was much the same as in occupied Poland and the Baltic States. In the chaos that must follow the German forces' withdrawal, the NKVD was also responsible for countering looting, banditry and speculation. Particular attention was focused on protecting trains, stations, repair works, water supplies, railway bridges and telephone and telegraph lines. And, once again, police stations and prisons. Any radio sets or firearms that had got into the hands of the population were to be identified and removed.[58] As in 1939, the NKVD troops under control of front NKVD commanders were immediately committed to securing the military and civil infrastructure.

On 16 December, following Beria's orders from the centre, more detailed instructions were issued by the Ukrainian NKVD. Anyone who had not been living in an area before it was occupied required the most careful checking. Anyone who might have deserted from the Red Army – which included any male of remotely military age, including those in their thirties or forties – was to be checked out and if a 'deserter', arrested. Anyone who had helped German administration, for example, local administrators and police, was to be identified and 'extracted' (iz'yaty). Ukrainian nationalists and churchmen were to be subject to renewed scrutiny. All documents left behind by the withdrawing Germans and produced in collaboration with them had to be seized, including not only the official papers of military and official administration, but also all newspapers, magazines, posters, books and so on, published during the 'temporary occupation'. And so it went on. It was bad enough to be overrun by withdrawing Red Army troops and deserters and then by the advancing Wehrmacht and SS. If you survived that, would you survive the return of the Red Army and the NKVD? Many did not. In his instructions, Sergey Savchenko, the Deputy People's Commissar for State Security of Ukraine, began to sound paranoid, but we must remember that the Soviet Russian Government in Moscow had a particular problem with Ukraine.

> When moving into the area, liberated from enemy forces, it is essential to establish and fix the political mood of all layers of the population in relation to the restoration of Soviet power. At the same time as doing this we have the opportunity to document, (using the statements of witnesses and survivors, photographs, records of actions and so on), the most characteristic details of the evils, destruction, repression and plunder which took place on the side of the fascist occupiers.[59]

There is a clear sense of fear that the presence of German forces and administration, albeit in some cases for only a short time, had immediately and maybe irrevocably tainted those in the occupied areas. Such fears, if exaggerated, were not utterly without foundation. But the orders to the NKVD were also rather premature. In Ukraine, before very long, the Germans would roll back.

The territory recaptured in the Moscow counteroffensive had all remained part of the German active operational area. The German civil administration, *Reichskommissariat Ostland*, stretching east to the old 'Stalin Line', had largely been formed by 1 September, with Estonia being added to it on 5 December. South from a line running just north of the Pripyeat river, corresponding to the former area of Army Group South, *Reichskommissariat Ukraine* was formed, stretching, again, to the old Stalin Line, on 1 September. It was extended to the middle reaches of the Dnepr on 20 October, and to the Dnepr in its entirety on 15 November (see Figure 12.5).[60] East of here the territory was under the control of 'Rear Army Areas' North, Centre and South. In the autumn of 1941, as the front-line German troops were increasingly stretched, the Germans started recruiting small numbers from Soviet prisoners of war. Initially, on 6 October, the three Rear Army Areas were allowed to recruit one experimental 'cossack' squadron each, for employment against partisans. Initially, the Germans favoured Belorussians and Ukrainians but it soon became obvious that there were just as many disaffected Russians as other Slavic nationalities and, conversely, that Belorussians and Ukrainians could not always be trusted. 'No prisoners at all would make their way to service in the German Wehrmacht for intellectual reasons,' argued the commander of Ninth Army's rear area on 7 December. 'The reason why they will be ready is terror of the prison camps, and the prospect of a better life with the German troops.'[61] Others disagreed, recommending that prisoners of war could make up a quarter of the supply services, and on 9 January OKH authorized each army to set up a unit of 'reliable' prisoners of war and locals to ensure local security and help fight the partisans. It remained a contentious issue. But all this happened deep within areas conquered by the Germans. The 'Operational Chekist' units, moving in the immediate wake of the Red Army Moscow counter-attack, probably had little to worry about.

The Soviet counteroffensive around Moscow also meant that German army and Waffen-SS units as well as police battalions had to be pushed forward from Rear Army Area Centre to stem the Soviet attacks. As a result, Soviet partisans were able to expand their control over large areas of the territory.[62]

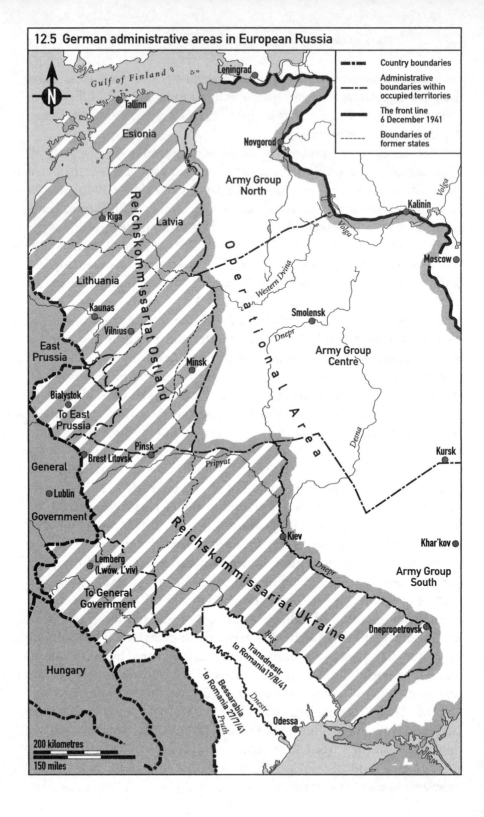

12.5 German administrative areas in European Russia

Legend:
- — · · — Country boundaries
- — · — Administrative boundaries within occupied territories
- ——— The front line 6 December 1941
- - - - - Boundaries of former states

Gulf of Finland

N

Leningrad

Tallinn

Estonia

Novgorod

Army Group North

Riga

Latvia

Kalinin

Volga

Operational

Western Dvina

Volga

Moscow

Lithuania

Kaunas

Vilnius

East Prussia

Minsk

Smolensk

Dnepr

Army Group Centre

Bialystok

To East Prussia

Pinsk

Brest Litovsk

Pripyat

Desna

Kursk

General

Lublin

Government

Lemberg (Lwów, L'viv)

To General Government

Reichskommissariat Ostland

Reichskommissariat Ukraine

Kiev

Dnepr

Khar'kov

Army Group South

Dnepropetrovsk

Bug

Transdnestr to Romania 19/8/41

Bessarabia to Romania 27/7/41

Dnestr

Prut

Odessa

Hungary

200 kilometres

150 miles

Further north, in the Tula area, the NKVD recorded a major triumph on 19 December when partisan units, including 221 Partisan Detachment and other groups, under direction from the NKVD's 4th Section, 'according to incomplete data', burned or destroyed 15 tanks; one armoured personnel carrier; 102 cars and trucks, with munitions, fuel and food; and 35 motorbikes, killing 1,200 Axis soldiers and knocking out or capturing 5 guns, 19 machine guns, 20 sub-machine guns and 85 rifles. The commander of Fiftieth Army, Lt Gen. Boldin, reported that the 4th Section had provided him with information about German troop concentrations in hundreds of villages, 16 airfields, headquarters in 194 villages, and 950 fire positions. It had also helped identify about 300 'traitors to the motherland'. It was quite unusual for a Red Army commander to issue a citation like this on behalf of the NKVD. Among those commended for directing the partisans were the commanders of 2nd and 3rd NKVD subsections, Junior Lieutenants of State Security (Senior Lieutenants) Mikhail Mokrinskiy and Vasiliy Grechikhin, both born in 1916. Both, and all the others nominated, survived the war, Mokrinskiy becoming a colonel in the KGB.[63]

New Year's Day . . .

On New Year's Day 1942, an hour after midnight, Hoepner received a telex message confirming that Hitler had forbidden all troop withdrawals. The grandiose Soviet plan to encircle Army Group Centre was just becoming apparent to the Germans. Zhukov's Tenth and Fiftieth Soviet armies in the south were doing well, and by 14 January Tenth Army had encircled Sukhinichi and got behind the south end of the Königsberg Line (see Figure 12.5). On New Year's Day, probably to bolster morale, the weathered German Third and Fourth Panzer Groups were renamed 'Armies' – which they had been, although by now they were barely of corps strength. Zhukov's most promising axis remained on his left flank, as Tenth Army prised open the gap between the German Fourth Army and Second Panzer Army until it was 80 kilometres wide. On 3 January 1942, Tenth Army trapped 4,000 German troops in Sukhinichi, and Hitler ordered them not to break out. By 9 January, they were trapped. The weather forecasters knew that, throughout Russian history, the cold got even worse in January, and on 9 January a blizzard completely stopped the war. Neither side could move: the Russians, who until now had moved with relative comfort in the open, or the Germans, who were hunkered down in isolated fortlets, wooden cabins in villages which – though inflammable – provided the best available protection against the elements and enemy fire, bearing in mind that the ground was frozen rock-hard.[64]

For the Russians, it was a good day to start again. When we survive a catastrophe, it is tempting to think nothing else can ever be as bad, and to be over-optimistic. After the mid October panic, key Soviet officials returned to Moscow in November, like Berezhkov (see Chapter 11). With the knife withdrawn from Moscow's throat after 5 December, government agencies returned to the capital from Kuybyshev en masse, although elements of the British embassy (not the Ambassador) remained there until 1943.[65] In its New Year editorial, *Pravda* predicted victory over Germany during the year, assisted by British and US aid.[66] With hindsight it was wildly optimistic, but it was not utterly ridiculous at the time. And what else could anybody tell the Russian people?

On the evening of 5 January 1942 Zhukov was summoned to a Stavka meeting with Stalin. The cadaverous but still urbane Shaposhnikov outlined the situation at the fronts, and then Stalin spoke. 'The Germans are in disarray after the defeat at Moscow. They were not prepared for winter. Now is the right moment to go over to a general offensive (*obshcheye nastupleniye*).'[67] This was not just a counteroffensive in the Moscow area: that had already been done. This was a massive general offensive across the entire front, from Leningrad, whose survival chances had been improved by the recapture of Tikhvin, to the Black Sea. The Germans were counting on holding Russian attacks until the spring, Stalin said, in order to resume the offensive in the summer. 'He wants time and a rest.'[68]

> We're not going to give the Germans this rest. We're going to
> chase them to the west with no rest. We're going to make
> them expend their reserves *until the summer* . . .[69]

Stalin emphasized the words '*until the summer*'. Zhukov knew what he meant. Stalin continued: 'Until we have new reserves, and the Germans have no reserves.' For anyone naïve enough to think that 'manoeuvre' and 'attrition' are opposed concepts, this makes it abundantly clear. They are utterly interdependent, and attrition would facilitate manoeuvre, just as manoeuvre had facilitated attrition.[70]

Stalin's concept was to exploit the successful counteroffensive in the western strategic direction and expand it with a general offensive on all fronts. The main blow of the 'general offensive' would fall on the German military-strategic centre of gravity – Army Group Centre. The Northern and Volkhov Fronts would smash Army Group North and break the Leningrad blockade. The South-Western, Southern and Caucasian Fronts, plus the Black Sea fleet, would recapture the Donbass industrial regions and the Crimea. Like all good military plans, it was very simple, but the simplest thing was very difficult.[71] Voznesenskiy, now a member of GKO, supported Zhukov, saying that the Russians still did not have enough people or equipment to sustain an offensive on all fronts. Timoshenko had suggested an offensive in the south-western direction, but Stalin gave no opinion, and disappeared. Shaposhnikov then emerged from his office.

'You argued in vain,' he said to Zhukov. 'The supreme commander already made his mind up.' 'So why did they ask our opinion?' Zhukov asked. 'I don't know. I don't know, my dear.'[72]

Zhukov's Western Front received the Directive for the general offensive on 7 January 1942. The Moscow strategic counteroffensive operation officially ended on that day,[73] although operations in the area continued until 20 April and are sometimes included within the broad heading of the Moscow operation. Within the Moscow strategic *offensive* operation, Russian sources identify the Klinsk-Solnechnogorsk Operation (6–25 December 1941), the Kalinin [Tver'] Operation (5 December 1941–7 January 1942), the Tula Counteroffensive Operation (6–17 December 1941), the Yeletsk Counteroffensive Operation (6–16 December 1941), the Kaluga Offensive Operation (18 December 1941–6 January 1942), and the 'Development of the offensive on the Sukhinichi direction' (18 December 1941–5 January 1942).[74]

However, although operations continued, the defence of Moscow and the two critical phases of the counteroffensive were successfully concluded by 7 January, even though Army Group Centre was not destroyed, as Stalin had hoped. General Zhukov – he was still not a Marshal – could breathe a sigh of relief. At some point, just before Christmas, Zhukov, who had been working all hours, surviving on black coffee and restoring his alertness by taking short but intensive breaks on skis in the refreshing Russian winter, went to bed and crashed. That night Stalin called, but was told, 'We can't wake him.' Stalin, not one for sleeping himself, understood. 'Let him sleep.'[75] Russia was saved – for the moment.

Pushing on. Rzhev-Vyaz'ma, 8 January to 20 April 1942

The Rzhev-Vyaz'ma Strategic Offensive Operation was the central component of the 'General Offensive'. The main Soviet forces involved were the Western and Kalinin Fronts, plus Third and Fourth Shock Armies and 29 other divisions and 39 brigades (see Figure 12.6).[76] Although it was planned as a separate operation, to the Germans, and the vast majority of Russian soldiers, it appeared as a continuation of the Moscow counteroffensive, rolling on without a break. On 22 December Russian forces had started to advance towards Rzhev, and by early January the German Ninth Army was in danger of being encircled, as the Soviet pincers menaced Fourth Army's *Rollbahn* – the German term for the main supply route (MSR). Fourth Army's *Rollbahn* was the Warsaw–Moscow highway – one of the few all-weather roads from the west. XX Corps, part of Fourth Army, was in particular danger of being trapped. Hoepner, Fourth Army's commander, contacted Kluge, asking permission to pull the corps out before it was totally cut off. Kluge contacted Halder, who took the decision himself, and ordered XX Corps to pull out. At 23.30 he was relieved of his command, as Guderian had been before. XX Corps passed into Fourth Panzer's area, leaving four corps being encircled by the Soviet Forty-Third and Fiftieth Armies crammed into a 40 by 30-kilometre area east of Yukhnov.[77]

On 21 January General Walter Model's Ninth Army managed to close the massive gap between itself and Third Panzer which had opened up west of Rzhev. Although it brought Model promotion to Colonel-General, and added oak-leaves to his Knight's Cross, Ninth Army's situation remained precarious. To the north and west there was no 'front line' – Soviet forces were spilling round and on 18 January cut the *Rollbahn* in two places. Fourth Shock Army reached Demidov, 140 kilometres almost due west of Vyaz'ma (see Figure 12.6). But in the

12.6 Winter operations on the Eastern Front, 5 December 1941 to 31 March 1942

Lake Ladoga

Leningrad Front
XXXXX

Leningrad
Puskin
Volkhov
Tichvin

Volkhov Front
XXXXX

Vologda

Army Group North HQ
XXXXX

Novgorod

Northwest Front
XXXXX

Danilov

Pskov

Volga

Demjansk

Kalinin Front
XXXXX

Stavka
XXXXX

Cholm
Ostaskov

Kalinin

Klin
Volokolamsk

West Front
XXXXX

THIRD

REICH

Sycevka

Vitebsk
Smolensk
Army Group Centre HQ
XXXXX
Dorogubuz

Vyaz'ma

MOSCOW

Moscow

Oka

Rjazan

Suchinici

Stalinogorsk

Zukovra

Briansk

Bryansk Front
XXXXX

Orel

Kursk

SOVIET

Army Group South HQ
XXXXX

South West Front
XXXXX

UNION

Khar'kov
Poltava
Krasnograd

Don

Losovaga

Donec

Dnepropetrovsk

Gorlovka

South Front
XXXXX

▬▬▬	Front line 5 December 1941
▪▪▪▪▪▪▪	Front line 7 January 1942
▬▬▬	Front line 31 March 1942
⬤	Soviet reserves
⬤	Partisan activity
→→→	Russian attack
▪▪▪▪▪▪	Railway line

Tagonrog
Rostov

Nikolaev

Dnepr

Transcaucasian Front
XXXXX

Odessa

Crimean Front
XXXXX

Caucasian Front
XXXXX

150 kilometres

100 miles

Sevastopol

knee-deep snow and with temperatures now falling as low as − 40 °F it was as difficult for the Russians to fight as the Germans and men's endurance quickly evaporated, making it essential to plan and time every move meticulously.[78]

South and west of Vyaz'ma large areas were controlled by Soviet partisans and, to make matters worse for the Germans, the Russians decided to drop airborne troops (paratroops), to link up with the partisans and accelerate their encirclement of German forces, near Kirov, between Vyaz'ma and Bryansk, on 20 January. At the same time, Fourth Shock Army would cut south across the Moscow–Warsaw highway west of Smolensk and seize the critical 'land bridge' between the Dnepr and Western Dvina, which had played such a crucial part in German planning during the summer – now a distant and unreal memory. Between 18 and 22 January two battalions of 21 Parachute Brigade and and 250th Air Assault Regiment were dropped south of Vyaz'ma in the Zhelan'ye area to cut the Germans' rearward communications. On 27 January Major-General P. A. Belov's I Guards Cavalry Corps cut the Warsaw highway. To reinforce Belov and also to link up with XI Cavalry Corps, Stavka planned to drop IV Airborne Corps, comprising three brigades – 6,000 men in total – in the Kirov area. However, only one brigade – 2,000 men of 8th Airborne – was actually dropped, according to Zhukov, 'because of lack of air transport'. Either Stavka got their sums wrong, which sounds most unlikely, or the air transport was urgently diverted somewhere else. It was probably to supply Thirty-Ninth Army, which was cut off when Model closed the Rzhev gap. The Germans reported that it was being resupplied by air drop three days after the Rzhev gap was closed, on 24 January.[79]

Although the Russians were close to achieving their aim of encircling Army Group Centre, they failed. In spite of the enormous emphasis they had placed on airborne forces in the pre-war period, they still lacked the aircraft to deliver them in decisive numbers. The landings south of Vyaz'ma were some of the last to be attempted. Airborne forces were henceforward employed as elite infantry who stayed on the ground, a role which they have acquired in many other armies.

The Rzhev-Vyaz'ma Operation was also the setting for other conceptual changes, although they affected all fronts. On 10 January Stavka issued a directive to all fronts and armies on principles of offensive operations which would remain essentially unchanged for the rest of the war. The Germans defended in depth. No sooner had they established a defence line, than a second and a third would spring up. In order to maintain momentum through several defence lines, therefore, Soviet troops had to amass a decisive superiority on narrow sectors. Each army needed to create a 'shock group' of three or four divisions 'concentrated for a blow on a given sector of the front'. Secondly, artillery, always the Russians' favourite arm, had to be much better coordinated with the advance of the attacking troops. The old term 'artillery preparation' was relegated to just one phase of the 'artillery offensive'.

> This means, first, that artillery cannot limit itself to 'one way' actions in the course of the hour or two before an offensive, but must attack together with the infantry, must bring fire down with small breaks during the entire time of the offensive, until the enemy defence line is broken through its entire depth.
>
> Second, it means that infantry must not attack after artillery fire has stopped, as takes place with so called 'artillery preparation', but attack together with the artillery, under the thunder of artillery fire, to the rhythm of artillery music.
>
> Third, it means that artillery must not be deployed scattered about, but in a concentrated fashion, and it must be concentrated not just on any bit of the front, but in the area of action of the shock group of the army or front, and only in that area. Without these conditions, an artillery offensive is unthinkable.[80]

On 1 February Stavka also reactivated the Western Strategic Direction, placing Zhukov in command at what would now be considered 'six-star' level, and thereby giving him authority to coordinate multi-front operations against the German military-strategic centre of gravity: Army Group Centre. By the beginning of February the front lines were a nightmarish tangle of isolated pockets and wide snowy gaps (see Figure 12.7).[81] The Germans had managed to pull their forces out of Sukhinichi against Hitler's orders, after re-establishing contact on 24 January, and also to pull Third Panzer west to establish a front from Velikiye Luki to Bely, where it held Fourth Shock Army in a stalemate for the rest of the winter. If Zhukov was going to encircle Army Group Centre he needed all his forces to do it, but on 19 January he had been ordered to transfer First Shock Army to the Stavka reserve, an order he

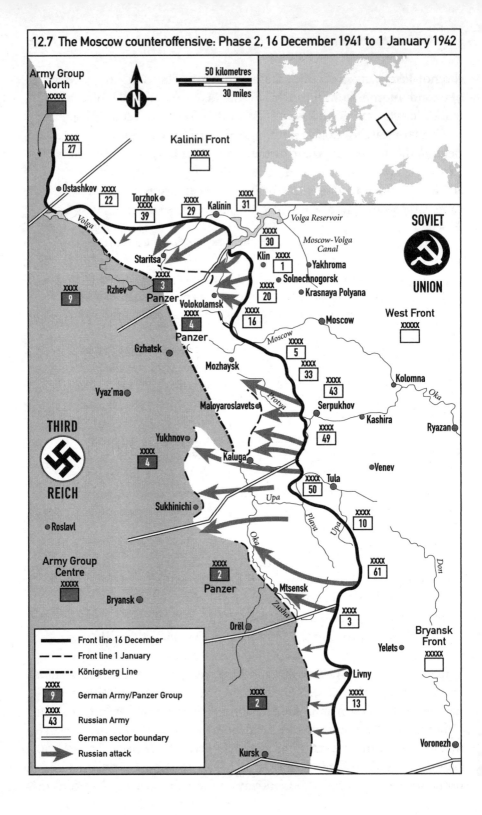

12.7 The Moscow counteroffensive: Phase 2, 16 December 1941 to 1 January 1942

50 kilometres

30 miles

Army Group North
XXXXX

Kalinin Front
XXXXX

XXXX
27

Ostashkov
XXXX
22

Torzhok
XXXX
39

XXXX
29

Kalinin
XXXX
31

Volga

Volga Reservoir

Staritsa

Rzhev
XXXX
3

Panzer

XXXX
9

Volokolamsk

XXXX
4

Panzer

Gzhatsk

Vyaz'ma

Moscow-Volga Canal

XXXX
30

Klin
XXXX
1

Yakhroma

Solnechnogorsk
XXXX
20

Krasnaya Polyana

Moscow

XXXX
16

SOVIET UNION

West Front
XXXXX

Moscow

XXXX
5

XXXX
33

XXXX
43

Kolomna

Oka

THIRD REICH

Mozhaysk

Maloyaroslavets

Prova

Serpukhov

Kashira

Ryazan

Yukhnov
XXXX
4

Kaluga

XXXX
49

Venev

Sukhinichi

Upa

XXXX
50

Tula

Roslavl

Oka

Plava

Upa

XXXX
10

Army Group Centre
XXXXX

XXXX
2

Panzer

Bryansk

Mtsensk

Zusha

XXXX
61

Don

Orël

Bryansk Front

Yelets

XXXXX

Livny

XXXX
3

XXXX
2

XXXX
13

Kursk

Voronezh

——	Front line 16 December
- - -	Front line 1 January
-·-·-	Königsberg Line
XXXX **9**	German Army/Panzer Group
XXXX 43	Russian Army
=	German sector boundary
➤	Russian attack

did not take lying down. But Stalin, the seven-star, was unmoved. Once again, Shaposhnikov counselled him. 'My dear. There was nothing I could do. A personal decision of the boss.'[82]

Zhukov also had Twenty-Ninth and Thirty-Ninth Armies trapped behind the German curtain which had closed over the former Rzhev gap.

On 15 January Hitler had finally authorized a withdrawal to the K-Line, albeit 'in small steps'. But with the Soviet Twenty-Ninth and Thirty-Third Armies cut off, the Russians were also in trouble. Stavka told Zhukov to mobilize all the strength of the Western and Kalinin Fronts, smash the Germans in the Rzhev-Vyaz'ma-Yukhnov area and drive them back 100 kilometres to Olenino, the Dnepr, and Yel'naya. Given the Russians' efficient destruction of locomotives and rolling-stock, and their brilliantly non-conformist five-foot rail gauge, the Germans had a plan to bring up more motor transport. Operations Elefant and Christophorus, were supposed to bring up thousands of trucks from occupied Europe but only a quarter made it. The others had broken down or been frozen into submission on icy roads all the way back to Poland.[83]

February turned to March, and the onset of the *rasputitsa* (which, given the millions of men, horses and vehicles who had fought over the roads, might be even muddier than the last) was difficult to predict. Normally, it would come in the third week of March. A week or two earlier in Ukraine, a week or so later in the north.[84]

Germany's first great defeat on land in the Second World War

While the Battle of the Atlantic would go on until 1943, Germany's first great defeat, in the air, was at the hands of the countries of the British Empire and their Polish and Czech allies in the Battle of Britain in 1940. However, the first great German defeat on land, which had a far greater impact on Germany's ability to continue the war, was the defeat before Moscow. After the 'panic' of mid October, as Stalin said (and there is no reason to doubt it), 4 December was the worst day for the Russians.

Then came the counteroffensive, Phase One, on 6 December and then Phase Two, on 16 December. Rzhev-Vyaz'ma on 16 January was effectively Phase Three. Stavka had identified the German military-strategic centre of gravity, and was trying to cut it off, but, in practice, it was not an easy thing to do and would take another two-and-a-half years to achieve.

Rokossovskiy, whose Sixteenth Army headquarters was pulled out on 21 January, and who was ordered to Sukhinichi to take command of Tenth Army units,[85] was highly critical of Soviet policy in the excised – now (2002) restored – sections of his memoirs.

> In the counter-offensive [my] army's forces were allowed no pauses. The further we got from Moscow, the stronger the enemy resisted. Right up to the point where we hit the Volokolamsk defence line the Front command [Zhukov] resorted to creating groupings for the breakthrough of this or that sector, for which purpose some unit or other from one army was moved to another ... The moment had come when it was incumbent on our high command to think about drawing conclusions from the established results and to start serious preparations for the summer campaign of 1942 ...
>
> Too many losses had been sustained by the armed forces from the first day of the war. In order to recoup these losses, time was necessary. We understood, that the war, in its essence, had only just begun, that our victory in this grandiose battle before Moscow where forces of three fronts had participated, was a paradigm shift in the course of the entire war, that this victory had accorded us a breathing-space, which we needed as much as air itself.
>
> ... Why did our high command, the General Staff, and Front commanders keep on with these pointless offensive operations? You see, it was all completely clear, that the enemy, although he had been thrown back from Moscow, for a hundred kilometres or so, had still not lost his combat capability, that he still had enough capability for organising a reliable defence, and, in order to accomplish a truly 'destructive' (razgromny) assault, it was necessary to amass forces, equipped with adequate quantities of armaments and equipment. We didn't have any of that in January 1942. Why, in such circumstances, did we did not use the time we

had won back from the enemy for the preparation of our armed forces for the operations planned for the summer, but continue to wear out, not so much the enemy, as ourselves in offensives lacking any perspective? This was the most crass (*grubeyshaya*) mistake of the Stavka of the Supreme High Command and of the General Staff. To a significant degree it relates to the commanders of the Western and Kalinin Fronts, who didn't succeed in convincing Stavka of the insolvency of the schemes which proved profitable only when the enemy, having gone onto the defensive, having prepared themselves according to Hitler's directive to his forces about decisive action for the campaign of summer 1942. I can't keep quiet about all this . . .

That severe, snowy winter counted in our favour in defence, and not theirs. So there was a kind of a paradox. The stronger side defended [the Germans], and the weaker – attacked.[86]

So Rokossovskiy, too, acknowledged in the censored part of his memoirs that the 1941–2 winter was '[unusually] severe'. His criticism of Stavka's policy of attacking, wherever, whenever, and whatever makes total sense, and is in accord with the spirit of the man. Rather like Wellington, he would flog a horse – or a soldier – to death to win a crucial race, but otherwise care for it, or him, as a most valued treasure.

While Rokossovskiy, the 'people's Marshal', as he later became, bemoaned the waste of life and resources, Zhukov recorded the undoubted triumph. In the Battle for Moscow, which must have included the defensive operation from 30 September and the Rzhev-Vyaz'ma operation to 20 April, the Germans lost 'half a million men' – killed, prisoners, and possibly wounded, 1,300 tanks, 2,500 guns, more than 15,000 trucks and other unarmoured vehicles, and had been forced to withdraw 150 to 300 kilometres. The latter includes the gains made in the Moscow counteroffensive (100 to 250 kilometres) and the Rzhev-Vyaz'ma offensive (a further 80 to 250 kilometres, on varying sectors).[87] The Russians suffered 514,338 irrecoverable losses in the sixty-seven days of the Strategic Defensive Operation from 30 September to 5 December, but a remarkably modest (by comparison) 139,586 in the thirty-four days of the Strategic Counteroffensive Operation, from 5 December to 7 January. In the Rzhev-Vyaz'ma Operation, from 8 January to 20 April, they suffered a further 272,320 irrecoverable losses.

The sick and wounded who recovered, amounted to 143,941, 231,369 and 504,569, respectively. All told, 926,244 irrecoverable losses and 1,806,123, including sick and wounded who recovered.[88] At best, on the basis of Zhukov's figures, the Russians were losing two soldiers for every German, at worst – three to four. For the Russians, the loss ratios were improving.

It is hard to disagree with the Russian verdict on the great Battle – *Bitva* – before Moscow – *Bitva pod Moskvoy*. The Strategic Defensive Operation stopped the Germans, and probably saved the country. The counteroffensive inflicted on the Germans the first major defeat on land and smashed the *Wehrmacht*'s reputation for invincibility. The Rzhev-Vyaz'ma Operation, while 'the Soviet Command was not entirely successful in carrying out its intended plan'[89] – a massive encirclement to destroy Army Group Centre – nevertheless pushed the Germans between 80 and 250 kilometres further back and liberated the Moscow and Tula regions, plus parts of Kalinin and Smolensk. Most importantly, for the spring, Army Group Centre now had Russian forces sticking forward into both flanks, with Ninth and Fourth Armies precariously holding a pocket centred on Rzhev-Sychevka and Vyaz'ma, halfway between the land bridge and Moscow.[90]

On 8 May 1965, twenty years after the Allied victory in Europe, Moscow was made a 'hero city', one of twelve cities to be so honoured, along with the 'Hero-Fortress' – Brest.[91] Zhukov had kept his promise – he had held Moscow. Napoleon had taken it. Hitler had failed.

13

WHITE NIGHT: LENINGRAD, SEPTEMBER 1941 TO FEBRUARY 1944

'The iron ring is closed'

By 8 September 1941 German forces were not only within 16 kilometres of Leningrad, but they had also cut off all the city's land communication with the rest of Russia. That day, the German OKW – the higher command controlling the entire war, not just the eastern front – sent an ominous signal. 'The iron ring around Leningrad has been closed.'[1] (See Figures 13.1, 13.2.) But that was slightly premature. A tiny chink remained in the iron ring which staggering Russian courage, effort and ingenuity would corrode and expand and which would eventually cause the ring to break.

On 7 September 1941, after a week's heavy fighting, the German 20th Motorized and 12th Panzer Divisions had cracked open the Soviet Forty-Eighth Army's defence south-east of Leningrad. Having crossed a narrow stretch of the Fiver Neva at Mga, the 20th Division captured Sinyavino on 7 September, and Shlisselburg, on Lake Ladoga, on 8 September (see Figure 13.1). They had torn a gap between the 1st NKVD Division, which fell back westwards to the River Neva, and thus into the Leningrad perimeter, and 1st Independent Mountain Rifle Brigade, which fell away east of Sinyavino as far as the Lake, splintering Leningrad from the rest of the country (*bol'shaya zemlya*).

The Germans had, however, missed a possible opportunity to cross the Neva further north, and to break on to the Karelian isthmus and link up with the Finns. The Soviet forces on the north bank of the Neva

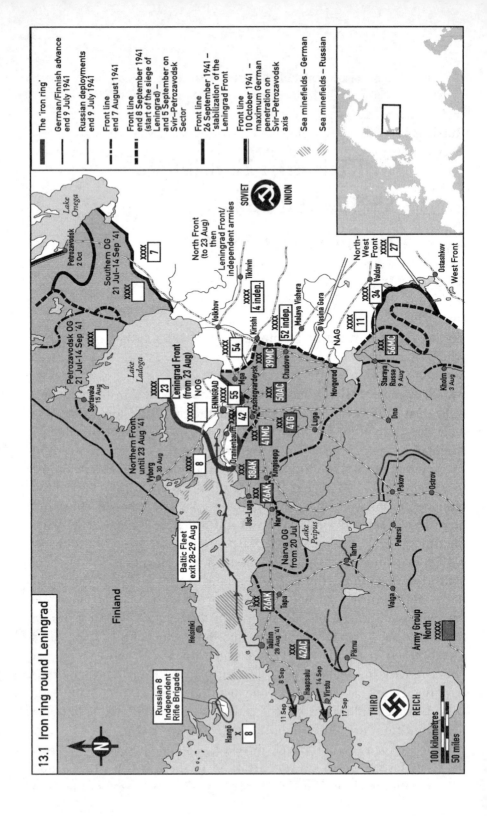

13.1 Iron ring round Leningrad

The 'iron ring'

German/Finnish advance
end 9 July 1941

Russian deployments
end 9 July 1941

Front line
end 7 August 1941

Front line
end 8 September 1941
(start of the siege of
Leningrad) –
and 5 September on
Svir–Petrozavodsk
Sector

Front line
26 September 1941 –
'stabilization' of the
Leningrad Front

Front line
10 October 1941 –
maximum German
penetration on
Svir–Petrozavodsk
axis

Sea minefields – German

Sea minefields – Russian

SOVIET UNION

Lake Onega

Petrozavodsk 2 Oct

Southern OG
21 Jul–14 Sep '41

XXXX 7

XXXX

Petrozavodsk OG
21 Jul–14 Sep '41

Sortavala 15 Aug

XXXX

Lake Ladoga

North Front (to 23 Aug)
then
Leningrad Front/
independent armies

Volkhov

Tikhvin

XXXX 4 indep.

Kirishi

52 indep.

Malaya Vishera

Vasina Gora

NAG

XXXX 11

Staraya Russa 9 Aug

XXX 56MC

North-West Front

Valday

XXXX 27

XXXX 34

Ostashkov

West Front

Kholm 3 Aug

Leningrad Front (from 23 Aug)

XXXX 23
NOG

Northern Front until 23 Aug '41

Vyborg 30 Aug

XXXX 8

Baltic Fleet exit 28–29 Aug

Finland

Helsinki

Mga

XXXX 54

XXX 39MC

Chudovo

XXXX 55

Krasnogvardeysk

XXXX 42

XXX 50AC

Novgorod

XXX 41TG

Luga

Dno

XXX 41MC

Oranienbaum

LENINGRAD

XXX 38AK

Kingisepp

XXX 28AK

Narva

Ust-Luga

Narva OG from 20 Jul

Lake Peipus

Tartu

Pskov

Ostrov

Petseri

XXX 26AK

Tapa

Tallinn 28 Aug 41

XXX 42AC

Haapsalu 14 Sep

Virstu

11 Sep   8 Sep   17 Sep

Pärnu

Valga

Army Group North
XXXX

THIRD REICH

Russian 8 Independent Rifle Brigade

Hangö
X
8

N

100 kilometres
50 miles

had been shattered by constant fighting with the Germans, were poorly equipped and, most critically, almost out of ammunition. However, in that area the river varies between 200 and 600 metres in breadth, the Russians had successfully blown all the bridges and the Germans had no river-crossing equipment with them. Leeb may have ordered an attack across the river on 9 September, but it was easily frustrated. On the 5th, anticipating the isolation of the city, Halder had already claimed that 'our objective has been achieved'.[2] Had the Germans been really determined to draw the ring tighter and link up with the Finns, completely severing the lifeline across Lake Ladoga, they probably could have done so early in September.

Leningrad, Russia's greatest port, centre for much industry, including arms manufacture, cradle of the Revolution and a cultural and intellectual powerhouse, was nonetheless now on its own. The population of the city had been officially assessed on 22 June 1941 as 2,812,134, which by 8 September had reduced only a little, to 2,457,605.[3] But, in addition to an official city population of roughly 2.5 million, there were 343,000 people in the suburban areas within the blockade ring. There must also have been about 100,000 refugees who had fled before the advancing Germans, plus the entire surviving Baltic fleet, and the troops defending the city. The total number trapped in the city and its immediate surroundings must therefore have reached about 3,400,000.

At 59° 55' N 30° 25' E, St Petersburg is the most northerly of the world's great historic cities, and the most northerly capital or ex-capital, apart from Oslo and Rejkjavik, lying on the same latitude as Britain's Shetland Islands or Yakutat Bay, Alaska. Hence its famous winter white nights, its penetrating damp cold, and perhaps, therefore, the compensating burning intensity of its intellectual, scientific and literary life. The icy, starving, disease-ridden, explosive horror of the siege of Leningrad was witnessed and recorded by some of the country's greatest writers and poets, like Anna Akhmatova who was, reluctantly, evacuated in October, and Vera Inber and Olga Berggolts, both of whom experienced and survived the whole siege. The composer Dmitry Shostakovich's mighty Seventh Symphony, *Leningrad*, completed during the siege, records the agony which did not end in January 1943, when the close land blockade was broken, but carried on until the Germans were pushed further back, at the end of January 1944. A total of 880 – nearly '900' – legendary days.[4]

A special place?

The Soviet Union was run from the Kremlin. Leningrad, the country's second city and former capital of Russia, was run from the Smolny, the former smart finishing school for Imperial Russia's debutantes, which had become the Bolsheviks' headquarters in the November 1917 Revolution. Leningrad was always bound to be a special case, and the fact that the Russian President from 2000, Vladimir Putin, made his power base there underlines the point. As the Germans advanced and threatened to cut off the city in August 1941, relations between the Kremlin and the Smolny became tense. The State Defence Committee, which had been made omnipotent, wanted strict control over everything, but geographical and military realities meant that by mid August Leningrad was left very much to its own devices. Moscow's iron rule was relaxed, and in time this led to extreme tension between Stalin and the Leningrad leaders. That finally boiled over in the purge of the Leningrad leadership in the 'Leningrad Affair' which began after the siege ended and continued after the war. On 24 August Leningrad's bosses formed a Leningrad Military Defence Soviet. This immediately provoked Stalin's ire, delivered in a somewhat comical message:

> Comrades Voroshilov, Zhdanov, Kuznetsov, Popov and staff. Hello. This is Stalin, Molotov, Mikoyan.
> 1. You have created a Leningrad Military Defence Soviet. You must understand, that only the Government can create a Military Soviet or, with its delegated authority, Stavka. We ask you not to commit such an offence again . . .[5]

Leningrad's special position worried the Germans as well. Hitler's Directive No. 35 of 6 September had addressed the future fate of Leningrad. If the city surrendered, the Germans would have to feed the population. In a note of 21 September, the OKW's Department for Home Defence presented several options. It is a measure of Leningrad's importance that although OKH ran the eastern front, the fallout from Leningrad would be so great that it might affect German domestic security and thus became a concern for OKW, which ran the rest of the war.

The city should not, therefore, be occupied. The *Wehrmacht* was already starting to have trouble feeding itself, never mind 2.5–3.5 million Leningraders and Soviet prisoners of war. The city, OKW reasoned, could be isolated with an electric fence, covered by machine guns. But within this 'deadline' the weak would starve, the strong would take all available food, and there was a danger of epidemics which could spread to the German forces hemming it in. One of the very few reports of the possible use of bacteriological warfare occurred in the Leningrad area. (Whether bacteria are distributed deliberately or naturally is difficult to establish.) Women, children and the elderly might be removed through openings in the encirclement, and the rest left to starve. But this so-called 'solution' would also involve the danger of epidemics and leave some of the most robust to fight on 'for some time'. Or the Germans could retire behind the Neva and leave the city to the Finns. The Finns officially stated that they would like the Neva, south of Leningrad and running through it to the Gulf of Finland, to be their state frontier, but that in that event, Leningrad 'would have to be removed'.[6] They never really meant that, as their conduct of the war subsequently bears out.

When dealing with an international city of at least 2.5, and very possibly 3.4 million people, of staggering historical and cultural significance, the equivalent of what would now be a 'world heritage site', even the Germans could not afford to ignore international opinion. Even though the United States was still neutral, the American Red Cross had campaigned in favour of the USSR and the Germans had an intelligence report of that campaign. A group of 120 US missionaries was on its way to Vladivostok and another group was about to be sent via the main route for US aid to Russia during the war – through Iraq and Iran, which were friendly with the British. The Germans expected these missions to be accompanied by photographers who would 'present Germany as a barbaric country in the USA'. The Germans contemplated the possibility of President Roosevelt taking responsibility for the population of Leningrad, either by supplying the inhabitants or by removing them 'to his part of the world'.[7]

No such offer was actually made. The idea of evacuating the entire population of Russia's second city to the US and, probably, Canada, would be one of the most ambitious refugee projects ever contemplated. It would certainly have caused great problems with the subsequent onset of the cold war. The Germans concluded that 'such an offer could not, of course, be accepted, and should be treated only as propaganda'.[8] The Germans should declare to the world that Leningrad was 'being defended as a fortress and that therefore the city and its inhabitants should be treated as military targets'. Leningrad should therefore be 'isolated hermetically' and 'as far as possible', pounded 'to dust with artillery and air attacks'. Once it had been worn down by terror and hunger, a few passages were to be opened and defenceless people let out, and deported 'to the interior of Russia', which at that time the Germans confidently expected to capture. Others would be scattered across the interior of the country. The rest would be left to freeze and die during the winter, and in the spring the Germans would force their way into the city, if the Finns had not done so already. Leningrad should then be levelled with demolition charges and the big smoking hole left north of the Neva should be handed over to the Finns.[9] It was a plan of stupendous ambition, but also stupendous naivety.

Leningrad's unique position as Russia's 'window on the west', largely isolated by water or ice on the very north-west edge of the empire, made it uniquely suited to some special status within the context of the wider war. The fact that the two sides immediately involved were content to let 3.5 million people starve and freeze to death is perhaps just another indicator of the 'absolute' nature of the war. On 21 September Stalin wrote to the Leningrad command team and to Merkulov, the head of the NKGB, that he understood the Germans heading for Leningrad – 'nasty bits of work' (*merzavtsy*) – had sent ahead of their troops old men, women and children from occupied areas to plead for Leningrad to surrender and to achieve some sort of local ceasefire. 'They say', Stalin continued,

> that among the Bolsheviks in Leningrad there are those who don't consider it possible to use weapons against messengers such as this. I consider that if such there are such people among the Bolsheviks, then they should be exterminated straight away, as they are more dangerous than the German fascists. My advice: don't get sentimental, but smash in the teeth of the enemy and their helpers, whether voluntary helpers or not. War is pitiless, and it brings destruction, first of all, to those who show weakness and permit wavering. If there's anyone in our ranks who permits wavering, then they will be responsible for the fall of Leningrad. Smash the

Germans, and as for those 'delegates', whoever they are, wipe them out as enemies, whether they be willing or unwilling enemies. There must be no mercy, either to the filthy Germans, or to their delegates, whoever they may be. Pass this on to divisional and regimental commanders and also to the Baltic Fleet, captains and commissars.[10]

The Leningrad team – Zhukov, Zhdanov, Kuznetsov and Merkulov – duly did so, appending a supplementary order to 'open fire immediately on anyone approaching the front line and prevent them getting close to our positions. Negotiations with the civil population are not permitted.' The Germans captured a copy, which was an absolute gift to their propaganda department.[11]

The stories of old men women and children being used as 'envoys' mirror Zhukov's report that earlier in the month the Germans attempting to cross the River Neva had herded local people in front of them as 'human shields'. Zhukov's comment is telling. 'To avoid hitting our people, our mortar and artillery fire had to be conducted especially accurately, against enemy troops further back.'[12] Zhukov did not show much sign of 'wavering'.

In late January 1942, the Party Committee and the City Council began to receive letters – apparently proposals from Leningrad citizens – that Leningrad be made an 'open city' and that German troops be allowed in. Obviously, this was the last thing the Germans wanted until resistance in the city was crushed. Soviet and Russian sources agree that while the Germans never wanted to take responsibility for a vast urban area with millions of people, they might nevertheless employ the suggestion as a ruse to get in, just as the Mongols had often done with Russian cities in the Middle Ages. The Germans, Russian historians surmise, were trying to stir up a 'hunger revolt' in which food shops would be attacked and in which women would then march to the outskirts and demand that the men gave up resistance and let the Germans in. Shades of psychological and sexual pressure, as well.[13] But by now the women of Leningrad hated the Germans just as much as the men did, and the newly revealed archives of the NKVD tend to support the Russian line.

A city unprepared

The closing of the German pincers on 8 September (see Figure 3.1) caught the Soviet planners in Leningrad and Moscow by surprise. On 26 August the Military Soviet of the Leningrad Front recommended evacuating the ethnic Germans and Finns in the Leningrad region (Oblast'), and two days later a plan to move out the 88,700 Finns and 6,700 Germans (the latter figure later revised down to 6,500), according to the 1939 census, was signed by Nikitin, the Secretary of the Leningrad Communist Party, and by Merkulov. The plan – one of many to evacuate suspect minorities to remote areas in Siberia and Kazakhstan – was to be completed by 7 September.[14] Two days later, on 30 August, Merkulov, now Deputy Head of the NKVD, passed the plan on to Beria, although Merkulov added that the numbers of Germans and Finns had probably increased significantly since 1939. Clearly, the danger of sabotage and diversion posed by the Germans and Finns was considered more pressing than the welfare of the overwhelming majority of its inhabitants, who were Russian. To do this a *troika* – 'threesome' – to supervise evacuation would be created: Kubatkin, the Leningrad region NKVD chief, Drozdetskiy, who had come from Ukraine, and Makarov, Deputy Chief of the Leningrad NKGB.[15] Once again, the Soviet security apparatus was not being completely paranoid. The first communication from 'Petersburg' – as the Germans still called it – by the Command of the German Eighteenth Army, dated 2 October, reported that a large element of the intelligentsia and the 30,000 to 40,000 'Germans' whom they believed to be in the city – half the total number of Germans and Finns reported by the Soviet authorities – would be willing to give up the city without a fight. However, the German command recognized a 'strong terror' had, from the start, paralysed the motivation of this group.[16] The courage, determination and resilience of most of the population sustained Leningrad, as it sustained the whole country. As for anyone tempted not to be brave and resilient, terror was usually an effective deterrent.

But by then, it was already too late to get the Germans and Finns out, and there were far greater priorities. On 17 and 18 March 1942 some 6,888 Germans and Finns would be evacuated in five trains, after the first, terrible winter of the Leningrad siege. It is quite possible that they were the survivors among the 95,000 or so who had been there in August.[17]

Normal rail communications with the rest of the Soviet Union were severed on 27 August 1941. The city immediately sent a telegram to the GKO in Moscow asking for emergency food supplies, but they had left that too late as well. Then, on 8 September the Germans, following Hitler's orders to starve the city out, rather than assaulting it directly, struck. German aircraft attacked the Badayev warehouses in the south-west part of the city (see Figure 13.2), where much of the city's food supplies were stored, with incendiaries. The compound around Boro-vaya station contained wooden buildings which were only 7–9 metres apart. It was a disaster waiting to happen. Three thousand tonnes of flour were burned, and 2,500 tonnes of molten sugar flowed into the cellars. About 900 tonnes of the blackened, melted sugar and 1,000 tonnes of flour would later be 'reclaimed'. You will eat anything when you are starving. The Badayev fire was but one of many reasons for the shortage of food, but at the time it seemed an utter and inexcusable disaster. Dmitry Pavlov, the city's food chief, downplayed the effect of the fire, but that is understandable. Immediately, he ordered the remaining food supplies to be dispersed, and started compiling an inventory of food stocks. The German aircraft returned on 10 September, and incinerated three more of the Badayev warehouses, but by now they were empty.[18]

Although rationing had been in force since June, the rations in Leningrad were no lower than in other major cities and there was a thriving black market. More prosperous Leningraders stocked up on caviare and champagne.[19] On 12 September Pavlov made the first of several radical cuts to the bread ration, reducing it to 500 grams for manual workers and 300 for office workers and children under twelve. On that day there were enough grain, flour and biscuits left for 35 days, cereals and pasta for 30, meat, including live cattle, for 33, fats for 40 and sugar for 60.[20] Trains that might have been used to bring in extra food had been used to evacuate industry.

Another commodity was also crucial. Firewood, which was harvested from the surrounding forests every autumn. But by 8 September, when the city was cut off, the annual wood-cutting had not begun. Two-and-a-half million people, a Russian winter, and none of the usual massive stocks of firewood . . .

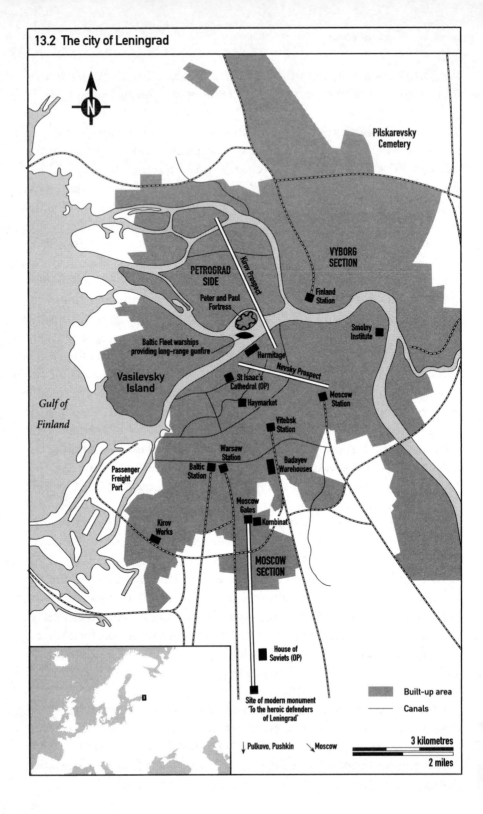

13.2 The city of Leningrad

Pilskarevsky Cemetery

VYBORG SECTION

PETROGRAD SIDE

Kirov Prospect

Peter and Paul Fortress

Finland Station

Smolny Institute

Baltic Fleet warships providing long-range gunfire

Hermitage

Nevsky Prospect

Vasilevsky Island

St Isaac's Cathedral (OP)

Moscow Station

Gulf of Finland

Haymarket

Vitebsk Station

Warsaw Station

Badayev Warehouses

Passenger Freight Port

Baltic Station

Moscow Gates

Kirov Works

Kombinat

MOSCOW SECTION

House of Soviets (OP)

Site of modern monument 'To the heroic defenders of Leningrad'

↓ Pulkovo, Pushkin   ↘ Moscow

■ Built-up area

— Canals

3 kilometres

2 miles

Zhukov takes command

On 10 September General Zhukov, with Major-General Fedyuninskiy and Lt Gen. Khozin, flew into Leningrad. Zhukov carried a note from Stalin, authorizing him to take command of the Leningrad Front from Marshal Voroshilov, who had been in charge for just five days. Their plane made its final approach low over Lake Ladoga hotly pursued by two Messerschmitts. Having landed, the Russian generals then headed for the Leningrad Front headquarters. This was alongside the Leningrad regional government in the Smolny Institute. Zhukov wryly recalled how he and his team, who had just flown in from Moscow dodging German fighters, arrived without the appropriate passes. Zhukov, no doubt fuming, was kept waiting for fifteen minutes while an officer was summoned to issue him with one. 'Well, that's the Army for you,' Zhukov later recalled, philosophically, although the officer concerned probably got a tongue-lashing he never forgot.[21]

Voroshilov was having a meeting with Andrei Zhdanov, the Leningrad Party Secretary and effective boss of the city, and Zhukov asked if he might attend. He then handed Voroshilov the note from Stalin. This indicated that Zhukov would be taking over, which he claims he did that night 'by authority of the Supreme Commander's note', although the Stavka order appointing him was not signed until the next day, and some sources say he took command on the 12th.[22] Knowing Zhukov, he would not have waited for the red tape to be tied. Fedyuninskiy took over command of the Front from Zhukov on 10 October, when Zhukov returned to deal with another crisis at Moscow, and Khozin from him on 26 October.

The Leningrad Front military council comprised Zhdanov, Zhukov, Aleksey A. Kuznetsov, Zhdanov's deputy and Leningrad Party secretary,[23] Shtykov, secretary of the Leningrad Party committee, Solovëv, secretary of the Regional Executive committee, and Popkov, chairman of the City committee. They agreed that if the city could not be held, all installations of any military or industrial value should be destroyed.[24] On 13 September Admiral Ivan Isakov, the First Deputy Minister for the navy, issued a complementary order saying that in the event of a 'forced withdrawal from Leningrad', all warships, merchant ships, commercial vessels and specialist craft were to be blown up. They could not sail east. There was only land, that way. He issued detailed instructions for their destruction and appointed a number of flag officers to supervise scuttling the Red Banner Baltic fleet (KBF), under its commander, Vice-Admiral Vladimir Tributs. Rear-Admirals and Captains First Rank would oversee the destruction of the fleet. Rear Admiral Yuri Panteleyev was earmarked to oversee the destruction of the ships at the great island fortress of Kronshtadt, and others were posted at the mouths of the various tributaries of the Neva.[25]

But the fleet did not have to be destroyed. Some of the ships' guns, including those of the cruiser *Aurora*, which had signalled the Revolutionary attack on the Winter Palace in November 1917, were taken off and used on land – in the case of the *Aurora* guns, on the Pulkovo heights, the limit of German advance south of the city. Other warships were moored and used as almost invulnerable floating batteries to fire back at the German siege guns. Artillery General Nikolai Voronov, who had been the Soviet military adviser during the siege of Madrid in the Spanish Civil War, was a Leningrader. He returned to his home city and climbed to the cupola of St Isaac's cathedral, which he used as an observation post just as he had used the Telefonica Central telephone exchange in Madrid. From 85 metres up he could see the anti-aircraft guns on the roofs of the taller buildings, and the Baltic fleet ships which had been pulled back into the Neva. To the south and south-west he could see the flashes of the German guns firing on the city.

> Again and again my thoughts returned to Madrid and what that city had survived. There also the enemy had closed in on all sides [in fact, three out of four]. But here it was all repeated on an even grander scale – the city was greater, the intensity of the battle, the size of the forces. Here everything was infinitely more complicated.[26]

The main artillery and air defence 'Command Observation Post' was in fact set up on the roof of the Council of People's Commissars' building, a huge, yellow-grey brick-shaped 1930s edifice, which, like the Cathedral, is still there, but further south, nearer the enemy, on the left of the road out towards Pushkin (see Figure 13.2).

On 15 September, in moves similar to those imposed in Moscow, NKVD troops in Leningrad were placed under unified command, in order to be better able to police another city in a 'state of siege'. Merkulov ordered 34-year-old Kombrig Arseniy Kurlykin to take command and to form an NKVD operations staff, using personnel from the security directorate and rear services (NKVD) of the Northern Front and the headquarters of 2nd [NKVD] Division.[27] By mid September there were reports of groups of deserters and troops fleeing in panic, sometimes having removed their insignia, and on 18 September Zhdanov issued an order to reinforce the fight against 'desertion and the penetration of enemy elements'. Some blamed the Badayev fire on saboteurs, or thought they had seen German agents signalling to the attacking aircraft. Zhdanov ordered regular NKVD patrols of the main streets and around key installations and the creation of four 'blocking detachments' to check out any servicemen who did not have the right documents.[28] Anyone caught panicking or running away who did not immediately surrender to the NKVD patrols, was shot.[29]

The fear of German spies and diversionary troops was not pure paranoia. In the first week of the war the Germans had overrun no fewer than sixty Red Army warehouses containing more than 400,000 Red Army uniforms in the Western Front sector alone.[30] These were not fakes, which would have been easy to make, anyway, but the genuine article. While the Soviet forces who were being rapidly reconstituted after losing millions of men were short of uniforms, the Germans had plenty of them. On 11 September an NKVD patrol arrested a man in Red Army uniform who turned out to be a Russian-speaking Romanian NCO from a Romanian reconnaissance company. On 17 September they arrested another man in Red Army uniform, who turned out to be a German 'saboteur' (diversant), one of a group of six inserted into the Leningrad area.[31] In spite of these measures, however, many civilians and Soviet soldiers continued to flee, and since their treatment within Leningrad was so uncompromising, they often went the other way. By October, the Germans reckoned 100 to 120 Red Army men were deserting daily.

At this point, in September, the Germans were still undecided about how to deal with great urban areas. It was not until 12 October (see Chapter 10) that OKW issued the definitive order that, following experience in Kiev, no German soldier was to enter downtown Moscow or Leningrad.[32]

Attempts to break the ring

Zhukov was not going to allow the city to be strangled without one hell of a fight. German shelling settled down into a pattern, concentrating on the busiest thoroughfares. According to evidence given at the Nuremberg Trials after the war, the Germans shelled with Teutonic punctuality. They opened fire from 08.00 to 09.00 (the morning 'rush hour', 11.00 to 12.00 (lunchtime), 17.00 to 18.00 (the evening 'rush hour'), and 20.00 to 22.00 (dinnertime, and evening entertainment).[33] By 9 September the German part of the ring stretched more or less eastwards along the southern edge of what would become the 'Oranienbaum bridgehead', on the coast of the Gulf of Finland, west of the city, which never fell to the Germans. It then looped south, along the Pulkovo heights, which give a splendid view of the city lying to the north, and also of the deadly, flat fields of fire between those heights and the suburbs. Then it ran north-east, to Shlisselburg, where the Germans had reached Lake Ladoga.

North of the Pulkovo heights, the ground is extremely flat, a perfect killing-ground running north to the outer suburbs, past where St Petersburg's Pulkovo international airport now lies. Just inside the modern suburbs you can see massive concrete permanent fire points – DOTs – from which high-velocity guns could be trained across the flat killing-ground. One can see why the Germans never made it across this last stretch. A railway runs round the outside of the southern suburbs, and the defenders used that to carry armoured trains, which were thus able to bring their firepower to bear on any part of that perimeter relatively quickly. Further east, the Germans were stopped on the River Neva but at one point the Russians maintained a bridgehead on the eastern bank: a tiny enclave around the hamlet of Moskovskaya Dubrovka, which they hung on to with grim determination. The troops in the bridgehead were relieved every couple of days. They called it 'pyatichëk' – a five-kopeck piece, a 'sixpence' or a 'dime'. It was never taken.

On 13 September the Germans launched a ferocious attack from the west towards Uritsk (Ligovo). Zhukov responded with his last reserve,

10th Rifle Division. It was a risk, but it worked. The Russians counter-attacked on the 14th, and pushed the Germans back. They had reached Krasnoye Selo, about 26 kilometres from the centre of Leningrad, and on 14 September Zhukov told Shaposhnikov that he planned to drive them out. The 1st NKVD Rifle Division, which had been formed on the orders of the Leningrad Front Military Soviet,[34] was deployed in the southern outskirts of Leningrad. In order to draw German forces away from the Pulkovo area, the bumbling Marshal Grigoriy Kulik's Fifty-Fourth Army would attack south-westwards to clear the enemy from the Mga-Shlisselburg area, where they were cutting Leningrad off from the east. The right-hand German pincer, cutting Leningrad off from the 'mainland', was only about 15 to 20 kilometres wide here, and Zhukov could see that it was the 'most favourable place to break the blockade'. But Kulik was not ready, and wittered on about not having enough artillery.

Marshal Kulik was by now commanding only an army. Zhukov, still only an Army General, was commanding a front. But Kulik's army was not subordinate to Zhukov's front. Kulik was actually senior to Zhukov in rank – not that that mattered unduly in the Soviet system – but, more to the point, Kulik was a creature and protégé of Stalin. Zhukov, who did not suffer fools – at all, never mind gladly – lost his temper. Kulik was putting the welfare of his miserable army before that of the country's second city, and frustrating the man who was emerging as – who probably already was – the country's top military commander. 'It seems to me', said Zhukov, with razor-like malice and contempt, 'that Suvorov, if he were in your place, would have acted differently ... Pardon me for being direct, but I'm not much of a diplomat. Best wishes ...'[35]

In spite of all Zhukov's efforts, and those of Stavka, especially Marshal Shaposhnikov, the Germans pressed on and by 16 September had pushed the Russians back to a perimeter running through Pushkin, about 26 kilometres from the centre of Leningrad. On 17 September the fighting reached maximum intensity with six German divisions, strongly supported by Army Group North's Luftflotte 1, trying to break through from the south. On 19 September the artillery bombardment of Leningrad went on for eighteen hours – from 01.05 until 19.00, instead of the usual five, and on 21, 22 and 23 September the Germans mounted massive air raids with hundreds of bombers against the unsinkable island battleship of Kronshtadt and the great grey warships further east.

The Baltic fleet was a formidable force, and little substantial damage was done to it, while the Soviet anti-aircraft guns and fighters took a heavy toll of German aircraft. The Baltic fleet mustered 338 guns in shore batteries, mounted on railway wagons or in warships, mostly ranging from 100mm to 180mm calibre. Some seventy-six were 180mm to 305mm, plus one 356mm and one 406mm, with ranges from 30 to 45 kilometres.[36] Like most Russian guns, they had extremely long range, and the effect of weapons like this on German armour, even firing indirect, was awesome, especially when well directed, as they usually were.

There were more intensive attacks on the Pulkovo heights and towards Oranienbaum from 23 to 26 September. By 7 October the Germans had reached the coast between the Oranienbaum bridgehead (*platsdarm*), due south of Kronshtadt, cutting it off from besieged Leningrad, but like Leningrad, it never fell. Meanwhile, on 20 September Stavka (Stalin) told Kulik he had to re-establish contact with Leningrad. Otherwise, 'the Germans will turn every village into a fortress and you will never be able to join the Leningraders'. Kulik, who was probably the last pre-war buffoon to survive in a senior command position, failed to carry out the order. On 29 September he was relieved of his command, and subsequently demoted to major-general, but remained in the area to irritate his colleagues in the counter-attack on Tikhvin the next month.[37] The front line around Leningrad had 'stabilized' for the best part of sixteen months, until January 1943, when the immediate blockade of Leningrad was broken. On 30 September the 'Leningrad Strategic Defensive Operation' came to an end. Out of 517,000 Soviet troops involved from the Northern, North-Western and Leningrad Fronts, 214,078 had become 'irrecoverable losses' and 130,848 sick and wounded. All in eighty-three days, from 10 July to 30 September.[38]

Wilderness, east of Leningrad

Some 120 kilometres east of the centre of Leningrad the River Volkhov enters the Gulf of the same name, on the eastern side of Lake Ladoga. The town of Volkhov lies 20 kilometres south of here. The 'Volkhov

Front' would be of key importance to Germans and Russians for the next fifteen months. Some 75 kilometres east-south-east of Volkhov town lies a road and rail junction called Tikhvin, 190 kilometres east of central Leningrad. The main rail line from Moscow to Leningrad had been cut by 26 August (see Figure 13.1), and a short length of the line running from the east, from Vologda through Cherepovets and Volkhov, was also cut, west of Tikhvin, by 9 September. As long as the Russians held Tikhvin, however, they at least had road links from that railhead north and north-west to Lake Ladoga, through Koskovo and Kolchanovo (Pul'nitsa) – where there was also another rail line heading north – to Syasstroi on the Lake. If they lost Tikhvin, however, the next usable railheads back were Podborov'ye and Zabor'ye, and a long trail would have to be cut through the forest, as far as Karpino – Pashskiy perevoz – on Lake Ladoga, to open up potential communication with the city, and even then only across the Lake. (See Figure 13.3.)

Leeb's Army Group North struggled north-eastwards, and having been ready to fall back towards the Volkhov river, summoned a superhuman effort and reached the outskirts of Tikhvin on 8 November. On 9 November, Tikhvin fell to the Germans. Leeb observed that '[Leningrad] is now also cut off from contact across Lake Ladoga.'[39] Almost, but not quite.

Now, the Russians were forced to build a new, 320-kilometre forest supply road, skirting round the north of the new German positions: Route 102. Some sources say that the Leningrad Military Council issued the order on 8 November: others, not until the 14th. Either way, the 'lifeline' road – a 'corduroy road', because of its appearance, surfaced with felled trees – would run along an ancient Russian forest road from Novaya Ladoga east, then south, through local hamlets so obscure they do not feature on maps. Karpino, Yamskoye, Novinka, Yeremina Gora, Shugozero, Nikolskoye, and on to Zabor'ye (see Figure 13.3).[40] Thousands died building it. They included peasants and people from collective farms – effectively forced labour – plus rear area troops and construction battalions and almost certainly GULag prisoners. Those who died building it were buried under the logs. It was finished on 6 December. Yet in one of the many ironies of the war, on 9 December Tikhvin was recaptured. After all the sacrifices made to build the forest road, it quickly fell out of use.

But that was a month ahead. In the interim, as Moscow steeled itself for the final German assault, the Russians struck back anywhere they

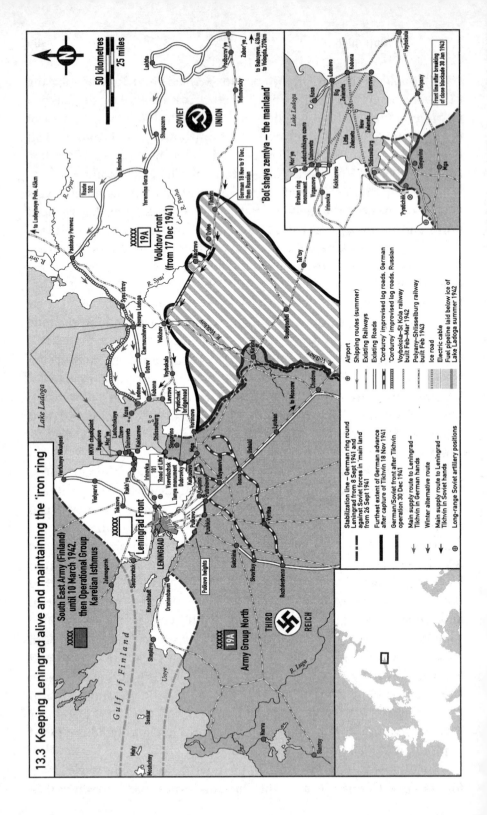

13.3 Keeping Leningrad alive and maintaining the 'iron ring'

Legend:

- ⊕ Airport
- Shipping routes (summer)
- Existing Railways
- Existing Roads
- 'Corduroy' improvised log roads. German
- 'Corduroy' improvised log roads. Russian
- Voybokola–St Kola railway built Feb–Mar 1942
- Polyany–Shlisselburg railway built Feb 1943
- Ice road
- Electric cable
- Fuel pipeline laid below ice of Lake Ladoga summer 1942

- Stabilization line – German ring round Leningrad from 8 Sept 1941 and against Soviet forces in 'main land' from 26 Sept 1941
- Furthest extent of German advance after capture of Tikhvin 18 Nov 1941
- German/Soviet front after Tikhvin operation 30 Dec 1941
- ↓ Main supply route to Leningrad – Tikhvin in German hands
- ↓ Winter alternative route
- ↓ Main supply route to Leningrad – Tikhvin in Soviet hands
- ⊕ Long-range Soviet artillery positions

50 kilometres
25 miles

N

South East Army (Finland) until 10 March 1942, then Operational Group Karelian Isthmus

XXXX

Volkhov Front (from 17 Dec 1941)

XXXXX 19A

German 18 Nov to 9 Dec, then Russian

'Bol'shaya zemlya – the mainland'

Leningrad Front

XXXXX

LENINGRAD

Army Group North

XXXX 19A

THIRD REICH

SOVIET UNION

Lake Ladoga

Gulf of Finland

Front line after breaking of close blockade 30 Jan 1943

could, and Leningrad was an obvious place. It was clear that, having expended so much energy to get to Tikhvin, and given that town's critical importance for the survival of Leningrad, the Germans would fight hard to defend it. On 19 November General Kirill Meretskov who, like Rokossovskiy, had been horribly beaten up by the NKVD, but was now back in uniform and commanding Fourth Army (and would soon be commanding the Volkhov Front), attacked with an infantry division and two tank battalions – all he had. But Army Group North held the critical town.

While Leningrad held, the big Soviet counter-attack to break or, as it turned out, mitigate the strangulation of the city was scheduled to coincide with the counteroffensive at Moscow. On 1 December a German push towards Lake Ladoga was stopped at Volkhov (see Figure 13.3). The next day German air reconnaissance reported twenty-nine trains heading west on the Vologda–Tikhvin line. It was obvious that if the Germans did not maintain strong pressure on Moscow, the Russians would be able to spare forces to try to break the siege of Leningrad.[41] On 5 December Meretskov directed forces in towards Tikhvin from three sides. On 7 December, in a blizzard, mirroring one at Moscow, 650 kilometres to the south, the Russians encircled the Germans holding Tikhvin. Hitler had promised around 100 tanks and 22,000 troops. In fact, the Russians faced just five German tanks and some freezing, exhausted infantry. On 7 December Leeb ordered Tikhvin evacuated. The Germans had lost 7,000 casualties and were pushed back westwards, across the River Volkhov.

The Russian recapture of Tikhvin on 9 December, although nowhere near breaking the blockade of Leningrad,190 kilometres to the west, at least opened up a major railhead and cut the remaining road route to the edge of Lake Ladoga from 320 to about 100 kilometres. It helped and probably saved Leningrad, just for the moment. But it was no final solution. And there was no guarantee that the Germans might not take Tikhvin back. Pavlov, Leningrad's food chief, was nevertheless greatly relieved. 'Without exaggeration,' he wrote, 'the defeat of the German Fascist forces at Tikhvin and the recapture of the northern railway line up to Mga station saved thousands of people from starvation.'[42] Or maybe a million.

More than that, the counteroffensive which retook the vital junction at Tikhvin on 9 December 1941 was the first major successful counter-offensive against the *Wehrmacht* by any combatant in the Second World

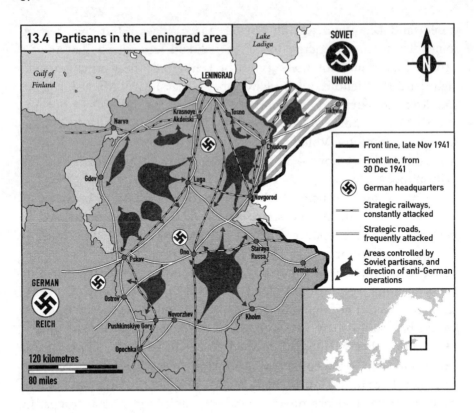

13.4 Partisans in the Leningrad area

War. Besides the regular forces, the Russian recapture of a triangular area 150 kilometres wide and 100 deep owed much to the activity of partisans in the area (see Figure 13.4).

The Germans, too, had communication problems. In the Leningrad area 'there was not a single serviceable hard-surface road leading eastward towards the German front' recalled a group of former German generals and staff officers (see also Figure 13.3).[43] The Volkhov area was swampy forest, and the Germans, too, found that 'corduroy roads', made from the copious supplies of logs, were the only possible substitute for concrete or paved roads, which, they soon discovered were 'impossible' to build. Huge amounts of timber were required. Where possible, the Germans used logs about 30 centimetres in diameter, in several layers. In the Leningrad area, the logs were about half that diameter – 15 centimetres, but even this limited the width of the roadway to a single lane for trucks, so passing places were constructed about every kilometre. The passage of traffic along these bumpy, corrugated strips necessitated careful traffic control, as was also the case on the Russian side, the Road of Life. Ideally, the top layer of logs would be smoothed off, but otherwise they had to be topped with sand, cinders or rubble. Even so, the constant concussions as traffic bumped over the uneven surface meant that the vehicles, and any sensitive equipment they might be carrying, suffered. Their speed was limited to about 8 kilometres per hour, and marching troops could manage, at most, a half to two-thirds of their normal marching speed. The main German corduroy roads, as well as Russian Routes 101 and 102, are shown in Figure 13.3. The local German commander was utterly dependent on the two corduroy roads running from the nearest hardstanding at Sivoritsy and Rozhdestveno, covering a total distance of 120 kilometres.

In these conditions the Germans, like the Russians, found that old methods worked best. At first the Germans had been bemused – and amused – by the prevalence of the tiny Russian 'Panje' steppe ponies they encountered across the eastern front, pulling lightweight peasant carts and, once the freeze came, sleighs. Even compared with the big, carefully bred German horses, never mind the mechanical tractors, these were regarded as 'a hundred years behind the times'. And yet, the mud and the snow soon saw off the big German horses and motor vehicles. By early 1942 some Panzer divisions were using up to 2,000 Panje horses to move supplies, and to evacuate the wounded, while having scarcely a single serviceable motor vehicle.[44] A hundred years behind the times they might have been, but they worked.

Feeding a frozen city

With the closure of the German iron ring round Leningrad on 8 September 1941, the final approach to the city from the 'mainland' was either by air, in the face of German air superiority, or across Lake Ladoga. The latter, first of all by boat, and then, as the inland sea froze, over the ice. The main landfall was at the small village, one of several fishermen's villages, now with a small marina, appropriately named Ladozhskoye Ozero ('Lake Ladoga'). It stands on the lake shore, 40 kilometres east-north-east of the city centre, where a tall and prominent red-and-white-striped lighthouse marks the spot. The lighthouse was there in 1941, but, being an obvious landmark and target for air attack, was camouflaged. From there, running south and then west-south-west, the 'Road of Life' – *doroga zhizni* – runs to the city, through the vast expanses of birch trees which, at this latitude, extend from here to the Pacific. There are now stones marking each kilometre along the way – 46 kilometres in all. A single-track railway also ran from Ladozhskoye Ozero to the city, 57 kilometres long in all. The enveloping forests at least provided wood to fuel the steam trains which helped carry supplies in, and people out. At the Ladozhskoye Ozero station a carefully restored olive-green locomotive still stands guard, marked 'Everything for Victory. Everything for the Front'.

The Road of Life is now roughly asphalted, but in 1941 it was gravel, with pot-holes. It still has pot-holes. It began to operate in earnest from late November 1941. As supplies were brought in, across the Lake and then down the 45-kilometre road, people were evacuated the other way. A million were evacuated, in all. Evacuees travelled in open-topped trucks, but there were stopping points along the way where people could get a hot drink and warm up. At Irinovka the NKVD stopped vehicles and trains to check people's identities, and those who died working on the Road of Life were buried. Some 9 kilometres out, at Vsevolozhsk, there was a military airfield. As the road going out from the city approaches Lake Ladoga, just past Vaganovo, one first sees the edge of the inland sea, full of tall rushes. Here, there is a simple but huge monument in the form of a low concrete arch, broken into two parts, but overlapping in the centre. The 'ring' was never completely sealed, as the concrete graphic explains, and this 46-kilometre road and the frozen lake beyond were the reason why.

'Sanitary detachments' were employed to bury the corpses of those who died maintaining and moving along the road, in the siege, and from German attack. In the freezing winter it was impossible to dig into the ground, and in February 1942 explosives were used to blast out the graves.

The most evocative memorial lies close to the city, however. It commemorates the thousands of children – there were about 400,000 in the city when the siege started – who fought and died in the 'blockade'. Many youngsters were in summer camps around the city when the Germans approached, and they joined the partisans. Some of these, and some who were trapped in the city – 15,000 children and youngsters in all – were awarded medals for their part in the Battle for Leningrad. In belated recognition of their services, these young war veterans received their 'passports' – adults' ID cards – two years later. At the memorial on the left (north) of the Road of Life, a few kilometres out from the city, some of their names are recorded, some – incongruously, perhaps, in a supposedly egalitarian society – made 'Knights' of Soviet orders. As winter set in, without fuel or food, children started to die, but often lasted longer than their parents. Here also, in masonry, are reproduced the notes from a child's exercise book, that of Tanya Savicheva, an 11-year-old schoolgirl. It records the deaths of each member of her family during December 1941 and from January to May 1942, until, under the letter 'S' there is the entry, 'Savichevs died. All died. Only Tanya remains.' By another one of those tragic historical ironies, Tanya herself survived to be evacuated in the spring, probably after her mother died on 13 May 1942. But she was by then suffering from chronic dysentery, and died a year later, in summer 1943.[45] That was after the Leningrad close blockade had been broken and as the Germans were about to start falling back along the entire front.

Route 101: the ice war

The Russians knew about fighting – and logistics – on and over ice. In 1242 Prince Aleksandr Nevskiy had defeated the Teutonic Knights in the great 'Ice Battle' (*ledovoye poboishche*) on Lake Peipus (Chud). This was in part, allegedly, because the German crusaders ('*Nemtsy*'), being heavier, fell through the ice, while his Russian forces, more lightly armoured in the oriental fashion, did not. Whether that is true or not is less relevant than the fact that everyone had seen it in Eisenstein's 1938 *Aleksandr Nevskiy* movie, to the accompaniment of screeching, ice-breaking musical sound effects by Prokofiev. In 1808, the Russians had marched across the frozen Gulf of Bothnia to attack Sweden, and before the section of the Siberian Railway round Lake Baikal was completed in 1904, during the Russo-Japanese war, they had constructed a railway across the ice of the world's greatest freshwater lake to maintain their precarious 6,000-kilometre supply line to the Far East. In 1921 Tukhach-evsky had suppressed the Kronshtadt rebellion attacking over the ice of the Gulf of Finland, and in the 1939–40 Soviet–Finnish war (see Chapter 4) the Russians had attacked Vyborg (Viipuri) over the same frozen waters. But remarkable though these feats were, none was as urgent, complex or needed to be sustained for anywhere near as long as supplying millions of people (as it turned out) through two ferocious winters.[46]

Lake Ladoga, lying east of Leningrad, was subject to dramatic changes in temperature, winds and storms. The Lake extends roughly 400 kilometres from south to north and 112 kilometres west to east, and falls to 220 metres in depth, although the southern part, which was the area of key interest, is only 20 to 50 metres deep (see Figures 13.1 and 13.3). The surface ice needed to be 12 centimetres thick to carry a horse, 18 centimetres thick to take a horse and a loaded sledge, and a uniform 20 centimetres thick, at least, before it could carry a truck carrying a 1-tonne load. The Leningraders knew roughly when Lake Ladoga would freeze, and one of their scientists calculated exactly how long it would take, subject to the unpredictable winds and depths involved. Calculations were still done in Fahrenheit (see Chapter 12), but at 5 °F above zero (− 15 °C), it would take eight days to create the critical foot of ice.[47]

The plan for the ice road began to take shape in mid October. Lt Gen. F. N. Lagunov – the chief of rear services – had already put 20,000 people to work improving the port and storage facilities at Osinovets and Kokorevo on the western shore and Kobona, Lavrova and Novaya Ladoga on the 'mainland' side. From 8 November Russian reconnaissance aircraft began to fly over Ladoga looking for promising signs of ice formation. The northern part of the Lake was freezing up nicely but an infuriating watery black hole lay across the proposed route. Then, pretty well on schedule, on 15 November a north wind started the big freeze.[48]

On 17 November, at this northerly latitude, the sun did not rise until after nine in the morning. An hour before, reconnaissance teams had moved out to test the ice and mark the routes from Kokorevo to the island of Zelenets and thence to Kobona, on the 'mainland' side. They were due to report back by 18.00, but it was not until 04.00 the next morning that Zhdanov, waiting at the Front headquarters at the Smolny Institute, received word that a route looked feasible. On 19 November Lagunov himself arrived at Konkorevo and set out in a scout car – an M-1, the equivalent of a modern 'Hummer' (a high-mobility wheeled vehicle) – to follow the precariously designated route. Crevasses continued to appear in the ice, but that evening the Leningrad Military Soviet took the decision to open a road across it. The next day, the ration was cut to 500 grams of bread per day for fighting soldiers, 250 grams for manual workers and 125 grams for everyone else. Captain Murov and a team of drivers and skin-and-bone horses assembled on the lake shore to head across the still-thin ice – about 12 centimetres thick – via Karedzhskiy island to Kobona, to pick up life-saving supplies, and come back. A political commissar approached him.

> There are supplies in the city for two more days. After that, there is nothing more. The ice is very young and not very strong. But we can't wait. Each hour is dear.[49]

In two days, Leningrad, already starving, would start an irrecoverable spiral downwards to an icy, malnourished death. Crevasses kept opening up in the ice, but Murov's teams dodged them, and by the evening they had reached Kobona, where the drivers and horses were fed. Murov feared that the poor animals, covered in frost, would not make the 30 to 50 kilometres back to the Leningrad side. Remembering an old Russian Civil War practice, having reached the eastern landward side, he ordered the snow to be scraped away, so that the horses could feed on the old grass beneath. The drivers, who had been given 800 grams of bread each – nearly twice a soldier's daily ration and a week's worth for an ordinary citizen of the great city – shared their rations with the horses as well. Then they headed back over the grey ice through the black night carrying flour and high-nutrition food. Early in the morning of 21 November, they made it back to the Leningrad side.

Route 101, comprising the Ladoga ice road (*Ladozhskaya ledovaya trassa*) and the Road of Life, *doroga zhizni*, overland into the city of Leningrad, was *open*.

Although the ice road was crystallizing, ships still made their way through. In October and November ships carried nearly 60,000 tonnes of supplies – 44,000 of them food; the rest fuel, ammunition and sundries.[50]

The ice rapidly reached the thickness needed to carry motor vehicles. The first substantial, scheduled cargo convoy – sixty trucks carrying 33.5 tonnes, of which 33 tonnes was flour – crossed in a snowstorm on 22 November and reached Leningrad on 23 November.[51] An absolute minimum of 100 tonnes a day was needed to keep the city alive, although Leningrad's daily consumption was nearer 600 tonnes. As the ice thickened, the Russian engineers created new roads further north. With the recapture of Tikhvin on 9 December a more reliable route across Lake Ladoga (now frozen, although the ice was still far from uniformly secure), was established. On 29 October an underwater signals cable had been laid across the bottom of the lake to link with the encircled area at Konkorevo, and once the ice hardened, some sixty ice roads or tracks (*trassy*) were formed across the frozen lake (see Figure 13.3).

A bizarre war on the ice developed. The Germans sent out ski patrols, to try to cut the Soviet supply columns traversing the frozen lake, but the Russians built pillboxes from blocks of ice, cemented rock hard by pouring water over them. On a perfectly flat and exposed surface, the German ski patrols were picked off like surfers assailing icy battleships. The 350 anti-aircraft guns and machine guns and the 100 searchlights along the ice road were protected by ice revetments, and the crews' accommodation reinforced by outer igloos.[52] As the snow fell, it was piled up into high white walls to protect the ice road. The trucks carried light loads, in case they broke the ice, and the drivers were always on the alert to jump out. Just like the 'Road of Life' on land, the ice roads had points with tents where people could warm up. Traffic control was vital and initially there were twenty control points, between 300 and 400 metres apart. By 1 January 1942 there were seventy-five traffic control points, manned by 350 people. When the scheme was completed the ice roads – *trassy* – extended 1,770 kilometres – 1,100 miles.[53]

Like any great project, the Road of Life grew in efficiency and effectiveness. As on the land road, the ice road was quickly provided with medical tents for people to thaw out and for the numerous casualties to be treated. At kilometre 7, Ol'ga Pisarenko, a nurse, was proudly photographed outside her 'medical tent'.[54] By the end of December the ice had become a metre thick, and could therefore carry just about any amount of traffic, including the massive KV heavy tanks. A thaw at the end of November reduced the supplies brought in to a catastrophically inadequate 61 tonnes on 30 November, and every soldier and civilian faced starvation and hypothermia. Then the cold returned, and on 22 and 23 December the ice road carried 687 and 786 tonnes of supplies, respectively, for the first time ever exceeding the daily rate of consumption in the city.[55] About 500 tonnes of bread alone was needed every day to keep the city alive on minimum rations in winter.[56] It was not a happy Christmas.

The 'Road of Life' Museum at the landing point at Ladozhskoye Ozero reveals other pieces of Russian – and German – ingenuity. When the ice was melted, from May through to November, the Germans deployed catamarans powered by aircraft engines with propellors, carrying anti-aircraft guns, some of which the Russians captured. On the ice the Russians used small, lightly armoured craft armed with machine guns, called 'Aerosani' – 'aerosleighs'. These ran on skis, and were again powered by aircraft engines with propellors at the back.[57] It was a bizarre testament to man's infinite adaptability, made more tragic by the appalling circumstances that made it necessary.[58]

Winter hell

The opening of the ice road was not enough to maintain any semblance of normality, health, law and, in some inevitable cases, human decency. In any great city subject to natural or man-made disaster, people fight to survive. The supreme 'plus' was the application of Leningrad's scientific ingenuity and inventiveness. On 23 September beer production was halted and all malt, barley, soya beans and bran used in brewing beer were diverted to make bread. Different baking methods were used to make the bread denser and more nutritious. And then a scientist at the Leningrad Scientific Institute devised a way of making the cellulose from the congealed paste and size on the back of stripped wallpaper edible. By the end of November a fifth to a half of every loaf consisted of edible cellulose. But even this measure extended the bread supply only by a month or two, and in any case, men and women cannot live on bread alone. Scurvy, caused by lack of vitamin C, became common. To get over this the Russian scientists started to produce vitamin C from pine needles – one commodity, at least, not scarce in Leningrad and its environs in autumn and winter. In the first half of 1942, more than 700,000 litres of pine extract were produced.[59]

In spite of all these efforts, and for the best reasons, any meat or

Table 13.1 – Leningrad bread ration, 1941–3 (grams)

From date	Fighting troops	Rear echelon troops, manual workers	Factory and other high-priority workers	Office workers	Dependants and children
8 Nov 1941	600 (from 800)	400	400	200	200
13 Nov 1941	600	400	300	150	150
20 Nov 1941	500	300	250	125	125
Route 101 up and running, recapture of Tikhvin					
25 Dec 1941	500	475	350	200	200
24 Jan 1941	600	575	400	300	300
10 Feb 1942	800	600	400	300	300
Inner ring broken 18 January 1943					
22 Feb 1943	800	700	600	500	400

Source: Salisbury, *900 Days*, pp. 377, 387–8, 411, Glantz, *The Siege* . . . pp. 91–2, 144–5.

meat substitutes went to the fighting troops. Variation in the bread ration are shown in Table 13.1.[60] A 125-gram slice of bread is often portrayed as the standard daily bread ration for the siege. That is not strictly accurate. It was the ration for those not directly involved in productive work for five weeks in winter 1941. But it was abysmally inadequate.

Even the most ingenious triumphs of the ice road engineers and the nutritional experts could not solve the most critical problem in the city itself. Water. Water is not only the most essential commodity, after air, for human survival: it was also necessary to put out the fires started by German attacks on the city. Air and artillery strikes smashed water mains, and the population had to draw water from the Neva in buckets.

All food was rationed, although there was a thriving black market. At first, people were mugged for their ration cards. Pavlov had issued strict rules that no replacement ration cards were to be issued, because otherwise many people would claim they had been stolen or lost in air or artillery raids, and get a second – or third – maybe even fourth – ration. As a result the injured, sick, exhausted or unwary fell prey to thieves.

After the widespread theft of ration cards, people started to eat the crows. Then came gulls, pigeons and much-loved dogs and cats. Anna Akhmatova, the famous poetess, wrote of pigeons in the square in front of the Kazan Cathedral, but was savagely criticized by a Leningrad survivor after the war. There were no pigeons, the survivor explained. They had already been eaten. And then people began to kill and eat an abundant and less loved food source – rats.

And then it got worse. As early as November there were stories of children disappearing. And then parents started to keep them off the streets because of rumours of cannibalism. Harrison Salisbury, author of the classic *900 Days*, cites the story. The Soviet rejection of Harrison Salisbury's book probably owed much to his reports of the practice. But when people are starving, and there are many dead – as we know from stories of air crashes in remote mountain ranges – people driven to extremes will, under duress, eat the dead of their own kind. In a city of 2.5 million people, subsisting on a slice of bread a day in temperatures of $-20°$ C, it must have happened, on occasions.

According to the accounts, the Haymarket – *Sennoy Rynok*, where Dostoyevskiy's character Raskol'nikov had spent a good deal of time in *Crime and Punishment* – was the centre for a suspicious trade in meat patties (burgers), which people convinced themselves were made from horses, dogs, cats, rats – anything but humans, although the rumours circulated. There were also stories that children were preferred, because they tasted better, and then women. Certainly there were plenty of dead bodies around. But there were also stories of people being murdered to be eaten. Especially soldiers, briefly off duty, who, being better fed, had more flesh on them. Salisbury cites the story of one witness, 'Dmitry', who was lured upstairs to an apartment by a well-fed and well-dressed man who said to his colleague inside, 'It's me. With a live one.' From inside, he smelt the warm, sweet stench of human flesh and saw human limbs hanging from hooks, and ran. Fortunately, outside, he encountered a truck full of Red Army soldiers. 'Cannibals,' he shouted. Two of the soldiers moved in and two shots rang out. The soldiers then returned, one carrying a loaf of bread. They said they had found parts of five bodies, gave him the bread, and headed for the Road of Life.[61]

Such sensational reports must be treated with extreme caution. In every great city, a tiny proportion of people will do terrible things – war or no war, siege or no siege. Interestingly, the newly released selections of NKVD and NKGB documents for 1941 and 1942 published by the

FSB Academy contain no documents, no reports, not even any speculation about cannibalism.[62] However, other selections of documents do.
An army food supply officer confirmed there was a gang of cannibals
who killed and ate military messengers, south of the city, and according
to an archivist at the Central State Archive of St Petersburg, 1,500
people were arrested for cannibalism during the siege, 886 of them
during the first, terrible winter, between the start of December 1941 and
15 February 1942.[63] At the end of November the number of crimes
committed on account of hunger showed an inexorable increase, including 'incidents of cannibalism'.[64] However, the most chilling reference
comes from June 1942. According to NKVD records,

> in connection with improvement in the food situation in
> June the death rate went down by a third. In addition, the
> number of incidents of *use of human flesh in food* sharply
> decreased. Whereas 226 people were arrested for this crime in
> May, then in June, it was just 56.[65]

It happened.

They seek him here . . .

In this situation, the population could be highly susceptible to German
propaganda, raising the spectre of revolt and the Leningraders then
opening the gates to the Germans. Rumours also spread that the
authorities were hoarding supplies while the ordinary people starved. In
January 1942 the NKVD's worst nightmare threatened to unfold. On 9
January eighty copies of a leaflet from someone signing him or herself
'Rebel' or 'Insurgent' (*Buntovshchik*) were left on a platform at Leningrad's Moscow Station.

> Citizens! Down with the power which makes us die of
> hunger! Citizens, destroy the warehouses and shops, the
> scoundrels who rob us, making us die from hunger. Down
> with hunger. We, the people still alive, must be determined
> . . . Citizens! The armed forces are leaving the city, and
> leaving us to die of hunger. Down with our leaders![66]

This was not the kind of thing any wartime government needs, and not something people in Stalin's Russia were used to. It was the first of many leaflets and anonymous letters from the 'Rebel' over the next twenty-one months. Leningrad under siege, under German bombardment, its population dying of starvation and cold, the survivors sustained by a thread across ice and water, became the desperate setting for a fascinating detective story.

The NKVD was desperate to track down the 'Rebel'. At first the internal security and police forces concentrated on the October Station area, and on the 18,000 people employed there. The syntax of the leaflets was clumsy, suggesting the author was not an educated person, but that could have been to throw them off the scent – like Jack the Ripper's ungrammatical 'Dear boss' letters.[67] The NKVD checked the handwriting of all 18,000, including the office workers. But they drew a blank.

Another lead took the NKVD to the Kartontol' factory, and the 'Horse traction' workers' cooperative, with a total of 227 employees. All their handwriting was checked but that, too, produced no results.[68] Early in 1942, the 'Rebel' was still at large.

The first winter

Although Leningrad endured two war winters under close siege, the first was unquestionably the worst. In December 1941 the city's population was estimated at 2,280,000. By April 1942, it had fallen to 1,100,000. Russian statistics are in the main pretty reliable, though not always complete, and we know that 440,000 people were evacuated that winter. That is probably the origin of the 620,000 dead which was the original Soviet count for civilian deaths in the siege. The total cost in Soviet lives, bearing in mind military deaths in the same period and civilian deaths the following winter, is likely to have totalled a million, or even more.[69] German senior officers reckoned that in the first war winter – 1941–2 – 'the city of Leningrad came close to extinction, one million civilians being starved or frozen to death. Even the Russian soldiers were inadequately fed and equipped and by the end of the winter half of them were dead.'[70]

Further attempts to break the siege – the Volkhov Offensive, January–June 1942

Even the most cynical Soviet planner in Moscow, dismissive of its eccentric, 'intellectual' image, could not have written Leningrad off. It was a hugely important armaments centre, and after the ice froze really hard in December, the evacuation of its industry, interrupted in August, started again. Between December 1941 and April 1942 no fewer than 3,677 railway freight cars, capable of carrying more than 100,000 tonnes of machinery, were dispatched from the city across the ice road to the mainland.[71] The resources needed to keep the ice road open were also colossal. It would be far cheaper and easier to supply the city and extract its resources for redeployment into the vastness of Asia if a land route with proper railways were re-established.

The Soviet leadership therefore decided that Leningrad must be relieved at all costs. A new staff was formed under Meretskov and the Fifty-Ninth and Second Shock Armies were moved in to reinforce the Fifty-Second on the Volkhov river. The Soviet Fifty-Fourth Army, reinforced by another six divisions, would attack southwards across marshy terrain north of Kirishi towards Lyuban'. The plan was for it to link with Vlasov's Second Shock Army, cutting into the rear of the German Eighteenth and severing the Chudovo–Tosno Main Supply Route (*Rollbahn*)[72] (see Figure 13.5) – although the thrusts from north and east together formed the Lyuban' offensive, from 7 January to 30 April 1943. However, the southern component of this is known as the Volkhov offensive, and this and its consequences carried on until 28 June.[73]

Second Shock Army's attack across the Volkhov between 10 and 13 January 1942 succeeded and the army cut into the German rear areas, its spearheads advancing 80 kilometres, threatening to cut off Eighteenth Army (see Figure 13.4). The Germans just held on, although they had nothing to match Fifty-Fourth Army's main striking force of 200 tanks, mostly the formidable T-34 which was at home in winter and on the marshy, albeit now frozen, terrain. Second Shock Army got within a few kilometres of the *Rollbahn* when it was stopped. Then, on 15 March,

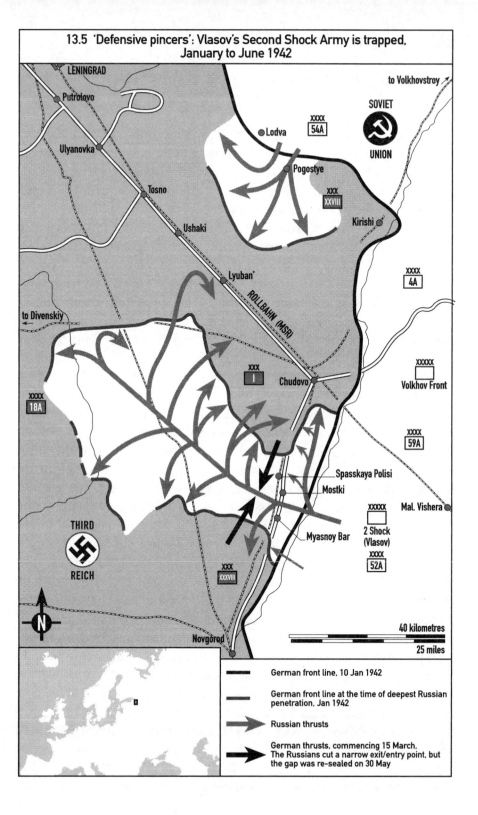

13.5 'Defensive pincers': Vlasov's Second Shock Army is trapped, January to June 1942

LENINGRAD
Putrolovo
Ulyanovka
Tosno
Ushaki
to Divenskiy
Lyuban'
ROLLBAHN (MSR)

Lodva
Pogostye
Kirishi

to Volkhovstroy

SOVIET
UNION

XXXX
54A

XXX
XXVIII

XXXX
4A

XXX
I
Chudovo

XXXXX
Volkhov Front

XXXX
59A

Spasskaya Polisi
Mostki

Mal. Vishera

XXXXX
2 Shock
(Vlasov)

XXXX
52A

Myasnoy Bar

THIRD
REICH

XXX
XXXVIII

N

Novgorod

40 kilometres

25 miles

German front line, 10 Jan 1942

German front line at the time of deepest Russian penetration, Jan 1942

Russian thrusts

German thrusts, commencing 15 March, The Russians cut a narrow exit/entry point, but the gap was re-sealed on 30 May

XXXX
18A

the Germans attacked across Second Shock's supply lines in a manoeuvre known as a 'defensive pincer', cutting it off with a 'finger' nowhere more than 4 kilometres wide. The Russians were able to cut a small gap in the 'finger', about 3 kilometres wide, and to lay two narrow-gauge railways through it, but these were nowhere near enough to keep the 180,000 Russian troops encircled in the pocket resupplied. It was an exact mirror, on a smaller scale, of the situation around Leningrad to the north-west.

On 20 April Stavka ordered the deputy commander of Meretskov's Volkhov Front, Lt Gen. Andrey Vlasov, into the pocket to take over command of Second Shock from its ailing commander, Gen. Klykov. Vlasov's orders were to extricate Second Shock Army – preferably by moving forwards and linking up with other Soviet formations but, if not, then backwards, out of encirclement.[74] Three days later the Volkhov Front was temporarily downgraded to the Volkhov Operational Group, one of two groups within an enlarged Leningrad Front, the other part of which became the Leningrad Group of Forces. This creation of an intermediate level of command between army and front was highly unusual, and Shaposhnikov objected, but Stalin agreed. The arrangement did not last long: the Volkhov Front was re-established as a Front, now led by Meretskov, on 9 June.[75] Vlasov (1900–46) was at this time regarded as one of the Red Army's best generals, and was one of its youngest. It was perhaps a mistake to give a Shock Army, which was designed to force a breakthrough at the price of heavy casualties and was relatively poorly equipped, to such a talented and ambitious commander, especially since it was now in deep trouble.

Unlike Leningrad itself, Vlasov's Army could not hold. On 15 May the Russians started to try to withdraw, but the Germans pursued relentlessly. Winter favoured the Russians. Now it was late spring. On 24 May the commander of the 'operational group' – the new, intermediate level between Army and Front – Lt Gen. Mikhail Khozin, reprimanded Vlasov for losing control of his forces and ordered him to stop the Germans cutting across his line of withdrawal.[76]

On 30 May the Germans once again managed to seal the escape route near Myasnoy Bor. Disparate Russian groups managed to escape, however. By 25 June Second Shock Army had ceased organized resistance, but the Soviet reports indicate that it was not until 1 June that the escape route was totally cut off.[77] In all, some 60,000 Russian troops were killed or taken prisoner in the pocket, including Vlasov, who was captured on 12 July, and his army headquarters.[78] On 1 June there were 40,157 men in the pocket, of whom 13,018 escaped, leaving, with the usual baffling Soviet precision in the midst of turmoil, 27,139 killed and prisoners.[79]

The Soviet command tried to get Vlasov and his staff out, but they had lost track of him and were too late. On 17 July Stavka ordered Meretskov, commander of the now re-established Volkhov Front, to evacuate 'Vlasov and his people' – the commander, chief-of-staff and signals chief of Second Shock Army – no later than 19 July. They thought he was with the local partisan commander, F. I. Sazonov, but if he had been, he was no longer.[80] On 21 July Beria, no less, reported the NKVD's assessment of what had happened to Second Shock Army to the GKO – the State Defence Committee. The report concluded with a radio intercept from the Germans. On 14 July they reported that 'during the mopping-up of the recent Volkhov encirclement we discovered in his shelter the commander of Second Shock Army, Lt Gen. Vlasov, and took him prisoner.'[81]

It is clear that Stavka had made a real effort to sustain Second Shock Army and, when that failed, to get Vlasov out. The volume of correspondence in the NKVD archives shows that, by now, losing an Army was a major issue – more so than in 1941. Stavka had also tried to resupply the trapped Army by air. The Russians dropped more than a million rounds of small-arms ammunition and about 2,000 artillery shells, but only a little over a half of them reached Second Shock Army: the Germans, presumably, got some of the rest.[82]

Second Shock Army therefore lost 60,000 men in all, 27,000 of them after 1 June. Six Russian infantry divisions and six brigades were totally destroyed and another nine divisions partially. In total, twenty Russians divisions had been expended in a six-month battle to try to relieve Leningrad.[83] Vlasov, the bookish commander with his thick, heavy spectacles, passed into German captivity and into history not as one of the most talented Red Army commanders who, like Rokossovskiy, had commanded one of the great mechanized corps in the frontier battles and played a key role in the critical defence of Moscow, but as a traitor. In captivity, expecting the Germans to win the war, he soon became an ardent anti-communist and volunteered to raise an army from Russian prisoners to fight against his homeland. Hitler allowed him to raise the Russian National Liberation Army (KONR), but used it mainly for its propaganda value rather than in combat. Most of the Russian and other

Soviet prisoners who fought for the Germans did so in German units or, in the case of certain nationalities, the SS. In 1945 Vlasov was captured by the US Army, who handed him over to the Russians, where he was tried and met a grisly end on the gallows on 1 August 1946.[84]

The (second) Sinyavino Operation, August–September 1942

With German forces moving successfully east from Ukraine in the summer of 1942 (see Chapters 15 and 16), the Germans began to plan new offensives in the Leningrad area, where they had been desperately holding on against the Russian counter-attacks during the winter and spring. One aim was to destroy the large Russian bridgehead around Oranienbaum, which was supplied across the Gulf of Finland from the fortress island of Kronshtadt. Von Manstein's Eleventh Army with six divisions was moved up from the Crimea, along with the massive siege guns Dora, Gamma and Karl, to help smash Kronshtadt – and possibly Leningrad as well. At the end of July this plan became Operation 'Nordlicht'. On 23 August, in an unusual fit of mission command-style delegation, Hitler ordered Manstein to do whatever he liked in order to link up with the Finns and raze Leningrad to the ground. The Russians clearly divined German intent. Stavka ordered the re-established Volkhov Front under Kirill Meretskov and the Leningrad Front, now under Leonid Govorov, to pre-empt any such German attack and, if possible, to break the blockade.

The next attempt to break the 'iron ring' therefore came less than two months after Second Shock Army's destruction, although the formation was reconstituted. The main offensive was due to start on 28 August, just five days after Manstein received his orders from Hitler, although Govorov was to secure bridgeheads over the Neva before that, on 19 August.

The Soviet offensive is shown in Figure 13.6. Govorov's initial attacks out of Leningrad failed, but they diverted the Germans. The main striking force was to be Eighth Army, part of Meretskov's Volkhov Front, commanded by Major-General Filipp Starikov. It attacked at

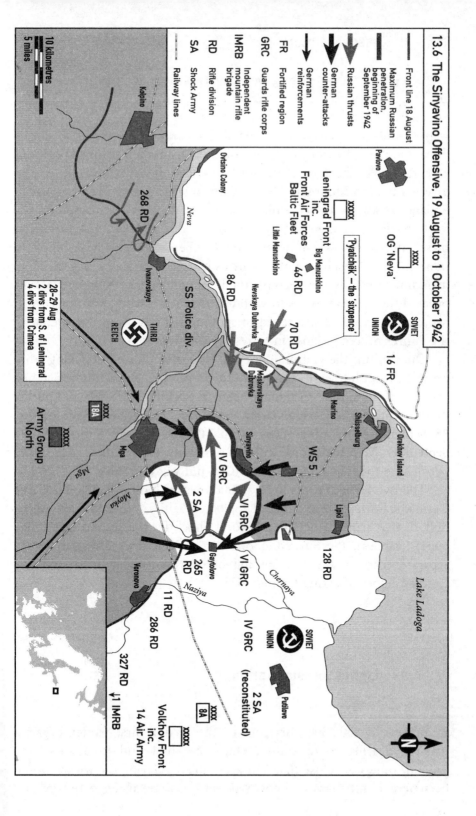

13.6 The Sinyavino Offensive, 19 August to 1 October 1942

Legend:
- Front line 18 August
- Maximum Russian penetration, beginning of September 1942
- German counter-attacks
- Russian thrusts
- German reinforcements
- **FR** Fortified region
- **GRC** Guards rifle corps
- **IMRB** Independent mountain rifle brigade
- **RD** Rifle division
- **SA** Shock Army
- Railway lines

10 kilometres
5 miles

Map labels:
Kolpino, Pavlovo, Ovtsino Colony, Neva, 268 RD, Ivanovskoye, REICH, THIRD, SS Police div., Mga, Moyka, Mga, Army Group North, 18A, Voronovo, Naziya, 11 RD, 286 RD, 327 RD, 1 IMRB, Volkhov Front inc. 14 Air Army, 8A, 2 SA (reconstituted), Putilovo, SOVIET UNION, IV GRC, Chernaya, 128 RD, Lake Ladoga, Lipki, Gaytolovo, 265 RD, VI GRC, 2 SA, VI GRC, IV GRC, Sinyavino, WS 5, Shlisselburg, Orekhov Island, Marino, Moskovskaya Dubrovka, Nevskaya Dubrovka, 70 RD, '*Pyatichok*' – the 'sixpence', 16 FR, SOVIET UNION, OG 'Neva', 86 RD, 46 RD, Little Manushkino, Big Manushkino, Leningrad Front inc. Front Air Forces Baltic Fleet

28–29 Aug
2 divs from S. of Leningrad
4 divs from Crimea

N

02.10 on 27 August, prising between two German infantry divisions, and rapidly capturing Tortolovo. By 31 August it was only seven kilometres from the Neva. The Germans could see what the Russians were trying to do and also feared that Operation Nordlicht would be disrupted. Two divisions had been diverted from their planned positions as part of Nordlicht to repel the Sinyavino offensive, and Hitler also diverted the 3rd Mountain Division which was heading from Norway to Finland by sea. By 12 September four of the divisions earmarked for the final attack on Leningrad had been diverted, and Hitler was furious at these 'atrocious developments'. Meanwhile, Meretskov was piling in more forces to sustain Eighth Army as it tried to battle its way through, including most of the reconstituted Second Shock. Although Stavka ordered the Russian forces to withdraw to their starting positions on 12 September, they had succeeded in spoiling Hitler's plans. 'Exasperated', the Fuhrer ordered Manstein to restore the situation.

Once again, the Germans used a 'defensive pincer', attacking from north and south towards Gaitolovo to cut off the penetration which had come so close to the Neva. Once again, a pocket – the Sinyavino pocket – was created. The German defensive pincers closed near Gaitolovo on 25 September, trapping most of Eighth and Second Shock. On 29 September Meretskov ordered his remnants to withdraw. He asked permission to launch another offensive, but was told 'no'.

The two Soviet Fronts lost 114,000 men including 40,085 dead. The Germans, however, had suffered 26,000 casualties. Whilst the loss of the bulk of two armies (including Second Shock for the second time) may appear careless, the Sinyavino offensive, which does not even rate a separate entry in the Russian log of operations, had frustrated any German hopes of taking Leningrad.[85]

Lights, music, action . . .

In the spring, 300,000 survivors of the terrible first winter began a massive clearing-up operation. Once the snow and ice thawed, the million tonnes of refuse that had accumulated during the winter would become a health hazard. Enormous efforts were made to restore and maintain morale, and to reintroduce a semblance of normality after a winter in which nearly a million might have died. The Soviet authorities also tried to project an image of normality to the rest of the country, and its allies. To convince the Leningraders, the country, the allies and the Germans that Leningrad was unbowed, they hit upon a wonderfully Russian, superbly flamboyant piece of psychological warfare. To stage and broadcast around the world a performance of Shostakovich's new Seventh Leningrad Symphony, which had first been staged far away in central Asia. The score was flown into the besieged city in late June. After six weeks of rehearsals, on 9 August, the Leningrad Philharmonic opened for the performance. There were some lights in chandeliers although the windows were all boarded up with plywood. Lt Gen. of Artillery Govorov, commanding the Leningrad Front, was there in his best uniform, with Kuznetsov, the Party Secretary. Many soldiers and sailors had tickets, and they wore uniform, but everyone else was in their best suit or silk dress. As the chords, like workmen hammering to construct a vast edifice, became louder, in a slow but inexorable build-up of strength and intensity, General Friedrich Ferch, Eighteenth Army's Chief-of-Staff, started getting reports that his troops were listening on the radio. The performance was being relayed across the Soviet Union and by short-wave radio to the rest of Europe and the United States. The Germans later banned the symphony from being played in any territory they occupied. But for now, Ferch sensed an opportunity. He ordered his long-range artillery to zero in on the Philharmonic.

But Govorov had anticipated him. The siege of Leningrad was very much an artillery battle and the Germans knew the whereabouts of any significant buildings in the city. Their bombardment timetable had always targeted people who might be going to the theatre. However, the Russians had always been very good gunners, and Govorov, a specialist in counter-battery fire – silencing the enemy's artillery with your own – knew where the German batteries were. As the majestic symphony played on, a massive and precisely targeted Russian artillery strike paralysed the German guns. There is no doubt about this. Ferch ordered the initial German strike, but all the witnesses – and the elite of Leningrad were all there – confirm that no German shells landed anywhere near the concert hall.[86] As the entire orchestra in the Philharmonic joined in, building the volume of the symphony, other parts of a wider 'orchestra', Leningrad's guns, joined in, too. Land-based artillery and the grey Baltic fleet battleships, their fire superbly directed, belched shell at the German positions. The moral and physical components of a nation's soul and fighting power fused in harmony, and the German guns were silenced. The words of Aleksandr Tvardovskiy's poem come to mind: '*nashi byut, teper' kayuk*...' – 'those are *ours* firing. Now it's – curtains...'[87]

Not quite. It would be another eighteen months before the curtains finally closed on the siege.

Another winter approaches...

As conditions improved, many Leningraders felt the end of the siege was imminent, but it was not to be. The heaviest German air attacks on Leningrad occurred in the autumn of 1942, after Hitler's uncharacteristic order to Manstein to do anything he wanted to flatten the city. They also tried to attack the ship-borne traffic across Lake Ladoga, but failed to have any significant effect, reducing shipments by less than half of 1 per cent, but at a cost of 160 German aircraft. The Germans held a portion of the south shore of the Lake, but a Soviet naval garrison continued to hold the little island fortress of Orёshek just off Shlisselburg, which, among other distinctions, had been the place where Vladimir Ulyanov (Lenin's brother) had been executed as a terrorist. The Russians, Finns and Germans all engaged in naval and amphibious actions on the Lake, using conventional warships and fast craft powered by aircraft engines.

After the Sinyavino Operation ensured that Leningrad would survive, but failed to break the blockade, another siege winter looked inevitable. This time, however, the Russians had plenty of warning and had made extensive preparations. During the summer ships had evacuated nearly 540,000 people and 290,000 tonnes of industrial plant across the inland sea, and taken 310,000 reinforcements back in. Winter in that great, freezing city under attack with any kind of blockade or rationing is still an experience no one would want to endure. But compared with the indescribable horrors of 1941–2, things were a lot less bad.

Firstly, after perhaps a million deaths in 1941–2, there were fewer people in the city. In November 1942 there were just 700,000 civilians and 420,000 armed forces and NKVD, perhaps a third of the number in November 1941.

Secondly, much larger food and fuel reserves had been stockpiled. During the summer the remaining population was ordered to start growing vegetables in every available garden space. Every park and garden became a kitchen garden. Unlike the post-war city, today's city, many of the buildings outside the centre were wooden. With hundreds of thousands dead or evacuated, many were empty. The authorities therefore ordered them to be torn down and chopped up for fuel. In addition, a million cubic metres of coal, peat and other fuels were gathered. On 25 April 1942 the State Defence Committee (GKO) ordered a fuel pipeline to be laid along the bottom of Lake Ladoga. It became operational on 18 June, and carried 295 tonnes of fuel per day to the city. The western Allies would use a similar idea to support their massive and stupendously ambitious invasion of Normandy to open the second front in 1944, the Pipeline Under the Ocean (PLUTO). Then, in September 1942, the Volkhov power station, which was relatively safe from German artillery and, by now, air bombardment, started sending electricity across the lake through an underwater cable (see Figure 3.3).[88]

Thirdly, the winter of 1942–3 was far less severe than the previous one. The freeze did not come until 27 November and some sea traffic continued on the Lake until 7 January 1943. If you want to transport a lot of material, put it in a ship. During the entire blockade, more than 2.25 million tonnes of cargo were transported by water across the Lake – more than along the ice road and the re-established land routes. However, once the land routes were re-established they took most of the military traffic.[89]

Fourthly, once the freeze came, the Russian authorities had been through a steep learning curve with the ice road, and could run it much more efficiently, right from the start. The fifth reason was that, this winter, the ice road would be the city's exclusive lifeline only for a month and a half. After the late freeze, it opened for business on 19 December. . . .[90]

The accursed circle broken . . . Operation 'Spark'

On 14 October 1942 the German OKH ordered Army Group North to adopt a defensive posture for the winter. Operation Nordlicht – the capture of Leningrad – remained a future option, but on 20 November Manstein's Eleventh Army was ordered south to help deal with the Russian counteroffensive at Stalingrad, which had burst on the Germans the previous day. By the start of 1943, things were not as bad in Leningrad as they had been and the threat of a major German offensive had receded, but the city was still isolated apart from slender communications across or under the ice and under German artillery and air attack. Furthermore, German artillery was close enough to bombard the ice road. Stavka determined to end the siege or, at least, to open up a much more efficient land route and push the Germans further away.

On 8 November 1942 the Soviet government marked the twenty-fifth anniversary of the Russian Revolution. A reception was held at the Smolny, now brightly lit thanks to the electricity coming through the underwater cable. In his speech, broadcast from Moscow, Stalin said there would soon be a 'holiday in our streets'. That was a reference to the forthcoming counteroffensive at Stalingrad. No one noticed an aide-de-camp quietly tell Govorov that there was a phone call for him on the high-frequency line from Moscow. It was Stalin, who was characteristically brief.

'Proceed with war game Number Five'[91]

That was the code for the offensive to break the blockade – the fifth attempt. There had been the first Sinyavino offensive in October 1941; the second attempt, which recaptured Tikhvin, in December; the Lyuban' offensive early in 1942; and then the second Sinyavino offensive in the autumn. This, attempt number five, would be the *third* Sinyavino offensive. On 2 December Stavka assigned it a less prosaic codename: *Iskra* – 'Spark'. That was no coincidence. The operation to free Lenin's city bore the name of the revolutionary Bolshevik newspaper.

This time, the attack out of Leningrad was to be as powerful as the one from the east (see Figure 13.7), and the two fronts would attack

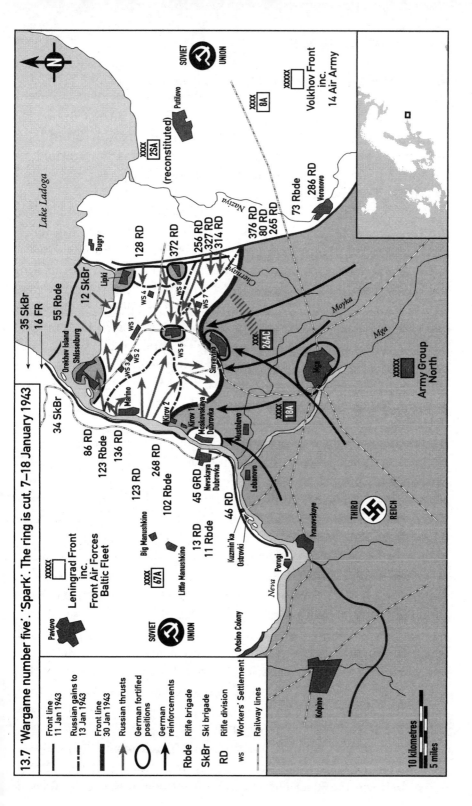

13.7 'Wargame number five'. 'Spark'. The ring is cut, 7–18 January 1943

Legend:

Front line 11 Jan 1943
Russian gains to 13 Jan 1943
Front line 30 Jan 1943
Russian thrusts
German fortified positions
German reinforcements

Rbde Rifle brigade
SkBr Ski brigade
RD   Rifle division
ws   Workers' Settlement
      Railway lines

10 kilometres
5 miles

Lake Ladoga

SOVIET UNION

Volkhov Front inc. 14 Air Army

XXXXX 8A

Putilovo

XXXX 2SA (reconstituted)

286 RD
Voronovo

73 Rbde

Naziya

265 RD
80 RD
376 RD

314 RD
327 RD
256 RD

372 RD

128 RD

Bugry

Chernaya

Lipki

35 SkBr
16 FR

55 Rbde

12 SkBr

Orekhov Island
Shlisselburg

ws 4
ws 6
ws 8
ws 7
ws 1
ws 2
ws 3
ws 5

34 SkBr

Sinyavino

XXX 26AC

Moyka

Mga

Mga

XXXX Army Group North

XXXX 10A

Malmo

Kirov 1
Kirov 2
Moskovskaya Dubrovka

Mustolovo

Lobanovo

86 RD
123 Rbde
136 RD

123 RD

268 RD
102 Rbde

45 GRD
Nevskaya Dubrovka

46 RD

13 RD
11 Rbde

Big Manushkino

Little Manushkino

Kuzmin'ka
Ostrovki

Neva

Porugi

Ivanovskoye

THIRD REICH

Pavlovo

Leningrad Front inc.
Front Air Forces
Baltic Fleet

XXXXX

SOVIET UNION

XXXX 67A

Ovtsino Colony

Kolpino

N

simultaneously. Govorov's Leningrad Front had to cross the Neva, and the offensive was postponed because the ice was not thick enough. The T-34s proved too heavy, in spite of experiments to spread the weight using wooden outriggers, so Govorov used light tanks, of which there were still plenty.[92] The forested, marshy terrain was not suitable for large armoured formations, and the tanks were dispersed and mainly used to support the infantry.

Stalin sent Zhukov back to Leningrad to coordinate the actions of the two fronts. By now it was standard procedure to send a Stavka representative to oversee and advise in multi-front operations. Zhukov had just experienced his only (and little-publicized) defeat, coordinating the Western and Kalinin Fronts' failed attempt to destroy Army Group Centre – or part of it – in the Rzhev-Sychevka operation, Operation Mars (see Chapter 16). He left on 9 January and stayed in Leningrad from 12 to 24 January, sometimes bullying commanders who seemed insufficiently aggressive, and began to develop plans for a more ambitious offensive to drive the Germans right away from Leningrad – an operation named, in accordance with the cosmic fashion of the time, Polar Star.[93]

But the immediate priority was breaking the iron ring. At 09.30 on 12 January 1943, with a temperature of $-25\,°C$, more than 4,500 Russian guns opened fire on the German forces. The critical area, the Mga-Sinyavino salient (see Figure 13.6) was held by three divisions of XXVI Army Corps of the German Eighteenth Army. The Russian guns blazed away for two hours and 20 minutes on the Leningrad side, one hour 45 minutes on the Volkhov Front side. Then the Russians moved in. It was a very different Red Army from that of a year or eighteen months before. The bombardment ended at 11.45 with a massive salvo from the *Katyusha* multiple rocket-launchers which had been so effective at Stalingrad. A green signal rocket appeared above the Neva at 11.42, which the Russian troops mistook for the signal to attack. Before the rain of rockets with their massive 132mm calibre warheads abated, they were on their way across the ice. But by moving sooner than planned, before the Germans had time to poke their heads up again, they were able to get across with very few casualties.[94]

Zhukov positioned himself with Second Shock Army, the northern-most of the Volkhov Front's armies. The main feature of the German salient between the River Neva and the front line of the Soviet Russian 'mainland' to the east was a number of 'workers' housing estates', some of which the Germans had fortified as effective defensive positions. By 14 January Soviet troops had reached the area between estates five and six, and a report came in that they had knocked out a tank of 'unusual design' which the Germans were trying desperately to recover from no man's land. 'We found this interesting,' Zhukov recalled. They formed a special group to go and get the abandoned tank. In the small hours of 17 November Lt Kesarev led the recovery team, heavily supported by artillery and mortar fire, to seize the tank, which was then dragged back to Russian positions. They also found the tank's logbook in the snow nearby. It was a new, heavy tank – the Tiger, Mark 1, which the Germans had been trying out on the Volkhov Front. With the formidable 88mm gun – originally an anti-aircraft gun – and a maximum 110mm of armour, the Tiger 1 was a revolutionary new machine which would greatly concern the Russians at Kursk the next summer. Although writing with the benefit of hindsight, Zhukov was obviously delighted to have been involved in capturing one of the first specimens, which was of huge value to Russian technical intelligence.[95]

After just two days the two Russian fronts were only a few kilometres apart and on 15 January, just a kilometre. That day, Stalin promoted Govorov to Colonel General (of Artillery). On 17 January Govorov ordered his front to close with the Volkhov Front using all necessary means. Shlisselburg, the key town at the point where the Neva met Lake Ladoga, was surrounded. At 09.30 on 18 January forces of the two fronts met just east of Workers' Settlement Number One. Sixty-Seventh Army's 123rd Rifle Division from Leningrad met 372nd Rifle Division from the Second Shock Army, now in its third incarnation. But that was not quite enough to secure the corridor into Leningrad. Less than an hour later the Leningrad Front's 136th Rifle Division captured Workers' Estate Number Five, 4 kilometres to the south (see Figure 13.7), and soon after made contact with troops from the Volkhov Front.[96]

All day, Leningrad waited for news. Although war correspondents had been precluded from accompanying the Russian troops until the very last minute, and the preparations for Iskra had been made in the strictest secrecy, informed rumours were still circulating. People waited all day by the public loudspeakers – private radios had been handed in in June 1941. Then came a snowy, moonlit night, bitterly cold, as always. Finally, at 23.00 on the evening of 18 January, Yuri Levitan,

Moscow's premier announcer, came on the air: 'Troops of the Leningrad and Volkhov Fronts have joined together and at the same time have broken the Siege of Leningrad.'[97]

The same day Zhukov was made Marshal of the Soviet Union.[98]

In reality, there was no guarantee that the Russians could re-establish, let alone hold, reliable land communications with the city. After seventeen months – 506 days – it was still too soon to celebrate. Olga Berggolts warned:

> My dear ones, my far ones, have you heard?
> The accursed circle is broken . . .
> I am not dreaming – it will happen,
> The long-awaited moment is close.
> But the heavy howling of angry guns
> Can still be heard: we're still in battle.
> The blockade is not completely broken.
> Farewell, my loved ones. I am going
> To my ordinary, terrible work
> In the name of Leningrad's new life.[99]

Although breaking the blockade was a clear military success for the Russians, it was a disappointing one. At this stage the land corridor was only about 10 kilometres wide and anyone moving in or out of the city was vulnerable to murderous German artillery fire. Sinyavino, and the Sinyavino heights, which commanded the route into Leningrad, were still in German hands (see Figure 13.6). Zhukov had berated Major-General Simoniak, commanding 136th Division, for not attacking the high ground, but Simoniak had argued that it was just not possible. There was no existing railway line across the ground the Russians had taken, so they had to build a new one, and a new bridge across the Neva near Shlisselburg. Work started on 21 January. This new 33-kilometre line ran only 6 to 8 kilometres from the front line to the south. However, although constructed under German fire, the new bridge and line were ready by 6 February. But the main railway line between Leningrad and Volkhov ran through Mga, which remained in German hands.

The German observers on the Sinyavino heights could see the new railway track, and in the remaining eleven months of 1943 they cut it 1,200 times, heavy artillery shells mangling the rails and sleepers. Sometimes trains were delayed for days. The narrow corridor was known as the 'corridor of death'. An elite unit of railway troops, Special Engine Column 48, was sent in to improve the service, and they did. By the end of 1943 some 4.5 million tonnes of freight had been delivered. Meanwhile the Germans had not given up their hopes of reimposing the blockade, and Zhdanov and Govorov knew it.[100]

Nevertheless, on 7 February 1943, with great ceremony, the first train to run across the land route to the 'mainland' since 27 August 1941, number 719, left the Finland station en route for Volkhovstroi. The routes across the Lake, combined with the new line, could now meet all of Leningrad's needs. Another line, closer to the Lake – and further from the Germans – was completed in May.[101] In spite of the problems, the new land routes still carried far more cargo than the ice and water routes. By September 1943 the Lake route was losing its military importance.[102]

On 22 February 1943 the rations were increased, to a relatively generous 700 grams of bread a day for workers in heavy industry, 600 for other workers, 500 for office workers, 400 for dependents and children. Later in 1943 US lease-lend supplies started to appear: the ubiquitous Second World War staple, Spam (a canned meat product, 'shoulder pork and ham'), canned butter, powdered milk, eggs and sugar. The Leningraders were grateful. But the sudden and dramatic increase they had expected in their quality of life had not occurred, and the German air and artillery bombardment continued. In July 1943, 210 people were killed and 921 wounded; in September, the casualties were 124 and 468. The continuing artillery bombardment became the main concern, and there was reason to think that German spies in the city were passing corrections to the gunners.[103]

The hunt for German agents, spies and saboteurs continued to be a high priority. The Red Army, which had been destroyed and rebuilt in 1941 and was being destroyed and rebuilt again, was engaged in titanic, strategically and operationally ambitious but tactically still rather clumsy efforts on the battlefield against a superbly professional *Wehrmacht*. Meanwhile, the NKVD and the Abwehr were playing a very different war. A war of extraordinarily complex and devious schemes to identify and outsmart each other. A besieged but still sophisticated and intellectual Leningrad, with the possibility, as the Germans saw it, of being turned, was the ideal place. On 27 April 1942 the NKVD 5th Rifle Division in Tikhvin picked up a German spy dressed as a Red Army junior lieutenant called Ivan Golovanov. He was the first of many to be seized in a major nationwide operation codenamed 'Quartz', although the Leningrad area was a focus for the action.[104]

Having captured the German agents, the NKVD 'turned' them into double agents – which was probably not very difficult – and engaged in 'radio games' with the Germans to lure more agents into traps. The Germans used the same phrase – *Funkspiele* – as they tried to do the same thing.[105] On 2 June two more German agents who had been landed by plane were picked up in the Vologda area, well east of Leningrad and Moscow.[106] The most promising catch, however, was a German agent codenamed 'Malakhov' who was caught on 26 April with two former Red Army soldiers whom the Germans had taken prisoner and then turned into agents. Using 'Malakhov's' hand-held radio set, the Russians were able to work out the necessary codes and establish 'business communications' with the Germans. 'Malakhov' requested new batteries for his radio, new documents and so on. On 29 June the Germans replied, 'Don't despair. Help is on its way.' The deputy head of the fifth section of the counter-espionage department of the Leningrad NKVD, State Security Lieutenant Yevgeniy Serebrov, now concocted a wonderful plan to draw German agents in. 'Malakhov' would appear to be able to organize the theft of important documents from one of the Soviet military commands which would be passed to the Germans by one of the NKVD's own most trusted agents. The latter's name was to be added in manuscript on certain copies, but is omitted from the published version of the document. If the Germans then took the bait and sent someone in he – one assumes it would be a he – would then be drawn into a 'honey trap'. He would be introduced to a lady doctor at one of the hospitals for Red Army officers, who, he would be told, was

> a bit of a flirt, a lover of a good time and presents, not
> interested in politics, and unhappy with her current situation,
> and with her life but, thanks to her external appearance,
> having great influence on men and, in this regard, enjoying
> good connections in the Army including senior and higher
> commanders.[107]

Serebrov's plan was countersigned by his boss, the chief of counter-intelligence for the Leningrad region, State Security Major Semën Zanin. One wonders if the strain of the siege was beginning to get to them. But Operation Quartz continued with the arrest of another spy, Nikolay

Yarmolenko, at Tikhvin on 2 August, trying to make contact with another agent, Golovanov, who had been caught in May. He was carrying two sets of batteries for Golovanov's radio, a revolver, a compass and nearly 16,000 roubles in cash – then, a huge amount of money. He had been taken prisoner by the Germans in November 1941, and trained at a German spy school at Vladimir-Volynsk from May 1942. Then, on 25 July, he had been taken to an airfield near Poltava, in the German-occupied area, and flown in a bomber to the Mytishchi area, near Moscow, where he parachuted into a wood. He then travelled by train to Tikhvin.[108]

It seems clear that, while the gigantic conventional war in the east was raging in the air and on the ground, both sides on the eastern front were putting at least as much effort into an underground war of spies, signals and intelligence as their Allies and the Germans were in the west. It must be remembered that at this time there was no second, western, front on land in Europe, so the western Allies and the Germans in the west had relatively more resources to devote to unconventional operations than the Russians and Germans did in the east. The eastern front did not enjoy a single identifiable intelligence coup comparable with Bletchley Park's cracking of the German Enigma and, later, Lorentz codes, giving rise to the vital Ultra intelligence. Nevertheless, the imagination, ingenuity and effort that went into the shadowy secret war in the east was certainly comparable, even if the results were not quite so spectacular. The Soviet NKVD's approach to captured spies was also similar to that of its British equivalent, MI5. When they caught German spies, they made good use of the intelligence derived and turned them into double agents, if they could. If not, they shot them.

They seek him there . . .

Meanwhile, in Leningrad itself, the less horrific conditions of summer 1942 and the energetic if ominous preparations made for the second winter of the siege had not diminished the 'Rebel's' activities. He or she kept up a stream of leaflets and, increasingly, anonymous letters. In spite of the partial evacuation of the city, the siege and the continuing artillery and air bombardment, a relatively normal postal service was maintained – in itself a colossal achievement.

On 30 September 1942 an anonymous letter addressed to Zhdanov was intercepted by the military censor. A check of the handwriting revealed that it was the 'Rebel's'. Then, on 6 November, another seditious letter arrived at Zhdanov's address, in a pink envelope called a *sekretka* – 'little secret', of the type used by the 'Rebel'. The name suggests they may have been marketed as envelopes for love letters. But in wartime Leningrad they were only available in two areas: Smolny and Volodar. The censors started filtering all the civilian correspondence out of those postal districts, and as a result the NKVD checked out 1,023 correspondents and their families, but again without result.[109]

The break in the close blockade of January 1943 did nothing to reduce the 'Rebel's' grievances. One of three 'Rebel' letters seized by the censor on 30 January 1943 complained about the decision to make infractions of employment regulations a criminal offence. The NKVD therefore checked out all the 753 people who had been charged with such offences in the courts in those two districts, and their families – another 2,100. By this time it appeared from the letters that the rebel was someone with 'medium technical qualifications' – a skilled worker or junior technician. Some 5,732 people who fitted this description in the two suspect Smolny and Volodar districts had their handwriting checked. With the help of the Workers' Deputies' Soviets of the Districts, another 13,000 people's handwriting was examined. The police also examined 27,860 people's writing when they applied for military registration. Finally, at sixteen major factories or enterprises a further 64,770 workers' files and property were checked: 112,000 more people in all.[110] But still the 'Rebel' remained elusive.

But the elusive dissenter was getting careless. At last, on 27 September 1943, the 'Rebel' sent three subversive documents to Zhdanov and Popkov, the President of the Leningrad Soviet. In one, he said he was a worker in a 'hot' workshop in a factory and that he was unhappy with the way food coupons were distributed. That focused enquiries on factories in Volodar district, and all efforts were concentrated there. Checks on the property of workers in the Bolshevik steelworks homed in on steelworker number 42, one Sergey Luzhkov, aged about forty. A graphics expert confirmed the similarity between Luzhkov's handwriting and that of the 'Rebel', and he was arrested.

Given the treatment meted out to distinguished generals who were merely suspected of incompetence or disloyalty, Luzhkov's interrogation was probably horrendous. Or maybe, for a change, the NKVD figured he would talk, anyway. The charges were so dire that the NKVD did not have to make anything up, and this time they really needed to know exactly who or what was driving Luzhkov. In custody, he admitted writing and distributing 'counter-revolutionary' leaflets and letters. In spite of pressure, no doubt, to name others, there were none. He had done it all himself. There were no accomplices.

In his statement Luzhkov admitted that he had intended to stir the Leningrad population to open the city gates to the Germans and that he had 'extolled' the virtues of the 'German fascist invaders', who would be 'our liberators'. However, there was no suggestion that he had been directly employed, sponsored or aided by the Germans.[111] Kubatkin declared the case closed in a report to Kuznetsov of 12 December. In a short note written on the report Kuznetsov asked how Luzhkov had come to be working in the steelworks and what the Party Organization knew about him. 'Report to me orally.'[112] In a city under siege, under such tight control, it seems extraordinary that someone did not suspect Luzhkov and whisper his name to the authorities. The story is a fascinating insight into the Soviet Russian security system. It shows that it was far from purely arbitrary, pulling people in on flimsy evidence, even in the darkest hours of the most terrible – or certainly the greatest – siege in history. It had taken the NKVD and police twenty-one months of painstaking police work, psychological profiling, and checks on nearly one in five of the surviving Leningrad population, but they had finally got their man.

Breaking the wider blockade

Even after the land route to the 'mainland' was reopened, the Germans were still too close for comfort. Marshal Timoshenko, so prominent in the first months of the war, was, by 1943, somewhat past his 'sell-by date'. Not only had the pre-war Red Army been destroyed in 1941 and its successor in the savage battles of 1942, particularly in the south, but new commanders like Zhukov and Rokossovskiy were showing far more mettle than the old Bolsheviks. Timoshenko was nevertheless still commander of the North-West Front. Now that the Leningrad and Volkhov Fronts had linked up, he would have to transcribe a wider arc round to their south. In accordance with the then prevailing Russian fad for astronomical codenames, after the disastrous Mars, and the triumphant Uranus and Little Saturn, this one was called Polar Star.[113]

Like Uranus and Little Saturn at Stalingrad, Polar Star was envisioned as a 'double encirclement'. The Leningrad and Volkhov Fronts would attack on 8 February, creating a shallow encirclement of the German forces in the Mga-Sinyavino region, still irritatingly close to Leningrad's umbilical cords, and also draw Eighteenth Army's reserves northwards. Then, a week later, on 15 February, the North-West Front would attack from the east to cut off and destroy the German Eighteenth Army. The plan is shown in Figure 13.8. The problem was that the third Sinyavino operation, Iskra, while relatively small in scale, had still been extremely costly for the Russians, with nearly 34,000 killed or captured out of 300,000 engaged. Govorov's Leningrad Front and Meretskov's Volkhov were just too exhausted and depleted to achieve Zhukov's ambitious aims. However, the fact that Stavka assigned Zhukov and Timoshenko to participate suggests that it set great store by the operation.

But the operation was a failure. Fifty-Fifth Army attacked out of Leningrad on 10 February and, in one of the more cosmopolitan episodes of the war, encountered the 250th Spanish 'Blue' division, comprising volunteers from Franco's Spain, which was actually neutral in the war. The Spanish division, which had no tanks, stopped the Russians along the Izhora river, and was able to hold with help from German reinforcements. Although the shallow encirclement failed, it diverted the Germans sufficiently for Zhukov to launch the wider one on 15 February, but that also failed. On 27 February Stalin halted the attacks. The deteriorating situation around Kursk required Stavka's attention elsewhere.[114]

19. Armies march on their stomachs. A field kitchen in winter.

20. 'Destroy the German monster': Leningrad poster, 1941–2.

21. Leningrad
fire-fighter.

22. Victims of
an air-raid on
Leningrad.

23. Suspected
'collaborators'
in the hands of
the NKVD.

24. Woman sniper.

25. Po-2 night bomber of the 46th Guards 'night witches' regiment.

26. Women pilots, Novorossiysk, 1943.

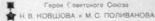

27. Heroines of the Soviet Union
N. V. Kovshova and M. S. Polivanova.

28. Women snipers, 1945.

29. Khrushchev and
Brezhnev, 1942.

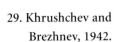

30. Russian map of northern Stalingrad.

31. Lt Gen. Vasiliy Chuikov, commanding Sixty Second Army, drawn by Finogenov.

32. Chuikov's command bunker, dug into the Volga bank behind the Red October factory.

33. Chuikov and his staff holding central Stalingrad.

34. Still a secret weapon: a *Katyusha* multiple rocket launcher fires in the distance.

35. Rokossovskiy, during the Moscow winter offensive the year before.

36. Surrender at Stalingrad.

Допрос Паулюса в Бекетовке.
Штаб 64 армии. Шумилов, Абрамов, сердюк, Чуянов.

37. Paulus's interrogation.
38. Paulus (left) and his Chief of Staff, Lt Gen. Schmidt (right)
   under interrogation after Stalingrad.

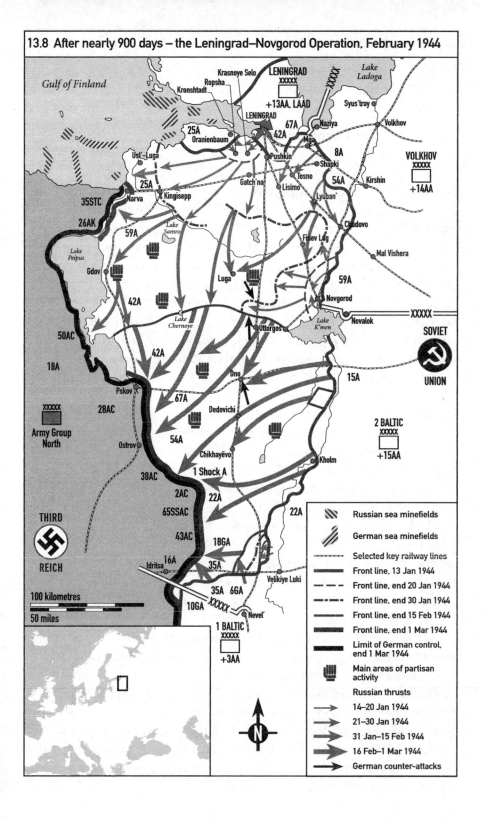

13.8 After nearly 900 days – the Leningrad–Novgorod Operation, February 1944

Gulf of Finland

Lake Ladoga

LENINGRAD
XXXXX
+13AA, LAAD

Krasnoye Selo
Ropsha
Kronshtadt
Syus'troy
Volkhov

LENINGRAD
25A
Oranienbaum
67A
42A
Naziya

Pushkin
Mga
8A

Ust'-Luga
Gatch'na
Shapki
VOLKHOV
XXXXX

25A
Lisimo
Tosno
54A
Kirshin
+14AA

Narva
Kingisepp
Lyuban'

35STC
Chudovo

26AK
59A
Lake Samro
Finev Lug
Mal Vishera

Lake Peipus
Gdov
Luga
59A

42A
Novgorod

Lake Chernoye
Uttorgos
Lake K'men
Novalok
SOVIET

50AC
42A
15A
UNION

18A
Uno

Pskov
67A
Dedovichi
2 BALTIC
XXXXX

Army Group North
XXXXX
54A
+15AA

Ostrov
Chikhayëvo
Kholm

38AC
1 Shock A

2AC
22A

THIRD
65SSAC
22A

43AC

REICH
18GA
16A
35A

100 kilometres
Idritsa
Velikiye Luki

50 miles
35A 6GA
10GA
XXXXX
Nevel'

1 BALTIC
XXXXX
+3AA

Russian sea minefields	
German sea minefields	
Selected key railway lines	
Front line, 13 Jan 1944	
Front line, end 20 Jan 1944	
Front line, end 30 Jan 1944	
Front line, end 15 Feb 1944	
Front line, end 1 Mar 1944	
Limit of German control, end 1 Mar 1944	
Main areas of partisan activity	
Russian thrusts	
14–20 Jan 1944	
21–30 Jan 1944	
31 Jan–15 Feb 1944	
16 Feb–1 Mar 1944	
German counter-attacks	

N

403

The second circle

The siege of Leningrad mirrored the course of the war on the entire eastern front. Although the cursed circle, the first circle, was broken in January 1943, it was not until after the Russians seized the strategic initiative at Kursk in July 1943 that they were really in a position to advance on a broad front, and only that would finally free Leningrad. The main German offensive in 1942 had been towards Stalingrad and the Caucasus, and that was therefore the principal theatre of war. While the Germans held the strategic initiative, and Leningrad was, for them, a secondary priority (which it was), the Russians had to treat it as a second priority as well. But at the end of 1943 Stavka was in a position to contemplate driving the Germans from all Soviet territory and Leningrad, as *Russian* territory, took priority.

The German Army Group North was slightly slow on the uptake. Colonel-General Georg Kuechler, who had commanded the army group through the entire siege, since Leeb was relieved of command in January 1942, surmised that any Russian offensives in 1944 would be no greater in scale than earlier ones, and Lindemann, still commanding Eighteenth Army, confirmed that he could hold any imminent Soviet attack. They believed that any Soviet attacks would be 'staggered' – because they had been before, one of the reasons why Polar Star failed – and Hitler ordered them to hold on at all costs. As an insurance policy, however, Kuechler secretly made plans to withdraw and set up new supply bases in Estonia for this purpose. As the map in Figure 13.8 shows, the Germans were still, at the closest point, 10 kilometres from Leningrad on 14 January 1944. From a political viewpoint, having enemy ground forces 10 kilometres from your second city was becoming slightly unacceptable for a nation that was, by now, winning the war. Also, on 12 October 1943, Stavka approved the Front commanders' recommendations that the attack should take place in January 1944, not least because they feared the Germans might evacuate the area and thus escape with their main forces intact. But Kuechler's Northern Army Group was dug in, holding strongly fortified positions, and would still put up serious resistance.

Govorov, who had suffered Zhukov's anger at Moscow, had obviously done well to survive as Leningrad Front commander since June 1942. He had started planning his offensive, Operation Neva, on 6 October 1943. The Russian operations are shown in Figure 13. 8. One of the most ambitious moves was the transfer of the Second Shock Army, now living yet another life, to the Oranienbaum bridgehead, the isolated pocket west of Leningrad which had long been sustained over the ice or water of the Gulf of Finland. Every night from 5 November barges set out from the quay at the Kanat factory and secretly ferried 30,000 troops, 47 tanks, 400 guns 1,400 trucks, 3,000 horses and 10,000 tonnes of ammmunition across the Gulf of Finland and into the pocket. When the Gulf froze, another 22,000 troops, 140 tanks and 380 guns were sent across the ice.

This time, the Russians would not fail. By the time the operation started, on 14 January, the Leningrad and Volkhov fronts between them had 21,600 guns 1,500 *Katyusha* multiple rocket-launchers, 1,475 tanks and self-propelled guns and 1,500 planes. That was a greater concentration of fighting power than the Russians had deployed for the counteroffensive at Stalingrad.[115]

The Leningrad–Novgorod Strategic Offensive Operation involved three Fronts in all: Leningrad, Volkhov and Second Baltic, plus, of course, the mighty Baltic fleet. The total Russian strength was 822,000, not much more than Kuechler's 741,000. But with 10,070 Russian guns, 385 tanks and 370 planes, the Germans were massively outgunned by between two and four to one.

The attack out of the Oranienbaum bridgehead started on 14 January, the 867th day of the siege. The next morning, at 09.30, a 100-minute artillery barrage heralded the attack from Pulkovo. Unlike the guns and rocket-launchers firing in support out of the Oranienbaum bridgehead, these could easily be heard by the people of Leningrad. 'Those are ours . . .'

By 27 January the Soviet forces had moved through Pushkin, also known as Tsarskoye Selo – the Tsar's village, just south of the city. It is now, once again, a fairytale collection of palaces reflecting Russia's great imperial past and literary genius. The Catherine Palace, now fully restored, iridescent blue with white columns and gold onion-domes, appeared largely undamaged from the outside. But it was an illusion. Inside, it was completely gutted. Among the priceless treasures that had vanished was the exquisite 'amber room'. The room contained amber

panels given, ironically, by Frederick I of Prussia, which Russian crafts-
men had then surrounded with a stunning mosaic of thousands of
pieces of translucent amber laid on a background of silver foil to reflect
light back through them. As soon as they had captured the area the
Germans had removed all the amber panels and taken them to Königsberg (Kaliningrad) where they had arrived by 5 December, and were
reassembled in the Royal Palace.[116] Königsberg was stormed by the
Russians between 9 and 11 April 1945, and the Royal Palace destroyed
by fire. The amber room appears to have been destroyed with it.
However, detailed photographs of the room – Russian and German –
survived and in 1999 a German firm, Ruhrgas AG, put up 3.5 million
dollars to re-create the room exactly as it had been, using vast quantities
of the semi-precious amber which is found in the Baltic region. On 31
May 2003 the re-creation was opened to the public as part of the 300th
anniversary of St Petersburg celebrations. It was a symbolic act of
closure.

In January 1944 that closure was still nearly sixty years away. The
last German shells fell on the city on 23 January. Then, there was
relative silence, suggesting the Germans had been pushed right away. At
20.00 on 27 January the black winter sky over Leningrad lit up with red,
white, blue and gold rockets and 324 guns fired a salute. After 880 days
the longest and worst siege in modern history – possibly all history –
finally came to an end. But people were too exhausted to celebrate. Vera
Inber, a professional writer who survived the siege, wrote in her diary
that she had 'no words for it. I simply say: Leningrad is free.'[117] Olga
Berggolts visited Pushkin on 25 January, and dared to look ahead,
foreseeing what it is like now. 'Again from the black dust, from the
place / Of death and ashes, will arise the garden as before.'[118]

Although the Leningrad–Novgorod operation lasted until 1 March,
the siege of Leningrad was now really over. In two weeks the Russians
had driven the Germans 100 kilometres south and south-west from
Leningrad and 80 kilometres west of Novgorod. In all, the Soviet forces
advanced between 220 and 280 kilometres, averaging 5 to 6 kilometres
per day. But Soviet casualties up to 1 March were heavy: nearly 77,000
dead or prisoners out of 822,000 engaged, but they had also mauled the
Germans savagely. Three German divisions were destroyed and seventeen severely damaged. During the operation Hitler replaced Kuechler
with one of his favourite commanders, Field Marshal Model, but even
Model was unable to restore the position, although he succeeded in

pulling most of the Eighteenth Army back into Estonia. The next phase lasted until 10 August, as the Russians swung their attention northwards to drive the Finns out of the Leningrad region, as far as the 1939 Finnish–Soviet border. On 10 August the whole Leningrad region was back in Soviet hands, and, as a result of this military-strategic victory, the political conditions were in place for Finland's withdrawal from the war.[119]

Epitome of the war

The siege of Leningrad is remembered, rightly, as a stupendous, if horrific, triumph of human endurance, resilience and ingenuity. There are good reasons for treating it as a self-contained story. However, the operations around Leningrad were always dependent on, and themselves influenced by, those elsewhere. The movement of Manstein's forces (including gigantic siege guns) north from the Crimea, once Sevastopol had fallen in early July 1942, and then south again to deal with a looming German catastrophe at Stalingrad, is but one example. Even after the close blockade was broken, in January 1943, it took another year for the city to be fully liberated by Russian successes on a much wider front.

The battles around Leningrad also exhibited many important aspects of warfare, some also encountered elsewhere, some unique. The universal importance of logistics was underlined, in the Leningrad case, by the effort and ingenuity expended in the creation and maintenance of ice roads, not only across Lake Ladoga but also from the city and Kronshtadt into the Oranienbaum bridgehead, and the construction of 'corduroy roads' through the marshy wilderness north and east of Tikhvin, by the Russians, and south of there, by the Germans. The way scientific expertise was used to create new foodstuffs from wallpaper paste, to pump fuel and electricity under Lake Ladoga to plot the thickening of the ice, mirror that of the western Allies in planning D-Day. The traditional Russian emphasis on, and superiority in, artillery was utterly crucial in such a siege situation. Intelligence – human intelligence, through the spy networks and clandestine struggle waged by both sides, and signals intelligence – was also critical, and were a constant preoccupation of the German and Soviet intelligence services. Whilst there were several attempts to break the inner and then the outer blockade physically, both sides waged an ingenious and continuous information and psychological warfare campaign throughout the whole siege.

Moving more widely, the survival and resilience of Leningrad mirrored that of the whole nation. Without the tight political and security control exercised through and by the NKVD, neither Leningrad nor the whole country might have survived. Leningrad's battle, like that of Moscow, of the Soviet Union, of the United Kingdom and the United States, and of Germany, was not just a military one. The creative interaction of all agencies, from soldiers to scientists, from artists and composers to policemen, was essential. The extraordinarily assiduous pursuit of the 'Rebel' is a detective story that would match up to any policeman's professional criteria. That person was dangerous to physical security, morale and political stability. He had to be caught. But, even in the midst of a horrendous siege, and the biggest and worst war in history, only proper police work would catch him. And what better example of the interaction of moral, physical and conceptual components of a whole nation's fighting power could there be than the coordination of an artillery counter-bombardment with the broadcast across the world of the first performance in Leningrad of its eponymous Seventh Symphony? Leningrad's story is a microcosm of Soviet Russia's. The words of Olga Berggolts, the Leningrad poetess, are etched on the granite wall of St Petersburg's Piskarevskiy Cemetery, where hundreds of thousands of victims of the siege are buried:

> Here lie the people of Leningrad . . .
> We cannot number the noble
> Ones who lie beneath the eternal granite,
> But of those honoured by this stone,
> *Let no one forget, let nothing be forgotten.*[120]

She was writing about the million or more who died in the siege of Leningrad. But the last line – *Nikto ne zabyt. Nichto ne zabyto* – also provides the words on every Russian war memorial. To the twenty-seven million.

14

THE 'GRAND ALLIANCE'

'An alliance of sorts'[1]

The diplomatic links between the United Kingdom and the Soviet Union hurriedly improvised after 22 June 1941 can best be described as 'an alliance – of sorts'. On Foreign Office advice, Churchill carefully avoided the word 'ally' in his speech that evening.[2] In the week before Barbarossa, the Foreign Secretary, Anthony Eden, had stressed that rather than becoming 'allies of the Soviet Union' – as the British government now knew that the Soviet–German war was imminent – the UK and Russia would 'have a common enemy and a common interest – i.e. to do Germany all the harm we can'.[3] They were not 'allies' but 'co-belligerents'. Even after the German attack, however, prejudice against the Russians continued unabated among senior British officers. 'I avoid the expression "Allies",' wrote Lt Gen. Sir Henry Pownall, the Vice-Chief of the Imperial General Staff, 'for the Russians are a dirty lot of murdering thieves themselves and double-crossers of the deepest dye. It is good to see the two biggest cut-throats in Europe, Hitler and Stalin, going for each other.'[4]

The British attitude was shaped by the prevailing view that Soviet Russia would soon collapse and that the best that could be done was to prolong Russian resistance as far as possible. Churchill offered 'whatever help we can', but technical and material aid was limited to 'whatever is in our power'. Unlike the mighty economic powerhouse of the United States, which was not yet a combatant in the war, the British were already stretched to the limit. For the moment, the only help they could offer was moral support and encouragement. The British had decided to send a 'military mission' – in fact, a joint service mission, comprising members of all three armed services – to Moscow on 13 June. It received its instructions on 23 and 24 June, before heading for Arkhangel'sk (Archangel) on the White Sea in Catalina flying boats, to make a nineteen-hour flight round the top of German-occupied Norway.

The head of mission was an eccentric intelligence officer, Lt Gen. Noel Mason Macfarlane, which probably did nothing to assuage Russian suspicions that the members of the British mission were all spies. Admiral Nikolay Kuznetsov, the Navy Minister, met them at Arkhangel'sk, and by 26 June they were in Moscow. The Russians remained anxious that the British might now make a separate peace with the Germans, although they reckoned, quite rightly, that the constant British quest for intelligence was to evaluate the length of the breathing space available before Germany smashed Russia and turned back against Britain. The Russians quickly managed to strike the right balance between reassuring the British that they could hold out, and alerting them to the dire predicament in which they found themselves. Macfarlane and his team had no access to first-hand information about the situation at the front, but were soon convinced by the confidence they found in the Kremlin.

At the end of June the British line remained the same. But trying to prolong Soviet resistance as far as possible did not mean sending material aid which, they thought, would probably just fall straight into German hands. Instead, the British sought to collate intelligence and, above all, to ensure that the Germans did not seize the Caucasus oilfields. If that looked likely, and the Russians did not destroy them, then the British would.[5]

On 12 July 1941 Molotov and British Ambassador Cripps signed the agreement – not a treaty – between the British and Soviet governments on mutual action in the war against Germany.[6] It was extremely vague, committing both governments to give each other mutual assistance and support 'of any kind'. Given the continuing concern, particularly among the Russians, that the other party might conclude a separate peace, both governments undertook not to conduct any negotiations or conclude any peace treaty without the agreement of the other. Four days later Maisky asked Eden for a cross-Channel operation by British forces, saying that the Soviet government expected 'an important land invasion' in the light of the shift of German divisions east. Although Lord Beaverbrook, the *Daily Mail* newspaper tycoon, also supported the idea, it was completely out of the question, not only then, but throughout 1942.[7] On 19 July Stalin himself broke his month-long diplomatic silence and also begged for help, with an uncharacteristic apology for past actions. If the Soviet Union had not occupied part of the former state of Poland and the Baltic States, 'the [initial] position of the German forces would have been many times more favourable', Stalin explained. That is debatable (see Chapter 4). However, 'the military situation of the Soviet Union, as well as of Great Britain, would be considerably improved if there could be established a front against Hitler in the West – Northern France – and in the North – the Arctic'.[8] But there was absolutely no way.

Meanwhile a Soviet military mission headed by General Filipp Golikov – also an intelligence officer and the former head of the Red Army's Intelligence Directorate, the GRU – arrived in London on 8 July. Stalin had told Golikov to concentrate on securing the sea route from the British Isles and North America to Russia by securing the occupation of Spitsbergen, part of the Svalbard archipelago, and Bear Island (see Figure 14.1). The British military was deeply prejudiced against the Russians. It was only twenty-three years, after all, since the Bolsheviks had murdered the Tsar and his family – the Tsar being a close relative of the British Royal Family, which had a particular connection with the Royal Navy. Admiral of the Fleet Sir Dudley Pound, the Chief of the Naval Staff, gave the impression that he was 'horrified' to be in the Russians' company, and that he had far more important things to do than embark on 'harebrained schemes with Bolsheviks'.[9] The next day Pound easily persuaded the other Chiefs-of-Staff to join him in rejecting the Soviet ideas for large-scale operations which 'amounted to a considerable commitment' and would pose great administrative problems.

However, the Americans were in a quite different position. From a geographical point of view, they had more secure – though longer – communications with the western Soviet Union through Alaska and across Siberia. The main routes for Allied aid into Russia during the war are shown in Figure 14.2. The Russians had worked out that the British, who were co-belligerents in the war, would need to coordinate transport and military matters, but that the Americans could supply the goods. Harry L. Hopkins, Roosevelt's adviser, who played a major role in facilitating US aid to Russia throughout the war, told the Soviet Ambassador in Washington that the British should understand that the Russians were entitled to a share of American aid. The US General Staff also had a more optimistic view of the Russian situation than the British did. Churchill realized, as he had all along, that the longer the Russians held on the better, particularly if they could hold out until winter. He

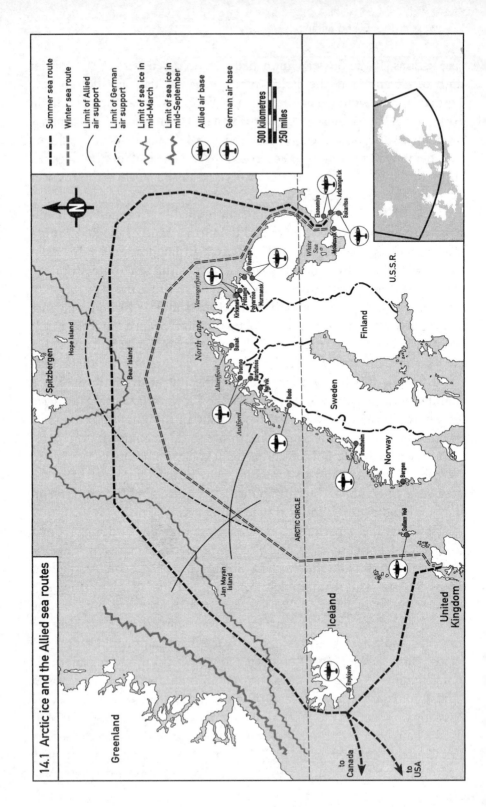

14.1 Arctic ice and the Allied sea routes

Legend:
- Summer sea route
- Winter sea route
- Limit of Allied air support
- Limit of German air support
- Limit of sea ice in mid-March
- Limit of sea ice in mid-September
- Allied air base
- German air base

500 kilometres
250 miles

Greenland

Spitzbergen

Hope Island

Bear Island

Jan Mayen Island

North Cape

Varangerfjord

Altenfjord

Andfjord

Iceland

Reykjavik

United Kingdom

to Canada

to USA

ARCTIC CIRCLE

Norway

Bergen

Trondheim

Stadlandet

Bodo

Narvik

Bardufoss

Tromso

Banak

Kirkenes

Petsamo

Polyarnoe

Murmansk

Vaenga

Molotovsk

Archangel'sk

Ekonomiya

Bakaritsa

White Sea

Sweden

Finland

U.S.S.R.

N

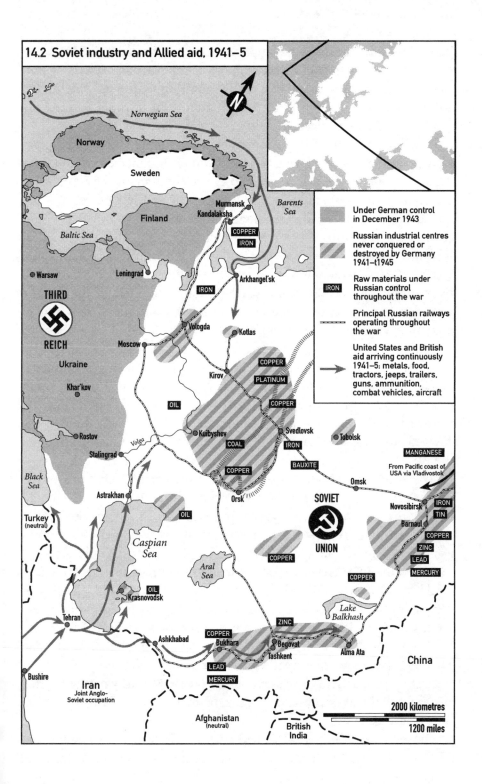

14.2 Soviet industry and Allied aid, 1941–5

Norwegian Sea

Norway

Sweden

Finland

Baltic Sea

Barents Sea

Murmansk
Kandalaksha

COPPER
IRON

Warsaw

Leningrad

Arkhangel'sk

THIRD

IRON

REICH

Vologda

Kotlas

Moscow

Ukraine

Kirov

COPPER
PLATINUM

Khar'kov

OIL

COPPER

Rostov

Kuibyshev

Svedlovsk

Tobolsk

Volga

COAL

IRON

MANGANESE

Stalingrad

Astrakhan

Orsk

COPPER

BAUXITE

Omsk

From Pacific coast of
USA via Vladivostok

Black
Sea

Turkey
(neutral)

OIL

Caspian
Sea

Aral
Sea

COPPER

SOVIET

UNION

Novosibirsk

IRON
TIN

Barnaul

COPPER

ZINC

LEAD

MERCURY

COPPER

OIL
Krasnovodsk

ZINC

Lake
Balkhash

Tehran

Ashkhabad

COPPER
Bukhara

Begovat

Tashkent

Alma Ata

China

Bushire

LEAD

MERCURY

Iran
Joint Anglo-
Soviet occupation

Afghanistan
(neutral)

British
India

Under German control in December 1943

Russian industrial centres never conquered or destroyed by Germany 1941–t1945

IRON **Raw materials under Russian control throughout the war**

Principal Russian railways operating throughout the war

United States and British aid arriving continuously 1941–5: metals, food, tractors, jeeps, trailers, guns, ammunition, combat vehicles, aircraft

2000 kilometres

1200 miles

therefore chose the least bad option: massive material aid, but only limited military action in direct support of the Russians, like it or not. Pound was ordered to send a small naval squadron to the Arctic. Golikov was then sent on to Washington, which could release the supplies the Russians needed.

The Russian objective was commendably simple and showed great strategic vision. By occupying stepping stones on Spitsbergen and Bear Island the 'allies' – of a sort – would create the framework for massive and continuous cooperation with both the UK and, via Greenland, the United States and Canada (see Figures 14.1 and 14.2). But that vision was lost on the British. Churchill kept telling Stalin that the practical difficulties were too great and that unless such operations were allocated massive forces, which were not available, they would inevitably fail disastrously. In fact Churchill was far more interested in the Middle East, and welcomed the joint occupation of Iran, which the Iranian government accepted at the end of August. This fitted in very well with his Middle Eastern strategy. Churchill was using all his rhetorical powers to soften the blows to Stalin, but Eden despaired. All this 'sentimental and florid' talk would have 'the worst effect on Stalin who will think guff no substitute for guns'. Given that Stalin did not speak English, most of it would be lost in translation, anyway. Eden also thought the slowness and lack of imagination of Chiefs-of-Staff 'enough to frighten one'.[10]

David Lloyd George, the former UK Minister of Munitions in the First World War, and then Prime Minister from 1916 to 1922, could also see the folly of such a myopic approach. On 22 August the NKVD man in London reported a conversation between Lloyd George and agent 'Kay', in which Lloyd George said that Britain could now do nothing without Soviet help. Like Russia in the previous war, the USSR would 'save the United Kingdom'. But, Lloyd George said, the British were doing nothing to establish a western front on the ground on the Continent. Even if attempts to establish a second front were unsuccessful, they would at least decrease pressure on the Red Army. 'The outcome of the entire war', the great statesman said, 'now depends on the USSR.' Lloyd George was telling the NKVD's man what he wanted to hear, but he was probably right and many senior British political figures agreed.[11]

By the end of July 1941 it had become clear to the Russians that there was, for the moment, no prospect of any sort of 'second front' in

France, which would become a major point of dispute in 1942–3, or even of a permanent British presence in the Arctic Ocean. Sending material assistance on board the Arctic convoys was the best the British could do. At the beginning of August the Americans set up independent arrangements to discuss the Russians' requirements and this also had influence on the British. In August 1941 the first British convoy carrying aircraft arrived in Arkhangel'sk.[12]

Cripps, who was very close to what the Russians thought, railed at the government for 'underestimating the enormous and absolutely vital importance of this front [the eastern front] to [Britain] as our one insurance against the future'.[13] He was absolutely right. The British had expected the Russians to collapse at any moment, and waited to see where the next German success would be so that they could make arrangements to counter the next one. This piecemeal approach meant postponing aid until it was too late to be of the decisive value that it might have been. At the end of August, Stalin said exactly the same thing to Maisky, his Ambassador in London:

> Your discussion with Eden [26 August 1941] on British
> strategy reflects the mood of the Soviet people [!] . . . in
> essence, the British Government, by its passive, waiting policy
> is helping the Nazis. The Nazis want to knock their enemies
> off one at a time – today the Russians, tomorrow the British.
> The situation, where Britain applauds us, and the Germans
> swear at us using the same words, doesn't change matters in
> the least. Do the British understand this? I think they
> understand. What do they want out of this? They want us to
> be weakened. If this suggestion is right, then we must be very
> severe in our relations with the British.[14]

By 'the Soviet people', Stalin meant 'me'. But he was absolutely right, and, now realizing that Russia's fate was increasingly *their* fate, the British were already trying to supply what Eden had described as 'guns', not 'guff'.

Pay attention, Commander . . .

However, old habits died hard and the British naval mission which would now bear the brunt of cooperation with the Russians was already in serious trouble. On 6 September 1941 Soviet naval counter-intelligence reported that members of the British naval mission were spying. Commander Derek Wyburd, deputy head of the naval mission, had arrived in Arkhangel'sk on 24 June, presumably in a Catalina with the other members of the 'military [tri-service] mission'. He then went to Sevastopol between 11 and 21 August, where he made contact with two other British naval officers, a Captain John Fox and Commander George Ambrose. Wyburd and Ambrose were friends and had both studied Russian, first in London, then at Tallinn, the capital of the then independent Estonia. Ambrose's Russian was not very good, however. Fox was a submariner, and asked 'naive' questions about shipbuilding techniques, the Sevastopol fortifications and Soviet navy conditions of service. Wyburd attracted attention by complaining about being 'imprisoned' in Sevastopol, by saying that the people were not told what was going on at the battlefronts and by asking why they had had their radios taken away for the duration. There was also a Lt Cdr John Powell, who was an expert on minesweeping. The Russians concluded that Fox, Ambrose and Powell had all come to Russia to spy on them, and should therefore be kept under careful surveillance. Wyburd, who had a diplomatic visa, was eventually declared *persona non grata*, and deported back to Britain on 6 December.[15]

Before that, however, Wyburd headed back to Arkhangel'sk where, in the last days of September, he left one of the jetties in a Soviet motor launch heading for the island of Yagodnik, and was observed making sketches of industrial sites on both banks of the Northern Dvina river. He asked the Russian minder looking after him how deep the anchorage was at the island, and whether it was deep enough for big ships, to which the Russian replied, 'Deep enough for our launch.' The Russian was in fact naval security's agent 'Shilov'. After that diplomatic reply, Shilov reported, Wyburd 'stopped asking such questions'.[16]

Meanwhile, Fox and Ambrose remained in Sevastopol. They took great interest in the Soviet minesweeper *Bodry*, and thought its 37mm rapid-firing cannon outstanding. Fox was also very impressed by the Soviet M-class submarine. He asked why the Russians had not bombarded the Bulgarian ports of Burgas and Varna. The Russians replied, 'The Bulgarians aren't fighting us.' Fox then said the Russians were stupid for not doing so. However, the Russians were getting good value for money, and took down his opinions on everything, including his assessment of what the British would do if Germany attacked Turkey. Because that was politico-strategic intelligence, the naval security report went straight to the Navy Minister, Admiral Kuznetsov.[17]

Clearly, it was part of the British mission's job to report on the military situation on the eastern front – hence Wyburd's exasperation about the unavailability of news – and on where convoys coming into the White Sea might be able to moor their ships. But it is hard to disagree with the Russian assessment of these would-be James Bonds as rather naive buffoons. They were certainly not diplomats. Most importantly, that opinion was not limited to the low-level counter-intelligence people whose job it was to report on everything they did and said. The Soviet Navy Minister knew about it, too.

The very uneasy 'alliance of sorts' with the British gave the Russians intelligence opportunities as well. On 21 November 1941 Senior Political Adviser Smyslov – equivalent to a navy lieutenant – of the Counter-Intelligence Section of the White Sea Flotilla reported that on 13 November he had had a fleeting opportunity – fifteen to twenty minutes – to go through the British secret report on the Kola peninsula and Arkhangel'sk on board the minesweeper *Bramble*. How a Russian officer was allowed to be alone with such a document for so long is puzzling. It may be that, as an act of good faith, the British captain thought there was no harm in letting the Russians know about their own country, and that the document was probably over-classified anyway. Smyslov must have had very good English and written very fast, or both, or else must have had more time than he said. Most important were the maps which bore instructions to officers visiting Russia to report back and provide corrections and amplification.[18]

More significant, however, were events between 8 and 15 November. The loading and unloading areas in the Arkhangel'sk commercial port were known locally as 'the Economy'. Three British warships – *Bramble*, *Sigal* [sic] and *Lida* were moored here. Commander Wyburd, shortly to be deported, also turned up. The Deputy Political Director of the Soviet navy, Vinogradov, was also there. On 11 and 12 November, Vinogradov said, the British sailors on board the ships threw bread – whole loaves in some cases – and cigarettes from their vessels to a number of 'prisoners' or 'convicts' (probably forced labourers), and took photographs. The 'prisoners' included a number of English-speaking Estonians who had been working in the 'Economy' area, whom the British sailors had managed to befriend. The Russian authorities had tried to stop such fraternization, but were unable to do so. Lt Cdr Benson said that the bread had been stale, and that no photographs had been taken, but later added that they had taken some photographs of Soviet warships as they passed, though none of the 'Economy' area. Smyslov asked if he could have the film, but Benson told him it included a number of pictures taken back in England and in Iceland, and therefore that he could not. Smyslov reported to the Military Commissar and the Deputy Chief-of-Staff of the White Sea Flotilla, warning that the same could happen again when the British moved to the nearby naval base of Molotovsk – modern Severodvinsk, now the main base of the Northern Fleet, named after the Northern Dvina at whose mouth it lies.[19]

By now the Russians were convinced that the British naval missions operating in the Arkhangel'sk and Murmansk areas included serious spies. Even more worrying, according to Deputy Commissar for Internal Affairs Kruglov, 'the lack of day-to-day contact between the counter-intelligence departments of the Arkhangel'sk and Murmansk regions prevents us using all our agents and operational capabilities to deal with British spies operating in our northern region.'[20] The Arkhangel'sk Military District, Northern Fleet and White Sea Flotilla were all told to keep their military secrets secret when dealing with the British.

Most significantly, any problems or delays with the unloading or transport of loads out of the White Sea ports were to be corrected *immediately*. Whatever the Russians thought of some pompous British naval officers, they clearly knew that other British sailors were risking, and sometimes meeting, a horrible, icy death bringing vital supplies round through the Arctic Ocean, dodging German submarines and aircraft and the cruellest weather conditions on the planet. The Russians did not want the British thinking they were inefficient, ungrateful, or that they were to blame for holding up the onward progress of those precious supplies down the single railway line due south to Moscow. Those were the kind of reports they were most worried about. Kruglov, one of Beria's deputies, saw the bigger political picture very clearly.[21]

With Soviet counter-intelligence stretched to the limit dealing with the British – and that was the implication of Kruglov's report – who needed the Germans? However, the top management of the NKVD saw the way ahead, as Stalin, Churchill, Cripps and Eden all had. The longer the war went on, the more the British and Americans could help. Whatever the low-level problems, when Allied aid arrived, it had to be seen to be well used. Through force of circumstance, and contact at all levels, the 'alliance of sorts' was slowly evolving into an alliance of substance.

Direct military involvement on land in the west was out of the question, for the moment, and the eastern front was the principal land theatre of war. As Churchill said in December 1941, just after the Moscow counteroffensive, which had finally quelled earlier British fears that Russia was about to collapse:

> Hitler's failure and losses in Russia are the prime fact in the war at this time . . . Neither Great Britain nor the United States have any part to play in this event, except to make sure that we send, without fail and punctually, the supplies we have promised. In this way alone shall we hold our influence upon Stalin and be able to weave the mighty Russian effort into the general texture of the war.[22]

'Guns, not guff'. The First (Moscow) Protocol, October 1941

At the end of June the Russians had presented the British with a request for 3,000 fighters, 3,000 bombers, 20,000 light anti-aircraft guns, bombs, flamethrowers, submarine detection equipment, magnetic mines, machine tools, raw materials, wheat, sugar, meat, 3 million pairs of boots and 10 million metres of woollen cloth. The British, who still feared an invasion as soon as Russia collapsed, said no.[23] At the beginning of July 1941 Roosevelt proposed a three-nation committee to sort out the division of US resources between the Russians and the British. Anastas Mikoyan was the member of the GKO who oversaw these negotiations and their results. He was a key player in the first tripartite lease-lend conference.

The British hoped that the Americans would eventually be able to supply most of Russia's needs, but US production was still gearing up – the United States was not yet a combatant in the war. Just after Barbarossa, an opinion poll showed that 54 per cent of those questioned opposed sending munitions to Russia. Cordell Hull, the Secretary of State, advised Roosevelt to give Russia 'all aid to the hilt' and so did Joseph Davies, former US Ambassador to Moscow. They told the Russian Ambassador Konstantin Umanskiy that they would be generous and within four days he responded with a request for more than 1.8 billion dollars' worth of aircraft, guns, ammunition and industrial plant. By August the British and Americans were beginning to come to some agreement on what each could provide, though at great cost to their own armed forces.[24]

On 29 September 1941 Mikoyan sent a memorandum to the Central Committee of the Communist Party with a list of supplies to be delivered between October 1941 and June 1942. The priorities, logically enough, were aeroplanes, tanks, anti-aircraft guns, anti-tank weapons, aluminium, tin, lead, steel, machine tools, wheat and sugar. The previous day a British delegation led by the press baron Lord Beaverbrook, who actively advised Churchill, and an American delegation led by the US diplomat Averill Harriman, had arrived in Moscow. The Soviet team was headed by Molotov, assisted by Voroshilov; Kuznetsov, the Navy Minister who was responsible for the service most involved in the aid effort; Golikov; Mikoyan, who was the Commissar for Foreign Trade, and others.[25]

Although Churchill later described the British and Americans' reception as 'bleak', he was not there. In fact, the Russians pulled out all the stops, with their usual spectacular ability to impress and convince. The western delegations had been tasked to get maximum information about the military situation and Soviet war production to ensure that what was requested was really needed. But they did not press. The Russians were in crisis and the requests seemed reasonable. Therefore, the western Allies did not make their offers conditional on the Russians disclosing information.[26]

The Moscow Conference lasted from 29 September to 1 October. On 1 October the tripartite commission concluded an agreement guaranteeing that the USA and the UK would send every month, starting immediately, 400 aeroplanes, 500 tanks, 300 anti-tank guns, plus aluminium, tin, lead, molybdenum, cobalt, copper and zinc, and other 'equipment'. The US would supply 1,250 tons of toluol – used to make high-grade aviation fuel – per month, and 100 tons of phosphorous, while the UK would supply $150,000 worth of (industrial) diamonds.[27]

In fact, only half a million dollars' worth of aid arrived in November and December – 1 per cent of the amount promised. According to Mikoyan, all the other recipients of lease-lend aid received nearly 62 million dollars' worth of aid every month. However, the initial difficulties of establishing the aid route and working relations should not be underestimated.[28] Although well intentioned, the undertakings made in the First October (Moscow) Protocol were impossibly optimistic.

The first problem was providing the material in the first place. At first, the Americans could not meet their undertakings and in late 1941 the British tried to substitute for them in return for the Americans making up the balance later. Secondly, it was difficult to get the military equipment, spare parts, ammunition and supplies to their destination. Murmansk was ice-free, but Arkhangel'sk was not. Several British ships which had taken supplies to Russia were trapped in the ice during the severe 1941–2 winter – the Battle of Moscow winter, the worst for fifteen years. In order to keep their propellors below the ice, ships needed to be low in the water. The Russians made sure that there were cargoes to put in the ships on their return trips, but did not always provide enough ballast to keep the ships down. The extreme cold also caused problems, cracking propellors and freezing any water that might remain in a Matilda tank engine block, cracking it. Arkhangel'sk had been mainly a timber port, and when a 68-tonne American machine arrived there was only one crane, which could lift one end of it. So it had to be jacked up alternately at each end, with logs jammed underneath, to get it off the ship.[29] Kruglov's orders that unloading the incoming ships should be as slick as possible showed that he was very much on the ball.

There were two other ways into the Soviet Union. The first was via Vladivostok, the great naval base in the Soviet far east, which could take 220,000 tonnes of goods per month, and then to destinations in Russia somewhere along the 6,400 kilometres of the Siberian railway. However, Stalin was anxious not to provoke the Japanese and after 7 December 1941 any British or US ships approaching Vladivostok would face Japanese attack. Soviet Russia remained at peace with Japan and there was discussion about re-flagging British and US ships as Soviet vessels.

It was not until October 1942, by which time Russia's crisis was nearly past, that events in the Pacific War enabled the Americans to operate this route.[30] The Russians were extremely sensitive about Japanese attitudes and concerned to keep them out of their war with Germany, even though the Japanese were now at war with two of Russia's Allies, and could therefore be considered as co-belligerents with Germany. On 7 March 1942 Beria sent the GKO a summary of a report that the British Admiralty had cabled to the British naval mission in Washington, asking for information about Vladivostok. The information requested included: warehouse facilities, fuel storage, airfields, rail links, defences against attack from sea and land, and the available Pacific Fleet warships, particularly minesweepers and submarines. And, 'especially important', whether the port could handle between ten and thirty ships, and anti-submarine defences. Clearly, the British were evaluating it as a point of entry for aid to the USSR. Nothing sinister, but it was Beria's job to report it.[31]

In the interim, the only other route was via the Persian Gulf, Iraq and Iran. The UK and USSR had occupied Iran with the consent of the new Iranian government in August and September 1941. Iraq, the former British mandate, had the best port – Basra, which the British had built in 1916 to feed their war against the Turks. But communications from here had been directed north-west, through Mesopotamia, not north-east, into Iran. The two Iranian ports of Khorramshahr and Bushire were even more rudimentary than Arkhangel'sk, and the railway from the coast to Tehran could carry only two trains a day. It also stopped 480 kilometres short of Tabriz, just south of the Soviet–Armenian border, where the railway south from the Caucasus terminated. The initial estimates made at the Moscow Conference that the route could carry 60,000 tonnes a month, raised to 100,000 after Pearl Harbor, proved wildly over-optimistic. In reality, the Arctic convoys were the only real option.

Even when it got there, the Allied aid did not always live up to expectations. At first, the British offered the Russians Hurricane fighters, which had been the mainstay of the RAF in the Battle of Britain, but were already obsolescent.[32] The Russians much preferred Spitfires, but they were not available in the same numbers and a mix of Spitfires and Hurricanes would create maintenance and logistic problems. The next British offer was 200 US-built P-40C Tomahawk aircraft (a variant of the P-40 Curtis Kittyhawk), which were being phased out in the Middle

East. This would let the British get rid of planes they no longer wanted, and the Americans could carry the burden of maintenance and spare parts. The Russians were very particular about the military equipment they wanted. They liked the US P-39 Airacobra and Kingcobra fighters, the A-20 Boston and B-25 Mitchell bombers.[33] One of the problems with the British fighters was that the Hurricanes and Spitfires were armed with eight .303 inch (7.69mm) machine guns,[34] whereas the Russians, like the Germans, much preferred smaller numbers of cannon. Cannon had longer range and a hit from a single cannon round – typically 20mm, nearly an inch, in calibre, was likely to destroy, or at any rate bring down an enemy aircraft. The Airacobra had cannon and also the same Allison engine as the P-40. The Russians have always liked firepower, in the air as well as on the ground.[35] To simplify maintenance and supply, they also liked standardization, and were very good at it. The Russians used a relatively small number of weapons with inter-changeable parts and ammunition, as opposed to the bewildering variety of machines and components which hindered the German forces.

'Hold on Russia'

Measured against the titanic war under way on the eastern front, the British and US commitments to deliver military, industrial and food aid, while overambitious on their part, might seem trivial compared with Soviet losses and Soviet war production as measured later in the war. But in 1941–2, it will be remembered, most of Russian war industry was either 'on wheels', having been evacuated from everywhere west of Moscow and out of Leningrad, or had recently arrived by train at greenfield sites in Siberia. Russian war industry was by now at its lowest ebb, and although the British, Canadian and US aid during the war as a whole might appear relatively insignificant, certainly as far as aircraft, tanks, artillery and other weapons are concerned, it was very significant in these critical years, and would remain so in certain areas throughout the entire war.

The Russians were not very interested in western artillery, because their own was probably the best in the world, and production in 1941 and 1942 remained high. Their tanks would be among the best, too, but in 1941 and 1942 the superb T-34 was only starting to be produced in significant numbers. In the interim, British tanks like the Valentine and Matilda had to help replace the vast numbers of Soviet tanks, many of them obsolescent, destroyed in the frontier battles. On 3 December Stalin asked for as many Valentines as possible, since they seemed to work better in Russian winter conditions than the Matildas did. Even at Kursk, in July 1943, some of the Soviet tank brigades deployed entire battalions of Valentines and Matildas.[36]

With the Japanese attack on Pearl Harbor, the British and Americans faced a complete change in the political and strategic situation. The Moscow protocol, however, remained carved in stone. Any failure to deliver on the promises made would greatly upset the Russians, who had survived – but only just. In spite of everything, then, the British tried very hard to honour their commitments in the first half of 1942.

Partly due to the efforts of Lord Beaverbrook and his media empire, British admiration and enthusiasm for the Russian war effort reached a crescendo in 1942. 'Hold on Russia: guns from Britain are coming', cried one poster. Maisky was invited to the exclusive Athenaeum club; Mrs Clementine Churchill's Aid to Russia fund raised £25,000, and in February 1942 Beaverbrook resigned from the War Cabinet to campaign for a 'second front' in the West. Some 43,000 people attended a second-front rally in London's Trafalgar Square at the end of March and 50,000 attended one in May. Communist Party membership rose by 25,000 in January and February. In June the first anniversary of the 'alliance of sorts' saw an unlikely confluence of pro-Russian enthusiasm at the Earl's Court exhibition centre. Two communist-backed organizations combined with Sir Stafford Cripps, a bishop, and the band of the Coldstream Guards to rouse support for Britain's Russian allies. It may not be too much to suggest that the socialist victory in the 1945 general election and the subsequent creation of the Welfare State owed something to the upsurge of pro-Russian, and therefore, at that time, pro-communist – certainly socialist – feeling among the British people during the war. After all, the British had faced the Germans alone for a year in 1940–41, and the Russians had held them and knocked them back, pretty well alone, apart from the limited support the western Allies could send, in 1941–2.[37]

The United Nations is created

Following the Japanese attack on Pearl Harbor, a three-week conference codenamed 'Arcadia' opened in Washington on 22 December 1941. Churchill and Roosevelt were both present. Roosevelt reaffirmed his 'Europe first' strategy, although many in the US remained sceptical, since it was the Japanese, not the Germans, who had attacked them. The conference set up the Combined Chiefs-of-Staff (multinational) organization and signed the Declaration of the United Nations. The latter was a statement of western Allied war aims, but its significance is often overlooked. All subsequent multinational Allied operations during the Second World War were conducted in the name of the United Nations. Not the United States; not the United Kingdom; but the United Nations which, by the end of the war, would embrace the Soviet Union as well, and would come into its modern form headed by the five victorious powers. The conference agreed to Operation Sledgehammer – the build-up of US forces in the UK, and to Super-Gymnast – a US landing in North Africa to help the British. The western Allies also tried to do something to help the Russians, who were in dire straits. In April 1942 the US Chief of Staff, General George C. Marshall, came to London with Roosevelt's adviser, Harry Hopkins, to discuss the possibility of a cross-Channel landing in 1942. If that happened, it would rule out the planned landing in north Africa, Operation Torch. In May, Molotov visited London and then Washington. The London negotiations lasted from 21 to 26 May. On the last day a treaty was signed between the Soviet Union and the United Kingdom. Molotov had met Churchill, but the signatories to the twenty-year agreement were Eden and Molotov, the Foreign Secretary and Minister, respectively. The associated communiqué said that 'full understanding was reached with regard to the urgent task of creating a second front in Europe in 1942'. The Russians, understandably, interpreted this as a firm commitment. Molotov was even more encouraged by his conversations with Roosevelt in Washington, which he interpreted as 'the president's firm promise to open the second front in 1942'.[38]

However, no sooner was the ink dry on the Soviet–British Treaty than Churchill headed to Washington to meet Roosevelt for the Second Washington Conference from 18 to 27 June. There, he went some way to persuading the Americans to buy his Mediterranean strategy, offering Operation Torch – the invasion of north Africa – as an alternative to an invasion of France. They also agreed to share information on nuclear research – the origins of the Manhattan project. In discussions in London between 18 and 25 July the Americans finally agreed with Churchill. However, this would not please the Russians, who were now suffering enormous losses again in the face of a determined German attack heading for the Volga and Stalingrad and, more critically, the Caucasus and the oilfields. In order to demonstrate determination to open the 'second front' – eventually – a cross-Channel raid was mounted against the port of Dieppe. It was allegedly to gain intelligence about German Atlantic and Channel wall defences. It was a disaster. Out of 6,000 troops, 3,600 were killed or captured before the landing zone could be evacuated. Most of the troops were Canadian. Whether intentionally or not, it served as a demonstration to everyone – especially the Americans and, probably, the Russians – how difficult an opposed amphibious assault on a defended enemy coast was, although the Russians already had some experience in their amphibious counter-attack on the Kerch' peninsula (see Chapter 15).[39]

Beaverbrook had pressed for a second front immediately after the German attack on Russia and did so again after the First Moscow Conference finished at the start of October 1941, but the Cabinet did not consider his paper.[40] The NKVD obviously took a huge interest in these discussions. After Churchill's meeting with Roosevelt in late June 1942, the NKVD reported that the British and American leaders had already decided to make their main effort against the Axis in north Africa.[41] US forces were beginning to move into Britain – 350,000 to 400,000 in July and August, and there were also 150,000 US troops in Iceland. These numbers were nowhere near adequate for a 'second front', and, by eastern front standards, were trifling. Beria also reported to the GKO that the western Allies expected the Japanese to attack the Soviet Union in summer or, at the latest, autumn 1942, and were holding back their own troops in the Pacific so that they could exploit this when it happened.[42]

Convoys in crisis

With the Arctic as the principal route for Allied aid, on 15 January 1942 the Luftwaffe hit and damaged the icebreaker *Stalin*. Besides its symbolic value, the strike meant that ice-bound Arkhangel'sk would effectively be closed until June. Realizing that Allied aid to Russia was helping weave the mighty Russian effort into the wider texture of the war, the Germans concentrated land-based air forces, submarines, fast surface attack craft and major surface combatants: the battleship *Tirpitz*, which reached Trondheim on 14–15 January, pocket battleships *Lutzow* and *Admiral Scheer* and the heavy cruiser *Admiral Hipper*. The western Allies asked the Russians to provide air cover east of Bear Island, but they did not do so. It appears they felt that the convoys were the western Allies' only contribution to the principal theatre of war – theirs – and that they should escort their convoys themselves. As the weather improved a little, losses among the convoys, which had been negligible during the winter, began to rise. Convoy PQ13 was scattered by a gale, and five ships – a quarter of the convoy – were lost to German aircraft and destroyers. The Russians demanded an increase in the number of convoys to three a month, to accelerate the arrival of supplies before the German summer offensive. Of 24 ships which sailed on 8 April 1942, only 7 reached north Russia. One was sunk and 16 turned back to Iceland.

As Figure 14.1 shows, until the Arctic ice receded northwards, convoys would have to sail relatively close to German-occupied Norway and would thus be within range of shore-based aircraft. Allied air cover from the UK and Iceland ran out just north of Bergen. Churchill asked Stalin for more air and naval support on 9 May. Stalin replied that he would do what he could but that 'our naval forces are very limited and ... our air forces in their vast majority are engaged at the battlefront'.[43] Pound, the Chief of the Naval Staff, decided that under the circumstances Convoys PQ16, due to leave on 18 May, and PQ17, to leave on 3 June, should be postponed until 1 July when bigger convoys could sail further north. Churchill was acutely conscious, however, of the political consequences, both with the Russians and the Americans, of letting the

Russians down. So PQ16 had to sail, and, depending on what happened, that would decide whether PQ17 should follow.

Convoy PQ16 did not suffer the catastrophe which Pound had feared. Only seven of its fifty ships were lost, and, conscious of the risk that the British might halt the convoys if losses were too high, the Russians sent a fighter escort to meet the convoy eleven hours out of the Kola inlet, and two Russian destroyers also met the convoy. In addition, the Russians launched air attacks on German airfields at Banak, Kirkeness and Petsamo. The British admitted that 'they really tried quite hard this time', and were encouraged by Russian promises to bomb further afield, including Tromso, next time.[44]

However, PQ17, which sailed on 17 June, was a disaster. Only 11 of the 34 ships reached Arkhangel'sk, 9 of them British. The British received intelligence of an attack by the battleships Tirpitz and Hipper, and ordered the convoy to scatter, making it vulnerable to attack by submarines and aircraft. Furthermore, most of the supplies that did arrive were American. Only 53 out of 215 British aircraft and 40 out of 245 tanks reached Russia. The British had lost 400,000 tons of shipping in one week. On 13 July the Defence Committee decided to suspend the sailing of convoy PQ18. Roosevelt reluctantly agreed, and Stalin was told on the 17th.[45]

On 15 July 1942 Churchill held a press conference in order to make a statement on ship losses. Inevitably, Allied aid to Russia and the question of the second front were linked. One of the journalists asked if a second front would be opened that year, to which Churchill replied that he knew the Russians wanted 'to see us in France'. However, although the Russians were suffering, that was no reason for the British to suffer in vain. What was important was to make the enemy suffer. Everyone took this to mean that there would be no second front soon.[46]

The Russians took careful note of Beaverbrook's efforts, however, and also those of Harry Hopkins whom Beaverbrook said was the USSR's 'greatest friend' in the United States.[47] On 31 July an NKVD agent sent a terse two lines reporting the British and US decision of 25 July, following a week-long conference in London from 18 July, that a second front would not be opened that year.[48] On 4 August, Beria passed the message on to the GKO, having checked the information which was now 'underlined by a source from circles in the American embassy': 'At its session on 25 July the British War Cabinet took the decision not to open a second front this year.'[49]

'Welcome to Moscow, Mr Prime Minister.'
August 1942

In order to break the news to the Russians, Churchill felt he had to go himself. At very short notice a 'summit' between Churchill and Stalin was organized. The Russians, of course, knew what Churchill was coming to say. When Molotov had been in London in May he had asked Churchill how Britain would react if Russia did not hold out through 1942 – and there was a real prospect it might not, as we shall investigate further in the next chapter. Churchill said that eventually the combined power of Britain, its Empire and the United States would prevail. However, he added, 'the British nation and its army [armed forces] were eager to engage the enemy as soon as possible and thereby help the Soviet army and its people in their glorious struggle'.[50] To the Russians, who had lost their entire pre-war army in 1941 – millions of men and women, the equivalent of a small nuclear attack – and who were now facing a German attack towards the Volga and the Caucasus that might yet dwarf the catastrophes of 1941, that might appear to mean men on the ground. There can be no question that the prospect of western aid was a major morale-booster for the Russian people. Stalin and the GKO knew the decision that had been made and what Churchill was going to say, but the Russian people, as yet, did not.

On the afternoon of 12 August 1942 Churchill's plane landed at the Moscow Central ('City') airport at Leningradskiy Prospekt. It was a sultry day, without wind, and Berezhkov recalled the smell of hot wormwood and the sound of birds and bees.[51] But Russia was in the middle of the worst year of its titanic war. Churchill had tried to strangle the Soviet Union at birth, and was unapologetic about that.[52] Now he was here to give them more bad news, although he wished it could have been different.

Churchill's bulky frame eventually appeared, climbing down a ladder from a hatch in the bottom of the plane. Molotov greeted Churchill like an old friend. He introduced Marshal Shaposhnikov, just eight years Churchill's junior and a fellow combatant in the First World War.[53] By an intriguing coincidence, the plane carrying Churchill's military advisers – Wavell and Sir Alan Brooke – and the Permanent Secretary at the Foreign Office, Alexander Cadogan, had to turn back to Tehran because of mechanical problems, and they did not arrive until the next day. Berezhkov describes Cadogan, a top civil servant, as the 'Deputy Foreign Minister' – incorrect, but not inaccurate. However, Churchill had with him Averill Harriman, the formidable US diplomat who was Roosevelt's personal representative, and who would become US Ambassador to the Soviet Union in October 1943.[54] Knowing Churchill, he was probably happy to be unencumbered by military top brass.

Churchill had not known quite what to expect in the land of workers and peasants which was bearing the brunt of the war with Germany, so he brought some sandwiches. He had eaten some of them on the plane from Tehran. Harriman was taken to a private residence in Ostrovskiy Street, while the other delegates were put up in the National Hotel and Churchill was taken to a dacha at Kuntsevo, right next to Stalin's. After a hot bath and a sumptuous late lunch – *zakuski* (hors d'oeuvres), red and black caviare, cold suckling pig and the usual alcoholic accompaniments served on or in exquisite plates and glassware – he was ready to face Stalin that night. Although Russia had its back to the wall and food for the masses was strictly rationed, these were luxuries they had, and could make available to one of the 'big three' Allied heads of state. Time was a luxury they did not have.[55] When Molotov had visited Churchill in May, he had been given standard wartime British food, which was consummately uninspiring, and a coffee substitute made from barley. When Molotov told Stalin, the dictator chuckled. 'A cheap show of democracy, Vyacheslav.' Churchill, furthermore, had 'not got that paunch of his eating nothing but sandwiches'. Stalin, for all his faults, had a great sense of humour and 'always had a twinkle in his eye'.[56]

Just after 19.00 that summer evening Churchill's car entered the Kremlin citadel through the Spasskaya gate and arrived outside Stalin's apartment. With him were Harriman and Sir Archibald Clark Kerr, the British Ambassador, plus Pavlov, the interpreter, and four others including Inspector Walter Thompson of Scotland Yard, his bodyguard. Stalin's diary records that the British party was there from 19.00 to 22.40.[57] Churchill apparently scanned the portraits of past Russian commanders – Aleksandr Nevskiy, Suvorov and Kutuzov of whom, as a military historian of great distinction, he knew. 'Welcome to Moscow, Mr Prime Minister,' said Stalin, hoarsely.[58]

After the usual polite questions about the flight and the accommodation, Stalin explained how Russia was still in peril from the German push towards Baku and Stalingrad. The reason why the Germans could easily mass twenty divisions or so at any given point, Stalin hinted, was because there was no land front anywhere else in Europe. Churchill took the hint. He said he believed Stalin wanted to hear about the second front. Stalin knew what Churchill was going to say, and listened. Churchill told Stalin about the landings in north Africa, Operation Torch, which was then scheduled for October. A large-scale incursion into Europe would not be possible until spring 1943, at the earliest.[59] Surprisingly, Stalin understood that this might take some of the strain off Russia. Churchill was tired, and withdrew to bed.[60]

The atmosphere remained strained. The next night Stalin saw the British delegation, now reinforced by the arrival of the military representatives who had been delayed. The formal meeting was from 23.15 to 01.40 the next morning. Churchill and Harriman were joined by their colleagues: General Wavell, who had visited Russia in 1936 and had met Tukhachevskiy; Brooke, the Chief of the Imperial General Staff; and Cadogan.[61] Stalin had just had a meeting with Stavka to discuss the appalling situation in the south, as the Germans pushed towards Stalingrad, and earlier in the evening had seen members of GKO – Molotov, Beria, Malenkov, Voroshilov and Mikoyan – individually, sometimes more than once.[62] He was not in a good mood, and the British generals also behaved abominably. Marshal Shaposhnikov, who was not well, went to Moscow airport to meet them but, Clark Kerr recalled, was left to one side while they fussed about their luggage. Eventually Kerr grabbed Wavell, who spoke Russian, and told him to be polite to the distinguished Russian Marshal. At the Kremlin dinner that night, before the meeting with Stalin, Wavell made a 'competent' speech in Russian, but made no effort to speak to Malenkov who was sitting next to him, and Brooke concentrated on chewing his food rather than making any effort to engage Voroshilov (who was always good value) in conversation.[63]

However, in spite of the British generals' contemptuous attitude to their hosts, by the time of the last meeting, which began at 19.00 on 15 August 1942, the two national leaders, at least, were acting like old friends. By this time Stalin had apparently resigned himself to the Allied landings in north Africa. Churchill then apologized for the abortive

British and French mission in 1939 and Stalin told Churchill about the Molotov–Ribbentrop Pact.[64]

Then, at about 20.30, Stalin suggested they retire to his private apartment for a drink. Churchill said he never refused offers like that. It was the first time Stalin had accorded any foreign head of state that honour. Churchill later described the apartment as 'modest in style and size, with a dining room, a living room, a study and a large bathroom'. It had been Bukharin's but Stalin moved in there after his wife, Nadezhda, committed suicide. Stalin's beloved and striking school-age daughter, the red-haired Svetlana – from the Russian for 'light' – joined them. Like many widowed men, Stalin had let his young daughter take over as the 'mistress of the house'. Molotov also joined the party, and acted as toastmaster. Churchill asked Stalin whether the war, so far, had been as much of a strain as the collectivization of agriculture in the 1930s. 'Oh, no,' replied Stalin. Collectivization had been a 'terrible struggle'. Ten million small landholders – *kulaks* (from the Russian word for a [tight] 'fist'), or relatively prosperous peasants – had been affected. Six million, more recent figures suggest, had died: the rest had been deported. 'It was very hard, but necessary,' Stalin repeated. He claimed that those deported did not always get on with their new neighbours and that many had been killed by local people. This was nonsense, but Churchill listened politely.[65]

Stalin and Churchill spent almost seven hours together – 20.30 in the evening until 03.00 in the morning. Churchill returned to his own dacha at about that time on 16 August and at 05.30 his plane took off from the Central airport and headed back to the relatively relaxing (though very hot) haven of Tehran. If Churchill ever suffered from hangovers, he probably had one after nearly seven hours with Stalin. The discussions, the communiqué later recorded, had been 'cordial and very frank' – which was obviously true. The next day, 17 August, Churchill cabled Roosevelt. The Russians, he said, had 'swallowed this bitter pill',[66] but they had not, entirely, and never would. Two days later, on 19 August, the Dieppe raid took place. Although it might have been better timed before Churchill's visit, the timing was nonetheless quite good. However, in spite of this brave if militarily futile demonstration, the western Allies' reputation in the Kremlin was reduced in the months after Churchill's visit.

The Second (Washington) Protocol, 6 October 1942

The First Protocol had highlighted two big problems with planning Allied aid to Russia. The first was the Russians' unwillingness – or practical inability – to let the British and Americans see what they were doing with the aid and to provide convincing evidence of what they really needed. The second was the totally unpredictable and rapidly changing character and strategic course of the war – like all wars. For this reason, aid had been determined as much by what the western Allies had and could ship, as by what the Russians wanted.

Early in 1942 the British and Americans proposed a conference, again in Moscow, to discuss the second supply protocol. With a second front in Europe in 1942 still an option at that stage, tank numbers were limited. US aircraft sent to Russia would not go to Britain, but the British maintained their aircraft offer, supplementing it with 6,000 tonnes of aluminium – the most useful metal for making aeroplanes. When Molotov arrived in Washington at the end of May 1942, Roosevelt told him Russia could not have its cake and eat it. If they wanted a second front, that would mean more supplies for the US and Britain and fewer for Russia. Whereas the First Protocol had been largely British in origin and emphasis, therefore, the Second Protocol was predominantly American. It was finally signed in Washington on 6 October 1942, but the Russians had agreed to it, and it was implemented, from early July. That was before the Russians received final confirmation of no second front in 1942. And then the Germans came within an ace of destroying the Soviet Union, which was on the verge of economic collapse (see Chapter 15), at Stalingrad. The British promised up to a million tonnes of supplies. The Americans promised seven times as many – 7.2 million short tons.[67] Taken together, the western Allies had offered about 8 million tonnes. They could not ship this, however, and asked the Russians to choose the 4.4 million short tons' worth of aid they most wanted – just over half. Of these 4.4 million short tons, the document stipulated, three-quarters – 3.3 million short tons – would go by the hazardous northern, Arctic route and one-quarter – 1.1 million short tons – via the Persian Gulf.[68]

The great Allied conferences of 1943:
Casablanca, Washington, Quebec, Cairo, Tehran . . .

On 8 November 1942 the British and Americans invaded western north Africa – Operation Torch. On 12 November the American Associated Press correspondent Henry C. Cassidy interviewed Stalin, who said the campaign showed that the Allies could mount 'a serious military operation' and might lead to a split in the German–Italian coalition in the near future. Asked what effect it would have in drawing German forces away from the Russian front, he suggested it was too early to say. Stalin knew, although Cassidy did not, that the counteroffensive at Stalingrad would be launched in a week. Following the interview, the Leningrad NKVD reported public reaction to it, and to Stalin's answers, in the city, which was entering its second agonizing winter of siege. Some thought the north African landings were the start of the 'second front'. Others were not so sure. Many thought north Africa was too far away to make any difference to them and that landings in northern or, at the least, southern France would be more help. Sister Emel'yanova, at the garrison clinic, thought 'the Allies' military action in north Africa is only a wretched pretence at a second front. It's too early to get excited, since it scarcely makes much difference to our situation.'[69]

Not only was north Africa an awfully long way from Leningrad – and Stalingrad – but the Allied landings could potentially backfire on the Russians. If the north African invasion succeeded, which it did, the western Allies would be tempted to reinforce success and carry on via Italy rather than landing in France, which was the shortest route to Germany itself and would divert far more German troops from the Russian front.

From 14 to 24 January 1943 Roosevelt and Churchill met at Casablanca, the first of many conferences that year. Here, Roosevelt and Churchill agreed that, despite the British and US victories in north Africa, the Red Army remained 'the greatest single drain on the power and hope of Germany'.[70] In mid 1943, just before the great Battle of Kursk, the Red Army still faced 216 Axis divisions on the eastern front as against 103 Axis divisions faced by the western Allies in southern (primarily south and south-eastern) Europe and just 71 north of the Alps. But in February 1943 the British Chiefs-of-Staff could still not predict with confidence what the outcome of the next summer campaigns in the east might be. Therefore, given that the most overwhelming expenditure of blood and materiel on land – and hence, the destruction of German military power – was in the East, aid to Russia remained the best (indeed, the only available) way of influencing the key theatre of war. Public and military opinion in the West remained steadfastly pro-Russian through 1943. However, in March 1943 there were those in the US who favoured making continued aid conditional on Russian cooperation – essentially, on bargaining.[71]

The British doubted whether the second front, which was to be created by a cross-Channel invasion of France, was feasible before 1944, and Roosevelt agreed. It was here, at Casablanca, that Roosevelt, almost casually, introduced the concept of 'unconditional surrender'. Nothing less would be accepted from the Axis powers. No negotiations, no conditions – nothing except unconditional surrender. For the Russians, although Stalin may have considered terms for surrendering to Germany in July and/or October of 1941, German surrender terms had never been an issue. From day one of the Great Patriotic War the message was simple. Germany would be destroyed, erased, annihilated, conquered.

From 11 to 27 May 1943 Roosevelt and Churchill met again, in Washington – the 'Trident' conference. Here, they agreed that the second front should be opened on 1 May 1944, and that a force of twenty-nine divisions should be assembled for this. After the invasion of Sicily (Operation Husky) in July 1943, the fall of Mussolini and Italy's change of sides, conditions were favourable for development of the campaign in Italy. To work out the details of continued operations in Italy and to reconcile the conflicting demands of the invasion of France, the Mediterranean and the Pacific, Roosevelt and Churchill met again at Quebec on 17 August – the 'Quadrant' conference. In March the British and Americans had already agreed that a landing should take place in Normandy. At Quebec they discussed more details of the plan, which acquired its final flamboyant codename – a close second to Barbarossa – Operation Overlord, and agreed to name the commanders. There were also further discussions on the Manhattan atomic bomb project. Although the Russians were not involved in the discussions, the NKVD were fully aware of most of the details.[72]

Although Stalin knew that the second front would not now be

established until summer 1944, he was no longer so worried. The invasion of Sicily had coincided with the Battle of Kursk (Chapter 17), where the last great German offensive in the east was halted and thrown back. From now on, the Germans were on the defensive. Whilst British, US, Canadian, Free French and other military action on the far side of Germany was welcome, Stalin was now winning the war on the eastern front largely on his own. This gave the Russians enormous political leverage. Roosevelt and Churchill, probably unaware of how much the Russians knew, felt it was necessary to reassure Stalin about the second front and also to tie up arrangements for Soviet involvement in the war in the Pacific. Before meeting Stalin, however, Roosevelt and Churchill flew to Cairo for the 'Sextant' conference, where they met the Chinese nationalist leader Chiang Kai-Shek, whose forces had been fighting the Japanese since the latter's full-scale invasion and conquest of northern and central China in July 1937. The Cairo declaration of 1 December set out terms for Japanese surrender; for the return of Manchuria, which had been a Japanese puppet state since 1931, to China; and independence for Korea.

Roosevelt and Churchill then headed to Tehran for their conference with Stalin, the 'Eureka' conference from 28 November to 1 December 1943. It was the first time that the 'big three' all met together. That was preceded by a Foreign Ministers' conference in Moscow from 19 to 30 October, attended by Eden for the UK, Cordell Hull for the US and Molotov for the USSR. The Foreign Ministers agreed many details for the post-war administration of Europe, including the renewed independence of Austria, a European Advisory Commission in London to discuss the future of Germany, and the occupation and government of Italy. The Italian fleet had surrendered in September and the Russians asked for a share of the spoils: a battleship, a cruiser, eight destroyers, four submarines for use in the Arctic and 40,000 tons of merchant shipping for the Black Sea. The British accepted the Soviet claim to compensation but needed all the ships for operations in the Mediterranean or for Overlord and, in any case, the warships were not suitable for Arctic conditions. Nevertheless, they agreed to the Russians having a 'reasonable share', and at Tehran Roosevelt offered the Russians a third of the Italian fleet – which was more than they had asked for. Instead of giving the Russians the Italian ships, the British and Americans offered to lend them their own, instead, and the Russians accepted. After the war, the Russians returned the British and US ships and the Italian vessels were transferred to them. It is no coincidence that many post-war Soviet and Russian warship designs have an elegance and stream-lined shape that is very Italian.[73]

At the Moscow meeting, the Russians let the western Allies know that they would enter the war against Japan once Germany was defeated. This was music to Hull's ears, as the Americans had been waiting for this news for a long time. If an amphibious invasion of France was going to be difficult, a landing in Japan was expected to cost hundreds of thousands of American lives. Although the western Allies could not be absolutely sure that the Soviets would intervene until Stalin confirmed that the attack was imminent at Potsdam in late July 1945, Stalin nevertheless confirmed this promise at Tehran. By this time, the Red Army had achieved two stupendous victories, at Stalingrad and Kursk, and so, even if the Japanese learned of the likelihood of Soviet attack, they were unlikely to try to pre-empt it by invading the Soviet Union's Pacific maritime provinces. They would try to postpone the evil day as long as possible – just as Stalin had in 1939–41. Secondly, by linking a Soviet attack on Japanese-held territory and forces with the defeat of Germany, Stalin made the point that the sooner the second front was launched, the sooner his country would be able to join the war against Japan. This may well have added to the western Allies' sense of urgency with regard to Overlord. Stalin said he was satisfied with progress on the second front, but by now, he was probably gaining confidence that, even if the Allies did not invade France in 1944, he could eventually defeat Germany on his own.[74]

The other big issue was the fate of eastern Europe. The Allies came to an understanding, though not a formal agreement, that Poland should be reconstituted as a state with the addition of former German territory in the west, which contained a good deal of industry, as compensation for the loss of eastern territory to the USSR.[75]

Tehran was in some ways the high point of the Grand Alliance. Stalin praised the British and American contribution to the war and US war production, without which, he said, the war would have been lost. In the first months of 1944 the Soviet press published extensive details of British and US supplies sent to the Russians. However, this public praise, which peaked at the time of the Normandy landings, postponed from 1 May to 5 June and, finally, 6 June 1944, concealed two growing areas of disagreement and potential conflict. The first was Soviet policy towards 'liberated' countries in eastern Europe. In January 1944 *Pravda* published an article claiming that it had evidence of secret British–German negotiations. Relations with the Polish government in exile in London steadily deteriorated, and the Russians put pressure on it to accept the 'Curzon line' – essentially the post 28 September 1939 division of former Polish territory – as the eastern frontier. 'I confess to growing apprehension', Eden said on 3 April 1944, 'that Russia has vast aims and that these may included the domination of eastern Europe and the "communising" of much that remains.'[76]

When Stalin arrived in Tehran, he also could not fail to notice the extent of the American presence and influence in Iran. During 1942 and 1943 the Russians had reined back their political propaganda and attempts to undermine the Iranian government in the interests of the 'alliance of sorts' with the west. However, probably as a direct result of Stalin's observations, in 1944 Russian interference increased again, and in the autumn they tried to obtain exclusive rights to petroleum and mineral exploration.[77]

However, the war was not yet won and during early 1944 the Russians still attached great importance to the 'alliance', even though there were points of disagreement. Most importantly, the western aid provided to the USSR consisted, increasingly, of industrial supplies which would be of value for post-war reconstruction, rather than war materiel.

By the end of 1943, after Tehran, a rough understanding had emerged between the 'allies'. The western Allies, while exploiting any success in Italy, and fighting a separate war in the Far East, would concentrate overwhelming force and expertise to launch a cross-Channel invasion in summer 1944. In return, the Soviet Union would be free to occupy whatever the Red Army conquered. Henceforward, 'Allied' agreement would focus on the division of spoils, rather than on saving Russia. Churchill and Roosevelt met again at the Second Quebec Conference 'Octagon' from 10 to 16 September 1944. At the Third Moscow Conference, from 9 to 20 October 1944, Churchill, Eden and Stalin discussed the partition of eastern Europe. At Yalta, in the Crimea 'Argonaut', from 21 February to 18 March 1945, and at Potsdam, just west of Berlin, optimistically but prematurely codenamed 'Terminal', from 17 July to 2 August 1945, the 'big three' shaped the post-war world.[78] It was only at Yalta that they agreed that the advancing Allied armies would respect a division of Germany along the Elbe, and even then the Russians did not trust the western Allies. Had the Allies not invaded in June 1944, the Russians might well have conquered all Germany, possibly even got to the Channel. After Russia survived in 1942, and seized the initiative in 1943, the course of the Second World War had changed. We shall therefore return to that part of the story later.

From war to reconstruction:
The Third and Fourth Protocols

The Third Supply Protocol was first presented to the Russians on 9 June 1943 and signed as the London Protocol of 19 October 1943. Because it was so difficult to predict what Soviet requirements would be and to check on what lease-lend deliveries might be used for, Roosevelt ordered 'unconditional aid'. In effect, he signed a blank cheque. As the British and US Chiefs-of-Staff had agreed at Casablanca, it contained the proviso that deliveries would depend on variations in production facilities, shipping losses and other unpredictable factors. The main difference from the earlier protocols, however, was that, rather than war materiel, it provided food, trucks and industrial plant needed for reconstruction. By now American aid vastly outstripped British. The Third Protocol expired on 30 June 1944, by which time the western Allies were in France and close to breaking out from Normandy, while the Russians were close to reconquering Belarus and destroying the German military-strategic centre of gravity, Army Group Centre (see Chapter 18). Negotiations on the Fourth Protocol had begun but the British were already facing bankruptcy and were shipping raw materials back to the United States under 'reverse lease-lend', to start paying the Americans back for what economist John Maynard Keynes called 'financial imprudence which [had] no parallel in history'.[79] But they were not alone in that. In order to win the war, the Russians had also thrown resources to the winds with no regard for the future. The Fourth Protocol was finally signed on 17 April 1945, the month before victory in Europe, and five and a half months before victory over Japan.

The diversion of US, British and Canadian resources to aid Russia was a contentious issue during the war, and became a highly political one afterwards. As early as the beginning of 1942, British politicians used the resources diverted to Russia as an excuse for losing Singapore, the great fortress captured by the Japanese on 15 February 1942. Churchill and Eden both said they had given to Russia what they had really needed for the defence of the Malay peninsula. This was untrue. British and Australian ground forces had been poorly trained and equipped for jungle warfare and were simply outmatched and outfought by aggressive Japanese troops enjoying superior morale, while the loss of the battleships *Prince of Wales* and *Repulse*, a cardinal blow, reflected an outdated appraisal of naval warfare.[80]

During the cold war, Soviet commentators emphasized that the planes and tanks provided by Britain, Canada and the US were second-rate, obsolescent and, given the gigantic scale of the war on the eastern front, relatively few in number. Again this was understandable, but actually wrong, and also misses the real point. The Head of the State Planning Centre, Nikolay Voznesenskiy, who was a member of the GKO during the war, said in 1948 that western supplies made up only 4 per cent of the Soviet Union's war production between 1941 and 1943. However, Voznesenskiy did not mention the supplies received in 1944 and 1945, under Roosevelt's 'unconditional aid' mandate. By the late 1970s, Soviet scholars were revising their assessment to be more generous to the West, admitting that the western Allies provided, or contributed substantially to, 10 per cent of tank production and 12 per cent of aircraft production. Again, it is difficult to pin down exactly what these figures mean and to which years they refer, but other research, including research by a senior officer for his thesis as part of the two-year course at the Voroshilov General Staff Academy, corroborates this figure.[81]

Furthermore, the first western war materiel started arriving in August 1941, just as Soviet war industry was being evacuated eastwards. In 1942, Soviet war production dropped dramatically, as industry was either 'on wheels' or being reassembled in Siberian fields. So at that point the provision of British and US tanks and aircraft, plus, in some cases, three months' worth of spares, insignificant though they might later have appeared, really mattered. Although no British or US tank was comparable with the T-34, that was not the point in 1942. The Matilda tank did not perform well, but the Valentine was not bad, and the Sherman, sent by the United States, could match the German Pzkw-III. The Kittyhawk and Hurricane were obsolescent and could not match the German Me-109, but they were still better than a lot of the Soviet fighters of 1941 and 1942. The Soviet air force, it will be remembered, had lost 1,800 planes in the first eight hours of Barbarossa and a further 3,200 planes in the next four months while their aircraft production fell dramatically. At that time, even obsolescent aircraft were better than none.

More importantly, however, throughout the war, the western Allies filled key gaps in areas where Soviet industry was less able to meet the armed forces' and the nation's needs or where western designs and expertise were particularly useful.

The most obvious and prevalent western contribution to the Soviet war effort was in the form of trucks and jeeps. At the end of the war the Soviet armed forces had 665,000 motor vehicles, of which 427,000 were western – mostly American. In addition to those made in the United States, the Russians also produced copies – notably the 'Willys' (*Villis*) jeep. Between 1942 and 1944 the Soviet Union manufactured just 128,000 trucks. As Khrushchev said, 'just imagine how we would have advanced from Stalingrad to Berlin without them. Our losses would have been colossal because we would have had no manoeuvrability.'[82] Between 11 March 1941 and 1 October 1945 the United States sent the Russians, in addition to 7,537 tanks: 51,503 jeeps; 35,170 motorbikes; 8,701 'tractors', including half-tracks, with tracks at the back and wheels at the front, which would be used to pull Russian artillery; and a staggering 375,883 trucks. While the jeeps – one for every 200 of the 11 million Russian soldiers in the field at the end of the war – motorized Russian command and control, the trucks – one for every 30 Russian soldiers (whereas Russian production would have provided one per 100) – helped motorize Russian logistics.[83] To keep the jeeps and nearly 376,000 trucks on the road, the Americans also supplied 3,786,000 tyres. Although there was no direct correlation, that worked out at about 10 tyres per truck.

American technology features prominently in film footage of the war. Marshal Zhukov regularly arrives at conferences in a Douglas DC3 'Dakota' transport plane, cunningly disguised with a couple of red stars. Out of the 14,795 aircraft which the United States sent to Russia between March 1941 and October 1945, 67 per cent were fighters and 26 per cent bombers, leaving only 7 per cent for transport and miscellaneous. But this was still a thousand planes. In the final attacks on East Prussia, East Pomerania and the northern wing of the Berlin operation, Rokossovskiy's troops nimbly negotiated the rivers in DUKW amphibious craft made in the USA – the oddly appropriate letters standing for '1942 – six-wheeled amphibious'.[84]

During the Soviet period there was a natural tendency to suppress evidence of western Allied aid and its significance. For example, most of the published pictures of *Katyusha* multiple rocket-launchers show them on Soviet-made trucks whereas a vast number of the rocket-launcher racks, certainly, were mounted on American Studebakers. One of the most eloquent testimonials to the sharing of expertise comes from the writer Aleksandr Solzhenitsyn, who served as an artillery officer in the Red Army until he was arrested by the NKVD at the end of the war and sent to the GULag Archipelago. The Russians were proud of their guns, but even Solzhenitsyn recognized that it sometimes took two to tango . . .

> See those Yankee half-tracks pulling
> Russian BS-3 type guns . . .[85]

Stepan Mikoyan, the eldest of Anastas's five sons, was one of three who served as fighter pilots. He crashed and was injured towards the end of the Battle of Moscow, then fought at Stalingrad and eventually returned to the Moscow air defence command. By this time it was 1943. The younger Mikoyan said the Russian aircraft were equipped with American radios and artificial horizons, and were vectored on to their targets by British radars. The Russian pilots also wore western flying suits.[86] British records confirm that the War Office did indeed send the Russians 1,474 radar sets, and the Admiralty another 329, but there is no record of radars from the Air Ministry.[87]

As Russian war production geared up, western aircraft, tanks and armaments became less significant, although there were a few exceptions. Most extraordinary was the request in the Fourth (1944) Supply Protocol for two US 240mm howitzers and two 203mm guns. These would have been shipped after January 1945. Given that the Red Army had 53,100 guns, 227,300 mortars and 4,800 multiple rocket-launchers available on 1 January 1944, increasing to 328,700 guns and mortars and 6,700 multiple rocket-launchers on 1 January 1945, including about 1,000 guns of 203mm calibre and above, a request for *four* heavy American guns at this stage of the war makes very little sense. Why on earth did they need them? It is pretty obvious that the Russians wanted to evaluate them for intelligence purposes. They had always preferred more, but less heavy, guns, since they were more manoeuvrable, and there is evidence that they drew on the design of the American weapons after the war.[88]

The most significant US and British contributions were in the field of communications and command and control. The Americans alone sent over more than 1.5 million kilometres of telephone cable, and between them the British and Americans provided 247,000 telephones. The US also provided half a million tons of railway tracking, 1,155 rail flatcars and wagons and 1,981 locomotives. Given that the Germans had destroyed 65,000 kilometres of railway track and more than 2,300 bridges in Soviet territory, the US contribution to rebuilding and expanding the Soviet railway system which was so critical to feeding the war, was enormously significant.[89]

Most basic, however, was food. By 1942 only 58 per cent of the land cultivated in the Soviet Union before the war was still in Russian hands. And that means *Russian* hands, because the Baltic States, Belarus and most of Ukraine were gone, under German control. Compared with 1940 – the last year, obviously, for which full statistics were available, Soviet grain production had fallen by two-thirds, cattle herds were reduced by 48 per cent, milk production – an associated activity – by 45 per cent, sheep and goat flocks by a third – 33 per cent – and pig production, which had been concentrated in the west, by a staggering 78 per cent. America provided more than 5 million tons of food, the value of all food shipments exceeding 1.3 billion dollars at 1946 prices. British Empire food shipments, while less significant in volume, were probably equally important for Russian morale. Like the British soldier, the Russian finds it difficult to function without tea. Some £8 million worth of food supplies came from the British Empire, including tea from Ceylon (modern Sri Lanka) and Africa; cocoa beans, oil and palm kernels from west Africa, coconut oil from Ceylon, pepper and spices.

In addition to government-funded supplies, in a mirror of the 'complex emergencies' of our own day, where non-governmental organizations are equally important, British charitable organizations spent £5,260,000 on surgical and medical items and clothing.[90]

Overall, the British contribution was valued at £45.6 million, the American at $11.26 billion. More than sixty years later it is probably futile to try to equate these prices with modern equivalents, especially given the quite different economic circumstances. However, one statistic stands out. The United States' contribution was enough to provide half a pound of concentrated battlefield rations for the Soviet armed and security forces' 12 million men and women for every day of the war.[91] The Americans also provided 49,000 tons of leather and 15 million pairs of boots. Armies march on their feet, as well as on their stomachs, and leather comes from cattle. The Russians, it will be recalled, had lost nearly half their cattle to the German invasion by 1942. Those boots would provide one pair for every two men of the total of 34,476,700 called up during the conflict.[92]

Other western supplies were either highly sophisticated and specialized or filled further key gaps in Soviet production. The Soviet government later dismissed total US deliveries of 2.67 million tons of petroleum as insignificant compared to their own output of 30 million tons per year, but the American fuel included high-octane aviation fuel which was scarce in the Soviet Union. Lease-lend provided three-quarters of Soviet aluminium and copper between 1941 and 1944.[93] Among other raw materials supplied were rubber, graphite and tin.

There was another, critical effect of Allied aid. It hugely complicated German calculations about Soviet industrial resilience and potential. The Germans underestimated what the Soviet Union could carry on producing. For example, in March 1942 they estimated Soviet steel production at 8 million tons a year, whereas, even in 1942, the worst year (see Chapter 15), it was 13.5 million. Secondly, they overestimated the effect that massive allocation of available steel would have on the rest of the economy. Steel that went into gun barrels could not also go into railway tracking or rolling stock. In fact, the Russians did much better than the Germans expected. The only exception was the motor vehicle sector. But what was the most significant form of western Allied aid? In addition to that compound error, the third source of German miscalculation about Russia's ability to continue the war was lease-land itself. They hugely underrated the impact of lease-land supplies and especially the delivery of the key raw materials which, as we have seen, included high-quality alloyed steel, aluminium, copper and industrial plant. The Germans could have forecast Soviet production of 128,000 trucks between 1942 and 1944. They did not forecast the number the Americans would provide in the same period – the best part of 376,000. This miscalculation formed part of a bigger miscalculation about Russia's ability to survive and fight on.[94] If war is a clash of wills, then it is as much about what the enemy thinks you may have, as about what you have. And western Allied aid, in addition to its obvious moral and physical importance, and its value in implementing Russian concepts, very significantly upset German calculations.

It is clear, therefore, that although the relocation of Soviet industry to the east – to the Urals and beyond – was a critical factor in the Soviet victory, western Allied aid also played a much bigger part than the trifling '4 per cent' publicly admitted by Soviet commentators. If key aspects of your air support, your battlefield rations, your trucks, your general's jeep, even your boots, come from the United States, then that is very important. However, that does not in any way diminish the importance of the brilliantly designed, robust and interchangeable mass-produced weaponry with which the Red Army was lavishly equipped. Still less, even though communications and logistics owed much to the western Allies' contribution, does it in any way diminish the Russians' record of resilience, fighting spirit, tactical ingenuity and innovation, and operational and strategic leadership.

A doomed alliance?

Some historians have suggested that the debates over the second front in 1942 led to a rift in the 'Alliance' which never really healed, and was the basis for the split which underpinned the subsequent 'cold war'. However, the 'alliance of sorts' never had much of a chance. The British and Americans had done their best to destroy the Soviet Union from the moment the communist government took over in Russia in 1917, and Churchill had never concealed his abiding opposition to communism. The Molotov–Ribbentrop Pact had not helped, either. Churchill made much of the warnings he had given to Stalin, starting in his speech on the evening of 22 June 1941. 'I gave clear and precise warnings to Stalin,' he said, 'Staleen . . ., as I have given warnings to others, before . . .' – a self-indulgent reference to his own domestic political campaign against appeasement. When Hitler attacked Russia, the event was regarded as a welcome but probably brief respite, and British policy was to keep the Russians going as long as possible, which was not expected to be very long. The American attitude was more distant, and perhaps more mature. As Russian resistance stiffened, public opinion in

Britain, certainly, became enthusiastically pro-Russian, and Churchill had to move with it. But the disagreements over the second front in 1942 and 1943 were merely symptoms of a much wider conflict of interests.[95] Russian tactics were simple from the start of the war and through 1942. They used their demands for a second front as moral blackmail to get supplies. At Tehran, in 1943, although the British and Americans had already agreed to invade France as soon as possible, Churchill still pushed hard for an invasion of the Balkans. Stalin could read his mind. Churchill wanted to insert his own forces into the Balkans, to stop the Russians getting in there.[96] If the Russians won the eastern front war largely on their own – which they ought to have been able to do, given the potential they displayed in the 1930s, and the balance of forces in 1941, then western Allied aid stopped them losing it in 1942, and provided the basis for recovery from then on. The Russians succeeded in diverting American resources to their front, using lease-lend, and also used a measure of moral blackmail to encourage and secure a British commitment to the second front in France which Churchill would probably rather have avoided.[97] But circumstances dictated that the overwhelming burden of fighting would fall on the Russians.

By early 1945, from 4 to 11 February, Churchill and Roosevelt could visit Yalta, in the Crimea, and divide the post-war world, and certainly post-war Europe, with Stalin. But at the beginning of 1942, that was still three years ahead. Allied aid would add approximately 5 per cent to Soviet resources in 1942 and 10 per cent in 1943 and 1944.[98] It might not sound much, but it probably made all the difference.

15

TO THE EDGE OF THE ABYSS:
THE WORST YEAR – 1942

'War will be decided in the east': German plans
for 1942 – the genesis of Operation *Blau*

As winter turned to spring in early 1942, many parts of the front from the Baltic to the Black Sea were eerily stable. Soviet and German forces viciously battered away at each other around Leningrad, but south of there the German forces held a series of defended areas known as 'hedgehogs'. Hitler ordered them to stand firm, using explosives to blast defensive positions in the rock-hard, frozen ground. Realizing that he had dispersed and diluted his offensive power by attacking in three directions in 1941, Hitler decided to concentrate in the south. The Germans would advance through the economically vital Donets basin into the Don bend, west of Stalingrad, and then south to the Caucasus and the coveted oilfields to the east. Militarily and economically that was the best option. And it nearly succeeded.[1]

In this area, the Germans had already pushed furthest east, holding three 'hedgehogs', with about 200 kilometres between them, at Khar'kov, Artemovsk and Taganrog, which lay in a German salient around Rostov-on-Don (see Figure 15.1). The Germans also controlled the whole of the Crimea, apart from the fortress of Sevastopol itself, which was still under siege. Sevastopol, on the Russian left flank, was a southern mirror of Leningrad on the other flank, 1,800 kilometres to the north. The Russians also held the Kerch' peninsula, the eastern Crimea. They had recaptured it after the Kerch'-Feodosiya landings, which started on Christmas Day, 1941. More than 250 naval and merchant vessels and 660 aircraft had taken part, and by 30 December the Russians had

20,000 troops ashore. On 29 December they had captured the port of Feodosiya, level with the isthmus leading to the peninsula, and by 2 January had driven the Germans back nearly 100 kilometres from the Kerch' strait. The Germans did not succeed in driving the Russians off it until Operation *Bustard*, from 8 to 18 May. After that, the Germans renewed their assault on Sevastopol.

The terrain in the south was also more suitable for large-scale manoeuvre battles, once the spring *rasputitsa* – the thaw, which turned the top layer of frozen soil to mud – had passed, and Hitler's plan was therefore to repeat the great successes of summer 1941, take much of the Soviet economic base – or, at any rate, deny it to the Russians, and then possibly swing north to take Moscow. According to Halder, the aim was to 'definitively destroy what vital defensive strength was left to the Soviets and, as far as possible, to deprive them of the most important energy sources for their war effort.'[2]

The model for the outflanking movements to trap successive concentrations of Russian forces was the twin battle of Vyaz'ma-Bryansk in October 1941. Against this background Hitler approved plan *Blau* ('Blue') on 5 April in Directive No. 41. Although Leningrad remained as an objective, priority was given to the southern front. A series of options – *Blau* I to *Blau* IV – were worked out (see Figure 15.1). The *Blau* Directive, No. 41, is a key document, because it proves Hitler's determination that the war as a whole – as Halder predicted at the 28 March conference which led to the Directive – would be decided in the east. As Figure 15.1 shows, there were four phases. The first would culminate in the capture of Voronezh. Then those forces would join with others breaking through from Khar'kov to the east. Then, in phase three, those forces would advance following the south bank of the Don and link with others moving up from the Taganrog-Rostov area. Furthermore, 'an attempt must be made to reach Stalingrad itself or, at least, to bring the city under fire from heavy artillery so that it may no longer be of any use as an industrial or communications centre.'[3]

The die was cast. If Barbarossa had been Hitler's first great campaign in the east, *Blau* was the second.[4]

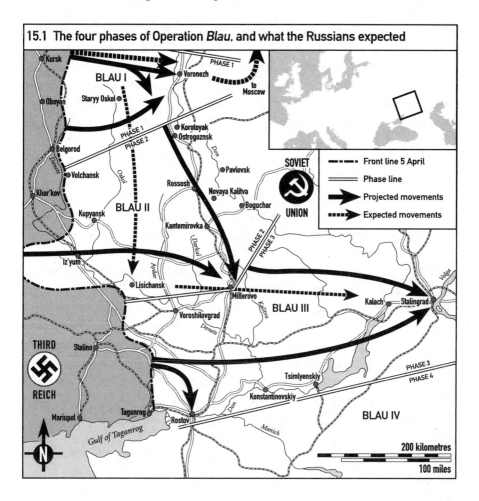

15.1 The four phases of Operation *Blau*, and what the Russians expected

Russian plans

Meanwhile Stalin, according to Zhukov, thought the Germans could launch substantial operations on *two* of the three axes, not just one, and was particularly concerned about the central one – Moscow – where seventy German divisions were available.[5] The main German effort was therefore going to take place in the south, but the Russians were going to make theirs in the centre. It was conceivable either that they would go right past each other, or that a massive revolving door movement would develop. German plans and Russian expectations are shown in Figure 15.1.[6]

Shaposhnikov and the Chief of his Operations Department of the General Staff, Aleksandr Vasilevskiy, argued that, for the moment, the best thing would be to hold on in the centre. Zhukov agreed, but nevertheless argued for a pre-emptive strike against the Germans in this area, not unlike his plan of May 1941 to deal with German forces in Poland. Stalin, however, supported by Timoshenko, who was then commanding both the South-West Front and also the still extant South-West Strategic Direction, remained over-optimistic. Stalin ordered the General Staff and fronts to plan local offensives in seven areas between the Baltic and Black Seas including Khar'kov (modern Kharkiv).

Stalin therefore issued a wonderfully confusing order that 'simultaneously with the shift to a strategic defence, I foresee the conduct of local offensive operations along a number of axes to fortify the success of the winter campaign ... to seize the strategic initiative [is that strategically 'defensive'?] and to disrupt German preparations for a new summer offensive'. Vasilevskiy, a fine staff officer, mused over the feasibility of Stalin's decision to 'defend and attack simultaneously'.[7]

Stalin's attention had been focused on the latter region by counter-offensives during the late winter. On 1 January 1942 the South-Western Front had launched an attack in the Kursk area, just north of Belgorod and Khar'kov, which lasted more than two months. From 18 to 31 January, Sixth and Fifty-Seventh Armies carved out a 30-kilometre-deep breakthrough (the Barvenkovo-Lozovaya operation).[8] The German divisions on either side held on to the 'shoulders' of the breakthrough, in what would become the classic German response to such penetrations of their front. Nevertheless, the Russian attack created the 'Iz'yum bulge', south of Khar'kov, so called because Iz'yum was at the centre of its base, the eastern end. It was also known as the Barvenkovo bridgehead. This would be the only significant shift in the front line in the south in early 1942. Then a small counter-attack was launched into the Donbass in March when Kirill Moskalenko's Thirty-Eighth Army captured a bridgehead across the Northern Donets river.

During the Russian discussions in March, an offensive against Khar'kov emerged as the favoured option for disabling any German attack on Moscow to the north-west, while, at the same time, interrupting any 'secondary' objective the Germans might have had of attacking south-eastwards towards the Don bend (in fact it was their main objective). The Khar'kov offensive was therefore planned for May 1942. The planners were Front and Strategic Direction Commander Timoshenko, his Chief of Operations Lt Gen. Ivan Bagramyan, and the Military Commissar for the Strategic Direction – the 'viceroy of Ukraine' – Nikita Khrushchev. What they proposed was no mere local counteroffensive. It was massive.

On 1 April Lt Col. Reinhard Gehlen had taken over as head of German military intelligence on 'Foreign Armies East' (*Fremde Heere Ost*). He estimated that Timoshenko had 620,000 men, 1,300 tanks, 10,000 guns and mortars and 926 planes. Although Timoshenko did not get all the reinforcements he had asked for, with three Russian armies in the Iz'yum bulge, south of Khar'kov, and three due east of it, those estimates were about right.[9] Shaposhnikov, meanwhile, disliked the idea of attacking out of a 'sack' – the Iz'yum salient.[10]

On 10 April Timoshenko and his staff presented the plan for defeating German forces in the Khar'kov region. It was not only to 'secure' the region, but 'by a subsequent attack in the direction of Dnepropetrovsk and Sinel'kinovo station', to 'deprive the enemy of important crossing sites over the Dnepr'.[11] Those sites were, at least, 200 kilometres further south-west of Khar'kov. Timoshenko planned to seize Khar'kov by envelopment and then use that as a launch pad towards the Dnepr river.

Another Russian disaster: Khar'kov, 11–29 May 1942

The overambitious Russian attack to seize Khar'kov, as a jumping-off point to regain the Don, began after an hour's artillery and air attack on 12 May 1942 (see Figure 15.2). The southern wing of the attack, out of the 'sack', was the larger: the northern wing launched a smaller attack out of a much shallower bulge south of Volchansk. In the first three days the Russians penetrated nearly 50 kilometres. Meanwhile, however, on 25 March, Army Group South had issued the Directive for Operation Fridericus, a 'defensive pincer' movement, like the one which would cut off Vlasov south-east of Leningrad. There were two variants: Fridericus

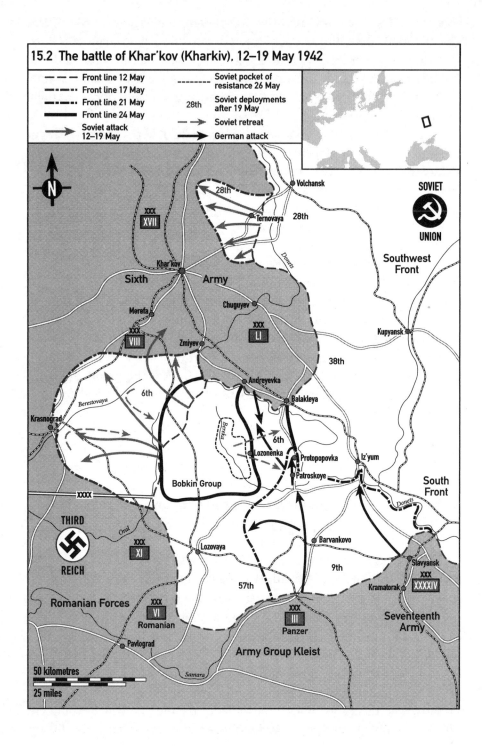

15.2 The battle of Khar'kov (Kharkiv), 12–19 May 1942

Legend:
- Front line 12 May
- Front line 17 May
- Front line 21 May
- Front line 24 May
- Soviet attack 12–19 May
- Soviet pocket of resistance 26 May
- 28th Soviet deployments after 19 May
- Soviet retreat
- German attack

SOVIET UNION

Southwest Front

Volchansk
28th
Ternovaya
28th

Khar'kov
Sixth   Army
Merefa
Chuguyev
Zmiyev
XXX
VIII
XXX
LI
38th
Kupyansk
Andreyevka
Berestovaya
6th
Balakleya
Krasnograd
Bereka
6th
Lozonenka
Protopopovka
Iz'yum
Patroskoye
South Front
Donets
Bobkin Group
XXXX
THIRD
REICH
Oral
XXX
XI
Lozovaya
Barvankovo
Slavyansk
XXXX
XXXXIV
9th
Kramatorak
57th
Romanian Forces
XXX
VI
Romanian
XXX
III
Panzer
Seventeenth Army
Pavlograd
Army Group Kleist
Samara

50 kilometres

25 miles

I and II. Both involved German attacks from the north-west and south-east to cut the salient off. Eliminating the 'bulge' was essential to regain freedom of manoeuvre to implement *Blau*. Fridericus I was a shallower encirclement, west of the Donets, to trap the Russians in the area of Lozovaya and Barvenkovo: Fridericus II was a bigger one, with the main effort east of the Donets, aiming to capture Izyum as quickly as possible. Bock argued for the 'lesser' solution, but OKH favoured Fridericus II. In the event, the Russians forced the Germans' hand, and Fridericus I was implemented.[12] The Russians had noticed German forces concentrating around Khar'kov, but not those south of the salient. Khar'kov itself was held by Paulus's Sixth Army, which would later become used to Soviet encirclements. The German forces to the south belonged to Seventeenth Army.

Even in spite of the Germans' excellent intelligence, the scale and scope of the Russian attack took them by surprise. Nevertheless, in accordance with Operation Fridericus, but with some desperation, on 17 May 1942, having weathered the Russian attack for five days, Kleist, commanding his own Army Group in the south of the theatre, attacked into the south of the Iz'yum bulge.

Meanwhile Timoshenko delayed committing his armoured reserve, XXI Tank Corps, on 14 May, because of bad intelligence. His intelligence people told him there was a big concentration of German armour at Zmiyev, which could slam into his right flank. That was wrong. Then, when the Germans attacked on 17 May, Stalin refused to break off the offensive to defend his three armies' lines of supply against the well-prepared German 'defensive pincers', and the Russians were cut off. By 19 May the forward Russian elements had been only 20 kilometres from Khar'kov.[13] On 23 May, however, Army Group Kleist and Paulus's Sixth Army, part of Army Group South, met south of Bakleya.

It was another catastrophic encirclement, 1941 style. When this 'battle of annihilation' ended two days later, only 22,000 Russians managed to make it out, eastwards, back to the northern bank of the Northern Donets, whence they had come. The Red Army had lost parts of four armies: 22 rifle divisions, 7 cavalry divisions and 15 tank brigades, 540 aircraft, 1,200 tanks and 2,000 guns. An estimated 240,000 were taken prisoner, and more than a quarter of a million lost altogether.[14] A number of generals were killed and Gorodnyanskiy, commanding Sixth Army, committed suicide rather than be captured. On a number of the Soviet gun positions the Germans found all the artillery officers dead. Again, they had shot themselves rather than face capture.

Kleist, a highly experienced commander, wrote:

> the battlefield testifies to the fierceness of the fighting: at the focal points the ground, as far as the eye can see, is so thickly covered with the cadavers of men and horses that it is difficult to find a passage through for one's command car.[15]

History, he wrote to his brother, 'probably never witnessed such a battlefield'.[16] Again, the odds were not good for the Russians, although 20,000 Germans from Sixth Army alone were killed and wounded. Having annihilated the Iz'yum bulge, the Germans then switched their attention to the shallower Volchansk salient, on 10 June. Although the operation was another German success, and provided a jumping-off point for Operation *Blau*, this time the Russians managed to extract most of their soldiers. Only 21,000 were captured.[17]

For the Russians, Khar'kov was another disaster on a stupendous scale. After the resilience they had shown in recovering from the German invasion in the winter of 1941–2, the catastrophe which met by far the most ambitious of German counter-attacks of early to mid 1942, at Khar'kov, was a huge political blow to the Soviet Union. Zhukov noted the January 1942 declaration by twenty-six countries that they would conclude no separate peace with the Axis powers and would combine all their strength against them. Although the Soviet Union would subsequently be severely disappointed, as we saw in the last chapter, in early 1942 the prospect of a second front in Europe that year appeared quite real.[18] Coming after a tide of Soviet optimism, Khar'kov was a huge blow, and like many 'dislocations of expectation', perhaps appeared worse than it really was. Compared with 1941, the loss of a quarter of a million soldiers might not seem so bad. But it came at a time of optimism, renewed confidence and hope, so the Khar'kov offensive and the formidably professional German response struck home to the Soviet leadership. Stalin, Stavka and the senior military command became much more realistic and cautious as a result. Finally, Khar'kov had obvious international political repercussions. The western Allies, as seen in Chapter 14, had been reassured by Soviet resilience during the winter. After another Soviet calamity, there was renewed impetus to accelerate the implementation of the second front.

On 22 June 1942 – exactly a year after Barbarossa – the Germans continued their attack with Fridericus II, cutting more deeply into Soviet-held territory, as far as the River Oskol. But this time, the German success owed a lot to the Russians pulling back to avoid another disastrous encirclement on the scale of Khar'kov, and Hitler's stated aim of trapping and destroying 'the vital striking force of the enemy' was not achieved. Bock warned OKH that this sudden and unexpected willingness of the Russians to withdraw might be 'intended also on the larger scale not to expose [themselves] to a decisive defeat at the moment, in order to gain time for the intervention of the Americans'. He was right. Gehlen's *Fremde Heere Ost* Department warned on 28 June that the Red Army was turning away from the 'tactic of an uneconomical ruthless employment of men and material'. In future the Red Army could be expected to 'withdraw most of its forces at the front from German surprise thrusts and attempts at encirclement, and to contain the German advances from the depth of its territory by attacks against the German flanks'.[19] Times were changing, but the warning was not heeded.

The Crimea and German recovery of the Kerch' peninsula

The battles in the Crimea in early 1942 were among the most savage of the war, with many unique characteristics. Historically, the Crimea had been the key to dominance of the Black Sea.[20] Sevastopol was the base for the Black Sea fleet, still the most formidable of the three Russian fleets. In Russian hands the peninsula constantly threatened any eastward German advance bypassing it to the north, and the Crimea was essential as a base and staging post for any further German advance into the Caucasus. Hitler saw the Crimea as 'the German Gibraltar' and 'the German south'. Like British-held Gibraltar and, perhaps, later, parts of the British-populated Costa del Sol, the Crimea would become a disembodied part of Germany which, for military and political reasons, could not establish a 'Gibraltar' or 'Costa' on the Mediterranean coast. Renamed '*Gau Gotenland*' – 'Goth land' – it would be linked to the heartland of the Reich by an autobahn and cleansed of its native population who would be replaced by 'pure Germans'. However, although the Germans expelled the Russians from eastern Crimea and finally captured Sevastopol after a 250-day siege on 4 July 1942, the more grandiose plans for *Lebensraum* in the sun worked out by Himmler and others had to be shelved until after the war, and therefore, thankfully, forever.[21]

Even before the Iz'yum bulge collapsed, the Germans launched a new attack to dislodge the Russians from the Kerch' peninsula. The Eleventh Army in the Crimea was commanded by General Erich von Manstein, who had taken command in October 1941 after his predecessor General von Schobert was killed when his plane crash-landed, carelessly, in a Russian minefield. From January to the end of April the Red Army had regained the initiative, and Manstein was too weak to contain Sevastopol and retake the Kerch' peninsula. In order to support the attack on the Kerch' peninsula Hitler ordered the Luftwaffe to massively reinforce the Crimea, at the expense of everywhere else in Army Group South. Goering privately admitted that the Luftwaffe was so stretched that it 'was no longer sufficient for the great tasks'.[22]

The German Operation Bustard (*Trappen*) was originally fixed for 5 May but postponed until the 8th. At its narrowest point, the isthmus leading to the Kerch' peninsula was a mere 19 kilometres wide – so there was no 'room for manoeuvre' and the Germans had to attack frontally. Having postponed the attack from 5 to 8 May because of the weather, they did, and they won. The Germans encircled Soviet troops on the northern wing of the Kerch' peninsula. Manstein was very skilful: the Russians, in the Crimea, were not. In 'a nightmare of confusion and incompetence',[23] the Russians fell back, defeated by a numerically inferior enemy. On 10 May, Stalin ordered Soviet troops to retire back to the 'Turkish wall' across the peninsula. On 15 May, Halder noted 'the Kerch' offensive may be considered closed'. Russians sources say it ended on 18 May and fighting in the area finally came to an end on 21 May, six days after Halder's note. Of the Soviet forces trapped on the peninsula, 170,000, according to German records, went into captivity.[24] Some 7,558 Germans were killed in action, while 120,000 Russians – according to Soviet records – escaped across the Kerch' strait to the Taman peninsula on the other side. The Germans also claimed to have taken 258 tanks and more than 1,100 guns.[25] The pictures taken in 1942 of Soviet prisoners tramping westwards, hands up, mirror those of Iraqis in the 1991 and 2003 wars (see Plate 15). Lt Gen. Kozlov, the commander of the Front responsible for the Kerch' peninsula, was reprimanded by his political commissar, Army Commissar Lev Mekhlis, who was technically superior in rank. But Stalin was unimpressed and replied sarcastically that Mekhlis should not have blamed Kozlov, but taken responsibility himself.[26] Times were changing here too.

Khar'kov and Kerch' in perspective

The Russian defence of the Kerch' peninsula and the Battle of Khar'kov were probably the most stupendously costly front operations the Russians ever engaged in. It all depends, of course, on how you measure it. They were the most costly locally, and in terms of losses per day, rather than over a longer period. In the first two weeks of the war, in June–July 1941, the Western Front had suffered 23,207 losses a day in the face of the German onslaught. In western Ukraine, in the same period, the South-Western and Southern Fronts had taken 16,106 losses per day. But these were operations over a much bigger area, involving bigger groups of forces. By comparison, in the Kerch' defensive operation from 8 to 9 May 1942, the Russians lost 14,714 people a day, and in the Battle of Khar'kov, from 12 to 29 May, 15,399 per day. Overall, however, we are looking at 177,000 lost on the Kerch' peninsula and 277,000 at Khar'kov. These compare with 418,000 for the Western Front in the first two weeks of the war and 242,000 for the two fronts in western Ukraine. By comparison, again, the daily loss in the defensive phase at Stalingrad between July and November 1942 would be just 5,151 and in the offensive phase, from November 1942 to February 1943, 6,392. And even at Moscow the daily losses were fewer – although, again, much greater forces were involved overall. The defensive phase cost the Russians 9,825 losses a day, although across four fronts and over more than two months, while the counteroffensive cost 10,910 a day from four fronts, again, over about a month.[27]

You could therefore argue that Kerch' and Khar'kov in early summer 1942 were the hardest, most intense hits the Russians ever took. It was about to change.

'Magnificent city': Sevastopol

By 16 November 1941 the Germans had isolated Sevastopol. When Suvorov took the Crimea from the Turks in the eighteenth century, using his famous *glazomer* – '*coup d'oeil*', he had instantly seen the bay where the fortress harbour dominating the Black Sea would be sited, as a perfect naval base. It was immediately named after the Greek: *sevastos* – 'magnificent' – *polis* – 'city'. It is now in Ukraine, because Khrushchev transferred the Crimea to the Ukrainian SSR when the borders within the Soviet Union did not much matter. Today, once again, Sevastopol is a particularly neat city, showing all the influence of naval discipline, with a pleasant climate, and popular with tourists. But in its short history it endured two terrible sieges. The British and French had had a hard time taking the key base from the Russians in 1855,[28] and in 1941–2 the Red Army and navy gave the German Eleventh and the Romanian Third Armies an even harder time. The fortress was surrounded by three main lines of fortification: an outer ring of entrenchments and dugouts, and a second ring of massive underground forts and gun batteries in armoured emplacements buried in concrete and rock. The third ring comprised pillboxes – the usual concrete 'DOTs', ringing the city centre itself. Its defences are mapped in Figure 15.3. When the defence of Sevastopol officially began on 30 October 1941 there were just 52,000 defenders.[29] With troops who had escaped the Germans and fallen back into the Sevastopol fortress complex, the strength of the defending force rapidly rose to 106,000. And then there were the civilians. They had 600 guns, including fortress guns in armoured turrets, but only a few dozen tanks and just over 50 aircraft. However, the garrison was not completely cut off as the Soviet navy retained supremacy in the Black Sea and the German and Italian naval units could do little to interdict those communications. The Germans had air supremacy, which made things dangerous for Soviet surface vessels, but they got round the problem by using submarines to reinforce the largely subterranean, labyrinthine defences of the most powerful fortress on earth.[30]

After breaking into the Crimea, the Axis forces began to bombard

Sevastopol on 17 December 1942, but the Russians decided to try to relieve the city with a huge amphibious assault to the east, the attack on the Kerch' peninsula on 25 December. Soviet forces remained locked in Sevastopol, however, although there was only one German corps and one Romanian division to contain them. Having recaptured Kerch' itself on 18 May, the German Eleventh Army renewed its efforts to take the fortress, which was still obstinately holding on the Russian left flank of an 1,800-kilometre Baltic to Black Sea front.[31]

With the Kerch' peninsula recaptured by 15 May 1942, the Germans and their Romanian allies could swing back to deal with Sevastopol. It was believed to be the strongest fortress in the world. Manstein concentrated most of Eleventh Army's formations – seven-and-a-half German and one-and-a-half Romanian divisions – round the 35-kilometre land perimeter running from 10 kilometres north of the city centre, round to Balaklava.[32]

The Germans codenamed their operation Störfang – 'Sturgeon Catch', a reference to the capture of the fish which provides caviare. Once again, the eastern front produced its world-record-breaking superlatives. While VIII Air Corps supplied extra planes, 600 artillery pieces with six times the normal ammunition supply were sent to Sevastopol, including two huge guns: the 600mm 'Thor' and the 800mm 'Dora'. The latter was the biggest mobile gun ever built. It had been tested at the Rugenwalde range in Hitler's presence. The Iraqi 'supergun' discovered in 1990 was bigger, but that was designed to be buried on a mountainside.[33] 'Big Dora' was officially known as 'Gustav-ordnance' (*Gustav-Gerät*), but the German soldiers irreverently renamed it, as soldiers do. It was mounted on a railway carriage with eighty wheels which straddled two parallel railway lines to carry its 1,350-ton overall weight. To move it, sixty locomotives were needed. It could fire a 7-ton armour- or concrete-piercing shell 38 kilometres or a 5-ton high-explosive shell to a maximum range of 54 kilometres. The only record of its being used in anger was at the siege of Sevastopol, although there would not have been much time to do so before Sevastopol fell in June 1942. To emplace, man, maintain and provide local security for this monster – which would have been a wonderful target for air attack – some 4,120 men were required, who worked for five weeks, as new rail track had to be laid. They were commanded by a major-general. This added up to half a division. A mere 250 to 500 men, commanded by a colonel, were needed actually to fire it.

The massive gun on double railway tracks was reportedly sited at Bakhchisaray, in central Crimea, and fired 30 to 40 rounds at Sevastopol. One of these rounds reportedly penetrated 30 metres of earth to destroy an underground Soviet ammunition bunker at Severnaya Bay. Its eventual fate is unknown but it was presumably captured by the Red Army.[34] Although intriguing for the record books, superguns like this were an evolutionary dead end. It was already perfectly possible to put a 5-ton bomb in a plane and to fly it a lot further than the comparatively limited range of the world's biggest gun, although improved ammunition designs could, theoretically, have enabled it to fire up to perhaps 160 kilometres. Furthermore, had the Russians enjoyed air supremacy at this stage, the 1,350-ton leviathan would have become an equivalent volume of scrap metal even sooner than it did. On the other hand, once the gun's projectile was airborne nothing could stop it, and its 5- or 7-ton shells may have enjoyed greater penetrating power against underground targets than an air bomb. Hitler, whose passion for the grandiose is well known, was enthusiastic about the monster. Halder, on the other hand, was sceptical. 'An extraordinary piece of engineering', he wrote in his diary on 7 December 1941, 'but useless.'[35]

The attack on Sevastopol proper began on 2 June with five days of air and artillery strikes intended to destroy Russian artillery positions and erase the outer defences, and to shatter the defenders' morale. Even after five days' bombardment, however, Eleventh Army reported that the advancing infantry found the enemy 'tougher than expected'.

Eventually, on 17 June, the German LIV Corps broke through the outer defence line in the north and captured most of the terrain north of Severnaya Bay. This gave Manstein a problem. The second line of defence surrounded an area to the south, so to repeat the strategy of blasting it to pieces would have meant transferring artillery infantry to the south over very difficult, hilly terrain with goat tracks as the main means of communication. Then he had a brainwave. His troops would attack across Severnaya Bay with no preparation, and take the second line of defences along the Sapun Heights from behind. On the night of 28 to 29 June XXX Corps feigned an attack with the biggest unreinforced artillery and air strike it could manage, while troops in a hundred assault boats stormed across the bay and then swarmed up the steep shore on the other side. The Russians were completely taken by surprise.

At this point the battle should have been nearly over, but the Russians' annoying habit of not realizing they were beaten once again came into play. On the night of 30 June 1942 many of the commanders, senior party officials and key combatants were evacuated by submarine. Those who remained – soldiers, sailors and naval infantry (marines) and civilians, including many women – fought on from the labyrinth. Having suffered enormous casualties and expended inordinate amounts of ammunition, the Germans resorted to desperate measures to subjugate the Russians still fighting from caves and bunkers underground.

'Weapons of mass destruction': chemical

Faced with the Russian resistance, the Germans used toxic smoke to try to clear them out of the caverns below Sevastopol – one of the few times that chemical weapons were used in the Second World War and a breach of the 1925 Protocol.[36] Given the circumstances, these were probably 'non-persistent agents' – quick-acting gases whose effect would diminish very quickly. These were clearly ideal conditions for using chemical weapons, and there were other instances of the Germans using asphyxiating gas in similar circumstances. They reportedly used them against the Odessa catacombs – another naval base, when they captured it in November 1941, and at the end of May 1942, in the recapture of the Kerch' peninsula, against fighters in Adzhimushkay quarry outside the city of Kerch'.[37]

The use of chemical weapons appears to have been most widespread round the Black Sea coast, simply because the caves and catacombs of that coastline made it expedient. However, on 11 July 1942, just after the last Soviet resistance in Sevastopol ceased, an NKVD agent reported that Manstein was in Berlin with General Schultz for discussions with Nazi party officials in which Schultz emphasized that 'the losses suffered by the German Army at Sevastopol would have been halved if the Army command had given permission to use chemical weapons'. Given that they were used in the final stages, the Germans presumably meant 'use more widely'. The Germans enjoyed a superiority in chemical weapons and Manstein had also advocated their use on several occasions, as had Halder. The ban – or severe limitation – on their use was purely down to political considerations. Halder had apparently told the Nazi Ministry of Information that the use of chemical weapons was the most 'humane' form of war as the losses from gas would actually be 'unexpectedly small'.[38]

However, reports of the Germans using chemical weapons coincided with the first reports of the Russians doing the same, though this time – it is generally agreed – in error. Because chemical weapons were not widely used in the Second World War, the high awareness of a 'chemical threat' among the fighting troops – every single one carried a gas mask – has been overlooked in accounts and, of course, in the movies. All the troops attacking on D-Day carried respirators and were fully trained for, and half expecting, chemical attack.[39] The German troops attacking Russia in June 1941 were briefed about the Russian emphasis on chemical warfare, and told that if the Russians resorted to it, then the Germans would retaliate in kind – and better.[40]

There were five cases where the Germans alleged that the Russians used chemical weapons up to 1 August 1941. Four of them were dismissed, after it was established that they probably resulted from smoke from ordinary high explosive shells or the combustion of burning tanks. The fifth report was more serious, involving the alleged dropping of twenty-five aerial bombs filled with lewisite – a persistent chemical agent. Although fourteen men of the German Eleventh Army head-quarters – coincidentally the army which took Sevastopol in 1942 – were injured, tests ruled out lewisite and suggested that the bombs were training weapons containing a minor skin irritant which had been dropped in error. The Germans, punctilious as ever, ruled out a deliberate chemical attack and 'no further steps were taken by the German high command'.[41]

Another report of December 1941 suggested the Russians were using a chemical agent that caused vomiting. Again, this proved to be wrong: it was a side effect of the smoke of large-calibre high explosive rounds.[42]

The most serious potential violation of the 1925 Protocol, which had the potential to generate a downward spiral into chemical warfare, was reported on 6 June 1942, at Sevastopol. A captured Russian officer of 54th Gas Battalion, who was being held in the German PoW camp outside the besieged city (which was going to be attacked in earnest the next day), told his German captors that in the first half of April he had fired three lewisite shells from 120mm mortars at Martynevskaya Balka, near Severnaya Bay, north-eastwards towards German troops who were holding a dairy farm. The mortar bombs were marked with two red bands round the middle – lewisite. One red band meant mustard gas, another persistent agent; and three red bands, a mustard and lewisite mix.[43] They came in boxes of two, he said, and there were fifty boxes on the position. Possibly faced with a shortage of ammunition, soldiers sent to collect it might bring up anything that was available, not necessarily recognizing the stripes indicating what they were, and officers might, not unreasonably, fire it. The Russian officer said that the Red Army had immediately launched an investigation, sending the Chief of the Corps Ammunition Service, an artificer and an artillery technician. Although the Germans could have made much out of this reported incident, they did not. The German command 'refused to take any steps whatever, evidently being convinced that there was no *planned* and *premeditated* use of war gases'.[44]

What is striking is the extreme care taken by the Red Army, in the midst of one of the bloodiest campaigns in the world's worst war, to verify the details of what happened in this alleged breach of the laws of warfare, and, correspondingly, the legalistic care the Germans took not to convict until proven guilty. Whatever the horrors of the war, the military machines on both sides were behaving very professionally. That should not be surprising, but it is, nonetheless, perhaps oddly reassuring.

Another potential incident occurred in 1944, when Russian partisans blew up a German ammunition dump which produced irritation to people's throats and noses. Analysis showed a high arsine content, but this would be consistent with the incineration of candles designed to produce smoke. Again there was no evidence of 'war gases' that had been planned and ordered by the Russian command. As far as the Germans were concerned, then, the Soviet forces made 'no *planned* and *premeditated* use of war gases during the whole Russian campaign'.[45]

No mere city . . .

The Russian defenders carried on fighting in the vicinity of the Maksim Gor'kiy II fortifications, among the most formidable of all the defensive works, on the Khersones peninsula, until 5 July 1942. The last of them carried on their fatal struggle in the caves on the same outcrop, to the west of the city, until 9 July. They hoped to be evacuated, but mostly hoped in vain. Of Maksim Gor'kiy II's garrison of 1,000, only 50 men were taken prisoner. All were wounded. According to a German Luftwaffe captain serving with a Stuka formation,

> they were bombed again and again; one explosion next to another, like poisonous mushrooms, shot up between the rocky hideouts. The whole [Khersones] peninsula was fire and smoke – yet in the end thousands of prisoners were taken, even there. One can only stand amazed at such resilience – it is unbelievable in the truest sense of the word. That is how they defended Sevastopol all along the line and the whole time, and that is why it was a very tough nut. The whole country had to be literally ploughed over by bombs before they yielded a short distance.[46]

The Germans had taken Sevastopol after a total of nine-and-a-half months. Its fall was almost simultaneous with that of the British fortress of Tobruk, in Cyrenaica (Libya), which fell to the Germans on 21 June 1942. At Sevastopol, in the final battle from 2 June until 9 July 1942, the Red Army, navy and air force had lost tens of thousands killed and 95,000 taken prisoner. The Russian records for the Sevastopol defended area for the entire period from 30 December 1941 to 4 July 1942 give 156,800 'irrecoverable losses', plus 53,601 sick and wounded – a total of 200,000. However, the latter covers a period of eight months, whereas the Germans were just talking about the last month. Interestingly, however, the Russians' *average* daily losses over the longer period were a little over 800 – far fewer than in the catastrophic battles in the open field.[47] Fortresses had always been good ways of tying down large enemy forces for relatively small losses. That has always been their function.

The German Eleventh Army's war diary for 4 July 1942 recorded that 'The City of Sevastopol is a heap of rubble.' In this heap of rubble one-sixth of the city's pre-siege population of 200,000 survived. Hitler ordered that at the end of the war Sevastopol would become a completely German city and would be the main base for the German fleet in the Black Sea. Until then, any reconstruction was limited to what the German navy needed.

The defence of Sevastopol, however, had tied down an entire German army and stupendous resources. Nearly 25,000 Germans were killed. Eleventh Army had by far the highest casualties of any army in

Bock's command. Between 22 June 1941 and March 1942 it lost nearly 70,000 men including 2,000 officers, an average of about 10,000 per division – so that by March 1942 each division had been pretty much replaced. To maintain the besieging forces and supply them with food, medical supplies, building materials and six times the usual complement of ammunition required 135 railway wagons a day – four-and-a-half trains. During the siege, the Germans consumed 50,000 tonnes of ammunition – 100 trainloads. All this had to be carried down just two lines. As with the fall of Tobruk, the Germans capitalized on the fall of the great fortress after the catastrophic failure to take Moscow and months on the strategic defensive. Manstein was promoted to Field Marshal, and both the Germans and the Russians issued campaign medals: the German one for the Crimea, the Russian one specifically for the defence of Sevastopol.

The fact that Eleventh Army was tied down around Sevastopol for so long significantly weakened the rest of the German Army Group Centre's effort and delayed the start of the second phase of the main strategic operation, *Blau*, possibly with disastrous consequences for the Germans at Stalingrad. Manstein asked the 'vital question' whether it was right to commit an entire army – his – to an attack on Sevastopol in the brief window of opportunity between recapturing the Kerch' peninsula and launching phase two of *Blau*. Would it not have been enough just to mask the fortress, and keep its defenders in, rather than launching a stupendously costly and bloody attack? Given the Soviet ability to resupply Sevastopol by sea, the answer may be 'no', but given German control of the entire rest of the Crimea and air superiority, Sevastopol was not as much of a threat to the German rear as it had been.[48]

For the Germans, however, there was another worrying development. German soldiers started talking about how much they respected the Russian defenders, which Dr Goebbels, the propaganda Minister, immediately moved to stop. The Russian defence was not superhumanly brave, he said, but 'nothing other than the primitive animal instincts of Slavdom, organised into resistance by ferocious terror'.[49]

That was not how the Russians saw it. 'The Germans boasted: "we shall drink champagne on June 15 on the Grafskiy embankment",' wrote Il'ya Ehrenburg.

> But they forgot one thing. Sevastopol is not merely a city. It
> is the glory of Russia, the pride of the Soviet Union. We have

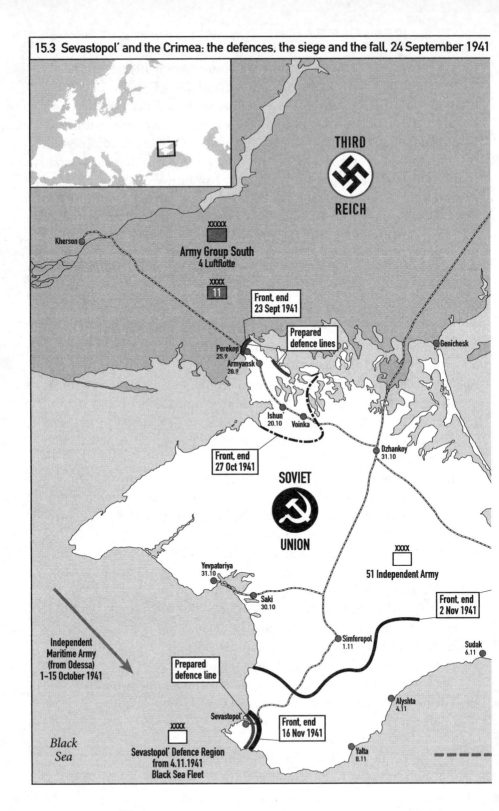

15.3 Sevastopol' and the Crimea: the defences, the siege and the fall, 24 September 1941

THIRD REICH

XXXXX
Army Group South
4 Luftflotte

XXXX
11

Kherson

Front, end
23 Sept 1941

Prepared
defence lines

Perekop
25.9

Armyansk
28.9

Genichesk

Ishun'
20.10

Voinka

Front, end
27 Oct 1941

Dzhankoy
31.10

SOVIET UNION

XXXX
51 Independent Army

Yevpatoriya
31.10

Saki
30.10

Front, end
2 Nov 1941

Independent
Maritime Army
(from Odessa)
1–15 October 1941

Simferopol
1.11

Sudak
6.11

Prepared
defence line

Alyshta
4.11

Sevastopol'

Front, end
16 Nov 1941

Black
Sea

XXXX
Sevastopol' Defence Region
from 4.11.1941
Black Sea Fleet

Yalta
8.11

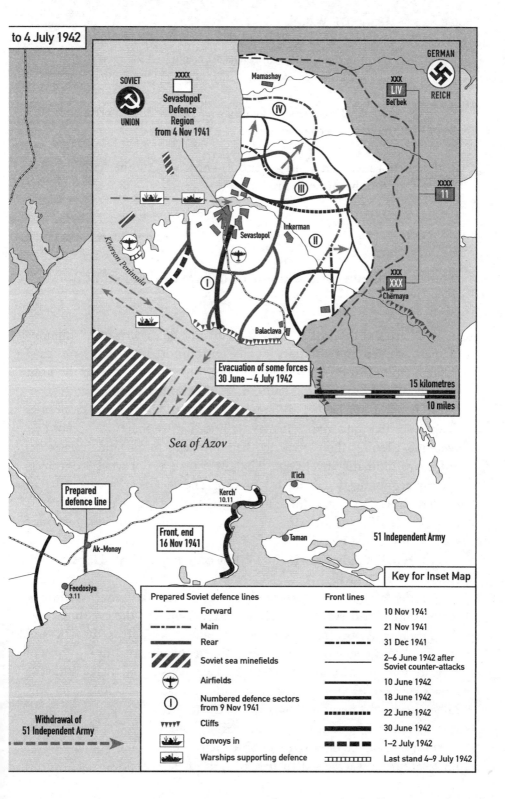

SOVIET
UNION

XXXX

Sevastopol'
Defence
Region
from 4 Nov 1941

Mamashay

GERMAN
REICH

XXX
LIV
Bel'bek

XXXX
11

IV

III

II

Inkerman

Sevastopol'

Kherson Peninsula

Chernaya

Balaclava

**Evacuation of some forces
30 June – 4 July 1942**

15 kilometres

10 miles

Sea of Azov

**Prepared
defence line**

Il'ich

Kerch'
10.11

**Front, end
16 Nov 1941**

Taman

Ak-Monay

51 Independent Army

Feodosiya
3.11

Key for Inset Map	
Prepared Soviet defence lines	**Front lines**
– – – Forward	– – – – – 10 Nov 1941
–·–·–· Main	——— 21 Nov 1941
▬▬▬ Rear	–·–·–·– 31 Dec 1941
▨▨▨ Soviet sea minefields	——— 2–6 June 1942 after Soviet counter-attacks
✈ Airfields	▬▬▬ 10 June 1942
① Numbered defence sectors from 9 Nov 1941	▬▬▬ 18 June 1942
▼▼▼ Cliffs	▪▪▪▪▪ 22 June 1942
🚢 Convoys in	▬▬▬ 30 June 1942
⛴ Warships supporting defence	▬ ▬ ▬ 1–2 July 1942
	⊥⊥⊥⊥ Last stand 4–9 July 1942

**Withdrawal of
51 Independent Army**

467

> seen the capitulation of towns, of celebrated fortresses, of
> states. But Sevastopol is not surrendering. Our soldiers do
> not play at war. They fight a life-and-death struggle. They do
> not say 'I surrender' when they see two or three more enemy
> men on the chessboard.[50]

It was not just a city, but a symbol. There was another city like that, too. And it, too, began with an 'S'.

Russia on the point of collapse – economic?

In 1942, around the world, and especially on the eastern front, millions of men, women and children fought, and hundreds of thousands died or were wounded, on both sides. On both sides they strove to the limit of their physical and moral endurance and employed stupendous ingenuity. Economists have a different take on it. 'Ultimately, economics determines the outcome.'[51] It may well do. Do we therefore accept that everyone pushing themselves to their physical, moral and intellectual limits was ultimately irrelevant? That, of course, is not what economists – even economic determinists – mean. The fact is, however, that in modern interstate wars, the countries with the biggest gross domestic product (GDP) tend to win in the end – assuming, always, that they survive in the first place.

The GDP ratios drawn up by the economist Mark Harrison are shown in Table 15.1.

On the face of it, the Axis powers did not stand a chance of winning the Second World War – at least, with hindsight. On the eve of the war the Molotov–Ribbentrop Pact was announced. Whereas the UK and France had enjoyed superior GDP to Germany and Austria – a ratio of 1.25 to 1 – the Molotov–Ribbentrop Pact neutralized that. With the Soviet Union effectively cooperating with Germany – certainly economically – the ratio became 0.64 to 1, and the Allies thought they might lose. When Italy joined the war and France fell, the UK alone faced an unenviable balance of 0.51 to 1, which fell to 0.38 when France's GDP, now captured, was added to that of the other Axis powers. However,

Table 15.1 – GDP ratios between the combatants, 1941–5

	GDP in 1990 prices (billions of dollars)							
	1938	*1939*	*1940*	*1941*	*1942*	*1943*	*1944*	*1945*
USA	800	869	943	1094	1235	1399	1499	1474
UK	284	287	316	344	353	361	346	331
France	186	199	164*	130	116	110	93	101
Italy	141	151	147	144	145	137	117	92
USSR	*359*	*366*	*417*	*359*	*274*	*305*	*362*	*343*
Germany	*351*	*384*	*387*	*412*	*417*	*426*	*437*	*310*
Austria	24	27	27	29	27	28	29	12
Japan	169	184	192	196	197	194	189	144
	GDP ratio							
	1938	*1939*	*1940*	*1941*	*1942*	*1943*	*1944*	*1945*
Allied/Axis	2.4	2.3	2.1	2.0	2.1	2.3	3.1	5.0
USSR/Germany	*1.0*	*1.0*	*1.1*	*0.9*	*0.7*	*0.7*	*0.8*	*1.1*

Source: Harrison, Table 1, 'The USSR and total war: why didn't the Soviet economy collapse in 1942?' Adapted (emphasis added) by the author.[52]
* France's GDP for 1940 is allocated half to the Allies, half to the Axis.

although technically neutral, the US was already helping Britain. When Germany attacked Russia the balance suddenly shifted back to 1.31 to 1 in the Allies' favour. Two major powers still remained neutral: the United States and Japan. Japan's entry to the war on the Axis side was inadequate to counterbalance the entry of the United States and from December 1941 the Allied–Axis ratio of GDP became 1.83 to 1. From this perspective, after the United States joined the war on 7 December 1941 and the Russians counter-attacked at Moscow, (starting in earnest the same day), the Allies were bound to win.

The figures do reflect the reality of the war to an extraordinary extent. In 1940, the Soviet Union was prospering, relatively speaking, with a greater GDP than Germany or the United Kingdom, whose GDP had increased substantially since the outbreak of war ended the Depression. In 1941 the same thing happened to the United States. Just six months of war shattered the Soviet Union's GDP in 1941, however, and in 1942 – the worst year, as this chapter makes clear – it plummeted to a mere 70 per cent of Germany's. In 1943 it recovered very slightly, but not enough to offset an increase in Germany's, and it did not exceed Germany's until 1945.

However, it was not quite that simple. The initial success of the Axis powers – certainly of Germany and Japan – can only be explained by the superior professional quality of their armed forces and, at least initially, the rapid decision-making advantages of their totalitarian leadership. As Mark Harrison has explained, absolutely rightly, 1942 was the best year for the Axis powers. If they could not win then, they never could. Soviet GDP had been greater than Germany's in 1940 but in 1941 vast Soviet resources, especially in Belarus, Ukraine and western Russia, fell into German hands, significantly shifting the advantage towards the Germans and their allies. In 1942 and 1943, Russian GDP was about 70 per cent of Germany's. In 1944 it rose to 80 per cent. In spite of that, however, and despite catastrophic losses, the Russians managed to maintain more troops in the field than Germany and to produce more weapons. The role of Allied aid in all this, as we saw in the last chapter, was certainly significant, but not overwhelming.

By all the normal rules, the Soviet economy should have collapsed in 1942. The weaker economies of Italy and Japan collapsed when they were attacked by stronger opponents. The Soviet Union's did not. The reasons why not go back to the preparations for war which are explored in Chapter 2. Even before the war, the USSR was relatively poor and the burden of rearmament in 1940 was much greater than it was for Germany, Britain or the United States. With the German attack, household consumption fell to 40 per cent below the pre-war level, which had been pretty low anyway. In 1942, as war production and the diversion of labour struggled to keep up with catastrophic losses of men and materiel, the civilian infrastructure fell away, and many civilians starved or froze to death. In these circumstances, society breaks into two sorts of people. Harrison calls them 'mice' – hard-working honest people who do their duty, and 'rats', who look after themselves. At first, a few rats make off with the richest pickings, and that is normal in war – the 'black market' phenomenon which attracted so much concern and official condemnation in Britain and the United States.[53] On a small scale, it may not do excessive harm, but as the number of rats increases and that of the productive mice diminishes, there is less to steal. When the returns to rats and mice reach equilibrium again, the state is close to collapse.

Hitler and the Soviet government between them stopped this happening. The Soviet government made it absolutely clear that any potential collaboration with the Germans was punishable by death. The Moscow 'panic' of October 1941 offers the clearest example. With the Germans close, and people believing, wrongly, that Stalin had left the city, there was some rioting and looting. But the NKVD was able to counter such 'panic' and suppress information about what was happening very effectively. Controls over the movement of people within the country, and especially evacuees, helped. Stalin's order No. 270 of 6 August 1941 which made it a 'betrayal of the Motherland' to be captured, and punished the families of those taken prisoner,[54] and the 'not a step back' order No. 227 of 28 July 1942 were also very effective at deterring the 'rats'.[55]

> It is time to stop withdrawing. Not a step back! [*Ni shagu nazad!*] That must now be our main clarion call. It is vital to defend every position, every metre of Soviet territory, to the last drop of blood, to cling to every sod of Soviet soil and to save it to the very limit of what is possible.[56]

Ironically, by this time, the Red Army was starting to conduct clever tactical withdrawals to prevent catastrophic encirclements like those experienced at Vyaz'ma-Bryansk and Khar'kov. The implementation of the order, which also confirmed the formation of punishment battalions and blocking detachments (see below), depended very much on who was giving the orders, and where.

The Germans' attitude to the people in the occupied territories also rebounded against them. The peoples of western Ukraine, Belarus and the Baltic States welcomed the Germans as liberators in many cases. But the Germans treated them badly, and many ethnic Russians who were dispersed through those territories, in many cases as local leaders and managers, had nothing to hope for from the Germans. Some of the people, expecting the Germans to win, risked reprisals by Soviet authorities or, once they had withdrawn, the partisans. They expected the Germans to recognize their efforts and their status, possibly as new landlords including, in some cases, forged or stolen property deeds. They were in for a rude awakening.

So there was no point being a 'rat' because, if the Russian authorities didn't get you (and they were determined to do so, whether through the partisans or the NKVD after reoccupation), and the Germans won, you would still not be allowed to keep your ill-gotten gains. Both Stalin and Hitler helped eliminate the possibility of any form of 'honourable surrender' and collaboration. The very absoluteness of the war therefore helped determine its outcome.

The final key factor was western Allied aid. This perhaps accounted for only an extra 5 per cent added to Soviet resources in 1942 and 10 per cent in 1943 and 1944. But it may have been crucial. When your bank account is frozen, fifty pounds – or dollars – in cash is worth more than five hundred, or a thousand, transferred to an account you cannot use. The lease-lend supplies, while directed specifically at the military sector, must have released some resources to other sectors as well, and may have shifted the 'bottom line' – where military and civilian collapse would reinforce each other – to the other side of the survival threshold.[57]

By the economists' calculations, then, Soviet Russia should have collapsed in 1942. The Russians were at a massive disadvantage compared with Germany according to the iron law of GDP – even given that a significant, but (at least initially) not overwhelming amount of western Allied aid came to Russia. But the Russians *did* win, in circumstances where they should normally have lost. A hundred million people made individual choices, based, perhaps, on the fact that a 'mouse' might survive, but a 'rat' might well be caught, either way. As Mark Harrison puts it, 'The battle of motivations took place in the context of a balance of resources between the two sides that was indecisive.' Thus the decisions made by Stalin, Hitler, Roosevelt and Churchill all made a difference. ' "Moral, political and organizational factors" decided the outcome.'[58] So, the economists' calculations prove that the Russians were at a disadvantage in conducting a traditional, big-power war against the Germans. The cost of victory was appalling. But to win, they must have been either significantly tougher and more resilient than other peoples; or were better led, fought better and more skilfully, using an asymmetric approach; or, perhaps, all of them.

In 1933 most Soviet war industry had been concentrated in Moscow and Leningrad, with tank building in Khar'kov and shipbuilding at Nikolayev on the Black Sea. Guns and ammunition were, however, already being built at Perm and Nizhny Tagil in the Urals and facilities were under construction at Sverdlovsk and Chelyabinsk. By 1941 there were major facilities in the Donbass region, which was rapidly captured by the Germans. The loss of the Donbass also deprived Russia of coal, while the Maykop and Grozny oilfields (see Chapter 16) were threatened. Khar'kov, a major centre of tank and gun production, was lost and, later in the year, Stalingrad's production was severely diminished. The balance of resources switched temporarily to Germany's advantage. However, during the first half of 1942 1,200 enterprises evacuated from the west resumed production in the Urals and further east. In addition, 850 new factories, machine shops, mines and power stations opened up. The results of this unprecedented migration, conversion and birth of new industry are shown in Figure 15.4. The Urals, safely out of range of German bombs, became the country's main military-industrial centre, with 450 evacuated enterprises. Another 250 were evacuated to Central Asia, with Kazakhstan becoming a major production centre for non-ferrous metals, including molybdenum, tin and zinc. The German invasion had also destroyed or captured precious agricultural land and livestock. In 1942 2.8 million more hectares of land in eastern Russia came under cultivation than in 1941, although total grain production dropped from 95.5 million metric tonnes in 1940 to 29.7 million in 1942. The development of industry and agriculture had to be accompanied by frantic railway construction, even though steel for rails could not also go into guns or ammunition. In the Volga, north and east Russian areas, the length of railway track increased by 8.7 per cent in 1942. Factories and farms needed people to work them, and as just about every able-bodied man was at the front or acting in some other security or administrative capacity, women, children and the elderly were recruited and trained as skilled and semi-skilled workers.[59]

Russia on the point of collapse – military?

In the second half of 1941 Soviet Russia juddered under an attack which eliminated forces equivalent to its entire pre-war army, and caused 27.8 per cent of its total irrecoverable losses (dead and prisoners) in the war against Germany. (The losses against Japan in August–September 1945 are excluded from these figures.) But 1942 would be worse – albeit slower – than 1941. In the twelve months of 1942, rather than the six of

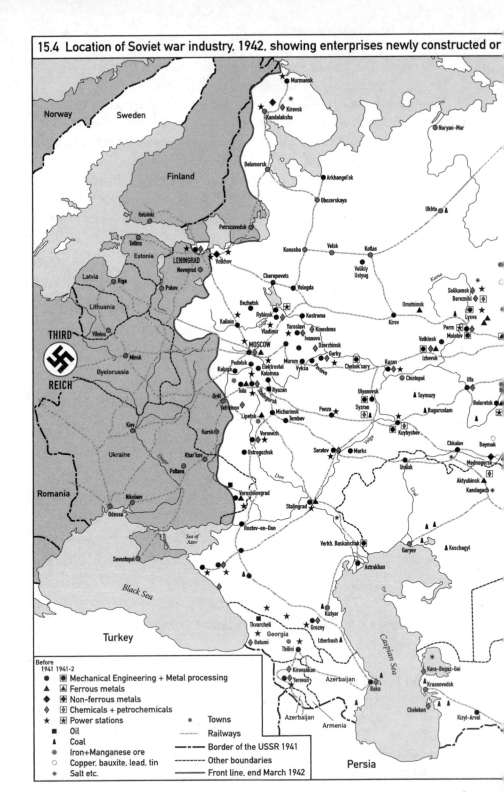

15.4 Location of Soviet war industry, 1942, showing enterprises newly constructed or

Before 1941 | 1941-2

- ● ◉ Mechanical Engineering + Metal processing
- ▲ ◮ Ferrous metals
- ◆ ◈ Non-ferrous metals
- ◆ ⊡ Chemicals + petrochemicals
- ★ ⊞ Power stations
- ■ Oil
- ▲ Coal
- ● Iron+Manganese ore
- ○ Copper, bauxite, lead, tin
- ✳ Salt etc.

- ● Towns
- ⋯ Railways
- —·—· Border of the USSR 1941
- ----- Other boundaries
- —— Front line, end March 1942

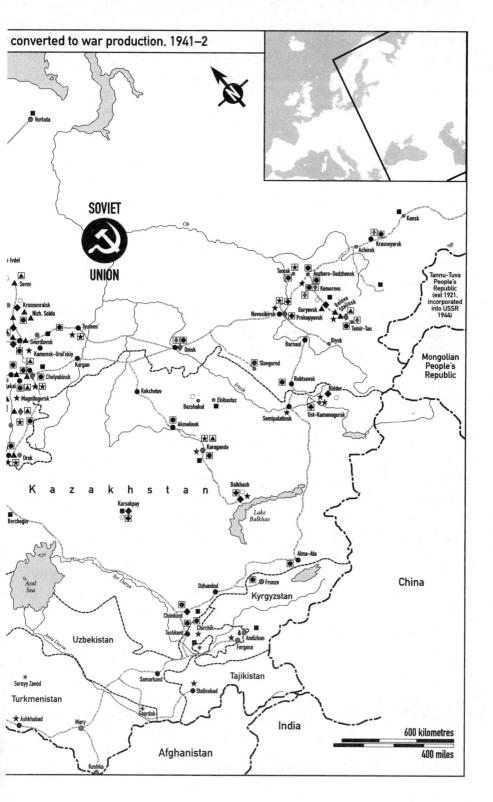

converted to war production, 1941–2

SOVIET UNION

Vorkuta

Ob

Kansk

Achinsk

Krasnoyarsk

Tannu-Tuva People's Republic (est 1921, incorporated into USSR 1944)

Ivdel

Serov

Tomsk

Anzhero-Sudzhensk

Kemerovo

Krasnonralsk

Nizh. Salda

Novosibirsk

Guryevsk

Prokopyevsk

Belovo

Stalinsk

Tyumen'

Temir-Tau

Sverdlovsk

Mongolian People's Republic

Kamensk–Ural'skiy

Kurgan

Omsk

Barnaul

Biysk

Chelyabinsk

Slavgorod

Irtysh

Rubtsovsk

Ridder

Magnitogorsk

Kokchetav

Ekibastuz

Bozshakul

Ust-Kamenogorsk

Akmolinsk

Semipalatinsk

Orsk

Karaganda

K a z a k h s t a n

Balkhash

Berchogur

Karsakpay

Lake Balkhas

Aral Sea

Syr-Darya

Alma-Ata

China

Dzhambul

Frunze

Kyrgyzstan

Chimkent

Amu Darya

Uzbekistan

Tashkent

Chirchik

Andizhan

Fergana

Samarkand

Tajikistan

Sernyy Zavod

Turkmenistan

Stalinabad

Ashkhabad

Mary

Gaurdak

India

600 kilometres

Afghanistan

400 miles

Kushka

Table 15.2 – Soviet war losses by year 1941–5

| | By year, as percentage of entire war | | | | | |
	1941*	1942	1943	1944	1945**	Total
Irrecoverable losses (a)	27.8	28.9	20.5	15.6	7.1	100
Sick and wounded (b)	7.3	22.4	30.2	27.9	12.1	100
Total (a + b ÷ 2)	17.5	25.7	25.4	21.8	9.6	100

Source: Bar chart in Krivosheyev, ed., *Soviet Casualties . . .*, p. 99, adapted by the author.
 * 22 June to 31 December 1941.
** 1 January to 9 May 1945.

1941, Russia suffered a further 28.9 per cent of her entire irrecoverable wartime losses against Germany. These can be seen in Table 15.2.

With an average strength of just over half a million, the Western Front which faced the centre of the German attack suffered more than 956,000 irrecoverable losses in the terrible second six months of 1941. That was 191 per cent of its strength, and with the sick and wounded, some of whom did come back, it lost 259 per cent of its strength. In other words, it was completely wiped out nearly twice over. The front lost 40 per cent of its strength every month. Across all fronts, during 1941, 142 per cent of Soviet personnel became casualties. In real terms, therefore, the Red Army was destroyed between one and one and a half times. In 1942, irrecoverable losses dropped to 56 per cent, but sick and wounded increased to 77 per cent. In all, then, the casualty rate was 133 per cent. So, in 1942, the Red Army suffered one and a third times its strength at the beginning of that year killed or wounded.[60] Without colossal reinforcement and 'force generation', no army can sustain that level of attrition and the country replacing the losses does so at the expense of other war-winning priorities.

'Not a step back': punishment battalions and blocking detachments

In the 28 July 1942 'not a step back' order, Stalin authorized fronts to form up to three 800-man 'punishment battalions' – *shtrafnye batal'ony*, known as *shtrafbats* – each depending on the local situation, and the availability of suitable cannon fodder. Stalin's order explained that after being forced back during the winter, the Germans restored discipline, in part, by creating more than a hundred punishment companies and about ten punishment battalions from officers, and he decided to do much the same.[61] The Soviet *shtrafbats* would be manned by former 'middle-ranking and senior commanders' – officers – and political officers at corresponding levels, who had infringed discipline by coward-ice or lack of resolution. These would be sent to the 'most difficult parts of the front, to give them the possibility to redeem their crimes against their country with their blood'. The order, like so much about the entire eastern front, was a chilling mixture of mid twentieth century and medieval, but a study of the *shtrafbats* shows that they were a very scarce – and in some ways very valuable – asset to be deployed on the orders of the front – army group – commander. The fact that all – or at least many – members of a *shtrafbat*, as it would appear from Stalin's order, were former officers, also gave them a perversely elite status. They might have fallen from grace, their missions might well be suicidal, but there were not many of them, and they would be used only on key sectors where the risks – and potential gains – for the front commander were extremely great.

At the same time, armies were to create, again depending on the circumstances, five to ten punishment companies (*shtrafroty*) made up of miscreant soldiers and 'junior commanders' (NCOs) who, like their more senior colleagues in the front-level *shtrafbats*, would also have the unenviable opportunity to 'purge their crimes in blood'.[62] The preoccu-pation with rank – even former rank – is intriguing. Front commanders sent former officers on suicide missions: army commanders sent ordi-nary soldiers and former NCOs. Of course, it made little difference to the men so condemned – or, perhaps briefly, empowered. The legal status of those condemned was confirmed by Defence Ministry orders of 28 September and 16 October.[63]

Although the *shtrafbats'* existence was officially denied in the Soviet period, it is now acknowledged, and in 2004 Russian television screened a remarkable drama-documentary film, *Shtrafbat*.[64] Between the battle episodes, the film re-creates conversations between the soldiers: where they came from, how they came to be in a *shtrafbat*, and why they were fighting for a regime they hated. The film accurately reports that there was at least one *shtrafbat* per front and 1,049 penal companies (*shtrafroty*) altogether. After Stalin's initial order to form punishment battalions at front level, however, *shtrafbats* do appear at army level as well. Thus, the Volkhov Front, which was engaged in heavy fighting near Leningrad, had a first and a second *shtrafbat*, but Second Guards Army got through *seven* of them.[65]

In the same order Stalin also instructed army commanders each to form between three and five 'well-armed blocking detachments' (*zagraditel'nye otryady*). This was very much a reinforcement of earlier orders issued by Shaposhnikov at Stavka to Yeremenko, on the Bryansk Front, and to Timoshenko's South-Western Strategic Direction, in September 1941.[66] At that stage 'blocking detachments' had been formed only within divisions. Now each army was to have three to five such detachments to be positioned in the rear of 'unreliable units', to shoot 'panic-mongers' and 'cowards', if necessary.

The partisan war

The blocking detachments were – perversely, perhaps – hand-picked Red Army personnel, and quite different from the 'destroyer battalions' which were under NKVD control but were formed mainly from civilians. The latter took responsibility for dealing with spies, saboteurs and looters in wider society, but their formation was closely linked to that of partisan detachments, and in many cases they soon became indistinguishable. When the areas in which the 'destroyer battalions' initially operated were overrun by the Germans, they often re-emerged as partisans. In Ukraine, for example, between July and September 1941,

118,000 people were formed into no fewer than 651 destroyer battalions. Between them, the NKVD's main armaments supply department, the Border Guards' supply department, the Kiev Special Military District and 'local procurement' provided more than 96,000 rifles, 1,150 sub-machine guns and 27 heavy machine guns, plus more than 43,500,000 rounds of ammunition. Most of these were foreign weapons – the rifles were German Mausers. It therefore made sense to give them to units which were not operating as part of the main Red Army effort.[67]

During 1942, the partisan groups which had formed in the vast spaces of the east after the initial German assault became far more operationally effective. On 30 May the Communist Party and the GKO formed a combined command of the partisan movement. The Central Staff of the partisan movement in Moscow exercised control through partisan movement headquarters at each front, to partisan headquarters behind German lines. The mission was clearly set out. Targets to be destroyed were physical communications – railways, bridges, rolling-stock and motor transport – telephone, telegraph and radio links, ammunition, fuel and food supply dumps, German headquarters, and airfields. In addition, the partisans were to furnish the Red Army – via the NKVD, although that was not spelled out in the order – with intelligence on German deployments, numbers and movements.[68] The front headquarters were staffed by a Communist Party official, an NKVD man and the chief of intelligence of the front equivalent organization.[69]

Hitler responded to the increase in partisan activity with Directive No. 46 of 18 August, in which he stormed:

> the bandit monstrosity in the east has assumed a scope which is no longer tolerable and has become a serious danger to supplies for the front and to the economic exploitation of the country. By the beginning of winter these bandit gangs must be substantially exterminated, so that order may be restored behind the Eastern Front and severe disadvantages to our winter operations avoided.[70]

He gave Himmler, Chief of the SS, responsibility for suppressing partisan activity. Himmler had already begun to respond, first of all (and more modern, 'democratic' governments are not immune to this) by banning the use of the word 'partisan'. He said the Russians were trying to adopt the term as a designation for a respectable branch of the armed forces – which, in the Russian view, they undoubtedly were. It was a 'propaganda swindle of the Bolshevik sub-humans'. Henceforward, 'partisan' was no longer to be used. He did not much like '*franctireur*', the phrase the Germans had picked up from invading France in 1870, either, but in his Order No. 65 of 12 August he said they were to be referred to as 'bandits' or '*francs-tireurs*'.[71]

In 1942 the partisan war – the war on the German 'inner front' – became as important as the conventional military operations, at least in Hitler's view. That is consistent both with Hitler's paranoia and with the emphasis the Russians were laying on it.[72] The fight against 'banditry', Hitler said, 'is as much a matter of strategy as the fight against the enemy at the front. It will therefore be organised and carried out by the same staffs.' However, Nazi policy was starting to sound unfeasibly reasonable. Realizing at last, perhaps, that a measure of carrot could be as valuable as the same amount of stick, Directive No. 46 recognized that:

> In the struggle against the bandits the cooperation of the
> local population is indispensable. Deserving persons should
> not be parsimoniously treated; rewards should be really
> attractive. On the other hand, reprisals for action in support
> of the bandits must be all the more severe.[73]

Himmler's involvement in the anti-partisan campaign is ironic, given that strenuous efforts had been made to exclude him from the eastern front in 1941. Nevertheless, he was now in charge and in September 1942 the Reichsführer SS and the chief of the German police jointly issued the first manual on *Bandenbekämpfung* – what would now be called counter-insurgency warfare.[74] It opened with a quotation from Stalin's July 1941 speech calling for a guerrilla war, and then detailed measures for dealing with the 'bandits'. It stressed the need to distinguish between partisan (sorry – 'bandit') – groups and regular Soviet forces and also between organized 'bandit' groups and individual opportunists. Himmler subsequently measured his success through body counts – and could not understand why Stalin was prepared to sacrifice 'bandits' in such large numbers. Firstly, because the Soviet authorities' control over the partisans was, inevitably, limited, and secondly because, if they were not a proper part of the Soviet war effort (which they were, but Himmler did not admit it), then why should Stalin care, anyway?[75]

The lessons the Germans learned from their campaign mirror those of every counter-insurgency campaign since, Iraq included.

Weapons of mass destruction – nuclear

The terrible year of 1942 also saw the inception of Russia's nuclear bomb project. Russian scientists had been as active as their international peers in work on nuclear energy during the 1930s. However, as so often happens, the prophets were without honour in their own country until Beria got wind of other countries working in the area. On 4 October 1941 the NKVD reported that its agent in the United Kingdom had obtained a secret War Cabinet paper, presented on 24 September, on the potential for use of nuclear energy from uranium to achieve an explosive effect.

> Even taking into account the weight of the ballistic
> mechanism [the conventional explosive charges, shielding
> and bomb casing], a nuclear bomb will produce about a
> thousand times the explosive yield of a conventional bomb of
> the same weight . . .
>   A uranium bomb can deliver a double effect. In addition
> to the destructive effect of the shock wave, on account of the
> massive gas cloud, a huge area will be saturated with
> radioactive particles. Every living thing in the area of action
> of these particles, for a few minutes, will inevitably be
> killed.[76]

The source was most probably John Cairncross, one of the 'Cambridge Five', along with Philby, Burgess, Maclean and Blunt. Cairncross had transferred from the Foreign Office to the Treasury in 1938, and in September 1940 was made private secretary to Lord Hankey, Minister without Portfolio in Churchill's War Cabinet. Hankey had access to most secret War Cabinet papers (the British only adopted the American 'top secret' in 1945) and also chaired the Scientific Advisory Committee.[77]

Whoever passed the report to Moscow, it was a remarkable description of the effects of a nuclear explosion: flash, blast and immediate radiation. The effects of residual radiation were less well understood, and would remain so until after the first demonstrations of nuclear bombs. The prediction of a yield a thousand times greater than a conventional bomb of the same weight was pretty accurate, if slightly conservative. The biggest conventional bombs dropped in the Second World War weighed 10 tons. Little Boy, dropped on Hiroshima on 6 August 1945, weighed 8,900 pounds (just over 4 tons) and Fat Man, dropped on Nagasaki on 9 August, 10,000 pounds – closer to 5 tons. Their yield is estimated at between 10 and 12.5 kilotons and 20 kilotons, respectively – more than *two* thousand times that of a conventional bomb of the same weight.[78]

US President Harry Truman told Stalin at the Potsdam Conference in July 1945 that the United States possessed a new weapon of enormous power . Some have suggested that Stalin did not understand the impact of what he was saying. Stalin knew all about the Manhattan Project, obviously. But it is now clear that he must also have been well briefed on exactly what Truman was talking about, although, as we know, he did not always want to hear the intelligence he was given.

By early 1942 Beria was getting so much information about American, British, French and German research on nuclear weapons that he could not ignore it. In March he signed a report to Stalin, summarizing what the NKVD had learned about foreign research. They knew about British and American plans to cooperate, but, in contrast to the first NKVD report, considerably underestimated the significance of the developments.[79] British estimates of the cost of enriching uranium-235 led Beria, in bean-counting mode, to calculate that one nuclear bomb would cost £236,000 compared to 1,500 tons of TNT, to which other British reports suggested it would be equivalent, at a cost of £326,000. It was, therefore, a worthwhile investment. However, Beria had underestimated the power of the first atomic bombs by a factor of ten.

On 11 March 1942 Roosevelt enthusiastically embraced the atomic bomb project. 'I think the whole thing should be pushed ... Time is of the essence.' But America was wealthy and spared the direct hand of war. Russia, we know, was on the brink of collapse. Moscow was still on the front line, the Germans were cutting south, towards the oilfields of Asia, and the eventual Russian victory at Stalingrad was still a long way off. In April 1942, however, a Red Army colonel in charge of one of the partisan detachments charged with gathering all possible intelligence sent a captured document to Sergei Kaftanov, the

Minister of Higher Education and also chief scientific adviser to the GKO. The Ukrainian partisans had brought him a notebook taken from a dead German officer who had been sent to Ukraine to look for – uranium. Kaftanov passed it on to nuclear experts, who were sceptical, believing that nuclear fission might not be achieved for another ten to fifteen years and that there were far more important things to worry about in the midst of the war which was threatening to topple Soviet Russia.

But another physicist, Georgiy Flërov, who had been jointly nominated for the Stalin prize in 1940 with Konstantin Petrzhak for discovering spontaneous nuclear fission, had other ideas. At the start of the war he had joined the air force, but at the end of 1941 he proposed a design for a 'gun-assembly' nuclear weapon – like the American 'Little Boy' – in which two lumps of uranium would be driven together to form the critical mass necessary for a nuclear fission chain reaction to take place. He was now serving as a lieutenant, in a reconnaissance squadron at Voronezh, south of Moscow. The University at Voronezh had been evacuated but the library had been left behind. In his spare time, Flërov checked out the most recent physics journals which the University had received.

All the top American nuclear physicists had stopped publishing articles. It was blindingly obvious. Everything to do with nuclear physics had been classified. The Americans were developing an atomic bomb. Flërov threw caution to the winds, and in April he wrote to Stalin, saying that 'a revolution will occur in military hardware', and warning that 'it may take place without our participation'.

Stalin summoned Kaftanov and other experts, including Peter Kapitsa, a pupil of Ernest Rutherford, and asked their opinion. They said the work was important. Two of them said that to build the bomb would cost as much as the entire Soviet war effort – and the Soviet Union was on the verge of cracking. But Kaftanov argued in favour of the project, whatever the cost. Otherwise, the Germans might have the bomb – which is what all the intelligence told Stalin the British and Americans feared – while the Russians did not.

After some hesitation, according to Kaftanov, Stalin said: 'We should do it.'[80]

In order to do it, at minimum cost, the NKVD's excellent spy network was mobilized. Throughout the 1920s and 1930s the Russians had cleverly exploited any captured science or technology, and now the potential gains were greater than ever. On 14 June 1942 a coded message was sent to NKVD 'residents' in Berlin, London and New York ordering them to use all necessary means to obtain information on theoretical and practical aspects of nuclear bomb projects, including methods of separating uranium isotopes, other nuclear fuels – plutonium – and likely changes in British and American policy connected with development of the atomic bomb. Klaus Fuchs, a German émigré with a communist past, and a Soviet spy, had already started work on the British atom bomb project in Birmingham in May 1941.[81] On 6 October Beria reported back to Stalin that the British War Cabinet was paying enormous attention to the use of nuclear energy for military purposes because it feared the Germans might get there first. Beria said that Peter Kapitsa, at the Academy of Sciences Dmitry Skobel'tsyn, in Leningrad, and Abram Slutskin, of the Khar'kov Institute, were all working on nuclear fission.[82]

The Russians also needed someone to direct their atomic bomb project. Beria suggested Kapitsa or Abram Ioffe, an eminent Leningrad academic. But, Stalin shrewdly observed, they were both internationally renowned scientists and if they disappeared into top secret work the world would notice – just as Lieutenant Flërov had noticed the sudden disappearance of the American scientists from the peer-reviewed literature. Kaftyanov suggested Ioffe, but Ioffe said that, at 63, he was too old to act as the dynamic leader of a demanding project. Kapitsa was also approached, but was sceptical about the feasibility of the project. Attention therefore focused on two young and little-known scientists, Abram Alikhanov (39) and Igor Kurchatov (40). Alikhanov was already quite well known, and initially had the advantage, but for some reason the tall, bearded Kurchatov got the job.[83] He appears to have impressed everyone, including Molotov, with his tremendous charisma and energy, and had worked with uranium. He proved to be a great scientific leader. Once again, the Soviet Russian system, while appearing vast and anonymous, depended and pivoted to an extraordinary extent on individuals. For apparently inexplicable reasons, the right person often came through. By September 1942, the Russians had picked Kurchatov as the right man to lead and manage the building of the Red bomb.

On 15 May 1942 the first Russian rocket aircraft, the BI-1 interceptor, was also tested. Designed by V. F. Bolkhovitinov, it was, like its German equivalent, designed to climb very fast to intercept incoming bombers. The Russians did produce some jet aircraft during the war, but nowhere near as many as the Germans or even the British. Right to the end, they relied on the tried and tested piston-engined aircraft.[84] But, as with nuclear bombs, the programmes to develop weapons which would revolutionize the post-war military world were begun in the darkest hour of the war, in 1942. On 6 June Stalin saw Bolkhovitinov for fifteen minutes. He was obviously interested in all new technological developments.[85]

There were also weapons of minor or small destruction, of which there would be many. Again, 1942 was a critical year for future developments. In the Vyazma-Bryansk encirclement of October 1941 a tank commander had been badly wounded and burned. As one of nearly 144,000 sick and wounded who survived the entire Moscow defensive operation, and very lucky to have got out of the German trap, his story might seem insignificant against the much wider canvas of the war. He was evacuated to Siberia and spent six months recovering. In a system which so often sacrificed its own people so ruthlessly, the care, attention and resources which could be devoted to bringing a wounded tank commander sergeant back to health seem extraordinary. While confined to the hospital, he doodled, recalling his interest in designing gadgets and guns. In 1942 he was assigned to join the well-known designers Georgiy Degtyarev and Georgiy Shpagin, to work on new sub-machine guns – *avtomaty*. His energy and originality attracted attention. On 23 September 1942 there is an entry in Stalin's diary. At 21.30 the 'Boss' saw the former sergeant for five minutes. His name: Mikhail Kalashnikov, billed as 'constr [uctor] of small arms'. He would design the AK-47, the first in the most numerous, rugged and popular series of small arms ever made.[86]

Deadlier than the male . . .

Of all the images – and facts – of the Second World War, the presence of significant numbers of women as fighting soldiers in the Red Army is among the most striking. It is even more striking because the moment the crisis of national survival passed, women disappeared from very active roles in the Soviet and Russian armed forces. In 1945 cinema audiences were transfixed by images of the glorious Red Army's drive into Germany facilitated by women traffic control police, snapping smartly to attention, swirling balletically and directing the flow of jeeps and trucks with precise flag movements.

The large-scale employment of women in the Soviet forces in the war was a response to the gravest national emergency, and started in earnest at the end of 1941, gaining momentum in 1942. The 'Amazons' of Greek mythology had, it is true, populated the south Russian steppe, and archaeology confirms that warrior women were part of society among central Asian tribes like the Sarmatians and Scythians. The Russian Revolution was supposed to bring about a new order which would include complete equality for women. But practice lagged a long way behind such Utopian hopes. Soviet Russian society remained 'pronatalist [and] sexist', and was also suspicious of any kind of initiative.[87] But absolute war would change that – if only temporarily.

In its 1945 *Order of battle for USSR military forces*, British Intelligence estimated that between one and two million women were in active service, and that is about right, certainly at the bottom end of that scale.[88] A massive mobilization of women began in spring 1942. On 25 March GKO ordered the Defence Ministry to mobilize 100,000 young women members of Komsomol, the communist youth league, to replace Red Army male soldiers in air defence and early warning units. While some were assigned non-combat duties, others were specifically designated as anti-aircraft gunners and the order directed that the male soldiers so released should be used to fill out rifle divisions and brigades that had been withdrawn from the front. On the basis of this GKO order and another one on 23 April, more than 550,000 female Komsomol members became soldiers. It is not clear how many, if any, of these were among the 300,000 women who were called up into the air defence forces during the rest of the war, making up one-quarter of the entire strength of that arm. They mainly manned searchlights and anti-aircraft guns, but some also flew fighters. Women were also particularly prominent as members of the medical services. Some 300,000 became nurses, 300,000 medical orderlies and 500,000 medical assistants. In May 1942 GKO ordered the conscription of a further 25,000 women into the navy. Overall, the British assessment of 'one to two million' women on active service in 1944 appears fairly accurate.

Women acted as radio and telephone operators, as part of the 'road service' – military policewomen upon whom the smooth movement of hundreds of thousands of troops in operations of great complexity depended – and the most front-line specialities of all: tank commanders, snipers, and the three women's aviation regiments. Some 220,000 young women snipers and signallers were trained in young people's units under the *Vsevobuch* – Universal Military Education[89] – scheme introduced by the GKO on 17 September 1941. A further 100,000 women were members of partisan and other underground organizations.[90]

The colossal contribution of women and girls to the real 'front-line' fighting effort, as well as to the security of the homeland and to the maintenance of the economy, has still not been properly acknowledged in Russian sources, never mind anywhere else. Many of the women concerned were not employed in the traditional roles which women had long fulfilled with armed forces as nurses and cantinières, or even in those which they came to fill in other theatres in the First and Second World Wars, as drivers, signallers, clerks, administrators, interpreters and doctors. These women *fought*. And they often fought better than men.

The all-women fighting formations included the three aviation regiments, the 1st Independent Women's Volunteer Rifle Brigade, based in Moscow, the 1st Women's Reserve Rifle Regiment and the Central Women's School for Sniper Training. Because women breathe better than men, they make better shots – and because they are more patient, and resistant to cold, they are particularly suitable as snipers.[91]

Many women had become interested in flying through the Osoaviakhim organization in the 1930s. Stalin encouraged the development of aviation and there was propaganda value in promoting women pilots as examples of the superiority of the new order. In September 1938 a three-woman crew, including two of the very few women who had managed to obtain commissions in the Red air force, Marina Raskova and Polina Osipenko, established a world record for the longest ever straight-line flight by a female crew, from Moscow to Komsomolsk – the full, and not inconsiderable, extent of the Soviet Union. Stalin was invited to the dinner at which Osipenko made a short speech drawing a parallel between the work that women were doing on collective farms and what they might do in the military. Stalin appeared to agree.[92]

That may have been the reason why the creation of three all-women aviation regiments preceded the mass induction of women into the armed forces, which began in 1942. Marina Raskova's dogged persistence eventually paid off.[93] On 8 October 1941, in GKO order 0099, Stalin authorized the formation of the 586th Fighter, 588th Night Bomber and 587th Short-Range Bomber (Dive-Bomber) Aviation Regiments. The 587th later became 125th Guards Dive-Bomber Regiment, and 588th became 46th Taman Guards Night Bomber regiment. The fighter regiment had Yak-1s, the dive-bomber regiment SU-2s and the night bomber regiment old U-2 (Po-2) biplanes. At the time they were called U-2s, designed by Polikarpov, and were renamed Po-2s in July 1944 after his death.[94]Together, the three regiments would make up Aviation Group 122. Marina Raskova, the famous, record-breaking woman pilot, would command the Group. The idea was for it to be staffed entirely by women. Not just the pilots and navigators, but mechanics, armourers – everyone. In fact, the dive-bomber and fighter regiments did have some male personnel and both later had male commanders. The night-bomber regiment had one female commander, Yevdokia Bershanskaya, and consisted entirely of women throughout the war. The best way of getting the right people, in terms of education and loyalty, was through the Young Communist League. On 10 October, a message went round the university students digging anti-tank ditches west of Moscow that females were being recruited for aviation units. It sounded better than digging ditches, and young women flocked to sign up. It seems to have been done by word of mouth, and there was no widespread publicity.[95]

On 17 October all the women selected to make up Aviation Group 122 boarded a train in Moscow for a secret location. Once the train was moving, they were told it was Engels, on the other side of the Volga. They spent nine days on the train, and food was scarce. At one station there were piles of fresh cabbage, and they ate it there and then 'just like rabbits'.[96] From then on, for the rest of the war, they called each other 'brother rabbit'.

The combat record of all three 'rabbit' units, who also often referred to themselves as 'Raskova's Regiments', was outstanding. The 46th Guards, as the 588th Regiment became in February 1943, became the most famous, perhaps, in part, because it was the worst equipped. The Po-2 (U-2) biplane was a flimsy wood-and-canvas contraption. Flying it at night must have been a terrifying experience. The regiment got the name 'the night witches', apparently because that was what the Germans called them. One reason may be that in order to hit targets by surprise, bearing in mind the Po-2 biplanes were tinderboxes and carried no defensive armament, the pilots would sometimes cut the engine and then glide in to deliver their bombs before restarting it.[97] This was a standard tactic used by all Soviet light bombers at night. It 'increased the unexpectedness of the attack and reduced losses'.[98] The result, in the Po-2s' case, was a whooshing sound, like a witch's broomstick in the night, and then explosions. Soldiers are superstitious people.

During the war, the 'night witches' earned twenty-one Hero of the Soviet Union medals – the highest award for gallantry and effectiveness.[99]

The most famous woman pilot actually served with three others in an otherwise all-male squadron. Lidiya Litvak had been a flying instructor and joined Raskova's group, but was later assigned to 437th Fighter Regiment, one of four women in an otherwise all-male unit. The male fighter pilots did not trust them to be their 'wingmen' so they formed their own flight, fighting at Stalingrad.[100] Litvak achieved twelve personal and four shared kills, plus a reconnaissance balloon. She was reported missing on 1 August 1943.[101]

The most effective woman sniper was Lyudmila Pavlichenko, who killed a total of 309 Axis troops before finding herself in Sevastopol in June 1942. She was one of those considered valuable enough to be evacuated by submarine, just before the fortress fell. Snipers often worked in pairs. Between them, Mariya Polivanova and Natalya Kovshova (see plate 27) scored more than 300 kills before German troops surrounded them in fighting near Novgorod, south of Leningrad, on 14 August 1942. They fired until they ran out of ammunition, and then waited for the Germans to come forward. Then then blew themselves up with hand grenades, taking some of the enemy with them.[102] They became two of the total of ninety-two Soviet women who were made Heroes of the Soviet Union during the war or later.

After the large-scale induction of women in 1942, from 1943 to 1945 there was an average of 2,000 to 3,000 women soldiers per field army, with around 20,000 women per front.[103] The Germans' views on the role of women in war were considerably less 'modern' than the Russians', although the Russian use of women fighters was a temporary aberration. The Germans, and especially the SS, were appalled to find the corpses of dead women combatants on the field. As some of the photographs in this book show, although they were effective and sometimes highly decorated combat soldiers, and in spite of the intensity and brutality of the fighting and the primitive conditions in the field on the eastern front, many of the women soldiers do not seem to have lost their femininity. And they may have had some civilizing influence on their male colleagues. They certainly had an effect on logistics. In April 1943, with the worst of the war over, GKO authorized an extra 100 grams of soap per month for women soldiers, over and above the norm for male soldiers which had been established in 1941.[104]

Force generation

Although women fighters played a heroic role, the mass induction of women was principally designed to release men from other duties for front-line fighting. In order to feed the front's insatiable appetite for manpower, other pre-war assumptions were also ditched. Non-Slavic nationalities and religious groups including Jews and Muslims had been exempt from service before the war because of reservations about their political reliability. But they were called up, starting in November 1941, and an estimated 8 million of them served during the war. Any territory from the Germans was considered ripe for exploitation: in February 1942 Stavka ordered fronts to conscript anyone eligible between 17 and 45 – that is, anyone who passed a rudimentary medical and who had not already been called up. In fact, German successes as part of Operation *Blau* made this order largely inapplicable. Finally, the huge pool of GULag inmates was a promising source of man – and woman – power. An estimated 975,000 were freed from the camps during the war. The GKO wanted to remove their and their families' names from the lists of NKVD deportees after a year's service, but to boost morale in October 1942 the NKVD ordered them to be taken off the list immediately. Restrictions on conscripting former ordinary criminals were also lifted.[105]

While the Soviet system became much less choosy about whom it allowed to carry weapons on its behalf, it was also learning how to fight differently. 1942 was 'the learning year'.[106] As the Red Army fell back in the south in summer 1942, Stavka and the Defence Ministry had begun rebuilding the Red Army and other fighting and security services. The pre-war army had been destroyed in 1941: the hastily raised replacements were largely destroyed in the summer battles of 1942. But in the spring a third army was growing, which would be much better suited to offensive operations.

In April and May 1942 some 25 new tank corps were formed, 11 allocated to fronts and the other 14 in the Stavka reserve. Each comprised 7,300 men and 168 tanks. And more and more of the tanks were excellent KVs and T-34s, although light tanks continued to be manufactured until the end of 1943 and British Matildas and American Shermans were still used at Kursk. Although the new tank corps were committed in dribs and drabs at first, the Russians quickly learned that they needed to commit these hard, fast-moving formations altogether, rather than split up into their three component brigades, and preferably grouped with others. That was the message of NKO Order 325, issued in October. In September 1942 new mechanized corps with 13,500 men and 175 tanks were also formed. These and the tank corps were robust, highly mobile players on the battlefield, and were first used in accordance with the NKO instruction in the counteroffensive at Stalingrad.[107] And, reflecting the tipping point in the battle between the two greatest land–air forces on earth, just as the Russian mobile formations entered the game, the Germans were desperately short of them. If you are advancing, but cannot kick out at your flanks using mobile formations, you have to hunker down in the centre and leave your flanks exposed. The enemy, newly provided with mobile formations, will then exploit them to the maximum, attacking your flanks to multiply your problems and drive the point home.[108] It is all about 'freedom of action' and 'room for manoeuvre'.

The increased emphasis on concentrating combat power was also reflected in the organization of artillery, which had been fragmented at the outset of the war. The proportion of artillery which came under the High Command reserve, so it could be concentrated where it was most needed, at key strategic points along the front, increased throughout the war from 8 per cent in 1941 to 35 per cent by August 1945. In autumn 1942 artillery divisions – numbering hundreds of guns – were reintroduced, to provide massive firepower in support of army attacks.[109] As part of the front stabilized, and as the German thrust to the south and the oilfields of Asia was identified, it became possible to concentrate force more rigorously. But that simple concept required a physical component, which Siberia was beginning to churn out and lease-lend was helping – more tanks, more guns – and more responsive organization. It was starting to happen.

Holding on . . .

The Germans were now becoming very interested in Russia's remaining reserves. Having hoped for a quick victory, *Fremde Heere Ost* had not thought it necessary to do any in-depth analysis until February 1942. Not until 23 March, with *Blau* already inevitable in some form, did the department submit its first estimate of the most critical element of Russia's war-making potential. People. With a current strength of 7.8 million in all the Soviet services, there would be a manpower pool of 1.93 million left, and that pool would reduce by 250,000 to 300,000 a month with the stupendous casualties the Russians were expected to take. Therefore, the Germans concluded, the Russians had enough manpower to cope with the current shortfall but reserves were by no means inexhaustible. Calling up potentially unreliable ethnic minorities and women were regarded as temporary 'expedients', and would result in 'a further decline in quality'. Gehlen, who took over as head of *Fremde Heere Ost*, told the War Academy on 9 June that it was 'unlikely' that the Russians would be able to cope with losses like those sustained at Vyaz'ma and Bryansk again 'without great efforts'. The Russians would not, he said, 'be able to throw into Battle again such voluminous reserves as during the winter of 1941–42'.[110] However, these assessments underestimated the flexibility of the Soviet system to draw on the wider pool of man- and womanpower, and also assumed that the Russians would go on taking casualties at the 1941 rate.[111]

Furthermore, as the Germans had advanced into Soviet territory, Stalin feared that ethnic minorities who had been persecuted under Soviet rule would welcome the invaders. Only the Chechen–Ingush actually began an open rebellion as the Germans approached, but four ethnic groups were later deported in reprisal. The deportations of the war years, and immediately before and after, are depicted graphically in Figure 15.5.

On 15 July 1942 British Intelligence issued a gloomy report of the situation in south Russia, filed under *Possible action in the event of Soviet collapse*.[112] Significantly, the previous entry on the file is July 1941. For a year, embracing the drama and relief of the Battle of Moscow, the

British were relatively confident in their 'ally of sorts'. But suddenly, another most pessimistic document appeared on the file. It mirrors everything we now know. Following the loss by the Red Army of their 'regular formations' (the entire peacetime army) in 1941; the irreplaceable loss of heavy equipment; the views of General Anders, of the Polish government in exile; 'the physical lack of trained manpower for hole-plugging'; and the need to use all available forces to hold the crust of the defence against the Germans, 'MI3c' (a major in the MI3 Intelligence Directorate of the General Staff) concluded:

> I have had the inescapable feeling that much as the Germans may have lost, the Red Army has lost more.
>
> The test in 1942 began at KERCH, which was overrun by the Germans in a matter of days, and continued in the Soviet offensive and German counter-offensive at KHARKOV, which was a fairly disastrous battle for the Red Army. Both these actions took place in the open conditions of the Southern Russian plains and augured very badly for the Red Army in the coming German offensive.
>
> SEVASTOPOL was, on the other hand, a fair feat of Soviet arms and demonstrated the enormous power of the Red Army on the defensive – given the right conditions of terrain.
>
> The answer is therefore that, in spite of the elimination of the element of surprise and its war experience, the Red Army is still not capable of dealing with the Germans in the open terrain of South Russia which is suitable for the use of A.F.Vs [Armoured Fighting Vehicles – *sic*].[113]

On 1 June the Joint Intelligence Committee had forecast that the Germans might reach the River Donets by the beginning of August. On 15 July they had already passed this line, much sooner than expected. The Germans had been 'underestimated': the Red Army 'overvalued'. 'MI3c' therefore suggested that:

> On the whole the Germans have most things in their favour. Their preliminary dispositions are generally more favourable for attack than those of the Russians for defence: the ground favours them; they possess a better fighting machine than the Russians. Any possible Russian numerical superiority is

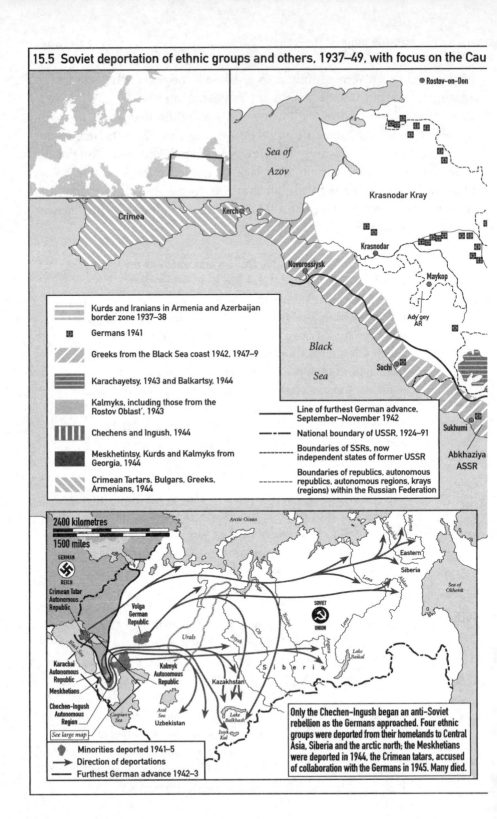

Rostov-on-Don

Sea of
Azov

Crimea

Kerch

Krasnodar Kray

Krasnodar

Novorossiysk

Maykop

Adygey
AR

Black

Sea

Sochi

Sukhumi

Abkhaziya
ASSR

Kurds and Iranians in Armenia and Azerbaijan border zone 1937–38

Germans 1941

Greeks from the Black Sea coast 1942, 1947–9

Karachayetsy, 1943 and Balkartsy, 1944

Kalmyks, including those from the Rostov Oblast', 1943

Chechens and Ingush, 1944

Meskhetintsy, Kurds and Kalmyks from Georgia, 1944

Crimean Tartars, Bulgars, Greeks, Armenians, 1944

Line of furthest German advance, September–November 1942

National boundary of USSR, 1924–91

Boundaries of SSRs, now independent states of former USSR

Boundaries of republics, autonomous republics, autonomous regions, krays (regions) within the Russian Federation

2400 kilometres

1500 miles

GERMAN
REICH

Crimean Tatar
Autonomous
Republic

Black Sea

Karachai
Autonomous
Republic

Meskhetians

Chechen-Ingush
Autonomous
Region

See large map

Volga
German
Republic

Urals

Kalmyk
Autonomous
Republic

Kazakhstan

Caspian
Sea

Aral
Sea

Uzbekistan

Lake
Balkhash

Issyk
Kul

Arctic Ocean

Kolyma

Indigirka

Eastern

Siberia

Sea of
Okhotsk

SOVIET
UNION

Ob

Irtysh

Yenisei

Lena

Angara

Lake
Baikal

S i b e r i a

Aldan

Minorities deported 1941–5

Direction of deportations

Furthest German advance 1942–3

Only the Chechen-Ingush began an anti-Soviet rebellion as the Germans approached. Four ethnic groups were deported from their homelands to Central Asia, Siberia and the arctic north: the Meskhetians were deported in 1944, the Crimean tatars, accused of collaboration with the Germans in 1945. Many died.

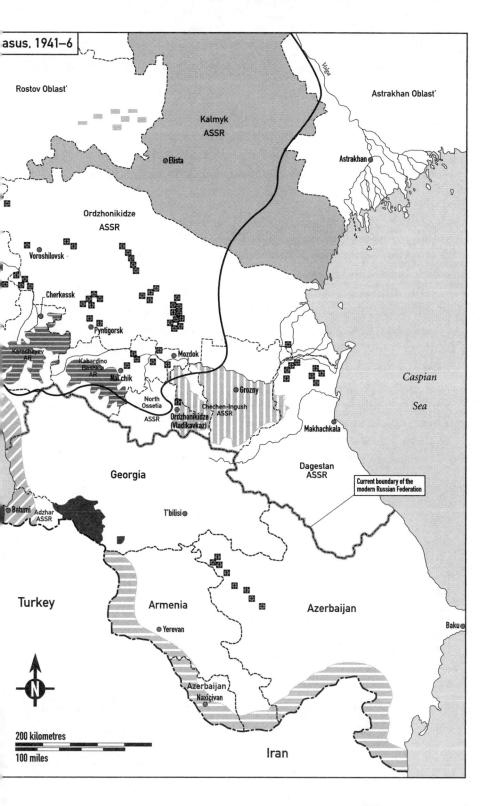

asus, 1941–6

Rostov Oblast'

Astrakhan Oblast'

Kalmyk
ASSR

● Elista

Astrakhan ●

Volga

Ordzhonikidze
ASSR

Voroshilovsk

Cherkessk

Pyntigorsk

Karachayev
AR

Kabardino
Bashkia
AR
Nalchik

Mozdok

North
Ossetia
ASSR

Ordzhonikidze
(Vladikavkaz)

Chechen-Ingush
ASSR

● Grozny

Makhachkala ●

Caspian

Sea

Georgia

Dagestan
ASSR

Current boundary of the
modern Russian Federation

● Batumi

Adzhar
ASSR

T'bilisi ●

Turkey

Armenia

Azerbaijan

Baku ●

● Yerevan

Azerbaijan
Naxiçivan

Iran

N

200 kilometres

100 miles

495

undoubtedly set off by the better equipment, training and mobility of the Germans.

It is probable that the initial German attack will succeed. How far the Germans will be able to exploit their success will depend on the ability of the Red Army to retain some form of cohesion in retreat until they have gone back behind great natural obstacles or into country more suitable for the defence.[114]

The last sentence is prophetic: '... great natural obstacles or ... country more suitable for the defence.' Nothing could match this description better than a sprawling city, smashed to rubble, on a river which is a kilometre wide.

The British report was uncannily prescient, perhaps deliberately so, in spite of an obvious omission. Numbers, equipment, training, mobility ... all were there. But where was the moral component? The Russian economy and state apparatus should have collapsed in 1942, but the Russians forced their heart and nerve and sinew to serve their turn, long after they were gone. Thanks in part (but probably critically) to lease-lend, they still held on when all reserves of strength were exhausted. There was nothing, except the will – and the political control – that said to them, 'Hold on!'[115]

There are no more enclosures on that British file.

16

FROM DEFENCE TO ATTACK: THE CAUCASUS, STALINGRAD AND MARS

The strategic situation in the second half of 1942

From the very start of 1942 Hitler's main objective had been to seize the oilfields of the Caucasus and the Caspian in order to be able to carry on fighting the war, in which the Americans were now involved. 'If I do not get the oil of Maykop and Grozny [the two principal cities lying about a hundred kilometres north of the Caucasus mountains]', he reportedly said, 'then I must end this war.'[1] Oil was also produced at Baku on the Caspian coast. The oil of this area, and also natural gas, remain of crucial importance today, and were not irrelevant to Russia's determination to hold on to Chechnya when it declared independence after the break-up of the Soviet Union in 1992. Stalin's decision to deport the Chechens, among other nationalities, for alleged disloyalty in 1944 also contributed to bitterness and resentment against the Russians which exploded into armed revolt fifty years later.

For Hitler, seizing the oilfields would not only help in the global war: it would also be a body blow to the Russians. By 1942 the Germans occupied territory which had held 40 per cent of the country's population and a third of its gross industrial output. In 1940 the Donets basin had produced 57 per cent of the Soviet Union's coal. In 1942 this fell to just 5 per cent. The Russians had to hang on to the oilfields for the very reasons the Germans wanted them.[2]

However, the Russians most feared another, possibly successful, attack on Moscow. Hitler's strategic-economic aim was clear, but he allowed himself to be distracted from it. That, and the Russian preoccupation with an attack either on Moscow itself or round to the east of it, to cut the capital off from the rest of the country, explains what happened in the second half of 1942. Even while the Russians hung on by the skin of their teeth at Stalingrad, the city bearing Stalin's name, they were equally concerned about the capital and in November launched not one but two huge counteroffensive operations. The one at Stalingrad is well known, because the Russians won. The other one, the Rzhev-Sychevka operation, west of Moscow, codenamed Mars, is not.[3] Like the counteroffensive at Stalingrad, it was also designed to cut off a German army – the Ninth – and perhaps destroy Army Group Centre, the German military-strategic centre of gravity. It remained virtually unknown for fifty years, not because the linked place-names are less catchy – though they are – but because it failed. The two great counteroffensives, and what led up to them, must therefore be considered together.

Blau I – the advance to the Don

On 19 June 1942 the Russians had a remarkable stroke of luck. Major Reichel, Chief of Staff of the German 23rd Armoured Division, was in a plane flying over its deployment area near Belgorod carrying orders and situation maps for *Blau* I. He was shot down and the top secret documents fell into the hands of the Red Army. The same day they were passed to Moscow but Stalin, whose distrust of intelligence reports was now well known, clearly believed in the old maxim that if it seemed too good to be true, then it probably was. The German divisional commander and his Chief-of-Staff, and their boss, the commander of XXXX Motorized Corps (part of Sixth Army), were all fired, but Stalin probably thought the documents were a German ruse. Even though other intelligence backed up the evidence of the captured plans, and even though he knew how desperate Germany was for oil, Stalin continued to believe that any German attack towards the south and the Caucasus would be, at most, a secondary objective. He, and Colonel-General Aleksandr Vasilevskiy, newly appointed as Chief of the Soviet General Staff,

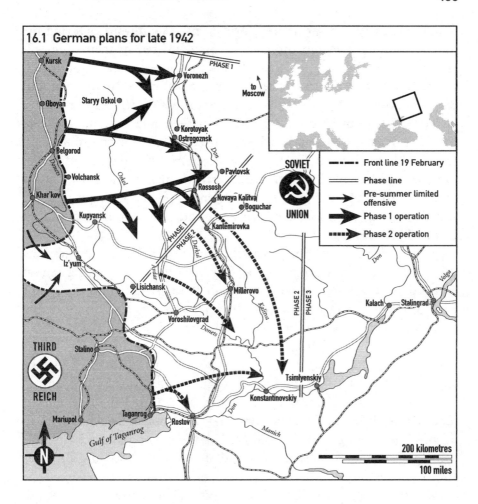

16.1 German plans for late 1942

believed the aim might be to draw reserves away from Moscow, which, they thought, was still the Germans' main objective.[4]

On 28 June 1942 the Germans launched *Blau* I, as shown in Figure 16.1. They stormed towards Voronezh, which the Russians saw as the start of the dreaded drive on Moscow. Local Russian counter-attacks proved futile and by early July the Germans had reached the Don. More counter-attacks were launched in the Orël area, further to the north, but the Germans held these off, too. However, although Bock, commanding Army Group South, had captured the ground envisaged in the plan, he had failed to trap and annihilate vast Russian forces. On 2 July he was told that capturing Voronezh itself was not particularly important. In complete conformity with the original aim of the operation, set out in Directive 41, Hitler wanted to swing the maximum force possible

– and particularly the armoured formations – southwards. During the next few days Hitler and the General Staff differed in their opinions, Hitler putting the race for the oilfields first, the generals wanting to secure the Voronezh area. The city was captured on 6 July without much opposition, but the four divisions of XXXXVIII Panzer Corps, including one Panzer division, one motorized infantry and the elite Großdeutschland[5] division which were needed for the swing south-east, remained bogged down for days. The Russians, believing this to be the Moscow attack, sent seven armoured corps to the area and Vasilevskiy himself turned up to supervise the defence. On the German side the situation brought tensions between Bock and Halder to a head and on 13 July Bock was sacked.[6]

On 6 July, the day Voronezh fell, the Russians began to withdraw from the area. What happened next became the first strategic retreat ever ordered by Stavka. In fact, the South-Western and Southern Fronts were ordered to pull back about 100 kilometres, to the Don, but the order did not apply in the Voronezh area. The idea was to hold Voronezh to allow Timoshenko to pull back in the south. The withdrawal there may have been more spontaneous, and given Stavka authority later, after front and army commands apparently lost control. The change in Russian strategy nevertheless confused the Germans at first. On 6 July the Russian withdrawal tempted Weichs's Group northwards (see Figure 16.1), but OKH refused to be drawn.[7] Golikov, commanding the Bryansk Front, had not done a bad job, but was effectively demoted. On 7 July Golikov's three armies were renamed the Voronezh Front and Rokossovskiy was put in command of the Bryansk Front in his place. The Russians were clearly still concerned about an attack towards Moscow, and were sending in their best people. Further north, Zhukov launched an offensive towards Orël, again to disrupt a German drive towards Moscow, but it was halted after five days.

By now it was becoming obvious to the Russians that the main German thrust had turned south-east (see Figure 16.1). On 10 July Army Group South was split in two. Bock would command Army Group B (for just four days, it turned out, before being relieved of command). This comprised a German, an Italian, a Hungarian and a Romanian army. Army Group A, commanded by List, was all-German. It initially consisted of just one army, Seventeenth, but after 14 July the First and Fourth Panzer Armies were added.[8] Army Group A was heading south, to the Caucasus, Army Group B to the Don. On 22 July the Germans flanked Rostov-on-Don and the city fell on the 25th. Timoshenko was severely criticized in the press for allowing the city, which should have been a real centre of resistance, to fall. There were suggestions that his costly – indeed, disastrous – spring offensive at Khar'kov had cost precious troops who would have been very useful later in the summer, fighting further south.[9] That was probably right. However, by the time Rostov fell, Timoshenko had already been very effectively demoted to command the new Stalingrad Front, comprising three reserve armies – Sixty-Second, Sixty-Third and Sixty-Fourth – on 12 July. He lasted nine days, before being replaced by General Vasiliy Gordov. Timoshenko probably feared for his life but in early July 1942 the idea that defending every morsel of ground was a sacred duty was giving way. 'Major evasive movements' – living to fight another day, an idea favoured by Vasilevskiy, the Chief of the General Staff – were briefly back in favour.[10]

The offensive splits

With the new Russian 'evasive movements', *Blau* II never happened. Neither did *Blau* III, which had Stalingrad as its objective. Instead of *Blau* III – Stalingrad – and *Blau* IV – the Caucasus and the oilfields – happening consecutively, as originally planned, they would be subsumed by two prongs of a split offensive, attacking outwards at right angles. Directive No. 45 of 23 July, the day Rostov fell, confirmed the decision.[11] The various directives are shown in Figure 16.1. In Operation Edelweiss, Army Group A would take Batum and seize 'the entire eastern coastline of the Black Sea', thereby eliminating the Black Sea ports and the Russian Black Sea fleet. Other forces would strike towards the Grozny oilfields. Army Group B would take Stalingrad and then prepare defensive positions along the Don against possible counter-attack, assuming the Russians had any fight left in them. It was an impossibly grandiose plan. The main effort lay towards the Caucasus, and Hitler assumed that Stalingrad could be taken easily.

Hitler had been running the war on the eastern front from the fortress-like Wolf's Lair – *Wolfsschanze* – at Rastenburg in East Prussia

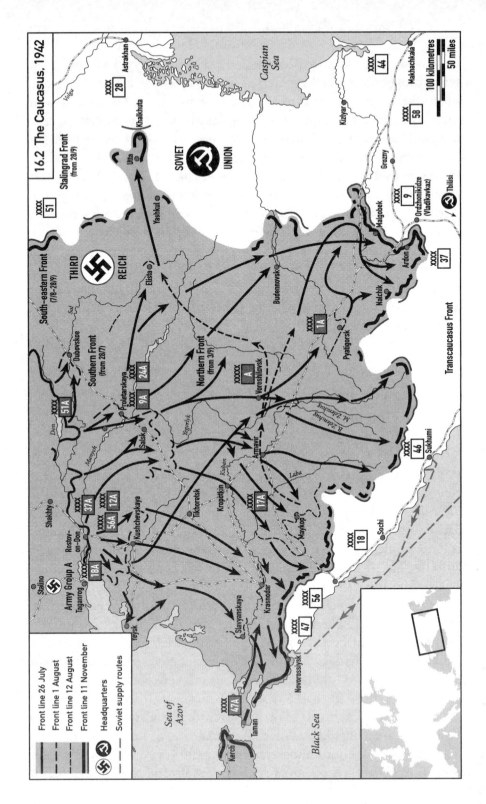

16.2 The Caucasus, 1942

Legend:
- Front line 26 July
- Front line 1 August
- Front line 12 August
- Front line 11 November
- Headquarters
- Soviet supply routes

Stalingrad Front (from 28/9)

South-eastern Front (7/8–28/9)

Southern Front (from 28/7)

Northern Front (from 3/9)

Transcaucasus Front

THIRD REICH

SOVIET UNION

Army Group A

Caspian Sea

Sea of Azov

Black Sea

Volga

Don

Manych

Sal

Yegorlyk

Kuban

Laba

B. Zelenchug

M. Zelenchug

Astrakhan
Khalkhuta
Utta
Yashkul
Elista
Makhachkala
Kizlyar
Grozny
Ordzhonikidze (Vladikavkaz)
Tbilisi
Malgobek
Nalchik
Ardon
Budennovsk
Pyatigorsk
Voroshilovsk
Sukhumi
Sochi
Armavir
Kropotkin
Maykop
Tikhoretsk
Salsk
Proletarskaya
Dubovskoe
Shakhty
Rostov-on-Don
Stalino
Taganrog
Yeysk
Slavyanskaya
Krasnodar
Novorossiysk
Taman
Kerch
Kushchevskaya

Unit markers:
- 51 (xxxx)
- 28 (xxx)
- 44 (xxxx)
- 58 (xxx)
- 9 (xxx)
- 37 (xxxx)
- 1A (xxxx)
- A (xxxxx)
- 24A (xxxx)
- 9A (xxxx)
- 51A (xxxx)
- 37A (xxxx)
- 12A (xxxx)
- 56A (xxxx)
- 1BA (xxxx)
- 17A (xxxx)
- 46 (xxxx)
- 18 (xxxx)
- 56 (xxxx)
- 47 (xxxx)
- 47A (xxxx)

Scale: 100 kilometres / 50 miles

but, on 14 July, he moved to a new field headquarters at Vinnitsa in western Ukraine, codenamed *Werwolf*. It consisted mainly of prefabricated wooden cabins, plus two concrete bunkers in case of attack. It was still 1,000 kilometres west of Stalingrad and in practical terms he could probably have supervised operations just as well from Rastenburg, but it certainly made the point about the priority he attached to the drive for the oilfields, and particularly Operation Edelweiss. The same day Stalingrad was put on a war footing, two days after the creation of the Stalingrad Front: on 25 August it would come under a 'state of siege'.[12]

The weaknesses of Hitler's overambitious plan were obvious to any trained staff officer. Halder tried to persuade Hitler to concentrate the offensive against Stalingrad initially, and to postpone the attack on the Caucasus until the left (northern) flank was secured and any threat to its rear removed. Hitler seemed to be losing concentration and drastically underestimating what the Russians could do. The new Russian willingness to conduct deliberate withdrawals appeared to Hitler to indicate Russian weakness: *Fremde Heere Ost* and the German generals were not fooled. As early as 3 July Bock allegedly told Hitler that the Russians were 'gradually getting smart'.[13]

Another distraction which diverted Hitler in these crucial weeks was the possibility that as Russian resistance in the east was cracking (as Hitler believed it was), the British and Americans might be more likely to invade France. After explaining this on 9 July Hitler immediately transferred the two senior SS divisions – Leibstandarte Adolf Hitler and Das Reich – to the west, followed, two weeks later, by the Army Großdeutschland division. A month later he also ordered the creation of the Atlantic wall along the Atlantic and Channel coasts, which would consume vast resources, including the very fuel he was now also heading for the Caucasus to replenish.[14]

Drive to the Caucasus

Besides the oil of Maykop, Grozny and Baku, the capture of the Caucasus and the transcaucasian republics of the Soviet Union beyond offered other dazzling potential rewards. Turkey might be persuaded to join the Axis and the British possessions in the Middle East would be encircled, while one of the key routes for Allied aid to Russia could also then be cut off. For the relatively weak force available to Army Group A, however, the distances and the terrain ultimately proved too great. From the German starting point at Rostov to Baku was as far as the Germans had come from the pre-war German–Soviet border to Rostov. And the army group soon found that the Fourth Luftflotte, which provided tactical air support, was diverted increasingly to Stalingrad. In 1942, Hitler would prove as bad at 'selection and maintenance of the aim' as he had the previous year.

List's Army Group comprised the First Panzer Army under Kleist, the Fourth Panzer Army under Hoth, and the Seventeenth Army under Ruoff. First Panzer would head for Maykop, with Fourth Panzer covering it to the east, heading for Voroshilovsk, a small town 40 kilometres east of Armavir. The first troops of Kleist's army were across the River Don, east of Rostov, on 25 July but most of the heavy tanks did not get to the southern side until the 27th, while Hoth's tanks did not get across until the 29th. The Russian forces faced an impossible dilemma. If they held, they would probably be encircled. But Stalin's 'not a step back' order, No. 227, issued on 28 July, forbade withdrawal. The same day Budenny, commanding the 'North Caucasus Theatre' – a Strategic Direction command – was ordered to combine the Southern and North Caucasian Fronts into just one (the North Caucasus). Its commander, Tyulenev, was to fortify the passes through the Caucasus, while two groups of armies, Malinovskiy's Don Group and Chevrevichenko's Coastal Group, covered Stavropol' and Krasnodar, respectively.

Kleist made terrific progress, coming within sight of the derricks of the Maykop oil wells on 9 August. But the vital oilfields were in flames. Hoth's Fourth Panzer which according to the original plan should have led Paulus into Stalingrad, and was level with the Stalingrad–Krasnodar railway line, was ordered north, back to Stalingrad, on 31 July (see Figure 16.3).[15]

Vast though the distances were, and although now deprived of one of the two Panzer armies, and with air support increasingly diverted to Stalingrad, the Germans made incredible progress. There are no continuous front lines on the maps recording their progress, just isolated indications of German forces moving south and east in a country too big for armies. By mid August the Germans were close to Novorossiysk in the west and Mozdok in the east. Refugees crammed the trains heading south-east, towards Baku and the Caspian.

Stalin, who was from Georgia, knew full well the political dangers that military defeat in that area might bring. It had always been turbulent. The Caucasian tribes had chosen the Russians as overlords in marginal preference to the Ottoman Turks, and the Turks were interested in cultivating the Turkic peoples of the region. He therefore sent his fellow-Georgian, Beria, to the Trans-Caucasus Front at the end of August. Beria, and some of his NKVD 'heavies' including Kobulov and Tsanava, who had been a key player in the occupation of the former Poland, were to suppress any nascent revolt in the Caucasus and the Volga delta area. They immediately fell out with Malinovskiy and Beria threatened to have him arrested. The military men asked for more Red Army soldiers to fight the Germans: Beria moved in more NKVD troops. Beria's personal involvement in the Caucasus at this time led directly to the deportations of whole ethnic groups – Crimean Tartars, Chechens, Ingush, Kalmyks and Volga Germans – in 1943 and 1944. Even if people had not been collaborating – or trying to collaborate – with the Germans, the fact that the Germans found the Muslim peoples of this area the most amenable did the others no good. During August Karanadze, the People's Commissar for Internal Affairs for the Crimean ASSR, issued a lengthy report on the various nationalities in the Crimea now under German occupation. Whereas the Russians, Ukrainians, Greeks, Bulgarians and Armenians were 'patriotic', the Germans were making efforts to cultivate the Tatars who were, in the main (though not exclusively, he admitted), hostile to the Soviet government.[16]

Beria also interfered in military matters, but as a member of GKO, that was his prerogative. To the military men trying to fight the Germans it was an extreme version of the all-too-familiar 'long screwdriver concept' – political control imposed very directly and, in this case, by a member of the war cabinet, who was also a head of the secret police, physically present in an army group headquarters.

In mid August 1942, Army Group A began the second stage of its advance. First Panzer would head towards Baku, in the flat country either side of the River Terek, through Grozny, while Seventeenth Army would follow the Black Sea coast. The Caucasus mountains forced both sides to split their forces. Tyulenev's front formed Forty-Sixth Army to block the German attack down the coast, but Beria insisted on getting involved. The Germans sent their LXXIX Jäger Corps – specialized mountain troops – to take the Caucasian passes, which Yulenev's men were defending. Beria ordered the creation of a Caucasus Range Operational Group, made up of NKVD men headed by himself, to which the troops defending the passes would report. Beria was back in Moscow by 18 August but on that day Kobulov ordered a ten-man headquarters to oversee 'operational-chekist detachments' to be established in Tbilisi and a twenty-four-strong headquarters with 464 troops to cover the 'principal passes across the Caucasus mountain range'.[17] Effectively, he removed the Forty-Sixth Army Staff. As the German alpine Jägers, expert climbers with ropes and climbing boots, moved into the high mountains – and remember that Mount Elbrus, to the east of the area where they were operating, is the highest in Europe – Beria's men were not the best people to be in charge of the Soviet defence. Stalin realized that this was a catastrophic mistake, and ordered Beria's plan to be changed.

Beria was away from Moscow only from 23 August until 17 September 1942. He normally saw Stalin every day, but did not between those dates.[18] On 13 September he wrote a letter warning that as the Germans approached the mountains they were dropping diversionary forces by parachute, and that the NKVD had picked up more than fifty of them. There was to be constant surveillance of the air; factories and power stations were to be guarded, and the population kept under extra surveillance.[19]

While Beria was still in the Caucasus at the end of August, German troops crossed from Kerch' to the Taman peninsula to reinforce German forces assailing Novorossiysk. The Germans captured Novorossiysk after heavy street fighting in the first week of September. Soviet naval infantry were pulled out by boat. Once the Germans got a hold on the shoreline, there were few obstacles to stop them slipping round, south of the Caucasus mountains, and rolling up (or down) the entire eastern Black Sea coast. But they did not. Seventeenth Army reached Novorossiysk on 6 September. The town and port fell, but the German advance stopped at a cement factory just to the east, north of the bay. The Germans were to be stuck there for a year, until on 9 September 1943 an amphibious landing recaptured the city. Tuapse, the next port, did not fall. As the alpine Jägers tried to push through the high mountain passes to the north, worsening weather and the overstretch of the supply lines halted the German advance. In the blizzards and snow of the mountains, operations stopped on 9 November.[20] But two months before this, most attention had switched to the lesser objective, which had become the focus of the most iconic battle, probably, of the entire war.[21]

Drive to the Volga and Stalingrad

Paulus's Sixth Army had reached the Don bend by 23 July 1942 (see Figure 16.3).[22] On that day Hitler ordered him to try to take Stalingrad in a surprise attack, but that proved impossible. The Russian Sixty-Second and Sixty-Fourth Armies held a bridgehead on the west bank, inside the bend, and refused to give way. A lull followed as Paulus waited for Hoth's Fourth Panzer Army to work its way up from the south, and also for more fuel and ammunition. They struck again on 7 August and trapped some Russian troops west of the Don. By 23 August they had crossed the narrow land bridge between the two rivers and reached the Volga north of Stalingrad. On the same day the first really major German bombing raid on the city took place, with 2,000 sorties, killing up to 40,000 people and wounding 150,000. The effects of the bombing were made worse by the summer weather. Down there on the steppe the daytime temperature soared to more than 100 °F (38 °C), and fires broke out all over the city. The Germans hit fuel storage tanks to the north of the city and fuel poured into the Neva, the flames rising 200 metres high.[23] Although Stalin's order of 28 July, 'not a step back', was addressed to his armed forces everywhere, it applied particularly to Stalingrad. It did not apply to civilians, and thousands of them headed for the shore of the Volga, hoping to get across to the safety of the east. Here, and crossing the river in small steamers, they were easy meat for the German air force, and – not for the last time – the shoreline was 'slippery with blood'.[24] Mostly civilian blood.

Meanwhile, on 1 August, General Yeremenko was summoned from hospital, where he had been recovering from wounds, to the Kremlin, and told that the defence of Stalingrad was to be conducted by two fronts. The former Stalingrad Front would be split into a Stalingrad Front to the north and the South-eastern Front to the south. Yeremenko

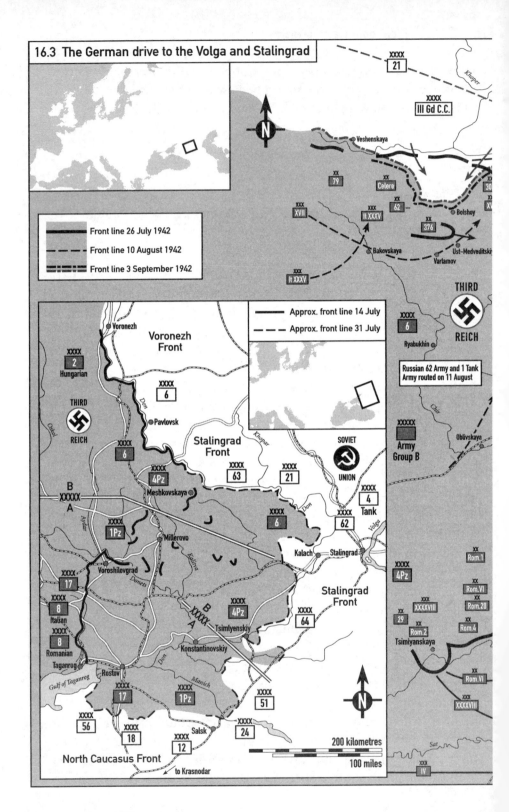

16.3 The German drive to the Volga and Stalingrad

Front line 26 July 1942
Front line 10 August 1942
Front line 3 September 1942

Approx. front line 14 July
Approx. front line 31 July

Russian 62 Army and 1 Tank Army routed on 11 August

THIRD REICH

SOVIET UNION

Army Group B

Voronezh Front

Stalingrad Front

Stalingrad Front

North Caucasus Front

200 kilometres
100 miles

to Krasnodar

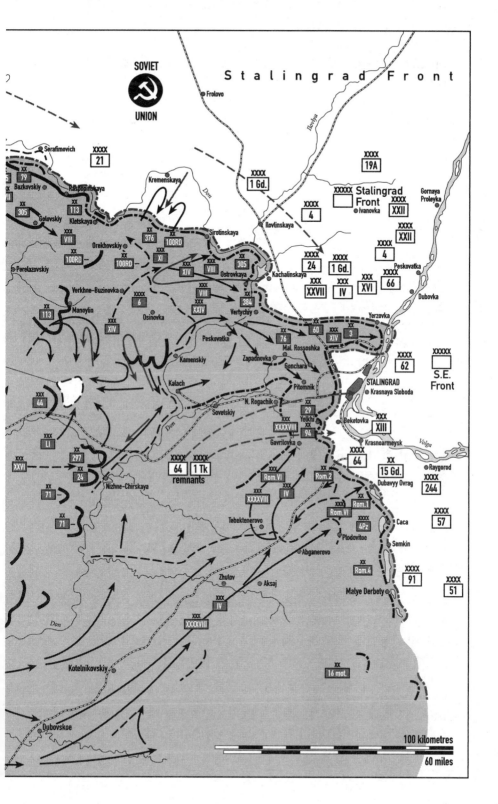

SOVIET UNION

S t a l i n g r a d   F r o n t

Frolovo

Serafimovich

XXXX
21

XXXX
19A

XXXX
1 Gd.

XXXXX
Stalingrad
Front

XXXX
4

Ivanovka

Gornaya
Proleyka

XXXX
XXII

79

Bazkovskiy

Raspopinskaya

Kremenskaya

Don

XX
305

Golovskiy

Kletskaya

XX
113

Sirotinskaya

Ilovlinskaya

XXXX
4

XXXX
XXII

XXX
376

XX
100RD

Orekhovskiy

XXX
VIII

XX
100RD

XX
100RD

XX
XI

Ostrovskaya

XXX
XIV

XX
VIII

XX
305

Kachalinskaya

Peskovatka

XXXX
24

XXXX
1 Gd.

XXX
XVI

XXXX
66

Dubovka

Perelazovskiy

Verkhne-Buzinovka

XXXX
6

XXX
XIV

Manoylin

Osinovka

XX
VIII

XX
XXIV

XX
384

Vertychiy

XXX
XXVII

XXX
IV

XX
113

Peskovatka

Zapadnovka

XX
76

Mal. Rossoshka

Gonchara

XX
60

XX
XIV

XX
3

Yerzovka

XXXX
62

XXXXX

S.E.
Front

Kamenskiy

Kalach

Don

Sovetskiy

Pitomnik

N. Rogachik

XX
29

Yelkhi

XXXXVIII

XX
94

STALINGRAD
Krasnaya Sloboda

Beketovka

XXX
XIII

Volga

XX
44

XXX
LI

Gavrilovka

Krasnoarmeysk

XXXX
64

XXX
XXVI

XX
297

XX
24

Nizhne-Chirskaya

XXXX
64
remnants

XXXX
1 Tk

Rom.VI

Rom.2

XX
15 Gd.

Dubavyy Ovrag

Raygorod

XXXX
244

XX
71

XXXXVIII

XX
IV

Rom.1

Rom.VI

Caca

XXXX
57

XX
71

Tebektenerovo

XX
4Pz

Plodovitoe

Semkin

Zhutov

Aksaj

Abganerovo

XX
Rom.4

Malye Derbety

XXXX
91

XXXX
51

Don

Kotelnikovskiy

XXX
IV

XXXXVIII

XX
16 mot.

Dubovskoe

100 kilometres

60 miles

would command the latter. The boundary would run along the Tsaritsa river, in the middle of the city. Yeremenko suggested it might be better to have just one front responsible for the city but Stalin and Vasilevskiy told him that, with German attacks now expected from north and south, it had already been decided.

The straggling city

In 1942 Stalingrad, former Tsaritsyn, straggled for almost 50 kilometres along the western (right) bank of the Volga, with the city centre stretching for nearly 20. But it was nowhere more than 4 kilometres wide (see Figure 16.4). As a visitor flies from the north-west over the Don towards the city, which was renamed Volgograd in 1961, the country looks much like Spain. Along the Volga, there are yellow sandbanks and beaches, and the soil is yellowy brown. The western bank of the Volga here is much higher than the eastern, and on a clear day there is a good view across the great river (which is in places a kilometre wide), far to the east, towards Asia. The Volga sometimes appears silver or grey, sometimes yellow, its flowing water coloured by the local clay. That is why they called it Tsaritsyn. The name had nothing to do with the Tsar but comes from the Tatar, Sari-Su – 'Yellow River'. On one occasion this author was in a plane climbing away from the city, out of the dawn in the east. He looked for the Volga, but could see only sky. Then the aircraft banked, and he realized he had been looking at water. The river is that big.

During the civil war, from July 1918 to February 1919, Red forces in Tsaritsyn, led by Stalin and Voroshilov, had faced three major attacks by White Guards.[25] Stalin's name was therefore given to the city. It was developed after the civil war, and by summer 1942 had a population of 525,000. In its centre lies Mamayev Kurgan – Mamay Hill, named after one of the Khans of the Golden Horde who had ruled Russia, in his case until defeated by Dmitry of the Don at the great battle of Kulikovo in 1380. Codenamed Hill 102 during the battle, it was a grassy hillock, 102 metres high, much of which was a huge, ancient Scythian burial mound. During the battle, fighting for the hill lasted 200 days and it is

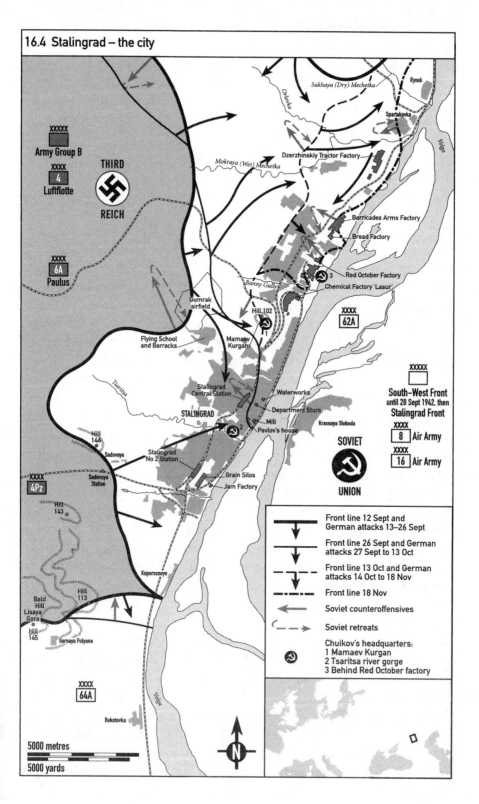

16.4 Stalingrad – the city

Army Group B
XXXXX

4 Luftflotte
XXXX

THIRD REICH

6A Paulus
XXXX

Orlovka
Sukhaya (Dry) Mechetka
Rynok
Spartakovka
Dzerzhinskiy Tractor Factory
Mokraya (Wet) Mechetka
Barricades Arms Factory
Bread Factory
Red October Factory
Chemical Factory 'Lasur'
Banny Gully
Gumrak airfield
Hill 102
62A
XXXX
Flying School and Barracks
Mamaev Kurgan
Tsaritsa
Stalingrad Central Station
Waterworks
STALINGRAD
Department Store
Mill
Pavlov's house
Krasnaya Sloboda
Hill 146
Sadovaya
Stalingrad No 2 Station
4Pz
XXXX
Sadovaya Station
Grain Silos
Jam Factory
Hill 143
Kuporosnoye
Hill 113
Bald Hill Lisaya Gora
Hill 145
Gornaya Polyana
64A
XXXX
Beketovka
Volga

South-West Front
until 28 Sept 1942, then
Stalingrad Front

8 Air Army
XXXX

16 Air Army
XXXX

SOVIET UNION

Front line 12 Sept and German attacks 13–26 Sept

Front line 26 Sept and German attacks 27 Sept to 13 Oct

Front line 13 Oct and German attacks 14 Oct to 18 Nov

Front line 18 Nov

Soviet counteroffensives

Soviet retreats

Chuikov's headquarters:
1 Mamaev Kurgan
2 Tsaritsa river gorge
3 Behind Red October factory

5000 metres

5000 yards

N

said that, even in the ferocious Russian winter, the snow never settled, because the constant shellfire melted it off.

The old city of Tsaritsyn lay south of there, and featured attractive old red-brick buildings, of which only one, a big shell-spattered warehouse, survives. The old town, in turn, was split by the Tsaritsa, coming in from the west. South of there were railway yards, grain silos, grey apartment blocks and the massive, towering 'grain elevator' close to Number Two station. The freight station was surrounded by the Germans in September but held out for several more days. North of the river was the administrative centre of the city including Red Square, the main railway station, imaginatively named 'Number One', a power station and more blocks of post-civil war apartments. The railway then turned north to run between the Kurgan and an oil refinery on the river. North of the Mamay Hill was new industry, a series of steel and masonry factories stretching north along the bank: the Lazur chemical plant, the Krasny Oktyabr (Red October) metal works, a bakery, the Barrikady (Barricades) gun factory and, finally, the Dzerzhinskiy Tractor Factory. The Red October works, Barricades factory and tractor factory each extend for about a kilometre, parallel with the river, and are between 500 and 1,000 metres wide (see Figure 16.4). The tractor factory, established in 1930, under the first Five-Year plan, had switched to making tank chassis. Even before the war these three massive enterprises formed a linked arms production facility and were connected by underground tunnels with secure telephone lines. Thus, they formed a ready-made defensive system. Furthermore, the factory staff, who were formed into 'workers militia' units, knew plenty about how weapons worked, which made them more effective fighters than other hastily mobilized civilians. Close to the factories, and nestling against the modern concrete buildings around the city were wooden cottages, mostly one storey high, where the workers lived.

Running down to the Volga are a number of ravines or mechetkas, which are shown very clearly in Finogenov's excellent drawings of the time (see Plates 31, 32, 34, 36, 37). During the fighting 91 per cent of the city was destroyed and it was rebuilt largely as a memorial, which makes a visit there to follow the course of the action exactly less valuable than it might be. However, the sandy gullies leading into the river, the great river itself and the commanding height of Mamayev Kurgan have not changed much, apart from the fact that the hill is now largely buried under concrete and has to be climbed via ramps and steps. It is topped by a monument with an eternal flame and, further on, the vast and imposing concrete figure of Mother Russia, summoning her millions of people – men, women and children – to defend her. Mother Russia and her mighty upraised rallying sword rise another 102 metres above the summit of the hill.

A Soviet military map of the time, 1:50,000 scale, which was used in the battle, is reproduced as Plate 30. It shows the northern part of the city, with Mamayev Kurgan to the bottom left, grid 6501.[26] To the extreme south of the extended city, beyond the grain silos, there was another hill (see Figure 16.4). Bald Hill – *Lysaya Gora* – was the extreme south of the city, the southern flank. Sixty-Second Army fought over Mamayev Kurgan for 200 days. Sixty-Fourth fought for Bald Hill for even longer. It was the southern flank of the position – the equivalent of Little Round Top at Gettysburg – and it never fell. At 145 metres it commanded the south of the city, and although the Germans reached the river to the north, Bald Hill remained a thorn in the German side.

When the Germans reached the Volga on 23 August it galvanized Stalin into further action. In the city, more than a thousand workers were mobilized into militia units to reinforce Red Army troops, and the City authorities ordered every factory and industrial enterprise to be turned into a fortress. A state of siege was declared on 25 August.[27] Lopatin, commanding Sixty-Second Army, thought he could pinch out the salient which had appeared north of the city, but failed. On 27 August he received a phone call from Poskrebyshev, the head of Stalin's secretariat, saying he had been made Stalin's deputy. It was an amazing honour for one who was not yet a Marshal. But he did get results. By a strange coincidence Zhukov was west of Moscow, in charge of two armies which were to attack into the south of the German salient there and cut the Germans off in the Rzhev-Sychevka area, an operational idea which would raise its head again later. Poskrebyshev refused to answer the barrage of questions from Zhukov, saying that Stalin would answer them himself. That afternoon, Stalin duly called. Stalin told him to report to Stavka in Moscow immediately, as the situation in the south was looking critical.

Moskalenko's First Guards Army was directed to attack south, to link up with Sixty-Second and cut off the German penetration to the Volga. Delayed by fuel shortages, Moskalenko attacked on 3 September, but his troops advanced only a few kilometres towards Stalingrad. Stalin was very worried.

'The enemy is three *vërsts* from Stalingrad [a *vërst* is an old Russian measure, effectively a kilometre]', he said. That was right: they were 3 kilometres north of Rynok, the most northerly suburb (see Figure 16.4). 'They can take Stalingrad today or tomorrow, unless the northern group gives help urgently.'[28] Zhukov ordered an attack as soon as possible, on 5 September, and the Russians battered away for a week, but could not cut off the tentacle which had reached the Volga. Then, at 08.00 on 13 September, a massive German air and artillery attack, with large numbers of Stuka dive-bombers, opened up against the city of Stalingrad itself.

Lopatin had been dismissed from command of Sixty-Second Army which had fallen back into Stalingrad on 10 September, and was replaced by Vasiliy Chuikov, who arrived on the 13th. Finogenov's portrait (Plate 31) tells much about him. He was a tough street-fighter, described by one of his staff officers as a 'coarse' man – *gruby* – who had been known to hit officers whose performance displeased him with a big stick he carried. Whatever faults we might perceive in his managerial style from a modern viewpoint, he was the right man, at the right place, at the right time.

War of the rats

On the morning of 13 September Chuikov was in Sixty-Second Army's headquarters, a dugout on Mamay Hill. It was a good place for an army headquarters, well forward and on high ground, but German artillery of LI Corps opened fire from behind Razgulyayevka station (see Figure 16.4) and the corps moved in to within 1,500 metres or so. Brave though he was, Chuikov had no intention of being captured and moved the command post to a bunker close to the Tsaritsa river in the side of the Tsaritsa gorge, about a kilometre west of the Volga. It had more than 10 metres of hammered earth and clay overhead but was right between LI Corps and XXXXVIII Panzer, which was also heading for the Volga. The German troops hacked their way into the city with unparalleled savagery and determination. On 14 September they got close to Stalingrad Central station, occupying some of the railway workers' houses, having moved in from Gumrak between the Tsaritsa and Mamayev Kurgan. According to the official Soviet history the station changed hands five times on the 14th, and had changed hands another thirteen times by 17 September.[29] There is no reason to doubt it. From 14 September the Germans found the Russians were contesting every building, sometimes floor by floor. On the 15th the German LI Corps took Mamayev Kurgan, so Chuikov had moved just in time. On the 17th he moved again, to near the Red October factory, and stayed there, on the edge of Volga, in a bunker cut into the high bank of the river (see Finogenov's sketch, Plate 32) until January.

On 16 September Voronin, head of the Stalingrad NKVD, sent a cool report to Beria, saying that the Germans had broken into the city from the west. The Germans were attacking the Barricades and Red October factories, and NKVD troops had joined Red Army soldiers to identify and destroy groups of German machine-gunners who had occupied buildings on the bank of the river. There were, however, 'no anti-Soviet incidents among the population', and most of the population had been evacuated *in an organised fashion behind the Volga*.[30] That was not quite true. It was only after the terrible German raid on 23 August that evacuation started, on the 24th. By 10 September some 300,000 civilians had been evacuated, but 50,000 remained.[31]

As the Russians fell back into the city, the urban landscape helped them. The Germans could not use their armour freely, and the Russian lack of available armour and air power did not matter so much. The Germans called it the 'rat war'. A German group might spend a whole day clearing a street, from one end to the other, and establish blocks and fire points at the far end, but the next day the Russians would reappear behind them. It took the Germans a while to discover the trick. The Russians had knocked holes in the walls dividing up the terraces, usually between the attics, which were too high to be vulnerable to direct tank fire at close range, and during the night they would run back along the terraces 'like rats in the rafters'.[32]

The fighting continued without any respite amidst the glow of burning buildings and illuminating shells, while small boats ferried ammunition and supplies, including vodka, from the east bank across the yellow river which now burned orange with flaming oil. The ferries across the Volga, maintaining the stubborn Russian bridgehead on the west bank, were crucial. One factor which the Germans were slow to recognize was that, as can be seen from the maps, there was a very slight convex curve in the west (right) bank, which made it difficult for the Germans to enfilade all the crossings – that is, fire at them from the side down the river. They held positions to the north and south of Stalingrad, but were still clawing away, block by block, at the centre. The German army was not designed for this kind of fighting and, as General Dörr admitted,

> Despite the concentrated activity of aircraft and artillery it was impossible to break out of the area of close fighting. The Russians surpassed the Germans in their use of the terrain, and in camouflage and were more experienced in barricade warfare [sic] for individual buildings.[33]

'Pavlov's House' – a four-storey yellow building just north of the department store in the old downtown area – became a strong point. It stood just opposite the old red-brick mill and the museum. Its role in autumn 1942 exemplifies the skill and tenacity of the Russian defence. On 28 September Sergeant Jakob Pavlov of 42nd Regiment and his team of twenty-three soldiers occupied the house and turned it into a small fortress covering all the approaches. Officially, Pavlov was only in command for three days, until a lieutenant, Afanas'yev, arrived. However, the officer was wounded and Pavlov remained the inspiration – and effective leader – of the defence for the remaining 56 days: Afanas'yev 'commanded', Pavlov led. They beat off every German attack for 59 days between the end of September and the end of November. On Paulus's map, captured when his headquarters in the department store just to the south fell at the end of January, it was circled in red and marked 'castle'. When Pavlov's men moved in there were a large number of women, plus a few old men and children, in the building. Including Pavlov's team, but excluding occasional visitors – snipers and scouts – there were about sixty people in the embattled building. The house was destroyed but has been restored, with the addition of a red-brick monument.

The Luftwaffe had already been largely diverted from the original grand-strategic objective – the Caucasus – to deal with Stalingrad. Although a relatively important regional capital and centre of manufacturing, including some armaments, the city was hardly a war-winner. The only reason it became such a focus of fire, and the worst battle of attrition, probably, in history, was Hitler's determination to destroy the city named after his arch-enemy. The Russians, meanwhile, realized that they had the Germans exactly where they wanted them, in that 'unfavourable terrain' – urban terrain – which the British intelligence officer had presciently identified, writing of the 'possibility of Russian collapse' on 15 July.

Air power and artillery

At the time of the Battle of Stalingrad the Luftwaffe and Allied air forces, principally the Romanians and Finns, had 3,300 aircraft on the entire eastern front. They were stretched, but of very high quality. Modified or new aircraft – the Bf (Me-)109G and the Focke-Wulf 190 arrived. However, by November 1942 the Red air force had numerical superiority.

At Stalingrad the Luftwaffe could have done better. Had Richthofen used his considerable air power, and air supremacy, at that stage, for what we now call 'interdiction', he might have 'shaped' the urban battlefield to the point that the Russian forces on the west bank were isolated and cut off. He could have done more against the critical Volga ferries, and against the Soviet artillery group on the east bank – with 300 guns, 250 of them 76.2mm, but also with 50 heavy guns. These had the double advantage of firing from relative safety – the other side of a river a kilometre wide – but nonetheless, relatively close in terms of artillery range. In mid October more heavy 203mm and 280mm guns were moved in to intensify the firepower available.

In November there were three air armies – Seventeenth, Sixteenth and Eighth, assigned to the South-Western, Don and Stalingrad Fronts, respectively. The Second Air Army of the Voronezh Front was also assigned to the South-Western Front. The four air armies were all placed under the command of General Aleksandr Novikov, who was the Stavka representative – air – for the Stalingrad counteroffensive. As the Russian ground forces held on, the balance of air power was beginning to swing towards the Russians. They had 1,414 aircraft ready for the opening of the counteroffensive. The Germans and Romanians had 1,216. More than 400 of the Russian aircraft operated only at night, as they were so vulnerable to the German fighters by day, but in the four air armies there were 575 Ilyushin-2 Shturmoviks. The 'flying tanks' had already made a formidable reputation for themselves. And for this counteroffensive there would be plenty of them. Reconnaissance was extremely important, and in spite of German air superiority Russian reconnaissance planes managed to take photographs enabling the image analysts at the front headquarters to plot precise numbers of motor vehicles, tanks and aircraft and machine-gun nests, artillery, mortar, anti-tank, anti-aircraft positions, and also fuel dumps. These can all be seen marked up on the map at Plate 30 which resulted from photo-reconnaissance from mid September to 1 October.

It was during the Battle of Stalingrad that the concentrated, massed firepower of the *Katyusha* rocket-launchers became legendary. With relatively short range they were nevertheless ideal for bringing down huge concentrations of firepower – eight rockets with 132mm calibre warheads in a single salvo from each truck. By 14 October they were having to be backed into the Volga to get the necessary angle of fire. The Russian troops loved them – hence the nickname – but they remained a 'secret' weapon. In spite of their importance, they do not feature in any of Finogenov's January 1943 sketches of Stalingrad, apart from the tail flares of a salvo – nothing else – in the distance, shown in Plate 34.

There were renewed German surges on 27 September, when eighty tanks moved against the Red October factory, once again ruining Lt Gen. Chuikov's night. The Soviet 193rd Rifle Division was ferried across the Volga to retake it. The Russians also tried to attack from the north, into the German wedge to the north of Stalingrad, which, at its narrowest, was only 8 kilometres wide along the Volga bank between Rynok and Yerzovka. In the map at Plate 30 we can see a planned attack by 84th Rifle Division, south of Yerzovka, on a 2-kilometre-wide front, with 99th Rifle Division on its left and 126th on its right. By 5 October the Germans had occupied the northern landing stages and Stalin ordered them to be prised away by massed artillery fire. A bombardment by 300 guns and five regiments of *katyusha* multiple rocket-launchers lasting forty minutes smashed German units preparing to break into the Tractor Factory and the Barricades gun factory. The Germans attacked again, even more fiercely, and by 16 October had taken the Tractor Factory and looked set to take the Barricades, but the Russians held on to parts of the factory until 23 October. On 17 October, Herbert Pabst, a Stuka pilot, recalled:

we ploughed over the blazing fields of the Stalingrad battlefield all day long. It is incomprehensible to me how people can continue to live in that hell, but the Russians are firmly established in the wreckage, in ravines, cellars, and in a chaos of twisted steel skeletons of the factories.[34]

The 10th Order of Lenin NKVD Division

The defence of the very centre of the city was in the hands of the 10th NKVD Division which had been brought in from Saratov, in Siberia, after the creation of the Stalingrad Front on 12 July. It comprised five rifle regiments (269th to 272nd and 282nd) under the overall command of Colonel Aleksandr Sarayev (1902–70). On 9 August Sarayev was named commander of the Stalingrad garrison. Although an NKVD officer, he had attended the Frunze Academy in 1938 alongside the most promising Red Army officers. He had commanded the 10th Division since January 1942 and, significantly, after the German defeat at Stalingrad, two Red Army rifle divisions, 181st and then 99th.[35] Coming from the Urals and Siberia, his men were good shots, and good at fieldcraft. The divisional headquarters took command of all blocking detachments, an armoured train detachment, organized two tank training battalions and, most critically, took charge of the two-way traffic across the Volga.[36] Reinforcements, ammunition and supplies in: civilians and wounded out. While NKVD blocking detachments watched for any unauthorized Red Army withdrawals, 10th Division's rifle regiments took their place alongside Red Army units. 272nd Rifle Regiment took its place on 23 August with 271st Regiment on its left and no one on its right.[37]

By 23 September 1942, according to a report from Beria to the GKO and the General Staff, the 13th Guards Rifle Division of the Red Army was down to just 500 'active bayonets' – fighting soldiers – a twentieth of its official fighting strength. The 10th NKVD was down to 60. The 13th Guards, he continued, had begun to retreat. Blocking detachments of Sixty-Second Army shot one Lieutenant Mirolyubov, accused of 'panicking', in front of his men. One wonders whether Beria's creative writing skills were being exercised. It seems a remarkable coincidence that Mirolyubov means 'peace lover'. According to Beria, the Sixty-Second and Sixty-Fourth Army blocking detachments had detained 659 people in the preceding twenty-four hours, and shot seven 'cowards' and one 'enemy of the people' in front of the troops. Another twenty-four were arrested: one spy, three betrayers of the motherland, eight cowards, four deserters and eight enemies of the people.[38]

The 10th NKVD Division was therefore in charge of the defence of the city and the logistics which made it possible, and also played a direct part in the battle. In mid October Aleksey Kostesnitsyn, commanding 271st Regiment, reported how one of his men had rallied Red Army soldiers who were pulling back in the grain elevator area and launched a counter-attack.[39] On 12 November the 10th NKVD Division was awarded the Order of Lenin for heroism shown in the battles for Stalingrad. Their achievements were listed as arresting and processing 63,547 people, of whom 1,146 were spies, people who had given themselves up to the Germans or escaped from encirclement, and deserters. On 23 and 24 August, with a total of just over 7,500 men, the division had pushed German forces back from the city, covering the redeployment of Sixty-Second Army. During the whole period it had killed about 15,000 German soldiers and – this is a Stalingrad statistic – captured twenty-four. It had also destroyed about 100 German tanks and two aircraft, at a cost of 1,227 killed and 2,756 wounded. For all that, Yeremenko and Khrushchev signed the citation for the award of the Order of Lenin.[40] There could be no doubting the courage and military professionalism of this elite Siberian Interior Ministry division. But its record also underscores the inescapable truth that for Russian soldiers the choice was very much one between German bullets and Russian ones. That alone would not, and could not, hold Stalingrad.

Women at Stalingrad

For all his 'coarseness', General Chuikov was the most feminist of Russian commanders when it came to acknowledging the role that women played in this battle. And, as commander of Sixty-Second Army, holding the city centre, he was in the thick of it.

> Remembering the defence of Stalingrad, I can't overlook the very important question which, in my opinion, is still weakly covered in military literature, and at times unjustifiably forgotten in our reports and work on the generalisation of the experience of the Great Patriotic War. I have in mind the question about the role of women in war, in the rear, but also at the front. Equally with men they bore all the burdens of combat life and together with us men, they went all the way to Berlin.[41]

Chuikov seems an unlikely male feminist but he made the point many times. 'Women soldiers proved themselves to be just as heroic in the days of fighting as men,' he wrote in 1968.[42] And in his book on the battle published in 1960 he had an entire chapter specifically devoted to women's roles in the battle.[43] Yeremenko also made the point, rubbishing the idea (still current today) that women's roles in the war were primarily limited to supporting ones, including the traditional *métiers* (though hazardous as any) of medical staff and signallers and – not so traditional – air defence crews. Yeremenko, commanding the front holding the southern half of Stalingrad, said there was hardly 'any military specialism which our brave women did not handle just as well as their brothers, husbands and fathers'.[44]

With most of the men fighting further forward, the initial weight of German air attacks fell on the city's women, who had already provided most of the labour that had built the three lines of defence around the Stalingrad – 478 kilometres of trenches, dugouts, firing points and anti-tank ditches and obstacles – during the summer. But as the Germans advanced on the city the Russian efforts to recruit women made in the spring were beginning to have a real impact. The Stalingrad air defence (PVO) corps had recruited more than 8,000 female volunteers in April. With these, and the women soldiers in the thirteen field armies, it seems certain that between 20,000 and 60,000 servicewomen, in uniform, were involved in the battle altogether.[45]

Many of the women recruited to air defence units in April were assigned to the forward VNOS posts – air observation, warning and communications. These were, by their nature, widely separated, far out on the steppe. Each post had a detachment of five people, mostly young women. With German advance patrols probing across the porous vastness of the steppe, these were highly exposed positions. On 31 August the Germans captured three VNOS detachments, made them dig a trench and stand next to it, and then shot them in turn – five men and thirteen women – as they refused to tell the Germans the shortest route to their next destination. Vera Nikonovaya survived by playing dead, though wounded. She crawled from among the bodies of her comrades and headed for a neighbouring post, which she reached after five days.[46]

The air defence observers were sometimes called *Vnosovtsi*, which might have helped dispel the confusion that arose because a 'reconnaissance person' – *razvedchik* – could be either an air defence observer or, very different, a combatant. A *razvedchik* could also be a behind-the-lines operative, effectively what are now known as special forces or 'sneaky-beakies', used for deep (strategic) reconnaissance and for capturing *yazyky* – 'tongues' – prisoners to talk.[47]

The anti-aircraft units soon found themselves on the front line against German tanks, as well as against Stukas. One battery kept up a continuous battle against oncoming tanks and Stukas for 24 hours. The gunners, observers, fire control instrument operators, and signallers were all women. None of them would take cover. The German accounts of these battles vary. Some reports speak of fighting against 'enemy anti-aircraft positions, manned by tenacious women'. Others speak of civilian women lying dead in bloodstained summer cotton dresses – strange, since women wearing military uniform had been at air defence posts for several months before the Germans approached Stalingrad in late August. It may be that civilians attempted to help out the air defence units when their people were killed or wounded.[48] One only has to recall the tragic chaos at the Beslan school siege in September 2004, when local civilians, men and women, grabbed their own rifles to try to help Russian special forces rescue their children. 'Just leave it to the professionals' is not – and, it appears, never has been – a Russian concept.[49]

Of women – and snipers

The 'rat war' among the chimneys, the garrets, the cellars, the high windows in gutted warehouses and factory buildings, was also the ideal environment for snipers. Of all the stories associated with the smashed and smouldering city of Stalingrad, the sniper war is among the most fascinating, but one where the truth is as elusive as the rats. 'Sniperism' became a cult, and on 10 November it was ordered that, when a marksman or woman achieved forty kills, the 'For Bravery' medal and the title 'noble sniper' would be awarded.[50]

Women had been operating as snipers since the start of the war. As the Stalingrad fighting reached its fiercest intensity, Ludmila Pavlichenko, with 309 kills and a submarine ticket out of Sevastopol to her credit, had already been invalided out of service. The fact that the Central Women's School for Sniper Training was not established until May 1943 has led some to question as to whether there were any women snipers at Stalingrad. There were. The Battle of Stalingrad underlined women's aptitude for this role, which not only required a good eye and good breathing but the ability to lie stone-still in the freezing cold for hours, awaiting the moment to squeeze the trigger. The Central Women's School was headed by N. P. Chegodaeva, who had been one of the Soviet 'advisers' in the Spanish Civil War, and turned out 1,061 women snipers and 407 instructors. The graduates, it is claimed, killed about 12,000 German soldiers.[51]

The most famous, though not the most deadly, Stalingrad woman sniper was Tanya Chernova. She is alleged to have fought with partisans in Belarus and Ukraine, and, aged 20, arrived on 24 September with 284th Siberian Division commanded by Colonel Nikolai Batyuk.

Tanya Chernova's career at Stalingrad has been linked with that of a fellow sniper, Vasiliy Zaytsev, who had arrived with the same division on 20 September. The tale is based entirely on the testimony of William A. Craig, who interviewed Chernova for his book, *Enemy at the Gates*. According to Craig, in ten days Zaytsev had killed forty Germans and was already a celebrity, although, with 149 kills by 7 November, he was not the highest scoring Russian sniper during the battle. That honour went to one 'Zikan', who killed 224.[52] In late September an ad hoc sniper school for Sixty-Second Army was set up in the Lazur chemical plant, between Mamayev Kurgan and the Red October factory, and Chernova became one of about thirty students there, along with Zaytsev, an instructor. Craig alleges they become lovers – that is the only basis for the story.

In three months Chernova killed eighty Germans. During the Russian counteroffensive, she was on a mission which Craig alleges may have been to kill the German commander, Paulus, when another woman sniper stepped on a mine. She was 'slightly hurt' but Chernova was seriously wounded in the gut, and nearly died. The next day, she was evacuated across the Volga – and invalided out of the war, cursing the 'stupid cow' who had trodden on the mine.[53]

When interviewed in the 1970s, Chernova said she had believed that Zaytsev had been killed, and that she only learned of his survival in 1969. Zaytsev does not mention Chernova in his memoirs but in a 1991 interview admitted that she was 'one of our female snipers' and was 'a fine sniper'. It may be that Zaytsev omitted any mention of Tanya Chernova from his memoirs so as not to upset his wife.[54]

The other story is that, within the vast, apparently impersonal, fiery maelstrom of Stalingrad, Zaytsev became involved in a personal duel with a German sniper. Because Zaytsev was killing so many German officers and was such a Russian propaganda asset, the Germans sent their top sniper to eliminate him. Allegedly it was the aristocratic Major König, who had won a rifle-shooting gold medal at the 1936 Berlin Olympics and had become the head of the German sniper school at Zossen-Wünsdorf, the OKH headquarters complex south of Berlin. No Major König won any shooting medal at Berlin for sure. After a sniper duel in the ruins of the city, Zaytsev tracked him to his lair under a sheet of corrugated iron, and shot him dead. It is a great story but probably, like that of the twenty-eight Panfilovtsy at the battle of Moscow, completely untrue. Furthermore, unlike the Panfilovtsy story, it was never promulgated by the Soviet authorities. There is no mention of it in the surviving Soviet correspondence which, given the assiduous reporting of all 'sniperism' issues, seems surprising if there was any evidence that it happened.[55] Zaytsev retired to Kiev but asked to be buried in the city on the Volga. The break-up of the Soviet Union made this impossible, but he was eventually reburied in Volgograd in January 2006.

To the wire

On 11 November the last great German attempt to break through to the Volga split for the third time Chuikov's precarious bridgehead holding on to the west bank, with its army command post dug into the clayey cliff riverside. The Red October factory was in German hands. Soviet units and formations were, at best, down to a tenth of regulation strength, and running out of ammunition and food. By 17 November, the Russian situation was desperate, and the Volga was starting to freeze. Meanwhile, however, the German High Command was receiving reports of Russian redeployments north of the Don.

The final words on the battle for the city itself remain with those who were there. Like the great Aleksandr Suvorov, Chuikov, who commanded Sixty-Second Army's defence, issued no-nonsense orders which any soldier could understand:

> At every step danger lurks. No matter – a grenade in every corner of the room, then forward! A burst from your *avtomat* (tommy gun) around what's left, a bit further – a grenade, then on again! Another room – a grenade. A turning – another grenade! Rake it with your tommy gun! And get a move on![56]

The Germans had forced their way forward against fanatical and skilful resistance, and paid a terrible price. A lieutenant of XXIV Panzer Division recalled:

> We have fought for fifteen days for a single house, with mortars, machine guns, grenades and bayonets. The front is a corridor between burnt-out rooms: it is the thin ceiling between two floors . . . imagine Stalingrad: eighty days and eighty nights of hand-to-hand struggles. The street is no longer measured in metres, but in corpses.
>
> Stalingrad is no longer a town. By day it is an enormous cloud of burning, blinding smoke; it is a vast furnace lit by the reflection of the flames. And when night arrives, one of those scorching, howling, bleeding nights, the dogs plunge

into the Volga and swim desperately for the other bank. The
nights of Stalingrad are a terror for them. *Animals flee this
hell; the hardest stones cannot bear it for long; only men
endure.*[57]

And women.

The Gods strike back . . .

The Germans were now 'fixed'. They were locked into a battle in a city,
exactly where the Russians wanted them. As early as the middle of
September the Reich Press Chief Dietrich launched a number of releases
saying that the 'Battle for Stalingrad' was now in its 'final stage'. The
press had duly picked these up and published them on 15 and 16
September.[58] Although the German Propaganda Ministry called it 'the
greatest battle of attrition the world has ever seen', and it must also
have seemed like that to the Russians who were there, Zhukov had in
fact been very sparing about the reinforcements he sent in. In the two
months from 1 September to 1 November only five infantry divisions
were ferried across the Volga to reinforce Sixty-Second Army – a tiny
force compared with the usual expenditure of forces on the eastern
front and only just enough to cover 'wastage' (casualties) within the
city. The difficulty of getting people across the Volga, and especially
heavy weapons, forced the Russians to be judicious about what they
sent. Meanwhile, the Germans had poured in huge numbers of troops,
who were absorbed in the great urban sponge. The assault on the factory
districts which began on 14 October had used three infantry divisions
and more than 300 tanks.

On 12 September Zhukov saw Stalin and Vasilevskiy in Moscow,
although the meeting, like many of the most important, is not recorded
in his appointments diary. Paulus, coincidentally, went to see Hitler at
Vinnitsa the same day. In Moscow, Stalin asked what was needed to
break through to Stalingrad from the north. 'A lot,' was the answer. He
told Zhukov and Vasilevskiy to go away and think about it. The next
day the generals returned to see Stalin. Their visit coincided with the

first day of an all-out German attack on the city. All became clear. With the Germans fixed in Stalingrad, their extended flank along the Don guarded by brave but weaker and relatively poorly equipped satellite armies, the way was open for a spectacular encirclement. The idea of the Stalingrad counteroffensive was born. Zhukov, as usual, was thinking big: a huge encirclement, west of the Don. Stalin thought they did not have enough troops for that, and that the Germans should be cut off east of it by an attack from north and south level with the Don river, closer to Stalingrad. Zhukov then explained that an attack so close to the existing German positions would enable them to swing around their armoured forces in Stalingrad, quickly, to counter it, whereas one further to the west – a wider swing – would hit the less reliable satellite formations and prevent the Germans from bringing up reserves. Meanwhile, a day before, Paulus had been explaining to Hitler that his forces in Stalingrad were overextended and their flanks exposed.[59]

For Stalin and for Zhukov, however, the immediate priority was to hold on to Stalingrad. But planning for a great, wider-ranging counteroffensive also began to take shape. The Russian forces would not have the troops or equipment in place for two months, until mid November, but that would coincide conveniently with the onset of the first snow. Rokossovskiy was summoned to the Kremlin on the 22 September.[60] He already knew that a powerful German grouping occupied the area between the Volga and the Don, but said he was personally called to see the Boss 'several days later' – that is, on the 22nd. The idea of attacking the vulnerable German flank from the north was 'alluring', he recorded. 'The only problem was whether it would be dangerous for Stavka to spend the time concentrating the forces and launching them into action.'[61]

On 26 September it is likely that Stavka met to consider not one but two major counteroffensives. David Glantz suggests that the decision to launch twin counteroffensives around Stalingrad, to encircle the German Sixth Army, and south of Rzhev, to encircle Ninth Army, was made then, and approved by Stalin early the next morning.[62] According to Glantz, Stalin told his commanders, 'You may continue to plan your offensive. Conduct two efforts. Zhukov will control the Rzhev operation and Vasilevskiy the operation at Stalingrad.'[63] According to Stalin's diary the Boss certainly saw Zhukov at the Kremlin in the small hours of 27 September, along with Molotov and Beria, joined shortly afterwards by Voroshilov and Andrey Khrulev – a former chief of Red Army logistics

Table 16.1 – Comparison of forces available for counteroffensives west of Moscow and around Stalingrad

	Kalinin, Western Fronts, Moscow Defence Zone (*Mars, 'Jupiter'*)	South-Western, Don, Stalingrad Front (*Uranus, Saturn*)
Troops	1.9 million	1 million
Guns and mortars	24,000	15,000
Tanks	3,300	1,400
Aircraft	1,100	900

and now Minister for Communications. If the planning of two huge counteroffensives were being discussed, that would make sense.[64]

The metaphysical codenames mirrored the grandiose nature of the attacks. They were named as planets, circling from the north and around Moscow, roughly in the order of their orbits from the sun. There definitely was an operation called Mars, attacking the Ninth Army from the north-west and north. Even references to Mars are scarce but in his official history of the war Marshal Grechko confirmed that:

> In October–November 1942 the North-Western, Kalinin and Western Fronts were to conduct a combined offensive operation along the Moscow axis to destroy the enemy in the Rzhev and Novo-Sokol'nikov regions. The code-name of the operation was 'Mars'. . . . its aim was not only to tie down enemy forces and defeat them in the region but also to draw additional enemy reserves to that region.[65]

Between the three of them these fronts had roughly half the tanks and 35 per cent of overall Russian strength on the eastern front on just 17 per cent of its extent.[66] But then, they were defending Moscow. The comparison between them and the forces available around Stalingrad is shown in Table 16.1.[67]

David Glantz surmises that the Western Front's operation to follow Operation Mars, and to meet up with the Kalinin Front's advance, which would take place subsequently, was called Jupiter, although there is no firm evidence of this. Further to the south, the initial encirclement of Sixth Army, which the Russians had 'fixed' in Stalingrad, was called

Uranus. There would also be a wider outer encirclement, appropriately named Saturn, with its big rings. The Russian concept was as awesome in its ambition as the codenames it was given. It was to be a counter-offensive of the classical gods, starting in the north with the Roman god of war. The two sets of operations are shown, with some speculation, in Figure 16.5.

Grechko's comments suggest, as Zhukov did, that 'Mars' was, at least in part, a diversion, which would undoubtedly draw German forces away from Stalingrad. The order went out on 28–29 September, with an initial D-Day of 12 October,[68] whereas Russian forces would not be ready to attack around Stalingrad until mid November – although that might have been good timing, drawing maximum forces away before a strike in the outer orbits a month later. However, the numbers of forces involved suggest that if Mars (and a possible concomitant which logically would have been Jupiter) was a diversion, it was some diversion.

Table 16.2 compares the forces actually involved in the two pairs of operations.

The two sets of operations, assuming there was a 'Jupiter', look fairly evenly matched. The planets circling close to the Moscow sun had more rifle divisions and mobile brigades, and potentially more soldiers, whereas the Stalingrad counteroffensive had more mobile forces, artillery and specialist forces. Overall, they were about the same. If Rzhev-Sychevka was merely a 'diversion', it was, indeed, an astronomical diversion.

The orders for Mars were issued on 1 October but the counter-attack had to be postponed from 12 October because of bad weather. The weather dogged the preparations, and at the end of October Zhukov flew to Moscow to discuss the two great counteroffensives with Stalin. Uranus was scheduled for around 19 November, but now Mars was pushed back – unavoidably – until the 25th. As Deputy Supreme Commander Zhukov was responsible for both operations, although given Army Group Centre's strategic significance and its proximity to Moscow – at its closest it was only 300 kilometres away – and the big Soviet forces in the area, he may have felt it was the more important of the two. If he did, he said nothing about it when it failed.

The obscurity which cloaked Mars and a possible Jovian successor for fifty years did not just result from Soviet censorship. To be fair to the Russians, they covered it up very well. Western intelligence at the time seems to have been completely unaware of Zhukov's unsuccessful

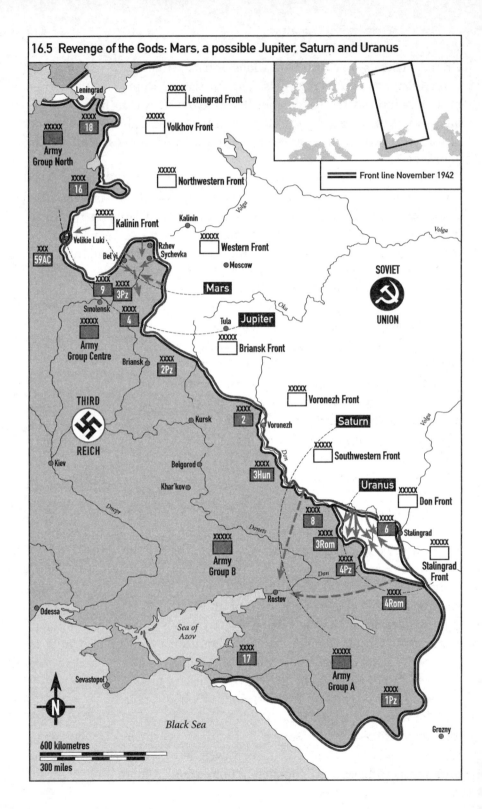

16.5 Revenge of the Gods: Mars, a possible Jupiter, Saturn and Uranus

Front line November 1942

Leningrad

XXXXX Leningrad Front

XXXXX Volkhov Front

XXXXX Army Group North

XXXX 18

XXXX 16

XXXXX Northwestern Front

XXXXX Kalinin Front

Kalinin

Velikie Luki

XXX 59AC

Bel'yi

Rzhev
Sychevka

XXXXX Western Front

Moscow

XXXX 9

XXXX 3Pz

Mars

XXXX 4

Smolensk

XXXXX Army Group Centre

Briansk

XXXX 2Pz

Tula

Jupiter

XXXXX Brjansk Front

THIRD

REICH

Kiev

Kursk

Belgorod

Khar'kov

Odessa

Sevastopol'

Voronezh

SOVIET

UNION

Oka

Volga

Volga

XXXX 2

XXXXX Voronezh Front

Saturn

XXXXX Southwestern Front

Don

XXXX 3Hun

Uranus

XXXXX Don Front

XXXX 8

XXXX 3Rom

XXXX 6

Stalingrad

XXXXX Army Group B

Donets

XXXX 4Pz

XXXXX Stalingrad Front

Don

Rostov

XXXX 4Rom

Dnepr

Sea of
Azov

XXXX 17

XXXXX Army Group A

XXXX 1Pz

Grozny

Black Sea

N

600 kilometres

300 miles

Table 16.2 – Comparison of forces employed in Mars and 'Jupiter' with those employed in Uranus and Saturn, 1942[69]

	Mars and 'Jupiter'*	Uranus and Saturn
Men and women available in sector November 1942	1,890,000	1,103,000
Armies	10[†]	10[†]
Rifle divisions	65	53.5
Mobile brigades	76	62.5
Artillery regiments	88	92
Anti-tank regiments	36	40
Anti-aircraft regiments	26	33
Engineer battalions	31	45

* Includes Moscow Defence Zone.
† Includes one tank army.

attempt to cut off and kill Ninth Army and possibly rupture Army Group Centre. The excellent and wonderfully concise American account of operations for November 1942 to January 1943 concentrates on those south of Leningrad, and on the divergent Stalingrad and Caucasus axes. As for the centre, 'Only local operations took place with no important change in the situation.'[70]

Meanwhile the build-up for Uranus continued, in great secrecy. According to Soviet reports, some 160,000 men, 10,000 horses, 430 tanks, 6,000 guns and mortars, and 14,000 other vehicles were ferried across the Volga between 1 and 20 November. There were nine crossings over the Volga, and more over the Don – twenty bridges and twenty-one ferries in the areas of the South-Western and Don Fronts.[71] A simple but brilliant operational plan is one thing: logistics is everything.

An icy planet: Uranus

Back in an outer orbit, in the more southerly city of Stalingrad, Chuikov was still hanging on with his Sixty-Second Army, holding four bridgeheads precariously clinging to the west bank of the Volga. Desperate to take the city before winter, Paulus's troops launched another attack on 17 November. The day before that, the first wisps of snow had fallen. The summer had been baking hot, and the heat of the gunfire and blazing oil had never gone away. But during the night of 18–19 November thick snow clouds brought their white cargo, and freezing fog, 'as thick as milk'.[72] The German and Romanian sentries could see no more than a few metres. During the night Chuikov had been told to stand by for further orders.

At 07.20 Russian time, 05.20 German time – either way, it was still dark – at least 3,500 of the 13,000 Russian guns, heavy mortars and 'Guards mortars' – *Katyushas* – available for the entire counteroffensive were loaded. That was just the artillery to support the first pincer, from the north. At 07.30 they fired, on what became, from 1944, 'artillery day' in Russia, and at 08.50 the infantry attack went in.

The initial target was Third Romanian Army, under General Petre Dumitrescu, but German soldiers 50 kilometres to the south were wakened by the ground shaking.[73] Units of the Russian South-West Front ripped a 12-kilometre gap in the defences and although the Romanians fought valiantly they were soon being pursued across the now white steppe by formidable 30-tonne T-34 and 62-tonne KV2 tanks. The Russian attack trapped five Romanian divisions in the Don bend, where they held on until 24 November.

Once again the Russians had exploited the weather to their advantage. 'Richthofen could only get one or two planes airborne, and could not attack the crossings over the Don by which the attacking Russian troops of the South-Western Front were supplied.'[74] On 20 November the Stalingrad Front attacked south of the city, into the Romanian Fourth Army, commanded by Constantin Constantinescu-Klaps, which was under command of Hoth's German Fourth Panzer Army. The Romanian Fourth Army, one of two in south Russia, therefore often does not feature on historical maps, but they took the brunt of the attack.[75] It was delayed two hours from 08.00 to 10.00 because the weather was so bad that the Russians could not observe their fire in the morning murk, but by that evening Constantinescu's forward Romanian troops had collapsed, and a 30-kilometre rip had appeared. Into that breach, in what would become classic fashion, the Russians pushed two mobile corps, IV Cavalry and IV Mechanized, towards Plodovitoye (see Figure 16.6).

On 14 October, in Operational Order No. 1, Hitler had brought the wider German summer offensive to a close, apart from the attack into Stalingrad itself. As with the planned assault on Moscow the previous winter, capturing the city before the winter set in would give the troops somewhere, however bomb-blasted, to shelter. But now it was winter and the bomb-blasting was still going on. On 23 October, Kurt Zeitzler, Chief of the Army General Staff, said the Russians were 'in no position to mount a major offensive with any far reaching objective'.[76] It was Zeitzler who, on the morning of 19 November, had to break the bad news to Hitler.

Not only had Zeitzler been wrong, but on 16 August Hitler had actually expressed concern that Stalin might repeat what had happened in the Civil War in 1920 and attack across the Don. He had therefore ordered the Don front to be 'fortified as strongly as possible and mined'.[77] It was mined, but the Russians had skilfully cleared the minefields on the narrow attack sectors during the night of 18 to 19 November. It seems that it was the *Wehrmacht*, not Hitler, who neglected the flanks. Hitler must now have realized that the entire German position in south Russia was at risk but brazened it out. On the next day he ordered Manstein south to take command of a new army group, Don, with a view to breaking the threatened Russian encirclement. Manstein later said that the attempt to gain the Volga through an urban battle in Stalingrad would only have worked if it had been over quickly and that to have a major force bogged down there for weeks with inadequately protected flanks was a 'cardinal error'.[78]

On Sunday, 22 November, the 19th Tank Brigade of the Russian XXVI Tank Corps, coming from the north, seized the bridge over the Don at Kalach. The next day, 23 November, the two pincers actually met as planned at the village of Sovietskiy, a little under 20 kilometres to the south-east. No film was taken that day, but the Russians staged a dramatic re-enactment later, with cheering waves of soldiers running

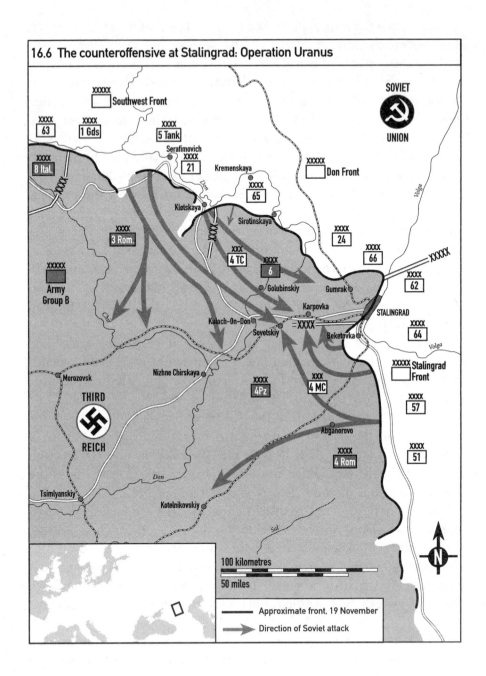

16.6 The counteroffensive at Stalingrad: Operation Uranus

SOVIET UNION

XXXXX Southwest Front

XXXX 63

XXXX 1 Gds

XXXX 5 Tank

Serafimovich XXXX 21

Kremenskaya

XXXXX Don Front

XXX Don

XXXX 65

Kletskaya

Sirotinskaya

XXXX 24

XXXX 66

XXXXX

XXXX 62

Volga

XXXX 8 Ital.

XXXX

XXXX 3 Rom.

XXX 4 TC

XXXX 6

XXXXX Army Group B

Golubinskiy Gumrak

Karpovka

STALINGRAD

Chir

Kalach-On-Don

Sovetskiy

=XXXX

Beketovka

XXXX 64

Volga

XXXXX Stalingrad Front

Morozovsk

Nizhne Chirskaya

XXXX 4 Pz

XXX 4 MC

XXXX 57

THIRD REICH

Abganerovo

XXXX 51

XXXX 4 Rom

Don

Tsimlyanskiy

Kotelnikovskiy

Sal

N

100 kilometres

50 miles

——— Approximate front, 19 November

⇒ Direction of Soviet attack

towards each other through the snow. In fact, the first men to meet were tank crews from IV and XXVI Tank Corps, which had covered 130 kilometres since crossing the start line to the north-west four days before, and IV Mechanized Corps, which had come 80 kilometres from the south-east in three days. Dwarfed by the vastness of the landscape, they fired green flares periodically so that they did not miss each other, or think the other force were Germans.[79]

By this time the Germans realized they were 'temporarily' encircled. Their resupply and exit routes were blocked. Along with the Carthaginians' encirclement and annihilation of the Romans at Cannae in 216 BC, Zhukov's destruction of the Japanese at Khalkin Gol in 1939, and Schwarzkopf's Hail Mary of 1991, it was from a purely military point of view one of the greatest encirclements of history.[80] But its staggering scale, in spatial and human terms, especially given the very thin margins available to the Soviet High Command, and its strategic and political consequences must make it the greatest encirclement of all time. And, as it would later turn out, a double encirclement, at that.

Initially, the Russians thought they might have trapped 85,000 to 90,000 Germans and Romanians. They soon realized they had trapped far more. At first, the German High Command thought 400,000 might have been trapped – both sides were using 'worst-case scenarios'. However, Manstein reckoned that estimates over 300,000 were exaggerated – the official Soviet estimate was 330,000. Some 250,000 to 275,000, including not only Germans but Italians, Romanians and the wretched Hiwis – Russians forced to serve the Germans, who now stood no chance – seems a reliable figure.[81] That would be consistent with the 91,000 prisoners the Russians took when the Germans finally surrendered at the end of January and the beginning of February. The balance would have been killed, have died of disease or exposure, or been evacuated as wounded or critical personnel.[82] The Russian pincers around this huge force – 'a tiger by the tail' – were also dangerously fragile: in places a few kilometres between the 450-kilometre arc of the outer ring of the encirclement, and the inner face, enclosing the Germans.

The arrival of Russians at Kalach was a nasty shock for Paulus and his Chief of Staff, Lt Gen. Arthur Schmidt. Their headquarters at Golubinskiy, on the Don, was only about 25 kilometres north of there. On 21 November, even before the outer Russian embrace was locked, Paulus and Schmidt flew to Nizhne-Chirskaya, at the confluence of the

Don and the Chir, and outside the encirclement, so that they could use secure communications with the Führer. Well, that was their story. Meanwhile, the Germans on the run or trapped in the closing bear hug seem to have shown the same mixture of courage and cowardice, panic and resilience, desperation and determination, and indifference to civilians or prisoners of war, as the Red Army had in 1941.[83]

On the 22nd Paulus and Schmidt flew back to a new headquarters at Gumrak, much closer to Stalingrad – a mere 12 kilometres from its centre (see Figures 16.6, 16.9). The meeting of the bear's paws the next day sealed the already obvious encirclement of the remnants of Sixth Army in an area which John Erickson has described as a 'crushed skull', with its nose on the Volga.[84] If you can envision a skull slammed against the Volga, then the River Tsaritsa flowed from one of its nostrils (see Figure 16.9).

By 24 November, then, the Russians had encircled the German Sixth Army and elements of the Fourth Panzer Army close to Stalingrad, destroyed the Fourth Romanian Army and pushed Third Romanian back to the Chir (see Figure 16.6), and created a massive gap between Army Group B to the north and Army Group A in the Caucasus. Manstein considered it imperative to get Sixth Army out. The Russians would obviously do everything they could to destroy Sixth Army and might also push fast-moving forces across the Don further west towards Rostov, threatening to cut off Army Group A as well. While Manstein planned to extract the encircled army, Hitler investigated the idea of resupplying Sixth Army by air. The Luftwaffe promised that it could, 'on a temporary basis'. He sounded out Hans Jeschonnek, the Luftwaffe Chief of Staff, and told Zeitzler there might be another way. The encircled force said it needed 750 tonnes of supplies a day – 380 tonnes of food, 250 of ammunition and 120 of fuel, but might make do with 400 in the short term, given the rations already in the pocket. Goering ignored this and told his Luftwaffe commanders 500. They replied that they could manage 350, although that made no allowance for the Russian winter and the increasingly active, numerous and competent Russian air force. Nor did it envisage further, wider encirclement by Russian ground forces.[85] In fact, Goering had 298 planes available per day, enough to deliver, at best, half of the inadequate 350 tonnes, but was hoping to bring in extra big planes from other theatres. The average daily delivery was just over 100 tonnes. Hopes of extraction were dashed. At 08.30 on 24 November, Sixth Army headquarters at Gumrak, where

Paulus had had the prescience to take a good supply of red wine and champagne, received a message from Hitler. There would be no withdrawal. 'Fortress Stalingrad' was a fact.[86]

The German supply flights began at Tatsinskaya airfield, 225 kilometres from the final airfield in the pocket, at Pitomnik (see Figures 16.7, 16.9). As the inadequate attempts to resupply the pocket by air progressed, the Russians launched their first main attack against the trapped Sixth Army on 2 December. On 4 December Stalin assigned extra forces to the Don Front, including the Red Army's strongest, Second Guards Army from the Stavka Reserve. Second Guards, it will be remembered, got through more than its fair share of penal battalions during the war. A few days later the operation to strangle the trapped Sixth Army received its apposite if rather obvious codename: *Kol'tso* – 'Ring'.[87]

Winter Storm, *Donnerschlag* and Little Saturn

On 12 December Manstein's attempt to relieve Sixth Army, Operation *Wintergewitte* (Winter Storm), got under way (see Figure 16.7). It was not a moment too soon, but it was doomed to failure from the outset.[88] On 26 November rations for the German soldiers in the Stalingrad *Kessel* – cauldron – had been reduced to 350 grams of bread, 120 grams of meat (including horses, who died in their thousands) and 30 grams of fat per day. Ten days later the bread ration was again cut, to 200 grams – little more than civilians got in the worst days of the siege of Leningrad. Extra food was brought in between 18 and 22 December, but at the expense of equally vital fuel and ammunition.[89] No one could survive like this in a Russian winter, especially fighting soldiers. The encircled Sixth Army reported its first deaths from starvation on 21 December. As Christmas approached, it was starving and freezing to death. Stalingrad was the new Leningrad.

To break in and relieve the Stalingrad *Kessel*, Manstein reckoned he needed a force equivalent to an army, and the number of formations available was well below that.[90] Furthermore, Paulus's force was getting so weak that, paradoxically, the 'breakout' option was looking unattrac-

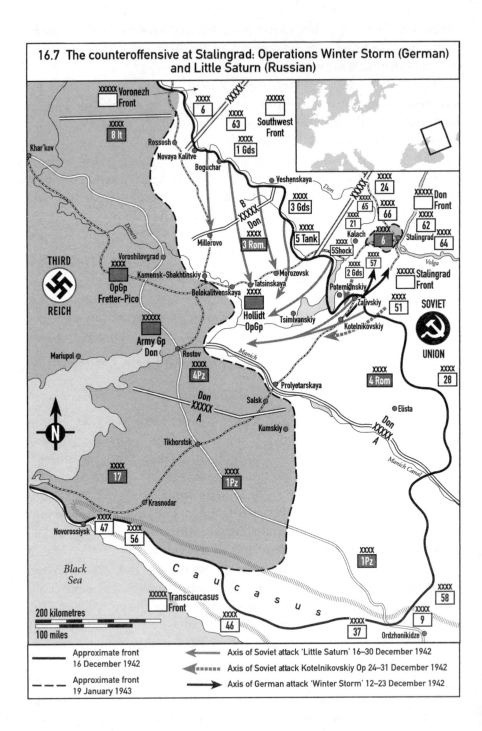

16.7 The counteroffensive at Stalingrad: Operations Winter Storm (German) and Little Saturn (Russian)

XXXXX Voronezh Front

XXXX 6

XXXX 63

XXXXX Southwest Front

XXXX 8 lt

Rossosh

Novaya Kalitve

XXXX 1 Gds

Boguchar

Khar'kov

Veshenskaya

Don

XXXX 24

XXXXX Don Front

B XXXXX Don

XXXX 3 Gds

XXXX 65

XXXX 66

Millerovo

XXXX 3 Rom.

XXXX 21

5 Tank

Kalach

XXXX 5Shock

XXXX 62

Stalingrad

XXXX 64

Donets

Voroshilovgrad

THIRD REICH

XXXX OpGp Fretter-Pico

Kamensk-Shakhtinskiy

Belokalitvenskaya

Tatsinskaya

Morozovsk

Volga

XXXX 57

XXXXX Stalingrad Front

XXXXX Army Gp Don

XXXX Hollidt OpGp

Tsimlvanskiy

Potemkinskiy

Zalivskiy

XXXX 2 Gds

SOVIET

Mariupol

Rostov

XXXX 4Pz

Manich

Kotelnikovskiy

XXXX 51

UNION

Don XXXXX A

Salsk

Prolyetarskaya

XXXX 4 Rom

XXXX 28

Kumskiy

Elista

Don XXXXX A

Tikhorstsk

XXXX 17

XXXX 1Pz

Manich Canal

Krasnodar

Novorossiysk

XXXX 47

XXXX 56

C a u c a s u s

XXXX 1Pz

Black Sea

N

200 kilometres

100 miles

XXXXX Transcaucasus Front

XXXX 46

XXXX 37

Ordzhonikidze

XXXX 58

XXXX 9

Volga

Approximate front 16 December 1942

⟵ Axis of Soviet attack 'Little Saturn' 16–30 December 1942

Approximate front 19 January 1943

⟵••••• Axis of Soviet attack Kotelnikovskiy Op 24–31 December 1942

⟶ Axis of German attack 'Winter Storm' 12–23 December 1942

tive. On 18 December Army Group B proposed a breakout and issued a draft directive, Operation *Donnerschlag* (Thunderclap). Hitler, however, refused to countenance any withdrawal. Paulus therefore had a choice. He could try to break out, as his immediate boss wanted, or obey Hitler and hold on. Guderian's 'Winter Storm' stalled 50 kilometres from its final objective. Paulus and his advisers, mindful of Hitler's views, and seeing the exhausted state of their troops, felt the lesser evil was to stay put.[91]

One can understand Hitler's feelings at this time. Given the vast expenditure of blood and treasure at Stalingrad, and the heavy weapons that would have to be left behind if the Germans pulled out, it would be a crippling waste. As he said to Zeitzler on 12 December:

> We must not give up now, in any circumstances. We won't win it back again ... we can't possibly replace the stuff we have inside. If we give that up we surrender the whole meaning of this campaign. We are not coming back here a second time. That is why we must not leave here. Because too much blood has been shed for that.[92]

He was right about one thing. They were not coming back.

Manstein's attempted relief of Sixth Army inevitably affected Russian plans for the second part of the double encirclement. Operation Saturn was to accomplish a wider pincer movement – bear hug – by the South-Western and Voronezh Fronts west of the Uranus trap. The original idea, discussed back in September and put forward in more detail by Vasilevskiy on 26 November, was to seize the Donets industrial area, which the Russians desperately needed, and to cut off Army Group A in the Caucasus. The economic and strategic aims were grandiose, mirroring the original variant of *Blau*. Saturn was intended to destroy Eighth Italian army, the army group 'Hollidt' and the remnants of Third Romanian Army. However, while the German *Blau* had been confounded by over-optimism and an obsession with Stalingrad, the Russians realistically pulled in their horns to take account of Manstein's counteroffensive. A new variant, 'Little Saturn', would concentrate on the elimination of the newly created Army Group Don, and a narrower encirclement which would reinforce the attempts to eliminate the Sixth Army trapped in Stalingrad.[93]

Stavka met in late December to discuss the elimination of Sixth Army. Stalin said that Operation 'Ring' needed one man in command:

at the moment, two fronts, Rokossovskiy's Don and Yeremenko's Stalingrad, were involved. The Boss decided to put Rokossovskiy in charge and subordinate the Stalingrad Front to him. Zhukov pointed out that Yeremenko would be hurt if his front was put under Rokossovskiy, but Stalin snapped, 'It's not the time for feeling hurt.'[94] On 30 December three Stalingrad Front armies – Sixty-Second, which had held the city centre, Sixty-Fourth and Fifty-Seventh, were transferred to Rokossovskiy's Don Front.

Besides commanding Operation 'Ring', Rokossovskiy had strong views on the downgrading of Saturn. In his memoirs he made an uncharacteristically bitchy attack on Vasilevskiy, in a chunk cut out and now reinstated:

> A brave variant would have opened up huge possibilities for future action on the southern wing of the Soviet–German front. The game, as they say, is worth the candle provided the risk is not too great. Several enemy groupings which had hastened to the defence of the encircled [Sixth Army], having appeared overwhelming to those who reported them, couldn't provide any help. They were made up of smashed up units and rear-area commands. Of course, I can say that now that everything has become clear . . . Stavka preferred the variant suggested by Vasilevskiy. They considered that he was more reliable. But you see, even this variant did not exclude an element of risk. So the lovely operation envisaged by Stavka, heading in the Rostov direction, could not happen . . . The operation was narrowed down because all attention and significant forces were diverted to the so-called Manstein Group. That helped the Germans escape an even worse fate. I am convinced that if Vasilevskiy had not been with us then, at Zavorykino [Don Front headquarters], but in his own place in Moscow, at the General Staff, then the question of using Second Shock Army would have been resolved as Stavka wanted, that is, the army would have been used to reinforce a blow by the South-West and Voronezh Fronts towards Rostov.[95]

'Little Saturn', known more prosaically, and no doubt for security reasons, as the 'Middle Don' operation, was launched on 16 December, southwards towards Millerovo and the airfields at Tatsinskaya and

Morozovsk which lay along the air corrridor into Stalingrad (see Figure 16.7). The latter airfields were the objectives for XXIV and XXV Tank Corps, which were committed on 18 and 17 December, respectively. Their mission was to seize the airfields and destroy everything. That included 180 Ju-52 transport planes at Tatsinskaya and He-111 bombers at Morozovsk: pretty well all the assets available for the Stalingrad airlift. The XXIV Tank Corps was destroyed, but not before it had wrecked 431 German planes. Little Saturn, the outer encirclement, had also been a success.[96]

The red planet: Mars

On 25 November Operation Mars against Ninth Army's salient west of Moscow finally began with an attack by Twentieth Army, from the east of the Rzhev-Sychevka salient, and Twenty-Second and Forty-First, from the west. Further out on the western flank, attacks by Third Shock on Velikiye Luki suggest there was a wider aim, to encircle Army Group Centre (see Figure 16.8). The weather was as bad as that for the start of Uranus, a week before, and severely hampered the accuracy of the Russian artillery. In spite of the problems the initial Russian attacks penetrated at most of the chosen points of attack. The Germans counter-attacked at Bely on 7 December and routed Forty-First Army.[97] German attention remained focused on Stalingrad, and on 15 December the Russians retook Velikiye Luki – Rokossovskiy's birthplace – in a smaller-scale version of the nightmare which would befall the Germans in Stalingrad. The Russians failed in their aim of encircling Ninth Army and as a result the wider encirclement, which may have been called Jupiter, was never attempted. The final and ironic difference from Uranus and Saturn was that, in contrast to his determination to hold on in Stalingrad, and perhaps as a result of its consequences, on 6 February – three days after the end at Stalingrad – Hitler approved the withdrawal of the Fourth and Ninth Armies to the Kirov–Velizh line, the base of the salient which the Russians had hoped to cut off.[98] Again, the gigantic Mars effort failed to register with western intelligence. 'After a long period of relative inactivity,' one report concluded,

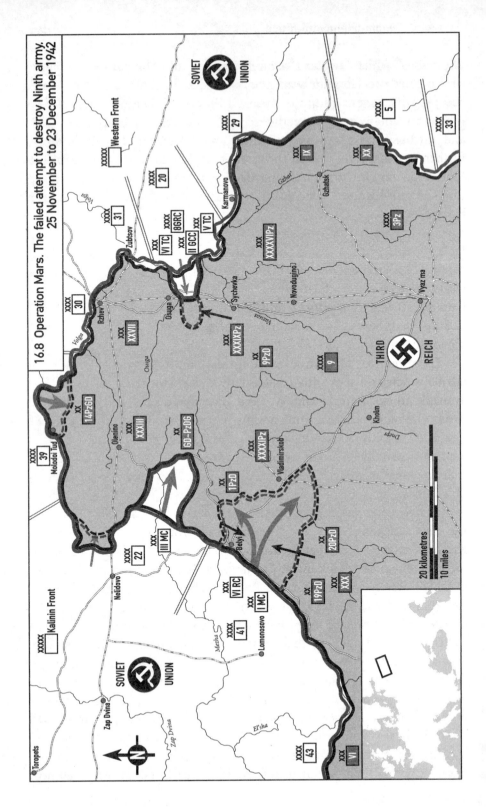

16.8 Operation Mars. The failed attempt to destroy Ninth army, 25 November to 23 December 1942

'the Soviets went over to the offensive west of Moscow and in early March took two German strong points of Rzhev and Gzhatsk.'[99] These had been the targets of Mars, and now the Germans just vacated them, to shorten their defensive perimeter and to release troops to go south and threaten the north side of the Kursk salient (which is explored further in Chapter 17). However, later in March 1943, the Russians took Vyaz'ma and the remaining danger of a renewed German attack threatening Moscow was removed. By default, one of Mars's objectives had been achieved.[100]

Zhukov, understandably, devotes little space to Mars in his memoirs. He explains the reasons for the Russian failure, emphasizing the strength of the German defence on difficult terrain. Given the comparative weakness of the Romanian forces who were the target of the Russian flanking attacks in Uranus, that is not unreasonable.[101] Furthermore, if Uranus had failed, there would have been no Little Saturn. Mars obviously failed, so there was no Jupiter . . . that is war.

The seven Russian Armies committed to Operation Mars numbered 667,000 men and more than 1,900 tanks, over one-third of the forces available to the Kalinin and Western Fronts and the Moscow defence zone. German sources estimate that the Russians lost about 200,000 people, 100,000 of them dead. Russian tank losses were huge – at least 1,600 out of 1,900 committed to the operation initially. That was more than the total number of tanks – 1,400 – committed by Vasilevskiy for Operation Uranus.

In spite of its scale, Mars does not feature as a discrete operation in the new Russian count of casualties and combat losses.[102] General Krivosheyev explained that he had only managed to compute the tallies for forty-three out of seventy-three large independent operations. However, he later estimated that the Rzhev-Sychevka operation accounted for 70,374 dead and 145,300 wounded, which, even if it is wrong, corresponds pretty well to the German estimate.[103]

David Glantz suggests that 'in terms of scale, scope, strategic intent and consequences, Operation Mars was analogous to the circumstances Allied military leaders would have faced should Operation Overlord (the Normandy Landings) [1944] have failed'.[104] This author is sceptical about that. Mounting an attack over the sea is far more complicated than one over land, as Stalin, understandably, did not completely appreciate. Furthermore, the western Allies only had one shot at the main route to Berlin – Normandy. In 1942, the Russians, who had not even recovered from the Barbarossa blow a year before, had two shots. Each shot might eliminate an army. Eliminating an entire army group proved overambitious, in both cases. One of the shots – the Stalingrad counter-offensive – succeeded in eliminating an army and smashing parts of four others. But what a shot.

Weapons of mass destruction – chemical and biological?

With Stalingrad hanging on like grim death and possibly about to fall to the Germans before 19 November 1942, and the German Sixth Army encircled soon after that, the fate of both combatants in this worst of all wars was looking grim. On 26 December Beria told the GKO that the NKVD London 'resident' had passed on one of his agents' reports from early November. Why it took so long is a mystery, but the timing is extraordinary. As Sixth Army began to starve and die at Christmas, Beria reported that British intelligence received by the Foreign Office – presumably Maclean was the source – had reliable information from Polish sources of a discussion between Hitler and Himmler.

> In the event of a significant worsening of the German situation, the German command would use poison gases and bacteria. Here it was underlined that Germany would in no instance consider itself defeated until all means at its disposal had been used. As a result of this meeting German industry, it is said, must be given authorisation to produce large amounts of poison substances and apparatus for chemical and biological warfare.
>
> In the report the Polish agent doesn't indicate on which bit of the Front the Germans suggest using gas and bacteria first. Nevertheless, the British Foreign Office is taking this report seriously. Cadogan [the Permanent Secretary, who had accompanied Churchill to Moscow in August] personally told Eden about this. The British Foreign Office opinion is that Germany is not yet in quite such a tough position, that it will use such desperate measures.[105]

However, the Russians too were desperate. They had a huge arsenal of chemical weapons and had also paid great attention to developing biological weapons during the 1920s and 1930s.[106] If there was ever a time to break international treaties (and if they lost, would it matter? or if they won, could anybody argue?) it might be now.

According to Ken Alibek, a defector and former head of the Soviet *Biopreparat* (biological warfare preparation) programme, there was a mysterious outbreak of tularaemia – a popular biological warfare agent – among German forces around Stalingrad in summer 1942. Alibek was instructed to investigate it by Colonel Absyonenko of the Tomsk Medical Institute. German Panzer troops fell ill in such large numbers that the advance came to a temporary halt. Thousands of Russians living in the Volga area also became victims. Whilst this could have been a natural outbreak of the disease, fanned by the terrible conditions of war in that area, Alibek notes that there were about 10,000 cases of tularaemia in the Soviet Union in 1941, but that in 1942, the year of the south Russian outbreak, the number soared to 100,000 – ten times the previous year's level. In 1943 it fell back to its former level of 10,000.[107]

Alibek became convinced 'that this epidemic was caused intentionally' – he does not say by whom, but it seems to have affected the Germans worse than the Russians. All German intelligence on biological weapons was passed to Professor H. Kliewe who was appointed by the Surgeon General in early 1942 to study chemical defence. Kliewe was captured in the American sector of Germany in spring 1945 and interrogated by a combined British and American team.[108] He was extremely glad to cooperate. He said that Hitler had issued a strict order that on no account was any work to be done on offensive biological warfare and that he understood Hitler was 'very annoyed' when he heard that any work at all was being done on the subject. Kliewe was therefore told to confine himself to defensive measures. Most of the reports he received came from Russia. These included reports that the Russians might use bacterial clouds of tularaemia and another favoured biological warfare agent, bubonic plague.[109] Tularaemia and plague remain high on the list of potential agents at the time of writing, and in the 1991 Gulf War British and American servicemen and women were inoculated against plague in case Saddam Hussein should use it.

Kliewe received sixteen reports from Russia, mostly dealing with plague. In 1942 the Germans received information from prisoners that the Russian forces in Stalingrad had all been recently inoculated against plague. Stalingrad was not normally a focus of plague infection, and to organize the vaccination of all the Russian forces in the city would have been a huge operation. The Red Army at this time had not even succeeded in getting most of its soldiers to wear identification 'capsules' – the equivalent of western armies' 'dog tags'. The troops thought they were bad luck, and very few wore them. According to archaeologists, very few of the bodies, or uniforms found near to remains, carried identification capsules. It seems extraordinary that an army as ferociously disciplined as the Russian one, constantly overseen by the NKVD, could have been so lax in enforcing a basic military procedure designed to identify and number casualties. That is another example of the erratic, contradictory nature of the Russian military system, and is also the reason why so many of the Russian dead lie unidentified in mass graves from Stalingrad to Berlin. The best way of getting your family notified if you were killed was joining the Communist Party, and getting a Party card. That was not considered bad luck, but it also imposed greater accountability.[110] Maybe the Red Army's aberrant failure to insist on everyone wearing identity 'capsules' had a certain logic to it.

Organizing a mass inoculation would certainly have taxed the Russian military medical services but, with the NKVD in control of logistics in the city, they might have done it. Kliewe thought the Russians might be about to use plague, and authorized the distribution of 3,000 litres of vaccine, enough for a million soldiers, from the IG plant at Marburg. It was kept at the front, but never actually used. As late as 1944, in Budapest, Kliewe also heard a report that the Russians might use plague. On the other hand, the one Russian doctor Kliewe was able to interview, in Warsaw, said he had never heard the subject mentioned in the Russian Army.[111]

It therefore seems that although the Germans may have discussed the use of chemical and biological weapons in the dark moments before Christmas 1942, Hitler, who had seen the effects of gas in the First World War, was always against its use (except on people in concentration camps, who could not fight back). As for Russian intentions, the evidence is contradictory.

The final mysterious piece of the picture appears in a British report from spring 1942. British Intelligence wrote to the Chemical Defence Research establishment at Porton Down about the prevailing winds on the eastern front. During the summer there was very little wind in the

European USSR. Only in the Leningrad sector would the prevailing winds favour the use of poison gas by the Germans, while in the southern half of the front, from Oboyan' to the Black Sea, the winds favoured the Russians.[112] Obviously there had been some report of the possible use of chemical weapons, by one side or the other. Once again, the date is highly revealing. If either side was going to break the 1925 international convention by which they *had* both agreed to abide (unlike the 1929 Geneva Convention), and use chemical or biological weapons on any scale, then 1942 was the most likely year.

The end at Stalingrad

The first ultimatum had been issued to the encircled Germans in Stalingrad on 30 November 1942, signed by Yeremenko, commanding the Stalingrad Front, and Rokossovskiy, commanding the Don Front. 'Choose between life and certain death,' was the message.[113] On 9 January the Russian command issued another ultimatum, signed by Voronov, the Stavka representative, and Rokossovskiy. If Paulus did not comply, it said, then the face of the German troops would be 'your responsibility alone'.[114] It was taken to the Germans by two Russian officers, Major Aleksandr Smyslov of the GRU and Captain Nikolay Smyslenko of the NKVD. They were accompanied by a sergeant-major who had a talent for memorizing the ground he had crossed.[115] The Germans again refused the ultimatum.

On 10 December the Russian 'ring' began its final closure on Stalingrad (see Figure 16.10). The next day, Stavka issued a brief order saying the 'skull' would be crushed in two phases.[116] Paulus, sceptical of his forces' ability to fight in the open, was inclined to obey Hitler's order to hold. On 19 December Manstein, his immediate superior, told him to break out to the south-west. Manstein was right from a military point of view: leaving Sixth Army and a large part of Fourth Panzer tied down around Stalingrad placed Army Group B as a whole in a very vulnerable position. Sixth Army was rapidly becoming too weak not only to get out, but even to hold its ragged perimeter. Paulus wrote to Manstein outlining his dilemma in a letter which epitomizes the bizarre

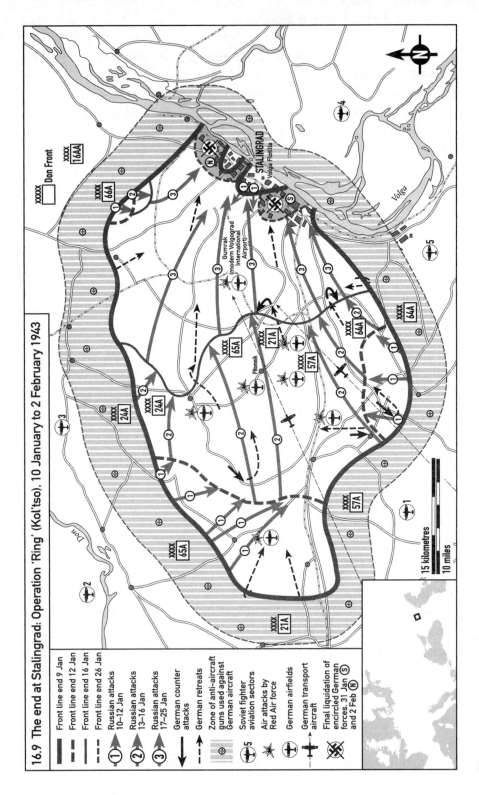

16.9 The end at Stalingrad: Operation 'Ring' (Kol'tso). 10 January to 2 February 1943

courtesy which attended the dealings of 'five-star' officers. This had been the bloodiest, most terrible battle of attrition in the biggest and worst war in history. Paulus's troops were dying of disease and starvation, if not from Russian bullets and shell fragments. 'My dear Field Marshal,' wrote Paulus, 'may I first of all apologize for the quality of the paper and the fact that this letter is handwritten...'[117] Given that he was surrounded by 47 Russian divisions, 5,600 guns, and 169 tanks supported by 300 aircraft, this professional concern about the quality of the paper and the absence of a typist seems quaint.[118]

On 26 December Paulus was radioing that he could not hold out for much longer and that he had received only 70 tonnes of supplies that day. By 24 January 1943 some 24,000 German wounded had been flown out and the Sixth Army was ordered to break up into small groups and try to escape. By the 28th they had been splintered into two pockets, either side of Mamayev Kurgan, which the Russians recaptured on the 26th. Troops of Sixty-Second Army coming through the city met those of the Twenty-First, which had come right across the 'flattened skull' from the west, on the slopes, and that is the moment depicted at the centre of the Stalingrad panorama in the museum close to Paulus's headquarters. Then, in a last, almost comic gesture, Hitler promoted Paulus, already a Colonel-General, to Field Marshal on 31 January. No German Field Marshal had ever surrendered. In addition, to be a Field Marshal in the German Army, unlike your counterpart in some others, you must normally have commanded an army in battle. And won.[119] It was obviously an invitation to Paulus to kill himself, but Paulus declined. He got the signal just before Russian troops arrived at his headquarters in the basement of the department store, ironically close to Pavlov's House, in the old, downtown Tsaritsyn area, at about 07.35 on 31 January. Troops from the Russian 39th Motor-Rifle Brigade, moving from the south, swung north-east across Fallen Heroes' Square. Having sealed off the block, they descended into the basement.

Paulus and Schmidt, his Chief-of-Staff, were taken by car to Sixty-Fourth Army headquarters and thence to the Don Front headquarters at Zavarykino, 80 kilometres from Stalingrad. Paulus was taken, with all the courtesy due to a senior officer, to an *izba* – peasant house or cottage. There, they were met by Marshal of Artillery (full General) Nikolay Voronov, whose residence it was, and Colonel-General Rokossovskiy, two of the key players in the Russian conduct of the war. They were joined by two NKVD men sent by Beria from Moscow. Dyatlenko, who had taken the ultimatum to the Germans on 9 January, acted as interpreter. Paulus was still dressed as a Colonel-General, but told the Russians he was now a Field Marshal. They smiled, because they already knew. They asked Paulus to sign an order to his men to surrender, but in spite of attempts to persuade him to avert further unnecessary bloodshed, he refused to do so. The southern part of the *Kessel* had already collapsed; the last segment holding out, to the north, between the Barricades factory and the Tractor Factory, surrendered on 2 February. Voronov asked if his accommodation was all right. It was the first interrogation, but would not be the last.[120]

The Russians took 91,000 prisoners at Stalingrad, including 2,500 officers and 22 generals. Paulus was the first Field Marshal they had captured. The drawing and photograph of a later interrogation (Plates 37 and 38), apparently in daylight, show how Field Marshals should be treated. This had been the most ghastly battle. According to their figures, 324,000 Russians had died or been taken prisoner in the four-month Stalingrad defensive operation, from 17 July to 18 November, and 320,000 had become sick or wounded – a complete travesty of the usual ratio of one dead to three wounded in a battle. In the counter-offensive, from 19 November 1942 to 2 February 1943, when the last Germans in Stalingrad surrendered, 155,000 Russians had been killed or taken prisoner and 331,000 were sick or wounded. In the two phases, that makes nearly 1,130,000 altogether. Zhukov reckoned the Germans suffered one and a half million casualties in both operations, and Russian figures give 800,000 for the counteroffensive phase alone.[121] It had been a filthy war, a 'rat-war' (*Rattenkrieg*), with no mercy for civilians and few prisoners taken – and then only for the information they might spill. But a Field Marshal deserves respect. In an airy, spacious room, with a fine table, there are flowers on the windowsill (at the beginning of February), and an exquisite carafe of water on the table, no doubt to ease Schmidt and Paulus's vocal chords. The Russians know how to look after guests. For the other German prisoners, only 5,000 of whom would return home alive, it would not be so gracious.

On 2 February a German reconnaissance plane flew over Stalingrad. Its message was similar to the one passed from Sevastopol nearly seven months before: 'No more sign of fighting in Stalingrad'.[122] The Soviet Information Bureau report in *Pravda* on 3 February said simply that on the morning of the previous day:

> Forces of the Don Front destroyed fragmented groups of
> Nazis, putting up resistance north of Stalingrad. After artillery
> bombardment of enemy defensive positions troops of N-unit
> captured a number of enemy anti-aircraft positions and dug-
> outs. Prisoners were taken.[123]

It was over. The battle had been raging for more than six months, and had been widely covered in the international press. In Germany, and occupied Europe, the news was met with shock and silence. In Britain, the King commissioned a great sword – the 'Sword of Stalingrad' – to be manufactured at the Wilkinson Sword factory in Acton. Churchill presented it to Marshal Voroshilov at the Tehran Conference on 29 November 1943.[124] The developing German catastrophe at Stalingrad 'disturbed the whole [German] nation', in the words of an SS report. 'Universally . . . there is a conviction that Stalingrad represents a turning point in the war.' Speculation about how long it would be before victory came gave way to anxiety about how long Germany could 'hang on in this war with the prospect of an honourable victory'.[125] If Stalingrad had a profound impact on public opinion and confidence in Germany, it had even more of an impact on Germany's allies. Romania, Hungary and Italy had all lost major parts of their armed forces and, to make it worse, were blamed by German commanders for not pulling their weight, which they had tried to do, valiantly.[126]

In terms of the Second World War as a whole, it could be argued that Stalingrad was not the turning point because once the United States became involved, Germany had no chance of winning, anyway. From that point of view 7 December 1941, whether in eastern front terms, with the Moscow counteroffensive, or in global terms, with Pearl Harbor, was the turning point. However, from December 1941, while it had gained a breathing space, Russia could still lose – or just collapse, as by all normal rules it should have done in 1942. Stalingrad was the last of a series of checks which progressively narrowed German options. The first was Smolensk, in July 1941, which fatally delayed the German advance. The next was Moscow in December 1941. Then there was the evacuation and re-establishment of Soviet industry – the 'economic Stalingrad'.[127] Next came Hitler's decision in July 1942 to split Operation *Blau* and, furthermore, to let himself be diverted to the lesser aim of capturing Stalingrad, rather than the Caucasus, the oilfields, and access to the wider world. At each point, there was less room for manoeuvre.

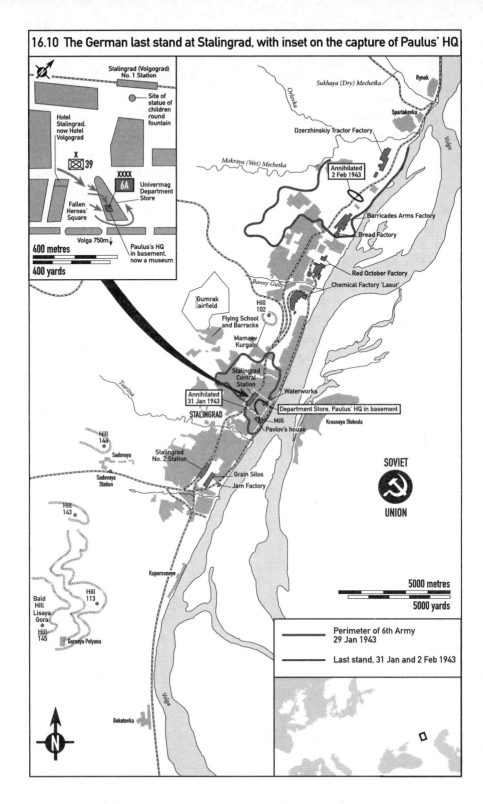

16.10 The German last stand at Stalingrad, with inset on the capture of Paulus' HQ

Inset:

Stalingrad (Volgograd) No. 1 Station

Hotel Stalingrad, now Hotel Volgograd

Site of statue of children round fountain

X ⊠ 39

XXXX 6A

Univermag Department Store

Fallen Heroes' Square

Volga 750m ↓

Paulus's HQ in basement, now a museum

400 metres

400 yards

Main map:

Sukhaya (Dry) Mechetka

Rynok

Orlovka

Spartakovka

Volga

Dzerzhinskiy Tractor Factory

Mokraya (Wet) Mechetka

Annihilated 2 Feb 1943

Barricades Arms Factory

Bread Factory

Red October Factory

Chemical Factory 'Lasur'

Banny Gully

Gumrak airfield

Hill 102

Flying School and Barracks

Mamaev Kurgan

Tsaritsa

Stalingrad Central Station

Waterworks

Annihilated 31 Jan 1943

STALINGRAD

Department Store, Paulus' HQ in basement

Mill

Pavlov's house

Krasnaya Sloboda

Hill 146

Sadovaya

Stalingrad No. 2 Station

Sadovaya Station

Grain Silos

Jam Factory

SOVIET UNION

Hill 143

Kuporosnoye

5000 metres

5000 yards

Bald Hill Lisaya Gora

Hill 113

Hill 145

Gornaya Polyana

Perimeter of 6th Army 29 Jan 1943

Last stand, 31 Jan and 2 Feb 1943

Beketovka

Volga

N

After the catastrophic defeat at Stalingrad, with German forces and those of their allies stretched to the limit, there was no hope of a German victory in the east.[128]

After Stalingrad, Germany could not win. But could Russia? And the Germans had one last card to play.

17

KURSK, AND A
NEW PROFESSIONALISM

All dressed up . . .

In the first quarter of 1943 there were nearly 6 million soldiers in the Red Army and, in that February, another 516,000 in the NKVD – a total of nearly 6.5 million.[1] With a German army in Stalingrad still surrounded by seven smaller Russian ones,[2] it might have seemed a touch premature to invest in a change of image. However, in spite of the obvious logistic challenges of introducing new uniforms, appearances matter. They are obviously very important in maintaining morale, but they can also make extraordinary political statements. Even before striking back at Stalingrad, Stavka had decided that the Workers' and Peasants' Red Army should be dressed like that of the Tsars. The Soviet military's greater professional competence was becoming apparent and as early as 9 October 1942, Stavka agreed a big change, although it was not approved by the Supreme Soviet until 6 January 1943 and implemented by the Defence Ministry on 15 January 1943.[3] On 9 October, new, far less proletarian uniforms had been provisionally approved for the Red Army and the NKVD. Instead of the rank insignia comprising sleeve chevrons and enamelled collar studs which had, admittedly, become increasingly elaborate with each change in military fashion – from 1919, through 1922, 1935 and 1940 – the Soviet security forces would once again wear the shoulder boards (*pogony*) of the Imperial Russian Army, with some slight modifications.[4]

The original idea had been to distinguish the units bearing the distinction 'Guards' from others by giving them different insignia, but that would have been monstrously inefficient and divisive. So all officers' full-dress shoulder boards were to include strips of gold braid, although in the field most seem to have worn a khaki drab cloth substitute, which is a fair imitation of 'gold'. On special occasions they did put on glittery gold shoulder boards – for example, when they met the Americans at Torgau on the Elbe in 1945, as the American colour film of the event makes clear. Only generals seems to have worn gold much in the field and even they generally wore a darker, embroidered cloth substitute instead.

It took some time to get everyone tricked out in the new kit, and the old insignia continued in use for months. There were also those old-school revolutionaries who refused to wear it, in protest.[5] It is said that the Russians put in an order for kilometres of gold braid from the British, as part of lease-land. Since the British were sending precious ships struggling through the Arctic Ocean to supply Russia with vital war materials, it would be understandable if they reacted to a demand for gold braid with incredulity and some anger.[6] Whether that is true or not, two things are clear. The design of the revived Imperial insignia did emphasize the distinction between officers – a word hitherto considered very politically incorrect, but now reintroduced – and other ranks.[7] Even more importantly, they were not stressing a Soviet or a communist identity. They were Russian. And they stressed Russia's great military past.

Rokossovskiy found it very amusing, in retrospect. On 4 February 1943 he and Voronov arrived in Moscow by plane, fresh from interrogating Paulus who had just surrendered at Stalingrad. Triumphant as they were, the victors of Stalingrad had no idea about spring fashions. Rokossovskiy confessed he was taken aback, even scared, by

> the sight of the generals and officers meeting us. They all wore gold-braided shoulder straps [*pogony*] on their shoulders. 'Look here, where have we come to?' I said to Nikolay Nikolayevich [Voronov]. He too was at a loss. However, we noticed familiar faces and soon the mystery was cleared up. It was simply that shoulder straps had been introduced in the Red Army in place of collar tabs: and we hadn't even known.[8]

The Russians bounce back: early 1943

The final destruction of Sixth Army made a renewed Russian advance possible. Little Saturn – the Middle Don operation – had taken Russian forces to a line just 80 kilometres east of Belgorod and Kursk. Once again, victory went to Stalin's head. Three fronts – Voronezh, South-Western and Southern – would 'liberate' the second largest political entity, and formerly the wealthiest region of the USSR, Ukraine. The inner blockade of Leningrad had also been broken, so to the north Russian forces would cut off the Demyansk salient (see Figure 17.1) and open the way to the complete relief of Leningrad.

The Russians started their attack with the Voronezh Front, plus an army each from the Bryansk and the South-Western Fronts, on 13 January, even before the complete collapse of Stalingrad, but capitalizing on the wider encirclement. The Russian advance completed the destruction of Eighth Italian Army, which had first been hit in Little Saturn, and also the Second Hungarian, to add to Third and Fourth Romanian, also destroyed in the Stalingrad counteroffensive.[9] On 6 February Manstein met Hitler to ask permission to withdraw from the eastern part of the 'balcony' between the Don and the Donets. By 9 February the Russians had retaken Belgorod and, to the north, Kursk. They were now threatening Khar'kov, which had been the fourth-largest city in the Soviet Union. On 13 February Hitler ordered it to be held at all costs but the SS Panzer Corps had no intention of being encircled there and withdrew two days later. The next day the Russians took it, creating a 160-kilometre gap between Army Group B and Manstein's Army Group Don, which had been renamed South on 13 February. It was close to what the original Operation Saturn had been designed to achieve. This very success invited a counterstroke, masterminded by Manstein.

On 19 February, just before the thaw would make mobile operations impossible, Fourth Panzer Army attacked from the west, to be joined by First Panzer Army from the south. The Germans mauled the Russians horribly again, counting 23,000 Russian dead, but only 9,000 prisoners. The Russians reckon they lost 45,000 killed and prisoners in defending Khar'kov.[10] Given the difficulty of establishing casualty figures on both sides, that is not surprising. It is also possible, as always, that some fell to blocking detachments. Certainly, many of the Russians were able to get away across the frozen Donets, and that accounts for the small haul of prisoners. On 4 March the Russians went on the defensive, but were forced to abandon Khar'kov on the 14th. The Donets was now thawing. The Voronezh Front had pulled back 100 to 150 kilometres, creating the southern face of the huge Kursk 'bulge', or salient, sticking out into territory now regained by the Germans. The salient – *Kurskaya duga* – provided a formidable springboard for future Russian attacks to the north, against Army Group Centre – the greatest prize – and south, against the Army Group of the same name (see Figures 17.1.2 and 17.1.3).

Meanwhile, throughout January, as the German Sixth Army and part of Fourth Panzer died at Stalingrad, the Russians had launched the North Caucasus Strategic Offensive Operation, optimistically code-named 'Don'. It did indeed push the Germans back between 300 and 600 kilometres, right back to the lower reaches of that river, in just thirty-five days between 1 January and 4 February. Although not completely successful, because most of the Germans managed to get away to the Donbass area, it was a remarkable achievement. With the ring of Little Saturn curving in to join Operation Don from the north, the approaches to the Caucasus and Caspian had been completely cleared. The North Caucasus operation cost the Russians just 70,000 killed and prisoners. An enormous number by most people's standards but relatively few, compared with what had gone before.[11]

The Russian advances had put a heavy strain on their logistics and in the face of German counter-attacks, including those in the Donbass in March, the Russians were forced to withdraw. The Germans recaptured Khar'kov and Belgorod and reached the Donets again. The Russians held on to Kursk, however. The spring thaw now began to hamper operations, and during April, May and June there was a slight 'lull' – by eastern front standards. However, a ferocious struggle continued to throw the Germans off the Taman peninsula.[12]

From Stalingrad to Khar'kov, from close to Grozny, which had never fallen, to the Don, the Germans had been thrown back 600 kilometres in three months. Now, the most obvious feature on the eastern front was the Kursk salient, sticking out more than 100 kilometres west of Kursk, and extending nearly 250 kilometres from north to south and 500 kilometres around its exposed perimeter (see Figure

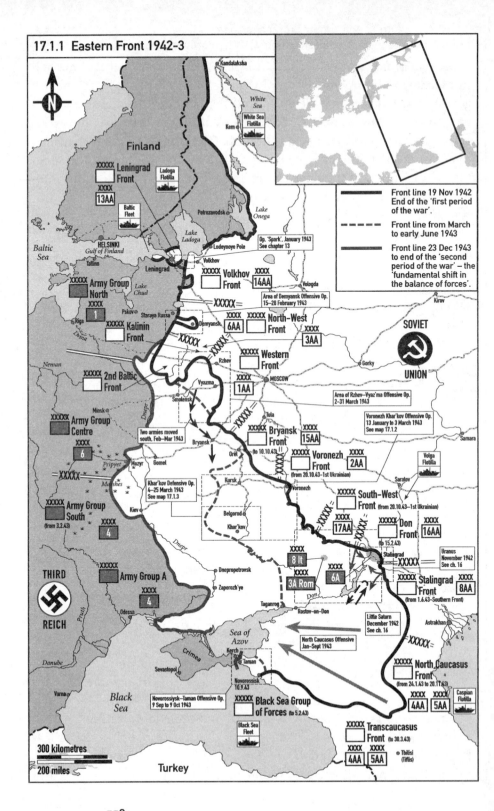

17.1.1 Eastern Front 1942–3

Front line 19 Nov 1942
End of the 'first period of the war'.

Front line from March to early June 1943

Front line 23 Dec 1943 to end of the 'second period of the war' – the 'fundamental shift in the balance of forces'.

Kandalaksha

White Sea

White Sea Flotilla

Kem

Finland

XXXXX Leningrad Front
XXXX 13AA

Ladoga Flotilla

Baltic Fleet

Petrozavodsk

Lake Onega

Lake Ladoga

Op. 'Spark', January 1943
See chapter 13

Lodeynoye Pole

HELSINKI
Gulf of Finland
Tallinn

Leningrad

Volkhov

Lake Chud

XXXXX Volkhov Front
XXXX 14AA

Vologda

Kirov

Baltic Sea

XXXXX Army Group North
XXXX 1

Riga

Pskov

Staraya Russa

Demyansk

Area of Demyansk Offensive Op.
15–28 February 1943

XXXXX =

XXXXX 6AA **XXXXX North–West Front**
XXXX 3AA

SOVIET

Duna

Neman

XXXXX Kalinin Front

Rzhev

XXXXX Western Front
XXXX 1AA

MOSCOW

Gorky

UNION

Samara

XXXXX 2nd Baltic Front

Vyazma

Smolensk

Minsk

XXXXX Army Group Centre
XXXX 6

Pripyet
Mozyr
Marshes

Gomel

Two armies moved south, Feb–Mar 1943

Bryansk

XXXXX =

XXXXX Bryansk Front
XXXX 15AA
(to 10.10.43)

Orel

Tula

Area of Rzhev–Vyaz'ma Offensive Op.
2–31 March 1943

Voronezh Khar'kov Offensive Op.
13 January to 3 March 1943
See map 17.1.2

Volga Flotilla

Saratov

XXXXX Army Group South
(from 3.2.43)
XXXX 4

Kiev

Dnepr

Kursk

Belgorod

Khar'kov

Khar'kov Defensive Op.
4–25 March 1943
See map 17.1.3

Voronezh

XXXXX Voronezh Front
(from 20.10.43–1st Ukrainian)
XXXX 2AA

XXXXX South–West Front
(from 20.10.43–1st Ukrainian)

XXXX 17AA

XXXXX Don Front
(to 15.2.43)
XXXX 16AA

THIRD

REICH

XXXXX Army Group A
XXXX 4

Dnepropetrovsk

Zaporozh'ye

Dnepr

Taganrog

XXXX 8 It

XXXX 3A Rom

XXXX 6A

Stalingrad

Uranus
November 1942
See ch. 16

XXXXX =

XXXXX Stalingrad Front
(from 1.6.43–Southern Front)
XXXX 8AA

Astrakhan

Rostov-on-Don

Don

Little Saturn
December 1942
See ch. 16

North Caucasus Offensive
Jan–Sept 1943

XXXXX =

Danube

Odessa

Pruth

Sea of Azov

Crimea

Kerch

Taman

Sevastopol

Novorossiysk
10.9.43

Novorossiysk–Taman Offensive Op.
9 Sep to 9 Oct 1943

XXXXX Black Sea Group of Forces (to 5.2.43)

XXXXX North Caucasus Front
(from 24.1.43 to 20.11.43)
XXXX 4AA **XXXX 5AA**

Caspian Flotilla

Varna

Black Sea

Black Sea Fleet

XXXXX Transcaucasus Front (to 30.3.43)
XXXX 4AA **XXXX 5AA**

Tbilisi (Tiflis)

300 kilometres

200 miles

Turkey

17.1.2 Formation of the Kursk salient (1): The Voronezh–Khar'kov Operation, 13 January to 3 March 1943

THIRD REICH

SOVIET UNION

XXXXX Bryansk Front

Livny
Sosna
Zadonsk

Sevsk
Dmitriev l'govskiy 2.3 Fatezh 7.2 Zolotukhino
Volovo
Kozynka
Olym

Shigry
Kursk 8.2
Kastornoye 29.1
Voronezh

L'gov
Tim
Seym
Don

Front line end 3 March 1943
Front line end 17 Feb 1943
Front line end 12 Jan 1943

Sudzha 3.3 Oboyan 18.2
Stary Oskol 5.2

Belopol'ye
Front line 1–2 Feb 1943
Liski

XXXXX Army Group Centre

Sumy
Krasnopol'ye Proletarskiy
Prokhorovka
Oskol

XXXXX Voronezh Front

Korocha 7.2
Novy Oskol
Pavlovsk

Tomarovka
Belgorod 9.2
Trostyanets
Grayvoron 16.2

XXXXX
Gadyach
Akhtyrka 23.2
Bogodukhov
Shebekino
Volchansk 9.2
Valuyki
Rossosh' 16.1
Don

XXXXX Army Group South
(From 21.2 Operational Group 'Kempf')

Lyebotin
Khar'kov 16.2
Chuguyev 10.2
Lozno–Aleksandovka

Valki Merefa
Zmiyev 16.2
Kupyansk
Pokrovskoya
Kartemirovka
N

Poltava
Krasnograd Alekseyevka
Balekleya 5.2
Svatovo
Chertkovo

Karlova Pervomayskiy
Iz'yum 6.2
Starobel'sk

100 kilometres
Sakhnovshch'ina

50 miles

XXXXX South-West Front

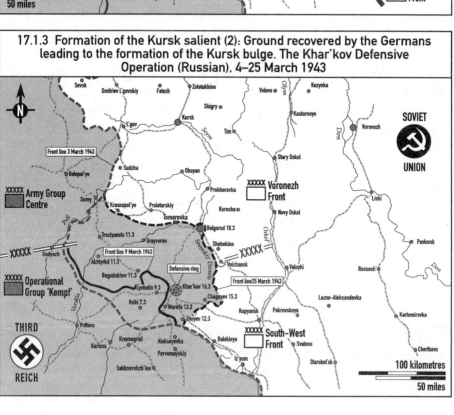

17.1.3 Formation of the Kursk salient (2): Ground recovered by the Germans leading to the formation of the Kursk bulge. The Khar'kov Defensive Operation (Russian), 4–25 March 1943

N

Sevsk
Dmitriev L'govskiy Fatezh Zolotukhino
Volovo
Olym
Kozynka

Shigry
Kursk
Kastornoye
Voronezh

SOVIET UNION

L'gov
Tim
Seym
Don

Front line 3 March 1943
Stary Oskol

Belopol'ye
Sudzha Oboyan

XXXXX Army Group Centre

Sumy
Prokhorovka
XXXXX Voronezh Front
Liski

Krasnopol'ye Proletarskiy
Korocha
Novy Oskol

Tomarovka
Pavlovsk

Trostyanets 11.3 Grayvoron
Belgorod 18.3
Oskol

XXXXX
Gadyach
Front line 9 March 1943
Shebekino
XXXXX
Akhtyrka 11.3
Volchansk
Valuyki
Rossosh'
Don

XXXXX Operational Group 'Kempf'

Bogodukhov 11.3
Defensive ring
Lyebotin 9.3
Khar'kov 16.3
Front line 25 March 1943

Valki 7.2 Chuguyev 15.3
Lozno–Aleksandovka
Kartemirovka

Merefa 13.3
Zmiyev 12.3
Kupyansk Pokrovskoya

THIRD REICH

Poltava
XXXXX South-West Front

Krasnograd Alekseyevka
Balekleya
Svatovo
Chertkovo

Karlova Pervomayskiy
Iz'yum
Starobel'sk

100 kilometres

Sakhnovshch'ina

50 miles

559

17.2). Besides threatening the German army groups to north and south, it also made their 'front line' – not that there ever really was such a thing, given partisan activity – 250 kilometres longer than it might be. That was the rationale behind the German plan to 'pinch out' the salient. The sooner the Germans attacked it, the less ready the Russian forces, exhausted and with their supply lines stretched, would be. Had they attacked in May, as they initially planned, it might have worked. But there would be a fatal delay. April, May and June were relatively quiet as both sides prepared to pit their latest and best equipment against each other in what has been seen – maybe wrongly – as a symbolic and final trial of strength.

The 'fiery salient'

Kursk is a sleepy provincial city close to the western border of Russia proper. To the south, Belgorod, just outside the Kursk 'bulge', is in Russia, but Khar'kov is in Ukraine. To the north of the salient lies Orël, also in Russia. Kursk is an old city – 'pre-Mongol', they say – the Russian equivalent of being in the English Domesday Book.[13] From the ancient city's heart on a hilltop, there is a good view of the surrounding countryside, ideal for spotting Mongol patrols. Kursk is pretty much in the centre of the 1943 bulge, and from there, by road, it takes a whole day to visit either the north or the south 'face' – *fas* – of the salient, and get back again. In area, the salient was nearly half the size of England, and a bit smaller than West Virginia. It is more wooded now than it was then, but still only 16 per cent of the country is covered by trees. Furthermore, one impression must be corrected. Even in hot July 1943, it was not a baked yellow expanse like the Canadian or American prairie or the steppe further east. It was, and is, largely green, well-cultivated, rolling land, although by early July the standing grain was turning yellow.

The Kursk salient rises gently, and is a natural watershed running north–south. The rivers, which are narrow, shallow and slow flowing, run off it to east and west, towards the Don and the Dnepr, respectively. That is important. A German assault from the north, through Ponyri

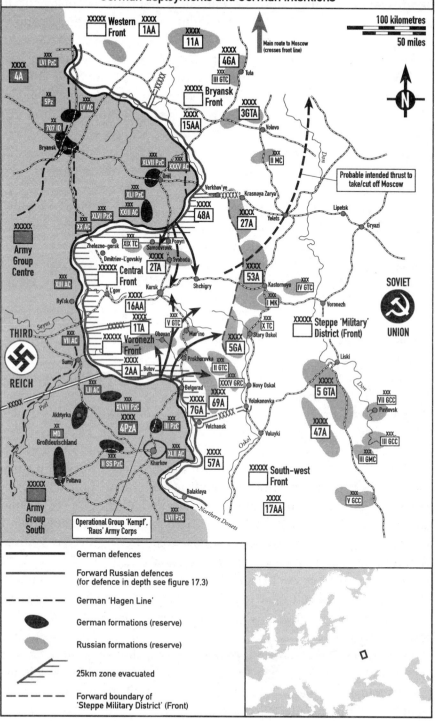

17.2 The Kursk salient. Situation at the end of 4 July 1942 showing Russian and German deployments and German intentions

German defences

Forward Russian defences
(for defence in depth see figure 17.3)

German 'Hagen Line'

German formations (reserve)

Russian formations (reserve)

25km zone evacuated

Forward boundary of
'Steppe Military District' (Front)

towards Kursk, could follow the watershed, and thus avoid having to cross any water obstacles.[14] To the south of the salient the Northern Donets river provided a strong natural defence against any German attack, in that area. At the beginning of April the Russian General Staff correctly predicted that the initial German attacks would be into the south and north of the bulge towards Oboyan' and Svoboda (see Figure 17.2). Oboyan' stands on the Psël river, which is surrounded on either side by a wide strip of marsh, and makes a very good obstacle, with perfect fields of fire. Even if the Germans had broken through from the south, it is likely that they would have been unable to force the river in that area.

The other peculiarity of the salient is the 'Kursk magnetic anomaly', caused by a large underground deposit of iron ore, between 250 and 500 metres below the surface. In some places it rises closer, and at Zheleznogorsk there are open-cast mines. It was discovered at the beginning of the twentieth century by a visiting team of German scientists, and has a dramatic effect on compasses. However, both the Germans and the Russians were fully aware of it and if there were navigation errors during the battle, the intriguing anomaly is unlikely to be responsible.

The Germans viewed the salient as a 'prepared starting point and gateway for the invasion of the Ukraine'.[15] They also saw the advantage of shortening their front by 250 kilometres, which would free eighteen to twenty divisions for subsequent offensive operations. Elsewhere, they shortened the front by pulling back. At Kursk, they would shorten it by moving forward and, in the process, destroying huge Russian forces. In the spring of 1943, the sensible German decision to pull back from Rzhev shortened the front by 300 kilometres and freed twenty to twenty-two divisions. Pulling back from the Demyansk bridgehead shortened the front by 250 kilometres and freed up to eight divisions. As a result, twelve divisions were moved from Army Group Centre's left wing to its right, on the north of the Kursk salient, in the Orël area.[16]

The Russians had a clear picture of what was going on. Starting on 15 March 1943, the Germans began moving troops, tanks and fuel to positions opposite the Bryansk, Central and Voronezh Fronts. According to partisan and 'other' sources – NKVD agents, and signals intelligence – they moved 170,000 men, 2,100 tanks, 2,100 guns, 16,000 soft-skinned vehicles and 1,500 fuel bowsers to face the three Russian fronts, two of them holding the salient.[17]

The German plan took shape in March 1943. The main strategic objective for summer 1943 was destruction of the Red Army's largest grouping, which was in the Kursk salient. Besides shortening the front and killing or capturing perhaps millions of Soviet soldiers, the aim was to restore the *Wehrmacht*'s (and Waffen-SS's) prestige; to restore the confidence of other Axis powers; and to re-establish Hitler's authority, if not in Germany, then among the increasingly jittery governments of Nazi-occupied Europe. The operation was given the provisional code-name *Zitadelle* – 'Citadel'.[18] That was pretty obvious for an attack on a fortress, and a fortress it was becoming.

A disastrous prelude

As a result of the winter and spring battles, the Voronezh Front, under Nikolay Vatutin, was responsible for the southern third of the salient, and the new Central Front, created in early February, and commanded by Rokossovskiy, the northern two-thirds. But Stalin had not given Rokossovskiy, the crusher of German resistance at Stalingrad, a new front as a prize, and nor did he intend Rokossovskiy to lie around until the summer. The new Central Front was to attack northwards and encircle German forces around Orël. The attack was planned for 15 February but postponed until the 25th. Most of the forces required were still stuck at Stalingrad and there was only one railway line into the salient to move all the supplies and equipment from Kastornoye westwards to Kursk (see Figure 17.2). The main line to Kursk from Moscow ran through German-held territory. Rokossovskiy, no doubt remembering his time in the GULag, recalled wryly that:

> The job of accelerating the troops' movements was given to
> the NKVD, and its men pitched into it with such zeal,
> clamping down so hard on the railway authorities that the
> latter lost their heads completely, and whatever timetables
> and schedules had existed until then now went up in smoke.
> Troops began to arrive at the concentration area all mixed up
> ... One unit's materiel [equipment, weapons] might be

unloaded at one station while men were detrained at
another.[19]

Even worse, Rokossovskiy's incomplete and improperly supplied
forces were to attack a German concentration which was now heavily
reinforced by southward movements from Rzhev and Demyansk, 400
kilometres to the north.[20] Stavka had 'evidently miscalculated' in undertaking such a large-scale operation.[21] The Germans counter-attacked
and, following a report by Rokossovskiy, in the second half of March
the Central Front was ordered to fall back on the defensive. The
Germans attacked, in a perfect prelude to the summer, from Orël in the
north and Belgorod in the south, but were held.

Rokossovskiy was furious, and what he said next was censored from
his memoirs.

> *In undertaking such a grandiose operation as a deep
> encirclement of the enemy's Orël grouping, Stavka committed a
> coarse misjudgement, having overestimated its own capabilities
> and underestimated those of the enemy.* And then, having
> already succeeded in repelling the blows of the Soviet forces
> directed against him, on the Bryansk and Khar'kov axes, he
> [the Germans] himself prepared to strike counter-blows . . .
> In the second half of March the Stavka of the Supreme High
> Command [Stalin] took the decision on the need to carry out
> an offensive against Orël. That decision was correct. We all
> took heart, *hoping that the mistakes, made by Stavka in the
> winter and spring of 1942, would not be repeated.*[22]

The attempted offensive in February and March was a disaster. Even
the 1993 Russian compendium of casualties does not mention it,
although, perhaps surprisingly, Rokossovskiy was allowed to say something.[23] But at least this initial disaster provided a clear blueprint for the
success that would follow.

Digging in

With nearly two years' experience of war, the USSR's leadership – Stalin and GKO – had three options available. They could launch more frantic counter-attacks, as they had done in 1941, 1942 and even that very spring, which would be very costly. They could trade space for military success, but it was their space, their land, their people, which had been defended to the last drop of blood, and regained at horrendous cost. Or they could dig in where they were and make the invaders fight for every metre of Russian – and it still was Russian – territory, and bleed the enemy to death in the process. Zhukov wrote to Stalin on 8 April, saying he thought it was 'inexpedient' to launch a pre-emptive offensive in the near future. 'It would be better for us to wear down the enemy on our defence, knock out his tanks, bring in fresh reserves, and finish off his main grouping with a general offensive.'[24]

Stavka was also very aware of the different – asymmetric[25] – characteristics of the armies. The Russians were pumping out equipment in vast quantities. It was simple, but it was superbly designed and it worked. The Germans were continuing to produce superb machines, but in relatively few numbers and in many variants. In order to counter the T-34, the Germans produced the Panther – the PzKFW-5, known to the Russians as the T-5, with a high-velocity 75mm gun, good mobility and thick armour, up to 120mm. However, at the Battle of Kursk in summer 1943, there were fewer than 200 Panthers available. Further-more, they had been rushed into service and were therefore unreliable, and needed highly trained and experienced crews. The same went for the mighty Tiger – the PzKFW-VI, known to the Russians as the T-VI, with its 88mm gun and 110mm armour. Again, fewer than 200 were available at Kursk. These, and the huge 65-ton Ferdinand self-propelled assault guns – a cheaper, turretless version of the Tiger but on the same chassis – would form the tip of an armoured wedge which would try to penetrate the Russian defences exactly as the Teutonic Knights had tried to penetrate Aleksandr Nevskiy's 700 years before.[26] The Russians upgraded the T-34 with an 85mm gun and a bigger turret to hold it, but those were not introduced until early 1944. At Kursk they still had only the excellent but rather crude T-34/76, with a low-velocity 76mm gun, and therefore short range, no floor to the turret, and poor visibility. And also whole battalions equipped with British Matildas.[27]

Unusually, Stalin chose to go with Zhukov's advice. It would be a battle of attrition – deliberately so, which the defender, skilfully dug in, was best suited to win. Stavka's orders as early as March 1943 were brutally clear:

> to meet the enemy attack in a well-prepared defensive
> bridgehead, to bleed attacking German groupings dry,and then
> to launch a general offensive. The defeat of enemy shock
> groups created favourable prerequisites for developing new
> extensive offensive operations. Thus our defence was prepared
> with the intention of a subsequent shift to the offensive. The
> concentration of forces and their grouping in the Kursk
> bridgehead attests to this.[28]

After wearing down the enemy attack, reserves would strike back to destroy the Germans' main army groups, Centre and South, and clear the approaches to Ukraine, the Donbass region, and eastern Belarus. They would then regain the line from Smolensk to the Dnepr.[29]

On 8 April Zhukov signalled Vasilevskiy, the Chief of the General Staff. 'I believe it inexpedient for our forces to launch a preventive offensive in the next few days, it being more to our advantage to wear the enemy down in defensive action, and destroy his tanks. Subsequently, by committing fresh reserves, we should asssume an all-out offensive completely to destroy the main enemy grouping.'[30]

In April 1943 the forces of the Central and Voronezh Fronts began digging in around and inside the massive perimeter of the 'bulge'. The defences are shown in Figure 17.3. They were massive. There were five to six successive 'belts' – three within armies' defence zones, and three in the fronts' zones of responsibility. Then there was a seventh belt, the boundary of the Steppe Military District, which had become the Steppe Front, and finally the eighth belt – the 'national defensive' or 'state' boundary. Each of the belts comprised two to three lines. All told, these massive complexes of minefields, gun positions, intermediate and cut-off positions extended back 240 to 320 kilometres. The Russians kept working on them until the eve of the German attack, on 5 July. The entire civilian population was evacuated from the outer 25-kilometre zone, to improve security and also so that the armed forces could

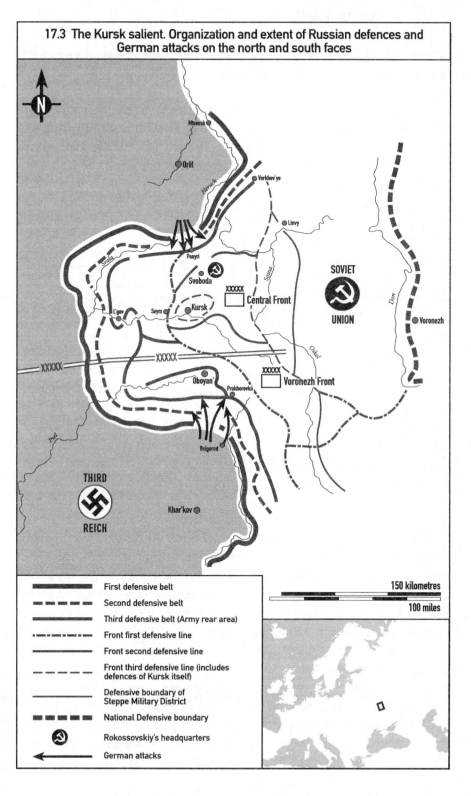

17.3 The Kursk salient. Organization and extent of Russian defences and German attacks on the north and south faces

Mtsensk

Orël

Verkhov'ye

Nerüch

Linvy

Ponyri

Svala

Svoboda

Seim

L'gov   Seym   Kursk

XXXXX   Central Front

SOVIET

UNION

Don

Voronezh

Oskol

XXXXX

XXXXX   XXXXX   Voronezh Front

Oboyan'   Prokhorovka

Psël   Belgorod

THIRD

REICH   Khar'kov

First defensive belt

Second defensive belt

Third defensive belt (Army rear area)

Front first defensive line

Front second defensive line

Front third defensive line (includes defences of Kursk itself)

Defensive boundary of Steppe Military District

National Defensive boundary

Rokossovskiy's headquarters

German attacks

150 kilometres

100 miles

prepare the villages as defensive points and also create 'operational obstacle zones'. In other words, minefields, which they did not want civilians or animals to tread on.

The Russians' main problem was the lack of communications and transport within the salient, which in those days meant railways. With the main line to Kursk from Moscow through Orël in German hands, the best line – double-tracked – ran from Moscow south through Tula, and thence to Kastornoye and Stary Oskol. That could take forty to forty-five pairs of trains a day. From Kastornoye, a line ran westwards through Kursk and L'gov, but that could only take twelve to eighteen pairs of trains a day. After heavy equipment, fuel and ammunition reached railway stations on those lines, transport was along dirt roads. The Germans had much better rail links, into Orël, Bryansk and Kharkov, and the Russians understood this. Signals went out to the partisans.[31]

The perimeter held by Vatutin's Voronezh Front extended for 245 kilometres; Rokossovskiy's Central Front, 308 kilometres. On the extreme left, the south face of the bulge, where the Germans were expected to try to break through, Vatutin concentrated most of his artillery – more than fifty guns per kilometre, or one for every 20 metres on much of Seventh and all of Sixth Guards' sectors. Although the Russians had initially expected an attack straight from the west as well, they had now ruled this out and spread their firepower relatively thinly along the west face of the salient. On the north face Rokossovskiy knew exactly where the Germans were coming from. Russian spies abroad, some of whom passed on British Ultra intelligence; partisans working behind German lines; and NKVD and Red Army signals intelligence, plus a soldier's instinct for terrain, all pinpointed two very narrow sectors as the paths for the German attack. So, too, did the bitter experience of the hasty Russian attacks and German counter-attacks in February–March. On Rokossovskiy's sector, either side of the expected attack, in Seventieth and Forty-Eighth Armies' sectors, there were about twenty-five guns supporting the infantry, and tanks on each kilometre of the front. On the critical Thirteenth Army sector there were nearly a hundred – one every 10 metres. The General Staff graphic from 1944, showing the rigorous concentration of firepower on the known directions of the German attack, is reproduced in Figure 17.4.

Most importantly, for the first time, the Russians could put an entire front in reserve. If the Germans had broken through Rokossovskiy's Central Front in the north or, more likely, Vatutin's Voronezh in

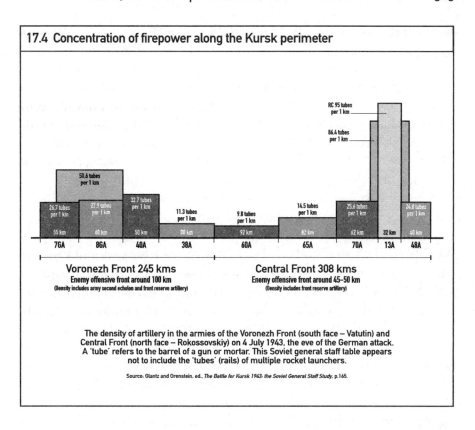

17.4 Concentration of firepower along the Kursk perimeter

The density of artillery in the armies of the Voronezh Front (south face – Vatutin) and Central Front (north face – Rokossovskiy) on 4 July 1943, the eve of the German attack. A 'tube' refers to the barrel of a gun or mortar. This Soviet general staff table appears not to include the 'tubes' (rails) of multiple rocket launchers.

Source: Glantz and Orenstein. ed.. *The Battle for Kursk 1943: the Soviet General Staff Study*, p.165.

the south, they would have had another backstop to beat: the Steppe Front, commanded by Ivan Koniev. The formation of this reserve front was largely complete by the end of April. However, on 13 April it was renamed the Steppe Military District. Military Districts normally became fronts on the outbreak of war. Now, in April 1943, the reserve front bolstering the Kursk bulge, behind the Kshen' and Oskol rivers, became an MD.[32] The Russians were remarkably sure of themselves. Or, perhaps, it was another shrewd piece of information warfare.

Know your enemy

The Russian defensive operation at Kursk was a triumph of good intelligence – their own and other people's. The Russians did not themselves emulate the spectacular British success, based on initial work by the Poles, in deciphering the codes produced by the German Enigma and, even more important, Lorentz machines. However, the NKVD/ NKGB intelligence operation abroad was so effective that the Russians benefited from British code-breaking, and especially in the run-up to Kursk. John Cairncross, one of the 'Cambridge Five' pro-communist intellectuals recruited to the NKVD (now, briefly, the NKGB) in the 1930s, was at Bletchley Park from summer 1942 to summer 1943. At Bletchley, the Enigma codes were broken and the information turned into intelligence bearing the caveat 'Ultra Most Secret' – hence 'Ultra'.[33] The value of the Bletchley decrypts is mentioned in a brief biography of Pavel Fitin, head of the Foreign Intelligence Department (INO) of NKGB/NKVD. Gorskiy, the NKVD London controller, gave Cairncross the money to buy a car so that he could take Ultra material to London on his days off. The deciphered Luftwaffe traffic was of particular value, and enabled the Russians to launch pre-emptive attacks on German airfields before the attack, which destroyed more than 500 aircraft.[34]

Even better, however, was the 'Lucy' spy ring, centred on Rudolf Rössler, a German refugee in Switzerland. Rössler was an anti-Nazi liberal who had fled after Hitler's accession. He had got to know a circle of friends while serving in the First World War, eight of whom stayed in the German military and were now working in OKW. They passed reports to Rössler, who passed them on to a Swiss officer, Major Haussmann. At first Rössler was highly protective of his information and the Swiss were far more willing to pass it to the western Allies than to the Russians. However, one of the nine copies of the Barbarossa plan reached a member of Rössler's ring. A young communist friend helped him make contact with Moscow and the NKGB agreed to pay Rössler for his cooperation. They gave him the codename 'Lucy'. The information on Barbarossa was ignored at the time, as we have seen, but 'Lucy's' credentials were now established. The increasingly successful extrication of Soviet forces from encirclement in 1942 may well owe something to 'Lucy'. Throughout the spring of 1943, Rössler provided Stalin, through Beria, with key decisions by OKW. 'Lucy' provided especially valuable information on the Caucasus area in January 1943 and detailed information about the movement of German divisions westward from Europe during the winter of 1942. 'Lucy's' biggest success, however, was Kursk, where the network provided the now trusting Russians with the position of supply depots, reinforcement and attack routes, and the numbers and quality of guns, armour and planes.[35] The NKVD had also sent agents into German-occupied south Russia, including N. I. Kuznetsov, posing as Oberleutnant Kurt Ziebert, who also passed on information on 'Citadel' – the German plan for Kursk. He found details of a German plan to kill the big three – Stalin, Churchill and Roosevelt – when they met in Tehran for the Eureka conference at the end of November. It must have been Lucy, however, who passed critical information to Stalin on 1 July 1943. That day, Hitler held the main conference giving instructions for the Citadel attack on 5 July. The next day Stalin signalled the commanders of the three fronts that 'according to information at our disposal the Germans may go over to the offensive on our front between 3 and 6 July'.[36]

In May, Stalin had also received a warning from the Americans, not that he particularly needed it. President Roosevelt proposed a meeting far away from embattled Europe, on one side or the other of the Bering Strait. He added that American 'estimates' were that Germany would launch an all-out attack on Russia in the summer, and the blow would fall 'against the middle of your line'. That could only be Kursk, but Stalin knew already. He replied that the Germans had already concentrated about 200 divisions and were expected to attack as early as June. Given that the German attack had originally been planned for May, his intelligence was better than the Americans'.[37]

In addition to top-level tip-offs, their own penetration of OKW through 'Lucy', and the feed of British Ultra intelligence, the Russians' battlefield intelligence benefited from lease-lend. After Stalingrad, they had begun to receive large numbers of radio sets from the Americans and the British. At the end of 1942 the Stavka set up 'special-purpose radio battalions' – electronic warfare units – each of which had eighteen to twenty receivers for radio intercepts and four direction-finding sets. Having captured the central command structure – the 'brains' – of an entire army at Stalingrad; they also had plenty of German signallers and cypher experts who had little option but to help them. The alternative was, after torture, summary execution by the NKVD.[38]

The Russians did not enjoy the luxury, available to the British, of being able to decode the widely used Enigma transmissions. Nor could they decode transmissions from the Lorentz system, with its twelve rotors, used to encode high-level messages between OKH, army groups and armies. However, direction-finding, traffic analysis and cracking lower-level manual cyphers told the Russians everything else they needed to know. Although code-breaking is the cream of the crop, most signals intelligence depends on intercepting radio signals and direction-finding to identify the position of units and formations – with which the lease-lend equipment helped enormously. There is also technical analysis of the radios concerned, which tells you the level of the headquarters you are dealing with, and traffic analysis to establish the pattern and identities of who is talking to whom. Even if you cannot read messages by deciphering and breaking the enemy's code, you can still learn a great deal. Finally, it is critical that, in gleaning the information, you do not let the enemy know that you have done so. Otherwise, he will unobligingly change his arrangements. The decision-maker then has to act on the intelligence in time to make a difference. However clever the code-breakers may be, it is a mistake to overlook the contribution of traffic analysis or direction-finding.

For example, the Germans always knew when a big air raid was on its way from the west by the chatter as the USAAF and RAF aircrews tested their radios before taking off. It was simple enough, but provided vital intelligence. On the eastern front, direction-finding and traffic analysis provided vast hauls of intelligence to both sides, without any need for code-breaking. Every headquarters transmitted signals from a location which could be pinpointed by taking a bearing and direction-finding by triangulation. Noting the call signs and who was talking and reporting to whom revealed the order of battle, and also showed the frequency or intensity of the traffic. The only way round this was almost complete radio silence. But it is very difficult for any mobile force to operate in those conditions and they greatly favour the defender, who can communicate using landline, rather than the attacker, who has to talk on the radio.

Traffic analysis identified the location of headquarters and units, the type of radios, their frequencies, and individual operators or commanders. It was obvious and apparent which units were subordinate to whom. So was the nature of their communications – for example, were they logistic or combat units? A typical example of traffic analysis as it might have applied at Kursk is shown in Figure 17.5.[39] Even if the Russians could not decode exactly what the Germans were saying – and to do so would have taken a long time, anyway – they could see what they were dealing with.

Intelligence reports captured by the Germans from the Red Army during the Kursk fighting indeed confirmed that Russian signals intelli-

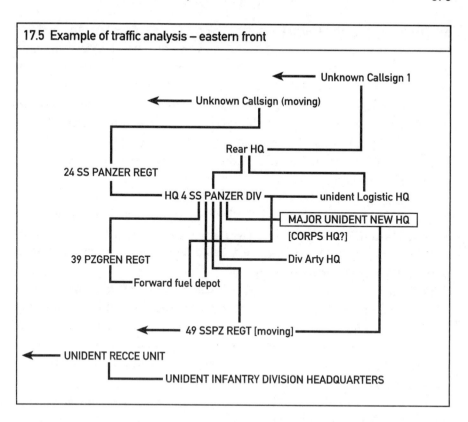

17.5 Example of traffic analysis – eastern front

gence had identified the deployment and headquarters of the 6th, 7th and 11th Panzer Divisions, II and XIII Panzer Corps and Second Army headquarters.[40]

Not only did the Russians know that the Germans were coming, and when, but they knew exactly where, and pretty well how many.

In the forest

During 1942 and early 1943 the partisan movement became increasingly well organized and better coordinated with the NKVD and Red Army, and partisan operations began to assume greater significance.[41] Following the creation of the Combined Command of the partisan movement on 30 May 1942, the Central Staff of the partisan movement in Moscow exercised control through partisan movement headquarters at each front.[42] On 5 September Stalin further clarified the partisans' aims, which again included sabotage and also intelligence on towns and populated areas, enemy troop movements, industry, civil administration, signals, deployments and boundaries between formations which Russian attacks might exploit and prise apart. Also, for the first time – a measure of growing Russian competence in the air – they included reporting the results of Russian air attacks.[43]

During 1943 the Soviet partisan movement in German-occupied eastern Europe increased in strength from 130,000 to perhaps 250,000 fighters. Whether Soviet claims (which always have to be treated with caution) are right or not,[44] the partisan units certainly played a huge part in the Battle of Kursk, though perhaps not initially. By summer 1943 Army Group Centre's rear area was 200 to 300 kilometres from north to south and extended 150 to 200 kilometres back from the forward fighting positions (see Figure 12.5). The most important German movement was from the Rzhev area down to the Kursk area in early March. The partisans warned Stavka, which duly ordered them to concentrate on cutting off ('interdicting', to use the military jargon) German communications north of the bulge. That was another factor in Rokossovskiy's favour. Although the railways available to the Germans were better than those available to the Russians, they were also utterly predictable – and therefore vulnerable. But it was not in the run-up to the Kursk offensive that the Russians would strike. They would wait.[45]

Rokossovskiy, commanding the Central Front, resented the continued interference from the top. Having been forced to undertake the disastrous but instructive offensive against the German forces to the north, he now found the 'long screwdriver' had been given a new name. Formerly there had been 'Strategic Directions'. At Stalingrad, and now, in the early summer of 1943, there were 'Representatives of the Stavka of the Supreme High Command'. At Stalingrad Rokossovskiy had got on all right with Stavka representative Voronov – another big man, humorous and humane, and a veteran of Spain – but he did not much like Zhukov. And Zhukov was sent as the Stavka representative to oversee Vatutin and Rokossovskiy's preparations. Stavka had got rid of the Directions, so 'why did they again start using them, but under another name – Stavka representatives to coordinate the operations of two fronts?' Rokossovskiy wanted freedom to command. And he fumed:

> Such a representative, arriving at the headquarters of one of the fronts, more often than not, interfered in the front commander's business, and undermined him. In addition, he had absolutely no actual responsibility for the way business was done on the ground. That was entirely the front commander's lookout, and often you got contradictory instructions on this or that question. From Stavka, you'd get one. From its representative – another. And lastly, being there as a coordinator, at one of the fronts, he naturally had a great interest in having the maximum force deployed where he was. This most often worked to the detriment of other fronts, who were charged with no less complex operations. Apart from that, the presence of a Stavka representative who was no less than the Deputy of the Supreme High Commander [Zhukov, Stalin's Deputy] at the front commander's headquarters cramped initiative, tied the front commander's hands and feet, as it were. It also raised questions about how much faith Stavka had in the front commander.[46]

Rokossovskiy recommended that when conducting a big, strategic operation involving the coordination of several fronts, the front commanders should all be summoned to Stavka and work it out there. That, as subsequent events proved, 'would be of great value'.[47]

The Russian divisions available to the Central Front were still very weak – 4,500 to 5,000 troops, according to Rokossovskiy, with some numbering 6,000 to 7,000. The German divisions had always been much more powerful, but in spite of terrible losses, those assembling on Rokossovskiy's front seemed to be at near full strength. German infantry divisions numbered 10,000 to 12,000, Panzer divisions 15,000 to 16,000, and motorized divisions 14,000. 'The clouds were gathering over the front,' Rokossovskiy recalled. 'At the end of June we started getting information about the movement of German tank, artillery and infantry formations into the forward area.'[48]

Why did the Germans try it?

If Rokossovskiy thought he had bad news, Stalin had already received worse – or so it seemed. Relations between Russia and its allies had already been shaken in April when, on the 13th, the Germans announced that they had found the mass graves of Polish officers at Katyn. The Poles in exile in London, including General Anders and Prime Minister Sikorskiy, were furious and deeply concerned, having attempted to track down the missing officers for three years. Relations between Soviet Russia and the London Poles virtually ceased. Meanwhile, in Russia, moves begun by the SPP – the Union of Polish Patriots, a group opposed to the 'London Poles' – were accelerated. The SPP had been formed in Moscow in early spring, to create a new Polish army linked to the Red Army. Then, at the Trident conference in Washington between 11 and 27 May, Churchill and Roosevelt had decided to postpone the cross-Channel invasion from late summer 1943 until May 1944. Stalin knew almost straight away, of course, but was told officially on 4 June. On 11 June he told his western allies that this created 'exceptional difficulties for the Soviet Union'. The Red Army would have to do the job 'almost single handed', and the Soviet people would be deeply disappointed. Kerr warned the British government that Stalin's icy politeness masked a very real lack of faith in the 'Grand Alliance'.[49]

While relations between the western Allies and the Russians quavered, the Germans were not happy, either. It is now widely acknowledged that in Hitler's mind, 'clear military victory over the Soviet Union was impossible to achieve'.[50] However, he wanted to conduct one more massive attack, perhaps to persuade his Quisling allies, and also continued diplomatic manoeuvres.[51] German agents approached Russian representatives in Sweden about a separate peace with Moscow, and also contacted the British and Americans. The first half of 1943 was therefore full of diplomatic tensions, although they abated after Quebec in August.

The Russian view, and the traditional view, is that Kursk was meant to restore German prestige and deal the Soviet Union a mortal blow by encircling and destroying the largest single grouping of Soviet forces on the eastern front. Subsequently, the Germans intended to regroup and drive through the Steppe Military District, north-north-east, cutting Moscow off from the rest of the country. It was meant not only to tidy up the battlefront and achieve attrition but, in so doing, to achieve a massive psychological victory. Its ultimate aim was 'shock and awe' or, as it is now called, 'effects-based warfare'.[52]

Some Germans now see it differently. Hitler and the German General Staff 'were fully aware of the fact that it was no longer possible to achieve a decisive victory on the eastern front, certainly not in a single battle'.[53] Therefore the OKH pursued only two, limited objectives. The first was to establish a shorter defensive line by pinching off the troops in the Kursk bulge, which might have released 20 divisions or so. The second was to weaken the Red Army, whose largest concentration of forces – estimated at 60 divisions – was concentrated in the salient.[54] Of 6 million troops on the eastern front, the Red Army had about 1.3 million from the Central and Voronezh Fronts in and close to the Kursk bulge for the defensive phase.[55] The Germans had 900,000 around it. Overall, however, there were more troops, perhaps 4 million altogether. The Germans concentrated about 10,000 artillery pieces, 2,700 tanks and assault guns and 2,000 aircraft for Operation Citadel – 70 per cent of their tanks and 65 per cent of their aircraft on the entire eastern front. The Russians had 20,000 artillery pieces, 3,600 tanks and assault guns and 2,400 aircraft. The five Russian fronts involved in the second phase – the counteroffensives to north and south – totalled more than 2.4 million troops – nearly a quarter of the Red Army's total strength on the eastern front at the time.[56] However, as in all battles, most of the manpower was not involved in fighting at the front. The assault forces which made up the German pincers may have comprised perhaps 250,000 men, 100,000 of them attacking the north face.

Hitler's order on 15 April does not give the impression of a limited offensive to straighten the line and pre-empt the expected Russian summer offensive.

> This offensive is of decisive importance. It must end in swift
> and decisive success. On the main axis the best formations,
> the better commanders and a large amount of ammunition
> must be used ... Victory at Kursk will be a beacon for the
> whole world.[57]

It would indeed. But the victory would not be Hitler's. He used the same words on 16 June, when Citadel was fixed for early July. But, he confessed to Guderian, the idea of this offensive 'made his stomach turn over'.[58]

A close-run thing . . .

Just before the great German attack Manstein visited Bucharest to award Romania's Marshal Antonescu a medal, which German radio trumpeted in a vain attempt to deceive the Russians. By 3 July Manstein was back in his Army Group South headquarters and Model, commanding Ninth Army, part of the northern pincer formed by Kluge's Army Group Centre, moved to his forward headquarters. Rokossovskiy, who would face Model's onslaught, was staying in a small white cottage with a red roof on the unmade-up main street of Svoboda, about halfway between Kursk itself and the north face of the salient. Opposite there stood an old monastery, which has now reopened and produces mineral water from an ancient spring. Beyond the monastery, the ground falls away steeply down to the River Seym, to the east.

German intelligence was good, too. Throughout May and June they had mounted heavy air attacks on Kursk itself, to disrupt Russian logistics and preparations. As for the Central Front headquarters, a combination of traffic analysis, probably, prisoner-of-war interrogation or maybe even a spy in town now gave the Germans a precision target. On the night of 3 July two planes came over. One dropped illuminating flares; the other scored a direct hit on the house. But Rokossovskiy was not there. Why he was out of the house is uncertain. He says he went to the senior officers' mess next door earlier than usual 'for some reason or other', and asked for decoded signals to be brought to him there, at about 23.00.[59] There is a story that the 'reason' was to avoid his doctor, a woman medical officer, who was looking for him. He would not be the only brave man who fears doctors. Then they heard the scream of falling bombs and dived for cover. Nobody in the mess was badly hurt. When they picked themselves up and went outside, they found that Rokossovskiy's house was completely flattened, and the sentry killed. Then one of his generals, N. G. Orël, appeared, somewhat confused, but very much alive. A bomb had hit the slit trench in which he should have been sheltering.

'Why weren't you in the trench?' grinned Rokossovskiy.

'I felt so cramped and cold,' replied Orël, flapping his arms like the eponymous bird. 'As though I'd been laid in a grave, and they were going to bury me. So I decided if I had to be killed, it might as well be in a warm, cosy room.'[60]

Generals, at least, sometimes had a choice. Most of the 2 million men waiting to do battle that night did not.

In the grounds of the former monastery, just opposite, the engineers immediately started to dig bunkers. Several layers of thick logs alternated with packed earth on top made secure but reasonably comfortable accommodation, lined with logs as well, and reached by a steep wooden stairway. A restored replica of Rokossovskiy's bunker is still there, in among the memorials to the divisions and regiments which fought at Kursk. Rokossovskiy kept his underground cavern fairly simple. One of his generals made his own quite luxurious, filling it with carpets, wall-hangings and fine furniture, and Rokossovskiy reportedly told him to move out to teach him a lesson.[61] The lesson about keeping the Red Army's best commanders alive was certainly learned. Henceforward not only Rokossovskiy, but also Zhukov would have well-appointed bunkers dug wherever they set up headquarters, even for a short time.

Rokossovskiy and Vatutin had received the warning of imminent attack on 2 July but were still anxious to know exactly when the attack would start because they planned to disrupt it with the biggest artillery 'counter-preparation' – smashing up the enemy when he is at his most vulnerable – in the history of war. That had to be timed very precisely, for when the Germans were in their final positions but before they actually attacked. On the eve of the battle – the evening of 4 July – Zhukov appeared at Rokossovskiy's headquarters. In spite of Rokossovskiy's occasional irritation with Zhukov, the Deputy Supreme Commander did not interfere. On the question of firing the counter-preparation, which would involve more than a thousand guns, mortars and rocket-launchers and half the artillery's allocation of ammunition,[62] Zhukov said simply, 'You're the front commander. It's up to you.' He then reported to Stalin that Rokossovskiy knew what he was doing, and asked permission to move on.[63] In spite of the tensions between the two men, it was a fine example of 'mission command' – letting trusted staff get on with it.

On the night of 4–5 July several German sappers were caught hacking their way through the minefields. They said 'H' hour was 03.00

Moscow time (02.00 German summer time). It was all down to Rokossovskiy's judgement. How reliable were the prisoners' statements? He immediately ordered the counter-preparation to be fired at 02.20. Some 500 guns, 460 mortars and 100 *Katyusha* rocket-launchers opened fire. Rokossovskiy claims to have anticipated the German artillery bombardment by just ten minutes. If that is so, then he succeeded in delaying the German bombardment by two hours. The Germans may have thought the Russians were launching an offensive, which, given all the experience from the previous year or so, would not have been unreasonable. It was not until 04.30 that the Germans opened fire. Meanwhile, 600 guns on Vatutin's front had already fired a counter-preparation on the night of 3–4 July and they fired another one an hour after Rokossovskiy's.[64] There is still argument about how effective the massive 'counter-preparation' was and whether it was perfectly timed. It seems certain, however, that it did shake the Germans very substantially.

Breaking the last great German offensive

Hoth's Fourth Panzer Army on the south face attacked at 05.00 on 5 July; Model's Ninth, on the north face, half an hour later. Hoth's 'wedge' had motorized infantry at the base, Panthers and Panzer IVs on the sides and Tigers and Ferdinands at the front. Many of the Panthers broke down, and the Germans drove into a barrage of fire from well-prepared positions. The Russians were using a technique which the Germans called the *Pakfront*: all the anti-tank guns would engage a single tank, and then move on to the next, in quick succession. By 10 July the attack in the south had stalled. The Germans had penetrated about 30 kilometres.

In the north, Rokossovskiy had correctly predicted the German attack towards Ponyri. The anti-tank guns were dug in on 'reverse slopes' – just behind the crests of the gently rolling hills, which were nevertheless sometimes scored by deep ravines. The maximum difference between the highest hill and the lowest valley bottom is about 40 metres. The anti-tank positions were often sited in woods, designed to fire into the more vulnerable sides of the German tanks as they attempted to flow past, although only 6 per cent of the land in the Ponyri area is wooded. The Russian Thirteenth Army put up particularly fierce resistance and by 10 July the Germans had only penetrated about 12 kilometres.

Of the eight lines of defence, stretching back to the Don, the Germans had reached the third.

Kursk was also an important air battle. The fiercest battles took place on the south face, as Second and Seventeenth Air Armies flew 19,263 sorties on the southern sector, from Kursk down to Belgorod, during the 'defensive' phase. The Red air force changed its tactics. Instead of flying ground-attack planes and bombers in groups of four or eight, they switched to big formations of thirty to forty. These proved much more effective against the targets, but were also better protected because it was easier for the fighters to cover one big group rather than several small ones. Also, some of the group could be used as a diversion, or to target ground-based anti-aircraft defences. It was very simple, but it made a huge difference. In this massed, multimillion man and woman battle, there might seem little room for individual performance, but individual performances add up. Close to the south face can be found the memorial to Lt Gorovets, who on 6 July had become separated from the rest of his flight. He noticed a large formation of enemy bombers flying towards the Russian positions, and shot down nine of them, before being shot down and killed himself. The monument stands by the side of the main road south from Kursk, through Oboyan'.[65] Interestingly, it does not mention the type of aircraft Gorovets was flying. It was an American Airacobra.

It was also here that Ivan Kozhedub, one of very few men to rival Zhukov as a three-times Hero of the Soviet Union, began his tally of kills, in a Russian La-5. He became the highest-scoring Russian fighter ace, with 62 kills from 520 sorties.[66]

The greatest tank battle?

In a final bid to break through the Soviet defences, outflank Kursk from the east and drive up the base of the salient, Hoth's Fourth Panzer Army with III Panzer Corps of the Operational Group Kempf to its right attacked on the south face on 11 July. It took them towards the little town of Prokhorovka, on the railway line from Kursk to Belgorod. Vatutin decided to try to outflank the attacking formations. The hot, dry weather had ended on 7 July and when 12 July dawned the sky above Prokhorovka field was piled high with ominous grey thunderclouds.

The II SS Panzer Corps, comprising the SS *Leibstandarte Adolf Hitler, Totenkopf* (Death's Head) and *Das Reich* Panzer divisions, was heading for Prokhorovka (see Figure 17.6). In equipment, as well as in the Nazi pecking order, it was the elite of the elite, numbering over 600 tanks and self-propelled guns including more than 100 Tigers, and also Ferdinands. On 5 July, Pavel Rotmistrov, commanding Fifth Guards Tank Army (part of the reserve formed by the Steppe Military District) had been ordered to head westwards to the Oskol in readiness to operate between Oboyan' and Kursk. On the night of 11 July Rotmistrov, now subordinated to Vatutin, commanding the Voronezh Front, received an order to deliver a counterstroke – an operational-level attack – towards the Komsomolets State farm, to destroy the enemy forces in the Kochetovka and Pokrovka area (see Figure 17.6), and prevent them from withdrawing south.

To do this, Fifth Guards Tank Army had 793 tanks, including 501 T-34s, 261 light T-70s, and, not to be forgotten, 31 British lease-lend Churchills. The portents were not good. As the Soviet General Staff study put it,

> Thus . . . the Fifth Guards Tank Army delivered a frontal
> attack against crack German Panzer divisions which, without
> an essential superiority in forces, could at best result in
> driving the enemy back. Since the Germans in turn were also
> assembling forces and were preparing to continue their

ongoing offensive, a large tank battle was in prospect, which, indeed, broke out during the day on 12 July.[67]

The General Staff Study blames the head-on collision between Fifth Guards Tank Army and II SS Panzer Corps on Rotmistrov, although he was carrying out Vatutin's orders. He could perhaps have done so more imaginatively. Rotmistrov's best tanks were the T-34s but even they were no match for the Tigers, except at very close range. He therefore ordered them to close with the Germans as fast as possible.

Even the classified Soviet General Staff study grossly overestimates the number of tanks involved. It says that 17th Panzer Division was 'in the immediate vicinity', but it never fought at Prokhorovka. The Soviet figures also count III Panzer Corps, which was well to the east. The total number of tanks is given as 1,200 to 1,300. The number actually engaged was about 850: 600 Soviet, from the corps of Fifth Guards Tank Army, and 250 German. At the end of 12 July, Soviet tank losses were about 400, as against 70 German.[68]

On that basis, Prokhorovka's claim to be 'the greatest tank battle in history' – or, perhaps, Rotmistrov's to have been its victor – begin to look shaky. There could have been ten tank battles on such a scale during the war. Stalin said that Rotmistrov was 'not very modest'.[69] Furthermore, the General Staff analysis was brutally unflattering:

> Thus on 12 July Fifth Guards Tank Army failed to accomplish its assigned mission. As a result of the frontal attack, the army's corps fought heavy battles against large enemy tank forces during which they were forced to assume the defence. On the night of 13 July the army's corps were given orders to consolidate on their achieved positions and regroup their units so that, by the morning of 14 July, they would be ready to assume the offensive.[70]

The last sentence is telling. It would be the beginning of the great Kursk counteroffensive.

Like so many of the stories from the Great Patriotic War, the story of Prokhorovka Field has been embellished and modified. There were three great 'field' (*pole*) battles in Russian military history: Kulikovo (1380), Borodino (1812), and Prokhorovka. None was really a victory: they were all bloody, messy, but highly symbolic draws. Today, over-looking what was the Komsomolets State Farm, close to the railway that

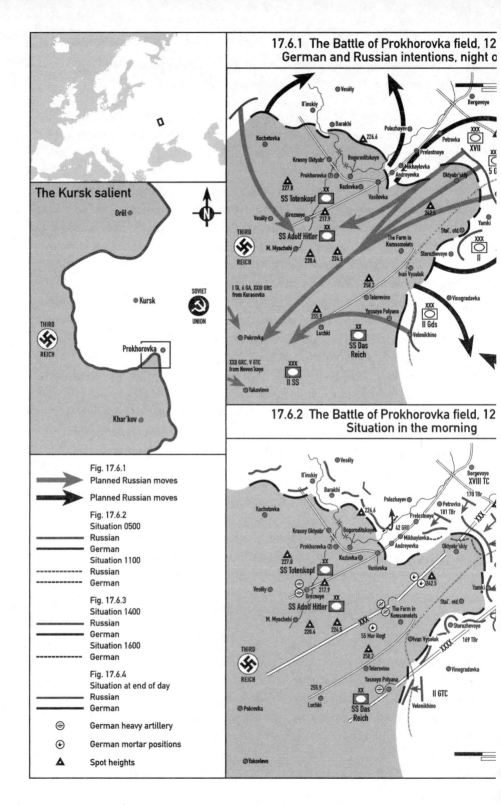

The Kursk salient

17.6.1 The Battle of Prokhorovka field, 12
German and Russian intentions, night o

17.6.2 The Battle of Prokhorovka field, 12
Situation in the morning

Fig. 17.6.1
Planned Russian moves

Planned Russian moves

Fig. 17.6.2
Situation 0500
Russian
German
Situation 1100
Russian
German

Fig. 17.6.3
Situation 1400
Russian
German
Situation 1600
German

Fig. 17.6.4
Situation at end of day
Russian
German

⊖ German heavy artillery

⊕ German mortar positions

▲ Spot heights

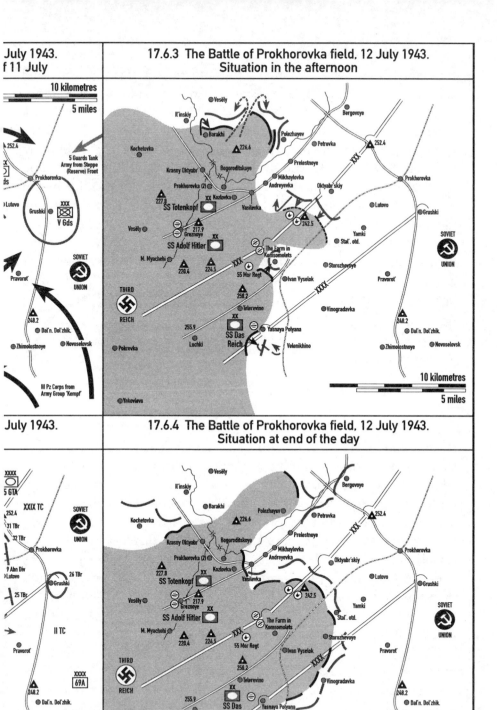

17.6.3 The Battle of Prokhorovka field, 12 July 1943.
Situation in the afternoon

10 kilometres

5 miles

17.6.4 The Battle of Prokhorovka field, 12 July 1943.
Situation at end of the day

runs north towards Prokhorovka itself, there is a gigantic white and gold memorial, a cross between Trajan's Column and a Russian Ortho-dox church tower, opened by President Yeltsin. Closer to the town, there is a vast new church with names of 9,000 soldiers killed in the battle inscribed in marble on the walls – one name for every three thousand Soviet people who died in the war. Back at the memorial, in the field which slopes down to the farm, you can still pick up bits of weapons, bits of ammunition. So much metal was expended there, on the wide field across which Fifth Guards Tank Army attacked the SS, that one could easily fill a suitcase, sixty years after. As for the men, their mangled and burnt remains were seared on to a reported 400 tank and armoured vehicle hulls – most, but far from all of which would have been Russian.[71]

Why did Hitler stop?

By the end of 12 July the Russians had fought the Germans to a standstill at Prokhorovka. The casualties on both sides are difficult to verify. The Russians claim that 70,000 German officers and men were killed in the defensive phase – bearing in mind, of course, that a considerable proportion of casualties would have been from 'friendly fire'. They also claim to have destroyed more than 3,000 tanks and assault guns, 844 artillery pieces, 1,392 planes and 5,000 trucks. The latest Russian statistics for the defence phase give 70,330 Russian killed, prisoners and missing, and 107,517 sick and wounded. The Germans claimed to have knocked out 1,800 tanks, 1,000 anti-tank guns and taken 24,000 prisoners on the south face alone.[72]

The results of the operation that had turned Hitler's stomach might be reason enough to stop, but there was another. Before Kursk, Hitler had said that if the western Allies landed in Italy, he would immediately halt the offensive. On 10 July, they did. At last, Churchill's Mediterra-nean strategy, with which Roosevelt was persuaded to agree, had a chance to show what it could do. The aims of the operation were limited to securing Mediterranean lines of communication, diverting German troops from the Soviet Union, detaching Italy from its alliance with Germany, and possibly bringing Turkey into the war on the Allied side.

The moment the British and Americans invaded Sicily, in Operation Husky, German troops were diverted from the Russian front. Indeed, some had already been diverted. More important, perhaps, was the diversion of air power. In July and August, according to German figures, the Luftwaffe lost 702 aircraft on the eastern front. During the same time, it lost 3,504 planes on other fronts, and most of them in Italy. Many of these were lost to accidents but in total they accounted for five times the Luftwaffe's losses in Russia.[73]

Although the Russians would, understandably, be sceptical about the idea, it may well be that Italy, and his alliance with Mussolini, was of greater importance to Hitler than the war on the eastern front which he was now losing. It is a persuasive thesis. With the British and American landfall in Europe, supported by increasingly superior naval and air power, the nature of the whole war was changing.

The 'rail war'

All the Soviet High Command's work organizing and cultivating the partisans behind the main German forces was now about to bear fruit. Stavka knew that the Germans enjoyed better rail and road communications on their side of the front. Partisan activity increased in June, but the real partisan offensive was held back until the Soviet counter-attack. On 14 July, two days after Prokhorovka, Stavka ordered the central partisan movement headquarters to carry out Operation 'Rel'sovaya voyna' – 'rail war'. It ran from 3 August to 15 September (see Figure 17.7). Stavka reckoned that to maintain their forces on either side of the salient against the Red Army striking back, the Germans would need 100,000 tonnes of supplies per day. After 397 attacks in January 1943, there were 1,092 attacks on communications in June and 1,460 in July. In June, in Army Group Centre's sector, pro-Soviet partisans blew up 44 railway bridges, damaged 298 locomotives and 1,233 railway wagons, and interrupted rail traffic 746 times. Even if a train and its cargo were not destroyed, having it sitting in a railway yard while the line was

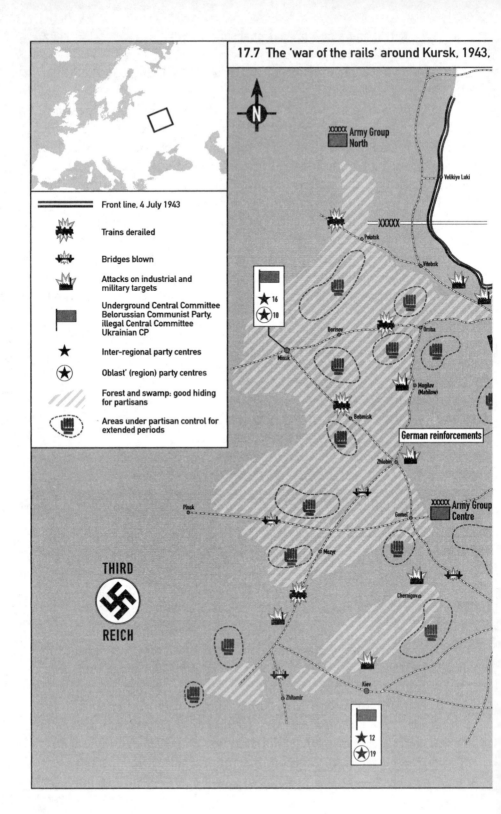

17.7 The 'war of the rails' around Kursk, 1943,

Legend:

Front line, 4 July 1943

Trains derailed

Bridges blown

Attacks on industrial and military targets

Underground Central Committee Belorussian Communist Party, illegal Central Committee Ukrainian CP

★ Inter-regional party centres

⊛ Oblast' (region) party centres

Forest and swamp: good hiding for partisans

Areas under partisan control for extended periods

Army Group North

Velikiye Luki

XXXXX

Polotsk

Vitebsk

★ 16
⊛ 10

Berisov

Orsha

Minsk

Mogilav (Mahilow)

Bobruisk

German reinforcements

Zhlobin

Pinsk

Gomel

XXXXX Army Group Centre

Mozyr

THIRD REICH

Chernigov

Kiev

Zhitomir

★ 12
⊛ 19

showing Partisan organization and activity in concert with main forces

Staraya Russa

200 kilometres

100 miles

Central Committee of Communist Party
Stavka
Central Staff of Partisan Movement

Moscow

SOVIET

UNION

Smolensk

Vyazma

Kaluga

Tula

★ 4

Bryansk

★ 3

Orël

20–21 July
11 Partisan brigades
430 demolitions

Unecha

Closed 21–23 July

Yelets

Khutor Mikhaylovskiy

Dmitrev-L'govskiy

Ponyri

Don

L'gov   Kursk   Shchigry   Kastornoye

Voronezh

★ 2
★ 1

Konotop

Seym

Vorozhba

Oboyan'

Stary Oskol

Liski

Sumy

Krasnopol'ye

Novy Oskol

Pavlovsk

XXXXX

Psël

XXXXX Army Group
South

Valuyki

Khar'kov

Poltava

Krasnograd

secured and repaired interrupted German operations significantly. The plan for the rail war included 96,000 partisan fighters who would cut between 200,000 and 300,000 sections of railway track. This huge sabotage operation would paralyse communications from the German Northern Army Group down into the Centre for several days and severely hamper the German response to the Soviet counteroffensive, at least north of the Kursk salient.[74]

With 12 partisan units operating behind German lines in the Leningrad area, 9 in the Kalinin district, 16 in Smolensk and 7 in Orël, the effort was concentrated in Belarus and north of there. There was a reason for that. In Ukraine, many of the partisans were against the Russians.[75]

In addition to destroying tracks and derailing trains, the partisans were ordered to inflict more permanent – and vindictive – damage by, first of all, killing the train crews. These were mainly former Soviet citizens who were willingly or, more probably, unwillingly working for the Germans. That mattered not a jot. Stalin had ordered that anyone surrendering to or cooperating with the enemy, whatever the reason, was a traitor and should die. Armour-piercing shells were very good for exploding the boilers of steam locomotives. After that, the coal tenders could be set on fire, as could any petroleum fuel the trains were carrying.

The first really big strike occurred on the night of 20 to 21 July, when eleven partisan brigades attacked the main railway south of Bryansk (Bryansk-L'gov) and other tracks supplying Army Groups Centre and South. That night the partisans fired 430 demolitions and the main line south of Bryansk, which was critical for the Germans, was blocked for two precious days. During August, partisan operations increased further and by 6 October Army Group Centre was reporting that that owing to 'lightning' partisan attacks, railway communications in the army group rear area were 'paralysed'. A report by the army group's commander of security forces added that trains could usually move only in daylight and that wagons filled with sand had to be pushed in front of the locomotives as protection again Russian mines. Partisan attacks focused on the main railway lines serving the German forces around the Kursk salient and in so doing undoubtedly prevented the Germans from manoeuvring to meet the Soviet counteroffensive. Paralysing the rail transport also had a big impact on the air war. In June the German Sixth Air Fleet, supporting the German offensive at

Kursk, used 8,600 tonnes of aviation fuel but received only 5,700. The rail war was a big success, and the Belorussian partisans recruited another 17,000 people.[76]

'Kutuzov', 'Rumyantsev': The counteroffensives

Rokossovskiy's forces in the north had taken less of a pounding, and on 12 July the counteroffensive to take Orël – codenamed 'Kutuzov', after the wily old field marshal of 1812, began (see Figure 17.8). The Germans attached great importance to Orël and held on stubbornly. However, Rokossovskiy's Central Front, with Popov's Bryansk and elements of Sokolovskiy's Western Front, began to gain ground. In a foretaste of the kind of war to come, Stavka ordered the front commanders to commit their tank armies to break up the German defence: Sokolovskiy's Front's Fourth Tank and the Bryansk Front's Third Guards tank. The Russians threatened to encircle German troops near Mtsensk, and Model, afraid of being trapped, asked for permission to withdraw. On 26 July, just after the rail war had begun in earnest, the German High Command resigned itself to withdrawing to the 'Hagen Line'. The Germans tried to withdraw in good order, but were by now utterly shattered, and on the night of 3 to 4 August Soviet troops recaptured Orël.[77]

'Kutuzov' lasted thirty-eight days. To the south, where the German attack had cut deeper and done more damage, Operation 'Rumyantsev', named after an eighteenth-century Russian field marshal,[78] began on 3 August. However, while starting later, it would be over more quickly. On 16 July Stavka had ordered the Steppe Military District to become operational – a front, again. By 23 July Koniev and Vatutin's fronts were back at the start line where the Germans had launched their attack on the 5th. German signals intelligence identified all the characteristics of an imminent Soviet attack, just as the Russians had before 5 July, and on 2 August Army Group South warned of an imment offensive west of Belgorod and south-east of Khar'kov. After a pause to bring up forces and supplies, Operation Rumyantsev began on 3 August. The Germans had fortified Belgorod and Khar'kov, and stiff resistance could be expected. Vatutin's forces were still reeling from repelling the German

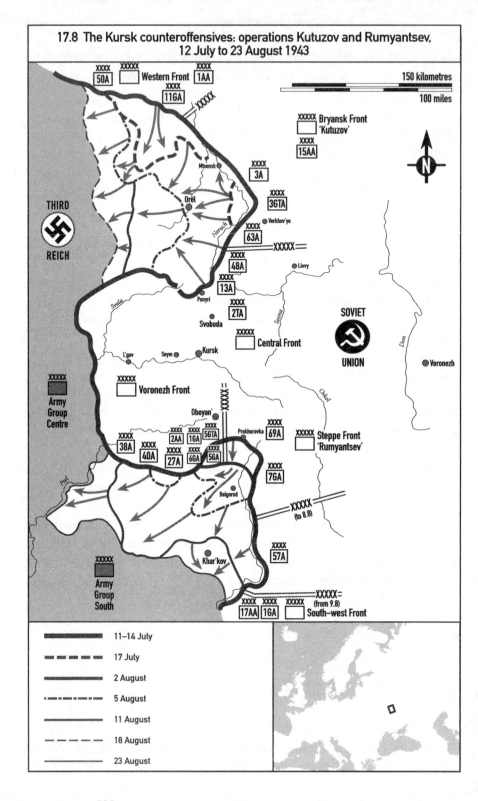

17.8 The Kursk counteroffensives: operations Kutuzov and Rumyantsev, 12 July to 23 August 1943

150 kilometres

100 miles

XXXX 50A   XXXXX   Western Front   XXXX 1AA

XXXX 116A

XXXXX

XXXXX Bryansk Front 'Kutuzov'

XXXX 15AA

Mtsensk

XXXX 3A

Orël

XXXX 3GTA

XXXX 63A   Verkhov'ye

XXXXX

XXXX 48A   Linvy

XXXX 13A

Ponyri

Svala

XXXX 2TA

Svoboda

Soma

XXXXX Central Front

SOVIET UNION

L'gov   Seym   Kursk

Don

Voronezh

THIRD REICH

XXXXX Army Group Centre

XXXXX Voronezh Front

Oboyan'

Oskol

XXXXX

XXXX 38A   XXXX 2AA   XXXX 16A   XXXX 5GTA   Prokhorovka   XXXX 69A

XXXXX Steppe Front 'Rumyantsev'

XXXX 40A   XXXX 27A   XXXX 66A   XXXX 56A

XXXX 76A

Belgorod

XXXXX (to 8.8)

Pul

XXXX 57A

Khar'kov

XXXXX Army Group South

XXXXX= (from 9.8)

XXXX 17AA   XXXX 16A   XXXXX   South-west Front

Neruch

	11–14 July
	17 July
	2 August
	5 August
	11 August
	18 August
	23 August

attack on the south face. Rotmistrov's Fifth Guards Tank Army had just 150 tanks left, out of the 793 it had on the morning of 12 July, at Prokhorovka, while Koniev's front had come up out of reserve very quickly, and had started to acquire the appropriate logistics for an army group only on 18 July. However, in order to coordinate Koniev's and Vatutin's efforts, Zhukov was sent in. The offensive against Belgorod and Khar'kov had much in common with offensives for the rest of the war. The attack was, like that in Operation Kutuzov, on a very wide front – 300 to 400 kilometres, and would penetrate even further – 250 kilometres, as opposed to just 150.[79] Zhukov was determined to have better artillery and air support, and in the Belgorod-Khar'kov operation he got it. The artillery would now put down a 'fire wall' to paralyse the entire forward defence line, back to about 1,500 metres, while each attacking army would get up to a corps of ground-attack planes. The Red Army was starting to fight as it would continue to do for the rest of the war.[80]

At 05.00 on 3 August the Russian artillery opened up with a very short barrage, and then silence. Then they switched to carefully selected targets. Finally, at 07.35 all the artillery and mortars opened up, followed ten minutes later by all the *Katyushas*. It worked. On the first day aircraft from the second air army flew 2,670 sorties in support of the ground troops, and they continued to take a heavy toll of German reinforcements, especially tank and motorized columns. By 5 August Belgorod was encircled (see Figure 17.8), and Russian troops entered the city the same day. When Belgorod was cleared there were more than 3,000 German dead in the ruins. On 22 August the Germans started pulling out of Khar'kov. To prevent the Germans from withdrawing, but also to protect property and pre-empt the demolition of the city, the Russians decided on a night attack. By midday on the 23rd Khar'kov was also in Russian hands.[81]

The 'first salute . . .'

On the evening of 5 August 1943, an unusual sound rumbled over Moscow. They were guns – 'our guns', again. Following the news of the recapture of Orël, after a relatively swift counteroffensive, and Belgorod the same day, Stalin ordered an artillery salute to be fired. Orël and Belgorod are known as the 'cities of the first salute'. From then on, every major victory would be greeted by a salute like that. It was another measure of the growing confidence of the government, Stavka, and the Red Army.

Although Russian losses were, again, greater than German, the German casualties were horrific, and they could afford them less. Of about seventy German divisions operating in the Kursk area, thirty had been destroyed and the German figures put their losses at more than half a million killed, seriously wounded, prisoners or missing in fifty days of fighting. That gives about 10,000 a day. The Russian figures show a remarkable shift from inordinate numbers of dead and missing to a more normal ratio of killed to wounded. During the defensive phase there were 70,000 'irrecoverable losses' against 107,517 sick and wounded. In Operation Rumyantsev the Russians lost 71,611 'irrecoverables' against 184,000 sick and wounded – closer to the one-to-three norm. In operation Kutuzov, the figures were 112,529 to 317,361, respectively, again, close to the norm of one-to-three. That must also be an indicator of improved Russian medical and evacuation procedures. Russian losses per day were 9,360 in the defensive phase, against a total of 23,483 in the two overlapping counteroffensives. With a very rough German toll of 10,000 killed, prisoners, sick, wounded and missing per day, that is close to the ratio of one German casualty to 1.5 Russian, which would apply for the rest of the war.[82]

So, was Kursk intended as an 'operational preventive blow from the strategic defensive', in which it succeeded to some extent, as it significantly weakened the punch of the summer offensive that followed?[83] Or was it Germany's last chance to win on the eastern front? From the military side, even if Army Groups Centre and South had met up on the gentle watershed running north–south across the salient and trapped some of the sixty divisions there, it is unlikely they could have done any more. By now, the Russians were getting wise and it was unlikely they would have got them all. A thrust north-east through the reserve (Steppe) Front to encircle Moscow would have been too much, and logistically unsustainable. It would have been a terrible disaster and tragedy for the Russians, but it would not have knocked them out of the war.

From the economic and production point of view, Germany had already lost the war. From that perspective the Battle of Kursk was not the turning point of the Second World War, which could be advanced to 7 December 1941. Nor was it the turning point of the war on the eastern front, which many would now consider to be the counteroffensive at Stalingrad or, at the latest, the destruction of Sixth Army. However, it did not seem like that at the time, either to the Russians, or the western Allies, or the Germans. Most German officers, from Keitel down to junior officers who served on the eastern front, considered Kursk to be the point after which Germany was bound to lose the war. Keitel testified that after the defeat of German forces in the summer of 1943 it became clear that Germany could not win the war by military means.[84] Churchill was more cautious. 'The three immense battles of Kursk, Orël and Khar'kov, all in the space of two months, heralded the downfall of the German army on the eastern front.'[85]

Heralding is not the same as doing. However, the Russians seemed very sure of themselves. In late 1943 they started building war memorials to their dead on the Kursk salient. They must have been very sure the Germans would not be coming back. And if, after Stalingrad, Germany could not win, then now the Russians could not lose. But they still had to fight their way to Berlin. In this absolute war, there was no chance of any peace deal. The British and Americans had already committed themselves to unconditional surrender at Casablanca in January, but that made no difference on the eastern front. It had been war to the death from the start. The Russians were going to annihilate Nazi Germany, albeit at great cost. And first, they would have to destroy the *Wehrmacht*.

18

DESTROYING THE *WEHRMACHT*.
UKRAINE, BELARUS AND THE BALTIC:
REASSERTING SOVIET CONTROL

The balance tips: the Battle of the Dnepr

Russian planning to reconquer Ukraine started even before the Battle of
Kursk was over, and was a natural development of the straightening of
the line to include Belgorod and Khar'kov. To the north of the salient,
the natural successor to Rumyantsev and Kutuzov was Operation
'Suvorov', named after Russia's greatest general, but not a well-known
operation. In the Smolensk Offensive, between 7 August and 2 October,
the Kalinin and Western Fronts pushed German forces back a further
200 to 250 kilometres, well clear of Moscow.[1]

The aim of the first phase was to 'liberate' (although many Ukrainians who had welcomed and cooperated with the Germans did not see it
that way) 'left-bank Ukraine'. That meant the *eastern* side of the Dnepr
– 'left', as seen from the direction of flow. No sooner had Koniev's
Steppe Front finished at Kursk than, on 13 August, parts of it pushed
south-west. The great 'Battle of the Dnepr' embraced several Strategic
Operations, to which the Russians were now getting increasingly accus-
tomed (see Figure 18.1). The Donbass Operation, in August and
September, was not officially part of the Dnepr battle, but was a crucial
jumping-off point, since it reached the river and even seized a bridgehead on the west bank. Equally – although from an industrial point of
view, more importantly – it regained the crucial Donbass industrial
area.[2] To the north, having straightened the line at the Germans'
expense, Rokossovskiy's Central Front now headed due west from the

former Kursk bulge and created a new salient, nearly 100 kilometres wide and 80 deep. During the second half of September Central Front continued westwards, arriving at the Dnepr north of Kiev.

To the south, the Voronezh Front sent a mobile group forward – a fast-moving formation intent on avoiding enemy defences and causing him to crack from the rear – which reached the Dnepr on the night of 21 to 22 September. On the next day, the Russians established small bridgeheads on the right (west) bank at Rzhishchev and Velikiy Bukrin (see inset to Figure 18.1) and then they tried dropping airborne (parachute) forces on the west bank to increase their hold – a variant of the same idea. Although the Russians had been pioneers in the experimental large-scale use of paratroops, their attempts to use them in the Second World War were pretty disastrous. 1st, 3rd and 5th Guards airborne 'brigades' were landed west of the river but only half of the 4,575 paratroops survived to fight their way out and continue offensive operations.[3] The Bukrin bridgehead battle would be the last Soviet attempt at an airborne assault landing in Europe, although they used paratroops quite successfully in Manchuria. As always, the successful delivery of paratroops depends on overwhelming air power. By this time the Russians had a slight numerical superiority in the air, but not enough to be significant.

Instead, in the old style, ground forces heading from the east reached the river on an 800-kilometre front between 22 and 30 September. After a delay while crossing points were secured, the Fifty-Second Army got across on 14 November. Meanwhile, on 12 October, the Voronezh Front attacked towards Kiev which was finally recaptured from the Germans after fierce fighting on 6 November.[4] The Kiev Operation, from 3 to 13 November 1943, not only recaptured the capital of Ukraine but also created a bridgehead 300 kilometres wide and 150 deep on the right-bank. This would prove an invaluable jumping-off point for the subsequent liberation of 'right bank Ukraine' in early 1944.[5]

In all, five fronts were involved in the Battle of the Dnepr: Central, Voronezh, Steppe, South-Western and South. From 20 October these were renamed Belorussian and First to Fourth Ukrainian, respectively. Overall, the operations which made up the 'Battle of the Dnepr' involved 2.6 million Soviet troops versus 1.24 million Germans.[6] The first and last component operations each involved about 1.5 million Soviet troops. The Chernigov-Poltava offensive from 26 August to 30 September, involving three fronts – Central, Voronezh and Steppe – deployed

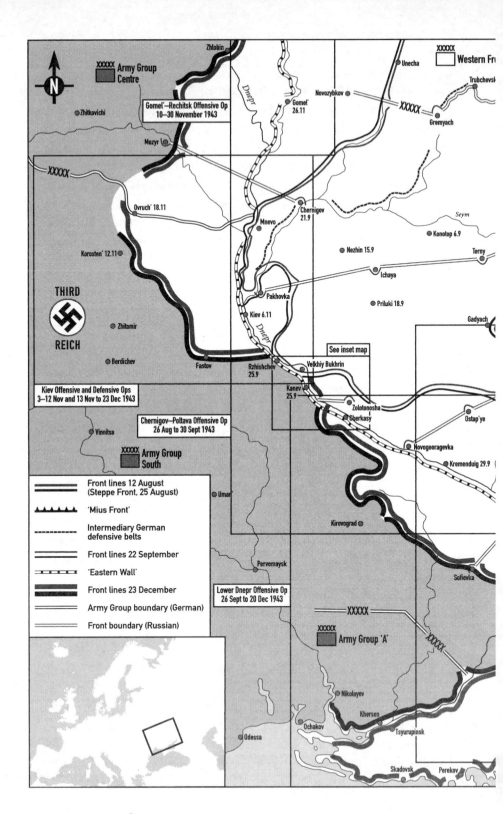

Army Group Centre

Gomel'–Rechitsk Offensive Op
10–30 November 1943

Zhlobin
Zhitkovichi
Mozyr
Dnepr
Gomel' 26.11
Novozybkov
Unecha
Trubchevs
Gremyach
XXXXX
XXXXX Western Fr

Ovruch' 18.11
Chernigov 21.9
Mnevo
Seym
Korosten' 12.11
Nezhin 15.9
Terny
Ichaya
THIRD
REICH
Zhitomir
Pakhovka
Priluki 18.9
Gadyach
Kiev 6.11
Dnepr
Berdichev
Fastov
Rzhishchev 25.9
Velkhiy Bukhrin
See inset map

Kiev Offensive and Defensive Ops
3–12 Nov and 13 Nov to 23 Dec 1943
Kanev 25.9
Zolotonosha
Cherkasy
Ostap'ye

Chernigov–Poltava Offensive Op
26 Aug to 30 Sept 1943
Vinnitsa
Novogeoragevka
Kremenduig 29.9

XXXXX Army Group South

Front lines 12 August
(Steppe Front, 25 August)

▲▲▲▲▲▲ 'Mius Front'

--------- Intermediary German
defensive belts

Front lines 22 September

'Eastern Wall'

Front lines 23 December

Army Group boundary (German)

Front boundary (Russian)

Uman'
Kirovograd

Pervomaysk
Sofievka

Lower Dnepr Offensive Op
26 Sept to 20 Dec 1943
XXXXX
XXXXX Army Group 'A'
XXXX

Nikolayev
Kherson
Ochakov
Tsyurupinsk
Odessa
Skadovsk
Perekov

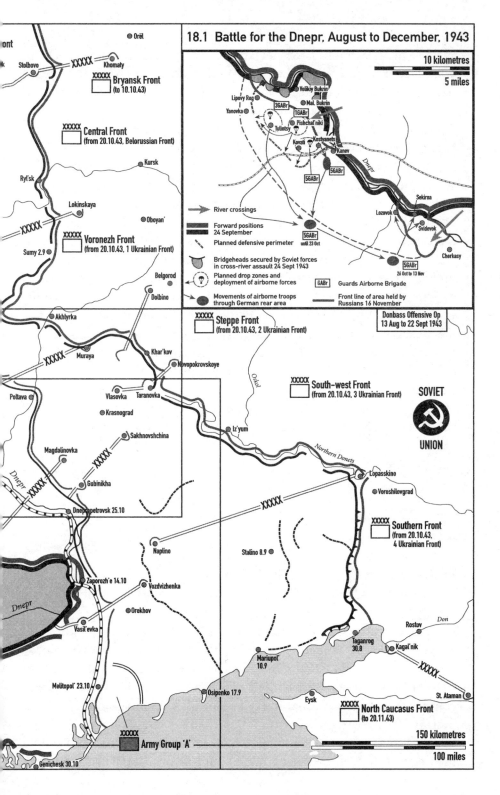

18.1 Battle for the Dnepr, August to December, 1943

10 kilometres

5 miles

Orël

Stolbovo

Khomaty

XXXXX

XXXXX Bryansk Front
(to 10.10.43)

XXXXX Central Front
(from 20.10.43, Belorussian Front)

Kursk

Ryl'sk

Lokinskaya

Oboyan'

XXXXX

Sumy 2.9

XXXXX Voronezh Front
(from 20.10.43, 1 Ukrainian Front)

Belgorod

Dolbino

Lipovy Rog

Velikiy Bukrin

3GABr

Mal. Bukrin

Yanovka

1GABr

Tulintsy

Pishchal'niki

Kovati

Kostyanets

Kanev

5GABr

5GABr

Sekirna

Lozovok

Svidevok

26 Oct to 13 Nov

Cherkasy

5GABr

Dnepr

River crossings

Forward positions
24 September

Planned defensive perimeter

until 23 Oct

5GABr

Bridgeheads secured by Soviet forces
in cross-river assault 24 Sept 1943

Planned drop zones and
deployment of airborne forces

GABr

Guards Airborne Brigade

Movements of airborne troops
through German rear area

Front line of area held by
Russians 16 November

Akhtyrka

XXXXX Steppe Front
(from 20.10.43, 2 Ukrainian Front)

Donbass Offensive Op
13 Aug to 22 Sept 1943

Muraya

Khar'kov

Novopokrovskoye

Oskol

XXXXX South-west Front
(from 20.10.43, 3 Ukrainian Front)

SOVIET

Vlasovka

Taranovka

Iz'yum

Poltava

Krasnograd

Sakhnovshchina

UNION

Northern Donets

Magdalinovka

Dnepr

Gubinikha

Lopasskino

XXXXX

Voroshilovgrad

Dnepropetrovsk 25.10

Naplino

Stalino 8.9

XXXXX

XXXXX Southern Front
(from 20.10.43,
4 Ukrainian Front)

Zaporozh'e 14.10

Vozdvizhenka

Dnepr

Orekhov

Don

Rostov

Vasil'evka

Taganrog
30.8

Kagal'nik

Melitopol' 23.10

Osipenko 17.9

Mariupol'
10.9

Eysk

XXXXX

St. Ataman

XXXXX North Caucasus Front
(to 20.11.43)

150 kilometres

XXXXX Army Group 'A'

Genichesk 30.10

100 miles

599

a total of 1.58 million Soviet troops.[7] The last, the Lower Dnepr offensive, from 26 September to 20 December, involving the Steppe (later Second Ukrainian), South-Western (Third Ukrainian) and Southern (Fourth Ukrainian) Fronts similarly called on 1.51 million soldiers.[8] First Ukrainian Front's operation to take Kiev, from 3 to 13 November, involved a total of 671,000 Soviet troops.[9]

By the end of December, the Russians had a strategic bridgehead across the Dnepr as far as Korosten, on the edge of the Pripyet marshes, which would also give them a springboard for the decisive Belorussian offensive in the summer. Russian historians divide the war into three main parts. The first period runs up to the counteroffensive at Stalingrad, when, in spite of energetic Russian counter-attacks, the strategic initiative was with the Germans. The second period – the 'fundamental shift in the correlation of forces' – runs from 19 November 1942 to the end of 1943. With the end of the Battle of the Dnepr at the end of 1943, this phase was complete. The next eighteen months would see the defeat of Germany.[10] During 1943 the Russian forces suffered most of their sick and wounded – 30 per cent of those in the entire war, but for the first time that percentage exceeded the irrecoverable losses. By the end of 1943 they had also suffered 77 per cent of their dead, missing and prisoners for the entire conflict. From now on, it was downhill.

Tehran

At the end of November Stalin flew to Tehran to meet his allies, Roosevelt and Churchill. Stalin's relationship with Churchill remained prickly, and they did not trust each other as much as Stalin and Roosevelt did. In fact, they hardly trusted each other at all. Churchill's proposal to move Poland westwards and to establish the Soviet–Polish border along the old Curzon line, which was pretty close to the 1939–41 frontier, went down rather well. That was understandable, since it compensated Poland for her losses in the East with much more valuable, industry-rich German territory. Berezhkov says Churchill was still opposed to a Normandy landing (which seems extraordinary, given that the decision had already been made), and favoured an invasion of the

Balkans. Nevertheless, Churchill did continue to argue that there would be advantages in 'stretching' the Germans in the Balkan theatre and trying to get Turkey into the war. It seems that, as Berezhkov argued, 'Stalin read Churchill's mind: he didn't want to let the Red Army into eastern Europe.'[11] However, the British and Americans did finally commit themselves to invading France in the summer of 1944. In March 1943 they had decided to head for Normandy rather than the shorter but more obvious crossing on the Pas de Calais. Having got a commitment from Roosevelt and Churchill that Overlord would be launched no later than May, Stalin then tried to get a better idea of the date by promising a simultaneous offensive from the East. Field Marshal Brooke, the British Chief of Staff, reported that he could see 'a military brain of the very highest calibre in action'. Stalin was also a brilliant negotiator.[12]

Hitler's eyes had remained largely fixed on the eastern front, even though he had diverted forces from there to Italy. But in November Führer Directive No. 51 gave a new priority to defending the Atlantic wall and put Rommel in charge of Army Group B, under Runstedt. Some fifty infantry and ten armoured divisions were in France and the Low Countries, and the Allies worked hard at deceiving the Germans about their likely invasion targets, ranging from southern France to Norway. However, there were still no western Allied troops in Europe, and more than 200 German divisions were still on the eastern front.[13] With the date for Overlord apparently firmly fixed – although it was postponed again – Stalin at last had reassurance that a major effort drawing German forces away was not far off, and it also kept rival Allied armies away from his southern flank, giving him a free hand in southeastern Europe. In return, Stalin promised to enter the war against Japan. On his return from Tehran, Stalin said that 'Roosevelt has given his word that large-scale action will be mounted in France in 1944.' He made no mention of Churchill. 'I believe he [Roosevelt] will keep his word. *But even if he doesn't, we have enough forces of our own to complete the rout of Germany.*'[14]

Tools for the job

In order to break the German defences as rapidly as possible, the Russians knew they would have to encircle large German groups, just as the Germans had done so effectively in 1941–2. If the German forces pulled back slowly, digging in again and again, the war would take forever. During the counteroffensive at Stalingrad, Manstein had noted how 'at each of the two points of penetration strong Soviet tank forces had immediately pushed through in depth – just as we had taught them to do'.[15] That was a touch arrogant: the Russians had developed a clear concept of deep operations in the 1930s, but had, admittedly, executed its leading advocate. Having experienced vast encirclements at the hands of the Germans and had millions of troops fall into captivity, the effectiveness of the concept was no longer in any doubt. The rapid advances of the Red Army in ensuing operations were therefore made possible by changes in the force structure during 1943. By that summer, in response to lessons from Stalingrad, the Red Army had formed and equipped five tank armies of a new design, each comprising two tank and one mechanized corps.[16] By summer 1943, responsibility for exploiting any breakthrough and driving fast and far into the enemy 'depth', in order to trap him before he could pull back, became the main responsibility of the front commanders, and the prime instrument became either the unified tank army or the cavalry–mechanized group (KMG).[17] The latter comprised an apparently anachronistic – but very effective – mix of cavalry and tank corps. These tank armies and KMGs had a 'different purpose' from the tank corps which were part of ordinary armies. Whereas the latter would help the armies break through, the tank armies and KMGs were to act as powerful, heavy-hitting spearheads under front control, to deal a 'strong determined tank strike' in the enemy's operational depth and to accomplish encirclement operations.[18] Sometimes tank armies received their orders directly from Stavka, and at Berlin both Zhukov and Koniev had to clear the use to which they put these armies with Stalin himself.[19] At Stalingrad, there had been only one tank army – Fifth. In the Kursk counteroffensives – Kutuzov and Rumyantsev – two tank armies had been available to each operation. Most of the major offensives thereafter had two or three tank armies available, and for the Vistula-Oder and Berlin offensives in 1945 there were four.[20]

In addition, eighteen heavy tank regiments were formed to reinforce ordinary armies and help the initial breakthrough of enemy defences. The air forces were reorganized and equipped with new planes including the La-5, YaK-9, Pe-2, Tu-2 and Il-4. Each front now had its own air army, with between 700 and 800 planes. Overall, the Russian air force had 8,300 combat planes available by the summer of 1943.[21]

An increasing amount of artillery was 'motorized', which usually meant pulled by (American) trucks, rather than horse drawn, but there was also an increased amount of self-propelled artillery. Like the Germans, the Russians favoured tank destroyers – effectively turretless tanks – as a cheap substitute for tanks. The first assault guns were only manufactured in 1942, and, according to the official Russian statistics, all 600 of them were lost in action. However, in 1943, 4,400 self-propelled guns were delivered and in 1944, 13,500.[22] In order to deal with the Panther, the T-34 tank was also up-gunned to 85mm, and these began to appear in early 1944. Furthermore, new heavy tank designs, the IS-2 and the the highly futuristic and streamlined IS-3, both named after Stalin, were entering production, although they would not become widely available until later.

Right-bank Ukraine and the Crimea

By 24 December 1943 the Russians had sealed off the Crimea, and on that Christmas Eve the Red Army renewed its attacks. The ensuing operations, ten of them, known collectively as 'right-bank Ukraine', lasted until 17 April 1944 and extended over a front of 1,250 kilometres (see Figures 18.2 and 18.4). A great offensive west of Kiev began on 26 December and early in January cavalry of the First Ukrainian Front crossed the old Polish border and then swung south to try to cut off the German armies in the Dnepr bend.

The German salient sticking out around Korsun-Shevchenkovskiy in Ukraine attracted special attention and between 24 January and 27

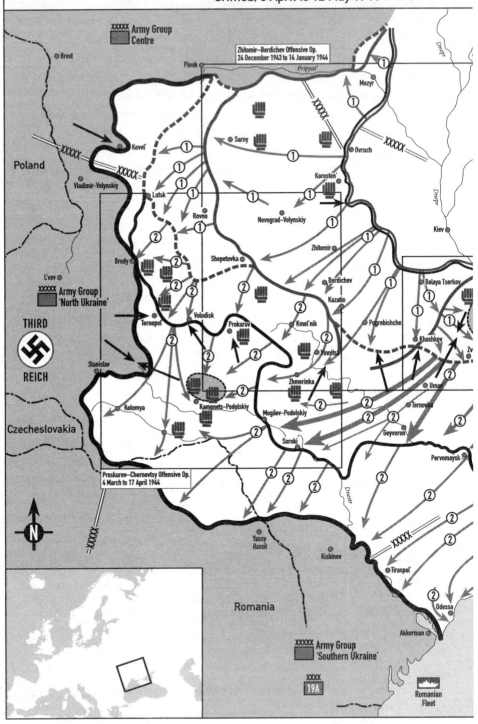

18.2 'Right Bank Ukraine' – the Dnepr-Carpathian Offensive Operation, 24 Dec 1943 to Crimea, 8 April to 12 May 1944

XXXXX Army Group
Centre

Brest

Pinsk

Pripyat

Mozyr

Zhitomir–Berdichev Offensive Op.
24 December 1943 to 14 January 1944

Sarny

Ovruch

Korosten'

Kovel'

Poland

Vladimir-Volynskiy

Lutsk

Rovno

Novograd-Volynskiy

Kiev

Zhitomir

Shepetovka

Berdichev

Belaya Tserkov

Brody

Kazatin

L'vov

XXXXX Army Group
'North Ukraine'

Volodisk

Pogrebishche

Khashkov

THIRD

Ternopol

Prokurov

Kmel'nik

Zv

Vinnitsa

Stanislav

REICH

Kamenets–Podolskiy

Zhmerinka

Uman

Ternovka

Kolomya

Mogilev–Podolskiy

Czecheslovakia

Soroki

Geyvoron

Pervomaysk

Proskurov–Chernovtsy Offensive Op.
4 March to 17 April 1944

Dnestr

N

Yassy
(Iassy)

Kishinev

Tiraspol'

Romania

Odessa

Akkerman

XXXXX Army Group
'Southern Ukraine'

XXXX
19A

Romanian
Fleet

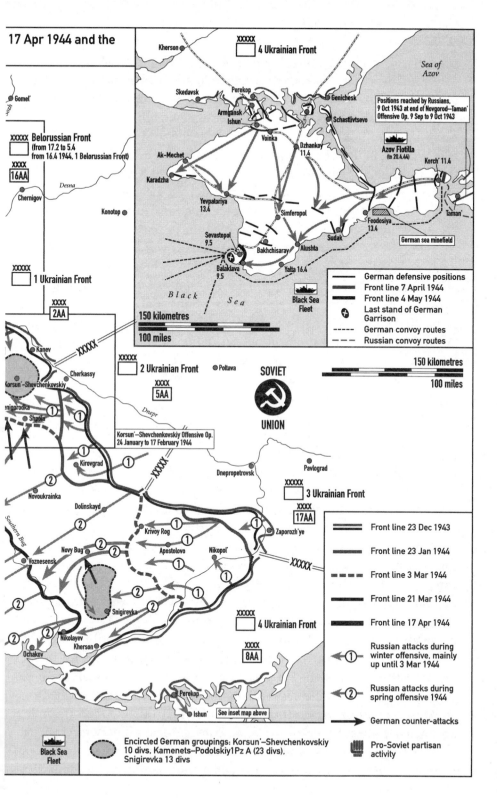

17 Apr 1944 and the

XXXXX 4 Ukrainian Front

Kherson

Sea of Azov

Skedavsk

Perekop

Genichesk

Armgansk
Ishun'

Schastlivtsevo

Voinka

Positions reached by Russians,
9 Oct 1943 at end of Novgorod–Taman'
Offensive Op. 9 Sep to 9 Oct 1943

Ak–Mechet

Dzhankoy
11.4

Azov Flotilla
(to 20.4.44)

Karadzha

Kerch' 11.4

Yevpatoriya
13.4

Simferopol

Feodosiya
13.4

Taman'

Sevastopol
9.5

Sudak

German sea minefield

Bakhchisaray

Alushta

Balaklava
9.5

Yalta 16.4

Black Sea

Black Sea
Fleet

German defensive positions
Front line 7 April 1944
Front line 4 May 1944
Last stand of German
Garrison
German convoy routes
Russian convoy routes

150 kilometres
100 miles

XXXXX Belorussian Front
(from 17.2 to 5.4
from 16.4 1944, 1 Belorussian Front)

XXXX 16AA

Gomel'

Desna

Chernigov

Konotop

XXXXX 1 Ukrainian Front

XXXX 2AA

Kanev

Cherkassy

XXXXX 2 Ukrainian Front

Poltava

XXXX 5AA

SOVIET
UNION

150 kilometres
100 miles

Korsun'–Shevchenkovskiy

Dnepr

Shenigorodka

Shpola

Korsun'–Shevchenkovskiy Offensive Op.
24 January to 17 February 1944

Kirovgrad

Dnepropetrovsk

Pavlograd

XXXXX 3 Ukrainian Front

XXXX 17AA

Novoukrainka

Dolinskayd

Southern Bug

Krivoy Rog

Zaporozh'ye

Novy Bug

Apostolovo

Nikopol'

Voznesensk

Front line 23 Dec 1943

Front line 23 Jan 1944

Front line 3 Mar 1944

Front line 21 Mar 1944

Front line 17 Apr 1944

Snigirevka

XXXXX 4 Ukrainian Front

XXXX 8AA

Nikolayev

Kherson

Ochakov

Russian attacks during
winter offensive, mainly
up until 3 Mar 1944

Russian attacks during
spring offensive 1944

German counter-attacks

Perekop

Ishun'

See inset map above

Black Sea
Fleet

Encircled German groupings: Korsun'–Shevchenkovskiy
10 divs, Kamenets–Podolskiy1Pz A (23 divs),
Snigirevka 13 divs

Pro-Soviet partisan
activity

February First and Second Ukrainian Fronts under Vatutin and Koniev, with Zhukov as the Stavka representative coordinating their work, tried to eliminate it. However, the salient was ably defended by eleven German divisions from First Panzer and Eighth German Armies. According to Zhukov, twenty-seven Soviet divisions were earmarked to take it out. The Russian attempts were frustrated by an untimely, early thaw which hampered their movement, while the Germans planned a rescue attempt. General Hube, commander of the First Panzer Army, sent a signal: 'I shall rescue you. Hube', which the Russians intercepted. On 8 February Zhukov issued an ultimatum to the encircled Germans, passed on by a German colonel called Fukke. It was rejected, and on the night of 11 to 12 February the Germans tried to break out under cover of a blizzard. Zhukov had caught the flu, and was put to bed. He was woken from a deep, sick sleep by a phone call from Stalin, who demanded to know what was going on. After Zhukov reported back, Stalin decided to put Koniev in overall charge of eliminating the group. Vatutin was 'a highly emotional man', in Zhukov's words, and was very upset. Again, the story underlines the rivalry between senior Russian commanders. On 17 February the encircled group surrendered, yielding 18,000 prisoners and most of their heavy equipment. A small number of senior officers and SS men managed to escape, but 18,000 prisoners is not much from eleven divisions, estimated at 73,000 men.[23] Most of the rest died, and the encirclement ended with carnage and debris strewn across the snow. Koniev got all the credit, which Zhukov said was very unfair. But then, Zhukov and Koniev were great rivals, as Stalin knew – a rivalry he played on at Berlin.

On 29 February – 1944 was a leap year – Zhukov received a message that Vatutin had been seriously wounded. He had been travelling in a car after inspecting Sixtieth Army, to the north of his sector. Another car with security guards was ahead of his. As they drove through a village, they were ambushed by a group of *Bandera* – Ukrainian nationalists ('bandits'). Vatutin and his fellow officers had jumped out of the car and exchanged fire with the partisans. Vatutin was hit in the hip, and badly wounded. He was flown to Kiev, but although the best medical specialists available were summoned to treat him, he died on 15 April. His untimely death is a reminder that this was not a simple, symmetric contest between two great, conventional military forces. This was a complicated war, with nationalist guerrillas who had their own agendas. Even a Soviet general, travelling from and army headquarters back to his front, with a security escort, was not necessarily safe.[24] It was a situation not dissimilar to Iraq in the early 2000s. The Russians, for all their talk of 'liberation', were not always welcome back in Ukraine.

Early in March Zhukov's two fronts launched a very powerful offensive which by 21 March had reached the Dnestr. This offensive finally cut the German eastern front in two, separating German troops in former Poland from those in south Russia. One month after the start of this offensive their troops had reached the Carpathians, retaken most of Bukovina and crossed the Dnestr to occupy the northern half of Bessarabia. They also had bridgeheads across the Pruth, in Romania proper. Large areas of the Soviet Union had been recaptured, and some Russian troops had even reached foreign soil. Separated from their colleagues to the north, Schörner's Army Group South Ukraine, formerly Army Group A, backed nervously on to the Danube.[25]

The Germans had held on to the Crimea for longer than might have been expected, given its strategic importance. Now that it was cut off by land, it was time for the Russians to retake it. They had retaken Novorossiysk on the Temryuk peninsula, further to the east – the last German stronghold in the North Caucasus–Kuban area – in an amphibious assault between 8 and 16 September 1943. The Germans started to withdraw to the Crimea. And by 10 October Russian territory east of the Sea of Azov had been completely cleared. With the Russians over the River Bug and into Romania, the Germans withdrew their forces from Odessa on 10 April. The operation to recover the Crimea began on 8 April. Nearly half a million Soviet troops backed by the Azov flotilla and the Black Sea fleet attacked 150,000 Germans and Romanians. Although strong defences had been built along the 'Turkish wall' – the historic name for the Perekop isthmus – and the 'tongue of Arabat' (see Figure 18.2 inset), the former crumbled quickly and the Russians never went near the latter. The Germans had been working on the Perekop defences for months but after a very accurate artillery barrage, troops of Tolbukhin's Fourth Ukrainian Front penetrated them in two days, and mobile troops – a tank corps and two independent brigades – broke out into the open territory beyond. Yeremenko's Independent Maritime Army, meanwhile, recaptured Kerch' on 11 April and by the beginning of May the Germans and Romanians had been pushed back to Sevastopol itself. The united Russian forces began a ferocious bombardment of the fortress city on 5 May and the Germans abandoned it after a week.[26]

Given Sevastopol's strategic importance, it does seem extraordinary that, while the Russians defended it for 250 days, the Germans vacated it after seven. Like the Russians before them, the last German defenders held out on the Khersones peninsula, west of the city. Vasilevskiy, the Stavka representative coordinating Third and Fourth Ukrainian Fronts' operations, came to watch. On 12 May, it was all over. Some 25,000 German and Romanian troops surrendered. Another 'hero city' was back in Russian hands.

The recapture of the Crimea was relatively inexpensive in Russian lives. The irrecoverable losses were 17,754, with 67,000 sick and wounded. Overall, the Russians lost 2,423 a day. The last big German bridgehead threatening the rear of the fronts pushing out of the Soviet Union was removed, and the Black Sea fleet could be reinstalled in its historic and secure base.[27] It also released two armies – Second Guards and Fifty-First – to move north for the next big challenge. It had all happened quite fast. But now the biggest task lay ahead.

Operation Bagration: the destruction of Army Group Centre in Belarus

Planning for the Belorussian operation began in spring 1944. Stalin had been told that the second front – 'D' Day, the Normandy invasion – was to open at the end of May, and his superb intelligence sources almost certainly confirmed that it would, within a few days. The actual date was 5 June, which was postponed, one more time, to 6 June, because of the weather. The position of the combatants on the eastern front in summer 1944 can be seen in Figure 18.3. The Germans had been pushed back from Leningrad and the Russians had rapidly reconquered Ukraine. Most of former Soviet territory had been retaken. As a result, there were two vast salients. In the south, to the edge of the Pripyet marshes, the Russians had advanced deeply and were well into Romania. North of the marshes Army Group Centre's forces jutted towards Moscow, still holding Orsha, that bitterly fought-over rail junction on the main line to Moscow, a little over 400 kilometres from Red Square.[28] Army Group Centre stuck out eastwards – it was known as the 'Belorussian balcony' by both sides – and Orsha was on the railings.

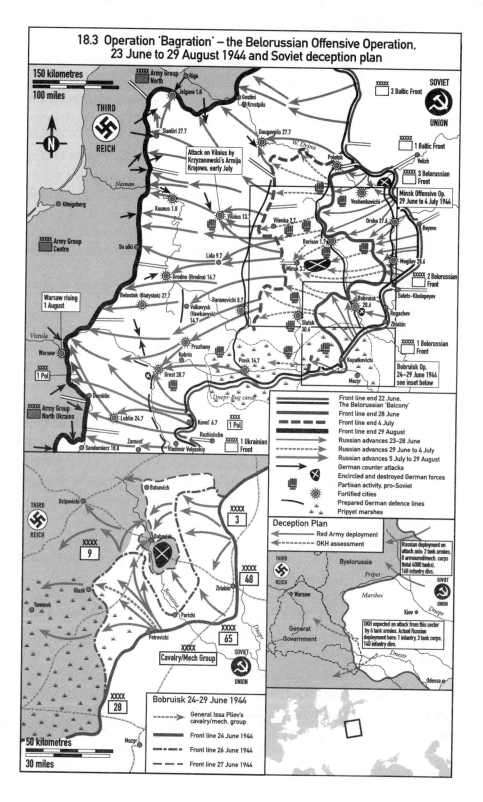

18.3 Operation 'Bagration' – the Belorussian Offensive Operation, 23 June to 29 August 1944 and Soviet deception plan

XXXXX Army Group North

THIRD REICH

SOVIET UNION

XXXXX 2 Baltic Front

Riga
Jelgava 1.8
Gostini
Krustpils
Siautiri 27.7
Daugavpils 27.7
W. Dvina
Polotsk
Velizh
XXXXX 1 Baltic Front

XXXXX 3 Belorussian Front

150 kilometres
100 miles

Neman

Königsberg

XXXXX Army Group Centre

Attack on Vilnius by Krzyzanowski's Armija Krajowa, early July

Kaunus 1.8
Vilnius 13.7
Vilenka 2.7
Orsha 27.6
Bayevo
Su alki
Borisov 1.7
Lida 9.7
Mogilev 28.6
Minsk 3.7
XXXXX 2 Belorussian Front
Grodno (Hrodna) 16.7
Veshenkovichi

Minsk Offensive Op. 29 June to 4 July 1944

Warsaw rising 1 August

Belostok (Bialystok) 27.7
Volkovysk (Vawkavysk) 14.7
Baranovichi 8.7
Bobruisk 28.6
Rogachev
Zhlobin
Selets–Kholopeyev

XXXXX 1 Belorussian Front

Vistula
Warsaw
XXXX 1 Pol
Pruzhany
Kobrin
Pinsk 14.7
Slutsk 30.6
Kopatkevichi
Mozyr

Bobruisk Op. 24–29 June 1944 see inset below

Brest 28.7

Demblin

XXXXX Army Group North Ukraine

Dnepr-Bug canal

Lublin 24.7
Kovel 6.7
XXXX 1 Pol
Rozhishche
Vladimir Volyaskiy
XXXXX 1 Ukrainian Front
Zamost'
Sandomierz 18.8

Front line end 22 June. The Belorussian 'Balcony'
Front line end 28 June
Front line end 4 July
Front line end 29 August
Russian advances 23–28 June
Russian advances 29 June to 4 July
Russian advances 5 July to 29 August
German counter attacks
Encircled and destroyed German forces
Partisan activity, pro-Soviet
Fortified cities
Prepared German defence lines
Pripyet marshes

THIRD REICH

Osipovichi
Batsevich
XXXX 3
XXXX 9
Bobruisk
Glusk
Yaminsk
Berezina
Parichi
XXXX 48
Zhlobin
Petrovichi
XXXX 65
XXXX 28
Mozyr

Cavalry/Mech Group

SOVIET UNION

Deception Plan
Red Army deployment
OKH assessment

Russian deployment on attack axis: 2 tank armies, 8 armoured/mech. corps (total 4000 tanks), 168 infantry divs.

THIRD REICH
Warsaw
General Government
Byelorussia
Pripet
Marshes
Kiev
SOVIET UNION
Dnepr
Dnestr
Odessa

OKH expected an attack from this sector by 6 tank armies. Actual Russian deployment here: 1 infantry, 3 tank corps, 140 infantry divs.

Bobruisk 24–29 June 1944
General Issa Pliev's cavalry/mech. group
Front line 24 June 1944
Front line 26 June 1944
Front line 27 June 1944

50 kilometres
30 miles

Belarus and the Baltic States were the last parts of the Soviet Union to remain in enemy hands. Army Group Centre – the centre of gravity of the German military effort, which Zhukov had tried to destroy at the end of 1941 and again with Mars at the end of 1942 – was in Belarus. There was therefore absolutely no choice. It had to be big, it had to work, and it had to be theatrical. On 20 May, having had no other suggestions, Stalin personally chose the codename: 'Bagration', a fellow Georgian, the Russian field marshal mortally wounded at Borodino.[29] And, with what John Erickson described as a sense of 'grand opera', it would begin on the third anniversary of the invasion of the Soviet Union, 22 June, although, in a final superb touch of irony, it had to be postponed one day – just like D-Day – to 23 June 1944.[30]

By mid April the General Staff had completed its outline plan, which was sent to Stavka at the end of the month. Just five men worked on it, and communications were strictly controlled to keep it as secret as possible. The only hint of its possible objectives was in Stalin's May Day speech, which spoke of liberating 'all Soviet territory, from the Barents Sea to the Black Sea'. However, that was addressed to his allies and his own people rather than the Germans, and might refer equally to the Baltic States and territory occupied by the Finns. Behind the scenes, Stavka knew it had to deceive the Germans as to the direction of the main thrust. The German OKH expected the main thrust in the south, to capitalize on the political weakness of Germany's allies, and because the Russians had already been successful in that direction, they thought they would keep on going. They therefore expected an attack by First and Second Ukrainian Fronts into the wall below the balcony (see Figure 18.3). North of the Pripyet marshes, *Fremde Heere Ost* predicted, the front would remain quiet.[31] However, in the third week of April the Russian Stavka decided to attack in the north, straight at the railings, with First, Second and Third Belorussian and First Baltic Fronts, while maintaining an elaborate deception which, like all good deceptions, told the Germans what they were expecting to hear.[32]

Stalin held his final planning conference on 22 and 23 May. The military objective was the destruction of German Army Group Centre with a simultaneous breakthrough on six sectors. A major argument blew up involving Rokossovskiy, commanding First Belorussian Front. Rokossovskiy wanted to advance on Bobruisk, on the way to Minsk, which was where the three Belorussian Fronts would aim to converge from two directions, either side of the Berezina. It had certain symbolic undertones, as the Berezina was the old Russian frontier, which Napoleon's frozen army had crossed in disarray after retreating from Moscow in 1812. But that was not the reason for doing it. Stalin wanted *one* blow – to the north of the river, from the Dnepr bridgehead held by Third Army. Rokossovskiy was sent out twice to think again, but each time came back and said he was right. Eventually Stalin said Rokossovskiy's robust defence of his position was 'a reliable guarantee of success'.[33] Rokossovskiy wanted '*two* main blows'.[34] And he got them. Bullies respect courage.

'Why did I defend the decision on two thrusts so vehemently?' Rokossovskiy asked in the censored part of his story. Because, he explains, only part of the Third and Forty-Eighth Armies' forces would be available to the north of the river and they would therefore be isolated by it. Also, north of there, the Germans were on both sides of the Dnepr (see Figure 18.3 (inset)). That meant they could cut down behind the single attack, and into Rokossovskiy's right flank. He had to ensure the security of his front, and by pushing Sixty-Fifth and Twenty-Eighth Armies up on the west (right) bank of the Berezina he could deny the Germans the freedom to do that. Furthermore, by attacking on both banks, Rokossovskiy could use the entire weight of the right flank of his front, whereas otherwise he could only use part of his available forces, in a limited area. Finally, success on either side of the river would achieve the desired result, but if the Germans saw that they were being attacked from two sides, they would be even more likely to collapse quickly. In conversations with Stavka, they worked out measures for cooperation with Chernyakovskiy's Third Belorussian, to the north, and Rokossovskiy's First, to which Stavka gave the principal task. The forces of both fronts were to strike west and close up west of Minsk, to destroy the encircled enemy forces.[35] That they would do.

One can see why Stalin listened, and why they made Rokossovskiy a marshal. But it is also clear how much thought and frank debate went into formulating the Russian war plans.

The mission was to 'liquidate the enemy salient in the Vitebsk, Bobruisk and Moisk area, destroy Army Group Centre, liberate the Belorussian Soviet republic, and then begin the liberation of fraternal Poland – and that would become a sore point, at Warsaw, and subsequently carry the war to Nazi Germany'.[36] It was truly a 'strategic' operation – the aims of which would directly influence political and economic considerations. It was also the first operation on the eastern front in which the Russians were not alone as land combatants.

On 6 June, after a fraught 24-hour delay, British, Canadian, American and Free French units and formations landed in Normandy. Churchill signalled Stalin, that same day. Everything was looking good, he said. Stalin signalled back. 'The summer offensive of the Soviet troops, to be launched in keeping with the agreement reached at the Tehran Conference, will begin in mid-June in one of the vital sectors of the front . . .'[37]

Vasiliy Grossman, who was to accompany the Russian troops to Berlin, noted initial enthusiasm among the Russian troops when the final opening of the 'second front' on 6 June was announced. 'Spontaneous meetings, shooting, saluting, then a sharp decrease of interest.'[38] Most people, understandably, were preoccupied with their immediate terrors. However, what really mattered to them was that whether the Normandy landings succeeded and established a foothold, or were driven back into the sea, the Germans were going to be fully preoccupied with them three weeks later. Bagration was perfectly timed. The Germans really were now fighting on two fronts.

The deception plan and the partisans

Knowing how the Germans would react, the Russians feigned a big concentration of forces in the southern area, where OKH was expecting an attack by six tank armies. In Rokossovskiy's sector, and further north, the real concentration was carefully concealed. The Germans were fooled – to some extent. Of thirty Panzer and mechanized divisions on the eastern front, twenty-four were south of the Pripyet marshes. Air forces in the south were also markedly stronger than in the north. The Germans assumed all five tank armies to be in the south.

The partisans were also important for the deception plan, as well as their other roles. By the summer of 1944 there were an estimated 143,000 members of partisan groups in Belarus, organized into 150 brigades and 47 independent detachments. On 8 June the Belorussian

Party Central Committee ordered the partisan formations, which were exceptionally active in Belarus, to attack German communications starting on 20 June. The 'rail war' began again. On that night alone the partisans derailed 147 trains. As at Kursk, the partisan operation was carefully coordinated with those of the regular Red Army formations.[39]

Shortly before Bagration began, Stavka ordered partisan attacks in the rear of Army Group Centre to stop. Then, Russian forces carried out a diversionary attack in the southern sector, where the Germans were expecting the main Russian blow. The Germans sent reserves south, while the partisans held off. The reinforcements for the southern sector arrived safely, and then the main Soviet attack fell in the north. When the reserves were sent north again, the partisans were waiting.[40] They brought rail traffic to a near-complete standstill.

The biggest battle yet

On the 'balcony', Army Group Centre had 1.2 million men in 63 divisions. Facing them, the Russians assembled nearly 2.4 million in 168 divisions, 12 'corps' – the tank formations equating to divisions – and 20 brigades. For the first time they also had the newly formed First Polish Army – 4 divisions and 2 brigades. The balance of forces was overwhelmingly in the Russians' favour: 36,400 guns and mortars against 9,500; 5,200 tanks against 900; and 5,300 aircraft against 1,350.[41]

As usual, there were battalion attacks on 22 June – 'reconnaissance by battle' – and Sixth Guards Army also attacked north-west of Vitebsk on the 22nd, but the main artillery barrage and the main offensive began on the 23rd, and that is the official date for the start of the operation.

To accelerate the attack, according to the now well-practised formula, there were three tank armies – Third and Fifth Guards, and Fourth, and also two cavalry–mechanized groups (KMGs). Pliev's KMG was with Rokossovskiy, and was an ideal formation to traverse the Pripyet marshes.[42] Pliev's KMG bypassed the Germans in Bobruisk and used its exceptional mobility in the wild terrain of the Pripyet marshes to cut south of the main body of Ninth Army, through Glutsk, and prevent it from escaping westwards. Further north, Oskilovskiy's KMG helped encircle Vitebsk (see Figures 18.4 and 18.5).

Rokossovskiy's attack from either side of the Berezina, converging on Minsk, began on the 24th. It was a spectacular success. Pliev's KMG, which had been waiting between Twenty-Eighth and Sixty-Fifth Armies, was pushed forward on the second day. By the end of the fourth day the Germans had committed all their reserves, without stopping the Russians anywhere. The Russians held the initiative, and also had overwhelming air superiority. The western Allied bombing offensive against Germany had drained the Luftwaffe, and the Germans had very few planes to oppose the British and Americans now fighting in Normandy, or the Red Army attacking from the east. That gave the Russians freedom to move, and to multiply their two-to-one overall superiority into a ten-to-one superiority in chosen areas. On the six breakthrough sectors the forward Russian division attacked on a front-age of just 1,500 metres. The tanks stayed out of sight until the infantry had cleared an opening, and then stormed straight through without bothering about their flanks. According to one account the German Sixth Luftflotte, supporting Army Group Centre, had only forty fighters in working order on 22 June, and not enough fuel to keep them in the air.[43] There were therefore no planes to oppose the armoured Shturmo-viks which pulverized German anti-tank positions.

By 26 June the Germans were completely encircled in Vitebsk and Rokossovskiy's men were behind Bobruisk. Early on the 27th the German Ninth Army received permission to withdraw, but before it could, another order came in, from Hitler, ordering them to hold it as one of four 'fortified places' (*feste Plätze*), along with Vitebsk, Orsha and Mogilev. It was too late anyway. Two corps – 70,000 German troops – were trapped in and east of the city of Bobruisk. On 28 June Field Marshal Ernst Busch, a slavish servant of Hitler's, commanding Army Group Centre, reported that Ninth Army was destroyed, Fourth Army was retreating and Third Panzer had one corps left out of three. He could not make contact with Mogilev, which also fell to the Russians that day.

OKH realized that the attack on Army Group Centre was more ambitious than they had previously assumed, but still feared an attack to the south, where they had expected it, against Army Group North Ukraine. Hitler put Model in charge of Army Group Centre as well as North Ukraine, to help move forces between the two, but it did no good. Minsk fell on 3 July and by 4 July Army Group Centre had lost twenty-five divisions. Fourth Army lost 130,000 out of its original strength of 165,000; Third Panzer lost ten divisions and of Ninth Army, perhaps 10,000 to 15,000 escaped.[44]

The second phase of Bagration began on 5 July. The grouping encircled east of Minsk was destroyed between 5 and 11 July. Hitler ordered Vilna (Vilnius, now the capital of Lithuania) to be held at all costs, but it fell on 13 July. Army Group North was in danger of being cut off, but Hitler refused to allow its withdrawal because Grand Admiral Dönitz wanted the Baltic ports kept open. The Russians, meanwhile, having pushed the Germans back across the 'balcony', planned to attack the wall below, heading into the 'General Government' area south of Warsaw. They no longer needed such massive artillery forces to the north, as the breakthrough had been accomplished and the Germans were on the run. So, between 5 and 13 July the Russians moved 3,500 artillery pieces with ten times that number of motor vehicles by rail and road south and then west, through the Pripyet marshes, as far as Kovel (Kowel), bolstering the artillery strength on First Belorussian's west face to 9,000. As a result, the front was able to push into Poland later in July, just ahead of the fronts which had cleared the 'balcony'.[45]

Hitler's insistence that the *feste Plätze* be held and his refusal to allow any withdrawal meant that huge German forces were trapped, just as the Russians intended. Army Group Centre had been destroyed in a huge 'cauldron battle' – *Kesselschlacht*. Some seventeen divisions had been totally annihilated and another fifty were down to half strength – the equivalent of losing forty-two divisions. Army Group Centre's destruction was sealed on 20 July, the very day that a group of German officers, appalled by Hitler's handling of the war and realizing they were going to lose, attempted to kill the Führer in the Stauffenberg bomb plot. It failed, and the conspirators were rounded up and died horribly. The attempt on Hitler's life made him even more paranoid, and almost certainly played into the Russians' hands for the remaining period of the war.

The Russian advance, inevitably, ran out of steam. After coming so far so fast, fuel, ammunition and human endurance were at their limit. They continued for another month, taking Kaunas and touching the border of East Prussia. Having reached the Vistula to the south by 28 July, they pushed on another 100 kilometres, in the area due west of Warsaw, and by 15 September were just 10 kilometres from the city.

For the Russians, too, the cost had been great. Out of nearly 2.4 million troops, 178,507 were killed, taken prisoner or went missing. Another 578,308 were wounded. The daily losses, at 11,262, were comparable with the counteroffensives at Kursk, but it lasted twice as long – 68 days.[46] But all Belorussia and parts of Lithuania and Latvia were restored to Soviet control. In order to stem the Russian onslaught, the Germans moved forty-six divisions from other sectors, some from Army Group North, but also taking some of the pressure off British and American troops in France.

If we compare the speed and scale of the Russian advances in Operation Bagration with the lengthy battle to break out of the Normandy bridgehead which was going on at the same time, the Russian performance is clearly superior.[47] They had been fighting the Germans on the ground a lot longer, but the 'European funnel' (see Figure 7.1) also had an effect. Despite the huge numbers of troops deployed, there was far more space here. There was nowhere near the density of force that resulted in the attritional battle of the Normandy breakout. In the east, on the other hand, because the Russians had air supremacy and held the initiative, as well as *space*, they could create the densities they needed pretty well anywhere they wanted.

The restoration of Soviet control was an important factor, and symbolic and significant in terms of prestige. But, most of all, Operation Bagration underlined a cardinal principle of war. The enemy's main forces must be the main objective.

And the enemy's main force had been destroyed.

Warsaw

As the Red Army pushed into former Polish territory, it encountered the *Armija Krajowa* – Polish Home Army (AK). The Soviet Union's aim with regard to Poland was clear. The Russians were very happy with Churchill's suggestion at Tehran that the whole country should be moved west, but they also wanted it to have 'firm friendly relations' with the USSR. In reality, that meant a communist government. The London-

backed AK, who had been fighting an increasingly well-organized guerrilla campaign against the Germans, which was growing into one more
reminiscent of a conventional army, did not want that at all.[48]

In early July Colonel 'Wilk' (Aleksandr Krzyzanowski) assembled
10,000 troops near Vilnius and attacked it from four directions. At this
stage all the AK units cooperated with the Red Army who provided
support with tanks, artillery and air. They liberated the city from the
Germans, and the surviving Polish inhabitants flew red and white Polish
flags to greet them. They controlled the city for two days before being
invited to a conference with Chernyakovskiy's Third Belorussian Front.
Wilk and his officers were arrested and deported to the Soviet Union.
About 6,000 AK men were ordered to assemble outside the city, where
the Russians surrounded and disarmed them. Most were loaded on to
trains and deported to Kaluga, but several hundred who tried to escape
were caught and massacred.

In Lwów an AK force of about 4,000 under Colonel 'Janka' (Wladysllaw Filipkowski) managed to seize the city from the Germans. He was
called to First Ukrainian Front for talks on 25 July, in which the NKVD
were heavily involved. The Russians told him to disband his troops,
who would have the choice, they said, of joining the First Polish Army,
led by General Zygmunt Berling, which was operating as part of the Red
Army. On 31 July the Russians invited about thirty senior AK officers
to a conference. They were immediately arrested as 'criminals and Polish
fascists'. The exiled Polish leaders in London continued to regard
themselves as the only legitimate Polish government but the reality was
that Poland was rapidly being overrun by the Russians. On 22 July a
Soviet-backed 'Committee of National Liberation' was formed in Lublin
and on the 26th Moscow recognized it as the sovereign body in all
reconquered parts of former Poland. The AK ordered all its units east
of the Curzon line – roughly the 1939 border – to accept the offer to
join up with Berling's First Polish Army. However, that still left the AK
units west of there with a choice.

Then, on 1 August, the Warsaw uprising broke out. It was bad news
for both the Germans and the Russians. Guderian realized that Warsaw
was very close to a front line which might collapse and it was the centre
of the German supply system. Rokossovskiy – who said he was a Pole,
and was certainly half-Polish – reported that he received news of the
uprising on 2 August and that it caused great alarm.

> It was so sudden that we were quite at a loss, and at first we
> thought the Germans might have spread the rumour . . .
> Frankly speaking, the timing of the uprising was just about
> the worst possible in the circumstances. It was as though its
> leaders had deliberately chosen a time that would ensure
> defeat.[49]

At the time Rokossovskiy's main forces were battling 100 kilometres away to the east and north-east. Rokossovskiy understood why 'certain carping critics in the western press' accused him of standing back and deliberately condemning the Warsaw insurgents 'to death and destruction'. He accused the AK, under 'orders from the people in London' of trying to seize power before the Russians got there. In fact, his troops were exhausted, and had other missions. He was particularly annoyed by a BBC broadcast on 18 August with a report from the Polish commander in Warsaw, Tadeusz Komorowski ('Bór'), known as Bór-Komorowski, that his operations were being coordinated with Rokossovskiy and that Russian planes were continually dropping arms, ammunition and fuel to the insurgent forces.

From an observation post at the top of a factory chimney, Rokossovskiy could see Warsaw, blazing with the flashes of bombs and shells and a dense pall of smoke. It would have been difficult for him to intervene, but he had no reason to do so. On 3 August Stalin saw the Prime Minister of the Polish government in exile in London, Stanisław Mikołajczyk, who had come to the Kremlin to ask him to help Warsaw. Stalin called the AK 'fascists' and said that they were preparing to fight the Soviet Union. 'I cannot trust the Poles,' he said. Mikołajczyk explained that the AK wanted good relations with the Red Army and came away thinking that Stalin was 'more positively inclined towards the AK' than before.[50]

Warsaw was right at the limit of western bomber range, but until 10 September the Russians refused to let the Americans use their airfields to help resupply the insurgents. On 14 September a force of 80 to 100 four-engined US bombers escorted by Mustang fighters appeared over Warsaw and dropped supplies, but fighting was already subsiding. They flew another supply drop on the 18th, but the areas under AK control were too small for accurate drops and 80 per cent of the supplies fell on the Germans.[51] On the night of 16 to 17 September the First Polish Army under Soviet command attacked across the Vistula into Warsaw, but it seems to have been a small gesture. The Germans estimated their strength at just a few companies. The Russians evacuated them on 26 September, and on 2 October Bór-Komorowski's representatives surrendered to the Germans.

There seems little doubt that Stalin decided it was not in his – or Russia's – interest to help the Warsaw rebels. He was not responsible for the outbreak of the revolt, which had been sanctioned in London by the exiled government. Stalin had stopped talking to them in 1943, apart from his chilly reception for Mikołajczyk. He had no intention of giving substantial help to the rebels, brave as they were. A victory by the AK would be very inconvenient for his plans for a pro-Soviet, communist Poland. He therefore let the Germans do his work for him.[52] The Red Army would move on when it was ready.

Ukraine, Moldova and political effects

There were more good reasons for the Russians to halt, temporarily, on the Vistula. To the south, parts of Ukraine were still to be recovered, and Romania was still in the war on Germany's side. On the same day that Vilnius fell, 13 July, the first of two other great operations began to unfold as part of the Russian westward thrust that would unroll from north to south. The pattern and sequence of the great Russian offensive operations is shown in Figure 18.6. The L'vov (Lwów)–Sandomir (Sandomierz) offensive was carried out by the million-strong First Ukrainian Front and took place in two phases. In the first, from 13 to 27 July 1944, the Russians encircled three groupings of German troops and recaptured Lwów and Przemysl, historic names on Russia's western border. In the second phase, from 28 July to 29 August 1944, the Red Army crossed the Vistula and established a bridgehead on its western bank, at Sandomierz. Then, on 20 August, the Second and Third Ukrainian Fronts launched the Yassy–Kishinev offensive. This is of great interest because it had grand-strategic and economic as well as purely military objectives. The aims were to destroy the German–Romanian Army Group Southern Ukraine, to reconquer the Moldavian Soviet Socialist republic (acquired in 1940 – modern Moldova) and thus to

18.4 Outline of major Russian offensive operations, 1943–5

1. Battle of the Dnepr 25 August to December 1943, see fig 18.1
2. Winter campaign, 'Right Bank Ukraine', 1943–4, see fig 18.2
3. Leningrad–Novogorod, 14 January to 1 April 1944, see fig 13.8
4. Crimea, 8 April to 12 May 1944, see fig 18.2
5. Vyborg–Petrozavodsk 10 June to 9 August 1944
6. Belorussia 23 June to 29 August 1944, see fig 18.3
7. Lwów–Sandomierz 13 July to 29 August 1944
8. Yassy–Kishinev (Iassi–Chisinau) 20–29 August 1944
9. East Carpathian 8 September to 28 October 1944
10. Budapest 29 October 1944 to 13 February 1945, see fig 19.1
11. Baltic 14 September to 24 December 1944 (Divided by Courland Peninsula, which remains in German hands until the end of the war)
12. Vistula–Oder 12 January to 3 February 1945, see fig 19.2
13. East Prussia 7 January to 25 April 1945
14. East Pomerania 10 February to 4 April 1945
15. Berlin 16 April to 8 May 1945, see fig 19.3
16. Prague 6–11 May 1945, see fig 19.5

300 kilometres
200 miles

XXXXX Army Group North
From 26.1.1945
'Courland Grouping' (33 divisions) remains until end of war

Operation Hannibal, 23 Jan to 8 May 1945 Grand Admiral Dönitz's evacuation of 2 million people

Sinking of Wilhelm Gustloff 30 January 1945 Greatest maritime disaster in history

SOVIET UNION

Destroyed 15 July 1944

Destroyed 15 July 1944

Destroyed 27 July 1944

Capitulated 11 May 1945

___ Front line Dec 1943

- - - - - Front line mid-June 1944 (Vyborg Petrozavodsk, 11 July)

– – – – Front line Dec 1944

–·–·–· Soviet front line April 1945

___ Soviet front line 7 May 1945

·········· Western Allies' front line 7 May 1945

═══ Agreed post war east-west dividing line (later 'Iron Curtain')

– – – Approximate divisions between main operations

Pockets of remaining German Axis troops

split the German–Romanian alliance. It succeeded. In just ten days the Russians quickly routed Army Group Southern Ukraine, destroying twenty-two German and almost all the Romanian divisions deployed on the eastern front. Moldavia was returned to Soviet control, and Romania withdrew from the Axis on 23 August 1944. King Michael had Marshal Antonescu, Hitler's client, and his brother Mihai arrested, and declared war on Germany on the 26th. On 31 August Malinovskiy's Second Ukrainian Front moved into Bucharest. Not only was Romania now on the Russian side, but any risk of Churchillian British–American interference was precluded.

The political shock effect continued. On 5 September 1944 the Soviet Union declared war on Bulgaria, which had been siding with Germany and was a formal enemy of Britain and the United States, but not an active participant in the war. On 7 September Bulgaria promptly declared war on Germany and the next day units of Third Ukrainian Front entered the country. On 9 September a coup placed communists in charge. Within two weeks, the greater part of the country was under Soviet occupation. A few days after the Soviet declaration of war, an armistice between Bulgaria and the Allies was in place.[53] The dominoes were falling.

Out of 1.3 million troops, the Russians suffered just 13,197 irrecoverable losses – 1 per cent. It was a telling reminder of the old military maxim that the faster you go, the more you save on casualties. In both operations the total losses per day, including sick and wounded, were 6,027 and 6,713 – little more than half the rate of loss in Bagration.

Panic and resistance in the Baltic States

Operation Bagration had already lapped into the formerly independent Baltic States, annexed by the Soviet Union in 1940. By 1 March 1944, having completely ended the siege of Leningrad, the Russians were on the border with Estonia. Having outflanked the Germans along the Baltic coast during the summer, the Russians launched the Baltic Strategic Offensive Operation on 14 September with four entire fronts – Leningrad and the First to Third Baltic Fronts, and an army from Third

Belorussian, plus the Baltic fleet. The Russian force totalled more than 1.5 million troops. On 16 September OKH approved the Aster plan, by which German forces would withdraw from Estonia, leaving Estonian forces to cover their withdrawal in the face of the Russians. They swung round the south end of Lake Peipus, and headed northwards towards Tallinn.

Marja Talvi's family had had a lucky escape in the spring, when the Russians had bombed Tallinn, in a big raid on 8–9 April. The eight-year-old had been asleep in a comfortable suburban house about 8 kilometres from the city centre when the bombs fell among the pine trees around the family home. 'The pine trees saved us,' she recalled, 'because it was forbidden to cut them down.' The other thing that saved them was the family skis, stacked in the hall between the bomb-blast and the kitchen. They stopped the bomb fragments, but that was the end of their career as skis. Marja was later told it was the 'night witches' who had attacked them. Could that have been? Early in 1944 the all-female 46th Guards Night Bomber Regiment had been in the Crimea. But by July, certainly, they were in north-east Poland, and then moved to East Prussia by January 1945.[54] So it could have been ...

In September, as the Russians approached from the south, the Talvis tried to get out. 'Leave the country' was the advice, and they headed west for a harbour from where they hoped to get a ship to neutral Sweden. 'There were so many people – there were people on the roof,' she recalled. 'Then the Russians started to bomb the train.' German officers ordered everyone off, but as people started to climb out with all their luggage, they changed their minds: '*Don't* get out.' The train then moved off, leaving some people behind. The Talvis had stayed on board, and the train stopped about 100 kilometres west of Tallinn. That was where the Russians were. They had moved round, west of the capital. She does not remember the first Russians she saw, but recalls Estonians working for the Russians, who arrived on bicycles – with no tyres. After about a week in a small village, they made their way back to Tallinn. Their house was intact, and undisturbed. The Russians billeted soldiers with local families, but because it was a small house the Talvis were exempt. The houses and apartments of the richer Estonians were all taken over by the Russians. Marja was lucky. The Soviet government later nationalized all the land, but let the family keep the house. Seven years after independence, in 1997, Marja finally got the land back.

While the Red Army had swung to the west, the NKVD reached

Tallinn first. When they took control of the offices vacated by the Abwehr – German Intelligence – they received a pleasant surprise. The Germans had removed most of their papers, but had left behind the archive dealing with resistance movements. They did the same thing in Lithuania, probably deliberately.[55] They would let their Russian counterparts finish the job, using the names and addresses of all known resistance leaders, friends and relatives.

The NKVD's first job was to stop anyone else escaping, so they placed a heavy guard along the coastline and wrecked or confiscated any boats they found. Refugees nevertheless got away, waiting to be picked up by speedboats based in Finland or Sweden. The NKVD also targeted members of the National Committee of the Republic of Estonia (EVRK), the main resistance organization. On the Soviet reoccupation, this operated from Sweden. At first, the final outcome of an Allied victory in the war was uncertain, and many hoped either that Estonia would gain independence as part of the final peace agreement, or that a new great war would start between East and West which would ultimately have the same effect. It did, but there was no shooting and it took forty-five years. The 'forest brothers', who had been active in 1941, lay low for the moment. Many of them could have pulled out with the Germans, but they preferred to stay and resist the Soviet reoccupation. When victory in Europe in summer 1945 did not bring the desired results, they renewed their armed campaign, focusing on killing senior armed forces and NKVD officers.[56]

In Latvia resistance was less resolute at first, because quite a few Latvians supported the reassertion of Soviet power. Nevertheless, during 1945 the Red Army combed the forests looking for partisans, in concert with the Baltic Region Staff of the NKVD based in Riga. The NKVD units, well equipped with dogs, radios, mortars, tanks and firearms with silencers, were the main anti-partisan force. There were, apparently, no Estonians, Latvians or Lithuanians among them. By the beginning of 1945 there were about 10,000 active members of resistance organizations. However, the NKVD signed separate ceasefire agreements with the partisan units in different villages, and the anti-Soviet movement did not become active until after the war's end.

Lithuania was different. Among the first troops into Lithuania in July 1944 were five NKVD rear defence regiments of Third Belorussian Front. They stayed in Lithuania until February 1945, when they were sent forward into East Prussia. A fortnight after the Red Army occupied

Vilnius on 13 July 1944, conscription was introduced. In August, only 14 per cent of those eligible responded to the summons. The 4th NKVD Rifle Division, nine NKVD regiments and the NKVD rear defence regiments of four Red Army corps were employed in tracking down draft-dodgers. By November, 33,000 men were in hiding. Over Christmas the Soviet internal security forces mounted seventy-four operations, killing more than 400 people. During 1944 and 1945; 82,000 Lithuanians were conscripted into the Red Army, more than half of them captured by force.[57] The Baltic States had, indeed, been 'liberated'.

The Baltic Sea and the war of superlatives

With the capture of Narva in Estonia in July 1944, and the Finnish withdrawal from the war on 19 September, which made bases along the northern shore of the Gulf of Finland, including Hangö, available to the Russians, the Baltic fleet was again free to break out into its watery domain. The Baltic operation from September to November had trapped Army Group North in the Courland peninsula, in western Latvia. This left a huge pocket with thirty-three divisions trapped to the north of the westward Russian advance. Stavka assessed, probably rightly, that while this huge pocket of German troops was an annoyance, it could be contained, and was less of a priority than the main thrust to destroy Germany proper. Between the time Army Group North was cut off by land, in October, and the end of the war, the Germans managed to evacuate twelve divisions as part of Grand-Admiral Dönitz's masterly operation to extract people and equipment from the Baltic coast. The force on the Courland peninsula was renamed Army Group Courland on 26 January 1945. Nevertheless, twenty-one divisions – some 149,000 officers and men, with 42 generals – remained on the peninsula to surrender on 9 May 1945. Had they been withdrawn back into Germany as well, they could have caused considerable problems for the Russians, British or Americans, or all three.

Nevertheless, Dönitz's operation – the greatest seaborne evacuation in history – was astonishingly successful. With stories of Russian atrocities preceding the Red Army, panic-stricken refugees were pouring into the Baltic ports: Königsberg, Gdynia, Danzig (Gdansk) and Pilau. The most efficient way of moving large numbers of people and stores is by sea. Between 23 January and 8 May 1945, Dönitz oversaw the evacuation of a reported 2,022,602 people from pockets along the Baltic coast as the Russians closed in: Courland, Königsberg, East and West Prussia and Pomerania.

The Soviet Baltic fleet was highly professional, but its core competencies had been severely impaired by more than three years of being cooped up in the shallow Gulf of Finland and used as part of land battles around Leningrad. It did not have the ships, the men or the expertise to take on first-rate German ships like the cruiser *Admiral Hipper*. However, in the interwar period it had placed great stress on submarine operations. Just as the Black Sea fleet had extracted people from Sevastopol in 1942 and then severely mauled the Germans as they tried to do the same in 1944, now the Baltic fleet could wage a *guerre de course*, harrying German withdrawals from the Baltic ports.

In Hangö, on the north side of the Gulf of Finland, the Baltic fleet was now a not particularly welcome guest of the Finns, after the September 1944 armistice agreement. One night Aleksandr Marinesco, captain of the 780-ton Soviet submarine S-13, did what many sailors do on a run ashore, especially in the Baltic in January, and got terribly drunk. The NKVD wanted to drag him back to Russia and punish him, but he was such a good submarine captain that the Baltic fleet persuaded them to give him another chance. On 11 January 1945 he took S-13 out to look for German targets. For nineteen days he saw nothing. But at 20.35 on 30 January he saw a faint glow on the horizon, and ordered battle stations. He did not know exactly what it was, but it was a ship. It was big. And it was German.

It was the *Wilhelm Gustloff*, a 26,000-ton cruise liner which was evacuating thousands of Germans from Gdynia, then known as Gotenhafen. It had been designed to carry about 2,000 people on 'strength through joy' holiday cruises. It was originally to be named *Adolf Hitler*, but Hitler was superstitious and when the head of the Swiss Nazi party, Wilhelm Gustloff, was assassinated, Hitler figured the name change could now do no harm. Now it carried many more, including 1,200 wounded submarine cadets being evacuated as part of Operation Hannibal to save precious U-boat personnel, and a large contingent of young female Luftwaffe staff. To get everyone in, they had drained the swimming pool, which is where the Luftwaffe girls were settling down for the night on what they hoped would be a swift run to safety.

Marinesco feared that the ship might be escorted by a destroyer, and therefore took what he considered an acceptable risk. Instead of attacking from the seaward side, he would get inside the target, and attack from the shore side. The water was shallow, and mines were a potential hazard. But the Baltic fleet had not saved him from the NKVD for nothing. Two torpedo boats were escorting *Wilhelm Gustloff*, but one developed a leak and had to turn back. Marinesco, on the landward side, closed to 1,000 metres and at 23.08 gave the order to fire three torpedoes.[58]

One torpedo chalked with 'for Stalin' failed to fire. Of the two that fired, and struck, one was chalked 'for Leningrad'.

The *Gustloff* sank in fifty minutes. Some 996 people survived, rescued from the icy Baltic. It was widely believed that more than 5,000, possibly 6,000, perished, unable to escape from the grossly overcrowded ship. However, new analysis, using computer modelling in concert with the very detailed blueprints of the ship, tells a different story. Based on analysis of photographs, the *Gustloff* was carrying 8,000 people more than it was designed to do. And with an estimate of 910 'virtual' survivors, close to the figure of 996 real survivors, it looks as if there were 10,600 or so people on board. A death toll, in other words, of 9,618.[59]

It was certainly the worst sea disaster in history. With 6,000 frozen dead bobbing in or trapped below the dark waters of the Baltic, it would have been the equivalent of four *Titanics*. In reality, it was probably more like six, brought about when a torpedo 'for Leningrad' hit a ship which might have been called *Adolf Hitler*.

All five of the the worst ship sinkings befell German vessels in 1945. They include the *Gustloff*, the *Goya*, the hospital ship *Steuben*, and the *Thielbeck*. However, the total losses in Dönitz's evacuation still number little more than 1 per cent of more than 2 million who got safely away.[60]

Dividing the world . . .

In October 1944 Churchill made his second visit to Russia. Relations at
Tehran had been tense, and on 29 November Churchill had stormed
out of a dinner after an apparently humorous comment by Stalin that
50,000 Germans – the elite of the General Staff – should be shot out of
hand when the war was over. Churchill had replied that he would rather
be shot himself than agree to such a thing, and left, to be coaxed back
by Stalin at his most charming, who explained, as we all do when we
have said something outrageous, that he was 'only joking'.[61] Now that
the western Allies were ashore in France, and doing quite well, relations
had, understandably, calmed a little. The main topic of discussion was
Poland. Churchill said that the Polish leadership in exile was being
difficult and that he was trying to get them to agree to the Soviet
demands. It was not inconceivable that Poland could have adopted a
benignly neutral position towards the Soviet Union like that of Finland
or Austria, although, given Russia's long and antipathetic relations with
the Poles, it seems unlikely the Russians would have been satisfied with
that. Mikołajczyk, the government-in-exile Prime Minister, was in
Moscow as well, but did not make any great effort to reach an agreement
with the Russians. It may be that the Americans were telling him not to
make any concessions. For once, Stalin seemed to believe Churchill.[62]

Averill Harriman, the new US Ambassador, was in attendance but
steered clear of the conversations between Churchill and Stalin so as not
to imply that America was party to any of the agreements. Churchill
kept him informed. On 9 October Churchill, Stalin and their respective
interpreters – nobody else – met in Stalin's office. Churchill explained
that they should talk about Romania, which had gone over to Stalin's
side, and Greece, in which Churchill, as a failed classical scholar,
nevertheless took quite an interest. According to Berezhkov, who may
have been the interpreter, and was an NKVD man, whom liberal sources
in Russia believe to be reliable, Churchill said: 'I have here this naughty
document with some ideas of certain people in London.' The piece of
paper was folded in four. Stalin could not read English but understood
the letters and numbers, as anyone would.

Romania: 90 per cent Russia
10 per cent Others

Greece: 90 per cent Great Britain (in accord with USA)
10 per cent Russia

Yugoslavia: 50–50

Hungary: 50–50

Bulgaria: Russia 75 per cent
Others 25 per cent

Berezhkov says Stalin looked at it for a while, then got out one of his favourite coloured pencils – not a green one, this time, but blue – and ticked the top left-hand corner. He pushed it back towards Churchill. 'Might it not be thought rather cynical if it seemed that we had disposed of these issues, so fateful to millions of people, in such an offhand manner?' Churchill is alleged to have said, 'Let us burn the paper.'

'No. You keep it.'

Stalin was quite used to deciding the fate of millions of people with the stroke of a coloured pencil. He had done so many times, sometimes wrongly.

The figures which Churchill and Stalin allegedly agreed and which Eden and Molotov argued over do explain a lot. They explain why the British crushing of communist insurgents in Greece elicited no great opposition from Stalin, and why, if Hungary was modified to 75:25, Stalin was annoyed at British attempts to interfere in the evolving situation there.[63]

Churchill left Moscow on 19 October on much better terms with Stalin, and with very perceptive presents. Churchill, whom the NKVD referred to as 'the boar', loved animals and often used them as metaphors in his correspondence. Clemmie, Churchill's wife, and the Prime Minister referred to Stalin as 'the Old Bear' in their private correspondence. Clemmie received a vase with a picture of the sternsman in a boat. 'Behind every great man . . .' Churchill's was called 'a hunter with a bow against a bear'. How could the Russians have known?[64]

Whether the report of Stalin and Churchill's secret meeting is exactly right or not, it underlines the cynicism that inevitably attended managing a war – and its consequences – on any scale, never mind this one. The Red Army's halt before Warsaw was cynical, too – but realistic. And, as well as the cynicism, and the symbolism in the timings and the codenames, 1944 had seen many superlatives. The biggest military operations, the destruction of Army Group Centre. And, with the dominoes falling in south-east Europe, Hitler's make-believe world was falling apart. The Russians just had to finish the job.

19

VICTORY

Back in the USSR...

So far, Valentin Berezhkov had experienced a very good war. He had been Molotov's interpreter, met Hitler and Ribbentrop, escaped from Germany after Barbarossa thanks to diplomatic immunity, and been present at meetings between the Politburo and Churchill. He worked for the NKVD, of course. Although as Molotov's assistant he now wore an embroidered shoulder board with a single star, equivalent to a major-general, he still ate in the NKVD Kremlin canteen, staying lean on the sausages they served. But in late 1944 his charmed life was in danger. An old NKVD report surfaced that ten years before he had paid a visit to a Polish friend at the Polish Consulate in Kiev. Intelligence agencies work like that. Why had he sneaked round the back of the Polish consulate? He was summoned to see Beria, and explained that the Pole was just an old friend. Beria seemed affable. But given what had happened at Warsaw, Stalin's distrust of the Poles and his determination to crush any independent Polish identity, it was not a good time for a Russian in a high-powered job to be linked with them, in any way. One night, Berezhkov was suddenly dismissed. Foreign Minister's assistant one moment, nobody the next. The guard took away his blue all-area Kremlin pass – a very prestigious piece of ID – and he was out on the street. He wandered those streets, terrified, for hours. Molotov probably protected him by getting him a posting away from the snakes in the Kremlin hot-house. He was assigned to a new job, working on a new official newspaper, *War and the Working Class*. Stalin did not like the title, and changed it to *New Times*. Berezhkov's incredible luck had held.[1] In spite of the great Russian military triumphs, the opening of the second front and the overwhelming material superiority now enjoyed by the Allies, life in Russia, even in Moscow, remained much as it had throughout the worst years of the war: beset by shortages, frugal, hard, and potentially brutish and short. No other country, except possibly Britain, had mobilized its economy so ruthlessly for war, but Soviet Russia had a far less varied economic base to start from, and had not been able to do so as efficiently as Britain. And there was still the same obsession with security and spies.

Rolling up the German right flank

By September 1944 the spectacular success of Bagration had created a salient threatened by German forces from north and south. To the south, by 24 September the Russians had overrun Romania and part of Hungary (see Figure 19.1). The Russians had managed to raise two divisions of troops from Romanian prisoners and when Romania switched sides, another fourteen became available. When Marshal Tolbukhin, commanding Third Ukrainian Front, drove through Romania and arrived in Bulgaria in October, Bulgaria also produced about fourteen divisions to fight with the Russians.[2] From 28 September to 20 October Tolbukhin's Third and Malinovskiy's Second Ukrainian Fronts in cooperation with the Yugoslav communists, who played a similar role to that of their own partisans in Belorussia, carried out the Belgrade Strategic Offensive. They quickly smashed the German Army Group Serbia and freed eastern and north-eastern Yugoslavia (modern Serbia) and the capital, Belgrade. The Serbs (whose ethnic and military affiliations with the Russians extend from the Russo–Turkish war of 1877–8, through bringing the great powers to war in 1914, to Pristina airport in 1999) were enthusiastic allies, although Tito, the leader of the communist partisan movement, was a Croat. The Yugoslav partisans operating in the mountains attacked German communications and reinforcements and severely hampered their efforts to resist the attack.[3] Stalin's eye was firmly on the Hungarian capital. The Russian conquest of Hungary fell into two main phases. The first was Operation Debrecen, from 6 to 28 October, in which Second Ukrainian Front, including two Romanian armies, aimed to destroy Army Groups South and F or, at least, distract

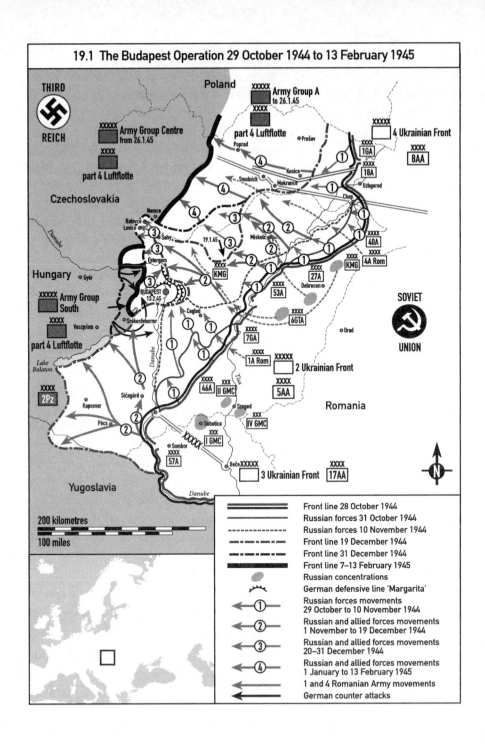

19.1 The Budapest Operation 29 October 1944 to 13 February 1945

	Front line 28 October 1944
	Russian forces 31 October 1944
	Russian forces 10 November 1944
	Front line 19 December 1944
	Front line 31 December 1944
	Front line 7–13 February 1945
	Russian concentrations
	German defensive line 'Margarita'
←①	Russian forces movements 29 October to 10 November 1944
←②	Russian and allied forces movements 1 November to 19 December 1944
←③	Russian and allied forces movements 20–31 December 1944
←④	Russian and allied forces movements 1 January to 13 February 1945
←	1 and 4 Romanian Army movements
←	German counter attacks

them to enable Fourth Ukrainian to cross the Carpathians. The Slovak revolt against the Germans had begun on 29 August and on 8 September the First Ukrainian Front (Koniev) and Fourth (Petrov) launched the East Carpathian operation. They seized the Carpathian passes and opened communications with Slovak partisans. By 28 October eastern Czechoslovakia (now Slovakia) was also in Soviet hands. At the same time, Second and Third Ukrainian Fronts pushed round south of Budapest. A particularly important role was played by the fronts' two KMGs, Pliev's and Gorshkov's, as front mobile groups to exploit the terrain and get behind the enemy. KMG Pliev got 100 kilometres behind enemy lines by day three, and cut off the retreat of two Hungarian and one German armies. Then on 29 October the two fronts, Second and Third, launched the second phase of the Soviet conquest of Hungary, Operation Budapest. Second Ukrainian headed straight north along the Kiskun watershed, much as the Germans would like to have done at Kursk. By 20 December they were just south of Budapest and on the 26th it was completely surrounded, trapping 188,000 men. However, the twin city of Buda – on the west bank of the Danube, and Pest – on the east, proved a very tough nut to crack. By 17 January almost all of Pest was in Russian hands and the garrison there surrendered the next day. But fighting for Buda, on the west bank, continued until 13 February, and concentrated especially on the castle district, rising high above the Danube which runs north–south at this point. The Budapest University Battalion was fighting with the Germans, and the Russians knew it. Some of these were potential future leaders of Hungary, and if they were with the Germans, that was no good. Using their usual good intelligence the Russians set a trap with machine guns and planned air strikes covering the possible exits. When it became obvious that the castle was about to fall, the University Battalion tried to break out to the north-west, but the Russians were waiting and they were massacred. Very few survived.[4]

Meanwhile, Hitler ordered a counter-attack, codenamed *Frühlingserwachen* ('Spring Awakening'), which began on 5 February. The Germans counter-attacked with three Panzer Corps against two Russian armies west of Budapest, between Lake Balaton and Széksfehérvár, and penetrated the hastily improvised Russian defences', but Tolbukhin's front swung round on their left and resumed its advance. By 4 April the Russians were within 8 kilometres of Vienna.

To the north of the Belorussian salient the Russians had forced the

Germans out of Estonia, western Latvia and western Lithuania in the second half of September and first three weeks of October 1944. By 23 October they had the Courland grouping bottled up, together with a tiny German bridgehead around Memel', and the Germans just holding the borders of their own East Prussia. On 16 October three Russian armies attacked towards Gumbinnen, scene of the first Russian victory in 1914, but the Germans held on. The next Russian thrust westwards, along the Baltic coast, the East Prussian Operation (7 January to 25 April 1945), would coincide with a bigger one to the south, and further west.[5]

From the Vistula to the Oder.
Through Poland to Berlin

The Germans collapsed so fast in Hungary and Czechoslovakia because, quite simply, their attention was focused elsewhere. Since the British, Canadians, Americans and Free French had stormed ashore in Normandy on 6 June 1944, the German war on the eastern front, already lost, had to be balanced against overwhelming western Allied superiority not only in the air and at sea, but, now, on the ground and approaching Germany. On 16 December American forces in the Ardennes forest in Belgium were taken by surprise by two Panzer divisions, preceded by diversionary groups dressed as American troops. The Battle of the Bulge had begun. Hitler's plan was to attack through the Ardennes, which the western Allies had discounted as unlikely, in spite of what had happened only four and a half years before. He aimed to split the British and Canadian armies in the north from the Americans in the south, and to recapture Antwerp, thus halting the western Allies' drive on Germany. He could then move forces back east, and do something similar to the Russians as they advanced towards Berlin. Initially Operation Autumn Mist, as the German offensive was known, made striking gains. Although the British had their Ultra decrypts, German radio silence gave them nothing to go on, and because the Germans were now fighting out of their own territory, they could use secure landlines.

However, thanks in part to decisive action by Eisenhower, the

Americans held in the west, and the Battle for Budapest became linked in the German High Command's mind with the Battle of the Bulge. Hitler had said that to lose Budapest would reduce the significance of a victory in the west by half, and so Budapest had to be held, even if, as Guderian warned, that meant diluting the offensive in the west.[6]

Between June and November 1944 German irrecoverable losses on all fronts were 1,457,000, of which 903,000 – two-thirds – were on the eastern front. On 1 October German eastern front strength had been 1,790,000, against about 6.4 million Soviet and Allied troops. Since Bagration, the situation had not changed much north of the Carpathians, with Army Group Courland successfully beating off Russian attacks. On 1 January half the German air force – 1900 planes – was facing the western Allies and very slightly fewer – 1,875 – facing the Russians. The Russians had more than 10,000.[7]

Stavka's plan for January 1945, which was accepted by Stalin at the end of November 1944,[8] was, quite simply, to end the war in about forty-five days. What was left of army Group Centre was weak and the threat from Army Group North, to the right, could be held (see Figure 19.2). The first phase – fifteen days – of the Russian operation was planned in detail, as always, but thereafter things were expected to take their own course and planning became difficult. Rokossovskiy's Second Belorussian would strike north-west towards the Baltic and cut off East Prussia. Zhukov's First Belorussian and Koniev's First Ukrainian would destroy German forces in the Kielce-Radom area and then advance side by side north and north-west towards the Oder. To Rokossovskiy's right, Chernyakovskiy's Third Belorussian would envelop the German Fourth Army in the area of the Masurian Lakes. Then, in the second phase, lasting thirty days, without any pause, Stavka intended to roll First Ukrainian and First Belorussian straight on to the capital of the Third Reich.[9]

In fact, it took nearly four months, and fell into four major component operations: the Vistula-Oder offensive, from 12 January to 3 February, the almost simultaneous East Prussian offensive, from 13 January to 25 February, the East Pomeranian offensive, from 10 February to 4 April, and the Berlin operation, from 16 April to 8 May. The Prague operation, from 6 to 11 May, was the final one of the European war, but had not been envisaged as part of the original, near-seamless descent on Berlin (see Figures 18.4, 19.2).[10]

The Russians' logistic preparations were unprecedented. The railways

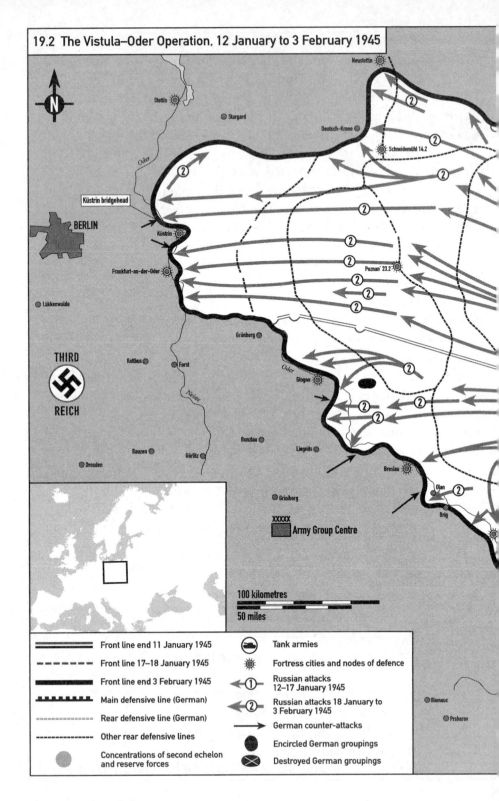

19.2 The Vistula–Oder Operation, 12 January to 3 February 1945

Neustettin

Stettin

Stargard

Deutsch-Krone

Schneidemühl 14.2

Küstrin bridgehead

BERLIN

Küstrin

Frankfurt-an-der-Oder

Poznań 23.2

Lükkenwalde

Grünberg

THIRD

Kottbus

Forst

Oder

Glogau

Neisse

REICH

Bunzlau

Bauzen

Görlitz

Liegnits

Breslau

Dresden

Grünberg

Olau

XXXXX
Army Group Centre

Brieg

100 kilometres

50 miles

Olomouc

Prsherov

	Front line end 11 January 1945		Tank armies
	Front line 17–18 January 1945		Fortress cities and nodes of defence
	Front line end 3 February 1945	①	Russian attacks 12–17 January 1945
	Main defensive line (German)	②	Russian attacks 18 January to 3 February 1945
	Rear defensive line (German)		German counter-attacks
	Other rear defensive lines		Encircled German groupings
	Concentrations of second echelon and reserve forces		Destroyed German groupings

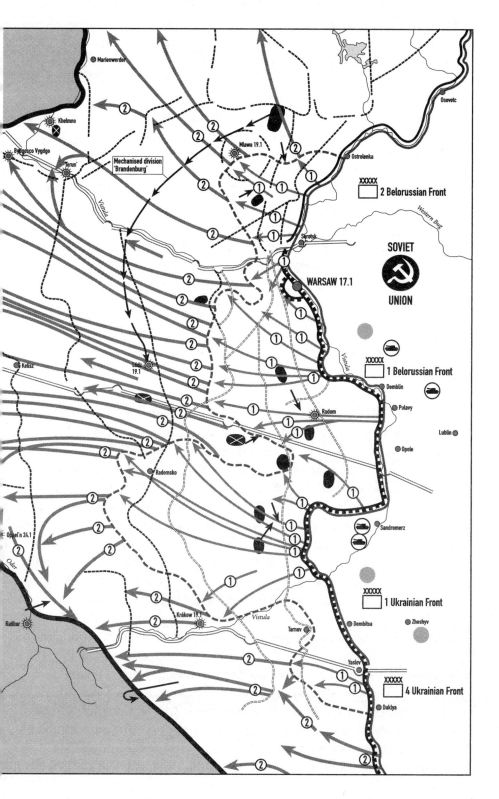

Mechanised division 'Brandenburg'

Marienwerder

Osovetc

Khelmno

Byldgosco Vygdgo

Torun'

Vistula

Mlawa 19.1

Ostrolenka

Western Bug

Sirotsk

XXXXX
2 Belorussian Front

SOVIET

WARSAW 17.1

UNION

Vistula

XXXXX
1 Belorussian Front

Demblin

Kelisz

Łódz 19.1

Pulavy

Radom

Opole

Lublin

Radomsko

Opoel'n 24.1

Sandromerz

Oder

XXXXX
1 Ukrainian Front

Ratibor

Kråkow 19.1

Vistula

Dembitsa

Zheshyv

Tarnuv

Yaslov

XXXXX
4 Ukrainian Front

Duklya

in eastern Poland were converted to the wider Russian gauge and extended across the Vistula to where the Red Army held bridgeheads on the other side. At the jumping-off point across the Vistula, south-west of Magnuszów, Zhukov piled up 2.5 million artillery shells and mortar bombs and in the Russian-held area on the west bank south of Pulawy, 1.3 million. For comparison, at Stalingrad the Don Front had fired fewer than a million rounds, all told. The two biggest fronts, Zhukov's and Koniev's, between them amassed 30 million gallons of fuel. During the operation, the Russians also made extensive use of captured fuel. Second and Third Belorussian fronts were less lavishly supplied with fuel, but compensated with ammunition. Between them they had 9 million artillery and mortar rounds.[11]

Fuelled by hate

It was not only preparations for the physical advance to Berlin that were well under way. There was also the moral component of the Red Army's final push. Because they were not intending to stop in Poland, the troops were already being psyched-up for the break-in to Germany. Liberating the motherland was no longer an issue. This was, at its best and most dignified, conquest. However, to motivate the ordinary Red Army soldier, who, it was believed, did not think much beyond the next meal and the next sleep, that would not do. In fact, Vasiliy Grossman, the war correspondent, found that the questions he was most often asked were surprisingly wide ranging, including the second front, Japan, Turkey and Iran, and 'hundreds of other issues'.[12]

Vengeance was the theme, stressed over and over again, with lurid tales of what the Germans had done to their people, and encouraged by the political officers backed up by Russia's top writers, notably Il'ya Ehrenburg. 'Germany,' Ehrenburg wrote, 'you can whirl round in circles, and howl in your deathly agony. The hour of revenge has struck!'[13] Many soldiers, probably all, felt grief and hatred against the Germans, but now they were also under orders. The political officers disseminated an instruction. 'The soldier's rage in battle must be terrible. He does not merely seek to fight; he must also be the embodiment of the court of his people's justice.'[14] The phrase is repeated in hundreds of letters from the time, written by Soviet soldiers but captured by the Germans. In the context of absolute war, that is very frightening.

It has been said that while the Soviet authorities, including the military command, did nothing to discourage the widespread and wanton rape and destruction, they did not actually order it. But that instruction from the political officers meant that revenge – cruelty over and above the already horrific and brutal necessities of war – was not merely condoned. It was a *duty*. There was a legal obligation for any soldier, as the representative of the 'court of people's justice', to exact retribution. The murder and rape that followed – and every account of the invasion of Germany stresses it – was an inevitable side effect for men not only under extreme pressure and constant danger, but also separated from their wives and girlfriends for years. And it was deliberately encouraged. When the Russians entered German territory, first of all in East Prussia, Lev Kopelev, writer turned officer, ordered his men to urinate on German soil. Another group, about to cross the border, had political officers crawling with them, repeating morale-boosting instructions. 'There is Germany. Over there in Germany our sisters are suffering in slavery ... onwards to the destruction of the enemy in his own lair.'[15] In fact, according to Vasiliy Grossman, the war correspondent, Soviet girls deported by the Germans for slave labour were often robbed and raped as well.[16] That was not in the orders. However, the fact that the Germans had captured the orders was also an incentive for them to fight harder.

There seems to have been a change in the behaviour of the Soviet troops after they had crossed out of their own territory. The first rumours of large-scale atrocities came out of Hungary. The fighting for Budapest had been long and hard and 80,000 Soviet troops were killed. On the Buda side, the Russian troops ransacked the city for food and alcohol before turning on the female population, some of whom were locked up in the soldiers' barracks and repeatedly raped.[17] When the Red Army moved into Poland, they had already been indoctrinated with the official 'revenge' creed, but it seemed to apply to everyone whose language they did not speak, including Poles, plus their own deportees. The fact that the indoctrination had taken place by early January is additional evidence, not that any is needed, that the plan was to drive straight through to Berlin.

The price of coalition war?

The Russian offensive was probably intended to start on 20 January, and that is what the Soviet accounts say. However, with the German Ardennes offensive the western Allies were in trouble. On 6 January Churchill asked Stalin what he could do to take some of the pressure off. Stalin brought the offensive forward eight days, to the 12th. The western Allies had been surprised by the relative passivity of the usually energetic Russian forces in December, and Harriman had asked Stalin when they were going to attack. Stalin said that a winter offensive would be launched, but nothing more. German intelligence reports indicate that the Russians were probably waiting for the weather to improve. On 15 January Sir Arthur Tedder, Eisenhower's deputy, visited Stalin and was told the offensive had been delayed by the weather but brought forward to help his coalition partners. Stalin then said something very significant. The Russian objective was now the Oder – 60 kilometres short of Berlin.[18] Bringing the offensive forward and limiting its objective may have cost the Russians a very early victory. If they had gone fully prepared on 20 January, in better weather which would aid artillery observation and air support, the 30-day plan – if it worked – would have put them in Berlin by the end of February. It was not to be.

However, the Yalta conference was due to take place from 4 to 11 February. Even with the more limited offensive, Stalin would still have Poland in his hand – which would strengthen it when negotiating on the awkward question of the fate of that country. There was also the potential problem of Germans still threatening his northern flank. The final division of Germany was not agreed until Yalta, so there might be some diplomatic gains to be made there. Finally, Stalin had done the western Allies a favour, which he could call in at a later date.

Poland overrun

The Russians launched their operation, slightly less ambitious than originally planned, on 12 January. The two fronts were roughly equal in strength: Zhukov's with 1,028,900 men and women soldiers, Koniev's with 1,083,800. There were also 91,000 in the First Polish Army.[19]

The two fronts were also similar in organization. There were three distinct components, or 'echelons' (not to be confused with troop trains, which is the same word in Russian). First Belorussian's first echelon comprised seven armies, with Third Shock as its second echelon. The mobile group, the third component, comprised First and Second Guards Tank Armies. Koniev's first echelon was six armies, with two in the second echelon and Third Guards and Fourth Tank Armies as the mobile group. This was the template, and these were the commanders, who were going all the way to Berlin.[20]

The density of artillery massed to blast a way through the forward German units exceeded that in any other operation, apart from Kiev in 1943. In Eighth Guards Army's Sector, part of Zhukov's First Belorussian Front and now under command of Chuikov, the defender of Stalingrad, there were 350 guns or heavy mortars for every kilometre of front. That is one every three metres – literally wheel to wheel. As usual, 'reconnaissance by battle' started in the small hours, battalions moving ahead of the main forces to get the Germans to reveal their positions. Then, at 10.00, now that it was just light, First Ukrainian's artillery opened up. A fifteen-minute deluge of intense fire, then forty minutes of slower, more deliberate shelling. Then a seven-minute strike on German artillery batteries, anti-tank positions and observation posts. It surgically cut out the German artillery command network. Then another thirty minutes of deliberate fire, a fifteen-minute intense strike, and the infantry went in, preceded by a double rolling barrage. At this stage the Germans started to run.

On Zhukov's front the initial artillery strike lasted just twenty-five minutes, during which they fired 315,000 projectiles weighing nearly 5,500 tonnes. Of these, 15 per cent were rockets from the BM-13 *Katyushas*, with 132mm warheads and BM-31 *Ivan Grozny* – 'Ivan the

Terrible' launchers, with great, bulbous 300mm warheads.[21] By noon, the Russians had opened up gaps that were wide enough for the tank formations to come through, and by 15 January the tank armies were moving fast into the German rear. On the 13th Hitler ordered two infantry divisions to be transferred from the west. On that and the following day, Guderian sent two messages to Hitler, warning that the eastern front could not survive without more reinforcements from the west, but no more were forthcoming.[22] On the 15th Hitler moved his headquarters for the last time, to the Reichs Chancellery in Berlin. That night Guderian called and, as Jodl recalled, 'requested urgently that everything be thrown east'. The next day, he said he would send two SS corps, not to Army Group A (renamed Army Group Centre on 26 January) which was being torn apart by the Russians, but to Army Group South. Hitler had decided that the war depended on holding on to the Hungarian oilfields.[23]

By 17 January the Russians had broken out of their bridgeheads and were motoring forward. Warsaw was recaptured on that day by Soviet-subordinated First Polish Army, showing rather more determination this time.[24] Krakow and Łódz were taken soon after. Although the relative lack of resistance suggests that the Germans had planned to withdraw, the rapidity of the Soviet advance cut off many of the German units in forward positions. However, just as the Germans had found in Russia, very rapid advance had left large pockets of German troops unbeaten, and able to fight their way back to their own lines.[25]

The tank armies which formed the mobile groups – two for each front – each comprised tank and mechanized corps, in a rough ratio of two to one. Koniev took a special interest in briefing these spearheads himself, so important were they to the successful outcome of the operation.[26]

In the Vistula-Oder offensive the Russian tank armies covered up to 500 kilometres in three weeks. Keeping the Red Army's highest-technology forces supplied at such distances over such a period of time presented huge problems. Four tank armies were operating as far ahead of the massed majority following behind as at any time during the war. That was typically 60 to 90 kilometres ahead of the reassuring presence of large numbers of other Russian troops. Across that distance, to keep going, each tank army needed 600 to 750 tonnes of fuel per day, which required 270 to 300 trucks to carry it.

In addition to the huge fuel reserves brought in before the attack, the Russians captured many fuel dumps as they outflanked the Germans before they could destroy them. However, this fuel could not be used until it had been tested to ensure that it had not been tampered with and that it worked in Red Army vehicles. That meant, in general, Russian tanks and self-propelled guns and American 'soft-skinned' jeeps and trucks. The Russians therefore set up army field laboratories (PL or PSL) at the Army Petrol, Oil and Lubricant (POL) depots. They tested for metallic particles and water in the fuel, and worked out its octane, and the viscosity of oil. Obviously, any high-octane fuel would be wasted in trucks and went to the air force. The Russians only permitted the use of captured fuel 'after all kinds of laboratory testing and this took some time'.[27] As for food, apart from American Spam, the Red Army expected to live off the land as much as possible, and did so whenever there was anything left to eat. Unlike the vehicles, the men's stomachs were expected to run on whatever was available. Ammunition was also a problem. Special motor transport units with about 600 trucks each were created for three of the four tank armies but even these could only carry half a 'unit of fire' and a third of a 'fill' of fuel for its army on each trip. With the tank armies moving 60 to 90 kilometres ahead, the Russians thanked God there was no longer any serious opposition in the air.[28] Once again, the Russian approach to logistics varied from the brutally casual (or casually brutal) – just nick it – to the meticulously scientific. It all depended on what you could get away with.

By 3 February the Russian advance had reached a line roughly level with a straight one drawn between the north-eastern border of modern Slovakia and the centre of Berlin. That line passes pretty well exactly through the junction of the Neisse, flowing from the south, and the Oder which, having flowed from the east, at this point turns north to Szczecin and the Baltic. To the east of the confluence of the Oder and the Neisse, the Russians had pushed beyond that straight line, capturing German 'fortress cities' at Kraków, Oppeln (Opole), Breslau (Wrocław) and Glogau (Głogów). During the last week of January units of the First Ukrainian Front fought their way through industrial Upper Silesia, which lies east of Opole, and west of Kraków (see Figure 19.2). During the late November 1944 briefings, Stalin had drawn Koniev's attention to the area. Wrocław would be First Ukrainian Front's main objective. It was not to be destroyed, however. It was too valuable industrially for that. It was to be taken intact. Stalin had made the point in a typically elliptical fashion. He had traced the area carefully on the map, and then said one word: *Zoloto* – 'gold'.[29] The industrial cities of upper Silesia had taken over from those of the Ruhr – which the British and Americans had bombed to bits – as Germany's main production centre for the very basics of industrial war: coal and ferrous metals. At the end of January, the foundries and mines were still producing but by 27 January four armies from fourth Belorussian Front had cut off the area and Koniev's Third Guards Tank Army was approaching from the north-west. Bearing in mind Stalin's instructions, the southern end of the pocket was left open to allow the Germans to withdraw, thus avoiding a battle which would destroy the precious factories. If this area was 'gold', then this was a military device sometimes called the 'golden bridge' – deliberately leaving the enemy a way out.[30]

In the afternoon of 27 January Koniev's forces reached the town of Oswiecim, west of Kraków, better known by its German name – Auschwitz. The Russians had been the first Allied power to come across a German concentration camp, at Maidanek, just outside Lublin, in July 1944. Then, the find was reported in *Pravda*, although the prevalence of Jews among its victims was not mentioned. Auschwitz, however, was something different. The Red Army found 2,819 surviving prisoners, many close to death, and grim evidence of the industrial mass slaughter that had gone on there. With the usual Russian precision, they counted 348,820 men's suits and 836,255 women's coats and dresses. Some of the surviving prisoners turned out to be Soviet citizens, and were, of course, interrogated by *Smersh*,[31] the military counter-espionage department set up in 1943. The Soviet troops who 'liberated' the camp – if that is the right word – were obviously shocked and their desire for revenge against the Germans was further fuelled. But the Soviet authorities did not broadcast what they had found until 7 May, the eve of final victory in the war. And, again, the Jewish angle was completely ignored. The victims were 'four million people from various European countries'.[32]

While Koniev was successfully gaining upper Silesia, Zhukov's front overran a fortified zone known as the 'Oder Quadrilateral'. The Quadrilateral comprised four fortress cities which were, running clockwise from the north-east: Schneidemühl, which fell on 4 February; Poznan, which fell on 23 February; Glogau (Głogów), which was then in Germany; and Küstrin, on the Oder. Although the area was overrun, Poznan held on for nearly a month and Glogau fell only on 31 March, while Breslau (Wrocław) held on until 15 April. That did not unduly bother Zhukov. By 31 January, I Mechanized Corps of First Belorussian Front was over the Oder. The Russians established a bridgehead north of Küstrin, and another one across the river south of Frankfurt-an-der-Oder (not to be confused with Frankfurt-am-Main, in western Germany). These two enclaves on the west bank would become the jumping-off point for Zhukov's front when the final attack on the capital began. The two bridgeheads, about 30 kilometres apart, were some 65 kilometres from Berlin. Zhukov, the rest of whose front had by 3 February closed on the river from Zehden to its southern boundary 60 kilometres south of Frankfurt, was in no mood to stop, having got so far.[33] On 26 January he had reported that if he was given four days to bring up reinforcements and supplies – until the day his forces actually crossed the Oder – he could be ready to attack towards Berlin on 1 or 2 February. Koniev said he could be ready to attack across the Neisse in his sector two or three days later.

So far, the offensive had gone stupendously well. In twenty-three days the Russians had advanced 500 kilometres on a front about as wide. Out of more than 2 million soldiers, 43,251 would never be seen alive again, and 150,000 were sick or wounded. Altogether, less than a 10 per cent loss rate, with 8,397 casualties a day. That was 20 per cent fewer than in the last operation on a comparably stupendous scale – Bagration.[34]

Zhukov and Koniev were raring to go on but their supplies and their troops were exhausted, and Stalin was concerned about the right flank. Meanwhile, Second and Third Belorussian and First Baltic Fronts were making slow progress in East Prussia. The question of whether the Front commanders – and Zhukov, as Deputy Supreme Commander, in particular – should have pressed for permission to carry on was first raised in a conference in Berlin in 1945. Twenty years later, Chuikov said it was he who raised it but Zhukov claims he said nothing on the subject at the time. In 1965 Chuikov caused a bit of a stir by saying that 'Berlin could have been taken as early as February and that, of course, would have brought the end of the war nearer.'[35] Zhukov said there was 'more to the Berlin offensive than Marshal Chuikov can see'. The German defences in front of Berlin were strong and Zhukov ordered two 'units of fire' for the guns and two 'fills' of fuel for the vehicles, and six for aircraft, to be brought up with a view to capturing Berlin by 15 or 16 February. However, there was a very real danger of an attack in his right flank from East Pomerania. The city of Poznan was still holding out and Chuikov's forces did not take it until 23 February. Zhukov's divisions were down to an average of 5,500 troops – half their official strength – and First Ukrainian Front's were in a similar state. Having advanced 500 kilometres in twenty-three days, the logistics on which the Red Army relied were lagging behind and, finally, the spring thaw had turned the grass airfields from which the rapidly advancing Russians had to operate into bogs, while the Germans were deploying what aircraft they had from concrete runways. Besides, Berlin was a gigantic city, the size of London or New York, and there were still about 2.5 million people living there, out of a pre-war population of 4,300,000. From their experience at Stalingrad, the Russians – and especially Chuikov – should have known how many troops a spacious city can absorb. Taking it 'in their stride', as Chuikov later suggested, was not an option.[36]

It was time for Stalin to go somewhere warmer. To what could now be restored as the Soviet Riviera, although it still had a very long way to go.

Yalta

The 'big three' had considered Scotland, Malta or Athens as the venue for the conference which would decide the fate of Europe, but on the advice of his doctors Stalin insisted on Yalta in the Crimea. With the Germans thrown out only nine months before, the place was still littered with the detritus of war. President Roosevelt, who had just two months to live – until 12 April – therefore had to travel a quarter of the way round the world to get there. The codename for the conference – Argonaut – was ironically appropriate. Roosevelt stopped off at Malta on the way, to meet Churchill. When he reached Saki airfield in the Crimea, and had completed the 110-kilometre journey to Yalta, he was put up in the pre-Revolution Livadia palace, surrounded by electronic bugging devices.[37] Livadia would be his residence and also the venue for the plenary conferences. Churchill's description of a 'beautiful Black Sea Riviera' where the Russians had restored Imperial palaces and villas to good order 'by extreme exertions and every form of thoughtfulness and ingenuity' probably put a very positive gloss on the physical environment. By that, he meant that the Russians had plundered the surrounding countryside for every ashtray, coat hanger and other necessity. And so, 'on this shore we laboured for nine days and grappled with many problems of war and policy while friendship grew'.[38]

In fact, mistrust was growing. On the surface, it all seemed very comradely. Stalin arrived with Poland and south-eastern Europe – Romania, the Balkans and much of Hungary – in his possession. However, he wanted to woo the western Allies for a continuation of lease-lend aid, not so much to win the war, which he was doing rather convincingly, but for post-war reconstruction. The participants in the Yalta conference agreed that Germany should be divided between the three, and that France should also have a zone, and be a member of the Allied Control Commission, if it wanted. War criminals would be brought to trial, and the western Allies agreed that, as part of a general agreement to hand back one another's citizens, Soviet citizens found in Germany (including those in German military uniform) should be repatriated. It was at Yalta that, unknowingly, Churchill and Roosevelt signed the death warrant of many Russians and other Soviet people whom they would pick up in France and Germany.

The British and Americans finally withdrew recognition for the lame-duck Polish government in exile in London and recognized the de facto supremacy of the Moscow-backed Polish provisional government, following Poland's complete 'liberation' by the Red Army. The western leaders extracted a promise of 'free and unfettered elections', in Poland and elsewhere in eastern Europe, but Stalin refused to allow supervision. Moving Poland west, at Germany's expense, was agreed in principle. Finally, Stalin reaffirmed that he would join the war against Japan, which he had already agreed to do at Tehran. In return, he got south Sakhalin, which had been Japanese since 1904, and the Kuriles, right down to Hokkaido. The big three also agreed to hold a United Nations conference in San Francisco, on 25–6 April 1945, which would be attended by the countries which are now permanent members of the UN Security Council. The UN Charter, first drafted at Dumbarton Oaks by representatives of the 'big three' between 21 August and 29 September, 1944 and considered by their heads of government at Yalta, was signed at San Francisco on 26 April 1945.

The Crimea Declaration of 12 February 1945 concluded with the commitment to 'a secure and lasting peace' which, in the words of the

Dumbarton Oaks draft charter, would 'afford assurance that all men in all the lands may live their lives in freedom from fear and want'. Those words – 'freedom from fear and want' are one definition of what, since 1994, has been the UN's definition of 'human security'. For the moment, however, all three leaders were still preoccupied with a more immediate concern. The first section of the Declaration was called 'defeat of Germany'. It concluded: 'Nazi Germany is doomed. The German people will only make the cost of their defeat heavier to themselves by attempting to continue a hopeless resistance.'[39]

Given that the big three agreed on the division of Germany, a provisional demarcation line between the western Allies and Stalin down the line of the River Elbe was reached at Yalta, although it does not, understandably, appear in the published statements. The Soviet zone of occupation would therefore extend far west of Berlin.[40] However, neither side trusted the other, and it was the western Allies who, later, finally decided to halt on the Elbe. Assuming the Elbe was the dividing line, then there was no point in fighting and dying for territory one was not going to keep. When a nation's armed forces seize an area, they may be reluctant to withdraw, whatever their previous agreements – precisely the argument that impelled the Russians into Poland, rather prematurely, from their point of view, on 14 September 1939. Nevertheless, the question of whether the western Allies or the Russians would take Berlin was far from settled. On 28 March Eisenhower sent a personal telegram to Stalin ruling out any direct British–US advance on the German capital. Instead the western Allies would head for the Erfurt-Leipzig-Dresden area, in part because of (false) rumours that Hitler would dig himself into a redoubt in Bavaria. In fact, Hitler was in a bunker below the Reichs Chancellery in Berlin and would not come out much. Eisenhower asked for information about Russian plans so that the movements of the armies advancing from east and west could be coordinated. At a very practical level, when armies who have never seen each other before meet in the forlorn loneliness of wide contested spaces, 'friendly fire' is a real and lethal possibility. Stalin considered Eisenhower's telegram, and agreed the course of action, saying that his forces would head in that direction. 'Berlin has lost its former strategic importance,' he said.[41] It was the main German forces, not a political symbol, that mattered. That was a splendid lie. Politically, militarily and, not least, because Hitler was there and the Russians wanted to stop him getting out, Berlin was the principal objective. Recent Allied successes had made the Russians suspicious, and, whatever might happen in Berlin itself, in order to secure the 'agreed' occupation zone east of the Elbe the Russians would have to overrun it as soon as possible. And they could not do that without taking Berlin.

While Russian suspicions fuelled the planning for Berlin, there was also an argument between the Allies because British and American diplomats in Berne, Switzerland, had started talks about the surrender of German forces in Italy, without consulting the Russians. Understandably, at the end of March, the Russians went ballistic. To them it looked as if the western Allies were trying to engineer a separate peace. As a result, Stalin told the dying US President that Molotov would not attend the world-shaping San Francisco conference.[42]

On 28 March, the day Eisenhower penned his message about his planned thrust east of the Elbe, Zhukov was briefing Stavka on the very operation which Stalin had claimed did not interest him – the capture of Berlin. The next day he flew to Moscow and supposedly met Stalin although, as so often, this meeting is not in Stalin's diary.[43] On 31 March Koniev also arrived in Moscow to talk to the General Staff. That night Stalin met with US Ambassador Harriman and British Ambassador Kerr, plus other westerners including John R. Deane, the head of the US Military Mission. They presented him with Eisenhower's proposal for an advance along the Erfurt–Leipzig–Dresden line. Stalin replied to Eisenhower the next day, dismissing Berlin as a major objective and fixing a big Russian offensive for later in May, by which time the war in Europe would be over.[44] After his first visit to Russia, in August 1942, Churchill had applauded the 'great rugged war chief', Stalin, saying that 'above all he is a man with that saving sense of humour which is of high importance to all men and all nations, but particularly to great men and great nations'.[45] Stalin sent his message to Eisenhower on 1 April.[46]

Into the lair of the fascist beast[47]

For all the reasons given by Zhukov, the Red Army paused on the Oder and the Neisse during March, to build up its strength for the crowning – though not the final – battle of the European war. To the north, bitter fighting continued on the edge of the Baltic, with the Courland Group still holding out. On 30 March Rokossovskiy's troops took Danzig (Gdansk). Meanwhile, on 5 March Hitler called up the 'class of 1929' – fifteen-year-olds.[48] On 20 March the Führer made his last public appearance to award medals to children who had distinguished themselves at the front. 'It was one of the most moving situations I ever witnessed,' recalled Secretary of State Naumann. The youngest was a twelve-year-old, who had caught a spy. Hitler asked him how he had discovered the enemy agent. 'He wore his corporal's stripe on the wrong arm, my Führer.'[49] It is unclear whether the 'Bohemian corporal' appreciated the inadvertent irony.

On 1 April, having told Eisenhower he had lost interest in Berlin and would restart his offensive in late May, Stalin eyed his main planning conference: the seven members of the GKO, plus the the two leading front commanders, Zhukov and Koniev, General Aleksey Antonov from the General Staff and Colonel-General Sergey Shtemenko, head of the Main Operations Directorate. Rokossovskiy, commanding Second Belorussian, the third front that would be involved, was not there. He had to finish the Germans in East Pomerania and East Prussia. The three fronts had their own air armies and in addition they would be supported by Eighteenth Long-Range Air Army with medium bombers.

'So, who is going to take Berlin, we or the Allies?' said Stalin. Whatever had been agreed at Yalta, Stalin and his advisers were distrustful. Koniev fell into the trap. 'We will,' he said. How was he going to move his forces, most of which were still engaged to the south, Stalin asked. Zhukov said his front was now ready and was pointed straight at the city. First Belorussian was the most powerful military formation in the world, with 908,000 men and women to Koniev's 550,900 and Rokossovskiy's 441,600. Zhukov had 3,155 tanks and self-propelled guns and 16,934 artillery pieces. The German Ninth Army and Fourth Panzer Army, opposing him, had 754 tanks between them and Ninth Army had about 750 guns, including 300 to 400 anti-aircraft guns. All told, the three Soviet fronts to be launched at Berlin had about two million men and women, 6,250 tanks, 7,500 aircraft, 41,600 guns and mortars, 3,255 multiple rocket-launchers and 95,383 motor vehicles.[50] But there were still a million German troops around Berlin and within the city there were a further 200,000 *Volksturm* – essentially a home guard, but still dangerous, particularly when armed, as they were, with large numbers of *Panzerfaust* disposable anti-tank weapons. There were also fanatical units of the Hitler Youth. The battle for Berlin, which is probably the most written-about battle in recent history, was by no means just a contest with old men and children, and the capture of the city would be no walkover.[51] Although Hitler, now in denial, fantasized about a great battle at the gates of Berlin, for the Russians – and most of the Germans – the outcome was not in doubt.

Back in November Stalin had promised that Zhukov would take Berlin. But to effectively exclude from the city Koniev's force, which enjoyed a very important advantage, would be absurd. The boundaries between the fronts were marked with a red 'Oxford rule' – one thick, one thin line. Stalin scrubbed out the line from Lubben, 60 kilometres east of the Nazi capital. From there on in, Zhukov and Koniev, who were rivals, would race. 'Whoever breaks in first, let him take Berlin.'[52] Rokossovskiy's Second Belorussian would stand by to swing west and move across the devastated country of East Prussia, to attack north of Berlin.

All three marshals were popular, but, given Rokossovskiy's GULag record, Stalin did not regard him as a threat. Zhukov and Koniev were a different matter. That is almost certainly why he pitted them against each other. Zhukov had been promised the prize, but now it was all to play for. And Zhukov had the harder job. The rival commanders approached their tasks in very different ways. Ahead of First Belorussian Front, the German Ninth Army blocked Zhukov's path (see Figure 19.3). His plan could be likened to banging one's head through a brick wall. Into the tiny bridgehead across the Oder near Küstrin, he brought 8,000 guns across twenty-five bridges. There was no way this could be done without the Germans' knowledge. Spring came late that year and the leafless trees and and sodden low-lying ground by the river made both camouflage and digging difficult. Soviet troops, many still wearing their winter fur hats, dug in their guns under the nose of the enemy, and brought 7 million rounds of artillery ammunition to Zhukov's front-line dumps. Since he had to attack head-on, Zhukov came up with a novel plan to blind the German defenders with 140 anti-aircraft searchlights. Like most anti-aircraft units, these were operated by women, whose arrival in the tightly packed bridgehead was apparently something of a morale-booster. The artillery barrage would be short – only thirty minutes.

Zhukov decided to direct the operation from the only piece of high

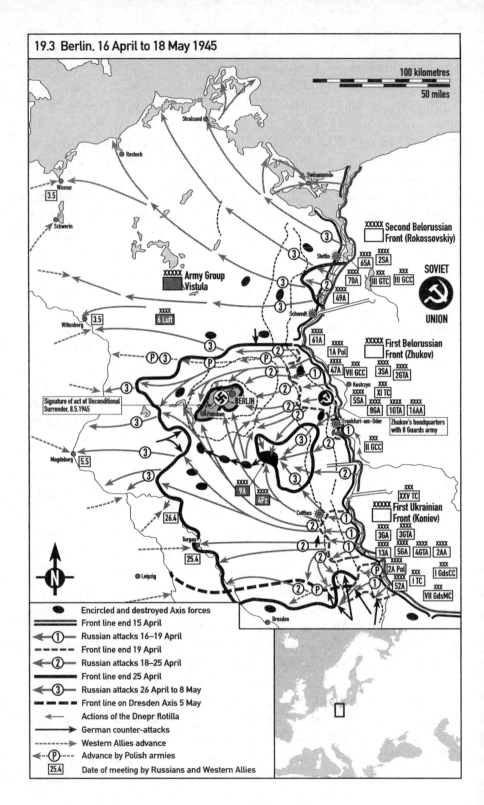

19.3 Berlin, 16 April to 18 May 1945

100 kilometres

50 miles

Stralsund

Rostock

Wismar
3.5

Schwerin

Swinamünde

XXXXX Second Belorussian
Front (Rokossovskiy)

Stettin

XXXX 65A   XXXX 2SA

XXXX 70A   XXX III GTC   XXX III GCC

XXXX 49A

SOVIET UNION

Schwedt

XXXXX Army Group
Vistula

Wittenberg
3.5   XXXX 6 Luft

3

3

3

3

XXXX 61A

XXXX 1A Pol

XXXXX First Belorussian
Front (Zhukov)

XXXX 47A   XXX VII GCC   XXXX 3SA   XXXX 2GTA

Kostrzyn   XXX XI TC

XXXX 5SA   XXXX 86A   XXX 1GTA   XXXX 16AA

BERLIN

Potsdam

Frankfurt-am-Oder

Zhukov's headquarters
with 8 Guards army

XXX II GCC

Signature of act of Unconditional
Surrender, 8.5.1945

Magdeburg
5.5

XXXX 9A   XXXX 4Pz

XXX XXV TC

First Ukrainian
Front (Koniev)

Cottbus

XXXX 3GA   XXXX 3GTA

26.4

Torgau

25.4

Leipzig

XXXX 13A   XXXX 5GA   XXXX 46TA   XXXX 2AA

XXXX 2A Pol   XXX I GdsCC

XXXX 52A   XXX I TC

XXX VII GdsMC

Dresden

Legend

- ● Encircled and destroyed Axis forces
- ═══ Front line end 15 April
- ◁―① Russian attacks 16–19 April
- – – – Front line end 19 April
- ◁―② Russian attacks 18–25 April
- ═══ Front line end 25 April
- ◁―③ Russian attacks 26 April to 8 May
- – – – Front line on Dresden Axis 5 May
- ←···· Actions of the Dnepr flotilla
- ➤ German counter-attacks
- ···▷ Western Allies advance
- ◁··(P)·· Advance by Polish armies
- 25.4 Date of meeting by Russians and Western Allies

ground the Russians held – the Reitwein ridge or 'spur' which sticks out north-east, parallel with the river. It is like a fish-hook, curving up as a continuation of the Seelow heights. The Russians held only about 6 kilometres of the ridge: German forces were dug in where the hook curves, to the south-west, south of the main road from Kostrzyn to Berlin. An engineer battalion was brought in and excavated a bunker deep in the clay of the ridge. Today, 'Zhukov's bunker' is well signposted – you approach from the north. Tank scrapes guard the approaches. With the Germans 6 kilometres away, the commander of the world's most powerful army group and Stalin's deputy would be a fine prize for any German special forces unit. From the bunker, officers could ascend to the neat command–observation post just below the crest, on the forward slope. Any fool can be uncomfortable, and to make the bunker habitable the Russian engineers had a stroke of genius. Using flame-throwers, they fired the clay walls of the bunker and turned them into terracotta. The bunker lasted for about forty years, but finally became unsafe to enter. Today, the Reitwein spur is heavily wooded, including the area around the observation post. But in April 1945 there was a good view of the first high ground on the axis of attack – the Seelow heights, the shank of the fish-hook, about 10 kilometres away.

Zhukov's plan was to attack frontally, across the few kilometres of flat, low-lying ground crossed by numerous ditches, and up on to the heights. It might seem extraordinary that the Russians did not try to work their way round to the left, from the Reitwein ridge, part of which they held, on to the Seelow heights, and roll them up from the south. The occupied villages were strong defensive positions, to be sure, but surely driving straight at the Seelow feature would be madness. Zhukov probably decided that the assembled forces, a juggernaut of tanks and artillery, could not execute anything subtler. Eighth Guards Army's combat power was on the northern side, and could not easily be transferred south. Instead of working round the left flank, a frontal attack, straight down the road from Küstrin to Berlin, it would be.

Koniev's approach was quite different. He did not have a bridgehead on the west side, and would therefore have to cross the River Neisse in the Cottbus area (see Figure 19.3). It was imperative to get his tanks across as soon as possible, as in front of him, behind belts of prepared defences, elements of Fourth Panzer Army were waiting. He opted for *Nacht und Nebel*: under cover of darkness and smokescreens his infantry would swim the river or cross in small boats, then get small bridges across, then big bridges that could carry tanks. His artillery barrage would last 145 minutes.

The bombardment and assault on both fronts were targeted and organized with ruthless precision. Zhukov used a huge, elaborate scale model of the city for briefing and both fronts used air reconnaissance photographs of the German defences to a depth of 100 kilometres beyond the target city. Soviet aircraft overflew some sectors eight times. The engineers built their own model to study problems of street fighting.

Meanwhile the British and Americans had been making good progress in the West. On 3 September 1944 Stalin had written to Roosevelt complaining about the suspected 'separate peace' negotiations in Switzerland. Stalin accused the British and Americans of making an agreement with Kesselring, the German commander in the West, to 'open the front' to their troops in exchange for easier armistice terms.[53] That was not true but individual Germans, realizing what was to come, were much more willing to surrender to the western Allies than to the dreaded and vengeful Russian bear (see Plate 46). By 14 April 1945 some US forces were already on the eastern bank of the Elbe, and Eisenhower ordered a halt. General Simpson, commanding the US Ninth Army, told one of his generals, commanding 2nd US Armoured Division, Brigadier-General Sidney R. Hinds: 'We're not going to Berlin, Sid. This is the end of the war for us.'[54] Bearing in mind the Yalta agreement, the Americans stopped on the Elbe, and Eisenhower, the supreme commander of all western Allied forces, planned to push north into Denmark and southeast, down the Danube, to link up with the Russians there.

On the German side, General Gotthard Heinrici, the commander of Army Group Vistula, which had been falling back in the north, was a valuable asset. He was one of the few German generals who was a real expert on defence. Heinrici knew how the Russians operated. They would blast and incinerate the forward German trenches, so he planned to pull his forward troops back just before they did so. To do that, he needed perfect timing. He was not deceived when shelling and attacks by rifle battalions began on the 14th. That was 'reconnaissance by battle'. A Red Army soldier captured south of Küstrin on 15 April said a gigantic attack on Berlin would start the next day. That night, 15 to 16 April, General Busse, commanding Ninth Army, pulled his men back to the second line of defence.[55]

Of the eleven armies on Zhukov's front, the Eighth Guards, under Chuikov, was in the centre of the action. Zhukov arrived there at 03.00, two hours before First Belorussian Front's artillery attack was to commence.

> The hands of the clock seemed to be moving slower than ever before. To kill the remaining 15 minutes we all decided to have some hot strong tea which was made right there in the dug-out by a young girl. I remember that, rather strangely, she sported the very un-Russian name of Margo. We sipped our tea in silence, each of us deeply engrossed in his thoughts.[56]

At 05.00 Moscow time, flares lit up the sky, signalling the start of the artillery attack. 'It seemed that no living being could have survived in the enemy positions,' Zhukov wrote in his memoirs.[57] He was right. There was hardly anyone there. Heinrici had pulled them out. As the half-hour initial bombardment was about to end, a searchlight shone its beam vertically, a signal for the other 140 or so to switch on and light up the battlefield with a billion candlepower. But the searchlights, meant to blind the defenders, blinded the Soviet troops instead, as so much smoke and debris was thrown up by the massive bombardment. Heinrici had done brilliantly. This massive Soviet blow had struck thin air.

While Zhukov's men moved forward in confusion, asking for the lights to be switched off, Koniev awaited the start of his bombardment, at 06.15. The smoke laid by artillery and aircraft hung at just the right height, and this artificial smoke was soon supplemented by smoke from the burning forests. Along this sector, between Forst and Muskau – now the border between Germany and Poland – a flood plain several hundred metres wide separates the west bank of the Neisse from slightly rising wooded ground. You can still find German trenches and machine-gun positions there, with a good field of fire across to the river. But all the luck was with Koniev that day. At 150 points along the Neisse, engineers were waiting with boats and bridges. Once the leading battalions had crossed in boats, small bridges were thrown across. By 09.00 the first of the bigger bridges, able to carry 30-tonne loads, was across, and next came 60-tonne bridges able to carry tanks and heavy artillery.

By the next day Koniev's front was halfway to Cottbus, while Zhukov's forces were still struggling across the open killing-field, impeded by drainage ditches, under murderous fire from the Seelow heights. Zhukov's people had advanced only 3 to 8 kilometres. Zhukov threw his two tank armies forward to try to blast a way through, which was not what they were meant for. The result was an ever more horrendous traffic jam in full view of German artillery and observers with a grandstand view from the heights. Stalin was furious with Zhukov for committing the tank armies without his permission, and Zhukov took it out on his commanders. Stalin toyed with Zhukov, reminding him that he could give Koniev permission to take the prize. The point was not lost on Zhukov. During 17 April Koniev's units forced the River Spree (see Figure 19.3). The bridging equipment had not caught up with them but there was talk of a ford, and a single T-34 with a hand-picked crew chanced it. The water turned out to be only a metre deep, and tank brigade after tank brigade followed.

Koniev's position – and accommodation – could not be more different from Zhukov's. While Zhukov moved from clay bunker to clay bunker with Stalin's ire and threats hanging over him, the aristocratic-looking Koniev found himself appropriately put up in a castle near Cottbus. Now that his forces were well past the Spree, he called Stalin, and asked for permission to turn his two tank armies, Lelyushenko's Third and Rybalko's Fourth Guards, on Berlin, by way of Zossen-Wünsdorf. Stalin asked if Koniev knew that Zossen was the headquarters of the 'German General Staff' – OKH, in fact. Koniev said he did. 'Very well,' said Stalin. 'I agree. Turn your tank armies on Berlin.'[58]

Zhukov's delay in capturing the Seelow heights, at enormous cost, and Koniev's incredibly rapid swing around the German right, raise two questions. Given that Zhukov was, effectively, stuck for three days, while Koniev had sailed past Lubben and was moving rapidly north into Berlin, a more forgiving regime might have accepted the flow of events and let Zhukov go over to the defensive, while reinforcing the spectacular success of Koniev's front. But even without Stalin in charge, who had pitted his top commanders against each other, Zhukov's personality would not have let that happen. He was competing with Koniev for the greatest prize of the war. Not only was he racing his Russian rival, but he may also have thought he was racing the British and Americans, although the US implementation of Eisenhower's directive on 14 April may have been communicated to him. (If Stalin had anything to do with it, it may not have been, providing another incentive.) Zhukov was supremely ambitious, and the idea of conceding the race would have been unthinkable. If he had to batter through the wall with his men's heads, then he would. Another national leader, and another commander, might well have agreed that First Belorussian should halt, and let First

Ukrainian take the city. But with Stalin, Zhukov and Koniev involved – no way.

The other question is why Koniev sped forward so much faster than Zhukov. The answer lies on the ground. In 2000 the author was reconnoitring a 'staff ride' – a battlefield tour – for the British Army. We headed from Berlin south-east, towards Koniev's crossing point over the Neisse, near Cottbus. The autobahn took us almost straight there. Strange, I thought, looking at the map, that the autobahn seemed to follow the axis of Koniev's advance, although, obviously, in the opposite direction. Surely there was no autobahn here in 1945? There was. A 1938 map showed that this was one of the first autobahns ever built. Marshal Koniev had 15,000 American lease-lend trucks, and an autobahn. No wonder he could move.

The next day, 18 April, Zhukov's troops finally fought their way off the Seelow heights, and on the 19th took Müncheberg. The day after, Rokossovskiy's Second Belorussian attacked in the north, across the Oder between Schwedt and Sczecin, securing several bridgeheads. Film of the river crossing shows them using American DUKW amphibious troop carriers, which came in very handy. The same day, Zhukov's front at last came within artillery range of Berlin and the Russian artillery opened a murderous fire on the German capital. Koniev's forces, approaching Berlin from the south, closed up to the German screening forces about 15 kilometres south of Zossen.

Koniev's swing around the German defences had trapped Busse's Ninth Army south-east of Berlin, in the Halbe area. On 22 April, Heinrici phoned General Hans Krebs, the OKH Chief of Staff, to say that unless Ninth Army was allowed to withdraw by nightfall, it would be split in two. That same Sunday Stavka ordered Zhukov and Koniev to complete the encirclement of the German group south-east of the capital by the 24th at the latest and prevent it from withdrawing west. Some of Ninth Army did break out, cutting across Koniev's northward approach to the city, but many died in the attempt. Konstantin Simonov, the writer and war correspondent (see Plate 51) encountered the results on the autobahn as he drove into the city just after the fighting ended:

> The German troops that had been fighting on the Oder when
> the fighting in Berlin had already started had used this route
> to try and thrust their way across the autobahn . . . amid this

chaos of iron, wood, weapons, baggage, papers, lay burnt and blackened objects that I couldn't identify, a mass of mutilated bodies. And this carnage extended across the cutting as far as I could see. All around in the woods there dead, dead and yet more dead, the corpses of those who fell while running under fire. Dead, and as I then saw, some alive among them . . . the whole of this vast column had come under fire from several regiments of heavy artillery and a few regiments of *Katyushas* that had previously been concentrated in the vicinity and had fired on the cutting on the assumption that the Germans would try to break through here . . .[59]

Simonov had been as much a supporter of the 'revenge' message as anyone. But even he was clearly appalled at what the Russians had done to their nearly vanquished foe. Out of 140,000 German soldiers in the pocket, between 30,000 and 60,000 were killed, plus thousands of civilians. They perished in yet another eastern front encirclement, but it was almost the last.[60] The German Twelfth Army moved from the west to try to extricate the Ninth, but failed.

The next day, 21 April, Koniev's forces captured the massive concrete bunkers of the OKH headquarters. at Zossen. The German armed forces had fled, leaving the deep and oppressive concrete catacombs strewn with printouts from teleprinters, maps and bits of German uniform. The telephones continued to ring, the remaining parts of the military command not realizing that the headquarters of the Supreme Command of the Army – responsible for the war against Russia – was now in Russian hands. A telephone rang, and the person on the other end asked to speak to a German general. A Russian soldier, probably drunk, answered. '*Vot Ivan. Vy mozhete* . . .' – 'Ivan here. You can . . .'[61]

The British and Americans had bombed Zossen just once, but mostly left it alone, probably deliberately. The German high command had to be based somewhere, and since the British were now decoding not only Enigma messages but also, with the aid of the world's first computer, Colossus, the twelve-rotor Lorentz system, there was no point in killing the goose that was laying golden eggs.[62] The Russians now took over the headquarters complex, which dated back to the Kaiser's day, and later turned it into the headquarters of the Group of Soviet Forces, Germany. Since the end of the cold war, and German reunification, it has been redeveloped as a dormitory for Berlin professionals,

39. Zhukov (right) and Koniev (centre).

40. Ilyushin-2 Shturmovik ground attack planes over Berlin.

41. German prisoners being marched through the streets of Moscow.

42. Rokossovskiy in the new, post-15 January 1943, uniform.

43. The cruiser *Paris Commune* firing in defence of Sevastopol, 1941.

44. Churchill and Molotov, during Molotov's visit to Britain, May 1942.

45. The 'big three': Churchill, Roosevelt, and Stalin at Yalta, February 1945.

46. Revenge of the bear: after the destruction of the Army Group Centre, illustrated by the broken rifle, vengeful Russia advances on Hitler's Germany.

47. Red flag over the Reichstag. Re-enactment of 2 May
– the unretouched version. Note the watches.

48. Yevgeniy Khaldei,
war photographer,
in Berlin. The tank
behind him is the
new JS-II.

49. Victory in Berlin. Maria Shalneva, Soviet traffic policewoman, in Berlin.

50. German prisoners of the Russians at the end of the war.

51. The writer Konstantin Simonov, with the Soviet forces as a war correspondent.

52. Unconditional surrender: Keitel signs for Germany at one of the ceremonies. The official capitulation was signed by Jodl, the designated representative of the German 'state' – what was left of it.

53. The 'United Nations' – the four powers that will occupy Germany –
witness the surrender. Zhukov represents the Soviet Union.

54. Stalin and his generals.

55. Zhukov, Rokossovskiy, Sokolovskiy and Vasilevskiy in Berlin after the award of British honours.

56. The end of Nazi Germany – and Austria.

and the oppressive and claustrophobic bunkers which the Russians took over in April 1945 or built afterwards are open to the public.[63]

On 24 April at 06.00, units of the two Russian fronts made contact near the Schonefeld airfield: Chuikov's Eighth Guards from Zhukov's front and Rybalko's Third Guards Tank from Koniev's. In a careless but perhaps understandable manifestation of the fog of war, none of the front or army headquarters knew where the other front's people were, and there were serious 'friendly fire' incidents. Zhukov demanded to know about Koniev's advance into Berlin – the professional relationship between senior commanders was as good as ever. A few hours later Rybalko arrived at Chuikov's headquarters and phoned Zhukov, who was no doubt gratified to know the reports were true.

Zhukov could feel more secure now. The day before, Stalin had confirmed that the boundary between the fronts would run just 150 metres west of the Reichstag, the final objective of the Soviet forces, effectively shutting Koniev out of the prize-winning position.[64]

The next day brought even bigger link-ups. West of Berlin, the outer pincers of the fronts met at Ketzin, completing the encirclement of Berlin. The Russians did not want German forces, and particularly Hitler's ruling elite, to get away. On the same day, 25 April, the Americans of 69th Infantry Division met up with Soviet troops from 58th Division of Zhadov's Fifth Guards Army at three places along the river near Strela and Torgau, 30 kilometres to the north. Koniev's report to Stalin was very precise about times and places. The Americans had colour film cameras on hand to record the official link-up between the two future superpowers, or, as it was described then, the *United Nations*, at 16.40, German time, on 25 April 1945. The film is very moving. The Russians, their officers wearing shoulder boards with real gold braid, carried sophisticated cameras, probably looted. But for all the faults of both parties, for a brief moment, the world was in unison against evil.[65]

Hitler's last appearance in the public eye was on his fifty-sixth birthday on 20 April. He refused to take his last chance to escape from Berlin on 22 April, but let his OKW staff escape to the north and join OKH – who had vacated Zossen – and Grand-Admiral Dönitz, who would succeed Hitler as Führer. They set up headquarters at Mürwik in Schleswig-Holstein. After Hitler's death on 30 April this little-known place became the last capital of the Third Reich, for the remaining week of its monstrous twelve-year existence. On 26 April nearly half a million

Russian troops broke into the central area of Berlin (see Figure 19.3). Here, the high concrete flak towers, built to give anti-aircraft guns a better field of fire at American B-17s and British Lancasters, and also containing massive air-raid shelters, acquired a new purpose. The guns could also fire down into the streets, and were a major hazard to the attackers. The zoo flak tower had eight 128mm anti-aircraft guns, which could also take out any tank in existence – today, as well as then – and twelve multi-barrelled 20mm or 37mm cannon. But inside, and in cellars throughout the spacious, elegant, once ultra-modern city, German civilians now sheltered, some driven insane by the intensity of shellfire, others fearing a horrible death at the hands of the avenging Russians, or Nazi werewolf units ready to string up anyone who showed the slightest inclination to give in. And for the women, in particular, there was the hideous spectre of multiple rape, not only condoned but, we can be pretty sure, legally sanctioned by the political officers speaking for the Soviet government.[66]

The Russian soldiers did not limit themselves to German women, either, and nor, even, did the 'gentlemen correspondents' accompanying the glorious Red Army. 'Soviet girls liberated from the camps are suffering a lot now,' Grossman, a war correspondent, recalled, even before reaching Berlin. 'Tonight, some of them are hiding in our correspondents' room. During the night, we were woken up by screams: one of the correspondents couldn't resist the temptation . . .'[67] It has long been thought that the atrocities were committed mainly by follow-on units and that the front-line soldiers were too busy – and too tired – to get involved. But that is not so. Grossman was accompanying units of the elite Eighth Guards Army, who would storm the centre of Berlin. Even they committed atrocities.

The Russian plan to capture the city centre envisaged breaking it up into blocks and then working through them, 300 per day. They used their artillery – even the heaviest – to fire straight at buildings. One technique was to work in teams of three guns, two light and one heavy. The lighter guns would fire smoke rounds to mask a building, and then a massive 203mm howitzer would be rolled out to demolish the building with a round or two. The Germans fought on fanatically, but the Russians, scenting imminent victory, piled resources in. Along the Unter den Linden, 500 guns were drawn up along a one-kilometre stretch – wheel to wheel – and fired. Sometimes a hail of a thousand shells would crash on a target. So terrifying was the effect of this constant hail of

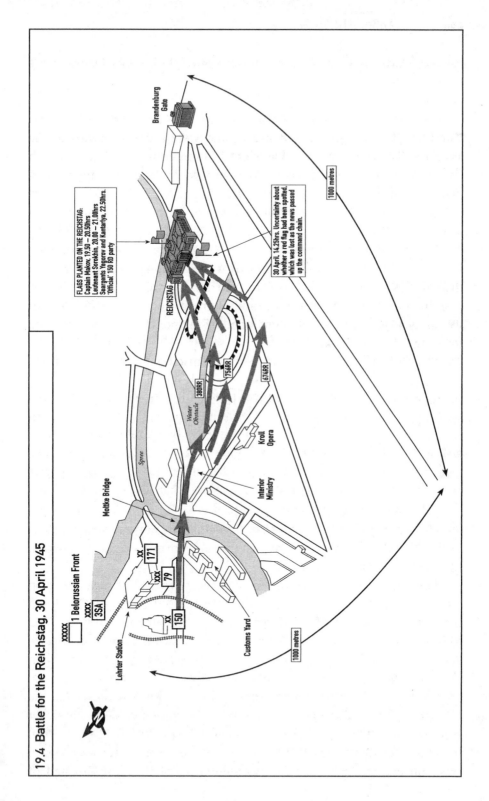

19.4 Battle for the Reichstag, 30 April 1945

Lehrter Station

XXXXX
◻ 1 Belorussian Front

XXXX
◻ 3SA

XXX
◻ 79

XX
◻ 171

XX
◻ 150

Customs Yard

Moltke Bridge

Spree

Interior Ministry

Kroll Opera

Water Obstacle

380RR

756RR

674RR

REICHSTAG

FLAGS PLANTED ON THE REICHSTAG:
Captain Makov, 19.50 – 20.50hrs
Lieutenant Sorokhin, 20.00 – 21.00hrs
Seargents Yegorov and Kantariya, 22.50hrs.
'Official' 150 RD party

30 April, 14.25hrs. Uncertainty about whether a red flag had been spotted, which was lost as the news passed up the command chain.

Brandenburg Gate

1000 metres

1000 metres

shot and shell that out of 130 prisoners taken in the cellars of the Air Ministry, 'seventeen *had gone mad*'.[68]

On 28 April the Russians seized the bridge on the Potsdamerstraße, to the south of the central sector, and began to fight their way through the zoo – the *Tiergarten* – where one of the huge flak towers stood, in the face of ferocious SS opposition. That evening, forces of First Belorussian Front seized the Moltke Bridge over the Spree, now the Willy Brandt Bridge, north-west of the Reichstag (see Figure 19.4). The Germans had tried to blow it, but failed. On 29th Soviet artillery based in the Customs Yard area north of the Spree opened fire on the Interior Ministry building at 07.00, while infantry broke into the zoo area, where they could fire up at the flak tower from the hippopotamus house, one of whose occupants survived.

Hitler was by now firmly underground, in his hermetically sealed bunker under the Reichs Chancellery, just south of the Branbdenburg Gate. On the evening of 28 April Weidling, the commander of the Berlin garrison, reported to Hitler. He later told a Russian interrogator that Hitler was, by then, 'a sick, broken man'.[69] The final battle conference in the *Führerbunker* took place the next evening. Weidling told Hitler that there was no ammunition, no more *Panzerfausts*, no way of repairing tanks, and no air resupply. The fighting was bound to end within the next twenty-four hours. In a tired voice, Hitler asked what SS Colonel Mohnke, the commander of the *Führerbunker*, thought. He said he could only agree. Weidling asked what should happen when the defenders ran out of ammunition. 'Break out in small groups,' said Hitler. But Berlin was *not* to be surrendered. That was all.[70]

Why the Reichstag?

Why was the Reichstag, the German parliament building, the Russians' prime objective? Target number 105, in fact, on the Red Army's target list. The answer is that in any war, especially a big war against a powerful country, the moment of 'victory' is hard to define. It is even more difficult now than it was at the time.[71] The Reichstag had been a burnt-out shell for twelve years, since 1933, and the history of 'parliamentary

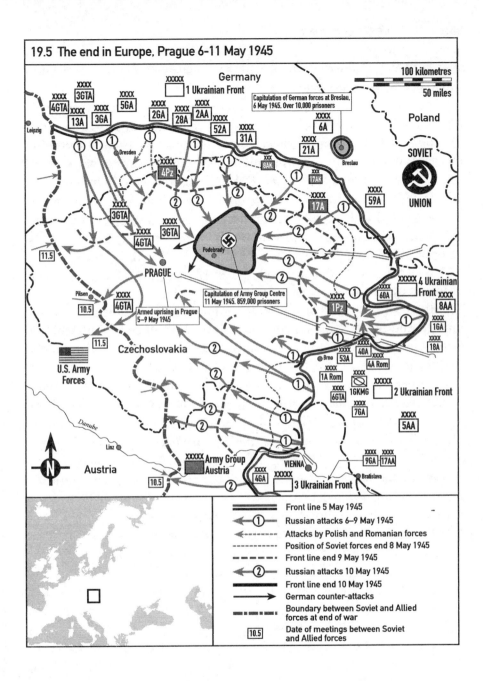

19.5 The end in Europe, Prague 6–11 May 1945

Germany

1 Ukrainian Front

Unit label	Designation
XXXX	3GTA
XXXX	4GTA
XXXX	13A
XXXX	5GA
XXXX	3GA
XXXX	2GA
XXXX	28A
XXXX	2AA
XXXX	52A
XXXX	31A

Capitulation of German forces at Breslau, 6 May 1945. Over 10,000 prisoners

XXXX 6A

XXXX 21A

Breslau

Leipzig

Dresden

4Pz

XXX 8AK

XXX 17AK

Poland

100 kilometres

50 miles

SOVIET

UNION

XXXX 3GTA

XXXX 3GTA

Podebrady

XXXX 4GTA

11.5

PRAGUE

Capitulation of Army Group Centre 11 May 1945. 859,000 prisoners

XXXX 17A

XXXX 59A

Pilsen

10.5

XXXX 4GTA

Armed uprising in Prague 5–9 May 1945

11.5

Czechoslovakia

U.S. Army Forces

Danube

Linz

Austria

N

Army Group Austria

1Pz

XXXXX 4 Ukrainian Front

XXXX 60A

XXXX 8AA

XXXX 16A

XXXX 18A

Brno

XXXX 53A

XXXX 1A Rom

XXXX 4A Rom

XXXX 6GTA

XXXX 1GKMG

XXXX 76A

XXXXX 2 Ukrainian Front

XXXX 5AA

VIENNA

Bratislava

XXXX 96A

XXXX 17AA

XXXX 4GA

3 Ukrainian Front

10.5

Legend	
———	Front line 5 May 1945
←—①	Russian attacks 6–9 May 1945
←----	Attacks by Polish and Romanian forces
----------	Position of Soviet forces end 8 May 1945
—·—·—	Front line end 9 May 1945
←—②	Russian attacks 10 May 1945
———	Front line end 10 May 1945
→	German counter-attacks
■—■—■	Boundary between Soviet and Allied forces at end of war
10.5	Date of meetings between Soviet and Allied forces

democracy' in Germany, whether under the Kaiser, when it was built in 1894, or under Hitler, was hardly a glorious one.

The cry 'on to the Reichstag' first became widespread after Kursk. The burnt-out bricked-up old shell was pretty meaningless in terms of Germany's ability to fight the war, which had largely been destroyed in Belarus in 1944; to organize resistance, which was in tatters and eliminated after the capture of OKH headquarters at Zossen; and even in terms of its top political leadership, which was high on drugs metres below ground and about to commit suicide. According to political logic, the Reichs Chancellery and Hitler's bunker below it, to the south, beyond the Brandenburg Gate, should have been the priority target. However, the Reichstag had all the attributes needed for an iconic victory symbol. It was a huge and imposing building, even if charred and bricked up. It was isolated, and therefore identifiable, clearly separate from the surrounding buildings and streets. It was also a formidable fortress and the obvious Russian intention to take it made it a focus for SS and Hitler Youth fighters, thousands of whom had pulled back to the Reichstag as the Russians closed in. But the catalyst, perhaps, is the inscription above the main entrance: *Dem deutschen Volke* – 'To the German people'. Given what the 'German people' had done to Russia, where better to give them the final payback?

When it comes to 'defining victory', images and icons matter – the raising of the US flag over Iwo Jima, the felling of Saddam Hussein's statue in Baghdad in 2003. There were dozens of statues of Saddam Hussein in Baghdad. But the world's cameras needed just one.

The attack on the Reichstag was therefore a genuine military necessity. But it would also be the most effective demonstration to the Germans, to the Russians – military and civilian – and to the Russians' Allies and the rest of the world, that Russia had beaten Nazi Germany. In the current scientific jargon, it was an 'effects-based operation'. The effect? *Let the world know we've won.*

The Reichstag and its surroundings are shown in Figure 19.4. The Spree curves round to the north, and to the north-west of the Reichstag there was a huge hole, which had been the beginnings of a monstrous dome, one of Hitler's architectural schemes, so big that clouds would have formed inside it. Before the war, the Germans had also started excavating an underground (tube or subway) line to the new monstrosity, which, like the big hole, had filled with water, creating a major obstacle.

The Russians approached the Reichstag from the west and north-west, working through the Interior Ministry and the Kroll Opera. Soviet estimates of the opposition in the area were about 5,000 German fighters of various kinds, although German estimates are much lower: an unknown number of Allgemeine SS in the Interior Ministry, a company of a hundred potential NCOs between the bridge, the Reichstag and the Brandenburg Gate. The Reichstag was a substantial fortress, however, and even a few German troops could inflict disproportionate damage on attackers.

Stalin wanted the Reichstag taken by May Day, and nearly a million troops of Zhukov's Belorussian Front just wanted it all to end. At midday on 30 April troops of 150th and 171st Rifle Divisions of LXXIX Corps, Third Shock Army, took up their final assault positions. Each of the nine rifle divisions in Third Shock had been issued with a specially made, adapted Soviet flag. As Plate 47 shows, the hammer and sickle was much larger than on the normal Soviet Union flag. The whole world would be watching, and this was a hammer and sickle on steroids. The first man or woman to raise the Soviet flag over the Reichstag would get the gold star medal of a Hero of the Soviet Union. By noon on 30 April, 150th Division had earmarked two sergeants, Yegorov and Kantariya, as the 'official' red banner party. But there were plenty of other people willing to have a go. The first attempt was by the Soviet air force. The 115th Fighter Regiment managed to drop some 6-metre-wide red silk panels with *pobeda* – 'victory' – on them onto the roof, but they slid off, and that probably did not count, anyway. At 13.00, under a blanket of covering fire from *Katyusha* rocket launchers, heavy guns and even captured *Panzerfausts*, three rifle regiments of 150th Division careered across the deadly ground, littered with debris, barbed wire and mines, west of the great charred shell of a building. From his head-quarters in the Customs Yard area, Major-General Shatilov, command-ing 150th Rifle Division, was watching from about 600 metres away (see Figure 19.4). At 14.25 he reported that he *thought* he saw, through the smoke and explosions, a red flag flying from the right-hand side of the columned entrance. That went straight up the chain of command to LXXIX Corps, Third Shock Army, and Marshal Zhukov, Stalin's Deputy. Zhukov, who was waiting to tell the world, did so: 'Units of the Third Shock Army, having broken the resistance of the enemy, have captured the Reichstag and hoisted our Soviet flag on it today, April 30th 1945 at 14.25 hours.'[72]

The message went round the world, to TASS, and to Reuters. But Zhukov was wrong. When the war correspondents descended on the area, they found the Russian troops still pinned down only halfway across the approach to the building, the Königsplatz.

Shatilov probably came close to living up to his name. Zhukov had said it had happened. Therefore it must happen. 'Somehow you have to hoist a flag or a pennant, screamed Shatilov, 'even on the columns at the main entrance. Somehow!'[73]

The men of 150th Division, with a picked team including Yegorov and Kantariya clutching the red banner, somehow got over the flooded excavation for the thousand-year Reich underground railway project, and charged into the Reichstag up the central staircase. Yegorov and Kantariya were not, in fact, the first to raise a red banner. A group of Russian artillerymen – who regarded themselves as the elite – under Captain Makov raised a flag on the Goddess of Victory statue on the front of the building at around 21.00, to be followed fifteen minutes later by a team from Lt Sergey Sorokhin's reconnaissance platoon. Makov, being a gunner, had a radio which enabled him to report to the corps commander. Both these groups got the Order of the Red Banner but the coveted gold stars still went to the 'official' party. Yegorov and Kantariya were recorded as signalling victory at 22.50, within the deadline and before May Day in Moscow.[74] There were still German troops inside the building, and fighting continued for another twenty-four hours.

Well before Yegorov and Kantariya had raised their flag, it was dark. Early on the morning of 2 May, Yevgeniy Khaldei, the pre-eminent Soviet photographer of the war, who was with the Red Army in uniform, secured a dizzy re-enactment. He shot a whole sequence of photographs, one of which is shown at Plate 47. The flag was raised at the highest point, but the photographer and the two sergeants have changed places, so Khaldei is looking down on them. That way, he gets the wonderful detail of the Brandenburg gate and people moving apparently peaceably through a now quiet city. These photographs are among the most famous of the entire war. In terms of communicating the victory message, they are masterly. However, the photograph here shows the man holding his colleague's legs wearing two watches, one on each wrist. They are obviously 'liberated' from some German citizens, or a jeweller's. That same night Khaldei flew to Moscow with the reel of 36 photographs, and they were published immediately. A few months later a TASS editor noticed the additional watch. That was not the message Stalin or the Red Army wanted to send out, so Khaldei was ordered to paint out the watch on the right wrist.[75]

The end in Berlin

Khaldei could not re-enact the event sooner, because fighting was still going on. That same night, 30 April, the Russians learned of Hitler's suicide. At 01.00 on 30 April Keitel had reported that all the German forces attempting to relieve Berlin had stopped and been encircled and forced onto the defensive. Hitler then decided to kill himself. The day before, he had dictated his 'political testament', dismissed Albert Speer, the industry tsar, who had ultimately failed to deliver the impossible in the face of Allied (including Soviet) production superiority, and appointed Dönitz as his successor. Then he married his long-standing girlfriend, Eva Braun, in a bizarrely normal ceremony. Goebbels and his wife and children were there. The next day, the 30th, about an hour after the first sighting of an illusory red flag around the second floor of the Reichstag, Hitler and Eva Braun retired to his study, and bit into cyanide capsules. Their bodies were then taken up to the surface, and burned. There have been many stories that Hitler escaped, that the body found was a 'double', and so on. All can be dismissed. An NKVD forensic team later analysed the evidence. Hitler, who had so misguidedly attacked Russia, was dead.

At 23.30 on 30 April a German lieutenant colonel, Seifert, approached the Russian lines between Fifth Shock and Eighth Guards Armies. He said he had 'important papers for the attention of the Soviet command'. Arrangements were made for Krebs, OKH Chief of Staff, to meet the Eighth Guards' commander, Chuikov. The man who had held the centre at Stalingrad had planned a celebration dinner with his colleagues. Now, desperate for sleep, he would conduct negotiations for the German surrender. Krebs eventually reached Chuikov's headquarters at 03.50 on 1 May. He said that Hitler had committed suicide on 30 April, about twelve hours before.

'We know that,' said Chuikov.

They did now.

The negotiations continued until the middle of 1 May when Chuikov, exasperated, ordered every single Russian gun, mortar and rocket-launcher within range to blast the Reichstag, where SS men were still skulking in the basement, the Chancellery and government office buildings. Then, after further German equivocation, an even bigger bombardment ensued. The Germans in the basement of the Reichstag said they would only surrender to a Russian general, so Lieutenant Berest, a suitably big and imposing man, played the part. The Russians also learned that Goebbels had killed himself on 1 May. Eventually, around 07.00 on 2 May, Weidling, commander of the Berlin garrison, came to see Chuikov. The Russians persuaded him to draft an order to all German forces in Berlin to 'cease resistance forthwith'. Weidling picked up a pen, and started to write. The Führer had committed suicide, so oaths of loyalty to him no longer applied, and ammunition had run out. Further resistance was senseless. Sokolovskiy, the Chief of the General Staff and Chuikov said it was all right. At 15.00 on 2 May Russian guns ceased fire in Berlin.[76] The Third Reich was destroyed, and in the absolute war between the world's most absolute powers, accelerated by the opening of the second front nearly a year before, the Russians had won.

In order to take Berlin as fast as possible, the Russians had not worried about casualties – not that they ever did, much. In the twenty-three days of the Berlin operation they suffered 78,291 irrecoverable losses, and with the expected three-to-one ratio of sick and wounded – 274,184. Overall, their casualties were 15,325 a day. That was more than Belorussia, nearly double Vistula-Oder, more than either of the Kursk counteroffensives, half as many again as the Moscow counteroffensive and, with one exception, the highest daily loss rate overall since the frontier battles of 1941. Zhukov's First Belorussian Front, which had been hurled at the brick wall of the Seelow heights, lost a total of 37,610 killed, prisoners and missing; Koniev's First Ukrainian 27,580.[77] The price of victory – and of bull-headed determination to beat the other guy – was very high.

It was not quite the end. To the south, Schörner's Army Group Centre was effectively encircled east of Prague by Soviet and, more distantly, American forces (see Figure 19.5). Whereas the demarcation line in the north had been clearly marked on the Elbe, that in the south was more fuzzy and the Russians resolved to eliminate the last German groupings as swiftly as possible. At the beginning of May nationalist risings broke out all over Czechoslovakia and on 5 May there was a popular rising in Prague. Eisenhower proposed to the Russians that the Americans might now head that way, but was told sharply to stay out. The situation in Prague was particularly messy because among the German-controlled forces were Vlasov's KONR – Russian 'liberation army' divisions. They had helped put down the 1944 Warsaw rising. The Czechs appealed to them, as fellow Slavs, to join them, but Vlasov wanted to stay with the Germans. Uppermost in all their minds, undoubtedly, was the desperate wish to surrender to the Americans, rather than be caught by the Russians who would have no mercy on them. The 1st KONR division had an exceptionally hard time, joining the Czechs, and then being trapped and forced to fight alongside the Waffen SS. Schörner's troops were the last Germans to keep fighting. The Germans surrendered unconditionally at Reims on 7 May but there was no guarantee that German forces would obey the order. On 8 May at 20.00 Koniev transmitted surrender terms to all German units in western Czechoslovakia and gave them three hours to respond. When they did not, he did what the Russians had done in Berlin, and ordered a massive artillery strike. The Russians resumed their operations. To the West the war was over, but the Russians had to keep fighting for another day, until 9 May, which is one of the two reasons why they celebrate VE day a day later than the British and Americans do. And also, there was the time difference. By the time peace was initially signed, late on the German western front on 8 May, it was already 9 May in the east. In the early hours of 9 May, Lelyushenko's Fourth Guards Tank Army which, not long before, had been in Berlin, raced into Prague.

Lelyushenko reported: 'remaining fascist resistance destroyed. Many prisoners . . . there are no American forces'.[78] The Great Patriotic War – the worst ever war – really was over. There was just a little more business to attend to.

20

NEW WORLD ORDER

Picking up the pieces

The first troops into Berlin had been from Colonel-General Nikolay Berzarin's Fifth Shock Army. Berzarin had been with Chuikov during the negotiations with Weidling. Zhukov made him commandant of the fallen city – an inspired choice. Grossman had been in Moscow, but was called back to Berlin for the big story. The Front military council member, Telegin, who was in charge of media handling, told the correspondents they could choose to accompany any army. But, he said, 'please don't all go to Chuikov'.[1] Grossman attached himself to Berzarin. He described him as 'fat, brown-eyed, arched over, with white hair, although he is young. He is clever, very calm and resourceful.'[2] Even before the fighting stopped in Berlin on 2 May Berzarin took measures to start restoring essential services. The Red Army brought up its soup kitchens to feed the shell-shocked Berliners. The looting and rape gradually subsided, and the Russians appointed 'reliable' Germans to head each city block, and organize the clearing-up. The Berliners loved Berzarin, and when he was killed in a motorbike accident some weeks later it was rumoured that he had been removed by the NKVD.

The Russians, like the western Allies, had carefully planned the rebuilding and de-Nazification of Germany. German communists came out of hiding, expecting to be welcomed by the Russians, but instead were ignored or treated with contempt. Why had they not resisted the Nazis, as partisans? That aroused suspicion. The Russians were also overwhelmed by the wealth – or remains of wealth – they found in this sophisticated city. 'Our soldiers have seen the two-storey suburban houses with electricity, gas, bathrooms and beautifully tended gardens,' wrote Berzarin. 'Our people have seen the villas of the rich bourgeoisie in Berlin, the unbelievable luxury of castles, estates and mansions. And thousands of soldiers repeat these angry questions when they look around here in Germany. "But why did they come to us? What did they want?" '3

At Tehran the big three had set up a European Advisory Commission on what to do with Germany when it was defeated. In March 1944 the Commission had completed its plan, with Germany divided into three zones corresponding to the likely direction of the approaching armies. The Russians got the east, the British the north of the other side and the Americans the south. That went back to the planning for D-Day because the British were on the left of the Allied landings and the Americans, who had arrived in England later and also had to cross the Atlantic, were on the right. When they swung through 90 degrees, that put the British in the north and the Americans in the south. The British and American zones were reduced when, at Yalta, France was also given a share. Berlin was to be divided between the four powers, although a proposal by Roosevelt to give the western Allies a corridor to Berlin from the Elbe, also agreed at Yalta as the demarcation line between east and west, was overlooked. The western Allies took possession of their zones of Berlin on 9 July, after the city had been completely under Russian control for two months. The Allied Control Commission for Germany had come into operation on 22 June. In the immediate aftermath of the war, all of Germany was a dangerous place: there was massive violence and disorder, and foreign civilian visitors were warned how dangerous it was. The western Allies began a process of de-Nazification, while the Russians concentrated initially on plundering their sector for industrial and military equipment. In early 1945 they had overrun a complete German rocket factory in Thuringia and 200 rocket scientists were transported back to the Soviet Union. The Americans allowed elections in their sector in January 1946, the beginning of a process which led to the formation of the Federal Republic of Germany on 21 September 1949. On 7 October the German Democratic Republic, under communist government, was formed in the Russian occupation zone. The surrender signed by German representatives on 7 May 1945 had only been an armistice. Britain and America ended their state of war with the Federal Republic in 1951: the USSR followed in 1955.4 The erasure of Nazi Germany and its short-lived dominions in the east created an enormous political and ethnic minefield, which the victors agreed to address at the Terminal conference in the Cecilienhof palace at Potsdam, just outside Berlin, from 17 July to 2 August 1945.

Black and white knights

Meanwhile, back in Moscow, Yuri Levitan had announced the news of the German surrender early on 9 May. As in London, Paris, New York and countless other great cities, Moscow had a party. An estimated 3 million people thronged the streets and squares around the Kremlin during the next day, and when the sun set the searchlights were turned on the Kremlin, turning the formidable citadel into a passable antici-pation of a Disneyland fantasy. The government had long expected and prepared for this day. Its stage management was always very good. A spectacular firework display, preceded by planes dropping flares, had been organized. For a day or so everyone celebrated, before they came to face the cost of victory.[5]

Soviet Russia's role in the victory over the Third Reich, a triumph which far eclipsed that of Tsar Alexander in the victory over Napoleon, also demanded a traditional military celebration. The victory parade in Moscow was set for 24 June. Stalin was going to take the salute, but military tradition dictated he should do so on horseback, and he was not the world's best horseman. The Russians found a beautiful white Arab stallion, called Kumir – 'Beloved'. Stalin could not master the fiery steed, and it may have thrown him, which could have been very dangerous for the 66-year-old dictator and, given the way Stalin treated people who upset him, possibly also for the horse. Stalin must have been very shaken, because he let Zhukov take the salute instead. The Imperial Russian cavalry knew how to teach its NCOs to ride, and Zhukov recalls the arduous brutality of the process in his memoirs. The cavalryman mastered the Arab easily. As for the parade commander, who better than another cavalryman whose torture, humiliation, sur-vival, resilience and ultimate military greatness mirrored the experience of Soviet Russia herself. Marshal Konstantin Rokossovskiy would com-mand the parade on a black horse, perhaps an allusion to his comeback from the GULag, called Polus – 'Pole'. As the film of the parade shows, both Marshals were superb horsemen. In the face of thunderous shouts from thousands of assembled troops, they controlled their horses in a meticulous display of dressage.

The day of the victory parade dawned grey and wet. Rain poured down on the Red Square cobbles. All along the front of the GUM shopping arcade facing the Kremlin across Red Square ranks of soldiers beneath their Fronts' banners stood to attention. Banners bearing the badges of all the Soviet republics hung from the front of the building while, across the square, on Lenin's Mausoleum, Stalin and the Politburo watched. Zhukov and Rokossovskiy emerged from the Kremlin's Spasskaya tower gate at 10.00. Zhukov galloped along the line. Khaldei had been on the Spasskaya tower but somehow got down to ground level and released the shutter, one of just two shots he took of the entire parade. Years later, in 1972, Marshal Zhukov asked him for an enlargement. 'Why so few?' he asked.

'My knees were shaking. I couldn't run any more. My legs betrayed me,' replied the photographer.

'Do you think that I felt any different?' said Zhukov. 'The horse seemed to move by itself through Red Square. It was as if there was a fog all around. I thought of the soldiers who had fallen and could not be there at the parade. Now I'll tell you why I like the photograph. In your picture the horse has all four legs in the air, so that I am floating, too.'[6]

Maybe Zhukov had mellowed a little with age. But, in contrast to much that has been said about him, this was not a man without sensitivity.

At the end of the parade there was a spectacular piece of theatre. A group of 200 soldiers – many of them officers – had been selected and for some time before the parade they practised, day and night, throwing poles at the Kremlin wall. Onlookers, and the soldiers themselves, must have wondered what on earth this was for. On 24 June they were formed up, but instead of poles they were each given a captured German ensign or standard. Fëdor Legkoshur was given Hitler's personal standard, with the words 'Adolf Hitler' beneath a swastika ringed by a laurel wreath and surmounted by an eagle. He did not want it, saying the thought of touching it disgusted him. It was explained that this was a mark of special esteem, so he took it. At the end of the parade, at 11.25, Moscow radio called a minute's silence. Some eighty drums began to beat. The drummers moved forward, followed by the 200 men. Starting with Hitler's, they hurled the captured flags end standards contemptuously towards the wall in a flawless, now perfectly practised manoeuvre and then, having thrown them, moved smartly aside.[7]

The captured standards can now be seen in the Central Museum of the Armed Forces in Moscow, beneath a huge photograph of the final humbling of the Third Reich. The immaculate standard bearers are often described as members of the Red Army. They were not, and that says something very important about the entire conduct of Soviet Russia's war effort. They were from the 1st Division of the NKVD – another reminder that more than half a million NKVD troops were crucial to the war effort, and the final guarantee of Russia's state security.

By the time Zhukov and Rokossovskiy rode their white and black horses across the square, they were also recognized as knights by their 'class enemies'. Soon after the fall of Berlin, the British Field Marshal Bernard Montgomery had presented orders of chivalry to the senior Soviet commanders.[8] Only just over a month before, Stalin and his commanders had been worried that Montgomery or Bradley might take Berlin. Again, mistrust and suspicion were forgotten in a good-humoured moment (captured in Plate 55). It would not last for long.

Potsdam

The final Allied conference of the war opened at Potsdam on 17 July. Roosevelt was dead and the new President of the United States, Harry S. Truman, arrived with his Secretary of State, James Byrnes. Stalin came by train, in one of Beria's most elaborate security operations, and Churchill was accompanied by Foreign Secretary Eden and also, in a sensible move, Clement Attlee, who would become Prime Minister when Churchill lost the 1945 general election. In the Declaration of Potsdam on 26 July the leaders of the big three called on Japan to surrender. The Japanese, who were not at war with Russia, accepted via Moscow but with so many conditions that it amounted to a refusal. Many questions on post-war Europe were referred to a new Council of Foreign Ministers, but the main issue to emerge was Japan and the atomic bomb. The

Americans had successfully test-fired their complex plutonium bomb, the 'Gadget', at Alamogordo, New Mexico, on 16 July. Stalin had been kept fully informed of western bomb developments through the NKGB since 1942, but decided to play dumb. On 24 July Truman told him 'casually' that 'we had a new weapon of unusual destructive force'. Stalin, Truman recalled, 'showed no special interest. All he said was he was glad to hear it and hoped we would make "good use of it against the Japanese".'[9] According to Burns, Truman was afraid that if Stalin knew the power of the weapon and its potential to terminate the conflict in the Pacific, he might be tempted to declare war on Japan sooner and gain successes which the President felt the Russians did not deserve. Zhukov, who was not in on all the meetings, but was there, said that many British and American authors assumed Stalin had not appreciated the significance of what he had been told. Of course he had. He did not even need to be an actor to appear unimpressed, since he knew already. Later, in Zhukov's presence, Stalin told Molotov about the conversation. 'They're raising the price,' he said. 'Let them. We'll have a talk with Kurchatov and get him to speed things up.'[10] Molotov let slip that 'they couldn't yet unleash a war, that they had only one or two atomic bombs'. Even if they had a few more, that was still not enough to pose a significant threat to the Soviet Union. So, at the end of July 1945 the Russians knew roughly how many bombs the US had in its arsenal.[11] The reason why the Soviet intelligence was so good went back to a far-sighted decision made at Quebec in August 1943. They had agreed that not only would Britain, Canada and the US not use atomic bombs against each other – which showed great foresight, as the things did not yet exist – but they would also not use them against third parties without the others' consent. Britain and Canada therefore had a veto on the American use of nuclear weapons. Before the first bombs were dropped, the Combined Policy Committee (CPC) had to meet to approve it. Among the British representatives on the CPC and probably present at the meeting was a certain young British diplomat called Donald Maclean – an NKGB agent.[12]

Manchuria

Following their non-aggression treaty of 1941, Japan and the Soviet Union enjoyed the benefits of each other's neutrality in their own wars. The fact that the Soviet Union was not at war with Japan helped American aid reach it. But in April 1945 the Russians indicated that they would not renew the non-aggression treaty with Japan when it expired in a year's time. The Japanese correctly deduced that the Soviet Union would join the war against them as soon as it had finished with Germany in Europe. Stalin had committed himself at Yalta to war with Japan and by the Potsdam conference Russian plans had firmed up. Soviet Russia would attack Japan three months, to the day, after victory in Europe. That meant the night of 8 to 9 August, and the morning of the second atomic bomb strike on Nagasaki.

While the western Allies planned a massive amphibious operation, scheduled for 1946, the Russians did not need to cross the sea to destroy a very significant component of Japanese military power. Since 1941 they had kept a wary eye on the massive Kwantung Army which occupied the Japanese puppet state of Manchukuo, headed by the last Emperor of China who had been thrown out in 1911. Russian concern about the offensive potential of the Kwantung Army led them to retain forty divisions in the Far Eastern and Trans-Baikal Military Districts during the war. The 1941 treaty provided nominal protection but so had the Molotov-Ribbentrop Pact, and look what had happened to that. The Kwantung Army was in fact a theatre command, comprising two 'Area Armies' or army groups, equivalent to Soviet fronts, and a separate Combined Army (see Figure 20.1). In addition to Japanese troops there were also Manchukuoan and Inner Mongolian auxiliaries. All told, the forces facing the Russians in the Far East in August 1945 numbered 1.2 million men.[13] These included not only forces in Manchuria proper, but also those in Japanese-held south Sakhalin. Japanese forces were also in China, fighting Mao Tse Tung (Mao Zhedong) and Chiang Kai-Shek. The Soviet operation would therefore spill over into China. Manchuria covers 1.5 million square kilometres – making it about three times the size of France. The terrain of the area is extraordinarily varied, from the

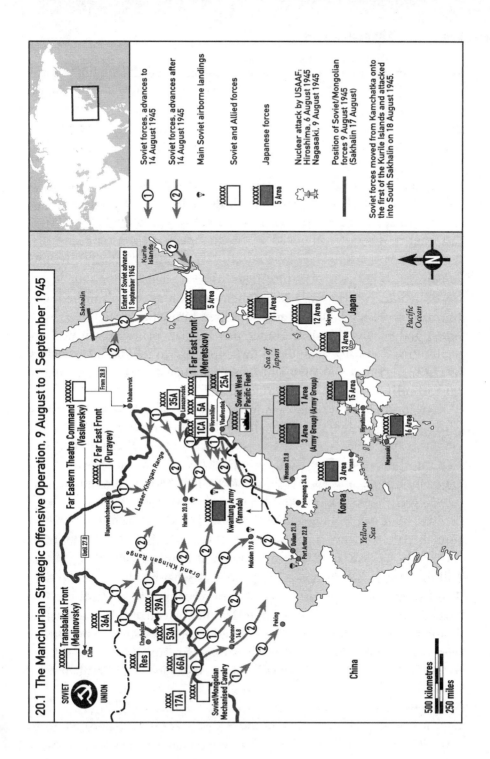

20.1 The Manchurian Strategic Offensive Operation. 9 August to 1 September 1945

Soviet forces, advances to 14 August 1945

Soviet forces, advances after 14 August 1945

Main Soviet airborne landings

Soviet and Allied forces

Japanese forces

Nuclear attack by USAAF: Hiroshima. 6 August 1945 Nagasaki. 9 August 1945

Position of Soviet/Mongolian forces 9 August 1945 (Sakhalin 17 August)

Soviet forces moved from Kamchatka onto the first of the Kurile Islands and attacked into South Sakhalin on 18 August 1945.

Grand Khingan mountains to the west and the jagged Tunghua mountains on the Korean border, to low-lying marshy terrain, sand dunes, grassy plains and bluffs, to two deserts. Across this spectacular canvas the Red Army, well practised in large-scale operations, would execute its grandest and swiftest triumph in a final 'special period' of the war, also known as 'the rout of Imperial Japan'.[14]

Soviet planning started in March 1945, after Stalin's commitment at Yalta. The Russians started shifting troops, supplies and equipment east in April. It would take three months to move Russia's mighty war effort east, and it was not completed when the operation started. Generally, the Russians stockpiled equipment first, and also re-equipped units already there, and sent the troops later. Stavka chose formations which had relevant experience. Thus, Thirty-Ninth Army, which had experience in the savage fighting for the heavily fortified city of Königsberg, which had fallen on 9 April, would attack the Halung-Arshaan fortified region of Manchuria. The Fifth Army, also engaged in the fortress battle for Königsberg, would attack the heavily fortified Japanese defensive zone in eastern Manchuria. Sixth Guards Tank Army, which had fought its way through the Carpathian Mountains, would do the same thing with the Grand Khingan mountains. Fifty-Third Army, also with Carpathian experience, would attack Japanese forces in the mountains of western Manchuria. Two front headquarters, the Karelian – which had experience of dealing with endless lakes – and Second Ukrainian, were moved east to provide the right balance of experience.

The offensive would require doubling Soviet forces in the Far East from forty to eighty divisions. For the 9,000- to 12,000-kilometre journey from eastern Europe to Manchuria the Russians used 136,000 railway wagons. In June and July 1945, twenty to thirty trains were moving along the trans-Siberian railway each day. Once they reached their railheads there was often still a long way to go, as Zhukov had discovered at Khalkin Gol in 1939. It was 500 kilometres by smaller railway and road from the trans-Siberian to Choybalsan in Mongolia, the last town of any significance behind Sixth and Fifty-Third Armies. In May and June 1945, thirty divisions moved across the country, involving, with army and support troops, about one million in all. The total forces for the operation numbered 1,669,500 Soviet troops from three fronts: Trans-Baikal, First and Second Far Eastern, supported by the Amur flotilla and the Pacific fleet.[15] In addition, there were 16,000, mostly cavalry, on the right flank from the Mongolian People's Army.

In order to manage an operation on this scale so far from Moscow, the Russians set up a theatre command above the three fronts, under Vasilevskiy. At first he was sent as a Stavka coordinator but it soon became obvious that fighting on three fronts in an operation on this scale needed more than just coordination, and on 30 July the 'Far East Command' was created. Although the Russians had experimented with theatre commands early in the Great Patriotic War, they had always proved redundant. The creation of a fully fledged, independent theatre command with its own staff – almost its own Stavka – was a first in the Russian experience during the Second World War.[16]

Deception was also vital. Units assembled as far away from the borders as possible but that meant that when the attack was launched they would have to move over long distances. The large numbers of new staff officers and senior commanders necessary to double Soviet forces in the Far East often moved into the area under assumed names and wearing the insignia of junior officers. The Japanese did not believe the Russians were ready to attack on 9 August, but expected a possible attack in the autumn, when the ground would have dried after the seasonal summer rains, or even in spring 1946.[17]

The 16,000 Mongolians would form part of the formation on the extreme right of the Soviet forces, Issa Pliev's Soviet–Mongolian cavalry-mechanized group (KMG), part of the Trans-Baikal Front. Once again, the Russians picked Pliev because of his reputation and relevant experience commanding KMGs in Bagration and other operations in Europe.

Vasilevskiy briefed him on the plane on the flight to Ulan Bator. It was not a mission for the faint-hearted.

> You, Issa Aleksandrovich, will execute a raid in your
> favourite style, across the Gobi Desert and the Grand
> Khingan mountains. Your cavalry-mechanised group will
> conduct a vigorous offensive on the axis Kalgan–Beijing, and
> will subsequently exploit success as far as the Gulf of
> Liaodong. That is where our main forces will concentrate . . .
> your mission – to secure the front's forces against attack
> from the south.[18]

At first Pliev's KMG – equivalent to an army – would cross grassy steppe. Then there were rocky heights and great stretches of quicksand which glistened in the sun. After that came the foothills of the Great Khingan range, and then the mountains themselves, and the passes through them. The end of the route, the Kalgan road, extended by the Japanese, ran along the Great Wall of China.

The unprecedented international force encountered unexpected problems. Pliev recalled that the Mongolians, brought up on a diet of milk and meat, were dismayed by Soviet Army rations. 'What do we do with it?' they said. 'This shchi [cabbage soup] and kasha [buckwheat porridge]?'[19]

The main effort would be made by the Trans-Baikal Front from the west with Pliev protecting its flank, and a secondary effort by First Far Eastern in the east, specially strengthened with artillery, engineers and infantry to overcome the border defences. The Second Far Eastern would hold the Amur river.

The Soviet declaration of war, three months after victory in Europe, and the start of the offensive occurred within hours of each other on the night of 8–9 August. The timing was perfect, allowing the Soviet Union to enter the war before Japan could leave it. The Japanese had not only misjudged the timings, but also significantly underestimated the Russians' speed and logistics. They thought the Russians would have to stop after 400 kilometres to resupply, although they had covered more than that in the Vistula-Oder offensive. Within a week, as Soviet columns bit deep into Manchuria, Japan announced its decision to surrender, and on 17 August, following a direct order from Emperor Hirohito, the Kwantung Army signed the instrument of capitulation at Khabarovsk.[20] However, as elsewhere in the Pacific campaign, not all the Japanese got the message and fighting continued in Manchuria and the Kuriles right up to 1 September. On 18 August Pliev's forces reached the edge of the Khalgan fortified region, and although the Japanese High Command announced the capitulation of the Kwantung Army that day, fighting continued there until 21 August.

Pliev's group is an extraordinary amalgam of styles and combined the characteristics of widely differing eras. In that sense, it was another epitome of the Soviet war effort. Mongolian cavalry and the latest Russian tanks moved together, effectively, as part of a theatre strategic operation under a headquarters which was directing three army groups. The techniques of Genghis Khan merged, imperceptibly, into the nuclear age.

As might be expected, given the rapidity of the advance and the speed of the Japanese collapse, Soviet casualties were relatively light – just 12,031 irrecoverable losses out of 1,669,500 Soviet troops committed. Out of 16,000, the Mongolians lost 72. Average daily losses, even though it was really over in ten days, were 1,458 over the twenty-five-day period from 9 August to 2 September inclusive.[21] Soviet Russia had learned a lot about war, and the Manchurian operation gave Nato military planners a great deal to think about in the forty or so years of cold war that followed. It was studied as the prototype 'theatre strategic operation', with many lessons for what the Soviet Union might do in a war in Europe. In the twenty-first century (2003), we have seen a spectacularly swift and successful conventional military operation in Iraq, but on a much smaller scale. Two corps. As for battles with millions on each side, like Manchuria, let them remain history.

The destruction of the Kwantung Army in Manchuria also drew the teeth of the divisions in south Sakhalin, northern Korea and the Kurile islands. In addition, Japan lost its military-economic base in China and Korea. Even if there had been no atomic bombs, the Russian victory in Manchuria would have meant that Japan had lost its largest body of armed forces and much of its economic base. It could not have continued the war. In discussion with a visiting Russian admiral, the author asked him whether the Soviet Union ever intended to invade Japan. It was perhaps a naive question. Unlike the British and Americans, there would have been no need for a vast amphibious assault. From Kamchatka, and from northern Sakhalin, the Russians could have island-hopped down to Hokkaido. For them, there were stepping stones straight to Japan. Had the Americans not had the bomb, it could well be that the Soviet Union would have invaded Japan first.

The final Japanese surrender – the end of the Second World War – took place on board the battleship USS *Missouri* on 2 September 1945, in Tokyo Bay. The Japanese signatory was Mamoro Shigemitsu, the Foreign Minister, attired in formal diplomatic garb: a wing collar and tails. On board the great ship there were British, Dutch, American and Soviet Russian representatives. The western footage of the event is dignified, showing Shigemitsu, seated at a desk, signing the instrument of surrender with Yoshijiro Umezu, of the Imperial General Headquarters. It is timed 09.08, on 2 September 1945. The Russians took film as well. Shigemitsu appears to have had a wooden leg. Getting him up to the deck of the battleship from the cutter which brought him from Tokyo meant he had to climb a very steep ladder. The western newsreels did not show any of this. The Russian film, however, shows everything, as the poor man struggled valiantly to get on board the battleship. The Russians had no compunction about humiliating those they defeated, whether by hurling captured standards down before the Kremlin or by filming the Japanese Foreign Minister's extreme embarrassment. Nevertheless, among the Soviet servicemen on board the *Missouri* that day, and across a sixth of the earth's land surface, the restored territory of the Soviet Union, and in newly occupied Europe as far west as the Elbe, no one would have laughed at the next words, from US General Douglas MacArthur, which formally ended the Second World War: 'These proceedings are now closed.'[22]

Such a victory as this

For the Soviet people, there would be little rest. Reconstruction would prove to be as demanding as war. And the Soviet Union had to capitalize on its new international position, and could not ignore the new fact of nuclear weapons. Stalin's May Day order of 1945 called upon the people to 'heal wounds of war quickly' and to 'increase the power of the Soviet state'. Frank Roberts in Moscow reported that newspapers repeatedly stressed the enormity of the task ahead. Immediately after the end of the war in Europe there was no relaxation of efforts and peace did not bring any tangible advantages.[23] On 23 June the Supreme Soviet passed a law demobilizing the thirteen oldest groups on active service – men between the ages of forty and fifty-two, stipulating that they should receive work within one month, at least as good as before enlistment, and specifying gratuities to be paid, food rations, coupons for meals and loans for house-building. A Soviet journalist, asked 'how things were going', told a member of the British embassy staff, 'Peace has come but it has not yet turned into something tangible.' Citizens would have to wait some years before they could enjoy the fruits of their labours and the government's long-term planning, wrote the Chargé d'Affaires. 'But they are buoyed up by pride in their recent victory, by confidence in the wisdom of their leaders, by the conviction that one day things will be better, if not for them, at least for their children.'[24]

By July 1945 the Soviet Union had total armed forces – not just the 6.5 million combat soldiers who had won on the Soviet–German front

– of 11,365,000. Demobilizing and absorbing such a number of returning soldiers – 7 to 8 million by March 1946 – proceeded less smoothly than expected. Some were dissatisfied with the new jobs found for them, others found they were not treated with the respect which they felt they had earned. Kerr, the British Ambassador, noted on 4 December, 'Moscow is now experiencing a real wave of hooliganism.' The more unruly elements among the demobilized soldiers were partly to blame, but in the wake of amnesties for prisoners declared after the war it was likely that 'habitual criminals and amnestied jailbirds are taking advantage of the situation to operate even more actively than before'.[25]

The mood of disappointment was very clear.

> People seem to have hoped that in some mysterious way the war would lead to an immediate and great improvement in the standard of living. Now that they realise that this improvement will inevitably be much slower than they had imagined, and that the main emphasis in the new five-year plan is to be reconstruction, capital goods industries and the development of railways, their spirits have sunk, and at the moment there is certainly a mood of depression, even protest.[26]

However, such discontent was unlikely to make the leadership modify its chosen course. The prestige of the victory and other factors – the stoic Russian tendency to put up with it, and the grip of the NKVD, which had got stronger during the war – were all important points on the government's side.[27]

On 26 May 1945 the GKO ordered the gradual conversion of military to civilian production but this process of 'conversion' – a phrase that returned at the end of the cold war – was slow to begin, and arguably never happened. Defence output fell by 68 per cent in the last quarter of 1945 but civilian production rose by only 21 per cent. It would take years to turn the oil tanker round, and in fact they never did. 'It is probable, in view of the re-equipment of the armed forces, the slowness of reconversion of war factories and new preparations for the production of the atomic bomb', Frank Roberts wrote from the British embassy in March 1946, 'that armaments account for a higher proportion of total production now than in 1940.'[28]

Returning soldiers faced a difficult time. Those who had joined the Germans, whether willingly or not, who had been been taken prisoner, or even valiantly wounded and saved by German medical staff, were quietly passed to the GULag as 'special prisoners'. In all, about 1.8 million were processed in this way.[29] For those not disgraced, those who had not fallen foul of the system, it was often tough as well. There were no social services for those who had lost limbs; no counselling for those traumatized.

The million or so women with the Red Army and air forces faced the biggest change of all. Most women serving in the services, including those in the air force, were demobilized as soon as possible after the victory over Germany. Although they had done almost everything that the men did, their enormous wartime contribution was not seen as a catalyst for a change in their role in society. There were, perhaps, pragmatic reasons behind this. With so many men killed, 'pro-natalism' demanded that women return to family life. Many of the women who had had extraordinary wartime careers were happy to give them up. But the military also took a decision to exclude women from promotion to senior ranks. When two selected pilots from the 'night witches', both Heroines of the Soviet Union, turned up at the Zhukovskiy Aviation Academy in Moscow they were taken aside by the commanding general and politely told to register at a civilian university instead. Although women could fulfil combat roles when called on in times of extreme national emergency, they could not expect full or permanent careers in the military. Their achievements had been acknowledged during the war, but were soon relegated to celebrations on International Women's Day. As Reina Pennington put it, 'where the Americans had Uncle Sam, the Soviets had Mother Russia. Soviet women were constantly reminded – and many believed – that their true place was on the home front, not the battlefront'.[30]

Conclusion

In 1945, and for the next forty years, Soviet Russia probably appeared stronger to foreigners than she really was. By a chance chain of events, the Second World War and Hitler's arrogance and misjudgement had turned the country which before the war had been an aberrant 'pariah state' into the strongest land power, one of the three strongest air powers and the very successful exponent of a new political and economic system.[31] Soviet Russia was also the heir to the Russian Imperial past, and behaved as such throughout the war. The analogies with 1812–15 are obvious. Furthermore, Soviet Russia's new status in the international system forced it on to greater technological achievements as a nuclear and a space power. But it would be inaccurate to think that this greatness was unexpectedly thrust on the Soviet Union. Had it been, its position as one of the five permanent members of the UN Security Council would still have been assured, but it would not have been the pre-eminent power apart from the United States, and the only one that could repeatedly challenge the US. The foundations for that position had been laid in military-economic planning since 1925.

It could be argued that Nazi Germany and Soviet Russia really destroyed each other in the Second World War, but that while Germany collapsed under hammer blows from all sides, Soviet Russia survived because the western Allies needed it. Then, when a critical margin of Allied aid and good will was removed, Russia began to struggle, but it took another forty-five years to succumb to the long-term effects of the intolerable exertions it had undergone. That would be a neat theory but the facts do not fit. Very slowly, life in the Soviet Union did get better after the war. In the immediate aftermath, the Stalinist terror got worse, but after Stalin's death in 1953 the 'thaw' did bring progress. The late 1950s and 1960s saw extraordinary Soviet achievements, most of which could trace their origins to the Great Patriotic War. Soviet scientific expertise and the emphasis which a planned economy could place on such critical projects as the nuclear and space programmes focused effort where it was needed, at the expense, admittedly, of huge other areas of the economy. Putting the first artificial satellite and the first man into space were both direct results of a heady mix of native Russian and Soviet scientific talent, espionage and wartime booty. What destroyed the Soviet Union, in the end, was not a delayed-action effect from the Second World War, but the continuing and increasing pressure of an arms race with the world's greatest economic power, the United States.

As for the war itself, the scale of the Soviet sacrifice and casualties is almost incomprehensible. But while we might shudder at the suffering and marvel at the resilence of the Soviet people and the Red Army, it is perhaps even more difficult to understand what kept the Germans going for so long. They had lost their chance to win a quick victory at Moscow. After Stalingrad, they could not win. After Kursk, the Russians could not lose, and once the western Allies were ashore in June 1944 – compounded by the destruction of Army Group Centre in Operation Bagration, starting later that month – it was only a matter of time. For those reasons, this book has concentrated on the critical years of 1941 and 1942, when the very survival of Soviet Russia hung in the balance. By the end of 1942, all the critical elements of Soviet success including the main administrative structures, most of which were introduced in 1941, the creation of a 'third generation' Red Army, and the mass recruitment of women, were all in place. So, too, crucially, were the blueprints for Soviet military and political advances after the war: nuclear weapons, rockets and jets, and such international exports as Kalashnikov's famous small arms.

Russia's war effort between 1941 and 1945 actually reveals many things which are relevant to our own security dilemmas today, even in so-called 'peacetime'. Although often thought of as a straight, first-division contest between the Red Army and the *Wehrmacht* and Waffen SS – epitomized, perhaps, by the collision of armour at Prokhorovka – the Soviet–German war was a highly complex, multidimensional con-flict. The Russians were not always regarded as liberators and Russian generals, like Vatutin, could be killed by Ukrainian nationalist partisans. Besides organizing partisan operations, especially after 1942, the NKVD – the Interior Ministry – had its own troops: half a million and more, and their role has been neglected. Although usually derided in western sources as 'secret police' and so on, they were probably better trained, better disciplined and more highly motivated than most Red Army units, and this showed at Leningrad and Stalingrad. Furthermore, the meticulous Soviet arrangements for 'state-building' and establishing security in the immediate wake of military conquest or reconquest – for example, in Poland, the Baltic States and post-war Germany – compare quite favourably, in terms of their organization and effectiveness, with recent efforts in Iraq. The role of the State Defence Committee – GKO – in coordinating every aspect of national security, from conventional armaments to the Moscow fire services, is an object lesson for our own endeavours to guarantee 'homeland security' and 'resilience' in the face of different threats in the twenty-first century. The maintenance of 'normal' peacetime procedures, and proper police work, to catch the right people, even in the appalling circumstances of the Siege of

Leningrad, is also, perhaps, a warning not to respond too hastily to new threats. The role of women, which has been grossly understated, has also played a part in this story. And finally, no one nowadays can look at a catastrophe, whether man-made or natural, without considering the effects on the environment. When Stalingrad was ablaze, the dogs dived into the Volga and tried to swim east to escape the inferno. Then the Russians started pushing the Germans the other way and more than twenty years later rabid wolves and foxes reached the English Channel. The German officer's words at Stalingrad say it all: 'Animals flee this hell; the hardest stones cannot bear it for long; only men endure.'[32] Men and women, some of them, did endure, and built another world. The modern international system, with its five permanent members of the UN Security Council and, to a very large extent still, the world we live in now.

The survival of the Soviet Union in 1941–2 and its resilience in the face of shattering defeats can be ascribed to the character and patriotism of its people, especially the Russians, or to the draconian measures imposed by Stalin, Beria and their Lieutenants. In fact, it must be ascribed to both. During the war, an already authoritarian system became more so. In spite of the catastrophic errors that led to the events of 1941 and 1942, the system was able, using a mixture of terror and propaganda, to mobilize the latent patriotism of the nation. One recent analysis acknowledged that 'without Stalin, we would not have won. But if it had not been for Stalin, in all probability the war would not have happened.'[33] The latter is perhaps debatable: Hitler might have been as determined to destroy any other Soviet Russian leader or government. Had he not, had Tukhachevskiy perhaps survived to overthrow Stalin and come to some accommodation with Hitler, then Nazi Germany and the Soviet Union might have presented a united front against the free world. What might have happened then is perhaps even more terrible to contemplate.

Select bibliography

Primary sources

ARCHIVES

Presidential Archive of Russia (AP RF)
Fond 3, Opis 64, delo 675, map dividing Poland between Soviet Russia and Germany, 28 September 1939 (Plate 1).
Fond 3, Opis 50, delo 450, TASS broadcast, 22 June 1941 and Party Directive.
Fond 3, Opis 50, delo 415, NKGB report on imminent German attack with Stalin's comments, 17 June 1941 (Plate 2).
Central Committee to Zhdanov, 13 VI 1948 (Plate 6).

Author's own archive
M-38-114-A (Yerzovka), General Staff of the Red Army, RSFSR Stalingrad Oblast', map, 1:50,000 1937, revised 22 April to 10 July 1942 (Plate 30).

Die Bahn – German railways museum in Nürnberg
Deutsches Kursbuch (National Railway Timetable), summer 1941 (valid from 5 May 1941).

UK National Archives (UKNA), Kew
MAF 287/433, esp. Enclosure 24a, Central Veterinary Laboratory, MAFF Weybridge. CUST 49/5099.
FO/371/43335, Some Probable Post-War Tendencies in Soviet Foreign Policy as Affecting British Interests, Foreign Office, 29 April 1944, N1008/183/38.
FO 371/47924, Roberts to Bevin N 10185/627/38, printed 11 August 1945.
FO/371/47925, Roberts [Frank (later Sir Frank)] to Ernest Bevin, 21 September 1945, printed 29 September 1945.
FO 371/47925, despatch of 4 December 1945.
FO 371/47925, Clark Kerr to Bevin N 17305/627/38, printed 9 December 1945.
FO 371/56831, No. 1090, 21 March 1946.
FO 371/56831, N 3799/605/938, dated 24 March 1946.
FO 800/279.

WO 33/1684, *Order of Battle of Military Forces in USSR 1941.*

WO 33/1828A, 1829 (summary), *Order of Battle of Military Forces in USSR 1945.*

WO 193/642, 'The Foreign Relations of USSR', paper by Military Intelligence MI2(b), 2 November 1940.

WO 208/1757.

WO/208/1758.

WO/208/1777, *Effects of a Possible Soviet Collapse and Possible Action Required*, 1941–2.

W0 208/1790, *Soviet Ground Operations 1941–45.*

WO 208/1802, *Possible use of gas, prevailing winds*, 28 March 1942, to CDR 5 Porton, dated 1 April 1942.

WO 208/4277, *Report on the Interrogation of Professor H. Kliewe May 7th–11th 1945* by Major H. M. B. Adam, Major J. M. Barnes, Capt W. J. Cromartie, Capt Carlo Henze and Lt J. W. Hofer, Ref. A-B-C-H-H/149, dated 13 May 1945.

Operational Records Book for Bomber Command, entry for 13/14 November 1940.

Blomberg, Werner von, *Report on Visit of the Chief of the Army Board to Russia, August to September 1928, Staff* (Reichswehr Ministerium, 17 November 1928), trans. W. R. Newby-Grant, RMA Sandhurst, 1970s.

US National Archives

Hirsch, *Soviet BW and CW Preparation and Capabilities (The Hirsch Report)*, National Archives, Washington DC, Reference *NAW RG 319 GZ, P-Project file*, Box 13.

PUBLISHED DOCUMENTS – RUSSIAN

Filatov, V. P., President of the Editorial Committee, ed., *Moskovskaya Bitva v Postanovleniyakh Gosudarstvennogo Komiteta Oborony: Dokumenty I Materialy 1941–42 (The Battle of Moscow in Announcements of the State Defence Committee: Documents and Materials)*, henceforward *Moscow Documents* (Institute for Military History/Russian Federal Archive Service/Moscow Committee of Culture, Moscow, 2001).

FSB Archives see Stepashin, below.

Gor'kov, Yuri, ed., *Gosudarstvenny Komitet Oboorony Postanovlyayet (The State Defence Committee [War Cabinet](GKO, Orders)* (Olma Press, Moscow, 2002).

Lomagin, N. A., ed., *Neizvestnaya blokada*, 2 vols (Olma Press, Moscow/Neva Press, St Petersburg, 2002).

Moscow Documents – see Filatov, above.

Stalingradskaya Bitva: Khronika, fakty, lyudi. Arkhiv (The Battle of Stalingrad: the Story, the Facts, the People. Archives) (2 vols, Olma Press, Moscow, 2002).

Stepashin, Lt Gen. S. V., ed., *Organy Gosudarstvennoy Bezopasnosti SSSR v Velikoy Otechestvennoy Voyne. Sbornik documentov (Organs of State Security of the USSR in the Great Patriotic War. A Collection of Documents).*

 Tom I. Nakanune (Volume One. *On the Eve*). Bk 1: November 1938 – December 1940, Bk 2: 1 January–21 June 1941 (FSK Academy, Russia, 1995, 20,000 copies).

   Tom II. *Nachalo* (Volume Two. *The Beginning*). Bk 1: 22 June–31 August 1941, Bk 2: 1 September–31 December 1941 (Rus' publishers, Moscow, 2000).

   Tom III (Volume Three). Bk 1: *Krushcheniya 'Blitzkriga'(Breaking the 'Blitzkrieg'*), 1 January–30 June 1942, Bk 2: *Ot oborony k nastupleniyu* (*From the Defensive to the Offensive*), 1 July–31 December 1942 (Rus', Moscow, 2003). Referenced as *FSB Archives*.

SSSR–Germaniya 1939: Dokumenty I materialy o sovetsko-germanskikh otnosheniyakh s aprelya po oktyabrya 1939 g.(USSR–Germany 1939. Documents and Materials on Soviet-German Relations from April to October 1939) (Mosklas, Vilnius, 1989).

USSR Germany 1939 see *SSSR–Germaniya*, above.

Zakharov, M. V., Samsonov, Aleksandr and Pechorkin, Vitol'd, ed., *Stalingradskaya epopeya: Vpervye publikuyemye dokumenty rassekrechennye FSB RF . . . (The Stalingrad Epic: a Collection of Documents First Declassified by the Federal Security Service of the Russian Federation . . .)* (Zvonnitsa-MG, Moscow, 2000).

Zhilin, V. A., ed., *Bitva pod Moskvoy: Khronika, Fakty, Lyudy (The Battle of Moscow: Chronicles, Facts, People)*, 'Archive' Series, 2 vols (Olma Press, Moscow, 2002).

PUBLISHED DOCUMENTS – OTHER

Documents on German Foreign Policy 1918–1945, Series D, Vol. XII, *The War Years*, February 1, 1941 to June 2, 1941 (Her Majesty's Stationery Office, London, 1962).

Roberts, Adam and Guelff, Richard, ed., *Documents on the Laws of War* (Third Edition, Oxford University Press, 2000).

Torr, Dona, ed., *Karl Marx and Friedrich Engels Correspondence* (Martin Lawrence, London, 1934).

Hugh Trevor-Roper, *Hitler's War Directives, 1939–1945* (London, 1960).

USSR–Germany see *SSSR–Germaniya*, above.

Wartime International Agreements: Soviet Supply Protocols (US Department of State, Publication 2759, European Series 22, Washington DC, 1948).

EYEWITNESS INTERVIEWS

Interview with Prof. Marja Talvi (b. 1935) of Tallin University, International Border Security Conference, Budapest, 30 August 2003.

Interview with Norwegian air force generals, Royal Norwegian Air Force Conference, Trondheim, February 1999.

WORKS OF MILITARY THOUGHT

Clausewitz, Carl von, *On War* (1832), trans. and ed. Michael Howard and Peter Paret (Princeton University Press, 1976).

Ludendorff, Erich von, *The Nation at War*, trans. from *Der totale Krieg* (Munich, 1935) by Dr A. S. Rapoport (Hutchinson, London, 1936).

Sokolovskiy, Vitaliy D., *Voyennaya Strategiya (Military Strategy)* (Voyenizdat, Moscow,

1962, 1963, 1968), trans. as *Soviet Military Strategy* by Harriet Fast Scott and William F. Scott (Macdonald and Jane's, London, 1975).

Sun Tzu, *The Art of War*, trans. and ed. Samuel B. Griffith (Oxford University Press, 1963).

Svechin, Maj. Gen. A. A., *Strategiya* (2nd edn, Voyenny Vestnik Press, Moscow, 1927). Preface to 1st edn (1926) was written in 1925.

Tukhachevskiy, Mikhail, *O kharaktere sovremennykh voyn v svete resheniy VI Kongressa Kominterna (On the Character of Contemporary Wars in the Light of the VI Comintern Congress)*, in *Kommunisticheskaya Akademiya, sektsiya po izucheniyu problem voyny* (Communist Academy, Section for the Study of the Problems of War), *Zapiski* (Notes), Vol. 1 (*Izd. Kommunisticheskoy Akademii*, Moscow, 1930), pp. 6–29, stenographic record of paper to the Leningrad branch of Komakad, pp. 3, 9,14,19. Known as 'the Komakad speech'.

MEMOIRS AND SPEECHES – RUSSIAN

Berezhkov, Valentin, *Stranitsy diplomaticheskoy istorii (Pages from Diplomatic History)* (Mezhdunarodnye otnosheniya, Moscow, 1982).

Chuikov, Vasiliy, and Paderin, Ivan, *Nachalo puti (The Start of the Journey)*, (Military memoirs series, Voyenizdat, Moscow, 1959).

Eranburg, Il'ya, ed. B. Ya Frezinskiy, *Voyna 1941–1945 (War 1941–1945)*, (Astral', Moscow, 2004) (Anthology of wartime writings).

Pliev, Issa Aleksandrovich, *Pod gvardeyskim znamanem (Under the Guards' Banner)* (Ordzhonikidze, 1976).

Konets kvantuinskoy armii. Zapiski komanduyushchego konno-makhanizirovannoy gruppy sovetsko-Mongol'skikh voysk) (The End of the Kwantung Army. Notes of the Commander of the Soviet-Mongolian Cavalry-Mechanized Group) (Ir, Ordzhonikidze, 1969).

Rokossovskiy, Konstantin, *Soldatskiy dolg (A Soldier's Duty)* (Olma Press, Moscow, 2002).

Voronov, Nikolai Nikolayevich, *Na sluzhbe voyennoy (In Military Service)* (Voyenizdat, Moscow, 1963).

Yeremenko, Andrey, *Stalingrad. Zapiski komanduyushchego frontom (Stalingrad. Memoirs of a Front Commander)* (Voyenizdat, Moscow, 1961).

Zhukov, Georgiy, *Vospominaniya I Razmyshleniya (Reminiscences and Reflections)*, 13th edn, unexpurgated, 2 vols (Olma Press, Moscow, 2002).

MEMOIRS AND SPEECHES – OTHER

Berezhkov, Valentin, trans. Sergey M. Mikheyev, *At Stalin's Side: His Interpreter's Memoirs from the October Revolution to the Fall of the Dictator's Empire* (Birch Lane Press, New York, 1994).

Churchill, Randolph S., compiler, *Into Battle. War Speeches by the Right Hon. Winston S. Churchill* (Cassell, London, February 1941).

Eade, Charles, compiler, *The End of the Beginning. War Speeches by the Right Hon. Winston S. Churchill, 1942* (Cassell, London, 1943).

Eade, Charles, compiler, *The Dawn of Liberation. War Speeches by the Right Hon. Winston S. Churchill, 1944* (Cassell, London, 1945).

Eade, Charles, compiler, *Victory. War Speeches by the Right Hon. Winston S. Churchill, 1945* (Cassell, London, 1946).

Guderian, Heinz, *Panzer Leader* (Ballantine, New York, 1965).

Hitler, Adolf, *Hitler's Mein Kampf [My Struggle]*, Unexpurgated Edition, trans. James Murphy (Hurst and Blackett, London, 1939).

Khrushchev, Nikita, *Khrushchev Remembers* (London, 1971).

Manstein, Field Marshal Erich von, *Lost Victories (Verlorene Siege)* trans. Anthony Powell (London, 1958).

Rokossovskiy, Konstantin Konstantinovich, *A Soldier's Duty*, trans. of the abridged edition of *Soldatskiy dolg* (Progress, Moscow, 1985).

Zhukov, Georgiy, *The Memoirs of Marshal Zhukov* (Jonathan Cape, London, 1971).

COLLECTIONS OF PHOTOGRAPHS AND DRAWINGS

Erickson, John and Erickson, Ljubica, *The Eastern Front in Photographs 1941–45* (Carlton, London, 2001).

Leutov, V. E., ed., *Parod Pobady (Victory Parade)*, (LIK, St Petersburg, 2005). Boxed set.

Rachel Schnold, ed., *Icons of War: Yevgeny Khaldei, Soviet Photographer, World War II* (Beth Hatefutsoth, Nahum Goldmann Museum of the Jewish Diaspora and Ministry of Defence Publishing House, Tel Aviv, 1999).

Stalingrad: Dekabr' 1942g. – fevral' 1943g. Frontovy dnevnik khudozhnika K. I. Finogenova (Stalingrad: December 1942–February 1943. The front-line diary of artist K. I. Finogenov) (Iskusstvo, Moscow/Leningrad, 1948).

OFFICIAL HISTORIES/REPORTS

Armata Romana in al Doilea Razboi Mondial (Romanian Army in World War II) (Editura Meridiane, Bucharest 1995).

Germany and the Second World War. See Militärgeschichtliches Forschungsamt (below).

Glantz, David M. and Orenstein, Harold, trans. and ed., *The Battle for Kursk 1943: the Soviet General Staff Study* (Frank Cass, London, 1999). Originally published as part of *Collection of Materials for the Study of War Experiences*, No. 11 (Military Publishing House of the People's Commissariat of Defence, Moscow, 1944).

Glantz, David M. and Orenstein, Harold L., trans. and ed., *Belorussia 1944: the Soviet General Staff Study*. Originally published as Soviet General Staff study No. 18 (Frank Cass, London and Portland, Oregon, 2001).

Grechko, Marshal A. A., ed., *Istoriya Vtoroy Mirovoy voyny (A History of the Second World War)*, Vol. 6 (Voyenizdat, Moscow, 1976).

Lederrey, Col. E., *Germany's Defeat in the East, 1941–45* (Official History, War Office, London, 1955).

Militärgeschichtliches Forschungsamt (Research Institute for Military History), Potsdam, *Germany and the Second World War*, published in German by Deutsche Verlags-Anstalt GmbH, Stuttgart (henceforward DVAG), and in English by the Clarendon Press, Oxford. Of particular value are Vol. IV, *The Attack on the Soviet Union* (DVAG, 1996), by Horst Boog, Jürgen Förster, Joachim Hoffmann, Ernst Klink, Rolf-Dieter Müller and Gerd R. Ueberschär, trans. Dean S. McMurray, Ewald Osers and Louise Willmot, and Vol. VI, *The Global War* (DVAG and OUP, 2001), by Horst Boog, Werner Rahn, Richard Stumpf and Bernd Wegner, trans. Ewald Osers, John Brownjohn, Patricia Crampton and Louise Willmot. Introducing Volume IV, Manfred Messerschmidt says it is 'once more no "official" publication'. Referenced as *Germany and the Second World War*.

Harris, Air Chief Marshal Sir Arthur, *Despatch on War Operations*, 23rd February 1942–8th May 1945 (October 1945), Preface and Introduction by Sebastian Cox, and *Harris – a German View* by Horst Boog (Frank Cass, London, 1995).

Secondary sources

BIBLIOGRAPHIES

Erickson, John and Erickson, Ljubica, *The Soviet Armed Forces, 1918–1992: A Research Guide to Soviet Sources* (Greenwood Press, Westport and London, 1996).

ATLASES

Gilbert, Martin and Banks, Arthur, *Soviet History Atlas* (Routledge and Kegan Paul, London and Henley, 1979).

Keegan, John, ed., *The Times Atlas of the Second World War* (Times Books, 1989).

Magocsi, Paul Robert, Matthews, Geoffrey J., *Historical Atlas of East Central Europe* (University of Washington Press, Seattle and London, 1993).

Maksimov, Lt Gen. I. I., Lobov, Army Gen. N. N., Zolotarev, Maj. Gen. V. A., *Velikaya Otechestvennaya voyna 1941–45 (The Great Patriotic War, 1941–45)*, (DIK Press, Moscow, Military Cartographic Department of the General Staff, VS RF, and OOO Drofa, Moscow, 2005).

Tsutsiyev, Artur, *Atlas Etnologicheskoy Istorii Kavkaza (1774–2004) (Atlas of the Ethnographic History of the Caucasus (1774–2004)*, (Yevropa, Moscow, 2006).

OFFICIAL REPORTS AND MANUALS – UK AND US

Pamphlet No. 20–201, *Military Improvisations During the Russian Campaign* (US Department of the Army, August 1951, facsimile edition Center of Military History, US Army, Washington DC, 1983).

Pamphlet No. 20–233, *German Defense Tactics against Russian Break-Throughs*, (Department of the Army, Washington DC, October 1951).

British Army Field Manual *D/DAT/13/34/25, The Army Field Manual*. Vol. 1. The Fundamentals. Part 1. *The Application of Force*. Code 71344 (Pt 1), 1985.

BOOKS – RUSSIAN

Anikin, V. I., *Brestskaya krepost' – krepost'-geroi (Brest Fortress – Hero-Fortress)* (Stroiizdat, Moscow, 1985).

Beshanov, V. V., *God 1942 – 'Uchebny' (1942 – 'The Learning Year')* (Kharvest, Minsk, 2004.

Cherepanov, Viktor, *Vlast' I Voyna: Stalinskiy mekhanizm gosudarstvennogo upravieniya v Velikoy Otechestvennoy voyne (Power and War: the Stalinist Mechanism for State Direction in the Great Patriotic War)*, (Izvestiya, Moscow, 2006).

Drobyazko, Sergey, *Pod znamenami vragi. Antisovetskiye formirovaniya 1941–45, (Under Enemy Banners. Anti-Soviet Formations 1941–45)* (Dom knigi, Moscow, 2004).

Ehrenburg, Il'ya, ed. B Ya Frezinskiy, *Voyna 1941–1945 (War 1941–1945)* (a collection of writings from those years) (Astrel', Moscow, 2004).

Galagan, Valentina Ya, *Ratny podvig zhenshchin v gody Velikoy Otechestvennoy voyny (The Triumph of Women in the Great Patriotic War)* (Vysshaya shkola, Kiev /Ki'iv, 1986).

Gorodetsky, Gabriel, *Mif 'Ledokola': nakanune voyny (The 'Icebreaker' Myth: on the Eve of War)* (Moscow, 1995).

Kazakov, Marshal of Artillery K. P., *Artilleriya i rakety (Artillery and Rockets)* (Voyenizdat, Moscow, 1968).

Krasnov, Valeriy, *Neizvestny Zhukov: Lavry I Ternii polkovodtsa (The Unknown Zhukov: Laurels and Thorns of a Military Leader)* (Olma Press, Moscow, 2002).

Krivosheyev, G. F., ed., *Grif sekretnosti snyat. Poteri vooruzhennykh sil SSSR v voynakh, boyevykh deystviyakh i voyennykh konfliktakh (The 'Secret' Stamp is Lifted. Losses of USSR Armed Forces in Wars, Military Actions and Armed Conflicts)* (Voyenizdat [Military Press], Moscow, 1993).

Lelyushenko, Army General D. D., *Moskva-Stalingrad – Berlin-Praga: Zapiski komandarma (Moscow-Stalingrad-Berlin-Prague: Notes of an Army Commander)* (3rd edn, Nauka, Moscow, 1985).

Losik, Marshal of Tank Troops O. A., (ed.), *Stroitel'stvo I boyevoye primeneniye Sovetskikh tankovykh voysk v gody Velikoy Otechestvennoy voyny (The Composition and Operational Employment of Soviet Tank Forces in the Great Patriotic War)*, (Voyenizdat, Moscow, 1979).

Mikhalev, Sergey, *Voyennaya Strategiya. Podgotovka I vedeniye voyn Novogo i Noveyshego vremeni (Military strategy. The Preparation and Conduct of War in Recent and Most Recent Times)*, ed. V. A. Zolotarev (Zhukovskiy, Kuchkovo Pole, Moscow, 2003).

Plaude, V., et al., *Yantarnaya Komnata – Ekaterinskiy dvorets (The Amber Room – the Catherine Palace)* (Izd. Ivan Fedorov, St Petersburg, 2004).

Pliev, Issa Aleksandrovich, *Pod gvardeyskim znamenem (Under the Guards' Banner)* (Ordzhonikidze, 1976).

Pliev, Issa Aleksandrovich, *Konets kvantunskoy armii. Zapiski komanduyushchego konno-mekhanizirovannoy gruppy sovetsko-Mongol'skikh voysk (The End of the Kwantung Army. Notes of the Commander-in-Chief of the Soviet-Mongolian Cavalry–Mechanized Group)* (Ir, Ordzhonikidze, 1969).

Radzievskiy, Gen. A. I., *Tankovy udar (Tankovaya armiya v nastupatel'noy operatsii fronta po opytu Velikoy otechestvennoy voyny) (Tank Strike. (The Tank Army in the Front Offensive Operation as experienced in the Great Patriotic War))*, (Voyenizdat, Moscow, 1977).

Rokossovskiy, Marshal Konstantin, *Velikaya Pobeda na Volge (Great Victory on the Volga)*, 2 vols (Voyenizdat, Moscow, 1965).

Samsonov, A. M., (ed.), *Stalingradskaya epopeya* (Nauka, Moscow, 1968).

Saparov, A. V., *Doroga Zhizni: Dokumental'naya povest' (The Road of Life: a Documentary Tale)* (Lenizdat, Leningrad, 1959).

Sherstnev, Vladimir, *Tragediya Sorok Pervogo: Dokumenty I Razmyshleniya (The Tragedy of 'Forty-One: Documents and Reminiscences)* (Rusich, Smolensk, 2005).

Zakharov, M. V., *General'ny shtab v predvoyennye gody (The General Staff in the Pre-War Years)* (Voyenizdat, Moscow, 1989).

BOOKS – OTHER

Alibek, Ken and Handelman, Stephen, *Biohazard* (Hutchinson, London, 1999).

Applebaum, Anne, *GULag: a History* (Doubleday, New York, 2003).

Andrew, Christopher and Mitrokhin, Vasiliy, *The Mitrokhin Archive: The KGB in Europe and the West* (Penguin, London, 2000).

Anusauskas, Arvydas, ed., *The Anti-Soviet Resistance in the Baltic States* (Genocide and Resistance Research Centre of Lithuania / Du Ka, Vilnius, 1999).

Bacon, Edwin, *The GULag at War. Stalin's Forced Labour System in the Light of the Archives* (Macmillan, London, 1996).

Beaumont, Joan, *Comrades in Arms: British Aid to Russia 1941–45* (Davis Poynter, London, 1980).

Beevor, Antony, *Stalingrad* (Viking, London, 1998) and *Berlin 1945: the Downfall* (Viking, London, 2002).

Beevor, Antony, and Vinogradova, Luba, trans. and ed., *A Writer at War: Vasily Grossman with the Red Army 1941–1945* (Harvill Press, London, 2005).

Bellamy, Christopher D., *Red God of War: Soviet Artillery and Rocket Forces* (Brassey's, London, 1986).

Bellamy, Christopher D., *Expert Witness: a Defence Correspondent's Gulf War* (Brassey's, London, 1993).

Blood, Phillip W., *Hitler's Bandit Hunters: the SS and the Nazi Occupation of Europe* (published version of his PhD – see Theses below) (Potomac Books, Washington, 2006).

Bobbit, Philip, *The Shield of Achilles – War, Peace and the Course of History* (Penguin, London, 2002).

Borowiec, Andrew, *Destroy Warsaw! Hitler's Punishment, Stalin's Revenge* (Praeger, Westport and London, 2001).

Churchill, Winston S., *The Second World War*, 6 vols (Cassell, London, 1948–54).

Churchill, Winston S., *The World Crisis*, 5 vols (Thornton Butterworth, London, 1923–1931).

Churchill, Winston S., *The World Crisis: the Eastern Front* (Thornton Butterworth, London, 1931).

Davies, Norman, *Rising '44: 'The Battle for Warsaw'* (Macmillan, London, 2003).

Dollinger, Hans, trans. Pomerans, Arnold, *The Decline and Fall of Nazi Germany and Imperial Japan. A Pictorial History of the Final Days of World War II* [1945] (Gramercy Books, New York, 1995).

Duffy, Christopher, *Red Storm on the Reich. The Soviet March on Germany, 1945* (London 1991).

Duffy, Christopher, *Russia's Military Way to the West. Origins and Nature of Russian Military Power, 1700–1800* (Routledge & Kegan Paul, London, 1981).

Ehrenburg, Il'ya, *Russia at War*. Collection of articles, with an Introduction by J. B. Priestley (London, 1943).

Ely, Louis B., *The Red Army Today*, first pub. 1949 (Military Service Publishing Co., Harrisburg, PA, 1953).

Engle, Eloise and Paananen, Lauri, *The Winter War: the Russo-Finnish Conflict 1939–40* (Military Book Society/Sidgwick & Jackson, London, 1973).

Erickson, John, *The Soviet High Command: a Military-Political History, 1918–1941*, (3rd. edn, Frank Cass, London and Portland, Oregon, 2001).

Erickson, John, *The Road to Stalingrad. Stalin's War with Germany, Vol. 1* (Weidenfeld & Nicolson, London, 1975) and *The Road to Berlin. Stalin's War with Germany, Vol. 2* (Weidenfeld & Nicolson, London, 1983).

Erickson, John and Dilks, David, ed., *Barbarossa: the Axis and the Allies* (Edinburgh University Press, 1994), p. 227.

Erickson, Ljubica and Erickson, Mark, ed., *Russia: War, Peace and Diplomacy* (Weidenfeld & Nicolson, London, 2005).

Ezell, Edward, *The AK-47 Story: Evolution of the Kalashnikov Weapons* (Harrisburg, PA., 1986).

Feltzer, Leland, trans. and Wegner, Ray, ed., *The Soviet Air Force in World War II* (David & Charles, London, 1974, trans. from the Soviet Official History).

Fitzgibbon, Louis, *The Katyn massacre. The shocking truth behind the world's worst unjudged mass murder* (Corgi, 1979).

Gareyev, Col. Gen. Makhmut, *M. V. Frunze, Military Theorist* (Pergamon-Brassey's, London, 1988).

Glantz, David M., *Zhukov's Greatest Defeat. The Red Army's Epic Disaster in Operation Mars, 1942* (University of Kansas, 1999/Ian Allen, London, 2000).

Glantz, David M., *Atlas of the Battle of Smolensk* (Self-published, Carlisle PA, 2001).

Glantz, David M., *August Storm: the Soviet 1945 Operational and Strategic Offensive in Manchuria* (Leavenworth Paper No. 7, US Army Command and General Staff College, Fort Leavenworth, 1983).

Glantz, David M., *August Storm: Soviet Tactical and Operational Combat in Manchuria, 1945* (Leavenworth Paper No. 8, US Army Command and General Staff College, Fort Leavenworth, 1983).

Glantz, David, *Barbarossa: Hitler's Invasion of Russia 1941* (Tempus, Charleston SC, 2001), p. 31.

Glantz, David, ed., *The Initial Period of the War on the Eastern Front 22 June – August 1941. Proceedings of the Fourth Art of War Symposium, Garmisch, October 1987* (Frank Cass, London and Portland, Oregon, 1993).

Glantz, David M., *Kharkov 1942: Anatomy of a Military Disaster through Soviet Eyes* (Ian Allan, London, 1998).

Glantz, David, *The Siege of Leningrad 1941–1944. 900 Days of Terror* (Cassell, London, 2004).

Glantz, David, *Colossus Reborn: The Red Army at War, 1941–1943* (Kansas University Press, 2005).

Gorodetsky, Gabriel, *Grand Delusion. Stalin and the German Invasion of Russia,* (Yale University Press, 1999).

Gray, Colin S. and Sloan, Geoffrey, ed., *Geopolitics: Geography and Strategy* (Frank Cass, London and Portland, Oregon, 1999).

Grenkevich, Leonid D., *The Soviet Partisan Movement 1941–1944* (Frank Cass, London and Portland, Oregon, 1999).

Harrison, Mark, *Accounting for War: Soviet Production, Employment and the Defence Burden, 1940–45* (Cambridge University Press, 1996, 2002).

Harrison, Mark, ed., *The Economics of World War II: Six Great Powers in International Comparison* (Cambridge University Press, 1998).

Hastings, Max, *Armageddon* (Macmillan, London, 2004).

Haupt, Werner, *Army Group Center: The Wehrmacht in Russia 1941–45* (Schiffer Military History, Atgen, PA, 1997).

Hayward, Joel S., *Stopped at Stalingrad: The Luftwaffe and Hitler's Defeat in the East, 1942–43* (Kansas University Press, 1998).

Higham, Robin and Kagan, Frederick W., ed., *The Military History of the Soviet Union* (Palgrave, New York, 2002).

Holloway, David, *The Soviet Union and the Arms Race* (Yale University Press, 1983).

Holloway, David, *Stalin and the Bomb* (Yale University Press, 1994).

Holmes, Richard, ed., *The Oxford Companion to Military History* (Oxford University Press, 2001).

Howse, Derek, *Greenwich Time and Longitude* (Royal Observatory, London, 1997).

Hughes-Wilson, John, *Military Intelligence Blunders and Cover-Ups* (Revised and updated edition, Robinson, London, 2004).

Jenkins, Barries, ed., *Purnell's History of the Second World War* (BBC Publishing, London, 1966/1972).

Jones, Robert Huhn, *The Road to Russia: United States Lend-Lease to the Soviet Union* (Oklahoma, 1969).

Kershaw, Ian, *Hitler 1889–1936: Hubris* (Penguin, London, 2001).

Krivosheyev, G. F., *Soviet Casualties and Combat Losses in the Twentieth Century* (trans. Lionel Leventhal Ltd, 1997, pub. with a foreword by Prof. John Erickson, Greenhill Books, London and Stackpole, Pennsylvania, 1997).

Le Tissier, Tony, *Race for the Reichstag: the 1945 Battle for Berlin* (Frank Cass, London and Portland, 1999).

Le Tissier, Tony, *Slaughter at Halbe: the Destruction of Hitler's 9th Army, April 1945* (Sutton, Stroud, 2005).

Liddell Hart, Basil, *This Expanding War* (Faber & Faber, London, 1942).

Loring, Nancy, ed., *Female Soldiers – Combatants or Noncombatants? Historical and Contemporary Perspectives* (Greenwood, Westport, 1982).

Magenheimer, Heinz, *Die Militärstrategie Deutschlands 1940–45* (F. A. Herbig Verlag, Munich, 1997), trans. as *Hitler's War* by Helmut Bögler (Arms and Armour 1998/ Cassell Military Paperbacks, London, 2002).

Merridale, Catherine, *Ivan's War: The Red Army 1939–1945* (Faber, London, 2005; Metropolitan, New York, 2006).

Nemecek, Vaclav, *The History of Soviet Aircraft Since 1918* (Collins, London, 1986), trans. from the Czech *Sovetska Letadla*.

Niepold, Gerd, trans. Simpkin, Richard, *Battle for White Russia: The Destruction of Army Group Centre, June 1944* (Brassey's Defence Publishers, London, 1987).

Pavlov, Dmitry, *Leningrad, 1941: The Blockade* (Chicago UP, 1964).

Pennington, Reina, *Wings, Women and War: Soviet Airwomen in World War II Combat* (University Press of Kansas, 2001).

Pilsudski, Marshal of Poland Jozef, *Year 1920 and its Climax Battle of Warsaw during the Soviet–Polish War 1920 with the Addiition of M. Tukhachevskiy's March Beyond the Vistula* (Pilsudski Institute of America, London and New York, 1972).

Pleshakov, Konstantin, *Stalin's Folly: the Secret History of the German Invasion of Russia, June 1941* (Weidenfeld & Nicolson, 2005).

Rees, Lawrence, *War of the Century*. Series first broadcast on BBC2 in 1999 and published as *War of the Century: When Hitler fought Stalin* (BBC Worldwide, London, 1999).

Rhodes, Richard, *Dark Sun: the Making of the Hydrogen Bomb* (Simon & Schuster, New York and London, 1995).

Rohwer, Jürgen and Monakov, Mikhail S., *Stalin's Ocean-Going Fleet: Soviet Naval Strategy and Shipbuilding Programmes 1935–53* (Frank Cass, London, 2001), pp. 135–46.

Sakaida, Henry, illust. Hook, Christa, *Heroines of the Soviet Union 1941–45* (Osprey, Oxford, 2003).

Salisbury, Harrison E., *The 900 Days. The Siege of Leningrad* (First published Secker and Warburg, London, 1969; author used Pan, London, 2000 edition).

Samuelson, Lennart, *Plans for Stalin's War Machine. Tukhachevskii and Military-Economic Planning 1925–1941* (Macmillan, London and St Martin's Press, New York, 2000).

Schofield, Brian B., *The Russian Convoys* (London, 1964).

Sebag Montefiore, Simon, *Stalin. The Court of the Red Tsar* (Knopf, New York, 2004).

Silverlight, John, *The Victors' Dilemma, Allied Intervention in the Russian Civil War* (Barrie & Jenkins, London, 1970).

Steiner, Jean-François, *Treblinka: the Extraordinary Story of Jewish Resistance in the Notorious Nazi Death Camp* (Simon & Schuster, New York and London, 1967).

Stephan, Robert W., *Stalin's Secret War: Soviet Counterintelligence against the Nazis 1941–45* (University Press of Kansas, 2004).

Stone, Norman, *The Eastern Front, 1914–17* (London, 1974).

Suvorov, Viktor [Rezun], *Icebreaker: Who Started the Second World War?* (1990), published in Russian as *Ledokol* (1992).

Taylor, Brian, *Barbarossa to Berlin: A Chronology of the Campaigns on the Eastern Front 1941 to 1945* (Spellmount, Staplehurst, 2003).

Thurston, Robert W. and Bonwetsch, Bernd, ed., *The People's War: Responses to World War II in the Soviet Union* (University of Illinois, 2000).

Tolstoy, Leo, *War and Peace* (1869), trans. and with an introduction by Rosemary Edmonds (Penguin, London, 1982).

Van Dyke, Carl, *The Soviet Invasion of Finland, 1939–40* (Frank Cass, London and Portland, Oregon, 2001).

Woodward, Sir Llewellyn, *British Foreign Policy in the Second World War*, 3 vols (HMSO, London, 1970–72).

Ziemke, Earl F., *Moscow to Stalingrad: Decision in the East* (Center of Military History, US Army, Washington DC, 1987).

Ziemke, Earl F., *Stalingrad to Berlin: The German Defeat in the East* (Center of Military History, US Army, Washington DC, 1987).

ARTICLES AND CHAPTERS – RUSSIAN

Dorofeyev, Col. M., '*O nekotorykh prichinakh neudachnykh deystvii mekhaniizirovannykh korpusov v nachal'nom periode Velikoy Otechestvennoy voyny*' ('On certain causes of unsuccessful actions by mechanized corps in the opening period of the Great Patriotic War'), *Voyenno–Istoricheskiy Zhurnal* (Military Historical Journal) *VIZh*, 3/1964, pp. 32–44.

Gareyev, Gen. Makhmut A., '*Yeshchë raz k voprosu: gotovil li Stalin preventivny udar v 1941 g.*' ('Once again the question: whether Stalin was preparing a Preventive Strike in 1941'), *Novaya I noveyshaya istoriya (Recent and Most Recent History)(NNI)* 2/1994, pp. 198–202.

Gor'kov, Yu. A., '*Gotovil li Stalin uprezhdayushchiy udar protiv Gitlera v 1941 g.*' ('Whether Stalin was preparing a pre-emptive strike against Hitler in 1941'), *Novaya I noveyshaya istoriya (Recent and Most Recent History)(NNI)*, 3/1993, pp. 29–45.

Hoffman, I., '*Podgotovka Sovetskogo Soyuza k nastupatel'noy voyne. 1941 god.*' ('Preparation of the Soviet Union for an offensive war. 1941'), *Otechestvennaya istoria (Motherland History)*, 4/1993, pp. 19–31.

Karpov, Vladimir, '*Marshaly Velikoy Otechestvennoy – Zhukov*' ('Marshals of the Great

Patriotic [War] – Zhukov'), *Kommunist Vooruzhennykh Sil (Communist of the Armed Forces) (KVS)*, 5/1990, pp. 62–8.

Kireyev, Col. N., Dobenko, Lt Col. N., *'Iz opyta boyevogo primeneniya peredovykh otryadov tankovykh (mekhanizirovannykh) korpusov'* ('From the experience of employing forward detachments of tank (mechanized) corps in combat'), *VIZh*, 9/1982, pp. 20–7.

Kir'yan, Lt Gen. M. M., *'Nachal'ny period Velikoy Otechestvennoy voyny'*('The Opening Period of the GPW'), *VIZh*, 6/1988, pp. 11–17.

Kokoshin, Andrey, and Larionov, Maj. Gen. Valentin, *Problems of Preventing War*, in summer 1987, extracts from which were published in *Mirovaya ekonomika I mezhdunarodnye otnosheniya (World Economy and International Affairs)(MEMO)*, 6/1988, pp. 23–31.

Kurochkin, P., *'Deystviya tankovykh armiy v operativnoy glubine'*('Action of tank armies in the operational depth'), *Voyennaya Mysl'(Military thought)(VM)*, 11.1964, pp. 55–73.

Lelyushenko, Army General D. Didem, *'1-ya I 3-ya gvardeyskiye armii v kontrnastuplenii pod Stalingradom'* ('First and Third Guards armies in the counteroffensive at Stalingrad'), in A. M. Samsonov (ed.), *Stalingradskaya epopeya* (Nauka, Moscow, 1968).

Nevzorov, Col. B. I., *'Dostizheniye uspekha pri obshchem prevokhodstve protivnika v silakh I sredstvakh'* ('Attaining success in the presence of a general enemy superiority in forces and means [men and equipment]'), (*Tenth Army in the Moscow counteroffensive, VIZh*, 12/1986, pp. 22–9.

Pokazaniya marshala Tukhachevskogo ('Plan porazheniya'), *Voyenno-istoricheskiy zhurnal (Military Historical Journal) VIZh*), 8/1991, p. 48.

Polukhin, Col. N. F. and Patychenko, Lt Col. Yu. D., *''Material'noye obespecheniye podvyzhnykh grupp frontov v Vislo-Oderskoy Operatsii'* ('Logistic support of Front Mobile Groups during the Vistula-Oder operation'), *VIZh*, 1/1987, pp. 30–6.

Porfir'yev, Maj. Gen. E. V., *'Reyd k. Tatsinskoy'* ('Raid to Tatsinskaya'), *VIZh* 11/1987, pp. 63–71.

Sokolov, Lt Gen. A. A., *'Dostizheniye vysokykh tempov nastupleniya v khode frontovykh operatsii Velikoy otechestvennoy voyny'* ('Attaining High Tempos of the Offensive in the Course of Front Operations in the GPW'), *VIZh* 12/1985, pp. 8–13.

ARTICLES AND CHAPTERS – OTHER

Bellamy, Christopher D., 'Stalin's Plan to Cripple Germany', *Independent*, Saturday 14 April 1990, p. 12.

Bellamy, Christopher D., 'Brute Force and Genius. The View from the Soviet Union' in Richard Cobbold, ed., *The World Reshaped. Volume 1. Fifty Years After the War in Europe* (Macmillan, London and St Martin's Press, New York, 1996).

Bellamy, Christopher D., 'Red Star in the West: Marshal Tukhachevskiy and East-West Exchanges on the art of War', *RUSI Journal*, December 1987, pp. 63–73.

Cornford, Stan, *D-Day: the Role of the Met Office* (HMSO, 1994).

Cornford, Stan, *With Wind and Sword: the Story of Meteorology and D-Day* (Met Office internal publication).

Coyle, Capt. Harold W., 'Tatsinskaya and Soviet OMG Doctrine', *Armor*, Jan–Feb 1985.

Ellman, Michael, 'Soviet Repression Statistics: Some Comments', *Europe–Asia Studies* [formerly *Soviet Studies*], Vol. 54, No. 7, 2002, pp. 1151–72.

Ellman, Michael and Maksudov, S., 'Soviet Deaths in the Great Patriotic War: a Note – World War II', *Europe-Asia Studies*, July 1994.

Erickson, John, 'Barbarossa, June 1941: Who attacked whom?', *History Today*, Vol. 51(7), July 2001, pp. 11–17.

Erickson, John, 'Soviet Women at War' in John Garrard and Carol Garrard, eds., *World War 2 and the Soviet People* (St Martin's Press, London, 1993), pp. 50–76.

Erickson, John, ' "Russia will not be trifled with": Geopolitical Facts and Fantasies' in Colin S. Gray and Geoffrey Sloan, *Geopolitics: Geography and Strategy* (Frank Cass, London, 1999), pp. 242–68.

Frieser, Karl-Heinz, Kulikov, Pavel, Bellamy, Christopher, Vesey-Holt, Geoffrey and Hughes-Wilson, John, in 'Kursk–Sixty Years On', *RUSI Journal*, Vol. 148, No. 5 (October 2003), pp. 78–88.

Frisby, E. M., 'Russian Ideas on Long-Range Weather Forecasting', a review of *Basic principles of the synoptic method of long-range weather forecasting* (Hydrometeorological Publishing House, Moscow and Leningrad, 1940), in *Weather*, Vol. 12, No. 12, December 1947, p. 365.

Harrison, Mark, 'The USSR and Total War: Why Didn't the Soviet Economy Collapse in 1942?', draft chapter for Roger Chickering and Stig Förster, ed., *A World at Total War: Global Conflict and the Politics of Destruction 1939–45* (Cambridge University Press). Revised 13 February 2002.

Glantz, David M., 'Forgotten Battles of the Soviet-German War', *Journal of Soviet Military Studies*, Vol. 8, No. 4, December 1995, pp. 768–808; Rzhev-Sychevka pp. 784–89.

Gorodetsky, Gabriel, 'Was Stalin planning to attack Hitler in June 1941?', *RUSI*, 131/3 (1986), pp. 19–30.

Hole, N. H., 'Rabies and Quarantine', reprinted from *Nature*, Vol. 224, No. 5216, pp. 244–6.

Maslov, A. A., 'Tried for Treason against the Motherland: Soviet Generals Condemned after Release from German Captivity', Part 1, *Journal of Slavic Military Studies*, Vol. 13, No. 2 (June 2000), pp. 111–15.

Milligan, Timothy P., 'Spies, ciphers and "Zitadelle". Intelligence and the Battle of Kursk 1943', *Journal of Contemporary History*, Vol. 22 (1987), No. 2.

Nevezhin, V. A., 'The Pact with Germany and the Idea of an "Offensive War" (1939–1941)', *Journal of Slavic Military Studies*, Vol. 8, No. 4 (December 1995), pp. 809–43.

Pennington, Reina, 'Women and the Battle of Stalingrad' in Ljubica Erickson and Mark Erickson, ed., *Russia: War, Peace and Diplomacy: Essays in Honour of John Erickson*, (Weidenfeld & Nicolson, London, 2005), pp. 169–211, 327–33.

Snow, Edgar, 'The Red Army's Flying Tank' (Interview with Lt Gen. Sergey Ilyushin, *Saturday Evening Post*, 10 March 1945.

Stoeckli, Fritz, 'Soviet and German Loss Rates during the Great Patriotic War. The Price of Victory', *JSMS*, Vol. 3, no. 4 (Dec 1990), pp. 645–51.

Stolfi, Russel H. S., 'Chance in History: the Russian Winter of 1941–42', *History*, Vol. 65 (1980), pp. 214–28.

Whaley, Bart, 'Toward a general theory of deception', in a special issue of the *Journal of Strategic Studies, Issue on Military Deception and Strategic Surprise* (March 1982), pp. 178–92.

THESES

Blood, Philip Warren, *Bandenbekämpfung. Nazi occupation security in Eastern Europe and Soviet Russia 1942–45* (Ph.D., Cranfield University, 2003).

Raymond, Ellsworth Lester, *Soviet Preparation for Total War 1925–51*, (Ph.D., University of Michigan, 1951).

Wadley, Patricia Louise, *Even One is Too Many: An Examination of the Soviet Refusal to Repatriate Liberated American World War II Prisoners of War* (Ph.D., Texas Christian University, May 1993).

Wilkinson, Mark, *The Soviet Biological Weapons Programme from 1918 to 1945* (M.Sc. Global Security dissertation, Cranfield University, 2005).

TV PROGRAMMES, VIDEO AND DVD

Dostal, Nikolai, *Shtrafbat (Punishment Battalion)*, which the author believes to have been well researched, available on DVD, *Shtrafbat 1* and *Shtrafbat 2*, 2004.

Nazi Sea Disaster, a documentary originally made for UK Channel 4 (Termite Art Productions, Erik Nelson producer, 2002).

INTERNET

Eastern Front (World War II) in http://en.wikipedia.org/wiki/World_War_II_casualties, accessed 12 January 2007.

Gregorovich, Andrew, 'World War II in Ukraine: Ukraine's Population Losses in World War II: 7.5 million or 13,614,000?', accessed on <http://www.infoukes.com/history/ww2>'.

Harrison, Mark, 'The USSR and Total War: Why Didn't the Soviet Economy Collapse in 1942?', p. 6. Retrieved from <http://www.warwick.ac.uk/uk/fac/soc/economics/staff/faculty> 9 Dec 2005.

Kappes, Irwin J., 'The Greatest Maritime Disaster in History . . . and why you probably never heard of it' <http://www.militaryhistoryonline.com / wwii/articles/wilhelmgustloff.aspx>.

Prociuk, Stephan G., in *Annals of the Ukrainian Academy of Arts and Sciences in the US*, Vol. 13, no. 35–6, pp. 23–50 (New York, 1977)<http://www.infoukes.com/history/ww2>.

Der Untergang der "Wilhelm Gustloff", NDR 1 Radio MV on <http://www1.ndr.de/ndr>.

UN Population Fund on <www.unfpa.org>.

DaVanzo, Julie, Olinker, Olga and Grammich, Clifford, 'Too Few Good Men. The Security Implications of Russian demographics' <www.rand.org/popmatters/pubs.html>.

Sellwood, A.V., *The Damned Don't Drown. The Sinking of the Wilhelm Gustloff.* See <http://www.amazon.com>.

Memoirs of Roza Weintraub – oral history prepared 26 June 1986, accessed on <http://www.shtetlinks.jewishgen.org/kibart/rozamem.html> 6 August 2005.

<http://nuclearweaponarchive.org/Usa/Med/Lbfm.html> retrieved 13 December 2005.

<http://mothra.rerf.or.jp/ENG/A-bomb/History/Damages.html>, retrieved 13 December 2005.

<www.historyontheweb.com>.

Notes and references

Preface and acknowledgements

1 Carl von Clausewitz, *On War* (1832), trans. and ed. Michael Howard and Peter Paret (Princeton University Press, 1976), Bk 1, ch. 3, 'On Military Genius', p. 102.
2 Clausewitz, 'Plan of Operations', *Strategie aus dem Jahr 1804* (Strategy in 1804) (Hamburg, 1937), p. 51, cited in Peter Paret, 'The Genesis of *On War*', in Clausewitz, *On War*, op. cit., p. 21.
3 John Erickson, *The Road to Stalingrad. Stalin's War with Germany, Vol. 1* (Weidenfeld & Nicolson, London, 1975) and *The Road to Berlin. Stalin's War with Germany, Vol. 2* (Weidenfeld & Nicolson, London, 1983).
4 Militärgeschichtliches Forschungsamt (Research Institute for Military History), Potsdam, *Germany and the Second World War*, published in German by Deutsche Verlags-Anstalt GmbH, Stuttgart (henceforward DVAG), and in English by the Clarendon Press, Oxford. Of particular value are Vol. IV, *The Attack on the Soviet Union* (DVAG 1996), by Horst Boog, Jürgen Förster, Joachim Hoffmann, Ernst Klink, Rolf-Dieter Müller and Gerd R. Ueberschär, trans. Dean S. McMurray, Ewald Osers and Louise Willmot, and Vol. VI, *The Global War* (DVAG and OUP, 2001), by Horst Boog, Werner Rahn, Richard Stumpf and Bernd Wegner, trans. Ewald Osers, John Brownjohn, Patricia Crampton and Louise Willmot. Introducing Volume IV, Manfred Messerschmidt says it is 'once more no "official" publication' (p. 8).
5 G. F. Krivosheyev, ed., *Grif sekretnosti snyat. Poteri vooruzhennykh sil SSSR v voynakh, boyevykh deystviyakh i voyennykh konfliktakh (The 'Secret' Stamp is Lifted. Losses of USSR Armed Forces in Wars, Military Actions and Armed Conflicts)*(Voyenizdat [Military Press], Moscow, 1993), signed to press 10 December 1992, 30,000 copies. Translated as *Soviet Casualties and Combat losses in the Twentieth Century* (trans. Lionel Leventhal Ltd, 1997, pub. with a foreword by Prof. John Erickson, Greenhill Books, London and Stackpole, Pennsylvania, 1997).
6 Anthony Beevor, *Stalingrad* (Viking, London, 1998) and *Berlin 1945: the Downfall* (Viking, London, 2002).
7 Max Hastings, *Armageddon* (Macmillan, London, 2004).
8 Lt Gen. S. V. Stepashin, ed., *Organy Gosudarstvennoy Bezopasnosti SSSR v Velikoy Otechestvennoy Voyne. Sbornik dokumentov (Organs of State Security of the USSR in the Great Patriotic War. A Collection of Documents). Tom I. Nakanune* (Volume

One. *On the Eve*). Bk 1: November 1938–December 1940, Bk 2: 1 January–21 June 1941 (FSK Academy, Russia, 1995, 20,000 copies). *Tom II Nachalo* (Volume Two. *The Beginning*). Bk 1: 22 June–31 August 1941 Bk 2: 1 September–31 December 1941 (Rus' publishers, Moscow, 2000). *Tom III* (Volume Three). Bk 1 *Krushcheniya 'Blitzkriga'(Breaking the 'Blitzkrieg')*, 1 January–30 June 1942, Bk 2: *Ot oborony k nastupleniyu (From the Defensive to the Offensive)*, 1 July–31 December 1942 (Rus', Moscow, 2003).

9 See Sergey Drobyazko, *Pod znamenami vragi. Antisovetskiye formirovaniya 1941–45 (Under Enemy Banners. Anti-Soviet Formations 1941–45)* (Dom knigi, Moscow, 2004).

10 V. A. Zhilin, ed., *Bitva pod Moskvoy*, 2 vols (Olma Press, Moscow, 2002).

11 N. A. Lomagin, ed., *Neizvestnaya blokada*, 2 vols (Olma Press, Moscow/Neva Press, St Petersburg, 2002).

12 Georgiy Zhukov, *Vospominaniya I Razmyshleniya (Reminiscences and Reflections)*, 13th edn, unexpurgated, 2 vols (Olma Press, Moscow, 2002).

13 Konstantin Rokossovskiy, *Soldatskiy dolg (A Soldier's Duty)* (Olma Press, Moscow, 2002).

14 Viktor Cherepanov, *Vlast, I Voyna: Stalinsky mekhanizm gosudarstvennogo upravieniya v Velikoy Otechestvennoy voyne (Power and War: the Stalinist Mechanism for State Direction in the Great Patriotic War)* Izvestiya, Moscow, 2006).

15 Lt Gen. I. I. Maksimov, Army Gen. N. N. Lobov, Maj. Gen. V. A. Zolotarev, *Velikaya Otechestvennaya voyna 1941–45 (The Great Patriotic War, 1941–45)* (DIK Press, Moscow, Military Cartographic Department of the General Stafgf, VS RF, and OOO Drofa, 2005).

16 V. E. Levtov, ed., *Parad Pobedy (Victory Parade)* (LIK, St Petersburg, 2005). Boxed set.

17 Catherine Merridale, *Ivan's War: The Red Army 1939–1945* (Faber, London, 2005; Metropolitan, New York, 2006).

18 Konstantin Pleshakov, *Stalin's Folly: the Secret History of the German Invasion of Russia, June 1941* (Weidenfeld & Nicolson, 2005).

19 Gabriel Gorodetsky, *Grand Delusion. Stalin and the German Invasion of Russia* (Yale University Press, 1999).

20 Simon Sebag Montefiore, *Stalin. The Court of the Red Tsar* (Knopf, New York, 2004).

21 Norman Davies, *Rising '44: 'The Battle for Warsaw'* (Macmillan, London, 2003).

22 Lennart Samuelson, *Plans for Stalin's War Machine. Tukhachevskii and Military-Economic Planning 1925–1941* (Macmillan, London and St Martin's Press, New York, 2000).

23 Edwin Bacon, *The GULag at War. Stalin's Forced Labour System in the Light of the Archives* (Macmillan, London, 1996). *GULag* should be written like that, as it stands for *Glavnoye Upravleniye LaGerey* – Main Directorate of Camps.

24 See Valentina Ya. Galagan, *Ratny podvig zhenshchin v gody Velikoy Otechestvennoy voyny (The Triumph of Women in the Great Patriotic War)*, (Vysshaya shkola, Kiev [Ki'iv], 1986); also Reina Pennington's superb *Wings, Women and War: Soviet Airwomen in World War II Combat* (University Press of Kansas, 2001), and

'Women and the Battle of Stalingrad' in Ljubica Erickson and Mark Erickson, ed., *Russia: War, Peace and Diplomacy: Essays in Honour of John Erickson* (Weidenfeld & Nicolson, London, 2005), pp. 169–211, 327–33. Also John Erickson, 'Soviet Women at War' in John Garrard and Carol Garrard, eds, *World War 2 and the Soviet People* (St Martin's Press, London, 1993), pp. 50–76.

25 Michael Ellman, 'Soviet Repression Statistics: Some Comments', *Europe–Asia Studies* [formerly *Soviet Studies*] Vol. 54, No. 7, 2002, pp. 1151–72.

26 Mark Harrison, *Accounting for War: Soviet Production, Employment and the Defence Burden, 1940–45* (Cambridge University Press, 1996, 2002). See also 'The USSR and Total War: Why Didn't the Soviet Economy Collapse in 1942?', draft chapter for Roger Chickering and Stig Forster, eds, *A World at Total War: Global Conflict and the Politics of Destruction 1939–45* (Cambridge University Press). Revised 13 February 2002.

27 Carl Van Dyke, *The Soviet Invasion of Finland, 1939–40* (Frank Cass, London and Portland, Oregon, 2001).

28 One of the best sources of information was the Russian TV drama, directed by Nikolai Dostal, which the author believes to have been well researched, available on DVD, *Shtrafbat 1* and *Shtrafbat 2*, 2004.

29 Philip Warren Blood, *Bandenbekämpfung. Nazi Occupation Security in Eastern Europe and Soviet Russia 1942–45* (Ph.D., Cranfield University, 2003). Published as *Hitler's Bandit Hunters: the SS and the Nazi Occupation of Europe* (Potomac, Washington, 2006).

30 *Stalingrad: Dekabr' 1942g. – fevral' 1943g. Frontovy dnevnik khudozhnika K. I. Finogenova (Stalingrad: December 1942–February 1943. The front-line diary of artist K. I. Finogenov)* (Iskusstvo, Moscow/Leningrad, 1948).

1. Flight of the rabid wolf

1 UK National Archives (UKNA) (formerly the Public Record Office), Kew, *MAF 287/433*, esp. Enclosure 24a, Central Veterinary Laboratory, MAFF Weybridge, N. H. Hole, 'Rabies and Quarantine', reprinted from *Nature*, Vol. 224, No. 5216, pp. 244–6. 'Today rabies is epizootic in many countries . . . Sylvatic rabies occasionally assumes epizootic proportions, resulting in an alarming spread of infections such as has occurred in western Europe since 1945.' The last major outbreak of rabies in the UK had been the result of 300 dogs being smuggled in after the First World War. See CUST 49/5099. The number of reported cases in the Union of Soviet Socialist Republics (USSR) had peaked at a relatively modest 910 in 1967.

2 Hole, ibid., p. 2 (of 3).

3 When the Berlin Wall was suddenly erected in 1961, wild boar which normally lived around West Berlin but which had headed down seasonal 'runs' were trapped in East German territory – behind the 'Berlin Wall'. Happily, when the Wall came down in 1989, the wild boar remembered their seasonal routes from twenty-eight years before, and returned. Conversation with Colonel Christopher Langton who served in Berlin, 1 November 2004.

4 Introduction to 'Conflict, Compromise, Cost', Part 3 of John Erickson and David Dilks, ed., *Barbarossa: the Axis and the Allies* (Edinburgh University Press, 1994), p. 227.

5 The Kwantung Army signed the instrument of surrender at Khabarovsk on 17 August 1945, following a direct order from Tokyo. See the entry in John Keegan, ed., *The Times Atlas of the Second World War* (Times Books, 1989), p. 198. Colonel David Glantz, *August Storm: the Soviet 1945 Strategic Offensive in Manchuria* (Leavenworth Paper No. 7, Fort Leavenworth, Kansas, 1983) is the classic on this operation.

6 John Erickson, 'Soviet War Losses. Calculations and Controversies', in Erickson and Dilks, ed., *Barbarossa*, pp. 255–77. On German losses, the best estimate is 4 million killed and missing on the eastern front, plus 374,000 out of 3.3 million prisoners who died in captivity. In addition, at least 360,000 German civilians may have died in eastern Europe and the Soviet invasion of Germany. See Dr Rüdiger Overmans of the German Military History Office in Potsdam, cited in Eastern Front (World War II) in http://en.wikipedia.org/wiki/World_War_II_ casualties, accessed 12 January 2007.

7 Christopher Duffy, *Red Storm on the Reich. The Soviet March on Germany, 1945* (London, 1991), pp. 93–4.

8 Valentin Berezhkov, trans. Sergey M. Mikheyev, *At Stalin's Side: His Interpreter's Memoirs from the October Revolution to the Fall of the Dictator's Empire* (Birch Lane Press, New York, 1994), p. 310.

9 Based on a conversation with Richard Overy, Professor of Modern History at King's College London. See also Richard Overy's entry 'World War II', in Richard Holmes, ed., *The Oxford Companion to Military History* (Oxford University Press, 2001), pp. 1004–7.

10 Robert Harris, *Fatherland*, is an interesting counter-factual historical novel, set in Germany in the 1960s. The Germans have repelled the western Allied invasion in June 1944, and have just reopened dialogue with the United States twenty years later. But Germany continues to be engaged in a war deep in Russia.

11 Air Chief Marshal Sir Arthur Harris, *Despatch on War Operations*, 23 February 1942–8 May 1945 (October 1945), Preface and Introduction by Sebastian Cox; and *Harris – a German View* by Horst Boog (Frank Cass, London, 1995), p. 12. 'The force available for bombing Germany during 1942, therefore, remained inadequate for the task.'

12 See *The Times Atlas of the Second World War*, pp. 108–9 (Battle of the Atlantic), 122–3 (South West Pacific), 130–1 (Sicily). 'D' Day for 'Husky', the invasion of Sicily, was 10 July: on 12 July the Battle of Kursk reached its climax with the clash of armour at Prokhorovka. Furthermore, 'August 1943 marked the real Allied victory in the Battle of the Atlantic' (p. 108).

13 Introduction to *Germany and the Second World War* (1996), Vol. IV, p. 8.

14 *Time* magazine, New York, 4 January 1943, with cover painting. Churchill, who was half American, had, slightly less surprisingly, been 'man of the year' in 1942 (for 1940). The Nazi-Soviet pact had also earned Stalin the title for 1939.

15 'Hour of Our Greatest Effort is Approaching', 26 March 1944, in Charles Eade, ed., *The Dawn of Liberation. War Speeches by the Right Hon. Winston S. Churchill,*

1944 (Cassell, London, Toronto, Melbourne and Sydney, 1945), p. 41. Emphasis added.

16 UKNA, *WO/208/1777, Effects of a Possible Soviet Collapse and Possible Action Required.*

17 UKNA, *FO/371/43335, Some Probable Post-War Tendencies in Soviet Foreign Policy as Affecting British Interests*, Foreign Office 29 April 1944, N1008/183/38.

18 See John Erickson, ' "Russia will not be trifled with": Geopolitical Facts and Fantasies', in Colin S. Gray and Geoffrey Sloan, *Geopolitics: Geography and Strategy* (Frank Cass, London, 1999), pp. 242–68, esp. pp. 248, 252–63.

19 Michael Ellman and S. Maksudov, 'Soviet Deaths in the Great Patriotic War: a note – World War II'. *Europe–Asia Studies*, July 1994. This examines all the estimates in great detail. See also Erickson, 'Soviet War Losses', in Erickson and Dilks, ed., *Barbarossa*, esp. pp. 256–8.

20 See especially the introduction to Krivosheyev, *Soviet Casualties and Combat Losses*, p. 4.

21 David M. Glantz, *Zhukov's Greatest Defeat. The Red Army's Epic Disaster in Operation Mars, 1942* (University of Kansas, 1999/Ian Allen, London, 2000).

22 Anton Antonov-Ovseenko, *The Time of Stalin – Portrait of a Tyranny*, trans. from the Russian by George Sanders with an introduction by Stephen F. Cohen (New York, 1981), cited in <http://www.databank.neu.edu/census.htm>; 1939 USSR census. <http://www.eastview.com/xq/ASP/sk>

23 *Pravda*, 26 September 1937, cited in Antonov-Ovseenko, above.

24 1939 census on <eastview.com> (see reference 22).

25 197 million in Michael Ellman and S. Maksudov, 'Soviet Deaths in the Great Patriotic War: a Note – World War II', p. 2; Otto von Erdmannsdorf, German Minister in Hungary, to the [German] Foreign Ministry, Budapest, 22 June 1941, Telegram No. 681, in *Documents on German Foreign Policy 1918–1945*, Series D, Vol. XII, *The War Years*, February 1 1941 to June 2 1941 (Her Majesty's Stationery Office, London, 1962), pp. 1077–8, 'One hundred and eighty million Russians . . .'.

26 Ellman and Maksudov, 'Soviet Deaths . . .', p. 1.

27 Ibid.

28 Ibid., p. 3.

29 Erickson's foreword to Krivosheyev, *Soviet Casualties and Combat Losses . . .*, pp. vii–xii.

30 Ibid., esp. pp. x–xi.

31 Ibid., p. x.

32 Ibid., p. xi.

33 Ibid., and Reina Pennington, *Wings, Women and War*, op.cit.

34 Andrew Gregorovich, 'World War II in Ukraine: Ukraine's Population Losses in World War II: 7.5 million or 13,614,000?', accessed on <http://www.infoukes.com/history/ww2>.

35 *A Short History of Ukraine*, published by the Ukrainian Academy of Sciences in Kiev in 1986, says that as a result of the Second World war the population contracted by 13,614,000. In 1977 Stephan G. Prociuk estimated that Ukraine lost 11 million as a result of the war. See *Annals of the Ukrainian Academy of Arts and*

Sciences in the US, Vol. 13, no. 35–6, pp. 23–50 (New York, 1977). <http://www.infoukes.com/history/ww2>.

36 In addition to the direct losses, the 'birth deficit' – babies not born between 1941 and 45 – is estimated at 10 million and there was also a lower post-war birth rate because of the imbalance in the sex ratios among people of child-rearing age. Erickson, in Erickson and Dilks, ed., *Barbarossa*, p. 258. Ellman and Maksudov mention a 'hypothetical demographic loss' of 40 million by 31 December 1945 (p. 2).

37 See *The Times Atlas*, p. 173. 350,000 orphans, Erickson, 'Soviet War Losses', p. 273.

38 A. V. Sellwood, *The Damned Don't Drown. The Sinking of the Wilhelm Gustloff.* See <http://www.amazon.com>. Also Irwin J. Kappes, 'The Greatest Maritime Disaster in History . . . and why you probably never heard of it', <http://www.militaryhistoryonline.com/wwii/articles/wilhelmgustloff.aspx>. Originally 6,000 to 7,000 were thought to be on board, of whom 996 are known to have survived. However, *Nazi Sea Disaster*, a documentary originally made for UK Channel 4 (Termite Art Productions, Erik Nelson, producer, 2002) used eyewitness accounts, blueprints and computer modelling of the ship and the events, based on evacuation patterns in similar disasters, and produced an estimate of 10,614 on board, giving 9,618 deaths. See also 'Der Untergang der "Wilhelm Gustloff"', NDR 1 Radio MV on <http://www1.ndr.de/ndr> (10,000 refugees: hence, perhaps, 9,000 dead).

39 The UN Population Fund on <www.unfpa.org> estimates the Russian population at the time of writing to be just below 144 million. The Russian State Statistics Committee, quoted by Nicholas Eberstadt in 'The emptying of Russia', *Washington Post*, 13 February 2004, estimated the population in mid 2003 as 144.5 million. See also Julie DaVanzo, Olga Olinker and Clifford Grammich, 'Too Few Good Men. The Security Implications of Russian Demographics', <www.rand.org/popmatters/pubs.html>.

40 UKNA, *FO 371/43335, Some Probable Post-War Tendencies*, p. 3.

41 UKNA, *FO/371/47925*, Roberts, Frank (later Sir Frank) to Ernest Bevin, 21 September 1945, printed 29 September 1945.

2. Absolute and total war

1 Engels to Sorge, London, 7 January 1888, in Dona Torr, ed., *Karl Marx and Friedrich Engels' Correspondence* (Martin Lawrence, London, 1934), p. 455.

2 Adam Roberts and Richard Guelff, ed., *Documents on the Laws of War* (Third Edition, Oxford University Press, 2000), esp. pp. 67–84, 1907 Hague Convention IV, Laws and Customs of War on Land, pp. 196–7 relating to 27 July 1929 *Geneva Convention for the Relief of the Wounded and Sick in Armies in the Field* and p. 244 relating to the *Convention* (also of 27 July) *Relative to the Treatment of Prisoners of War*. These conventions were superseded by the expanded 1949 Geneva Conventions, and Roberts and Guelff therefore only refer to the 1929 Conventions in passing. The signatories to the 1929 Conventions can be found,

however, on <www.historyontheweb.com>. In 1941 the USSR announced that it would observe the terms of the Hague Convention of 1907, which did not provide (as the 1929 Geneva Convention does) for neutral inspection of prison camps, for the exchange of prisoners' names, and for correspondence with prisoners. The Soviet Union did sign the 1949 revision of the Geneva Conventions in 1955, when it also acknowledged itself as the successor state to Russia regarding the 1907 Hague Convention.

3 Clausewitz, *On War*, trans. Howard and Paret, Bk 1, ch. 1, part 3, p. 75. For a critical view of Clausewitz, in the Russian context, see Andrei Mertsalov, 'Jomini versus Clausewitz' in Erickson and Erickson, *Russia: War, Peace and Diplomacy*, pp. 11–19, 300–1.

4 Winston S. Churchill, 'Their finest hour'. Speech to the House of Commons and also broadcast, 18 June 1940, in *Into Battle* (War Speeches), compiled by Randolph S. Churchill (Cassell, London, February 1941), p. 234.

5 Clausewitz, *On War*, trans. Howard and Paret, Bk 1, ch. 1, part 3, p. 77.

6 Ibid., part 4, p. 77.

7 Ibid., part 5, p. 77.

8 UKNA, *FO/371/43335, Some Probable Post-War Tendencies in Soviet Foreign Policy*, p. 5.

9 Clausewitz, trans. Howard and Paret, Bk 1, ch.1, part 6, p. 78.

10 Ibid., part 12, p. 82.

11 Ibid., part 2, p. 75.

12 Ibid., part 8, p. 79.

13 Ibid., Bk 1, ch. 7, 'On friction in war', pp. 119–21.

14 Ibid., Bk 1, ch.1, part 6, p. 78.

15 Ibid., part 8, p. 79.

16 Krivosheyev, ed., *Casualties and Combat Losses*, pp. 111–13, 124–5, 126–8, 157–9. Total Soviet losses in the race for Berlin are given as 78,291 irrecoverable and 274,184 wounded. But the daily rate of losses, killed and wounded was 15,325. Although overall losses at Stalingrad were greater – 323,856 irrecoverable losses in the defensive phase and 154,885 in the offensive phase (post 19 November 1942), Stalingrad went on for much longer and the daily loss rate (killed and wounded) was a relatively modest 5,151 and 6,392, respectively. The Berlin loss rates were only just exceeded by those in the frontier battles of 1941, when Soviet forces lost 23,210 per day in Belarus between 22 June and 9 July and 16,106 per day in western Ukraine between 22 June and 6 July.

17 Clausewitz, trans. Howard and Paret, Bk 1, ch. 1, part 28, 'The Consequences for Theory', p. 89, is the classic Clausewitzian 'Trinity'. The idea is often misunderstood and misquoted. The basic Trinity is primordial violence; luck and chance; and subordination to political aims. The people, the military command(ers) and the government are the agencies principally, though never exclusively, concerned with these interlocking areas.

18 Roberts and Guelff, pp. 67–84; *Germany and the Second World War*, Vol. IV, p. 841.

19 'World War Two: the Geneva Convention', at <www.historyonthenet.com>. The forty-three included 'Ireland and British Dominions' as one signatory (Ireland

was then a 'Free State' and, although a sovereign nation like Australia or Canada, did not finally shake off its British dependency until 1949). Of the other combatants involved on the eastern front, Poland, Finland, Hungary, Latvia and Estonia signed, but not Lithuania or Romania.

20 Roberts and Guelff, pp. 156–73.

21 Patricia Louise Wadley, *Even One is Too Many: An Examination of the Soviet Refusal to Repatriate Liberated American World War II Prisoners of War* (Ph.D., Texas Christian University, May 1993), accessed on internet, ch. II.

22 Ibid.

23 *Germany and the Second World War*, Vol. IV, pp. 841(17 July note), 914 (17 July and 1 July), citing V. V. Pozdnyakov '*Sovetskaya agentura v lageryakh voyennoplennykh v Germanii, 1941–45 gg.*' ('The Soviet Secret Service in Prisoner of War Camps in Germany 1941–45), *Novy zhurnal*, 101 (1970), pp. 156–71, and *Polozheniya o voyennoplennykh*, Postanovleniye SNK SSSR, 1 July 1941, 1798–1800s, Bundesarchiv-Militararchiv (BA-MA), Freiburg, RW 2.v, 158, fo. 128.

24 Wadley, ch. II.

25 Vladimir Sherstnev, *Tragediya Sorok Pervogo: Dokumenty I Razmyshleniya (The Tragedy of 'Forty-One: Documents and Reminiscences)* (Rusich, Smolensk, 2005), p. 108.

26 *Germany and the Second World War*, Vol. IV, p. 841, citing Karl Fricke, *Politik und Justiz in der DDR* (Cologne, 1979). On Article 58 see also Aleksandr Solzhenitsyn, *The GULag Archipelago*.

27 *Germany and the Second World War*, Vol. IV, p. 849.

28 The Soviet government's lack of interest in the prisoner-of-war conventions is noted in *Rapport du Comité International de la Croix Rouge sur son activité pendant la seconde guerre mondiale, 1 septembre 1939–30 juin 1947, i, Activités de la caractère général* (Geneva, 1948), 419–53, cited in *Germany and the Second World War*, Vol. IV, p. 842.

29 *Germany and the Second World War*, Vol. IV, p. 487, citing OKH/GenStdH/ GenQu/Qu 1/Abt Kriegsverwaltung (Qu 4) No. I/0050/41 VII Angelegenheit, 4 March 1941, BA-MA RH 3/v.132.

30 *Germany and the Second World War*, Vol. IV, p. 849.

31 Ibid., p. 487.

32 Ibid., p. 482, citing *KTB OKW*i. 341 (3 March 1941).

33 Blood, *Bandenbekämpfung*, pp. 40–7.

34 *Germany and the Second World War*, Vol. IV, p. 504.

35 Ibid., p. 505.

36 Ibid., p. 514 (Jurgen Förster). In 'The Brutalisation of Warfare, Nazi Crimes and the Wehrmacht', in Erickson and Dilks, ed., *Barbarossa*, pp. 229–37, on p. 230 Klaus-Jurgen Müller dates the Guidelines as 15 May, which is equally correct.

37 *Germany and the Second World War*, Vol. IV, pp. 514–15, citing OKW/WFSt/Abt. L(IV Qu) No. 44560/41 g.Kdos. Chefs 19 May 1941, emphasis in original. Also referred to in Müller, in Erickson and Erickson, *Barbarossa*, p. 230.

38 Blood, p. 100.

39 *Germany and the Second World War*, Vol. IV, p. 510.

40 Ibid.

41 Müller in Erickson and Dilks, p. 231.

42 Ibid., p. 232; Canaris's statement used in his defence at the Nuremberg war trials: Quoted in Judgment, IMT, *Trials of the Major War Criminals*, Vol. XXII, p. 475

43 Müller in Erickson and Dilks, p. 232.

44 *Germany and the Second World War*, Vol. IV, p. 497, citing Franz Halder, *Kriegstagebuch* (War Diaries) (Stuttgart 1962–4), trans. and ed. Trevor N. Dupuy, *The Halder Diaries 1939–1942* (2 vols, Boulder, Colorado, 1975), pp. 846–7.

45 Ibid., p. 911, citing Stalin, *Velikaya Otechestvennaya Voyna Sovetskogo Soyuza (On the Great Patriotic War of the Soviet Union)* (Moscow, 1946).

46 Ilya Ehrenburg, *Russia at War*. Collection of articles, with an Introduction by J. B. Priestley (London, 1943), pp. 97, 130.

47 Ibid., pp. 97, 189.

48 *Germany and the Second World War*, Vol. IV, p. 913, citing Alfred Maurice de Zayas, *Die Wehrmacht-Untersuchungstelle: Deutsche Ermittlungen über Alliierte Völkerrechtsverletzungen im Zweiten Weltkrieg* (Munich, 1980).

49 Ibid.

50 Ibid., p. 914, citing Shaposhnikov to Army and Front Chiefs of Staff, Bundesarchiv-Militärarchiv, Freiburg, captured Soviet orders on prisoner handling BA-MA RW 2/v, 158, folio 103.

51 Ibid., p. 914.

52 Ibid., p. 916.

53 Ibid., pp. 917–18.

54 Ibid., p. 918.

55 Lawrence Rees, *War of the Century*. Series first broadcast on BBC2 in 1999 and published as *War of the Century. When Hitler fought Stalin* (BBC Worldwide, London, 1999), pp. 165–8. On *Smersh*, see Robert W. Stephan, *Stalin's Secret War: Soviet Counterintelligence against the Nazis 1941–45* (University Press of Kansas, 2004). This is the first comprehensive survey in English of the work of Soviet state security services in the war and contains essential information on the organization of the NKGB, NKVD and *Smersh*.

56 Robert W. Stephan, *Stalin's Secret War*. The author is employed by the CIA, which might cause some readers to question his deductions about the scale of the Soviet effort, but the research is impeccable.

57 Elena Vasilevna (surname not recorded), on visit to the Museum of the Road of Life, Mor'ye, Lake Ladoga, 1 March 2004, and again, 6 March 2005.

58 Norbert Wallbaum and guide Kirill Kirillovich, visit to Museum of the Defence of Moscow, 11 March 2005.

59 *Clausewitz, On War*, Bk 1, ch. 1, part 2, p. 75.

60 Valentin Berezhkov, *Stranitsy diplomaticheskoy istorii (Pages from Diplomatic History)* (Mezhdunarodnye otnosheniya, Moscow, 1982), pp. 51–76.

61 Engels to Danielson, London, 22 September 1892, cited in Torr, p. 498.

62 Erich von Ludendorff, *The Nation at War*, trans. from *Der totale Krieg* (Munich, 1935) by Dr A. S. Rapoport (Hutchinson, London, 1936).

63 S. Vishnev and A. Shpirt, '*Voyna motorov I rezervov*', *Pravda*, 23 March 1941. Includes figures on the energy armament of the world's leading military powers.

64 Ellsworth Lester Raymond, *Soviet Preparation for Total War, 1925–51*, (Ph.D., University of Michigan, 1951) p. 4.

65 Norman Stone, *The Eastern Front, 1914–17* (London, 1974).

66 See the author's entry in Holmes, ed., *The Oxford Companion to Military History*, pp. 338–9. See also Col. Gen. Makhmut Gareyev, *M. V. Frunze, Military Theorist* (Pergamon-Brassey's, London, 1988).

67 Raymond, p. 37, citing Frunze, 'The Front and Rear in Future War', preface to P. Karatygin, *Mobilizatsiya promyshlennosti dlya nuzhd voyny (Mobilization of Industry for War Needs)*, (Voyenny Vestnik Press, Moscow, 1925).

68 Raymond, pp. 43–4, citing *Collection of Laws and Edicts of the USSR Government*, Vol. 1, No. 35, June 1925.

69 Samuelson, *Plans for Stalin's War Machine: Tukhachevskiy and Military Economic Planning*, p. 19. On Tukhachevskiy see the author's 'Red Star in the West: Marshal Tukhachevskiy and East–West Exchanges on the Art of War', *RUSI Journal*, December 1987, pp. 63–73.

70 Samuelson, pp. 31–3.

71 Werner von Blomberg, *Report on Visit of the Chief of the Army Board to Russia, August to September, 1928 Staff* (Reichswehr Ministerium, 17 November 1928), trans. W. R. Newby-Grant, RMA Sandhurst.

72 Raymond, pp. 72, 77.

73 *Strategiya* (2nd edn, Voyenny Vestnik Press, Moscow, 1927). Preface to 1st edn (1926) was written in 1925.

74 Ibid., p. 173.

75 Ibid., pp. 46–7.

76 Ibid., p. 38.

77 Ibid., pp. 46–7.

78 Probably best documented in *Moskovskaya bitva v postanovleniyakh Gosudarstvennogo komiteta oborony. Dokumenty I materialy 1941–1942 (The Battle of Moscow in Proceedings of the State Defence Committee: Documents and Materials 1941–1942)*,. (Moscow Government Cultural Committee/Institute of Military History of the Ministry of Defence/Russian Federal Archival Service, Moscow, 2001). The book includes a facsimile of the GKO order to evacuate Moscow of 15 October 1941.

79 V. D. Sokolovskiy, *Voyennaya Strategiya* (Voyenizdat, Moscow, 1962, 1963, 1968), trans. as *Soviet Military Strategy* by Harriet Fast Scott and William F. Scott (Macdonald and Jane's, London, 1975). The volume has the changes between the three editions helpfully indicated by underlining.

80 Mikhail Tukhachevskiy, *O kharaktere sovremennykh voyn v svete resheniy VI Kongressa Kominterna (On the Character of Contemporary Wars in the Light of the VI Comintern Congress)*, in *Kommunisticheskaya Akademiya, sektsiya po izucheniyu problem voyny (Communist Academy, Section for the Study of the Problems of War)*, *Zapiski* (Notes), Vol. 1 (*Izd. Kommunisticheskoy Akademii*, Moscow, 1930), pp. 6–29, stenographic record of paper to the Leningrad branch of Komakad, pp. 3, 9, 14, 19. Known as 'the Komakad speech'.

81 *Germany and the Second World War*, Vol. IV, pp. 908–10.

82 Ibid., p. 910.

3. 'A cruel romance'

1 Berezhkov, *At Stalin's Side* (1994), pp. 45–6; *Stranitsy Diplomaticheskoy Istorii*, (1982), p. 54; Geoffrey T. Waddington, 'Barbarossa and the Soviet Union', in Erickson and Dilks, ed., *Barbarossa*, pp. 7–33, this p. 7. The German documents say the meeting occurred at 0400 hours. Berezhkov says that the time of the initial phone call – 03.00 German time – equated with 05.00 Moscow, which it normally would, but may have forgotten that the Germans had put their clocks forward by an hour to German summer time. (See the end of Chapter 6.) The phrases 'concentrations on the eastern border' and 'military countermeasures' are taken from subsequent (later on 22 June) documents 664 and 665 in *Documents on German Foreign Policy*, Series D, Vol. XII, 1 February 1941–22 June 1941 (HMSO, London, 1962), pp. 1074–5.

2 Minister Schmidt, Doc. 664 in *Documents on German Foreign Policy*, Series D, Vol. XII, p. 107. 'The Foreign Minister added that he regretted very much this development in German-Russian relations as he in particular had made every attempt to bring about better relations between the two countries.' That sounds like a very diplomatic 'for the record' version of what Berezhkov reported Ribbentrop as saying.

3 See the excellent study by Heinz Magenheimer, *Die Militärstrategie Deutschlands 1940–45* (F. A. Herbig Verlag, Munich, 1997), trans. as *Hitler's War* by Helmut Bögler (Arms & Armour 1998/Cassell Military Paperbacks, London, 2002). On the lateness of Hitler's final decision, pp. 44–5.

4 Philip Bobbit, *The Shield of Achilles – War, Peace and the Course of History* (Penguin, London, 2002), p. 819.

5 Leo Tolstoy, *War and Peace* (1869), trans. and with an introduction by Rosemary Edmonds (Penguin, London, 1982), pp. 715–17.

6 Adolf Hitler, *Hitler's Mein Kampf [My Struggle]*, unexpurgated edition, trans. James Murphy (Hurst & Blackett, London, 1939).

7 Ian Kershaw, *Hitler 1889–1936: Hubris* (Penguin, London, 2001), p. xix.

8 In 1917 the western powers – still not yet victors – to be fair, had sought to re-establish the eastern front against Germany. See John Silverlight, *The Victors' Dilemma, Allied Intervention in the Russian Civil War* (Barrie & Jenkins, London, 1970). The Soviet Union, ultimately comprising fifteen Soviet socialist republics, which became independent states after 1991, coalesced around the Russian Soviet Federated Socialist Republic. It was formed in 1922 from four republics: Russia, Belarus, Ukraine and Transcaucasia (Armenia, Azerbaijan and Georgia). Other republics joined later, with the first USSR Constitution coming into force on 31 January 1924.

9 'The Foreign Relations of USSR', Paper by Military Intelligence MI2(b), 2 November 1940, British War Office, in UK NA, *WO 193/642*, this pp. 1–2.

10 Blomberg, *Report*, trans. Newby-Grant.

11 Christopher Duffy, *Russia's Military Way to the West. Origins and Nature of Russian Military Power, 1700–1800* (Routledge & Kegan Paul, London, 1981), p. 241.

12 See, for example, Berezhkov, *At Stalin's Side*, in particular 'In That Moment Before the War', pp. 227–35.

13 Alan Bullock, *Hitler and Stalin: Parallel Lives* (third edition, Fontana, 1998).

14 Ibid., p. 1.

15 In 1876 Hitler's father Alois had changed his name from Schicklgruber to Hitler. Although this point is often raised by Hitler's critics, for various reasons, it is irrelevant to Hitler's life and career. Kershaw, *Hitler . . . Hubris*, p. 3.

16 Phrase from Berezhkov, *At Stalin's Side*, pp. 52–8.

17 *Mein Kampf*, pp. 430–41.

18 Ibid., pp. 537–42. On Russia, see also Kershaw, *Hitler . . . Hubris*, pp. 248–50.

19 See Holger H. Herwig, '*Geopolitik*: Haushofer, Hitler and Lebensraum', in Colin S. Gray and Geoffrey Sloan, ed., *Geopolitics: Geography and Strategy* (Frank Cass, London and Portland, Oregon, 1999), pp. 218–41, and Kershaw, *Hitler . . . Hubris*, pp. 159, 248–9.

20 See Geoffrey Sloan, 'Sir Halford J. Mackinder: the Heartland Theory Then and Now', in Gray and Sloan, ed., *Geopolitics*, pp. 15–38.

21 Geoffrey T. Waddington, 'Ribbentrop and the Soviet Union, 1939–1941', in Erickson and Dilks, ed., *Barbarossa*, p. 9. Yes, he does mean China, although the reward, Hong Kong, seems negligible.

22 They included George Orwell from the UK and the journalist and writer Ernest Hemingway from the US.

23 Krivosheyev, *Soviet Casualties and Combat Losses*, p. 46.

24 The display of some of Voronov's possessions is in the hall devoted to the Great Patriotic War. Memoirs: Nikolai Nikolayevich Voronov, *Na sluzhbe voyennoy (In Military Service)* (Voyenizdat, Moscow, 1963), esp. p. 88, 165.

25 Blomberg, trans. Newby Grant, and the author's 'Red Star in the West: Marshal Tukhachevskiy and East–West Exchanges on the Art of War', *RUSI Journal*, Vol. 132, No. 4 (December 1987), pp. 63–73; this, p. 63.

26 *Ogonëk*, No. 26 (3127), 27 June–5 July 1987, p. 6.

27 Berezhkov, *At Stalin's Side*, p. 11.

28 John Hughes-Wilson, *Military Intelligence Blunders and Cover-Ups* (Revised and updated edition, Robinson, London, 2004), pp. 41–2.

29 Waddington, in Erickson and Dilks, ed., *Barbarossa*, p. 13.

30 Ibid., pp. 13–14.

31 Berezhkov, *At Stalin's Side*, pp. 11–12, 24.

32 Ibid., p. 12. Cable No. 166 of 3 August 1939 15.47 hrs (received Moscow 4 August 04.30 hrs) in *SSSR-Germaniya 1939: Dokumenty I materialy o sovetsko-germanskikh otnosheniyakh s aprelya po oktyabrya 1939 g.(USSR–Germany 1939. Documents and Materials on Soviet-German Relations from April to October 1939)* (Mosklas, Vilnius, 1989), Doc. 12, pp. 27–8. Henceforward referred to as *USSR–Germany 1939*.

33 The Japanese had attempted to encircle a Soviet–Mongolian force on 28 May. Zhukov was ordered to Mongolia on 2 June and began his classic encirclement battle on 19 August. See 'Khalkin-Gol, Battle of', in Richard Holmes, ed., *The Oxford Companion to Military History*, pp. 474–5.

34 Berezhkov, *At Stalin's Side*, p. 23.

35 Ibid. Cable No. 175 of 14 August, Doc. 14 in *SSSR–Germaniya 1939* (hence forward) *USSR–Germany 1939*, pp. 30–2, sent 14 August 22.53.

36 Berezhkov, *At Stalin's Side*, p. 25.

37 Schulenberg to Ribbentrop, No. 189 of Cable 19 August, Doc. 22 in *USSR–Germany 1939*, pp. 46–7.

38 Hitler's personal message was passed to Stalin via Ribbentrop and the German ambassador in Moscow in Cable No. 189, 20 August 16.35, Doc. 24 in *USSR–Germany 1939*, pp. 51–2. Also Berezhkov, *At Stalin's Side*, pp. 26–39.

39 Schulenberg to Ribbentrop, Cable No. 199 of 21 August, Doc. 27 in *USSR–Germany 1939*, p. 54.

40 Schulenberg to Ribbentrop, Cable No. 200 of 21 August 19.30 hrs, Doc. 28 in *USSR–Germany 1939*, p. 55.

41 Doc. 30 in *USSR–Germany 1939*, p. 58.

42 Ribbentrop to Foreign Ministry, Cable No. 204 of 23 August 1939, 20.05 hrs. Document 31 in *USSR–Germany 1939*, pp. 58–60.

43 Transcript of telephone call, Cable No. 205, 23 August 1939 23.00, 'Yes. Agreed.' Doc. 32 in *USSR–Germany 1939*, p. 60.

44 Berezhkov, *At Stalin's Side*, pp. 40–1; Stalin's speech to the XVIII Congress of the Soviet Communist Party, 10 March, 1939 cited in *USSR–Germany 1939*, p. 7.

45 Berezhkov, *At Stalin's Side*, p. 42.

46 *Pravda*, 24 August 1939, cited in *USSR–Germany 1939*, pp. 60–2.

47 'Secret Additional Protocol', Doc. 33 in *USSR–Germany 1939*, pp. 62–4.

48 Doc. 56 in *USSR–Germany 1939*, pp. 109–10; Berezhkov, *At Stalin's Side*, p. 43.

49 Ribbentrop to Schulenberg, Cable 253 of 3 September 1939 18.50 hrs, Doc. 37 in *USSR–Germany 1939*, pp. 80–81.

50 Schulenberg to Ribbentrop, Cables 264 of 5 September and 308 of 9 September 1939, Docs 38 and 43 in *USSR–Germany 1939*, pp. 81, 86.

51 Schulenberg to Ribbentrop, Cables 371 of 16 September and 372 of 17 September, Docs 48 and 49 in *USSR–Germany 1939*, pp. 94–6.

52 Erickson, *The Soviet High Command*, p. 539.

53 Robin Higham and Frederick W. Kagan, ed., *The Military History of the Soviet Union* (Palgrave, New York, 2002), p. 103.

54 Krivosheyev, *Soviet Casualties*, pp. 57–60.

55 Albert Axell interview with General Krivosheyn, cited in Axell, *Russia's Heroes 1941–45* (Robinson, London, 2001), pp. xiii–xiv. In his memoirs, Guderian makes no mention of the diplomatic incident, only that the demarcation line on the Bug was 'disadvantageous' for Nazi Germany.

56 *Ob'yedinennoye Gosudarstvennoye Politicheskoye Upravleniye* – Unified State Political Directorate.

57 *Organs of State Security of the USSR in the Great Patriotic War: a Collection of Documents*, henceforward *FSB Archives*, Vol. I, *Nakanune (On the Eve)*. Bk 1: November 1938–December 1940, Doc. 29, '*Iz Prikaza NKVD SSSR No. 001064 . . .*' ('From USSR NKVD Order No. 001064 . . .'), 8 September 1939, pp. 70–3.

58 Ibid., Doc. 33, 'Iz direktivy NKVD SSSR Narodnym Komissariatam Vnutrennykh Del USSR I BSSR ob Organizatsii Raboty v Osvobozhdennykh Rayonakh Zapadnykh Oblastey Ukrainy I Belorusii', 15 September 1939, pp. 79–81.

59 Ibid., p. 80.

60 Ibid., p. 81.

61 Ibid., Doc. 35, 'O deystviyakh pogranichnykh otryadov v periode perekhoda granitsy chastyami krasnoy armii na territoriyu Pol'shi, 17 September 1939, pp. 85–7.

62 Ibid., Doc. 37, 'Iz doklada . . . o deyatel'nosti operativno-chekistskikh grupp na osvobozhdennoy territorii Zapadnoy Ukraini', 19 September 1941, pp. 88–90.

63 Ibid., p. 89.

64 Ibid., p. 90.

65 Louis Fitzgibbon, The Katyn massacre. The shocking truth behind the world's worst unjudged mass murder (Corgi, 1979), pp. 29, 312, citing 'A significant anniversary', Editorial, Krasnaya Zvezda, (Red Star), No. 210, 17 September 1940.

66 Fitzgibbon, p. 194, citing Sir Owen O'Malley (former British Ambassador to Poland), reports of 1943 and 1944, released January 1972.

67 Krivosheyev, Soviet Casualties, p. 57.

68 There is an old black-humoured Polish joke about what you do when trapped between the Germans and the Russians. Whom do you shoot first? Answer: 'The Germans.' Why? Answer: 'Business before pleasure.'

69 Fitzgibbon, p. 33, citing Jozef Czapski, a Polish officer and writer who survived, Memoirs of Starobielsk.

70 FSB Archives, Vol. 1, Bk 1, Doc. 48, 'Direktiva NKVD SSSR No. 807 Opergruppe NKVD na Belorusskom Fronte ob Organizatsii Priyema ot Germanskogo Komandovaniya I Proverki Voyennoplennykh Belorusov i Ukraintsev, imeyushchikh Sem'I na Sovetskoy Territorii', 16 October 1939, p. 109.

71 'The Red Army'. Paper dated 22 November 1939, in UKNA, WO 193/642, p. 1.

72 Ibid., p. 2. Emphasis added.

73 Ibid., pp. 3–4. Emphasis added.

74 Schulenberg to Ribbentrop, Cables 395 of 20 September 02.23 hrs and 442 of 25 September 22.58 hrs, Doc. 52 and 54 in USSR–Germany 1939, pp. 103–6.

75 See Pravda, 23 September 1939, p. 5; 26 September, p. 5; 28 September, p. 5.

76 Timetable is Doc. 59 in USSR–Germany 1939, p. 113.

77 Pravda, 29 September 1939, in USSR–Germany 1939, pp. 107–8.

78 Doc. 56 in USSR–Germany 1939, pp. 109–10.

79 Berezhkov, At Stalin's Side, p. 52.

80 Doc. 57 in USSR–Germany 1939, p. 110.

81 Berezhkov, At Stalin's Side, p. 42.

82 Fitzgibbon, p. 34.

83 Map in USSR–Germany 1939, p. 111. It is difficult to follow the demarcation line on many of the modern maps, especially given the different borders before and since. The Soviet sector effectively embraced the Suwalki, Bialystok and Lomza województwa (counties), in the north-east of modern Poland. The best guide to the line is probably in the German intelligence maps drawn up prior to Barbarossa and reproduced in the maps appended to Germany and the Second

World War, Vol. IV, especially maps 1 and 3, but, failing that, the principal line is along the River Bug.

84 Professor Sir Douglas Savory, Speech to the UK House of Commons, 6 November 1952, cited in Fitzgibbon, *Katyn*, pp. 220–9; this, p. 222.

85 Berezhkov, *At Stalin's Side*,., p. 43, map on p. 111.

86 *FSB Archives*, Vol. 1, Bk 1, Doc. 42, '. . . O rezultatakh raboty operativno-chekistskikh grupp na territorii Zapadnoy Ukrainy', pp. 96–7.

87 *FSB Archives*, Vol. 1, Bk 1, Doc. 49, 19 October 1939, pp. 110–13; this, footnote on p. 112.

88 Erickson, *The Soviet High Command*, p. 540.

89 'The Red Army', *WO 193/642*, 22 November 1939, pp. 1–3, 5.

90 Ibid., pp. 5, 6.

4. Further Soviet expansion and cooperation with Germany

1 Carl Van Dyke, *The Soviet Invasion of Finland*, pp. 1–3; Tukhachevskiy 'testament', '1937. *Pokazaniya marshala Tukhachevskogo ('Plan porazheniya'), Voyenno-istoricheskiy zhurnal (Military Historical Journal) (VIZh)*, 8/1991, p. 48.

2 Eloise Engle and Lauri Paananen, *The Winter War: the Russo-Finnish Conflict 1939–40* (Military Book Society/Sidgwick & Jackson, London, 1973), p. 12.

3 Van Dyke, pp. 17–19 and note 73. Quotation from K. Simonov, '*Glazami cheloveka moego pokoleniya: Besedy s marshalom sovetskogo soyuza A. M. Vasilevskim*' (Through the eyes of someone of my generation: Conversations with Marshal of the Soviet Union A. M. Vasilevskiy'), *Znamya*, 5/1988, p. 79.

4 Van Dyke, p. 27.

5 Krivosheyev, *Soviet Casualties . . .*, pp. 60–82, this p. 61.

6 Ibid., pp. 35–40; Erickson, *Soviet High Command*, pp. 542–4. The Soviet Union's expansion in the north cut Finland off from the Barents Sea and brought the Soviet Union into contact with Norway.

7 Krivosheyev, *Soviet Casualties*, p. 65; lakes in Engle and Paananen, p. 5.

8 Voronov, *Na sluzhbe voyennoy*, pp. 136–7.

9 Van Dyke, p. 86, citing Central State Archive of the Soviet Army (TsGASA), *fond* 34980, *opis'* 5, *delo* 53 II, 'Mekhlis report to Stavka on the incompetence of the chief of operations, Ninth Army Staff'.

10 Maj. Gen. J. W. Hägglund, commanding IV Army Corps, explained: 'People are talking about motti tactics as if the main objective of the Finns was to create them. This is not so. The only one that was planned before the battle was the so-called "great motti" in the area of Kitelä-Koirinoja. The smaller nests seemed to form as chips falling this way and that, as the wood carver created his main pieces of art.' Cited in Engle and Paananen, p. 107.

11 Van Dyke, p. 87. Van Dyke's sources say Chuikov asked permission from *Stavka* – the supreme high command – which seems strange as the Leningrad Military District was still running the war. *Stavka* ran the 1941–5 war but is hardly ever mentioned in the context of the Winter War. However, this must be correct.

Stavka is sometimes written, incorrectly, as STAVKA in non-Russian works, as if it were an acronym or set of initials. It is not, but rather an old Russian word for a warrior chief's encampment or headquarters.

12 Van Dyke, p. 186.

13 O. A. Dudorovna, '*Stranitsy "neizvestnoy voyny". Iz istorii Sovetsko-finlandskoy voyny*' ('Pages from an "unknown war". From the history of the Soviet–Finnish War'), manuscript in possession of Carl van Dyke and cited in *The Soviet Invasion of Finland*, p. 88 and notes 181, 187. Emphasis added.

14 Van Dyke, p. 103.

15 Ibid., pp. 103–5.

16 Although western armies, notably the British, now praise and pay lip service to 'mission command' (directive control), the increasingly litigious nature of modern society and the 'long screwdriver' wielded by politicians actually make it increasingly difficult for a commander to do what he thinks best without the risk of being sued by his soldiers or sacked by his political boss. The latter problem would not have been unfamiliar to senior German or Soviet officers between 1939 and 1945.

17 Engle and Paananen, pp. 134–5, 143.

18 Ibid., p. 144.

19 Krivosheyev, *Soviet Casualties*, p. 78, citing *Za rubezhom* 48/1989 on Finnish casualties.

20 UKNA, *WO/208/1758*, E.19A, MI2b, report of conversation with Sir Paul Dukes (expert on Russia), 12 January 1941.

21 Krivosheyev, *Soviet Casualties*, pp. 60–78, esp. pp. 69–70.

22 Van Dyke, p. 202, and note 64, p. 217.

23 Van Dyke, p. 201.

24 Ibid., pp. 201–2 and notes 52 and 60, pp. 216–17.

25 Ibid., p. 43 and note 26, p. 95, citing Voroshilov papers.

26 Basil Liddell Hart, *This Expanding War* (Faber & Faber, London, 1942), p. 72.

27 Voronov, *Na sluzhbe voyennoy*, pp. 153–7.

28 Van Dyke, p. 109.

29 Ibid., p. 169.

30 Ibid., pp. 209–10; p. 219, note 100.

31 Ibid., p. 212.

32 Ibid., p. 193, citing *Sovetsko-finlyandskaya voyna 1939–1940 gg. Na more* (The 1939–40 Soviet-Finnish War at Sea), p. 146.

33 Van Dyke, p. 197.

34 Voronov, *Na sluzhbe voyennoy*, pp. 153–7.

35 Krivosheyev, *Soviet casualties*, pp. 51–7.

36 Mary Habeck, 'Dress Rehearsals 1937–1941', in Higham and Kagan, ed., *The Military History of the Soviet Union*, pp. 93–107; this, pp. 98–100.

37 'Khalkin-Gol', in Holmes, ed., *The Oxford Companion to Military History*, pp. 474–5.

38 Habeck, in Higham and Kagan, ed., pp. 100–2.

39 UKNA, *WO 33/1684, Order of Battle of Military Forces in USSR 1941*, p.1, para. 3.

40 Van Dyke, p. 224.

41 Erickson, *The Soviet High Command*, pp. 553–5.

42 Ibid., p. 557.

43 Author's conversation with Norwegian air force general, Air Power Conference, Trondheim, Norway, February 1999.

44 Fitzgibbon, pp. 37, 174–6.

45 Ibid.

46 Information received in the Genocide Museum in the former NKVD/Gestapo/ NKVD/MGB/KGB Headquarters, Vilnius. Author's visit in 1999/2000.

47 Genocide and Resistance Research Centre of Lithuania, *The Anti-Soviet Resistance in the Baltic States* (Du Ka, Vilnius, 1999), pp. 6–10, 122–3; 186–7.

48 This had a slightly bizarre consequence during the cold war. US propaganda directed towards the Soviet Union was normally the responsibility of 'Radio Liberty', but Estonia, Latvia and Lithuania, like the non-Soviet Warsaw Pact States of eastern Europe, came under Radio Free Europe.

49 UKNA, WO 33/1684, *Order of Battle of Military Forces in USSR 1941* (reflecting changes in 1940), p. 1, para. 3.

50 Gabriel Gorodetsky, *Grand Delusion: Stalin and the German Invasion of Russia* (Yale University Press, New Haven and London, 1999), pp. 29–33; this, p. 33 citing GRU GSh RF, *op.* 918, *d.* 4, report by RKKA 5th Department, 23 June 1940.

51 *FSB Archives*, Vol. 1, Bk 1, Doc. 97, '... *O khode operatsii po linii 5-ogo Otdela UPB NKVD USSR v zanimayemykh rayonakh Bessarabii I Bukoviny*', 29 June 1940, pp. 203–5.

52 Ibid., Doc. 98, 3 July 1940, '... *O Rabote operativno-chekistskikh grupp na Territorii Bessarabii*', pp. 205–8.

53 Ibid., Doc. 100, 3 July 1940, '*O neobkhodimosti srochnogo vydvizheniya pogranychnykh voysk NKVD na Liniyu novoy Gosudarstvennoy Granitsy SSSR s Rumyniey*', pp. 210–11.

54 I am grateful to Tatiana Anton of the Moldovan Ministry of Defence Military Policy and Foreign Relations Department for her advice and assistance.

55 Paul Robert Magocsi, Geoffrey J. Matthews, *Historical Atlas of East Central Europe*, (University of Washington Press, Seattle and London, 1993), p. 152.

56 Information provided by Tatiana Anton.

57 Waddington, in Erickson and Dilks, ed., *Barbarossa*, p. 20.

58 Ibid., p. 21.

59 Berezhkov, *At Stalin's Side*, pp. 8–9; *Stranitsy diplomaticheskoy*, pp. 9–10.

60 Berezhkov, *At Stalin's Side*, p. 9.

61 Ibid. A reference to the infamous lampshades given by Himmler, which were made from the skin of concentration camp victims. This comment may be fanciful, as large-scale atrocities of this type occurred later in the war.

62 Berezhkov, *At Stalin's Side*, pp. 46, 298 (Churchill–Stalin meeting of 15 August 1941), also Winston S. Churchill, *The Second World War*, Vol. II, *Their Finest Hour* (Cassell, London, 1949), pp. 517–18.

63 *Operational Records Book for Bomber Command*, entry for 13/14 November 1940. I am grateful to Dr Anna Maria Brudenell for her research on this British raid.

64 Churchill, *The Second World War*, Vol. II, pp. 517–18.

65 Berezhkov, pp. 46–7.
66 Ibid.
67 Waddington, in Erickson and Dilks, ed., p. 22; Gorodetsky, *Grand Delusion*, p. 51; *Germany and the Second World War*, Vol. IV, p. 45.
68 *Germany and the Second World War*, Vol. IV, p. 119, citing OKW report *Germany's mineral oil supplies in the war* (note!), April 1939.
69 Ibid., pp. 120–3, citing Hitler's address to commanders-in-chief of 22 August 1939; the Kiel *Weltwirtschafsinstitut* study of September 1939, *Russian economic potential and the feasibility of intensifying German-Russian trade relations*, and meeting of ministerial council for Reich Defence of 16 October 1939.
70 Ibid., pp. 124–5, 133, 136.
71 *DGFP* D.XII, Doc. 13, record of Interministerial meeting of 4 February 1941, pp. 19–21.
72 Berezhkov, *At Stalin's side*, pp. 90–2.
73 *DGFP* D.XII, Doc. 157, Berlin, 12 March 1941, pp. 282–3.
74 Ibid., Doc. 280, Memorandum by Minister Schnurre, 5 April 1941, pp. 474–5.
75 Ibid., Doc. 369, 18 April 1941, pp. 579–80.
76 Ibid., Doc. 380, 21 April 1941, p. 602.
77 Ibid., Doc. 521, 15 May 1941, pp. 826–7.
78 Berezhkov, *At Stalin's side*, p. 31, citing Molotov interview with Feliks Chuyev, 29 November 1974.

5. Who planned to attack whom, and how?

1 Tolstoy, *War and Peace*, trans. Edmonds, Bk 3, Part 1, ch. I, p. 717.
2 The historiography of the question is excellently summarized in Manfred Messerschmidt's introduction to *Germany and the Second World War*, Vol. IV, pp. 1–9.
3 Harry Hinsley, 'British Intelligence and Barbarossa', in Erickson and Dilks, ed., *Barbarossa*, pp. 43–75, this p. 43.
4 Ibid., citing Joint Intelligence Committee (JIC) report of 2 July, UKNA, *CAB 80/14*.
5 Ibid., citing JIC (40)225.
6 Field Marshal and Generalissimus Aleksandr Vasilevich Suvorov (1730–1800) is revered as Russia's greatest military commander. The only other person to take the title Generalissimus was Stalin.
7 Viktor Suvorov, *Icebreaker: Who Started the Second World War?* (1990), published in Russian as *Ledokol* (1992); Suvorov followed this with *Den' M (M-Day)* (Moscow, 1994). For discussion of the debate see John Erickson, 'Barbarossa, June 1941: who attacked whom?', *History Today*, Vol. 51(7), July 2001, pp. 11–17.
8 The test case was the *Caroline* (1837), a US ship assisting Canadian rebels, which the British captured and pushed over Niagara Falls, much to the Americans' chagrin. Since then, however, the Americans have been less insistent that the threat should always be immediate, imminent and overwhelming, as demonstrated in 2003. The question of 'offensive' versus 'defensive' defence at the

military-strategic and operational levels was considered at the end of the Soviet period in Andrey Kokoshin and Maj. Gen. Valentin Larionov's *Problems of Preventing War*, in summer 1987, extracts from which were published in *Mirovaya ekonomika I mezhdunarodnye otnosheniya (World Economy and International Affairs) (MEMO)*, 6/1988, pp. 23–31. They identified four options: the pre-emptive strike or immediate counter-attack (not very 'defensive'!); initial defence with the specific objective of wearing the enemy down and then a counteroffensive, of which Kursk (see Chapter 17) was the prime example; destruction of the invading enemy within your own territory, of which Zhukov's victory at Khalkin Gol (see Chapter 4) was the classic example; and a defensive defence, like the Maginot Line, which could be described, perhaps somewhat cynically, as 'digging big holes and hiding in them'. Had they been writing now they would have been forced to consider a new first option: a 'preventive' war against a threat not yet fully formed, as set out in the US National Security Strategy of 20 September 2002.

9 *Polevoy ustav Raboche-Krest'yanskoy Krasnoi Armii (proyekt), (Field Service Regulations of the Workers' and Peasants' Red Army – provisional)* (Moscow, 1939), p. 9.

10 V. A. Nevezhin, 'The Pact with Germany and the Idea of an "Offensive War" (1939–1941)', *Journal of Slavic Military Studies* (JSMS), Vol. 8, No. 4 (December 1995), pp. 809–43, this p. 809.

11 I. Hoffman. '*Podgotovka Sovetskogo Soyuza k nastupatel'noy voyne. 1941 god*'('Preparation of the Soviet Union for an offensive War. 1941'), *Otechestvennaya istoria (Motherland History)*, 4/1993, pp. 19–31. Magenheimer, *Hitler's War*, pp. 51–64, strongly supports the idea of a planned Soviet attack in 1941, without going all the way to espousing Suvorov's wider thesis.

12 Gabriel Gorodetsky, 'Was Stalin planning to attack Hitler in June 1941?', *RUSI*, 131/3 (1986), pp. 19–30; *Mif 'Ledokola': nakanune voyny (The 'Icebreaker' Myth: on the Eve of War)* (Moscow, 1995); Erickson and Dilks, 'Barbarossa June 1941 . . .', p. 17; Yu. A. Gor'kov, '*Gotovil li Stalin uprezhdayushchiy udar protiv Gitlera v 1941 g.*' (Whether Stalin was preparing a pre-emptive strike against Hitler in 1941), *Novaya I noveyshaya istoriya (Recent and Most recent History)(NNI)*, 3/1993, pp. 29–45; Gen. Makhmut A. Gareyev, '*Yeshchë raz k voprosu: gotovil li Stalin preventivny udar v 1941 g*' ('Once again the question: whether Stalin was preparing a preventive strike in 1941', *NNI* 2/1994, pp. 198–202.

13 Erickson and Dilks, 'Barbarossa June 1941 . . .', p. 14.

14 Doc. 664, Berlin, 22 June 1941 in *DGFP* D.XII, p. 1074.

15 Doc. 659, Ribbentrop to Schulenberg personally, 21 June 1941in *DGFP* D. XII, pp. 1063–65, this p. 1065.

16 *VIZh*, 12/1991, pp. 2–20, plans for deployment in west, pp. 19–20. See also *VIZh* 1/1992 and 2/1992.

17 Ibid., p. 20.

18 The best and most convincing account of these deliberations, with which the present author concurs, is Constantine Pleshakov, *Stalin's Folly: The Secret History of the German Invasion of Russia, 1941* (Weidenfeld & Nicolson, London, 2005), this pp. 55–7.

19 Jürgen Rohwer and Mikhail S. Monakov, *Stalin's Ocean-Going Fleet: Soviet Naval Strategy and Shipbuilding Programmes 1935–53* (Frank Cass, London, 2001), pp. 135–46.

20 M. V. Zakharov, *General'ny shtab v predvoyennye gody (The General Staff in the Pre-War Years)* (Voyenizdat, Moscow, 1989), p. 240.

21 Ibid., p. 247.

22 Ibid. See also Gorodetsky, p. 127, for a very thorough account.

23 Zakharov, *General'ny shtab . . .*, p. 249.

24 Gorodetsky, p. 229. Magenheimer, p. 54, agrees. 'The original document of May 1940 [*sic* – he means 1941] revealed by Valery Danilov in 1992–3 . . . differs in one significant aspect from that of its predecessors.'

25 Pleshakov, *Stalin's Folly*, p. 77, citing *1941 God. Dokumenty (1941: a collection of documents)*, 2 vols (Demokratiya, Moscow, 1998), this Vol. 2, pp. 215–20.

26 Vladimir Karpov, '*Marshaly Velikoy Otechestvennoy – Zhukov*' ('Marshals of the Great Patriotic [War] – Zhukov'), *Kommunist Vooruzhennykh Sil (Communist of the Armed Forces) (KVS)*, 5/1990, pp. 62–8, details pp. 67–8. When it appeared, this prompted the author's first article as Defence Correspondent: 'Stalin's Plan to Cripple Germany', *Independent*, Saturday 14 April 1990, p. 12.

27 Magenheimer, p. 54.

28 Translated in Gorodetsky, p. 239.

29 Pleshakov, pp. 78–9, and the map in Mikhalev, *Voyennaya Strategiya, Skhema* 12, p. 470.

30 Pleshakov, p. 80. See also Andrei Mertsalov, 'The Collapse of Stalin's Diplomacy and Strategy', in Erickson and Dilks, ed., *Barbarossa*, pp. 134–49, this pp. 145–6.

31 Zhukov, *Vospominaniya . . .* Vol. 1, p. 342; Karpov, '*Marshaly Velikoy Otechestvennoy . . .*'; Gorodetsky, p. 240.

32 Conversation with Lt Gen. Sir John Kiszely, Director of the Defence Academy of the UK, 28 July 2005.

33 V. A. Nevezhin, 'The Pact with Germany and the Idea of an "Offensive War (1939–1941)"', *Journal of Slavic Military Studies (JSMS)*, Vol. 8, No. 4 (December 1995), pp. 809–43, this p. 810.

34 Ibid., p. 810.

35 Ibid., p. 819.

36 Ibid., pp. 815.

37 Cited in Nevezhin, p. 822.

38 Ibid., pp. 813–14.

39 *Pravda*, 2 August 1940.

40 Nevezhin, p. 831, citing Ehrenburg's memoirs and the Russian State Archive of Literature and Art (RGALI). St Augustine famously prayed, 'Give me chastity and continence – but not yet!' Cited in *The Oxford Dictionary of Phrase, Saying and Quotation* (Oxford University Press, 1997), p. 393.

41 *Germany and the Second World War*, Vol. IV, p. 257–74, this p. 271.

42 Ibid., pp. 271–2.

43 Ibid., pp. 267–8.

44 Ibid., p. 274.

45 Magenheimer, p. 62, citing Halder, *Diaries*, p. 353.

46 Erickson and Dilks, 'Barbarossa', p. 13.

47 Also modified and reproduced as map 1 in the Maps volume appended to Volume IV of *Germany and the Second World War*.

48 I am grateful to Lt Gen. Sir John Kiszely, late SG; Professor and former Brigadier Richard Holmes, late PWRR; Brigadier John Keeling, late RA; and Lt Col. Iftiar Zaidi, Pakistan Army, for their expert opinions.

49 Erickson and Dilks, 'Barbarossa', p. 15.

50 S. N. Mikhalev, *Voyennaya strategiya. Podgotovka I vedeniye voyn Novogo I Noveyshego vremeni (Military strategy. The Preparation and Conduct of War in Recent and Most Recent Times)*, ed. V. A. Zolotarev (Zhukovskiy, Kuchkovo Pole, Moscow, 2003), p. 595.

51 Ibid., citing *IVI MO RF (Ministry of Defence of the Russian Federation), Documents and Materials*, Inv. No. 7811, p. 2. and uncensored version of Zhukov's *Memoirs*, Moscow, 1990, Vol. 1, p. 307; Nevezhin, p. 833, says 800,000 were called up.

52 UKNA *WO 193/642* MA Moscow to War Office. Secret Cipher Telegram No. 36 dated 2015 7 April 1941, received 0045 8 April 1941.

53 UKNA *WO 193/642* MA Moscow to War Office. Secret Cipher Telegram No. 38 dated 2035 11 April 1941, received 0045 12 April 1941.

54 Nevezhin, p. 833.

55 UKNA *WO 193/642* Cipher Telegram 04820 20 May 1941.

56 Nevezhin p. 833, citing Vyshnevskiy diary in RGALI, f. 1038, op. 1, d. 2079, 1. 32. Also *Pravda*, 21 May 1941.

57 *Germany and the Second World War*, pp. 321–2.

58 Magenheimer, p. 48, citing Valery Danilov, '*Iyun' 1941 . . .*' ('June 1941 . . .') in *Poisk (The Search)*, 25/1996, p. 3.

59 Magenheimer, pp. 51–3.

60 Magenheimer, p. 63, citing Volker Heydorn, *Der sowjetische Aufmarsch im Bialystoker Balkon bis zum 22. June 1941 und der Kesel von Wolkowysk (Soviet Deployment in the Bialystok Salient up to 22 June 1941 and the Volkovysk pocket)*, (Munich, 1989), p. 77.

61 *Germany and the Second World War*, Vol. IV, pp. 226–30.

62 Erickson and Dilks, 'Barbarossa . . .', p. 13.

63 Col. M. Dorofeyev, '*O nekotorykh prichinakh neudachnykh deystvii mekhaniizirovannykh korpusov v nachal'nom periode Velikoy Otechestvennoy voyny*' ('On certain causes of unsuccessful actions by mechanized corps in the opening period of the Great Patriotic War'), *VIZh* 3/1964, pp. 32–44, this pp. 35–7; Lt Gen. M. M. Kir'yan '*Nachal'ny period Velikoy Otechestvennoy voyny*'('The Opening Period of the GPW'), *VIZh*, 6/1988, pp. 11–17.

64 Pleshakov, pp. 75, 77–81, 94, 180.

65 Andrei Mertsalov, 'The Collapse of Stalin's Diplomacy and Strategy', in Erickson and Dilks, ed., *Barbarossa*, pp. 134–49, this p. 146.

66 *Germany and the Second World War*, Vol. IV, p. 253. Erickson, *The Road to Stalingrad*, p. 20, correctly describes Hitler's 21 July instructions as to undertake 'preliminary studies'. On 31 July Hitler's intentions became clear.

67 *Germany and the Second World War*, Vol. IV, pp. 253–4.

68 Ibid.

69 Ibid, p. 306.

70 Ibid., p. 254, note 75.

71 Ibid., pp. 335–6.

72 Ibid., pp. 258–62.

73 Ibid., p. 262.

74 Ibid., p. 263.

75 Ibid., p. 239. For Tukhachevskiy's *March Beyond the Vistula* in English, see Marshal of Poland Jozef Pilsudski, *Year 1920 and its Climax Battle of Warsaw during the Soviet-Polish War 1920 with the Addition of M. Tukhachevskiy's March Beyond the Vistula* (Pilsudski Institute of America, London and New York, 1972).

76 He was not (as often, erroneously, described), a 'von'. He came from a relatively humble Prussian family. I am grateful to Dr Beatrice Heuser, now director of the Military Archives at Potsdam, professional colleague and scholar, and Paulus's niece, for her confirmation of this fact.

77 *Germany and the Second World War*, Vol. IV, pp. 262–6.

78 Ibid., p. 275.

79 Ibid., p. 278.

80 British Army Field Manual *D/DAT/13/34/25, The Army Field Manual.* Vol. 1. The Fundamentals. Part 1. *The Application of Force.* Code 71344 (Pt 1), 1985, pp. 133–140, this pp. 133–4.

81 *Germany and the Second World War*, Vol. IV, p. 281.

82 Ibid., p. 282.

83 *D/DAT/13/34/25, The Army Field Manual.* Part 1. *The Application of Force*, pp. 133–40. 'Selection and Maintenance of the Aim. A Failure . . .'

84 Erickson, *The Road to Stalingrad*, p. 21. On Barbarossa, man and operation, see the entries by Richard Holmes and Jurgen Förster, *The Oxford Companion to Military History*, pp. 121–2.

85 UKNA, *WO 193/642, The Foreign Relations of U.S.S.R.*, 2.11.1940, p. 1.

86 Hinsley, in Erickson and Dilks, *Barbarossa*, p. 45.

87 Ibid., p. 46.

88 Ibid., p. 47, citing MI 14 Appreciation of 31 October, *WO 190/891.*

89 Hinsley, in Erickson and Dilks, *Barbarossa*, p. 49.

90 Ibid., pp. 49–54.

91 Ibid., p. 51.

92 Churchill, *Second World War*, Vol. III, p. 317.

93 Gorodetsky, p. 157, citing sources from March 1941. The phrase 'war of nerves' was used in a War Office intelligence summary as late as 9 April, and on 10 April a JIC report still maintained that rumours of armed action were probably designed to frighten Russia into doing what Germany wanted. See Hinsley in Erickson and Dilks, *Barbarossa*, p. 59.

94 Churchill, *Second World War*, Vol. III, p. 319.

95 Hinsley, in Erickson and Dilks, *Barbarossa*, p. 62. My gratitude also to the Bletchley Park Trust, who have hosted visits by my Global Security degree students over the past years.

96 Gorodetsky, p. 159. Ultra is the generic classification given to information derived from Bletchley decrypts of signals intelligence. In order to help analyse the results,

the decrypts were given an initial 'star' rating of one, for routine transmissions, to five, for those which appeared to be extremely important. To break Lorentz, the British had to develop Colossus – the world's first electrical computer. By D Day on 6 June 1944, ten Colossus machines were in operation.

97 Gorodetsky, pp. 160–1.
98 Churchill, *Second World War*, Vol. III, p. 319.
99 PREM 3/510/11 Churchill to Eden 30 March 1941, cited in Churchill, *The Second World War*, pp. 319–20; Gorodetsky, p. 160; Hinsley in Erickson and Dilks, *Barbarossa*, p. 57.
100 L. Woodward, *British Foreign Policy in the Second World War* (HMSO, London, 1970), Vol. 1, p. 604, cited in Gorodetsky, p. 162 and Hinsley in Erickson and Dilks, *Barbarossa*, p. 57.
101 Gorodetsky, pp. 162–3.
102 Ibid., p. 177, citing Martin Van Creveld, *The Balkan Clue: Hitler's Strategy 1940–41* (Cambridge University Press, 1973), pp. 149, 151.
103 Gorodetsky, pp. 163–4.
104 Woodward, *British Foreign Policy*, Vol. I, pp. 608–9.
105 Hinsley, p. 61, citing MI14 and War Office *Weekly Intelligence Summary*.
106 Gorodetsky, p. 176, citing *FO 371 29465*, 17 and 19 April 1941.
107 Gorodetsky, p. 178.
108 Ibid., pp. 246–74, this pp. 246–8. In his conversation with Stalin during Churchill's visit to Moscow in October 1944, Churchill dismissed Hess as crazy. Stalin then proposed a toast to the British [Secret – Foreign] Intelligence Service, which had induced Hess to come to Scotland. Stalin believed Hess could not have made it without signals and that, therefore, the Intelligence Services must have been behind the flight or cooperated in its successful arrival.
109 Gorodetsky, p. 267.
110 *FSB Archives*, Vol. 1, Bk 2, Doc. 159, 1 March 1941, '*Iz direktivy NKVD SSSR I NKGB SSSR No. 782/B/265/M o Zadachakh Organov Vnutrennykh Del I Gosbezopasnosti v Svyazi s Razdeleniyem NKVD SSSR na Dva Narkomata*' ('From NKVD and NKGB Directive . . . on the Tasks of Organs of Internal Affairs and State Security in Connection with the Division of the NKVD into Two People's Commissariats'), pp. 40–3.
111 Gorodetsky, p. 268, citing *Central Archive of the FSB*, Russian Federation, *fond 338 d. 20566*, l. 71, 80, and 82–3 of 13 May 1941. These documents are not in the FSB archives published so far.
112 Gorodetsky, p. 274.

6. The war's worst-kept secret

1 *FSB Archives*. Vol. I, Bk 1, Doc. 103, 9 July 1940, '*Pis'mo Nachal'nika Vneshney Razvedki GUGB NKVD SSSR No 5/8175 v Razvedyvatel'noye Upravleniye RKKA s Pros'boy dat' otsenku poluchennym agenturnym materialam o podgotovke Germanii k Voyne protiv SSSR*', pp. 215–16.
2 Ibid., Docs. 110 (14 July 1940), 111 (15 July 1940), pp. 228–30.

3 Ibid., Doc. 128, 18 September 1940 '. . . *ob Osnovakh Strategicheskoogo Rezvertivaniya Vooruzhennykh Sil Sovetskogo soyuza na Zapade I na Vostoke na 1940 I 1941 gg*', pp. 253–9.

4 Ibid., Doc. 132 [*Ne ranee oktyabrya 1940 g.*], p. 269, including details of 'Corsican'.

5 Zakharov, *General'ny shtab . . .*, p. 251.

6 *FSB Archives*, Vol. 1, Bk 2, Doc. 149, 3 February 1941, p. 24.

7 Ibid., Doc. 159, '*Iz direktivy NKVD SSSR I NKGB SSSR No 782/B/265/M o Zadachakh Organov Vnutrennykh Del I Gosbezopasnosti v svyazi s razdeleniyem NKVD SSSRT na dva Narkomata*', pp. 40–3.

8 UKNA WO 287/135 *Notes on the Red Army* (handbook), March 1940, pp. 149–61, Plate XXI, Note 2 (at the very back).

9 *FSB Archives*, Vol. 1, Bk 2, Doc. 159, p. 41.

10 Ibid., pp. 42–3. Merkulov was one of those executed in the immediate aftermath of Stalin's death in 1953.

11 Ibid., Doc. 163, 11 March 1941, pp. 47–9, signed by Merkulov. The correspondents were Alfred Chollerton of the *Daily News, Daily Telegraph* and *Morning Post*; Maurice Lovell of Reuters; Henry Cassidy of Associated Press; Walter Duranty of the *New York Times*; Henry Shapiro of United Press and Robert Magidov of the *Exchange Telegraph, Associated Press* and *Business Week*.

12 Ibid., pp. 48–9; Bulgaria – *The Times Atlas of the Second World War*, pp. 54–5.

13 Gorodetsky, pp. 184–5. FO weekly summary is UKNA *FO 371 29135*.

14 FSB Archives, Vol. 1, Bk 2, Doc. 273, '*Kalendar soobshcheniy agentov Berlinskoy rezidentury NKGB SSSR "Korsikanetsa" I "Starshiny" o podgotovke Germanii k voyne s SSSR . . .*' pp. 286–96.

15 Details of *Starshina*, ibid., Doc. 161, p. 45.

16 Gorodetsky, pp. 207–10. The report is in *FSB Archives*, Vol. 1, Bk 2, Doc. 197, pp. 128–9.

17 *Germany and the Second World War*, Vol. IV, p. 341, citing BA-MA RL 3/2245.

18 *FSB Archives*, Vol. 1, Bk 2, Doc. 197, p. 128.

19 Note to *Kalendar . . .* (see note 6/14), p. 296.

20 *DGFP*, XII, Doc. 381, The Chargé d'Affaires in the Soviet Union to the Foreign Ministry about the Soviet note verbale of 21 April 1941.

21 Ibid., p. 603.

22 Translated by Gorodetsky, p. 232, citing GRU Archives.

23 Gorodetsky, p. 235.

24 Ibid., pp. 181–2.

25 Hinsley, in Erickson and Dilks, *Barbarossa*, p. 71.

26 *FSB Archives*, Vol. 1, Bk 2, Doc. 200, 5 May 1941, *Iz Soobshcheniya NKGB SSSR No 1452/M v TsK VKP(B), CNK, NKO I NKVD SSSR o Voyennykh Prigotovleniyakh Germanii na Okkupirovannykh Territoriyakh Pol'shi*, pp. 135–6.

27 Ibid., Doc. 201, 5 May 1941, '*Iz Spetssoobshcheniya Razvedyvatel'nogo Upravleniya RKKA No 6604777 ss v Ts K VKP(B), SNK, NKO I NKVD SSSR o Gruppirovke Nemetskikh voysk . . .*', pp. 136–7. Out of the RAF's eyes: David Glantz, *Barbarossa: Hitler's Invasion of Russia 1941* (Tempus, Charleston SC, 2001), p. 31;

Brian Taylor, *Barbarossa to Berlin: A Chronology of the Campaigns on the Eastern Front 1941 to 1945*, Vol. 1 (Spellmount, Staplehurst, 2003), p. 12.

28 Ibid., Doc. 206, 14 May 1941, '. . . *o Dislokatsii I stroitel'stve Nemetskimin Vlastyami Aerodromov I Posadochnykh Ploshchadok . . .*', pp. 142–3.

29 Ibid., Doc. 210, 21 May 1941, '. . . *Razvedyvatel'nogo Upravleniya General'nogo Shtaba Krasnoy Armii No 660533 v NKGB SSSR s Otsenkoy Poluchennykh Organami Gosbezopasnosti Razvedyvatel'nykh Dannykh . . . o Peredvizhenii Nemetskikh Voysk*', pp. 150–2.

30 Ibid., p. 151.

31 Ibid., Doc. 214, 24 May 1941, '. . . *Nachal'nika Vneshney Razvedki NKGB SSSR No 2/7/6358 Narkomam Bezopasnosti . . . o Kontsentratsii Germanskikh Voysk v Prigranichnoy s SSSR Polose*' pp. 157–8.

32 Magenheimer, p. 54.

33 Gorodetsky, pp. 238–9.

34 Ibid., p. 242.

35 *FSB Archives*, Vol. 1, Bk 2, Doc. 192, pp. 117–18.

36 Ibid., Doc. 242, '. . . *O narusheniyakh Gosudarstvennoy granitsy SSSR so Storony Germanii . . .*', pp. 220–1.

37 Ibid., Docs. 243, 244, '. . . *o voyennykh meropriyatiyakh Germanii so sostoyaniyu na 12 Iyunya 1941 g.*', pp. 221–4, and '*Iz spetssoobshcheniya UNKGB USSR po L'vovskoy Oblasti No 16/15602 v NKGB USSR o Voyennykh meropriyatiyakh Germanii*', pp. 224–5.

38 The Foreign Office talked of his 'piggery' – *FO 800/279* Su/41/1, 26, 29 and 30 April 1941, while in late 1940 the War Office opined that 'stalemate' in relations between the British and Soviet military was 'due to the personal pique of Sir S. Cripps, who is sulky' in Minute 22 to file UKNA *WO 208/1757*.

39 Gorodetsky, pp. 287–93. The author's brother-in-law, Ian Kerr, was born in Iran in 1942, and his mother told stories of a civilized émigré lifestyle. To my knowledge they were not closely related to Sir Archibald Clark Kerr, who succeeded Cripps as ambassador in Moscow.

40 TASS's informational web continued to link all fifteen former Soviet states after 1991.

41 Hinsley, in Erickson and Dilks, *Barbarossa*, pp. 71–2; Gorodetsky, pp. 287–93.

42 G. Kumanev, '"22-go" na rassvete' ('"Twenty-second" in a new light'), *Pravda*, 22 June 1989, cited in Gorodetsky, pp. 296–7.

43 I am grateful to Dr Teri McConville, an expert on 'organizational behaviour' in Cranfield's Defence Management department, for her insights.

44 *FSB Archives*, Doc. 250, 16 June 1941, '*Soobshcheniye Rezidenta NKGB SSSR v Berline o Srokakh Napadeniya Germanii na Sovetskiy Soyuz*', pp. 236–7.

45 Ibid., p. 237.

46 Ibid., Doc. 251, '*Soobshcheniye iz Berlina*', top secret, no later than 16 June 1941, pp. 237–8. The original, reproduced here in colour, is in the Presidential Archive in the Kremlin, *fond* 3, 17 June 1941, No. 2279/sh, 1170, Merkulov to Stalin and Molotov. The Svir' Z electric power station was on the the River Svir' (not the Belorussian place Svir), which is north-east of Lake Ladoga. Although not

particularly large, it was one of very few in northern Russia and provided power
for a large area in the Russian hinterland behind Leningrad.

47 Ibid. Emphasis added to reflect Stalin's hand. The printed version in *FSB Archives*
(Doc. 251) is annotated with most of Stalin's comment, but it is tactfully
abbreviated. 'You can tell your source . . . to . . .' Stalin's comment is now widely
reported, in Gorodetsky, p. 296, citing *Izvestiya Ts K KPSS*, 4 (1990), p. 221;
Simon Sebag Montefiore, *Stalin: The Court of the Red Tsar* (Knopf, New York,
2003), p. 354, and Lawrence Rees, *War of the Century* (BBC Worldwide, 1999),
p. 33. Only Sebag Montefiore translates it with its full literal coarseness. The
reader can now see for him or herself.

48 Cited in Gorodetsky, p. 299. Timoshenko signed statement to General
Lyashchenko. Also cited in Sebag Montefiore, p. 355.

49 Two of Genghis's generals, Chebe and Subedei, deliberately attacked Russia in
winter because the rivers and swamps would be frozen. They were the only two
who ever achieved much success. On the First World War see Stone, *The Eastern
Front*, and Alan J. P. Taylor, *War by Timetable*.

50 Gorodetsky, pp. 297–8.

51 *FSB Archives*, Vol. 1, Bk 2, see Docs 257, 18 June (NKVD), pp. 252–3 and 259, 19
June, '*Spetssoobshcheniye NKGB SSSR No 1/545 v NKGB SSSR O Voyenno-
Mobilizatsionnykh Prigotovleniyakh Fashistskoy Germanii k Voyne protiv SSSR*,
pp. 254–64, this p. 260.

52 Gorodetsky, pp 244–5.

53 *Germany and the Second World War*, Vol. IV, map supplement, 2, 'Schematische
Kriegsgliederung Stand: B-Tag 1941 (22.6) "Barbarossa"'. Besides the formations
(brigade, division, corps, army, army group and OKH), the schematic shows
heavy equipment and specialized assets allocated to corps, armies and army
groups.

54 *FSB Archives*, Vol. 1, Bk 2, Docs 207(16 May), 208 (17 May), 209 (19 May),
pp. 144–50; Docs 211 (22 May), 212 (23 May), 213 (24 May), pp. 152–6.

55 Ibid., Doc. 254, 17 June 1941, '. . . *NKGB SSSR No 2288/M v TsK VKP(B) SNK
SSSR I NKVD SSSR ob Itogakh Operatsii po Iz'yatiyu antisovetskogo Ugolovnogo I
Sotsial'no Opasnogo Elementa v Litve, Latvii, I Estonii*', pp. 247–8.

56 Ibid., Doc. 272, 20 June 1941, '*Prikaz Nachal'nika Pogranichnykh voysk NKVD
Belorusskogo Okruga ob Usilenii Okhrana Granitsy*', pp. 284–5.

57 Hinsley, in Erickson and Dilks, pp. 70–1.

58 Gorodetsky, pp. 303–6; Hinsley in Erickson and Dilks, *Barbarossa*, pp. 71–2.

59 Hinsley, ibid., citing JIC (41) 234.

60 *Germany and the Second World War*, Vol. IV, p. 767.

61 Jurgen Förster, 'The German Military's Image of Russia', in Ljubica Erickson and
Mark Erickson, ed., *Russia: War, Peace and Diplomacy. Essays in Honour of John
Erickson* (Weidenfeld & Nicolson, London, 2005), pp. 117–29, 320–2, this pp.
123–4, citing Halder, *War Diary*.

62 *Germany and the Second World War*, Vol. IV, p. 235, citing *OKH/GenStdH/
OquIV, Abt. Frd Heere Ost (II) No 100/41*, pts 1 and 2. The official publication
was issued in 2,000 copies and is available for consultation in the Bundesarchiv-
Militärarchiv (BA-MA) in Freiburg.

63 *Germany and the Second World War*, Vol. IV, pp. 236–9.

64 Förster, in Erickson and Erickson, p. 123.

65 Sebag Montefiore, pp. 355–6.

66 Ibid., p. 356; Berezhkov, *At Stalin's Side*, p. 55.

67 Berezhkov, *At Stalin's Side*, p. 6.

68 *FSB Archives*, Vol. 1, Bk 2, Doc. 276, 21 June 1941, 'Verbal'naya nota Polpredstva SSSR No 013166 Germanskomu Pravitel'stvu', p. 300.

69 Pleshakov, p. 94.

70 Ibid., pp. 93–5.

71 Sebag Montefiore, p. 357, says that Stalin first told Molotov to summon Schulenberg at about 19.00, which ties in with the timing of the meeting at 21.00 reported in *DGFP*, Vol. XII, Doc. 662, pp. 1071–2.

72 Erickson, *The Road to Stalingrad*, p. 156.

73 *DGFP* XII, Doc. 660, June 21 1941, Adolf Hitler to Benito Mussolini, pp. 1066–9.

74 In *Stranitsy diplomaticheskoy istorii*, p. 53. Berezhkov says 03.00 Berlin equates with 05.00 Moscow time, and that is normally so. However, he may just have forgotten about the peculiar daylight-saving measures used by Germany and the UK in the world wars – and, in the UK's case, ever since. 'Spring forward – fall [autumn] back.'

75 Gorodetsky, p. 311. Gorodetsky says NKGB border police: they were NKVD, at that point.

76 Pleshakov, p. 97.

77 Liskow is the only individual 'line-crosser' (*perebezhchik*) mentioned in the published *FSB Archives*, Vol. II, Bk 1, Doc. 287, 22 June 1941, p. 38. This report reached NKGB headquarters at 03.10, Moscow time – 02.10 German time.

78 Erickson, *The Road to Stalingrad*, pp. 150–1.

79 *FSB Archives*, Vol. II, Bk 1, Doc. 330, '*Iz zapisey, sdelannykh dezhurnymi sekretaryami, o posetitelyakh I V Stalina za period s 21 po 28 Iyunya 1941 g*'. Not earlier than 28 June 1941, pp. 98–113, this p. 98.

80 Erickson, *The Road to Stalingrad*, p. 359; Gorodetsky, pp. 310–11.

81 *FSB Archives*, Vol. 1, Bk 2, Doc. 275, '*Direktiva Narodnogo Kommisara Oborony S. K. Timoshenko I Nachalnika General'nogo Shtaba G K Zhukova Komanduyushchim prigranichnymi Ohrugami I Privedenii v Boyevuyu Gotovnost' Voysk v Svyazi s vozmozhnym Napadeniyam Fashistskoy Germanii na SSSR*', p. 298.

82 Glantz, *Barbarossa*, p. 35.

83 Erickson, *The Road to Stalingrad*, pp. 160–1, 163–4.

84 Berezhkov, *Stranitsy diplomaticheskoy istorii*, p. 53. Berezhkov says 03.00 Berlin equates with 05.00 Moscow time. See note 6/74, above.

85 *DGFP* XII, Doc. 662, 'The Foreign Minister to the Embassy in the Soviet Union'. Most Urgent. Top Secret, Berlin 21 June 1941, pp. 1063–65. Confirmation of events in Berlin, Doc. 664,'Memorandum by an Official of the Foreign Minister's Secretariat', 22 June 1941, conversation between the Foreign Minister and Soviet Russian Ambassador Dekanozov in the Foreign Ministry at 4.00 a.m. on 22 June. Moscow meeting: time confirmed, *FSB Archives*, Vol. II, *Nachalo (The Beginning)*, Bk 1, 22 June 1941–31 August 1941, Doc. 281, 22 June 1941, '*Zapis' besedy narodnogo komissara inostrannykh del SSSR V M Molotova s poslom Germanii v*

Mosckve F V Shulenbergom, (Iz dnevnika Molotova), pp. 11–13. 1941. The account in Molotov's diary corroborates the *Documents on German Foreign Policy* in just about every detail. This account also confirms the German attack as 04.00 Moscow time (03.00 German – H-30).

86 Werner Haupt, *Army Group Center: The Wehrmacht in Russia 1941–45*, (Schiffer Military History, Atgen PA, 1997), pp. 23–7.

87 Sebag Montefiore, pp. 363–4, Erickson, *Soviet High Command*, pp. 586–7, *The Road to Stalingrad*, pp. 155–67.

88 Erickson, *The Road to Stalingrad*, pp. 160–1.

89 *FSB Archives*, Vol. II, Bk 1, Doc. 281, p. 11, see note 180.

90 Ibid., *DGFP* XII, Doc. 659, p. 1065.

91 Berezhkov, *At Stalin's Side*, p. 56; *FSB Archives*, Vol. II, Bk 1, Doc. 281, p. 11.

92 Ibid.

93 *Protivo-vozdushnaya oborona*. The term also embraces air-defence fighter planes, but they were under separate command at this stage.

94 The most graphic account is in Sebag Montefiore, pp 363–5.

95 Glantz, *Barbarossa*, p. 31.

96 Ibid., pp. 31–2.

97 Lt Gen. Nikolay Kirillovich Popel', 'Barbarossa: the Shock', in *Barbarossa!: Purnell's History of the Second World War*, No. 22 (BBC Publishing, 1972), pp. 590–1. Popel's description of the formations tallies exactly with the German picture in *Germany and the Second World War*, Vol. IV, Map Annex, Plate 2.

98 Popel', p. 591; on political officers/commissars, *WO 287/135* March 1940, Plate XXI.

99 Erickson, *The Soviet High Command*, Preface to the Third Edition, 2001, p. xx, 1960s conversation between the late John Erickson and Marshal Voronov.

7. Iron road east: the country, the forces

1 With gratitude to Anna Ivanovna and Lyuba Shevardina, successive heads of the Kursk Centre for Youth Education and Tourism, and to those of the author's MSc students rash enough to elect to study Russian military history with him over the four years 2002–5.

2 Berezhkov, *At Stalin's Side*, p. 55; Erickson, *The Road to Stalingrad*, p. 153.

3 Erickson, *The Road to Stalingrad*, p. 153, widely repeated by other authors.

4 Memoirs of Roza Weintraub – oral history prepared 26 June 1986, accessed on <http://www.shtetlinks.jewishgen.org/kibart/rozamem.html> 6 August 2005.

5 The change of time is a pity, as '18.12 Express' would have made a great chapter title. But then, the train never made it, anyway. I am grateful to Norbert Wallbaum, who kindly researched this issue with Andreas Engwert of the Die Bahn (DB – Railway) Museum in Nürnberg. Letter from Andreas dated 1 April 2005, enclosing extracts from *Deutsches Kursbuch* (National Railway Timetable), Summer 1941 (valid from 5 May 1941).

6 Berezhkov, *At Stalin's Side*, p. 132.

7 Ibid.

8 Jean-Francois Steiner, *Treblinka: the Extraordinary Story of Jewish Resistance in the Notorious Nazi Death Camp* (Simon and Schuster, 1967), pp. 51–2. Treblinka did not become a work camp until August 1941, and a death camp until 1942.

9 *Deutsches Kursbuch* (National Railway Timetable), Summer 1941, timetables 65, Berlin–Moscow and 50, Berlin–Insterberg.

10 *The World Crisis* (1931), p. 83, start of the masterly chapter on 'The Fronts and the Combatants'.

11 Soviet regulations of the time laid down a frontage of 8 to 12 kilometres. Erickson, *The Soviet High Command*, p. 591. Also conversation with Charles Dick, Director, Conflict Studies Research Centre, Defence Academy of the UK, April 2005.

12 David Glantz, ed., *The Initial Period of the War on the Eastern Front 22 June–August 1941. Proceedings of the Fourth Art of War Symposium, Garmisch, October 1987* (Frank Cass, London and Portland, Oregon, 1993), pp. 29, 31; Mikhalev, *Voyennaya Strategiya* (2003), p. 604, table 6.6.

13 Ibid.; *Germany and the Second World War*, Vol. IV, map volume, item 2, *Schematische Kriegsgliederung*, gives 91 German and 9 Romanian divisions up front, but more divisions followed behind.

14 *Germany and the Second World War*, Vol. IV, p. 362.

15 General Sir Rupert Smith's phrase, used in the context of the 2003 invasion of Iraq. I am grateful to him for this simple but illuminating idea about the eastern front in the Second World War.

16 Glantz, *Barbarossa*, p. 22.

17 On the partisan movement on the eastern front 1915–18 see Blood, *Bandenbekämpfung . . .*, pp. 40–8.

18 Churchill, *The World Crisis* (1931), pp. 85–6, provides a magnificent description: things had not changed much ten years after Churchill wrote.

19 *Germany and the Second World War*, Vol. IV, p. 260; Martin Gilbert and Arthur Banks, *Soviet History Atlas* (Routledge & Kegan Paul, London, 1972), map 42.

20 *Germany and the Second World War*, Vol. IV, pp. 260–4.

21 Ibid., p. 297.

22 Ibid., pp. 265–6.

23 Glantz, *Barbarossa*, pp. 19–20.

24 Ibid., pp. 20–1; Taylor, *Barbarossa to Berlin*, p. 27; Kenneth Macksey, 'The German Army in 1941', in David Glantz, ed., *The Initial Period of the War on the Eastern Front . . .*', pp. 55–65, this pp. 57–62.

25 Horst Boog, 'The German Air Force', in *Germany and the Second World War*, Vol. IV, pp. 370–1. Taylor, *Barbarossa to Berlin*, p. 27. Estimates of the number of combat aircraft available to the Germans on the eastern front vary from 2,770 to 2,840, of which about 2,000 were operational.

26 Mikhalev, *Voyennaya Strategiya* (2003), p. 600.

27 Glantz, *Barbarossa*, p. 35; Taylor, p. 27.

28 Mikhalev, p. 329.

29 Ibid., p. 353.

30 Ibid., pp. 372–3.

31 Taylor, p. 31; Glantz, *Barbarossa*, pp. 22–3; Glantz, 'Prelude to Barbarossa', in

Glantz, ed., *The Initial Period of the War on the Eastern Front*, p. 29; Mikhalev, p. 600.

32 Glantz, *Barbarossa*, p. 16. On formation of Stavka, *FSB Archives*, Vol. II, *Nachalo*, Bk 1, Doc. 293, '*Iz postanovelniya SNK SSSR I TsK VKP(B) o sozdanii Stavki Glavnogo Komandovaniya Vooruzhennykh Sil Soyuza SSSR*, 23 June 1941, p. 51.

33 Glantz, *Barbarossa*, p. 16; Glantz, in Glantz, ed., *The Initial Period . . .*, p. 32.

34 Glantz, in Glantz, ed., *The Initial Period . . .*, pp. 6–9, 29, 33, 34, 39, 48; Glantz, *Barbarossa*, p. 24; Mikhalev, *Voyennaya Strategiya* (2003), p. 598. Glantz, *Initial Period* gives 1,475 of the new KV-1 and T-34 tanks overall, which out of an overall Soviet tank park of 17,000 seems pretty consistent. Mikhalev gives 27 Mechanized Corps on 22 June; the intention was to form 29. Of that 29, 20 in the west, seven in the centre of the country and two in the Far East.

35 See the author's *Red God of War: Soviet Artillery and Rocket Forces* (Brassey's Defence Publishers, London, 1986).

36 Glantz, *Barbarossa*, p. 27.

37 *Germany and the Second World War*, Vol. IV, p. 351, citing Bundesarchiv-Militärarchiv (BA-MA) RM 7/25, 275 (1,300 bombers and 1,500 fighters), and Gerhard Hümmelchen, '*Die Luftstreitkrafte der UdSSR am 22 Juni 1941 im Spiegel der sowjetische Kriegsliteratur*', *WWR* 20 (1970), pp. 325–31, this p. 331.

38 *Germany and the Second World War*, Vol. IV, pp. 351–2; Glantz, *Barbarossa*, pp. 27–28; PhD . . .

39 Boog, in *Germany and the Second World War*, Vol. IV, pp. 373, 813–14.

40 Edgar Snow, 'The Red Army's Flying Tank'. Interview with Lt Gen. Sergey Ilyushin, *Saturday Evening Post*, 10 March 1945, pp. 18–19, 102, this p. 18, col. 2.

41 Ibid., p. 19. The best single account of Soviet aircraft development is probably Vaclav Nemecek, *The History of Soviet Aircraft Since 1918* (Collins, London, 1986), trans. from the Czech *Sovetska Letadla*.

42 *Germany and the Second World War*, Vol. IV, pp. 376–85.

8. Barbarossa unleashed

1 Ibid., p. 290.

2 Ibid., p. 525 ; Glantz, *Barbarossa*, p. 35.

3 *Germany and the Second World War*, Vol. IV, p. 290.

4 Pavlov was later shot for failing to stem the German advance. For the full detail of the indictment, for which earlier alleged suspicions were dragged up, see *FSB Archives*, Vol. II, *Nachalo*, Bk 1, Doc. 378, '*Postanovleniye 3-go Upraveleniya NKO SSSR na arest Pavlova D.G.*', 6 July 1941, pp. 210–16, and Doc. 408, '*Postanoveleniye Gosudarstvennogo komiteta Oborony . . . ob areste I predanii sudu voyennogo tribunala byvshego komanduyushchego Zapadnym frontom general armii Pavlova D.G., byvshego nachal'nika shtaba Zapadnogo fronta general-mayora Klimovskikh V. E., I drugikh*', 16 July 1941, pp. 332–5.

5 Glantz, *Barbarossa*, pp. 37–8 ; Taylor, pp. 17–20; *Voyenno-Entsiklopedicheskiy Slovar'* (*VES*), p. 532.

6 Glantz, *Barbarossa*, pp. 46–7; Taylor, pp. 20–4 ; *VES*, p. 332.

7 Taylor, pp. 23–24; *VES*, p. 759.

8 *Germany and the Second World War*, Vol. IV, p. 290.

9 Glantz, *Barbarossa*, pp. 42–3; Taylor, pp. 13–16; *VES*, p. 381.

10 *Germany and the Second World War*, Vol. IV, pp. 290–1.

11 Ibid., p. 291.

12 Ibid.

13 Taylor, pp. 25–7; *VES*, pp. 397, 576.

14 Erickson, *The Road to Stalingrad*, p. 156, plus map, Plate 2.

15 Pleshakov, pp. 111–12, P. M. Kurochkin, '*Svyaz' Severno-Zapandnogo Fronyta*', ('Communications on the North-West Front'), in *Na Severno-Zapadnom Fronte (On the North-West Front)* (Nauka, Moscow, 1969), pp. 192, 197.

16 Ibid.

17 Erickson, *The Road to Stalingrad*, p. 165.

18 On the defence of Brest, see V. I. Anikin, *Brestskaya krepost' – krepost'-geroi (Brest Fortress – Hero-Fortress)* (Stroiizdat, Moscow, 1985); Glantz, *Barbarossa*, pp. 35, 216 n.2/ 3; Werner Haupt, *Army Group Center: the Wehrmacht in Russia 1941–45* (Schiffer Military History, Atglen, PA, 1997), pp. 26–30. Haupt's books, including also *Army Group North* . . . (other details as for *Army Group Center* . . .), are extremely detailed chronological accounts from German archival sources.

19 Haupt, *Army Group Center* . . ., p. 35, gives 30 June; Glantz, *Barbarossa*, p. 35 gives 12 July. *VES* gives 20 July. If some stragglers survived until 20 July, it is unlikely they were causing the Germans too many problems.

20 Axell, *Russia's Heroes*, pp. 21–42, is a gripping and authoritative account.

21 Haupt, *Army Group Center* . . ., pp. 30, 35; 45th Division report cited in Axell, p. 30.

22 Haupt, *Army Group Center* . . ., p. 30.

23 Glantz, *Barbarossa*, p. 39, Appendix II, item 3; pp. 242–3.

24 Glantz, *The Initial Period* . . ., p. 87.

25 Glantz, *Barbarossa*, pp. 242–3, citing *NKO Directive No. 3 to the Military Councils of the Northwestern, Western, Southwestern and Southern Fronts*, 21.15 hrs, 22 June, 1941.

26 Glantz, *The Initial Period*, p. 112.

27 Ibid., p. 113.

28 Ibid.

29 Mikhalev, *Voyennaya Strategiya* (2003), p. 602.

30 Pleshakov, p. 215.

31 Glantz, *Barbarossa*, pp. 38–40; *The Initial Period* . . ., pp. 200–23, for a much more detailed account of 'The border battles on the Bialystok-Minsk axis'.

32 *Germany and the Second World War*, Vol. IV, pp. 770–2.

33 Glantz, *Barbarossa*, p. 40.

34 Taylor, p. 19.

35 Glantz, *Barbarossa*, p. 40; Sebag Montefiore, pp. 367–71.

36 Pleshakov uses the date of Pavlov's arrest as an example of the problems of reconciling different sources in *Stalin's Folly*, pp. 280–2. He concludes that Pavlov was removed from command on 30 June, and arrested almost immediately, on 1 July. Sebag Montefiore, p. 371, gives 4 July. Two documents in the *FSB Archives*,

Vol. II, Bk 1, Docs 378 and 379, sanctioning the arrest, are both dated 6 July but the date in July when it actually occurred is left blank between square brackets. See pp. 210–17.

37 *FSB Archives*, Vol. II, Bk 1, Doc. 378, 6 July 1941, pp. 210–13. Doc. 408 (16 July 1941), pp. 332–4. (*Obvinitel'noye zaklyucheniye*). Quoted segment, p. 333, centre.

38 Ibid., Doc. 436, 21 July 1941,'*Obvinitel'noye zaklyucheniye po delu Pavlova D.G., Klimovskikh V.E., Grigor'eva A.T. i Korobkova A.A.*', pp. 378–80.

39 Ibid., Doc. 437, '*Protocol sudebnogo zasedaniya Voyennoy kollegii Verkhovnogo suda SSSR po delu Pavlova ...*' 22 July 1941, pp. 381–92, gives details of the trial, and Doc. 438 '*Prigovor Voyennoy kollegii Verkhovnogo suda*', pp. 392–4 gives the sentence.

40 Pleshakov, pp. 222–3.

41 Taylor, p. 54; *Times Atlas*, p. 56

42 Ernst Klink, in *Germany and the Second World War*, Vol. IV, pp. 532–3.

43 Krivosheyev, *Soviet Casualties and Combat Losses . . .* , pp. 111–12, includes 625,000 Western Front, plus 2,300 Pina flotilla. Compare with Taylor, p. 20–647,000 to start.

44 Krivosheyev, *Soviet Casualties . . .* , pp. 111–12. Glantz, *Barbarossa*, p. 40, gives the same figures, citing Soviet official statistics.

45 Haupt, *Army Group Center . . .*, p. 31, citing General Geyer, commanding IX Army Corps on the evening of 22 June.

46 Haupt, *Army Group North . . .* , p. 29.

47 Valentinas Brandisauskas, 'Anti-Soviet Resistance in 1940 and 1941 and the Revolt of June 1941', in Arvydas Anusauskas, ed., *The Anti-Soviet Resistance in the Baltic States* (Genocide and Resistance Centre of Lithuania, Du Ka, Vilnius, 1999), pp. 8–22, this p. 16.

48 Ibid., p. 19.

49 Brandisauskas, 'Anti-Soviet Resistance . . .' in Anusauskas, ed., *The Anti-Soviet Resistance in the Baltic States*, pp. 15–17; Glantz, *The Initial Period . . .* , p. 175.

50 Brandisauskas, in Anusauskas, ed., *The Anti-Soviet Resistance . . .*, pp. 17–19; Haupt, *Army Group North . . .*, pp. 31–2.

51 Haupt, *Army Group North . . .*, p. 31.

52 Ibid., p. 32, citing Rolf O. Stoves, First Panzer Division 1939–1945 (Podzun, Bad Neuheim, 1962), p. 882.

53 Juris Ciganovs, 'The Resistance Movement against the Soviet Regime in Latvia between 1940 and 1941', in Anusauskas, ed., *The Anti-Soviet Resistance . . .*, pp. 122–30, this p. 127.

54 Ibid., pp. 127–9.

55 Ibid., p. 129.

56 Tiit Noormets, 'The Summer War: the 1941 Armed Resistance in Estonia', in Anusauskas, ed., *The Anti-Soviet Resistance . . .*, pp. 186–208, this pp. 190–2.

57 Ibid., pp. 192, 195–6.

58 Ciganovs, in Anusauskas, ed. *The Anti-Soviet Resistance . . .*, p. 131.

59 Glantz, *Barbarossa*, pp. 45–6.

60 Ibid., pp. 46–7; *The Initial Period . . .*, pp. 248–52; Catherine Andreyev, *Vlasov and the Russian Liberation Movement* (Cambridge University Press, 1987).

61 Pleshakov, p. 162.

62 NKO Directive No. 3, 21.15 hrs 22 June 1941, reproduced in Glantz, *Barbarossa*, Appendix II.

63 Russian '*osobo sekretnogo*'. Top secret would have been *sovershenno sekretnogo*.

64 Rokossovskiy, *Soldatskiy dolg (A Soldier's Duty)*, revised and unexpurgated edition (Olma Press, Moscow, 2002). This section of the previously expurgated text is on pp. 28–34, this reference p. 30. All such sections are identified in the new edition by italics ('*kursiv*'). This book's emphasis added. This first, formerly expurgated, section starts with clear observation of German war preparation and the fact that this had all been reported to Moscow.

65 Ibid., p. 30.

66 Ibid.; see also Pleshakov, p. 181. Also Steven Walsh's research on Rokossovskiy and interviews with Rokossovskiy's other daughter for his forthcoming PhD. Adya was born around 1926, to Rokossovskiy's wife Yulya, whom Rokossovskiy married in 1923. However, it is believed that Adya died in the mid 1970s.

67 *FSB Archives*, Vol. II, Bk 1, Doc. 330, list of Stalin's meetings, 21–8 June 1941 (no later than 28 June), pp. 98–9; Pleshakov, pp. 164–8.

68 Mikhalev, *Voyennaya Strategiya*, p. 603; Pleshakov, esp. p. 170.

69 Pleshakov, pp. 172–3; Anne Applebaum, *GULag: a History* (Doubleday, New York, 2003), p. 416; and Popel', *V Tyazhku poru (In Tough Times)* (AST, Moscow, 2002), pp. 30–57.

70 Glantz, *Barbarossa*, pp. 46–51.

71 Pleshakov, p. 177, citing Popel', *V tyazhkuyu poru*, pp. 93–5.

72 Pleshakov, pp. 181.

73 Rokossovskiy, *Soldatskiy dolg (A Soldier's Duty)* (Olma Press, Moscow, 2002), restored section, pp. 28–34, this p. 33.

74 Ibid., second restored section, pp. 47–54 (italicized), this p. 48.

75 Ibid., pp. 48–9, '*ego vid I ton bukval'no vzorvali menya*'. One can see why this was cut from the Soviet edition.

76 Pleshakov, pp. 181–4.

77 Krivosheyev, *Soviet Casualties and Combat Losses . . .*, pp. 111–13.

78 Taylor, p. 57.

79 German casualties in the first three weeks, *The Times Atlas*, p. 58. This figure seems about right, if conservative. If we take 25,000 German dead in June and a quarter of the 63,000 dead in July in its first week, we get about 40,000 dead. Assuming the usual one-to-three ratio of dead to wounded, we might reckon that the *Wehrmacht* lost about 40,000 dead and 120,000 wounded in the 'frontier battles'. 60,000 French casualties in three weeks from 10 to 31 May 1940, Brian Bond, 'France, fall of (1940)', in Holmes, ed., *The Oxford Companion to Military History*, pp. 307–16, this, p. 316.

80 *Germany and the Second World War*, Vol. IV, p. 764, citing German Luftwaffe situation reports Ob.d.L./Fu.Stab Ic, 23–27 June, Nos 653–7 and 24 June–1 July, Nos 654–61, in BA-MA RL 2.

81 Attributed to Wellington, at Waterloo.

9. Kremlin at war

1 *FSB Archives*, Vol. II, Bk I, Doc. 330, Stalin's appointments, p. 98.
2 Sebag Montefiore, pp. 365–7.
3 Reproduced in Glantz, *Barbarossa*, p. 242.
4 *FSB Archives*, Doc. 330, p. 99; Sebag Montefiore, p. 367.
5 Pleshakov, pp. 107–8.
6 Speech in *FSB Archives*, Vol. II, Bk I, Doc. 282, 22 June 1941, 12.15 hrs, pp. 14–15. Emphasis added.
7 Sebag Montefiore, pp. 367–8.
8 Gabriel Gorodetsky, 'An Alliance of Sorts', in Erickson and Dilks, *Barbarossa*, pp. 101–22, this p. 104, and note 20, p. 119, citing FO 371/29466 N3018/3/38. Baggallay to Eden.
9 If the time is double British summer time, one hour behind Moscow, the news would have reached the British at about the same time as the Soviet mission in Berlin were told, and half an hour before Schulenberg told Molotov. It may be that the times given are Greenwich Mean Time, two hours behind (08.00 GMT = 10.00 DBST/GST = 11.00 Moscow time: 04.00 GMT = 07.00 Moscow time), which would make more sense. During the Second World War the British operated extreme daylight-saving measures, one hour ahead of GMT during the winter and *two* hours ahead (double summer time) in the summer, changing around the equinoxes. See Derek Howse, *Greenwich Time and Longitude* (London, 1997). I am grateful to the Royal Observatory, Greenwich and the National Maritime Museum for their advice on this key matter.
10 Gorodetsky, in Erickson and Dilks, *Barbarossa*, p. 104; *The Daily Worker*, 23 June 1941, p. 102, extracts on display in the Central Museum of the Armed Forces, Moscow; Churchill's speech in *The Grand Alliance* (Houghton Mifflin, Boston, 1948), pp. 370–1.
11 Gorodetsky, in Erickson and Dilks, pp. 105 and 120, citing CAB 80/58 COS (41)116(0), 23 June 1941.
12 Berezhkov, *Stranitsy Diplomaticheskoy Istorii . . .*, p. 56.
13 Ibid., p. 62, 'Tall, hefty and not young'. Described as an 'Oberleutnant' – SS Obersturmführer.
14 Ibid., p. 69. Emphasis added.
15 Ibid., p. 70; *At Stalin's Side* (1994), pp. 180–95.
16 Ibid., pp. 71–6.
17 *FSB Archives*, Vol. II, Bk I, Doc. 330, pp. 98–9, 105–6.
18 Ibid., pp. 99–100, 105–6.
19 Ibid., Doc. No. 293, '. . . o sozdanii Stavki Glavnogo Komandovaniya Vooruzhennykh Sil Soyuza SSR', 23 June 1941, pp. 51–2.
20 Ibid., Doc. 280, Telegram from Timoshenko, 22 June 1941, p. 10.
21 Ibid., Doc. 277, 'Ukaz Prezidiuma Verkhovnogo Soveta SSSR o veyennom polozhenii', 22 June 1941 pp. 5–7.
22 Ibid., Doc. 285, '. . . o perevode lagerey, tyurem I koloniy na voyennoye polozheniye . . .', 22 June 1941, p. 36.

23 Ibid., Doc. 284, '. . . *o meropriyatiyakh organov gosbezopasnosti v svyazi s nachavshimsya voyennymi deystviyami s Germaniyey*', 22 June 1941, 09.10 hrs, p. 35.

24 Ibid., Doc. 289, '*Plan agenturno-operativnykh meropriyatiy UNKGB I UNKVD po g. Moskve i Moskovskoy oblastij . . .*' and Doc. 290, '*Dokladnaya zapiska nachal'nikov UNKGB I UNKVD po g. Moskve i Moskovskoy oblastii . . . o provedennykh meropriyatiyakh po obespecheniyu poryadka v g. Moskve I Moskovskoy oblasti*', both 22 June, pp. 44–9. 'Confined to barracks' from the former, other details from the latter. Both documents signed by Commissar of State Security 3rd Class (Lt Gen., equivalent) Petr Nikolayevich Kubatkin (1907–50), head of the UNKGB for Moscow and Moscow Region and Senior Major of State Security (Maj. Gen., equivalent) Mikhail Ivanovich Zhuravlëv (1911–76), head of the UNKVD for the same. For equivalent ranks see Ibid., '*Perechen' spetszvaniy nachal'stvuyushchego sostava organov NKVD-NKGB SSSR i ikh sootvetstviye voynskim zvaniyam nachal'stvuyushchego sostava Krasnoy armii (1935–1945)*', p. 659. UShOSDOR stands for *Upravleniye Shosseynikh Dorog* – Directorate of Roadways. Later GAI – as in a traffic-calming hump – *spyayushchiy gaishchik* – 'sleeping policeman'(!)

25 Ibid., Doc. 310, '*Dokladnaya zapiska UNKGB I UNKVD po g. Moskve I Moskovskoy oblasti . . . o polozhenii v g. Moskve v svyazi s nachalom voyny*', pp. 68–72, this pp. 68–71.

26 Ibid., Doc. 313, '. . . *o sdache naceleniyem radiopriyemnykh I peredayushhchikh ustroystv*', 25 June 1941, pp. 75–6.

27 Ibid., Doc. 300, '*Direktiva TsK KP(b) Belorussii . . . o bor'be s vrazheskimi parashyutnymi desantami*', 23 June 1941, p. 58.

28 Ibid., Doc. 307, '. . . *o meropriyatiyakh po bor'be s parashyutnymi desantami I diversantami protivnika v prifrontovoy polose*', 24 June 1941, pp. 64–6, and Doc. 315, Prikaz NKVD SSSR No. 00804 . . .', 25 June 1941, pp. 77–9.

29 Ibid. Note to Doc. 307.

30 See for example ibid., Doc. 369, on measures taken in Moscow and the Moscow area for dealing with enemy agent-signallers, 5 July 1941, pp. 197–8.

31 Ibid., Doc. 346, '*Pis'mo razvedyvatel'nogo upravleniya Genshtaba Krasnoy Armii narodnomu komissaru vnutrennykh del SSSR . . .*' [Beria], p. 141.

32 Ibid., Doc. 347, '*Spetsial'noye polozheniye o voyennoplennykh*', 1 July 1941, pp. 141–6. Army commands and handover to NKVD, p. 142, article II.7.b.

33 Ibid., Doc. 343, '*Spravka UPVN NKVD SSSR o soderzhashchikhsya v lageryakh voyernnoplennykh I internirovannykh*' [June 1941], pp. 133–5.

34 Ibid., see note 32, p. 141.

35 Ibid., Doc. 343, note on p. 134, and Doc. 347, p. 145.

36 Ibid., Doc. 387, 11 July 1941, p. 229.

37 Ibid., Doc. 336, '*Iz ukazaniya nachal'nika UNKGB po Kurskoy oblasti . . . o proizvodstve arestov tol'ko s sanktsii prokurora oblasti*', 28 June 1941, p. 121 and note.

38 Ibid., Doc. 305, '. . . *o sozdanii Soveta po evakuatsii*', 24 June 1941, p. 62, quotation from the commentary.

39 Ibid.

40 An excellent summary is in Glantz, *Barbarossa*, pp. 71–3.

41 This is Pleshakov's view in *Stalin's Folly*, p. 189.

42 *FSB Archives*, Vol. II, Bk 1, Doc. 330, pp. 101–3, and commentary pp. 106–9.

43 Ibid., pp. 108–9; Pleshakov, pp. 189–90, citing Sudoplatov's affidavit for the council of Ministers, 7 August 1953, in *1941 god. Dokumenty*, Vol. 2, pp. 487–90, and Pavel Sudoplatov, and Anatoly Sudoplatov, *Special Tasks: the Memoirs of an Unwanted Witness – a Soviet Spymaster* (Little, Brown, Boston, 1994), pp. 145–6; Laurence Rees, *War of the Century*, 53–6.

44 Rees, ibid., p. 53.

45 Ibid., p. 54; Pleshakov, pp. 190–1.

46 Rees, ibid.

47 *FSB Archives*, Vol. II, Bk I, p. 108, citing Russian edition of Sudoplatov's memoirs *Razvedka I Kreml' (Intelligence and the Kremlin)* (Geya, Moscow, 1996), pp. 173–6, and report from Korsikanets at end of July 1941.

48 Ibid., p. 109.

49 Ibid., Doc. 326, '. . . *o vyvoze iz Moskvy gosudarstvennykh zapasov dragotsennykh metallov, dragotsennykh kamney, Almaznogo fonda SSSR I Tsennostey Oruzhenoy Palaty Kremlya*', 27 June 1941, p. 89.

50 Ibid., Doc. 330, p. 102.

51 Pleshakov, pp. 187–9.

52 *FSB Archives*, Vol. II, Bk I, Doc. 330, pp. 103–5.

53 Ibid., p. 106, note.

54 Anastas Mikoyan, '*V pervye mesyatsy Velikoy Otechestvennoy voiny*', in *Novaya I Noveyshaya Istorya (Recent and Most Recent history)*, 6/1985, cited by his son, Stepan Mikoyan, who also edited the recollections for publication, in 'Barbarossa and the Soviet Leadership: a Recollection' in Erickson and Dilks, *Barbarossa*, pp. 123–33, this p. 127.

55 Ibid.

56 Pleshakov, pp. 212–14, is the most graphic account.

57 FSB Archives, Vol. II, Bk I, Doc. 330, note, p. 107.

58 Ibid., p. 107, note.

59 Mikoyan, '*V pervye mesyatsy* . . .' cited in Erickson and Dilks, p. 128.

60 Pleshakov, p. 219.

61 Mikoyan, '*V pervye mesyatsy* . . .', in Erickson and Dilks, p. 128.

62 Sebag Montefiore, p. 377.

63 Sun Tzu, *The Art of War*, trans. and ed. Samuel B. Griffith (Oxford University Press, 1963).

64 *FSB Archives*, Vol. II, Bk 1, Doc. 340, '*Postanovleniye Prezidiuma Verkhovnogo Soveta SSSR, Soveta Narodnykh Komissarov SSSR I Tsentral'nogo Komiteta VKP(b) ob obrazovanii Gosudarstvennogo Komiteta Oborony*', 30 June 1941, pp. 126–7.

65 Mikoyan, '*V pervye mesyatsy* . . .', in Erickson and Dilks, p. 128.

66 *FSB Archives*, Vol. II, Bk 1, Doc. 340, note on p. 127.

67 Ibid., note, p. 127.

68 Ibid.

69 Glantz, *Barbarossa*, p. 60.

70 Pleshakov, p. 258.

71 *FSB Archives*, Vol. II, Bk 1, Doc. 355, '*Vystupleniye po radio Predsedatelya Gosudarstvennogo Komiteta Oborony I. V. Stalina*' 3 July 1941, pp. 161–7, this p. 161.

72 Ibid., p. 163, reflecting, perhaps, Churchill in *The Grand Alliance*, p. 371.

73 Ibid.

74 Ibid., p. 164

75 Ibid.

76 Ibid., p. 165.

77 Ibid., Doc. 356, '*Spetsvodka UNKB po g. Moscke I Moskovskoy oblasti 1-mu sekretaryu MK I MGK VKP(b) A. S. Shcherbakovu o reagirovanii naseleniya na vystupleniya I V Stalina*', 3 July 1941, pp. 167–9.

78 Ibid., p. 168 (bottom).

79 Ibid.

80 Ibid., p. 169.

81 Ibid., final comment in document (not note).

82 Ibid., Doc. 357, '. . . *o porydke evakuatsii imushchestva iz ugrazhayemykh rayonov*', 3 July 1941, pp. 169–70.

83 Ibid., Doc. 358, '. . . *o polozhenii na zheleznodorozhnym transporte*', 3 July 1941, pp. 171–2.

84 Ibid., Doc. 324., pp. 87–8, Doc. 324, 26 June 1941. Example is troop train (*Eshelon*) No. 1042.

85 Ibid., Doc. 358, p. 171.

86 Ibid., Doc. 365, '. . . *ob evakuatsii arkhivov*', 5 July 1941, pp. 183–4. Also published in *Izvestiya TsK KPSS*, 1990, No. 7, pp. 197–8.

87 Summary in Glantz, *Barbarossa*, pp. 61–2. 'Higher level commands' are *Glavnye komandovaniya (Glavkomy)*.

88 *FSB Archives*, Vol. II, Bk I, Doc. 384, '*Postanovleniya Gosudarstvennogo Komiteta Oborony No. GKO – 83ss ob obrazovaniy Severo-Zapadnogo, Zaspadnogo i Yugo-Zapadnogo strategicheskikh napravleniy I preobrazovanii Stavki Glavnogo Komandovaniya v Stavku Verkhovnogo Glavnokomandovaniya*', 10 July 1941, pp. 224–5. The 'ss' with the GKO order number stands for *sovershenno sekretno* – top secret, like so many of the documents in the FSB archives.

89 *FSB Archives*, Vol. II, Bk I, p. 225, note.

90 Journalistic term, from the Latin 'voice of the people'.

91 On the split see *FSB Archives*, Vol. I, Bk II, Doc. 159, 1 March 1941, pp. 40–3; on Third Directorate see ibid., Doc. 165, 12 March 1941, pp. 55–7.

92 Ibid., Vol. II, Bk 1, Doc. 411, 17 July 1941, pp. 337–8.

93 See ibid, Doc. 443, 23 July 1941, pp. 400; Doc. 448, 25 July, p. 407. However, the surplus ink expended on writing 'NKGB *and* NKVD . . .' in many documents does decrease substantially after July.

94 Ibid., Doc. 431, '*Ukaz Prezidiuma Verkhovnogo Soveta SSSR ob ob'yedinenii Narodnogo komissariata vnutrennykh del I Narodnogo komissariata gosudarstvennoy bezopasnosti v ediny Narodny komissariat vnutrennykh del*', 20 July 1941, pp. 372–3, and note.

95 'As water to a thirsting soul, so is good news from a far country.' The Bible, Proverbs, 25:25.

96 *FSB Archives*, Vol. II, Bk I, Doc. 304, 23 June 1941, p. 61.

97 Ibid., Doc. 366, '*Postanovleniye Gosudarstvennogo Komiteta Oborony No. 27ss o naznachenii voyenoy missii v Angliyu*', 5 July 1941, pp. 184–5.

98 Ibid., Doc. 392, '*Soglasheniye mezhdu Pravitel'stvami SSSR I Velikobritanii o sovmestnykh deystviyakh v voyne protiv Germanii*', 12 July 1941, p. 301. On the full line-up, see the exhibition in the Central Museum of Armed Forces, Moscow.

10. Winning oneself to death

1 Halder, *Diaries*, 1000–1 (3 July 1941), cited in *Germany and the Second World War* Vol. IV, p. 569, also in Glantz, *Barbarossa*, p. 77. The best way to understand the dynamics of the manoeuvre battle of Smolensk is via David M. Glantz, *Atlas of the Battle of Smolensk* (self-published, Carlisle PA, 2001).

2 *Germany and the Second World War*, Vol. IV, p. 583.

3 Halder, *Diaries*, 1076–7 (26 July 1941), cited in *Germany and the Second World War*, Vol. IV, p. 577. The author commends the reader to the dramatic opening battle sequence of the film *Gladiator*. 'A people should *know* when they're conquered'. To which the Roman commanding general replies, 'Would you, Quintus? Would I?'. For Stalin's speech, see Chapter 9, and also *Germany and the Second World War*, Vol. IV, p. 582.

4 *Germany and the Second World War*, Vol. IV, pp. 569–70.

5 Ibid., p. 570.

6 Haupt, *Army Group Center*, p. 42.

7 Halder's words. *Diaries*, 986 (29 June 1941).

8 Haupt, *Army Group Center*, p. 47.

9 *Germany and the Second World War*, Vol. IV, p. 765, citing Kesselring, *Memoirs*, p. 90, and Hoffman von Waldau, *Diary*, p. 53 (3 July 1941), BA-MA RL 200–17.

10 Ibid., p. 767.

11 Heinz Guderian, *Panzer Leader* (Ballantine, New York, 1965), p. 144.

12 Cited in Glantz, *Barbarossa*, p. 82, emphasis added.

13 See the author's *Red God of War*, p. 152, citing Marshal of Artillery K. P. Kazakov, *Artilleriya i rakety (Artillery and Rockets)* (Voyenizdat, Moscow, 1968), pp. 76–7, and numerous other sources.

14 Glantz, *Barbarossa*, pp. 82–3.

15 Boog, in *Germany and the Second World War*, Vol. IV, p. 770. The figure of 100,000 is Field Marshal Kesselring's estimate.

16 Ibid.

17 Ibid., p. 771.

18 See V. P. Filatov, President of the Editorial Committee, *Moskovskaya Bitva v Postanovleniyakh Gosudarstvennogo Komiteta Oborony: Dokumenty I Materialy 1941–42 (The Battle of Moscow in Announcements of the State Defence Committee: Documents and Materials)*, henceforward *Moscow Documents* (Institute for Military History/Russian Federal Archive Service/Moscow Committee of Culture, Moscow, 2001), Doc. No. 24, Postanovleniye No. GKO-325ss, '*O smene*

nachal'nika General'nogo Shtaba, Reorganizatsii Zapadnogo Strategicheskogo Napravleniya i Obrazovanii rezervnogo Fronta' 29 July 1941, pp. 51–2.

19 Glantz, *Barbarossa*, p. 83.

20 Dr Jacob Kipp, 'Overview', part of the section 'The Smolensk Operation', in Glantz, ed., *The Initial Period . . .*, p. 354.

21 Glantz, *Barbarossa*, p. 84, citing Charles von Luttichau, *The Campaign in Russia, 1941.* (Office of Military History, Washington, 1985), Chapter VI, pp. 41–3.

22 Halder, *Diaries*, p. 506.

23 Glantz, *Barbarossa*, pp. 86–7.

24 Boog, in *Germany and the Second World War*, Vol. IV, p. 774. First air attack on Moscow, *FSB Archives*, Vol. II, Bk 1, Doc. 441, '*Doneseniye nachal'nika Upravleniya NKVD po g. Moskve I Moskovskoy oblasti M. N. Zhuraleva narkomu vnutrennykh del SSSR L. P. Berii o rezul'tatakh naleta vrazheskoy aviatsii na Moskvu v noch' na 22 Yulya 1941 g*' 22 July 1941, pp. 397–8.

25 Glantz, *Barbarossa*, p. 87. For a detailed survey of the Russian tradition of deep penetration by cavalry, see the author's 'Corps Volant to OMG' chapter in, idem, *The Evolution of Modern Land Warfare: Theory and Practice* (Routledge, London, 1990).

26 Ibid., pp. 89–90, citing Zolotarëv, *Stavka VGK*, 171.

27 *FSB Archives*, Vol. II, Bk 2, Doc. 528, '. . . *UNKVD po Smolenskoy oblasti . . . v Osoby otdel NKVD Zapadnogo fronta ob ispol'zovanii nemetskoy razvedkoy detey i podrostkov*', 4 September 1941, pp. 18–19.

28 Ibid., Doc. 537, '*Prikaz voyennogo soveta Rezervnogo Fronta voyskam v svyazi s pobedoy, oderzhannoy pod Yel'ney*', 7 September 1941, pp. 34–5.

29 Ibid., p. 34.

30 Krivosheyev, *Soviet Casualties . . .*, Table 75, p. 105. This table has been put in a different place in the translation (*before* losses in individual strategic operations), than in the original *Grif sekretnosti snyat*, where it comes on p. 224, *after* the Manchurian operation.

31 Krivosheyev, *Soviet Casualties . . .*, pp. 116–17.

32 Ibid.

33 Glantz, *Barbarossa*, pp. 64–5.

34 Interview with Professor Marja Talvi, from Tallinn, 30 August 2003, at International Border Guards Conference, Budapest, Hungary.

35 Anusauskas, ed., *The Anti-Soviet Resistance*, pp. 198–204.

36 Ibid., pp. 203–4.

37 Glantz, *Barbarossa*, pp. 100–1.

38 Ibid., pp. 102–4.

39 There is still an excellent sleeper service between Moscow and St Petersburg, whereas that between London and the Scottish capitals is constantly under threat.

40 Horst Boog, in *Germany and the Second World War*, Vol. IV, pp. 777, 800.

41 Ibid., p. 777.

42 Glantz, *Barbarossa*, p. 106.

43 Krivosheyev, *Soviet Casualties . . .*, pp. 115–16. The operation officially lasted from 10 July until 30 September.

44 Glantz, *Barbarossa*, pp. 104–6, citing Halder, *Diaries*, p. 524. See also the *Times Atlas*, pp. 64–5.

45 On the arguments about encircling Soviet forces versus taking Kiev, see *Germany and the Second World War*, Vol. IV, pp. 560–9.

46 Ibid., p. 780.

47 Glantz, *Barbarossa*, pp. 117–19.

48 On this cruel and vindictive judgment, see A. A. Maslov, 'Tried for Treason against the Motherland: Soviet Generals Condemned after Release from German Captivity', Part 1, *Journal of Slavic Military Studies*, Vol. 13, No. 2 (June 2000), pp. 111–15.

49 *Germany and the Second World War*, Vol. IV, p. 562.

50 Ibid., pp. 564, 568.

51 Ibid., pp. 592–3.

52 Glantz, *Barbarossa*, citing Zolotarëv, *Stavka VGK*, p. 380; *Times Atlas*, p. 58, shows it most graphically.

53 *Germany and the Second World War*, Vol. IV, p. 784.

54 Glantz, *Barbarossa*, pp. 141–2. On Zhukov's move to Leningrad, and Voroshilov's removal from command of the Leningrad Front, *FSB Archives*, Vol. II, Bk 2, Doc. 549, '. . . o naznachenii G.K. Zhukova komanduyushchim Leningradskim Frontom', 11 September 1941, pp. 84–5, issued at 19.10 hrs. Back on 29 July, Timoshenko had gone down from Defence Minister to a Strategic Direction Commander, Zhukov from Chief of General Staff to a front commander, Budënny from a Strategic Direction Commander to the same. It was a very flexible system. See GKO-325ss, cited as Doc. 24 in *Moscow Documents*, pp. 51–2 and note 18.

55 *FSB Archives*, Vol. II, Bk 2, Doc. 550, '*Direktiva Stavki VGK No 001919 komanduyushchim voyskami frontov, armii, komandiram diviziy, glavnokomanduyushchemu Yugo-Zapadnogo napravleniya o sozdanii zagraditel'nykh otryadov v strelkovykh diiviziyakh.*', 12 September 1941, pp. 85–6.

56 Glantz, p. 132, citing Zolotarëv, *Stavka VGK*, p. 198.

57 *Germany and the Second World War*, Vol. IV, p. 784.

58 Ibid., pp. 602–3.

59 Ibid., pp. 602–4.

60 Ibid., p. 132; Krivosheyev, *Soviet Casualties*, p. 114, which explains the figures.

61 *Germany and the Second World War*, Vol. IV, pp. 799–802.

62 *FSB Archives*, Vol. II, Bk 2, Doc. 556, '*Ukazaniye Stavki . . . No. 001980 komanduyushchemu 51-y armiyey F I Kuznetsovu o nedopustimosti I kategoricheskom zapreshchenii ispol'zovaniya khimicheskikh veshchestv*', 15 September 1941, pp. 104–5 and notes. Yperite, named after the Belgian town of Ypres, a persistent blister agent, was first used by the Germans on 12 July 1917. *VES*, p. 295 ('Iperit').

63 *FSB Archives*, ibid., note on Kuznetsov (1898–1961), p. 104. In 1940–1 he was head of the General Staff Academy, then Commander of Forces in the North Caucasus and Baltic Special Military Districts, and during the war, commander of the North-West Front, Twenty-First Army, the Central Front, and Fifty-First Army. He was later Chief-of-Staff of Twenty-First Army, deputy commander of

the Western Front, and commander of Sixty-First Army. From April 1942 he again commanded the General Staff Academy.

64 *Oruzhiya Massogo Porazheniya* – WMD. At the time of writing the preferred English acronym is CBRN.

65 See the author's *Expert Witness: a Defence Correspondent's Gulf War* (Brassey's Defence Publishers, London, 1993), and especially the transcript of US Gen. Norman Schwarzkopf's 27 February account of how the war was won (Appendix A), pp. 210–29, esp. p. 217 – 'The nightmare scenario . . . get hung up in this breach . . . and then have the enemy artillery rain chemical weapons down . . .' Just what Kuznetsov must have been thinking.

66 The quotation is from Wilfred Owen's First World War poem, *Dulce et Decorum Est*, a graphic portrayal of a chemical attack.

67 Roberts and Guelff, *Documents on the Laws of War*, Third Edition (Oxford University Press, 2000), Ch. 13, pp. 155–68. Lease-Lend, Ziemke, *Moscow to Stalingrad*, p. 3.

68 *Germany and the Second World War*, Vol. IV, pp. 613–16, citing H.Gr Süd/Ia KTB, 20, 22 and 25 October 1941 in BA-MA RH 19 I/74; also Glantz, *Barbarossa*, p. 157.

69 *FSB Archives*, Vol. II, Bk 2, Doc. 526, '*Spravka 4-go otdela NKVD USSR ob organizovannykh I deystvuyushchikh partizanskikh otryadakh po sostoyaniyu*', 3 September 1941, pp. 14–15.

70 Gerd R. Ueberschär, 'German Operations in the "Finland Theatre"' and 'Finnish Army Operations', in *Germany and the Second World War*, Vol. IV, pp. 941–83, this pp. 941–2.

71 Ibid., pp. 945–53, in particular p. 952, citing *Foreign Relations of the United States (FRUS)* (1941), i. 81–98.

72 *Germany and the Second World War*, Vol. IV, p. 588, citing Hitler's War Directives.

73 Ibid., p. 594, citing *DGFP*, Series D, Vol. XIII, No. 265, p. 431, and p. 684, citing OKH/GenStdH/Op.Abt. (IIb) Conference at the Office of the Deputy Chief of Staff, 24 October 1941, KTB OKW i. 1072–3 (105).

74 Ibid., p. 139.

75 *Germany and the Second World War*, Vol. IV, pp. 592–3, citing Halder, *Diaries*, 1195 (22 August 1941).

76 Ernst Klink, in ibid., p. 594.

77 A 'double envelopment' is an envelopment from two sides – a 'pincer movement' into the enemy's flanks. An encirclement is a double envelopment which cuts him off completely, preventing withdrawal. A double encirclement is two double envelopments, one overlapping the other. See the author's *The Evolution of Modern Land Warfare: Theory and Practice* (Routledge, London, 2000), pp. 17–23, and his 'Manoeuvre Warfare' entry in *The Oxford Companion to Military History*, (Oxford University Press, 2001), pp. 541–4, especially diagram on p. 543.

78 *FSB Archives*, Vol. II, Bk 2, Doc. 529, '*Direktiva Stavki VGK No. 001650 komanduyushchemu Bryanskim Frontom A. I. Yeremenko, razreshayushchaya sozdaniye zagraditelnykh otryadov*', 5 September 1941, p. 20.

79 Ibid., Doc. 533, '*Ukazaniye I.V. Stalina komanduyushchemi Bryanskim Fronton . . . ob uluchshenii organizatsii boyevykh deystvii I vyvode iz okruzheniya 108-ya tankovoy divizii*', 6 September 1941, pp. 26–7.

80 He lived from 1892 to 1970. *VES*, p. 253.

81 Boog, in *Germany and the Second World War*, Vol. IV, p. 793, citing General Wolfram von Richthofen, *Diary*, for 5, 9, 10 and 13 October 1941.

82 Joachim Hoffmann, in ibid., p. 891.

83 Rokossovskiy, *A Soldier's Duty*, trans. of the abridged edition of *Soldatskiy dolg* (Progress, Moscow, 1985), pp. 49–52, this on the latter. This account is not expanded in the unabridged 2002 Russian version, where it appears on pp. 84–5 (belfry) –6 . . .

84 Ibid., p. 54; unexpurgated Russian version 2002, pp. 88–9.

85 Ibid.

86 Hoffmann, in *Germany and the Second World War*, Vol. IV, p. 889.

87 Rokossovskiy, *A Soldier's Duty*, abridged trans., 1985, p. 57; unchanged in unexpurgated Russian version, 2002, pp. 91–2.

88 Glantz, *Barbarossa*, pp. 149–50, citing *Völkischer Beobachter*, 9 and 10 October 1941.

89 *Germany and the Second World War*, Vol. IV, p. 794, citing Richthofen's *Diary*, 11 October 1941. Freiherr (Baron) Manfred von Richthofen had been the famous 'Red Baron' of the First World War.

90 Ibid., p. 794.

91 Glantz, *Barbarossa*, p. 151, citing *VOV*, Vol. 1, p. 222.

92 Glantz, *Barbarossa*, pp. 144–53; Krivosheyev, *Soviet Casualties*, p. 118; *Times Atlas*, p. 61.

93 *Germany and the Second World War*, Vol. IV, p. 586. The modern, western democratic assumption is more conservative. According to Maj. Gen. Sebastian Roberts, friend and colleague, the 'Roberts rule of thumb' is that for a modern democratic society it takes 25 million of population to produce an armoured division and a carrier battle group. Thus, the UK and France can manage two of each (correct) and the United States – ten. On that (anachronistic) basis, even allowing for the different strength of divisions, the USSR would have been dead on day two or three.

94 Glantz, p. 149, citing A. M. Samsonov, *Proval Gitlerovskogo nastupleniya pod Moskvu* (The Defeat of the Nazi Offensive before Moscow) (Nauka, Moscow, 1966), pp. 20–1.

95 Filatov, ed., *Moscow Documents*, Doc. 15, *O Mozhayskoy linii oborony*, 16 July 1941, p. 41.

96 *Germany and the Second World War*, Vol. IV, pp. 675–6.

97 Ibid., p. 579.

98 Ibid., p. 685. OKH assessed 183 formations deployed in the east as equivalent to 136.

99 Glantz, *Barbarossa*, p. 161.

100 Ibid., p. 68.

11. Midnight in Moscow

1 *Moscow Documents*, Doc. 1, *Rasporyazheniye No. GKO –1s, 'Ob uvelicheniyi vypuska pozharnykh mashin na Moskovskom Zavode Protivopozharnogo Oboorudovaniya'*, 1 July 1941, p. 13.

2 Ibid., Doc. 2, *Postanovleniye No GKO-3ss, 'Ob usilenii protivopozharnoy oborony Moskvy I prigoorodnykh Gorodov Moskovskoy Oblasti'*, 2 July 1941, pp. 14–24.

3 Ibid., Doc. 4, *Postanovleniye . . . GKO-26* [unclassified!], *'O reorganizatsii Sluzhby MPVO g. Moskvy'*, 5 July 1941, pp. 26–7.

4 Ibid., Doc. 8, *Postanovleniye GKO-73s, O sozdanii sluzhby maskirovki pri Moskovskom Sovete'*, 9 July 1941, pp. 31–2.

5 In his seminal article, 'Toward a general theory of deception', in a special issue of the *Journal of Strategic Studies, Issue on Military Deception and Strategic Surprise* (March 1982), pp. 178–92, Bart Whaley typologizes deception into dissimulation – hiding the real, and simulation – showing the false. Dissimulation includes masking, repackaging and dazzling. Simulation includes inventing, imitating and decoying.

6 *Moscow Documents*, Doc. 9, *Postanovleniye GKO-74ss, 'O provedenii spetsial'nykh rabot'*, 9 July 1941, pp. 32–3.

7 Ibid. ANFO was widely used by the IRA in its UK campaign in the 1970s to 1990s.

8 Ibid., Doc. 10, *'Postanovleniye GKO-76ss, 'O meropriyatiyakh po bor'be s desantami i diversantami protivnika v Moskve i prilegayushchikh rayonakh'*.

9 Ibid., Doc. 11, *Postanovleniya GKO-77ss, 'O protivovozdushnoy oborony Moskvy'*, 9 July 1941, pp. 35–6.

10 Ibid., Doc. 14, *Postanovleniya GKO-172ss, 'O Mozhayskoy Linii Oborony'*, 16 July 1941, also reproduced in *FSB Archives*, Doc. 409, pp. 335–6, and *Moscow Documents*, Doc. 17, *GKO-183ss, 'Voprosy Mozhayskoy Linii Oborony'*, pp. 42–3, not in *FSB Archives*.

11 *Moscow Documents*, Docs 21–3, *GKO-246ss, 'Ob organizatsii bespereboynogo radioveshchaniya vsesoyuznogo radiokomiteta I radioperedach dlya TASS'*, 23 July 1941, pp. 46–9 (Molotov); *GKO-278ss, 'O rabote radiostantsii'*, 25 July 1941, p. 50 (Stalin) and Doc. 23, *GKO-290ss, 'O perevode TASS v g. Kuybyshev*, 26 July 1941, pp. 50–1(Molotov).

12 Ibid., Doc. 19, *GKO-211ss*, 'Ob evakuatsii sotrudnikov NKVD SSSR in NKGB', 20 July 1941, p. 44, signed by Molotov.

13 *FSB Archives*, Vol. II, Bk 1, Doc. 431, pp. 372–3.

14 Ibid., Vol. II, Bk 2, Doc. 525, 3 September 1941, p. 13.

15 *Moscow Documents*, Doc. 44, *Postanovleniye GKO-801ss, 'Ob evakuatsii stolitsy SSSR Moskvy'*, 15 October 1941, p. 70, signed by Stalin.

16 Ibid., Doc. 25, *GKO-377ss, 'Vopros NKVD'*, 2 August 1941, pp. 52–3 (self-inflicted wounds); Rokossovskiy, *Soldatskiy dolg*, unexpurgated 2002 edition, restored section pp. 129–38, this p. 131.

17 *Moscow Documents*, Doc. 26, *GKO-562ss*, 22 August 1941, p. 53 (vodka).

18 Ibid., Doc. 34, *GKO-690, 'O vseobshhchem obyazatel'nom obuchenii voyennomu delu grazhdan SSSR'*, 17 September 1941, p. 61.

19 Ibid., Vol. II, Bk 1, Doc. 507, '*Ukaz . . . o pereselenii nemtsev, prozhivayushchikh v rayonakh Povolzh'ya*', pp. 539–40.

20 Ibid., Vol. II, Bk 2, Doc. 554, *Spetssoobshcheniye . . . No. 1/154 o khode operatsii po vypolneniyu Ukaza Preziidiuma Verkhovnogo Soveta SSSR o vyselenii nemtsev Povolzh'ya*, 14 September 1941, p. 92.

21 Ibid., Doc. 570, '. . . *Zapiska NKVD SSSR No 2639/B v Gosudarstvennoy Komitet Oborony SSSR ob itogakh preseleniya nemtsev is Byvshey Respubliki Nemtsev podvolzh'ya, saratovskoy I Stalingradskoy oblastey*', 21 September 1941, pp. 124–5.

22 IDPs are displaced within a nation state, and the Volga Germans fall into this category. Refugees move between states, and have special (and probably more favourable) status in international law.

23 Ibid., Doc. 532, GKO-636ss, '*o pereselenii nemtsev iz g. Moskvy I Moskovskoy oblasti I Rostovskoy oblasti*', 6 September 1941, pp. 25–6 and Doc. 558, '*UNKVD po Moskovskoy oblasti No 1/692 v NKVD SSSR ob okonchanii pereseleniya lits nemetskoy natsional'nostiiz rayonov oblasti*', 15 September 1941, p. 106.

24 Ibid., Doc. 569, '. . . *o rezul'tatakh operatsii po pereseleniyu nemtsev iz Moskvy . . .*', 20 September 1941, p. 123.

25 See map 19 in the Annex to *Germany and the Second World War*, Vol. IV, '*Frontveränderungen der H.Gr Mitte und Nord vom 7.10 bis 5.12.1941*', for a very clear picture of the front lines on 7 and 24 October, 25 November and 5 December.

26 Ibid., Doc. 36, GKO-740ss, '*O podgotovke k vyvodu iz stroya promyshlennykh predpriyatii Moskvy i Moskovskoy oblasti*', 8 October 1941, pp. 62–3; also in *FSB Archives*, Vol. II, Bk 2, Doc. 598, pp. 185–6.

27 *Moscow Documents*, Doc. 37, '*O podgotovke predpriyatiy g. Moskvy i Moskovskoy oblasti k unichtozheniyu*', no GKO number but addressed to it and to Stalin and signed by the 'gang of five', 9 October 1941, pp. 63–4. Also in *FSB Archives*, Vol. II, Bk 2, Doc. 604, p. 196.

28 Ibid., Doc. 38, no GKO number, '*O prikrytii Moskvy po Mozhayskomu napravleniyu*', 10 October 1941, pp. 64–5.

29 Professor Viktor Anfilov, who befriended Zhukov in the 1960s when he was out of favour, cited in Rees, *War of the Century* (BBC, 1999), pp. 55–6.

30 *Moscow Documents*, Doc. 41, *GKO-768ss1*, '*O stroitel'stve 3-y Linii Oborony gor. Moskvy*', 12 October 1941, pp. 67–8.

31 Ibid., Doc. 42, *GKO-788ss*, '*Ob evakuatsii bol'shogo Gosudarstevnnogo Akademicheskogo Ordena Lenina Teatra . . .*' etc., 13 October 1941, pp. 68–9.

32 Gor'kov, *Gosudarstvenny Komitet Oborony Postanovlyayet*, Stalin's appointments diary, pp. 228–9, 255.

33 *SVE*, Vol. 1 (1976), p. 566. Neither this, nor the 1986 *VES*, p. 96, allude to the incident, although in a Soviet source, it is easy to see why they might not.

34 V. A. Zhilin, ed., *Bitva pod Moskvoy: Khronika, Fakty, Lyudy (The Battle of Moscow: Chronicles, Facts, People)*, 'Archive' Series, 2 vols (Olma Press, Moscow, 2002), Vol. 1, Docs 17 October 1941, '*Izvlecheniye iz operativnoy svodki No 223 General'nogo Shtaba Krasnoy armii na. 8.00 17.10.41 g*', pp. 345–8, this p. 348, and 18 October 1941, '*Izvlecheniye iz operativnoy svodki No. 234 . . . na 8.00*

18.10.41 g', pp. 355–7, this p. 356. The first is signed by Deputy Chief of Staff of the Red Army Maj. Gen. Vasilevskiy and regimental commissar Ryzhkov; the second by Colonel Kurasov, Deputy Chief of the Operations Directorate, and by Kurasov.

35 Ibid., Doc. 44, '*Postanovleniye Gosudarstvennogo Komiteta Oborony ob evakuatsii stolitsy SSSR g. Moskvy*', 15 October 1941, p. 70; also FSB Archives, Doc. 611, pp. 207–8.

36 Berezhkov, *At Stalin's Side*, p. 329.

37 Gor'kov, *Gosudarstvenny Komitet Oborony Postanovlyayet*, Stalin's appointments diary, p. 255.

38 *FSB Archives*, Vol. II, Bk 2, Doc. 619, '*Spravka nachal'nika UNKVD po g. Moskve i Moskovskoy oblasti M. I. Zhuravlëva o reagirovanii naseleniya na priblizheniya vraga k stolitse*', pp. 222–6.

39 Sebag Montefiore, p. 397.

40 *FSB Archives*, Vol. II, Bk 2, Doc. 619, p. 222.

41 Ibid., Doc. 625, '*Raport zamestitelya nachal'nika 1-go otdeleniya NKVD SSSR D N. Shadrina zamestitelyu narkoma vnutrennykh del SSSR V. N. Merkulovu o resul'tatakh osmotra pomeshcheniy zdaniya TsK VKP(b) posle evakuatsii apparata TsK VKP(b)*'.

42 '*Pospeshnaya evakuatsiya*', ibid., Doc. 619, note, p. 222.

43 Sebag Montefiore, pp. 398–9.

44 Ibid., pp. 399–402.

45 *Moscow Documents*, Doc. 47, GKO 808s [secret], '*O Rabote Metropolitena I Predpriyatii v Moskve*', 16 October 1941, p. 73.

46 *FSB Archives*, Vol. II, Bk 2, Doc. 613, '2*Boyevoy prikaz 2-y motostrelokovoy divizii voysk NKVD No 1 o prikritii podstupov k moskve s severa I severo-zapad*', 15 October 1941, pp. 206–10.

47 Ibid., Doc. 616, '*Prikaz nachal'nika UNKVD po g. Moskve I Moskovskoy oblasti o sformirovanii istrebitel'noogo motostrelkovogo Moskovskogo polka*', 17 October 1941, pp. 213–14. Zhuravlëv was a Senior Major of State Security, equivalent to a major-general.

48 Ibid., Docs. 628, '*Prikaz . . . o peredache lichnoogo sostava raygorotdelov NKVD I militsii v istrebnitel'nye batal'ony*', and Doc. 629, '*. . . o neobkhodimosti peredachi istrebiitel'nykh batal'onov, nakhodyashchikhsya v zone fronta, v sostav RKKA*', both 22 October 1941, pp. 235–6.

49 *FSB Archives*, Vol. II, Bk 2, Doc. 621 (19 October 1941), reporting on situation from 13 to 15 October, p. 228; Doc. 630 (23 October), reporting on 20 October situation, pp. 236–7; Doc. 634 (25 October), p. 243, and Doc. 723 (6 December), p. 392. On 20 October the Boykov factory had 160,000 artillery shells all ready, but with nowhere to go, and on 24 October Factory No. 58 had 516,000 RPG-40 anti-tank launchers, more than a million signal cartridges and millions of other cartridges and detonators. On 6 December, Factory No. 575 had 10,000 aviation bombs, 123,180 hand grenades and 8,000 anti-tank mines undelivered.

50 *Moscow Documents*, Doc. 49, *Postanovleniye GKO-813* [unclassified!], '*O vvedenii osadnogo polozheniya v Moskve I prilegayushchikh k gorody rayonakh*', 19 October 1941, pp. 74–5. Also in *FSB Archives*, Vol. II, Bk 2, Doc. 620, p. 227.

51 Note to the *FSB Archives* version, Doc. 620, p. 227.

52 Ibid., pp. 74–5 (*Moscow Documents*), 227 (FSB).

53 Ogryzko, interviewed as part of the BBC TV series *War of the Century: When Hitler fought Stalin* (1999), published as ibid. (BBC Worldwide, London, 1999), p. 72. Ogryzko later served with 1st NKVD Division.

54 *FSB Archives*, Vol. II, Bk 2, Doc. 626, 'Svodka voyennoy komendatury g. Moskvy', 21 October 1941, pp. 232–3.

55 Rokossovskiy, *Soldatskiy dolg*, unexpurgated 2002 version, restored section pp. 129–38, this pp. 132–4. The section starts with events of 14 October (p. 132), and therefore should, more logically, have been re-inserted between pp. 92 and 93 of the complete edition, but for some reason has been inserted – or was in the original manuscript – after events in November.

56 Raymond, *Soviet Preparation for Total War, 1925–51*, p. 11. As this is a quotation I have used his spelling Kuibyshev: elsewhere, I have used the Nato system, Kuybyshev. Hence the [*sic*].

57 David Lean's very British impression of Russia in the 1965 film based on Boris Pasternak's famous novel.

58 Raymond, pp. ii-iv. See also note 29.

59 Ibid., p. iv.

60 Ibid., p. v.

61 Sebag Montefiore, p. 395.

62 *FSB Archives*, Vol. II, Bk 2, Doc. 617, '*Predpisaniye narkoma vnutrennykh del SSSR No 2756/B sotrudniku osobykh porucheniy spetsgruppy NKVD SSSR o rasstrele 25 Zaklyuchennykh v g. Kuybysheve*, 18 October 1941, pp. 215–20, and Docs 638 and 639, confirming the execution of twenty of the twenty-five on 28 October, pp. 247–9.

63 Ibid., p. 219.

64 Berezhkov, *At Stalin's Side*, p. 330.

65 Ibid., pp. 330–1.

66 Ibid., pp. 331–2.

67 Glantz, *Barbarossa*, p. 161.

68 Klaus Reinhardt, 'Moscow 1941: the Turning Point', in Erickson and Dilks, ed., *Barbarossa*, pp. 207–24, this pp. 213–14.

69 Glantz, *Barbarossa*, p. 162.

70 Ibid., p. 68. By 31 December the Red Army had lost more than 4 million soldiers and 200 divisions, roughly equivalent to its entire pre-war peacetime strength, and yet was still fighting.

71 'When the iron dice roll – may God help us' – Bethmann Hollweg, German Chancellor, on 1 August 1914, at the outbreak of the First World War. The Germans lost that one as well, but, unlike the Second World War, the Russians did not win.

72 Glantz, p. 169, citing Halder, *Diaries*, pp. 555–6.

73 Glantz, *Barbarossa*, p. 162; Reinhardt, in Erickson and Dilks, *Barbarossa*, pp. 214–15.

74 Reinhardt, in Erickson and Dilks, *Barbarossa*, p. 215.

75 Ibid., p. 215, citing OKW, Doc. 3208/41 gKdos Wi, 2 October 1941, in file

Thomas in BA-MA Wi ID 73, pp. 41 ff.; *VerbStd/Ru Amt beim reichsmarschall*, 31 October 1941, file Nagel, in BA-MA: W 01-B/27 and OKW, Doc. 3409/41 gKdos, 22 October 1941, file Thomas, in BA-MA: Wi ID 73.

76 Reinhardt, in Erickson and Dilks, p. 215.
77 Glantz, *Barbarossa*, p. 162; Reinhardt, in Erickson and Dilks, *Barbarossa*, p. 215.
78 Sebag Montefiore, pp. 404–5, Details: VES, pp. 48 (Artem'ev), 114–16 (Revolution).
79 Red Square – *Krasnaya Ploshchad'*. The modern Russian words *krasny*, 'red', and *krasivy*, 'beautiful' derive from the same old Slavic root. The modern Russian colloquialism for 'gay', by the way, is 'goluboy' – 'light blue'. Could that owe anything to the distinctive light, bright blue colour worn by the NKVD/NKGB, MGB and KGB?
80 Sebag Montefiore, pp. 404–6, for a brilliant account.
81 Glantz, *Barbarossa*, pp. 162–7.
82 Ibid., p. 168.
83 *Germany and the Second World War*, Vol. IV, pp. 895–6.
84 Glantz, *Barbarossa*, pp. 166–7.
85 Ibid., p. 170.
86 *28 geroyakh panfilovtsakh*.
87 *TsK VKP(b) Tovarishchu Zhdanovu A. A.* (Central Committee of the Communist Party Comrade Zhdanov AA), 13. VI.1948, Top Secret, Central Committee archives, reproduced at Plate 5. The Russian alphabet does not have a 'V' character – therefore, V as Roman numeral 5, (which the Romans pronounced as a 'U') is rendered by cyrillic 'Y'(U). My thanks to Dr Sergey Kudryashëv.
88 'Japan: the Avenue to Germany', in Gorodetsky pp. 201, this, pp. 181, 197–8.
89 Ibid., pp. 181–2.
90 *FSB Archives*, Vol. II, Bk 1, Doc. 465, 1 August 1941, p. 443.
91 Ibid., Doc. 641, '*Soobshcheniye GUGB NKVD SSSR . . . v NKVD SSSR o provokatsionnykh deystviyakh yapontsev na sovetsko-yaponskoy granitse v perio s 1 po 28 octyabrya 1941*', 28 October 1941, pp. 250–1.
92 Ibid., Doc. 654, '*Dokladnaya zapiska GUGB NKVD SSSR v NKVD SSSR I Genshtab Krasnoy Armii ob izdanii prikaza po Kvantunskoy armii o zakhvate sovetskikh pogranichnykh naryadov*', 2 November 1941, p. 265. A *naryad* is a detail.
93 Erickson and Dilks, *Barbarossa*, p. 182.
94 Ibid., Andrei Mertsalov, pp. 134–49, this p. 137.
95 Glantz, *Barbarossa*, p. 68.
96 Ibid., p. 69, Table 1, 'Red Army Wartime Mobilization 1941'.
97 Ibid.
98 *Germany and the Second World War*, Vol. IV, p. 897, citing Shtemenko, *General'ny shtab*, Vol. I, p. 38.
99 Glantz, *Barbarossa*, p. 165.
100 An old Russian saying: 'one person who has been scared shitless is worth two who have not.' One *Spetsnaz* unit encountered by the author, used in the capture of the Presidential Palace in Grozny in January 1995, hailed from Brnaul, in Siberia.
101 Rokossovskiy, *Soldatskiy dolg*, unexpurgated 2002 edition, restored section, pp. 129–38, this p. 134.

102 Ibid., p. 136.

103 Ibid.

104 Ibid., pp. 137–8.

105 Ibid., p. 138. It is easy to see why this ten-page section was excised from the published Soviet version.

106 Zhukov, *Vospominaniya I Razmyshleniya (Reminiscences and Reflections)*, 13th edition, corrected and with additions from the author's manuscript (unexpurgated), 2 vols (Olma Press, Moscow, 2002), Vol. 2, ch. 14, p. 55.

107 Zhukov, *Vospominaniya I Razmyshleniya* (2002), unexpurgated edition, p. 29; Sebag Montefiore, pp. 400, 406.

108 Rokossovskiy, *Soldatskiy dolg*, unexpurgated 2002 version, preface by Dr Aleksey Basov, pp. 8–9.

12. Black snow

1 Hoffmann, in *Germany and the Second World War*, Vol. IV, p. 894; Ziemke, p. 47, citing *IVOVSS*, Vol. II, p. 250 and Zhukov, *Memoirs*.

2 Haupt, *Assault on Moscow*, 1941, p. 140.

3 'Zapadny Front, 28 Noyabrya' ('Western Front . . .'), *Pravda*, 29 November 1941, reproduced in Zhilin, ed., *Bitva pod Moskvoy*, pp. 800–2.

4 Soviet General Staff Operational Reports Nos. 279 (2 December 1941, covering 0800 on 1 December to 0800 on 2 December), 280 (3 December), 281 (4 December) and 282 (5 December), in Zhilin, ed., *Bitva pod Moskvoy*, Vol. 1, pp. 843–6, 853–6, 866–9 and 876–80. These reports are extremely detailed and give the exact dispositions of Soviet Western Front forces day by day. The massive two-volume collection also includes German official reports for each day, and captured German documents. It is about the most detailed primary-source account of the Battle for Moscow available.

5 UKNA, *W0 208/1790, Soviet Ground Operations 1941–45*. Summary (20 pp.), p. 1–A3. 'The most critical day for Moscow . . .'

6 Cited in Haupt, *Assault on Moscow, 1941*, p. 152.

7 Ibid., pp. 152–3. Hitler order to OKH of 21 December, p. 183: 'Divest both prisoners and inhabitants of their winter clothing.' In other words, kill them – slowly.

8 Motorcycle battalion, Haupt, *Assault on Moscow*, p. 153. The single motorcyclist is the story told by many Moscow guides. The author has been unable to stand it up, but with forward German units 26 kilometres out, it could have happened.

9 Ibid., p. 154, citing combat diary of 87th Infantry Division.

10 Ibid., pp. 153–4, citing Sitrep of 30 November.

11 'Evaluation of the Position of Fourth Panzer Group', 3 December 1941, captured German despatch from *TsA MO RF fond* 500, opis. 12462, d. 565, p. 165, trans. into Russian and reproduced in Zhilin, ed., *Bitva pod Moskvoy*, Vol. 1, p. 856. Italics added.

12 Haupt, *Assault on Moscow*, p. 164. *Germany and the Second World War*, Vol. IV, p. 897.

13 *Germany and the Second World War*, Vol. IV, pp. 895–7.

14 *SVE*, Vol. 8 (1980), pp. 171–5 on Shock Army, as an idea, and the five Shock Armies formed in the Great Patriotic War. The lead formation in a possible Soviet invasion of western Europe in the 1970s and 1980s was Third Shock Army.

15 Ziemke, *Moscow to Stalingrad*, p. 61, citing Zhukov, *Memoirs*, and Sokolovskiy, *Soviet Art of War*.

16 Glantz, *Barbarossa*, pp. 182 (armed forces' losses), 187 (people, industry, terrain). Trotskiy, 'idealisation of our weakness', Erickson, *Soviet High Command*, p. 39, citing Trotskiy, *My Life*, p. 374.

17 Ibid., pp. 185–6, citing Zhukov, *Memoirs*, Vol. 1 (Progress, Moscow, 1974) (expurgated), p. 254.

18 *Germany and the Second World War*, Vol. IV, p. 898.

19 Zhukov, *Memoirs* (Progress, Moscow, 1974) (expurgated), p. 254. Ziemke, *Barbarossa to Stalingrad*, p. 61.

20 Letter from German soldier Haman, 6 December 1941, '*Iz pisem nemetskikh soldat I ofitserov*'. Zhilin, ed., *Bitva pod Moskvoy* (2002), Vol. 2, p. 31, document TsA MO RF f. 32, op. 11306, d. 65, p. 50.

21 The invasion was postponed from its planned date of 5 June 1944, because of appalling weather. Group Captain Stagg, the chief weather forecaster, predicted a window of opportunity on 6 June, and the decision was duly taken to 'go'.

22 Ziemke, *Moscow to Stalingrad*, pp. 65–6, citing Pz AOK 3, *Gefechtsbericht Russland, 1941–42*, Pz. AOK 3 21818/2 file.

23 Conversation with Stan Cornford, formerly Deputy Chief Meteorological Officer at RAF Strike Command, author of *D-Day: the Role of the Met Office* (HMSO, 1994) and *With Wind and Sword: the Story of Meteorology and D-Day* (Met Office internal publication), and Ian MacGregor of the Met Office Archives, Exeter.

24 See E. M. Frisby, 'Russian Ideas on Long-Range Weather Forecasting', a review of *Basic principles of the synoptic method of long-range weather forecasting* (Hydrometeorological Publishing House, Moscow and Leningrad, 1940), in *Weather*, Vol. 12, No. 12, December 1947, p. 365. With gratitude to Ian MacGregor, Met Office Archives, for scanning and transmitting the document.

25 Ibid.

26 Ziemke, p. 66, citing G. A. Deborin and B. S. Telpukhovskiy, *Itogi I uroki velikoy otechestvennoy voyny (Conclusions and Lessons from the GPW)* (Mysl', Moscow, 1975), p. 129.

27 Russel H. S. Stolfi, 'Chance in History: the Russian Winter of 1941–42', *History*, Vol. 65 (1980), pp. 214–28. The 1941 mean of $-28.6°C$ was cold, even by Russian standards. Details on the effects on equipment in Ziemke, pp. 64–7, 90, 118.

28 Stolfi, pp. 221, 225–6; Ziemke, p. 90 (T-34), p. 118 (turrets, constant running).

29 Zhilin, ed., *Bitva pod Moskvoy* (2002), Vol. 2, pp. 9–12, on the 'operational situation at the beginning of December 1941', this p. 11; Haupt, *Assault on Moscow*, p. 172.

30 Glantz, *Barbarossa*, pp. 188–9; Haupt, *Assault on Moscow*, p. 170.

31 Ziemke, pp. 67–8. Conversation between Field Marshal von Bock, commanding

Army Group Centre, and Field Marshal Günther von Kluge, commanding Fourth Army.

32 Stolfi, 'Chance in History . . .', p. 227, Table 3, last entry.

33 Ziemke, p. 70.

34 Haupt, *Assault on Moscow*, p. 174.

35 Glantz, *Barbarossa*, pp. 190–1; Ziemke, p. 70, citing Army Group Centre *Kriegstagebuch* for 7 December.

36 Ziemke, ibid.

37 Ibid.

38 'Pearl Harbor' entry in *The Oxford Companion to Military History*, pp. 696–9.

39 Japanese Admiral Yamamoto's famous words, 'I fear all we have done is awaken a sleeping dragon, who will exact a terrible revenge.' These words were often quoted again, after 11 September 2001. This paragraph with apologies to Rudyard Kipling, *Mandalay*.

40 Ziemke, p. 78.

41 Zhukov, *Memoirs*, unexpurgated 2002 edition, Vol. 2, p. 57, ch. 15, 'Severe Experiences Continue (1942)'.

42 See the note in *FSB Archives*, Vol. II, Bk 2, p. 415.

43 *Germany and the Second World War*, Vol. IV, p. 816.

44 *FSB Archives*, Vol. II, Bk 2, Enemy Documents, Doc. 127, '*Iz voyennogo dnevnika komanduyushhchego gruppoy armii "Tsentr" general-Fel'dmarshala Fedora fon Boka*', 7 December 1941, pp. 593–5.

45 Ziemke, p. 73.

46 See Stolfi, 'Chance in History . . .', p. 222, note 23.

47 Ziemke, p. 71.

48 Ibid., pp. 76–7. The first quotation, Bock's, is from Army Group Centre's *Kriegstagebuch* of 10 December 1941. The second is Ziemke's surmise, which seems logical.

49 Ziemke, p. 77, citing *VOV*, p. 114.

50 Ibid., p. 80, citing H. Gr. Mittel Ia, *Kriegstagebuch*, 14 December 1941.

51 Ibid., p. 82, citing OKW, OKH and Army Group Centre files.

52 Ibid., pp. 82–6.

53 Ibid., p. 90, citing *IVOVSS*, Vol. II, p. 288, and *IVMV*, Vol. IV, p. 291.

54 Zhukov, *Vospominaniya I Razmyshleniya* (2002), unexpurgated edn, Vol. 2, p. 41.

55 Col. B. I. Nevzorov, '*Dostizheniye uspekha pri obshchem prevokhodstve protivnika v silakh I sredstvakh*' ('Attaining success in the presence of a general enemy superiority in forces and means [men and equipment]'), Tenth Army in the Moscow counter-offensive, *VIZh* 12/1986, pp. 22–9, esp. pp. 25, 27.

56 Ziemke, pp. 97–104, particularly the former and the latter, citing *IVOVSS*, Vol. II, p. 292, and H. Gr. Mitte, *Kriegstagebuch*, 29, 30 and 31 December 1941 and 1 January 1942.

57 *FSB Archives*, Vol. II, Bk 2, Doc. 735, '*Prikaz NKVD SSSR No 001683 ob operativno-chekistskom obsluzhivanii mestnostey, osvobozhdennykh ot voysk protivnika*', 12 December 1941, pp. 413–15.

58 Ibid.

59 Ibid., Doc. 743, '*Iz direktivy NKVD USSR No 33881/CB o formirovanii I rabote*

organov NKVD na osvobezhdennoy ot protivnika territorii', 16 December 1941, pp. 429–31.

60 *Germany and the Second World War*, Vol. IV, Map Annex, map 27, *Ablösung der Militär- durch die Zivilverwaltung in ihrer zeitlichen Abfolge.*

61 Ibid., Vol. IV, Jurgen Förster, 'Pacification of Conquered Territories', text, pp. 1189–225, this pp. 1221–3, citing the commandant of army Rear area (Korück) 582 in BA-MA RH 23/219.

62 Ibid., p. 1224.

63 Ibid., Doc. 746, *'Prikaz komandovaniya 50-y armii No 23 s ob'yavleniem blagodarnosti sotrudnikam UNKVD po Tul'skoy oblasti, prinimavshim aktivnoye uchastiye v partizanskom dvizhenii'*, 19 December 1941, pp. 445–6.

64 Ziemke, pp. 118–32; Stolfi, p. 222, note 23.

65 See UKNA series *FO 371* for 1943. Correspondence of Sir Archibald Clark Kerr, Ambassador, etc.

66 *Pravda*, 1 January 1942.

67 Zhukov, *Vospominaniya I Razmyshleniya* (2002), unexpurgated edition, Vol. 2, p. 43. Trans. author.

68 Ibid.

69 Ibid.

70 Ibid., p. 44. See also author's *In Praise of Attrition*, inaugural lecture, Cranfield University/Royal Military College of Science, 14 June 2001.

71 Zhukov, *Vospominaniya . . .* (2002), unexpurgated edition, p. 44, and Clausewitz, *On War*, trans. Paret and Howard, 1976, Bk 1, ch. 7, 'On Friction in War', p. 119.

72 Zhukov, *Vospominaniya . . .* (2002), unexpurgated edition, pp. 44–5. 'My dear' – *golubchik* – literally 'my little dove'. John Erickson would also address his few protégés as 'my dear'. Perhaps acquired from studying Shaposhnikov? – although they could never have met.

73 Krivosheyev, ed., *Grif sekretnosti snyat*, pp. 174–5; *Soviet Casualties and Combat Losses*, pp. 120–1.

74 Zhilin, ed., *Bitva pod Moskvoy*, Vol. 2, pp. 12–22. The collection of documents on the counteroffensive (Vol. 2) covers the period from 5 December to 20 April.

75 Not in Zhukov's memoirs, but widely recounted, nonetheless. See Sebag Montefiore, pp. 406–7.

76 Krivosheyev, ed., *Grif sekretnosti snyat*, pp. 176–7, *Soviet Casualties . . .*, pp. 122–3.

77 Ziemke, pp. 161–6.

78 Ibid., pp. 166–70.

79 Zhukov, *Vospominaniya I Razmyshleniya* (2002), unexpurgated edition, Vol. 2, pp. 48–9; Ziemke, pp. 164, 170.

80 Zhukov, *Vospominaniya . . .* (2002), pp. 46–7, author's translation; Ziemke, p. 142.

81 Ziemke, pp. 173–5.

82 Zhukov, *Vospominaniye . . .* (2002), p. 49.

83 Ziemke, p. 177.

84 Ibid.

85 Ibid., p. 166.

86 Rokossovskiy, *Soldatskiy dolg* (2002), unexpurgated edition. Section pp. 170–7 was expurgated: restored section in italics, this, pp. 170, 172–4.

87 Zhukov *Vospominaniya . . .* (2002), Vol. 2, p. 53.
88 Krivosheyev, *Grif Sekretnosti snyat,* pp. 171, 174, 176; *Soviet Casualties . . .* pp. 118, 121, 122–3.
89 Ibid., *Grif . . .* p. 176, *Soviet Casualties . . .* p. 123.
90 Ibid.
91 Zhukov, *Vospominaniya . . .*(2002), p. 56; *VES,* (1986) p. 203.

13. White night: Leningrad, 1941–1944

1 David Glantz, *The Siege of Leningrad 1941–1944. 900 Days of Terror* (Cassell, London, 2004), pp. 32–3.
2 Ibid., p. 34; Harrison E. Salisbury. *The 900 Days. The Siege of Leningrad* (first published Secker and Warburg, London, 1969, author used Pan, London, 2000 edition), pp. 311–15.
3 Nikita Lomagin, ed., *Neizvestnaya blokada – Arkhiv (The Unknown Blockade – Archives),* (2 vols., Olma Press, Moscow, 2002), Vol. 2, Part 2, 'Political control', Doc. No 7, p. 34.
4 Salisbury, *The 900 Days,* is the classic. The book was banned in the Soviet Union, because it allegedly criticized the role of the Communist Party and contained some criticism of some of the people involved, including gruesome reports of incidences of cannibalism. It attracted some criticism from Zhukov. In fact, and especially given the constraints under which Salisbury was working, the people of Leningrad/St Petersburg, and of Russia, could not really have asked for a more fitting tribute. On the ice road in – and out – A V Saparov, *Doroga Zhizni: Dokumental'naya povest' (The Road of Life: a Documentary Tale),* Lenizdat, Leningrad, 1959). Although dating from Soviet times, this is still a stupendous tale and contains unique, albeit heavily screened photographs.; also Dmitry Pavlov, *Leningrad, 1941: The Blockade* (Chicago UP, 1964).
5 Lomagin, *Neizvestnaya blokada . . .* Vol. 1, Ch.1, '*Kreml' I Smol'ny,*' pp. 56–81, quotation p. 58.
6 *Germany and the Second World War,* Vol. IV, pp. 644–6, citing OKW and Army Group North documents, this p. 645.
7 Ibid., and note 397.
8 Ibid.
9 Ibid., p. 646.
10 Secret Document No. 252 Stalin to Zhukov, Zhdanov, Kuznetsov (AA) and Merkulov, 21 September 1941, reproduced in Valeriy Krasnov, *Neizvestny Zhukov: Lavry i Ternii polkovodtsa (The Unknown Zhukov: Laurels and Thorns of a Military Leader),* (Olma Press, Moscow, 2002), between pp. 352 and 353.
11 Lomagin, ed., *Neizvestnaya blokada* Vol. 2, Part 3, Doc No. 8, pp. 116–17 '. . . text of a captured Russian order . . .' The original, a German translation, is in the US National Archives, Eighteenth Army Command, microfilm T-312/1579–954–55. In Lomagin it is translated back into Russian, so the exact Russian wording is different from Stalin's original (ref. 9). It was distributed to 621 Propaganda

Company, Department 1c of Army Group North, the SS Sixteenth Army and the Abwehr.

12 Zhukov, *Vospominaniya I razmyshleniya*, (2002), Vol. 1, p. 388.

13 Salisbury, pp. 458–9. The Mongols, who were very cunning, took Moscow in 1382, by a ruse. See author's *Red God of War*, p. 10.

14 Lomagin, ed., *Neizvestnaya blokada*, Vol. 2, Doc. 1, pp. 23–6.

15 *FSB Archives*, Vol. II, Bk 1, Doc. 519, '*Soobshcheniye . . . V N Merkulova narkomu vnutrennykh del SSSR L P Berii s kratkim izlozheniyem plana . . . evakuatsii nemetskoogo I finskogo naseleniyya iz Leningradskoy oblasti*', p. 559.

16 Lomagin, *Neizvestnaya blokada*, Vol. 2, Doc. No. 9, pp. 118–21, *Komandovaniye 18-y armii, Soobshcheniye o Peterburge No. 1*, translated from the German, original in the US National Archives, Microfilm T-312/1579–944–950.

17 Lomagin, *Neizvestnaya blokada*, Vol. 2, pp. 35–6, Doc. 8, 'Directorate of the NKVD of the Leningrad Oblast' to Comrade Beria', 29 March 1942, signed by Kubatkin.

18 *Germany and the Second World War*, Vol. IV, pp. 293–7.

19 Salisbury, p. 292.

20 *Germany and the Second World War*, Vol. IV, p. 294.

21 Zhukov, *Vospominaniya i Razmyshleniya*, (2002), Vol. 1, p. 384. '*Sluzhba est' sluzhba . . .*'

22 Ibid., pp. 382–414, this pp. 382, 385. *VES* gives 12th, p. 397.

23 A party man, not to be confused with Lt Gen. Fëdor Isidorovich Kuznetsov, who had been in the area, commanding the Baltic Special Military District, now the North-West front, and would later command 51st Army in the Crimea (see Chapter Ten)

24 Zhukov, *Vospominaniya . . .* (2002), p. 385: . . . '*unichtozheniye vazhneyshikh voyennykh i industrial'nykh ob"yektov*'.

25 *FSB Archives*, Vol. II, Bk 2, Doc. 552, '*Doklad Zamestitelya narodnogo komissara VMF Verkhovnomu Glavnokomanduyushchemu plana meropriyatiy na sluchay vynuzhdennogo otkhoda iz Leningrada (po korablyam I sudam)*', 13 September 1941, pp. 88–90. Leningrad lies on a delta where the Neva enters the Gulf of Finland. Within the 'Venice of the North', it splits into a number of tributaries: the main Neva, the Big Neva, the Little Neva, and three *Nevkas* – little Nevas – the Big, Middle and Little *Nevkas*. Confusing. *Kapitan pervogo ranga* – Captain First Rank – might equate to either a senior captain or commodore in the US and UK navies. The Russians always insisted on the latter, but until recently Royal Navy Captains with more than five years' seniority were 'one star' officers anyway, equating to Army brigadiers. This practice has ceased, a casualty of 'jointery'.

26 Cited in Salisbury, *900 Days*, p. 299. Madrid from Voronov, *Na sluzhbe voyennoy*, pp. 87–9.

27 *FSB Archives.*, Vol. II, Bk 2, Doc. 557, '*Prikaz NKVD SSSRT No 001335 ob ob'yedinenii voysk NKVD g. Leningrada pod obshchim komandovaniyem I o sformirovanii operativnogo shtaba voysk NKVD*', 15 September 1941, p. 105.

28 Ibid., Doc. 565, '*Postanoveleniye voyennogo soveta Leningradskogo fronta No 00274 . . .* 18 September 1941, pp. 118–19.

29 Salisbury, *900 Days*, pp. 305–6, for a summary shooting incident at around this time.

30 Glantz, *Colossus Reborn: The Red Army at War, 1941–1943*, (Kansas University Press, 2005), p. 560.

31 *FSB Archives*, Vol. II, Bk 2, Doc. 578, '*Iz dokladnoy zapiski komandovaniya voysk NKVD po okhrane tyla Leningradskogo Fronta . . . so 2 po 20 sentyabrya 1941 g*', 26 September 1941, pp. 140–2.

32 *Germany and the Second World War*, Vol. IV, p. 646, citing *H.Gr Nord/Ia KTB*, 14–17 October 1941, BA-MA RH 19 III/168.

33 Zhukov, *Vospominaniya* (2002), Vol. I, p. 387, citing *Nyunrbergskiy protsess nad glavnymi nemetskimi voyennnymi prestupnikami*, (& Vols., Moscow, 1957), Vol. I, p. 594.

34 *FSB Archives*, Vol. II, Bk 2, Doc. 579, p. 140. The 1st NKVD Rifle Division was formed from the 3rd, 7th, 33rd and 102nd Border Guard Detachments and NKVD forces of the Leningrad garrison. The commander was Col. Semën Donskov (1907–1972), an NKVD cavalry officer. He finished as an MVD Lt Gen. as military commissar for the Moscow Military District (1960–72).

35 Zhukov, *Vospominaniya* (2000), Vol. I, pp. 394–6. '*Mne ne do diplomatii*'. The 1985 Novosti English translation has 'I have no time for diplomacy', which is not quite right.

36 Salisbury, *900 Days*, pp. 354–5.

37 Zhukov, *Vospominaniya* (2000), Vol. I, pp. 399–400; Salisbury, pp. 404–5.

38 Krivosheyev, ed., *Grif Sekretnosti* . . . pp. 167–8; *Soviet Casualties* . . . pp. 115–16.

39 Ziemke, p. 42.

40 Salisbury, p. 409, citing Saparov, p. 43, Kharitonov, *VIZh* 11/1966, p. 120; Lagunov, *VIZh* 12/1964, p. 95.

41 Ziemke, p. 57.

42 Cited in Salisbury, p. 413.

43 Pamphlet No. 20–201, *Military Improvisations During the Russian Campaign*, (US Department of the Army, August 1951, facsimile edition Center of Military History, US Army, Washington DC, 1983), p. 55.). These studies, which are invaluable, were compiled under US Army supervision by former German generals and general staff officers who had been fortunate enough to survive time on the eastern front and then to be captured by the Americans.

44 Ibid., p. 52.

45 The monument, marked by a concrete flower, lies left (north) of the outbound 'Road of Life', just east of the city. Diary details on monument and Salisbury, pp. 484–5.

46 See author's entries on the Russian Army and the Russo-Japanese War in Holmes, ed., *The Oxford Companion to Military History*, pp. 790–3, 795–8; *VES*, 26, 393–4, and Salisbury, p. 408.

47 Salisbury, p. 408.

48 Ibid., p. 410.

49 Ibid., p. 411.

50 Glantz, *The Siege*, p. 83.

51 Ibid., pp. 90, 247 n. 24. Salisbury gives 26 November.

52 'Ledyanoy domik' – 'ice houses'. See Saparov, *Doroga zhizni*, photographs.

53 Glantz, *The Siege*, p. 90.

54 '*Sanitarnaya palatka*', Saparov, *Doroga zhizni*, op. cit. Unfortunately the copyright rules, which the Russians signed retrospectively in 1974, precluded provision of the photograph.

55 Glantz, *The Siege* . . ., p. 91.

56 Ibid., p. 84.

57 Author's visits to the museum in March 2002, 2003, 2004, 2005; *Aerosani*, some of which were amphibious, able to slide on ice or or float on water, continue in use until the present day. See *VES* (1986), p. 58.

58 Author's visits; Glantz, *The Siege* . . ., pp. 93–4.

59 Glantz, *The Siege* . . ., p. 89.

60 Ibid., pp. 83–4; Salisbury, p. 411. 25 December is the Western Christmas Day, but not the Russian Orthodox, which is on 6 January.

61 Salisbury, pp. 478–83.

62 See *FSB Archives*, Vol. II, Bk 2 (winter, late 1941), Vol. III, Bk 1 (early 1942) and Bk 2 (winter, late 1942).

63 Richard Bidlack, 'Survival Strategies in Leningrad during the First Year of the Soviet–German War', in Robert W. Thurston and Bernd Bonwetsch, ed., *The People's War: Responses to World War II in the Soviet Union* (University of Illinois, 2000), pp. 107, this pp. 98–9, 107, citing N. Yu. Cherepenina and army food supply officer Vasiliy Yershov.

64 Lomagin, ed., *Neizvestnaya blokada*, Vol. I, p. 240.

65 Ibid., p. 298, '*Upotrebleniye chelovecheskogo myasa v pishche* . . .' For other recent research confirming this, A. R. Dzheniskevich, '*Banditizm (osobaya ketegoriya) v blokirovannom Leningrade*' ('Banditry (special category) in besieged Leningrad'), *Istoriya Peterburga (History of Petersburg)*, No. 1 (2001), pp. 47–51, and John Barber, ed., *Zhizn' I smert' v blokadnom Leningrade: Istoriko-meditsinskiy aspekt (Life and Death in Besieged Leningrad: the Medical-History Aspect)* (Dmitriy Bulganin, St Petersburg, 2001).

66 Lomagin, ed., *Neizvestnaya blokada*, Vol. 2, Part 3, Doc. 15, 'NKVD of Leningrad District and Leningrad City', Top Secret, pp. 57–60, citing Archive of the Directorate of the FSB, Leningrad Oblast', F.21/12, Opus. 2., P.n.31.D5, L. 146–50. Dated 12 December 1943.

67 The serial killer who murdered six prostitutes in the East End of London in autumn 1888. Ungrammatical and poorly spelt letters purporting to be from 'Jack' taunted the police, although there was speculation, and has been ever since, that the culprit was a member of the royal family, a doctor or even a writer.

68 Lomagin, ed., *Neizvestnaya blokada*, Vol. 2, Pt 3, Doc. 15, 12 December 1943, p. 58.

69 Glantz, *The Siege* . . ., p. 97.

70 Pamphlet No. 20–233, *German Defense Tactics against Russian Break-Throughs* (US Department of the Army, Washington DC, October 1951), p. 21. On the provenance of these excellent studies, see note 13/43.

71 Figures from Glantz, *The Siege* . . ., p. 93; analysis by author.

72 Pamphlet No. 20–233, *German Defense Tactics against Russian Break-Throughs*, (US DOA), p. 21.

73 *Times Atlas of the Second World War*, p. 65.

74 *FSB Archives*, Vol. III, Bk 1, *Krusheniye 'Blitskriga' (Destroying the 'Blitzkrieg')*, Doc. 898, '*Direktiva Stavki VGKNo 170282* . . .', 20 April 1942, pp. 370–1.

75 Ibid., Doc. 951, '*Prikaz komanduyushchego Volkhovskoy operativnoy gruppoy voysk* . . .', 24 May 1942, p. 484 and note; Glantz, *The Siege* . . ., pp. 113–14.

76 *FSB Archives*, Vol. III, Bk 1, Doc. 951, p. 484.

77 Ibid., Vol. III, Bk 2, Doc. 1073, '*Spravka Osobogo otdela NKVD Volkhovskogo fronta o polozhenii voysk I vooruzhenii 2-y Udarnoy armii s momenta okruzheniya yyeye protivnikom po sostoyaniyu na 1 Yuniya 1942 g.*', August 1942, pp. 189–90.

78 Glantz, *The Siege* . . ., p. 000.

79 *FSB Archives*, Vol. III, Bk 2, Doc. 1073, p. 190.

80 *FSB Archives*, Vol. III, Bk 2, *Ot oborony k nastupleniyu* . . . *(From the Defence to the Attack)*, Doc. 1014, '*Direktiva Stavki Verkhovnogo Glavnokomandovaniya No 170518 komanduyushchemu voyskami Volkhovskogo fronta* . . .', 17 July 1942, pp. 52–3.

81 Ibid., Doc. 1019, '*Dokladnaya zapiska NKVD SSSR v GKO o poluchennykh dannykh o nakhozhdenii v okruzhenii voysk protivnika komandovaniya 2-y Udarnoy armii Volkhovskogo fronta*', 21 July 1942, pp. 61–5, quotation on latter.

82 *FSB Archives*, Vol. III, Bk 2, Doc. 1045, pp. 120–8, '*Dokladnaya zapiska nachal'nika osobogo otdela Volkhovskogo fronta starshego mayora gosbezopasnosti D. I. Mel'nikova* . . . *Abakumovu o sryve boyevoy operatsii po vyvodu voysk 2-y Udarnoy armii iz vrazheskogo okruzheniya*', 6 August 1942, this p. 123.

83 Pamphlet No. 20–233, *German Defense Tactics against Russian Break-Throughs*, (US DOA), pp. 21–5.

84 See Holmes, *Oxford Companion to Military History*, p. 959; Catherine Andreyev, *Vlasov and the Russian Liberation Movement* (Cambridge University Press, 1987).

85 Glantz, *The Siege* . . ., pp. 127–32; Krivosheyev, ed. *Grif sekretnosti* . . . (1993) and *Soviet Casualties* . . . (1997) (would be pp. 122–6) does not identify the Lyuban' or Sinyavino offensives separately.

86 Salisbury, pp. 539–40, note 1, citing numerous witnesses who confirm that Ferch gave the order, no German shells fell, and the German guns were silenced. Ferch was sentenced to twenty-five years for war crimes but was turned over to the Federal Republic of Germany in 1955 and released soon after.

87 The narrative poem 'Vasiliy Tërkin' (1943), section translated by the author, in the author's *Red God of War*, p. 74. Other parts of same poem trans. endpapers.

88 Glantz, *The Siege* . . ., pp. 138–9.

89 Ibid., p. 145.

90 Ibid., p. 143.

91 Salisbury, p. 542.

92 Ibid., p. 547.

93 Glantz, *The Siege* . . ., pp. 160, 168–9; Salisbury, p. 548.

94 Salisbury, p. 547.

95 Zhukov, *Vospominaniya* (2000), Vol. 1, pp. 406–12, Tiger on the latter. Technical

details, Kenneth Macksey, 'The Tanks', in *History of the Second World War*, (BPC/ Purnell 1966/1974), No. 95, pp. 2633–41, this pp. 2640–41.

96 Salisbury, p. 548; Glantz, *The Siege* . . ., p. 159, 166.

97 Salisbury, p. 549.

98 Zhukov, *Vospominaniya* (2000), Vol. 1, p. 411.

99 Olga Berggolts, 'Tret'ye pis'mo na Kamu' (Third letter . . .), in *Izbrannye proizvedeniya* (*Selected Works*), (Sovetskiy pisatel', Leningrad, 1983), pp. 258–9. Part also cited in Salisbury, *900 Days*, pp. 549–50.

100 Salisbury, p. 551.

101 Ibid., p. 550; Glantz, p. 144.

102 Glantz, pp. 144–5.

103 Salisbury, pp. 552–5.

104 *FSB Archives*, Vol. III, Bk 1, Doc. 912, 30 April 1942, pp. 389–90; 'Quartz' first identified as such in ibid., Doc. 927, '*Iz dokladnoy zapiski UNKVD po Leningradskoy oblasti No. 776 v NKVD SSSR o rezul'tatakh rozyska nemetskikh agentov v rayone gorodov Tikhvina I Volkhova I provedenii radioigry s protivnikom (delo 'Kvarts')*, 11 May 1942, pp. 425–38.

105 Erickson, *The Road to Stalingrad*, p. 469.

106 *FSB Archives*, Vol. III, Bk 1, Doc. 977, 13 June 1942, pp. 538–9.

107 Ibid., Vol. III, Bk 1, *Ot oborony k nastupleniyu*, Doc. 1000, '*Plan egenturno-operativnykh meropriyatiy po delu 'Kvarts' KRO* [counter-espionage department] *NKVD po leningradskoy oblasti*', 6 July 1942, pp. 14–16, quotation from p. 16.

108 Ibid., Doc. 1074, August 1942, p. 191. On the earlier arrest of Golovanov, see Doc. 1050, 13 August 1942, pp. 135–6.

109 Lomagin, *Neizvestnaya blokada*, Part 2, Doc. 15 (NKVD report from FSB Archive, Arkhiv UFSB LO. F. 21/12 Op. 2. P.n.31.D.5. L. 146–50), 12 December 1943, p. 58.

110 Lomagin, *Neizvestnaya blokada*, p. 58.

111 Ibid., p. 59.

112 Ibid., p. 60.

113 Glantz, *The Siege* . . ., p. 171.

114 Ibid., pp. 171–6.

115 Salisbury, pp. 560–1.

116 V. Plaude et al., *Yantarnaya Komnata – Ekaterinskiy dvorets* (*The Amber Room – the Catherine Palace*) (Izd. Ivan Fedorov, St Petersburg, 2004), pp. 13–15, citing Königsberg Museum inventory of 5 December 1942, entry No. 200.

117 Vera Inber, trans. in Salisbury, p. 568.

118 Olga Berggolts, 'My prishli v Pushkin' ('We came to Pushkin'), in *Govorit Leningrad* (*Leningrad Speaks*) (Leningrad, 1946), pp. 109–17.

119 Glantz, pp. 213–16; Krivosheyev, *Soviet Casualties* . . ., pp. 141–2.

120 I. A. Wàlsh and V. P. Berkov, *Russko–anghyskiy slovar' krylatykh slov* (*Russian–English Dictionary of Quotations*) (Russkiy Yazyk, Moscow, 1984), p. 139. Also cited in Salisbury, p. 583.

14. The 'Grand Alliance'

1 Gabriel Gorodetsky, 'An Alliance of Sorts', in Erickson and Dilks, ed., *Barbarossa*, pp. 101–22.
2 Ibid., p. 105.
3 Ibid., p. 102, citing CAB 122/100, Eden to Halifax, 18 June 1941.
4 Pownall Diary 29 June 1941, cited in Joan Beaumont, *Comrades in Arms: British Aid to Russia 1941–45* (Davis Poynter, London, 1980), p. 26. Because British, US and Canadian aid to Russia was the subject of negotiations between all four countries, Beaumont's book gives an excellent picture of Allied aid in general, and Gorodetsky considered it the best account in his article in Erickson and Dilks, ed., *Barbarossa . . .* (1994), p. 122. Other key sources: Brian B. Schofield, *The Russian Convoys* (London, 1964); Robert Huhn Jones, *The Road to Russia: United States Lend-Lease to the Soviet Union* (Oklahoma, 1969). Principal primary sources are *Wartime International Agreements: Soviet Supply Protocols* (US Department of State, Publication 2759, European Series 22, Washington DC, 1948).
5 Ibid., pp. 108–10.
6 '*Soglasheniye mezhdu Pravitel'stvami SSSR I Velikobritanii o sovmestnykh deystviyakh v voyne protiv Germanii*', in *FSB Archives*, Vol. II, Bk 1, Doc. 392, 12 July 1941, p. 301. A treaty would have been a *dogovor*. See also Gorodetsky, in Erickson and Dilks, p. 111.
7 Beaumont, pp. 29–30.
8 Ibid., p. 30.
9 Gorodetsky, in Erickson and Dilks, p. 11, citing N. M. Kharlamov, *Trudnaya missiya (A Difficult Mission)*, (Moscow, 1983), p. 34. Kharlamov, an Admiral, later took over from Golikov. Golikov (1900–1980) also wrote an account of his mission, '*Sovetskaya voyennaya missiya v Anglii I SshA v 1941g*' ('The Soviet Military Mission to the UK and USA in 1941'), *Novaya I noveyshaya istoriya (Recent and Most Recent History)*, 3/1969.
10 Cited in Gorodetsky, p. 115.
11 *FSB Archives*, Vol. II, Bk 1, Doc. 500, '*Iz soobshcheniya Londonskoy rezidentury NKVD SSSR po voprosu ob otnoshenii Anglii k SSSR*', 22 August 1941, pp. 506–7.
12 Gorodetsky, in Erickson and Dilks, pp. 115–17.
13 Ibid., p. 116, citing Cripps to Eden, 14 August 1941.
14 *FSB Archives*, Vol. II, Bk 1, Doc. 516, '*Iz telegrammy Predsedatel'ya Soveta Narodnykh Komissarov SSSR I V Stalina poslu SSSR v Londone I M Mayskomu*', 30 August 1941, p. 554.
15 Ibid., Vol. II, Bk 2, Doc. 534, '*Soobshcheniye 1-go Upravleniya NKVMF SSSR No 54056-ss* [Top Secret] *v 3-Upraveleniye NKVMF SSSR o razvedyvatel'noy deyatel'nosti chlenov angliyskikh voyenno-morskikh missii I angliyskikh predstaviteley v SSSR*', 6 December 1941, pp. 27–30. Wyburd's seniority as a Commander dated from 31 December 1939.
16 Ibid., Doc. 661, 5 November 1941, pp. 275–6.
17 Ibid., Doc. 576, '*. . . narodnomu komissaru Voyenno-Morskogo Flota SSSR N. G. Kuznetsovu o provedenii razvedyvatel'noy deyatel'nosti na Chernomorskom Flote*

predstavitelyami angliyskoy voyenno-morskoy missii: Chto anglichanam izvestno ob Arkahngel'ske I Molotovske', 25 September 1941, pp. 133–5.

18 Ibid., Doc. 695, '*Donenseniye agenta 3-go otdela Belomorskoy voyennoy flotilii o deyatel'nosti angliyskoy razvedke v Arkahngel'ske'*, 21 November 1941, pp. 336–9. Much of the information was geographical, of the kind you can find on the internet nowadays. But there were also details of the British assessment of naval and air defences, with maps showing the position of air defence batteries. Since the Russians knew what they had, this may have seemed rather trivial.

19 Ibid., pp. 338–9. Both of the officers to whom Smyslov reported, Gavrilov and Blinov, respectively, were captains or equivalent – in the former's case, a brigade commissar.

20 Ibid., Doc. 702, '. . . *nachal'nikam UNKVD po Arkhangel'skoy I Murmanskoy oblastyam, nachal'nikam 3-x otdelov Severnogo flota I Belomorskoy voyennoy flotilii ob agenturno-operativnykh meropriyatiyakh po presecheniyu shpionskoy deyatel'nosti angliyskoy razvedki na Severe SSSR'*, 27 November 1941, pp. 357–8.

21 Ibid., p. 358, last paragraph (5). At first, this seems unrelated to the others. And then it makes sense.

22 Churchill, *The Second World War* (6 vols, London, 1948–54), Vol. III, p. 574, also cited in Beaumont, p. 88 and *The Times Atlas . . .*, p. 172.

23 Beaumont, p. 31.

24 Ibid., p. 35.

25 Stepan A. Mikoyan, son of Anastas Mikoyan, 'Barbarossa and the Soviet Leadership', in Erickson and Dilks, ed., *Barbarossa . . .*, pp. 123–33, this pp. 130–2.

26 Beaumont, pp. 52–5.

27 Mikoyan, in Erickson and Dilks, *Barbarossa*, p. 132; for the detail of what they asked for and what they were offered, see table 1 in Beaumont, pp. 58–60.

28 Mikoyan, in Erickson and Dilks, *Barbarossa . . .*, p. 132.

29 Beaumont, pp. 80–1.

30 Ibid., p. 82.

31 FSB Archives, Vol. III, Bk 1, Doc. 838, '*Soobshcheniye NKVD SSSR No 320/B v GKO s izlozheniem teksta telegrammy angliyskoooogo admiralteystva v adres angliyskoy morskoy missii v Vashingtone . . .*', 7 March 1942, pp. 234.

32 Although less famous than its more glamorous curved-wing competitor, the Hurricane was a more stable gun platform and could carry very slightly more ammunition. There were also more Hurricanes in the Battle of Britain.

33 Mikoyan, in Erickson and Dilks, p. 130: Beaumont, p. 66.

34 The eight machine guns on the British fighters could manage, in total, a 15-second burst of fire before the plane would have to land and rearm.

35 Beaumont, p. 67.

36 Ibid., pp. 65–6.

37 Ibid., p. 97. About this time, T.S. Eliot, the cat-loving poet who was now running Faber & Faber publishers, and who by no stretch of the imagination could be considered a communist, rejected George Orwell's *Animal Farm*, on the grounds that it might be construed as a criticism of the communist system (which it was).

38 Berezhkov, *At Stalin's Side . . .*, ch. 6, 'Stalin and Churchill', pp. 289–90.

39 *The Times Atlas* . . ., p. 86.

40 *FSB Archives*, Vol. II, Bk 2, '*Iz soobshcheniya Londonskoy rezidentury NKVD* . . .',
    25 October 1941, pp. 244–5.

41 Ibid., Vol. III, Bk 2, Doc. 1005, '*Soobshcheniye zakordonnoogo agenta NKVD SSSR
    o peregovorakh U. Cherchillya i F Ruzevel'ta v Vashingtone*', 9 July 1942, pp. 32–3.

42 Ibid., Doc. 1012, '*Soobshcheniye NKVD SSSR* . . . *s izlozheniyem dannykh,
    poluchennykh ot rezidenta NKVD v Londone, ob itogakh vashingtonskikh
    peregoovorov mezhdu F. Ruzevel'tom i. U. Cherchillem otnosotel'no planov
    dal'neyshego vedeniya voyny*', 12 July 1942, pp. 48–9.

43 Beaumont, p. 106.

44 Ibid., pp. 107–8.

45 Ibid., p. 108.

46 *FSB Archives*, Vol. III, Bk 2, Doc. 1025, '*Soobshcheniya zakordonnogo agenta
    NKVD SSSR o pozitsii U. Cherchillya po voprosu otkrytiya vtorogo fronta v Evrope*',
    24 July 1942, pp. 74–5.

47 Ibid., Doc. 1026, 24 July 1942, from NKVD agent, pp. 75–6, and Doc. 1030, 30
    July 1942, from Beria to GKO, pp. 82–4, Hopkins on the latter. Beaverbrook and
    Hopkins' positions were contrasted with that of William Bullitt, a US diplomat
    who often met Churchill and the Chiefs-of-Staff who was 'an enemy of the USSR
    and of Britain', from whom 'nothing good can be expected'.

48 Ibid., Doc. 1031, '*Soobshcheniye zakordonnogo agenta NKVD SSSR o reshenii
    pravitel'stva Velikobritanii ne otkryvat' vtorogo fronta v Evrope v 1942 g.*', 31 July
    1942, pp. 84–5.

49 Ibid., Doc. 1041, '*Soobshcheniye NKVD SSSR No 1420/B v GKO s izlozheniyem
    dannykh, poluchennykh ot rezidenta NKVD v Londone otnosiel'no reshseniya
    angliyskogo pravitel'stava ne otkryvat' vtorogo fronta v 1942 g.*', 4 August 1942,
    pp. 115–16. This corrected the original report of the 'War Committee' to 'War
    Cabinet'.

50 Berezhkov, *At Stalin's Side* . . ., p. 290.

51 Ibid. Berezhkov was still Molotov's 'assistant', but during the period of the
    Molotov–Ribbentrop Pact he had also been assistant to Mikoyan, who then
    became cardinal in handling aid from the West.

52 Ibid., pp. 290–2.

53 Churchill lived from 1874–1965; Shaposhnikov from 1882–1945. Having been
    First Lord of the Admiralty (Navy Minister) at the start of First World War,
    Churchill had left politics after the Dardanelles failure. In 1916 he took command
    of a battalion on the Western Front, as a lieutenant–colonel. Shaposhnikov,
    meanwhile, became a full colonel in the Imperial Russian Army. In 1918
    Shaposhnikov joined the Reds, whom Churchill, as one of the 'principal
    organizers of the foreign intervention', tried to strangle. *VES* (1986) pp. 809, 813.

54 Berezhkov, *At Stalin's Side* . . ., p. 292.

55 Ibid., p. 292. I make no apology for drawing on Khrushchev's attributed words in
    the 2000 film *Enemy at the Gates*.

56 Ibid., p. 293; 'twinkle in his eye', I am grateful to Dr Anna Maria Brudenell,
    whose grandfather was a member of the British delegation to Yalta, and said
    Stalin always had one.

57 Gor'kov, *Gosudarstvenny Komitet Oborony postanovlyayet* . . . (Archive), p. 315 (Stalin's diary, 12 August).

58 Berezhkov, *At Stalin's Side* . . ., p. 294.

59 *FSB Archives*, Vol. III, Bk 2, Doc. 1041, note, pp. 115–16, citing a note to the Soviet government on 14 August.

60 Berezhkov, *At Stalin's Side* . . ., pp. 295–7.

61 Gor'kov, pp. 315–16 (13–14 August).

62 Ibid., p. 315, first eleven entries for 13 August.

63 Beaumont, p. 121, citing Clark Kerr and John Reed in FO 800/300.

64 Berezhkov, *At Stalin's Side* . . ., p. 298.

65 Ibid., pp. 299–300.

66 Ibid., pp. 300–1; Gor'kov, p. 316 (15 August).

67 A ton (old British, still in use as a general term) is, strictly speaking, 2,260 pounds. A metric tonne – the EU measure – is 1,000 kilograms or 2,204.6 pounds. An American 'short ton' is 2,000 pounds.

68 Beaumont, pp. 113–21.

69 *FSB Archives*, Vol. III, Bk 2, Doc. 1198, '*Spetssoobshcheniye nachal'nika UNKVD po Leningradskoy oblasti P. N. Kubatkina . . . o vyskazyvaniyakh zhteley leningrada po povodu otvetov I. V. Stalina amerikanskomu korrespondentu v svyazi s voyennymi deystviyami soyuznikov v severnoy Afrike*', 15 November 1942, pp. 459–61.

70 Beaumont., p. 143; Michael Howard, *Grand Strategy, August 1942–August 1943, History of the Second World War*, UK Military Series (London, 1972), p. 602, citing COS (42) 466 (0), 31 December 1942.

71 Beaumont, pp. 145–6.

72 *The Times Atlas*, pp. 134–5. At the time of writing the *FSB Archives* for 1943 are still not available, but one can be certain that the NKVD 'sources', reporting on British and US discussions, remained as reliable, comprehensive and accurate as they had been in 1942.

73 Beaumont, pp. 219–20; see for example the *Kirov* class missile cruiser, introduced around 1980.

74 Berezhkov, pp. 263–4.

75 *The Times Atlas* . . ., p. 134.

76 Beaumont, p. 174, citing Sir Llewellyn Woodward, *British Foreign Policy in the Second World War*, Vols I–III (London 1970, 1971, 1972), this Vol. III.

77 Beaumont, p. 194.

78 *The Times Atlas* . . . p. 188.

79 Beaumont, p. 178 and pp. 240–1, note 4.

80 Ibid., pp. 203–8.

81 Interview with a retired Russian general, whose name, unfortunately, escapes me, at a conference organized by the International Institute for Strategic Studies on issues of military restructuring at a dacha outside Moscow in spring 2001.

82 Beaumont, p. 212, citing, *inter alia*, *Khrushchev Remembers* (London, 1971). Although there is slight doubt as to the veracity of 'Khrushchev's memoirs', Khrushchev had no reason to praise the West when it was not deserved, and all the evidence supports this assertion.

83 Beaumont, table 10, p. 208.

84 I am grateful to Peter Caddick-Adams for the origins of DUKW, and to David McWhinnie for his superb documentary films.

85 Solzhenitsyn, *Prusskiye nochi (Prussian Nights)*, a narrative poem, trans. Robert Conquest.

86 Mikoyan, in Erickson and Dilks, *Barbarossa . . .*, p. 130.

87 Beaumont, pp. 205–6, table 9.

88 Latest figures on Soviet equipment availability, Krivosheyev, *Soviet Casualties . . .*, table 95.II, Artillery, p. 251. Request to US: *Wartime International Agreements: Soviet Supply Protocols*, (US Department of State, Washington DC, 1948), 4th Protocol, pp. 95, 99, and Annex 2, analysed in the author's *Red God of War . . .* pp. 135–6.

89 Beaumont, pp. 212–13.

90 Ibid., p. 207, table 9.3.

91 Ibid., p. 213. The author attempted to apply the Nasa Consumer Price Index (CPI) comparing 1946 and 2004 prices – <http://www1jsc.nasa.govbu2/inflateCPI.html> – but decided that US domestic price indices over sixty years were, on balance, a pretty meaningless basis for comparison. The price of domestic goods typically increaséd by between twenty and fifty times during this period. The best comparison is probably to take the respective amounts spent on aid as a proportion of GDP.

92 Krivosheyev, *Soviet Casualties . . .*, p. 92.

93 Beaumont, pp. 213–14.

94 Bernd Wegner, 'The War against the Soviet Union 1942–1943', in *Germany and the Second World War*, Vol. VI, *The Global War*, pp. 841–1215, this pp. 897–9.

95 Gorodetskiy, in Erickson and Dilks, *Barbarossa . . .*, p. 118.

96 Berezhkov, *At Stalin's Side*, p. 301.

97 Gorodetsky, in Erickson and Dilks, *Barbarossa . . .*, p. 118.

98 Mark Harrison, 'The USSR and Total War: Why didn't the Soviet Economy collapse in 1942?', p. 6. Retrieved from <http://www.warwick.ac.uk/uk/fac/soc/economics/staff/faculty>; 9 Dec 2005.

15. To the edge of the abyss

1 *The Times Atlas . . .*, pp. 62–3; Ziemke, *Moscow to Stalingrad*, pp. 105–17; Glantz, *Kharkov 1942: Anatomy of a Military Disaster through Soviet Eyes* (Ian Allan, London, 1998), pp. 21–37; see also a particularly valuable, concise summary of operations throughout the war, UKNA, *WO 208/1790*, Appendix 1A, Soviet Ground Operations 1941–45, secret, 16 pp, plus another 4 pp. on naval operations. Although in the British National Archives, the style and spelling indicate it is American.

2 Bernd Wegner, 'The War against the Soviet Union 1942–43', in *Germany and the Second World War*, Vol. VI, *The Global War*, pp. 841–1215, this p. 843.

3 Ibid., p. 844, citing Halder, *Diaries*, 28 March 1941 and Directive 41 itself.

4 Wegner entitles the first part of his 'The War against the Soviet Union 1942–43', pp. 843 –903, 'Hitler's "Second Campaign"'.

5 Zhukov, *Vospominaniya* . . . (2000), Vol. II, pp. 59–60. See also Glantz, *Kharkov*, p. 22.

6 Wegner, in *Germany and the Second World War*, Vol. VI, p. 856, Map VI.I.2.

7 Glantz, *Kharkov 1942*, p. 25.

8 Ibid., p. 19; *The Times Atlas* . . ., p. 62.

9 Erickson, *The Road to Stalingrad*, p. 471.

10 Glantz, *Kharkov* . . ., p. 31.

11 Ibid., p. 30.

12 *Germany and the Second World War*, Vol. VI, pp. 942–50.

13 Glantz, *Kharkov* . . ., p. 242, citing Wilhelm Adams, a German military historian.

14 Ibid., p. 239.

15 Cited in *Germany and the Second World War*, Vol. VI, p. 950.

16 Ibid.

17 Ibid., p. 951.

18 Zhukov, *Vospominaniya*(2000), Vol. II, p. 57.

19 *Germany and the Second World War*, Vol. VI, pp. 951–4.

20 Ibid., VI, p. 929, cites César de Bazancourt, *Der Feldzug in der Krim* . . . (2 vols, Budapest and Vienna, 1856), on its geostrategic importance.

21 *Germany and the Second World War*, Vol. VI, p. 930. On the siege see also the excellent Col. Vasiliy Morozov, 'The Siege of Sebastopol' [*sic*], *Purnell's History of the Second World War* (1972/1966), pp. 961–9.

22 Ibid., p. 931, citing Gen. Milch, minute of conference on 19 April 1942, BA-MA RL 3/60.

23 Erickson, *The Road to Stalingrad* . . ., p. 347.

24 *Germany and the Second World War*, Vol. VI, pp. 932–3, citing AOK and Halder.

25 Ibid., p. 932.

26 Ibid., p. 934, citing Vasilevskiy.

27 Krivosheyev, *Soviet Casualties* . . ., table 75, Casualty Figures for Selected Army Group operations, pp. 107–8, on Sevastopol, Kerch' and the Battle of Khar'kov; pp. 111–12 on Western Front; 112 on Western Ukraine; and pp. 124–5 (Stalingrad defensive) and 126–8 (Stalingrad offensive). Moscow, pp. 118–19 and 120–1.

28 Among the defenders in 1855 was a young artillery lieutenant, Count Leo Tolstoy, whose autobiographical *Sevastopol' Stories* were a prototype for his subsequent accurate descriptions in *War and Peace*.

29 Krivosheyev, *Soviet casualties* . . ., table 75, Casualty Figures for Selected Army Group operations, p. 107.

30 *Germany and the Second World War*, Vol. VI, p. 935.

31 'Sevastopol, sieges of', in *The Oxford Companion to Military History*, p. 821.

32 *Germany and the Second World War*, Vol. VI, pp. 935–6.

33 See the author's account of the 'supergun' story in *Expert Witness* (Brassey's London, 1993), pp. 30–1. The biggest Iraqi 'supergun' was 1,000mm in calibre, but may have been designed to fire projectiles into space.

34 Ian Hogg, 'The guns', in Barrie Pitt, ed., *History of the Second World War*, (BPC/ Purnell, 1974/1966), No. 95, pp. 2642–52, this pp. 2645–9.

35 *Germany and the Second World War*, Vol. VI, pp. 940–1, citing Halder, *Diaries* . . . See also Von Manstein, *Lost Victories*, although Manstein's scepticism was with the benefit of hindsight.

36 'The 1925 Geneva Protocol for the Prohibition of the Use in War of Asphyxiating, Poisonous or Other Gases, and of Bacteriological Methods of Warfare', in Roberts and Guelff (3rd edition, 2000), pp. 155–67.

37 *FSB Archives*, Vol. III, Bk 1, Doc. 879, '*Ukazaniye NKVD SSSR . . . po sboru razvedyvatel'nykh dannykh o podgotovke nemtsev k vedeniyu khimicheskoy voyny, o vyyavlenii I unichtozhenii nemetskikh khimbaz I skladov, dislotsirovannykh na vremenno okkupirovannoy Ukrainy*', 9 April 1942, pp. 325–6, note.

38 Ibid., Vol. II, Bk 2, Doc. 1010, '*Soobshcheniye zakordonnogo agenta NKVD SSSR o podgotovke nemtsev k khimicheskoy voyne*', 11 July 1942, pp. 45–6.

39 General Omar Bradley, commanding First (US) Army on D-Day, said that 'there never was a greater temptation [for them to use chemical weapons] than the beaches of Normandy. Even the slightest sprinkling of persistent gas [such as mustard gas] on Omaha Beach would have cost us our footing there.' With hindsight, the two outstanding film renditions of this event – *The Longest Day* (Darryl Zanuck, 1962) and *Saving Private Ryan* (Steven Spielberg, 1998) completely ignore this key element of the 'threat'.

40 Walter Hirsch, *Soviet BW and CW Preparation and Capabilities (The Hirsch Report)*, National Archives, Washington DC, Reference *NAW RG 319 GZ, P-Project file*, Box 13, p. arabic 5 (the first 24 pp. are Roman numerals). Hirsch was a German officer who reported his knowledge to the Americans after the war. I am grateful to Major Mark Wilkinson, AGC(ETS), also a qualified Ammunition Technical Officer (ATO), graduate of the Global Security M.Sc., 2005, for obtaining the full report and for his help on these matters.

41 *Hirsch Report*, p. 6.

42 Ibid., p. 6.

43 Ibid., p. 43. Among the Russian markings were:

Type of chemical agent	Marking on shell
Chlorine	One green band
Phosgene	One blue band (green also found)
Smoke acids	One white, one green, one white band
Hydrogen cyanide	One yellow band
Mustard	One red band
Lewisite	Two red bands
Mustard and Lewisite mix	Three red bands

44 Ibid., p. 6.

45 Ibid.

46 *Germany and the Second World War*, Vol. VI, p. 938, citing Luftwaffe Captain Herbert Paber, *Berichte aus Rußland*, 10 (12 July 1942), BA-MA Lw 107/83.

47 Krivosheyev, *Soviet Casualties* . . ., table 75, p. 107.

48 *Germany and the Second World War*, Vol. VI, pp. 940–1.

49 Ibid., p. 939.

50 Ehrenburg, cited in Alexander Werth, *Russia at War*, and Col. Vasiliy Morozov, 'The Siege of Sebastopol' [*sic*], *Purnell's History of the Second World War*, No. 35, p. 969.

51 Mark Harrison, 'The Economics of World War II: an Overview', in Mark Harrison, ed., *The Economics of World War II: Six Great Powers in International Comparison*, (Cambridge University Press, 1998), p. 2, cited in idem, 'The USSR and Total War: Why Didn't the Soviet Economy Collapse in 1942?', p. 1, a chapter for Roger Chickering and Stig Förster, ed., *A World at Total War: Global Conflict and the Politics of Destruction, 1939–1945* (Cambridge University Press). Retrieved from <http://www.warwick.ac.uk/uk/fac/soc/economics/staff/faculty>; 9 December 2005. Also Mark Harrison, *Accounting for War: Soviet Production, Employment and the Defence Burden 1940–45* (Cambridge University Press, 1996).

52 Ibid.

53 The author remembers his mother telling him how, in London during the Blitz, her mother managed to secure a regular supply of Communion wine – the only fortified wine available – which went into her sherry trifle.

54 Harrison, 'The USSR and Total War: Why didn't the Soviet Economy Collapse in 1942?', p. 15. The order in full is in *FSB Archives*, Vol. II, Bk 1, Doc. 490, '*Prikaz No 270 Stavki Verkhovnogo Komandovania Krasnoy Armii*', 16 August 1941, pp. 482–6, signed by Stalin, Molotov, Budenny, Voroshilov, Timoshenko, Shaposhnikov and Zhukov.

55 *FSB Archives*, Vol. III, Bk 2, Doc. 1027, '*Prikaz narodnogo komissara oborony Soyuza SSR No. 227 o prinyatii mer po ukrepleniyu poryadki I povysheniyu distsipliny voyskakh*', 28 July 1942, pp. 76–80, signed by Stalin.

56 Ibid., p. 77. The key phrase comes in the middle of the document.

57 Harrison, 'The USSR and Total War . . .', pp. 7–17.

58 Ibid., p. 17.

59 Maksimov et al., *Velikaya Otechestvennaya* . . . (2005), p. 75. On the progressive development of Soviet war industry in the east, see ibid., pp. 20 (1933), 21 (1941) and 151 (1945). These maps show the number of people employed in each type of industry. On the wider Soviet economy during the war, ibid., p. 150.

60 Krivosheyev, *Soviet Casualties* . . ., p. 102.

61 *FSB Archives*, Vol. III, Bk 2, Doc. 1027, p. 78.

62 Ibid., p. 79.

63 NKO order 298 of 28 September and 323 of 16 October. See ibid., p. 80, note.

64 *Shtrafbat 1* and *Shtrafbat 2*, Nikolai Dostal, Director, available on DVD. I am grateful to Sir Rodric Braithwaite for his help on this matter and for compiling an Order of Battle of *shtrafbat* units.

65 Ibid.

66 *FSB Archives*, Vol. III, Bk 2, Doc. 1027, p. 79. See also Stavka's order to Yeremenko of 5 September 1941, in Vol. II, Bk 1, Doc. 529, p. 20, and to Timoshenko and his army and front commanders of 12 September 1941, Doc. 550, ibid., pp. 85–6.

67 *FSB Archives*, Vol. II, Bk 2, Doc. 596, '*Dokladnaya zapiska NKVD SSSR . . . v TsK KP(b) Ukrainy o deyatel'nosti istrebitel'nykh batal'onov i partizanskikh otryadov za yul' – sentyabr' 1941 g*', 6 October 1941, pp. 173–82.

68 Ibid., Vol. III, Bk 1, Doc. 961, '*Iz postanovleniya Gosudarstvennogo Komiteta Oborony SSSR No 1837ss [Top Secret] ob ob"yedinenii rukovodstva partizanskim dvizheniyem v tylu protivnika I yego dal'neyshem razvitii*', 30 May 1942, pp. 507–10.

69 Ibid. The document lists the Partisan Movement Headquarters for each front, with extensive biographies of all the people.

70 Cited in Philip Blood, *Bandenbekämpfung* . . . (PhD., Cranfield, 2003), also Glantz, *The Siege* . . ., pp. 146–7.

71 Ibid., p. 128, citing, *inter alia*, Hugh Trevor-Roper, *Hitler's War Directives, 1939–1945* (London, 1960).

72 Ibid., pp. 129–30. See, again, Trevor-Roper, *Hitler's War Directives* . . .

73 Ibid.

74 Der Reichsführer SS und Chef der Deutschen Polizei, *Bandenbekämpfung*, September 1942, reproduced in Blood, PhD., pp. 356–63.

75 Ibid., pp. 131–6.

76 *FSB Archives*, Vol. II, Bk 2, Doc. 594, '*Iz soobshcheniya rezidenta NKVD SSSR v Anglii ob ispol'zovaniyi atomnoy energii v voyennykh tselyakh*', 4 October 1941, p. 171.

77 Richard Rhodes, *Dark Sun: the Making of the Hydrogen Bomb* (Simon and Schuster, New York and London, 1995), pp. 52–3, and David Holloway, *The Soviet Union and the Arms Race* (Yale University Press, 1983) and *Stalin and the Bomb* (Yale University Press, 1994).

78 The 10-ton conventional bomb was the British 22,000-pound Grand Slam. Data on the yield of the nuclear bombs vary, but put those for Little Boy between 10 and 16 kT and for Fat Man 18–21 kT.: see <http://nuclearweaponarchive.org/Usa/Med/Lbfm.html>; and <http://mothra.rerf.or.jp/ENG/A-bomb/History/Damages.html>. Both retrieved 13 December 2005.

79 Rhodes, *Dark Sun* . . ., pp. 58–9.

80 Ibid., pp. 47–8, 60–1, citing an interview with Kaftanov in 1985. There is no record of a meeting between Stalin, Kaftanov, Kapitsa and others in Stalin's diary in Gor'kov, *GKO postanovlyayet*, between April 1942 and the end of the year, but special meetings often took place outside Stalin's main office, and may not be recorded.

81 Rhodes, *Dark Sun* . . ., p. 57.

82 *FSB Archives*, Vol. III, Bk 2, Doc. 1142, '. . . *o provodimykh v Anglii, SshA, Germanii I Frantsii intensivnykh nauchno-issledovatel'nykh rabotakh po sozdaniiyu atomnoy bomby*', 6 October 1942, pp. 341–2.

83 Rhodes, *Dark Sun* . . ., pp. 62–3.

84 Leland Feltzer, trans. and Ray Wegner, ed., *The Soviet Air Force in World War II* (David and Charles, London, 1974), (trans. from the Soviet Official History), pp. 91–2.

85 Stalin's diary in Gor'kov, p. 299. He is billed as designer of the first rocket engine.

86 On V'yazma-Bryansk see Krivosheyev, *Soviet Casualties* . . ., p. 118. From 30

September to 5 December 1941 the Russians suffered 514,338 irrecoverable losses as against 143,941 sick and wounded. On Kalashnikov, see Edward Ezell, *The AK-47 Story: Evolution of the Kalashnikov Weapons* (Harrisburg, PA., 1986); appointment with Stalin, Gor'kov, *GKO postanovlyayet*, p. 323.

87 Pennington, *Wings, Women and War* . . ., pp. 4–7. Quotation from Anne Elliot Griesse and Richard Stites, 'Russia: Revolution and War', in Nancy Loring, ed., *Female Soldiers – Combatants or Noncombatants? Historical and Contemporary Perspectives* (Greenwood, Westport, 1982), p. 68. An excellent pictorial history is Henry Sakaida, illust. Christa Hook, *Heroines of the Soviet Union 1941–45* (Osprey, Oxford, 2003).

88 UKNA, *WO 33/1828A, 1829* (summary), *Order of Battle of Military Forces in USSR 1945*, p. v. (reflects situation at end of 1944).

89 VSEobshcheyeo Voyennoye OBUCHeniye.

90 Glantz, *Colossus Reborn: The Red Army at War, 1941–43* (Kansas University Press, 2005), p. 551, citing VOV, and p. 721, n. 51.

91 Ibid., p. 721.

92 Pennington, *Wings* . . ., pp. 14–15.

93 There has been, perhaps inevitably, a suggestion that Marina Raskova and Stalin were close friends, but there is no serious evidence to support it. See Pennington, *Wings* . . ., p. 23.

94 Fetzer, *The Soviet Air Force*, pp. 14–15.

95 Pennington, *Wings* . . ., Ibid., pp. 26–35.

96 Ibid., p. 41, citing interview with Valentina Kravchenko-Savitskaya.

97 Sakaida, p. 13.

98 Fetzer, *The Soviet Air Force*, p. 120.

99 Sakaida, p. 4.

100 Pennington, 'Women and the Battle of Stalingrad', in Erickson and Erickson, ed., *Russia: War, Peace and Diplomacy*, pp. 169–211, 327–33, this pp. 198–9.

101 Ibid., pp. 13–14.

102 Ibid., pp. 29–31.

103 Pennington, 'Women and the Battle of Stalingrad', p. 170, citing John Erickson, 'Soviet Women at War', in John Garrard, ed., *World War II and the Soviet People* (St Martin's Press, New York, 1993), p. 68.

104 Glantz, *Colossus Reborn* . . ., p. 554.

105 Ibid., pp. 536–51.

106 V. V. Beshanov, *God 1942 – 'Uchebny' (1942 – 'The Learning Year')* (Kharvest, Minsk, 2004).

107 Marshal of Tank Troops O. A. Losik, ed, *Stroitel'stvo I boyevoye primeneniyeSovetskikh tankovykh voysk v gody VelikoyOtechestvennoy voyny (The Composition and Combat employment of Soviet tank Forces in the Great Patriotic war)* (Voyenizdat, Moscow, 1979), pp. 114–19; Gen. A. I. Radzievskiy, *Tankovy udar (Tankovaya armiya v nastupatel'noy operatsii fronta po opytu Velikoy otechestvennoy voyny), (Tank Strike. (The Tank army in the Front offensive Operation according to the Experience of the Great Patriotic war))* (Voyenizdat, Moscow, 1977), pp. 16–24.

108 *Germany and the Second World War*, Vol. VI, pp. 972–97.

109 Author's *Red God of War* . . ., p. 50.
110 *Germany and the Second World War*, Vol. VI, pp. 884–7.
111 Ibid., p. 889.
112 UKNA, *WO 208/1777, Effects of a Possible Soviet Collapse and Possible Action Required*, Most Secret, MI3c/Col/43/42, signed by a major, General Staff (illegible), to his Colonel, head of MI3.
113 Ibid., para. 3.
114 Ibid., paras 4–6, quotation from latter.
115 With some input from Rudyard Kipling, *If* . . .

16. From defence to attack

 1 Paulus's testimony to the International Military Tribunal (IMT) at Nuremberg, in 'Trial of Major War Criminals by the IMT . . .' (42 vols, London, 1947–9), Vol. VII, p. 260, cited in *Germany and the Second World War*, Vol. VI, p. 990.
 2 Ibid., p. 1022.
 3 David M. Glantz, 'Forgotten Battles of the Soviet–German War', *Journal of Soviet Military Studies*, Vol. 8, No. 4, December 1995, pp. 768–808; Rzhev-Sychevka, pp. 784–9; and Glantz, *Zhukov's Greatest Defeat: the Red Army's Epic Disaster in Operation Mars, 1942* (Kansas University Press 1999/Ian Allan, London, 2000).
 4 *Germany and the Second World War*, Vol. VI, pp. 958–63.
 5 Ibid., p. 969; Ziemke, *Moscow to Stalingrad*, pp. 333–40, maps on pp. 289, 35. The Großdeutschland division was *Wehrmacht* and not, as some assume, Waffen-SS.
 6 *Germany and the Second World War*, Vol. VI, pp. 969–72.
 7 Ibid., p. 971.
 8 Erickson, *The Road to Stalingrad* . . ., pp. 494–5.
 9 UKNA, *WO 208/1790, Soviet Ground Operations, 1941–1945*, p. 1A-4, para 6c. (2).
10 *Germany and the Second World War*, Vol. VI, pp. 970–1.
11 Ziemke, *Moscow to Stalingrad*, p. 351.
12 Ibid., pp. 351–2; *FSB Archives*, Vol. II, Bk 2, Doc. 620, p. 227.
13 Ziemke, *Moscow to Stalingrad* . . ., p. 344, citing Bock, Diary for 3 July; *Germany and the Second World War*, Vol. VI, pp. 986–7.
14 *Germany and the Second World War*, Vol. VI, pp. 988–89.
15 Ibid., p. 983; Erickson, *The Road to Stalingrad*, pp. 515–17.
16 *FSB Archives*, Vol. III, Bk 2, Doc. 1075, '*Iz dokladnoy zapiski NKVD Kryma*' [August, 1942], pp. 192–202.
17 *FSB Archives*, Vol. III, Bk 2, Doc. 1105, '*. . . ob organizatsii shtaba po rukovodstvu operativno-chekistskimi gruppami NKVD SSSR po oborone perevalov Glavnogo Kavkazskogo khrebta*', 18 September 1942, pp. 256–8.
18 Gor'kov, *GKO Postanovlyayet*, pp. 317–23 (Stalin's diary).
19 *FSB Archives*, Vol. III, Bk 2, Doc. 1075, '*Pis'mo NKVD SSSR o merakh po Krymskoy ASSR v NKVD SSSR o politiko-moral'nom sostoyanii naseleniya Kryma*' [August, 1942], pp. 192–202; Doc. 1105, '*. . . ob organizatsii shtaba po rukovodstvu operativno-chekistskimi gruppami NKVD SSSR po oborone perevalov Glavnogo Kavkazskogo khrebta*', 18 September 1942, pp. 256–8; and Doc. 1095, '*Pis'mo*

NKVD SSSR o merakh po usileniyu bor'by s nemetskimi parashyutistami-diversantami, zabrasivayemymi protivnikom na territoriyu respublik Zakavkaz'ya I Severenogo Kavkaza', 13 September 1942, pp. 240–1.

20 *The Times Atlas*, pp. 102–3.

21 Marshal Konstantin Rokossovskiy, *Velikaya Pobeda na Volge (Great Victory on the Volga)* (2 vols, Voyenizdat, Moscow, 1965); Army General D. D. Lelyushenko, *Moskva-Stalingrad – Berlin-Praga: Zapiski komandarma (Moscow–Stalingrad – Berlin–Prague: Notes of an Army Commander)* (3rd edition, Nauka, Moscow, 1985); idem., *'1-ya I 3-ya gvardeyskiye armii v kontrnastuplenii pod Stalingradom'* (First and Third Guards Armies in the Counter-Offensive at Stalingrad'), in A. M. Samsonov, ed., *Stalingradskaya epopeya* (Nauka, Moscow, 1968).

22 The documents, German and Russian, relating to the battle are available in two volumes, *Stalingradskaya Bitva: Khronika, fakty, lyudi. Arkhiv (The Battle of Stalingrad. The Story, the Facts, the People. Archives)* Olma Press, Moscow, 2002). Vol. 1, 17 July–18 November 1942, Vol. 2, 19 November–2 February 1943.

23 *FSB Archives*, Vol. III, Bk 2, Doc. 1063, 25 August 1942, pp. 166–7.

24 Pennington, 'Women and the Battle of Stalingrad', p. 178; William A. Craig, *Enemy at the Gates*, p. 70.

25 *VES* (1983), p. 799.

26 Using the British system – 'in the door (65 – eastings) and up the stairs (01 – northings)'.

27 *FSB Archives*, Vol. III, Bk 2, Doc. 1063, pp. 166–7.

28 Cited in Erickson, *The Road to Stalingrad*, p. 527.

29 Cited in Ziemke, *Moscow to Stalingrad . . .*, p. 394. It had changed hands four times between 08.00 and 13.20 on 14th: see Erickson, p. 551.

30 *FSB Archives*, Vol. III, Bk 2, Doc. 1103, *'Soobshcheniye UNKVD po Stalingradskoy oblast v NKVD SSSR o proryve nemetskikh voysk v g. Stalingrad I o polozhenii v gorode'*, 16 September 1942, p. 254.

31 Beevor, *Stalingrad*, p. 174.

32 German source, cited in Alan Clark, 'Stalingrad: the Onslaught', in *The Most Vicious Battle of the War: Stalingrad, Purnell's History . . .*, No. 38, pp. 1054–64.

33 Cited in Clark, ibid.

34 Herbert Pabst, *Berichte aus Rußland*, 65 (18 October 1942), BA-MA Lw 107/83, cited in *Germany and the Second World War*, Vol. VI, p. 1097.

35 *FSB Archives*, Vol. III, Bk 2, Doc. 1048, *'Direktiva Stavki VGK No 170562 komanduyushchim voyskami Yugo-Vostochnogo I Stalingradskogo frontov o reorganizatsii rukovodstva oboronoy Stalingrada'*, 9 August 1942, pp. 132–4.

36 Beevor, p. 75.

37 *FSB Archives*, Vol. III, Bk 2, Doc. 1120, pp. 289–300 gives a full account of 272nd Regiment's battles from 23 August to 26 September.

38 Ibid., Doc. 1116, *'Soobshcheniye NKVD SSSR No 1614/B v GKO I General'ny Shtab Krasnoy Armii ob obstanovke v Stalingrade'*, 23 September 1942, pp. 282–3.

39 Ibid., Doc. 1160, not earlier than 15 October 1942, p. 370.

40 Ibid., Doc. 1197, *'. . . o nagrazhdenii 10-y strelkovoy diviizii vnutrennykh voysk NKVD ordenom Lenina za otvagu I geroizm, proyavlennye yeye lichnym sostavom v boyakh za g. Stalingrad'*, 12 November 1942, pp. 457–8.

41 Vasiliy Chuikov and Ivan Paderin, *Nachalo puti (The Start of the Journey)*, (Military memoirs series, Voyenizdat, Moscow, 1959), p. 249. This and the next three references are from Reina Pennington, 'Women . . . Stalingrad', pp. 170, 211.

42 Chuikov, '*Razdum I o samykh tyazhelykh dnyakh Stalinfgrada*' ('Thoughts on the worst days of Stalingrad') in M. V. Zakharov, Aleksandr Samsonov, and Vitol'd Pechorkin, ed., *Stalingradskaya epopeya: Vpervye publikuyemye dokumenty rassekrechennye FSB RF . . . (The Stalingrad Epic: a Collection of Documents First Declassified by the Federal Security Service of the Russian Federation . . .)* (Zvonnitsa-MG, Moscow, 2000).

43 Chuikov, *Vystoyav, my pobedili: zapiski komandarma 62-y (Having held, we won. Notes of an Army Commander of the Sixty-Second)* (Sovetskaya Rossiya, Moscow, 1960), pp. 88–94.

44 Yeremenko, *Stalingrad. Zapiski komanduyushchego frontom (Stalingrad. Memoirs of a Front Commander)* (Voyenizdat, Moscow, 1961), p. 293.

45 Pennington, 'Women . . . Stalingrad', p. 170.

46 Ibid., p. 179.

47 'Sneaky-beaky' is a Royal Naval and Royal Marine term for Special (Purpose) Forces (SF UK, SPF US).

48 Pennington, 'Women . . . Stalingrad', pp. 180–1; Joel S. Hayward, *Stopped at Stalingrad: The Luftwaffe and Hitler's Defeat in the East, 1942–3* (Kansas University Press, 1998), pp. 187, 189.

49 In September 2004 members of a Chechen rebel group seized School No. 1 at Beslan in Stavropol' province and held hundreds of people hostage, mostly children. The terrorists started to kill hostages, the Russian forces had to move in, and in the ensuing chaos hundreds of people, mostly children, were killed. It was widely reported that local civilians tried to take matters into their own hands, and in the process accidentally hit members of the Russian Interior Ministry special forces (*Spetsnaz*) in the back.

50 Beevor, *Stalingrad*, p. 203, TsAMO 48/486/25, p. 122.

51 Erickson, *The Eastern Front in Photographs 1941–45* (Carlton, London, 2001), caption on p. 151.

52 Pennington, 'Women . . . Stalingrad', pp. 202–3, 332; Beevor, *Stalingrad*, p. 203.

53 Pennington, ibid., p. 203.

54 Ibid., It would not be the first time that a student had fallen for a teacher who was also a media celebrity, or that men and women sharing a disputed barricade had shed inhibitions.

55 Beevor, p. 204; http://en.wikipedia.org/wiki/shooting_at_the_1936_summer_ Olympics

56 Chuikov, 1960, op. cit.

57 Cited in Clark, 'Stalingrad: the Onslaught', p. 1064, emphasis added.

58 *Germany and the Second World War*, Vol. VI, pp. 1096–7.

59 Erickson, *The Road to Stalingrad*, pp. 530–4; *Germany and the Second World War*, Vol. VI, p. 1100. Stalin's diary, in Gor'kov, *GKO postanovlyaet . . .* (2002), pp. 321–2, lists no meetings at all for 12 September and only the usual series of

meetings with political and procurement people on the evening of the 13th. He probably saw Zhukov and Vasilevskiy at the Defence Ministry.

60 Gor'kov, *GKO Postanovlyayet* (Stalin's diary), p. 323.

61 Rokossovskiy, *Soldatskiy dolg* (unexpurgated, 2002), p. 243. It seems unclear why this restored section (pp. 243–52) was ever cut out in the first place. The two sensitive areas covered in the excised pages relate to Stalin's appointment of a special commission, headed by Bokov, 'to clean the forces and headquarters of unsuitable commanders and political staffs' (p. 243) and, secondly, to the problem over the name of the commander of Sixty-Sixth Army, A. S. Zhadov. His real name was 'Zhidov', which suggests Jewish antecedents, and that would not do. Stalin had suggested 'Zadov', which was also a bad name for a general, as it suggested 'backwards' – as in *ni shagu nazad* – 'not a step back', or *za* – behind. Eventually, the system agreed that the general would be called Zhadov (pp. 250–1).

62 Glantz, *Zhukov's Greatest Defeat . . .*, pp. 14–22. The first reference to this section relates to the formation of the first Soviet women's rifle brigade, which, while inspiring, is hardly relevant. The next is to Vasilevskiy's life and the third to Vatutin's. While all of these are important, none tells us that Stavka made this decision on that night.

63 Glantz, *Zhukov's Greatest Defeat . . .*, p. 20, no reference.

64 Gor'kov, *GKO postanovlyayet*, p. 324. Zhukov joined Molotov and Beria at 01.10, and they were joined by Voroshilov at 01.25 and Khrulev at 02.00, for forty minutes. Zhukov left at 03.40, the politburo members five minutes later.

65 A. A. Grechko, ed., *Istoriya Vtoroy Mirovoy voyny (A History of the Second World War)*, Vol. 6 (Voyenizdat, Moscow, 1976), pp. 29–30. See also M. E. Kayukov, *Na ostriye glavnogo udara (On the Point of the Main Attack)* (Voyenizdat, Moscow, 1976), p. 182.

66 Grechko, *Istoriya vtoroy . . .* Vol. 6, pp. 34–35.

67 Ibid., cited in Glantz, *Zhukov's . . .*, p. 19.

68 The orders, or fragments of them, from Russian archives are reproduced in Glantz, *Zhukov's Greatest Defeat . . .*, pp. 325–43.

69 Simplified from Glantz, ibid., Appendix D, Weighted Allocation of Forces in Selected Operations, p. 376. Also takes into account figures on p. 318. The number of people available in an area and to the formations involved is never the same as – and always greater than – the people actually committed to a particular offensive operation.

70 UKNA, *WO 208/1790, Soviet Ground Operations . . .*, p. 1A-5, para 7b.

71 *Germany and the Second World War . . .*, Vol. VI, p. 1101.

72 Cited in Beevor, p. 239.

73 On the role of the Romanians, with some excellent photographs and facsimiles of primary source material, see *Armata Romana in al Doilea Razboi Mondial (The Romanian Army in World War II)* (Editura Meridiane, Bucharest 1995), this pp. 79–88. Shaking ground, Beevor, p. 240.

74 Cited in Beevor, p. 244.

75 The *Oxford Companion . . .*, p. 870, does have it: most maps do not.

76 *Germany and the Second World War*, Vol. VI, p. 1117; *Times Atlas*, pp. 104–5.

77 *Germany and the Second World War*, Vol. VI, p. 1117.

78 *Times Atlas*, pp. 104–5.

79 Beevor, pp. 255–6; Erickson, *The Road to Berlin . . .*, pp. 1–2.

80 The Carthaginians lost, in the end; Khalkin Gol was significant and helped keep the Japanese out of the war, but was relatively small scale, and, though it was not his fault, the Iraqi Republican Guard were allowed to escape from Schwarzkopf's trap.

81 Beevor, *Stalingrad*, Appendix. B, pp. 439–40, discusses the various estimates. Estimates for the number encircled on 23 November sensibly vary from 220,000 to 290,000, with a ration strength in the *Kessel* on 6 December of 275,000. About 25,000 sick and specialists were flown out.

82 *The Times Atlas*, p. 105; *Germany and the Second World War*, Vol. VI, p. 1154; Erickson, *The Road to Berlin*, p. 2; Krivosheyev, *Soviet Casualties*, pp. 126–8.

83 Graphic account in Beevor, pp. 256–62.

84 Erickson *The Road to Berlin*, p. 2. John says the 'nose' protrudes to the 'south-west', but to this author, the 'face', looks east, and 'south-east' looks more appropriate, as well as more apposite.

85 Erickson, *The Road to Berlin*, pp. 4–5; Beevor, p. 270.

86 Ibid., pp. 4–5; *Germany and the Second World War*, Vol. VI, pp. 1130–1; Beevor, pp. 270–1.

87 *Germany and the Second World War*, Vol. VI, pp. 1154–5.

88 Ibid., p. 1145.

89 Ibid., p. 1152.

90 Ibid., p. 1143.

91 Ibid., pp. 1145, 1147, 1153.

92 Ibid., p. 1148, citing *Hitlers Lagebespechungen* 84 (12 December 1942), shorthand record of a situation conference.

93 *Germany and the Second World War*, Vol. VI, pp. 1155–6.

94 Zhukov, *Vospominaniya . . .* (2002), Vol. 2, p. 120; *The Memoirs of Marshal Zhukov* (1971), p. 420.

95 Rokossovskiy, *Soldatskiy dolg* (unexpurgated, 2002), p. 252.

96 Maj. Gen. E. V. Porfir'yev, 'Reyd k Tatsinskoy' ('Raid to Tatsinskaya'), *VIZh* 11/1987, pp. 63–71; Capt Harold W. Coyle, 'Tatsinskaya and Soviet OMG Doctrine', *Armor*, January–February 1985, pp. 33–8.

97 *Germany and the Second World War*, Vol. VI, p. 1194.

98 Ibid., pp. 1194–9.

99 UKNA, *WO 208/1790*, p. 1A-6, para 8b.

100 Ibid.

101 Zhukov, *Vospominaniya* (2002), pp. 112–15; *Memoirs* (1971), pp. 13–16; also Glantz, 'Operation Mars . . .', in *JSMS*, Vol 8 (December 1995), No. 4, pp. 788–9.

102 Krivosheyev, *Soviet Casualties . . .* If rated as a separate Strategic Offensive Operation, Mars would come after the Stalingrad Strategic Offensive Operation (pp. 126–8).

103 Glantz, *Zhukov's Greatest Defeat*, pp. 304, 318–19, 379 (Appendix E, with letter from General Krivosheyev).

104 Ibid., p. 320.

105 *FSB Archives*, Vol. III, Bk 2, Doc. 1247, '*Soobshcheniye NKVD SSSR No 2134/B v GKO s izlozhennym dannykh poluchennykh ot rezidenta NKVD v Londone, o podgotovke Germanii k primeneniyu khimicheskikh I bakteriologicheskikh sredstv vedeniya voyny*', 26 December 1942, p. 565, signed by Beria.

106 Mark Wilkinson, *The Soviet Biological Weapons Programme from 1918 to 1945*, M.Sc. Global Security dissertation, Cranfield University, 2005.

107 Ken Alibek and Stephen Handelman, *Biohazard* (Hutchinson, London, 1999), p. 29. Alibek became fascinated by 'what seemed an inexplicable sequence of events' after poring over the 25-volume *History of Soviet Military Medicine in the Great Patriotic War.*

108 UKNA, *WO 208/4277*, Report on the Interrogation of Professor H. Kliewe May 7th–11th 1945 by Major H. M. B. Adam, Major J. M. Barnes, Capt W. J. Cromartie, Capt Carlo Henze and Lt J. W. Hofer, Ref. A-B-C-H-H/149, dated 13 May 1945.

109 Ibid., pp. 5–6.

110 'Capsules' were similar to those we put on our pets – small tubes with a screw top into which a slip of paper with details on it was inserted. Conversation with guides at the German cemetery west of Volgograd, in the centre of the *Kessel* area, March 2001.

111 UKNA, *WO 208/4277*, p. 7.

112 UKNA, *WO 208/1802, Possible use of gas, prevailing winds*, 28 March 1942, to CDR 5 Porton, dated 1 April 1942.

113 *FSB Archives*, Vol. III, Bk 2, Doc. 1217, '*Listovka komandovaniya Stalingradskogo I Donskogo frontov k vrazheskim ofitseram i soldatam, okruzhennym v rayone Stalingrada*', 30 November 1942, pp. 499–500.

114 *Ul'timatum*, 8 January 1943, in *Stalingradskaya Bitva*, Vol. 2, pp. 396–7.

115 Beevor, pp. 322–30.

116 *FSB Archives*, Vol. III, Bk 2, Doc. 1230, Stalin to Head of Stavka (Vasilevskiy), '*o srokakh I etapakh operatsii "Kol'tso"*', 11 December 1942, pp. 524–5.

117 Manstein, *Lost Victories*, Appendix.

118 Russian figures: Beevor, p. 322.

119 I am grateful to Field Marshal Lord Inge for this observation.

120 Beevor, pp. 383–91.

121 Zhukov, *Vospominaniya* . . . (2002), Vol. 2, p. 122; *Memoirs* (1971), p. 423; Krivosheyev, *Soviet Casualties* . . ., pp. 124–5, 126–8.

122 Beevor, p. 396, citing German archive BA-MA RL30/6.

123 '*Ot Sovetskogo Informbyuro. Utrenneye soobshcheniye 2 fevralya*', *Pravda*, 3 February 1943, in *Stalingradskaya Bitva* . . . (2002), Vol. 2, p. 532.

124 Erickson and Erickson, *The Eastern Front in Photographs*, p. 169.

125 *Germany and the Second World War*, Vol. VI, pp. 1212–13.

126 Ibid., p. 1213.

127 Ibid., p. 1214, citing A. M. Belikov, 'Transfert de l'industrie Soviètique vers l'Est' (juin 1941–1942), *Revue d'istoire de la Deuxième Guerre Mondiale*, 43 (1961), pp. 35–50, this p. 48.

128 Bernd Wegner, in *Germany* . . ., Vol. VI, pp. 1214–15. This author agrees.

17. Kursk, and a new professionalism

1 Red Army, Krivosheyev, *Soviet Casualties* . . ., table 72, p. 101; NKVD, Glantz, *Colossus Reborn* . . ., p. 158.
2 Louis B. Ely, *The Red Army Today*, first pub. 1949, Military Service Publishing Co., Harrisburg, PA, 1953), pp. 16–17.
3 Erickson, *The Road to Berlin*, pp. 52–3; Gen. A. Khrulev, '*K istorii vvedeniya pogona*' ('On the story of introducing the shoulder board'), *VIZh*, 1/1963, pp. 109–16. The NKO Order was 15 January 1943. Khrulev was at the meeting on 9 October 1942: Gor'kov, *GKO Postanovlyayet*, p. 328, (Stalin's diary).
4 Officers in the Imperial Russian Army put away their tasselled epaulettes in the Caucasus and the Crimea because they made them easy targets for snipers. Instead, in the field, they sewed the silver or gold braid of their sword-belts onto their shoulder straps: two strips for junior officers and captains, three for more senior officers. This gave rise to a single long stripe between the strips of braid for subalterns and captains and two stripes, in the gaps, for colonels. Generals' shoulder boards were completely covered with diagonal criss-cross braid. After the First World War, in the Revolution and Civil War, shoulder boards were seen as a hated symbol of class oppression, worn by the White counter-revolutionaries. From 1919, the Bolsheviks adopted the system of geometrical shapes which lasted, but with increasing elaboration, until January 1943. The new shoulder boards were an adaptation of the Tsarist system, with some changes. The Tsarist army had no majors: the Red Army and NKVD did (or ranks equivalent to them). In the Imperial system, the highest rank in each category (captain, colonel, general) had no stars on the shoulder board at all. The Soviet system had one, two, three or four in each category, in ascending order of seniority. The Soviet system also had colonel-generals (three stars), and marshals (one very big star), unknown in the Imperial Army. Initially, full generals, like Rokossovskiy at Kursk, wore four stars. *VES* (1983), colour graphic between pp. 272 and 273.
5 Merridale, *Ivan's War*, p. 142.
6 Conversation with John Erickson, late 1980s; Erickson, *The Road to Berlin*, p. 53; Beevor, p. 405. That may be so, but this author has not found a reference in British sources relating to lease-lend.
7 Gold braid or not, generals had rich embroidery and stars, officers had stripes (usually red) running the length of the shoulder and also (smaller) stars. NCOs had broad cloth braid stripes running across the shoulder. *Starshinas* – sergeant majors – had a 'T' on the shoulder board. 'Ensign' (*praporshchik*) – Warrant Officer – was not introduced until 1972.
8 Rokossovskiy, *A Soldier's Duty* (1985), p. 174; *Soldatskiy dolg* (2002), p. 242.
9 Krivosheyev, *Soviet Casualties*, pp. 130–1.
10 Ibid. p. 131.
11 Ibid., pp. 128–9.
12 UKNA, *WO 208/1790*, p. 1A-6, para 8.
13 The Mongols first invaded the Russian principalities in 1223, and returned in 1240. They stayed for nearly 250 years. The Domesday Book itemized every bit of

land and property in England for its new Norman ruler, William the Conqueror, in the 1080s. For 'pre-Mongol' Kursk, my gratitude to Anna Ivanovna, Lyuba Sheverdina, Anya, and Heather Taylor.

14 Ibid., and Aleksandr, a former teacher of chemistry and biology, our guide.

15 David Glantz and Harold Orenstein, trans. and ed., *The Battle for Kursk 1943: the Soviet General Staff Study* (Frank Cass, London, 1999, originally published as part of *Collection of Materials for the Study of War Experiences*, No. 11, Military Publishing House of the People's Commissariat of Defence, Moscow 1944), p. 1.

16 Ibid., pp. 51–3.

17 Ibid., pp. 53–4.

18 Ibid., p. 54.

19 Rokossovskiy, *A Soldier's Duty*, pp. 175–83, this p. 176; *Soldatskiy dolg* (2002), pp. 253–62, this p. 254.

20 Ibid., *A Soldier's Duty*, p. 178; *Soldatskiy dolg* (2002), p. 257.

21 Ibid.

22 Ibid., *Soldatskiy dolg* (2002), pp. 262–3. Restored section. Emphasis added.

23 Krivosheyev, *Soviet Casualties . . .*, pp. 108–9, 130–1.

24 Cited in Lt Col. Pavel Kulikov, 'The Russian View', in 'Kursk – Sixty Years On', *RUSI Journal*, Vol. 148, No. 5 (October 2003), pp. 78–88, this p. 81.

25 The term 'asymmetric conflict' refers to combatants who have quite different characteristics and vulnerabilities. Of course, all war is 'asymmetric' – otherwise nobody could win. At the time of writing, however, it means conflict between quite different animals: suicide bombers against 'democratic' states, for example. For all its asymmetric elements (notably partisans), the war on the eastern front was predominantly symmetric: tanks, guns, aircraft, men and women in regular armed formations.

26 The battle on the ice of Lake Chud (Peipus), 5(11) April, 1242; see *VES* (1983), pp. 393–4.

27 Geoffrey Vesey Holt, 'Armoured warfare in 1943', in 'Kursk – Sixty Years On', pp. 83–8.

28 Glantz and Orenstein, *Kursk: The Soviet General Staff Study*, pp. 28–9. Emphasis is in original.

29 Kulikov in 'Kursk – Sixty Years On', p. 81.

30 Zhukov, *Memoirs* (1971), pp. 433–4; *Vospominaniya* (2002), pp. 130–1. Erickson, *The Road to Berlin*, pp. 87–9, 114.

31 *Soviet General Staff Study*, p. 5.

32 Ibid., p. 23.

33 Ultra was not a machine, as some have, understandably, assumed, but a clever cover for the source. The British classification was 'Most Secret': the American 'Top Secret' was adopted at the end of the war.

34 Christopher Andrew and Vasiliy Mitrokhin, *The Mitrokhin Archive: The KGB in Europe and the West* (Penguin, London, 2000), pp. 135, 156, 159.

35 John Vader, 'The Lucy Spy Ring', *Purnell's History . . .*, No. 50, *The Greatest Tank Battle in History*, pp. 1373–4.

36 Erickson, *The Road to Berlin*, pp. 85, 128–9.

37 Ibid., p. 119.

38 Andrew and Mitrokhin, pp. 135–6; Timothy P. Milligan, 'Spies, ciphers and "Zitadelle". Intelligence and the Battle of Kursk 1943', *Journal of Contemporary History*, Vol. 22 (1987), No. 2. Under the Lease-Lend agreements of 1941 the UK and the US were due to ship 35,000 radio sets, plus 380,000 field telephones and nearly 1.6 million kilometres of telephone cable. Andrew and Gordievskiy, p. 779, citing Overy, *Russia's War*, pp. 193–4. The British certainly sent 4,338 radio sets with about ten times that number of valves. Beaumont, *Comrades in Arms*, p. 205. Summary execution – testimony of a woman NKVD officer, Zinaida Pytkina, in Rees, *War of the Century*, pp. 165–8.

39 I am grateful to Col. John Hughes-Wilson for his advice.

40 Andrew and Gordievskiy, pp. 235–6; Milligan, ibid.

41 Leonid D. Grenkevich, *The Soviet Partisan Movement 1941–1944* (Frank Cass, London, 1999), pp. 7, 15.

42 *FSB Archives*, Vol. III, Bk 1, Doc. 961, '*Iz postanovleniya Gosudarstvennogo Komiteta Oborony SSSR No 1837ss [Top Secret] ob ob"yedinenii rukovodstva partizanskim dvizheniyem v tylu protivnika I yego dal'neyshem razvitii*', 30 May 1942, pp. 507–10.

43 Ibid., Vol. III, Bk 2, Doc. 1079, '*Prikaz narodnogo komissara oborony Soyuza SSR No. 00189 o zadachakh partizanskoogo dvizheniya*', 5 September 1942, pp. 208–12, esp. p. 211.

44 Grenkevich, p. 229, citing *Velikaya pobeda Sovetskogo naroda 1941–45 (The Great Victory of the Soviet People, 1941–45)* (Nauka, Moscow, 1976), p. 176, and other Soviet sources.

45 Grenkevich, pp. 239–42.

46 Rokossovskiy, *Soldatskiy dolg* (2002) (restored section), pp. 265–6.

47 Ibid., p. 293 (restored).

48 Ibid., restored, p. 266.

49 Erickson, *The Road to Berlin*, pp. 115–17.

50 Grenkevich, p. 225.

51 *Soviet General Staff Study*, p. 54.

52 Author's lecture to RUSI on 60th anniversary, in *RUSI Journal*, Vol. 148, No. 5 (October 2003), pp. 84–5.

53 Karl-Heinz Frieser, 'Turning Point of the War?' in 'Kursk – Sixty Years On', *RUSI Journal*, Vol. 148, No. 5 (October 2003), pp. 78–80, this p. 79.

54 Magenheimer, *Hitler's War*, p. 207.

55 Krivosheyev, *Soviet Casualties . . .*, gives 1.272 million as the strength before losses. This coincides very well with numbers given in general sources, such as *Purnell's History . . .* (1966/1972), which gives 1.3 million. The German figure of 900,000 is also well attested. *Purnell's History . . .*, again, and *Times Atlas*, p. 124.

56 Krivosheyev, *Soviet Casualties*, gives 1,144,000 for The Voronezh Front and Steppe MD during the Belgorod-Kharkov offensive (Rumyantsev) and 1,287,600 available for the Orël offensive (Kutuzov).

57 Col. G. A. Koltunov, 'Kursk: the Clash of Armour', *Purnell's History . . .*, pp. 1375–91, this p. 1376.

58 Erickson, *The Road to Berlin*, p. 114.

59 Rokossovskiy, *A Soldier's Duty*, p. 194; *Soldatskiy dolg* (2002), pp. 278–9. The unexpurgated version reveals nothing new here.

60 Ibid. Orël means eagle.

61 Story told by Aleksandr, my guide at Kursk.

62 *Boyevoy komplekt* – 'unit of fire'.

63 Rokossovskiy, *Soldatskiy dolg* (2002), p. 292, restored section. The censored version, p. 195, is more flattering to Zhukov and less to the author.

64 Ibid., pp. 280 and pp. 194–5, respectively.

65 Koltunov in *Purnell's History . . .*, p. 1383; Fetzer and Wagner, p. 175.

66 Fetzer and Wagner, ibid.

67 *Soviet General Staff Study*, pp. 98–102, 220–6, this p. 224.

68 Ibid., pp. 102, 128. Glantz's note on latter.

69 Conversation with Aleksandr, my Kursk guide.

70 *General Staff Study*, p. 226.

71 Erickson, *The Road to Berlin*, p. 149, citing Soviet after-action report.

72 Ibid., pp. 148–9; Krivosheyev, p. 132.

73 Karl-Heinz Freiser (Potsdam), in 'Kursk – Sixty Years On', *RUSI Journal*, Vol. 148, No. 5 (October 2003), p. 79.

74 Grenkevich, pp. 241–4.

75 Ibid., pp. 244–5.

76 Ibid., pp. 251–6.

77 Erickson, *The Road to Berlin*, pp. 149–53; Koltunov in *Purnell's History . . .*, pp. 1384–9.

78 Petr Rumyantsev-Zadunayskiy (1725–96). Rumyantsev had fought Prussia's Frederick the Great in the Seven Years' War and then the Turks, using innovative tactics (columns and dispersed formations) that are often associated with the French revolution.

79 Krivosheyev, *Soviet Casualties . . .*, pp. 132–4.

80 Erickson, *The Road to Berlin . . .*, pp. 154–9; author's *Red God of War*; Fetzer and Wagner, pp. 182–5.

81 Erickson, p. 158; Koltunov, p. 1390.

82 German casualties: Koltunov, p. 1390; Russian, Krivosheyev, pp. 132–4; German–Soviet casualty ratios, see Fritz Stoeckli, 'Soviet and German loss rates during the Great Patriotic War. The Price of Victory', *JSMS*, Vol. 3, no. 4 (December 1990), pp. 645–51. 'On average the Germans were more efficient than their Soviet counterparts in killing or wounding their opponents by a factor of approximately 1.5' (p. 650).

83 Frieser, in 'Kursk – Sixty Years On', *RUSI Journal*, October 2003.

84 Cited in Koltunov, p. 1391.

85 Ibid.

18. Destroying the *Wehrmacht*

1 Krivosheyev, *Soviet Casualties . . .*, pp. 134–5.

2 Ibid., pp. 135–6.

3 *Times Atlas*, pp. 126–7.

4 *Times Atlas*, p. 126; Krivosheyev, pp. 139–40.

5 Krivosheyev, pp. 139–40.

6 *Times Atlas*, p. 126.

7 Krivosheyev, pp. 136–7.

8 Ibid., pp. 138–9.

9 Ibid., pp. 139–40.

10 *VES*, pp. 116–19.

11 Berezhkov, p. 301; Erickson's masterly summary in *The Road to Berlin*, pp. 204–14.

12 Erickson, *The Road to Berlin*, p. 209.

13 Zhukov, *Memoirs* (1971), p. 443, gives 232 at the time of Kursk.

14 Cited in ibid., p. 493. Emphasis added.

15 Manstein, *Lost Victories*, p. 295.

16 Zhukov, *Memoirs* (1971), p. 441.

17 P. Kurochkin, '*Deystviya tankovykh armiy v operativnoy glubine*' ('Action of tank armies in the operational depth'), *Voyennaya Mysl' (Military thought) (VM)*, 11.1964, pp. 55–73, this p. 56. See also the table on pp. 62–3 which begins with Stalingrad. The other key sources are Marshal of Tank Troops O. A. Losik (ed.), *Stroitel'stvo I boyevoye primeneniye Sovetskikh tankovykh voysk v gody Velikoy Otechestvennoy voyny (The Composition and Operational Employment of Soviet Tank Forces in the Great Patriotic War)* (Voyenizdat, Moscow, 1979); and Gen. A. I. Radzievskiy, *Tankovy udar (Tankovaya armiya v nastupatel'noy operatsii fronta po opytu Velikoy otechestvennoy voyny) (Tank Strike (The Tank Army in the Front Offensive Operation as experienced in the Great Patriotic War)* (Voyenizdat, Moscow, 1977).

18 Radzievskiy, *Tank Strike . . .*, p. 123. See also Lt Gen. A. A. Sokolov, '*Dostizheniye vysokykh tempov nastupleniya v khode frontovykh operatsii Velikoy otechestvennoy voyny*' ('Attaining High Tempos of the Offensive in the Course of Front Operations in the GPW'), *VIZh*, 12/1985, pp. 8–13.

19 Losik, p. 121.

20 Radzievskiy, *Tank Strike . . .*, Appendix 3.

21 Zhukov, *Memoirs*, p. 442.

22 Krivosheyev, pp. 252–3; Zhukov, *Memoirs*, pp. 441–2.

23 Zhukov, *Memoirs*, pp. 503–9.

24 Ibid., pp. 511–12.

25 *Times Atlas*, pp. 146–7, WO 208/ 1790, pp. 1A-6–1A-9.

26 Ibid., Krivosheyev, pp. 137–8, 142–3.

27 Ibid., WO 208/1790, p. 1A-9, on Vasilevskiy's presence.

28 David M. Glantz and Harold L. Orenstein, trans. and ed., *Belorussia 1944: the Soviet General Staff Study*. (originally published as *Soviet General Staff Study no. 18) (Frank Cass, London and Portland, Oregon, 2001)*, p. 3; Ziemke, *Stalingrad to Berlin: the German Defeat in the East* (Center of Military History, US Army, US Government Printing Office, Washington DC, 1987, first published 1968), pp. 311–45; Gerd Niepold, trans. Richard Simpkin, *Battle for White Russia: The*

Destruction of Army Group Centre, June 1944 (Brassey's Defence Publishers, London, 1987).

29 Petr Ivanovich Bagration, 1765–1812. *VES*, p. 60; Erickson, *The Road to Berlin*, p. 265.

30 *Belorussia 1944: the Soviet General Staff Study . . .*, p. 3. Ziemke gives the date as 22 June, but then says all the Soviet accounts give the 23rd.

31 Ziemke, *Stalingrad to Berlin*, citing OKH GenStdH 1428/44.

32 Ibid., pp. 313–14; Krivosheyev, *Soviet Casualties*, pp. 144–6; *Times Atlas*, p. 149.

33 Rokossovskiy, *A Soldier's Duty* (1985), p. 255; *Soldatskiy dolg* (2002), p. 326.

34 Ibid. *Oba udara – glavnye* – 'both blows are main', pp. 231, 322, respectively.

35 Ibid., *Soldatskiy dolg* (2002), p. 327, restored section. This would have appeared on p. 235 of the 1985 censored version.

36 Ibid., pp. 327–8, 235, respectively.

37 Cited in Erickson, *The Road to Berlin*, p. 278. Those formations were accompanied, included and were supported by Poles, Czechs, Norwegians, Dutch and most of the countries of the British Commonwealth. If I have omitted anyone, I apologize.

38 Antony Beevor and Luba Vinogradova, trans. and ed., *A Writer at War: Vasily Grossman with the Red Army 1941–1945* (Harvill Press, London, 2005), p. 271.

39 Grenkevich, p. 259.

40 Ibid., pp. 259–60.

41 Ibid., p. 257; Krivosheyev, pp. 144–6. The First Polish Army comprised 79,900 men, in addition to the 2,331,700 in the four fronts, but was not included in the main operation.

42 Issa Aleksandrovich Pliev (1903–79), see Pliev, *Pod gvardeyskim znamanem (Under the Guards' Banner)* (Ordzhonikidze, 1976) and *Konets kvantuinskoy armii. Zapiski komanduyushchego konno-makhanizirovannoy gruppy sovetsko-Mongol'skikh voysk)(The end of the Kwantung Army. Notes of the Commander of the Soviet-Mongolian Cavalry-Mechanised Group)* (Ir, Ordzhonikidze, 1969).

43 Ziemke, *Stalingrad to Berlin*, p. 321, citing Tippelskirch, *Geschichte des Zweiten Weltkrieges*, p. 462.

44 Ibid., pp. 322–5.

45 On this and more about artillery and the Belorussian Operation, see author's *Red God of War*, pp. 57–63.

46 Krivosheyev, pp. 132–4, 144–6.

47 I am grateful to Charles Dick, Director of the Conflict Studies Research Centre, UK Defence Academy, for his presentation given to a Normandy staff ride comparing the two battles.

48 The definitive new work is Norman Davies, *Rising '44* (Macmillan, London, 2003). On the AK and the Warsaw rising, see Rokossovskiy, *A Soldier's Duty*, pp. 254–63, *Soldatskiy dolg* (2002), pp. 351–60. There is nothing new about Warsaw in the unexpurgated version. Also Andrew Borowiec, *Destroy Warsaw! Hitler's Punishment, Stalin's Revenge* (Praeger, Westport and London, 2001); Erickson, *The Road to Berlin*, pp. 329–88; Ziemke, *Stalingrad to Berlin*, pp. 344–5.

49 Rokossovskiy, *A Soldier's Duty*, p. 255.

50 Ibid., p. 257; Borowiec, p. 105.

51 Ziemke, p. 345; Rokossovskiy, *A Soldier's Duty* p. 257, says there were eighty and that they were 'flying fortresses' (B-17s). He says that two were shot down and the Americans made no more attempts. The flight on 18 September was probably the largest western military flight ever to land in Russia – 105 B-17s landed at the Soviet air base of Poltava, Davies, p. 377.

52 Ziemke, p. 345; Borowiec, p. 143; Davies, pp. 417–22.

53 UKNA, *WO 208/1790*, p. 1A-12.

54 Interview with Prof. Marja Talvi, Budapest, 30 August 2003; Pennington, *Wings . . .*, pp. 86–7.

55 Mart Laar, 'The Armed Resistance Movement in Estonia from 1944 to 1956', in Anusauskas, *The Anti-Soviet Resistance in the Baltic States*, pp. 209–41, this p. 211. Lithuania: interview at the Genocide Museum, Vilnius, December 2000.

56 Laar, in Anusauskas, pp. 211–14.

57 Heinrihs Strods, 'The Latvian partisan war between 1944 and 1956', in Anusauskas, ed., pp. 149–60, this pp. 151–4; Nijole Gaškaite-Zemataine, 'The Partisan war in Lithuania from 1944–1953', ibid., pp. 23–45.

58 See note 1/38; *Times Atlas*, p. 150; Irwin J. Kappes, 'The Greatest Marine Disaster in History', <www.militaryhistoryonline.com/wwii/articles/wilhelmgustloff.aspx>, retrieved on 29 December 2005.

59 *Nazi Sea Disaster* (see note 1/38).The computer modelling, using techniques developed for analysing disasters in football stadiums and so on, is reliable.

60 Kappes, op. cit.

61 Erickson, *The Road to Berlin*, p. 212.

62 Berezhkov, *At Stalin's Side . . .*, pp. 302–3.

63 Ibid., pp. 304–7.

64 Ibid., p. 312.

19. Victory

1 Berezhkov, *At Stalin's Side*, pp. 335–8.

2 Ely, pp. 199–200.

3 Krivosheyev, pp. 149–50.

4 Guide in Budapest Castle, visit during international border guards' conference, 29 August 2003.

5 *Times Atlas*, pp. 150–1 (Baltic), 178–9 (Hungary); Ziemke, *Stalingrad to Berlin*, pp. 365–409, esp. pp. 402 (map) –9.

6 Ziemke, *Stalingrad to Berlin*, p. 385.

7 Ibid., pp. 412, 418. Rüdiger Overmans gives German military losses against USSR (from 1941) as 2,742,909 until 31 December 1944, and 1,230,045 for final battles in Germany in 1945 (total). This seems to tally. See http://en.wikipedia.org/wiki/World_War_II_casualties, accessed 12 January 2007.

8 Erickson, *The Road to Berlin*, pp. 602–8.

9 Ziemke, p. 419, citing Shtemenko, '*Kak planirovalas' poslednaya kampaniya po*

razgromu gitlerovskoy Germanii' ('How the last operation to destroy Hitler's Germany was planned'), *VIZh*, 5/1965.

10 Krivosheyev, *Soviet Casualties . . .*, pp. 152–60.

11 Ziemke, *Stalingrad to Berlin*, p. 420.

12 Grossman, ed. Beevor and Vinogradova, p. 271.

13 Cited in Merridale, p. 261.

14 Ibid., citing Bundesarchiv, RH-2-2647, 82.

15 Ibid., p. 265, citing RH-2-2647, 9.

16 Grossman, ed. Beevor and Vinogradova, p. 321.

17 Merridale, p. 264.

18 Ziemke, pp. 420–1, citing Churchill, *Triumph and Tragedy*, pp. 278–80 and Forrest Pogue, *United States Army in World War II* (Washington DC, 1954), pp. 405–7.

19 Krivosheyev, pp. 152–3.

20 Sokolov, 'Dostizheniye vysokikh tempov . . .', *VIZh*, 12/1985, pp. 8–9.

21 Author's *Red God of War*, pp. 65–8.

22 Ziemke, pp. 421–2.

23 Ibid., p. 422, citing Jodl, Diary, 15 January 1945, and Guderian, *Erinnerungen eines Soldaten*, p. 357.

24 *Times Atlas*, p. 174.

25 UKNA, *WO 208/1790*, p. 1A-14.

26 Col. N. Kireyev, Lt Col. N. Dobenko, 'Iz opyta boyevogo primeneniya peredovykh otryadov tankovykh (mekhanizirovannykh) korpusov' ('From the experience of employing forward detachments of tank (mechanized) corps in combat'), *VIZh*, 9/1982, pp. 20–7, this p. 20.

27 Col. N. F. Polukhin and Lt Col. Yu. D. Patychenko, ''Material'noye obespecheniye podvyzhnykh grupp frontov v Vislo-Oderskoy Operatsii' ('Logistic Support of Front Mobile Groups during the Vistula-Oder operation'), *VIZh*, 1/1987, pp. 30–6.

28 Ibid.

29 Erickson, *The Road to Berlin*, p. 603, note on p. 1003.

30 Ziemke, p. 427, citing Zhilin, *Vazhneyshiye operatsii Velikoy otechestvennoy voyny (The Most Important Operations of the Great Patriotic War)*, p. 479.

31 From *SMERt' SHpionam* – 'Death to spies'.

32 Overy, *Russia's War*, pp. 260–1; Merridale, pp. 255–6.

33 Ziemke, pp. 428, 439.

34 Krivosheyev, pp. 144–6, 152–3.

35 Zhukov says it was a Maj. Gen. Yenyukov who raised it in 1945. See Zhukov, *Memoirs*, pp. 571–8, *Vospominaniya . . .* (2002), Vol. 2, pp. 274–80, Yenyukov on pp. 578, 280, respectively; Chuikov in *Novaya I noveyshaya istoriya*, No. 2, 1965, pp. 6–7 and discussion in *VIZh*, 3/1965, pp. 74–6, 80–1, 4/1965, pp. 62–4.

36 Zhukov, ibid., pp. 571–8, 274–80, respectively. Berlin: Tony Le Tissier, *Race for the Reichstag: the 1945 Battle for Berlin* (Frank Cass, London and Portland, 1999), p. 11.

37 Overy, pp. 252–4.

38 Churchill, 'Results of the three power conference. A speech to the House of

Commons, February 27, 1945', in Charles Eade, compiler, *Victory: War Speeches by the Right Hon. Winston S. Churchill, 1945* (Cassell, London, 1946), pp. 44–66, this p. 47.

39 'The Crimea Declaration', in ibid., pp. 31–7, signed by Winston S. Churchill, Franklin D. Roosevelt and J. V. Stalin, this p. 36.

40 Zhukov, *Memoirs*, p. 586, *Vospominaniya* (2002), Vol. 2, p. 287.

41 Erickson, *The Road to Berlin*, pp. 708–9.

42 Ibid., pp. 706–8.

43 Gor'kov, *GKO Postanovlyayet*, p. 460.

44 Ibid., p. 461; Ziemke, *Stalingrad to Berlin*, p. 467.

45 Churchill, 'The War Situation', 8 September 1942, in Charles Eade, compiler, *The End of the Beginning. War Speeches by the Right Hon. Winston S. Churchill, 1942*, pp. 163–76, this p. 174.

46 Erickson, p. 709; Gor'kov, p. 461. Harriman, Kerr, Deane and others were with Stalin from 20.00 to 20.50.

47 The phrase was widely used, and appeared on a poster which Soviet political officers put up on the German border. See the writer Vasiliy Grossman, in Beevor and Vinogradova, ed., *A Writer at War*, p. 325.

48 Hans Dollinger, trans. Arnold Pomerans, *The Decline and Fall of Nazi Germany and Imperial Japan. A Pictorial History of the Final Days of World War II* [1945] (Gramercy Books, New York, 1995), p. 78. This book is a goldmine of contemporary documents.

49 Ibid., p. 93.

50 Ziemke, *Stalingrad to Berlin*, pp. 470, 472, citing 'Berlinskaya operatsiya v tsifrakh' ('The Berlin operation in figures'), *VIZh*, 4/1965; personnel numbers, Krivosheyev, pp. 157–8.

51 In the last few years we have had Antony Beevor, *Downfall*, and Max Hastings, *Armageddon*. Cornelius Ryan, *The Last Battle*, is still excellent, as is John Erickson, 'No Time to Die', in *The Road to Berlin*, pp. 710–857. For the most authoritative and detailed coverage, see the numerous works of Le Tissier, who was the last British governor of Spandau prison. See *Race for the Reichstag*; *The Battle of Berlin 1945*; *Berlin Then and Now, Farewell*; *Zhukov and the Oder* and, most recently, *Slaughter at Halbe: the Destruction of Hitler's 9th Army, April 1945* (Sutton, Stroud, 2005). What follows in this book is largely based on research and exploration conducted by the author for two staff rides with the Logistic Brigade and the Divisional Headquarters and Signal Regiment of the First British Armoured Division in Germany during the early 2000s.

52 Zhukov, *Vospominaniya* (2002), Vol. 2, p. 293.

53 Ziemke, *Stalingrad to Berlin*, p. 469, citing Ministry of Foreign Affairs of the USSR, *Correspondence . . . 1941–1945* (Moscow, 1957), II, 160.

54 Erickson, *The Road to Berlin*, pp. 738–9.

55 Ibid., pp. 740–2.

56 Zhukov, *Memoirs*, p. 603; *Vospominaniya* (2002), Vol. 2, p. 305. The unexpurgated version adds nothing about the mysterious Margo. It is interesting, however, that this was at Chuikov's headquarters (see Chapter 16).

57 Ibid.

58 Erickson, *The Road to Berlin*, pp. 763–4.

59 Simonov, *War Diary*, cited in Le Tissier, *Slaughter at Halbe*, pp. 213–14.

60 For a minute analysis and graphic description, see Le Tissier, *Slaughter at Halbe*.

61 Erickson, *The Road to Berlin*, p. 778.

62 Colossus was in service for D-Day.

63 There is also a pleasant café, a restaurant, and a very good bookshop.

64 Erickson, *The Road to Berlin*, p. 785.

65 The colour film was used in the documentary *D-Day to Berlin*. I am grateful to Dan Plesch, of Birkbeck College, London, for pointing out that all the multinational operations in the later part of the Second World War were 'United Nations' operations.

66 Merridale, p. 261.

67 Beevor and Vinogradova, ed., *A Writer at War* . . ., p. 327.

68 Col. E. Lederrey, *Germany's Defeat in the East, 1941–45* (Official History, War Office, London, 1955), p. 219.

69 *Times Atlas*, pp. 182–3.

70 Erickson, *The Road to Berlin*, pp. 808–9.

71 I am grateful to Lt Col. Iftikhar Zaidi, Pakistan Army, who signed up with me to do a Cranfield PhD on 'Defining Victory'.

72 Le Tissier, *Race for the Reichstag*, pp. 167–8.

73 Ibid., p. 168.

74 Ibid., pp. 168–9.

75 Rachel Schnold, ed., *Icons of War: Yevgeny Khaldei, Soviet Photographer, World War II* (Beth Hatefutsoth, Nahum Goldmann Museum of the Jewish Diaspora and Ministry of Defence Publishing House, Tel Aviv, 1999), pp. 68–9.

76 Erickson, *The Road to Berlin*, pp. 813–28.

77 Krivosheyev, *Soviet Casualties* . . ., pp. 111–12, 120–1, 132–4, 144–5, 152–3, 157–9. The exception was the Voronezh-Voroshilovgrad defensive operation in the terrible summer of 1942 (28 June–24 July), as the Russians were falling back towards Stalingrad. The Russians suffered 21,050 losses a day, nearly two-thirds of them irrecoverable. Ibid., pp. 123–4.

78 Cited in *Times Atlas*, p. 186.

20. New world order

1 Beevor and Vinogradova, ed., p. 351. Telegin sounds just like any other official charged with herding the cats of the media. The author recalls attempting to get an assignment with the Parachute Regiment. 'We would not like that organization to be over-represented at the expense of the army as a whole . . .'

2 Beevor and Vinogradova, ed., p. 335.

3 Ibid., pp. 341–2.

4 *Times Atlas*, pp. 190–1.

5 Merridale, *Ivan's War*, pp. 290—320, 'Sheathe the old sword'.

6 Schnold, *Icons of War*, pp. 86–7.

7 Ibid., pp. 88–9; Levtov, *Parad pobady* (2005), pp. 114–43.

8 The British ranked their awards in a wonderfully Russian fashion. Zhukov got the Knight Grand Cross of the Order of the Bath (GCB), Rokossovskiy was made a Knight Commander of the Bath (KCB) and Sokolovskiy and Vasilevskiy Knights Commander of the British Empire (KBE).

9 Rhodes, *Dark Sun*, pp. 175–6.

10 Zhukov, *Memoirs* (1971), pp. 674–5.

11 Rhodes, p. 176.

12 Ibid., pp. 174, 276.

13 David M. Glantz, *August Storm: the Soviet 1945 Strategic Offensive in Manchuria* (Leavenworth Paper No. 7, US Army Command and General Staff College, Fort Leavenworth, 1983), pp. 25–9.

14 Ibid., pp. 5–24; 'special period', *VES* (1983), p. 119.

15 Krivosheyev, pp. 160–1.

16 Glantz, *August Storm . . .*, pp. 1–4.

17 Ibid., p. 4.

18 Pliev, *Konets kvantuinskoy armii. Zapiski komanduutushhchego konno-makhanizirovannoy gruppoy sovetsko-Mongol'skikh voysk (The end of the Kwantung Army. Notes of the Commander of the Soviet-Mongolian Cavalry-Mechanised Group)* (2nd edn, Ir, Ordzhonikidze [Vladikavkaz], 1969), p. 10.

19 Ibid.

20 *Times Atlas*, p. 198.

21 Krivosheyev, pp. 160–1.

22 Dollinger, pp. 402–3. On the film, I am grateful to David Black, for showing me the Russian footage.

23 UKNA, *FO 371/47924*, Roberts to Bevin N. 10185/627/38, printed 11 August 1945. Merridale, p. 291.

24 Ibid., pp. 1, 2, 5.

25 UKNA, *FO 371/47925*, Despatch of 4 December 1945. July 1945 strength, M. A. Garelov, '*Otkuda ugroza*' ('Whence the Threat?'), VIZh, 1/1989, p. 17. Seven to eight million demobilized, *FO 371/56831*, N 3799/605/938, dated 24 March 1946.

26 UKNA, *FO 371/47925*, Clark Kerr to Bevin N. 17305/627/38, printed 9 December 1945, p. 1.

27 Ibid., p. 2.

28 UKNA, *FO 371/56831*, No. 1090, 21 March 1946.

29 Merridale, pp. 303–6.

30 Pennington, *Wings . . .*, pp. 143–75, quotation on the latter.

31 UKNA, *FO 371/43335*, 'Probable post-war tendencies . . .', N 1008/183/38, 29 April 1944.

32 Lieutenant of XXIV Panzer Division, cited in *Purnell's History*, No. 38, p. 1064. See Chapter 16.

33 Cherepanov, *Vlast' i voyna . . .* (2006), p. 491.

Index

absolute war xvii, 18–19
Abwehr 151–3, 397
airborne operations 344, 597
air forces, *see* Luftwaffe; Soviet air force
Akhmatova, Anna 353
Aksenov, Pëtr 219
Alibek, Ken 545
Alikhanov, Abram 484
Allied Control Commission for Germany 671
Ambrazevicius, Jozas 194
Ambrose, Commander George 416–17
anti-Comintern Pact 51, 54
Antonov, General Aleksey 650
Arkhangel'sk, and Allied aid convoys 421
Arctic convoys 415, 427–8
Ardennes offensive (Battle of the Bulge) 634–5,
   640
armaments industry, Soviet
   and establishment of 34–5
   and Soviet–German co-operation 34, 41, 95, 96
Artem'yev, Pavel 282, 294, 303
artillery
   and German 'super-guns' 459–60
   and Soviet use of 176–7, 345
      Berlin offensive 655, 657, 660–2
      Leningrad 389–90
      reorganization 491
      against tanks 45
      Vistula–Oder offensive 641–2
   and Soviet–Finnish war 74
   and winter warfare 80
Astakhov, Georgiy 50, 51
Attlee, Clement 674
attrition 81, 340–1
Auschwitz 3, 644
Autumn Mist, Operation 634–5, 640
aviation, and Frunze reforms (1924–5) 33
Azovskiy, V 111

Bagramyan, Lt Gen. Ivan 451
Bagration, Operation 608–10, 613–16
   and deception plan 612–13

   and objectives of 610, 611–12
   and planning of 610–11
Balkans, and Germany 100
Baltic States
   and Baltic Strategic Offensive Operation
      621–4
   and German invasion 249–53
      frontier battles (June/July 1941) 193–8
   and German-Soviet Treaty (Sept 1939) 56–7,
      64–5, 66
   and incorporation into Soviet Union 88–9
   and Molotov–Ribbentrop Pact (1939) 54, 56
   and Soviet demand for military facilities 66–7
   and Soviet reoccupation of 621–4, 633–4
      resistance to 623
   and uprisings against Soviets 194–5, 196–7
Barbarossa, Operation
   and Battle of Smolensk (July–Sept 1941)
      240–8
   and changes in objectives 247, 251, 256–7,
      270
   and delay of 100
   and deployment of German and Soviet forces
      179–83
   and diversion of main effort 245
   and failure to exploit ethnic/linguistic tensions
      153
   and failure to exploit support for 195, 198,
      471
   and frontier battles (June/July 1941)
      Army Group Centre vs Western Front
         189–93
      Army Group North and Baltic states 193–8
      Army Group South and Ukraine 198–205
   and German intelligence on Soviet Union
      151–3
   and initial engagements 183–9
   and initial Soviet response 207–9
   and launch of 156, 159, 162–3
   and motives for 99–100
   and nature of 126–7
   and planning of 118–26

Barbarossa, Operation (*cont.*)
   21 July 1940 conference 118
   31 July 1940 conference 118–20
   aim of 126, 168
   changes in 126
   conflict of objectives 122
   Directive No. 21 123–5
   geographical assessments 168
   transport 168–9
  and pre-emptive war hypothesis
   assessment of 115–18
   circumstantial evidence 110–15
   covert Soviet mobilization 113–15
   German assessment of Soviet intent
     112–13, 116
   war plan evidence 104–10
  and Soviet intelligence on 136–43, 144,
     146–7, 149–50
   German deserters 155, 156–7
  and Soviet resistance 187, 188–9
  and starting time 156
Batyuk, Colonel Nikolai 523
Bear Island 411, 414
Beaverbrook, Lord 410, 420, 424, 426, 428
Beck, Colonel-General Ludwig 116
Belarus
  and loss of 223, 225, 226
  and Operation Bagration 608–10, 613–16
   deception plan 612–13
   objectives of 610, 611–12
   planning of 610–11
Belgrade Strategic Offensive 631
Belov, Major-General P A 344
Berezhkov, Valentin 31, 154, 159, 164, 211–13,
   290, 600
  and Beria's offices 299–301
  and Churchill–Stalin discussions (1944) 627,
    628
  and Churchill–Stalin meeting (1942) 429, 430
  and dismissal of 630
  and four-power pact negotiations 92–3, 94
  and Ribbentrop's opposition to war 39–40
Berggolts, Olga 353, 396, 406, 408
Berghof 118–19
Beria, Lavrenty Pavlovich 138, 139, 214, 216, 236
  and Caucasus 505, 506
  and chemical weapons 544
  on eve of war 154, 157
  and execution of prisoners 298
  and intelligence on German deployments 144
  and invasion of Poland 59–61, 62
  and leaves Moscow 290
  and liberated territories 335
  and nuclear weapons 481, 482, 484
  and offices of 299–300
  and peace feelers/disinformation 221–2

  and Stalingrad 519–20
  and State Defence Committee 227
  and Volkhov Offensive 385
Berlin
  and allied division of 671
  and British bombing of 93
Berlin offensive 635, 651–62
  and atrocities 660
   revenge as duty 638–9
  and attack on the Reichstag 662–7
  and capture of the city 660–2
  and German surrender 667–8
  and planning of 650–1
  and race for Berlin 651
  and Stalin 648–9, 650–1, 656, 659, 665
Berling, General Zygmunt 617
Bershanskaya, Yevdokia 488
Berzarin, Colonel-General Nikolay 670–1
Bessarabia 89–90
  and Molotov–Ribbentrop Pact (1939) 56, 90
  and Soviet occupation of 90–1
Bezymensky, Lev 147
Bezymyanny ('Nameless') 297–8
Bialystok pocket 190–1, 240
biological weapons
  and Hitler 545
  and Soviet Union 545–6
Bismarck, Otto von 41
Björkö islands 70
Black Sea 262–3
Blau, Operation 492
  and advance to the Don 498–501
  and changes in 501
  and delays in 465
  and drive to the Caucasus 503–7
  and Hitler's approval of 448
  and phases of 448
  and Sevastopol 458–65
  and split offensive 501
Bletchley Park 129–30
  see also Ultra intelligence
'blocking detachments' 203, 260, 271, 478
  and Stalingrad 519–20
Blomberg, General Werner von 34
Blunt, Anthony 139
Blyukher, Vasiliy 82–3
Bobbit, Philip 40
Bock, Field Marshal Fedor von 26–7, 112, 302,
   500
  and Battle of Moscow 326, 329, 330, 331
  and Operation Barbarossa 179
  and Operation Typhoon 271
Bogatsch, Lt Col. Rudolf 120
Bolkhovitinov, V F 484, 485
Bologoye 253
Borisov 193

Bormann, Martin 119
Borodino 288–9
Botman, Baron 213
Boysen, Harro Schulze ('Sergeant-Major') 140, 141, 146–7
Brauchitsch, Walther von 118
  and Battle of Moscow 331
  and 'Commisar Order' 26
  and Führer decree (1941) 24–5
  and planning of Barbarossa 119, 120
Braun, Eva 119, 667
Brest-Litovsk, and German assault on 184–7
Britain, Battle of 101, 347
British Intelligence
  and assessment of Soviet position (1942) 492–6
  and German intentions (1940) 101
  and German military preparations 139–41, 151
  and German use of chemical weapons 544
  and Red Army 67–8, 84
  and suspects German attack on Russia 127–8, 132
  and 'Ultra' intelligence 129–30, 570
Brooke, Sir Alan 430, 431
Bryansk encirclement 272, 276, 277
Budapest, Operation 633
Budënny, Semyon Mikhailovich 215
  and membership of Stavka 235
  and Reserve Front 260, 272
  and South-Western Strategic Direction 234–5
Bukovina 89–90
  and Soviet occupation of 90–1
Bulganin, Nikolay 236, 273, 275
Bulgaria 129, 621
Bulge, Battle of the 634–5, 640
Bullock, Alan 42
Bulvičius, Major Vytautas 195
Burandt, Wilhelm 146
Busch, Field Marshal Ernst 614
Bustard, Operation 456–7
Byrnes, James 674

Cadogan, Sir Alexander 131, 430, 431
Cairncross, John 481, 570
Cairo ('Sextant') conference 436
camouflage
  and defence of Moscow 281
  and Soviet–Finnish war 81
Canaris, Admiral Wilhelm 27
cannibalism, and Leningrad 379–80
Carol, King of Romania 90
Casablanca conference (1943) 434–5
Cassidy, Henry C 434
casualties
  and Germany 2

advance on Moscow 301, 318
Battle of Moscow 349
Berlin offensive 658
frontier battles (June/July 1941) 206, 245
June–November 1944 635
Kursk 586, 594
Operation Bagration 615
Sevastopol 464–5
Stalingrad 550
  and Soviet Union 2, 7, 9–11, 473–6
Battle of Moscow 349
Battle of Smolensk 247–8
Berlin offensive 668
Crimea 608
frontier battles (June/July 1941) 193, 198, 205, 206
Kerch' peninsula 457
Khalkin Gol 83
Khar'kov offensive 453–4, 457
Kiev encirclements 262
Kursk 586, 594
Leningrad 381
Leningrad counter-attacks 366
Leningrad–Novgorod Offensive 406
Manchurian offensive 680–1
North Caucasus operation 557
Operation Bagration 616
Operation Mars 543
pre-war 8
Rzhev-Vyaz'ma Strategic Offensive 349–50
Sevastopol 464
Soviet–Finnish war 78
Stalingrad 550
Vistula–Oder offensive 645
Vyaz'ma/Bryansk encirclements 277
Western Front 476
Caucasus
  and German drive to 503–7
  and oil-fields 497
cavalry, and Soviet use of 246, 248, 249, 289, 602
Battle of Moscow 330, 333
Manchurian offensive 679–80
Operation Bagration 613–14
Central Committee of the Communist Party, and analysis of conflicts 82, 84
Chamberlain, Neville 46
Chechnya 497
Chegodaeva, N P 523
chemical weapons
  and Frunze reforms (1924–25) 33
  and German use of 461–2
    British Intelligence on 544
    Sevastopol 461
  and investigations into alleged uses of 462–3, 545, 546–7
  and Soviet–Finnish war 77

chemical weapons (*cont.*)
  and suggested Soviet use of 264–6
  and troops' awareness of 462
Chernigov–Poltava offensive 597–600
Chernova, Tanya 523, 524
Chiang Kai-Shek 436, 676
children
  and German use of 247
  and Leningrad 372–3
Christie, Group Captain Malcolm 44
Chuikov, Vasiliy
  and Berlin offensive 645, 654–5
    German surrender 667–8
  and Soviet–Finnish war 75–6
  and Stalingrad 514, 515, 525, 532
    role of women 520–1
  and Vistula–Oder offensive 641
Churchill, Clementine 424
Churchill, Winston 409
  and aid to Soviet Union 411–14, 419, 427–8
  and allied conferences 438
    Cairo (1943) 436
    Casablanca (1943) 434–5
    Potsdam (1945) 438, 674–5
    Quebec (1943) 435
    Quebec (1944) 438
    Tehran (1943) 436–8, 600–1
    Washington (1941) 425
    Washington (1942) 426
    Washington (1943) 435, 576
    Yalta (1945) 438, 646–8
  and bombing of Berlin (1940) 93
  does not expect German–Soviet war 128–9
  on Hitler's intentions 130–1
  and meeting with Stalin (1942) 429–32
  on modern warfare 17
  and reaction to German invasion of Soviet
    Union 210–11
  and second front 428
  and size of eastern front 166
  on Soviet contribution to war 5
  and Stalin
    Poland 627
    post-war division of Europe 627–8
    warnings to 131, 445
Citadel, Operation 563
  and halted by Hitler 586–7
  and objectives of 563, 576–7
  and Soviet intelligence on 569–73
civilization, and warfare 16–17
Clark Kerr, Sir Archibald 430, 431
Clausewitz, Carl von 17, 32, 41
  and warfare 17–20
'Commisar Order' (1941) 25–6
  and protests against 26–7

communications, and German disruption of
  183–4, 189, 199
Communist International (Comintern) 46
concentration camps 644
conflict dynamics, and Clausewitz on 17
Constantinescu-Klaps, Constantin 532–3
'Corsican', *see* Harnack, Arvid ('Corsican')
counter-insurgency, and German anti-partisan
  campaign 480–1
counter-stroke, and Soviet forces 188–9
  and Barvenkovo–Lozovaya operation (1942)
    450
  and Battle of Moscow 320–1
    counteroffensive first phase 324–8, 329–31
    counteroffensive second phase 332–5,
      339–40
  and Battle of Smolensk (July–Sept 1941)
    240–4, 245–6
  and defence of Moscow 295–6
  and Finland 268
  and frontier battles (June/July 1941) 190, 193,
    199–200, 201, 202–3, 205, 223–5
  and Kursk 591–3
  and Lake Il'men 251
  and Leningrad 252, 364–6, 367–70
    Leningrad–Novgorod Offensive 404–8
    Operation Polar Star 401–2
    Operation Spark 392–6
    Sinyavino Operation 386–8
    Volkhov Offensive 382–6
  and Lithuania 252
  and Rzhev counteroffensive 527–8
  and Rzhev–Sychevka counteroffensive ('Mars')
    528, 529–31, 541–3
  and South-West Front 257
  and Stalingrad counteroffensive 526–8
    air power 517–18
    capture of Paulus 549–50
    end of fighting 550–1
    Operation Little Saturn 539, 540–1
    Operation Ring 537, 539–40
    Operation Saturn 529
    Operation Uranus 528–9, 531, 532–7
    ultimatum to Germans 547
Courland peninsula 624
Coventry 93
Craig, William A 523, 524
Crimea 263, 447
  and declared under siege 294
  and German attacks on 266–7
  and German plans for 455–6
  and Soviet recapture of 603, 607–8
Cripps, Sir Stafford 101, 132, 151
  and Anglo-Soviet agreement 410
  and delays delivering Churchill's message 131
  and importance of eastern front 415

and recall of 144–5
and Soviet–German relations 139
Czechoslovakia 633, 669

Davies, Joseph 420
Deane, John R 649
Debrecen, Operation 631–3
deep battle 79, 602
  and Khalkin Gol 83
  and Vistula–Oder offensive 642
defensive fortifications 81
  and Soviet Union 144, 148
defensive pincer
  and Operation Fridericus 451–5
  and Sinyavino Operation 388
  and Volkhov Offensive 384
Degtyarev, Georgiy 485
Dekanozov, Vladimir 39, 154, 155, 159
demobilization 682–3, 684
demography, and Great Patriotic War 7–13
Demyansk 252
Denmark 86
deportations, and ethnic minorities 492, 505
deserters, and Red Army 204–5
  and 'blocking detachments' 203, 260, 271, 478
  and 'destroyer battalions' 281–2
  and Leningrad 363
'destroyer battalions' 36, 217
  and defence of Moscow 281–2, 293–4
  and partisans 478–9
Dieppe raid 426, 432
Dill, Sir John 139
Dimitrov, Georgiy 208
diplomats 31
  and evacuation of 211–14
dive-bombing 79, 141
Dnepr, the
  Battle of 596–600
  and defence of 240, 259
Dobrovavin, Ivan Yevstavevich 307
Don, Operation 557
Donbass Operation 596
Dönitz, Grand-Admiral Karl 12, 624, 659, 667
  and Baltic evacuations 624–5, 626
Dovator, Major-General Lev 246, 289, 333
Dragun, Colonel Vasiliy 237
Dukhanov, A 75
Dumbarton Oaks 647
Dumitrescu, General Petre 532
Dunkirk 100
Dvina 240

East Pomeranian offensive 635
East Prussian Operation 634, 635, 645
economics, and outcome of war 468–70

economy, and impact of Great Patriotic War 13–14
Edelweiss, Operation 501, 503–7
Eden, Anthony 130, 139, 409, 674
  and Foreign Ministers' conference (1943) 436
  and Soviet Union 414, 425
  aims in eastern Europe 438
Edward VIII 136
Ehrenburg, Il'ya 28, 111, 465–8, 638
Einsatzgruppen 26
Eisenhower, Dwight D 634
  and Berlin 648
  and orders halt on the Elbe 654
Eisenstein, Sergei M 111, 373
encirclement
  and Battle of Moscow 333, 339
  and Bialystok pocket 191, 240
  and Bryansk 272, 276, 277
  and Kerch' peninsula 456
  and Kiev pocket 259–60
  and Operation Bagration 614–15
  and Operation Fridericus 451–3
  and Rzhev-Vyaz'ma Strategic Offensive 342, 344
  and Stalingrad counteroffensive 527
    capture of Paulus 549–50
    end of fighting 550–1
    Operation Little Saturn 539, 540–1
    Operation Ring 537, 539–40
    Operation Uranus 528–9, 531, 532–7
    ultimatum to Germans 547
  and Uman' pocket 257–9
  and Volkhov Offensive 384–5
  and Vyaz'ma 272–5, 276–7
Engels, Friedrich 16, 31–2
Enigma decoding 129–30
  see also Ultra intelligence
Environmental effect of war 1–2
Erickson, John 103, 116, 536, 610
Erna (Estonian commando group) 250–1
Estonia
  and arrests/deportations 150, 197
  and German invasion 197–8, 249–51
  and German withdrawal 622
  and incorporation into Soviet Union 89
  and Molotov–Ribbentrop Pact (1939) 56
  and NKVD 622–3
  and Soviet reoccupation of 622–3
    resistance to 623
  and Soviet–Estonian Pact on Mutual Cooperation (1939) 67
  and uprising against Soviets 197, 198
ethnic minorities
  and deportations 492, 505
  and ethnic minority Germans
    Leningrad 358–9

ethnic minorities (*cont.*)
    resettlement of 284–6
European Advisory Commission 671
Evacuation Soviet 220

Federal Republic of Germany 671
Feodosiya 448
Ferch, General Friedrich 389
Fibikh-Savchenko-Petrovskaya, Aleksandra 298
Filipkowski, Wladysllaw 617
'final solution' 2–3
Finland
    and Molotov–Ribbentrop Pact (1939) 56
    and Operation Barbarossa 182–3, 268–9
    and Soviet demands on 70
    and strategic importance of 69
    see also Soviet–Finnish war (1939–40)
Finnish army
    and 6th Division 268–9
    and III Corps 269
    and Karelian Army 182
    and Operation Barbarossa 182–3
    and South-Eastern Army 182
fire service 280
First World War, and industrial mobilization 32
Fitin, Pavel 570
Flërov, Georgiy 483
Forest Brother units 197, 250, 623
fortified regions 106
Fox, Captain John 416–17
France
    and defeat of 99, 100
    and Soviet Union 50
Franco, Francisco 45
Frederick I 'Barbarossa' 126
Frunze, Mikhail Vasilevich 32–3
Fuchs, Klaus 484

Gavrilov, Major Pëtr 185–7
Gehlen, Lt Col. Reinhard 451, 455, 492
generalship, and Soviet Union 5
Geneva Convention (1929) 16, 20, 22, 23, 65
    and Soviet failure to sign 20–1
Geneva Protocol on chemical and bacteriological
    warfare (1925) 20, 21, 264, 265–6, 462

GERMAN ARMY
    and assessment of Soviet reserves 492
    and deployment of forces 179–83
    and equipment 565
    and Finnish Front 182–3
    and infantry 169–72
    and limitation of military jurisdiction 24
    and Order of Battle 169, 170–1
    and strength of 172, 278, 301
    and supply problems 245, 256, 267, 279

'culminating point' 305, 318
and tanks 169
Army Groups
Army Group A 500
    Operation Edelweiss 501, 503–7
    Stalingrad 501
Army Group B 500
    Stalingrad 507
Army Group Centre
    Bialystok pocket 190–1, 240
    destruction of 613–16
    frontier battles (June/July 1941) 189–93
    Kursk 578
    losses 278
    Moscow 271, 313–17
    Moscow, Soviet counteroffensive 324–35,
        339–40
    Operation Barbarossa 122, 124–5, 179–81,
        187, 190–1, 240
    Operation Typhoon 272, 277, 301–2
    ordered on defence 245
    Rzhev-Vyaz'ma Strategic Offensive 342–4,
        345–7
Army Group Courland 624, 635, 650
Army Group Don 533, 539
Army Group East 127
Army Group North
    Courland peninsula 624
    frontier battles (June/July 1941) 193–8
    Leningrad 252–3, 256, 364–6, 367, 390
    Leningrad–Novgorod Offensive 404–6
    Operation Barbarossa 122, 124, 125, 181–2,
        251
    Sinyavino Operation 386–8
    Volkhov Offensive 382–6
Army Group Serbia 631
Army Group South
    Crimea 263, 266–7
    frontier battles (June/July 1941) 198–205,
        257
    Kursk 578
    Odessa 262–3
    Operation Barbarossa 122, 125, 181
    Operation Blau 498–9
    Operation Fridericus 451–5
    operational pause 267
Army Group South Ukraine 607, 619–21
Army Group Vistula 654
Armies
First Panzer Army 500
    Khar'kov 556–7
    Korsun-Shevchenkovskiy salient 606
    Operation Edelweiss 504, 505
Second Army 326, 330
Third Panzer Army 615
Fourth Army 179, 541, 615

Fourth Panzer Army 500
  Khar'kov 556–7
  Kursk 580, 582
  Operation Edelweiss 504, 505
  Stalingrad 507, 536
Sixth Army 181, 267
  air supply of 536, 537
  attempted relief of 537–9
  capture of Paulus 549–50
  encirclement of 532–7
  Operation Fridericus 453
  Soviet ultimatum to 547
  Stalingrad 507
  surrender 550
Eighth Army 606
Ninth Army 179, 541
  battle for Berlin 651, 654, 655, 657–8
  Battle of Moscow 326
  destruction of 614, 615
  Kursk 578, 580
  Rzhev-Vyaz'ma Strategic Offensive 342
Eleventh Army 181, 205, 392
  Crimea 266–7
  Kerch' peninsula 456–7
  Leningrad 386
  Odessa 263
  Sevastopol 459, 460, 464–5
  Uman' pocket 257
Twelfth Army 658
Sixteenth Army 182
Seventeenth Army 181, 267
  Operation Blau 500
  Operation Edelweiss 504, 505, 506
  Operation Fridericus 453
  Uman' pocket 257
Eighteenth Army 182
  Baltic States 253
  Operation Spark 394
  Volkhov Offensive 382
Panzer groups
First Panzer Group 181
  frontier battles (June/July 1941) 199, 202,
    257
  Kiev pocket 260
  Uman' pocket 257
Second Panzer Group 179, 271
  Battle of Moscow 326
  Battle of Smolensk 240, 243, 246
  frontier battles (June/July 1941) 190, 191,
    192, 193
  Kiev pocket 259–60
  Operation Typhoon 272, 305
Third Panzer Group 179, 245
  Battle of Moscow 313–15, 326, 327, 328–9,
    333, 339
  Battle of Smolensk 240, 243

  frontier battles (June/July 1941) 190, 191,
    192, 193
  Operation Typhoon 272
  Rzhev-Vyaz'ma Strategic Offensive 342, 345
  Vyaz'ma encirclement 273
Fourth Panzer Group 182
  Battle of Moscow 315, 317–18, 326, 328–9,
    333, 339
  Leningrad 256
  Operation Typhoon 272, 307
  Vyaz'ma encirclement 273
Corps
  II SS Panzer Corps 582, 583
  III Panzer Corps 267, 582
  XXIV Panzer Corps 277
  XXX Corps 460
  XXXVI Army Corps 182, 268–9
  XXXIX Panzer Corps 240
  XLI Motorized Corps 195–6
  XLI Panzer Corps 256
  XXXXI Motorized Corps 251
  XXXXVII Panzer Corps 240
  XXXXVIII Panzer Corps 500, 514
  LI Corps 514, 515
  LIV Corps 460
  LXXIX Jäger Corps 506
  Mountain Corps 182, 268
  SS Panzer Corps 556
Divisions
  1st Panzer Division 327
  3rd Motorized Division 251
  3rd Mountain Division 388
  3rd Panzer Division 261
  6th Panzer Division 188
  7th Panzer Division 272
  8th Panzer Division 251
  11th Panzer Division 202
  12th Panzer Division 351
  13th Panzer Division 203
  16th Panzer Division 202
  18th Panzer Division 242
  20th Motorized Division 351
  45th Infantry Division 185, 187
  46th Division 266
  73rd Division 266
  87th Infantry Division 317
  112th Infantry Division 305
  SS *Nordland* Division 268–9
  SS *Totenkopf* (Death's Head) Division 251
Special Forces
  Regiment 800 183–4

German Democratic Republic 671
German navy 178
  and Arctic convoys 427
  and Baltic evacuations 624–5, 626

German–Soviet Treaty on Friendship and the
  Frontier between the USSR and Germany
  (1939) 56–7, 63–6
  and secret protocols of 64–6
Germany
  and allied division of 647, 648, 671
  and de-Nazification 670, 671
  and evacuation of Soviet diplomats/citizens
    211–14
  and German–Soviet collaboration 44
    economic agreement (1940) 95
    economic agreement (1941) 95–6
    four-power pact negotiations 92–5
    German–Soviet Treaty (Sept 1939) 56–7,
      63–6
    Hitler's views 43–4
    military 34, 41
    Molotov–Ribbentrop Pact (1939) 50–7
    Poland 56, 57–9, 62
    raw material supplies 95–7
  and peace-feelers (1943) 576
  and similarities with Soviet Union 42
  and surrender of
    Berlin 667–8
    unconditional 669
Glantz, David 7, 527, 528, 543
Goebbels, Joseph 465, 667, 668
'golden bridge' 644
Golikov, Fillip Ivanovich 218, 500
  and Allied aid 420
  and Battle of Moscow 326, 333
  and German military preparations 141–2, 143,
    149–50
  and mission to UK 237, 411
Goloshchekin, Filipp 299
Golovanov, Ivan 397, 399
Gorbachëv, Mikhail 9, 56
Gordov, General Vasiliy 501
Göring, Hermann 134, 140, 253, 456
Gorodetsky, Gabriel 103, 116, 144, 147–8
Govorov, General Leonid 311, 312
  and Leningrad 389
    Leningrad–Novgorod Offensive 405
    Operation Spark 394–5
  and Sinyavino Operation 386–8
Great Patriotic War
  and brutality of 16, 30
  and comparison with Patriotic War of 1812 3
  and demographic impact of 7–13
  and economic impact of 13–14
  and historiography of 6–7
  and inevitability of 40–1
  and post-war legacy of 5–6, 684–5
  and scale of 2, 16
    territorial 164, 166–8
Grechikhin, Vasiliy 339

Greece 131
  and Churchill–Stalin discussions (1944) 627–8
  and German invasion 132
  and Italian attack on 122
Grigor'ev, Major-General Andrey 191
Grodno 190
gross domestic product (GDP), and Allied-Axis
  ratios 468–70
Grossman, Vasiliy 612, 638, 639, 660, 670
GRU (Main Intelligence Directorate of the Red
  Army) 236
  and German military preparations 136, 141–2,
    143, 145, 149–50
Guderian, Heinz 59, 159, 190, 191, 192
  and Battle of Moscow 331–2
  and Battle of Smolensk (July–Sept 1941) 240,
    243, 244
  and Kiev pocket 259–60
  and Operation Typhoon 272, 277
  on 'Timoshenko' offensive 242
  and Vistula–Oder offensive 642
Guernica 45
guerrilla movements, and Estonia 250–1
Guidelines for the Behaviour of the Fighting Forces
  in Russia 25
Guidelines on the Treatment of Political
  Commisars 25–6
  and protests against 26–7
GULag 37, 138
  as source of manpower 490
  and Soviet prisoners of war 22, 684
Gumbinnen 634
Gustloff, Wilhelm 625

Hague Conventions (1907) 16, 20, 21, 22, 24,
  218
Halder, Colonel-General Franz 27, 118, 342
  and assessment of Soviet intent 113, 116
  and Crimea 266–7
  on Leningrad 256
  and Operation Blau 503
  and Operation Typhoon 302
  and planning of Barbarossa 119, 120, 121,
    122, 125, 169
  and progress of invasion 239
  and underestimation of Soviet forces 245
Hamilton, Duke of 133
Hankey, Lord 481
Hanko peninsula 70, 78
Harnack, Arvid ('Corsican') 137, 140, 146
Harriman, Averill 3, 21, 265, 420, 430, 431, 627,
  640, 649
Harris, Air Chief Marshal Sir Arthur 4
Harrison, Mark 468, 470, 472
Haushofer, Karl 44, 133
heartland 44

'hedgehogs' 447
Heinrici, General Gotthard 654, 655, 657
Hess, Rudolf 44, 100
 and flight to United Kingdom 133–4
Hilger, Gustav 159
Himmler, Heinrich, and partisans 479–80
Hinds, Brig.-Gen. Sidney R 654
Hiroshima 19
Hitler, Adolf
 and assasination attempt 615
 and authorizes withdrawal to 'K' line 347
 and Battle of Moscow 330
  forbids withdrawal 331–2, 335, 339
 and Berlin offensive 662
 and biological weapons 545
 and Caucasus/Caspian oilfields 497
 and concentration on south 447, 448
 and declares war against USA 328
 and final public appearance 650, 659
 and four-power pact negotiations 92–3
 on German–Soviet alliance 43–4
 and ideological war 24
 and Kursk 577–8
  halts offensive 586–7
 and *Lebensraum* 44
 and Leningrad 354
 and Molotov–Ribbentrop Pact (1939) 50–4
 and Munich agreement 47
 and Operation Bagration 614, 615
 and Operation Barbarossa 239–40
  assessment of Red Army 152
  changes in objectives 251, 256–7, 270
  Führer directives 244–5, 251
  planning of 119–26
  use of air power 253
 and Operation Blau 448, 499–500
  changes in objectives 501–3
 and Operation Typhoon 270, 278, 303
 and partisans 479, 480
 and possible Allied landing in France 503,
  601
 and Soviet Union
  decision to attack 118–19, 155
  determination to destroy 94
  motives for attack on 99–100
 and Stalin
  respect for 43
  similarities with 42–3
 and Stalingrad 516, 533, 539
 and suicide of 667
 and treatment of conquered territory 24
 and Vistula–Oder offensive 642
 and war of extermination 27
Hoepner, Field Marshal Erich 256, 307
 and Battle of Moscow 317–18, 329–30, 339
 and Rzhev-Vyaz'ma Strategic Offensive 342

Hollidt, Major-General Karl 116
Holocaust 2–3
Hopkins, Harry L 411, 425, 428
Hoth, Colonel-General Herman 190, 192
 and Battle of Smolensk (July–Sept 1941) 242,
  243
 and Kursk 580, 582
 and Operation Edelweiss 505
 and Stalingrad 507
Hull, Cordell 21, 133, 420, 436
Hungarian army 556
Hungary
 and Churchill–Stalin discussions (1944)
  627–8
 and joins Axis powers 129
 and Soviet atrocities 639
 and Soviet conquest of 631–3

Ibarruri, Dolores 45
Inber, Vera 353, 406
industrial mobilization
 and armaments industry 34–5
 and Frunze reforms (1924–25) 32–3
 and industrialization 33
 and total war 31–2
 and Tukhachevskiy on 36–7
industry
 and destruction of 286
 and evacuation of 208, 214, 220–1, 233, 382,
  473
intelligence services
 and Kursk 569–73
 and role of 30
 and signals intelligence 571–3
 see also British Intelligence; GRU (Main
  Intelligence Directorate of the Red
  Army); NKGB (People's Commissariat
  for State Security); NKVD (People's
  Commissariat for Internal Affairs)
internal security, and Soviet Union
 and confiscation of radios 216–17
 and 'destroyer battalions' 36, 217
 and initial measures of 215–16, 219
 and inter-agency cooperation 217–18
 and Leningrad 362–3
 and liberated territories 335–7
 see also NKGB; NKVD
international law
 and diplomats 31
 and prisoners of war 20, 22, 23, 218–19
 and warfare 18, 20–1
Ioffe, Abram 484
Iran 422, 438
Iraq 422
Isakov, Admiral Ivan 81, 361–2
Italian army 556

Italy 435
    and invasion of 586–7
    and Second World War 3–4
Iz'yum bulge 450, 451

Jaik, Juhan 197
Japan
    and Cairo ('Sextant') conference 436
    and Khalkin Gol 83–4
    and Lake Khasan 82–3
    and Pearl Harbor 328
    and Second World War 4
    and Soviet Union 308–9
        Manchurian offensive 676–81
    and surrender of 681
    and Tehran ('Eureka') conference 437, 601
Jeschonnek, General Hans 120, 536
jet aircraft 484–5
Jodl, General Alfred 118, 331
    and planning of Barbarossa 119, 123–4
Joint Intelligence Committee (UK), and German
    intentions (1940) 101
Joyce, William 217
Junkers aircraft company 34
Jupiter, Operation 528

Kaftanov, Sergei 482–3, 484
Kaganovich, Lazar 208, 214, 220, 226, 229
Kalashnikov, Mikhail 485
Kalinin, and defence of Moscow 292, 306
Kamenev, Lev 298
Kameneva, Olga 298
Kapitsa, Peter 483, 484
Katyn massacre 87–8, 576
Katyusha 242–3
    and Stalingrad 518
Keitel, Field Marshal Wilhelm 667
    and Kursk 595
    and planning of Barbarossa 119
    and treatment of prisoners 27
Kerch' peninsula 457, 607
    and German offensive (Operation Bustard)
        456–7
    and Kerch'-Feodosiya landings 447–8
Kesselring, Field Marshal Albert 240
    and Operation Barbarossa 179, 246
Keynes, John Maynard 439
Khaldei, Yevgeniy 666–7, 673
Khalkin Gol 70, 83–4, 234, 309
    and casualties 83
    and lessons learned 83–4
Khar'kov 267
    and German counterstroke 556–7
    and German withdrawal 556
    and Kursk counteroffensive 593
Khar'kov offensive 450–4, 457

Kharlamov, Rear-Admiral Nikolay 237
Khasan, Lake 82–3
Kherson 263
Khozin, Lt Gen. Mikhail 361, 384
Khrulev, Andrey 527–8
Khrushchev, Nikita 7, 134, 153, 201, 214, 236,
        260–1, 451
Kiev 202, 259
    and encirclement of Soviet forces 259–60
    and execution of Jews by Germans 37–8, 262
    and executions by Soviets in 37–8
    and fire in 262
    and recapture of 597
    and withdrawal from 260–1
Kiev Operation 597
Kinzel, Colonel Eberhard 153
Kirhensteins, Augusts 89
Kirkenes 151
Kirponos, Colonel-General Mikhail 181, 184
    and counterstrokes 257
    and defence of Dnepr/Kiev 259
    and frontier battles (June/July 1941) 198, 199,
        201, 202, 203
    and withdrawal from Kiev 261
Kiryukhin, Major-General Nikolay 91
Kleist, Colonel-General Ewald 260
    and frontier battles (June/July 1941) 199, 202
    and Operation Edelweiss 504
    and Operation Fridericus 453, 454
    and Ukraine 257
Kliewe, H 545, 546
Klimovskikh, Major-General Vladimir 191, 192
Kluge, Field Marshal Günther von 192, 330, 332,
        342, 578
Kobulov, Amayak ('Zakhar') 146, 147
Koden 184
Kollontai, Aleksandra 86
Komorowski, Tadeusz 618
Koniev, Lt Gen. Ivan 199, 273, 275, 569, 635
    and Battle of Moscow 333
    and Battle of Smolensk (July–Sept 1941)
        240–2
    and Berlin offensive 650–1, 655–6, 657, 658,
        659
    and Korsun-Shevchenkovskiy salient 606
    and Kursk counteroffensive 593
    and Vistula–Oder offensive 641, 642, 644, 645
Kopelev, Lev 639
Korobkov, Major-General Aleksandr 191
Korpik, Wilhelm 156
Korsun-Shevchenkovskiy salient 603–6
Kostesnitsyn, Aleksey 520
Kosygin, Aleksey 220
Kotlyar, Major-General L Z 281
Kovshova, Natalya 489
Kozel'sk prisoner camp 87

Kozhedub, Ivan 581
Krebs, General Hans 657, 667
Kripens, Colonel Arvis 196
Krivosheyev, Colonel-General G F 9, 543
Krivosheyn, Semyon 59
Kronshtadt 386
Krupp, Gustav 96
Krzyzanowski, Aleksandr 617
Kuechler, Colonel-General Georg 404
Kulik, Gennady 74, 235
Kulik, Marshal Grigoriy 365, 366
Kurchatov, Igor 484
Kurganov, O 315
Kurile islands 2
Kurlykin, Kombrig Arseniy 363
Kursk 556, 560
Kursk, Battle of
    and German offensive 580–1
        halted by Hitler 586–7
        objectives of 563, 576–7
        preparations for 562, 575
    and Kursk salient 557–60
        features of 560–2
    and partisans 574
        'rail war' 587–91
    and Prokhorovka tank battle 582–6
    and Red Army
        artillery counter-preparation 579–80
        construction of defences 566–8
        counteroffensives 591–3
        defensive strategy 565, 566
        intelligence on German plans 569–73
        reserve front 568–9
        Soviet air force 581
        transport problems 568
    and significance of 594–5
Kutuzov, Operation 591
Kuybyshev (Samara) 296–7
    and evacuation to 289–90, 296, 299
    and execution of prisoners 298–9
    as reserve capital 283–4
Kuznetsov, Admiral Nikolay 158, 160, 214,
        237–8, 410, 417
    and Allied aid 420
    and membership of Stavka 215
Kuznetsov, Aleksey A 361
Kuznetsov, Colonel-General Fëdor 182
    and proposed use of mustard gas 264, 265
Kuznetsov, Lt Gen. Vasiliy 28, 320
Kuznetsov, N I 571
Kwantung Army, and Soviet Manchurian
        offensive 676–81

Lagunov, Lt Gen F N 374
Lake Khasan 82–3
    and lessons learned 83

Lake Ladoga 371–2, 374–5, 390, 391
Latvia
    and arrests/deportations 150, 196
    and incorporation into Soviet Union 88–9
    and Molotov–Ribbentrop Pact (1939) 56
    and Soviet demand for military facilities 67
    and Soviet reoccupation of 623
    and uprising against Soviets 196–7
Lebensraum 44
Leeb, Field Marshal Ritter von 181–2
    and Battle of Moscow 330
    and frontier battles (June/July 1941) 193
    and Leningrad 251–2, 367, 369
Legkoshur, Fëdor 673
Lelyushenko, Dmitry 326, 669
Leningrad 251, 253–6
    and breaking of siege 396, 406
    and children 372–3
    and counterattacks 364–6, 367–70
        Leningrad–Novgorod Offensive 404–8
        Operation Polar Star 401–2
        Operation Spark 392–6
        Sinyavino Operation 386–8
        Volkhov Offensive 382–6
    and deaths 381
    and defence of 362
    and deserters 363
    and evacuation of ethnic Germans/Finns
        358–9
    and evacuations from 372, 390
    and food supplies 369, 375–6
        animals 379
        cannibalism 379–80
        German attacks on 359
        increased rations 397
        production of 377
        rationing of 359, 375, 378
        second winter 391
        troops 377–8
    and German army
        advance of 252–3
        attacks by 364–6, 390
        communication problems 370–1
        encirclement by 351–3, 364
        shelling by 364, 365, 397
    and German policy towards 354–6
    and industrial evacuation 382
    and NKVD 362–3
        search for German spies 397–9
        search for 'Rebel' 380–1, 399–401
    and open city proposal 357
    and population of 353, 381, 390–1
    and Red Banner Baltic Fleet 362, 366
    and Shostakovich's Seventh Leningrad
        Symphony 389–90, 408
    and siege of 256

Leningrad (*cont.*)
  and Stalin 354, 356–7
  and supply routes
    fuel pipeline 391
    Lake Ladoga 371–2, 374–6, 390, 391
    railways 367, 369, 372, 396–7
    'Road of Life' 372–3, 375, 376–7
  and vulnerability of 69
  and water supplies 378
Levitan, Yuri 395–6, 672
Liddell-Hart, Basil 80
Liskow, Corporal Alfred 156, 157
Lithuania
  and arrests/deportations 150
  and German invasion 188, 194
  and German-Soviet Treaty (Sept 1939) 56–7,
    64–5
  and incorporation into Soviet Union 89
  and Molotov–Ribbentrop Pact (1939) 56
  and Soviet demand for military facilities 67
  and Soviet reoccupation of 623–4
  and uprising against Soviets 194–5
Lithuanian Activist Front (LAF) 194–5
Litvak, Lidiya 489
Lloyd George, David 414
Lower Dnepr offensive 600
'Lucy' spy ring 570–1
Ludendorff, Field Marshal Erich von, and total
    war 32
Luftwaffe
  and air attacks on Moscow 246
  and attacks on United Kingdom 172
  and limited range of 173
  and Operation Bagration 614
  and Operation Barbarossa 120, 179, 187
    attacks on Soviet aircraft 158
    Baltic States 252–3
    Battle of Smolensk 243–4
    Bialystok pocket 190–1
    encirclement battles 276
    ground support 240
    Kiev 261
    preparations for 151
  and pre-Barbarossa losses 172–3
  and Stalingrad 516, 517
    air supply of Sixth Army 536, 537
  and strength of 172
  and Uman' pocket 257
Lutzov (cruiser) 96
Luzhkov, Sergey ('Rebel') 400–1
  and search for 380–1, 399–400, 408
L'vov–Sandomir offensive 619
Lwów (L'viv) 617
  and Polish surrender 62
  and recapture of 619

MacArthur, Douglas 682
Macfarlane, Lt Gen. Noel Mason 410
Mackinder, Halford 44
Maclean, Donald 675
Magenheimer, Heinz 115–16, 117, 144
Main Intelligence Directorate of the Red Army
    (GRU) *see* GRU
Maisky, Ivan 47, 151, 210, 410, 424
Malenkov, Georgiy 157, 208, 229
Manchuria, and Soviet offensive 2, 19, 676–81
Manhattan Project 426, 435, 482
Mannerheim Line 71, 74, 75, 76, 81
manoeuvre, and warfare 81, 340–1
Manstein, Erich von 386, 392, 465, 533
  and encirclement of Sixth Army 535, 536, 547
    attempted relief of 537–9
  and Kerch' peninsula 456
  and Khar'kov 556–7
  and Kursk 578
  and Sevastopol 459, 460
Mao Tse Tung 676
Marcks, Major-General Erick 112, 118, 153
  and planning of Barbarossa 120–1, 168–9
Marinesco, Aleksandr 625, 626
Mars, Operation (Rzhev–Sychevka
    counteroffensive) 7, 528, 529–31, 541–3
Marshall, General George C 425
Mekhlis, Lev 110
  and defensive fortifications 81
  on eve of war 157
  and Kerch' peninsula 457
  and Soviet–Finnish war 74, 76, 77
memorials, and Great Patriotic War 15
Menzies, Major-General Sir Stewart 130
Meretskov, Kirill 85, 106, 330, 384, 386
  and Sinyavino Operation 388
  and Soviet–Finnish war 71, 74, 75, 81
  and Tikhvin 369
  and Volkhov Offensive 382, 385
Merkulov, Vsevolod 61, 66, 139, 141, 214, 356
  and German military preparations 142–3
  and Leningrad 358, 363
Mertsalov, Andrei 118
Mikhaidin, Major-General Ivan 192
Mikhalev, S N 114
Mikolajczyk, Stanisllaw 618, 619, 627
Mikoyan, Anastas 220, 225–6, 227–8, 229
  and Allied aid 419–20, 421
Mikoyan, Artem 140, 153, 208
Mikoyan, Stepan 442
militia units (Soviet Union)
Minsk
  and fall of 225
  and Soviet recapture of 615
mission command 77, 80, 84
  and Kursk 579

mobile groups
    and Battle of Moscow 334–5
    and use of mobile formations 491
Model, General Walter 342, 406–7, 614–15
    and Kursk 578, 580, 591
Mokrinskiy, Mikhail 339
Moldavian Soviet Socialist Republic, and creation
        of 91–2
Moldova
    and frontier battles (June/July 1941) 205
    and Yassy–Kishinev offensive 619–21
Molotov, Vyacheslav M 111, 214, 229, 275, 429
    and Allied aid 420
    and Anglo-Soviet agreement 410
    and announcement of war 209
    on eve of war 154, 157
    and Foreign Ministers' conference (1943) 436
    and four-power pact negotiations 92–4
    and German-Soviet Treaty (Sept 1939) 65
    and membership of Stavka 215, 235
    and Molotov–Ribbentrop Pact (1939) 50–4
    and nuclear weapons 675
    and Poland 57–8
    and response to German attack 160
    and Romania 90
    and Soviet–Finnish war 78
    and TASS 282–3
    and United Kingdom 425
Molotov Line 144
Molotov–Ribbentrop Pact (1939)
    and confusion caused by 111
    and negotiation of 50–4
    and Poland 56
    and provisions of 54–6
    and secret protocols of 56–7
Montgomery, Field Marshal Bernard 674
Moscow 280
    and air attacks on 246
    and declared under siege 294
    and defence of 277, 292–3, 306–7
        air defence 282
        anti-aircraft forces 282
        Camouflage Service 281
        construction of defences 287–8
        defence lines 306
        'destroyer battalions' 281–2, 293–4
        destruction of enterprises 286
        forces available 305
        Mozhaysk Defence Line 282, 288
        NKVD 293
        preparations for 280–4
        public order 294–5
        Red Army reinforcements 309–11
    and ethnic minority Germans 285–6
    and evacuation of 288, 289–91
    and fire service 280

    and German offensive against 270–1, 272
    and Local Air Defence Service (MPVO) 280–1
    and looting 290
    and panic in 289–90, 295
    and Red Square parade 303–4
    and Soviet fear of second attack 497, 498
    and victory parade 672–4
    see also Moscow, Battle of; Typhoon,
        Operation
Moscow, Battle of 350
    and German army
        'culminating point' 318
        first defeat on land 347–8
        Hitler forbids withdrawal 331–2, 335, 339
        limit of advance 318
        loss of combat power 317–18
        offensive by 313–17
        withdrawals 327, 328–9
    and Red Army
        counteroffensive first phase 324–8, 329–31
        counteroffensive planning 320–1
        counteroffensive second phase 332–5,
            339–40
        creation of reserve armies 318–20
        mobile groups 334–5
    and weather 313, 316, 317, 322–4, 340
        equipment failure 323–4
Moscow Local Air Defence Service (MPVO)
        280–1
Moskalenko, Kirill 450, 513
motti battle 75, 719n.
Mozhaysk Defence Line 282, 286, 288, 306
Mtsensk 277
Müller, Lt Gen. Eugen 24
Munich agreement (1938) 46–7, 51
Murmansk 182, 268–9
Mussolini, Benito 45, 122, 155, 435
mustard gas 264
    see also chemical weapons
Muzychenko, Lt Gen. Ivan N 162, 203, 257, 259

Nagasaki 19
Nameless 297–8
Napoleon 3, 11
Narodny Kommissariat Vnutrennykh Del, see
        NKVD
National Committee of the Republic of Estonia
        (EVRK) 623
national treasures, and evacuation of 223
navies, see German navy; Soviet navy
Nazi–Soviet Pact (1939), see Molotov–Ribbentrop
        Pact (1939)
Nesterenko, Mariya 298
Nikishev, D 76
Nikolayev 263
Nikonovaya, Vera 522

NKGB (People's Commissariat for State Security)
and action against insurgent elements 150
and amalgamation with NKVD 236
and German military preparations 137,
139–40, 142–3, 144, 146–7, 149
and Hess affair 134
and internal security measures 215–16, 219
and response to Stalin's speech (July 1941)
232–3
and responsibilities of 138
NKPS (People's Commissariat for
Communications) 216, 234
NKVD (People's Commissariat for Internal
Affairs) 7
and action against insurgent elements 150
and Caucasus 505, 506
and defence of Moscow 292–3
and Estonia 622–3
and ethnic minority Germans 285
and evacuation from Moscow 283
and evacuation of state archives 233–4
and execution of prisoners 298–9
and executions at outbreak of war 37
and forces of 185
1st NKVD Division 674
1st NKVD Rifle Division 365
2nd NKVD Motor-Rifle Division 293
4th NKVD Rifle Division 624
9th Dzerzhinskiy Division 293
10th NKVD Division 519–20
308th Rifle Regiment 293
'destroyer battalions' 36, 217, 293–4, 478–9
Moscow Motor-Rifle Destroyer Regiment
293
and German military preparations 136–7, 149
and German use of children 247
and internal security measures 215–16, 219
and invasion of Poland 59–61, 66
and Kursk 570
and Lake Khasan 82–3
and Latvia 623
and Leningrad 362–3
search for German spies 397–9
search for 'Rebel' 380–1, 399–401, 408
and liberated territories 335–7
and Lithuania 623–4
and nuclear weapons project 483–4
and partisans 339
and prisoners of war 218–19
and reorganization of 137–8
and responsibilities of 37, 138
and reunification of 236
and role of 686
and Romania 91
and Stalingrad 519–20
and strength of 554

and treatment of prisoners 29–30
Katyn massacre 87–8
Norway 86
Novgorod 253
Novikov, General Aleksandr 517
Novorossiysk 506, 607
nuclear weapons 674–5
and Soviet intelligence on 481–4, 675
and Soviet work on 481, 484

Oder Quadrilateral 644–5
Odessa 89–90
and defence/evacuation of 262–3
Odessa Defensive Region 263
Ogryzko, Vladimir 295
oil
and Caucasus 497
and German requirements 95
OKH (German Army High Command)
and assessment of Soviet forces 153
and capture of headquarters 658
and control of Barbarossa 127
and Kursk 577
and Moscow 278
OKW (German Armed Forces High Command)
127
and Leningrad 351, 354–5
Orël
and Kursk counteroffensive 591
and Soviet offensive 563–4
Orël, N G 578–9
Organization of Ukrainian Nationalists (OUN)
201
Orsha 242, 608
Ortenberg, David 231
Osipenko, Polina 487
Ostashkov prisoner camp 87
Overlord, Operation 435, 612
and Tehran conference (1943) 601
see also second front

Pabst, Herbert 518–19
Panfilov, Major-General Ivan Vasilevich 307
'Panfilovtsy', and myth of 307–8
panic
and Moscow 289–90, 295
and Red Army 203–4
Panteleyev, Rear-Admiral Yuri 362
partisans 478–81
and Battle of Moscow 337–9
and deployment of 268
and 'destroyer battalions' 478–9
and German campaign against 479–81
and growing significance of 573–4
and impact of 239
and Kursk 574

'rail war' 587–91
and Operation Bagration 612–13
and Organization of Ukrainian Nationalists
    201
and Rzhev-Vyaz'ma Strategic Offensive 344
and Soviet organization of 479, 574
and Stalin's call for creation of 231
and Stavka 230
and Ukraine 267–8
Patriotic War of 1812 3, 17
Paulus, Lt Gen., later Field Marshal Friedrich
    535–6
and planning of Barbarossa 121–2
and Stalingrad 507, 527, 539, 547–9
captured at 549–50
Pavlichenko, Lyudmila 489, 523
Pavlov, Army-General Dmitry 181
and arrest and execution 191–2
and frontier battles (June/July 1941) 190, 191
Pavlov, Dmitry (Leningrad's food chief) 359, 369
Pavlov, Jakob 516
Pearl Harbor 328
penal battalions 320
Pennington, Reina 684
People's Commissariat for Defence (GKO), see
    State Defence Committee (GKO)
People's Commissariat for Internal Affairs, see
    NKVD
People's Commissariat for State Security, see
    NKGB
People's Defence Commissariat (NKO) 282
and Directive No. 2 207–8
and Directive No. 3 188, 199, 200–1
People's Militia 232
Pervukhin, M G 220
Petrzhak, Konstantin 483
Petsamo (Pechenga) 78
pincer movement
and defensive pincer 384, 388
    Operation Fridericus 451–5
and Leningrad 358, 365
and Operation Typhoon 271
and Operation Uranus 532–7
Pisarenko, Ol'ga 376
plague 545–6
Platinum Fox, Operation 268–9
Pleshakov, Constantine 117–18, 200
Plesners, Colonel Alexander 197
Pliev, Issa 613, 614, 679–80
Poland
and Churchill–Stalin discussions 627
and Committee of National Liberation 617
and German invasion 3, 57
and German–Soviet partition of 63–6
and Molotov–Ribbentrop Pact (1939) 56
and Soviet offensive 57–9

assessment of Red Army 62–3, 67–8
NKVD operations 59–61, 66
prisoners of war 61–2, 65, 87–8
and Soviet Union's post-war aims 616, 619
and Vistula–Oder offensive 641–2, 643–5
and Warsaw uprising 617–19
and Yalta conference 647
Polish Home Army (AK) 616–17, 618
Polivanova, Mariya 489
Popel, Nikolay 162–3, 176
Popov, Lt Gen. Markian 183
Portal, Sir Charles 237
Potsdam conference 438, 672, 674–5
Pound, Admiral Sir Dudley 411, 414, 427
Powell, Lt Cdr John 416
Pownall, Lt Gen. Sir Henry 409
Prague 669
pre-emptive war hypothesis, and Operation
    Barbarossa 101–18
assessment of 115–18
circumstantial evidence 110–15
covert Soviet mobilization 113–15
German assessment of Soviet intent 112–13,
    116
Soviet war plans 104–10
preventive war 102
Pripyet marshes 168
and planning of Barbarossa 121
prisoners of war
and German treatment of
    Führer decree (1941) 23–5
    German protests against 26–7
    German troops 22
    Guidelines for the Behaviour of the Fighting
        Forces in Russia 25
    Guidelines on the Treatment of Political
        Commisars 25–7
    logistical problems 23
    numbers of prisoners 23
    recruitment of 337, 385–6
and international law 20, 22, 23
and Soviet treatment of 28–30, 218–19
    execution 28
    international law 20–1
    murder 29
    Polish 61–2, 65, 87–8
    Soviet troops 21–2, 683–4
Prokhorovka 582–6
public opinion
and response to Stalin's speech (July 1941)
    232–3
and response to war 216
Pugachëv, Colonel Grigory 237
punishment battalions and companies 477–8
Putin, Vladimir 98, 354
Pytkina, Zinaida 30

Quebec conference ('Octagon') 438
Quebec conference ('Quadrant') 435

rabies 1
radio communication 79
Raeder, Grand-Admiral Erich 118, 119, 178
'rail war', and pro-Soviet partisans 587–91
railways 164–5, 267
    and German attack on Murmansk route
        268–9
    and Leningrad 367, 369, 372, 396–7
    and planning of Barbarossa 169
    and scarcity of 166
Rank insignia 778n.
Rapallo, Treaty of (1922) 41
rape, and Red Army 660
Raskova, Marina 487, 488
raw materials, and Soviet supplies to Germany
    95–7
Raymond, Ellsworth Lester 296, 297–8
'Rebel' (Sergey Luzhkov) 380–1, 399–401, 408
reconnaissance flights, German 141, 144

RED ARMY
    and artillery strength 176–7
    and assessment of
        British Intelligence 67–8, 492–6
        German Intelligence 152, 492
        Hitler 152
        invasion of Poland 62–3
        Soviet–Finnish war 80
    and 'blocking detachments' 203, 260, 271, 478
        Stalingrad 519–20
    and conscription 490
    creation and re-formation of armies 310
    and demobilization 682–3, 684
    and deployment of forces 179–83
    and equipment 565–6, 603
    and eve of war orders 157–8
    and expansion of 309–10
    and initial deployment of 175–6
    and military doctrine 102, 110
    and mobilization of, covert 113–15
    and organization of 175
        changes in 248–9
        Representatives of the Stavka 574–5
        Strategic Directions 234–6
    and panic among 203–4
    and punishment battalions/companies 477–8
    and purge of senior officers (1937) 46, 109–10
    and rebuilding of (1942) 490–1
    and reforms of 84–5
        discipline 85
        officer training 79–80
        ranks and titles 85
        tank armies 602–3

    uniforms 554–5
    unitary command 86
    and reinforcements 309–11
    and revenge as duty 638–9
    and strength of 175, 278–9, 554
    and trials/executions of officers 191–2, 259
    and unpreparedness of 162, 176, 200
    and use of mobile formations 491
Theatre Commands
    Far East Command 679
Fronts
    Belorussian Front 58, 62
    Bryansk Front 246, 271, 277, 500, 556
        Battle of Moscow 324
        Kursk counteroffensive 591
        Operation Typhoon 272
    Central Front
        Battle of the Dnepr 596–7
        Kursk 563, 566, 568, 575
        Kursk counteroffensive 591
        Orël offensive 563–4
    Don Front 540
    First Baltic Front 621, 645
    First Belorussian Front 615, 635
        Berlin offensive 650–1, 654–7, 662
        Vistula–Oder offensive 641, 644–5
    First Far Eastern Front 678, 680
    First Ukrainian Front 617, 633, 635
        Berlin offensive 650–1, 655–7, 659
        Korsun-Shevchenkovskiy salient 603–6
        L'vov–Sandomir offensive 619
        Vistula–Oder offensive 641, 643
    Fourth Belorussian 644
    Fourth Ukrainian Front 600, 607, 633
    Kalinin Front 276
        Battle of Moscow 321, 324
        Rzhev–Vyaz'ma Strategic Offensive 342
    Karelian Front 253
    Leningrad Front 183, 253, 256, 361–2
        Baltic Strategic Offensive Operation 621
        Leningrad–Novgorod Offensive 405–6
        Operation Polar Star 402
        Operation Spark 394–6
    North Caucasus Front 504
    Northern Front 183, 188, 253
    North-West Front 182, 253
        Operation Polar Star 402
        response to Barbarossa 188
        Soviet-Finnish war 77
    Reserve Front 247, 272, 277
    Second Baltic Front 405–6, 621
    Second Belorussian Front 635
        Berlin offensive 657, 659
        East Prussian Operation 645
    Second Far Eastern Front 678, 680
    Second Ukrainian Front 600, 631, 633

Korsun-Shevchenkovskiy salient 603–6
Yassy–Kishinev offensive 619–21
South-Eastern Front 507–10
Southern Front
frontier battles (June/July 1941) 198–205
Operation Blau 500
response to Barbarossa 188
Ukraine 556
South-West Front 113, 181, 184
Barvenkovo-Lozovaya operation 450
Battle of Moscow 321, 324
destruction of 261
encirclement of 259–60
Operation Blau 500
Operation Uranus 532
response to Barbarossa 188
Ukraine 556
Stalingrad Front 501, 507–10, 532
Steppe Front 569, 591, 596
Third Baltic Front 621
Third Belorussian Front 617, 621–2, 635, 645
Third Ukrainian Front 600, 619–21, 631, 633
Trans-Baikal Front 678, 680
Ukrainian Front 58, 61–2
Volkhov Front 366–7
Leningrad–Novgorod Offensive 405–6
Operation Polar Star 402
Operation Spark 394–6
Volkhov Offensive 382–6
Voronezh Front 500
Battle of the Dnepr 597
Kursk salient 563, 566, 568
Ukraine 556, 557
Western Front 113, 179–81, 277
Battle of Moscow 321, 324
Battle of Smolensk 240–8
defence of Moscow 301
frontier battles (June/July 1941) 189–93
general offensive 341
Kursk counteroffensive 591
losses 476
Operation Typhoon 272
reconstitution of 277
response to Barbarossa 188
Rzhev–Vyaz'ma Strategic Offensive 342
Military Districts
Far Eastern Military District 82–3
Leningrad Military District 89
Soviet–Finnish war 70–4, 76
Odessa Military District 91, 181
Pri-Baltic Military District 89
Armies
First Army Group 83–4
First Guards Army 513
First Guards Tank Army 641
First Polish Army 613, 617, 618–19, 641, 642

First Shock Army 320, 327
Second Guards Army 537, 608
Second Guards Tank Army 641
Second Shock Army 382–5, 388, 394, 395, 405
Third Army
frontier battles (June/July 1941) 189, 191
Operation Typhoon 272
Third Guards Tank Army 613, 641, 644, 659
Third Shock Army 342, 665
Operation Mars 541
Vistula–Oder offensive 641
Third Tank Army 656
Fourth Army
frontier battles (June/July 1941) 189, 191
Leningrad 369
Fourth Guards Tank Army 613, 656
Fourth Shock Army 342, 344, 345
Fourth Tank Army 641
Fifth Army 257
defence of Moscow 301
frontier battles (June/July 1941) 199
Manchurian offensive 678
Fifth Guards Tank Army 582–3, 586, 593, 613
Fifth Shock Army 670
Sixth Army
Barvenkovo–Lozovaya operation 450
encirclement 257–9
frontier battles (June/July 1941) 199, 203
Sixth Guards Army 613
Sixth Guards Tank Army 678
Seventh Army 75
Eighth Army 386–8, 654–5
Eighth Guards Army 641, 659
Ninth Army 75–6
Tenth Army
Battle of Moscow 326, 333–4, 339
frontier battles (June/July 1941) 189–90,
191
Twelfth Army 257–9
Thirteenth Army
frontier battles (June/July 1941) 189, 191
Kursk 568, 581
Sixteenth Army
Battle of Moscow 327
Battle of Smolensk 243
defence of Moscow 295–6, 301, 305, 306,
311, 315
frontier battles (June/July 1941) 198–9
Vyaz'ma encirclement 273
Eighteenth Army 205
Nineteenth Army 225
Battle of Smolensk 240–2, 243
frontier battles (June/July 1941) 198–9
Vyaz'ma encirclement 273
Twentieth Army
Battle of Moscow 320

RED ARMY (*cont.*)
    Battle of Smolensk 243
    Operation Mars 541
    Vyaz'ma encirclement 273
Twenty-First Army 225, 549
Twenty-Second Army 225, 240, 246, 541
Twenty-Fourth Army 225, 273
Twenty-Eighth Army 225
Twenty-Ninth Army
    Battle of Moscow 326
    Rzhev-Vyaz'ma Strategic Offensive 347
Thirtieth Army 246, 326, 327
Thirty-First Army 326
Thirty-Second Army 273
Thirty-Third Army 347
Thirty-Eighth Army 450
Thirty-Ninth Army 678
Forty-First Army 541
Forty-Third Army 301
Forty-Eighth Army 351, 568
Forty-Ninth Army 301, 305
Fiftieth Army
    Battle of Moscow 334–5, 339
    Operation Typhoon 272
Fifty-First Army 264, 608
Fifty-Second Army 382, 597
Fifty-Third Army 678
Fifty-Fourth Army 365, 382
Fifty-Fifth Army 402
Fifty-Seventh Army
    Barvenkovo–Lozovaya operation 450
    Operation Ring 540
Fifty-Ninth Army 382
Sixty-Second Army 501
    Operation Ring 540
    Stalingrad 507, 513, 514, 532, 549
Sixty-Third Army 501
Sixty-Fourth Army 501
    Operation Ring 540
    Stalingrad 507, 513
Seventieth Army 568
Corps
    I Guards Rifle Corps 277
    I Mechanized Corps 645
    III Mechanized Corps 195–6
    IV Cavalry Corps 533
    IV Mechanized Corps
        frontier battles (June/July 1941) 199
        Stalingrad counteroffensive 533, 535
    IV Tank Corps 535
    V Mechanized Corps 240
    VI Cavalry Corps 190
    VI Mechanized Corps 190
    VIII Mechanized Corps 240
        Battle of Smolensk 240
        frontier battles (June/July 1941) 199, 201–2

IX Mechanized Corps 199, 202–3
XI Mechanized Corps 190
XV Mechanized Corps 199, 201, 202
XVI Mechanized Corps 199
XIX Mechanized Corps 199, 202
XXII Mechanized Corps 199, 201, 203
XXII Rifle Corps 197
XXIV Mechanized Corps 199
XXIV Tank Corps 541
XXV Tank Corps 541
XXVI Tank Corps 533, 535
XXVII Rifle Corps 203
LXXIX Corps 665
Divisions
    1st Motor-Rifle Division 240
    6th Orël Red Banner Division 185
    10th Rifle Division 364–5
    10th Tank Division 201
    13th Guards Rifle Division 519
    42nd Rifle Division 185
    44th Division Division 75
    50th Cavalry Division 246
    53rd Cavalry Division 246
    84th Rifle Division 518
    99th Rifle Division 518
    150th Rifle Division 665, 666
    163rd Rifle Division 75
    171st Rifle Division 665
    193rd Rifle Division 518
    413th Rifle Division 305

Red Crescent 219
Red Cross 22, 219
Reichstag, and Berlin offensive 662–7
Reindeer, Operation 268
Reinhardt, Colonel-General Hans 329, 330
resettlement, and ethnic minority Germans
    284–6
resources, and warfare 18
revenge, and Berlin offensive 638–9, 660
Ribbentrop, Joachim von 154, 159
    and foreign policy goals 44
    and four-power pact negotiations 92–4
    and German–Soviet collaboration 44, 47
    and German–Soviet Treaty (Sept 1939) 64, 65,
        66
    and invasion of Poland 57
    and Molotov–Ribbentrop Pact (1939) 50–4,
        56
    and opposition to war 39–40
Richthofen, General Freiherr Wolfram von 276,
    517, 532
Ritgen, Colonel Helmuth 188–9
roads
    and bad condition of 267
    and Leningrad 370–1, 372

and planning of Barbarossa 168
and scarcity of 166
Roberts, Frank 682, 683
rocket aircraft 484
rocket launchers 242–3
and Stalingrad 518
Rokossovskiy, Konstantin 85–6
and Battle of Moscow 327
and Battle of Smolensk (July–Sept 1941) 243
and Battle of the Dnepr 596–7
and Berlin offensive 657
and Bryansk Front 500
and criticism of Soviet policy 348–9
and defence of Moscow 295–6, 305, 306, 312, 315
reinforcements 310–11
and deserters 204–5
and East Prussian operation 635
and frontier battles (June/July 1941) 199, 200, 202–3
and Kursk 563, 568
artillery counter-preparation 579–80
counteroffensive 591
headquarters attacked 578–9
and Operation Bagration 610–11, 614
and Orël offensive 563–4
and Representatives of the Stavka 574–5
and Stalingrad counteroffensive 527, 549
Operation Ring 540
and uniform changes 555
and victory parade 672–3, 674
and Vyaz'ma 272–6
and Warsaw uprising 617–18
and Zhukov 311–12
Romania 619
and joins Axis powers 129
and oil fields 95
and Soviet occupation of Bessarabia and Bukovina 90–1
and withdrawal from Axis 621
Romanian army
Fourth Army 181, 263, 532–3
Third Army 181, 532
Rommel, Erwin 601
Roosevelt, Franklin D 419
and aid to Soviet Union 439
and allied conferences 438
Cairo (1943) 436
Casablanca (1943) 434–5
Potsdam (1945) 438
Quebec (1943) 435
Quebec (1944) 438
Tehran (1943) 436–8, 600–1
Washington (1941) 425
Washington (1942) 426
Washington (1943) 435, 576

Yalta (1945) 438, 646–8
and 'Europe first' strategy 425
and nuclear weapons 482
and unconditional surrender 435
Rössler, Rudolf 570
Rostov 501
Rotmistrov, Pavel 582–3
Royal Navy 178
Rozova-Yegorova, Zinaida 298
Rumyantsev, Operation 591–3
Runstedt, Field Marshal Gerd von 601
and frontier battles (June/July 1942 198, 199, 205, 257
and Operation Barbarossa 181
Russian Federation, and demographic impact of Great Patriotic War 12–13
Russian National Liberation Army (KONR) 385, 669
Russo-Finnish War (1939–40) 4
Ryabishev, Lt Gen. Dmitriy 162, 163
and frontier battles (June/July 1941) 201, 202
Rychagev, Pavel 298
Ryti, Risto 78
Rzhev-Sychevka 181
Rzhev-Sychevka offensive (Operation Mars) 527, 529–31, 541–3
Rzhev-Vyaz'ma Strategic Offensive Operation 342–7

Saburov, M Z 220
Sakhalin 676, 681
Salisbury, Harrison 379
San Francisco conference (1945) 647, 649
Saturn, Operation 529
Savchenko, Sergey 336
Savicheva, Tanya 373
Sazonov, F I 385
Schlotterer, Gustav 146
Schmidt, Lt Gen. Arthur 535–6, 549
Schmundt, Major-General Rudolf 331
Schörner, Ferdinand 607, 668
Schulenberg, Count Werner von 50–1, 52, 53, 57–8, 63–4, 90, 104, 139, 155, 159, 160, 207
scorched earth policy, and destruction of enterprises 286
Sea Lion, Operation 101, 119
Sebag Montefiore, Simon 292
second front
and Beaverbrook campaigns for 424, 426
and Casablanca conference 435
and Churchill 428
and Churchill–Stalin meeting (1942) 429–32
and Dieppe raid 426, 432
and opening of 612
and Quebec ('Quadrant') conference 435
and Soviet calls for 410, 414–15

second front (*cont.*)
  and Soviet–British Treaty (1942) 425
  and Tehran conference (1943) 601
  and Washington ('Trident') conference 435,
    576 Second World War, and component
    wars of 3–4 Secret Intelligence Service
    (SIS)
  anticipates German attack on Russia 128
  on German intentions (1940) 127
  see also British Intelligence
Seidlitz und Gohlau, Colonel Baron von 262
Serebrov, Yevgeniy 397
'Sergeant-Major', *see* Boysen, Harro Schulze
Serov, Ivan 59, 61, 91, 286
Sevastopol 263, 447, 455, 458
  and defences of 458
  and German capture of 456, 460–1, 464
    resource implications of 464–5
    Soviet resistance 463–4
    use of chemical weapons 461
  and siege of 458–60
  and Soviet recapture of 607–8
Shaposhnikov, Marshal Boris 28–9, 84, 234, 238,
    259, 429, 431, 450
  and Battle of Moscow 321
  and Battle of Smolensk (July–Sept 1941)
    246–7
  and chemical warfare 264, 265
  and general offensive 341
  and invasion of Poland 58
  and Kiev pocket 259–60
  and membership of Stavka 215, 235
  and war plans against Germany 104
Shigemitsu, Mamoro 681
Shock Armies 320
Shostakovich, Dmitry 353, 389
Shpagin, Georgiy 485
Shpanov, N 111
Shtemenko, Colonel-General Sergey 650
Shtrafbat (drama-documentary) 478
Shvetsov, Major Boris 237
Sicily, and invasion of 587
signals intelligence 571–3
Siilasvuo, Colonel Hjalmar 75, 269
Simonov, Konstantin 657–8
Simpson, Wallis 136
Singapore 440
Sinilov, Major-General K R 294, 295
Sinyavino Operation 386–8
Sizov, Major Aleksandr 237
Skirpa, Kazys 194
Sklyarov, Colonel Ivan 237
Sledgehammer, Operation 425
Slezberg, Anna 298
Slutskin, Abram 484

Smersh 644
  and treatment of prisoners 29–30
Smolensk, Battle of (July–Sept 1941) 240–8
Smolensk Offensive 596
Smyslenko, Captain Nikolay 547
Smyslov, Major Aleksandr 547
snipers
  and Stalingrad 523–4
  and women as 489
Snow, Edgar 11
Society for Aviation and Chemical Defence 33
Sokolovskiy, Marshal Vitaliy 36, 320–1, 668
Solzhenitsyn, Aleksandr 442
Sorge, Richard 142, 145, 149, 308
Sorokhin, Lt Sergey 666
Soviet air force
  and attacks on German airfields 187
  and Battle of Smolensk (July–Sept 1941) 244
  and characteristics of 177–8
  and German advance on Leningrad 252–3
  and Kursk 581
  and reorganization of 249
  and Stalingrad 517–18
  and strength of 177, 603
  and women 487–9
Soviet General Staff 234
  and war games (1941) 105–6
Soviet navy 105, 158, 159, 178
  and Baltic fleet 362, 366, 622, 624, 625
  and Black Sea fleet 263, 607, 608
  and break-out from Tallinn 253
  and Leningrad 361–2
Soviet Union
  and Allied aid 411–14, 418–19, 439–45
    aircraft 422–3
    Arctic convoys 415, 427–8
    First (Moscow) Protocol 420–1
    food 443
    Fourth Protocol (1945) 439
    impact on German calculations 444–5
    intelligence use of 442–3
    Second (Washington) Protocol 433
    significance of 423, 440–2, 443–4, 445, 472
    supply routes 421–2
    tanks 424
    Third Protocol (1943) 439
  and Anglo-French negotiations 47–50
  and break-up of 6
  and economy
    gross domestic product (GDP) 468–70
    reasons for survival of 470–2
  and European distrust of 46
  and German–Soviet collaboration
    economic agreement (1940) 95
    economic agreement (1941) 95–6
    four-power pact negotiations 92–5

German–Soviet Treaty (Sept 1939) 56–7,
  63–6
  military 34, 41
  Molotov–Ribbentrop Pact (1939) 50–7
  Poland 56, 57–9, 62
  supply of raw materials 95–7
and Great Patriotic War
  defining impact of 5–6
  demographic impact 7–13
  economic impact of 13–14
and impact of German success in France 101,
  111
and intelligence on German deployments
  136–43, 144, 146–7, 149–50
  German deserters 155, 156–7
and Japan 308–9, 421–2
  agree to enter war against 437, 601
and Munich agreement 47, 51
and planning to attack Germany hypothesis
  101–18
  assessment of 115–18
  circumstantial evidence 110–15
  covert Soviet mobilization 113–15
  German assessment of Soviet intent
    112–13, 116
  war plan evidence 104–10
and population of 7–9
and post-war developments 685
and post-war disappointment 683
and post-war status 684–5
and similarities with Germany 42
and Spanish Civil War 45
and United Kingdom
  Anglo-Soviet agreement 410
  cooperation agreement 237–8
  Hess affair 133–5
  intelligence activities 416–18
  military mission from 409–10
  mission to 237, 411
  naval mission from 416–18
  Soviet–British Treaty (1942) 425
  suspicions of 100, 133, 135, 415
and warned of German attack
by United Kingdom 101, 131, 132
  by United States 128
Soviet–Finnish war (1939–40) 70–4
  and battle of Suomussalmi 75–6
  and casualties 78
  and change in Soviet organization 76–7
  and Finnish defences 71
  and lessons learned from 79–82
  and size of Soviet forces 71–4
  and Soviet miscalculations 74
  and Soviet prisoners of war 21
  and Soviet territorial gains 78
  and strategic/tactical lessons 76

Spanish Civil War 44–6
Spark, Operation 392–6
Speer, Albert 54, 667
Spitsbergen 411, 414
Spring Awakening 633
Stalin, Josef
  and allied conferences
    Moscow (1944) 438
    Potsdam (1945) 438, 674–5
    Tehran (1943) 436–8, 600–1
    Yalta (1945) 438, 646–8
  and Anglo-French negotiations 47–50
  and appeasement/deterrence strategy 140–1
  and Baltic States 66–7
  and Battle of Moscow 332
  and Berlin offensive 648–9, 656, 659, 665
    planning of 650–1
  and Caucasus 505, 506
  and Churchill
    meeting with (1942) 429–32
    Poland 627
    post-war division of Europe 627–8
    warned by 131, 445
  and establishment of Stavka 214–15
  on eve of war 154, 156–7
  and expansion of Soviet borders 97–8
  and expectations of German operations (1942)
    449–50
  and general offensive 340–1
  and Hitler
    respect for 43
    similarities with 42–3
  and impact of German success in France 101,
    111
  and industrialization 35
  and initial response to German attack 207–9,
    214–15
    coup possibility 227–8
    evacuation of national treasures 222–3
    loss of Belarus 226
    peace-feelers/disinformation 221–2
    speech to Russian people 231–2
    supposed nervous breakdown 226–7, 228
  and Kursk 566
  and Leningrad 354, 356–7
  and military advice from 271–2
  and military plans (1942) 450
  and military strategy 79
  and Molotov–Ribbentrop Pact (1939) 50–4
  and Moscow
    Battle of 315
    decides to remain 290, 292
    declared under siege 294
    evacuation of 288
    evacuation of theatres 288
    Red Square parade 303–4

Stalin, Josef (*cont.*)
  and nature of war 27–8
  and 'not a step back' order 471, 477
  and nuclear weapons 482, 483, 674–5
  and Operation Bagration 610
  and Operation Blau 498–9
  and Orël offensive 563, 564
  and outbreak of war 160–1
  and partisans 574
  and Patriotic War of 1812 3
  and peace feelers 221–2, 287
  and planning to attack Germany hypothesis
      101–18
    assessment of 115–18
    circumstantial evidence 110–15
    war plan evidence 104–10
  and Poland 58
    partition of 64
  and refuses to put armed forces on alert 147–8
  and role of 687
  and Soviet–Finnish war 76–7, 78
  and Stalingrad 513–14, 518, 527
    counteroffensive 527
    Operation Ring 539–40
  as *Time* 'man of the year' 5
  and treatment of prisoners 29
  and United Kingdom 410–11
    suspicion of 100, 133, 135, 415
  and victory parade 672, 673
  and Vistula–Oder offensive 643–4
  and warned of German attack 153–4
    in denial over 145–6, 147–8
    disbelief in 149
    Soviet intelligence 136–43, 144, 145,
      146–7, 149–50
  and Warsaw uprising 618–19
Stalin Line 144, 176, 203, 205
Stalingrad
  and Bald Hill 513
  and characteristics of 510–13
  and counteroffensive 526–8
    air power 517–18
    capture of Paulus 549–50
    end of fighting 550–1
    Operation Little Saturn 539, 540–1
    Operation Ring 537, 539–40
    Operation Saturn 529
    Operation Uranus 528–9, 531, 532–7
    ultimatum to Germans 547
  and declared under siege 294
  and defence of 507–10, 516
    NKVD 519
    reinforcements 526
    role of women 520–4
    snipers 523–4
    Soviet air force 517–18

  and evacuation of 515
  and German assault on 514–17, 518–19,
      525–6, 532
    air raids 507, 514
    Luftwaffe's role 517
  and Hill 102 510–12
  and impact of German defeat 551–2
  and Mamayev Kurgan 513, 515, 549
  and population of 510
  and siege declared 513
Stamenov, Ivan 221–2
Starikov, Major-General Filipp 386
Starobelsk prisoner camp 87
State Defence Committee (GKO)
  and Battle of Moscow
    creation of reserve armies 318–20
  and fire service 280
  and formation of 227–9
  and Leningrad 354, 391
  and membership of 229
  and mobilization of women 486
  and Moscow
    declared under siege 294
    defence of 287–8
    evacuation of 289–91
  and reconstruction 683
  and responsibilities of 229–30
  and role of 686
  and Strategic Directions 234–5
Stavka
  and Battle of Moscow
    counteroffensive planning 320–1
    reserve armies 318–20
  and Battle of Smolensk (July–Sept 1941) 242,
      245–6
  and Berlin offensive 649, 657
  and 'blocking detachments' 260
  and defence of Dvina and Dnepr 240
  and defence of Moscow 301
  and Directive No. 01 248–9
  and final offensives 635
  and formation of 175, 214–15
  and general offensive 340–1
  and Kiev 259
  and Kursk
    adopts defensive strategy 566
    counteroffensives 591
  and Leningrad 386
    Leningrad–Novgorod Offensive 404
    Operation Spark 392
    Sinyavino Operation 388
    Volkhov Offensive 384, 385
  and Manchurian offensive 678
  and membership of 235
  and Odessa Defensive Region 263
  and Operation Bagration 610

deception plan 612–13
  objectives of 610, 611–12
  planning of 610–11
and Orël offensive 564
and Representatives of 574–5
and responsibilities of 230
and Rokossovskiy's criticism of 348–9
and Rzhev counteroffensive 527–8
and Rzhev-Vyaz'ma Strategic Offensive 344,
    347
  offensive principles 344–5
and Stalingrad counteroffensive 527–8, 547
and Strategic Directions 234–6
and strategic retreats 500–1
Steinhardt, Laurence 128, 132–3
Stone, Norman 32
strategic bombing offensive 4, 173
Strategic Directions 234–6
Sudoplatov, Pavel 221, 222, 287
Suomussalmi 74
  and battle of (1939–40) 75–6
Super-Gymnast, Operation 425
Suvorov, Operation 596
Suvorov, Viktor (Rezun) 101–4
Svechin, Aleksandr 35–6, 137, 216

Tallinn 253
Talvi, Märja 249–50, 622
Taman peninsula 557
Tarnopol (Ternopil) 61
TASS 282–3
  and communiqué (June 1941) 145, 148, 155
    German reception of 145, 146, 147
Tedder, Sir Arthur 640
Tehran ('Eureka') conference 436–8, 600–1, 671
theatres, and evacuation from Moscow 288
Thompson, Walter 430
Tikhvin 367–9, 376
Time magazine, and Stalin 5
Timoshenko, Semyen 58, 62, 214, 501
  and appointed to command Western Front
    191, 192, 230–1, 234
  and Battle of Smolensk (July–Sept 1941) 242,
    243, 245–6
  on eve of war 154, 156, 157
    order alerting Soviet forces 157–8
  and Khar'kov offensive 451, 453
  and Leningrad 401–2
  and membership of Stavka 214, 235
  and Red Army reforms 84–5
  and South-Western Strategic Direction 260
  and Soviet–Finnish war 77, 79
  and war plans against Germany 104
  and warns Stalin 145
    requests full alert for forces 147–8
  and Western Strategic Direction 234

Tito, Josip Broz 631
Tobruk 464
Tolstoy, Leo 40, 99
Torch, Operation 425, 426, 431
  and Soviet reaction to 434
total war xvii, 31–7
  and conduct of 35–6
  and industrial mobilization 31–2
  and Soviet preparations for
    armaments industry development 34–5
    Frunze reforms (1924–25) 32–3
    industrialization 33
    integrated approach 35–6
    Svechin's Strategy 35–6
    Tukhachevskiy on nature of 36–7
Tributs, Vice-Admiral Vladimir 362
Trotsky, Leon 24, 34, 221
Troyanovskiy, P 312
Truman, Harry S 482, 674–5
Tsanava, Lavrenty 59
Tukhachevskiy, Mikhail Nikolayevich 33–5, 46,
    79, 121, 687
  and Finland 69
  and nature of total war 36–7
Tula 277
  and declared under siege 294
  and defence of Moscow 292, 306
Tupikov, General V I 142, 154, 260
Tvardovskiy, Aleksandr 390
Typhoon, Operation 256, 262, 271
  and advance on Moscow 288–9, 292, 301,
    306–7
  and Bryansk encirclement 272, 276, 277
  and 'culminating point' 305
  and German forces 272
  and impact of weather 302, 304–5
  and pause in operations 302–3
  and planning decisions 302–3
  and resumption of operations 303
  and Vyaz'ma encirclement 272–3, 276–7
  see also Moscow, Battle of
Tyulenev, Major-General Ivan 181, 504
  and frontier battles (June/July 1941) 205

Ukraine
  and Battle of the Dnepr 596–600
  and frontier battles (June/July 1941) 198–205,
    257
  and Great Patriotic War 11
  and internal security, liberated territory 336–7
  and oil fields 95
  and partisans 267–8, 478–9
  and right-bank Ukraine operations 603
  and Soviet resistance 257
Ultra intelligence 129–30, 151, 570
Uman' pocket 257–9

Umanskiy, Konstantin 420
Umezu, Yoshijiro 681
uncertainty, and warfare 17–18
Union of Polish Patriots (SPP) 576
United Kingdom
  and bombing of Berlin (1940) 93
  and invasion prospect 151
  and Soviet Union
    aid to 411–14, 418–19, 420–1, 424, 427–8,
      439–45
    Anglo-French negotiations with 50
    Anglo-Soviet agreement 410
    attitude towards 409, 445–6
    cooperation agreement 237–8
    danger of German–Soviet alliance 47, 145
    First (Moscow) Protocol 420–1
    intelligence activities 416–18
    military mission to 409–10
    mission from 237, 411
    naval mission to 416–18
    pessimism over prospects of 151
    popular enthusiasm for 424
    reaction to German invasion 210–11
    Second (Washington) Protocol 433
    Soviet–British Treaty (1942) 425
    suspicions of 100
    warnings to 101, 131, 132
  and United States
    First Washington Conference 425
    Second Washington Conference 426
  and withdrawal from Europe 100
United Nations conference (1945) 647
United Nations, Declaration of the (1941) 425
United States
  and Finland 269
  and Leningrad 355
  and Pearl Harbor 328
  and Second World War 4, 100
  and Soviet Union
    aid to 411–14, 419–21, 439–45
    anticipates German attack 132–3
    attitude towards 445
    First (Moscow) Protocol 420–1
    Second (Washington) Protocol 433
    warns of German attack 128
  and United Kingdom
    First Washington Conference 425
    Second Washington Conference 426
Uranus, Operation 528–9, 531
urban terrain
  and Berlin offensive 660–2
  and German policy towards 363
  and NKVD 293
  and siege of Leningrad 256
  and Stalingrad 515, 516, 517
USSR, foundation of 1917–24 715n.

Van Creveld, Martin 131
van Dyke, Carl 71, 84
Vansittart, Sir Robert 47
Vasilevna, Elena 30
Vasilevskiy, Aleksandr 450
  and Kiev pocket 259–60
  and Manchurian offensive 679
  and mobilization plan 113
  and Operation Blau 498–9
  and Stalingrad counteroffensive 527
  and war plans against Germany 104–5, 106–7
Vatutin, General Nikolay 143, 214
  and Korsun-Shevchenkovskiy salient 603
  and Kursk 563, 568, 582
    counteroffensive 591–3
  and Lake Il'men counter-stroke 251
Versailles, Treaty of (1919) 34, 41
Viipuri (Vyborg) 78
Vilnius 190
  and liberation of 617
Vinogradov, A 75, 76, 418
Vistula–Oder offensive 635, 641–6
  and supply problems 642–3
Vitebsk 242
Vladivostok 421–2
Vlasov, Major-General Andrey 199, 320, 669
  as traitor 385–6
  and Volkhov Offensive 382, 384–5
Volga Germans 284–5
Volkhov 366–7, 369
  and Volkhov Offensive 382–6
Volkogonov, Dmitry 225, 226
Volokolamsk 306
Voronezh 499, 500
Voronov, Nikolai 160, 549
  and Leningrad 362
  and Soviet–Finnish war 74, 80
  and Spanish Civil War 45
Voroshilov, Kliment 58, 84, 214, 275, 361
  and Allied aid 420
  and Anglo-French negotiations 50
  on eve of war 157
  and membership of Stavka 215, 235
  and North-West Strategic Direction 234, 251
  and officer training reforms 79–80
Voznesenskiy, Nikolay 220, 227, 229, 341, 440
Vyaz'ma
  and Rzhev-Vyaz'ma Strategic Offensive
    Operation 342–7
  and Vyaz'ma encirclement 272–5, 276–7
Vyshinskiy, Andrey 89, 132, 139, 208

Waldau, Major-General Hoffman von Waldau
  151–2
warfare
  and absolute war 18–19

and civilization 16–17
and conflict dynamics 17
and resources 18
and uncertainty 17–18
and will 18
Warsaw uprising 617–19
Washington ('Trident') conference (1943) 435, 576
Washington Conferences (1941–42) 425, 426
Wavell, Archibald 430, 431
weapons of mass destruction 265
  see also chemical weapons; nuclear weapons
Wehrmacht, see German army
wild boar 707n
Wilhelm Gustloff, and sinking of 12, 625–6
will, and warfare 18
Winter Storm, Operation 537–9
Winter War, *see* Soviet–Finnish war (1939–40)
winter warfare
  and Battle of Moscow 313, 316, 317, 322–4, 340
    equipment failure 323–4
  and Soviet preparations for 80
  and Soviet–Finnish war 74, 80
women
  and contribution to Soviet war effort 487
  and demobilization 684
  and executions in Kuybyshev 298
  and post-war role 684
  and role of 687
  in Soviet armed forces 10–11, 485–7, 489–90
    aviation regiments 487–9
    snipers 489, 523–4
    Stalingrad 520–2, 523–4
  and total war 32
Wroclaw 643–4
Wyburd, Commander Derek 416, 417–18

Yalta conference 438, 640, 646–8
  and Crimea Declaration 647–8
  and division of Germany 647, 648
  and Poland 647
  and repatriation of Soviet citizens 647
  and United Nations 647
Yarmolenko, Nikolay 398–9
Yassy–Kishinev offensive 619–21
Yel'nya bridgehead 246
Yeremenko, General Andrey 192
  and advice from Stalin 271–2
  and Battle of Smolensk (July–Sept 1941) 246
  and Kerch' peninsula 607
  and Stalingrad 507–10, 521
Yugoslavia 631
  and German invasion 100, 131–2

and joins Axis powers 129
and military coup 129

Zakharov, Matvey 105, 106, 137
Zanin, Major Semën 398
Zaytsev, Vasiliy 523, 524
Zeitzler, Kurt 533, 536
Zhdanov, Andrey 140, 153, 236, 307
  and Leningrad 361, 363
Zhukov, Georgiy 51, 85, 450, 635, 638
  and appointed Chief of the General Staff 106
  and ascendancy of 234
  and Battle of Moscow 341–2, 350
    counteroffensive first phase 330–1
    counteroffensive planning 320
    counteroffensive second phase 332, 339
  and Battle of Smolensk (July–Sept 1941) 243, 246, 247
  and Berlin offensive 645, 649, 650–4, 655–7, 659, 665
  and defence of Moscow 277, 294, 295–6, 305, 306, 311
  and defensive 'block' (June 1941) 223–5
  on eve of war 156, 157
    order alerting Soviet forces 157–8
  and frontier battles (June/July 1941) 200–1
  and general offensive 341
  and Khalkin Gol 83–4, 234
  and Korsun-Shevchenkovskiy salient 606
  and Kursk 579
    counteroffensive 593
    defensive strategy 565, 566
    Rokossovskiy's resentment of 574–5
  and Leningrad 357, 361
    counter-attacks 364–6
    Operation Spark 394–6
  and Leningrad Front 256, 260
  and management style 311–12
  and membership of Stavka 214–15, 235
  and outbreak of war 160–1
  and Rzhev–Sychevka counteroffensive ('Mars') 527, 529–31, 541–3
  and Rzhev-Vyaz'ma Strategic Offensive 347
  and Stalingrad 514, 526
  and Stalin's peace-feelers 287
  and victory parade 672–3, 674
  and Vistula–Oder offensive 641–2, 644–5
  and war games (1941) 105–6
  and war plans against Germany 106–9, 113, 143–4
  and warns Stalin 145
    requests alert for forces 147–8
  and Western Strategic Direction 345
Zhuravlëv, Mikhail 293
Zolotarëv, Major-General V A 114